MW00983688

Oracle Press™

Oracle Certified Professional™ DBA Certification Exam Guide

Jason S. Couchman

Tata McGraw-Hill Publishing Company Limited

NEW DELHI

McGraw-Hill Offices

New Delhi New York St Louis San Francisco Auckland Bogotá Caracas
Lisbon London Madrid Mexico City Milan Montreal
San Juan Singapore Sydney Tokyo Toronto

Tata McGraw-Hill

A Division of The **McGraw-Hill** *Companies*

Oracle Certified Professional DBA Certification Exam Guide

Copyright © 1998 by The McGraw-Hill Companies, Inc. All rights reserved.

No part of this publication may be reproduced or distributed in
any form or by any means, or stored in a database or retrieval system,
without the prior written permission of the publisher

Tata McGraw-Hill Edition 1999

Fourth reprint 2000
RAZYCRLCDZLXL

Reprinted in India by arrangement with The McGraw-Hill Companies, Inc.,
New York

For Sale in India Only

When ordering this title use ISBN 0-07-463556-5

Published by Tata McGraw-Hill Publishing Company Limited,
7 West Patel Nagar, New Delhi 110 008, and printed at
Pashupati Printers, Shahdara, Delhi 110 032

To Stacy

About the Author

Jason S. Couchman is an OCP-certified Oracle
DBA. He has led Oracle database projects with
Fortune 500 corporations and presented topics at
the North Carolina Oracle User Group. His articles
on Internet and intranet development have been
published internationally.

Contents

UNIT II
Preparing for OCP DBA Exam 2: Database Administration

UNIT III
Preparing for OCP DBA Exam 3:
Backup and Recovery Workshop

UNIT IV
Preparing for OCP DBA Exam 4: Performance Tuning Workshop

UNIT V
Preparing for OCP DBA Exam 5:
Oracle8 Features for Administrators

ORACLE®
Certified Professional

About the Oracle Certification Exams

Oracle Education is the largest IT training provider in the U.S. It has trained over 300,000 students worldwide in FY96 with over 304 education centers in over 70 countries worldwide.

Oracle Corporation produces a number of different software programs, but the company is best known for its Oracle database system. Oracle Education has launched The Oracle Certified Professional (OCP) program which offers the Certified Database Administrator credential.

Oracle Certified Professionals are eligible to receive use of Oracle Certified Professional logo and a certificate for framing.

The Certified Database Administrator credential demonstrates your skill and expertise in administering Oracle database systems. If you are already using Oracle7 at your company, it can help you move up to a position of greater responsibility and higher pay.

Requirements for Certification

To become an Oracle Certified Database Administrator, you must pass four tests. These exams cover knowledge of the essential aspects of the SQL language, Oracle7 administration, backup and recovery, and performance tuning of systems. The certification process requires that you pass the following four exams:

- Exam 1: Introduction to Oracle: SQL and PL/SQL exam.

- Exam 2: Oracle7 Database Administration exam.

- Exam 3: Oracle7 Backup and Recovery exam.

- Exam 4: Oracle7 Performance and Tuning exam.

If you fail a test, you must wait at least 30 days before you retake that exam. You may attempt a particular test up to three times in a twelve-month period.

Recertification

Oracle announces requirements for recertification based on the release of new products and upgrades. Previously-obtained certifications are valid for six months following an announcement of recertification requirements.

Exam Format

The computer-based exams are multiple-choice tests consisting of 60 to 70 questions that must be completed in 90 minutes.

Special 10% Exam Discount Offer

You can qualify for a special 10% discount when you register for the OCP Exam by contacting the number listed below. You must specifically request the discount and mention the publication that promoted the discount. Offer valid through December 31, 1998.

To register for an Oracle test, call Sylvan Prometric at 1-800-891-EXAM ext. 27 (1-800-891-3296 ext. 27).

For additional information, call Oracle at: 1-888-31-ORACL ext. 27 (1-888-316-7225 ext. 27)

The Oracle Web site offers a program guide that details the objectives for each exam. For more certification information, contact Oracle at **http://www.education.oracle.com/certification**.

Preface

y interest in Oracle certification began in 1996 when I read about the Oracle DBA certificate offered by the Chauncey Group. I found it difficult to prepare for that certification exam for two reasons. First, there was an absence of practice questions readily available. Second, preparation for the exam involved reviewing six or seven different manuals and Oracle Press books, none of which were particularly suited to the task. Judging from the response to this book so far, it would seem others have had similar experiences.

This book is divided into five units, one covering each exam. Each unit has several chapters covering the material you need to know in order to pass the exam. The body of each chapter follows the format described in this preface. At the end of the book, there is an appendix that covers the new scenario-based questions introduced by Oracle into the OCP exam.

Within each chapter, there are several section discussions. These section discussions correspond directly to subject areas tested in the OCP exams. The discussion presents facts about the Oracle database. Commands and keywords that the user enters are presented in **bold**, while new terms and emphasized facts are presented in *italics*. Particularly important facts and suggestions are set apart from regular text. They are preceded by the word TIP, and a special icon appears in the margin next to them.

At the end of each section are some exercises. Designed to reinforce the material you just read, these exercises are short answer questions. You should try to do *all* the exercises at the end of each discussion. If you can, try to answer each question without reviewing the chapter material, and write the answer in the book for later review.

A summary of the material presented appears near the end of each chapter. This digest information is designed for quick review after reading the chapter and doing the exercises. In the days prior to your OCP exam, you can reread the chapter summary to familiarize yourself with the information covered.

After the chapter summary, you'll find a short list of the key facts about Oracle presented in the chapter. This list, called a "Two-Minute Drill," is designed to be your final review for the OCP exam in the subject area covered in the chapter. Go over the Two Minute Drills in the unit corresponding to the OCP exam the night before you take the exam—as a memory jogger.

Each chapter also contains multiple choice and TRUE/FALSE questions patterned after the actual exam. These questions will familiarize you with the style of OCP questions. They will also test your knowledge of the Oracle material presented in the chapter. You should attempt to answer these questions after reviewing the chapter material. Finally, to help you understand the test material, each chapter contains the answers to the chapter questions, along with an explanation of each answer.

There are two ways to use this book. If you are a professional with beginner or intermediate level Oracle experience, you should use the standard method of studying the material in this book. Start at the beginning of each chapter, read it from start to finish, and *do the exercises*. Review the material by reading the chapter summary and Two-Minute Drill, and then answer the practice questions. The standard method should give you the facts you need to understand in order to pass the OCP exams, presented in several different ways to help you retain that information. If you have reviewed the material thoroughly, answering the exercise questions and studying the chapter summary and the drill for all chapters in the unit, you should do well on the OCP exam.

Advanced users of Oracle seeking to prepare for OCP exams quickly can also use the book's *accelerated reading method.* Skip directly to the chapter summary and read it to understand the content of the chapter. Then, review the Two Minute Drill, and try the chapter questions. If you find yourself getting most of the questions right, you may be ready to take the test. Even if you are missing questions, you will probably have a better idea of the areas you need review. You can then flip back to the specific area in the chapter content to help refresh your memory.

Good luck!

Acknowledgments

here are many people I would like to thank for their help with writing this book. Thanks go to Rob Pedigo, for without an early evening call from Rob several months ago, none of this would have happened. Much appreciation also to Brad Saffer, Joni Nakamura, Chris Pirie, Jim DiIanni, and Ulrike Schwinn for their feedback and assistance with the technical content review and with the material covering Oracle8.

Next, for the people who make the book possible. Thanks goes to Scott Rogers, whose enthusiasm made the project move along faster than I think any of us thought possible. I also thank Ann Sellers, Jeremy Judson, Ron Hull, Dennis Weaver, Marlene Vasilieff, and Robin Small, who kept things rolling and put it all together in the end. I would also like to thank Greg Zipes for his attention to detail and ability to ask the right questions, both of which gave me a lot of valuable insight.

Thanks to Liz Thompson who got me started with Oracle several years ago, to Deborah Tabacco, who got me started with IS as a profession, and to my father, Jack Couchman who bought me my first computer when I was 13.

A unique cross-pollination of educational influences at Vassar College gave me the idea of writing books about computers. Thanks to Joseph

XXV

Manning, Nancy Ide, Lou Voerman, and Sharon Tuggle and Winifred Asprey in computer science, and also to Julia and Albert Rosenblatt, who, along with *The Baker Street Journal*, gave me my first big publishing break. Thanks also to Joe Andrieu of Association of Internet Professionals who also gave me a chance to hone my writing craft, and an opportunity to be cyberbuds with Randy Hinrichs. Thanks to Randy for his entertaining advice along the way.

Most of all, thanks to my wonderful wife who tended to numerous details while I wrote. Stacy, you really are the greatest thing that ever happened to me.

Introduction

he Oracle Certified Professional DBA certification exam series is the latest knowledge good from Oracle Corporation. Called OCP, it represents the culmination of many people's request for objective standards in one of the hottest markets in the software field, Oracle database administration. The presence of OCP in the market indicates an important reality about Oracle as a career path. Oracle is mature, robust, and stable for enterprise-wide information management. However, corporations facing a severe shortage of qualified Oracle professionals need a measurement for Oracle expertise.

The OCP certification track for DBAs consists of four tests in the following areas of Oracle: SQL and PL/SQL, database administration, performance tuning, and backup and recovery. As of this printing, each test consists of about 60 multiple choice and TRUE/FALSE questions pertaining to the recommended usage of Oracle databases. You have about 90 minutes to take each exam. The current content of these four exams covers Oracle through version 7.3. A fifth exam is in the works to test DBAs on the new features available in Oracle8. Obtaining certification for Oracle7 is contingent on taking and passing *all four* examinations, while certification for both Oracle7 and Oracle8 requires taking and passing the fifth exam.

Why Get Certified?

If you are already an Oracle professional, you may wonder, "Why should I get certified?" Perhaps you have a successful career as an Oracle DBA, enjoying the instant prestige your resume gets with that one magic word on it. With market forces currently in your favor, you're right to wonder. But, while no one is saying your resume isn't already impressive, can you prove how well you *do* know Oracle without undergoing a technical interview? I started asking myself that question last year when Oracle certification began to emerge. I was surprised to find out that, after years of using Oracle, developing Oracle applications, and administering Oracle databases for Fortune 500 companies, there were a lot of things about Oracle I *didn't* know. And the only reason I know them now is because I took the time and effort to become certified.

If you're looking for another reason to become certified in Oracle, consider the example of computer professionals with Novell NetWare experience in the late 1980s and early 1990s. It seemed that anyone with even a little experience in Novell could count on a fantastic job offer. Then Novell introduced its CNE/CNA programs. At first, employers were fine hiring professionals with or without the certificate. As time went on, however, employers no longer simply asked for computer professionals with Novell NetWare experience—they asked for CNEs and CNAs. A similar phenomenon can be witnessed in the arena of Microsoft Windows NT, where the MCSE has already become the standard by which those professionals are measuring their skills. If you want to stay competitive in the field of Oracle database administration, your real question shouldn't be *whether* you should become certified, but *when*.

If you are not in the field of Oracle database management, or if you want to advance your career using Oracle, there has never been a better time to do so. OCP is already altering the playing field for DBAs by changing the focus of the Oracle skill set from "How many years have you used it?" to "*How well* do you know how to use it?" That shift benefits organizations using Oracle as much as it benefits the professionals who use Oracle because the emphasis is on *performance*, not attrition.

Managers who are faced with the task of hiring Oracle professionals can breathe a sigh of relief with the debut of OCP as well. By seeking professionals who are certified, managers can spend less time trying to determine if the candidate knows Oracle well enough to do the job, and more time assessing the candidate's work habits and compatibility with the team.

How Should You Prepare for the Exam?

If you spend your free time studying things like the name of the dynamic performance view that helps a DBA estimate the effect of adding buffers to the buffer cache, you are probably ready to take the OCP DBA exams right now. For the rest of us, Oracle and other companies offer classroom- and computer-based training options to learn Oracle. Now, users have another option—this book! By selecting this book, you demonstrate two excellent characteristics—that you are committed to a superior career in the field of Oracle database administration, and that you care about preparing for the exam correctly and thoroughly. And by the way, the name of the dynamic performance view that helps a DBA estimate the effect of adding buffers to the buffer cache is X$KCBRBH, and it is on the OCP DBA exam. That fact, along with thousands of others, is covered extensively in this book to help you prepare for, and pass, the OCP DBA certification exam.

DBA Certification Past and Present

Oracle certification started in the mid 1990s with the involvement of the Chauncey Group International, a division of Educational Testing Service. With the help of many Oracle DBAs, Chauncey put together an objective, fact-based and scenario-based examination on Oracle database administration. This test did an excellent job of measuring knowledge of Oracle7, versions 7.0 to 7.2. Consisting of 60 questions, Chauncey's exam covered several different topic areas, including backup and recovery, security, administration, and performance tuning, all in one test.

Oracle Corporation has taken DBA certification several giant leaps ahead with the advent of OCP. Their certification examination is actually four tests, each consisting of about 60 questions. By quadrupling the number of questions you must answer, Oracle requires that you have unprecedented depth of knowledge in Oracle database administration. Oracle has also committed to including scenario-based questions on the OCP examinations, and preparation material for these new questions is included in this book as well. Scenario-based questions require you not only to know the facts about Oracle, but also to understand how to apply those facts in real-life situations.

Oracle's final contribution to the area of Oracle certification is a commitment to reviewing and updating the material presented in the certification exams. Oracle-certified DBAs will be required to maintain their certification by retaking the certification exams about once a year—meaning that those who certify will stay on the cutting edge of the Oracle database better than those who do not.

There is one final bonus to beginning your certification process right now. You can leverage the knowledge you already have of Oracle7 to obtain a demonstrated credential of expertise on Oracle8. The OCP DBA certification series' fifth exam, Oracle8: New Features for Administrators, will allow those professionals who are already certified in Oracle7 to extend their certification to include Oracle8. In contrast, those who wait to become certified on Oracle8 when Oracle8 certification becomes available will have to take *five* exams to become certified instead of just one.

Taking the Oracle Assessment Test

It is essential that you begin your preparation for the OCP DBA certification exams by taking the Oracle Assessment Test. Developed by Self Test Software, the Oracle Assessment Test is a mock-up of the real exam, with questions designed to help you identify your personal areas of strength and weakness with Oracle. You can load the Oracle Assessment Test from the CD-ROM included with this book. You should load it onto your Windows-based computer and take the exams to determine which areas you need to study.

Figure I-1 shows the Assessment Test graphical user interface. The features of the interface are indicated in the figure. Several of the main features of the assessment test interface are explained here. The Assessment Test interface is highly similar to the actual Sylvan Prometric OCP DBA test driver, with a few exceptions as noted. At the top of the interface tells you how much time has elapsed and the number of questions you have answered. On the actual OCP exam only, there is also a checkbox in the upper left-hand corner of the interface. You can use this checkbox to mark questions you would like to review later. In the main window of the interface is the actual production question, along with the choices. The interface generally allows the user to select only one answer, unless the question directs you to select more answers. In this case, the interface will allow you to select only as many answers as the question requests. After answering a question, or marking the question for later review, the candidate can move on to the next question by clicking the appropriate button in the lower left-hand corner. The next button along the bottom allows you either to print on the assessment test or to return to the previous question on the OCP exam. Next, in the Assessment Test only, you can score your questions at any time by pressing the grade test button on the bottom right-hand side. The final point feature to cover is the exhibit button. In some cases, you may require the use of an exhibit to answer a question. If the question does not require use of an exhibit, the button will be grayed out.

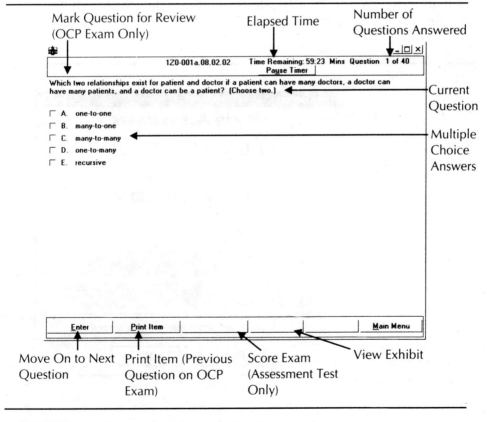

FIGURE I-I. *The Oracle Assessment Test User Interface*

The Assessment Test indicates your performance by means of a grade window, such as the one displayed in Figure I-2. It details the number of questions you answered correctly, along with your percentage score based on 100 percent. Finally, a bar graph indicates where your performance falls in comparison to the maximum score possible on the exam. The OCP exam reports your score immediately after you exit the exam, so you will know right then whether you pass or not in a similar fashion as the assessment test. Both interfaces offer you the ability to print a report of your score.

Taking the OCP Exams

The score range for each OCP Exam is between 200 and 800. Since there is a 600-point range for potential scores, and typically there are 60 questions, each question is worth about 10 points. There is no penalty for wrong answers. The OCP examinations required for the DBA track are listed

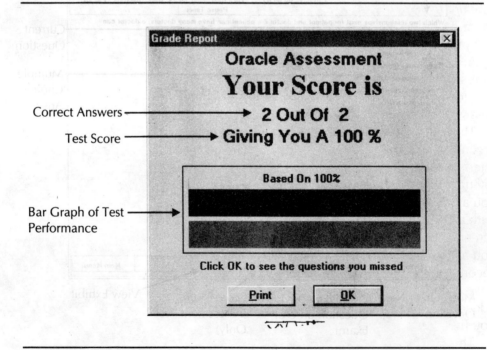

FIGURE I-10. *Grading Your Test Performance*

below. The OCP DBA certification exam is administered at Sylvan Prometric test centers. To schedule your OCP Exam in the United States, call Sylvan Prometric at **1-800-891-EXAM.** For contact information outside the USA, refer to the assessment test software. For Oracle's official information about OCP Certification, visit its website at **http://education.oracle.com/.** The exams in the OCP DBA series are as follows:

1. Oracle7: SQL and PL/SQL

2. Oracle7: Database Administration

3. Oracle7: Backup and Recovery

4. Oracle7: Performance Tuning

5. Oracle8: New Features for Administrators (not required for Oracle7 Certification)

Now here's some advice on taking the OCP exams. The first tip is, *don't wait until you're the world's foremost authority on Oracle to take the OCP Exam.* The passing score for most exams is 650. With each question worth 10 points, you have to get 45 questions right. That's about 75 percent of the exam. So, if you are getting about three questions right out of four on the assessment test or in the chapters (more on chapter format in a minute), you should consider taking the OCP exam. Remember, you're certified if you pass with a 650 or an 800.

The next piece of advice is, if you can't answer a question within 30 seconds, mark it with the checkbox in the upper left-hand corner of the OCP interface for review later. The most significant difference between the OCP interface and the assessment test interface is a special screen appearing after you answer all the questions. This screen displays all your answers, along with a special indicator next to the questions you marked for review. This screen also offers a button for you to click in order to review the questions you marked. You should use this feature extensively. If you spend only 30 seconds answering each question in your first pass on the exam, you will have at least an hour to review the questions you're unsure of, with the added bonus of knowing you answered all the questions that were easiest to you first.

Third, *there is no penalty for guessing.* If you answer the question correctly, your score goes up ten points, if not, your score does not change.

If you can eliminate any choices on a question, you should take the chance in the interest of improving your score. In some questions, the OCP exam requires you to specify two or even three choices—this can work in your favor, meaning you need to eliminate fewer choices to get the question right.

Finally, unless your level of expertise with Oracle is high in a particular area, *it is recommended that you take the exams in the sequential order listed above*. This is especially recommended for readers whose background in Oracle is more on the beginner/intermediate level, and even more important if you are using this Guide to prepare for the exam. This is because each subsequent chapter of the Guide builds on information presented in the previous chapters. As such, you should read the Guide from beginning to end, and take the test accordingly. Taking the exams in this manner will maximize your use of the Guide and your results on the tests.

The New Scenario-Based Questions on the OCP Exam

Oracle Corporation has announced its intention to include scenario-based questions in the OCP DBA certification exam series. These questions require you to take the facts about Oracle and apply those facts to real-life situations portrayed on the exam—complete with exhibits and documents to substantiate the example—and determine the correct answer based on those exhibits and documents. In order to assist you better in preparation for these new test questions, the appendix to this book contains information about the scenario-based portion of the exam. Some of the areas covered in this appendix include:

- Understanding the types of exhibits you will be presented.
- Strategies for putting the exhibits together to answer *more* questions *right*.

Finally, if you have comments about the book or would like to contact me about it, please do so by email at **jcouchman@mindspring.com**.

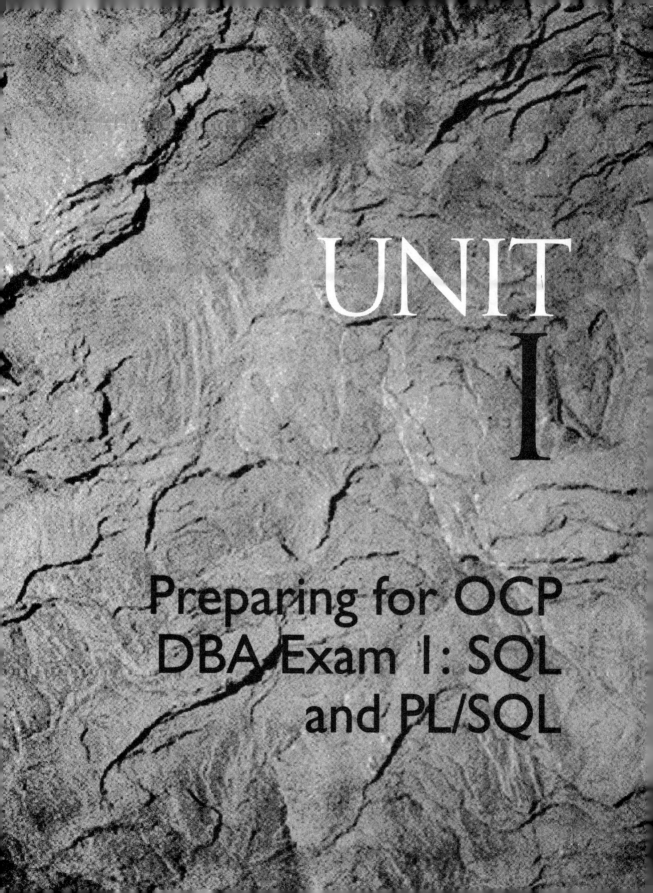

UNIT
I

Preparing for OCP DBA Exam 1: SQL and PL/SQL

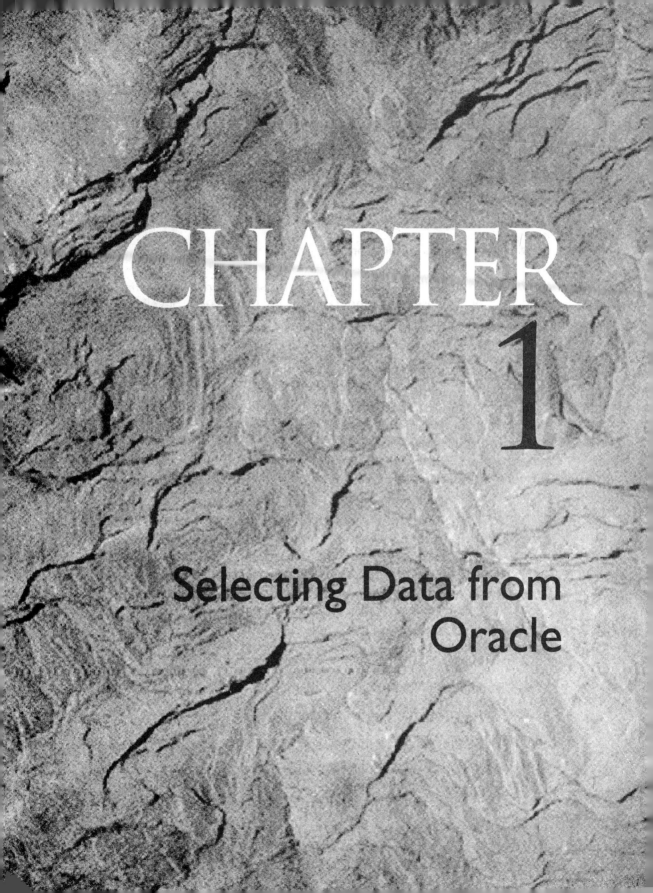

CHAPTER
1

Selecting Data from Oracle

n this chapter, you will understand and demonstrate knowledge in the following areas:

- Selecting rows
- Limiting selected output
- Using single-row functions

The first exam in the Oracle Certified Professional series covers many basic areas of database usage and design. Every Oracle user, developer, and DBA should have complete mastery in these areas before moving on into other test areas such as database design, administration, backup and recovery, and tuning. This unit assumes little or no prior knowledge of Oracle in order to help the user go from never using Oracle to having enough expertise in the Oracle server product to maintain and enhance existing applications and develop small new ones. The five chapters in this unit will function as the basis for understanding the rest of the book. This chapter will cover several aspects of data retrieval from the Oracle database, including selecting rows, limiting the selection, and single-row functions. The content of this chapter covers material comprising 17 percent of test content on OCP Exam 1.

Selecting Rows

In this section, you will cover the following areas related to selecting rows:

- Writing **select** statements
- Performing arithmetic equations
- Handling NULL values
- "Renaming" columns with column aliases
- Putting columns together with concatenation
- Editing SQL queries within SQL*Plus

Use of Oracle for many people begins with usage of an existing Oracle application in an organization. The first tool many people see for selecting data directly from the Oracle relational database management system is called SQL*Plus. When users first start SQL*Plus, in most cases they must enter their Oracle username and password in order to begin a session with the Oracle database. There are some exceptions to this rule that utilize the password authentication provided with the operating system. The next unit, covering OCP Exam 2, will explore the methods and implications of starting SQL*Plus sessions without supplying an Oracle username and password. The following examples show how you might begin a session.

```
$> sqlplus jason/athena
```

or

```
$> sqlplus /
```

A session is an interactive runtime environment in which the user enters a command to retrieve data and Oracle performs a series of activities to obtain the data that the user asked for. What does interactive mean? It means that Oracle and the user have an interactive "conversation" in which the user asks Oracle to provide certain pieces of information and Oracle provides it. Conversation implies language. In order for the user and Oracle to communicate, they must both speak the same language. The language users "speak" to Oracle in order to retrieve data is a special type of language called Structured Query Language, or SQL for short. SQL can be pronounced as three individual letters, or in the same way as "sequel." SQL is a "functional" language. A functional language is one that allows the users to specify the types of things they want to see happen in terms of the results they want. Contrast this approach to other languages you may have heard about or programmed in, such as C++ or COBOL. These other languages are often referred to as "procedural" programming languages because the code written in these languages implies an end result by explicitly defining the means, or the procedure, by which to get there. In contrast, SQL explicitly defines the end result, leaving it up to Oracle to determine the method by which to obtain the data. Data selection can be accomplished using the following code listing.

```
SELECT *
FROM emp
WHERE empid = 39334;
```

This SQL *statement* asks Oracle to provide all data from the EMP table where the value in a certain column called EMPID equals 39334. The following block of code from an imaginary procedural programming language similar to C illustrates how the same function may be handled by explicitly defining the means to the end.

```
Include <stdio.h>
Include <string.h>
Include <rdbms.h>

Int *empid;
Char *statement;

Type emp_rec is record (
Int            empid;
Char[10]       emp_name;
Int            salary; )

Void main()
{
  Access_table(emp);
  Open(statement.memaddr);
  Strcpy("SELECT * FROM EMP WHERE EMPID = 39334",statement.text);
  parse(statement);
  execute(statement);
  for (I=1,I=statement.results,I+1) {
    fetch(statement.result[I],emp_rec);
    printf(emp_rec);
  }
  close(statement.memaddr);
}
```

Of course, that C-like block of code would not compile anywhere but in the imagination of the reader, but the point of the example is clear—other languages define a means toward an end, while SQL allows the user to define the end in and of itself.

Writing SELECT Statements

The most common type of SQL statement executed in most database environments is the *query*, or **select** statement. **Select** statements are designed to pull requested data from the database. Where is data stored in the database? Data is stored in special database objects called *tables*. A table in Oracle is similar in concept to Table 1-1. It has columns and rows, each of which is meant to be unique. For more information about tables, see Chapter 3.

The user can issue a simple **select** statement that is designed to pull all data from the table shown in Table 1-1. When SQL*Plus is started, it produces several components of information, including the version of SQL*Plus being used, the date, the version of the Oracle database being accessed, the version of PL/SQL in use, and the server options available on the database. The following code block demonstrates SQL*Plus.

Empid	Lastname	Fname	Salary
39334	Smith	Gina	75,000
49539	Qian	Lee	90,000
60403	Harper	Rod	45,000
02039	Walla	Rajendra	60,000
49392	Spanky	Stacy	100,000

TABLE 1-1. *EMP*

```
SQL*Plus: Release 3.2.3.0.0 - Production on Tue Feb 03 18:53:11 1998
Copyright (c) Oracle Corporation 1979, 1994.  All rights reserved.
Connected to: Oracle7 Release 7.3.4.0.1
With the distributed and replication options
PL/SQL Release 2.3.0.0.0 - Production

SQL> SELECT * FROM HRAPP.EMP;

EMPID    LASTNAME    FIRSTNAME    SALARY
-----    --------    ---------    ------
39334    SMITH       GINA         75000
49539    QIAN        LEE          90000
60403    HARPER      ROD          45000
02039    WALLA       RAJENDRA     60000
49392    SPANKY      STACY        100000
```

The line in bold in this excerpt from a SQL*Plus session illustrates the entry of a simple SQL statement. The query requests Oracle to give all data from all columns in the EMP table. Oracle replies with the contents of the EMP table as diagrammed in Table 1-1. Note that the user did not tell Oracle how to retrieve the data, the user simply expressed the data they wanted using SQL syntax and Oracle returned it. Chapter 17 shows how Oracle performs these tasks behind the scenes. For now, make sure you understand how to specify a schema owner, the table name, and the column name in a **select** statement in SQL*Plus. The following code block demonstrates proper usage.

```
SELECT table_name.column_name, table_name.column_name …
FROM schema.table_name;
```

TIP
*Always use a semicolon (;) to end SQL statements when entering them directly into SQL*Plus.*

The main components of a **select** statement are outlined. The first component is the **select** clause. This part is required in order for Oracle to identify that it must now perform a **select** statement. The second component of a **select** statement is the list of columns from which the user would like to view data. In the statement issued in the example SQL*Plus session, the column listing as described in the statement format was substituted with a special *wildcard* (*) character, which indicates to Oracle that the user wants to view data from every column in the table. The user could have executed the following query and obtained different data instead. The last aspect of the **select** statement of importance is the **from** clause. This special clause tells Oracle what database table to pull the information from. Usually, the database user will need to specify the schema, or owner, to which the table belongs, in addition to naming the table from which the data should come.

```
SELECT empid, lastname, salary FROM HRAPP.EMP;

EMPID     LASTNAME    SALARY
-----     --------    ------
39334     SMITH        75000
49539     QIAN         90000
60403     HARPER       45000
02039     WALLA        60000
49392     SPANKY      100000
```

Notice in the statement issued that the table named in the **from** clause is HRAPP.EMP. This means that Oracle should pull data from the EMP table in the HRAPP schema. When a user is granted the ability to create database objects, the objects he or she creates belong to the user. Ownership creates a logical grouping of the database objects by owner, and the grouping is called a *schema*.

TIP
A schema is a logical grouping of database objects based on the user that owns the object.

Exercises

1. What is a **select** statement? Name the two required components of a **select** statement.

2. How should the user end a **select** statement in SQL*Plus?

3. What is a schema?

Performing Arithmetic Equations

In addition to simple selection of data from a table, Oracle allows the user to perform different types of activities using the data. The most basic of these activities is arithmetic. All basic arithmetic operations are available in Oracle, including addition, subtraction, multiplication, and division. The operators used to denote arithmetic in Oracle SQL are the same as in daily use.

To better understand use of arithmetic equations in Oracle, the following example is offered. Assume, for example, that the user of the database is performing a simple annual review that involves giving each user a cost-of-living increase in the amount of 8 percent of their salary. The process would involve multiplying each person's salary by 1.08. The user could execute the process manually with pencil or calculator, but look at how much easier it is for the user to execute a slightly more complicated query to determine the result with SQL:

```
SELECT empid, salary, salary*1.08 FROM HRAPP.EMP;

EMPID    LASTNAME    SALARY    SALARY*1.08
-----    --------    ------    -----------
39334    SMITH        75000         81000
49539    QIAN         90000         97200
60403    HARPER       45000         48600
02039    WALLA        60000         64800
49392    SPANKY      100000        108000
```

SQL allows the user to execute all types of arithmetic operations, including +, -, *, /. Oracle allows the user to execute special SQL statements designed to perform mathematical problems without selecting data as well. The feature of Oracle related to arithmetic functions of this type is a special table called DUAL. DUAL is an empty table that is used to fulfill the SQL **select from** construct.

```
SELECT 64+36 FROM DUAL;

64+36
-----
  100
```

2·

There is no data actually in DUAL; rather it simply exists as a SQL construct to support the requirement of a table specification in the **from** clause. Additionally, the DUAL table contains only one column and one row.

2·

TIP
*DUAL is a special table consisting of one column and all NULL values. DUAL is used to satisfy the SQL syntax construct stating that all SQL statements must contain a **from** clause that names the table from which the data will be selected. When a user does not want to pull data from any table, but rather wants simply to use an arithmetic operation on a constant value, the user can include the values, operations, and the **from DUAL** clause.*

Exercises

1. How can the user perform arithmetic on selected columns in Oracle?

2. What is the DUAL table? Why is it used?

3. How does the user specify arithmetic operations on numbers not selected from any table?

Handling NULL Values

Sometimes, a query for some information will produce a nothing result. In database terms, nothing is called *NULL*. NULL is an expression that represents a nothing value. In set theory, the mathematical foundation for relational databases, NULL represents the value of an empty dataset, or a dataset containing no values. Unless specified otherwise, a column in a table is designed to accommodate the placement of nothing into the column. An example of retrieving a NULL is listed in the following code block. Notice that some of the employees have no spouse. Nothing in Oracle is represented with the NULL value. NULL is similar to nothing in that it represents no data present for this column in the row.

```
SELECT empid, lastname, firstname, spouse FROM HRAPP.EMP;

EMPID        LASTNAME      FIRSTNAME      SPOUSE
-----        --------      ---------      ------
39334        SMITH         GINA           FRED
49539        QIAN          LEE
60403        HARPER        ROD            SUSAN
02039        WALLA         RAJENDRA       HARPREET
49392        SPANKY        STACY
```

1. However, there arise times when the user will not want to see nothing. Instead of retrieving an empty data field, there may be occasions where the user wants to see some default message. Oracle provides this functionality with a special function called **nvl( )**. This is the first function covered, so some extra attention will be paid to using it in Oracle. In this case, assume that the user does not want to see blank spaces for spouse information. Instead, the user wants the output of the query to contain the word "unmarried" instead. The query below illustrates how the user can issue the query against Oracle to obtain the desired result. The **nvl( )** function is used to modify the SPOUSE column such that if the value in the SPOUSE column is NULL, it will return the text string 'unmarried'. Text strings in Oracle must be enclosed in single quotes.

```
SELECT empid, lastname, firstname, NVL(spouse,'unmarried') FROM HRAPP.EMP;

EMPID        LASTNAME      FIRSTNAME      NVL(spous
-----        --------      ---------      ---------
39334        SMITH         GINA           FRED
49539        QIAN          LEE            unmarried
60403        HARPER        ROD            SUSAN
02039        WALLA         RAJENDRA       HARPREET
49392        SPANKY        STACY          unmarried
```

2. Notice, first of all, that if the column specified in **nvl( )** is not NULL, the value in the column is returned, while when the column is NULL, the special string is returned. The **nvl( )** function can be used on columns of all datatypes. A discussion of different datatypes will appear later. For now, it is important to understand that the syntax for **nvl( )** is as follows:

```
NVL(column_name, value_if_null)
```

Exercises

1. What does NULL mean in the context of Oracle SQL?
2. What is the **nvl( )** function? How is it used?

"Renaming" Columns with Column Aliases

As the user may have noticed in some of the earlier examples, when Oracle returns data to the user, Oracle creates special headings for each column so that the user knows what the data is. The heading returned corresponds directly with the name of the column passed to Oracle as part of the **select** statement:

```
SELECT empid, lastname, firstname, NVL(spouse,'unmarried') FROM HRAPP.EMP;

EMPID        LASTNAME    FIRSTNAME    NVL(spous
-----        --------    ---------    ---------
39334        SMITH       GINA         FRED
49539        QIAN        LEE          unmarried
60403        HARPER      ROD          SUSAN
02039        WALLA       RAJENDRA     HARPREET
49392        SPANKY      STACY        unmarried
```

The columns above correspond to the column names indicated in the **select** statement, including the **nvl( )** operation on SPOUSE. By default, Oracle reprints the column name exactly as it was included in the **select** statement. Unfortunately, although this method exactly describes the data selected in the query, it does not usually give a descriptive explanation of the column data. Compounding the problem is the fact that Oracle truncates the expression to fit a certain column length corresponding to the datatype of the column returned.

Oracle provides a solution to this situation with the use of column aliases in the **select** statement. Any column can be given another name by the user when the **select** statement is issued. This feature gives the user the ability to fit more descriptive names into the space allotted by the column datatype definition.

```
SELECT empid, lastname, firstname, NVL(spouse,'unmarried') spouse FROM HRAPP.EMP;
```

EMPID	LASTNAME	FIRSTNAME	**SPOUSE**
39334	SMITH	GINA	FRED
49539	QIAN	LEE	unmarried
60403	HARPER	ROD	SUSAN
02039	WALLA	RAJENDRA	HARPREET
49392	SPANKY	STACY	unmarried

As indicated in bold by this code, the SPOUSE column is again named SPOUSE, even with the **nvl( )** operation performed on it. The alias is specified after the column is named in the **select** statement according to the following method. In order to specify an alias, simply name the alias after identifying the column to be selected, with or without an operation performed on it, separated by white space.

Alternatively, the user can issue the **as** keyword to denote the alias. The column with the operation in it is specified as usual, but instead of naming the column alias as described in the preceding paragraph, the **as** keyword can clearly identify the alias for others reading the query. Note the use of **as** to denote the alias in the following code block:

```
SELECT empid, lastname, firstname, NVL(spouse,'unmarried')
AS spouse
FROM HRAPP.EMP;
```

EMPID	LASTNAME	FIRSTNAME	SPOUSE
39334	SMITH	GINA	FRED
49539	QIAN	LEE	unmarried
60403	HARPER	ROD	SUSAN
02039	WALLA	RAJENDRA	HARPREET
49392	SPANKY	STACY	unmarried

To summarize, column aliases are useful for identifying the data in the output from SQL queries with meaningful headings. Aliases can be specified in two ways, either by naming the alias after the column specification separated by white space, or with the use of the **as** keyword to mark the alias more clearly for other readers of the query, as shown here:

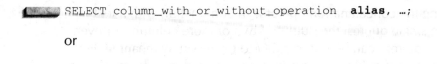

```
SELECT column_with_or_without_operation  alias, …;
```

or

```
SELECT column_with_or_without_operation  AS alias, …;
```

Exercises

1. What is a column alias? For what situations might column aliases be useful?

2. What are two ways to define aliases for columns?

Putting Columns Together with Concatenation

Renaming a column in a **select** statement and using the **nvl( )** operation are not the only things that can be done to change the output of a query. Entire columns can be put together to produce more interesting or readable output. The method used to merge the output of certain columns into something new is accomplished with a special operation called concatenation. The concatenation operator looks like two pipe characters put together, or | |. Consider the running example of output from EMP. In the following example, the user wants to change the name output to be in the format *lastname, firstname*.

```
SELECT empid, lastname||', '||firstname full_name,
NVL(spouse,'unmarried') spouse, FROM HRAPP.EMP;
```

EMPID	FULL_NAME	SPOUSE
39334	SMITH, GINA	FRED
49539	QIAN, LEE	unmarried
60403	HARPER, ROD	SUSAN
02039	WALLA, RAJENDRA	HARPREET
49392	SPANKY, STACY	unmarried

Again, by using the concatenation operator in conjunction with a text string enclosed in single quotes, the output of two or more columns, or even the output of one column, can be put together to express new meaning. For good measure, the use of column aliases is recommended in order to make the name of the concatenated columns more meaningful.

Exercises

1. What is column concatenation?

2. What special character sequence is used to concatenate columns?

Editing SQL Queries Within SQL*Plus

As the user gains more exposure to SQL*Plus, he or she will undoubtedly notice an annoying feature of the SQL*Plus command line—it is hard to back up to previous lines. In other words, the user must type in the query very carefully, making sure that each line of the statement is correct before pressing the ENTER key and moving on to type the next line. So far, this limitation of the SQL command line hasn't presented much difficulty. However, as the queries the user can write get more and more complicated, the user will grow frustrated. SQL*Plus does allow some correction of statement entry with the use of a special command called **change**, abbreviated as **c**. Consider the following example to illustrate the point:

```
SELECT empid, lastname||', '||firstname full_name,
NVL(sppuse,'unmarried') spouse, FROM HRAPP.EMP;

NVL(sppuse,'unmarried') spouse, FROM HRAPP.EMP;
      *
ERROR at line 2:
ORA-00904: invalid column name

SQL> 2

2> NVL(sppuse,'unmarried') spouse, FROM HRAPP.EMP;

SQL> c/sppuse/spouse

2> NVL(spouse,'unmarried') spouse, FROM HRAPP.EMP;
```

```
SQL> /

EMPID   FULL_NAME          SPOUSE
-----   ----------------   ---------
39334   SMITH, GINA        FRED
49539   QIAN, LEE          unmarried
60403   HARPER, ROD        SUSAN
02039   WALLA, RAJENDRA    HARPREET
49392   SPANKY, STACY      unmarried
```

In this example, the user issues a **select** statement containing a typographical error, **sppuse**. Oracle notices the error and alerts the user to it with **ORA-00904**. To change it, the user first references the line containing the mistake, in this case with the number 2. At this point, Oracle indicates the current version of the SQL statement. Then the user issues the **change** command, abbreviated as **c**. The old text appears after the first slash, and the new text follows the second slash. Oracle makes the change and then displays the new version of the line. The user can then execute the SQL statement, using the slash (/) command. Other errors that may be produced by the user are:

ORA-00923: FROM Keyword Not Found Where Expected
This error indicates that the **from** keyword was not included or was misspelled.

ORA-00942: Table or View Does Not Exist
This error indicates that the table or view typed in does not exist. Usually, the reason for ORA-00942 is a typo in the name of the table or view, or because the schema owner was not specified in front of the table name. This error is fixed either by correcting the typing problem or by adding the schema owner onto the front of the table name. An alternative solution exists for the latter cause in creating synonyms for tables that are accessible to other users. This solution will be discussed in a later section.

In any case, the method used to correct the typing problem is to first **select** the line number from the special buffer that SQL*Plus maintains the current query in. The name of the buffer is **afiedt.buf** on many operating systems. The line of the buffer is identified by entering the line number and pressing ENTER as indicated by the entry at the prompt as indicated. After that line is chosen, the change command is entered in the following syntax.

```
c/old_value/new_value
```

After making the change to the *first* appearance of *old_value* in the current line, Oracle redisplays the current line, with the change made. Note that the change will be made to the first appearance of *old_value* only. If the change must be made to a specific place in the line, more characters can be added to the *old_value* parameter as appropriate. Finally, the corrected text can be reexecuted by entering a slash (/) at the prompt as indicated.

It takes some acclimation before the user will use SQL*Plus line editor to change the command as freely as they would use their own favorite text editor. Fortunately, Oracle makes provisions for the users to utilize their favorite text editor to edit the statement created in afiedt.buf. Instead of entering all the additional commands to identify the line to be edited, followed by the exact character sequence to change, Oracle allows the user to type in the **edit** command (abbreviated **ed**). This action causes Oracle to bring up the SQL statement in afiedt.buf into the operating system's default text editor. On UNIX systems, that text editor is usually VI or EMACS, while Windows environments usually opt for the Notepad text editor. To change the text editor used, issue the **define_editor='***youreditor***'** statement from the prompt.

Using a text editor rather than the line editor native to SQL*Plus offers many benefits. First and foremost is the benefit of using a text editor the user knows well, creating a familiarity with the application that is useful in adapting to SQL*Plus quickly. Second, it is helpful with large queries to have the entire block of code in front of the user and immediately accessible.

TIP
When running SQL statements from scripts, do NOT put a semicolon (;) at the end of the SQL statement. Instead, put a slash (/) character on the line following the script.

One final word of note for using external editors to create SQL statements that will then be executed with Oracle SQL*Plus. It is possible to use the text editor of choice to write the entire query first and then load it

Into Oracle SQL*Plus. Two commands are available for this functionality. The first is called **get**. The **get** command opens the text file specified and places it in afiedt.buf. Once loaded, the user can execute the command using the slash (/) command. Alternatively, the user can simply load SQL statements from the file into **afiedt.buf** and execute in one step using the @ command.

```
SQL*Plus: Release 3.2.3.0.0 - Production on Tue Feb 03 18:53:11 1998
Copyright (c) Oracle Corporation 1979, 1998.  All rights reserved.
Connected to Oracle7 Release 7.3.4.0.0
With the distributed and replication options
PL/SQL Release 2.3.0.0.0 - Production

SQL> GET select_emp
SELECT * FROM emp
SQL> /

EMPID     LASTNAME     FIRSTNAME     SALARY
-----     --------     ---------     ------
39334     SMITH        GINA           75000
49539     QIAN         LEE            90000
60403     HARPER       ROD            45000
02039     WALLA        RAJENDRA       60000
49392     SPANKY       STACY         100000

5 rows selected;

SQL> @select_emp

SELECT * FROM emp

/

EMPID     LASTNAME     FIRSTNAME     SALARY
-----     --------     ---------     ------
39334     SMITH        GINA           75000
49539     QIAN         LEE            90000
60403     HARPER       ROD            45000
02039     WALLA        RAJENDRA       60000
49392     SPANKY       STACY         100000

5 rows selected;
```

In the first case illustrated by this example, the **get** command is used to pull in the contents of the select_emp.sql file into the afiedt.buf buffer. Notice that the **.sql** extension was left off. Oracle SQL*Plus assumes that all scripts containing SQL statements will have the **.sql** extension, so the extension can be omitted. Notice also that after the file is brought in using **get**, it can then be executed using the slash (/) command. In the second case, illustrated by the example, the same file is read into **afiedt.buf** and executed in one step, eliminating the need for the slash (/) command by using the @ command. Again, the .sql extension is omitted. Remember that when using the **get** or @ commands, if a full pathname is not specified as the filename, then Oracle SQL*Plus assumes the file is in the local directory.

Exercises

1. What two mechanisms are available to enter and modify SQL statements within SQL*Plus?

2. What is the edit command in the SQL*Plus command line? How can SQL scripts be loaded from files into SQL*Plus? How are they run?

3. What command is used to define a text editor for SQL*Plus to use?

Limiting Selected Output

In this section, you will cover the following areas related to limiting selected output:

- The **order by** clause
- The **where** clause

Obtaining all output from a table is a great feature, but in the reality of database applications, the user must be more selective in choosing output. The reason is because most database applications contain a lot of data. How much data can a database contain? Some applications contain tables with a million rows or more, and the most recent release of Oracle, Oracle8, will store up to 512 petabytes of data. Needless to say, manipulating vast amounts of data requires the user to be careful to ask for *exactly* what he or she wants.

The ORDER BY Clause

In our running example of data from the EMP table, a fundamental principle of relational data storage is illustrated. Data within a table need not have any order. Another quick look at the output from the EMP table will demonstrate:

```
SQL> /

EMPID   LASTNAME   FIRSTNAME   SALARY
-----   --------   ---------   ------
39334   SMITH      GINA        75000
49539   QIAN       LEE         90000
60403   HARPER     ROD         45000
02039   WALLA      RAJENDRA    60000
49392   SPANKY     STACY      100000
```

Notice that the data returned is in no particular order on any column, either numeric or alphabetical. Oracle allows the user to place order on output from **select** statements by issuing a special clause along with the statement already presented. That special clause is called **order by**. This clause can be included in **select** statements at the end of the statement. The general syntax for the **order by** clause is to include both the clause and the column(s) or column alias(es) on which Oracle will define order, optionally followed by a special clause defining the direction of the order. Possible directions are **asc** for ascending and **desc** for descending, as shown here:

```
SQL> SELECT * FROM emp ORDER BY empid DESC;

EMPID   LASTNAME   FIRSTNAME   SALARY
-----   --------   ---------   ------
60403   HARPER     ROD         45000
49539   QIAN       LEE         90000
49392   SPANKY     STACY      100000
39334   SMITH      GINA        75000
02039   WALLA      RAJENDRA    60000
```

In addition to providing order on one column, Oracle can provide order on many columns. If the user desires, he or she can include multiple column specifications, as well as ascending *or* descending order in each of the columns specified. The **order by** clause can be useful in simple reporting. It can be applied to columns that are of NUMBER, text (VARCHAR2 and

CHAR), and DATE datatypes. Finally, one can use numbers to indicate the column on which Oracle should order the output from a statement. The use of numbers depends on the positioning of each column. For example, if the user issues a statement similar to the one in the following code block, the order for the output will be as shown. The number 2 indicates that the second column should be used to define order in the output. But, since the second column is something different in each statement, the order of the output will be different as well.

```
SELECT empid, lastname FROM emp ORDER BY 2;

EMPID     LASTNAME
-----     --------
02039     WALLA
39334     SMITH
49392     SPANKY
49539     QIAN
60403     HARPER

SELECT lastname, empid FROM emp ORDER BY 2;

LASTNAME  EMPID
--------  -----
60403     HARPER
39334     SMITH
49392     SPANKY
49539     QIAN
02039     WALLA
```

Exercises

1. How can a user put row data returned from a **select** statement in order? What are the various orders that can be used with this option?

2. What are the two ways to specify the column on which order should be defined?

The WHERE Clause

The **where** clause in Oracle **select** statements is where the really interesting things begin. This important clause in **select** statements allows the user to single out a few rows from hundreds, thousands, or even millions like it. The **where** clause operates on a basic principle of comparison:

```
SELECT * FROM emp WHERE empid = 43932;

EMPID     LASTNAME    FIRSTNAME     SALARY
-----     --------    ---------     ------
49392     SPANKY      STACY         100000
```

Instead of pulling all rows from EMP, Oracle pulls just one row for display. To determine what row to display, the **where** clause performs a comparison operation as specified by the query—in this case, the comparison is an equality operation, **where** *empid* = 43932. However, equality is not the only means by which Oracle can obtain data. Some other examples of comparison are demonstrated in the following list:

x = y	Comparison to see if *x* is equal to *y*.
x > y	Comparison to see if *x* is greater than *y*.
x >= y	Comparison to see if *x* is greater than or equal to *y*.
x < y	Comparison to see if *x* is less than *y*.
x <= y	Comparison to see if *x* is less than or equal to *y*.
x <> y *x != y* *x ^= y*	Comparison to see if *x* is not equal to *y*.
like	A special comparison used in conjunction with the character wildcard (%) character to find substrings in text variables.
soundex	A special function used to introduce "fuzzy logic" into text string comparisons by allowing equality based on similarly spelled words.
between	A range comparison operation that allows for operations on dates that are similar to the following numeric comparison: *Y* "is between" *X* and *Z*.
in	A special comparison that allows the user to specify multiple equality statements by defining a set of values, any of which the value can be equal to. An example of its usage may be x **in** (1,2,3,4,5).

These six operations are the cornerstone of comparison. According to Boolean logic (one of the cornerstones of computing in a database or any other type of environment), every comparison between two values boils down to one or more of these operations. A **select** statement need not have only one comparison in it to determine what data should be returned. Multiple comparisons can be placed together using the following list of operations. The operator is listed along with the result that is required to fulfill the criteria based on the presence of this operator.

x **and** *y*	Both comparisons in *x* and *y* must be true.
x **or** *y*	One comparison in *x* or *y* must be true.
not *x*	The logical opposite of *x*.

Exercises

1. What is a **where** clause? On what principle does this clause operate to determine which data is selected?

2. What are some operations available to assist in the purpose of comparison? What are some operations that allow the user to specify more than one comparison in the **where** clause?

Using Single-Row Functions

In this section, you will cover the following areas related to using single-row functions:

- Various single-row functions explained
- Using functions in **select** statements
- Date functions

In addition to simple comparison, Oracle allows more complex comparison operations with the use of special functions. There are dozens of functions available in Oracle that can be used for many purposes. Some functions in Oracle are designed to alter the data returned by a query, such as the **nvl( )** function already presented. The functions in this category are designed to work on columns of any datatype to return information in a different way. For example, the **nvl( )** function can handle nulls appearing in any column, including dates, numbers, text strings, and others. One commonly used example of this type of function is **decode( )**. The **decode( )** procedure works on the same principle as an **if-then-else** statement works in many common programming languages, including PL/SQL, which will be discussed in Chapter 6.

```
SELECT DECODE(column, val1, return1, val2, return2, … ,return_default)
…
```

The **decode( )** function allows for powerful transformation of data from one value to another. Its scope encompasses the functionality provided by **nvl( )**, yet **decode( )** goes so much farther than **nvl( )** in its ability to return highly specialized data when given the right criteria. Furthermore, it allows for a default return value to be specified if the user so desires. Some examples of **decode( )** in action will appear later in the chapter.

Various Single-Row Functions Explained

From this point on, all functions described have limitations on the datatype they can perform their operations on. Related to the set of functions designed to convert data from one thing to another are several functions that manipulate text strings. These functions are similar in concept to **nvl( )** and **decode( )** in that they can perform a change on a piece of data, but the functions in this family can perform data change on only one type of data—text. As such, the functions in this family are often referred to as text, or *character functions*. In this family are several functions in Oracle, for which some of the highlighted functions that are most used are listed following this paragraph.

lpad(x,y[,z]) **rpad**(x,y[,z])	Returns the column "padded" on the left or right side of the data in the column passed as x to a width passed as y. The optional passed value z indicates the character(s) that **lpad** or **rpad** will insert into the column.
lower(x) **upper**(x) **initcap**(x)	Returns the column value passed as x into all lowercase or uppercase, or changes the initial letter in the string to a capital letter.

length(*x*)	Returns a number indicating the number of characters in the column value passed as *x*.
substr(*x*,*y*[,*z*])	Returns a substring of string *x*, starting at character number *y* to the end, which is optionally defined by the character appearing in position *z* of the string.

Others are designed to perform specialized mathematical functions such as those used in scientific applications like sine and logarithm, which should already be fairly well understood by those with a background in trigonometry. These operations are commonly referred to as math or number operations. The functions falling into this category are listed next. These functions are not all the ones available in Oracle, but rather are the most commonly used ones that will likely be used on OCP Exam 1.

abs(*x*)	Obtains the absolute value for a number. For example, the absolute value of (-1) is 1, while the absolute value of 6 is 6.
ceil(*x*)	Similar to executing **round** on an integer (i.e., **round(x,0)**, except **ceil** always rounds up. For example, **ceil(1.6)** = 2. Note that rounding "up" on negative numbers produces a value closer to zero (e.g., **ceil(-1.6)** = -1, not -2).
floor(*x*)	Similar to **ceil**, except **floor** always rounds down. For example, **floor(1.6)** = 1. Note that rounding "down" on negative numbers produces a value further away from zero (e.g., **floor(-1.6)** = -2, not -1).
mod(*x*,*y*)	The modulus of *x*, as defined by long division as the integer remainder left over when *x* is divided by *y* until no further whole number can be produced. An example is **mod(10,3)** = 1, or **mod(10,2)** = 0.
round(*x*,*y*)	Round *x* to the decimal precision of *y*. If *y* is negative, round to the precision of *y* places to the left of the decimal point. For example, **round(134.345,1)** = 134.3, **round(134.345,0)** = 134, **round(134.345,-1)** = 130.

sign(x)	Displays **integer** value corresponding to the sign of x, 1 if x is positive, -1 if x is negative.
sqrt(x)	The square root of x.
trunc(x,y)	Truncate value of x to decimal precision y. If y is negative, then truncate to y number of places to the left of the decimal point.
vsize(x)	The storage size in bytes for value x.

The final category of number functions that will be discussed here is the set of list functions. These functions are actually used for many different datatypes, including text, numeric, and date. The list functions are listed here.

greatest(x,y,...)	Returns the highest value from list of text strings, numbers, or dates (x,y...).
least(x,y,...)	Returns the lowest value from list of text strings, numbers, or dates (x,y...).

Another class of data functions available in Oracle correspond to another commonly used datatype in the Oracle database—the *DATE* datatype. The functions that perform operations on dates are known as date functions. Before diving into the functions, a useful item in Oracle related to dates will be presented. There is a special keyword that can be specified to give Oracle users the current date. This keyword is called **sysdate**. In the same way that the user calculated simple arithmetic in an earlier part of the chapter using the DUAL table, so too can the user execute a **select** statement using **sysdate** to produce today's date:

```
SELECT sysdate FROM DUAL;

SYSDATE
---------
15-MAR-98
```

With usage of **sysdate** established, the functions that can be used on DATE columns are listed in the following definitions:

add_months(*x,y*)	Returns a date corresponding to date *x* plus *y* months.
last_day(*x*)	Returns the date of the last day of the month that contains date *x*.
months_between(*x,y*)	Returns a number of months between *y* and *x* as produced by *y-x*. Can return a decimal value.
new_time(*x,y,z*)	Returns the current date and time for date *x* in time zone *y* as it would be in time zone *z*.

Why use functions at all? The functions available in Oracle are highly useful for executing well-defined operations on data in a table or constant values in an easy way. For example, if the user were working with a scientific organization to produce a report of data for that organization, the user may want to use some of the math functions available in Oracle. Rather than selecting data from a table and performing standard mathematical calculations using a scientific calculator, the user may instead execute the functions on that data and produce the report cleanly, in one step. The use of functions in Oracle often saves time and energy.

Exercises

1. Identify some of the character, number, and date functions available in SQL. What are two functions that allow the user to transform column values regardless of the datatype?

2. What are other types of functions that perform operations on columns of specific datatypes?

Using Functions in SELECT Statements

The previous section introduced the many functions available in Oracle. The definitions in that section should suffice for reference; however, there is no substitute for actual usage. This section will show the functions listed in action. The first example details use of the **decode( )** function. Assume that the user is selecting data from the EMP table. The data in the SEX column of EMP is populated with M for male and F for female. Instead of displaying a letter, the user wants to write out the full word for each sex.

```
SELECT empid, lastname, firstname,
DECODE(sex,'M','MALE','F','FEMALE') sex FROM emp
ORDER BY empid DESC;

EMPID       LASTNAME    FIRSTNAME   SEX
-----       --------    ---------   ------
60403       HARPER      ROD         MALE
49539       QIAN        LEE         FEMALE
49392       SPANKY      STACY       FEMALE
39334       SMITH       GINA        FEMALE
02039       WALLA       RAJENDRA    MALE
```

Notice that the **decode( )** command has five vaariables, the first of which is the name of the column. This column must always be present. The second variable corresponds to the value that could be found in the SEX column, followed by the value that **decode( )** should return if SEX in this row is equal to 'M'. The next set of variables answers the question of what **decode( )** should return if the value in the column is 'F'. This matching of column values with appropriate return values can continue until the user has identified all cases he or she would like **decode( )** to handle. The last variable according to the definition of **decode( )** is used for the default return value. No default value was specified in this example, as the default return value is optional.

The next section will present examples of text or character function examples. The first of these examples is for **rpad( )** and **lpad( )**. These two functions can be used to place additional filler characters on the right or left side of data in a column out to a specified column width.

```
SELECT empid, lastname, firstname,
RPAD(DECODE(sex,'M','MALE','F','FEMALE'),10,'-') sex FROM emp
ORDER BY empid DESC;

EMPID       LASTNAME    FIRSTNAME   SEX
-----       --------    ---------   ----------
60403       HARPER      ROD         MALE------
49539       QIAN        LEE         FEMALE----
49392       SPANKY      STACY       FEMALE----
39334       SMITH       GINA        FEMALE----
02039       WALLA       RAJENDRA    MALE------
```

An interesting property of Oracle SQL functions is displayed in this example. The output from one SQL function can be used as input for another. In this case, the **rpad( )** operation will pad the decoded SEX column out to ten characters with dashes. If the **lpad( )** operation had been used instead, the result would have been as follows:

```
SELECT empid, lastname, firstname,
LPAD(DECODE(sex,'M','MALE','F','FEMALE'),10,'-') sex FROM emp
ORDER BY empid DESC;
```

EMPID	LASTNAME	FIRSTNAME	SEX
60403	HARPER	ROD	------MALE
49539	QIAN	LEE	----FEMALE
49392	SPANKY	STACY	----FEMALE
39334	SMITH	GINA	----FEMALE
02039	WALLA	RAJENDRA	------MALE

Some of the simpler character functions are next. Two straightforward examples of SQL queries are sometimes referred to as "case translators," because they perform a simple translation of case based on the text string passed.

```
SELECT LOWER(title) TITLE_NOQUOTE,
UPPER(artist) ARTIST1, INITCAP(artist) ARTIST2 FROM SONGS;
```

TITLE_NOQUOTE	ARTIST1	ARTIST2
"happy birthday"	ANONYMOUS	Anonymous
"diamonds and rust"	ANONYMOUS	Anonymous
"amazing grace"	ANONYMOUS	Anonymous

Another straightforward and surprisingly useful character function is the **length( )** function, which returns the length of a text string.

```
SELECT title, LENGTH(title) LENGTH
FROM SONGS;
```

TITLE	LENGTH
"HAPPY BIRTHDAY"	16
"DIAMONDS AND RUST"	19
"AMAZING GRACE"	15

Note one interesting thing happening in this query—spaces and special characters are all counted as part of the length! This is an important facet to remember when dealing with text strings in Oracle. Blank spaces count as part of the length of the column value. Another extraordinarily useful function related to character strings is the **substr( )** function. This function is commonly used to extract data from a longer text string. Its syntax, though slightly more difficult to understand than some of the other commands in Oracle, is definitely worth mastering. **substr( )** takes as its first variable the full text string to be searched. The second variable contains an integer that designates the character number at which the substring should begin. The third parameter is optional and specifies how many characters to the right of the start of the substring will be included in the substring. Optionally, the final variable in the **substr( )** call could have been left off, producing the following output:

```
SELECT title, SUBSTR(title,5,5) CHARS
FROM SONGS;

TITLE                  CHARS
-------------------    -----
"HAPPY BIRTHDAY"       Y BIR
"DIAMONDS AND RUST"    ONDS
"AMAZING GRACE"        ING G

SELECT title, SUBSTR(title,5) CHARACTERS
FROM SONGS;

TITLE                  CHARACTERS
-------------------    ---------------
"HAPPY BIRTHDAY"            Y BIRTHDAY"
"DIAMONDS AND RUST"    ONDS AND RUST"
"AMAZING GRACE"            ING GRACE"
```

The number or math functions are frequently used in scientific applications, and as such may not be as familiar to developers with less mathematical experience. It is beyond the scope of this chapter to discuss the meaning of the math functions, particularly the logarithmic functions. The first function detailed here is the **abs( )** or absolute value function.

```
SELECT ABS(25), ABS(-12) FROM DUAL;

ABS(25)    ABS(-12)
-------    --------
25         12
```

The next single-value function that will be covered in this section is the **ceil( )** function.

```
SELECT CEIL(123.323), CEIL(45), CEIL(-392), CEIL(-1.12) FROM DUAL;

CEIL(123.323)    CEIL(45)    CEIL(-392)    CEIL(-1.12)
-------------    --------    ----------    -----------
124              45          -392          -1
```

The next single-value function is the **floor( )** function. The **floor( )** is the opposite of **ceil( )**.

```
SELECT FLOOR(123.323), FLOOR(45), FLOOR(-392), FLOOR(-1.12) FROM DUAL;

FLOOR(123.323)    FLOOR(45)    FLOOR(-392)    FLOOR(-1.12)
-------------     --------     ----------     -----------
123               45           -392           -2
```

The next function covered in this section is related to long division. The function is called **mod( )**, and it returns the remainder amount for a number and its divisor.

```
SELECT MOD(12,3), MOD(55,4) FROM DUAL;

MOD(12,3)    MOD(55,4)
---------    ---------
0            3
```

After that, the user should look at **round( )**. This important function allows the user to round a number off to a specified value of precision.

```
SELECT ROUND(123.323,2), ROUND(45,1), ROUND(-392,-1), ROUND
(-1.12,0) FROM DUAL;

ROUND(123.323,2)    ROUND(45,1)    ROUND(-392,1)    ROUND(-1.12,0)
----------------    -----------    -------------    --------------
123.32              45             -390             -1
```

The next function is called **sign( )**. It assists in identifying a number to be positive or negative. If the number passed is positive, **sign( )** returns 1, if the number is negative, **sign( )** returns –1.

```
SELECT SIGN(-1933), SIGN(55), SIGN(0) FROM DUAL;

SIGN(-1933)   SIGN(55)      SIGN(0)
----------    -----------   -------
-1            1             0
```

The next example is the **sqrt( )** function. It is used to derive the square root for a number.

```
SELECT SQRT(34), SQRT(9) FROM DUAL;

SQRT(34)    SQRT(9)
---------   ----------
5.8309519   3
```

The next single-value number function is called **trunc( )**. Similar to **round( )**, **trunc( )** truncates a value passed into it according to the precision that is passed in as well.

```
SELECT TRUNC(123.232,2), TRUNC(-45,1), TRUNC(392,-1), TRUNC(5,0)
FROM DUAL;

TRUNC(123.232,2) TRUNC(-45,1) TRUNC(392,-1) TRUNC(5,0)
---------------- ------------ ------------- ----------
          123.23         -45           390          5
```

The final single-row operation that will be covered in this section is the **vsize( )** function. This function is not strictly for numeric datatypes, either. The **vsize( )** function gives the size in bytes of any value for a text, number, date, or ROWID, and other columns.

```
SELECT VSIZE(384838), VSIZE('ORANGE_TABBY.'), VSIZE(sysdate) FROM DUAL;

VSIZE(384838)     VSIZE('ORANGE_TABBY')     VSIZE(SYSDATE)
-------------     ---------------------     --------------
            4                        12                  8
```

Exercises

1. What is the purpose of the **nvl( )** function? What datatypes does it accept? What is the purpose of a **decode( )** statement? What datatypes does it accept?

2. Name some character functions? Can two functions be combined? Why or why not?

3. Name some single-value number functions. What types of applications are these functions typically used in?

4. What function is used to determine the size in bytes of a given value or column?

Date Functions

There are several date functions in the Oracle database. The syntax of these functions has already been presented. This section will discuss each function in more detail and present examples of their usage. But first, the user should understand how dates are stored in Oracle. The Oracle database stores dates in an integer format, storing the date as the number of days from the beginning of the Julian calendar. This method allows for easy format changes and inherent millennium compliance.

The first function is the **add_months( )** function. This function takes as input a date and a number of months to be added. Oracle then returns the new date, which is the old date plus the number of months.

```
SELECT ADD_MONTHS('15-MAR-98',26)
FROM DUAL;

ADD_MONTHS('15
--------------
     15-MAY-02
```

The next date function, **last_day( )**, helps to determine the date for the last date in the month for the date given.

```
SELECT LAST_DAY('15-MAR-99') FROM DUAL;

LAST_DAY('15-M
--------------
 31-MAR-99
```

The next date function determines the number of months between two different dates given. The name of the function is **months_between( )**. The syntax of this command is tricky, so it will be presented here. The syntax of this command is **months_between(y,x)**, and the return value for this function is *y-x*.

```
SELECT MONTHS_BETWEEN('15-MAR-98','26-JUN-97') FROM DUAL;

MONTHS_BETWEEN
--------------
     8.6451613
```

The next and last example of a date function is the **new_time( )** function. This procedure accepts three parameters, the first being a date and time, the second being the time zone the first parameter belongs in, and the last parameter being the time zone the user would like to convert to. Each time zone is abbreviated in the following way: *X*ST or *X*DT, where *S* or *D* stands for standard or daylight savings time, and where *X* stands for the first letter of the time zone (such as *A*tlantic, *B*ering, *c*entral, *e*astern, *H*awaii, *M*ountain, *N*ewfoundland, *P*acific, or *Y*ukon). There are two exceptions: Greenwich mean time is indicated by GMT, while Newfoundland standard time does not use daylight savings. An example of the usage of **new_time( )** is as follows in this example. Another useful fact to know when using **new_time( )** is that the Oracle date format shown is not the only one available. Dates in Oracle are stored as numbers from the beginning of the Julian calendar (December 31, 4713 B.C.E.), down to the second. So far, none of the queries used to demonstrate the date functions have required that much precision, but the following example will. In order to demonstrate the full capability of Oracle in the **new_time( )** function, the NLS date format can be changed to display the full date and time for the query. The following example demonstrates both the use of **nls_date_format** to change the date format and the **new_time( )** function to convert a time stamp to a new time zone:

```
ALTER SESSION
SET NLS_DATE_FORMAT = 'DD-MON-YYYY HH24:MI:SS';
```

```
SELECT NEW_TIME('15-MAR-1998 14:35:00','AST','GMT')
FROM DUAL;

NEW_TIME('15-MAR-199
--------------------
15-MAR-1998 18:35:00
```

Exercises

1. What is **nls_date_format**? How is it set? How is it used?

2. Which date functions described in this section return information in the DATE datatype? Which one returns information in a datatype other than DATE?

3. How are dates stored in Oracle?

Conversion Functions

Still other functions are designed to convert columns of one datatype to another type. As these functions are simply designed to change the datatype of the column value, not actually modify the data itself, the functions are called conversion functions. There are several different conversion functions available in the Oracle database. The ones available appear in the following list:

to_char(x)	Converts noncharacter value x to character
to_number(x)	Converts nonnumeric value x to number
to_date(x[,y])	Converts nondate value x to date, using format specified by y
to_multi_byte(x)	Converts single-byte character string x to multibyte characters according to national language standards
to_single_byte(x)	Converts multibyte character string x to single-byte characters according to national language standards

chartorowid(*x*)	Converts string of characters *x* into an Oracle ROWID
rowidtochar(*x*)	Converts string of characters *x* into an Oracle ROWID
hextoraw(*x*)	Converts hexadecimal (base-16) value *x* into raw (binary) format
rawtohex(*x*)	Converts raw (binary) value *x* into hexadecimal (base-16) format
convert(*x*[,*y*[,*z*]])	Executes a conversion of alphanumeric string *x* from the current character set optionally specified as *z* to the one specified by *y*
translate(*x*,*y*,*z*)	Executes a simple value conversion for character or numeric string *x* into something else based on the conversion factors *y* and *z*

The following text illustrates the most commonly used procedures for converting data in action. These are the **to_char( )**, **to_number( )**, and **to_date( )** functions. The first one demonstrated is the **to_char( )** procedure. In the example of **new_time( )**, the date function described earlier, the **alter session set nls_date_format** statement was used to demonstrate the full capabilities both of Oracle in storing date information and Oracle in converting dates and times from one time zone to another. That exercise could have been accomplished with the use of the **to_char( )** conversion function as well, however. Using **to_char( )** in this manner saves the user from converting **nls_date_format**, which, once executed, is in effect for the rest of the user's session, or until the user executes another **alter session set nls_date_format** statement. Rather than using this method, the user may want to opt for a less permanent option offered by the **to_char( )** function.

```
SELECT TO_CHAR(NEW_TIME(TO_DATE('15-MAR-1998 14:35:00',
'DD-MON-YYYY HH24:MI:SS'),'AST','GMT')
FROM DUAL;

NEXT_DAY('15-MAR-9
------------------
15-MAR-98 18:35:00
```

Note that this example also uses the **to_date( )** function, another conversion function in the list to be discussed. The **to_number( )** function is very useful for converting numbers, and especially character strings, into properly formatted DATE fields.

```
SELECT TO_NUMBER('49583') FROM DUAL;

TO_NUMBER('49583')
--------------------
49583
```

Although there does not appear to be much difference between the output of this query and the string that was passed, the main difference is the underlying datatype. Even so, Oracle is actually intelligent enough to convert a character string consisting of all numbers before performing an arithmetic operation using two values of two different datatypes.

```
SELECT '49583' + 34 FROM DUAL;

'49583'+34
----------
     49617
```

Exercises

1. Identify some conversion functions. Which conversion functions are commonly used?

2. What is **nls_date_format**? How is it used?

Chapter Summary

This chapter provides an introduction to using Oracle by demonstrating basic techniques for use of **select** statements. The areas discussed in this chapter are selecting row data from tables using the **select from** statement, limiting the rows selected with the **where** clause of the **select from** statement, and using the single-row functions available in Oracle to manipulate selected data into other values, formats, or meanings. This chapter is the cornerstone for all other usage in Oracle, as well as for passing the OCP Exam 1. Material covered in this chapter comprises 17 percent of test content on OCP Exam 1.

The first area covered in this chapter is information about selecting data from Oracle. The most common manipulation of data in the Oracle database is to select it, and the means by which to select data from Oracle is the **select** statement. The **select** statement has two basic parts, the **select** clause and the **from** clause. The **select** clause identifies the column(s) of the table that the user would like to view contents of. The **from** clause identifies the table(s) in which the data selected is stored. In this chapter, data from only one table at a time was considered. In the next chapter, the concept of pulling or "joining" data from multiple tables will be considered.

Often, users will want to perform calculations involving the data selected from a table. Oracle allows for basic, intermediate, and complex manipulation of data selected from a database table through the use of standard arithmetic notation. These operators can be used to perform math calculations on the data **select**ed from a table or as math operators on numbers in calculator-like fashion. In order to perform calculations on numbers that are not selected from any table, the user must utilize the DUAL table. DUAL is simply an empty table with one column that fulfills the syntactic requirements of SQL statements like **select**, which need a table name in the **from** clause in order to work.

When manipulating data from a table, the user must remember to handle cases when column data for a particular row is nonexistent. Nonexistent column data in a table row is often referred to as being NULL. These NULL values can be viewed either as blank space, by default, or the user can account for the appearance of NULL data by using a special function that will substitute NULL fields with a data value. The name of this special function is **nvl( )**. The **nvl( )** function takes two parameters: the first is the column or value to be investigated for being NULL, and the second is the default value **nvl( )** will substitute if the column or value is NULL. The **nvl( )** function operates on all sorts of datatypes, including CHAR, VARCHAR2, NUMBER, and DATE.

When performing special operations on columns in a **select** statement, Oracle often displays hard-to-read headings for the column name because Oracle draws the column name directly from the **select** clause of the **select** statement. The user can avoid this problem by giving a column alias for Oracle to use instead. For example, the following **select** may produce a cryptic column heading: **select nvl(empid,'00000') EMPID ...**, while a column alias would allow Oracle to provide a more meaningful heading: **select nvl(empid,'00000') EMPID ...**. Column aliases are specified as character strings following the function and/or column name the alias will substitute. Be sure to include white space between the function and/or column name and the alias.

Concluding the introduction to SQL **select** statements, the use of concatenation and entering the actual statements was discussed. Columns can be concatenated together using the double-pipe (||) delimiter. This operation is useful for placing information closer together, or to use special characters to separate the output, such as commas or others. The SQL statement itself is entered using the SQL*Plus tool. If a user makes an error while typing in the line of SQL, the user can use the BACKSPACE key to erase characters until he or she reaches the mistake; however, this approach only works if the user is still on the same line in the SQL entry buffer. If the user has already proceeded to another line, or if he or she has already tried to execute the command, then he or she can type in the number corresponding to the line to be corrected to **select** that line for editing. Then, the user can type in the change command, abbreviated **c/old/new**, where **old** is the existing version of the string containing the mistake, and **new** is the correction. If this all sounds complicated, the user can simply type **edit**, or **ed** from the prompt in SQL*Plus, and Oracle will immediately bring up the user's favorite text editor. The text editor used here can be specified or changed with the **define_editor="**_youreditor_**"** command.

The number or order of selected rows from the database can be limited with various options. The first option discussed is **order by**. This is a clause that allows the user to specify two things—the first is a column on which to list the data in order, the second is whether Oracle should use ascending or descending order. Usage of the **order by** clause can make output from an Oracle **select** statement more readable, since there is no guarantee that the data in Oracle will be stored in any particular order.

The second means of limiting selected output is the **where** clause. Proper use of this clause is key to successful usage of Oracle and SQL. In the **where** clause, the user can specify one or more comparison criteria that must be met by the data in a table in order for Oracle to select the row. A comparison consists of two elements that are compared using a comparison operator, which may consist of a logic operator such as equality (=), inequality (<>,!=, or ^=), less than (<) or greater than (>), or a combination of less or greater than and equality. Alternatively, the user can also utilize special comparison operators that enable for pattern matches using **like %**, range scans using **between** x **and** y, or fuzzy logic with the **soundex**(x) = **soundex**(y) statement. In addition, one or more comparison operations may be specified in the **where** clause, joined together with **and** or the **or** operator, or preceded by **not**.

Data selected in Oracle can be modified with the use of several functions available in Oracle. These functions may work on many different types of data, as is the case with **nvl( )** functions called **decode( )**, **greatest( )**, or **least( )**. Alternatively, their use may be limited to a particular datatype. These functions may be divided into categories based on the types of data they can handle. Typically, the functions are categorized into text or character functions, math or number functions, and date functions.

Usage of Oracle built-in functions enables the user to perform many different operations. In general, the use of a function comprises specifying the name of the function and the passing of variables to the function. For example, to change the characters in a text string requires identifying the function that performs this task, followed by passing the function a value. To perform the task in this example, the following function call could be made: **upper**(*lowercase*).

The chapter also detailed the usage of all the functions available in Oracle, and provided examples for most of them. For brevity sake, they will not reappear here; however, it should be noted that many of the functions *can* be used together and in conjunction with the multitype functions like **decode( )**. For example, the usage of **decode(sqrt(x), 4, 'HARVEY',5,'JILL', 'BRAD')** is permitted. In essence, this functionality allows the user to incorporate the output from one function as input for another. An entire set of conversion functions are also available to change datatypes for values, or to create ciphers, or even to change the character sets used in order to move data onto different machines. Again, for the sake of brevity, the functions themselves are not listed here; however, it should be stated that the conversion functions can be used in conjunction with many of the other functions already named.

Two-Minute Drill

- Data is retrieved from Oracle using **select** statements.

- Syntax for a **select** statement consists of **select ...from...;**.

- When entering a **select** statement from the prompt using SQL*Plus, a semicolon(;) must be used to end the statement.

- Arithmetic operations can be used to perform math operations on data selected from a table, or on numbers using the DUAL table.

- The DUAL table is an empty table used to fulfill the syntactic requirements of SQL **select** statements.

- Values in columns for particular rows may be empty, or NULL.

- If a column contains the NULL value, the user can use the **nvl( )** function to return meaningful information instead of an empty field.

- Aliases can be used in place of the actual column name or to replace the appearance of the function name in the header.

- Output from two columns can be concatenated together using a double-pipe (||).

- SQL commands can be entered directly into SQL*Plus on the command line.

- If a mistake is made, the change (**c**/*old*/*new*) command is used.

- Alternatively, the **edit** (**ed**) command can be used to make changes in the user's favorite text editor.

- The user can specify a favorite text editor by issuing the **define_editor** command at the prompt.

- The **order by** clause in a **select** statement is a useful clause to incorporate sort order into the output of the file.

- Sort orders that can be used are **ascending** or **descending**, abbreviated as **asc** and **desc**. Order is determined by the column identified by the **order by** clause.

- The **where** clause is used in SQL queries to limit the data returned by the query.

- The **where** clauses contain comparison operations that determine whether a row will be returned by a query.

- There are several logical comparison operations, including =, >, >=, <, <=, <>, !=, ^=.

- In addition to the logical operations, there is a comparison operation for pattern matching called **like**. The % character is used to designate wildcards.

- There is also a range operation called **between**.

- There is also a fuzzy logic operation called **soundex**.

- Finally, the **where** clause can contain one or more comparison operations linked together by use of **and**, **or**, and preceded by **not**.

- Several SQL functions exist in Oracle.

- SQL functions are broken down into character functions, number functions, and date functions.

- A few functions are usable on many different types of data.

- There are also several conversion functions available for transforming data from text to numeric datatypes and back, numbers to dates and back, text to ROWID and back, etc.

Chapter Questions

1. **Which of the following statements contains an error?**

   A. select * from EMP where EMPID = 493945;

   B. select EMPID from EMP where EMPID = 493945;

   C. select EMPID from EMP;

   D. select EMPID where EMPID = 56949 and LASTNAME = 'SMITH';

2. **Which of the following correctly describes how to specify a column alias?**

   A. Place the alias at the beginning of the statement to describe the table.

   B. Place the alias after each column, separated by white space, to describe the column.

    C. Place the alias after each column, separated by a comma, to describe the column.

    D. Place the alias at the end of the statement to describe the table.

3. The NVL( ) function

    A. Assists in the distribution of output across multiple columns.

    B. Allows the user to specify alternate output for non-NULL column values.

    C. Allows the user to specify alternate output for NULL column values.

    D. Nullifies the value of the column output.

4. Output from a table called PLAYS with two columns, PLAY_NAME and AUTHOR, is shown next. Which of the following SQL statements produced it?

PLAY_TABLE

"Midsummer Night's Dream", SHAKESPEARE
"Waiting For Godot", BECKETT
"The Glass Menagerie", WILLIAMS

    A. select PLAY_NAME‖ AUTHOR **from** PLAYS;

    B. select PLAY_NAME, AUTHOR **from** PLAYS;

    C. select PLAY_NAME‖', ' ‖ AUTHOR **from** PLAYS;

    D. select PLAY_NAME‖', ' ‖ AUTHOR **play_table from** PLAYS;

5. Issuing the DEFINE_EDITOR="emacs" will produce which outcome?

    A. The emacs editor will become the SQL*Plus default text editor.

    B. The emacs editor will start running immediately.

    C. The emacs editor will no longer be used by SQL*Plus as the default text editor.

    D. The emacs editor will be deleted from the system.

6. Which function can best be categorized as similar in function to an IF-THEN-ELSE statement?

   A. sqrt( )

   B. decode( )

   C. new_time( )

   D. rowidtochar( )

7. Which three of the following are number functions? (Choose three of the four)

   A. sinh( )

   B. to_number( )

   C. sqrt( )

   D. round( )

8. The user issues the following statement. What will be displayed if the EMPID selected is 60494?

   SELECT DECODE(empid,38475, "Terminated",60494, "LOA", "ACTIVE") FROM emp;

   A. 60494

   B. LOA

   C. Terminated

   D. ACTIVE

9. SELECT (TO_CHAR(NVL(SQRT(59483), "INVALID")) FROM DUAL is a valid SQL statement.

   A. TRUE

   B. FALSE

10. **The appropriate table to use when performing arithmetic calculations on values defined within the SELECT statement (not pulled from a table column) is**

    A. EMP

    B. The table containing the column values

    C. DUAL

    D. An Oracle-defined table

11. **Which two of the following orders are used in ORDER BY clauses? (Choose two)**

    A. ABS

    B. ASC

    C. DESC

    D. DISC

12. **Only one column can be used to define order in an ORDER BY clause.**

    A. TRUE

    B. FALSE

13. **Which of the following lines in the SELECT statement here contain an error?**

    A. select decode(EMPID, 58385, "INACTIVE", "ACTIVE") empid

    B. from EMP

    C. where substr(LASTNAME,1,1) > to_number('S')

    D. and EMPID > 02000

    E. order by EMPID desc, lastname asc;

    F. There are no errors in this statement.

Answers to Chapter Questions

1. D. **select** EMPID **where** EMPID = 56949 **and** LASTNAME = 'SMITH';

Explanation   There is no **from** clause in this statement. Although a **select** statement can be issued without a **where** clause, no **select** statement can be executed without a **from** clause specified. For that reason, the DUAL table exists to satisfy the **from** clause in situations where the user defines all data needed within the statement.

2. B. Place the alias after each column, separated by white space, to describe the column.

Explanation   Aliases do not describe tables, they describe columns, which eliminates choices A and D. Commas in the **select** statement separate each column selected from one another. If a column alias appeared after a column, then Oracle would either select the wrong column name based on information provided in the alias or return an error.

3. C. Allows the user to specify alternate output for NULL column values.

Explanation   The **nvl( )** function is a simple **if-then** operation that tests column value output to see if it is NULL. If it is, then **nvl( )** substitutes the NULL value with the default value specified. Since this function only operates on one column per call to **nvl( )**, choice A is incorrect. Choice C is incorrect because it is the logical opposite of choice B. Choice D is incorrect because **nvl( )** is designed to substitute actual values for situations where null is present, not nullify data.

4. D. **select** PLAY_NAME||', ' || AUTHOR **play_table from** PLAYS;

Explanation   This question illustrates the need to do careful reading. Since the output specified for the question contained a column alias for the output of the statement, choice D is the only one that is correct, even though choice C also performed the correct calculation. Choice A is incorrect because it specified an inaccurate concatenation method, and choice B is wrong because it doesn't specify concatenation at all.

5. A. The emacs editor will become the SQL*Plus default text editor.

Explanation The **define_editor** statement is designed to define the default text editor in SQL*Plus. Changing the definition will not start or stop the editor specified from running, which eliminates B and D. Choice C is the logical opposite of choice A and therefore is incorrect.

6. B. decode( )

Explanation The **decode( )** function is a full-fledged **if-then-else** statement that can support manipulation of output values for several different cases plus a default. The **sqrt** statement simply calculates square roots, eliminating choice A. Choice C is incorrect because **new_time( )** is a date function that converts a time in one time zone to a time in another time zone. Choice D is incorrect because it is a simple conversion operation.

7. A, C, and D. sinh( ), sqrt( ), and round( )

Explanation The only function in this list is the **to_number( )** function, which is a conversion operation. Several questions of this type appear throughout the OCP exams, whereby the test taker will choose multiple answers. For more information about number functions, refer to the discussion or examples of their usage.

8. B. LOA

Explanation The **decode( )** statement has a provision in it that will return LOA if the *empid* in the row matches the **empid** specified for that case, which also eliminates choice D. Also, since a default value is specified by the **decode( )**, there will never be an EMPID returned by this query. Therefore, choice A is incorrect. Choice C is also eliminated because Terminated is only displayed when 38475 is the column value.

9. A.   TRUE

Explanation   Functions such as these can be used in conjunction with one another.

10. C.   DUAL

Explanation   When all data to be processed by the query is present in the statement, and no data shall be pulled from the database, users typically specify the DUAL table to fulfill the syntactic requirements of the **from** clause.

11. B and C.   ASC and DESC

Explanation   The **abs( )** function is the absolute value function, which eliminates choice A. The **disc( )** function is not an actual option either, eliminating choice D.

12. B.   FALSE

Explanation   Multiple columns can be used to define order in **order by** statements.

13. C.   **where substr(LASTNAME,1,1) > to_number('S')**

Explanation   Characters that are alphabetic like S cannot be converted into numbers. When this statement is run, it will produce an error on this line.

CHAPTER
2

Advanced Data
Selection in Oracle

n this chapter, you will understand and demonstrate knowledge in the following areas:

- Displaying data from multiple tables
- Group functions and their uses
- Using subqueries
- Using runtime variables

The previous chapter covered the basics of **select** statements in order to get the user started with SQL and with Oracle. Data selection is probably the most common operation executed by users of an Oracle database. There are many advanced techniques for selecting the data the user needs to understand. This understanding includes mastery of such tasks as ad-hoc reporting, screen data population, and other types of work that requires selecting data. This chapter will cover the advanced topics of Oracle data selection. The following areas of SQL **select** statements will be discussed. The first area of understanding discussed in this chapter is the table join. The chapter will cover how users can write **select** statements to access data from more than one table. The discussion will also cover how the user can create joins that capture data from different tables even when the information in the two tables does not correspond completely. Finally, the use of table self joins will be discussed. The chapter also introduces the **group by** clause used in **select** statements and group functions. Use of the subquery is another area covered in this chapter. The writing of subqueries and different situations where subqueries are useful is presented. Finally, specification and use of variables is presented. The material in this chapter will complete the user's knowledge of data selection and also comprises 22 percent of OCP Exam 1.

Displaying Data from Multiple Tables

In this section, you will cover the following areas related to displaying data from multiple tables:

- **Select** statements to join data from more than one table

- Creating outer joins

- Joining a table to itself

The typical database contains many tables. Some smaller databases may have only a dozen or so tables, while other databases may have hundreds. The common factor, however, is that no database has just one table that contains all data that the user will need. Oracle recognizes that the user may want data that resides in multiple tables drawn together in some meaningful way. In order to allow the user to have that data all in one place, Oracle allows the user to perform *table joins*. A table join is when data from one table is associated with data from another table according to a common column that appears in both tables. This column is called a *foreign key*. Foreign keys between two tables create a relationship between the two tables that is referred to as referential integrity.

TIP
*There must be at least one column shared between two tables in order to join the two tables in a **select** statement.*

Foreign keys work in the following way. If a column appears in two tables, a foreign key relationship can be defined between them if one of the columns appears as part of a primary key in one of the tables. A *primary key* is used in a table to identify the uniqueness of each row in a table. The table in which the column appears as a primary key is referred to as the *parent table*, while the column that references the other table in the relationship is often called the *child table*. Figure 2-1 demonstrates how the relationship may work in a database.

Select Statements That Join Data from More than One Table

When a foreign-key relationship exists between several tables, then it is possible to merge the data in each table with data from another table to invent new meaning for the data in Oracle. This technique is accomplished with the use of a table join. As described in the last chapter, a **select** statement can have three parts: the **select** clause, the **from** clause, and the **where** clause. The **select** clause is where the user will list the column names

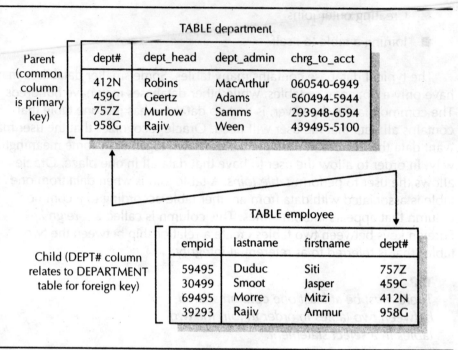

FIGURE 2-1. *Parent and child tables with foreign-key relationships*

he or she wants to view data from, along with any single-row functions and/or column aliases. The **from** clause gives the names of the tables from which the data would be selected. So far, data from only one table at a time has been selected. In a table join, two or more tables are named to specify the joined data. The final clause is the **where** clause, which contains comparison operations that will filter out the unwanted data from what the user wants to see. The comparison operations in a table join statement have another purpose—to describe how the data between two tables should be joined together.

```
SELECT a.antique_name, a.antique_cost,
a.storage_box_number, b.box_name, b.box_location
FROM antique a, storage_box b
WHERE a.antique_name in ('VICTROLA','CAMERA','RADIO')
AND a.storage_box_number = b.storage_box_number;
```

A.ANTIQUE_N	A.ANTIQ	A.STOR	B.BOX_NAME	B.BOX_LOCATION
VICTROLA	150.00	3	ALPHA-3	ALPHA BLDG
CAMERA	75.00	4	ALPHA-4	ALPHA BLDG
RADIO	200.00	4	ALPHA-4	ALPHA BLDG

Many important things are happening in this sample statement, the most fundamental of which is the table join. The **from** clause in this statement is the clearest indication that a table join statement is taking place. In this statement, the **from** clause contains two table names, each of which is followed by a letter. Table ANTIQUE in this example is followed by the letter A, while table STORAGE_BOX is followed by the letter B. This display demonstrates an interesting concept in Oracle—not only can the columns in a **select** statement have aliases, but the tables named in the **from** clause can have aliases as well. Table aliases have an important use in a table join statement, as given evidence in both the **select** and the **where** clauses of this example statement.

Often, tables with columns in common will have the same name for those columns. This common name can lead to ambiguity when the Oracle SQL processing mechanism attempts to parse the statement and resolve all database object names. If each column isn't linked to the particular tables identified in the **from** clause, Oracle will return an error. By specifying an alias for each table in the **from** clause, and then preceding each column in the database with the alias, the user can avoid ambiguity in his or her SQL statements while also avoiding the need to type out a table name each time a column is specified. The aliases, therefore, aren't necessary, but they do reduce the number of characters the user has to type each time a column is specified. The following code block illustrates the extra coding necessary when referencing columns if table aliases aren't used.

```
SELECT antique_name, antique_cost,
antique.storage_box_number, box_name, box_location
FROM antique, storage_box
WHERE antique_name in ('VICTROLA','CAMERA','RADIO')
AND antique.storage_box_number = storage_box.storage_box_number;
```

ANTIQUE_NAM	ANTIQUE	ANTIQU	BOX_NAME	BOX_LOCATION
VICTROLA	150.00	3	ALPHA-3	ALPHA BLDG
CAMERA	75.00	4	ALPHA-4	ALPHA BLDG
RADIO	200.00	4	ALPHA-4	ALPHA BLDG

As mentioned, eliminating ambiguity can be accomplished either by specifying the full table name before any column that appears in both tables or with the use of aliases. Remember also that neither the alias nor the full table name need be specified before a column that appears in only one table specified by the **from** clause. Ambiguity is only produced when the column appears in two or more of the tables specified in the **from** clause.

The next area to cover in creating queries that join data from one table to data from another table is the mechanism by which the join takes place. That mechanism is the use of comparison operations in the **where** clause of the statement. The **where** clause of the statement generally must include one comparison that links the data in one column of one table to the data from the same column in the other table. Without this link, all data from both tables is generated as output from the query in something referred to as a *Cartesian product*.

There are two possibilities available in order to link the data from one table column number to another. The alternatives are to perform equality comparisons or to perform inequality comparisons. The type of comparison used to produce the joined data often translates into the name of the join operation itself. In the situation where the tables are being joined based on an equality statement in the **where** clause, the join itself is often referred to as an "inner" join, or as an equijoin. An *inner join* will return data where the value in one column in one table equals the value in the column of the other table. In the situation where the tables are being joined based on an inequality statement in the **where** clause, typically the data returned may have less meaning unless a range of data is specified and the actual link between the two tables is an equality statement.

```
SELECT antique_name, antique_cost,
antique.storage_box_number, box_name, box_location
FROM antique, storage_box
WHERE antique_name IN ('VICTROLA','CAMERA','RADIO')
AND antique.storage_box_number < storage_box.storage_box_number;

ANTIQUE_NAM  ANTIQUE  ANTIQU  BOX_NAME  BOX_LOCATION
-----------  -------  ------  --------  ------------
VICTROLA     150.00   3       ALPHA-1   ALPHA BLDG
VICTROLA     150.00   3       ALPHA-2   ALPHA BLDG
VICTROLA     150.00   3       ALPHA-3   ALPHA BLDG
VICTROLA     150.00   3       ALPHA-4   ALPHA BLDG
```

```
CAMERA       75.00    4       ALPHA-1    ALPHA BLDG
CAMERA       75.00    4       ALPHA-2    ALPHA BLDG
CAMERA       75.00    4       ALPHA 3    ALPHA BLDG
CAMERA       75.00    4       ALPHA-4    ALPHA BLDG
RADIO       200.00    4       ALPHA-1    ALPHA BLDG
RADIO       200.00    4       ALPHA-2    ALPHA BLDG
RADIO       200.00    4       ALPHA-3    ALPHA BLDG
RADIO       200.00    4       ALPHA-4    ALPHA BLDG
```

How does Oracle determine what data should be returned by this query? When Oracle tries to evaluate the second clause in the statement, it may look at the data in the ANTIQUE table, one at a time, and determine which values in the STORAGE_BOX table have a greater values set for STORAGE_BOX_NUMBER. If the value for that column in the first row of ANTIQUE is 2, then there may be several rows in STORAGE_BOX that have STORAGE_BOX_NUMBER set to values greater than 2. However, in the second row of the ANTIQUE table, the value set to the STORAGE_BOX_ NUMBER might be 1, returning almost every row in the STORAGE_BOX table because the values for STORAGE_BOX_NUMBER in that table are all greater than 1. The point of this example is to illustrate that when an inequality operation is specified as part of the **where** clause joining data from one table to another, there is no way to guarantee that the inequality operation will be satisfied for *all* values in the column for *both* tables. There is also a high possibility that the data returned by an inequality join will look suspiciously like a Cartesian product.

A better alternative for drawing data from a table that satisfies an inequality operation but does not produce a Cartesian product is to specify the inequality operation outside the comparison that produces the join as shown here:

```
SELECT antique_name, antique_cost,
antique.storage_box_number, box_name, box_location
FROM antique, storage_box
WHERE box_location in ('VICTROLA','CAMERA','RADIO')
AND antique.storage_box_number = storage_box.storage_box_number
AND antique.storage_box_number > 3;

ANTIQUE_NAM  ANTIQUE  ANTIQU  BOX_NAME  BOX_LOCATION
-----------  -------  ------  --------  ------------
CAMERA       75.00    4       ALPHA-4   ALPHA BLDG
RADIO       200.00    4       ALPHA-4   ALPHA BLDG
```

This **select** statement will produce all results joined properly using the equality operation to link the rows of two tables in an inner join, while also satisfying the less-than comparison needed to obtain data for only those storage boxes less than box #2. In general, it is best to specify an equality operation for the two columns linking the tables for the join, followed by an inequality operation on the same column in *one* of the tables to filter the number of rows that will be linked in the join.

Generally speaking, the query used to produce a table join must contain the right number of equality operations to avoid a Cartesian product. If the number of tables to be joined equals *N*, the user should remember to include at least *N*-1 equality conditions in the **select** statement so that each column in each table that exists in another table is referenced *at least once*.

TIP

*For N joined tables, you need at least N-1 join conditions in the **select** statement in order to avoid a Cartesian product.*

Exercises

1. What is a table join? How is a table join produced?

2. Why is it important to use equality operations when creating a table join?

3. How many equality conditions are required to join three tables? Six tables? Twenty tables?

Creating Outer Joins

In some cases, however, the user needs some measure of inequality on the joined columns of a table join operation in order to produce the data required in the return set. Consider, for example, that the user in this antique store wanted to see all Victrolas not in storage boxes as well as those that are boxed. One limitation of "inner" join or equijoin statements is that they will not return data from either table unless there is a common value in both columns for both tables on which to make the join.

```
SELECT antique_name, antique_cost,
antique.storage_box_number, box_name, box_location
```

```
FROM antique, storage_box
WHERE box_location = 'VICTROLA'
AND antique.storage_box_number = storage_box.storage_box_number;
```

```
ANTIQUE_NAM  ANTIQUE  ANTIQU  BOX_NAME  BOX_LOCATION
-----------  -------  ------  --------  ------------
VICTROLA     150.00   3       ALPHA-3   ALPHA BLDG
```

Notice that in this example, only Victrolas that have corresponding storage box entries in the STORAGE_BOX table will be included in the return set. In an attempt to obtain a list of Victrolas that are not boxed, the user then issues the following nonjoin query:

```
SELECT antique_name, antique_cost
FROM antique;
```

```
ANTIQUE_NAM ANTIQUE
----------- -------
VICTROLA    150.00
VICTROLA    90.00
VICTROLA    45.00
```

This query is a little closer to the mark, returning data on antique Victrolas regardless of whether or not they are boxed, but the user still needs to see storage box information for those Victrolas that are boxed. In order to force the join to return data from one table even if there is no corresponding record in the other table, the user can specify an *outer join* operation. The previous inner join statement can be modified in the following way to show records in the ANTIQUE table that have no corresponding record in the STORAGE_BOX table:

```
SELECT antique_name, antique_cost,
antique.storage_box_number, box_name, box_location
FROM antique, storage_box
WHERE box_location = 'VICTROLA'
AND antique.storage_box_number = storage_box.storage_box_number (+);
```

```
ANTIQUE_NAM  ANTIQUE  ANTIQU  BOX_NAME  BOX_LOCATION
-----------  -------  ------  --------  ------------
VICTROLA     150.00   3       ALPHA-3   ALPHA BLDG
VICTROLA     90.00
VICTROLA     75.00
```

Outer join statements such as these produce result sets that are "outside" the join criteria as well as inside it. Notice the special **(+)** marker at the end of the comparison that forms the join. This marker denotes which column can have null data corresponding to the non-null values in the other table. In the previous example, the outer join marker is on the side of the STORAGE_BOX table, meaning that data in the ANTIQUE table can correspond either to values in STORAGE_BOX or to null if there is no corresponding value in STORAGE_BOX.

TIP
*For "inner" joins, there must be shared values in the common column in order for the row in either table to be returned by the **select** statement.*

Exercises

1. How does an outer join remedy the situation where a lack of corresponding values in the shared column of two tables causes rows from neither table to be selected?

2. What is the special character used to denote outer joins?

Joining a Table to Itself

In special situations, it may be necessary for the user to perform a join using only one table. This task can be useful in certain cases where there is a possibility that some slight difference exists between two rows that would otherwise be duplicate records. If the user wants to perform a self join on a table, the user should utilize the table alias method described earlier in the chapter to specify the same table for Oracle to understand that a self join is being performed.

The following example of a self join shows how to use this technique properly. For the example, assume that there is a table called TEST_RESULTS on which users at various locations administer a test for employees of a large corporation. The test is designed to determine if a given employee is ready for promotion. If an employee fails the test, he or she must wait a full year before taking the test again. It is discovered that there is a bug in the system that allowed some employees to circumvent the rule by taking the test at a different location. Now, management wants to find out which employees have taken the test more than once in the past year. The columns in the TEST_RESULTS table are listed as follows: EMPID, LOCATION, DATE, and SCORE. In order to determine if an employee has taken the test twice in the last year, the user could issue the following SQL **select** that uses self join techniques:

```
SELECT a.empid, a.location, a.date, b.location, b.date
FROM test_results a, test_results b
WHERE a.empid = b.empid
AND a.location <> b.location
AND a.date > sysdate-365
AND b.date > sysdate-365;
```

A.EMPID	A.LOCATION	A.DATE	B.LOCATION	B.DATE
94839	St. John	04-NOV-97	Wendt	03-JAN-98
04030	Stridberg	27-JUN-97	Wendt	03-AUG-97
59393	St. John	20-SEP-97	Wendt	04-OCT-97

The output from this self join shows that three employees took the test in different locations within the last 12 months. The clause used to determine DATE highlights the flexibility inherent in Oracle's internal method for storing DATE datatypes and **sysdate** as numbers representing the number of days since the beginning of the Julian calendar. The storage method Oracle uses allows the user to perform simple mathematical operations on dates to obtain other dates without worrying about taking into account factors like the number of days in months between the old date and new, whether the year in question is a leap year, etc.

Those users who must perform self joins on tables should be extremely cautious about doing so in order to avoid performance issues or Cartesian products. The required number of equality operations is usually at least *two* in the situation of self joins, simply because only using one equality condition usually does not limit the output of a self join to the degree that the output must be limited in order to obtain meaningful information.

TIP
*The number of equality operations required in the **where** clause of a self join should usually be greater than or equal to 2.*

It should be stated that a self join typically requires a long time to execute, because Oracle must necessarily read all data for each table twice sequentially. Ordinarily, Oracle will read data from two different tables to perform the join, but since the operation in this case is a self join, all data comes from one table. Also, the user must be careful with self joins to ensure that a Cartesian product is not produced. Without a proper comparison operation set up in the **where** clause, the user may wind up with many copies of every row in the table returned, which will certainly run for a long time and produce a lot of unnecessary output.

Exercises

1. What is a self join? How might a self join be used?

2. How many equality operations should be used to create a self join?

3. What performance issues do self joins present?

Group Functions and Their Uses

In this section, you will cover the following areas related to group functions and their uses:

-   Identifying available group functions
-   Using group functions
-   Using the **group by** clause
-   Excluding group data with **having**

A group function allows the user to perform a data operation on several values in a column of data as though the column was one collective group of data. These functions are called group functions also, because they are often used in a special clause of **select** statements called a **group by** clause. A more complete discussion of the **group by** clause appears in the second discussion of this section.

Identifying Available Group Functions

An important advantage group functions offer over single-row functions is that group functions can operate on several rows at a time. This advantage allows functions to be used that calculate figures like averages and standard deviation. The list of available group functions appears here:

avg(x)   Average for all x column values returned by the **select** statement

count(x)   A sum of all rows returned by the **select** statement for column x

max(x)   The maximum value in column x for all rows returned by the **select** statement

min(x)   The minimum value in column x for all rows returned by the **select** statement

stddev(x)   The standard deviation for all values in column x in all rows returned by **select** statements

sum(x)   The sum of all values in column x in all rows returned by the **select** statement

variance(x)   The variance for all values in column x in all rows returned by **select** statements

Exercises

1. What is a group function? How do they differ from single-row functions?

2. Name several group functions.

Using Group Functions

Examples of output from each of the following group functions appear over the next several pages. Since these functions require the use of several rows of data, the EMP table from the previous chapter will be used frequently. The EMP table appears in Table 2-1.

The first function considered is the **avg( )** function. The **avg( )** function takes the values for a column on rows returned by the query and calculates the average value for that column. Based on the data from the previous table, the **avg( )** function on the SALARY column produces the following result:

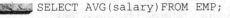

```
SELECT AVG(salary) FROM EMP;

AVG(salary)
-----------
74000
```

The second grouping function that will be illustrated is the **count( )** function. This function is bound to become the cornerstone of any Oracle professional's repertoire. The **count( )** function returns a row count for the table given certain column names and/or **select** criteria. It is worth learning the best way to use this command. There are many different ways to use the **count( )** function, three of which are listed next. Note that the fastest way to execute **count( )** is to pass a value that resolves quickly in the SQL processing mechanism. Some values that resolve quickly are integers and the ROWID pseudocolumn.

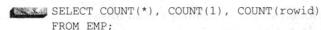

```
SELECT COUNT(*), COUNT(1), COUNT(rowid)
FROM EMP;

COUNT(*)   COUNT(1) COUNT(rowid)
--------   -------- ------------
5          5        5
```

Empid	Lastname	Firstname	Salary
39334	Smith	Gina	75,000
49539	Qian	Lee	90,000
60403	Harper	Rod	45,000
02039	Walla	Rajendra	60,000
49392	Spanky	Stacy	100,000

TABLE 2-1. *The EMP Table*

The asterisk (*) in the previous query is a wildcard variable that indicates all columns in all rows in the table. For better performance, this wildcard should not generally be used because the Oracle SQL processing mechanism must first resolve all column names in the table, a step that is unnecessary if one is simply trying to count rows. Notice that one of these examples uses the special pseudocolumn called ROWID. A ROWID is a special value that uniquely identifies each row. In the next unit covering OCP Exam 2, the use of ROWID to identify the location on disk of row data will be explained. Each row in a table has one unique ROWID. The ROWID is not actually part of the table; rather, ROWID is a piece of information stored internally within Oracle. Thus, it is considered a "pseudocolumn."

TIP
*Do not use **count(*)** to determine the number of rows in a table. Use **count(1)** or **count(ROWID)** instead. These options are faster because they bypass some unnecessary operations in Oracle's SQL processing mechanism.*

The next pair of grouping functions to be covered are the **max( )/min( )** functions. The **max( )** function determines the largest value for the column passed, while **min( )** determines the smallest value for the column passed.

```
SELECT MAX(salary), MIN(salary) FROM EMP;

MAX(salary)  MIN(salary)
-----------  -----------
100000       45000
```

Another group function details the **variance( )** of all values in a column. The variance of a set of numbers represents a measure of variability—the mean squared deviation from the expected value for the set.

```
SELECT VARIANCE(salary) FROM EMP;

VARIANCE(salary)
----------------
492500000
```

Related to **variance( )** is the next example in this section—the **stddev( )** function. It produces the standard deviation for values in the column specified. *Standard deviation* is the square root of the variance for the set—a measure of variability. The number produced represents the margin of variance or error for a set of numbers.

```
SELECT STDDEV(salary) FROM EMP;

STDDEV(salary)
--------------
22192.341
```

The final group function is used commonly in simple accounting reports. The **sum( )** function gives the total of all values in a column.

```
SELECT SUM(salary) FROM EMP;

SUM(salary)
-----------
370000
```

In general, the group functions will operate on columns of datatype NUMBER because many of the functions they represent in mathematics are numeric operations. For example, it makes little sense to take the standard deviation for a set of 12 words, unless the user wants to take the standard deviation of the length of those words by combining the use of the **length( )** function with the **stddev( )** function. There is one notable exception to this general rule, though—that exception is the **count( )** function. The **count( )** function will operate on a column of any datatype.

Exercises

1. How are group functions incorporated into **select** statements? How many rows of output can usually be expected from a query using a group function?

2. What is ROWID? Is ROWID stored in a table?

Using the GROUP BY Clause

Sometimes it gives more meaning to the output of a **select** statement to collect data into logical groupings. For example, to perform calculations on the populations of several cities in America, the user may issue a query against all records in the CITIES table. The **select** statements, such as ones containing **order by**, may work well for specific queries against particular cities in this table, such as listing data in order based on an alphabetized list of cities and states such as the SQL statement listed:

```
SELECT state, city, population
FROM cities
ORDER BY state, city;

STATE              CITY             POPULATION
---------------    --------------   ----------
ALABAMA            AARDVARK         12,560
ALABAMA            BARNARD          176,000
...
```

Consider the following example, however. There arises a situation where a user wants to perform specific calculations on the cities in each state separately. For example, assume the user wants to find out the average city population for each of the states listed on the table. This **select** statement works fine for producing the raw data the user needs to calculate the average city population for each state; however, there is an easier way for the user to determine this information based on usage of the **group by** clause in SQL statements.

```
SELECT state, AVG(population)
FROM CITIES
GROUP BY state
ORDER BY state;

STATE              AVG(POPULA
-----------------  ----------
ALABAMA            49494
```

```
ALASKA          14349
NEW YORK        85030
ARIZONA         35003
CALIFORNIA      65040
...
```

The **group by** clause in this example saves the user from performing a great deal of work by hand. Instead, Oracle shoulders most of the work and outputs to the user only the results he or she needs. The **group by** clause works well in many situations where a user wants to report calculations on data according to groups or categories. However, the user should be careful to always place the column on which the **group by** clause will group the data first in the list of columns specified by the **select** clause. If the columns being grouped using the **group by** clause are not in the same sequential order and first in the list of columns selected, then the user could encounter one of the most problematic Oracle error messages: **ORA-00937 – Not a single group set function**.

To illustrate the usage of **group by** in another example, assume that the user now wants to calculate the average salary for all employees in a corporation by department. The EMP table contains the following columns: EMPID, LASTNAME, FIRSTNAME, SALARY, and DEPT. However, in addition to obtaining the average employee salary by department, the user wants the information in order from highest average salary to lowest.

```
SELECT dept, AVG(salary)
FROM emp
GROUP BY dept
ORDER BY avg(salary) DESC;

DEPT   AVG(SALARY)
----   -----------
201B   103020
594C   94030
493W   71039
201C   50403
```

In this example, the **order by** clause was combined with the **group by** clause to create a special order for the output. This order gives the data some additional meaning to the user who requested its display. The user is not limited to grouping data by only one selected column, either. If the user desires, more than one column can be used in the **group by** statement—

provided that the order of columns specified in the **select** clause of the query matches the order of columns specified in the **group by** clause. The following example illustrates proper usage of **group by** with more than one column specified. It assumes the addition of a column, COUNTRY, which names the country containing the city. Notice that the columns named in the **group by** clause are in the same order as they are named in the **select** clause. It often must be set up in this way in order to avoid errors.

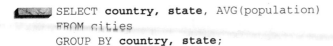

```
SELECT country, state, AVG(population)
FROM cities
GROUP BY country, state;
```

Exercises

1. How is the **group by** clause of a **select** statement used?

2. What happens when the columns being grouped using the **group by** clause are not in the same sequential order and first in the list of columns selected?

Excluding GROUP Data with HAVING

One initial problem encountered when using the **group by** statement is that once the data is grouped, the user must then analyze the data returned by the **group by** statement in order to determine which groups are relevant and which are not. It is sometimes useful to the user to *weed out* unwanted data. For example, in the final query from the previous section, suppose the user only wanted to see which departments paid an average salary of $80,000 per year. In effect, the user is attempting to put a **where** clause on the **group by** clause.

This effect can be gained with the use of a special clause in Oracle called **having**. This clause acts as a modified **where** clause that only applies to the resultant rows generated by the **group by** expression. Consider the application of the previous modifications to the query of employee salary by department. If the user wants to view only those departments whose employees make an average of $80,000 or more, the user may want to issue the following query. The **having** clause in this case is used to eliminate the departments whose average salary is under $80,000. Notice that this selectivity cannot easily be accomplished with an ordinary **where** clause, because the **where** clause is selective to the precision of individual rows while the user requires selectivity for eliminating groups of rows.

```
SELECT dept, AVG(salary)
FROM emp
GROUP BY dept HAVING avg(salary)>80000
ORDER BY avg(salary) DESC;

DEPT   AVG(SALARY)
----   -----------
201B   103020
705B   94030
```

In this query, the user has successfully limited output on the **group by** rows by using the **having** clause. But the **having** clause need not be limited by some arbitrary number that the user must key in manually. In addition to performing a comparison operation on a constant value, the **having** clause can perform a special operation to derive the required data with the use of a *subquery*. A subquery is another SQL query embedded within the overarching query being executed by the user that derives some special value required by a part of the entire query. Subqueries are useful to incorporate into **select** statements when there is a need for valid value data that the user does not actually know the value of, but knows the manner in which to obtain it. Take, for example, that the user in this situation would like to compare her salary with that of the rest of the departments in the company. Unfortunately, the user doesn't know her salary, but the user does know her empid is 49394. In order to execute the following query again, only modified according to the current needs of the user, the following statement can be utilized:

```
SELECT dept, AVG(salary)
FROM emp
GROUP BY dept HAVING AVG(salary)>(SELECT salary FROM emp WHERE empid=49394)
ORDER BY avg(salary) DESC;

DEPT   AVG(SALARY)
----   -----------
201B   103020
569A   96120
```

Exercises

1. What is the **having** clause, and what function does it serve?
2. How can the user specify values to fulfill **having** criteria without actually knowing what the values themselves are?

Using Subqueries

In this section, you will cover the following topics related to using subqueries:

■ Nested subqueries

■ Subqueries in other DML situations

■ Putting data in order with subqueries

The usage of subqueries need not be limited to the **having** clause of a **group by** statement. The power of subqueries to determine unknown criteria based on known methods for obtaining it can be used in many different ways. Of particular importance in using subqueries is incorporating them properly into comparison operations of the **where** clause. There are several different ways to include subqueries in **where** statements. The most common method used is through the equality comparison operation, or with the **in** comparison, which is in itself similar to a **case** statement offered in many programming languages because the equality can be established with one element in the group. Another useful item for inclusion of a subquery in the **where** clause of a **select** statement is the **exists** clause. When a user specifies the **exists** operation in a **where** clause, the user must include a subquery that satisfies the **exists** operation. If the subquery returns data, then the **exists** operation returns TRUE. If not, the **exists** operation returns FALSE. These and other uses for subqueries will be discussed shortly.

TIP
*A subquery is a "query within a query," a **select** statement nested within a **select** statement designed to limit the selected output of the parent query by producing an intermediate result set of some sort.*

Nested Subqueries

Subqueries can be used to obtain search criteria for **select** statements. The way subqueries work is as follows. The **where** clause in a **select** statement has one or more comparison operations. Each comparison operation can contain the name of a column on the left side and a given search method to obtain unknown data on the right side by means of a subquery.

```
SELECT empid, dept, salary
FROM emp
WHERE dept = (select dept from emp where empid = 78483);
```

The portion of the SQL statement that is highlighted is the subquery portion of the statement. On one side is the DEPT column, on which a comparison will be based to determine the result dataset. On the other side is the unknown search criteria, defined by the subquery. At the time this **select** statement is submitted, Oracle will process the subquery *first* in order to resolve all unknown search criteria, then feed that resolved criteria to the outer query. The outer query then can resolve the dataset it is supposed to return.

Similar to the outer query, the subquery itself can contain subqueries. This process is known as nested subqueries. Consider the following example. There is a user trying to determine the salary of employees in the same department as an employee who has submitted an expensive invoice for payment on the company's relocation expenditure system. The tables involved in this **select** statement are the EMP table, which has been described, and the INVOICE table, which consists of the following columns: INVOICE_NUMBER, EMPID, INVOICE_AMT, and PAY_DATE. The only information the user has about the employee they are looking for is the invoice number the employee submitted for relocation expenses, which is 5640.

```
SELECT e.empid, e.salary
FROM emp e
WHERE e.dept =
(SELECT dept FROM emp WHERE empid =
(SELECT empid FROM invoice WHERE invoice_number = 5640));
```

In this statement, there are two subqueries, the subquery to the main **select** statement highlighted in **bold**, and the nested subquery in *italics*. Each subquery produces unknown criteria to fulfill the main search occurring in the **select** statement, the first producing the department information and the second producing the employee ID for the person submitting the invoice. These two details are crucial for completing the **select** statement, yet the data is unknown to the user at the time the **select** statement is issued. Oracle must first resolve the innermost nested subquery in *italics* to resolve the next level. After that, Oracle will resolve the subquery level in **bold** to resolve the outermost level of the **select** statement issued.

Subqueries can be nested to a surprisingly deep level. The rule of thumb used to be that the user could nest 16 or more subqueries into a **select** statement. In reality, the number of nested subqueries can be far higher. However, if a user needs to nest more than five subqueries, he or she may want to consider writing the query in PL/SQL or in a programming language like PRO*C or PRO*COBOL or some other programming language that allows embedded SQL statements and cursors. At the very least, the user may want to consider rewriting a query that makes heavy use of subqueries into a query that performs extensive join operations as well. The reason these recommendations are made is because database performance degrades substantially after about that level when processing nested subqueries on all but the most powerful database servers and mainframes. At the very least, the user should check carefully to ensure that there are no performance issues within the nested query that may slow down database performance significantly.

Exercises

1. What is a subquery? When might a user want to incorporate a subquery into a database **select** statement?

2. What are some situations where a **where** clause may be sufficient in place of a subquery?

3. What performance issues might revolve around the use of subqueries?

Subqueries in Other DML Situations

The previous discussion covered many areas of using subqueries in data manipulation statements. However, that discussion barely scratches the surface on the power of subqueries. A subquery can be used for complicated step-by-step joins of data that use data from one subquery to feed into the processing of its immediate parent. However, subqueries also allow the user to "jump" subquery levels to perform incredibly complex, almost counterintuitive processing that necessarily must involve some discussion of a programming concept known as *variable scope*. For those users not familiar with the term, variable scope refers to the availability or "viewability" of data in certain variables at certain times.

Sometimes a variable has a local scope. That is to say that the variable can only be seen when the current block of code is being executed. For the purposes of this discussion, the user can consider the columns in comparison operations named in subqueries to be variables whose "scope" is *local* to the query. Additionally, there is another type of scope, called global scope. In addition to a variable having local scope within the subquery where it appears, the variable also has *global* scope in all subqueries to that query. In the previous **select** statement example, all variables or columns named in comparison operations in the outermost **select** operation are local to that operation and global to all nested subqueries, given in **bold** and *italics*. Additionally, all columns in the subquery detailed in **bold** are local to that query and global to the subquery listed in *italics*. Columns named in the query in *italics* are local to that query only; since there are no subqueries to it, the columns in that query cannot be global. The nested query example from the previous discussion is featured in Figure 2-2.

TIP
The scope of a variable defines which code blocks will have the variable and its defined value available to it. There are two different types of variable scope—local and global. If a variable has global scope, then it and its value are available everywhere in the code block. If a variable has local scope, then it and its value are available only in the current code block running in the memory stack.

In certain cases, it may be useful for a subquery to refer to a global column value rather than a local one to obtain result data. The subquery architecture of Oracle allows the user to refer to global variables in

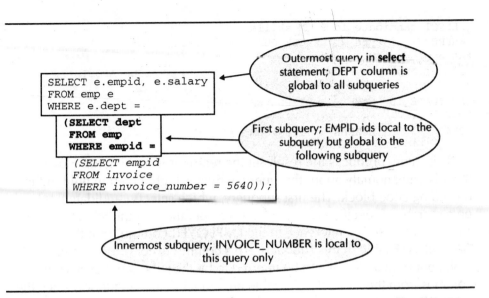

FIGURE 2-2.   *Nested subqueries and variable scope*

subqueries as well as local ones to produce more powerful queries. An example of this type of global scope usage, sometimes also referred to as *correlated subqueries*, is as follows. Assume that there is a recruiter for a national consulting firm who wants to find people in Minneapolis who are proficient in Oracle DBA skills. Furthermore, the recruiter only wants to see the names and home cities for people who are certified Oracle DBAs. The recruiter has at her disposal a nationwide resume search system with several tables. These tables include one called CANDIDATE, which contains the candidate ID, candidate name, salary requirement and current employer. Another table in this example is called SKILLS, where the candidate ID is matched with the skill(s) the candidate possesses. A third table, called COMPANIES, contains the names and home cities for companies that the consulting firm tries to draw their talent from. In order to find the names and locations of people who possess the abilities the recruiter requires, the recruiter may issue the following **select** statement against the national recruiting database:

```
SELECT  candidate_id, name, employer
FROM candidate
WHERE candidate_id IN
```

```
(SELECT candidate_id FROM skills
 WHERE skill_type = 'ORACLE DBA' AND certified = 'YES')
AND employer IN
(SELECT employer FROM companies WHERE city = 'MINNEAPOLIS');

CANDIDATE_ID  NAME      EMPLOYER
------------  --------  ---------------
60549         DURNAM    TransCom
```

This query produces the result set the recruiter is looking for. However, there is one anomaly about this query, which is highlighted in **bold** in the preceding code block. The first subquery, which selects candidate IDs based on a search for specific skills, performs its operation on the SKILLS table. Notice that there is a reference to the EMPLOYER column from the CANDIDATE table in this subquery. This column is not present in the SKILLS table, but nonetheless it can be referred to by the subquery because the columns from the CANDIDATE table are global to all subqueries, since the CANDIDATE table is in the outermost query of the **select** statement. Notice in the last subquery the use of the **in** keyword. Recall from Chapter 1 that the **in** operation allows the user to identify a set of values, any of which the column named in the **in** clause can equal in order to be part of the result set. Thus, if the **where** clause of the **select** statement contains **and** *number* **in (1,2,3)**, that means only the rows whose value in the NUMBER column are equal to 1, 2, or 3 will be part of the result set.

Another complicated possibility offered by subqueries is the use of the **exists** operation. Mentioned earlier, **exists** allows the user to specify the results of a **select** statement according to a special subquery operation. This **exists** operation returns TRUE or FALSE based on whether or not the subquery obtains data when it runs. An example of the usage for the **exists** subquery is related to a previous example of the relocation expenditure tracking system. The tables involved in this system are the EMP table, which has been described, and the INVOICE table, which consists of the following columns: INVOICE_NUMBER, EMPID, INVOICE_AMT, and PAY_DATE. Let's assume that the user wants to identify all the departments that have employees who have incurred relocation expenses in the past year.

```
SELECT distinct e.dept
FROM emp e
WHERE EXISTS
(SELECT i.empid FROM invoice i
  WHERE i.empid = e.empid AND i.pay_date > SYSDATE-365);
```

There are several new things that are worthy of note in this **select** statement. The first point to be made is that global scope variables are again incorporated in the subquery to produce meaningful results from that code. The second point to make is more about the general nature of **exists** statements. Oracle will go through every record in the EMP table to see if the EMPID matches that of a row in the INVOICE table. If there is a matching invoice, then the **exists** criteria is met and the department ID is added to the list of departments that will be returned. If not, then the **exists** criteria is not met and the record is not added to the list of departments that will be returned.

Notice that there is one other aspect of this query that has not been explained—the **distinct** keyword highlighted in bold in the **select** column clause of the outer portion of the query. This special keyword identifies a filter that Oracle will put on the data returned from the **exists** subquery. When **distinct** is used, Oracle will return only one row for a particular department, even if there are several employees in that department that have submitted relocation expenses within the past year. This **distinct** operation is useful for situations when the user wants a list of unique rows but anticipates that the query may return duplicate rows. The **distinct** operation removes duplicate rows from the result set before displaying that result to the user.

Exercises

1. Name a TRUE/FALSE operation that depends on the results of a subquery to determine its value.

2. What is variable scope? What is a local variable? What is a global variable?

3. What is the **distinct** keyword, and how is it used?

Putting Data in Order with Subqueries

As with other types of **select** statements, those statements that involve subqueries may also require some semblance of order in the data that is returned to the user. In the examples of subquery usage in the previous discussion, there may be a need to return the data in a particular order based on the columns selected by the outermost query. In this case, the user may simply want to add in the usage of the **order by** clause. The previous example of selecting the departments containing relocated employees could be modified as follows to produce the required department data in a particular order required by the user:

```
SELECT distinct e.dept
FROM emp e
WHERE EXISTS
(SELECT i.empid FROM invoice i
 WHERE i.empid = e.empid AND i.pay_date > SYSDATE-365)
ORDER BY dept;
```

As in using the **order by** statement in other situations, the data returned from a statement containing a subquery and the **order by** clause can be sorted into ascending or descending order. Furthermore, the user can incorporate order into the data returned by the subquery.

```
SELECT distinct e.dept
FROM emp e
WHERE EXISTS
(SELECT i.empid FROM invoice i
 WHERE i.empid = e.empid AND i.pay_date > SYSDATE-365)
ORDER BY i.empid;
```

In this example, the data returned from the **exists** subquery will appear in ascending order. However, since the fundamental point of the **exists** subquery is to determine whether the data exists that the subquery is looking for, it is probably considered overkill to return data in order from most subqueries. However, for those times when it might be useful, the user should understand that the potential does exist for returning data from a subquery in order.

In another example, the points made before about global and local scope will be reinforced. A recruiter from the national consulting firm mentioned

earlier tries to issue the following **select** statement, similar to the original
one discussed with that example:

```
SELECT candidate_id, name, employer
FROM candidate
WHERE candidate_id IN
(SELECT candidate_id FROM skills
 WHERE employer IN
   (SELECT employer FROM companies
    WHERE city = 'MINNEAPOLIS'))
ORDER BY skill_type;
```

When the recruiter attempts to issue the preceding **select** statement,
Oracle will execute the statement without error because the column
specified by the **order by** clause need not be part of the column list in the
select column list of the outermost **select** statement. However, within a
subquery it is possible for the user to create order based on the column
"variables" from the outer query. Order, then, can only be made on the
columns local or global to the query on which the **order by** clause is placed.

Exercise

What special clause is used to determine the order of output in a
select statement containing a subquery?

Using Runtime Variables

In this section, you will cover the following topics related to using
runtime variables:

- Entering variables at run time
- Automatic definition of runtime variables
- The **accept** command

SQL is an interpreted language. That is, there is no "executable code"
other than the statement the user enters into the command line. At the time
that statement is entered, Oracle's SQL processing mechanism works on
obtaining the data and returning it to the user. When Oracle is finished

returning the data, it is ready for the user to enter another statement. This interactive behavior is typical of interpreted programming languages.

```
SELECT name, salary, dept
FROM emp
WHERE empid = 40539;

NAME        SALARY    DEPT
--------    -------   ----
DURNAP      70560     450P
```

In the previous statement, the highlighted comparison operation designates that the data returned from this statement must correspond to the EMPID value specified. If the user were to run this statement again, the data returned would be exactly the same, provided that no portion of the record had been changed by the user issuing the query or any other user on the database. However, Oracle's interpretive SQL processing mechanism need not have everything defined for it at the time the user enters a SQL statement. In fact, there are features within the SQL processing mechanism of Oracle that allow the user to identify a specific value to be used for the execution of the query as a runtime variable. This feature permits some flexibility and reusability of SQL statements.

Entering Variables at Runtime

Consider, for example, the situation where a user must pull up data for several different employees manually for the purpose of reviewing some aspect of their data. Rather than rekeying the entire statement in with the EMPID value hard-coded into each statement, the user can substitute a variable specification that forces Oracle to prompt the user to enter a data value in order to let Oracle complete the statement. The earlier statement that returned data from the EMP table based on a hard-coded EMPID value can now be rewritten as the following query that allows the user to reuse the same code again and again with different values set for EMPID:

```
SELECT name, salary, dept
FROM emp
WHERE empid = &empid;

Enter value for empid: 40539
Old 3: WHERE empid = &empid;
```

```
New 3: WHERE empid = 40539;

NAME      SALARY    DEPT
------    -------   ----
DURNAP    70560     450P
```

After completing execution, the user now has the flexibility to rerun that same query, except now that user can specify a different EMPID without having to reenter the entire statement. Notice that a special *ampersand* (**&**) character precedes the name of the variable that will be specified at run time. The actual character can be changed with the **set define** command at the prompt. The user can reexecute the statement containing a runtime variable declaration by using the slash (/) command at the prompt in SQL*Plus.

```
Enter value for empid: 99706
Old 3: WHERE empid = &empid;
New 3: WHERE empid = 99706;

NAME      SALARY    DEPT
-------   -------   ----
MCCALL    103560    795P
```

This time, the user enters another value for the EMPID, and Oracle searches for data in the table based on the new value specified. This activity will go on as listed above until the user enters a new SQL statement. Notice that Oracle provides additional information back to the user after a value is entered for the runtime variable. The line as it appeared before is listed as the old value, while below the new value is presented as well. This presentation allows the user to know what data was changed by his or her input.

Exercises

1. What special character is used to specify a runtime variable?

2. How does Oracle prompt for runtime variable change?

3. What special character is used to reexecute a statement in SQL*Plus if the statement is stored in the current buffer? Can you recall the name of the file in which the SQL*Plus statement buffer is stored?

Automatic Definition of Runtime Variables

In some cases, however, it may not be useful to have the user entering new values for a runtime variable every time the statement executes. For example, assume that there is some onerous reporting process that a user must perform weekly on every person in a company. A great deal of value is added to the process by having a variable that can be specified at run time because the user can now simply reexecute the same statement over and over again, with new EMPID values each time. However, even this improvement is not streamlining the process as much as the user would like. Instead of running the statement over and over again with new values specified, the user could create a script that contained the SQL statement, preceded by a special statement that defined the input value automatically and triggered the execution of the statement automatically as well. Some basic reporting conventions will be presented in this example, such as **spool**. This command is used to designate to the Oracle database that all output generated by the following SQL activity should be redirected to an output file named after the parameter following **spool**:

```
SPOOL emp_info.out;
DEFINE VAR_EMPID = 34030

SELECT name, salary, dept
FROM emp
WHERE empid = &var_empid

UNDEFINE VAR_EMPID
DEFINE VAR_EMPID = 94059

SELECT name, salary, dept
FROM emp
WHERE empid = &var_empid
```

When the user executes the statements in this script, the time spent actually keying in values for the variables named in the SQL **select** statement is eliminated with the **define** statement. Notice, however, that in between each execution of the SQL statement there is a special statement using a command called **undefine**. In Oracle, the data that is defined with the **define** statement as corresponding to the variable will remain defined for the entire session unless the variable is undefined. By *undefining* a variable, the user allows another **define** statement to reuse the variable in another execution of the same or a different statement.

Exercises

1. How are variables defined within the SQL*Plus session to be used by **select** statements?

2. How can the user change a value set for a defined variable?

ACCEPT: Another Way to Define Variables

After executing a few example SQL statements that incorporate runtime variables, the user will notice that Oracle's method for identifying input, though not exactly cryptic, is fairly nonexpressive.

```
SELECT name, salary, dept
FROM emp
WHERE empid = &empid
AND dept = '&dept';

Enter value for &empid: 30403
Old 3: WHERE empid = &empid
New 3: WHERE empid = 30403

Enter value for &dept: 983X
Old 4: WHERE dept = '&dept'
New 4: WHERE dept = '983X'

NAME        SALARY      DEPT
--------    --------    ----
TIBBINS     56700       983X
```

The user need not stick with Oracle's default messaging to identify the need for input from a user. Instead, the user can incorporate into scripted SQL statements another method for the purpose of defining runtime variables. This other method allows the creator of the script to define a more expressive message that the user will see when Oracle prompts for input data. The name of the command that provides this functionality is the **accept** command. In order to use the **accept** command in a runtime SQL environment, the user can create a script in the following way. Assume for the sake of example that the user has created a script called **name_sal_dept.sql**, into which the following SQL statements are placed:

```
ACCEPT var_empid PROMPT 'Enter the Employee ID Now:'
ACCEPT var_dept PROMPT 'Enter the Employee Department Now:'

SELECT name, salary, dept
FROM emp
WHERE empid = &var_empid
AND dept = '&var_dept'
```

At this point, the user can run the script at the prompt using the following command syntax:

```
SQL> @emp_sal_dept
```

or

```
SQL> start emp_sal_dept.sql
```

Oracle will then execute the contents of the script. When Oracle needs to obtain the runtime value for the variables that the user identified in the SQL statement and with the **accept** statement, Oracle will use the prompt the user defined with the **prompt** clause of the **accept** statement.

```
SQL> @emp_sal_dept
Enter the Employee ID Now: 30403

SELECT name, salary, dept
FROM emp
WHERE empid = &var_empid
AND dept = '&var_dept'

Old 3: WHERE dept = '&dept'
New   3: WHERE empid = 30403

Enter the Employee Dept Now: 983X

SELECT name, salary, dept
FROM emp
WHERE empid = 30403
AND dept = '&var_dept'
```

```
Old 4: WHERE dept = '&dept'
New    4: WHERE dept = '983X'

NAME      SALARY   DEPT
--------  -------  ----
TIBBINS   56700    983X
```

Using the **accept** command can be preferable to Oracle's default output message in situations where the user wants to define a more accurate or specific prompt, or the user wants more output to display as the values are defined. In either case, the **accept** command can work well. Oracle offers a host of options for making powerful and complex SQL statements possible with runtime variables. These options covered can be used for both interactive SQL data selection and for SQL scripts.

Exercises

1. What is the **accept** command and how is it used?

2. What benefits does using the **accept** command offer?

Chapter Summary

This chapter continues the discussion presented last chapter of using the **select** statement to obtain data from the Oracle database. The **select** statements have many powerful features that allow the user to accomplish many tasks. Those features include joining data from multiple tables, grouping data output together and performing data operations on the groups of data, creating **select** statements that can use subqueries to obtain criteria that is unknown (but the method for obtaining it is known), and using variables that accept values at run time. Together, these areas comprise the advanced usage of SQL **select** statements. The material in this chapter comprises 22 percent of information questioned on OCP Exam 1.

The first area discussed in this chapter is how data from multiple tables can be joined together to create new meaning. Data in a table can be linked if there is a common or shared column between the two tables. This shared column is often referred to as a foreign key. Foreign keys establish a relationship between two tables that is referred to as a parent/child relationship. The parent table is typically the table in which the common column is defined as a primary key, or the column by which uniqueness is identified for rows in the table. The child table is typically the table in which the column is not the primary key, but refers to the primary key in the parent table.

There are two types of joins. One of those types is the "inner" join, also known as an equijoin. An inner join is a data join based on equality comparisons between common columns of two or more tables. An "outer" join is a nonequality join operation that allows the user to obtain output from a table even if there is no corresponding data for that record in the other table.

Joins are generated by using **select** statements in the following way. First, the columns desired in the result set are defined in the **select** clause of the statement. Those columns may or may not be preceded with a table definition, depending on whether or not the column appears in more than one table. If the common column is named differently in each table, then there is no need to identify the table name along with the column name, as Oracle will be able to distinguish which table the column belongs to automatically. However, if the column name is duplicated in two or more tables, then the user must specify which column he or she would like to obtain data from, since Oracle must be able to resolve any ambiguities clearly at the time the query is parsed. The columns from which data is selected are named in the **from** clause, and may optionally be followed by a table alias. A table alias is similar in principle to a column alias, which was discussed in the last chapter. The **where** clause of a join statement specifies how the join is performed. An inner join is created by specifying the two shared columns in each table in an equality comparison. An outer join is created in the same way, with an additional special marker placed by the column specification of the "outer" table, or the table in which there need not be data corresponding to rows in the other table for that data in the other table to be returned. That special marker is indicated by a (+). Finally, a table may be joined to itself with the use of table aliases. This activity is often done to determine if there are records in a table with slightly different information from rows that otherwise are duplicate rows.

Another advanced technique for data selection in Oracle databases is the use of grouping functions. Data can be grouped together in order to provide additional meaning to the data. Columns in a table can also be treated as a group in order to perform certain operations on them. These grouping functions often perform math operations such as averaging values or obtaining standard deviation on the dataset. Other group functions available on groups of data are **max( )**, **min( )**, **sum( )**, and **count( )**.

One common grouping operation performed on data for reporting purposes is a special clause in **select** statements called **group by**. This clause allows the user to segment output data and perform grouping operations on it. There is another special operation associated with grouping that acts as a **where** clause for which to limit the output produced by the selection. This limiting operation is designated by the **having** keyword. The criteria for including or excluding data using the **having** clause can be identified in one of two ways. Either criterion can be a hard-coded value or it can be based on the results of a **select** statement embedded into the overarching **select** statement. This embedded selection is called a subquery.

Another advanced function offered by **select** statements is the use of subqueries in the **where** clause of the **select** statement. A **select** statement can have 16 or more nested subqueries in the **where** clause, although it is not generally advisable to do so based on performance. Subqueries allow the user to specify unknown search criteria for the comparisons in the **where** clause as opposed to using strictly hard-coded values. Subqueries also illustrate the principle of data scope in SQL statements by virtue of the fact that the user can specify columns that appear in the parent query, even when those columns do not appear in the table used in the subquery.

Another use of subqueries can be found in association with a special operation that can be used in the **where** clause of a **select** statement. The name of this special operation is **exists**. This operation produces a TRUE or FALSE value based on whether or not the related subquery produces data. The **exists** clause is a popular option for users to incorporate subqueries into their **select** statements.

Output from the query can be placed into an order specified by the user with the assistance of the **order by** clause. However, the user must make sure that the columns in the **order by** clause are the same as those actually listed by the outermost **select** statement. The **order by** clause can also be used in subqueries; however, since the subqueries of a **select** statement are usually used to determine a valid value for searching or as part of an **exists** clause, the user should be more concerned about the existence of the data than the order in which data is returned from the subquery. Therefore, there is not much value added to using the **order by** clause in subqueries.

One final advanced technique covered in this chapter is the specification of variables at run time. This technique is especially valuable in order to provide reusability in a data selection statement. In order to denote a runtime variable in SQL, the user should place a variable name in the comparison operation the user wants to specify a runtime value for. The name of that variable in the **select** statement should be preceded with a special character to denote it as a variable. By default, this character is an ampersand (**&**). However, the default variable specification character can be changed with the use of the **set define** command at the prompt.

Runtime variables can be specified for SQL statements in other ways as well. The **define** command can be used to identify a runtime variable for a **select** statement automatically. After being defined and specified in the **define** command, a variable is specified for the entire session or until it is altered with the **undefine** command. In this way, the user can avoid the entire process of having to input values for the runtime variables. The final technique covered in this chapter on **select** statements is the usage of **accept** to redefine the text displayed for the input prompt. More cosmetic than anything else, **accept** allows the user to display a more direct message than the Oracle default message for data entry.

Two-Minute Drill

- **Select** statements that obtain data from more than one table and merge the data together are called joins.

- In order to join data from two tables, there must be a common column.

- A common column between two tables can create a foreign key, or link, from one table to another. This condition is especially true if the data in one of the tables is part of the primary key, or the column that defines uniqueness for rows on a table.

- A foreign key can create a parent/child relationship between two tables.

- One type of join is the inner join, or equijoin. An equijoin operation is based on an equality operation linking the data in common columns of two tables.

- Another type of join is the outer join. An outer join returns data in one table even when there is no data in the other table.

- The "other" table in the outer join operation is called the outer table.

- The common column that appears in the outer table of the join must have a special marker next to it in the comparison operation of the **select** statement that creates the table.

- The outer join marker is as follows: (**+**).

- Common columns in tables used in join operations must be preceded either with a table alias that denotes the table in which the column appears, or else the entire table name if the column name is the same in both tables.

- The data from a table can be joined to itself. This technique is useful in determining if there are rows in the table that have slightly different values but are otherwise duplicate rows.

- Table aliases must be used in self join **select** statements.

- Data output from table **select** statements can be grouped together according to criteria set by the query.

- A special clause exists to assist the user in grouping data together. That clause is called **group by**.

- There are several grouping functions that allow the user to perform operations on data in a column as though the data were logically one variable.

- The grouping functions are **max( )**, **min( )**, **sum( )**, **avg( )**, **stddev( )**, **variance( )**, and **count( )**.

- These grouping functions can be applied to the column values for a table as a whole or for subsets of column data for rows returned in **group by** statements.

- Data in a **group by** statement can be excluded or included based on a special set of **where** criteria defined specifically for the group in a **having** clause.

- The data used to determine the **having** clause can either be specified at run time by the query or by a special embedded query, called a subquery, which obtains unknown search criteria based on known search methods.

- Subqueries can be used in other parts of the **select** statement to determine unknown search criteria as well. Including subqueries in this fashion typically appears in the **where** clause.

- Subqueries can use columns in comparison operations that are either local to the table specified in the subquery or use columns that are specified in tables named in any parent query to the subquery. This usage is based on the principles of variable scope as presented in this chapter.

- Data can be returned from statements containing subqueries with the **order by** clause.

- It is not typically recommended for users to use **order by** in the subquery itself, as the subquery is generally designed to test a valid value or produce an intermediate dataset result. Order is usually not important for these purposes.

- Variables can be set in a **select** statement at run time with use of runtime variables. A runtime variable is designated with the ampersand character (**&**) preceding the variable name.

- The special character that designates a runtime variable can be changed using the **set define** command.

- A command called **define** can identify a runtime variable value to be picked up by the **select** statement automatically.

- Once defined, the variable remains defined for the rest of the session or until undefined by the user or process with the **undefine** command.

- A user can also modify the message that prompts the user to input a variable value. This activity is performed with the **accept** command.

Chapter Questions

1. **Which of the following is not a group function?**

   A. avg( )

   B. sqrt( )

   C. sum( )

   D. max( )

2. **In order to perform an inner join, which criteria must be true?**

   A. The common columns in the join do not need to have shared values.

   B. The tables in the join need to have common columns.

   C. The common columns in the join may or may not have shared values.

   D. The common columns in the join must have shared values.

3. **Once defined, how long will a variable remain so in SQL*Plus?**

   A. Until the database is shut down

   B. Until the instance is shut down

   C. Until the statement completes

   D. Until the session completes

4. **To alter the prompt Oracle uses to obtain input from a user:**

   A. Change the prompt in the **config.ora** file.

   B. Alter the **prompt** clause of the **accept** command.

   C. Enter a new prompt in the **login.sql** file.

   D. There is no way to change a prompt in Oracle.

5. Which two of the following options is appropriate for use when search criteria is unknown for comparison operations in a SELECT statement? (Choose two)

   A. select * from emp where empid = &empid;

   B. select * from emp where empid = 69494;

   C. select * from emp where empid = (select empid from invoice where invoice_no = 4399485);

   D. select * from emp;

6. The default character for specifying runtime variables in SELECT statements is

   A. Ampersand

   B. Ellipses

   C. Quotation marks

   D. Asterisk

7. A user is setting up a join operation between tables EMP and DEPT. There are some employees in the EMP table that the user wants returned by the query, but the employees are not assigned to departments yet. Which SELECT statement is most appropriate for this user?

   A. select e.empid, d.head from emp e, dept d;

   B. select e.empid, d.head from emp e, dept d where e.dept# = d.dept#;

   C. select e.empid, d.head from emp e, dept d where e.dept# = d.dept# (+);

   D. select e.empid, d.head from emp e, dept d where e.dept# (+) = d.dept#;

8. SELECT statements with many layers of nested subqueries generally perform better than SELECT statements with few layers of subqueries.

   A. TRUE

   B. FALSE

9. Which three of the following uses of the HAVING clause are appropriate? (Choose three)

   A. To put returned data into sorted order

   B. To exclude certain data groups based on known criteria

   C. To include certain data groups based on unknown criteria

   D. To include certain data groups based on known criteria

10. A Cartesian product is

   A. A group function

   B. Produced as a result of a join **select** statement with no **where** clause

   C. The result of fuzzy logic

   D. A special feature of Oracle Server

11. The default character that identifies runtime variables is changed by

   A. Modifying the init.ora file

   B. Modifying the login.sql file

   C. Issuing the **define** *variablename* command

   D. Issuing the **set define** command

12. **Which line in the following SELECT statement will produce an error?**

    A. **select** dept, **avg**(salary)

    B. **from** emp

    C. **group by** empid;

    D. There are no errors in this statement.

13. **A table may not be joined to itself.**

    A. TRUE

    B. FALSE

Answers to Chapter Questions

1. B. **sqrt( )**

Explanation Square root operations are performed on one column value. Review the discussion of available group functions.

2. B. The tables in the join need to have common columns.

Explanation It Is possible that a join operation will produce no return data, just as it is possible for any **select** statement not to return any data. Choices A, C, and D represent the spectrum of possibility with regard to the shared values that may or may not be present in common columns. However, joins themselves are not possible without two tables having common columns. Refer to the discussion of table joins.

3. D. Until the session completes.

Explanation A variable defined by the user during a session with SQL*Plus will remain defined until the session ends or until the user explicitly undefines the variable. Refer to the discussion of defining variables from earlier in the chapter.

4. B. Alter the **prompt** clause of the **accept** command.

Explanation Choice D should be eliminated immediately, leaving the user to select between A, B, and C. Choice A is incorrect because **config.ora** is a feature associated with Oracle's client/server network communications product. Choice C is incorrect. **login.sql** is a special file Oracle users can incorporate into their usage of Oracle that will automatically configure aspects of the SQL*Plus session, such as the default text editor, column and NLS data formats, and other items. This file does not configure input prompts, however. Only **accept** does that. Refer to the description of the use of the **accept** command.

5. A and C.

Explanation Choice A details usage of a runtime variable, which can be used to have the user input an appropriate search criteria after the statement has begun processing. Choice C details usage of a subquery, which allows the user to select unknown search criteria from the database using known methods for obtaining the data. Choice B is incorrect because the statement simply provides a known search criteria, while choice D is incorrect because it provides no search criteria at all. Review the discussion of defining runtime variables and subqueries.

6. A.   Ampersand

Explanation The ampersand (**&**) character is used by default to define runtime variables in SQL*Plus. Review the discussion of the definition of runtime variables and the **set define** command.

7. C.   **select** e.empid, d.head **from** emp e, dept d **where** e.dept# = d.dept# (+);

Explanation Choice C details the outer join operation most appropriate to this user's needs. The outer table in this join is the DEPT table, as identified by the (+) marker next to the DEPT# column in that table in the comparison operation that defines the join.

8. B.   FALSE

Explanation The more nested subqueries there are in a **select** statement, the worse the statement typically performs. Review the discussion of subqueries.

9. B, C, and D.

Explanation All exclusion or inclusion of grouped rows is handled by the **having** clause of a **select** statement. Choice A is not an appropriate answer because sort order is given in a **select** statement by the **order by** clause.

10. B. Produced as a result of a join **select** statement with no **where** clause.

Explanation A Cartesian product is the result dataset from a **select** statement where all data from both tables is returned. Some potential causes of a Cartesian product include not specifying a **where** clause for the join **select** statement. Review the discussion of performing join **select** statements.

11. D. Issuing the **set define** command.

Explanation Choice A is incorrect because a change to the **init.ora** file will alter the parameters Oracle uses to start the database instance. Use of this feature will be covered in the next unit. Choice B is incorrect because although the **login.sql** file can define many properties in a SQL*Plus session, the character that denotes runtime variables is not one of them. Choice C is incorrect because the **define** command is used to define variables used in a session, not an individual statement. Review the discussion of defining runtime variables in **select** statements.

12. C. GROUP BY empid;

Explanation Since the EMPID column does not appear in the original list of columns to be displayed by the query, it cannot be used in a **group by** statement. Review the discussion of using **group by** in **select** statements.

13. B. FALSE

Explanation A table may certainly be joined to itself. Review the discussion of joining tables.

CHAPTER
3

Creating the Oracle Database

n this chapter, you will understand and demonstrate knowledge in the following areas:

- Overview of data modeling and database design
- Creating the tables of an Oracle database
- The Oracle data dictionary
- Manipulating Oracle data

At this point, you should feel comfortable with the idea of database usage via data selection. Now, in order to move forward on the road to becoming an Oracle DBA, you must immerse in the subject of Oracle database creation. This chapter will do just that. The topics covered in this chapter include data modeling, creating tables, the data dictionary, and data manipulation beyond **select** statements. With mastery of these topics, the user of an Oracle system moves more into the world of application development. Typically, it is the application developer who creates database objects and determines how users will access those objects in production environments. The DBA is then the person who is responsible for migrating developed objects into production and then managing the needs of production systems. This chapter will lay the foundation for discussion of Oracle database object creation and other advanced topics, so it is important to review this material carefully. The OCP Exam 1 will consist of test questions in this subject area worth 22 percent of the final score. With these thoughts in mind, move on now to the topic at hand.

Overview of Data Modeling and Database Design

In this section, you will cover the following topics related to data modeling:

- The stages of system development
- The basic types of data relationships

- The relational database components
- Reading an entity-relationship diagram

Computer programs are the most animate of inanimate objects. Like the people who use, develop, and maintain them, software applications are dynamic creatures that are subject to the same constraints and realities as the very realities they try to model. Software applications are also subject to economic constraints, as any analyst who has spent months planning a project only to have the project's funds pulled at the last minute will attest. In so attempting to model reality, software applications become reality.

Stages of System Development

The first part of the software development life cycle is generally the one that most people pay attention to. This period of development is followed by a production phase, which may or may not involve the creation of enhancements. As time goes on, the users and developers of the project attempt to incorporate features into the production system. After quite a long time, usually, advances in the industry or the emergence of system requirements that the original technology cannot handle will cause the system's use to wane, until finally the data from the system will be archived and the system itself retired. The steps involved in the software development life cycle are as follows:

- Needs assessment
- Database design
- Application development
- Performance tuning
- Enhancements

Needs Assessment

A database system begins as an idea in someone's head. At this early stage in the game, a database application's possibilities can seem endless— however, this stage is as wrought with danger as other stages in the model. *Many questions should be answered by the end of this planning stage.* The first question that can be asked about an application is—will this application support large-volume data entry, or is the fundamental point of this application to make data viewable to users? In many cases, the answer is both. By the end of needs assessment, the designer of an application should have a clear idea about the following questions:

- Who will use the application?
- What use will the application fill in the organization?
- How do people plan on using the application?

Recent successes involving user-facilitated meetings show that the success of a project can often be improved with the early and frequent involvement of users on the project. Once the users' needs have been assessed, there is an activity that takes place allowing the developers to determine what data and tools are available for use. In this phase of software development, the developers of a software application must assess many things, such as process flow for data within the system and the method by which to present data to the user both on the screen and in reports. Generally, a software application involving a database involves three parts, all of which should be planned before creating them. The three components of a database application generally consist of user interface, the database, and reports. For our purposes, we focus on database design.

Database Design

This activity in creating a database application lays the groundwork for success in supporting current and future needs of the application. To design a database requires two steps. The two steps of designing a database are

- Creating an entity-relationship diagram
- Translating an entity-relationship diagram into a logical data model

Creating an entity-relationship diagram and translating it into a logical data model is an involved process. The steps to execute this process, however, are important to ensure correct design of the tables that will support both the user interface and the reports. So, even though the users will interface with the database in a controlled manner via the application, it is still important for the success of the application to have a strong database design. More on this process will appear later in the discussion.

Application Development

Once the users' needs are assessed and the database design in place, the building of the application logic can begin. Some components of the application that may be placed within the database include integrity constraints and triggers, stored procedures and/or packages, and SQL tuning features such as the shared pool and the SQL statement optimizer. Application development is often a task that involves stepwise refinement. As needs arise, or as hidden intricacies of a current process are uncovered, the application software that models business rules will undoubtedly grow complex. PL/SQL, the programming language of Oracle database packages, supports many constructs that allow for modularization and abstract datatypes, as well as other useful programming constructs that will simplify the logic used to represent complex business rules.

Performance Tuning

No application is harder to use than a slow one. As will be discussed in Unit IV, covering performance tuning and optimization, the source of most performance issues in applications using Oracle databases is the application code itself. The application developers should, wherever possible, explore alternative methods for providing the same data to the user interface or reports in order to find the method that performs best. This step may involve development of alternative blocks of code that pull the same data from the database and executing benchmark tests to compare performance. This step may also involve the maintenance of two different databases, or at the very least, the need to maintain and use different database configurations to determine which methods work best. A fuller discussion of what performance tuning for an application entails appears in Unit IV.

Database Security

The guarded usage of the database application created will ensure that its use is appropriate. Database security is an important factor in any database, allowing the developers and managers for the database system to handle large user populations, if necessary, and to limit database access to those users that require it. One key activity that should occur early on in the development of an application is the determining of levels of data access that will be afforded to each user or type of user in the system. At this early stage of the project, users should be divided into rough categories for the purpose of determining what data they need access to in order to perform their tasks. Furthermore, once general access and usage levels for various users are established, there are features within the Oracle database that allow the developer or the DBA to limit users to only their access level or to restrict their usage of the database to only what they need. Some key terms to know here are privileges and roles for managing user access, and resource profiles to manage system hardware usage. A more complete discussion of these features appears in Unit II.

Enhancements

Enhancements are often as important as the actual application in the minds of the users, because they represent an evolution of the business process that must be modeled by the application supporting that business process. However, in some ways developing enhancements is often riskier than developing the application itself. Some of the advantages of the initial application development, such as reduced production burden on the developers of the application, a structured project plan, funding, and management attention, are lost once the application sees its first few months of successful production life. When enhancements are requested, the developers often have to do double duty—they are both the enhancement developer who has to rework existing code *and* the analyst that has to handle the production issues of the application as they arise. However, these obstacles represent as much of an opportunity for success as they do for failure. Strong project management in these situations generally helps the enhancement development effort to succeed.

Exercises

1. What are the stages of the software development life cycle?

2. What important questions should be answered before the application is developed?

Basic Types of Data Relationships

The focus of this discussion is to present the areas of data modeling and database design. In order to model data, there must be relationships between the various components that make up a database design. These components are stored as data, while the relationships between data can be defined explicitly via the use of integrity constraints and/or database triggers that model business rules, or implicitly by the data manipulation statements that select data for viewing or populate the database with new data. The following list of data relationships will be discussed in this section:

- Primary keys

- Functional dependency

- Foreign keys

One type of data relationship starts in the tables that comprise the Oracle database. So far, we have seen many tables containing data. One common element in all the tables seen is that they contain multiple columns that "hang" off of one main column, called a primary key. This primary key is the column(s) that determines the uniqueness of every row in the database. In the primary key, there can be no duplicate value for any row in the entire table. Each column that is not part of the primary key is considered to be "functionally dependent" on the primary key. This term simply means that the dependent column stores data that relates directly to or modifies directly each individual row.

One other relationship to discuss in this section is the idea of a foreign key. This relationship is often referred to as a parent/child relationship because of where the data must appear in each table to create the foreign-key relationship. In the "child" table, the data can appear either as part of the primary key or as a functionally dependent column. However, in the "parent" table, the referenced column must appear in the primary key.

Exercises

1. What are three types of data relationships?

2. What is functional dependency?

3. What is required of two tables in order for the tables to be related?

Relational Database Components

A relational database consists of many components, some of which already have been covered. These components include objects to store data, objects to aid in accessing data quickly, and objects to manage user access to data. Additionally, there are objects in the database that contain the code that is used to manipulate and change data, produce reports of data, and otherwise use data to produce the desired result. Some of the objects that are part of the relational database produced by Oracle that are used in the functions mentioned earlier are listed as follows:

- **Tables, views, and synonyms**   Used to store and access data

- **Indexes and the SQL processing mechanism**   Used to speed access to data

- **Triggers and integrity constraints**   Used to maintain the validity of data entered

- **Privileges, roles, and profiles**   Used to manage database access and usage

- **Packages, procedures, and functions**   Used to code the applications that will use the database

A relational database works on principles of relational data within tables. The relational data models real-world business situations through the use of datasets called tables that can contain different elements or columns. These columns then are able to relate to other columns in other tables, or simply to the primary key via functional dependency.

Exercises

1. What is a relational database model?

2. What are the components of a relational database? How are they used?

Reading an Entity-Relationship Diagram

Every database starts out as an entity-relationship diagram. In order to model a business process, the developers of an application must first map out the different components of a system. This map of a business process is often referred to as the entity-relationship diagram, or *ERD* for short. The ERD consists of two different components, which are listed here.

■ **Entity**   A person, place, thing, or idea involved in the business process flow

■ **Relationship**   The ties that bind entities together

In order to understand the process of creating an ERD, an example will be presented. This example is of a business process used by employees of an organization to obtain reimbursement for expenses that they may have incurred on behalf of their employer. See Figure 3-1. Already, a few entities have emerged in the description of the application to be created, namely *employee* (a person), *expenses* (things), and the *employer* (a person or group of people). A relationship has also been identified, *obtain reimbursement*, or "pay," which is an activity.

Often, a database application begins with looking at the process as it already exists. For this example, assume there is inefficiency in the current process. There may be several different points of entry of data, and there is the possibility that copies will get lost. Finally, there is the turnaround lag in paying employees, during which time the employee is basically owed money by the employer. If there is a problem, the employee will not know about it for several weeks. On top of that, it may take several more weeks for the problem to be corrected. These reasons are enough to justify the need for a more automated process, and the ERD is the mechanism to model that process.

From ERD to LDM

An entity-relationship diagram is helpful to understand the process flow of data through the system. Once an entity-relationship diagram is created, the developer must then create a special diagram that models the data stored in a database to represent the entities and relationships in the ERD. The name of this special diagram is a logical data model, or LDM for short. The LDM

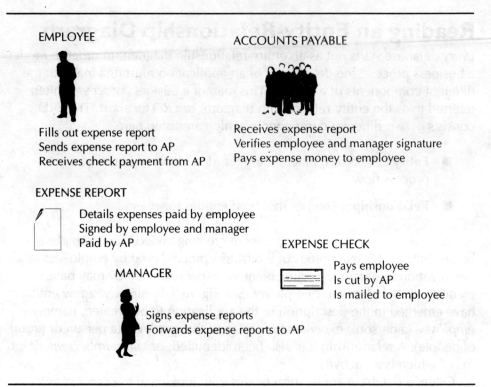

EMPLOYEE

Fills out expense report
Sends expense report to AP
Receives check payment from AP

ACCOUNTS PAYABLE

Receives expense report
Verifies employee and manager signature
Pays expense money to employee

EXPENSE REPORT

Details expenses paid by employee
Signed by employee and manager
Paid by AP

EXPENSE CHECK

Pays employee
Is cut by AP
Is mailed to employee

MANAGER

Signs expense reports
Forwards expense reports to AP

FIGURE 3-1. *An entity-relationship diagram of the employee expense system*

will be used to display how all data relating to the business process being modeled is stored in the database. A logical data model consists of a diagrammatic representation of tables in a database. Some of the tables for the example are EMPLOYEE, EXPENSE, BANK_ACCOUNT, and PHONE_NUMBER.

The first step in creating a list of table columns is to determine what will be the unique characteristic of any row in the table. The unique identifier for all employees may be a social security number or some other unique integer assigned by the company to an employee for the term of that employee's employment. Following the determination of the primary key is determining what items could be included in the EMPLOYEE table—the developer will need to determine what features about employees must be stored in the database. The determination about whether to incorporate data as a column into the table should rest on two conditions:

- Is this data functionally dependent on the primary key?
- Will there be only one copy of this data per appearance of the primary key?

Once these factors are determined, the designer will know if he or she should include the column in the table or whether the column should be used to define another table. In this example of defining the EMPLOYEE table, the designer may want to include a few different elements, such as the person's name, hire date, age, spouse name, various telephone numbers, and supervisor's name.

In the case of bank accounts, employees may have several, each with a set of corresponding information such as bank name and ABA routing number. The additional storage overhead makes it difficult to store all bank account information in the EMPLOYEE table. Data components that have no functional dependency to the other data in a table record should be placed in separate tables. The designer may create a separate table containing bank account information, called BANK_ACCOUNT. The primary key of this table may be the bank account number and the associated employee who owns the account. In addition, there may be several columns that share a common functional dependency on the primary key. One final point is that since the bank account does eventually get associated back to an employee, it is required that there be some method to associate the two tables—a foreign key.

TIP
Data normalization is the act of breaking down column data to place in tables where each column in the table is functionally dependent on only one primary key. This process reduces data storage costs by eliminating redundancy and minimizes dependency of any column in the "normalized" database to only one primary key.

Role of Ordinality

Related to the discussion of foreign keys and table relationships is an aspect of data relationships relating to a special term called *ordinality*. This term represents two important features about a relationship between two tables. The ordinality of a table relationship is a message the designer uses to identify two facts about the relationship:

- Is the relationship mandatory or optional for these objects?

- Does one record in the table correspond to one or many records in the other table?

The ordinality of a table relationship contains two elements and is generally represented on the logical data model as an "ordered pair," usually (0,N) or (1,1), or (1,N), etc. In some cases, the relationship between two entities may not be required. Consider the following example of employees and expenses. This relationship works in two directions, from employees to expenses and from expenses to employees. In the direction of employees to expenses, the relationship is optional. That is to say, an employee need not have ever incurred expenses on behalf of the company. However, in the other direction, from expenses to employees, the relationship is mandatory because each and every expense submitted to the employee expense system will correspond to an employee. To answer the second question, in the direction of employees to expenses there is a one-to-many relationship, as each employee in the company may have submitted one or more expense reports in the course of their employment, or none at all. In contrast, on the other direction, each expense submitted will always have one and only one employee who submitted it, as shown in Figure 3-2.

In summary, the creation of quality data models is more a product of experience than formula. Even though there are many theories on data normalization, the process of it is fairly arbitrary. In fact, most database designers break the so-called "rules" of normalization constantly in an attempt to improve performance. As the saying goes, "normalize until it hurts, denormalize until it works."

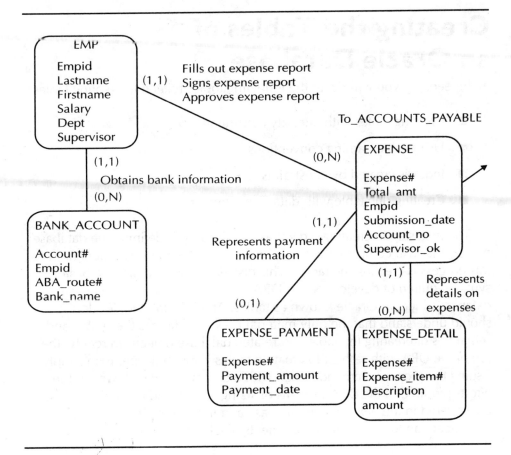

FIGURE 3-2.   *The logical data model for the employee expense system*

Exercises

1. What is an entity-relationship diagram and how is it read?

2. What is a logical data model? Identify some methods used to translate an entity-relationship diagram into a data model.

3. What is ordinality and how is it significant?

Creating the Tables of an Oracle Database

In this section, you will cover the following topics related to creating tables:

- Creating tables with integrity constraints

- Using table naming conventions

- Indexes created by constraints

- Creating one table with data from another

The next step in creating a database application is defining the database objects that will comprise the logical data model. A major component in this process is creating the tables. This discussion will explain the basic syntax required of developers and DBAs in order to produce the logical database object in Oracle known as tables. At this point, the developer should understand that the only material presented here is the syntax and semantics of creating the table and related database objects. In reality, the job of the DBA with respect to creating tables is much deeper than simply issuing the proper command syntax with a column listing. However, the efforts required of the DBA in terms of sizing a table and managing its usage are covered in the next unit on database administration. For now, the developer can focus on the requirements of table creation.

Creating a Table with Integrity Constraints

The basic creation of a table involves using the **create table** command. This statement is one of many database object creation statements known in Oracle as the data definition language, or *DDL*. Within SQL*Plus, the developer can issue the following command to create the EMPLOYEE table described in the previous section on data modeling. Tables created can contain integrity constraints, or rules that limit the type of data that can be placed in the table, row, or column. There are two types of integrity constraints table constraints and column constraints. A column can have a table constraint on it, limiting the data that can be put into the table. The table constraints available in Oracle are primary keys and unique constraints. Column constraints limit the type of data that can be placed in a specific column. These constraints include foreign keys, check constraints and table constraints.

```
CREATE TABLE employee
(empid            NUMBER(10),
lastname          VARCHAR2(25),
firstname         VARCHAR2(25),
salary            NUMBER(10,4),
CONSTRAINT        pk_employee_01
PRIMARY KEY       (empid));
```

What does this **create table** statement tell the developer about the table being created? First of all, there are several columns, each with a corresponding datatype, or a specification of the "type" of data that can be stored in this column. The types of data available in an Oracle database will be described shortly. There are four columns defined, which correspond to the four columns that the data modeling session from the previous discussion identified. Finally, the statement scratches the surface of data relationships by defining the EMPID column to be the primary key. This definition means that data in the EMPID column can be used to identify every row in the table as a unique row.

The definition of a column as the primary key in a table produces a few noticeable effects within the database itself. The term "primary key" itself refers to a special designation for a constraint that says to Oracle, "don't let any row insert a column value for EMPID that is NULL or that is the same as a column value that already exists for another row." There are some special methods Oracle will use to enforce this integrity constraint. Column values that are part of primary keys have the following conditions enforced on them. Any value in the column for any row must be unique. That is to say that no two rows in the EMPLOYEE table can have the same value for EMPID defined. Secondly, no row can define the value in a column as NULL if that column is part of the primary key. This means that no employee in the EMPLOYEE table can have a NULL value defined for EMPID.

TIP

Integrity constraints are rules that are defined on table columns that prevent anyone from placing inappropriate data in the column. There are five types of integrity constraints: primary key, foreign key, unique, NOT NULL, and check.

Take another moment to review the definition that was determined for the BANK_ACCOUNT table. Remember that the BANK_ACCOUNT table was supposed to have the BANK_ACCT_NO column be its primary key, because that column defines the data that is unique about each row in the table. However, remember also that there is a special relationship between the BANK_ACCOUNT table and the EMPLOYEE table.

```
CREATE TABLE bank_account
  (bank_acct_no        VARCHAR2(40),
  empid                NUMBER(10),
  BANK_ROUTE_NO        VARCHAR2(40),
  BANK_NAME            VARCHAR2(50),
  CONSTRAINT           pk_bank_acct_01
  PRIMARY KEY          (bank_acct_no),
  CONSTRAINT           fk_bank_acct_01
  FOREIGN KEY (empid) REFERENCES employee (empid));
```

Notice that in addition to the definition of a primary-key constraint, this table also has a foreign-key constraint. The syntax for the definition allows the column to reference another table's column, of either the same or a different name. In order for a foreign-key constraint to be valid, the columns in both tables must have exactly the same datatypes. A fuller discussion of datatypes and their significance will appear later in the chapter. The designation "foreign key" tells Oracle that the developer would like to create referential integrity between the EMPID column in the BANK_ACCOUNT table and the EMPLOYEE table. This fact prevents a column in the child table from containing a value that does not exist in the referenced column in the parent table.

An option that can be specified along with the foreign key relates to the deletion of data from the parent. If someone attempts to **delete** a row from the parent table that contains a referenced value from the child table, Oracle will block the deletion unless the **on delete cascade** option is specified in the foreign-key definition of the **create table** statement. When the **on delete cascade** option is used, Oracle will not only allow the user to **delete** a referenced record from the parent table, but the deletion will cascade into the child table as well.

```
CREATE TABLE bank_acct
  (bank_acct_no          VARCHAR2(40),
   empid                 NUMBER(10),
   BANK_ROUTE_NO         VARCHAR2(40),
   BANK_NAME             VARCHAR2(50),
   CONSTRAINT            pk_bank_acct_01
   PRIMARY KEY           (bank_acct_no),
   CONSTRAINT            fk_bank_acct_01
   FOREIGN KEY (empid) REFERENCES employee (empid)
   ON DELETE CASCADE);
```

Other integrity constraints abound. There are five types of integrity constraints in all, including primary and foreign keys, unique constraints, NOT NULL constraints, and check constraints.

```
CREATE TABLE employee
  (empid         NUMBER(10),
   lastname      VARCHAR2(25),
   firstname     VARCHAR2(25),
   salary        NUMBER(10,4),
   home_phone    number(15),
   CONSTRAINT    pk_employee_01
   PRIMARY KEY   (empid),
   CONSTRAINT    uk_employee_01
   UNIQUE        (home_phone));
```

The definition of a unique constraint on HOME_PHONE prevents anyone from defining a row that contains a phone number that is identical to the phone number of anyone else already in the table. There are two weaknesses in this definition. The first is that having a unique constraint on a home phone number makes it difficult to store records for employees who are spouses with the same telephone number, or who are roommates. Another point to be made about unique constraints, and foreign-key constraints for that matter, is that there is no data integrity enforced on data in a row that has NULL defined for its value. This is a special case scenario that applies only to NULL data in columns with foreign-key, unique, and check constraints defined on them.

TIP

Foreign-key, check, and unique integrity constraints for a column are not enforced on a row if the column data value for the row is NULL.

The final two types of constraints are NOT NULL constraints and check constraints. The first type of constraint identified prevents the data value defined by any row for the column to be NULL if the column has the NOT NULL constraint defined on it. By default, primary keys are defined to be NOT NULL. All other constraints are NULLable unless the developer explicitly defines the column to be NOT NULL.

```
CREATE TABLE employee
(empid            NUMBER(10),
 lastname         VARCHAR2(25)      NOT NULL,
 firstname        VARCHAR2(25)      NOT NULL,
 salary           NUMBER(10,4)      CHECK(salary<500000),
 home_phone       number(15),
 CONSTRAINT       pk_employee_01
 PRIMARY KEY      (empid),
 CONSTRAINT       uk_employee_01
 UNIQUE           (home_phone));
```

Notice that in this table definition, there are *three* columns defined to be NOT NULL, including the primary key. The two others are the LASTNAME column and the FIRSTNAME column. When defined, the NOT NULL table constraint will be applied to the columns, preventing anyone from creating a row for this table that does not contain a first and last name for the employee.

Notice also that an additional constraint has been created on this table. The final integrity constraint that will be identified by this section is the check constraint. Check constraints allow Oracle to verify the validity of data being entered on a table against a set of constants. These constants act as valid values. If, for example, someone tries to create an employee row for the table defined earlier with a salary of $1,000,000 per year, Oracle will return an error message saying that the record data defined for the SALARY column has violated the check constraint for that column. Check constraints have a number of limitations, all centering around the fact that the constraint can only refer to a specific set of constant values or operations on those values. A check constraint cannot refer to another column or row in any table, including the one the constraint is defined on, and it cannot refer to special keywords that can have values in them, such as **user**, **sysdate**, or **rowid** (see following *TIP*). Thus, the check constraint in the table definition earlier is valid, but the one in the following excerpt from a table definition is not:

```
CREATE TABLE address
(...,
city        check(city in (SELECT city FROM cities))
...);
```

TIP
*There are some special keywords that contain information about certain database conditions. These keywords are **user**, **sysdate**, and **rowid**. The **user** keyword gives the username of the owner of the current session. The **sysdate** keyword gives the current date and time at the time the statement is issued. The **rowid** keyword gives the ROWID of the row specified. These keywords cannot be used in conjunction with a NOT NULL constraint.*

Exercises

1. What command is used to create tables?
2. What is an integrity constraint? What are the five types of integrity constraints?

Using Table Naming Conventions

There are many philosophies around the naming of variables, tables, columns, and other items in software that come from the early days of computing. More often than not, available memory and disk space was small on those early machines. As such, the names of variables in these environments was small. This cryptic method was born out of necessity. In many systems today, however, developers are not faced with that restriction. As a result, the names of variables, columns, and tables need not be bound by the naming rules of yesteryear. However, some standard for naming tables and columns still has value, if only for the sake of readability.

Keep Names Short and Descriptive

A naming convention used in the Oracle database may be compact, but someone viewing variables in the database for the first time should also have some idea of what the variable is supposed to represent. For example, using the name EMP_LN_FN_SAL instead of EMPLOYEE for the table created previously would not be as easily understood as simply calling the table EMPLOYEE, or even EMP.

Relate Names for Child Tables to Their Parent

In certain situations, the developers of an application may find themselves creating multiple tables to define a logical object. The developer may have a logical entity that is represented by several tables, which have a one-to-many relationship among them. Consider the EXPENSE table, which was defined to hold the expense summaries that employees submit in order to generate a feed to the AP system. The developer could define a second table in conjunction with the EXPENSE table called EXPENSE_ITEM, which stores detail information about each expense incurred. Both are descriptive names, and it is obvious by those names that there is some relationship between them.

Foreign-Key Columns Should Have the Same Name in Both Tables

In the case of creating foreign-key relationships between columns in two different tables, it also helps if the referring and the referenced columns in both tables share the same name, making the potential existence of a foreign key a bit more obvious.

Names of Associated Objects Should Relate to the Table

Other naming conventions in the database related to tables include giving all integrity constraints, triggers, and indexes meaningful names that identify both the type of constraint created and the table to which the constraint belongs. Consider some of the names chosen in the previous examples.

They include: PK_EMPLOYEE_01, which is a primary key (PK) on the EMPLOYEE table; or FK_EMPLOYEE_01, which is a foreign key defined for the EMPLOYEE table. The name of the foreign key includes reference to the table to which the foreign-key constraint belongs.

Avoid Quotes, Keywords, and Nonalphanumeric Characters

You can't use quotes in the name of a database object. Nor can you use a nonalphanumeric character. This rule has three exceptions: the dollar sign ($), the underscore (_), and the hash mark (#). The dollar sign is most notable in the use for naming dynamic performance views. In general, the DBA should steer clear of its use. The underscore is useful for separating two words or abbreviations, such as EXPENSE_ITEM, or BANK_ACCOUNT.

Exercises

1. Describe some table naming conventions.

2. What should be included in the name of a table that has a referential integrity constraint with another table, in which the table referring to the other table is the child table?

Datatypes and Column Definitions

The usage of datatypes to identify the "type" of data a column can hold has been mentioned a few times so far. At this point, it is necessary to discuss the available datatypes in the Oracle database. A few obvious ones should come to mind, as there have already been several tables defined and discussed in the preceding few chapters. Loosely speaking, the "type" of data a column will allow that have been used so far are alphanumeric datatypes that store text strings such as CHAR and VARCHAR2, the NUMBER datatype that stores numeric data only, and the DATE datatype.

Here's a list of datatypes and their descriptions:

VARCHAR2	Contains text strings of up to 2000 bytes
CHAR	Contains text strings of up to 255 bytes
NUMBER	Contains numeric data

DATE	Contains date data
RAW	Contains binary data of up to 2000 bytes
LONG	Contains text data of up to 2 gigabytes
LONG RAW	Contains binary data of up to 2 gigabytes
ROWID	Contains disk location for table rows

Some other datatypes may not be so obvious. For example, the alphanumeric datatypes identified here are not one simple datatype, but two—a CHAR datatype and a VARCHAR2 datatype. Some people may ask, why does VARCHAR2 have the "2" on the end, and the reason is that there may be a VARCHAR datatype defined in future releases of Oracle; so, although VARCHAR and VARCHAR2 for now are synonymous, they may not be in the future. Both the CHAR and the VARCHAR2 variable datatypes can be defined to hold character strings, but there are some subtle differences. First, the CHAR datatype only supports character strings up to a length of 255 bytes in Oracle7 (2,000 for Oracle8), while the VARCHAR2 datatype supports character strings up to a length of 2,000 characters in Oracle7 (4,000 for Oracle8). Second, and perhaps most important, when Oracle stores data in a CHAR datatype, it will pad the value stored in the column up to the length of the column as declared by the table with blanks. In contrast, Oracle will not store padded blank spaces if the same value is stored in a column defined to be datatype VARCHAR2. To illustrate, if a column called LASTNAME was defined as CHAR(50) and the value someone attempted to store in it was "BRADY," the value Oracle would store would actually be "BRADY" with 45 blank spaces to the right of it. That same value stored in a column that was defined as datatype VARCHAR2 would be stored simply as "BRADY."

The NUMBER datatype that is used to store number data can be specified either to store integers or decimals with the addition of a parenthetical precision indicator. For example, if the value 49309.593 were stored in a column defined as datatype NUMBER with no precision identified, the number would be stored as shown: 49309.593. However, in a column defined to be datatype NUMBER(15,2), the same number would be stored as 49309.59, because the number specified after the comma in the parenthetical precision definition of the datatype represents the number of places to the right of the decimal point that will be stored. The number on the left of the comma shows the total width of allowed values stored in this column, including the two decimal places to the right of the decimal point. Finally, a column declared to be of type NUMBER(9) will not store any decimals at all. The number 49309.593 stored in a column defined in this way will appear as 49310, because Oracle automatically rounds up in cases where the value in the precision area that the declared datatype will not support is 5 or above.

Another type that has already been discussed is the DATE datatype, which stores date values in a special format internal to Oracle represented as the number of days since December 31, 4713 B.C.E., the beginning of the Julian date calendar. This datatype offers a great deal of flexibility to users who want to perform date manipulation operations, such as adding 30 days to a given date. In this case, all the user has to do is specify the column declared as a DATE datatype and add the number of days. Of course, there are also numerous functions that handle date operations more complex than simple arithmetic. Another nice feature of Oracle's method for date storage is that it is inherently millennium compliant.

Beyond these datatypes, there is an entire set of important options available to the developer and DBA with respect to type declaration. In Oracle7, these datatypes include LONG, RAW, LONG RAW, and MLSLABEL. RAW datatypes in Oracle store data in binary format up to 2,000 bytes long in version 7. It is useful to store graphics and sound files when used in conjunction with LONG to form the LONG RAW datatype, which can accommodate up to 2 gigabytes of data. The developer or DBA can declare columns to be of LONG datatype, which stores up to 2 gigabytes of alphanumeric text data. There can be only one column declared to be of type LONG in the database as of version 7. The entire operation of storing large blocks of data has been reworked significantly for Oracle8. For a full treatment of the options available in that version for large object data storage, refer to the last unit of this text, which discusses the new features of Oracle8 in conjunction with preparing for certification in that area.

Finally, the ROWID datatype is considered. This datatype stores information related to the disk location of table rows. Generally, no column should be created to store data in type ROWID, but this datatype supports the **rowid** virtual column associated with every table.

Exercises

1. Name several different datatypes available in Oracle7.

2. What are some of the differences between the CHAR and the VARCHAR2 datatype?

3. How is data stored in the DATE datatype? What is the ROWID datatype?

Indexes Created by Constraints

Indexes are created in support of integrity constraints that enforce uniqueness. The two types of integrity constraints that enforce uniqueness are primary keys and unique constraints. Essentially, unique constraints in Oracle are the same as primary-key constraints, except for the fact that they allow NULL values. When the primary-key or the unique constraint is declared, the index that supports the uniqueness enforcement is also created, and all values in all columns are placed into the index.

The name of the index depends on the name given to the constraint. For example, the following table definition statement creates one index on the primary-key column EMPID. EMPID cannot then contain any NULL values or any duplicates. The name of the index is the same as the name given to the primary key. Thus, the name given to the index created to support uniqueness on the primary key for this table is called PK_EMPLOYEE_01. There are performance benefits associated with indexes that will be discussed in the next chapter, but for now it is sufficient to say that the creation of an index in conjunction with the definition of a primary key is a handy feature of table declaration in Oracle.

```
CREATE TABLE employee
(empid          NUMBER(10),
lastname        VARCHAR2(25)    NOT NULL,
firstname       VARCHAR2(25)    NOT NULL,
salary          NUMBER(10,4)    CHECK(salary<500000),
home_phone      number(15),
CONSTRAINT      pk_employee_01
PRIMARY KEY     (empid),
CONSTRAINT      uk_employee_01
UNIQUE          (home_phone));
```

Another important case to consider is the unique constraint index. If the unique constraint is defined in the manner detailed in the previous code example, then the name of the corresponding index in the database created automatically by Oracle to support enforcement of the uniqueness of the column will be UK_EMPLOYEE_01. However, there is another method for declaring a unique constraint on a column such that the index created will remain somewhat anonymous.

```
CREATE TABLE employee
(empid          NUMBER(10),
lastname        VARCHAR2(25)      NOT NULL,
firstname       VARCHAR2(25)      NOT NULL,
salary          NUMBER(10,4)      CHECK(salary<500000),
home_phone      number(15)        UNIQUE,
CONSTRAINT      pk_employee_01
PRIMARY KEY     (empid));
```

The unique constraint created in this situation will have the same properties as the unique constraint created in the previous code example. It will also enforce uniqueness on that column just as well as the constraint defined in the previous example. The main difference, however, is the fact that the associated index with the unique constraint created as a result of executing the previous code will have a relatively anonymous name associated with it. This name is usually something similar to SYSXXXXXXX, where XXXXXXX is equal to some long string of numbers designed to uniquely identify the index name.

In summary, indexes are used to support the enforcement of unique integrity constraints, such as the primary-key and the unique constraints. The associated indexes can either be named with something corresponding to the name given to the constraint if the constraint is explicitly named, or the constraint can be given a relatively anonymous name automatically by Oracle when the unique index is created. In Unit II, the text will discuss some sizing considerations associated with creating a table. It is important to bear in mind that with the creation of a table comes the creation of an associated primary-key index. The DBA should bear this fact in mind when creating a table.

TIP
When a table is created, an index
corresponding to the primary key of the table is
also created to enforce uniqueness and to
speed performance on data selection that uses
*the primary key in the **where** clause of the*
***select** statement.*

Exercises

1. Identify two constraints that create indexes.

2. What determines the name given to an index created automatically?

3. What two purposes does the index serve in the enforcement of its associated constraint?

Creating One Table with Data from Another

The final area of discussion in this section on creating tables is one on how to create a table with prepopulated data. In most cases, when a developer or the DBA creates a table in Oracle, the table is empty—it has no data in it. Once created, the users or developers are then free to populate the table as long as proper access has been granted. However, there are some cases in which the developer can create a table that already has data in it. The general statement used to create tables in this manner is the **create table as select** statement.

```
CREATE TABLE employee
(empid          NUMBER(10),
 lastname       VARCHAR2(25)    NOT NULL,
 firstname      VARCHAR2(25)    NOT NULL,
 salary         NUMBER(10,4)    CHECK(salary<500000),
 home_phone     number(15)      UNIQUE,
 CONSTRAINT     pk_employee_01
 PRIMARY KEY    (empid))
AS SELECT * FROM hrglobal.empl;
```

The final **as select** clause instructs Oracle to insert data into the table it just created from the HRGLOBAL.EMPL table specified. In order to use **select ***, the columns in the table from which data will be selected must be identical to the column specification made in the table just created. Alternately, an exact copy of a table can be made without declaring any columns at all with the code block shown following this paragraph:

```
CREATE TABLE employee
AS SELECT * FROM hrglobal.empl;
```

Finally, it is also possible for the developer or DBA to specify any option in the **select** statement that makes a copy of data that the developer could use in any other **select** statement in the database. This feature includes the specification of column concatenation, selecting only a limited number of columns, limiting the number of rows returned with the **where** clause, or even using arithmetic and other single-row operations to modify data in virtually any way available on other **select** statements.

Exercises

1. How can a table be created with data already populated in it?

2. What limits are there on the data that can be selected in creating a table from existing data?

The Oracle Data Dictionary

In this section, you will cover the following topics related to the Oracle data dictionary:

- Available dictionary views
- Querying the data dictionary

Few resources in the Oracle database are as useful as the Oracle data dictionary. Developers, DBAs, and users will find themselves referring to the data dictionary time and time again to resolve questions about object availability, roles and privileges, and performance. Whatever the perspective,

Oracle has it all stored in the data dictionary. This discussion will introduce the major components of the data dictionary in the Oracle database, pointing out its features and the highlights in order to set groundwork for fuller discussions on the data dictionary in later chapters. It is worth having the major concepts related to the data dictionary down before moving on, as data dictionary views will be referred to in many other areas throughout the rest of the guide.

Available Dictionary Views

There are scores of dictionary tables available in the Oracle data dictionary, used to keep track of many of the database objects that have been discussed. The dictionary tells the user just about anything he or she needs to know about the database, including which objects can be seen by the user, which objects are available, the current performance status of the database, etc. There are a few basic facts about the data dictionary that the user should know. First, the Oracle data dictionary consists of tables where information about the database is stored. The SYS user in Oracle is the only user allowed to **update** those dictionary tables. It is not recommended that any other users update dictionary tables except to periodically **update** and purge records from the SYS.AUD$ table, which stores audit trail records.

Rather than having users manipulate the dictionary tables directly, Oracle has available several *views* on the dictionary tables through which users get a distilled look at the dictionary contents. A view is a database object loosely akin to the idea of a "virtual table." The data in a view is pulled from a real table by way of a **select** statement and stored in memory. Users can then **select** and even **insert** and update records from views. The views in the Oracle data dictionary allow users to see the available database objects to various depths, depending on their needs as users.

The views of the data dictionary are divided into three general categories to correspond to the depth of the database to which one is permitted to view. The three general categories of views are listed as follows, along with a general description of the objects the view will allow the user to see. The text in all caps at the beginning of each bullet corresponds to text that is prefixed onto the name of the dictionary view categories in question.

- **USER_** These views typically allow the user to see all database objects in the view that are owned by the user accessing the view.

- **ALL_** These views typically allow the user to see all database objects in the view that are accessible to the user.

- **DBA_** This powerful set of views allows those who may access them to see all database objects that correspond to the view in the entire database.

The USER_ views are generally those views with the least scope. They only display a limited amount of information about the database objects that the user created in his or her own schema. One way that tables can be referred to is by their schema owner. For example, assume there is a database with a user named SPANKY. SPANKY creates some tables in his user schema, one of which is called PRODUCTS, and then grants access to those tables to another user on the database called ATHENA. User ATHENA can then refer to SPANKY's tables as SPANKY.PRODUCTS, or SPANKY.*tablename* for a more general format. However, if user ATHENA attempts to look in the USER_TABLES view to gather more information about table PRODUCTS, she will find nothing in that view about it. Why? *Because the table belongs to user SPANKY.*

The next level of scope in dictionary views comes with the ALL_ views. The objects whose information is displayed in the ALL_ views correspond to any database object that the user can look at, change data in, or access in any way, shape, or form. In order for a user to be able to access a database object, one of three conditions must be true. Either the user herself must have created the object, or the user must have been granted access by the object owner to manipulate the object or data in the object, or the owner of the object must have granted access privileges on the object to the PUBLIC user. The PUBLIC user in the database is a special user who represents the access privileges every user has. Thus, when an object owner creates a table and grants access to the table to user PUBLIC, then every user in the database has access privileges to the table created.

The final category of data dictionary views available on the database is DBA_ views. These views are incredibly handy for developers and DBAs to find out information about every database object corresponding to the information the view captures in the database. Thus, as mentioned earlier, the DBA_TABLES view displays information about every table in the database. At this point, the developer should note that this view allows the user to see objects in the database that the user may not even have permission to use. It can be a violation of security concerns to have certain users even aware of the existence of certain tables. If the DBA is ever in doubt about a user requesting to have access to the DBA_ views, then it is usually a good idea not to give it to them.

The name of each view has two components, which are the scope or depth to which the user will be able to see information about the object in the database (USER_, ALL_, DBA_), followed by the name of the object type itself. For example, information about tables in the database can be found in the USER_TABLES, ALL_TABLES, or DBA_TABLES views. Some other views that correspond to areas that have been discussed or will be discussed, along with some information about the contents of the view, are listed here:

- **USER_, ALL_, DBA_OBJECTS**   Gives information about various database objects

- **USER_, ALL_, DBA_TABLES**   Displays information about tables in the database

- **USER_, ALL_, DBA_INDEXES**   Displays information about indexes in the database

- **USER_, ALL_, DBA_VIEWS**   Displays information about views in the database

- **USER_, ALL_, DBA_SEQUENCES**   Displays information about sequences in the database

- **USER_, ALL_, DBA_USERS**   Displays information about users in the database

- **USER_, ALL_, DBA_CONSTRAINTS**   Displays information about constraints in the database

- **USER_, ALL_, DBA_CONS_COLUMNS**   Displays information about table columns that have constraints in the database

- **USER_, ALL_, DBA_IND_COLUMNS**   Displays information about table columns that have indexes in the database

Exercises

1. What is the data dictionary?

2. What are the three categories of views that a user may access in the dictionary? How much information about the database is available in each view?

3. Who owns the data dictionary? Are users allowed to access the tables of the dictionary directly? Why or why not?

Querying the Data Dictionary

The introduction to the views available in the data dictionary now will be used to present ways for the user to select data from the dictionary to understand better how useful the data dictionary is in Oracle. Consider first the need to get information about tables. For the purposes of this presentation, the ALL_ views will be used, except where noted. The first thing every user should learn how to do related to the data dictionary is to list the columns available in a table. A listing of the columns in a table can be obtained from the dictionary with the use of the **describe** command often abbreviated as **desc**.

```
DESC spanky.products

NAME                  NULL?           TYPE
-----------------     ----------      -----------
PRODUCT#              NOT NULL        NUMBER(10)
PRODUCT_NAME          NOT NULL        VARCHAR2(35)
QUANTITY                              NUMBER(10)
```

The user can find out any information about the database tables that is available for their usage with the ALL_TABLES view. In order to apply the description of any of these views to its sibling in the USER_ or DBA_ family, substitute the scope "available to the user" with "created by the user" or "all those created in the database" for USER_ or DBA_, respectively. ALL_TABLES displays information about who owns the table, where the table is stored in the database, and information about storage parameters that a table is using.

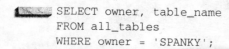

```
SELECT owner, table_name
FROM all_tables
WHERE owner = 'SPANKY';
```

Some of the other object views are similar to ALL_TABLES. For example, ALL_INDEXES contains information about the indexes on tables that are available to the user. Some of the information listed in this view corresponds to the features of the index, such as whether or not all values in the indexed column are unique. Other information in the view corresponds to the storage parameters of the index and where the index is stored.

```
SELECT owner, index_name, table_name, status
FROM all_indexes
WHERE owner = 'SPANKY';
```

The next data dictionary view represents a slight departure from the previous pattern. The ALL_VIEWS data dictionary view gives information about all the views in the database available to the user. It lists the schema owner, the view name, and the query that was used to create the view. The column containing the text that created the view is stored in LONG format. To obtain data from this column of the view, the user may need to issue the **set long** command to set the formatting that SQL*Plus will use to display to a LONG column to something large enough to display the entire query used to create the view. Typically **set long 5000** will suffice. More information about creating views in Oracle will be covered in the next chapter.

```
SET LONG 5000

SELECT owner, view_name, text
FROM all_views
WHERE owner = 'SPANKY';
```

The next view is the USER_USERS view. This view is used to tell the current user of the database more information about his or her environment. Contained in this view are the default locations where objects created by the user will be stored, along with the user profile this user will abide by. There are several other pieces of information that will be more useful in later discussions about users in the next chapter on user creation and in the next unit of this book, which discusses the management of users.

```
SELECT * FROM user_users;
```

The next few views discussed cover some more interesting material related to constraints. There are several views in this category that will be discussed, and the first one is the ALL_CONSTRAINTS view. This view is used to display information about the constraints that have been defined in the database. This view is particularly useful in determining the referenced column in cases where referential integrity constraints have been created on a table. This view gives the name of the constraint, the owner of the constraint, the name of the table the constraint is created on, and the name of the referenced table and column if the constraint created is a foreign key.

```
SELECT constraint_name, table_name, r_owner, r_constraint_name
FROM all_constraints
WHERE table_name = 'PRODUCTS' and owner = 'SPANKY';
```

The next view discussed also relates to constraints. The view is called ALL_CONS_COLUMNS, and it presents information about the columns that are incorporated into constraints on a table. For example, it is possible to create a primary key for a table that uses as its unique identifier two or more columns from the table. This definition of the primary key is sometimes referred to as a *composite primary key*. The ALL_CONS_COLUMNS view gives information about the columns that are in the primary key and which order they appear in the composite index.

```
SELECT constraint_name, table_name, column_name, column_position
FROM all_cons_columns
WHERE table_name = 'PRODUCTS' and owner = 'SPANKY';
```

The final dictionary view discussed in this section is related to the ALL_CONS_COLUMNS view, but extends the scope of that view by providing information about all the indexed columns on the database.

```
SELECT index_name, table_name, column_name, column_position
FROM all_ind_columns
WHERE table_name = 'PRODUCTS' and owner = 'SPANKY';
```

Exercises

1. Describe usage of object views. What purpose do the constraint views serve?

2. What is a composite index?

3. What purpose does the COLUMN_POSITION column serve in some of the dictionary views?

Manipulating Oracle Data

In this section, you will cover the following topics related to manipulating Oracle data:

- Inserting new rows into a table
- Making changes to existing row data
- Deleting data from the Oracle database
- The importance of transaction controls

In this section, an introduction to all forms of data change manipulation will be covered. The three types of data change manipulation that exist in the Oracle database include updating, deleting, and inserting data. These statements are collectively known as the data manipulation language of Oracle, or *DML* for short. Furthermore, a treatment of *transaction processing* will also be included. Transaction processing is a mechanism that the Oracle database provides in order to facilitate the act of changing data. Without transaction-processing mechanisms, the database would not be able to guarantee that the users would not overwrite one another's changes midprocess, or select data that is in the process of being changed by another user.

Inserting New Rows into a Table

The first data change manipulation operation that will be discussed is the act of inserting new rows into a table. Once a table is created, there is no data in the table, with the one exception of creating a table populated by rows selected from another table. Even in this case, the data must come from somewhere. This somewhere is from users who enter data into the table via **insert** statements.

An **insert** statement has syntax different from a **select** statement. The general syntax for an **insert** statement is listed in the following code block, which defines several rows to be added to the PRODUCTS table owned by SPANKY. This table has three columns, titled PRODUCT#,

PRODUCT_NAME, and QUANTITY. User SPANKY now wants to put some data in his table, so he executes the following statement designed to place one new row into the PRODUCTS table.

```
INSERT INTO products (product#,product_name, quantity)
VALUES (7848394, 'KITTY LITTER', 12);
```

Notice a few general rules of syntax in this statement. The **insert** statement has two parts, the first is one in which the table to receive the inserted row is defined, in conjunction with the columns of the table that will have the column values specified inserted into them. The second portion of the statement defines the actual data values that comprise the row to be added. This portion of the statement is denoted by use of the **values** keyword.

There are several variations Oracle is capable of handling in order to **insert** data on a table. For example, it is generally only required for the user to define explicit columns of the table in which to **insert** data when all columns of the table are not going to have data inserted into them. For example, if user SPANKY only wanted to define the product number and the name at the time the row was inserted, then SPANKY would be required to list the PRODUCT# and PRODUCT_NAME columns in the **into** clause of the **insert** statement. However, since he named column values for all columns in the table, the following statement would be just as acceptable for inserting the row into the PRODUCTS table:

```
INSERT INTO products
VALUES (7848394, 'KITTY LITTER', 12);
```

One important question to ask in this situation is how does Oracle know which column to populate with what data? Assume further about the table that the column datatypes are defined to be NUMBER for PRODUCT# and QUANTITY, and VARCHAR2 for PRODUCT_NAME. What prevents Oracle from placing the 12 in the PRODUCT# column? Again, as with the discussion of column positions in composite indexes as displayed by some of the views in the last section, position can matter in the Oracle database. The position of the data must correspond to the position of the column as it is created in the table. The user can determine the position of each column in a table by using the **describe** command. The order in which the columns are listed from the **describe** command is the same order that values should be placed in if the user would like to **insert** data into the table without explicitly naming the columns of the table.

Another variation of the **insert** theme is the ability **insert** has to populate a table using the data obtained from other tables using a **select** statement. This method of populating table data is similar to the method used by the **create table as select** statement, which was discussed earlier in the chapter. In this case, the **values** clause can be omitted entirely. Also, the rules regarding column position of the inserted data apply in this situation as well, meaning that if the user can select data for all columns of the table having data inserted into it, then the user need not name the columns in the **insert into** clause.

```
INSERT INTO products
(SELECT product#, product_name, quantity
 FROM MASTER.PRODUCTS);
```

In order to put data into a table, a special privilege must be granted from the table owner to the user who needs to perform the **insert**. A more complete discussion of object privileges will appear in the next chapter. Note also that data cannot be inserted into a table that allows only read-only access to its data.

Exercises

1. What statement is used to place new data into an Oracle table?

2. What are the three options available with the statement that allows new data to be placed into Oracle tables?

Making Changes to Existing Row Data

Often, the data rows in a table will need to be changed. In order to make those changes, the **update** statement can be used. Updates can be made to any row in a database, except in two cases. Data that a user does not have enough access privileges to **update** cannot be updated by that user, and data that is **read only** cannot be updated by any user. Data is updated by the user when an **update** statement is issued.

```
UPDATE spanky.products
   SET quantity = 54
   WHERE product# = 4959495;
```

Notice that the typical **update** statement has three clauses. The first is the actual **update** clause, where the table that will be updated is named. The second clause is the **set** clause. In the **set** clause, all columns that will be changed by the **update** statement are named, along with their new values. The list of columns in the **set** clause can be updated as long as there are columns in the table being updated. The final clause of the **update** statement is the **where** clause. The **where** clause in an **update** statement is the same as the **where** clause in a **select** statement. There are one or more comparison operations that determine which rows Oracle will **update** as a result of this statement being issued.

The **update** and **set** clauses are mandatory in an **update** statement. However, the **where** clause is not. Omitting the **where** clause in an **update** statement has the effect of applying the data change to every row that presently exists in the table. Consider the following code block that issues a data change without a **where** clause specified. The change made by this statement will therefore apply to every column in the table.

```
UPDATE spanky.products
   SET quantity = 0;
```

Every operation that was possible in the **where** clauses of a **select** statement are possible in the **where** clauses of an **update**. The **where** clause in an **update** statement can have any type of comparison or range operation in it, and can even handle the use of the **exists** operation or other uses for subqueries.

Exercises

1. What statement is used to change data in an Oracle table? What clauses in this statement are mandatory?

2. When can a user not change data in a table?

Deleting Data from the Oracle Database

The removal of data from a database is as much a fact of life as putting the data there in the first place. Removal of database rows from tables is accomplished with the use of the **delete** statement in SQL*Plus. The syntax for usage of the **delete** statement is detailed in the following code block. Note that in the next example there is no way to **delete** data from selected columns in a row in the table; this act is accomplished with the **update** statement where the columns that are to be "deleted" are set to NULL by the **update** statement.

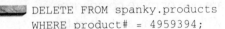

```
DELETE FROM spanky.products
WHERE product# = 4959394;
```

As in the case of database updates, **delete** statements use the **where** clause to help determine which rows are meant to be deleted. In the same way as an **update** or **select** statement, the **where** clause in a **delete** statement can contain any type of comparison operation, range operation, subquery, or any other operation acceptable for a **where** clause. In the same way as an **update** statement, if the **where** clause is left off the **delete** statement, then the deletion will be applied to all rows in the table.

Data deletion is a careful matter to undertake. It can be costly to replace data that has been deleted from the database, which is why the privilege to **delete** information should only be given out to those users who really should be able to **delete** records from a table. As in the case of updates, data cannot be deleted from a table by any user if that table is **read only**.

Exercises

1. What statement is used to remove data from an Oracle table? What clauses in this statement are mandatory?

2. When can a user not remove data in a table?

The Importance of Transaction Controls

One of the first realities that a user of the Oracle database must understand is that a change to data made in the Oracle database is not saved immediately. Oracle allows for a period in which a user can specify several changes to database data before saving those changes to the database, and thus making the changes available to other users on the database. This period allotted to a user to make changes is called a transaction.

Transaction processing consists of a set of controls that allow a user issuing an **insert**, **update**, or **delete** statement to declare a beginning to the series of data change statements he or she will issue. When the user has completed making the changes to the database, the user can save the data to the database by explicitly ending the transaction. Alternatively, if a mistake is made at any point during the transaction, the user can have the database discard the changes made on the database in favor of the way the data existed before the transaction began. This principle is known as statement-level read consistency, and it is a feature provided by Oracle as part of transaction-processing mechanisms.

Transactions are created with the usage of two different concepts in the Oracle database. The first concept is the set of commands that define the beginning, middle, and end of a transaction. These commands are listed in the following set of bullets. The second concept is that of special locking mechanisms designed to prevent more than one user from making a change to row information in a database at a time. Locks will be discussed after the transaction control commands are defined.

- **SET TRANSACTION** Initiates the beginning of a transaction and sets key features

- **COMMIT** Ends current transaction by saving database changes and starts new transaction

- **ROLLBACK** Ends current transaction by discarding database changes

- **SAVEPOINT** Defines "midpoint" for the transaction to allow partial rollbacks

SET TRANSACTION

This command is used to define the beginning of a transaction. If any change is made to the database after the **set transaction** command is issued but before the transaction is ended, all changes made will be considered part of that transaction. The **set transaction** command has several possible effects. The first effect that can be created by **set transaction** is that the transaction can be configured to use **read only** access to the database.

Alternatively, the transaction can state to Oracle that it plans to read and write data on the database.

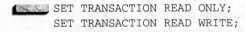
```
SET TRANSACTION READ ONLY;
SET TRANSACTION READ WRITE;
```

COMMIT

The **commit** statement in transaction processing represents the point in time where the user has made all the changes she wants to have logically grouped together, and since no mistakes have been made, the user is ready to save her work. The **work** keyword is an extraneous word in the **commit** syntax that is designed for readability. Issuing a **commit** statement also implicitly begins a new transaction on the database. It is important also to understand the implicit **commit** that occurs on the database when a user exits SQL*Plus or issues a DDL such as a **create table** statement.

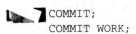
```
COMMIT;
COMMIT WORK;
```

ROLLBACK

If the user has at any point issued a data change statement that produces a mistake, the user can discard the changes made to the database with the use of the **rollback** statement. After the **rollback** command is issued, a new transaction is started implicitly by the database session. In addition to rollbacks executed when the **rollback** statement is issued, there are implicit **rollback** statements conducted when a statement fails for any reason or if the user cancels a statement with the CTRL+C **cancel** command.

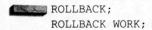
```
ROLLBACK;
ROLLBACK WORK;
```

SAVEPOINT

In some cases involving long transactions or transactions that involve many data changes, the user may not want to scrap all the change made simply because the last statement issued contains a mistake. Savepoints are special operations that allow the user to divide the work of a transaction into different segments. The user can execute rollbacks to the savepoint only, leaving prior changes intact. Savepoint usage is great for situations like this where part of the transaction needs to be recovered in an uncommitted transaction. At the point the **rollback to savepoint A1** statement completes

In the following code block, only changes made before the savepoint was defined are kept when the **commit** is issued.

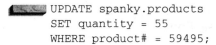

```
UPDATE spanky.products
SET quantity = 55
WHERE product# = 59495;

SAVEPOINT A1;

UPDATE spanky.products
SET quantity = 504;

ROLLBACK TO SAVEPOINT A1;
COMMIT;
```

Locks

The final aspect of the Oracle database that allows the user to have transaction processing is a lock, the mechanism by which Oracle prevents data from being changed by more than one user at a time. There are several different types of locks, each with its own level of scope. Locks available on a database are categorized into table-level locks and row-level locks. A table-level lock makes it so that only the user holding the lock can change any piece of row data in the table, during which time no other users can make changes anywhere on the table. A row-level lock is one that allows the user the exclusive ability to change data in one or more rows of the table. However, any row in the table that is not held by the row-level lock can be changed by another user.

TIP

*An **update** statement acquires a special row-level lock called a "row-exclusive" lock, which means that for the period of time the **update** statement is executing, no other user in the database can view OR change the data in the row. Another **update** statement, the **select for update** statement, acquires a more lenient lock called the "share row" lock. This lock means that for the period of time the **update** statement is changing the data in the rows of the table, no other user may change that row, but users may look at the data in the row as it changes.*

Exercises

1. What is transaction processing?

2. Identify the mechanisms that support transactions.

Chapter Summary

This chapter covered the foundational material for understanding the mechanics of creating an Oracle database. The material in this chapter corresponds to 22 percent of the test material in OCP Exam 1 and represents the foundation on which other exams will build. This understanding is required in order to move the casual user who understands material related to selecting data from an Oracle database to a full-fledged expert on the Oracle database server product. Understanding this material is crucial to understanding several areas in the rest of this guide, including the management of tables, using rollback segments, locks and the contention issues they often produce, and proper management of the data dictionary.

The first portion of this chapter discussed the concepts of data modeling. In order to create a database in Oracle, it is important that all stages of system development be executed carefully. Some of the stages covered include needs assessment, requirements definition, database design, application development, performance tuning, security enforcement, and enhancements development. The final stage in that life cycle is really a miniature version of the first several stages rolled into one. The needs assessment stage is a critical one. It is the period of time where the users of the system are identified, and the desired and required features of the system are documented. After needs assessment, a full list of requirements should be agreed upon and documented so as to avoid costly rework later. Once the requirements of the system are completely understood, the developers of the database portion of the application should model the business process required into an entity-relationship diagram, which consists of entities, or persons, places, things, or ideas involved in the process flow, and the relationships between each entity. This entity-relationship diagram will then be used to create a logical data model, or a pictorial diagram of the tables that will represent each entity and the referential integrity constraints that will represent each relationship. Ordinality is a key point here. Ordinality defines whether the relationship is mandatory for the entities partaking of the relationship, and the record-to-record correspondence of one record in a database. There are three types of record-to-record correspondence in the database—one-to-one, one-to-many, and many-to-many. A one-to-one correspondence means that one record of one table corresponds to one record in another. One-to-many correspondence means that one record from one table corresponds to many records of another table. Many-to-many correspondence means that several records from one table correspond to several records on another table.

Once the planning is complete, than developers and DBAs can move forward with the process of actually creating the database. The syntax for creating a table with column definitions and constraints is covered in this chapter. A table can be created with several different columns. The allowed datatypes for these columns in Oracle7 are VARCHAR2, CHAR, NUMBER, DATE, RAW, LONG, LONG RAW, MLSLABEL and ROWID. More datatypes are available in Oracle8. One or more of these columns is used to define the primary key, or element in each row that distinguishes one row of data from another in the table. A primary key is one type of integrity constraint. Another type of integrity constraint is the foreign key, which defines referential integrity on the table, creating table relationships and often modeling the relationships between entities from the entity-relationship diagram. Referential integrity produces a parent/child relationship between two tables. Sometimes it is useful to name tables according to conventions that have the child objects take on the name of the parent object as part of their own name. The three other constraints available on the database are unique, check, and NOT NULL. Unique constraints prevent duplicate non-NULL values from appearing in a column for two or more rows. Check constraints verify data in a column against a set of constants defined to be valid values. NOT NULL constraints prevent the entry of NULL data for a column on which the NOT NULL constraint is defined. Two of the five constraints create indexes to help enforce the integrity they are designed to enforce. Those two constraints are the ones designed to enforce uniqueness, the unique constraint and the primary key. Finally, a table is created with no data in it, except in the case of the **create table as select**. This statement allows the user to create a table with row data prepopulated from another table. All options available for regular **select** statements are available in this statement as well.

The next portion of this chapter discussed the Oracle data dictionary. The data dictionary contains information about all objects created in the database. It also contains a listing of available columns in each object created in the database. Information about table columns can be obtained using the **describe** command, followed by the name of the table the user wants to view the columns on. Information is kept in data dictionary tables about the objects created in Oracle, where they are stored, and performance statistics. However, the user will not usually access the tables of the data dictionary directly. Rather, the user generally will look at that data using data dictionary views. Data can be selected from views in the same way it can be selected from tables. No user is able to **delete** data from the data dictionary, because doing so could permanently damage the Oracle database. All tables and views in the Oracle data dictionary are owned by SYS.

Several data dictionary views are available to find out information about the objects discussed in this unit. Those views are divided into three general categories that correspond to the scope of data availability in the view. The USER_ views show information on objects owned by the user, the ALL_ views show information on all the objects accessible by the user, and the DBA_ views show information on all objects in the database. Data dictionary views are available on every type of object in the database, including indexes, constraints, tables, views, synonyms, sequences, and triggers. Additionally, information is available to help the user understand which columns are available in indexes or primary-key constraints. Several views exist to show the position of columns in composite indexes, which are indexes that contain several columns.

The remainder of the chapter discussed the usage of SQL statements for the purpose of changing data in a database. There are three types of data change statements available in the Oracle database. They are **update**, **insert**, and **delete**. The **update** statement allows the user to change row data that already exists in the database. The **insert** statement allows the user to add new row data records to the tables of a database. The **delete** statement allows the user to remove records from the database. The various data change operations are supported in Oracle with the usage of transaction-processing controls. There are several different aspects to transaction processing. These include the commands used to set the beginning, middle, and end of transactions, rollback segments designed to store uncommitted data changes, and the locking mechanisms that allow one and only one user at a time to make changes to the data in the database.

Two-Minute Drill

- The stages of system development include needs assessment, requirements definition, database design, application development, performance tuning, database security enforcement, and enhancement development.

- The basic types of data relationships in Oracle include primary keys and functional dependency within a table, and foreign-key constraints and referential integrity between two or more tables.

- A relational database is composed of objects to store data, objects to manage access to data, and objects to improve performance on accessing data.

- Within database planning, it is necessary to create an entity-relationship diagram that acts as a visual representation of the business process being modeled. The diagram consists of people, places, things, and ideas called entities, which are related to one another using activities or a process flow called relationships.

- Once an entity-relationship diagram has been created for an application, it must be translated into a logical data model. The logical data model is a collection of tables that represent entities and referential integrity constraints that represent relationships.

- A table can be created with five different types of integrity constraints: primary keys, foreign keys, unique constraints, NOT NULL constraints, and check constraints.

- Referential integrity often creates a parent/child relationship between two tables, the parent being the referenced table and the child being the referring table. Often, a naming convention that requires child objects to adopt and extend the name of the parent table is useful in identifying these relationships.

- The datatypes available in Oracle7 for creating columns in tables are CHAR, VARCHAR2, NUMBER, DATE, RAW, LONG, LONG RAW, ROWID, and MLSLABEL.

■ Indexes are created automatically in conjunction with primary-key and unique constraints. These indexes are named after the constraint name given to the constraint in the definition of the table.

■ Tables are created without any data in them, except for tables created with the **create table as select** statement. These tables are created with data prepopulated from another table.

■ There is information available in the Oracle database to help users, developers, and DBAs know what objects exist in the Oracle database. The information is in the Oracle data dictionary.

■ To find the positional order of columns in a table, or what columns there are in a table at all, the user can issue a **describe** command on that table. The Oracle data dictionary will then list all columns in the table being described.

■ Data dictionary views on database objects are divided into three categories: USER_, for objects created by or owned by the user; ALL_, for all objects accessible to the user; and DBA_, for all objects created of this type in the database.

■ New rows are inserted into a table with the **insert** statement. The user issuing the **insert** statement can **insert** one or more rows at a time with one statement.

■ Existing rows in a database table can be modified using the **update** statement. The **update** statement contains a **where** clause similar in function to the **where** clause of **select** statements.

■ Existing rows in a table can be deleted using the **delete** statement. The **delete** statement also contains a **where** clause similar in function to the **where** clause in **update** or **select** statements.

■ Transaction processing controls the change of data in an Oracle database.

■ Transaction controls include commands that identify the beginning, middle, and end of a transaction, locking mechanisms that prevent more than one user at a time from making changes in the database, and rollback segments that store uncommitted data changes made to the database.

Chapter Questions

1. **Which of the following integrity constraints automatically create an index when defined? (Choose two)**

   A. Foreign keys

   B. Unique constraints

   C. NOT NULL constraints

   D. Primary keys

2. **Which of the following dictionary views give information about the position of a column in a primary key?**

   A. ALL_PRIMARY_KEYS

   B. USER_CONSTRAINTS

   C. ALL_IND_COLUMNS

   D. ALL_TABLES

3. **Developer ANJU executes the following statement: CREATE TABLE animals AS SELECT * from MASTER.ANIMALS; What is the effect of this statement?**

   A. A table named ANIMALS will be created in the MASTER schema with the same data as the ANIMALS table owned by ANJU.

   B. A table named ANJU will be created in the ANIMALS schema with the same data as the ANIMALS table owned by MASTER.

   C. A table named ANIMALS will be created in the ANJU schema with the same data as the ANIMALS table owned by MASTER.

   D. A table named MASTER will be created in the ANIMALS schema with the same data as the ANJU table owned by ANIMALS.

4. User JANKO would like to insert a row into the EMPLOYEE table, which has three columns: EMPID, LASTNAME, and SALARY. The user would like to enter data for EMPID 59694, LASTNAME Harris, but no salary. Which statement would work best?

   A. insert into EMPLOYEE values (59694,'HARRIS', NULL);

   B. insert into EMPLOYEE values (59694,'HARRIS');

   C. insert into EMPLOYEE (EMPID, LASTNAME, SALARY) values (59694,'HARRIS');

   D. insert into EMPLOYEE (select 59694 from 'HARRIS');

5. Which two components are parts of an entity relationship diagram? (Choose two)

   A. Referential integrity constraints

   B. Entities

   C. Relationships

   D. Triggers

6. Which of the following choices is the strongest indicator of a parent/child relationship?

   A. Two tables in the database are named VOUCHER and VOUCHER_ITEM, respectively.

   B. Two tables in the database are named EMPOYEE and PRODUCTS, respectively.

   C. Two tables in the database were created on the same day.

   D. Two tables in the database contain none of the same columns.

7. The purpose of data normalization is to correct integrity problems that occurred during data entry.

   A. TRUE

   B. FALSE

8. **Which three of the following are valid database datatypes in Oracle? (Choose three)**

   A. CHAR

   B. VARCHAR2

   C. BOOLEAN

   D. NUMBER

9. **Omitting the WHERE clause from a DELETE statement has which of the following effects?**

   A. The **delete** statement will fail because there are no records to delete.

   B. The **delete** statement will prompt the user to enter criteria for the deletion.

   C. The **delete** statement will fail because of syntax error.

   D. The **delete** statement will remove all records from the table.

10. **Creating a foreign-key constraint between columns of two tables defined with two different datatypes will produce an error.**

    A. TRUE

    B. FALSE

11. **Which line of the following statement will produce an error?**

    A. **create table** GOODS

    B. (GOOD_NO **number**,

    C. GOOD_NAME **varchar2 check**(GOOD_NAME in (**select** NAME FROM AVAIL_GOODS)),

    D. **constraint** PK_GOODS_01

    E. **primary key** (GOODNO));

    F. There are no errors in this statement.

12. **A CREATE TABLE AS SELECT statement may not have any subqueries in its WHERE clause.**

    A. TRUE

    B. FALSE

13. **The transaction control that prevents more than one user from updating data in a table is called**

    A. Locks

    B. Commits

    C. Rollbacks

    D. Savepoints

Answers to Chapter Questions

1. B and D.   Unique constraints and primary keys

Explanation   Every constraint that enforces uniqueness creates an index to assist in the process. The two integrity constraints that enforce uniqueness are unique constraints and primary keys. Refer to the discussion of creating a table with integrity constraints.

2. C.   ALL_IND_COLUMNS

Explanation   This view is the only one listed that provides column positions in an index. Since primary keys create an index, the index created by the primary key will be listed with all the other indexed data. Choice A is incorrect because no view exists in Oracle called PRIMARY_KEYS. Choice B is incorrect because although ALL_CONSTRAINTS lists information about the constraints in a database, it does not contain information about the index created by the primary key. Choice D is incorrect because ALL_TABLES contains no information related to the position of a column in an index.

3. C.   A table named ANIMALS will be created in the ANJU schema with the same data as the ANIMALS table owned by MASTER.

Explanation   This question requires the user to look carefully at the **create table** statement in the question, and to know some things about table creation. First, a table is always created in the schema of the user who created it. Second, since the **create table as select** clause was used, choices B and D are both incorrect because they identify the table being created as something other than ANIMALS, among other things. Choice A identifies the schema into which the ANIMALS table will be created as MASTER, which is incorrect for the reasons just stated. Refer to the discussion of creating tables for more information.

4. A.   **insert into** EMPLOYEE **values** (59694,'HARRIS', NULL);

Explanation   This choice is acceptable because the positional criteria for not specifying column order is met by the data in the **values** clause. When a user would like to specify that no data be inserted into a particular column, one method of doing so is to **insert** a NULL. Choice B is incorrect because not all columns in the table have values identified. When using positional references to populate column data, there must be values present for every column in the table. Otherwise, the columns that will be populated should be named explicitly. Choice C is incorrect because when a column is named for data **insert** in the **insert into** clause, then a value must definitely be specified in the **values** clause. Choice D is incorrect because using the multiple row **insert** option with a **select** statement is not appropriate in this situation. Refer to the discussion of **insert** statements for more information.

5. B and C. Entities and Relationships

Explanation There are only two components to an entity-relationship diagram—entities and relationships. Choices A and D are incorrect because referential integrity constraints and triggers are part of database implementation of a logical data model. Refer to the discussion of an entity-relationship diagram.

6. A. Two tables in the database are named VOUCHER and VOUCHER_ITEM, respectively.

Explanation This choice implies the use of a naming convention similar to the one discussed in the guide. Although there is no guarantee that these two tables are related, the possibility is strongest with this option. Choice B implies the same naming convention, and since the two tables' names are dissimilar, there is little likelihood that the two tables are related in any way. Choice C is incorrect because the date a table is created has absolutely no bearing on what function the table serves in the database. Choice D is incorrect because two tables can NOT be related if there are no common columns between them. Refer to the discussion of creating tables with integrity constraints, naming conventions, and data modeling in the guide.

7. B. FALSE

Explanation The purpose of data normalization is to reduce the redundancy in the number of times a column is stored in the database, and to minimize the functional dependency of any column to be related to only one primary key. Review the discussion of data modeling in this guide.

8. A, B, and D.   CHAR, VARCHAR2, and NUMBER.

Explanation   BOOLEAN is the only invalid datatype in this listing. Although BOOLEAN is a valid datatype in PL/SQL, it is not a datatype available on the Oracle database, meaning that you cannot create a column in a table that uses the BOOLEAN datatype. Review the discussion of allowed datatypes in column definition.

9. D.   The **delete** statement will remove all records from the table.

Explanation   There is only one effect produced by leaving off the **where** clause from any statement that allows one—the requested operation is performed on all records in the table.

10. A.   TRUE

Explanation   A foreign-key constraint can only be created on columns in two tables with the same datatype. Refer to the discussion of creating tables with foreign-key constraints.

11. C.   GOOD_NAME **varchar2 check**(GOOD_NAME in (**select** NAME **from** AVAIL_GOODS)),

Explanation   A check constraint cannot contain a reference to another table, nor can it reference a virtual column such as ROWID or SYSDATE.

12. B.   FALSE

Explanation   The conditions that apply to the **select** portion in a **create table as select** statement are the same as those that apply to other **select** statements. Refer to the discussion of creating tables with data from other tables.

13. A.   Locks

Explanation   Locks are the mechanisms that prevent more than one user at a time from making changes to the database. All other options refer to the commands that are issued to mark the beginning, middle, and end of a transaction. Review the discussion of transaction controls as part of this guide.

CHAPTER
4

Creating Other Database Objects in Oracle

n this chapter, you will understand and demonstrate knowledge in the following areas:

- Altering tables and constraints
- Creating sequences
- Creating views
- Creating indexes
- Controlling user access

At this point, the user should know how to select data from a database, model a business process, design a set of database tables from that process, and populate those tables with data. These functions represent the cornerstone of functionality that Oracle can provide in an organization. However, the design of a database does not stop there. There are several features in the Oracle architecture that allows the user to give richer, deeper meaning to the databases created in Oracle. These features can make data "transparent" to some users but not to others, speed access to data, or generate primary keys for database tables automatically. These features are collectively known as the advanced database features of the Oracle database. This chapter covers material in several different areas tested in the OCP Exam 1. The material in this chapter consists of 17 percent of the material covered on the exam.

Table and Constraint Modifications

In this section, you will cover the following topics related to altering tables and constraints:

- Adding and modifying columns
- Modifying integrity constraints
- Enabling or disabling constraints
- Dropping tables

- Truncating tables

- Changing names of objects

- Dictionary comments on objects

Once a table is created, any of several things can happen to make the needs of the database change such that the table must be changed. The database developer and DBA will need to understand how to implement changes on the database in an effective and *nondisruptive* manner. Consider the implications of this statement. For example, there are two ways to cure an ingrown toenail. One is to go to a podiatrist and have the toenail removed. The other is to chop off the toe. Although both approaches work, the second one produces side effects that most people can safely do without. The same concept applies to database changes. The developer or DBA can do one of two things when a request to add some columns to a table comes in. One is to add the column, and the other is to re-create the entire table from scratch. Obviously, there is a great deal of value in knowing the right way to perform the first approach.

Adding and Modifying Columns

Columns can be added and modified in the Oracle database with ease using the **alter table** statement and its many options for changing the number of columns in the database. When adding columns, a column added with a NOT NULL constraint must have data populated for that column in all rows before the NOT NULL constraint is enabled, and only one column of the LONG datatype can appear in a table in Oracle7. The following code block is an example of using the **alter table** statement.

```
ALTER TABLE products
ADD (color VARCHAR2(10));
```

If the developer or the DBA needs to add a column that will have a NOT NULL constraint on it, then several things needs to happen. The column should first be created without the constraint, then the column should have a value for all rows populated. After all column values are NOT NULL, the NOT NULL constraint can be applied to it. If the user tries to add a column with a NOT NULL constraint on it, the developer will encounter an error stating that the table must be NULL.

Only one column in the table may be of type LONG within a table. That restriction includes the LONG RAW datatype. This restriction, as well as the entire usage of datatypes to store large amounts of data, was removed and remodeled as part of Oracle8. More details appear in Unit V. It is sometimes useful in Oracle7 databases to have a special table that contains the LONG column and a foreign key to the table that would have contained the column in order to reduce the amount of data migration and row chaining on the database. More details about row chaining and migration will appear in Unit IV.

Another important facet about table columns is the configuration of the datatype that is permitted for storage in the column. On a table called PRODUCTS, there is a column called SERIAL# of type VARCHAR2(10). The retailer has just begun to carry a new line of products whose serial number is substantially longer than the serial numbers of other products the store carries. The DBA is called in to determine if the longer serial number will present a problem to the database. As it turns out, the average serial number for this new line of products is 23 characters long. In order to resolve the issue, the DBA can issue a statement that will make the column length longer.

```
ALTER TABLE products
MODIFY (serial#  VARCHAR2(25));
```

Several conditions apply to modifying the datatypes of existing columns or to adding columns to a table in the database. The general rule of thumb is that increases are generally OK, while decreases are usually a little trickier. Some examples of increases that are generally acceptable are listed as follows:

- Increases to the size of a VARCHAR2 or CHAR column

- Increases in size of a NUMBER column

- Increasing the number of columns in the table

Decreasing the size of various aspects of the table, including some of the column datatypes or the actual number of columns in the table, requires special steps to accomplish. Usually, the effort involves making sure that the relevant column (or columns) has all NULL values in it before executing the change. In order to execute these types of operations on columns or tables that contain data, the developer or DBA must find or create some sort of temporary storage place for the data in the column. One acceptable method is creating a table using the **create table as select** statement where the **select** statement used draws data from the primary key and the column(s) in question that will be altered. Another method is spooling the data in a table to a flat file and reloading later using SQL*Loader. More information about this method will be discussed in Unit II. The following list details the allowable operations that decrease various aspects of the database:

- Reducing the number of columns in a table (empty table only)

- Reducing the size of a NUMBER column (empty column for all rows only)

- Reducing the length of a VARCHAR2 or CHAR column (empty column for all rows only)

- Changing the datatype of a column (empty column for all rows only)

Exercises

1. What statement is used to change the definition of a table?

2. What process is used to change a nullable column to one with a NOT NULL constraint?

3. What are some of the rules and guidelines for changing column definitions?

Modifying Integrity Constraints

There are several different changes that can be made to constraints. These changes include altering the constraint, disabling, enabling, or removing the constraint from the column or table of the database. These processes allow the DBA or developer to create, modify, or remove the business rules that constrain data. The first activity that a DBA or developer may need to do related to supporting constraints on a database is to add constraints to a database. This process can be easy or difficult, depending on the circumstances. If a constraint cannot be created with the database, it can be added to the database before data is populated into the database with the most ease of any scenario in which a constraint must be added to the database.

```
ALTER TABLE products
MODIFY (color  NOT NULL);

ALTER TABLE products
ADD (CONSTRAINT pk_products _01 PRIMARY KEY (product#));

ALTER TABLE products
ADD (CONSTRAINT fk_products _02 FOREIGN KEY (color)
REFERENCES (AVAIL_COLORS.color));

ALTER TABLE products
ADD (UNIQUE (serial#));

ALTER TABLE products
ADD(size CHECK (size in 'P,S,M,L,XL,XXL,XXXL'));
```

Notice that in the first statement in the list of examples that the **modify** clause is used to add a NOT NULL constraint to the column, while the **add** clause is used to add all other types of integrity constraints. The column must already exist in the database table. No constraint can be created for a column that does not exist in the table. Some of the restrictions on creating constraints are listed here:

■ **Primary keys** Columns cannot be NULL and must have all unique values.

■ **Foreign keys** Referenced columns in other tables must contain values corresponding to all values in the referring columns or the referring columns values must be NULL.

■ **Unique constraints** Columns must contain all unique values or NULL.

■ **Check constraints** The new constraint will only be applied to data added or modified after the constraint is created.

■ **NOT NULL** Columns cannot be NULL.

If any of the conditions for the constraints just listed are not met for the respective constraint to which the rule applies, then creation of the constraint *will fail*. The proper procedure the DBA should take to correct the situation where the creation of a constraint fails is detailed in Unit II.

Exercises

1. What are some of the ways integrity constraints can be changed on a table?

2. What are some rules that must be adhered to for modification of each type of constraint?

Enabling or Disabling Constraints

What happens to a constraint if the creation of the constraint fails? This question is answered by examining the concept of enabling or disabling a constraint. Think of a constraint as a switch. When the switch is enabled, the constraint will do its job in enforcing business rules on the data entering the table. If the switch is disabled, the rules defined for the constraint are not enforced, rendering the constraint as ineffective as if it had been removed. Examine the process of enabling a disabled constraint. This process may be executed after the DBA has taken steps to correct the reason the integrity constraint failed during creation in the first place. When the problem has been corrected or when the load completes, the DBA may want to take steps to put the constraints back in order again.

```
ALTER TABLE products
ENABLE pk_products_01;

ALTER TABLE products
ENABLE uk_products_03;
```

Note that in this situation, only constraints that have been defined and are currently disabled can be enabled by this code. A constraint that has not been created cannot be enabled. As just discussed, a constraint that fails on creation will automatically be disabled. There are situations where the DBA may want to disable a constraint for some general purpose. *BE CAREFUL WHEN USING THIS APPROACH, HOWEVER!* If data is loaded into a table that violates the integrity constraint while the constraint was disabled, the DBA's attempt to enable the constraint later will fail. Precautions should be taken to ensure that data loaded into a table that has disabled constraints on it does not violate the constraint rules so that the enabling of the constraint later will be a smooth process. If there are dependent foreign keys on a primary key, the **cascade** option is required for disabling or dropping a primary key.

```
ALTER TABLE products
DISABLE PRIMARY KEY;

ALTER TABLE products
DISABLE PRIMARY KEY CASCADE;

ALTER TABLE products
DISABLE UNIQUE (serial#);
```

TIP

Disabling a constraint leaves the table vulnerable to inappropriate data being entered into the table. Care should be taken to ensure that the data loaded during the period the constraint is disabled will not interfere with the DBA's ability to enable the constraint later.

The final aspect of constraint manipulation to be discussed is the removal of a constraint. There is generally nothing about a constraint that will interfere with the DBA's ability to remove a constraint, so long as the person attempting to do so is either the owner of the table or granted the appropriate privilege to do so. A full discussion of system and object privileges in Oracle appears in Unit II. When a constraint is dropped, any associated index with that constraint (if there is one) is also dropped.

```
ALTER TABLE products
DROP CONSTRAINT uk_products_01;

ALTER TABLE products
DROP PRIMARY KEY CASCADE;
```

TIP

*Several anomalies can be found when adding, enabling, disabling, or dropping NOT NULL constraints. Generally, the **alter table modify** clause must be used in all situations where the NOT NULL constraints on a table must be altered.*

Exercises

1. How does the DBA enable a disabled constraint?

2. What are some restrictions on enabling constraints?

Dropping Tables

Sometimes, the "cut off your toe" approach to database alteration is required to make sweeping changes to a table in the database. All requirements to executing that approach have been discussed so far except one—eliminating the offending table. In order to delete a table from the database, the **drop table** command must be executed.

```
DROP TABLE products;
```

If there are foreign key constraints on other tables that reference the table to be dropped, then the DBA can use **cascade constraints**. The constraints in other tables that refer to the table being dropped are also dropped with **cascade constraints**. There are usually some associated objects that exist in a database along with the table. These objects may include the index that is created by the primary key or the unique constraint that is associated with columns in the table. If the table is dropped, Oracle automatically drops any index associated with the table as well.

```
DROP TABLE products
CASCADE CONSTRAINTS;
```

Exercises

1. How is a table dropped?

2. What special clause must be used when dropping a table when other tables have foreign key constraints against it?

3. What happens to associated objects like indexes when a table is dropped?

Truncating Tables

There is a special option available in Oracle that allows certain users to delete information from a table quickly. Remember, in the last chapter the

delete statement was discussed. One limitation of the **delete** statement is the fact that it uses the transaction processing controls that were also covered in the last chapter. Sometimes, in large tables or when the DBA or privileged developer is sure he or she wants to remove the data in a table, the **delete** option is an inefficient one for accomplishing the job.

As an alternative, the DBA or developer may use the **truncate** statement. The **truncate** statement is a part of the data definition language of the Oracle database, unlike the **delete** statement, which is part of the DML. Truncating a table removes all row data from a table quickly while leaving the definition of the table intact, including the definition of constraints and indexes on the table. The **truncate** statement is a high-speed data deletion that bypasses the transaction controls available in Oracle for recoverability in data changes. Truncating a table is almost always faster than executing the **delete** statement without a **where** clause to delete all rows from the table, but once complete, the data cannot be recovered without having a backed up copy of the data. More information about backup and recovery will be discussed in Unit III.

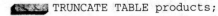 TRUNCATE TABLE products;

Exercises

1. What are two options for deleting data from a table?

2. Is truncating a table part of DML or DDL? Explain.

Changing Names of Objects

To change object names in Oracle is accomplished using the **rename** command. This command allows the DBA to change the name of one table to another by taking data from one table and automatically moves it to another that is called something else. Use of **rename** can take a long time, depending on the size of the table involved in the operation.

RENAME products TO objects;

The effect here can be duplicated through the use of synonyms. A synonym gives users an alternate name with which they can use to refer to the existing table. No actual data movement takes place, as in the **rename** command, which physically moves data in the Oracle database to an object with the new name. Renaming tables can be detrimental to performance, especially if the object being renamed is large.

TIP
Synonyms in Oracle are used to offer an alternate name to the table without altering the details of the table's definition. Synonyms can be public or private, as Oracle supports data privacy.

Exercises

   1. How is a database object name changed? What are some of the effects of renaming a table?

   2. What is another way to duplicate the effect of renaming a table?

Viewing Dictionary Comments on Objects

The Oracle data dictionary carries many different items about the table, including the description of the columns in the table. This is provided by the data dictionary with use of the **describe** command. More object information can be found in the data dictionary is the use of object commenting. Comments are useful for recording data modeling information or any other information about the database objects directly within the data dictionary. To add a comment to a table or column, use the **comment on** statement. To view these comments, query the ALL_TAB_COMMENTS for tables, or ALL_COL_COMMENTS for columns on tables.

```
COMMENT ON TABLE product IS your_comment;
COMMENT ON COLUMN product.serial# IS your_comment;
```

Exercises .

   1. How can table remarks be entered and where are they stored?

   2. How can the DBA reference comments on a database object?

Sequences

In this section, you will cover the following topics related to creating sequences:

- The use of sequences
- Creating sequences
- Using sequences
- Modifying the sequence definition
- Removing sequences

In database development, sometimes it becomes necessary to populate a column with a series of integers on an ongoing basis. These integers may be used as numbers to identify the records being entered as unique. For example, a doctor's office may have a client tracking system that assigns each new patient a unique integer ID to identify their records. There are several ways to produce this integer ID through programmatic means, but the most effective means to do it in Oracle is through sequences.

Role of Sequences

A sequence is a special database object that generates integers according to specified rules at the time the sequence was created. Sequences have many purposes in database systems, the most common of which is to generate primary keys automatically. This task is common in situations where the primary key is not important to use for accessing data to store in a table. The common use of sequences to create primary keys has some drawbacks, though. With the use of sequences for this purpose, the primary key itself and the index it creates is rendered somewhat meaningless. One other area of use for sequences is for random number generation.

Sequences operate on the following principle. Users select data from them using two special keywords to denote virtual columns in the database. The first virtual column is CURRVAL. This column can be used to see what the current value generated by the sequence is. The second virtual column is NEXTVAL. This column is the next value that the sequence will generate according to the rules developed for it. Selecting NEXTVAL on the sequence effectively eliminates whatever value is stored in CURRVAL. Data may only be drawn from a sequence, never placed into it. These virtual columns are available for **select** access, but users can incorporate a call on the sequence's CURRVAL or NEXTVAL to use the value in either of the two columns for insert or update on a row of another table.

Some restrictions are placed on the types of statements that can draw on CURRVAL and NEXTVAL of sequences as well. Any **update** or **insert** statement can make use of the data in a sequence. However, it generally is not advisable to set up an **insert** or **update** statement to do so in a trigger, as this has a tendency to cause the SQL*Plus session that fires the trigger to end abnormally with the ORA-03113 error. In addition, subqueries of **select** statements (including those with **having**), views, **select** statements using set operations such as **union** or **minus**, or any **select** statement that requires a sort to be performed are not able to contain reference to a sequence.

Exercises

1. What is a sequence? What are some ways a sequence can be used?

2. What are CURRVAL and NEXTVAL? What happens to CURRVAL when NEXTVAL is selected?

Creating Sequences

Many rules are available on sequences that allow the developer or DBA to specify how the sequence generates integers. These rules are useful for the definition of sequences that produce integers in special order, or with increments in a certain way. There is even a feature related to sequences that allows the developer to improve performance on a sequence. The explanation of each clause in the statement along with some options for configuring that clause appear in the following list:

- **start with _n_**   Allows the creator of the sequence the ability to identify the first value generated by the sequence. Once created, the sequence will generate the value specified by **start with** the first time the sequence's NEXTVAL virtual column is referenced.

- **increment by _n_**   Defines the number by which to increment the sequence every time the NEXTVAL virtual column is referenced.

- **minvalue** *n*   Defines the minimum value that can be produced by the sequence as a value for the sequence. If no minimum value is desired, the **nominvalue** keyword can be used.

- **maxvalue** *n*   Defines the maximum value that can be produced by the sequence as a value for the sequence. If no maximum value is desired, the **nomaxvalue** keyword can be used.

- **cycle**   Allows the sequence to recycle values produced when the **maxvalue** or **minvalue** is reached. If recycling is not desired, the **nocycle** keyword can be used.

- **cache** *n*   Allows the sequence to cache the specified number of values at any time in order to improve performance. If caching is not desired, the **nocache** keyword can be used.

- **order**   Allows the sequence to assign sequence values in the **order** the requests are received by the sequence. If **order** is not desired, the **noorder** keyword can be specified.

Consider now some various examples for defining sequences. The integers that can be specified for sequences as they are created can be negative as well as positive. Consider the following example of a sequence that generates decreasing numbers into the negatives. The **start with** integer in this example is positive, but the **increment by** integer is negative, which effectively tells the sequence to decrement instead of incrementing. When zero is reached, the sequence will start again from the top. This sequence can be useful in countdowns for programs that require a countdown before an event will occur.

```
CREATE SEQUENCE countdown_20
START WITH 20
INCREMENT BY -1
NOMAXVALUE
CYCLE
ORDER;
```

The final example offered is useful for generating completely random numbers. When **noorder** is used in conjunction with no value specified for **start with** or **increment by**, then the sequence is left to its own devices for generating random numbers every time NEXTVAL is referenced. The next code block illustrates a sequence that generates random numbers between zero and 1,000 without repeating a sequence value during the life of the sequence:

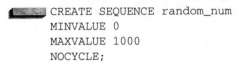

```
CREATE SEQUENCE random_num
MINVALUE 0
MAXVALUE 1000
NOCYCLE;
```

Exercises

1. What statement is used for creating a sequence?

2. What are the options used for sequence creation?

Using Sequences

Once the sequence is created, it is referenced using the CURRVAL and NEXTVAL virtual columns. This reference may occur in a few different ways. Sometimes the users of the database may want to view the current value of the sequence by means of a **select** statement. The next value generated by the sequence can be generated with a **select** statement as well. Notice the reappearance of the DUAL table. Since sequences themselves are not tables, only objects that generate integers via the use of virtual columns, the DUAL table acts as the "virtual" table to pull virtual column data from. As stated earlier, values cannot be placed into the sequence, only selected from the sequence. Once the NEXTVAL column is referenced, the value in CURRVAL becomes the value in NEXTVAL, and the prior value in CURRVAL is lost.

```
SELECT random_num.currval CURRENT,
random_num.nextval NEXT,
random_num.currval CURRENT
FROM dual;

CURRENT     NEXT        CURRENT
---------   ---------   ---------
59496       9382        9382
```

Generally, however, users do not use **select** statements to draw data from sequences. Instead, that functionality can be incorporated directly into data changes made by **insert** or **update** statements. The statements here illustrate usage of sequences directly in changes made to tables:

```
INSERT INTO expense(expense_no, empid, amt, submit_date)
VALUES(expense_sequence_01.nextval, 59495, 456.34, '21-NOV-98');

UPDATE_product
SET product_num = random_num.currval
WHERE serial_num = 34938583945;
```

This direct usage of sequences in **insert** and **update** statements is the most common use for sequences in a database. In the situation where the sequence generates a primary key for all new rows entering the database table, the sequence would likely be referenced directly from the **insert** statement. Note however, that this approach sometimes fails when the sequence is referenced by triggers. Therefore, the best method to use when referencing sequences is within the user interface or within stored procedures.

Exercises

1. Identify a way to refer to a sequence with the **select** statement. Why is use of the DUAL table important in this method?
2. Identify a way to refer to a sequence with the **update** and **insert** statements.

Modifying a Sequence Definition

Like tables, there may come a time when the sequence of a database will need its rules altered in some way. For example, in the employee expense application, the users may want to start the box numbering at some different number in order to start a new fiscal year. For another example, a sequence may have generated several primary keys for the rows in a database. When the sequence is re-created, the DBA may need to set the first value produced by the sequence in order to avoid primary key constraint violations. Any parameter of a sequence can be modified by the DBA or owner of the sequence with the issuance of the **alter sequence** statement.

```
ALTER SEQUENCE decrement_sequence_01
INCREMENT BY  4;
```

The effect is immediate—the statement will change the DECREMENT_SEQUENCE_01 to decrement each NEXTVAL by 4. Any parameter of a sequence that is not specified by the **alter sequence** statement will remain unchanged. The COUNTDOWN_20 sequence will now be changed to run through one countdown from 20 to zero only. After the sequence hits zero, no further references to COUNTDOWN_ 20.NEXTVAL will be allowed.

```
ALTER SEQUENCE countdown_20
NOCYCLE;
```

The final example of usage for the **alter sequence** statement involves the RANDOM_NUMS sequence created earlier. The next code block is designed to change the range of values that can be generated by the sequence from 1,000 to 10,000.

```
ALTER SEQUENCE random_nums
MAXVALUE 10000;
```

Modification of sequences is a relatively simple process. However, the main concern related to changing sequences is monitoring the effect on tables or other processes that use the values generated by the sequence. For example, resetting the value returned by the sequence from 1,150 back to zero is not a problem to execute. Once performed, there could be repercussions if the sequence was used to generate primary keys for a table, of which several values between zero and 1,150 were already generated. When the sequence begins generating values for **insert** statements that depend on the sequence for primary keys, there will be primary key constraint violations on the table inserts. Although these problems don't show up when the sequence is altered, the only way to solve the problem (other than deleting the records already existing in the table) is to alter the sequence again.

Exercises

1. What statement is used to modify a sequence definition?

2. When do changes to a sequence take effect?

Removing Sequences

Removing a sequence may be required when the sequence is no longer needed. In this case, the DBA or owner of the sequence can issue the **drop sequence** statement. Dropping the sequence renders its virtual columns CURRVAL and NEXTVAL unusable. However, if the sequence was being used to generate primary key values, the values generated by the sequence will continue to exist in the database. There is no cascading effect on the values generated by a sequence when the sequence is removed.

 DROP SEQUENCE random_nums;

Exercises

1. How are sequences dropped?
2. What are the effects of dropping a sequence?

Views

In this section, you will cover the following topics related to creating views:

- Data dictionary views
- Creating simple and complex views
- Creating views that enforce constraints
- Modifying views
- Removing views

It has been said that eyes are the windows to the soul. That statement may or may not be true. What is definitely true is that eyes can be used to view the data in a table. In order to make sure the right eyes see the right things, however, some special "windows" on the data in a table can be created. These special windows are called *views*. A view can be thought of as a virtual table. In reality, a view is nothing more than the results of a **select** statement stored in a memory structure that resembles a table. To the user utilizing the view, manipulating the data from the view seems identical to manipulating the data from a table. In some cases, it is even possible for the user to insert data into a view as though the view *was* a table. The relationship between tables and views is illustrated in Figure 4-1.

Data Dictionary Views

The use of views in the data dictionary prevents the user from referring to the tables of the data dictionary directly. This additional safeguard is important for two reasons. First, it underscores the sensitivity of the tables that store dictionary data. If something happens to the tables that store dictionary data that should cause either data to be lost or the table to be removed, the effects could seriously damage the Oracle database, possibly rendering it completely unusable. Second, the dictionary views distill the information in the data dictionary into something highly understandable and useful. Those views divide information about the database into neat categories based on viewing scope and objects referred to.

Dictionary views are useful to draw data from the data dictionary. Some of the following examples illustrate selection of data from the data dictionary views that have already been identified in the previous chapter as ones containing information about the objects covered in this chapter:

```
SELECT * FROM all_sequences;
SELECT * FROM dba_objects;
SELECT * FROM user_tables;
```

Other dictionary views provide information about the views themselves. Recall that a view is simply the resultant dataset from a **select** statement, and

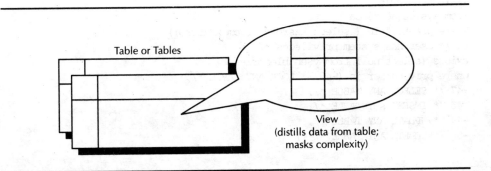

Table or Tables

View
(distills data from table;
masks complexity)

FIGURE 4-1. *Tables and views*

that the data dictionary actually contains the **select** statement that creates the view. As shown, view definitions can be quite complex. There are several functions specified in the **select** statement that produce ALL_TABLES.

```
SET LONG 9999;
SELECT text FROM all_views WHERE view_name = 'ALL_TABLES';

TEXT
----------------------------------------------------------------------
select u.name, o.name, ts.name, co.name,
t.pctfree$, t.pctused$,
t.initrans, t.maxtrans,
s.iniexts * ts.blocksize, s.extsize * ts.blocksize,
s.minexts, s.maxexts, s.extpct,
decode(s.lists, 0, 1, s.lists), decode(s.groups, 0, 1, s.groups),
decode(bitand(t.modified,1), 0, 'Y', 1, 'N', '?'),
t.rowcnt, t.blkcnt, t.empcnt, t.avgspc, t.chncnt, t.avgrln,
lpad(decode(t.spare1, 0, '1', 1, 'DEFAULT', to_char(t.spare1)), 10),
lpad(decode(mod(t.spare2, 65536), 0, '1', 1, 'DEFAULT',
to_char(mod(t.spare2, 65536))), 10),
lpad(decode(floor(t.spare2 / 65536), 0, 'N', 1, 'Y', '?'), 5),
decode(bitand(t.modified, 6), 0, 'ENABLED', 'DISABLED')
from sys.user$ u, sys.ts$ ts, sys.seg$ s, sys.obj$ co, sys.tab$ t, sys.obj$ o
where o.owner# = u.user#
and o.obj# = t.obj#
and t.clu# = co.obj# (+)
and t.ts# = ts.ts#
and t.file# = s.file# (+)
and t.block# = s.block# (+)
and (o.owner# = userenv('SCHEMAID')
or o.obj# in
(select oa.obj#
from sys.objauth$ oa
where grantee# in ( select kzsrorol from x$kzsro))
or /* user has system privileges */
exists (select null from v$enabledprivs
where priv_number in (-45 /* LOCK ANY TABLE */,
-47 /* SELECT ANY TABLE */,
-48 /* INSERT ANY TABLE */,
-49 /* UPDATE ANY TABLE */,
-50 /* DELETE ANY TABLE */)))
```

Exercises

1. Why are views used by Oracle in the data dictionary?

2. What are two reasons for using views, both in the data dictionary and elsewhere?

Creating Simple and Complex Views

One example statement for creating a view has already been identified. To delve further into the requirements for creating views, the following discussion is offered. Creating a view is accomplished by using the **create view** statement. Once created, views are owned by the user who created them. They cannot be reassigned by the owner unless the owner has the **create any view** system privilege. More about privileges will be covered in a later section of this chapter.

There are different types of views that can be created in Oracle. The first type of view is a *simple view*. This type of view is created from the data in one table. Within the simple view, all single-row operations are permitted. In addition, data can be placed in specific order or into groups by the **group by** or **order by** clause of the **select** statement. The only option that is not allowed for a simple view is reference to more than one table. The following code block demonstrates creation of a simple view.

```
CREATE VIEW employee_view
AS (SELECT empid, lastname, firstname, salary
FROM employee
WHERE empid = 59495);
```

Users of a simple view can insert data in the underlying table of the view if the creator of the view allows them to do so. A few restrictions apply. First, the data that the user attempts to **insert** into an underlying table via the view must be data that the user would be able to select via the view if the data existed in the table already. However, updating or inserting data on rows or columns on a table that the view itself would not allow the user to see is only permitted if the **with check option** is not used. The following statement demonstrates data change via a view.

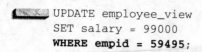
```
UPDATE employee_view
SET salary = 99000
WHERE empid = 59495;
```

The restrictions on inserting or updating data to an underlying table through a simple view are listed here:

- The user may not insert, delete, or update data on the table underlying the simple view if the view itself is not able to select that data for the user if the **with check option** is used.

- The user may not insert, delete, or update data on the table underlying the simple view if the **select** statement creating the view contains **group by** or **order by,** or a single-row operation.

- No data may be inserted to simple views that contain references to any virtual column such as ROWID, CURRVAL, NEXTVAL, and ROWNUM.

- No data may be inserted into simple views that are created with the **read only** option.

Users will have problems inserting data into views if the underlying table has NOT NULL constraints on it. This can be eliminated with use of a default value for the NOT NULL column in the table definition.

Complex views have two major differences from simple views. Complex views draw data from more than one table in addition to possibly containing single-row operations and/or references to virtual columns. No data may be inserted, updated, or deleted from underlying tables for complex views under most circumstances. Complex views are excellent for hiding complicated data models and/or conversion operations behind a simple name for the user to reference the view. The complex view allows data to be joined from multiple tables in addition to all the features of simple views, such as using **order by** or **group by** in the **select** statement that creates the view.

```
CREATE VIEW employee_view
AS (SELECT e.empid empid, e.lastname lastname, e.firstname firstname,
e.salary salary, a.address, a.city, a.state, a.zipcode
FROM employee e, employee_address a);
```

Complex views cannot allow data to be changed on the underlying table because of the join that is performed in order to obtain the result set displayed in the view. As such, it is not necessary for the creator of the view to specify the **read only** option on the view, as the view already is assumed to be read only.

Exercises

1. What is a simple view? How does it differ from a complex view?

2. Which view allows the user to insert data into the view's underlying table? Explain.

Creating Views that Enforce Constraints

Tables that underlie views often have constraints that limit the data that can be added to a table. Views have the same limitations placed on data that may enter the table. In addition, the view can define special constraints for data entry. The option used to configure view constraints is the **with check option**. These special constraints force the view to review the data changes made to see if the data being changed is data the view can select. If the data being changed will not be selected by the view, then the view will not let the user make the data change. The following view will now guarantee that any user who tries to insert data into EMPLOYEE_VIEW for an employee other than EMPID# 59495 will not be able to do so:

```
CREATE VIEW employee_view
AS (SELECT empid, lastname, firstname, salary
FROM employee
WHERE empid = 59495)
WITH CHECK OPTION;
```

Exercises

1. How can constraints be created and enforced on views?

2. On what principle does a view constraint operate?

Modifying Views

There may be situations where the creator of a view may need to change the view. However, views don't follow the syntax conventions of other database objects. While there is an **alter view** statement in the Oracle SQL language, used to recompile or revalidate all references in the view *as it exists already*, the statement used to alter the definition of a view is the **create or replace view** statement. When a **create or replace view** statement is issued, Oracle will disregard the error that arises when it encounters the view that already exists with that name, overwriting the definition for the old view with the definition for the new. The following code block illustrates the use of the **create or replace view** statement.

```
CREATE OR REPLACE VIEW employee_view
AS (SELECT empid, lastname, firstname, salary
FROM employee
WHERE empid = user)
WITH CHECK OPTION;
```

TIP
*If a view should become invalid due to the redefinition or deletion of a table that underlies the view, the view will become invalid. To fix, the creator of the view must either re-create the underlying table and issue the **alter view** command, or modify the view with the **create or replace view** statement.*

The invalidation of a view as a result of the removal of the underlying table illustrates an example of object dependency in the Oracle database. That is to say, certain objects in Oracle depend on others in order to work. Some examples of object dependency that have been presented so far are indexes depending on the existence of the corresponding tables and views depending on the existence of underlying tables.

Exercises

1. What statement is used to recompile or revalidate an existing view definition?

2. What statement is used to alter the definition of a view?

3. What is object dependency?

Removing Views

Like other database objects, there may come a time when the view creator needs to remove the view. The command for executing this function is the **drop view** statement. There are no cascading scenarios that the person dropping a view must be aware of. The following code block illustrates the use of **drop view** for deleting views from the database:

```
DROP VIEW employee_view;
```

Exercise

How are views dropped?

Indexes

In this section, you will cover the following topics related to creating indexes:

- Manual and automatic indexes
- Uses for indexes
- Index structure and operation
- Creating indexes
- Removing indexes
- Guidelines for creating indexes

Indexes are synonymous with performance on the Oracle database. Especially on large tables, indexes are the difference between an application that drags its heels and an application that runs with efficiency. However, there are many performance considerations that must be weighed before making the decision to create an index. This discussion focuses on introducing the usage of indexes on the database. Some usage of indexes has already been presented with the discussion of constraints. However, the indexes that are created along with constraints are only the beginning. In Oracle7, indexes can be created on any column in a table except for columns of the LONG datatype. However, performance is not improved simply by throwing a few indexes on the table and forgetting about it. The following section will discuss the usage of indexes.

Manual and Automatic Indexes

So far, the indexes that have been presented have been ones that are created automatically via the primary key or unique constraints on tables. Those indexes are identified in the data dictionary in the DBA_INDEXES view. Their name corresponds to the name of the primary key or unique constraint that can be given if the creator of the table chooses to name indexes. Alternatively, if the creator of the table chooses to use unnamed constraints (possible for unique constraints only), then the name given to the constraint and the index will be something akin to SYS_C*XXXXX*, where *XXXXX* is an integer. However, there are many more indexes that can exist on a database. These indexes are the manual indexes that are created when the table owner or the DBA issues the **create index** command to bring indexes into existence. Once created, there is little to distinguish an index that was created automatically by Oracle from an index that was created manually by the DBA.

The most commonly used way to distinguish automatic from manual indexes is through naming conventions. Take, for example, the table EMPLOYEE. The primary key constraint on this table might be named EMPLOYEE_PKEY_01, while an index created on some other column in the table might be called EMPLOYEE_INDX_01. In this fashion, it is easier for the DBA or creator of the database objects to distinguish which objects are which when selecting dictionary data.

Another way for the DBA to distinguish manually created indexes from automatically created ones is by looking at the actual columns in the index. The information about the columns in an index can be found in the DBA_CONS_COLUMNS data dictionary view. The columns in an index can give some indication as to whether the index was created automatically to someone who is familiar with the design of the database tables. Finding indexes automatically created for columns that have unique constraints can be trickier. It may require an in-depth knowledge of the application or an additional call to the DBA_CONSTRAINTS table to verify the name of the constraint generated automatically by Oracle, if not named explicitly by the creator of the table.

Exercises

1. What are some differences between manual and automatic indexes?

2. How can the DBA distinguish between indexes created manually and those created automatically?

Uses for Indexes

Indexes have multiple uses on the Oracle database. Indexes can be used to ensure uniqueness on a database. Indexes also boost performance on searching for records in a table. This improvement in performance is gained when the search criteria for data in a table includes reference to the indexed column or columns. So far, all uses for indexes discussed involved unique indexes, where all the values in the column indexed are unique. However, data in this form is not required for creating an index of the table. Although the best performance improvement can be seen when a column containing all unique values has an index created on it, similar performance improvements can be made on columns containing some duplicate values or NULLS. However, there are some guidelines to ensure that the traditional index produces the performance improvements desired. The guidelines for evaluating performance improvements given by traditional indexes and whether it is worth the storage trade-off to create the index will be presented later in this discussion. Up to 16 columns in a table can be included in a single index on that table.

Exercises

1. Identify two reasons for using indexes.
2. Must all the data in an index be unique? Explain.

Index Structure and Operation

When data in a column is indexed, a special structure is created that allows Oracle to search for values in that column quickly. This discussion will highlight the features of the index structure, explaining why it works and what works best with it. This discussion covers traditional indexes and bitmap options that are available in Oracle 7.3. The traditional index in the Oracle database is based on the principle governing a highly advanced algorithm for sorting data called a binary search tree, or a *B-tree* for short. A B-tree contains data placed in layered, branching order, from top to bottom, resembling an upside-down tree. The midpoint of the entire list is placed at the top of the "tree" and called the "root node." The midpoints of each half of the remaining two lists are placed at the next level, and so on, as illustrated in Figure 4-2.

It has been proven by computer scientists that this mechanism for searching data can produce a match for any given value from searching a list containing one million values in a *maximum* of 20 tries. By using a "divide and conquer" method for structuring and searching for data, the values of a column are only a few hops on the tree away, rather than several thousand sequential reads through the list away. However, B-tree indexes work best when there are many distinct values in the column, or when the column is unique. This algorithm works as follows:

■ Compare the given value to the value in the halfway point of the list. If the value at hand is greater, discard the lower half the list. If the value at hand is less, then discard the upper half.

■ Repeat the process on the half remaining until a value is found or the list exhausted.

Along with the data values of a column, the individual nodes of an index also store a piece of information about the column value's row location on disk. This crucial piece of lookup data is called a "ROWID." The *ROWID* for

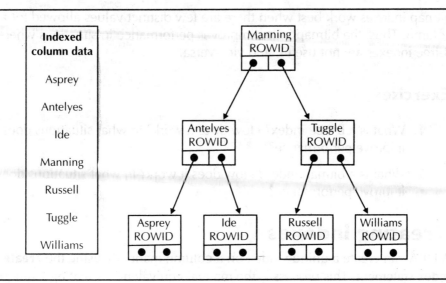

FIGURE 4-2.   *A B-tree index, displayed pictorially*

the column value points Oracle directly to the location on disk in the table of the row corresponding to the column value. A ROWID consists of three components to identify the location on disk of a row—down to the row in the data block in the datafile on disk. With this information, Oracle can then find all the data associated with the row in the table.

TIP

The ROWID for a table is an address for the row on disk. With the ROWID, Oracle can search for the data on disk rapidly.

The other type of index available in Oracle is the bitmap index. The principle of a bitmap index is the use of a matrix, which has columns corresponding to all data values in the column. Thus, if the column contains only three distinct values, the bitmap index can be visualized as containing a column for the ROWID and three columns, one for each distinct value. Figure 4-3 displays a pictorial representation of a bitmap index containing three distinct values. The physical representation of the bitmap index is not far from the picture. Since each distinct value adds to the size of the index, bitmap indexes work best when there are few distinct values allowed for a column. Thus, the bitmap index improves performance in situations where B-tree indexes are not useful, and vice-versa.

Exercises

1. What is a B-tree index? How does it work? In what situations does it improve performance?

2. What is a bitmap index? How does it work? In what situations does it improve performance?

Creating Indexes

A DBA can create a unique index on a column manually using the **create index** statement. This process is the manual equivalent of creating a unique constraint or primary key on a table. Remember, unique indexes are created automatically in support of that task. The index created is a B-tree index. The **create index** statement used to create a unique index must contain the

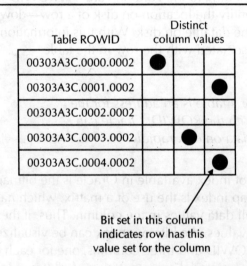

Table ROWID	Distinct column values		
00303A3C.0000.0002	●		
00303A3C.0001.0002			●
00303A3C.0002.0002			
00303A3C.0003.0002		●	
00303A3C.0004.0002			●

Bit set in this column
indicates row has this
value set for the column

FIGURE 4-3. *A bitmap index, displayed pictorially*

unique keyword. The DBA can index a column that contains NULL values as well, simply by eliminating the **unique** keyword. Creating a composite index with more columns named is possible as well. Finally, the DBA can create a bitmap index by substituting the **unique** keyword with the **bitmap** keyword.

```
-- unique indexes
CREATE UNIQUE INDEX employee_lastname_indx_01
ON employee (lastname);

-- nonunique indexes
CREATE INDEX employee_lastname_indx_01
ON employee (lastname);

-- composite indexes
CREATE UNIQUE INDEX employee_last_first_indx_01
ON employee (lastname, firstname);

-- bitmap indexes
CREATE BITMAP INDEX employee_status_indx_01
ON employee (empl_status);
```

Once created, there can be little altered about an index other than some storage parameters. In order to replace the definition of the index, the entire index must be dropped and re-created. Once the index is created, there are several different ways to find information about it. The DBA_INDEXES dictionary view displays storage information about the index, along with the name of the table to which the index is associated. The DBA_OBJECTS dictionary view displays object information about the index, including the index status. The DBA_IND_COLUMNS view displays information about the columns that are indexed on the database. This last view is especially useful for determining the order of columns in a composite index.

Exercises

1. What method is used to create a unique index? A nonunique index?

2. How does the DBA create a bitmap index?

3. In unique indexes containing more than one column, how do you think uniqueness is identified? Explain.

Removing Indexes

When an index is no longer needed in the database, the developer or DBA can remove it with the use of the **drop index** command. Once an index is dropped, it will no longer improve performance on searches using the column or columns contained in the index. No mention of that index will appear in the data dictionary any more, either. Additionally, if the index is used in relation to a primary key or unique constraint, then the index will no longer continue to enforce that uniqueness constraint. The syntax for the **drop index** statement is the same, regardless of the type of index being dropped. If the developer or DBA wishes to rework the index in any way, he or she must first drop the old index and then create the new one.

```
DROP INDEX employee_last_first_indx_01;
```

Exercises

1. How is a bitmap index dropped? How is a unique index dropped?

2. What are the effects of dropping an index?

Guidelines for Creating Indexes

The usage of indexes for searching tables for information can provide incredible performance gains over searching tables using columns that are not indexed. However, care must be taken to choose the right index. Although a completely unique column is preferable for indexing using the B-tree structured index, a nonunique column will work almost as well if only about 10 percent of its rows have the same value. "Switch" or "flag" columns, such as ones for storing the sex of a person, are a bad idea for B-tree indexes. So are columns used to store a few "valid values," or columns that store a token value representing valid or invalid, active or inactive, yes or no, or any type of value such as these. Bitmap indexes are more appropriate for these types of columns.

TIP
The uniqueness of the values of a column is referred to as cardinality. Unique columns or columns that contain many distinct values have **high cardinality**, *while columns with few distinct values have* **low cardinality**. *Use B-tree indexes for columns with high cardinality, bitmap indexes for columns with low cardinality.*

Exercises

1. What is cardinality?

2. When might the DBA use a B-tree index to improve performance? When might the DBA use a bitmap index to improve performance?

User Access Control

In this section, you will cover the following topics related to controlling user access:

- The database security model
- System privileges
- Using roles to manage database access
- Object privileges
- Changing passwords
- Granting and revoking object privileges
- Using synonyms for database transparency

The most secure database is one with no users, but take away the users of a database and the whole point of creating a database is lost. In order to address the issues of security within Oracle, a careful balance of limiting access to the database and controlling what a user can see once connection is established is required. Oracle provides a means of doing so with its security model. The Oracle database security model consists of several options for limiting connect access to the database and controlling what a user can and cannot see once connection is established. This section will focus on the presentation of security on the Oracle database, from user creation to password administration to administering security on individual objects in the database.

Database Security Model

Oracle security consists of two parts. The first part of the Oracle database security model consists of password authentication for all users of the Oracle database. Password authentication is available either directly from the Oracle server or from the operating system supporting the Oracle database. When Oracle's own authentication system is used, password information is stored in Oracle in an encrypted format.

The second part of the Oracle security model consists of controlling what database objects a user may access, the level of access a user may have to the object, and the authority to place new objects into the Oracle database. At a high level, these controls are referred to as privileges.

The key to giving database access is creating users. Users are created in Oracle with the **create user** command. Along with a password, several storage and database usage options are set up with the creation of a user. The following statement can be issued by a user with the **create user** privilege in Oracle to create new users:

```
CREATE USER athena IDENTIFIED BY greek#goddess
```

Security in the database is a serious matter. In most organizations, it is a set of functions handled either by the DBA or, more appropriately, by a *security administrator*. This person is the one with the final say over creating new users and determining the accessibility of objects in the database. As a general rule, the larger the organization is and the more sensitive the information, the more likely it is that security will be handled by a special security administrator. However, it is important that the DBA understand the options available in the Oracle security model.

Exercises

1. What are the two parts of database security?

2. Who should manage database security such as user and password administration?

Granting System Privileges

System privileges grant the user the ability to create, modify, and eliminate the database objects in Oracle that store data for the application. In fact, in order to do anything in the Oracle database, the user must have a system privilege called **create session**. Within the scope of system privileges, there are two categories. The first is the set of system privileges that relate to object management. These objects include tables, indexes, triggers, sequences and views, packages, stored procedures, and functions. The three actions on objects managed by system privileges are defining or creating the object, altering definition, and dropping the object.

The other category of system privileges refers to the ability of a user to manage special system-wide activities. These activities include functions such as auditing database activity, generating statistics to support the cost-based optimizer, to setting up Oracle to allow access to the database only to users with a special system privilege called **restricted session**. These privileges should generally be granted only to the user or users on the database who will be performing high-level database administration tasks.

All granting of system privileges is managed with the **grant** command. In order to grant a system privilege, the grantor must either have the privilege granted to himself or herself **with admin option**, or the user must have **grant any privilege** granted to them. Granting a privilege **with admin option** signifies that the grantee may further grant or revoke the system privilege to any user on the database, with or without the **with admin option**. Users can create objects in their own schema with a system privilege such as **create table**. However, the user can create objects in any schema if the **any** keyword is added to the system privilege when it is granted, as in **create any table**.

```
GRANT CREATE PROCEDURE, CREATE FUNCTION, CREATE PACKAGE TO spanky;
GRANT CREATE TABLE, CREATE VIEW, CREATE TRIGGER, CREATE SEQUENCE TO athena;
GRANT CREATE TABLE TO athena WITH ADMIN OPTION;
```

Revoking system privileges is handled with the **revoke** command. In general, there are no cascading concerns related to revoking system privileges. For example, user ATHENA created 17 tables with the **create table** privilege while she had it, and granted the **create table** privilege with and without the **with admin option** to several users as well. Another user revokes the privilege from her, along with the **with admin option**. The revocation of **create table** from user ATHENA would have no effect either on the tables she created or the users to which she granted the **create table** privilege.

Exercises

1. What is a system privilege? What abilities do system privileges manage?

2. How are privileges granted and revoked?

3. What does **with admin option** mean, and how is it used?

Using Roles to Manage Database Access

When databases get large, privileges can become unwieldy and hard to manage. DBAs can simplify the management of privileges with the use of a database object called a *role*. Roles act in two capacities in the database. First, the role can act as a focal point for grouping the privileges to execute certain tasks. The second capacity is to act as a "virtual user" of a database, to which all the object privileges required to execute a certain job function can be granted, such as data entry, manager review, batch processing, and others.

The amount of access to the objects of the database can be categorized using database roles to administrate the privileges that must be granted for database usage. In order to use roles, two activities must occur. The first is that the DBA must logically group certain privileges together, such as creating tables, indexes, triggers, and procedures. Using the privileges that are granted to a role can be protected with a password when a special clause, called **identified by**, is used in role creation.

```
CREATE ROLE create_procs IDENTIFIED BY creator;
GRANT create any procedure TO create_procs WITH ADMIN OPTION;
```

The second aspect of work the DBA must complete is logically grouping the users of a database application together according to similar needs. The most effective way to manage users is to identify the various types of users that will be using the database. The DBA determines the activities each type of user will carry out, and lists the privileges that each activity will require. These types or categories will determine the access privileges that will then be granted to roles on the database. The next step is to create roles that correspond to each activity, and to grant the privileges to the roles. Once this architecture of using roles as a "middle layer" for granting privileges is established, the administration of user privileges becomes very simply granting the appropriate role or roles to the users that need them

```
CREATE ROLE empl_submt;

GRANT insert, select, update ON expense TO empl_submt;
GRANT select ON employee TO empl_submt;
GRANT empl_submt TO spanky;
GRANT empl_submt TO athena;
GRANT empl_submt TO dinah;
```

Roles can be altered to support the requirement of a password using the **alter role identified by** statement. Deleting a role is performed with the **drop role** statement. These two options may only be executed by those users with the **create any role**, **alter any role**, or **drop any role** privileges, or by the owner of the role. Privileges can be revoked from a role in the same way as they can be revoked from a user. When a role is dropped, the associated privileges are revoked from the user granted the role. Figure 4-4 shows how privileges can be managed with roles.

In order to use the privileges granted to a user via a role, the role must be enabled for that user. In order for the role to be enabled, it must be the default role for the user, or one of the default roles. The status of a role is enabled usually, unless for some reason the role has been disabled. To change the status of a role for the user, the **alter user default role** statement can be issued. Some of the keywords that can be used in conjunction with defining roles are **all**, **all except**, and **none**; these keywords limit the roles defined for the **alter user** statement.

```
ALTER USER spanky DEFAULT ROLE ALL;
ALTER USER spanky DEFAULT ROLE ALL EXCEPT sysdba;
ALTER USER spanky DEFAULT ROLE app_dev, sys_aly, unit_mgr;
ALTER USER spanky DEFAULT ROLE NONE;
```

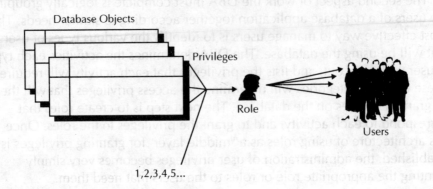

FIGURE 4-4. *Using roles to manage privileges*

Exercises

1. What is a role? How are privileges granted to a role?

2. What is a default role? Can a user exercise privileges granted through a role if the role is disabled? Explain.

Granting Object Privileges

Once an object in the Oracle database has been created, it can be administered by either the creator of the table or by a user who has **grant any privilege** available to them. Administration of a database object consists of granting privileges that will allow users to manipulate the object by adding, changing, removing, or viewing data in the database object. Sometimes, object privileges are referred to by developers as *SUDI* (Select, Update, Delete, Insert) privileges. Other object privileges refer to the ability to refer to database objects, or to use them in some way that will not drop or change them in any way. These object privileges are **references** and **execute**. The **references** privilege allows the grantee of the privilege to create foreign key constraints on the referenced column of a table. The **execute** privilege allows the user to run a compiled stored procedure, package, or function. Other object privileges manage the alteration and creation of certain database objects. These include the **alter table**, **alter sequence**, and **index table** privileges.

The object privileges for any database object belong to that user and to users with appropriate **any** system privileges granted to them. Object privileges can be granted to other users for the purpose of allowing them to access and manipulate the object, or to administer the privileges to other users. The latter option is accomplished via a special parameter on the privilege called **with grant option**.

Exercises

1. What are object privileges? Name some of the object privileges?

2. What option is used to grant an object privilege with the ability to grant the privilege further to others?

Changing Passwords

Once the user ID is created, the users can change their own passwords by issuing the following statement:

```
ALTER USER athena IDENTIFIED BY black#cat;
```

Exercise

How is the user password changed?

Granting and Revoking Object Privileges

All granting of object privileges is managed with the **grant** command. In order to grant an object privilege, the grantor must either have the privilege granted to himself or herself with the **grant option**, or the user must have **grant any privilege** granted to them, or the user must own the object. Granting an object privilege must be managed in the following way. First, the grantor of the privilege must determine the level of access a user requires on the table. Then, the privilege is granted. Granting object privileges can allow the grantee of the privilege the ability to administer a privilege as well when **with grant option** is used. Administrative ability over an object privilege includes the ability to grant the privilege or revoke it from anyone, as well as the ability to grant the object privilege to another user with administrative ability over the privilege.

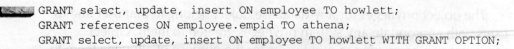

```
GRANT select, update, insert ON employee TO howlett;
GRANT references ON employee.empid TO athena;
GRANT select, update, insert ON employee TO howlett WITH GRANT OPTION;
```

Revoking object privileges is handled with the **revoke** command. In general, there are no cascading concerns related to revoking object privileges. For example, user HOWLETT creates the EMPLOYEE table and inserts several rows in it. She then grants the **select** privilege along with the **with grant option** on the EMPLOYEE table to user ATHENA. User ATHENA then revokes the privilege from user HOWLETT, along with the **with grant option**. The revocation of these privileges from user HOWLETT would have no effect either on the data she created or on user ATHENA's continued ability to use the privileges granted by user HOWLETT.

Using Synonyms for Database Transparency

Database objects are owned by the users who create them. The objects are available only in the user's schema unless the user grants access to the objects explicitly to other users or to roles granted to other users. However, even when granted permission to use the object, the user must be aware of the boundaries created by schema ownership in order to access the data objects in Oracle. For example, assume the EMPLOYEE table exists in user SPANKY's schema, and user ATHENA attempts to access the table. Instead of returning the data associated with EMPID 96945, however, Oracle tells the user that the object does not exist. The reason this user could not see the table in the SPANKY schema is because user ATHENA did not refer to the table as being in the schema owned by SPANKY.

```
SELECT * FROM employee
WHERE empid = 96945;

SELECT * FROM employee
              *
ORA-00942: table or view does not exist.

SELECT * FROM spanky.employee
WHERE empid = 96945;
```

If that extra piece of information seems to be unnecessary to remember, public synonyms may be used on the database. A synonym allows the users of the database to refer to the objects of a database with some word other than the official name of the object. For example, a synonym can be created on the EMPLOYEE table. After creating a synonym, user ATHENA can access the table by use of it.

```
-- Executed by SPANKY
CREATE PUBLIC SYNONYM emp FOR employee;

-- Executed by ATHENA
SELECT * FROM employee
WHERE empid = 96945;

EMPID       LASTNAME      FIRSTNAME     SALARY
---------   -----------   -----------   ----------
96945       AHL           BARBARA       45000
```

Exercises

1. What is schema transparency?

2. How are synonyms used to facilitate schema transparency?

Chapter Summary

This chapter covered several sections of required information for OCP Exam 1 related to the advanced creation of database objects. Some of the areas this chapter covered were altering tables and constraints, creating sequences, creating views, creating indexes, and controlling user access. The material in this chapter comprises about 17 percent of OCP Exam 1 and builds the foundation of discussion for managing the schema objects that will be presented in Unit II.

The first area of discussion for this chapter is the altering of tables and constraints. There are several activities a developer or DBA can do in order to alter tables and constraints. Some of these activities include adding columns or constraints, modifying the datatypes of columns, or removing constraints. Adding and modifying columns is accomplished with the **alter**

table command, as are adding or modifying constraints on the table. There are several restricting factors on adding constraints, centering around the fact that adding a constraint to a column means that the data already in the column must conform to the constraint being placed upon it.

With respect to adding columns or changing the datatype of a column, there are some general rules to remember. It is easier to increase the size of a datatype for a column, and to add columns to the table. More difficult is changing the datatype of a column from one thing to another. Generally, the column whose datatype is being altered must have NULL values for that column specified for all rows in the table. A table can be dropped with the **drop table** statement. Once dropped, all associated database objects like triggers and constraints, and indexes automatically created to support the constraints, are dropped as well. Indexes that were manually generated by the DBA to improve performance on the table will also be dropped.

There are several other tricks to table alteration. If the user wants to delete all data from a table but leave the definition of the table intact, the user can use the **truncate** command. A database object can be renamed with use of the **rename** command. Alternatively, the DBA can create a synonym, which allows users to reference the database object using a different name. One final option offered to the DBA is to make notes in the database about objects by adding comments. Comments are added with the **comment on** statement.

Creation of sequences is another important area of advanced Oracle object creation. A sequence is an object that produces integers on demand according to rules that are defined for the sequence at sequence creation time. Some uses for a sequence include using a sequence to generate primary keys for a table or to generate random numbers. Creating a sequence is accomplished with the **create sequence** command in Oracle. To use a sequence, the user must reference two virtual columns in the sequence, known as CURRVAL and NEXTVAL. The CURRVAL column stores the current value generated by the sequence, while referencing NEXTVAL causes the sequence to generate a new number and replace the value in CURRVAL with that new number. Several rules can be used to govern how sequences generate their numbers. These rules include the first number the sequence should generate, how the sequence should increment, maximum and minimum values, whether values can be recycled, and others. Modifying the rules that govern sequence integer generation is accomplished with the **alter sequence** statement, while removal of the sequence is accomplished with the **drop sequence** statement.

Creating views is another area of database object creation covered in this chapter. Views are used to distill data from a table that may be inappropriate for use by some users. Other uses for views include the creation of views that mask the complexity of certain data (such as joins from multiple tables), data that has single-row operations performed on it, and other things. One common example of view usage is the data dictionary, which stores all data about the Oracle database in tables but disallows direct access to the tables in favor of providing views through which the user can select data. There are two categories of views, simple and complex. A simple view is one that draws data from only one table. A complex view is one that draws data from two or more tables. Simple views sometimes allow the user to insert, update, or delete data from the underlying table, while complex views never allow this to occur. A view can also have the option of enforcing a check on the data being inserted. This means that if the user tries to make a change, insertion, or deletion to the underlying table, the view will not allow it unless the view can then select the row being changed. Modifying the definition of a view requires dropping the old view and re-creating it or, alternatively, creating the view again with the **or replace** option. The **alter view** statement is used for recompiling an existing view due to a problem with the object dependencies of the database. Removing a view from the database is done with the **drop view** statement.

Creating an index is another area covered in this chapter. There are several indexes created automatically to support enforcement of uniqueness constraints such as the primary key or the unique constraint. However, the DBA can also create nonunique indexes to support performance improvements on the database application. The traditional index consists of a binary search tree structure. The search algorithm supported by this structure operates by dividing a sorted list of elements in half and comparing the value at hand to the midpoint value, then searching the greater or lesser half depending on whether the value at hand is greater or less than the midpoint value. This process is repeated until the index values are exhausted or the value is found. Studies have shown that this algorithm can find a value from a list of one million elements in 20 or fewer tries. In order for a column to be indexed and used effectively using the B-tree index, the cardinality, or number of distinct values in the column, should be high. To change storage parameters about the index, the DBA can issue the **alter index** statement.

To change the number of columns in an index, the index must be dropped and rebuilt. To drop an index, use the **drop index** statement.

Another index available in Oracle is the bitmap index. This index stores each ROWID in the table along with a series of bits, one for every distinct value in the column. The values that are not used in the column are set off, while the value that is present in the column is set on. Bitmap indexes work well for improving performance on columns with few distinct values.

Controlling user access on the database is the final area covered by this chapter. The Oracle database security model contains three major areas—user authentication, system privileges to control the creation of database objects, and object privileges to control usage of database objects. To change a password, the user can issue the **alter user identified by** statement, specifying the person's username and the desired password. System privileges govern the creation of new database objects, such as tables, sequences, triggers, and views, as well as the execution of certain commands for analyzing and auditing database objects. Three general object maintenance activities are governed by system privileges, and they are the creation, change, and dropping of database objects. Object privileges govern access to an object once it is created, such as selects, updates, inserts, and deletes on tables, execution of packages or procedures, and reference of columns on tables for foreign key constraints.

In situations where there are many users and many privileges governing database usage, the management of privilege granting to users can be improved using roles. Roles act as "virtual users" of the database system. The DBA first defines the privileges a user may need, groups them logically by function or job description, then creates an appropriate role. Privileges to support the function or the job description are then granted to the role, and the role is granted to the user. Roles help to alleviate the necessity of granting several privileges each time a user is added to an application.

Finally, the use of synonyms for data transparency is discussed. Database objects are owned by users and accessible to their schema only, unless permission is explicitly granted by the owner to another user to view the data in the table. Even then, the schema owning the object must be referenced in the statement the user issues to reference the object. Public synonyms can eliminate that requirement, making the schema ownership of the database object transparent. A public synonym is created with the **create public synonym** statement.

Two-Minute Drill

- Adding or modifying a table column is done with the **alter table** statement.

- Columns can be added with little difficulty, if they will be nullable, using the **alter table add** *column_name* statement. If a NOT NULL constraint is desired, add the column, populate the column with data, and then add the NOT NULL constraint separately.

- Column datatype size can be increased with no difficulty using the **alter table (modify** *column_name datatype***)** statement. Column size can be decreased or the datatype can be changed only if the column contains NULL for all rows.

- Constraints can be added to a column only if the column already contains values that will not violate the added constraint.

- Adding a constraint is accomplished with the **alter table add** *constraint_name* statement.

- Dropping a constraint is accomplished with the **alter table drop** *constraint_name* statement.

- If a constraint is dropped that created an index automatically (primary keys and unique constraints), then the corresponding index is also dropped.

- If the table is dropped, all constraints, triggers, and indexes created for the table are also dropped.

- Removing all data from a table is best accomplished with the **truncate** command rather than the **delete from** *table_name* statement because **alter table truncate** will reset the table's highwatermark, improving performance on **select count()** statements issued after the truncation.

- An object name can be changed with the **rename** statement or with the use of synonyms.

- A comment can be added to the data dictionary for a database object with the **comment on** command. The comment can subsequently be viewed in DBA_TAB_COMMENTS or DBA_COL_COMMENTS.

- A sequence generates integers based on rules that are defined by sequence creation.

- Options that can be defined for sequences are the first number generated, how the sequence increments, the maximum value, the minimum value, whether the sequence can recycle numbers, and whether numbers will be cached for improved performance.

- Sequences are used by selecting from the CURRVAL and NEXTVAL virtual columns.

- The CURRVAL column contains the current value of the sequence.

- Selecting from NEXTVAL increments the sequence and changes the value of CURRVAL to whatever is produced by NEXTVAL.

- Modifying the rules that a sequence uses to generate values is accomplished using the **alter sequence** statement.

- Deleting the sequence is accomplished with the **drop sequence** statement.

- A view is a virtual table defined by a **select** statement.

- A view is similar to a table in that it contains rows and columns, but different because the view actually stores no data.

- Views can distill data from tables that may be inappropriate for some users, or hide complexity of data from several tables or on which many operations have been performed.

- There are two types of views—simple and complex.

- Simple views are those that have only one underlying table.

- Complex views are those with two or more underlying tables that have been joined together.

- Data cannot be inserted into complex views, but may be inserted into simple views in some cases.

- The **with check option** clause on administering any object privilege allows the simple view to limit the data that can be inserted or otherwise changed on the underlying table by requiring that the data change be selectable by the view.

- Modifying the data selected by a view requires re-creating the view with the **create or replace view** statement, or dropping the view first and issuing the **create view** statement.

- An existing view can be recompiled if for some reason it becomes invalid due to object dependency by executing the **alter view** statement.

- A view is dropped with the **drop view** statement.

- Some indexes in a database are created automatically, such as those supporting the primary key and the unique constraints on a table.

- Other indexes are created manually to support database performance improvements.

- Indexes created manually are often on nonunique columns.

- B-tree indexes work best on columns that have high cardinality, or a large number of distinct values and few duplicates in the column.

- B-tree indexes improve performance by storing data in a binary search tree, then searching for values in the tree using a "divide and conquer" methodology outlined in the chapter.

- Bitmap indexes improve performance on columns with low cardinality, or few distinct values and many duplicates on the column.

- Columns stored in the index can be changed only by dropping and re-creating the index.

- Deleting an index is accomplished by issuing the **drop index** statement.

- The Oracle database security model consists of two parts—limiting user access with password authentication and controlling object usage with privileges.

- Available privileges in Oracle include system privileges for maintaining database objects and object privileges for accessing and manipulating data in database objects.

- Changing a password can be performed by a user with the **alter user identified by** statement.

- Granting system and object privileges is accomplished with the **grant** command.

- Taking away system and object privileges is accomplished with the **revoke** command.

- Creating a synonym to make schema transparency is accomplished with the **create public synonym** command.

Chapter Questions

1. **Dropping a table has which of the following effects on a nonunique index created for the table?**

   A. No effect.

   B. The index will be dropped.

   C. The index will be rendered invalid.

   D. The index will contain NULL values.

2. **Columns with low cardinality are handled well by B-tree indexes.**

   A. TRUE

   B. FALSE

3. **To increase the number of nullable columns for a table**

   A. Use the **alter table** statement.

   B. Ensure that all column values are NULL for all rows.

   C. First increase the size of adjacent column datatypes, then add the column.

D. Add the column, populate the column, then add the NOT NULL constraint.

4. **To add the number of columns selected by a view**

   A. Add more columns to the underlying table.

   B. Issue the **alter view** statement.

   C. Use a correlated subquery in conjunction with the view

   D. Drop and re-create the view with references to select more columns.

5. **A user issues the statement SELECT COUNT(*) FROM EMPLOYEE. The query takes an inordinately long amount of time and returns a count of zero. The most cost-effective solution is**

   A. Upgrade hardware.

   B. Truncate the table.

   C. Upgrade version of Oracle.

   D. Delete the highwatermark.

6. **MAXVALUE is a valid parameter for sequence creation.**

   A. TRUE

   B. FALSE

7. **The following statement is issued against the Oracle database. Which line will produce an error?**

   A. **create view** EMP_VIEW_01

   B. **as select** E.EMPID, E.LASTNAME, E.FIRSTNAME, A.ADDRESS

   C. **from** EMPLOYEE E, EMPL_ADDRESS A

   D. **where** E.EMPID = A.EMPID

   E. **with check option;**

   F. This statement contains no errors.

8. **The following statement is issued on the database: COMMENT ON TABLE empl IS 'Do not use this table.' How can this data be viewed?**

   A. Using the **describe** command

   B. Issuing a **select * from empl** statement

   C. Selecting from ALL_COMMENTS

   D. Selecting from ALL_TAB_COMMENTS

9. **Which system privilege allows the user to connect to a database in restricted session mode?**

   A. create table

   B. create user

   C. restricted session

   D. create session

10. **A simple view may use the WITH CHECK OPTION to constrain data being entered to the underlying table.**

    A. TRUE

    B. FALSE

11. **Which of the following statements is true about roles? (Choose three)**

    A. Roles can be granted to other roles.

    B. Privileges can be granted to roles.

    C. Roles can be granted to users.

    D. Roles can be granted to synonyms.

12. **User MANN has granted the CREATE ANY VIEW WITH ADMIN OPTION privilege to user SNOW. User SNOW granted the same privilege WITH ADMIN OPTION to user REED. User MANN revokes the privilege from user SNOW. Which statement is true about privileges granted to users REED, MANN, and SNOW?**

    A. REED and MANN have the privilege, but SNOW does not.

    B. REED and SNOW have the privilege, but MANN does not.

    C. MANN and SNOW have the privilege, but REED does not.

    D. MANN has the privilege, but SNOW and REED do not.

13. After referencing NEXTVAL, the value in CURRVAL

    A. Is incremented by one

    B. Is now in PREVVAL

    C. Is equal to NEXTVAL

    D. Is unchanged

14. Indexes improve performance in queries using the indexed column in the WHERE clause.

    A. TRUE

    B. FALSE

Answers to Chapter Questions

1. B. The index will be dropped.

Explanation Like automatically generated indexes associated with a table's primary key, the indexes created manually on a table to improve performance will be dropped if the table is dropped. Choices A, C, and D are therefore invalid. Refer to the discussion of dropping indexes in the chapter summary.

2. B. FALSE

Explanation Columns with low cardinality are the bane of B-tree indexes. Review the discussion of how B-tree indexes work.

3. A. Use the **alter table** statement.

Explanation The **alter table** statement is the only choice offered that allows the developer to increase the number of columns per table. Choice B is incorrect because setting a column to all NULL values for all rows does simply that. Choice C is incorrect because increasing the adjacent column sizes simply increases the sizes of the columns, and choice D is incorrect because the steps listed outline how to add a column with a NOT NULL constraint, something not specified by the question.

4. D. Drop and re-create the view with references to select more columns.

Explanation Choice A is incorrect because adding columns to the underlying table will not add columns to the view, but will likely invalidate the view. Choice B is incorrect because the **alter view** statement simply recompiles an existing view definition, while the real solution here is to change the existing view definition by dropping and re-creating the view. Choice C is incorrect because a correlated subquery will likely worsen performance and underscores the real problem—a column must be added to the view. Review the discussion of altering the definition of a view.

5. B. Truncate the table.

Explanation Choices A and C may work, but an upgrade of hardware and software will cost far more than truncating the table. Choice D is partly correct, as there will be some change required to the highwatermark, but the change is to reset, not eliminate entirely, and the method used is to truncate the table.

6. A. TRUE

Explanation The **maxvalue** option is a valid option for sequence creation. Review the discussion on creating sequences.

7. F. This statement contains no errors.

Explanation Even though the reference to **with check option** is inappropriate, considering that inserts into complex views are not possible, the statement will not actually produce an error when compiled. Therefore, there are no errors in the view. This is not something that can be learned. It requires hands-on experience with Oracle.

8. D. Selecting from ALL_TAB_COMMENTS

Explanation Choice A is incorrect because comments will not appear in the description of the table from the data dictionary. Instead, the user must select comments from the ALL_, USER, or DBA_TAB_COLUMNS view. Choice C is incorrect because ALL_COMMENTS is not a view in the Oracle data dictionary, while choice B is incorrect because selection of data from the table commented yields only the data in that table, not the comments. Refer to the discussion of adding comments to tables.

9. C. RESTRICTED SESSION

Explanation Choice A is incorrect because the **create table** privilege allows the user to create a table, while choice B is incorrect for a similar reason—**create user** allows the user to create new users. Choice D is required for establishing connection to an open database, while choice C is the only privilege listed that allows the user to connect to a database in **restricted session** mode. Refer to the discussion and review of roles and privileges.

10. A. TRUE

Explanation The **with check option** is entirely appropriate for simple views. Refer to the discussion of simple and complex views.

11. A, B, and C.

Explanation Choice D is the only option not available to managing roles. Roles cannot be granted to synonyms. Refer to the discussion of roles and privileges in this chapter.

12. A. REED and MANN have the privilege, but SNOW does not.

Explanation The only result of revoking a system or object privilege in Oracle is that the user the privilege is revoked from is the only user who loses it. If the user has granted the privilege to someone else, that other user will still have the privilege. Review the discussion of cascading effects of granting privileges.

13. C. Is equal to NEXTVAL.

Explanation Once NEXTVAL is referenced, the sequence increments the integer and changes the value of CURRVAL to be equal to NEXTVAL. Refer to the discussion of sequences for more information.

14. A. TRUE

Explanation The purpose of indexes is to improve performance on **select** statements that refer to the column in their **where** clause. For more information, refer to the discussion of indexes.

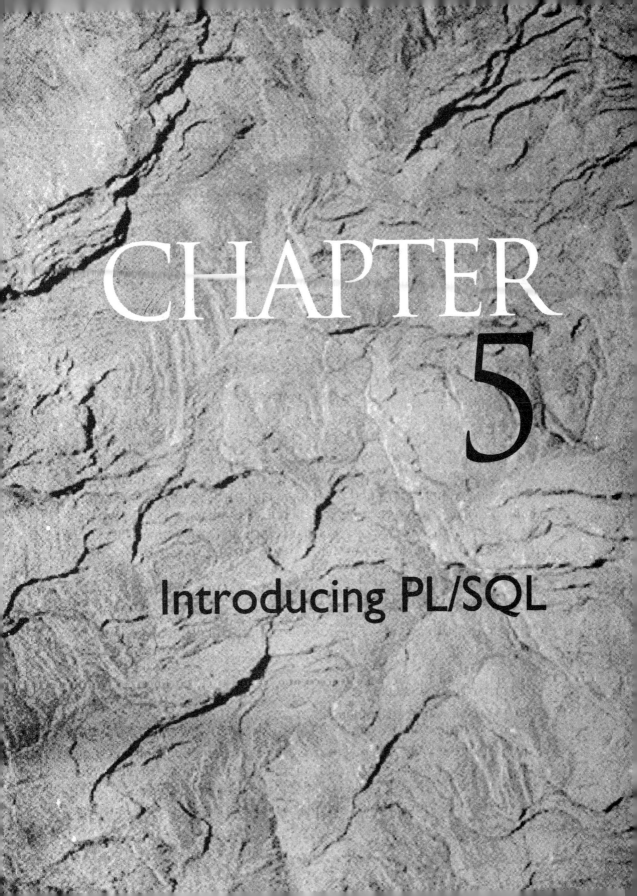

CHAPTER

5

Introducing PL/SQL

n this chapter, you will understand and demonstrate knowledge in the following areas:

- Overview of PL/SQL

- Developing a PL/SQL block

- Interacting with the Oracle database

- Controlling PL/SQL process flow

- Explicit cursor handling

- Error handling

In Oracle, there is a special language available for developers to code stored procedures that seamlessly integrate with database object access via the language of database objects, SQL. However, this language offers far more execution potential than simple updates, selects, inserts, and deletes. This language offers a procedural extension that allows for modularity, variable declaration, loops and other logic constructs, and advanced error handling. This language is known as PL/SQL. This chapter will present an overview of PL/SQL syntax, constructs, and usage. This information is tested on OCP Exam 1, and comprises 22 percent of the test material.

Overview of PL/SQL

In this section, you will cover the following topics related to overview of PL/SQL:

- Using PL/SQL to access Oracle

- Variable value assignment

PL/SQL offers many advantages over other programming languages for handling the logic and business rule enforcement of database applications. It is a straightforward language with all the common logic constructs associated with a programming language, plus many things other languages don't have, such as robust error handling and modularization of code blocks. The PL/SQL code used to interface with the database is also stored directly on the Oracle database, and is the only programming language that interfaces with the Oracle database natively and within the database environment. This overview will cover the details of benefits associated with using PL/SQL in the Oracle database and the basic constructs of the PL/SQL language.

Using PL/SQL to Access Oracle

Many applications that use client/server architecture have one thing in common—a difficulty maintaining the business rules for an application. When business rules are decentralized throughout the application, the developers must make changes throughout the application and implement system testing that will determine whether the changes are sufficient. However, in tight scheduling situations, the first deployment item to get left off is almost invariably testing. One logical design change that should be implemented in this scenario is the centralization of logic in the application to allow for easier management of change. In systems that use the Oracle database, a "middle layer" of application logic can be designed with PL/SOL. The benefits are as follows:

- PL/SQL is managed centrally within the Oracle database. The DBA manages source code and execution privileges with the same syntax used to manage other database objects.

- PL/SQL communicates natively with other Oracle database objects.

- PL/SQL is easy to read and has many features for code modularity and error handling.

The features of PL/SQL that manage centralized code management make PL/SQL the logical choice for a database-centric client/server application that uses stored procedures for business logic and allows the client application developer to focus mainly on the user interface. Storing application logic centrally means only having to compile a change once, and then it is immediately accessible to all users of the application. With business logic stored in the client application, the effort of distributing code includes the recompilation of the client application (potentially on several different platforms). There is an additional distribution cost to getting the new executable version of the client on every user's desktop, as well as overhead for communication and support to make sure all users of the application are on the right version. Decentralized computing has increased the capacity of organizations to provide easy-to-use and fast applications to their customers. But some centralization improves the job even further by allowing the application development shop the ability to eliminate distribution channels for business logic changes and focus the client-side developers' efforts on the client application. Figure 5-1 shows an example of the difference between centralized and decentralized business logic code management.

Exercises

1. What are some advantages of using PL/SQL to access the database?

2. Where is PL/SQL compiled and stored?

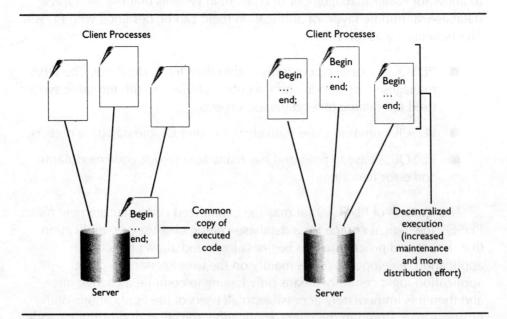

FIGURE 5-1. *Centralized vs. decentralized business logic code management*

PL/SQL Program Constructs

There are many different programming constructs to PL/SQL, from the various types of modules available, to the components of a PL/SQL block, to the logic constructs that manage process flow. This section will identify each component of the PL/SQL language and give some highlights about each area of the language.

Modularity

PL/SQL allows the developer to create program modules to improve software reusability and to hide the complexity of the execution of a specific operation behind a name. For example, there may be a complex process involved to an employee record to a corporate database, which requires records to be added to several different tables for several different applications. Stored procedures may handle the addition of records to each of the systems, making it look to the user that the only step required is entering data on one screen. In reality, that screen's worth of data entry may call dozens of separate procedures, each designed to handle one small component of the overall process of adding the employee. These components may even be reused data entry code blocks from the various pension, health care, day care, payroll, and other HR applications, which have simply been repackaged around this new data entry screen. Figure 5-2 shows how modularity can be implemented in PL/SQL blocks.

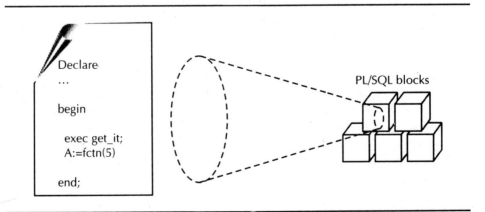

FIGURE 5-2. *Modularity and PL/SQL blocks*

Procedures, Functions, Triggers, and Packages

The modules of PL/SQL code are divided into four categories. Those categories are stored procedures, functions, packages, and triggers. To summarize, the four types of PL/SQL code blocks are as follows.

- *Procedure*—A series of statements accepting and/or returning zero or more variables.

- *Function*—A series of statements accepting zero or more variables that returns one value.

- *Package*—A collection of procedures and functions that has two parts, a specification listing available procedures and functions and their parameters, and a body that contains the actual code for the procedures and functions.

- *Trigger*—A series of PL/SQL statements attached to a database table that execute whenever a triggering event (**select**, **update**, **insert**, **delete**) occurs.

Components of a PL/SQL Block

There are three components of any PL/SQL block named in the previous section. Those components are the *variable declaration section*, the *executable section*, and the *exception handler*. The declaration section contains identification of all variable constructs that will be used in the code block. A variable can be of any datatype available in the Oracle database, as well as of some other types exclusive to PL/SQL. The executable section of a PL/SQL block starts with the **begin** keyword and ends either with the **end** keyword for the entire code block or with the **exceptions** keyword. The final component of a PL/SQL block is the exception handler. This code portion defines all errors that may occur in the block and specifies how they should be handled. The exception handler is optional in PL/SQL. There are two types of code blocks in PL/SQL—named blocks and anonymous blocks. The first example in this section is a named block of PL/SQL code—a function. It contains a declaration block, an executable block, and an exception handler.

```
FUNCTION convert_money
(amount          IN NUMBER,
from_currency    IN VARCHAR2(5),
```

```
to_currency      IN VARCHAR2(5)
)  IS   /* denotes the beginning of the declaration section—if no */
        /* variables to declare, use the AS keyword instead of IS. */
   My_new_amt number := 0;
BEGIN   /* begins the executable section of a code block. */
    IF (My_new_amt>3) THEN
      . . .
    ELSE
      . . .
    END IF;
EXCEPTIONS  /*Begins the Exception Handler */
    WHEN bad_data THEN
       DBMS._OUTPUT.PUT_LINE('Error condition');
END;
```

The other class of PL/SQL blocks is known as an unnamed or *anonymous*
block. It is easier to identify the declaration section of an anonymous
PL/SQL block because the declaration section is preceded by the **declare**
keyword. It too contains a declaration section, an executable section, and
an exception handler.

```
DECLARE   /* begins the declaration section in an anonymous block */
    My_convert_amt         NUMBER;
    My_convert_currency    VARCHAR2(5);
    My_old_currency        VARCHAR2(5);
BEGIN /* begins the executable section of a code block. */
    IF (My_convert_amt=6) THEN
      . . . .
    ELSE
      . . .
    END IF;
EXCEPTIONS  /*Begins the Exception Handler */
    WHEN bad_data THEN
       DBMS._OUTPUT.PUT_LINE('Error condition');
END;
```

TIP
*The call to DBMS_OUTPUT.**put_line( )** in one
of the code blocks is used to write a line of
output to the SQL*Plus interface. In order to
view the line of output produced, use the set
serveroutput on command.*

Process Flow and Logic Constructs

PL/SQL offers the programmer logic constructs such as **for** loops, **while** loops, **if-then-else** statements, assignments, and expressions. Other logic constructs include PL/SQL tables and records. These "procedural" constructs are the items in PL/SQL that allow it to be both a programming language for supporting business rules and a functional language for providing data.

Cursors

One of the real strengths of PL/SQL, however, is its ability to handle cursors. A cursor is a handle to an address in memory that stores the results of an executed SQL statement. They are extremely useful for performing operations on each row returned from a **select** statement. Therefore, the PL/SQL programmer often finds herself using the looping procedural constructs of PL/SQL in conjunction with cursor manipulation operations.

Error Handling

Errors are called *exceptions* in PL/SQL, and they are checked implicitly anywhere in the code block. If at any time an error occurs in the code block, the exception corresponding to that error can be raised. At that point, execution in the executable code block stops and control is transferred to the exception handler. There are many different types of exceptions in Oracle, some of which are user defined. Others are defined by the Oracle PL/SQL engine.

Exercises

1. What is PL/SQL? Name some benefits to accessing the Oracle database with PL/SQL.

2. What are the three parts of a PL/SQL code block? Name four different types of code blocks in Oracle. What are some program constructs available in PL/SQL?

3. What is the difference between a named and an anonymous code block?

Developing a PL/SQL Block

In this section, you will cover the following topics related to developing a simple PL/SQL block:

- Declaring and using variables

- Variable value assignment

A sample PL/SQL block has already been offered. This section will cover in more detail some of the technical aspects of creating PL/SQL blocks. The topics that will be covered in this section include advanced usage and declaration of variables and constants in the declarative section of the PL/SQL block, and a refresher on assigning values to variables in the executable section.

Declaring and Using Variables

PL/SQL offers a great deal of flexibility in variable declaration. So far, two examples of variable declaration in different code blocks have been presented. Both of these examples used simple declaration of datatypes. The ones used were datatypes that have been presented as valid datatypes on the Oracle database.

Database Datatypes

There are several datatypes that can be used in PL/SQL that correspond to the datatypes used on the database. These types are as follows:

- **NUMBER**   Used to store any number.

- **CHAR(*size*), VARCHAR2(*size*)**   Used to store alphanumeric text strings. The CHAR datatype pads the value stored to the full length of the variable with blanks.

- **DATE**   Used to store dates.

- **LONG**   Stores large blocks of text, up to 2 gigabytes in length.

- ■ **LONG RAW** Stores large blocks of data stored in binary format.

- ■ **RAW** Stores smaller blocks of data stored in binary format.

- ■ **MLSLABEL** Used in Trusted Oracle.

- ■ **ROWID** Used to store the special format of ROWIDs on the database.

Nondatabase Datatypes

There are also several other PL/SQL datatypes that are not designed for use in storing data to a table:

- ■ **DEC, DECIMAL, REAL, DOUBLE_PRECISION** These numeric datatypes are a subset of the NUMBER datatype that is used for variable declaration in PL/SQL.

- ■ **INTEGER, INT, SMALLINT, NATURAL, POSITIVE, NUMERIC** These numeric datatypes are a subset of the NUMBER datatype that is used for variable declaration in PL/SQL.

- ■ **BINARY_INTEGER** This datatype is considered separately from the others, because it is stored in binary format. A variable in BINARY_INTEGER format cannot be stored in the database without conversion first.

- ■ **CHARACTER** Another name for the CHAR datatype.

- ■ **VARCHAR** Another name for the VARCHAR2 datatype.

- ■ **BOOLEAN** Stores a TRUE/FALSE value.

- ■ **TABLE/RECORD** Tables can be used to store the equivalent of an array, while records store variables with composite datatypes.

%TYPE

In general, the variables that deal with table columns should have the same datatype as the column itself. Rather than look it up, the developer can use PL/SQL's special syntactic feature that allows the developer simply to identify the table column to which this variable's datatype should correspond. This syntax uses a special keyword known as **%type**. When using the **%type** keyword, all the developer needs to know is the name of the column and the table to which the variable will correspond. Additionally, a variable can be declared with an initialization value by setting it equal to the value in the declaration section. Notice the characters used to set the variable to a value:

```
DECLARE
    My_employee_id       employee.empid%TYPE;
BEGIN …
```

```
DECLARE
    My_salary        employee.salary%TYPE   := 0;
    My_lastname      employee.lastname%TYPE:= 'SMITH';
BEGIN …
```

%ROWTYPE

There is another variable declaration method that uses the same reference principle described in the previous text. It is called **%rowtype**, and it permits the developer to create a composite datatype in which all the columns of a row in the table referenced are lumped together into a record. For example, if the EMPLOYEE table contains four columns—EMPID, LASTNAME, FIRSTNAME, and SALARY—and the developer wants to manipulate the values in each column of a row using only one referenced variable, the variable can be declared with the **%rowtype** keyword. Compare the use of **%rowtype** to manual record declaration:

```
DECLARE
    My_employee        employee%ROWTYPE;
BEGIN …
```

or manually:

```
DECLARE
    TYPE t_employee IS RECORD (
    My_empid        employee.empid%TYPE,
    My_lastname     employee.lastname%TYPE,
    My_firstname    employee.firstname%TYPE,
    My_salary       employee.salary%TYPE);

    My_employee    t_employee;
BEGIN …
```

TIP
Blocks of PL/SQL code can be nested, that is to say that a procedure can have subprocedures. In which case, the same principles of variable scope discussed in Chapter 2 also apply to nested PL/SQL blocks.

Constant Declaration

It may be useful for a developer to declare constants in the declaration section of the PL/SQL blocks developed as well. Constants make a good substitute for the use of hard-coded values, or "magic numbers." A magic value in programming is a value that is required to perform an operation or calculation but does not have any sort of meaning in the code block to help others identify why the value is there. Take, for example, a function that calculates the area of a circle, which is the number pi times radius squared. The number pi is well known to most people, but imagine if it was not, how difficult it would be to understand the reason for having the number 3.14159265358 in the middle of the function.

```
CREATE FUNCTION find_circle_area (
    p_radius   IN   circle.radius%TYPE
  RETURN NUMBER IS
    My_area    number := 0;
    Pi         constant number  := 3.14159265358;
BEGIN
    My_area := (p_radius*p_radius)* Pi;
    Return my_area;
END;
```

Exercises

1. Identify some of the database and nondatabase datatypes in PL/SQL that can be used.

2. How can the developer declare PL/SQL variables without explicitly identifying the datatype?

3. How does the developer declare a variable with an initialized value?

4. How does the developer declare a constant? Why might the developer use a constant?

Variable Value Assignment

As noted, it is possible to assign an initial value to a variable in the declaration section of the code block, and it is also possible to assign a value to a variable at any point during execution by using the assignment character—the colon followed by an equals sign. Note that the use of the equality (=) operation is for comparison only. Note also that variable assignment can be accomplished in a variety of ways in the executable section, including the use of the return value from a function call to populate a variable, or the use of the current value in a variable in an arithmetic equation to produce a new value.

```
DECLARE
    My_area     circle.area%TYPE := 0;
BEGIN
    My_area := find_circle_area(493);
    My_area := my_area + 45;
END;
```

Exercises

1. Where can a variable be assigned a value?

2. What is the assignment operator? How does it differ from the equality operator?

Interacting with the Oracle Database

In this section, you will cover the following topics related to interacting with Oracle:

- Using **select**, **insert**, **update** and **delete** in PL/SQL code
- Using implicit cursor attributes
- Transaction processing in PL/SQL

No usage of PL/SQL is complete without presenting the ease of use involved in interacting with the Oracle database. Any data manipulation or change operation can be accomplished within PL/SQL without the additional overhead typically required in other programming environments. There is no ODBC interface, and no embedding is required for use of database manipulation with PL/SQL.

Using SQL Statements in PL/SQL

Using a **select** statement in a PL/SQL code block shows how seamless the integration of PL/SQL and the Oracle database is. Note that there are no special characters that must precede the PL/SQL variables in SQL statements. The one concession PL/SQL must make is the **into** clause, which places the return values from the **select** statement into the **%rowtype** record created in the declaration section. Even so, the utility for declaring a complex record with **%rowtype** has already been proven to be more efficient than manual record declaration. The same ease of use can be seen in **update** statements. The use of the *record.element* notation to refer to the components of a record variable is illustrated as well. Using **insert** statements in PL/SQL is as straightforward as the other statements available in PL/SQL. The same is true for the **insert** statement. And, as one might expect, the usage of **delete** is as straightforward as the usage of other SQL statements in PL/SQL.

```
DECLARE
    My_employee        employee%ROWTYPE;
    My_lastname        VARCHAR2     := 'SAMSON';
    My_firstname       VARCHAR2     := 'DELILAH';
    My_salary          NUMBER       := 49500;
BEGIN
    SELECT *
    INTO my_employee
    FROM employee
    WHERE empid = 49594;

    UPDATE employee
    SET salary = my_employee.my_salary + 10000
    WHERE empid = my_employee.my_empid;

    INSERT INTO employee (empid, lastname, firstname, salary)
    VALUES (emp_sequence.nextval, my_lastname, my_firstname, my_salary);

    My_empid := 59495;
```

```
DELETE FROM employee
WHERE empid = my_empid;
END;
```

Exercises

1. What special characters are required for using data manipulation statements in PL/SQL?

2. Explain how Oracle assigns values to elements in a record.

Using Implicit Cursor Attributes

After the SQL statement executes, several things can happen that a developer may care about. For example, assume that a block of code is designed to select data from a table. If there is no data selected, then a special message should appear to let the user of the PL/SQL block know that no data was found. There are two ways to handle this situation. The first option is straightforward enough. Check the variable into which data from the **select** statement will be placed. If the variable is NULL, no data was found. However, the second option is the more powerful and elegant of the two. The developer can use cursor attributes. Cursor attributes are a set of built-in "checks" that a developer can use to identify when certain situations occur during SQL statement processing in PL/SQL blocks. The cursor attributes that will be discussed in this chapter are listed in the following series of bullets:

- **%notfound** Identifies whether the fetch executed on the cursor did not return a row. Returns a TRUE or FALSE value, the opposite of that which is returned by **%found**.

- **%rowcount** Identifies the number of rows that were processed by this cursor. Returns a numeric value.

- **%found** Identifies whether the fetch executed on the cursor did not return a row. Returns a TRUE or FALSE value, the opposite of that which is returned by **%notfound**.

- **%isopen** Identifies whether the cursor referred to is opened and ready for use. Returns a TRUE or FALSE value.

In order to understand fully the use of cursor attributes, a discussion of cursor processing is required. For now, it is sufficient to know that cursors are generally named something, and that the syntax for using the cursor attributes just identified is to identify the cursor name, followed by the attribute. This syntax is similar to that used for the **%type** and **%rowtype** variable declaration attributes. For example, the open or close status of cursor EMPLOYEES can be referred to by its cursor attribute, with the user entering EMPLOYEES**%isopen**, which will return TRUE if the cursor is open or FALSE if the cursor is closed. More details about using cursor attributes and general cursor processing are discussed later in the chapter.

Exercises

1. What value can implicit cursor attributes serve in PL/SQL code?

2. What are some of the implicit cursor attributes a developer can use in PL/SQL?

Transaction Processing in PL/SQL

The same options for transaction processing that are available in SQL statement processing are available in PL/SQL processing. Those options include specifications that name the beginning, middle, and end of a transaction. The database options that provide lock mechanisms to ensure that only one user at a time has the ability to change a record in the database is still available within the database, regardless of whether SQL or PL/SQL is used to reference the database objects.

The three transaction specifications available in PL/SQL are **commit**, **savepoint**, and **rollback**. An important distinction to make between executing SQL statements in PL/SQL blocks and the iterative entering of SQL statements with SQL*Plus is that the beginning and end of a PL/SQL block does not generally denote the beginning or end of a transaction. The beginning of a transaction in the PL/SQL block is the execution of the first SQL data change statement. In general, in order to guarantee that statements executed that make changes in the database have those changes saved, the PL/SQL code block should explicitly contain a **commit** statement. Likewise, to discard changes made or to specify a midpoint in a transaction, the developer should code in **rollback** and **savepoint** operations appropriately.

Also, the **set transaction** statement is available in PL/SQL to denote the beginning of the transaction, to assign the transaction to a rollback segment, or to set the transaction's database access to **read only**. One final option for controlling transactions is the DBMS_TRANSACTION package. Within this package, there are several different functions that allow the user to start, end, and moderate the transaction processing within PL/SQL blocks.

Exercises

1. What transaction processing features are available in PL/SQL?

2. What is DBMS_TRANSACTION?

Controlling PL/SQL Process Flow

In this section, you will cover the following topics related to controlling PL/SQL process flow:

- Conditional statements and process flow

- Using loops

No programming language is complete without the use of semantic devices to control the processing flow of its code. Some mention has already been made of the two categories of PL/SQL process flow statements, which are conditional expressions and loops. This section will cover the details of using both conditions and loops to moderate the processing of a PL/SQL block. As these concepts are fairly standard among procedural programming languages such as COBOL or C, most developers with programming experience should have no problem with the concepts. The more specific area of the chapter, and the one that will be tested in OCP Exam 1, is the area of syntax and appropriate usage. The developer should focus on these areas to gain the best background in preparation of the test.

Conditional Statements and Process Flow

A condition in a program equates directly with the idea of making a decision. The fundamental idea behind conditional processing is that of Boolean logic. Boolean logic, named for Charles Boole, a mathematician from the 19th century, is TRUE or FALSE logic. Some of the questions at the end of this chapter illustrate the idea behind TRUE or FALSE logic. The values TRUE and FALSE are conditions that can be applied to certain types of statements, called *comparison operations*. Some comparisons are as folows:

- $3 + 5 = 8$

- Menorahs hold ten candles

- $4 = 10$

- Today is Tuesday

Note that these comparison operations can all be evaluated for their validity, or whether they are TRUE or FALSE. In the first case, the statement is TRUE because 3 plus 5 equals 8. In the second, a menorah (used to commemorate the Jewish Feast of Lights around the same time as Christmas) usually contains eight or nine candles, but never ten. Therefore, the statement is FALSE. In the third example, 4 definitely does not equal 10, so the statement is FALSE. The final example illustrates an interesting principle about comparison operations; sometimes today is Tuesday, but sometimes it is not. The validity of the statement, then, depends on the day on which the comparison is made.

Conditional statement processing mechanisms allow the developer to structure code such that certain statements may or may not execute based on the validity of a comparison operation. The general syntax for conditional statements is "**if** the comparison is TRUE, **then** do the following." PL/SQL also offers an optional add-on, called **else**, which says essentially, "otherwise, do whatever the **else** clause says."

```
DECLARE
    My_hypotenuse    NUMBER := 0;
BEGIN
    IF TO_DATE(sysdate, 'DAY') = 'TUESDAY' THEN
        Execute find_hypotenuse(56,45,my_hypotenuse);
    ELSE
        My_hypotenuse := derive_hypotenuse(56,45);
    END IF;
END;
```

Note that single-row operations are allowed in comparison statements, so long as they resolve to a datatype that can be compared properly. If, for example, one side of the comparison operation resolves to a number and the other side is a text string, then that will be a problem. Additionally, note that the **else** statement can contain another **if** statement, allowing for nested **if** statements that amount to a **case** operation.

```
DECLARE
     My_hypotenuse      NUMBER;
BEGIN
     IF TO_DATE(sysdate, 'DAY') = 'TUESDAY' THEN
          Execute find_hypotenuse(56,45,my_hypotenuse);
     ELSIF TO_DATE(sysdate, 'DAY') = 'THURSDAY' THEN
          My_hypotenuse := derive_hypotenuse(56,45);
     ELSE
          My_hypotenuse := 0;
     END IF;
END;
```

Once again, if the first condition is TRUE, the first block of PL/SQL will execute. If the second condition is TRUE, then the second block of PL/SQL code will execute. If neither of the preceding code blocks is TRUE, then the third PL/SQL block will execute. To end an **if** statement, there must be the **end if** keywords. Otherwise, the code after the conditional expression will be treated as part of the **else** clause, which will cause the PL/SQL compiler to error out.

Exercises

1. What statement allows the developer to handle conditional statement processing?

2. What is a comparison operation? What is Boolean logic?

Using Loops

Another situation that arises in programming is the need to execute a set of statements repeatedly. The repetitions can be controlled in two ways: the first is to repeat the code for a specified number of times, and the second is to repeat the code until some condition is met, thus rendering a comparison operation to TRUE. The types of loops that are available in PL/SQL are listed as follows.

- **Loop-exit** statements

- **While-loop** statements

- **For-loop** statements

LOOP-EXIT Statements

The **loop-exit** statement is the simplest type of loop that can be written in PL/SQL. The **loop** keyword denotes the beginning of the code block that will be repeated, and the **end loop** keywords denote the end of the code block that will be repeated. The **exit** keyword specified by itself denotes that process should break out of the loop, while the **exit when** keywords denote a comparison operation that will test whether the statement is finished executing.

```
DECLARE
    My_leg              NUMBER := 0;
    My_hypotenuse       NUMBER := 0;
BEGIN
    LOOP
      My_leg := my_leg + 1;
      Execute find_hypotenuse(my_leg,my_leg,my_hypotenuse);
      IF my_leg = 25 THEN
        EXIT;
      END IF;
    END LOOP;
END;
```

The **if-then** statement is designed to determine if the conditions within the loop are such that the loop should terminate. The **exit** statement instructs the PL/SQL execution mechanism to leave the loop. An alternative to setting up an **if-then** statement to determine if the loop should end is to add a **when** condition to the **exit** statement. The **when** condition contains the comparison operation that the **if-then** statement would have handled. An example of a simple **loop** statement that uses an **exit when** statement is listed in the following code block. Note that the code is essentially a revision of the simple **loop** block.

```
DECLARE
    My_leg              NUMBER := 0;
    My_hypotenuse       NUMBER := 0;
BEGIN
    LOOP
       My_leg := my_leg + 1;
       Execute find_hypotenuse(my_leg,my_leg,my_hypotenuse);
       EXIT WHEN my_leg = 25;
    END LOOP;
END;
```

The **when** clause is very useful for the developer because it offers an elegant solution to defining when the loop will end, as opposed to hiding an **exit** statement inside an **if-then** statement. However, there are other possibilities for developing loops to handle repetition in coding.

WHILE-LOOP Statements

The next type of loop that approximates the usage of a **loop-exit when** statement is the **while loop** statement. The code in the previous block can be rewritten to include the **while loop**. The only difference between the **while loop** statement and the **loop-exit when** statement is where PL/SQL evaluates the **exit** condition. In a **while loop** statement, the exiting condition is evaluated at the beginning of the statement, while in the **loop-exit when** statement, the **exit** condition is evaluated wherever the **exit when** statement is placed. In one sense, the **loop-exit when** statement offers more flexibility than the **while loop** statement does because **loop-exit when** allows the developer to specify the **exit** condition wherever he wants. However, the flexibility that the **while-loop** statement may lack is made up for by its comparative elegance, in that there is no need for an **exit** statement.

```
DECLARE
    My_leg              NUMBER := 0;
    My_hypotenuse       NUMBER := 0;
BEGIN
    WHILE my_leg < 25 LOOP
       My_leg := my_leg + 1;
       Execute find_hypotenuse(my_leg,my_leg,my_hypotenuse);
    END LOOP;
END;
```

FOR-LOOP Statements

The final example of looping constructs to be presented is the **for-loop** statement. This type of loop allows the developer to specify exactly the number of times the code will execute before PL/SQL will break out of it. To accomplish this process, the **for-loop** statement specifies a loop counter and a range through which the counter will circulate. Optionally, the developer can circulate through the loop counter in reverse order, or in numeric descending order. The loop counter is then available for use by the statements in the **for-loop** statement.

```
DECLARE
    My_leg            NUMBER := 0;
    My_hypotenuse     NUMBER := 0;
BEGIN
    FOR my_leg IN 1..25 LOOP
      Execute find_hypotenuse(my_leg,my_leg,my_hypotenuse);
    END LOOP;
END;
```

Notice that the use of a **for-loop** statement made this code block even more elegant. No longer necessary is the statement that increments the *my_leg* variable, since the **for-loop** statement handles the incrementation activity automatically. There is another type of **for-loop** statement related to cursor handling that offers the same elegance and utility as the **for-loop** statement detailed in the previous code block. Its usage, as well as the more general usage of cursors will be covered in the next section of this chapter.

Exercises

1. How is nested conditional statement processing handled?

2. What are three different types of loops? What is an **exit when** statement? What is a loop counter, and for which type of loop is it most commonly used? Which type of loop doesn't require an explicit **exit** statement?

Explicit Cursor Handling

In this section, you will cover the following topics related to using cursors in PL/SQL:

- Implicit vs. explicit cursors

- Declaring and using explicit cursors

- Parameters and explicit cursors

- Writing **cursor for** loops

The definition of a cursor has already been presented. To recap, a cursor is an address in memory where a SQL statement is processed. Cursors are frequently used in PL/SQL to handle loop processing for a set of values returned by a **select** statement, and they have other uses as well. This discussion will present the uses for cursors, along with the different types of cursors available in Oracle. Creation of all types of cursors will be presented, along with a more detailed discussion of creating the special **for** loop for cursor data handling.

Implicit vs. Explicit Cursors

Every time a user executes SQL statements of any sort, there is activity on the database that involves cursors. There are two types of cursors in PL/SQL—implicit and explicit cursors. The implicit cursor is an unnamed address where the SQL statement is processed by Oracle and/or the PL/SQL execution mechanism. Every SQL statement executes in an implicit cursor, including **update**, **insert**, and **delete** statements, and **select** statements that do not execute in explicit cursors.

 TIP
Every SQL statement executed on the Oracle database is an implicit cursor, and any implicit cursor attribute can be used in conjunction with them.

An explicit cursor is one that is named by the developer. The cursor is little more than a **select** statement that has a name. Any sort of **select** statement can be used in an explicit cursor using the **cursor** *cursor_name* **is** syntax. When a **select** statement is placed in an explicit cursor, the developer has more complete control over the statement's execution.

```
DECLARE
    CURSOR employee_cursor IS
        SELECT * FROM employee;
    END;
BEGIN …
```

There is really no such thing as determining "the best time" to use an implicit cursor, but the developer can determine the best time to use an explicit one. Every time a SQL operation is requested, an implicit cursor is used. When the developer wants to perform some manipulation on each record returned by a **select** operation, she will use an explicit cursor. Most serious processing of data records is done with explicit cursors; however, there are some operations that work with implicit cursors as well. For example, many of the cursor attributes identified in an earlier section of this chapter can be applied to implicit cursors with useful results. To refresh the discussion, the list of cursor attributes available are **%notfound**, **%found**, **%rowcount**, and **%isopen**. **%notfound** identifies whether the fetch executed on the cursor did not return a row. The return value is the opposite of that which is returned by **%found**, which identifies whether the fetch executed on the cursor returned a row. These two attributes return a TRUE or FALSE value. **%rowcount** identifies the number of rows that were processed by this cursor and returns a numeric value. **%isopen** identifies whether the cursor referred to is opened and ready for use, and returns a TRUE or FALSE value.

Using an implicit cursor in conjunction with cursor attributes may consist of executing some statement and then finding out if the results were successful. In the following example, a user attempts to update an employee salary record. If there are no employees in the EMPLOYEE table that correspond with the EMPID he would like to modify, then he wants the process to add an employee record.

```
DECLARE
    My_empid     employee.empid%TYPE;
    My_salary    employee.salary%TYPE;
```

```
      My_lastname employee.lastname%TYPE;
BEGIN
      My_salary    := 99000;
      My_empid     := 59694;
      My_lastname := 'RIDDINGS';

      UPDATE employee
      SET salary = my_salary
      WHERE empid = my_empid;

      IF SQL%NOTFOUND THEN
          INSERT INTO EMPLOYEE (empid, lastname, salary)
          VALUES(my_empid, my_lastname, my_salary);
      END IF;
END;
```

There are two implicit cursors in this example. The first is the **update** statement, and the second is the **insert** statement. If the **update** statement produces a change on no rows, the **if sql%notfound then** statement will trap the error and force some operation to happen as a result of the condition. Note that in the situation of an implicit cursor, there is no name to use to precede the cursor attribute. In this situation, the developer should specify **sql%notfound**, or **sql%found**, or use "SQL" followed by the cursor attribute. That "SQL" represents the most recently-executed SQL statement producing an implicit cursor.

Exercises

1. What is an implicit cursor and what is the syntax for creating one?

2. What is an explicit cursor? Why might a developer use an explicit cursor rather than an implicit one?

3. What is the syntax for creating an explicit cursor?

Declaring and Using Explicit Cursors

Most of the time, developers spend their efforts working with explicitly defined cursors. These programming devices allow the developer to control processing outcome based on manipulation of individual records returned by a **select** statement. As stated, a cursor is defined with the syntax **cursor**

cursor_name **is**, which is then followed by a **select** statement. Once defined, the cursor allows the developer to step through the results of the query in a number of different ways.

```
DECLARE
    /* extract from a salary review program */
    High_pctinc   constant   number      := 1.20;
    Med_pctinc    constant   number      := 1.10;
    Low_pctinc    constant   number      := 1.05;
    My_salary     number;
    My_empid      number;
    CURSOR employee_crsr IS
        SELECT empid, salary
        FROM employee;
BEGIN …
```

Consider the definition of EMPLOYEE_CRSR. The two keywords used are **cursor** and **is**. Note that the syntactic requirements of the **select** statement are fairly standard. The declaration of a cursor does not actually produce the cursor, however. At this point, the cursor definition simply stands ready for action. The cursor will not actually exist in memory until it is opened and parsed by the SQL execution mechanism in Oracle. Data will not populate the cursor until the cursor is executed.

Attention should turn now to the process of invoking the cursor in memory. In this example, the employees of the company will be selected into the cursor for the purpose of salary review. Once selected, the review will be conducted as follows. Every employee of the company will obtain a midlevel raise as defined by the percentage increase listed for *mid_pctinc*. There are four exceptions: two employees will get a large raise as defined by the percentage increase listed for *high_pctinc*, while two other employees will get low performance increases as defined by *low_pctinc*. The process flow will be governed by a conditional statement, along with a loop.

```
DECLARE
    /* extract from a salary review program */
    High_pctinc   constant   number      := 1.20;
    Med_pctinc    constant   number      := 1.10;
    Low_pctinc    constant   number      := 1.05;
    My_salary     number;
```

```
    My_empid     number;
    CURSOR employee_crsr IS
        SELECT empid, salary
        FROM employee;
BEGIN
    /* The following statement creates and */
    /* executes the cursor in memory */
    OPEN employee_crsr;

    LOOP  /* sets a loop that allows program to step through */
          /* records of cursor */
        FETCH employee_crsr INTO my_empid, my salary;
        EXIT WHEN employee_crsr%NOTFOUND;  /* stop looping when no */
                                           /* records found */
        IF my_empid = 59697 OR my_empid = 76095 THEN
            UPDATE employee SET salary = my_salary*high_pctinc
            WHERE empid = my_empid;
        ELSIF my_empid = 39294 OR my_Empid = 94329 THEN
            UPDATE employee SET salary = my_salary*low_pctinc
            WHERE empid = my_empid;
        ELSE
            UPDATE employee SET salary = my_salary*mid_pctinc
            WHERE empid = my_empid;
        END IF;
    END LOOP;
END;
```

The main cursor manipulation operations are the **open, loop-exit when, fetch,** and *cursor*%**notfound** statements. The cursor is first opened with the **open** command, which implicitly parses and executes the statement as well. The loop is defined such that it should run until all records from the cursor are processed. The **exit** condition uses the %**notfound** attribute, preceded by the name of the explicit cursor. Pay particular attention to the **fetch** statement. This operation can only be performed on explicit cursors that are **select** statements. When a call to **fetch** is made, PL/SQL will obtain the next record from the cursor and populate the variables specified with values obtained from the cursor. If the **fetch** produces no results, then the %**notfound** attribute is set to TRUE. The cursor **fetch** statement can handle variables of two sorts. The **fetch** command in the preceding code block illustrates use of stand-alone variables for each column value stored in the cursor. The **fetch** statement depends on positional specification to populate the variables if this option is used. Alternately, the use of a record that contains the same attributes as those columns defined by the cursor is also handled by **fetch**. Positional specification is used here as well, so it is required for the order of the variables in the declared record to match the order of columns specified in the cursor declaration.

```
DECLARE
    /* extract from a salary review program */
    High_pctinc  constant   number   := 1.20;
    Med_pctinc   constant   number   := 1.10;
    Low_pctinc   constant   number   := 1.05;
    TYPE t_emp IS RECORD (
        T_salary   number,
        t_empid    number);
    my_emprec  t_emp;
    CURSOR employee_crsr IS
        SELECT empid, salary
        FROM employee;
BEGIN
    /* The following statement creates and executes the cursor in memory */
    OPEN employee_crsr;
    LOOP  /* sets a loop that allows program to step */
          /* through records of cursor */
        FETCH employee_crsr INTO my_emprec;
        EXIT WHEN employee_crsr%NOTFOUND;  /* stop looping when no */
                                           /* records found */
        IF my_emprec.t_empid = 59697 OR my_emprec.t_empid = 76095 THEN
            UPDATE employee SET salary = my_emprec.t_salary*high_pctinc
            WHERE empid = my_emprec.t_empid;
        ELSIF my_emprec.t_empid = 39294 OR my_emprec.t_empid = 94329 THEN
            UPDATE employee SET salary = my_emprec.t_salary*low_pctinc
            WHERE empid = my_emprec.t_empid;
        ELSE
            UPDATE employee SET salary = my_emprec.t_salary*mid_pctinc
            WHERE empid = my_emprec.t_empid;
        END IF;
    END LOOP;
END;
```

The additional code required to support records in this case may well be worth it if there are many variables in the PL/SQL block. Records give the developer a more object-oriented method for handling the variables required for cursor manipulation.

Exercises

1. What must be done in order to make a cursor exist in memory?

2. What step must be accomplished to put data in a cursor?

3. How is data retrieved from a cursor?

Parameters and Explicit Cursors

At times, there may be opportunities for the reuse of a cursor definition. However, the cursors demonstrated thus far either select every record in the database or, alternately, may be designed to select from a table according to hard-coded "magic" values. There is a way to configure cursors such that the values from which data will be selected can be specified at the time the cursor is opened. The method used to create this cursor setup is the use of parameters. For example, assume the developer wanted to set up so that the cursor would select a subset of values from the database to run the salary review program on, based on the first letter of the last name. This process could be accomplished with the use of cursor parameters. The developer could allow the cursor to accept a low and high limit, and then select data from the table for the cursor using that range.

```
DECLARE
/* extract from a salary review program */
   High_pctinc   constant   number    := 1.20;
   Med_pctinc    constant   number    := 1.10;
   Low_pctinc    constant   number    := 1.05;
   TYPE t_emp IS RECORD (
       T_salary    number,
       t_empid     number);
       my_emprec   t_emp;
   CURSOR employee_crsr(low_end VARCHAR2, high_end VARCHAR2) IS
       SELECT empid, salary
       FROM employee
       WHERE substr(lastname,1,1) BETWEEN UPPER(low_end) AND UPPER(high_end);
BEGIN …
```

With the parameter passing defined, the developer can set up the cursor with more control over the data that is ultimately processed. For example, if the developer wants only to process salary increases for employees whose last names start with A through M, she can develop the following code block:

```
DECLARE
/* extract from a salary review program */
    High_pctinc    constant    number    := 1.20;
    Med_pctinc     constant    number    := 1.10;
    Low_pctinc     constant    number    := 1.05;
    TYPE t_emp IS RECORD (
        T_salary    number,
        t_empid     number);
    my_emprec  t_emp;
    CURSOR employee_crsr(low_end VARCHAR2, high_end VARCHAR2) IS
        SELECT empid, salary
        FROM employee
            WHERE substr(lastname,1,1) BETWEEN UPPER(low_end) AND UPPER(high_end);
BEGIN
/* The following statement creates and executes the cursor in memory */
    OPEN employee_crsr('A','M');
    LOOP  /* sets a loop that allows program to step */
            /* through records of cursor */
        FETCH employee_crsr INTO my_emprec;
        EXIT WHEN employee_crsr%NOTFOUND;  /* stop looping when no */
                                           /* records found */
        IF my_emprec.t_empid = 59697 OR my_emprec.t_empid = 76095 THEN
            UPDATE employee SET salary = my_emprec.t_salary*high_pctinc
            WHERE empid = my_emprec.t_empid;
        ELSIF my_emprec.t_empid = 39294 OR my_emprec.t_empid = 94329 THEN
            UPDATE employee SET salary = my_emprec.t_salary*low_pctinc
            WHERE empid = my_emprec.t_empid;
        ELSE
            UPDATE employee SET salary = my_emprec.t_salary*mid_pctinc
            WHERE empid = my_emprec.t_empid;
        END IF;
    END LOOP;
END;
```

Notice that this code block—the **open** statement that opens, parses, and executes the cursor—now contains two values passed into the cursor creation as parameters. This parameter passing is required for the cursor to resolve into a set of data rows.

Exercises

1. What value does passing parameters to a cursor provide?

2. How can a cursor be defined to accept parameters?

Writing CURSOR FOR Loops

As given evidence in the previous examples, quite a bit of usage surrounding cursors involves selecting data and performing operations on each row returned by the cursor. The code examples presented thus far illustrate how to perform this activity. However, each one of the examples illustrates also that there is some overhead for handling the looping process correctly. Depending on the type of loop used, the overhead required can be substantial. Take, for example, the use of a simple **loop-exit** statement. Not only must the code that will execute repeatedly be enclosed in the **loop** syntax construct, but the test for the **exit** condition must be defined explicitly. Other looping statement examples do simplify the process somewhat.

There is one other loop that is ideal for the situation where a developer wants to pull together some rows of data and perform a specified set of operations on them. This loop statement is called the **cursor for** loop. The **cursor for** loops handle several activities implicitly related to loop creation. The items handled implicitly by a **cursor for** loop are the opening, parsing, executing, and fetching of row data from the cursor, and the check to determine if there is more data (and thus if the loop should exit). Moreover, the declaration of a record variable to handle the data fetched from the cursor by the **cursor for** loop is also handled implicitly. The sample PL/SQL block is reprinted with the addition of a **cursor for** loop statement to handle all cursor processing:

```
DECLARE
/* extract from a salary review program */
   High_pctinc   constant   number   := 1.20;
```

```
Med_pctinc    constant    number    := 1.10;
Low_pctinc    constant    number    := 1.05;
CURSOR employee_crsr(low_end VARCHAR2, high_end VARCHAR2) IS
     SELECT empid, salary
     FROM employee
     WHERE substr(lastname,1,1) BETWEEN UPPER(low_end) AND UPPER(high_end);
BEGIN
/* The following statement creates and executes the cursor in memory */
/* sets a loop that allows program to step through records of cursor */
  FOR my_emprec in employee_crsr('A','M') LOOP
    IF my_emprec.empid = 59697 OR my_emprec.empid = 76095 THEN
       UPDATE employee SET salary = my_emprec.salary*high_pctinc
       WHERE empid = my_emprec.empid;
    ELSIF my_emprec.empid = 39294 OF my_emprec.empid = 94329 THEN
       UPDATE employee SET salary = my_emprec.salary*low_pctinc
       WHERE empid = my_emprec.empid;
    ELSE
       UPDATE employee SET salary = my_emprec.t_salary*mid_pctinc;
       WHERE empid = my_emprec.t_empid;
    END IF;
  END LOOP;
END;
```

Take an extra moment to review the code block detailing a **cursor for** loop and confirm the following features the loop handles implicitly. Note that the benefit of using a **cursor for** loop is that there are fewer requirements to set up the loop, resulting in fewer lines of code, fewer mistakes, and easier-to-read programs. The features that **cursor for** loops handle implicitly are listed here:

- The **cursor for** loop handles opening, parsing, and executing the cursor automatically.

- The **cursor for** loop fetches row data implicitly for each iteration of the loop.

- The **cursor for** loop handles the *cursor_name*%**notfound** condition implicitly and appropriately terminates the loop when the attribute is TRUE.

- The **cursor for** loop handles the definition of a record to store the row values returned by the cursor fetch automatically, resulting in a smaller declaration section.

Exercises

1. What steps in cursor loop handling does a **cursor for** loop handle implicitly?

2. How is the **exit** condition defined for a **cursor for** loop?

Error Handling

In this section, you will cover the following areas related to error handling:

- The three basic types of exceptions

- Identifying common exceptions

- Coding the exception handler

The handling of errors in PL/SQL is arguably the best contribution PL/SQL makes to commercial programming. Errors in PL/SQL need not be trapped and handled with **if** statements directly within the program, as they are in other procedural languages like C. Instead, PL/SQL allows the developer to *raise exceptions* when an error condition is identified and switch control to a special program area in the PL/SQL block, called the *exception handler*. The code to handle an error does not clutter the executable program logic in PL/SQL, nor is the programmer required to terminate programs with **return** or **exit** statements. The exception handler is a cleaner way to handle errors.

Three Basic Types of Exceptions

The three types of exceptions in Oracle PL/SQL are *predefined* exceptions, *user-defined* exceptions, and *pragma* exceptions. Exception handling in PL/SQL offers several advantages. These advantages are simplicity and flexibility. Predefined exceptions offer the developer several built-in problems that can be checked. User-defined and pragma exceptions allow for additional flexibility to build in a level of support for errors defined by the user into PL/SQL. The following discussions will illustrate the use of predefined, user-defined, and pragma exceptions.

Predefined Exceptions

In order to facilitate error handling in PL/SQL, Oracle has designed several "built-in" or predefined exceptions. These exceptions are used to handle common situations that may occur on the database. For example, there is a built-in exception that can be used to detect when a statement returns no data, or when a statement expecting one piece of data receives more than one piece of data. There is no invoking a predefined exception—they are tested and raised automatically by Oracle. However, in order to have something done when the predefined error occurs, there must be something in the exception handler both to identify the error and to define what happens when the error occurs. Later, in the section "Identifying Common Exceptions," several of the most common exceptions will be presented.

TIP

In order to trap a predefined exception, there must be an exception handler coded for it in the exceptions section of the PL/SQL block.

User-Defined Exceptions

In addition to predefined exceptions, there can be created a whole host of user-defined exceptions that handle situations that may arise in the code. A user-defined exception may not produce an Oracle error; instead, user-defined exceptions may enforce business rules in situations where an Oracle error would not necessarily occur. Unlike predefined exceptions, which are implicitly raised when the associated error condition arises, a user-defined exception must have explicit code in the PL/SQL block designed to raise it. There is code required for all three sections of a PL/SQL block if the developer plans on using user-defined exceptions. The required code is detailed in the bullets that follow:

■ **Exception declaration**   In the declaration section of the PL/SQL block, the exception name must be declared. This name will be used to invoke, or *raise*, the exception in the execution section if the conditions of the exception occur.

- **Exception testing** In the execution section of the PL/SQL block, there must be code that explicitly tests for the user-defined error condition, which raises the exception if the conditions are met.

- **Exception handling** In the exception handler section of the PL/SQL block, there must be a specified **when** clause that names the exception and the code that should be executed if that exception is raised. Alternately, there should be a **when others** exception handler that acts as a catchall.

The following code block provides an example for coding a user-defined exception. In the example, assume that there is some problem with an employee's salary record being NULL. The following code will select a record from the database. If the record selected has a NULL salary, the user-defined exception will identify the problem with an output message.

```
DECLARE
    My_empid            number;
    My_emp_record       employee%ROWTYPE;
    My_salary_null      EXCEPTION;
BEGIN
    My_empid := 59694;
    SELECT * FROM employee
    INTO my_emp_record
    WHERE empid = my_empid;

    IF my_emp_record.salary IS NULL THEN
        RAISE my_salary_null;
    END IF;
EXCEPTION
    WHEN NO_DATA_FOUND THEN
        DBMS_OUTPUT.PUT_LINE('No Data Found');
    WHEN my_salary_null THEN
        DBMS_OUTPUT.PUT_LINE('Salary column was null for employee');
END;
```

Note that code must appear for user-defined exceptions in all three areas of the PL/SQL block. Without one of these components, the exception will not operate properly and the code will produce errors.

The EXCEPTION_INIT Pragma

Sometimes a user-defined exception will occur in conjunction with an Oracle error. In the case where the PL/SQL block experiences errors and the developer would like to code some exception in conjunction with the error, the developer can use the **exception_init** *pragma*. The *pragma* statement allows the developer to declare the Oracle-numbered error to be associated with a named exception in the block. This usage allows the code to handle errors that it might not have handled previously. For example, assume that the developer is inserting data on the EMPLOYEE table, and this table defined a NOT NULL constraint on SALARY. Instead of allowing the PL/SQL block to terminate abnormally if an **insert** occurs that does not name a value for the SALARY column with an **ora-01400** error, the declaration of an exception allows the PL/SQL block to handle the error programmatically.

```
DECLARE
    My_emp_record         employee%ROWTYPE;
    PRAGMA EXCEPTION_INIT(my_salary_null, -1400);
BEGIN
    My_emp_record.empid := 59485;
    My_emp_record.lastname := 'RICHARD';
    My_emp_record.firstname := 'JEAN-MARIE';

    INSERT INTO employee(empid,lastname,firstname,salary)
    VALUES(my_emp_record.empid, my_emp_record.lastname,
           my_emp_record.firstname, my_emp_record.salary);
EXCEPTION
    WHEN NO_DATA_FOUND THEN
        DBMS_OUTPUT.PUT_LINE('No Data Found');
    WHEN my_salary_null THEN
        DBMS_OUTPUT.PUT_LINE('Salary column was null for employee');
END;
```

An advantage to using the **exception_init** pragma when the user-defined error produces some Oracle error is that there is no need for an explicit condition test that raises the exception if the condition is met. Exceptions defined with the **exception_init** pragma enjoy the same implicit exception handling as predefined exceptions do.

Exercises

1. What is a predefined error? How are they invoked?

2. What is a user-defined error? Where must code be defined in order to create a user-defined exception?

3. What can be used to associate an Oracle error with a user-defined error?

Identifying Common Exceptions

There are many common exceptions that Oracle PL/SQL allows developers to define and handle in their programs. Some of the predefined cursors are listed here:

- **invalid_cursor**   Occurs when an attempt is made to close a nonopen cursor.

- **cursor_already_open**   Occurs when an attempt is made to open a nonclosed cursor.

- **dup_val_on_index**   Unique or primary key constraint violation.

- **no_data_found**   No rows were selected or changed by the SQL operation.

- **too_many_rows**   More than one row was obtained by a single-row subquery, or in another SQL statement operation where Oracle was expecting one row.

- **zero_divide**   An attempt was made to divide by zero.

- **rowtype_mismatch**   The datatypes of the record to which data from the cursor is assigned are incompatible.

- **invalid_number**   An alphanumeric string was referenced as a number.

Of these operations, the developer may expect to use the **no_data_found** or **too_many_rows** exceptions most frequently. In fact, the user can incorporate checks for these areas using cursor attributes. As mentioned, in order to use an exception, the developer must *raise* it. Raising an exception requires usage of the **raise** statement. However, one of the best features about the predefined exceptions is that there is no need to raise them. They must simply be included in the exception handler for the PL/SQL block, and if a situation arises where the error occurs, then the predefined exception is raised automatically. The following code block illustrates the use of an exception handler, along with a predefined exception:

```
DECLARE
    My_empid    number;
BEGIN
    My_empid := 59694;
    SELECT * FROM employee
    WHERE empid = my_empid;
EXCEPTION
    WHEN NO_DATA_FOUND THEN
        DBMS_OUTPUT.PUT_LINE('No Data Found');
END;
```

Notice that there is no code that explicitly tells PL/SQL to write the output message if no data is found in the particular **select** statement in the executable portion of the block. Instead, the exception is implicitly raised when a predefined exception condition occurs. This layer of abstraction is useful because the additional **if** statement required for checking this condition manually is unnecessary.

Exercises

1. What predefined exception is used to identify the situation where no data is returned by a **select** statement?

2. What predefined exception is used to identify when the datatype of the information returned is not the same datatype as the declared variable?

Coding the Exception Handler

Special attention should be paid now to the actual code of the exception handler. So far, the exceptions handled in previous code blocks have had simple routines that display an error message. There are more advanced options than those presented, of course. This discussion will focus on a few of the options provided.

A named or user-defined exception in the declaration and executable section of the PL/SQL block should have an associated exception handler written for it. The best way to handle an exception is to name it specifically using the **when** clause in the exceptions block of the PL/SQL program. Following the **when** clause, there can be one or several statements that define the events that will happen if this exception is raised. If there is no code explicitly defined for the exception raised, then PL/SQL will execute whatever code is defined for a special catchall exception called **others**. If there is no explicit code defined for a particular exception and no code defined for the **others** exception, then control passes to the exception handler of the procedure that called the PL/SQL code block. The exception handler is perhaps the greatest achievement gained by using PL/SQL to write stored procedures in Oracle. Its flexibility and ease of use make it simple to code robust programs.

```
EXCEPTION
    WHEN NO_ROWS_FOUND THEN …
        /* does some work when the NO_ROWS_FOUND predefined exception is
           raised implicitly. */
    WHEN OTHERS THEN …
        /* this code will execute when any other exception is raised,
           explicitly or implicitly. */
END;
```

TIP
Once an exception is raised, PL/SQL flow control passes to the exception handler. Once the exception is handled, the PL/SQL block will be exited. In other words, once the exception is raised, the execution portion of the PL/SQL block is over.

Exercises

1. What are the components of an exception handler?

2. What is the **others** exception, and how is it used?

Chapter Summary

PL/SQL programming is the topic of this chapter. The subject areas discussed include overview of PL/SQL, modular coding practices, developing PL/SQL blocks, interacting with Oracle, controlling process flow with conditional statements and loops, cursors, and error handling. The PL/SQL areas of OCP Exam 1 comprise about 22 percent of the overall test. PL/SQL is the best method available for writing and managing stored procedures that work with Oracle data. PL/SQL code consists of three subblocks—the declaration section, the executable section, and the exception handler. In addition, PL/SQL can be used in four different programming constructs. The types are procedures and functions, packages, and triggers. Procedures and functions are similar in that they both contain a series of instructions that PL/SQL will execute. However, the main difference is that a function will always return one and only one value. Procedures can return more than that number as output parameters. Packages are collected libraries of PL/SQL procedures and functions that have an interface to tell others what procedures and functions are available as well as their parameters, and the body contains the actual code executed by those procedures and functions. Triggers are special PL/SQL blocks that execute when a triggering event occurs. Events that fire triggers include any SQL statement.

The declaration section allows for the declaration of variables and constants. A variable can have either a simple or "scalar" datatype, such as NUMBER or VARCHAR2. Alternatively, a variable can have a referential datatype that uses reference to a table column to derive its datatype. Constants can be declared in the declaration section in the same way as variables, but with the addition of a **constant** keyword and with a value assigned. If a value is not assigned to a constant in the declaration section, an error will occur. In the executable section, a variable can have a value assigned to it at any point using the assignment expression (:=).

Using PL/SQL allows the developer to produce code that integrates seamlessly with access to the Oracle database. Examples appeared in the chapter of using all SQL statements, including data selection, data change, and transaction processing statements. There are no special characters or keywords required for "embedding" SQL statements into PL/SQL, because SQL is an extension of PL/SQL. As such, there really is no embedding at all. Every SQL statement executes in a cursor. When a cursor is not named, it is called an implicit cursor. PL/SQL allows the developer to investigate certain return status features in conjunction with the implicit cursors that run. These implicit cursor attributes include **%notfound** and **%found** to identify if records were found or not found by the SQL statement; **%notfound**, which tells the developer how many rows were processed by the statement; and **%isopen**, which determines if the cursor is open and active in the database.

Conditional process control is made possible in PL/SQL with the use of **if-then-else** statements. The **if** statement uses a Boolean logic comparison to evaluate whether to execute the series of statements after the **then** clause. If the comparison evaluates to TRUE, the **then** clause is executed. If it evaluates to FALSE, then the code in the **else** statement is executed. Nested **if** statements can be placed in the **else** clause of an **if** statement, allowing for the development of code blocks that handle a number of different cases or situations.

Process flow can be controlled in PL/SQL with the use of loops as well. There are several different types of loops, from simple **loop-exit** statements to **loop-exit when** statements, **while loop** statements, and **for loop** statements. A simple **loop-exit** statement consists of the **loop** and **end loop** keywords enclosing the statements that will be executed repeatedly, with a special **if-then** statement designed to identify if an **exit** condition has been reached. The **if-then** statement can be eliminated by using an **exit when** statement to identify the **exit** condition. The entire process of identifying the **exit** condition as part of the steps executed in the loop can be eliminated with the use of a **while loop** statement. The **exit** condition is identified in the **while** clause of the statement. Finally, the **for loop** statement can be used in cases where the developer wants the code executing repeatedly for a specified number of times.

Cursor manipulation is useful for situations where a certain operation must be performed on each row returned from a query. A cursor is simply an address in memory where a SQL statement executes. A cursor can be explicitly named with the use of the **cursor** *cursor_name* **is** statement, followed by the SQL statement that will comprise the cursor. The **cursor** *cursor_name* **is** statement is used to define the cursor in the declaration section only. Once declared, the cursor must be opened, parsed, and executed before its data can be manipulated. This process is executed with the **open** statement. Once the cursor is declared and opened, rows from the resultant dataset can be obtained if the SQL statement defining the cursor was a **select** using the **fetch** statement. Both individual variables for each column's value or a PL/SQL record may be used to store fetched values from a cursor for manipulation in the statement.

Executing each of the operations associated with cursor manipulation can be simplified in situations where the user will be looping through the cursor results using the **cursor for** loop statement. The **cursor for** loops handle many aspects of cursor manipulation explicitly. These steps include opening, parsing, and executing the cursor statement, fetching the value from the statement, handling the exit when data not found condition, and even implicitly declaring the appropriate record type for a variable identified by the loop in which to store the fetched values from the query.

The exception handler is arguably the finest feature PL/SQL offers. In it, the developer can handle certain types of predefined exceptions without explicitly coding error-handling routines. The developer can also associate user-defined exceptions with standard Oracle errors, thereby eliminating the coding of an error check in the executable section. This step requires defining the exception using the **exception_init** pragma and coding a routine that handles the error when it occurs in the exception handler. For completely user-defined errors that do not raise Oracle errors, the user can declare an exception and code a programmatic check in the execution section of the PL/SQL block, followed by some routine to execute when the error occurs in the exception handler. A special predefined exception called **others** can be coded into the exception handler as well to function as a catchall for any exception that occurs that has no exception-handling process defined. Once an exception is raised, control passes from the execution section of the block to the exception handler. Once the exception handler has completed, control is passed to the process that called the PL/SQL block.

Two-Minute Drill

- PL/SQL is a programming environment that is native to the Oracle database. It features seamless integration with other database objects in Oracle and with SQL.

- There are three parts to a PL/SQL program: the declaration area, the execution area, and the exception handler.

- There are four types of PL/SQL blocks: procedures, functions, packages, and triggers

- Procedures allow the developer to specify more than one output parameter, while functions only allow one return value. Other than that, the two PL/SQL blocks are similar in function and usage.

- Variables are defined in the declaration section.

- Variables can have a scalar datatype like NUMBER or VARCHAR2, or a referential datatype defined by use of a table and/or column reference followed by **%type** or **%rowtype**.

- Constants are declared the same way as variables, except for the fact that the **constant** keyword is used to denote a constant and the constant must have a value assigned in the declaration section.

- Variables can have values assigned anywhere in the PL/SQL block using the assignment operator, which looks like (**:=**).

- Any SQL statement is valid for use in PL/SQL. This includes all SQL statements such as **select** and **delete**, and transaction control statements such as **set transaction** or **commit**.

- Conditional processing is handled in PL/SQL with **if-then-else** statements.

- **If-then-else** statements rely on Boolean logic to determine which set of statements will execute. If the condition is TRUE, the statements in the **then** clause will execute. If the condition is FALSE, the statements in the **else** clause will execute.

- The **if** statements can be nested into one another's **else** clause.

- Several loops also control the repetition of blocks of PL/SQL statements.

- The **loop-exit** statement is a simple definition for a loop that marks the beginning and end of the loop code. An **if-then** statement tests to see if conditions are such that the loop should exit. An **exit** statement must be specified explicitly.

- The **if-then** statement can be replaced with an **exit when** statement, which defines the **exit** condition for the loop.

- The **while** statement eliminates the need for an **exit** statement by defining the **exit** condition in the **while loop** statement.

- If the programmer wants her code to execute a specified number of times, the **for loop** can be used.

- Every SQL statement executes in an implicit cursor. An explicit cursor is a named cursor corresponding to a defined SQL statement.

- An explicit cursor can be defined with the **cursor** *cursor_name* **is** statement. Cursors can be defined to accept input parameters that will be used in the **where** clause to limit the data manipulated by the cursor.

- Once declared, a cursor must be opened, parsed, and executed in order to have its data used. This task is accomplished with the **open** statement.

- In order to obtain data from a cursor, the programmer must **fetch** the data into a variable. This task is accomplished with the **fetch** statement.

- The variable used in the **fetch** can either consist of several loose variables for storing single-column values or a record datatype that stores all column values in a record.

- A special loop exists to simplify use of cursors, the **cursor for** loop.

- The **cursor for** loop handles the steps normally done in the **open** statement, and implicitly fetches data from the cursor until the **data**

not found condition occurs. This statement also handles the declaration of the variable and associated record type, if any is required.

- The exception handler in PL/SQL handles all error handling.

- There are user-defined exceptions, predefined exceptions, and pragma exceptions in PL/SQL.

- Only user-defined exceptions require explicit checks in the execution portion of PL/SQL code to test to see if the exception condition has occurred.

- A named exception can have a **when** clause defined in the exception handler that executes whenever that exception occurs.

- The **others** exception is a catchall exception designed to operate if an exception occurs that is not associated with any other defined exception handler.

Chapter Questions

1. **Which of the following lines in this PL/SQL block will return an error?**

   A. CREATE FUNCTION add_numbers (var_a IN NUMBER,

   B. var_b IN OUT NUMBER) RETURN NUMBER IS

   C. BEGIN

   D. RETURN (var_a + var_b);

   E. END;

   F. There are no errors in this statement.

2. **Developer JANET receives an error due to the following statement in the DECLARATION section:**

   PI CONSTANT NUMBER;

   The problem is because

   A. There is not enough memory in the program for the constant.

    B. There is no value associated with the constant.

    C. There is no datatype associated with the constant.

    D. PI is a reserved word.

3. **Which statement most accurately describes the result of not creating an exception handler for a raised exception?**

    A. The program will continue without raising the exception.

    B. There will be a memory leak.

    C. Control will pass to the PL/SQL block caller's exception handler.

    D. The program will return a **%notfound** error.

4. **Which of the following statements is true about implicit cursors?**

    A. Implicit cursors are used for SQL statements that are not named.

    B. Developers should use implicit cursors with great care.

    C. Implicit cursors are used in **cursor for** loops to handle data processing.

    D. Implicit cursors are no longer a feature in Oracle.

5. **Which of the following is not a feature of a CURSOR FOR loop?**

    A. Record type declaration.

    B. Opening and parsing of SQL statements.

    C. Fetches records from cursor.

    D. Requires **exit** condition to be defined.

6. **A developer would like to use referential datatype declaration on a variable. The variable name is *EMPLOYEE_LASTNAME*, and the corresponding table and column is EMPLOYEE, and LNAME, respectively. How would the developer define this variable using referential datatypes?**

   A. Use employee.lname%**type**.

   B. Use employee.lname%**rowtype**.

   C. Look up datatype for EMPLOYEE column on LASTNAME table and use that.

   D. Declare it to be type LONG.

7. After executing an UPDATE statement, the developer codes a PL/SQL block to perform an operation based on SQL%ROWCOUNT. What data is returned by the SQL%ROWCOUNT operation.

   A. A Boolean value representing the success or failure of the **update**.

   B. A numeric value representing the number of rows updated.

   C. A VARCHAR2 value identifying the name of the table updated.

   D. A LONG value containing all data from the table.

8. Which three of the following are implicit cursor attributes?

   A. %found

   B. %too_many_rows

   C. %notfound

   D. %rowcount

   E. %rowtype

9. If left out, which of the following would cause an infinite loop to occur in a simple loop?

   A. LOOP

   B. END LOOP

   C. IF-THEN

   D. EXIT

10. The OTHERS exception handler is used to handle the OTHERS raised exception.

    A. TRUE

    B. FALSE

11. Which line in the following statement will produce an error?

    A. **cursor** action_cursor **is**

    B. **select** name, rate, action

    C. **into** action_record

    D. **from** action_table;

    E. There are no errors in this statement.

12. The command used to open a CURSOR FOR loop is

    A. **open**

    B. **fetch**

    C. **parse**

    D. None, **cursor for** loops handle cursor opening implicitly.

13. EXIT statements are required in WHILE loops.

    A. TRUE

    B. FALSE

Answers to Chapter Questions

1. B.   var_b IN OUT NUMBER) RETURN NUMBER IS).

Explanation   The parameters of a function cannot be specified as OUT parameters.

2. B.   There is no value associated with the constant.

Explanation   A value must be associated with a constant in the declaration section. If no value is given for the constant, an error will result.

3. C.   Control will pass to the PL/SQL block caller's exception handler.

Explanation   If the exception raised is not handled locally, then PL/SQL will attempt to handle it at the level of the process that called the PL/SQL block. If the exception is not handled there, then PL/SQL will attempt to keep finding an exception handler that will resolve the exception. If none is found, then an error will result.

4. A.   Implicit cursors are used for SQL statements that are not named.

Explanation   Implicit cursors are used for all SQL statements except for those statements that are named. They are never incorporated into **cursor for** loops, nor is much care given to using them more or less, which eliminates choices B and C. They are definitely a feature of Oracle, eliminating choice D.

5. D.   Requires **exit** condition to be defined.

Explanation   A **cursor for** loop handles just about every feature of cursor processing automatically, including **exit** conditions.

6. A.   Use employee.lname%**type**.

Explanation   The only option in this question that allows the developer to use referential type declaration for columns is choice A. Choice B uses the

%**rowtype** referential datatype, which defines a record variable, which is not what the developer is after.

7. B. A numeric value representing the number of rows updated.

Explanation %**rowtype** returns the numeric value representing the number of rows that were manipulated by the SQL statement.

8. A, C, D. %**found**, %**notfound**, %**rowcount**.

Explanation These three are the only choices that are valid cursor attributes.

9. D. EXIT

Explanation Without an **exit** statement, a simple loop will not stop.

10. B. FALSE

Explanation There is no **others** exception. The **others** exception handler handles all exceptions that may be raised in a PL/SQL block that do not have exception handlers explicitly defined for them.

11. C. **into** action_record

Explanation The **into** clause is not permitted in cursors.

12. D. None, **cursor for** loops handle cursor opening implicitly.

Explanation The **cursor for** loops handle, among other things, the opening, parsing, and executing of named cursors.

13. B. FALSE

Explanation There is no need for an **exit** statement in a **while** loop, since the exiting condition is defined in the **while** statement.

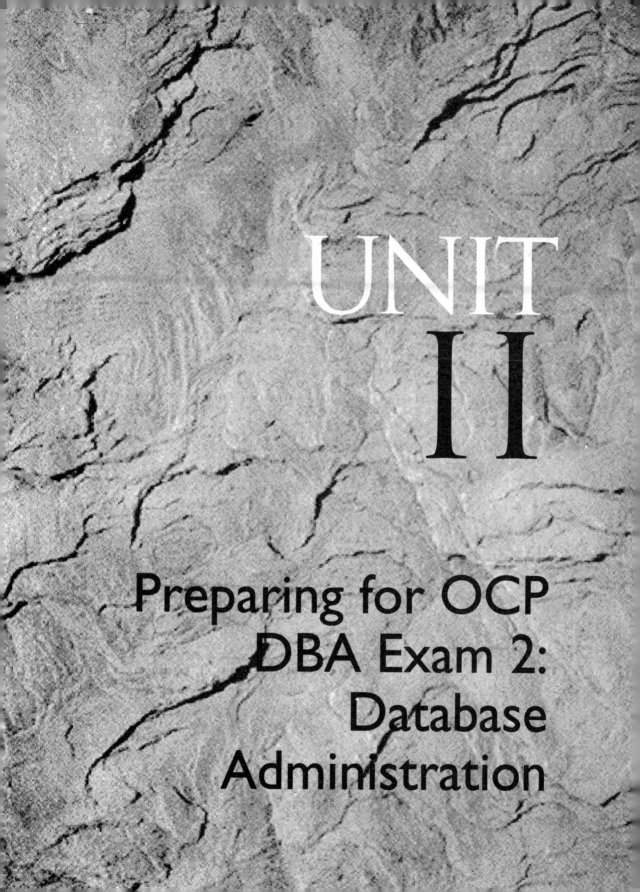

UNIT II

Preparing for OCP DBA Exam 2: Database Administration

CHAPTER
6

Basics of the Oracle Database Architecture

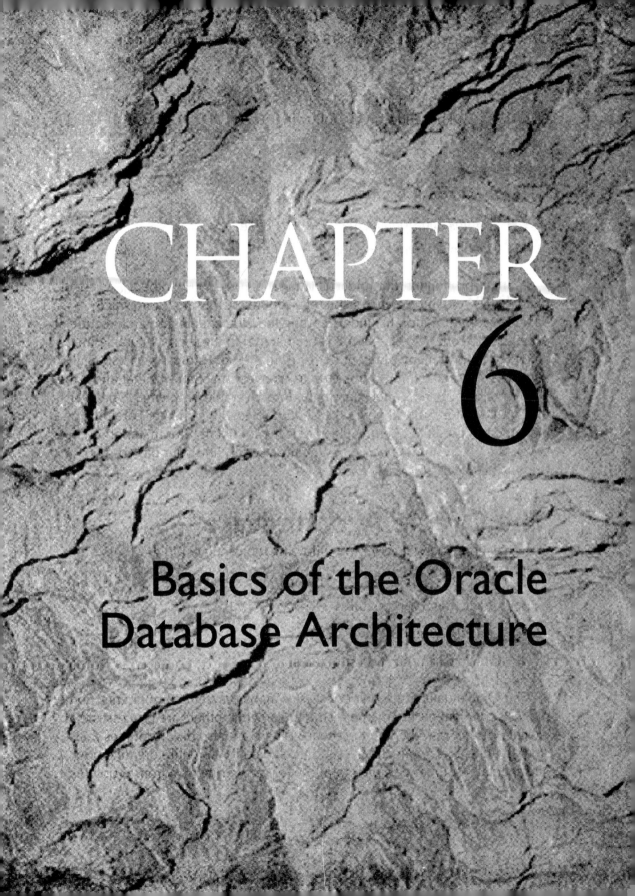

n this chapter, you will understand and demonstrate knowledge in the following areas:

- The Oracle architecture
- Starting and stopping the Oracle instance
- Creating an Oracle database

A major portion of your understanding of Oracle, both to be a successful Oracle DBA and to be a successful taker of the OCP Exam 2 for Oracle database administration, is understanding the Oracle database architecture. About 22 percent of OCP exam 2 is on material in these areas. Oracle in action consists of many different items, from memory structures, to special processes that make things run faster, to recovery mechanisms that allow the DBA to restore systems after seemingly unrecoverable problems. Whatever the Oracle feature, it's all here. You should review this chapter carefully, as the concepts presented here will serve as the foundation for material covered in the rest of the book, certification series, and your day-to-day responsibilities as an Oracle DBA.

The Oracle Architecture

In this section, you will cover the following topics related to the Oracle architecture:

- Oracle memory structures
- Oracle background processes
- Oracle disk utilization structures

The Oracle database server consists of many different components. Some of these components are memory structures, while others are processes that execute certain tasks behind the scenes. There are also disk resources that store the data that applications use to track data for an entire organization, and special resources designed to allow for recovering data from problems ranging from incorrect entry to disk failure. All three structures of the Oracle database server running together to allow users to read and modify data are referred to as an Oracle *instance*. Figure 6-1 demonstrates the various disk, memory, and process components of the Oracle instance. All of these features working together allow Oracle to handle data management for applications ranging from small "data marts" with fewer than five users to enterprise-wide client/server applications designed for online transaction processing for 50,000+ users in a global environment.

Oracle Memory Structures

Focus first on the memory components of the Oracle instance. This set of memory components represents a "living" version of Oracle that is available only when the instance is running. There are two basic memory structures on the Oracle instance. The first and most important is called the System Global Area, which is commonly referred to as the SGA. The other memory structure in the Oracle instance is called the Program Global Area, or PGA. This discussion will explain the components of the SGA and the PGA, and also cover the factors that determine the storage of information about users connected to the Oracle instance.

The Oracle SGA

The Oracle SGA is the most important memory structure in Oracle. When DBAs talk about most things related to memory, they are talking about the SGA. The SGA stores several different components of memory usage that are designed to execute processes to obtain data for user queries as quickly as possible while also maximizing the number of concurrent users that can access the Oracle instance. The SGA consists of three different items, listed here.

- The buffer cache
- The shared pool
- The redo log buffer

The buffer cache consists of buffers that are the size of database blocks. They are designed to store data blocks recently used by user SQL statements in order to improve performance for subsequent selects and data changes.

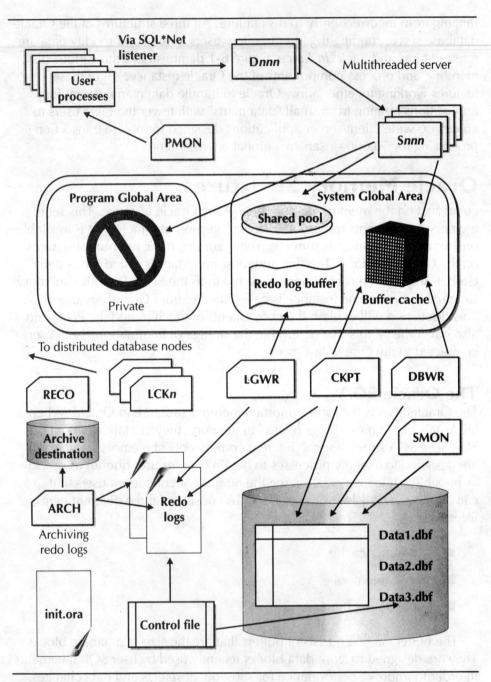

FIGURE 6-1. *The Oracle database architecture at a glance*

The shared pool has two required components and one optional component. The required components of the shared pool are the library cache and the dictionary cache. The optional component of the shared pool includes session information for user processes connecting to the Oracle instance. The final area of the SGA is the redo log buffer, which stores online redo log entries in memory until they can be written to disk.

Explore the usage of the shared pool in the Oracle database architecture. The library cache is designed to store parse information for SQL statements executing against the database. Parse information includes the set of database operations that the SQL execution mechanism will perform in order to obtain data requested by the user processes. This information is treated as a shared resource in the library cache. If another user process comes along wanting to run the same query that Oracle has already parsed for another user, the database will recognize the opportunity for reuse and let the user process utilize the parse information already available in the shared pool. Of course, the specific data returned by the query for each user will not reside in the shared pool, and thus not be shared, because sharing data between applications represents a data integrity/security issue.

The other mandatory component of the shared pool is dictionary cache, also referred to by many DBAs as the "row" cache. This memory structure is designed to store data from the Oracle data dictionary in order to improve response time on data dictionary queries. Since all user processes and the Oracle database internal processes use the data dictionary, the database as a whole benefits in terms of performance from the presence of cached dictionary data in memory.

The redo log buffer allows user processes to write their redo log entries to a memory area in order to speed processing on the tracking of database changes. One fact that is important to remember about redo logs and user processes is that every process that makes a change to the database must write an entry to the redo log in order to allow Oracle to recover the change. When the database is set up to archive redo logs, these database changes are kept in order to rebuild database objects in the event of a disk failure. The availability of a buffer for storing redo information in memory prevents the need for user processes to spend the extra time it takes to write an entry directly to disk. By having all user processes writing those redo log records to memory, the Oracle database avoids contention for disk usage that would invariably cause database performance to slow down. Since every data change process has to write a redo log entry, it makes sense that processes be able to write that change as quickly as possible in order to boost speed and avoid problems.

The final SGA resource is the buffer cache. This area of memory allows for selective performance gains on obtaining and changing data. The buffer cache stores data blocks that contain row data that has been selected or updated recently. When the user wants to select data from a table, Oracle looks in the buffer cache to see if the data block that contains the row has already been loaded. If it has, then the buffer cache has achieved its selective performance improvement by not having to look for the data block on disk. If not, then Oracle must locate the data block that contains the row, load it into memory, and present the selected output to the user. There is one overall performance gain that the buffer cache provides that is important to note. *No user process ever interfaces directly with any record on a disk.* This fact is true for the redo log buffer as well.

After the user's **select** statement has completed, Oracle keeps the block in memory according to a special algorithm that eliminates buffers according to how long ago they were used. The procedure is the same for a data change, except that after Oracle writes the data to the row, the block that contains the row will then be called a *dirty buffer*, which simply means that some row in the buffer has been changed. Another structure exists in the buffer cache, called the *dirty buffer write queue*, and it is designed to store those dirty buffers until the changes are written back to disk.

The Oracle PGA

The PGA is an area in memory that helps user processes execute, such as bind variable information, sort areas, and other aspects of cursor handling. From the prior discussion of the shared pool, the DBA should know that the database already stores parse trees for recently executed SQL statements in a shared area called the library cache. So, why do the users need their own area to execute? The reason users need their own area in memory to execute is that, even though the parse information for SQL or PL/SQL may already be available, the values that the user wants to execute the **select** or **update** upon cannot be shared. The PGA is used to store real values in place of bind variables for executing SQL statements.

Location of User Session Information

The question of location for user session information is an important one to consider. Whether user session information is stored in the PGA or the shared pool depends on whether the multithreaded server (MTS) architecture is used. MTS relates to how Oracle handles user processes connecting to the database. When the DBA uses MTS, all data is read into the database buffer cache by *shared* server processes acting on behalf of user processes. When the DBA uses the MTS configuration, session information is stored in the shared pool of the SGA. When MTS is not used, each user process has its own dedicated server process reading data blocks into the buffer cache. In the dedicated server process configuration, the PGA stores session information for each user running against Oracle. More information about shared vs. dedicated servers, the MTS architecture, and the purpose of the server process appear in this discussion, Unit IV, and Unit V of this book.

Exercises

1. What is the name of the main memory structure in Oracle, and what are its components?

2. What is the function of the PGA?

3. Where is user session information stored in memory on the Oracle instance? How is its location determined?

Oracle Background Processes

A good deal of the discussion around users thus far speaks of processes—user processes doing this or that. In any Oracle instance, there will be user processes accessing information. Likewise, the Oracle instance will be doing some things behind the scenes, using *background processes*. There are several background processes in the Oracle instance. It was mentioned in the discussion of the SGA that no user process ever interfaces directly with I/O. This setup is allowed because the Oracle instance has its own background processes that handle everything from writing changed data blocks onto disk to securing locks on remote databases for record changes in situations where the Oracle instance is set up to run in a distributed environment. The following list presents each background process and its role in the Oracle instance.

DBWR
:   The *database writer* process. This background process handles all data block writes to disk. It works in conjunction with the Oracle database buffer cache memory structure. It prevents users from ever accessing a disk to perform a data change such as **update**, **insert**, or **delete**.

LGWR
:   The *log writer* process. This background process handles the writing of redo log entries from the redo log buffer to online redo log files on disk. This process also writes the log sequence number of the current online redo log to the datafile headers and to the control file. Finally, LGWR handles initiating the process of clearing the dirty buffer write queue. At various times, depending on database configuration, those updated blocks are written to disk by DBWR. These events are called checkpoints. LGWR handles telling DBWR to write the changes.

SMON
:   The *system monitor* process. The usage and function of this Oracle background process is twofold. First, in the event of an instance failure—when the memory structures and processes that comprise the Oracle instance cannot continue to run—the SMON process handles recovery from that instance failure. Second, the SMON process handles disk space management issues on the database by taking smaller fragments of space and "coalescing" them, or piecing them together.

PMON
:   The *process monitor* process. PMON watches the user processes on the database to make sure that they work correctly. If for any reason a user process fails during its connection to Oracle, PMON will clean up the remnants of its activities and make sure that any changes it may have made to the system are "rolled back," or backed out of the database and reverted to their original form.

RECO   (optional) The *recoverer* process. In Oracle databases using the distributed option, this background process handles the resolution of distributed transactions against the database.

ARCH   (optional) The *archiver* process. In Oracle databases that archive their online redo logs, the ARCH process handles automatically moving a copy of the online redo log to a log archive destination.

CKPT   (optional) The *checkpoint* process. In high-activity databases, CKPT can be used to handle writing log sequence numbers to the datafile headers and control file, alleviating LGWR of that responsibility.

LCK0..   (optional) The *lock* processes, of which there can be as
LCK9   many as ten. In databases that use the **parallel server** option, this background process handles acquiring locks on remote tables for data changes.

S000..   The *server* process. Executes data reads from disk on
S999   behalf of user processes. Access to server processes can either be shared or dedicated, depending on whether the DBA uses MTS or not. In the MTS architecture, when users connect to the database, they must obtain access to a shared server process via a dispatcher process, described here.

D001..   (optional) The *dispatcher* process. This process acts as
D999   part of the Oracle MTS architecture to connect user processes to shared server processes that will handle their SQL processing needs. The user process comes into the database via a SQL*Net listener, which connects the process to a dispatcher. From there, the dispatcher finds the user process a shared server that will handle interacting with the database to obtain data on behalf of the user process.

Exercises

1. Name the background process that handles reading data into the buffer cache. Which process handles writing data changes from the buffer cache back to disk?

2. Which process handles writing redo log information from memory to disk? Which process can be configured to help it?

3. Which background processes act as part of the multithreaded server (MTS) architecture? Which background process coalesces free space on disk?

Oracle Disk Utilization Structures

In addition to memory, Oracle must execute disk management processing in order to create, access, store, and recover an Oracle database. There are structures that are stored on disk that the DBA must understand how to manage, and this section will identify and discuss the meaning of each structure in kind. To begin, the DBA must first understand that there are two different "lenses" through which he or she must view the way Oracle looks at data stored on disk. Through one lens, the DBA sees the disk utilization of the Oracle database consisting of logical data structures. These structures include tablespaces, segments, and extents. Through another, the DBA sees the physical database files that store these logical database structures. Figure 6-2 demonstrates the concept of a logical and physical view of storage in the Oracle instance.

A tablespace is a logical database structure that is designed to store other logical database structures. A *segment* is a logical data object that stores the data of a table, index, or series of rollback entries. An *extent* is similar to a segment in that the extent stores information corresponding to a table. However, the difference is that an extent handles table growth. When the row data for a table exceeds the space allocated to it by the segment, the table acquires an extent to place the additional data in. The objects a DBA may place into a tablespace are things like tables, indexes, rollback segments, and any other objects that consist of segments and extents. A logical database object such as a table or index can have multiple extents, but those extents and segments can be stored in only one tablespace.

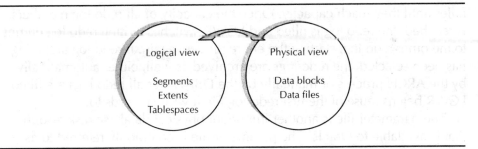

FIGURE 6-2.   *The logical and physical views of a database*

The other lens through which the DBA will view the data stored on disk is the physical lens. Underlying all the logical database objects in Oracle disk storage are the physical methods that Oracle uses to store those objects. The cornerstone of the physical method that Oracle uses to store data in the database is the Oracle data block. Data blocks store row data for segments and extents. In turn, the blocks are taken together to comprise a *datafile*. Datafiles correspond to the tablespace level of the logical Oracle disk storage architecture in that a tablespace may consist of one or more datafiles. The objects in a tablespace, namely segments and extents corresponding to different tables, can span across multiple datafiles, provided that all datafiles are part of the same tablespace. Just as a table, index, or rollback segments cannot span across multiple tablespaces, any datafile on the database can contain data for only one tablespace. Individual data objects, such as tables and indexes, however, can have their segments and extents span across multiple datafiles belonging to that one tablespace.

In addition to datafiles, the structures that Oracle uses to store information about the database on disk include: *control files, parameter files, password files,* and *redo log files*. Redo log files are used to store information about the changes users make to the database. These files are generally large enough to store many entries. There are generally two (minimum) redo logs available to the LGWR process of the Oracle instance for the purpose of storing redo log entries. Each redo log can consist of one or more redo log files, also referred to as redo log "members." The operation of online redo logs occurs in this way: LGWR writes entries to the files of one of the two (or more) online redo logs. As the redo log entries are written to the logs, the files that comprise the current online redo log get fuller and fuller until they reach capacity. Once the capacity of all redo log members is reached, the redo log is filled and LGWR switches writing redo log entries to the other redo log, starting the entire process again. If redo log archiving has been selected, the redo logs are archived as well, either automatically by the ARCH process or manually by the DBA. After all redo logs are filled, LGWR begins reuse of the first redo log file it wrote records to.

The parameter file is another important physical database disk resource that is available to Oracle. The parameter file is commonly referred to as **init.ora**. Used upon database startup, this file specifies many initialization parameters that identify the database as a unique database, either on the machine or on the entire network. Some parameters that **init.ora** sets include the size of various objects of the SGA, the location of the control file, the database name, and others. The database cannot start without **init.ora**, so it is imperative that the file be present at database startup.

Another database disk resource that is used by Oracle is the password file. This resource stores passwords for users who have administrative privileges over the Oracle database. The password file is only used on Oracle databases that use database authentication. The use of operating system authentication will be covered in more detail in the next section, "Starting and Stopping the Oracle Instance." In cases where operating system authentication is used, the password file is not present on the Oracle database.

The final database disk resource that will be covered in this section is the control file. The control file to the physical structure of the Oracle database is like the data dictionary to the logical structure. The control file tells Oracle what the datafiles are called for all tablespaces and where they are located on the machine, as well as what the redo log member filenames are and where to find them. Without a control file, Oracle database server would be unable to find its physical components, and thus it is imperative to have a control file. The name of the control file is specified in the **init.ora** file for the database instance. To recap, the main disk resources of Oracle are listed here:

- Datafiles
- Redo log files
- Control files

Exercises

1. Name five physical disk resources on the Oracle instance.

2. What are the three logical resources on the Oracle instance?

3. Explain the difference between a logical view of disk resources and a physical view of disk resources. How are the two linked?

Starting and Stopping the Oracle Instance

In this section, you will cover the following topics related to starting and stopping the instance:

- Selecting an authentication method
- Starting an Oracle instance and opening the database
- Shutting down the Oracle instance
- Altering database mode and restricting login

The first order of business for the DBA in many environments is to install the Oracle software. The act of installing the Oracle software is specific to the operating system on the machine used to host the Oracle database. Once installation is accomplished, the DBA will start working on other aspects of the Oracle server before actually creating his or her first database. The first step of configuring the Oracle server is managing the creation and startup of the Oracle instance, and the first step for managing the instance is password authentication.

Selecting an Authentication Method

In order to determine what method of authentication to use for the Oracle database, the DBA must first answer an important question. That question is "How do I plan to support this database?" The answer to that question usually boils down to whether the DBA will be working on the same site as the host machine running Oracle primarily to support database administration tasks, or whether the DBA plans to monitor the site remotely, with a monitoring server that manages the database administration for many other databases in addition to the one being set up.

Security in Oracle server consists initially of user authentication. The users of an Oracle system each have a username that they enter, along with a password, in order to gain entry into the database. Just as users supply a password, so too must the DBA. However, Oracle offers two options with respect to password authentication. The use of either depends on the answer to the question of whether the DBA will administer the database locally or remotely, and also on a matter of preference. The two methods available are to either allow Oracle to manage its own password authentication or to rely on the authentication methods provided by the operating system for Oracle access.

The decision-making flow may go something like this. If the database administrator is planning to administer the database from a remote location, then the question of whether or not a secure connection can be established with the host system running Oracle must be answered. If the DBA can in fact obtain a secure connection with the host system running Oracle, then the DBA can use either the Oracle method of authentication or the operating system authentication method. If the DBA cannot obtain a secure connection remotely, then the DBA must use the Oracle method of user authentication. If the DBA plans to administer the database locally, then the choice of whether to use operating system authentication or Oracle authentication is largely a matter of personal preference.

Operating system authentication presents some advantages and disadvantages to using Oracle's methods for user authentication. By using operating system authentication, the DBA thereby requires Oracle users to provide a password only when logging into the operating system on the machine hosting Oracle. When the user wants to access the Oracle database, he or she can simply use the "/" character at login time and Oracle will verify with the operating system that the user's password is correct and allow access. Similarly, if the DBA logs onto the machine hosting Oracle and wants to execute some privileged activities such as creating users or otherwise administrating the database, the DBA will be able to log onto the database simply by using the "/" character in place of a username and password. For example, in a UNIX environment, the login procedure for the DBA using operating system authentication may look something like the following:

```
UNIX® SYSTEM V TTYP01 (23.45.67.98)
Login: bobcat
Password:
User connected. Today is 12/17/99 14:15:34
[companyx] /home/bobcat/    --> sqlplus /
SQL*PLUS Version 3.2.3.0.0
(c) 1979,1996 Oracle Corporation(c) All rights reserved.
Connected to Oracle 7.3.4 (23.45.67.98)
With the parallel, distributed, and multithreaded server options
SQL>
```

Operating system authentication allows the user or DBA to access the database quickly and easily, with minimal typing and no chance that a password can be compromised at any time during the Oracle login process. However, using the operating system to perform authentication on the Oracle database leaves Oracle's data integrity and security at the level that the operating system provides. If for some reason a user's ID is compromised, not only is the host machine at risk to the extent that the user has access to the machine's resources, but the Oracle database is at risk as well to the level that the user has access to Oracle resources. Therefore, it is recommended that where it does not hinder usage of the database and where it improves security, use the Oracle methods of user authentication.

To use operating system authentication first requires that a special group be created on the operating system level if that feature is supported, or to grant the DBA special prioritization for executing processes on the host system for Oracle. This step of some other operating system requirements must be fulfilled in order to connect to the database for startup and shutdown as **internal**. The **internal** privilege is a special access method to the Oracle database that allows the DBA to start and stop the database. One additional constraint for connecting to the database as **internal** (in addition to having group privileges and proper process execution prioritization) is that the DBA must have a dedicated server connection. In effect, the DBA cannot connect as **internal** when shared servers are used in conjunction with the MTS architecture, rather than dedicated servers, for handling database reads for user processes.

The ability to connect as **internal** is provided for backward compatibilit'' In the future, the DBA can connect to the database for the purposes of administration using the **connect** *name*/*pass* **as sysdba** command. The **sysdba** keyword denotes a collection of privileges that are akin to those privileges granted with the **internal** keyword.

Once the DBA is connected as **internal** and the database instance is started, the DBA can then perform certain operations to create databases and objects with operating system authentication. The performance of these functions is contingent upon the DBA having certain roles granted to their userid. The roles the DBA must have granted to them in this case are called **osoper** and **osdba**. These two privileges are administrated via the operating system and cannot be revoked or administrated via Oracle, and are used in conjunction with operating system authentication. They have equivalents used with Oracle authentication—**sysoper** and **sysdba**, respectively—and from here on this book will assume the use of Oracle authentication; thus, the use of **sysoper** and **sysdba**. When the DBA connects to the database as **internal**, the **sysdba** and **sysoper** privileges are usually enabled as well. Therefore, it is possible for the DBA to simply connect as **internal** when the need arises to do any DBA-related activities. However, this is not advised in situations where the database is administered by multiple database administrators who may have limited access to accomplish various functions. In this case, it is better simply to grant **sysdba** or **sysoper** directly to the user who administers the system.

Choosing which privilege to grant to the user depends on what type of administrative functions the DBA may fulfill. The **sysoper** and **sysdba** privileges provide some breakout of responsibilities and function with the privileges they allow the grantee to perform. The **sysoper** privilege handles administration of the following privileges:

- Starting and stopping the Oracle instance
- Mounting or opening the database
- Backing up the database
- Initiating archival of redo logs
- Initiating database recovery operations
- Changing database access to **restricted session** mode

As shown by the types of privileges granted with **sysoper**, **sysdba** is a DBA privilege that is granted to the DBA for startup and shutdown recovery and backup, and other availability functions. The **sysdba** privilege administers certain other privileges as well. Those privileges are listed as follows:

- The **sysoper** privilege
- All system privileges granted **with admin option**
- The **create database** privilege
- Privileges required for time-based database recovery

Obviously, this is the role granted to the DBA ultimately responsible for the operation of the database in question. In addition, there is another role that is created upon installation of the Oracle software. This role is called DBA, and it also has all system privileges granted to it.

Oracle's method of user authentication for database administrators when operating system authentication is not used is called a *password file*. The DBA first creates a file to store the authentication passwords for all persons that will be permitted to perform administrative tasks on the Oracle database. This functionality is managed by a special utility called ORAPWD. The name of the password file can vary according to the operating system used by the machine hosting the Oracle instance. First, a filename for the password file that stores users that can log in as DBA must be specified. The location for the password file varies by database, but for the most part it can be found in the **dbs** subdirectory under the Oracle software home directory of the machine hosting the Oracle database. The filename for the password file is usually **orapw***sid*, where the database name is substituted for *sid*.

The password for administering the password file is the next parameter that the ORAPWD utility requires. By specifying a password for this file, the DBA simultaneously assigns the password for **internal** and SYS. After creating the password file, the DBA connects as **internal** and SYS and issues the **alter user** *name* **identified by** *password* command in order to change the password, and the user's and the password file's passwords are changed.

The final item to be specified to the ORAPWD utility is the number of entries that are allowed to be entered into the password file. This number will determine the number of users that will have administrator privileges allowed for their ID. Care should be taken when specifying this value. If too few values are specified and the DBA needs to add more, he or she will not be able to do so without deleting and re-creating the password file. This process is dangerous, and should be executed with care to ensure that the DBA does not log off before the process is complete. If the DBA does log off after deleting the password file, the database administrator will be unable to execute administrative operations on the database. Entries can be reused as members of the DBA team come and go. The actual execution of ORAPWD may look something like this from within Oracle:

```
SQL> ORAPWD FILE=/home/oracle/dbs/orapworgdb01.pwd PASSWORD=phantom
ENTRIES=5
```

Once this password file creation is complete, several items must be completed in order to continue with using Oracle's authentication method to allow DBA access to the database without allowing access as **internal**. The first step is to set a value for an initialization parameter in the **init.ora** file. This parameter is called REMOTE_LOGIN_PASSWORDFILE, and its permitted settings are *NONE*, *EXCLUSIVE*, and *SHARED*. These various settings have different meanings with respect to allowing remote database administration on the Oracle instance. The *NONE* setting means that the database will not allow privileged sessions to be established over nonsecured connections because no password file exists. When operating system authentication is used on the database, the REMOTE_LOGIN_ PASSWORDFILE parameter may be set to *NONE* to disallow remote access to the database for administration purposes. The following code block shows how the DBA can set this parameter in the **init.ora** file:

```
REMOTE_LOGIN_PASSWORDFILE=none
REMOTE_LOGIN_PASSWORDFILE=exclusive
REMOTE_LOGIN_PASSWORDFILE=shared
```

The *EXCLUSIVE* setting indicates that the password file developed by the ORAPWD utility for security use on that database instance can be used for that instance and that instance only. In this configuration, the DBA will add users who will administer the Oracle instance to the password file and grant the **sysoper** and **sysdba** privileges directly to those userids, allowing the DBAs to log into the database as themselves with all administrator privileges. When using password file authentication to administer a database remotely via a nonsecure connection, the REMOTE_LOGIN_PASSWORDFILE parameter should be set to *EXCLUSIVE*.

The final option is *SHARED*, which means that the password file allows access only by SYS and the DBA connected as **internal**. All administrative operations on the database must happen by a DBA who logs into the instance as SYS or as **internal** when this option is set.

After creating the password file with the ORAPWD utility and setting the REMOTE_LOGIN_PASSWORDFILE parameter to *EXCLUSIVE* in order to administer a database remotely, the DBA can then connect to the database as some user with **sysdba** privileges. One such user that is created when Oracle is installed is SYS. The DBA can log into the database as user SYS and create the database and other usernames as necessary, or simply mount the existing database. Then, the other users that will administer the instance can log onto it as themselves and execute DBA tasks as needed.

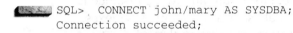

```
SQL> CONNECT john/mary AS SYSDBA;
Connection succeeded;
SQL>
```

There are two important key points to remember with respect to password files. One is gaining information about the users listed in them, the other is related to schema ownership. To find out which users are in the database password file, the DBA can query a dynamic performance view from the Oracle data dictionary on the password file called V$PWFILE_USERS. More on the data dictionary will be presented in this chapter. The other feature is that any object created in any login as **sysdba** or **sysoper** will be owned by the SYS schema. While this fact of ownership may not be all that important, especially given the ability to create and use public synonyms to obtain data without regard to schema ownership, it is an important point to make that the DBA should not look for objects they may create using their own username as the owner. In the event that the DBAs simply log in as themselves without the **as sysdba** trailer, the objects they create will be owned by their schemas.

Exercises

I. What two methods of user authentication are available in Oracle? Explain some advantages and disadvantages for each.

2. What is the name of the utility used to create a password file? Describe its usage, parameters, and the related parameter that must be set in INIT.ORA in order to use a password file for authentication.

3. What are the two Oracle roles granted to DBAs in order to perform database administration?

4. What is SYS? How is it used?

Starting the Oracle Instance and Opening the Database

There is an important distinction that sometimes gets blurry in the minds of DBAs and especially Oracle developers who don't work with Oracle internals often enough to notice a difference. The distinction is between an Oracle instance and an Oracle database. First of all, an Oracle instance is *NOT* an Oracle database. The Oracle database is a set of tables, indexes, procedures, and other data objects that store information that applications place into storage in the Oracle product. The Oracle instance is the memory structures, background processes, and disk resources, all working together to fulfill user data requests and changes. With those points made, it should also be said that the Oracle instance is *very close* in similarity to the Oracle database.

With that distinction made, attention should now turn to starting the Oracle instance. This step is the first that should be accomplished when creating a new database or allowing access to an existing database. To start the Oracle database instance, the DBA should do the following:

1. Start the appropriate administrative tool and connect as **sysdba** or **internal**. The appropriate tool in this case is Server Manager or Enterprise Manager.

2. Using Server Manager, use the **startup** *start_option* command to start the instance. The DBA must supply the name of the database (also known as the SID) and the parameter file Oracle should use to start the database. There are several different options the DBA can use to specify the startup status of the database.

Within the Server Manager tool there are several different options for database availability at system startup. These different options correspond to the level of access to the database once the database instance is running. Each startup feature has several associated facts about the access level permitted while the database is running in that mode. The options available for starting up an Oracle database are starting the database without mounting it, with mounting but not opening, mounting and opening in **restricted session** mode, mounting and opening for anyone's use, performing a forced start, or starting the database and initializing recovery from failure. This set of options is listed here:

- **Startup nomount**

- **Startup mount**

- **Startup open**

- **Startup restricted**

- **Startup force**

The first option available is starting up the instance without mounting the database. In Server Manager, the command used for starting any database is the **startup** command. For starting the instance without mounting the database, the **startup** command can be issued with an option called **nomount**. This option will start the instance for database creation, but will not open any other database that may be available to the Oracle instance. This option is used for preventing any problems with existing databases that are mounted at the time that a new database is created. Another recommended safety measure for creating new databases in the same instance that already owns a database is to back up the existing database before creating the new one. A complete discussion of backup and recovery occurs in Unit III.

In other situations, the DBA may want to start the instance and mount but not open an existing database for certain DBA maintenance activities. In this case, the DBA may need to work on some aspect of the physical database structure, such as the movement of redo log file members, data files, or to specify the usage of Oracle's archival of redo logs feature. In situations where the DBA needs to perform a full database recovery, the DBA should mount but not open the database. The same **startup** command is used for starting the database in all modes, but the mode option used in this situation is the **mount** option. The DBA will need to specify the database name and the parameter file for this option to mount the database to the instance for the physical database object maintenance activities previously described. A nonmounted database can be mounted to an instance after creation of that database using commands described in the section of this chapter titled "Changing Database Availability and Restricting Login."

TIP
*In a database that is mounted, the DBA can
alter the control file.*

All other options for starting a database will allow access to the database in one form or another. Hence, the options considered now are called opening the database. The DBA will open the database for many reasons, first and foremost so that users and applications can access the database in order to work. In order for the DBA to start the instance and then mount and open the database, the DBA must use the **startup open** option. Once the DBA has opened the database, any user with a valid username and password who has been granted the **create session** privilege or the CONNECT role can access the Oracle database.

In some cases, the DBA may want to open the database without letting users access the database objects. This is the most common situation for a DBA to start the database in when there is DBA maintenance activity required on the logical portion of the Oracle database. In this case, the DBA will execute the **startup** option as before. However, in addition to starting and opening the database, the DBA will execute a special command that restricts database access to only those users on the system with a special access privilege called **restricted session**. From database startup, the DBA can execute the **startup restrict** command within Server Manager. Although any user on the database can have this privilege granted to them, typically only the database administrator will have it. In some cases, such as in the case of reorganizing large tables that involves a large-volume data load, the DBA may grant the **restricted session** privilege to a developer who is assisting in the database maintenance work. In these situations, the DBA may want to consider a temporary grant of **restricted session** to the developer, followed by a revocation of the privilege afterward to prevent possible data integrity issues in later maintenance cycles. This method is generally preferable to a permanent grant of **restricted session** to someone outside the DBA organization. Typically, the DBA will want to use the **restrict** option for logical database object maintenance such as reorganizing tablespaces, creating new indexes or fixing old ones, large-volume data loads, reorganizing or renaming objects, and other DBA maintenance activities.

There are two special cases for database startup left to consider, both of which are used for circumstances outside of normal database activity. One of those two situations is when the database has experienced a failure of some sort that requires the DBA to perform a complete database recovery of the database and the instance. In this case, the DBA may want the instance to initiate its complete recovery at the time the instance is started. To accomplish the task, the DBA can issue the **startup recover** command from the Server Manager tool, and Oracle will start the instance and initiate the complete recovery at instance startup. In cases where archiving is used, Oracle may require certain archived redo logs to be present for this option to complete successfully. In any event, the use of this option will be more carefully considered in the next unit, the treatment of OCP Exam 3 on database backup and recovery.

The final option for database startup is used in unusual circumstances as well. Sometimes (rarely) there is a situation where the Oracle database cannot start the instance under normal circumstances or shut down properly due to some issue with memory management or disk resource management. In these cases, the DBA may need to push things a bit. The DBA can give database startup an additional shove with the **startup force** command option. This option will use a method akin to a **shutdown abort** (see the next section on database shutdown) in order to end the current instance having difficulty before starting the new instance. It is not recommended that the DBA use this option without extreme care, as there is usually a need for instance recovery in this type of situation.

Exercises

1. What is the tool used for starting the Oracle database? What connection must be used for the task?

2. What are the five options for database startup?

Shutting Down the Oracle Instance

Shutting down the Oracle instance works in much the same way as starting the instance, with the requirement to cease allowing access to the database and the requirement to accomplish the task while being logged on as **internal**. The task must also be accomplished from the Server Manager, either graphically with the use of the Shut Down menu under the Instance menu or with the **shutdown** command in line mode. The options for database shutdown are listed below:

- **Shutdown normal**
- **Shutdown immediate**
- **Shutdown abort**

There are three priorities that can be specified by the DBA for shutting down the database. The first and lowest priority is **normal**. It is the lowest priority because Oracle will wait for many other events to play themselves out before actually shutting down the connection. In other words, the database will make the DBA wait for all other users to finish what they are doing before the database will actually close. The following description of events illustrates specifically how the shutdown process works under **normal** priority:

1. DBA issues **shutdown normal** from Server Manager at 3 P.M.

2. User X is logged onto the system at 2:30 and performs data entry until 3:15 P.M. User X will experience no interruption in database availability as a result of **shutdown normal**.

3. User Y attempts to log into the database at 3:05 P.M. and receives the following message: **ORA-01090: shutdown in progress—connection is not permitted**.

4. User Z is the last user logged off at 3:35 P.M. The database will now shut down.

5. When the DBA starts the database up again, there will be no need to perform a database recovery.

There are three rules that can be abstracted from this situation. The first is that no new users will be permitted access to the system. The second is that the database does not force users already logged onto the system to log off in order to complete the shutdown. Third, under normal shutdown situations, there is no need for instance recovery.

Normal database shutdown may take some time. While Oracle attempts to shut down the database, the DBA's session will not allow the DBA to access any other options or issue any other commands until the shutdown process is complete. The time the process can take depends on several factors. Some of the factors that the database shutdown will depend on are whether many users have active transactions executing at the time the **shutdown** command is issued, how many users are logged on to the system and on the shutdown priority issued by the DBA.

A higher-priority shutdown that the DBA can enact in certain circumstances is the **shutdown immediate** command. Shutting down a database with **immediate** priority is similar to using the **normal** priority in that no new users will be able to connect to the database once the shutdown command is issued. However, Oracle will not wait for a user to log off as it did in points 2 and 4 earlier. Instead, Oracle terminates the user connections to the database immediately and rolls back any uncommitted transactions that may have been taking place. This option may be used in order to shut down an instance that is experiencing unusual problems, or in the situation where the database could experience a power outage in the near future. A power outage can be particularly detrimental to the database; therefore, it is recommended that the DBA shut things down with **immediate** priority when a power outage is looming. There are two issues associated with shutting down the database with **immediate** priority. The first is the issue of recovery. The database will most likely need instance recovery after an **immediate** shutdown. This activity should not require much effort from the DBA, as Oracle will handle the recovery of the database instance itself without much intervention. However, the other issue associated with shutting down the database immediately is that the effect of the shutdown is not always immediate! In some cases, particularly in situations involving user processes running large-volume transactions against a database, the rollback portion of the database shutdown may take some time to execute.

The final priority to be discussed with shutting down a database is the shutdown with **abort** priority. This is the highest priority that can be assigned a shutdown activity. In all cases that this priority is used, the database will shut down immediately, with no exceptions. Use of this priority when shutting down a database instance should be undertaken with care. The additional item that a **shutdown abort** uses to prevent the database from waiting for rollback to complete is not to roll back uncommitted transactions. This approach requires media recovery activity later when the instance is opened. Only in a situation where the behavior of the database is highly unusual or when the power to the database will cut off in less than two minutes should the **shutdown abort** option be employed. Otherwise, it is usually best to avoid using this option entirely, and use **shutdown immediate** in circumstances requiring the DBA to close the database quickly.

Exercises

1. What connection must be used for the task of database shutdown?

2. What are the three options for database shutdown?

Changing Database Availability and Restricting Login

During the course of normal operation on the database, the DBA may require changing the availability of the database in some way. For example, the DBA may have to initiate emergency maintenance on the database, which requires the database to be unavailable to the users. Perhaps there are some problems with the database that need to be resolved while the instance is still running but the database is unavailable. For this and many other reasons, the DBA can alter the availability of the database in several ways. The following discussion will highlight some of those ways.

The first way a DBA may want to alter the status and availability of the database instance is to change the **mount** status of a database. In some situations, the DBA may need to start a database with the **nomount** option, as discussed earlier in the section on starting the database. After the activities that required the database not to be mounted are complete, the DBA will want to **mount** the database to the instance, but have the database still be closed and therefore unavailable to the users. To change the status of a database to be mounted, the DBA can use either the graphical interface of Server Manager to **mount** the database or use the **alter database mount** statement to achieve that effect. Mounting the database allows the DBA to do several database maintenance activities without allowing users the chance to access the database and cause contention.

After database work, or in the course of a manual startup, the DBA will want to allow the users access to the database. This step can be accomplished in two ways. Like mounting the database manually, the DBA can use the graphical user interface to open the database for user access. Alternatively, the DBA can issue the **alter database open** statement from the SQL command prompt and open the database for user access. When the database is in **open** mode, then a database user with the **create session** privilege, or the CONNECT role, can access the database. One fact that is important to remember about the Oracle database is that it can be accessed by multiple instances.

The final option to be covered corresponds to situations where the DBA has the database open for use, and needs to make some changes to the database. Some of these changes may include re-creating indexes, large-volume data loads, tablespace reorganization, and other activities that require the database to be open but access to the data to be limited. This option is called the **restricted session**. In cases where the DBA wants to limit access to the database without actually closing it, the DBA can enable the database's **restricted session** mode. This option prevents logging into the database for any user that does not have the **restricted session** privilege granted to the user. Although any user on the database can have this privilege granted to them, typically only the database administrator will have it. In some cases, such as in the case of reorganizing large tables that involves a large-volume data load, the DBA may grant the **restricted session** privilege to a developer who is assisting in the database maintenance work. In these situations, the DBA may want to consider a temporary grant of **restricted session** to the developer, followed by a revocation of the privilege afterward to prevent possible data integrity issues in later maintenance cycles. This method is generally preferable to a permanent grant of **restricted session** to someone outside the DBA organization. This option is handled for the most part in one way. The method used to close access to the database to all users except those with the **restricted session** privilege is **alter database enable restricted session**. In order to restore access to the database to all users without the **restricted session** privilege is to issue the following command: **alter database enable restricted session.**

Exercises

1. What statement is used to change the status of a database?
2. Explain the use of the **restricted session** privilege.

Creating an Oracle Database

In this section, you will cover the following topics related to creating an Oracle database:

■ Entity relationships and database objects

■ Creating a database in Oracle

■ Creating the Oracle data dictionary

Once the DBA has set up some necessary preliminary items for running the Oracle instance, such as password authentication, the DBA can then create the database that users will soon utilize for data management. Creating a database involves three activities that will be discussed in this section. The first activity for creating a database is mapping a logical entity-relationship diagram that details a model for a process to the data model upon which the creation of database objects like indexes and tables will be based. The second activity that the DBA will perform as part of creating a database is the creation of physical data storage resources in the Oracle architecture, such as datafiles and redo log files. The final (and perhaps the most important) aspect of creating a database is creating the structures that comprise the Oracle data dictionary. A discussion of each element in the database creation process will be discussed now in detail.

Entity Relationships and Database Objects

The first part of creating a database is creating a model for that database. One fundamental tenet of database design is remembering that every database application is a model of reality. Most of the time, the database is used to model some sort of business reality, such as the tracking of inventory, payment of sales bonuses, employee expense vouchers, and customer accounts receivable invoices. The model for a database should be a model for the process that the database application will represent.

Now, explore the combination of those entities and their relationships. The concept of an entity maps loosely to the nouns in the reality the database application is trying to model. In the employee expenditure system mentioned previously, the entities (or nouns) in the model may include employees, expense sheets, receipts, payments, a payment creator such as accounts payable, and a payer account for the company that is reimbursing the employee. The relationships, on the other hand, map loosely to the idea of a verb, or action that takes place between two nouns. Some actions that take place in this employee expenditure system may be submits expense sheet, submits receipts, deducts money from account, and pays check. These entities and relationships can translate into several different types of visual representations or models of a business reality. Figure 6-3 illustrates each entity by a small illustration, with the relationships between each entity represented by an arrow and a description. The employee fills out the expense sheets for the expenses incurred on behalf of the company.

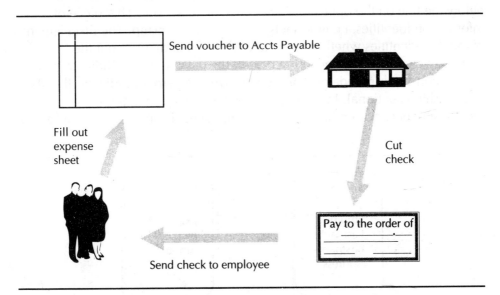

FIGURE 6-3.   *An entity-relationship diagram of process flow in the system*

Then, the employees send their vouchers to the accounts payable organization, which creates a check for the employee and mails the payment to the employee. The process is very simple, but it accurately models the business process within an organization to reimburse an employee for his expenses. When the developers of a database application create the employee expenditure system modeled by the entity-relationship diagram, they will first take those entities and map out the relationship, then take the entity-relationship diagram and create a logical data model out of those entities and processes. A logical data model is a more detailed diagram than the entity-relationship diagram in that it fills in details about the process flow that the entity-relationship diagram attempts to model. Figure 6-4 shows the logical data model of the employee table and the invoice table.

On the expense sheet, the employee will fill in various pieces of information, including the expense ID number, the employee ID number, and the expense amount. The line between the two entities is similar to a relationship; however, in the logical data model, the entities are called *tables* and the relationships are called *foreign keys*.

There is an interesting piece of information communicated above and below the line on the opposite side of each table as well. That piece of information identifies a pair of facts about the relationship. The first element of the pair identifies whether the relationship is mandatory from the perspective of the table appearing next to the pair. A one (1) indicates that the relationship is mandatory for the pair, while a zero (0) indicates that the relationship is optional. In the example in the previous diagram, the relationship between employee and expense sheet is optional for employees

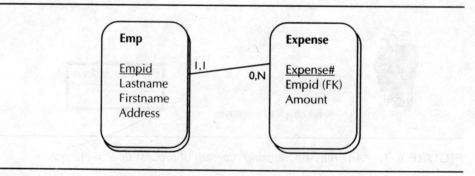

FIGURE 6-4. *Logical data model of employee table and invoice table*

but mandatory for expense sheets. This means that for any given record in the EMPLOYEE table, there may or may not be expense sheets in the EXPENSE table. However, every expense sheet record in the EXPENSE table will correspond to an employee record. The second component of that pair indicates whether there is a one-to-one, one-to-many, or many-to-many correspondence between records of one table and records of another table. In the previous example, records in the EMPLOYEE table have a one-to-many relationship with the records of the EXPENSE table, while the records of the EXPENSE table have a one-to-one relationship with records of the EMPLOYEE table. That is to say, each employee may have submitted one or more expense sheets, or none at all, while each expense sheet corresponds to one and only one employee. This pair of facts is referred to as the ordinality of the database tables.

   The relationship between columns to tables corresponds loosely to the activity or relationship that exists between the two entities that the tables represent. In the case of the table structure in Figure 6-5, the EMPID column in EXPENSE corresponds to the primary key column of the EMPLOYEE table. In terms of the entity-relationship diagram, the empid is the tie that binds an expense sheet to the employee who created it. Therefore, the relationship of one table to another through foreign keys should correspond somewhat to the relationship that occurs between two entities in the process flow being modeled.

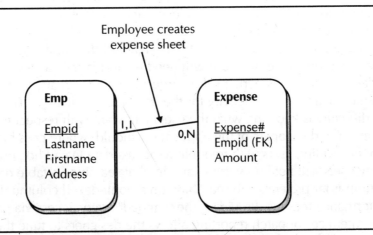

FIGURE 6-5.   *Detail of logical data model of EMPLOYEE and EXPENSE*

Creating a physical database out of the logical data model requires considering several issues. The database designer may ask several questions related to the physical design of that system as follows:

- How many employees will be allowed to use the system?

- What sort of company chargeback system will be used to take the employee expense payment from the budget of the department for which the expense was incurred on behalf of the employee?

- How many expense sheets will be submitted per month and per year?

The proper creation of a database in Oracle depends on answering these and many other questions regarding the physical relationship between the machine hosting Oracle and the data Oracle stores as part of the application model.

Some of these questions relate to Oracle-specific features. For example, the designer of the database should know row count estimates for each object to be created in Oracle. This estimate of row count should be something that is forecasted over a period of time, say two years. This forecast of sizing for the database will allow the DBA some "breathing room" when the database application is deployed, so that the DBA is not constantly trying to allocate more space to an application that continually runs out of it. Some objects that the designer will need to produce sizing estimates for are the tables and indexes, and the tablespaces that will contain those tables and indexes.

In a point related to indexes, the designer of the application should know what the users of the database will need regarding data access. This feature of database design is perhaps the hardest to nail down after the initial estimate of transaction activity for the database application. The reason for the difficulty is knowing what the users will want with respect to data access. The developers of the application should, where possible, try to avoid providing users with free rein to access data via ad hoc queries, as many users will not know, for example, that searching a table on an indexed column is far preferable to searching on a nonindexed column, for performance reasons. Providing the "canned" query access via graphical user interfaces or batch reporting allows the designers to tune the underlying queries that drive the screens or reports, scoring a positive response from the users while also minimizing the impact of application activity on the Oracle instance.

In addition, specifying the database's character set is critical to the proper functioning of the database. There are several different options for specifying character sets in the Oracle database, just as there are many different languages available for use by different peoples of the world. These languages fall into distinct categories with respect to the mechanisms on a computer that will store and display the characters that comprise those languages. The distinct categories are single-byte character sets, multibyte character sets, and languages read from right to left. Examples of single-byte character sets are any of the Romance or Teutonic languages originating in Western Europe, such as English, Spanish, French, German, Dutch, or Italian. Examples of the multibyte character sets available are the languages that originated in Eastern Asia, Southeast Asia, or the Pacific Rim. These languages include Mandarin, Japanese, and Korean. Examples of a language read right to left include Hebrew and Arabic.

One final, and perhaps the most important, area of all to consider at the onset of database system creation in the Oracle environment is how the user will preserve the data in the system from any type of failure inherent in the usage of computer machinery. Such methods may include full and partial backups for the database and the archiving (or storing) of redo logs created by Oracle to track changes made in the database. Backup and recovery are handled as a whole topic unto themselves in the OCP DBA Exam series, and also in this book. See Unit III covering OCP Exam 3, "Database Backup and Recovery."

There are three main steps in creating databases in the Oracle environment. The first is creating the physical locations for data in tables and indexes to be stored in the database. These physical locations are called *datafiles*. The second step is to create the files that will store the redo entries that Oracle records whenever any process makes a data change to the Oracle database. These physical structures are called the *redo log files*, or *redo log members*. The final step in creating an Oracle database is to create the logical structures of the data dictionary. The data dictionary comprises an integral portion of the database system. Both the users and Oracle refer to the data dictionary in order to find information stored in tables or indexes, to find out information about the tables or indexes, or to find out information about the underlying physical structure of the database, the datafiles, and the redo log files.

Exercises

1. What is an entity-relationship diagram? Explain both concepts of entities and relationships.

2. What is a logical data model? How does the logical data model correspond to the entity-relationship diagram? What structures in a data model relate loosely to the entities and the relationships of an entity-relationship diagram?

3. What is ordinality? Explain the concept of mandatory vs. optional relationships?

4. What is a foreign key? Is a foreign key part of the entity-relationship diagram or the logical data model? To what item in the other model does the foreign key relate to?

Creating a Database in Oracle

Creation of the Oracle database is accomplished with the **create database** statement. The first thing to remember about database creation is the Oracle recommended methodology for actually creating the database. The steps are as follows:

1. Back up existing databases.

2. Create or edit the **init.ora** parameter file.

3. Verify the instance name.

4. Start the appropriate database management tool.

5. Start the instance.

6. Create and back up the new database.

Step 1 in the process is to back up the database. This step prevents headaches later if there is a problem with database creation damaging an existing database, which can happen if the DBA attempts database creation without changing the DB_NAME parameter in the **init.ora** file. More details will be given shortly about the required parameters that must be unique for database creation. Steps 1 and 2 are critical in preserving the integrity of any existing databases that may already exist on the Oracle instance. Sometimes accidents do happen in database creation. The worst thing a DBA can face when creating a new database is when a datafile or log filename in a parameter file may not have been changed before creating the second database. This situation leaves the first database vulnerable to being overwritten when the second database is created, which causes the first database to be unusable. Always remember to back up any existing database that uses the same instance and host machine.

A critical resource used to start any instance is the file that contains any initialization parameter that the DBA cares to set for the Oracle database and instance being used. This file is generally referred to as the **init.ora** or parameter file. A parameter file is as unique as the database that uses it. Each database instance usually has at least one parameter file that corresponds to it and it only. Usually, a database instance will have more than one parameter file used exclusively for starting it, to handle various situations that the DBA may want to configure the instance to handle. For example, a DBA may have one parameter file for general use on starting the Oracle instance when users will access the system, one parameter file that is specifically configured to handle an increase in processing associated with heavy transaction periods at the end of the year, and another parameter file designed to start the instance in proper configuration for DBA maintenance weekends.

Oracle provides a generic copy of that parameter file **init.ora** in the software distribution used to install Oracle server on the machine hosting Oracle. Generally, the DBA will take this generic parameter file and alter certain parameters according to his or her needs. There are several parameters that *must* be changed as part of setting up and running a new Oracle database. The following list highlights key initialization parameters that have to be changed in order to correspond to a unique database. The list describes each parameter in some detail and offers some potential values if appropriate.

DB_NAME	The local name of the database on the machine hosting Oracle, and one component of a database's unique name within the network. If this is not changed, permanent damage may result in the event a database is created.

DB_DOMAIN	Identifies the domain location of the database name within a network. It is the second component of a database's unique name within the network.
CONTROL_FILES	A name or list of names for the control files of the database. The control files document the physical layout of the database for Oracle. If the name(s) specified for this parameter do not match filenames that exist currently, then Oracle will create a new control file for the database at startup. If the file does exist, Oracle will overwrite the contents of that file with the physical layout of the database being created.
DB_BLOCK_SIZE	The size in bytes of data blocks within the system. Data blocks are unit components of datafiles into which Oracle places the row data from indexes and tables. This parameter cannot be changed for the life of the database.
DB_BLOCK_BUFFERS	The maximum number of data blocks that will be stored in the database buffer cache of the Oracle SGA.
PROCESSES	The number of processes that can connect to Oracle at any given time. This value includes background processes (of which there are at least five) and user processes.
ROLLBACK_SEGMENTS	A list of named rollback segments that the Oracle instance will have to acquire at database startup. If there are particular segments the DBA wants Oracle to acquire, he/she can name them here.

LICENSE_MAX _SESSIONS	Used for license management. This number determines the number of sessions that users can establish with the Oracle database at any given time.
LICENSE_MAX _WARNING	Used for license management. Set to less than LICENSE_MAX_SESSIONS, Oracle will issue warnings to users as they connect if the number of users connecting has exceeded LICENCE_MAX_WARNING.
LICENSE_MAX_USERS	Used for license management. As an alternative to licensing by concurrent sessions, the DBA can limit the number of usernames created on the database by setting a numeric value for this parameter.

Following the creation of the appropriate initialization parameter file, the DBA will need to start the database instance while connected to the database as **sysdba** and while running Server Manager. The task of connecting to the database as **sysdba** has already been discussed. To start the instance, use the **startup nomount** command in order to run the instance without mounting a previously existing database. After starting the instance without mounting a database, the DBA can create the database with the **create database** command. In order to create a database, the user must have the **osdba** or **sysdba** granted to them and enabled. The following code block contains a **create database statement**:

```
CREATE DATABASE orgdb01
CONTROLFILE REUSE
LOGFILE GROUP 1 ('redo1a.log', 'redo1b.log', 'redo1c.log') SIZE 1M,
       GROUP 2 ('redo2a.log', 'redo2b.log', 'redo2c.log') SIZE 1M
MAXLOGFILES 2
DATAFILE 'data01.dat'  SIZE 30M AUTOEXTEND 10M MAXSIZE 100M,
        'index01.dat' SIZE 30M AUTOEXTEND 10M MAXSIZE 100M,
        'rbs01.dat'   SIZE 20M,
        'users01.dat' SIZE 30M,
        'temp01.dat'  SIZE 10M
MAXDATAFILES 20
ARCHIVELOG;
```

A new database is created by Oracle with several important features. The first item to remember about database creation is that the database will be created with two special users, which are designed to allow for performing important activities required throughout the life of a database. The names of the two users created by Oracle are SYS and SYSTEM. Both have many powerful privileges and should be used carefully for administrative tasks on the database. For now, the DBA should remember that when the users SYS and SYSTEM are created, the password for SYS is CHANGE_ON_INSTALL, and the password for SYSTEM is MANAGER.

Of the disk resources created, the one most central to database operation is the control file. As covered, the control file identifies all other disk resources to the Oracle database. If information about a datafile or redo log file is not contained in the control file for the database, the database will not know about it, and the DBA will not be able to recover it if the disk containing it is lost. The **controlfile reuse** clause is included in the **create database** statement to allow Oracle to reuse the file specified if it already exists. *BEWARE OF REUSING CONTROL FILES.* An existing database will need recovery if its control file is overwritten by the creation of another database. Control files are generally not very large, perhaps 250K for even a large database. This size of the control file is related to the number of datafiles and redo log files that are used on the Oracle database. Adding more datafiles and redo logs increases the size of a control file; fewer datafiles that grow larger with the **autoextend** option and fewer redo logs decrease the size of control files.

Other items created as part of the **create database** command are the datafiles and the redo log files. The datafiles are specified with the **datafile** clause, and they are where Oracle physically stores the data in any and all tablespaces. Redo logs are created with the **logfile** clause. Redo logs are entries for changes made to the database. If the **create database** statement specifies a datafile or a redo log file that currently exists on the system and the **reuse** keyword is used, then Oracle will overwrite that file with the data for the new redo log member or datafile for the database being created. This syntax is purely optional, and furthermore, if it is not used and the **create database** statement includes files that already exist, Oracle will overwrite them. In general, care should be taken when reusing files in order to prevent "accidental reuse" in a situation where a database already exists on the machine and the DBA creates another one that overwrites key files on the first database.

Another pair of options set at database creation time are called **maxdatafiles** and **maxlogfiles**. These are keywords specified in the **create database** statement, and they must be followed by integers. As its name implies, **maxdatafiles** indicates the maximum number of datafiles a database can have. This clause can be a potential limitation later when the database grows to a point where it cannot accommodate another datafile because the **maxdatafiles** value would be exceeded. A workaround for this problem is to use the **autoextend** option when defining datafiles. When **autoextend** is used, the datafiles will automatically allocate more space when the datafile fills, up to a total size specified by the **maxsize** keyword. The final and most important option included in the **create database** statement is the **archivelog** option. When **archivelog** is used, Oracle archives the redo logs generated. This feature should be enabled in all but **read only** databases.

Not only are physical database resources and database administrative passwords created as part of the **create database** command, but some important logical disk resources are created as well. One of these resources is the SYSTEM tablespace. Sometimes the SYSTEM tablespace is compared to the root directory of a machine's file system. The SYSTEM tablespace certainly is a tablespace in the Oracle system that is *HIGHLY* important to the operation of the Oracle database. Many important database objects are stored in the SYSTEM tablespace. Some of those objects are the Oracle data dictionary and rollback segments. There must be one rollback segment in the SYSTEM tablespace for Oracle to acquire at database startup, or else the database won't start. In the interests of preserving the integrity of the Oracle database, the DBA should ensure that only the data dictionary and system rollback segments are placed in the SYSTEM tablespace. In particular, no data objects such as tables or indexes should be placed in the SYSTEM tablespace.

Finally, the **create database** command specifies the character set used throughout the database. Like DB_BLOCK_SIZE, the character set specified for the database should not be changed at any point after the database is created. After database creation, the database that was just created is mounted and opened directly by Oracle for the DBA to begin placing data objects into it, such as tables, indexes, and rollback segments. Once the database is created, the DBA should consider some preliminary work on distributing the I/O load in order to simplify the maintainability of the database in the future. Some areas that the DBA may want to address right away are placement of redo logs and datafiles and the separation of tables from their corresponding indexes. Also, the DBA will find the further allocation of rollback segments in addition to the rollback segment in the SYSTEM tablespace to be an important initial consideration on creating the database. Generally, it is recommended to place the rest of the rollback segments available to the database in a special tablespace designed only to hold rollback segments.

Exercises

1. Name some of the steps in creating a new Oracle database. What resources are created as part of the creation of a database?

2. What is the SYSTEM tablespace? What is its significance?

3. What is a parameter file? What are some of the parameters a DBA must set uniquely for any database via the parameter file?

Creating the Oracle Data Dictionary

The data dictionary is the first database object created at the time a **create database** command is issued. Every object in the database is tracked in some fashion by the Oracle data dictionary. Oracle generally creates the data dictionary without any intervention from the DBA at database creation time with the use of **catalog.sql** and **catproc.sql**. The first script, **catalog.sql**, runs a series of other scripts in order to create all the data dictionary views, along with special public synonyms for those views. Within the **catalog.sql** script there are calls to several other scripts, which are listed here:

- **cataudit.sql**   Creates the SYS.AUD$ dictionary table, which tracks all audit trail information generated by Oracle when the auditing feature of the database is used.

- **catldr.sql**   Creates views that are used for the SQL*Loader tool, discussed later in this unit, which is used to process large-volume data loads from one system to another.

- **catexp.sql**   Creates views that are used by the IMPORT/EXPORT utilities, discussed in the unit covering OCP Exam 3, "Database Backup and Recovery."

The other script generally run by the Oracle database when the data dictionary is created is the **catproc.sql** script. This script calls several other scripts in the process of creating several different data dictionary components used in everything procedural related to the Oracle database. The code for creating these dictionary views is not contained in **catproc.sql**. The code that actually creates the objects is in several scripts called by this master script. Some of the objects created by the scripts called by **catproc.sql** are stored procedures, packages, triggers, snapshots, and certain utilities for PL/SQL constructs like alerts, locks, mail, and pipes.

Exercises

1. How is the data dictionary created?

2. What two scripts are used as part of database creation?

Chapter Summary

This chapter covered introductory material related to Oracle database administration. The topics covered in this chapter included an overview of the Oracle architecture, the process of starting and stopping access to a database and to an Oracle instance, and the tasks required for creating an Oracle database. The material in this chapter comprises about 22 percent of questions asked on OCP Exam 2.

The first area of discussion in this chapter was an overview of the various components of the Oracle database. Figure 6-1 gives a clear idea of the background processes, memory structures, and disk resources that comprise the Oracle instance, and also of the methods in which they act together to allow users to access information. Several memory structures exist on the Oracle database to improve performance on various areas of the database. The memory structures of an Oracle instance include the System Global Area (SGA) and the Program Global Area (PGA). The SGA, in turn, consists of a minimum of three components: the data block buffer cache, the shared pool, and the redo log buffer. Corresponding to several of these memory areas are certain disk resources. These disk resources are divided into two categories: physical resources and logical resources. The physical disk resources on the Oracle database are *datafiles, redo log files, control files, password files,* and *parameter files*. The logical resources are *tablespaces, segments,* and *extents.* Tying memory structures and disk resources together are several memory processes that move data between disk and memory, or handle activities in the background on Oracle's behalf. The core background processes available on the Oracle instance include data block writer (DBWR), log writer (LGWR), system monitor (SMON), process monitor (PMON), checkpoint (CKPT), archiver (ARCH), recoverer (RECO), dispatcher (D*nnn*), lock (LCK*n*), and server (S*nnn*).

These different processes have functions that are related to activities that happen regularly in Oracle against the memory structures, disk resources, or both. DBWR moves data blocks out of the buffer cache. LGWR writes redo log entries out of the redo log buffer and into the online redo log. SMON handles instance recovery at startup in the event of a failure, and periodically sifts through tablespaces, making large continuous free disk space out of smaller empty fragments. PMON ensures that if a user process fails, the appropriate cleanup activity and rollback occurs. CKPT handles writing new redo log number information to datafiles and control files in the database at periodic intervals during the time the database is open. ARCH handles the automatic archiving of online redo log files. RECO and LCK*n* handle transaction processing on distributed database configurations. Server processes read data into the buffer cache on behalf of user processes. They can either be dedicated to one user process, or shared between many processes in the MTS architecture. D*nnn* are dispatchers used to route user processes to a shared server in MTS configurations.

The next area covered by the chapter was on how to start the Oracle instance. Before starting the instance, the DBA must figure out what sort of database authentication to use both for users and administrators. The options available are operating system authentication and Oracle authentication. The factors that weigh on that choice are whether the DBA wants to use remote administration via network or local administration directly on the machine running Oracle. If the DBA chooses to use Oracle authentication, then the DBA must create a password file using the ORAPWD utility. The password file itself is protected by a password, and this password is the same as the one used for authentication as user SYS and when connecting as **internal**. To have database administrator privileges on the database, a DBA must be granted certain privileges. They are called **sysdba** and **sysoper** in environments where Oracle authentication is used, and **osdba** or **osoper** where operating system authentication is used.

In order to start a database instance, the DBA must run Server Manager and connect to the database as **internal**. The command to start the instance from Server Manager is called **startup**. There are several different options for starting the instance. They are **nomount**, **mount**, **open**, **restrict**, **recover**, and **force**. The **nomount** option starts the instance without mounting a corresponding database. The **mount** option starts the instance and mounts but does not open the database. The **open** option starts the instance, mounts the database, and opens it for general user access. The **restrict** option starts the instance, mounts the database, and opens it for users who have been granted a special access privilege called **restricted session**. The **recover** option starts the instance, but leaves the database closed and starts the database recovery procedures associated with disk failure. The **force** option gives the database startup procedure some extra pressure to assist in starting an instance that either has trouble opening or trouble closing normally. There are two **alter database** statements that can be used to change database accessibility once the instance is started as well.

Several options exist for shutting down the database as well. The DBA must again connect to the database as **internal** using the Server Manager tool. The three options for shutting down the Oracle database are **normal**, **immediate**, and **abort**. When the DBA shuts down the database with the **normal** option, the database refuses new connections to the database by users and waits for existing connections to terminate. Once the last user has logged off the system, then the **shutdown normal** will complete. The DBA issuing a **shutdown immediate** causes Oracle to prevent new connections while also terminating current ones, rolling back whatever transactions were taking place in the sessions just terminated. The final option for shutting down a database is **shutdown abort**, which disconnects current sessions without rolling back their transactions and prevents new connections to the database as well.

The final area covered in this chapter was the creation of a database. The steps of database creation were discussed. The first area covered was the process modeling that takes place when the database designer creates the entity-relationship diagram. After developing a model of the process to be turned into a database application, the designer of the application must then give a row count forecast for the application's tables. This row count forecast allows the DBA to size the amount of space in bytes that each table and index needs in order to store data in the database. Once this sizing is complete, the

DBA can then begin the work of creating the database. First, the DBA should back up existing databases associated with the instance, if any, in order to prevent data loss or accidental deletion of a disk file resource. The next thing that should happen is the DBA should create a parameter file that is unique to the database being created. Several initialization parameters were identified as needing to be set to create a database. They are DB_NAME, DB_DOMAIN, DB_BLOCK_SIZE, DB_BLOCK_BUFFERS, PROCESSES, ROLLBACK_SEGMENTS, LICENSE_MAX_SESSIONS, LICENSE_MAX_WARNING, LICENSE_MAX_USERS. After the parameter file is created, the DBA can execute the **create database** command, which creates all physical disk resources for the Oracle database. The physical resources are datafiles, control files, and redo log files, the SYS and SYSTEM users, the SYSTEM tablespace, one rollback segment in the SYSTEM tablespace, and the Oracle data dictionary for that database. After creating the database, it is recommended that the DBA back up the new database in order to avoid having to re-create the database from scratch in the event of a system failure.

Of particular importance in the database creation process is the process by which the data dictionary is created. The data dictionary must be created first in a database because all other database structure changes will be recorded in the data dictionary. This creation process happens automatically by Oracle. Several scripts are run in order to create the tables and views that comprise the data dictionary. There are two "master" scripts that everything else seems to hang off of. The first is **catalog.sql**. This script creates all the data dictionary tables that document the various objects on the database. The second is called **catproc.sql**. This script runs several other scripts that create everything required in the data dictionary to allow procedural blocks of code in the Oracle database, namely packages, procedures, functions, triggers, snapshots, and certain packages for PL/SQL such as pipes and alerts.

Two-Minute Drill

- Three major components of the Oracle architecture are memory structures that improve database performance, disk resources that store Oracle data, and background processes that handle disk writes and other time-consuming tasks in the background.

- Memory structures in the Oracle architecture are System Global Area (SGA) and Program Global Area (PGA).

- The SGA consists of: the buffer cache for storing recently accessed data blocks, the redo log buffer for storing redo entries until they can be written to disk, and shared pool for storing parsed information about recently executed SQL for code sharing.

- Disk resources in the Oracle architecture are divided into physical and logical categories.

- Physical disk resources are control files that store the physical layout of database, redo log files that store redo entries on disk, password files to store passwords for DBAs when Oracle authentication is used, parameter files, and datafiles that store tables, indexes, rollback segments, and the data dictionary.

- The fundamental unit of storage in a datafile is the data block.

- Logical disk resources are tablespaces for storing tables, indexes, rollback segments, and the data dictionary. The storage of these logical disk resources is handled with segments and extents, which are conglomerations of data blocks.

- DBWR writes data blocks back and forth between disk and the buffer cache.

- LGWR writes redo log entries between redo log buffer and online redo log on disk. It also writes redo log sequence numbers to datafiles and control files at checkpoints (also handled by CKPT when enabled) and tells DBWR to write dirty buffers to disk.

- CKPT writes redo log sequence numbers to datafiles and control files when enabled. This task can also be handled by LGWR.

- PMON monitors user processes and cleans up the database transactions in the event that they fail.

- SMON automatically handles instance recovery at startup when necessary, and defragments small free spaces in tablespaces into larger ones.

- ARCH handles archiving of online redo logs automatically when set up.

- RECO resolves in-doubt transactions on distributed database environments.

- LCKn obtains locks on remote databases.

- Dnnn receives user processes from SQL*Net listener in multithreaded server (MTS) environments.

- Snnn (server process) reads data from disk on the database on behalf of the user process.

- Two user authentication methods exist in Oracle: operating system authentication and Oracle authentication.

- There are two privileges DBAs require to perform their function on the database. Under OS authentication, the privileges are called **osdba** and **osoper**. In Oracle authentication environments, they are called **sysdba** and **sysoper**.

- To use Oracle authentication, the DBA must create a password file using the ORAPWD utility.

- To start and stop a database, the DBA must connect as **internal** or **sysdba**.

- The tool used to start and stop the database is called Server Manager.

- There are at least six different options for starting a database:

  - **Startup nomount**   Start instance, do not mount a database.

  - **Startup mount**   Start instance, mount but do not open the database.

  - **Startup open**   Start instance, mount and open database.

  - **Startup restrict**   Start instance, mount and open database, but restrict access to those users with **restricted session** privilege granted to them.

  - **Startup recover**   Start instance, leave database closed, and begin recovery for disk failure scenario.

- **Startup force** Make an instance start that is having problems either starting or stopping.

- When a database is open, any user with a username and password, with the **create session** privilege or the CONNECT role granted to them, may connect to the database.

- The database availability can be changed at any time using the **alter database** command.

- Options available for **alter database** are **mount, open,** and **enable (disable) restricted session.**

- Closing or shutting down a database must be done by the DBA while running Server Manager and while the DBA is connected to the database as **internal** or **sysdba.**

- There are three options for closing a database: **shutdown normal**— no new existing connections allowed, but existing sessions may take as long as they want to wrap up; **shutdown immediate**— no new connections allowed, existing sessions are terminated, and their transactions rolled back, **shutdown abort**—no new connections allowed, existing sessions are terminated, transactions are not rolled back.

- Instance recovery is required after **shutdown abort** is used.

- The first step in creation of a database is to model the process that will be performed by the database application.

- The next step in creating a database is to back up any existing databases associated with the instance.

- After that, the DBA should create a parameter file with unique values for several parameters, including the following:

  - DB_NAME The local name for the database.

  - DB_DOMAIN   The network-wide location for the database.

  - DB_BLOCK_SIZE   The size of each block in the database.

  - DB_BLOCK_BUFFERS   The number of blocks stored in the buffer cache.

- PROCESSES The maximum number of processes available on the database.

- ROLLBACK_SEGMENTS Named rollback segments that the database must acquire at startup.

- LICENSE_MAX_SESSIONS The maximum number of sessions that can connect to the database.

- LICENSE_MAX_WARNING The sessions trying to connect above the number specified by this parameter will receive a warning message.

- LICENSE_MAX_USERS The maximum number of users that can be created in the Oracle instance.

- LICENSE_MAX_SESSIONS and LICENSE_MAX_WARNING are used for license tracking or LICENSE_MAX_USERS is used, but not both, usually.

- After creating the parameter file, the DBA executes the **create database** command, which creates all physical database structures in the database, along with logical database structures like SYSTEM and an initial rollback segment, as well as the SYS and SYSTEM users. On conclusion of the **create database** statement, the database is created and open.

- The default password for SYS is CHANGE_ON_INSTALL.

- The default password for SYSTEM is MANAGER.

- The **create database** command also creates the Oracle data dictionary for that database. This task is done first to capture the other database objects that are created in the database.

- The number of datafiles and redo log files created for the life of the database can be limited with the **maxdatafiles** and **maxlogfiles** options of the **create database** statement.

- The size of a datafile is fixed, unless the **autoextend** option is used.

- The size of a control file is directly related to the number of datafiles and redo logs for the database.

- ■ At least two scripts are used to create the database:

  - ■ **catalog.sql**   Creates all data dictionary tables and views that track database objects like tables, indexes, and rollback segments.

  - ■ **catproc.sql**   Creates dictionary views for all procedural aspects of Oracle, like PL/SQL packages, procedures, functions, triggers, snapshots, and special utility PL/SQL packages such as those used to manage pipes, alerts, locks, etc.

Chapter Questions

1. **The background process that coalesces small blocks of free space into larger blocks of free space is**

   A. DBWR

   B. LGWR

   C. SMON

   D. PMON

   E. LMON

2. **In order to perform administrative tasks on the database using Oracle password authentication, the DBA should have the following two privileges granted to them:**

   A. sysdba or sysoper

   B. osdba or osoper

   C. CONNECT or RESOURCE

   D. restricted session or create session

3. **Which component of the system global area stores parsed SQL statements used for process sharing?**

   A. Buffer cache

   B. Private SQL area

    C. Redo log buffer

    D. Library cache

    E. Row cache

4. **A foreign key relationship between two tables with an ordinality of 0, N indicates that**

    A. The relationship is mandatory and one-to-many

    B. The relationship is optional and one-to-many

    C. The relationship is mandatory and one-to-one

    D. The relationship is optional and one-to-one

5. **The INIT.ORA parameter that indicates the size of each buffer in the buffer cache is the**

    A. DB_BLOCK_BUFFERS

    B. BUFFER_SIZE

    C. DB_BLOCK_SIZE

    D. ROLLBACK_SEGMENTS

6. **Which two of the following SQL scripts must be run as part of database creation?**

    A. utllockt.sql

    B. catalog.sql

    C. catalog6.sql

    D. utlmontr.sql

    E. utlestat.sql

    F. catexp.sql

7. **Changing the password used to manage the password file changes the password for which of the following?**

    A. SYSTEM

    B. RPT_BATCH

    C. CONNECT

    D. internal

    E. audit

8. The default password for the SYS userid is

    A. CHANGE_ON_INSTALL

    B. NO_PASSWORD

    C. MANAGER

    D. ORACLE

    E. NULL

9. DBAs who are planning to administer a database remotely should use operating system authentication.

    A. TRUE

    B. FALSE

10. Power will disconnect on the machine running Oracle in two minutes. How should the DBA shut down the instance?

    A. shutdown normal

    B. shutdown immediate

    C. shutdown abort

    D. shutdown force

    E. shutdown recover

11. What method should the DBA use to prevent access to the database while dropping and re-creating an index?

    A. Enable **restricted session** to prevent users from accessing the database.

    B. Shut down the database with the **abort** option to prevent users from accessing the database.

C. Execute an **alter database mount** to prevent users from accessing the database.

D. Execute a **connect internal** to prevent users from accessing the database.

Answers to Chapter Questions

1. C. SMON

Explanation SMON is the process that coalesces, or merges, smaller free space in tablespaces into larger spaces. Choice A, DBWR, moves data blocks between disk and the buffer cache, and therefore is not correct. Choice B, LGWR, copies redo entries from the redo log buffer to online redo logs on disk, and therefore is not correct. Choice D, PMON, performs cleanup on user processes that fail during transaction processing and is therefore wrong. LMON is not an Oracle background process and is therefore wrong. Refer to the discussion of the Oracle architecture.

2. A. **sysdba** or **sysoper**

Explanation Choice B is almost correct. **osdba** and **osoper** are the same roles DBAs need in Oracle authenticated environments for database administration. Choices C and D are incorrect. Each privilege listed has some bearing on access, but none of them give any administrative ability. Refer to the discussion of choosing an authentication method.

3. D. Library cache

Explanation Choice A is incorrect because the buffer cache is where data blocks are stored for recently executed queries. Choice B is incorrect because the private SQL area is in the PGA where the actual values returned from a query are stored, not the parse information for the query. Choice C is incorrect because the redo log buffer stores redo entries temporarily until LGWR can write them to disk. Choice E is incorrect because the row cache stores data dictionary row information for fast access by users and Oracle. Refer to the discussion of Oracle architecture.

4. B.   The relationship is optional and one-to-many

Explanation   Ordinality consists of two elements. The first element represents whether the relationship is optional (0) or mandatory (1). The second represents how many rows in each table correspond to one another. The relationship can be one-to-one (1) or one-to-many (N). A relationship with ordinality of (0,N) is optional and one-to-many. Refer to the discussion of logical data models and entity-relationship diagrams.

5. C.   DB_BLOCK_SIZE

Explanation   Since each buffer in the buffer cache is designed to fit one data block, the size of buffers in the database block buffer cache will be the same size as the blocks they store. The size of blocks in the database is determined by DB_BLOCK_BUFFERS. Refer to the discussion of initialization parameters to be changed during database creation.

6. B and F   **catalog.sql** and **catexp.sql**

Explanation   **catalog.sql** runs during database creation to create several data dictionary tables and views associated with database objects. **catexp.sql** is called by **catalog.sql** to create data dictionary views used by IMPORT/EXPORT. All others are optional startup scripts or utilities run for various tuning reasons. Refer to the discussion of how the data dictionary is created.

7. D.   **internal**

Explanation   Choice A is incorrect because the SYSTEM password has no affiliation with the password for the password file. SYS and **internal** do. Choice B is incorrect because RPT_BATCH is not a password created by Oracle in a **create database** statement. Choice C is incorrect because CONNECT is a role, not a user. Choice E is incorrect because **audit** is a command, not a user. Refer to the discussion of creating the password file as part of choosing user authentication.

8. A.   CHANGE_ON_INSTALL

Explanation   This is a classic piece of Oracle trivia. Memorize it.

9. B.   FALSE

Explanation   A DBA should use Oracle authentication when planning to administer a database remotely, due to the fact that most network connections over long distances are not secure, especially when the TCP/IP networking technology is being used. Refer to the discussion of choosing a user authentication method in starting and stopping the database.

10. C.   **shutdown abort**

Explanation   A power outage can cause damage to an Oracle instance if it is running when the power goes out. Choice C is the only way to guarantee that the database will shut down within two minutes. Choice A is definitely out, because Oracle will wait until the last user disconnects before shutting down the instance. Choice B will shut down the database more quickly; however, the DBA will still have to wait for the aborted transactions to roll back, which could take a long time if there were long-running transactions executing on the base. Choices D and E are not valid options for shutting down a database instance. Refer to the discussion of database shutdown.

11. A.   Enable **restricted session** to prevent users from accessing the database.

Explanation   Enabling **restricted session** keeps the database available for manipulating logical database objects like tables and indexes, but prevents all users except those with the **restricted session** privilege from connecting to the database. Choice B is wrong because **shutdown abort** prevents the DBA from accessing the index as well as preventing user access. Choice C is wrong because again the database is not open, therefore preventing the DBA from manipulating logical database objects like indexes. Choice D is wrong because although connect **internal** allows the DBA to execute powerful commands, it does nothing in and of itself to bar user access. Refer to the discussion of restricting user access via **startup restrict** or **alter database enable restricted session**.

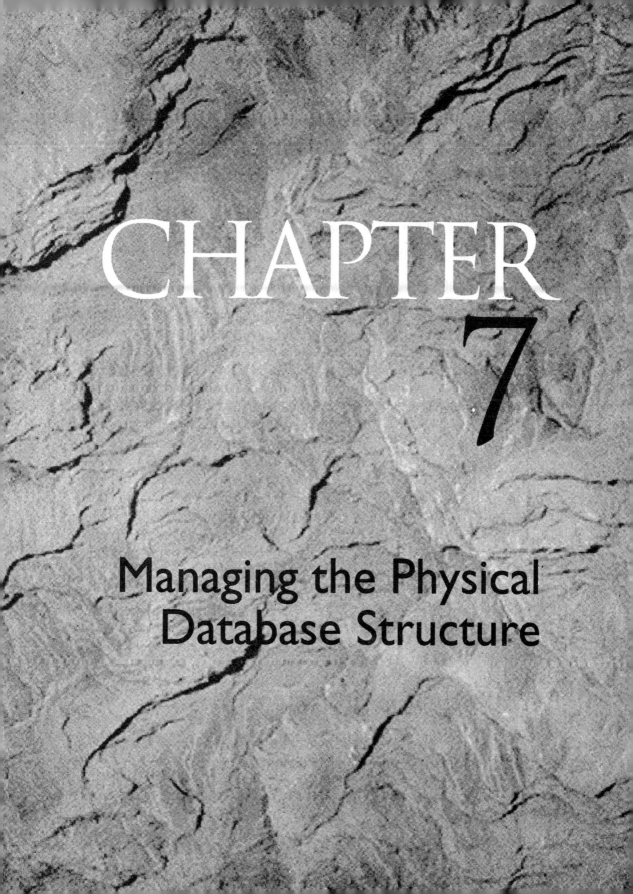

CHAPTER
7

Managing the Physical
Database Structure

n this chapter, you will understand and demonstrate knowledge in the following areas:

- Accessing and updating data
- Managing transaction concurrency
- Managing the database structure
- Managing storage allocation

Organizations use the Oracle database to manage their information. In order to work with a database, users in the organization must have some way to access the data in a database, and also some way to change the data in the database. The chapter at hand will cover how Oracle manages data change. The first area to be discussed will be accessing and updating data. How Oracle manages data access and data change will be presented, and the question of what happens when a user issues a data query or change request will be answered. Oracle also recognizes that data change in the database is never safe from the problems inherent in computer machinery that cause data loss. A discussion of how Oracle preserves data in the event that there is a problem will also appear in this chapter. Finally, the foundations of database management will be presented in a discussion of managing the database structure and storage allocation of various objects and resources in the database. These topics comprise 22 percent of the OCP Exam 2 on Oracle database administration.

Accessing and Updating Data

In this section, you will cover the following topics related to accessing and updating data:

- Steps in SQL statement processing
- The benefits of the shared SQL area
- The function and contents of the buffer cache

■ Role of the server process

■ Role of the DBWR process

■ Events triggering DBWR activity

Key to the use of an Oracle database is the ability to access and change data. Oracle simplifies the mechanics of accessing data in the database by providing mechanisms to access data and structures to manage access performance. With these built-in mechanisms handling the tasks of reading data from disk, saving it back to disk, and optimizing operation structure to improve SQL statement performance, the user can focus on more salient questions like "What data am I looking for?" This discussion will focus both on the mechanisms that process a user's request for data and on the mechanisms that work behind the scenes to make data available quickly.

Steps in SQL Statement Processing

SQL provides a method for obtaining data from a database by allowing the user to *define the data they need* and NOT a process by which to obtain it. Think about this difference by considering the following statement: *I'm thirsty.* To a person accustomed to dealing with thirst, the solution is obvious—get a glass of water and drink it. However, there are steps to be followed in order to fulfill that statement.

1. Get off the couch.

2. Walk to the kitchen.

3. Open a cupboard door.

4. Remove a glass from the cupboard.

5. Put the open end of it underneath the tap.

6. Turn the cold water knob on the side of the tap.

7. Fill the glass to capacity.

8. Turn off the water.

9. Raise the glass to my lips.

10. Ingest the water, being careful to not get any up my nose.

Notice, too, that each step in the process may have a procedure to be performed as well. Getting to the kitchen may require standing, putting the left foot in front of the right, then the right in front of the left, and repeating the loop, then going down the stairs, etc. So, while defining a "want," there is a procedure defined (perhaps implicitly) that is used to get it. Most programming languages provide the developer with mechanisms to define a procedure to obtain desired information. Unfortunately, when someone looks at the procedures another developer has created, the original developer's "want" gets lost in the details of how the developer obtained it.

SQL alleviates this situation by allowing a developer to define a desired outcome, and letting Oracle's relational database management system figure out the steps or operations to obtain it. Those operations fall into a pattern detailed in Figure 7-1. The flow of operation in processing a SQL statement is as follows:

- **Oracle opens the statement**   Oracle first obtains a *cursor*, or memory address in the library cache of the shared pool, where the statement will execute. Then Oracle obtains some space in the PGA called a private SQL area, where statement return values will be stored.

- **Oracle parses the statement**   Oracle creates a *parse tree*, or *execution plan*, for the statement and places it in the shared pool. The execution plan is a list of operations used to obtain data.

- **Oracle creates bind variables**   For **select** statements, bind variables for return values are created in the parsed SQL statement. This allows Oracle to share parsed operation, but not data, in the shared SQL area in the library cache of the shared pool. For **update**, **insert**, and **delete** commands, this step is omitted.

- **Oracle will execute the statement**   At this point, Oracle performs all processing to complete the specified operation.

In situations where a user making a data change via an **update**, **insert**, or **delete**, once the statement has been executed, the data is changed. On the other hand, if the user has issued a **select** statement, then the resulting set of the statement is available in the cursor at the end of the execution, and must

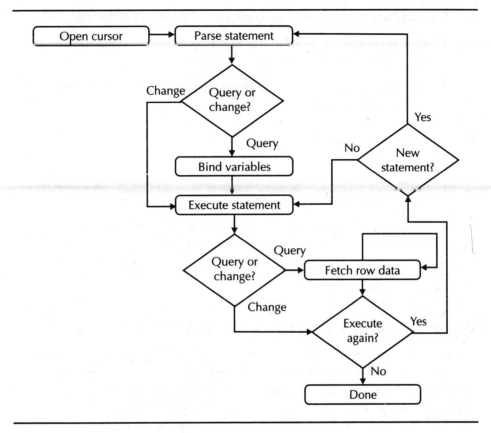

FIGURE 7-1. *SQL statement process flow*

be *fetched* from the cursor in order for the user to view it. The steps for executing SQL statements are as follows:

1. Open shared and private areas in memory for statement to use.

2. Parse statement to obtain execution plan.

3. Create bind variables for SQL parse information sharing while maintaining data privacy (**select** statements only).

4. Execute the SQL statement plan.

5. Fetch returned dataset into bind variables (**select** statements only).

6. Repeat process at step 4 if reprocessing the same statement, or at step 2 if processing a new one.

7. If no more processing, leave parse tree information in shared memory for execution plan reuse.

Exercises

1. Does SQL allow the user to define procedures or desired data for information retrieval? Explain.

2. What are the general tasks Oracle accomplishes to process SQL statements? Which are specific to **select** statements?

3. At what point in SQL statement processing is data updated or changed?

The Benefits of the Shared SQL Area

After execution, parse information for SQL statements stays in the shared SQL area for a short amount of time. If some user wants to reexecute a statement, the SQL processing mechanism will simply jump back to the execution phase of the previously parsed process. Thus, parse trees are reusable in Oracle. *Not only can a process reuse the execution plan it creates in the parse phase of its own execution, it can also reuse any parsed execution plan that is cached in the shared pool.* The criteria for reuse of an execution plan are as follows:

■ To reuse an execution plan in the shared pool, the current SQL statement must be identical to the already parsed statement, including white space and commas.

■ The execution plan must be in the shared pool at the same time that the current SQL statement trying to reuse it is looking for it.

There are two benefits to this setup for the entire database: increased statement performance and reduced memory. The performance gain is made both in the time it takes to open and parse the SQL statement. Thus, Oracle attempts to build on its own work as much as possible. The other benefit is that each iteration of the same statement in memory takes up that much less space under the shared model. Since there is only a finite amount of memory in the shared pool, the entire database would suffer if all processes had to wait for another process to finish in order to use the space in memory.

TIP

If a statement being executed in one process is identical to another process's statement whose parse tree still exists in the shared pool, the process will reuse the shared parse information, thus improving statement performance and reducing memory required for statement processing.

Exercises

1. What memory areas are involved in the processing of SQL statements?

2. Explain the benefits of shared SQL areas for SQL statement processing.

The Function and Contents of the Buffer Cache

In addition to defining operations required to obtain data, Oracle has special mechanisms for managing the rapid access of data stored on disk. The first component to the method Oracle uses to manage disk data is the buffer cache, a memory structure in the Oracle instance that stores data blocks that house rows involved in recently executed SQL statements. There are several components to the buffer cache, the main one being the database block buffers. This component consists of a number of buffers, each designed to hold one data block. Another one, called the *dirty buffer write queue*, is a list of data block buffers containing blocks that contain data changes made by user processes.

The buffer cache improves performance of SQL statement processing by providing a copy in memory of the data being used in the statement. Accessing data stored in memory is faster than accessing information stored on disk, so queries that have the blocks they need in the buffer cache will run much faster than the processes that do not. Once those blocks are in memory, the buffer cache keeps them for a certain period of time before eliminating them. The period of time is determined by a modified "least recently used" (LRU) algorithm in Oracle.

Additionally, the buffer cache releases SQL statements from being I/O bound in many cases. Data changes are made to blocks in memory, which are then held on the dirty buffer write queue until a background process called DBWR writes to disk. Having this special background process performing all disk writes frees user processes to do other things after making a data change instead of having to wait in line to write the data change to disk immediately. In addition, the block stays around for other processes to access it, potentially improving performance for other statements as well.

To see real performance gains, the buffer cache must be large, particularly if the database itself is large or experiences high-volume or long-running transactions. The number of buffers in the buffer cache is determined by the DB_BLOCK_BUFFERS initialization parameter of the Oracle instance. The size of the database buffer cache is determined by multiplying the number of buffers, DB_BLOCK_BUFFERS, by the size of each buffer, which is the same as DB_BLOCK_SIZE. *However, the DBA must be careful when configuring the buffer cache in order to avoid sizing the buffer cache out of real memory,* for reasons that will be discussed later.

Exercises

1. What is the buffer cache? What are the components of the buffer cache?

2. What function does the buffer cache serve? How is the size of the buffer cache determined?

Role of the Server Process

The server process accesses the database on behalf of user processes to read data from datafiles on disk into the buffer cache in the SGA. When SQL statements need to access certain data, Oracle places data into the buffer cache in the following way. If there is an index associated with the table that can be used by Oracle, the blocks for that index will be read into the buffer cache. Oracle then tracks down the appropriate ROWID corresponding to the data needed. As stated earlier, a ROWID is an exact location on disk for a row of data. There are three components of a ROWID: the *data block address*, the *block row number*, and the *block datafile number*. Memorize this information with the following acronym: *BRF, for block-row-file*. Once the ROWID for a block containing table data is identified, that block is read into memory. If many rows are to be read into memory, then all blocks containing those rows are placed into data block buffers of the database buffer cache. Figure 7-2 demonstrates the format for ROWID data in Oracle.

However, Oracle is not always able to bring data into memory in the most efficient way, as provided by some indexing mechanisms in Oracle. When there is no index on the table, or if the SQL statement does not make use of the index, Oracle has no choice but to read every data block associated with a table into memory to find the block(s) containing the data required for the user request. This method for obtaining data is called a *full table scan*. In this case, every data block in a table will be read into memory until the row containing the requested data is found.

Once in the buffer cache, that block will be held in the database buffer cache for a certain period of time. That time period is determined by the server process, the mechanism by which Oracle brought the data block into memory. If the data was brought into memory as part of an indexed search, the data block will be held in memory until the space is needed by another block, and the block in the buffer is the least recently used (LRU) block. In this way, frequently used blocks will stay in the buffer cache for a long time, while infrequently used buffers get eliminated to make way for more block storage. This method is often referred to as the LRU algorithm.

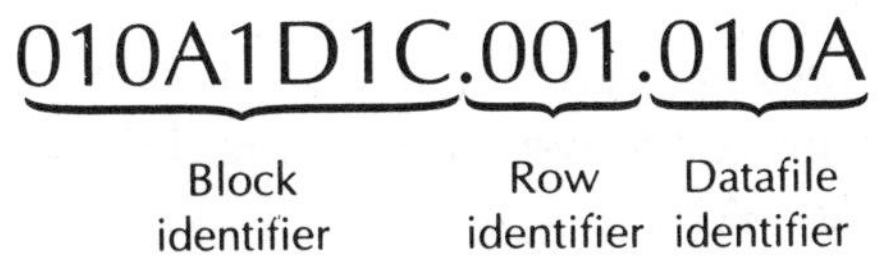

010A1D1C.001.010A

| Block identifier | Row identifier | Datafile identifier |

FIGURE 7-2.   *ROWID format in Oracle*

The method used to keep a data block in the buffer cache is slightly different if Oracle must use a full table scan to find the data the user requests. Oracle simply eliminates those buffers almost immediately after they are read by placing them on the least recently used end of the list of blocks slated for elimination from the buffer cache. Oracle doesn't simply use the LRU mechanism to hold data blocks brought in from full table scans because doing so would quickly fill the buffer cache with blocks from one table, eliminating blocks from other tables that may be in use by other queries. Without a modified LRU algorithm, full table scans will adversely impact performance not only for the query running the full table scan but for the entire database as well.

What often happens in the buffer cache is that blocks from indexes on tables commonly accessed stay in the buffer cache longest. Oracle's modified LRU algorithm facilitates this usage in the following ways. Index blocks are stored in the buffer cache, and frequent use will keep them in the buffer cache. Since an index block for a commonly used table is likely to be used frequently by users, the blocks of the index will likely live in the buffer cache for long periods of time. Storing the blocks of an index in memory is more effective than storing the actual rows of data in memory for two reasons. The first reason is that the index has many fewer blocks than the table, minimizing the number of blocks that need to be stored in memory in order to have easy access to a table. The second reason is that each index block stores searchable column values for table rows, plus an address on disk that will allow Oracle to know almost exactly where on disk to look for the full row data. The buffer cache then acts as a "superindex" of the data in the Oracle database.

Exercises

1. What process reads information into the buffer cache? What factor does the length of time a block stays in the buffer cache depend on?

2. In terms of improving performance, is storing a data block from an index more or less effective than storing data blocks from tables in the buffer cache? Why?

3. What is the algorithm called that is used to determine how long data stays in the buffer cache?

Role of the DBWR Process

Oracle uses the server process to move data blocks into the buffer cache in support of **select** and **update** statements. Oracle moves data block changes out of the buffer cache by means of the DBWR background process. DBWR is designed to minimize the dependency that database processes have on disk utilization. To understand the service the DBWR provides to all user processes on the database in order to improve performance, consider how the database would behave without having a special process earmarked to do nothing other than perform disk I/O. If there were no process to handle disk writes, then every user process that made changes to data would have to access disk resources individually to write those changes to disk. Since there is only one disk controller available to access the data blocks on any given disk drive, each process that wanted to write data blocks would have to wait in line to use the disk controller to find its data blocks.

This architecture has the potential for bottlenecks unless data for each user process could be placed on separate disks in order to relieve contention for the limited disk controller resources. This task is nearly impossible, however, due to the fact that extravagant numbers of disk controllers usually cannot be connected to one machine and, even if they could, there is really no way to predict accurately how user processes would want to access data in such a way so as to minimize contention for disk resources. Another problem inherent in this architecture of "every process for itself" is the fact that frequently run updates would line up to write exactly the same data, over and over again, bumping into one another and creating sticky situations related to read consistency with respect to the data on disk or in memory.

DBWR, then, minimizes the bottleneck or dependency that any process will have on writing data to disk. With one process putting data onto the disk resources, working with a cache of data blocks already stored in memory for easy access, other user processes run faster and complete sooner.

Exercises

1. What function does DBWR serve on a database?

2. What sort of scenario would occur if DBWR didn't exist?

Events Triggering DBWR Activity

Unless the database buffer cache is enormous enough to hold every data block cached in memory, and there is never a change to any data block that needs to be written to disk, chances are DBWR will be working quite frequently to write changes to disk. DBWR is triggered every three (3) seconds to write changed blocks to disk. This trigger mechanism is called a *timeout*.

Another event that triggers DBWR to do its job is caused by data changes on the system. When a user process issues a data change against the database, DBWR must find the data block containing the row to be changed and make that change to the row. Once the block is altered, it is called a *dirty buffer*. However, DBWR doesn't just run right out there and save the dirty buffer to disk. Rather, all the dirty buffers are gathered into the *dirty buffer write queue* and written to disk at one time. This way, disk I/O is further minimized in order to reduce the disk utilization requirements of any process accessing the database. When the number of buffers on the dirty buffer write queue reaches a threshold limit, DBWR flushes the entire queue at once and writes all the buffers to disk.

DBWR also writes changed blocks to disk at periodic intervals determined by the setup of another major disk resource on the Oracle architecture, called the online redo log. The periodic intervals at which the changed blocks are written to disk are referred to as *checkpoints*. A more complete discussion of the checkpoint process will appear later in this chapter in the discussion of the online redo logs, but for now it is important to know that the checkpoint process exists, and that at the time of a checkpoint, all data blocks that have been changed since the last checkpoint are written to disk.

Exercises

1. What events trigger the usage of DBWR?

2. What is the best performance scenario a DBA can realistically expect in the activities of DBWR and the buffer cache?

3. What is a dirty buffer? What is the dirty buffer write queue?

Managing Transaction Concurrency

In this section, you will cover the following topics related to managing transaction concurrency:

- The log writer process
- Components and purpose of the redo log
- The purpose of checkpoints
- Data concurrency and statement-level read consistency

In order to ensure the viability of any application using its database management system, the Oracle database has several special design features that allow for database recovery to be as thorough and complete as restoring committed transactions up to the moment of failure. The main feature that provides this data restorability is the ability Oracle has to keep redo logs. Redo logs can be thought of as a scroll upon which every process that makes a data change on the Oracle database must jot a note of key facts about the change they made to the system. If a user process cannot write a redo log entry for the data change it makes, then the transaction involving the data change cannot be completed. In addition to writing redo log entries, Oracle allows the DBA to choose whether or not to archive the redo log entries. In the event that the DBA does choose to archive redo logs, then the changes made to the database are stored on an ongoing basis, making recoverability a straightforward matter of applying redo log entries to a restored database up to the most recent redo log held in archive. This fact makes it possible to restore a database up to the moment in time the failure occurred. These mechanisms work together to achieve transaction concurrency in the Oracle database.

The Log Writer Process

Oracle writes redo log entries from memory to disk using the LGWR process. As with DBWR, LGWR is designed to free the user processes in the

Oracle database from having to write data to disk whenever they make a change to any information in the database. Oracle forces every process that makes a change to a database data component to write a change entry so that in case of an emergency the changes can be recovered. If not for LGWR, every process would have to write its own redo log entry to disk, causing severe bottlenecks. Instead, LGWR handles all redo log writes to disk. Without a queue of user processes waiting at the disk controller, LGWR can maximize its nearly private usage of particular disk controllers if the only contents of the disk are redo logs.

In addition to writing redo log entries from memory to disk, LGWR plays a critical role in actually writing the data changes made to the Oracle database. Every Oracle database has at least two redo logs available for the purpose of storing redo log entries. LGWR writes entries to the redo logs on disk, one entry to one log, until one log is filled. At the time that one log is filled, LGWR "switches" over to writing redo log entries to another log. This event is called a *log switch*. At the time a log switch occurs, LGWR declares a checkpoint to occur as well. When the checkpoint occurs, DBWR writes blocks in the dirty buffer write queue to their respective datafiles. In this way, LGWR rather directly determines when DBWR will write database changes to disk. At log switch event time, a checkpoint must occur, so LGWR will influence the saving of data blocks at least as often as it switches writing redo entries from one log to another. The LGWR process can specify other times a checkpoint can occur as well.

LGWR writes redo log information in the following way. When a transaction executes, it produces information that essentially states the changes the transaction is making to the database. This information is called *redo*. The redo information is collected in a part of the SGA called the redo log buffer. When the transaction commits, LGWR writes the redo information from the redo buffer to the online redo log.

Exercises

1. What is the log writer process? What function does LGWR serve on the database?

2. How does LGWR influence the behavior of DBWR?

3. When does LGWR write redo log information to the database?

Components and Purpose of the Online Redo Log

The components of a redo log are the redo log buffer, the online redo log files, and the LGWR process. The redo log buffer stores redo log entries created by user processes for a short period of time until LGWR can write more permanent redo log entries to the online redo log on disk. LGWR is the only process on the Oracle database that handles disk I/O related to writing redo log entries. These two components comprise the memory structures and process Oracle uses to save information in order to allow for recovery of that information in the event that the data on a disk becomes unavailable.

Typically, there are at least two online redo log *groups* available on the Oracle database to which LGWR writes redo log entries. Each redo log in the database consists of one or more files that store the redo entries, called *members*. In general, it is wise for the DBA to create multiple members for each online redo log group, as each member of an online redo log group contains the entire set of redo entries for the online redo log. *Multiplexing*, or making Oracle maintain multiple members (ideally on separate disks) for each online redo log group, is an important way to ensure the integrity of the online redo log against problems with disk failure. Again, the DBA should see the logical and physical component here. The logical component is the redo log group, while the physical components are the files, or "members," that comprise the actual redo log. The location of each redo log member and the name of the redo log to which the member belongs are determined by the **create database** statement, where the redo log names and member names are specified. Information about the physical location of redo log files is also stored in the control file. Figure 7-3 demonstrates the logical and physical view on redo logs.

Several important details surround how the DBA will configure the redo log files of a database. The first (and perhaps most important) detail addresses the importance of having redo logs available if a database disk failure were to ever occur. In order to ensure the probability of recovery in the event of disk failure, the DBA should configure Oracle to mirror redo logs. *Mirroring* is the act of storing multiple copies of redo information associated with each redo log. Figure 7-4 illustrates an important point—each redo log member in the redo log group contains a complete

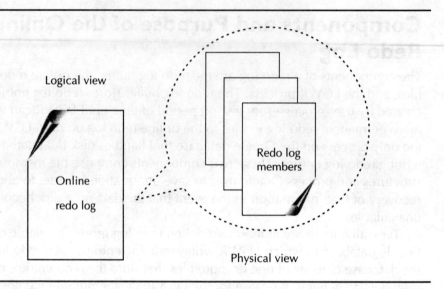

Logical view

Online
redo log

Redo log
members

Physical view

FIGURE 7-3. *Logical and physical view of redo logs*

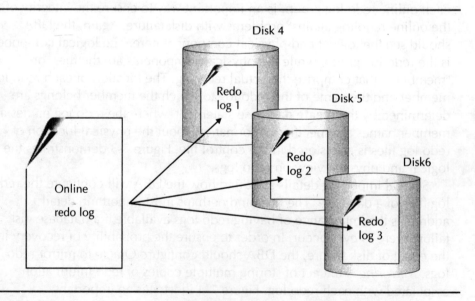

Disk 4

Redo
log 1

Disk 5

Online
redo log

Redo
log 2

Disk6

Redo
log 3

FIGURE 7-4. *Mirroring online redo logs*

copy of the online redo log. Thus, having multiple members of the redo log group allows the DBA to keep multiple copies of the redo log available to LGWR. Mirroring is the act of placing each redo log member on separate disks so that, in the event there is a disk problem with a disk that holds a redo log, the entire instance can continue running with another copy of the redo log in a separate member on a different disk. This process is also called multiplexing.

If mirrored online redo log members are not kept on multiple disks, there is significant risk posed to the instance by disk failure. If the disk containing the redo log that LGWR is writing experiences media failure, LGWR will not be able to write redo log entries and the Oracle instance will fail. Also, LGWR must write redo log entries to disk in order to clear space in the redo log buffer so that user processes can continue making changes to the database. Since LGWR cannot clear the space in memory if it cannot write the redo log entries to disk, the entire instance will fail.

The placement of redo log members on separate disks benefits the database in other ways. When archiving is enabled, and the DBA has specified that Oracle should run the ARCH process to automatically move archived redo logs to an archive destination, there can be contention at the time that a log switch occurs. If all members of the online redo log are on the same disk, ARCH and LGWR will contend for the disk controller resource because both processes need to execute activities on files on the same disk. With redo log members and the archive log destination spread across different disks, there is little possibility for ARCH and LGWR to contend because ARCH can work on what it needs to do using one disk while LGWR continues the switchover on another disk.

In order to enhance the recovery time of a database, the size of the redo log member should be as small as possible without causing excessive performance degradation. As stated before, when a redo log fills, LGWR conducts a log switch where it moves from writing redo entries from one redo log to another. At the time of a log switch, a checkpoint occurs on the database where DBWR writes changed data blocks to disk. It is important to have these activities occur in order to make sure that all data changes made are recorded on disk, both in live datafiles and in redo log files so that the DBA can recover in the event of a hardware problem. However, there are performance implications associated with these frequent saves. If redo log members are too small, LGWR spends excessive periods of time switching from one log to another. In heavy transaction environments, the database redo memory buffer may fill to capacity during the switch, causing user processes to wait for space in the redo memory buffer until LGWR starts clearing out redo entries to disk again. Also, the more time DBWR spends writing updated blocks to disk because of frequent checkpoints, the less time it has to retrieve blocks with data being requested by other user processes. In other words, both saving data and redo entries to disk and avoiding the performance degradation that these saves cause are important. But they give rise to the need for certain trade-offs in system performance for online transactions or performance in the event of requiring a database recovery.

The number of online redo log groups is also a factor in smooth redo log operation. Oracle sets a minimum for redo logs at two groups. LGWR writes to one group at a time until the group fills. At the time the group fills, a switch occurs and the LGWR process begins writing redo log entries to the other group. However, several factors may prevent LGWR from starting to write to another redo log group. One of the factors is that the other redo log group has not archived yet. Since there are only two groups online by default, LGWR recycles each group at switch time, overwriting the redo log entries in the other group. If archiving of redo logs is enabled, then the overwriting process cannot happen until ARCH has archived the redo log group. Switching may occur often on systems where redo log groups are too small or when there is a high transaction volume on the database. If switches occur frequently, the potential for contention between ARCH and LGWR over archiving and recycling the online redo log increases.

Two solutions exist for this problem. One solution is to increase the size of each redo log member. By increasing the size of each redo log member, switches occur less frequently because each redo log takes longer to fill. However, there is a performance cost to be paid when the DBA must attempt a recovery using large redo logs. It takes longer to restore the database when the redo logs are fewer and larger. An alternative to reducing the chance that LGWR will have to wait to begin writing entries to an online redo log when a switch occurs is to increase the number of online redo logs available on the Oracle instance. This can be set up at database creation time, or new redo log groups can be added after the fact with the **alter database add logfile group** statement. The only restrictions to this option are some options that are set by the **create database** command. These options limit the number and size of the redo logs that can be associated with a database. The options are called **maxlogfiles**, which limits the number of redo log groups, and **maxlogmembers**, which limits the size of each member or copy in the group. The only way to alter these options is to re-create the control file. In emergency situations only, and only for the lifetime of the current instance, the DBA can decrease the number of redo log groups that can be set for the instance by changing the LOG_FILES initialization parameter. However, this parameter offers little to the problem of wanting to add more redo log groups than **maxlogfiles** allows.

Exercises

1. What are the components of the Oracle redo log architecture? What are redo log groups? What are redo log members? How does this architecture limit I/O dependency of all user processes on the database? How often is redo log information moved from memory to disk?

2. What component of the buffer cache stores blocks containing changed data? What happens to that data during a checkpoint? What process initiates a checkpoint?

3. What is redo log mirroring? Why is it important for redo logs to be mirrored?

4. What is the effect of increasing the size of an online redo log group? What is the effect of increasing the number of redo log groups on the database? What parameters govern the maximum size and number of redo log groups and members?

The Purpose of Checkpoints

The checkpoint process has been mentioned several times in the discussion of transaction concurrency and the redo log architecture. During the course of regular database operation, users make changes to data. Blocks that have been changed while being stored in the buffer cache are stored in the dirty buffer write queue, a special part of the buffer cache where changed buffers are earmarked for a database save. A checkpoint is a point in time when DBWR writes all changes made to data blocks in memory to disk. The frequency of checkpoints is determined by many factors, one of which is directly attributed to the LGWR process. When LGWR fills an online redo log with redo entries from the redo memory buffer, LGWR performs a log switch; that is, it changes from writing redo entries from the online redo log it just filled to another redo log group. During the process of this log switch, a checkpoint occurs. At the time a checkpoint occurs, LGWR tells DBWR to write the blocks in the dirty buffer write queue to disk. Checkpoints, then, are points in time where changes to data block rows are written to disk.

Checkpoints occur at least as frequently as log switches. However, they can (and should) occur more frequently. If a database instance fails, the changes in blocks in the dirty buffer write queue of the database buffer cache that were not written to disk must be recovered from redo logs. Although this process happens automatically at startup with Oracle's instance recovery methods handled by the SMON background process, the process may take a long time if checkpoints happen infrequently and transaction volumes are large. The methods used to set checkpoints more frequently than log switches should be used only if the redo logs are sized to be very large. Typically, smaller redo logs fill faster, so checkpoints occur more often anyway when using small redo logs. But, if the redo log buffers must be large, then the DBA can specify more frequent checkpoints by using the LOG_CHECKPOINT_INTERVAL and/or LOG_CHECKPOINT_TIMEOUT initialization parameters of the **init.ora** file.

The two parameters that can be set to have checkpoints occur more frequently than log switches reflect two different principles upon which the frequency of checkpoints can be based—volume-based checkpoint intervals and time-based checkpoint intervals. The parameter called LOG_CHECKPOINT_INTERVAL sets checkpoint intervals to occur on a volume basis. The checkpoint happens at the point when LGWR writes a certain volume or number of redo entries to the redo log. When the capacity of the redo log reaches a certain point, the checkpoint occurs, and all the database blocks that are sitting in the dirty buffer write queue are written to the database. The process of writing data blocks in checkpoints continues on in this way. The principle behind setting checkpoint intervals to occur in this fashion is that during periods of high transaction volume, the dirty buffer write queue should be flushed more often because more changes are being made, and thus more redo log entries are being written to online redo logs. During periods of low transaction volume, fewer redo log entries will be written to online redo logs, and the LOG_CHECKPOINT_INTERVAL threshold will be crossed less frequently. As a result, there will be fewer checkpoints and fewer writes to disk. The principle of volume-based checkpoints with LOG_CHECKPOINT_INTERVAL is much the same as simply reducing the size of the online redo logs to have checkpoints occur at more frequent log switches. However, setting LOG_CHECKPOINT_INTERVAL to have checkpoints occur when threshold capacities of the redo log are exceeded offers an advantage over simply reducing the size of the redo log buffer. The additional overhead of a log switch, such as archiving the redo log, is avoided.

LOG_CHECKPOINT_INTERVAL is set as a numeric value representing the number of operating system blocks LGWR should write to the redo log after a log switch before a checkpoint should occur. This value is determined in the following way. If the DBA wants checkpoints to occur only as frequently as log switches, the value set for LOG_CHECKPOINT_INTERVAL is set to a value higher than the size of the redo log. If the DBA desires to set the LOG_CHECKPOINT_INTERVAL to effect a checkpoint at various thresholds in the writing of the current redo log, then the DBA must determine a few things. First, the DBA must divide the size of the redo log in bytes by the size of each Oracle block as specified at database creation with the DB_BLOCK_SIZE initialization parameter. Once this value is established, the DBA should then determine how frequently a checkpoint should occur between log switches, when checkpoints automatically occur. The last fact—and the fact that is most operating-system-specific—is that the DBA must find out how large the operating system blocks are for the machine hosting Oracle. After finding out the size of each operating system block, the DBA needs to figure out how many operating system blocks fit into one Oracle database block. Only when these values are obtained can the DBA specify the value for LOG_CHECKPOINT_INTERVAL using the formula in Figure 7-5.

$$\frac{\text{Size of redo log / DB\_BLOCK\_SIZE}}{\substack{\text{Desired frequency of} \\ \text{ckeckpoints between log} \\ \text{switches}}} * \substack{\text{Number of} \\ \text{operating system} \\ \text{blocks in one} \\ \text{Oracle block}}$$

FIGURE 7-5. *Use this formula to calculate checkpoint interval*

Using the formula above, assume that the DBA wants five checkpoints to occur on the database between log switches. The redo log is 1M in size, and the value set for DB_BLOCK_SIZE at database creation is 2K. Therefore, the size of the redo log in Oracle blocks is 1,024,000/2,048, or 500 blocks. Assume that the size of an operating system block in this case is 512 bytes, which is not uncommon for most UNIX environments. In this example, there are four operating system blocks in every Oracle block (2,048/512 = 4). With these values, the recommended setting according to the formula for LOG_CHECKPOINT_INTERVAL is (500/5) * 4, or *400*.

The other principle for identifying checkpoint times is the time-based checkpoint interval. Although using the volume-based checkpoint interval method fits well into the overall method of having checkpoints occur at log switches, assigning a time-based checkpoint interval is far simpler to configure. The LOG_CHECKPOINT_TIMEOUT initialization parameter is used for this configuration. The value set for LOG_CHECKPOINT_TIMEOUT is equal to the number of seconds that will transpire before another checkpoint will occur. The principle behind this method for specifying checkpoints is that the checkpoint process should occur at regular time intervals.

One concern that the DBA may have when specifying checkpoints to occur at regular intervals is that a checkpoint will always occur at the time of a log switch, whether the switch occurs at a regular time interval or not. In order to avoid a situation where a log switch causes a checkpoint to occur immediately before or after a checkpoint occurs as specified by LOG_CHECKPOINT_TIMEOUT, the DBA should try to determine the average amount of time it takes for the redo log to fill, and specify a time interval that is some fraction of that based on the number of times on average that the DBA wants a checkpoint to occur between the checkpoints that automatically occur at log switches.

To figure out the time it takes for a redo log to fill, a special file can be used. The special file used is called a trace file. Every process in the Oracle database, including all background processes and user processes, can generate a trace file that records the activities of the process. In order to determine the amount of time it takes for the transaction entries on the Oracle database to fill a redo log, the DBA can review the trace file associated with the LGWR background process to determine the time periods between log switches. To disable time-based checkpoints, the DBA should set the LOG_CHECKPOINT_TIMEOUT to zero (0).

Finally, there may be instances when the DBA wants to specify a checkpoint to occur. There are two ways to make a checkpoint occur. One is to force a log switch, and the other is to force a checkpoint. Both activities require the DBA to issue an **alter system** command. For a checkpoint to occur as part of a log switch, the option specified with the **alter system** command is **switch logfile**. For checkpoints to occur by themselves, without a log switch, the option specified with the **alter system** command is **checkpoint**. In this case, as in the case of any checkpoint that occurs without a corresponding log switch, that checkpoint is referred to as a *fast* checkpoint, while any checkpoint that involves a log switch is called a *full* (or *complete*) checkpoint.

Exercises

1. What is a checkpoint? When do checkpoints always occur?

2. What are two principles on which the DBA can specify more frequent checkpoints to occur regularly on the database? What parameters are used in this process?

3. What are two ways the DBA can force a checkpoint to occur?

4. How does the DBA configure the database to have checkpoints only at log switches?

Data Concurrency and Statement-level Read Consistency

Data concurrency and statement-level read consistency are provided by Oracle transaction processing. A transaction is a group of data change statements that are grouped together in a database designed to meet these needs. For example, imagine the storage of an invoice in a database. The invoice itself that contains the name and address of the purchaser, the total dollar amount, and the person's charge account number are stored on one table, while an itemized breakdown of goods purchased is stored on another. Figure 7-6 illustrates this configuration. The figure displays a typical parent-child table relationship used to map a one-to-many relationship of invoices to elements of the invoice.

Say, for example, that there is a user that must eliminate invoice #2 from the system. She issues the following statement to eliminate the data from INVOICE_ELEMENT. This is all well and good, except that if other users come into this process, they might think there was a problem with invoice #2 and attempt to add in the invoice elements again before the first user could issue the **delete** of invoice #2 from the INVOICE table.

```
DELETE FROM invoice_element
WHERE inv# = 2;
```

The concept of transaction processing can eliminate this problem. Just as the data in both tables is considered to be components in one logical object—namely an invoice—the removal of information from two tables of

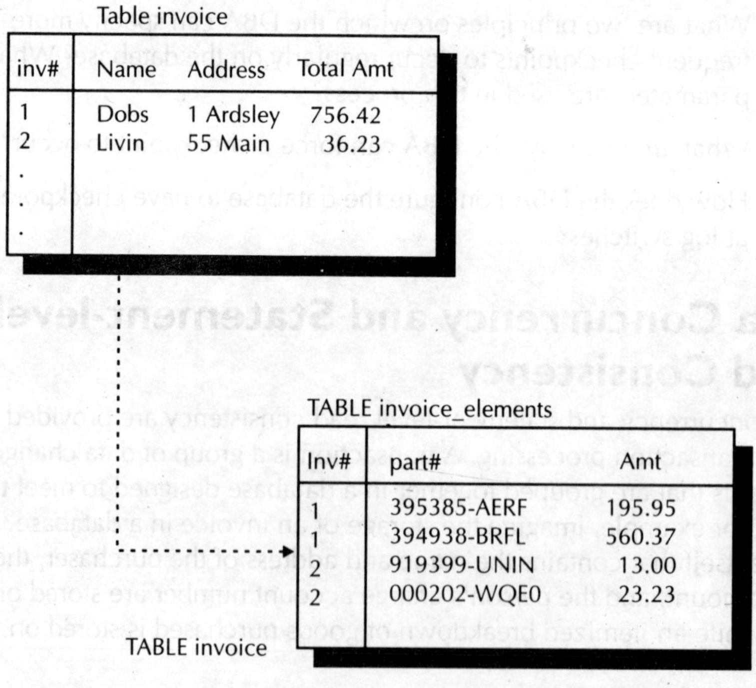

Table invoice

inv#	Name	Address	Total Amt
1	Dobs	1 Ardsley	756.42
2	Livin	55 Main	36.23

TABLE invoice_elements

Inv#	part#	Amt
1	395385-AERF	195.95
1	394938-BRFL	560.37
2	919399-UNIN	13.00
2	000202-WQE0	23.23

TABLE invoice

FIGURE 7-6. *When two tables represent one logical data object*

that logical object should also be treated logically as one act. This act can be called a transaction. Consider the following pseudocode:

```
"BEGIN TRANSACTION"

DELETE FROM invoice_element
WHERE inv# = 2;

DELETE FROM invoice
WHERE inv# = 2;

"END TRANSACTION;"
```

In this situation, the act of deleting from two tables is considered one event, or a transaction. The beginning of the transaction may consist of some mechanism ensuring that no other user may change this data, or perhaps even view the data, before the transaction is complete. The mechanism used for this act in place of a generic "**begin transaction**," is a *lock*. The process listed above may acquire a lock on the rows or the table before the **delete** commands are issued in order to prevent a misunderstanding over the status of the data.

The second point to be made here is that at any point during the transaction, the changes made can be discarded in favor of the way the data looked before the transaction began. *Oracle does not save the changes made by any changes to the database immediately.* Instead, the changes are marked as made, but the option is given to discard them until such point when the user issues a command to explicitly save the changes to the database. The mechanism through which Oracle explicitly saves data changes is called a **commit**, while the mechanism through which Oracle discards a data change is called a **rollback**. There is an associated concept in committing and rolling back transactions called a **savepoint**, whereby a transaction can be divided into portions for the purpose of committing or rolling back only part of a transaction at a time.

Transactions function as the cornerstone of data concurrency. In concurrent data change environments, locks and the **commit** and **rollback** statements provide the mechanisms necessary to allow for the logical grouping of database change activities that are transactions. With the concept of a transaction in place, the user is then able to earmark data for their exclusive access and change, and also may decide when the changes they make are finished and therefore ready for viewing by the rest of the system.

The final area of discussion concerns rollback segments and the idea of read consistency. By default, when a statement executes, Oracle ensures that the data viewed, retrieved, and changed by the statement will be consistent from the time the statement starts to the time the statement finishes. This is called *statement-level read consistency*. The same ability must exist at the transaction level in order to have multiple statements that can be made into components of some other atomic data operation. Recalling the earlier example, say that there are transactions on the system that are operating on the basis that invoice #2 exists on the database. During the course of activity in those other transactions, some records are written to other areas of the system that require data from those rows associated with invoice #2. Meanwhile, the user from before is on the system, and is currently running a transaction deleting invoice #2. In this situation, the user deleting invoice #2 may **commit** her transaction before the other users using invoice #2 data **commit** their own transactions. However, even though the data deletion is saved to the database, it still must exist somewhere for the transactions operating on the assumption that the rows corresponding to invoice #2 exist to have *transaction-level read consistency*. This read consistency at the transaction level is provided by a disk resource on the Oracle database called a rollback segment. The rollback segment holds a record of all uncommitted transactions and changes in the process of committing in order for other statements to rely on a read-consistent view of database. The locking mechanisms, commits, rollbacks, and the rollback segment disk resource all combine to make transactions possible on the Oracle database, which in turn allows for data concurrency and statement and transaction-level read consistency within and between transactions.

Exercises

1. What are some of the problems inherent in making data changes on systems with many users?

2. What is a transaction? What mechanisms make it possible to have transactions on the Oracle database?

3. Explain the function of each mechanism Oracle provides for transaction processing.

4. Explain how rollback segments make statement- and transaction-level read consistency possible in the Oracle database.

Managing the Database Structure

In this section, you will cover the following topics related to managing the database structure:

- Database storage allocation

- Customizing the database structure

- Preparing necessary tablespaces

- The different types of segments

With the discussion of how data is changed in the Oracle database, the DBA should turn attention to understanding how data is stored in the Oracle database. The various ways disk resources can be viewed in the Oracle architecture were introduced as part of the last chapter. Those two views are the logical view and the physical view. The physical view of the database consists of the physical files, such as datafiles, parameter files, control files and redo log files, that house Oracle data in Oracle-readable formats. The logical view of disk resources is the perspective of the logical objects being stored. Some examples of these objects are segments and extents that comprise tables, indexes, and rollback segments. Another logical database object that is available for data storage is the tablespace. Each of these logical objects corresponds in some way to a physical object. For example, the tablespace—a logical disk resource—consists of one or more datafiles that store tablespace data on disk. Other examples are the segments and extents that hold table data. Each segment and extent consists of data blocks that store table, index, or rollback segment data. The blocks, then, are components of the physical datafiles that store the segments and extents of a tablespace. A full treatment of these items appears in this section.

Database Storage Allocation

Each database has space allocated to it for storage. That space is determined either in the **create database** statement for datafiles and redo logs or in **alter database** where new datafiles or redo logs are created. Additionally, the objects in a database have space allocated to them for storage, too, as part of the **create** *object* or **alter** *object* statement that brings the object into being. The size of an object or file is specified either in kilobytes or megabytes. Storage allocation in Oracle has an underlying concept or idea. The idea is that Oracle simply allocates large blocks of a machine resource like memory or disk space, and deals with management of the utilization of that resource within the architecture of the Oracle database later. This design feature empowers the DBA in many ways, and also empowers the Oracle system in many ways. By simply obtaining large blocks of system resource from the machine when a database is created, Oracle minimizes its dependency on any particular operating system or machine configuration and sticks with some basic features that all machines provide, like memory, disk space, and processing power. All the rest of the resource management is handled by Oracle. In addition, Oracle avoids the "nickel and dime" effect of continuous creeping growth by getting all the space it needs for the database or an object within it, then filling that space as needed.

Logical database objects like tables and indexes generally reside within physical database objects like datafiles. Their existence and utilization are managed more directly by the Oracle architecture. As such, logical database objects generally have more extensive storage parameters for DBAs to configure and tune the objects in ways that allow applications to use the disk resources effectively. Some of the areas that can be configured in a logical database resource include the following:

- The maximum growth size of the object

- Space management within the data block

- Segment/extent allocation for the database object

- How Oracle manages free space in the object

- Default parameters for objects created within a tablespace

The basic object of storage within the logical disk resource usage architecture is the *data block*. Blocks are collected into segments, which can be used to build tables, indexes, and rollback segments. When the data stored in a table exceeds that capacity of the underlying segment that houses the table, the table can obtain additional data blocks collected into a logical storage object called an extent. Segments and extents that house data blocks storing table, index, and rollback segment data are collectively stored in tablespaces, which are the largest logical units of data storage on the Oracle database.

Exercises

1. Identify an underlying principle in the way Oracle allocates space. What are the types of things related to storage allocation that Oracle allows the DBA to manage?

2. What is a data block?

Customizing the Database Structure

The Oracle database offers a great deal of flexibility in how it can be configured in order to meet the storage needs of nearly every organization. There are some fundamental concepts behind customization on the database that the soon-to-be DBA must understand. Every Oracle database consists of several components. The first part that every Oracle database consists of is a host machine. Ultimately, it is the hardware constraints of the system running Oracle that will largely determine what the Oracle database is capable of handling. For example, a machine with only one hard drive with 2 gigabytes of space will not store a 10G database, no matter how well tuned the Oracle instance may be. Basic elements of customizing the Oracle database to meet the needs of the organization using Oracle begin with the customization of the hardware running Oracle. Some elements on a hardware platform that could be customized include the following:

- Available memory on the system, including cache memory
- Number of processors, or CPUs, on the machine hosting Oracle

■ Number of disk drives available on the machine

■ Offline storage capability; for example, tape drives or optical drives

While it is true that every machine hosting an Oracle database should have the above components available, the quality and/or quantity of devices of each type offers ample opportunity for customization. Of particular interest to most DBAs should be the number of available CPUs and disk drives on the machine hosting Oracle, as well as the available memory on the system. The daily production performance of the Oracle database depends heavily on each of these components being powerful and, if possible, plentiful. Much of the DBA's initial work on database installation and customization involves determining how to fit Oracle's need for fast, noncontentious access to its disk resources around the reality of the available drives on the hardware that hosts Oracle. Within reason, more is better in this area of customization.

Of great importance are the offline storage devices that will assist the DBA and/or system administrator in backing up and recovering the Oracle database. Although the performance offered by the world's greatest tape drive may not be noticed by the vast majority of users of the Oracle system in day-to-day production life, everyone will notice how slow the recovery is coming as a result of a poor choice in this department the day a disk drive crashes on the database. The recoverability of the Oracle database is the ultimate test of how well an organization can withstand its own need for electronic storage and retrieval of its mission-critical data. Besides, as in most support roles, the DBA gets no notice when everything related to the database runs smoothly. Superhuman recovery in emergency situations, however, is expected of every DBA, and nothing less.

Once a good machine with multiple processors to speed user access and multiple disk drives to prevent excessive dependence on any one drive is purchased, the DBA customizes the Oracle database around the hardware reality of its host machine. There is an entire school of thought on the physical layout of any Oracle database and its relationship to the performance of the Oracle database. Much of that school of thought appears on OCP Exam 4, Performance Tuning. For now, the DBA should be aware of the fact that having multiple disk drives available on the database means that the DBA should place each physical object—namely datafiles, redo logs, control files, parameter files, application software, archive log destination, and EXPORT dump destination—in such a way as to minimize the possibility that a failure of any one drive causes the failure of the entire database.

Proper use of the redo logs is key to the success of database recovery, as well as the performance of the database when recovery is not taking place. Loss of a drive that holds the only redo log for the database is a problem when a drive holding production data fails later. As mentioned before, mirroring redo information can spare the database the risks associated with no backups.

If possible, depending on the availability of multiple disk drives, the DBA may also want to store multiple copies of the control files and parameter files to minimize the risk of these important physical disk resources being lost by the failure of a disk drive on the database. Oracle recommends that the DBA maintain at least two control files for every Oracle database because loss of a sole control file or parameter file means that the instance will be unable to start. Having a copy of the control file and parameter file on different disks available to the database will minimize the possibility that any one disk failure will kill the system. A duplicate copy of the parameter file can be created with the use of operating system commands for copying flat files. To create additional control files for the database, the DBA can execute the following steps:

1. Shut down the database instance.

2. Copy the control file to another location (preferably on another disk).

3. Modify the CONTROL_FILES initialization parameter in **init.ora** to reflect the existence of the second control file.

4. Restart the instance. Oracle will now maintain two copies of the control file.

Finally, in terms of preserving backups in any database backup situation, it is important that the DBA copy any and all backups made to the backup disk destination off the machine entirely. This idea of backing up the database to offline storage media allows the DBA the peace of mind of knowing that the database is recoverable even if the entire machine fails. Making copies of backup media will also ensure a reduced dependency on any particular backup for the success of database recovery.

After these physical considerations related to failure, backup, and recovery are made, there are other aspects of database usage of its hardware that the DBA can address to achieve better performance. These are areas for customization of the database as well. A discussion of this area of customization must be prefaced with a discussion of efficient usage of *logical* database resources in light of constraints on *physical* resources.

Exercises

1. What are some of the hardware issues related to customizing the Oracle database structure?

2. What steps are required to create an additional control file on the database?

Preparing Necessary Tablespaces

With the idea that logical database structures can and should be built on the constraints of physical resources, the following discussion is offered on how to identify and prepare the logical storage components of the Oracle database.

When an Oracle database is installed, one tablespace is created to store a few logical database objects that Oracle needs to function. Those objects are the initial rollback segment of the database and all data dictionary objects for the database. This tablespace is called SYSTEM, and it is an incredibly important resource on the database, and its integrity on the system should be guarded carefully. As with any tablespace, the SYSTEM tablespace can contain any type of segment or extent used for any database object created. However, to put every database object that the database applications will use in the SYSTEM tablespace leaves the objects that *must* be in that tablespace vulnerable to storage needs, caused by the presence of those other objects. It is important to remember that if any damage should come to the SYSTEM tablespace, the database will need to be recovered.

By taking database objects and placing them in other databases designed to fit their storage needs, the DBA prevents the possibility of headaches related to storage needs. One of the first tasks the DBA should plan is how to store database objects like indexes, tables, temporary tablespaces, and rollback tablespaces. Each of these objects presents different needs that will be discussed in a moment. At this point, it is sufficient to say that these different types of database objects do exist, and that their storage needs are different. Therefore, the DBA should create appropriate tablespaces for each of these objects. A tablespace is created with the following command on the Oracle database:

```
CREATE TABLESPACE temp_01
DATAFILE 'db01_temp01.dbf' SIZE 10M
DEFAULT STORAGE (
INITIAL 100K NEXT 100K
MINEXTENTS 1 MAXEXTENTS 450
PCTINCREASE 10 )
ONLINE;
```

Notice that in the definition of the logical tablespace resource, there is a specification of a physical resource for that tablespace, a datafile. A size value is provided at tablespace creation as well, which specifies the total size of that tablespace. Additionally, there are default storage parameters associated with the tablespace. These default storage parameters are used for each database object that is placed in the tablespace that does not have storage parameters set explicitly by the database object **create** statement. When identifying default storage parameters for a tablespace, the DBA should attempt to set parameters that work well for a certain type of database object, and then within that type of object, the parameters set will be general guidelines for storage allocation.

Exercises

1. What tablespace is created with every Oracle database?

2. What storage parameters are set when a tablespace is created? What purpose do these parameters serve?

The Different Types of Segments

The DBA must recognize that different types of objects need different types of tablespaces to fit them. In order to understand the different types of tablespaces, the DBA must understand the different types of objects that a tablespace may store. Since every logical database object used by a database application will ultimately consist of segments and extents, the discussion will focus on the different types of segments available on the Oracle database.

The first, and perhaps most obvious, type of segment is the table segment. Table segments store data from tables. Each segment contains data blocks that store the row data for that table. How the data in a table fills is determined most closely by the type of role the data in that table will support. For example, if a table supports an application that accepts large volumes of data insertions, then the segments, extents, and blocks that comprise that table will fill at a regular pace and rarely, if ever, reduce in size. Therefore, the DBA managing that segment will want to create a structure that is conducive to regular growth, paying attention to the ever-increasing space requirements of that system. In this case, the DBA will want to pay attention to how the table will handle growth. Growth in a data segment is generally handled with extents. If the segment runs out of space to handle the size of the table, then the table will acquire an extent from the remaining free space in the tablespace. If, however, this table is designed for storing validation data, then the size requirements of the table may be a bit more static. In this case, the DBA may want to focus more on ensuring that the entire table fits comfortably into one segment, thus reducing the potential fragmentation that extent allocation may cause. A more complete discussion on extents and fragmentation will appear later in the chapter.

Another type of segment is the index segment. Similar to table segments, index segments can be classified according to the type of role they support in the database. If the table to which the index is associated is designed for volume transactions, as in the example above, then the index, too, should be planned for growth. By nature, the index will be smaller than the database. What does an index consist of, exactly? The standard types of indexes available on Oracle databases prior to Oracle8 are binary search tree, or B-tree, indexes and bitmap indexes. Indexes are much smaller than the tables they provide location data for, but the principles behind their growth are the same. If an index is associated with a validation table, then the size of the index may be relatively static.

Rollback segments offer a bit of a departure from the types of segments just discussed. The purpose of a rollback segment is to store change data from uncommitted transactions for the purpose of read consistency and transaction concurrency. In the previous two examples, the segments used to store data for tables and indexes are generally for one-time use. In other words, unless the data is deleted from the table, the storage allocated to the table will never be reused. In contrast, once a user process has written the changes it intends to make and commits the transaction, the space the uncommitted transaction information held in a rollback segment is no longer needed to hold that data. Oracle's rollback segment architecture is designed to allow the rollback segment to reuse that space at a later time. A rollback segment may have a few extents allocated to it in order to store uncommitted transactions. As the number of uncommitted transactions rises and falls; so, too, does the number of extents allocated to the rollback segment. Where possible, the rollback segment will try to place uncommitted transaction data into segments and extents allocated to it. For example, if the entire initial extent of a rollback segment contains data from committed transactions, the rollback segment will reuse that extent to store new data from uncommitted transactions.

Another type of segment available in the Oracle architecture is the cluster segment. Cluster segments are designed to support the use of clusters on the database. A cluster is a physical grouping of two or more tables around a common index. This grouping is done to enhance performance on searches that perform joins on the two tables. Sizing of cluster segments should be performed carefully, as each segment will essentially be storing data from two different tables in each block. A more complete discussion of cluster segments will appear in the next chapter.

The final type of segment to consider is the temporary segment. True to its name, the temporary segment is allocated to store temporary data for a user transaction that cannot all be stored in memory. One popular use for temporary segments in user processes is for sorting data selected into a requested order. These segments are allocated on the fly, and dismissed when their services are no longer required. Their space requirement is marked by short periods of high storage needs followed by periods of no storage need.

Each of these segment types presents very different, and often conflicting, storage needs on a tablespace that might house them. At this point, the DBA should understand why it is a bad idea to place all database objects in the SYSTEM tablespace. Instead, the DBA should create different tablespaces designed to hold each of the various types of segments and extents so as to keep them separated from one another and also to allow for storage allocation for each type that is appropriate for the needs of each type of segment.

Exercises

1. Identify four types of segments available to store database objects.

2. Why is it important not to put all database objects in the SYSTEM tablespace?

3. Should different types of database segments be stored in the same tablespace or in different tablespaces? Why or why not?

Managing Storage Allocation

In this section, you will cover the following topics related to managing storage allocation:

- Allocating extents to database objects
- Database storage allocation parameters
- Using space utilization parameters
- Displaying database storage information

Storage allocation is an ongoing maintenance task in the Oracle database. Tables and indexes will grow, and more space will be required to store them. The ongoing nature of storage allocation is the topic of the final areas of discussion in this chapter. Once the physical storage requirements of a system are determined in the configuration of physical database disk resources like datafiles and redo logs, the remaining maintenance activity is to allocate additional storage space to the logical structures, such as adding datafiles to tablespaces or obtaining extents for tables, indexes, or rollback segments.

Allocating Extents to Database Objects

Database objects are stored in segments of finite size. As new rows are added to tables, the space of the segment is used to store that new data. After some time, the segment will fill. At the time a new piece of data must be added to the table, if the segment storing the table data is full, the table

must allocate a new extent to store that data in. Figure 7-7 illustrates the
situation where extents are acquired on an Oracle database. When an
object requires a new extent, the size of the space obtained for the database
object depends on the storage parameters set for the database object or for
the tablespace containing the object. For reference, those parameters are
listed in the next discussion.

A new extent will be acquired for a database object only if there is no
room in any of the current extents for the data being inserted or updated.
Once acquired, an extent is never relinquished unless the DBA reorganizes
the table manually with the use of database tools like EXPORT, and
re-creates the object with only one extent. Oracle bases the size of the
extent on the value in the **next** clause if there is only one extent on the
database. If Oracle is getting ready to acquire a third extent or more, the size
of the extent will be the value of the **next** clause times the value specified
for the **pctincrease** clause. If the DBA would like to specify a different size

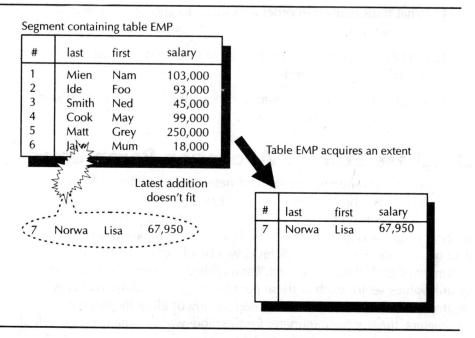

FIGURE 7-7. *Acquiring extents*

for an extent than the one that will be calculated, the DBA can issue the **alter** *object* statement to change the value specified for the **next** storage clause, substituting *object* with the name of the database object in question. The **next** clause informs Oracle of the size it should use for the next extent it allocates. Another way the DBA can manipulate the size of the next extent allocated is to change the **pctincrease** clause. This clause will change the percentage increase of the next extent over the size of the last one created when a new extent is issued.

```
ALTER TABLE employee
STORAGE (NEXT 10M);

ALTER TABLE employee
STORAGE (PCTINCREASE 50);
```

Exercises

1. What must happen in order for Oracle to allocate an extent to a database object?

2. On what parameters does the size of the extent allocated to a database object depend?

3. What statement can be used to change the size of the next extent allocated to a database object?

Database Storage Allocation Parameters

There are several different storage parameters associated with logical database objects. These parameters are associated with how the object manages segments and extents. Other parameters that can be set relating to specific database objects that deal with how the database object manages data on the more granular block level will be discussed later in the treatment of each database object. Each tablespace can be created with default values set for each of these parameters. If a database object is created with no value explicitly named for any or all of the storage parameters, the storage parameter for the table will be whatever the default value for that parameter was in the tablespace.

initial	Segment storage clause that determines the size (either in kilobytes or megabytes as determined by specifying K or M) of the initial extent comprising the database object.
next	Segment storage clause that determines the size (either in kilobytes or megabytes as determined by specifying K or M) of the second extent comprising the database object.
miniextents	Segment storage clause that determines the minimum number of extents a database object may have.
maxextents	Segment storage clause that determines the maximum number of extents a database object may have. A special keyword **unlimited** can be used to allow **unlimited** number of extents on the object.
pctincrease	Segment storage clause that specifies the permitted percentage of growth of each subsequent extent allocated to the database object. For example, if a table is created with **initial** 1M, **next** 1M, **minextents** 2 and **pctincrease** 20 storage clauses, the third extent created for this object will be 1.2M in size, the fourth will be 1.44M in size, etc. Oracle rounds up to the nearest block when use of this option identifies an extent size that is not measurable in whole blocks. The default value for this option is 50 percent. **Note: This option is NOT available for rollback segment creation.**
optimal	Segment storage clause that specifies the optimal number of extents that should be available to the rollback segment. **Note: This is ONLY available for rollback segment creation.**

freelists	Database object storage clause that specifies the number of lists in each freelist group that Oracle will maintain of blocks considered "free" for the table. A free block is one that either has not reached its **pctfree** threshold or fallen below its **pctused** threshold. A more complete discussion of **pctfree** and **pctused** will appear in the next chapter.
freelist groups	Database object storage clause that specifies the number of groups of freelists for database objects that Oracle will maintain in order to know which blocks have space available for row storage. *Note: This is available for Parallel Server Option usage.*

One critical way the DBA can limit the space usage of a particular database object is to restrict the number of extents a database object may allocate. For example, if a database object can only allocate a maximum number of 20 extents, chances are more favorable that the object will not go over its size limit than if the database object can allocate a maximum number of 100 extents. Another possibility for limiting space usage is to set tablespace default storage parameters to certain values, and use those default values for every object created in the tablespace by not specifying explicit storage parameter values in the object creation statement. This method allows for consolidation of all values specified for storage, and also allows the DBA to set standards in database object space allocation.

The best approach for designing storage accommodations on a database object is to have larger and fewer segments and extents available for a database object to use. There is some overhead involved in allocating extents that can be minimized if the frequency that a database object will need to extend is minimized. When the extents are larger, Oracle will be able to place more data in them, thus reducing the need to extend. Frequent allocation and deallocation of extents also has the tendency to fragment a tablespace, which can cause problems for the DBA when a tablespace requires reorganization. Although there are tools available for this task, it is time-consuming. Ultimately, larger extents are easier to manage.

A final area of space management that can be used to limit the amount of space allocated to the database object is limiting the percentage increase for each extent allocated to the database object. Specifying a percentage increase for each additional extent has positive effects and negative effects in reducing the maintenance burden of database object storage management. Consider the following example of using percentage increases for storage management. Table EMP has been created with a percentage increase of 50 percent on each extent allocated to it. The first extent is 1M, which fills quickly as employees are added to the company. The next extent is 1.5M. If the rate at which records are added to the database stays constant, it will take longer for the second extent to fill than it took the first extent. Each extent allocated will be 50 percent larger than the extent allocated before it, so the third extent will have 2.25M allocated to it, which takes even less time to fill. The benefit of specifying a percentage increase in this situation is that fewer extents are allocated to store 4.75M of data (three) by specifying the percentage increase. If no percentage increase had been permitted, the same data would have required five extents.

However, consider the following situation. The size of EMP has stabilized, with only a few rows needing to be added monthly. The size of the table has reached the 4.75M capacity of the three extents, but only a few more rows need to be added. With the percentage increase specified for each extent allocated, the next extent will be 3.375M. However, most of that space will be empty, as only a few rows will occupy that final extent allocated to the table. In some cases, specifying a percentage increase can cause too much space to be allocated to a database object. Of course, the only way a DBA could know that the high percentage increase was no longer necessary would be to carefully monitor the database tables to determine growth patterns and adjust values accordingly. In fact, careful monitoring is the only way a DBA can effectively manage the storage allocation in a database.

Each parameter above can be used by the DBA to manage the usage of a database's available space. One critical way the DBA can limit the space usage of a particular database object is to restrict the number of extents a database object may allocate. For example, if a database object can only allocate a maximum number of 20 extents, chances are more favorable that the object will not go over a certain size than if the database object can allocate a maximum number of 100 extents.

Another possibility for limiting space usage is to set tablespace default storage parameters to certain values, and use those default values for every object created in the tablespace by not specifying explicit storage parameter values in the object creation statement. This method allows for consolidation of all values specified for storage, and also allows the DBA to set standards in database object space allocation.

Exercises

1. Name the storage parameters that determine the number of extents that will be allocated for an object.

2. Name the storage parameters that determine the size of extents allocated for an object.

3. How can the DBA alter the size of the next extent allocated for a database object?

Using Space Utilization Parameters

The DBA should not only be concerned about the amount of space granted to a database object. The DBA must pay attention to see that the objects use the space they are given in an appropriate manner. Space usage is determined at the block level through use of the **pctfree** and **pctused** options. The appropriate manner for a database object to manage its space depends on how the object itself is utilized by the database applications. If the database object experiences a high update transaction volume that changes many fields from NULL to actual values, the storage within that database object should allow for additional growth per row. Conversely, if the object activity is marked by high insert volume of fairly static length rows, then the space usage within each block may try to place as many rows as possible into each block before allocating another one to fill. Finally, if a table's size is static and rows are infrequently added to the table, then the DBA may want to consider setting options for block space usage to put as many rows as possible in each block while also making sure that the entire table fits into one segment.

The **pctfree** option is used to specify the amount of space in each block Oracle should leave free for the growth of rows added to the block. For example, if a table has **pctfree** specified to be 10 percent, then Oracle will stop adding new rows to the block when there is only about 10 percent free space left in the block. A DBA may set this value high if it is determined that each row in the block will be updated often and each **update** will add several bytes to the total row length. Setting **pctfree** high prevents performance killers like chaining (where Oracle breaks a row apart because no data block can store the entire row) and row migration (where Oracle moves an entire row to another block because the original block doesn't have the room to store it anymore). Conversely, if the rows in the block will not be updated frequently, or if the updates that will occur will not affect the size of each row, the DBA may set the value for **pctfree** low on that database object.

The **pctused** option is used to specify a threshold by which Oracle will determine if it is acceptable to start adding rows to a block again. As data is deleted from a table, its space utilization may fall. There is a trade-off inherent in specifying this option because although it is good to utilize free space in a block to add row data, there is some overhead involved in marking a block as free and adding it to a freelist for that database object, especially if only one or two rows can even be added to the block. In many cases, the DBA may want it so that any block added to the freelist will have space available for 20 or more rows. In which case, the DBA will set the **pctused** option low. There are other performance trade-offs inherent in the use of **pctfree** and **pctused** that will be discussed in the next chapter.

Exercises

1. How is space usage within data blocks managed?

2. What are chaining and row migration? Which parameter should be set in order to prevent them from occurring? How should that parameter be set?

Displaying Database Storage Information

Several means exist for the DBA to determine storage information for database objects in the database. These methods center around the use of the data dictionary. There are three different classifications for data dictionary views associated with tracking information on logical database objects like tables, indexes, clusters, rollback segments, and temporary tables. The names of dictionary views are usually taken from the objects represented by the data in the dictionary view, preceded by classification on the scope of the data. Each segment has its own data dictionary view that displays the storage information. Assuming that the DBA wants to know the storage parameters set for all objects on the database, the DBA may use the following views to determine storage information for the segment types already discussed:

- **DBA_TABLES**   View contains information about all tables in the database.

- **DBA_INDEXES**   View contains information about all indexes in the database.

- **DBA_ROLLBACK_SEGS**   View contains information about all rollback segments in the database.

- **DBA_CLUSTERS**   View contains information about all clusters in the database.

- **DBA_SEGMENTS**   This summary view contains all types of segments listed by the data dictionary views above and their storage parameters.

- **DBA_TABLESPACES**   The DBA can use this view to see the default storage settings for the tablespaces in the database.

- **DBA_TS_QUOTAS**   The DBA can use this view to identify the tablespace quotas assigned for users to create objects in their default and temporary tablespaces.

Exercises

1. What dictionary view can be used to identify storage allocation for tables and indexes?

2. What dictionary view will tell the DBA the default settings for database objects in a tablespace?

3. What dictionary view tells the DBA the quotas for space on tablespaces each user has?

Chapter Summary

This chapter covered a great deal of information related to database administration on Oracle. The topics covered at a glance were how Oracle supports the accessing and updating of data, how Oracle manages transaction concurrency, how the DBA manages database structure, and how the DBA manages storage allocation. These areas consist of 22 percent of material tested on OCP Exam 2 and are key functions for understanding both how the Oracle database works and how to manage its efforts.

Accessing and updating data was the first area covered. Oracle allows users to access and change data via the SQL language. SQL is a unique language in that it allows users to define the data they want in terms of what they are looking for, not in terms of a procedure to obtain the data. Oracle manages the obtaining of data by translating SQL into a series of procedures Oracle will execute to fetch the data the user requested. The steps Oracle uses in SQL statement processing are opening the statement cursor, which is a memory address Oracle will use for storing the statement operation; parsing the statement into a series of data operations; binding variables in place of hard-coded values to allow for parse tree sharing; executing the statement; and fetching the results (query only). After the statement is executed, the parse information is left behind in the library cache of the shared pool in order to reduce the amount of memory required to handle user processes and also to boost performance of SQL statement processing.

In order to further boost performance, Oracle maintains an area of the SGA called the buffer cache, which is used to store data blocks containing rows from recently executed SQL statements. Part of this buffer cache contains an area called the dirty buffer write queue, which is a list of blocks containing row data that has been changed and needs to be written to disk. When users issue statements that require Oracle to retrieve data from disk, obtaining that data is handled by the server process. Another database process, DBWR, eliminates I/O contention on the database by freeing user processes from having to perform disk writes associated with the changes they make. Since users only deal directly with blocks that are in the buffer cache, they experience good performance while the server and DBWR processes handle all disk utilization behind the scenes.

The server process does its job whenever user processes need more blocks brought into the cache. In order to make room for the incoming data, the server process eliminates blocks from the buffer cache according to which ones were used least recently. One exception to this rule is made for blocks that were brought into the buffer cache to support full table scans. These buffers are eliminated almost immediately after they are scanned. The DBWR process will write buffers back to the database when triggered to do so by another process, called LGWR, during a special database event called a checkpoint. DBWR also writes data to the database every three seconds in a timeout.

Oracle handles the tracking of changes in the database through the use of the online redo log. There are several components to the online redo log. The first is an area in memory where user processes place the redo log entries they have to make when they write a change to the database. This area is called the redo log buffer. Another component of the online redo log is a set of files on disk that store the redo log entries. This is the actual "online redo log" portion of the architecture. There is a minimum of two online redo logs in the Oracle database. They consist of one or more files, called "members," that contain the entire contents of the redo log. For safety purposes, it is best to put each redo log member on a separate disk so as to avoid the failure of one disk causing the failure of an entire Oracle instance. The final component of the online redo log is the log writer process (LGWR), a background process mechanism that writes redo entries from the memory buffer to the online redo log.

The use of checkpoints has already been mentioned, and will now be explained. A checkpoint is performed every time LGWR fills an online redo log with redo entries and has to switch to writing entries to another redo log. A checkpoint is when LGWR sends a signal to DBWR to write all changed data blocks in the dirty buffer write queue out to their respective datafiles on disk. By default, checkpoints happen once every log switch, but can happen more often, depending on the values set for LOG_CHECKPOINT_INTERVAL or LOG_CHECKPOINT_TIMEOUT. These two parameters allow for transaction volume-based or time-based checkpoint intervals.

In multiple-user environments, it must be remembered that there are special considerations required to ensure that users don't overwrite others' changes on the database. In addition, users must also be able to have read-consistent views of the data, both for individual statements and for collections of statements treated as one operation. The key to transaction concurrency without overwriting another user's changes is the concept of transaction processing. Transactions are made possible in the Oracle database with the use of mechanisms that allow one and only one user at a time to make a change to a database table. These mechanisms are called locks. In addition, when the user makes a change to the database, that change isn't recorded on disk right away. Instead, the change is noted in a database object called a rollback segment. This mechanism allows the user to make a series of changes to the database and save or commit them once as one unit of work. Another feature this architecture allows for is the ability to discard the changes made in favor of the way the data used to look. This act is called a rollback. The rollback segment allows for read-consistent views of the data on the database at the transaction level.

Database structure was another aspect of OCP Exam 2 this chapter covered. There is a physical and a logical view of the database. The physical structure permits the database to grow to a certain size, while the logical structure regulates its setup. Storage is governed by parameters set at object creation. These parameters can be changed at various points in the maintenance of the object. Storage allocation should work around the reality of the physical database design in that the DBA should attempt to place objects over several disks to better utilize the physical resources available to Oracle.

At database creation, Oracle creates a special tablespace called SYSTEM to hold the data dictionary and the initial rollback segment of the database. There are several different types of segments on the database that correspond to the various types of database objects. Some examples are tables, indexes, rollback segments, clusters, and temporary segments. For the most part, these objects have different storage needs, and as such it is usually best for them to be in separate tablespaces.

When the data in a database object grows too large for the segment to store all the data, Oracle must acquire another extent for the object. The size of the initial extent, the acquired extent, the number of extents allowed, and possible percentage increases for each extent of an object are all governed by the use of storage parameters. Another aspect of database usage that is governed by storage parameters is how the data in each data block owned by the object will be stored. In order to find out the storage parameters and the overall space usage for a database object, the DBA can utilize several views in the data dictionary.

Two-Minute Drill

- The steps in SQL statement processing are as follows:

  - Open cursor in the shared pool library cache and create a private SQL area in PGA.

  - Parse statement into an execution plan.

  - Bind variables (**select** only).

  - Execute statement execution plan.

  - Fetch values from cursor (**select** only).

  - Leave execution plan available in shared pool library cache.

- The shared SQL area, in the library cache of the SGA's shared pool, has the following benefits:

  - Improves performance of subsequent executions of the same query by saving the previous work of developing an execution plan.

  - Saves space in memory by not storing duplicate execution plans.

- Oracle's buffer cache allows user processes to avoid I/O processing entirely by working off data contained in the buffer cache.

- The buffer cache contains blocks selected or changed in recent SQL statements.

- The server process reads data into the buffer cache when user processes request the data. When a block enters the cache, it will stay in the cache for as long as its data is recently used.

- Blocks in the buffer cache that contain changed row data are stored in the dirty buffer write queue.

- Blocks that are least recently used, or blocks read into the buffer cache as a result of full table scans, are eliminated from the buffer cache.

- Blocks are read into the buffer cache by the server process.

- The server process draws blocks into the cache whenever they are required by user processes.

- DBWR writes changed blocks out of the dirty buffer write queue whenever LGWR issues a checkpoint. The event of LGWR telling DBWR to write blocks out of the dirty buffer write queue and onto disk is called a checkpoint.

- DBWR also writes dirty blocks to disk every three seconds in an event called a timeout.

- The Oracle redo log architecture consists of the following components:

  - The LGWR process moves redo entries from memory onto disk.

  - The redo memory buffer stores redo entries from user processes, eliminating the need for user processes to handle I/O directly.

  - The online redo log is a group of one or more files, called members, where LGWR writes the redo log entries from memory. There are at least two online redo logs in the Oracle instance.

- Checkpoints are events in which LGWR tells DBWR to write all changed blocks to disk.

- Oracle handles data concurrency and statement- and transaction-level read consistency by using transaction processing.

- Components of transaction processing are as follows:

  - *Locks.* These prevent more than one user process from making data changes, and sometimes from even looking at changing data, at one time.

  - *The rollback segment architecture.* This architecture allows a user to determine when the changes they have made are acceptable for saving. A **commit** saves data changes, while a **rollback** discards data changes.

- Database storage allocation is handled in physical disk resource creation and logical disk resource creation.

- Physical database disk resources are as follows:

  - Datafiles
  - Redo log files
  - Control files
  - Parameter files
  - Data blocks

- Logical database disk resources are as follows:

  - Tablespaces
  - Segments
  - Extents

- The DBA can work around resource conflicts and improve performance with the right hardware available.

- It is important to customize a database around the need for good backups.

- The DBA should ensure that the redo log is adequately mirrored, or spread across disks so as to minimize the dependency of Oracle on any one disk on the machine hosting it.

- At database creation, there is one tablespace—SYSTEM. The DBA should NOT place all database objects into that tablespace. Instead, the DBA should create multiple tablespaces for the various types of objects on the database and place those objects into that tablespace.

- There are several different types of segments. They are as follows:

  - *Table*. Stores table row data.
  - *Index*. Stores index row data.

- *Rollback.* Stores data from uncommitted transactions until the transaction completes.

- *Cluster.* Stores cluster row data. A cluster is a special database object designed to enhance performance on selecting data from two closely related tables.

- *Temporary.* Stores data on a temporary basis from user SQL statements. In certain cases, Oracle needs extra space to perform special operations on selected data (such as a sort).

- When a segment containing a database object cannot store any more data for that table, Oracle will obtain an extent to store the data.

- There are several logical storage options that govern how Oracle obtains extents for segments. They are as follows:

  - **initial**   The size in K or M of the initial extent of a data object.

  - **next**   The size in K or M of the next extent allocated to a data object.

  - **minextents**   The minimum number of extents a data object will have.

  - **maxextents**   The maximum number of extents a data object will have.

  - **pctincrease**   A percentage increase in the next extent size that will be allocated for a database object.

  - **freelists**   The number of lists of free data blocks that will be maintained by Oracle in each **freelist groups** storage option (see below).

  - **freelist groups**   The number of groups of freelists Oracle will maintain for a data object. The default is one.

- If the DBA wants to size the next extent granted to a database object, she can alter the object to change the **next** option to set an explicit size for the next extent created. The change will take effect on the next extent granted.

- If the DBA wants to change the percentage increase of each extent obtained, she can alter the object to change the **pctincrease** option. The percentage increase change will take effect on the next extent created.

- Oracle allows the DBA to control how an object uses its space allocation at the block level. The options are as follows:

  - **pctfree** The amount of space left free for size increases of rows already added to the block via updates.

  - **pctused** A threshold that, once the block is filled to **pctfree**, the capacity held by that block must fall below in order for Oracle to add more row data to the block.

- Information for each storage parameter and for space parameters is available for specific types of objects in the following data dictionary view:

  - DBA_TABLES

  - DBA_INDEXES

  - DBA_CLUSTERS

  - DBA_ROLLBACK_SEGS

  - DBA_SEGMENTS

- Default settings for storage parameters as set by each tablespace can be found in the DBA_TABLESPACES view.

Chapter Questions

1. Examine the following statement and identify any errors.

   A. create rollback segment RBS_01

   B. tablespace ROLLBACK_SEGS

   C. storage (initial 10M next 10M

    D. minextents 5 maxextents 10

    E. pctincrease 10

    F. freelist groups 2);

    G. There are no errors in this statement.

2. **When a CREATE TABLE command is issued with no storage options specified, what storage options are used to create it?**

    A. The default options specified for the user in the tablespace.

    B. The default options specified for the table in the tablespace.

    C. The default options specified for the user in the database.

    D. The default options specified for the table in the database.

3. **A high PCTUSED**

    A. Increases performance costs by forcing Oracle to place the block on freelists frequently.

    B. Increases performance costs by forcing Oracle to place the block on freelists rarely.

    C. Decreases performance costs by forcing Oracle to place the block on freelists frequently.

    D. Decreases performance costs by forcing Oracle to place the block on freelists rarely.

4. **To control the storage allocation of a table or index: (choose two)**

    A. Specify a low **pctfree**

    B. Specify a high **pctused**

    C. Specify a low **maxextents**

    D. Specify a high **minextents**

    E. Specify a low **pctincrease**

    F. Specify a high **maxextents**

5. **Flushing the dirty buffer write queue is most directly handled by**

    A. PMON

    B. SMON

    C. ARCH

    D. RECO

    E. DBWR

6. **To decrease the number of checkpoints that occur on the database:**

    A. Set LOG_CHECKPOINT_INTERVAL to half the size of the online redo log.

    B. Set LOG_CHECKPOINT_INTERVAL to twice the size of the online redo log.

    C. Set LOG_CHECKPOINT_TIMEOUT to the number of bytes in the online redo log.

    D. Set LOG_CHECKPOINT_TIMEOUT to half the number of bytes in the online redo log.

7. **The following strategies are recommended when customizing the redo log configuration:**

    A. Store redo log members on the same disk to reduce I/O contention.

    B. Run LGWR only at night.

    C. Store redo log members on different disks to reduce I/O contention.

    D. Run DBWR only at night.

8. **By allowing user processes to write redo log entries to the redo memory buffer, Oracle reduces I/O contention for disks that contain redo log entries.**

    A. TRUE

    B. FALSE

9. At which point in an UPDATE is the data change actually made in the datafile?

   A. Parse step

   B. Execution step

   C. Commit step

   D. Checkpoint step

10. Which of the following best supports the concept of transaction concurrency?

   A. Read-only tablespaces

   B. Locking mechanisms

   C. Select statements issued by multiple users

   D. Distributing redo log members over multiple disks

11. By default, checkpoints happen at least as often as

   A. Redo log switches

   B. **update** statements are issued against the database

   C. The SYSTEM tablespace is accessed

   D. SMON coalesces free space in a tablespace

12. To determine the storage allocation for temporary segments, the DBA can access which of the following views?

   A. DBA_TEMP_SEGMENTS

   B. DBA_TABLES

   C. DBA_SEGMENTS

   D. DBA_TEMP_TABLES

13. If a redo log member becomes unavailable on the database,

   A. The instance will fail.

    B. The instance will continue to run, but media recovery is needed.

    C. The database will continue to remain open, but instance recovery is needed.

    D. The system will continue to function as normal.

14. **A read-consistent view of database data is**

    A. When data changes only when being read.

    B. Handled by rollback segments.

    C. When users execute the same query consistently.

    D. Not available in Oracle.

Answers to Chapter Questions

I. E. **pctincrease 10**

Explanation Percentage increase from one rollback segment extent to another is not allowed. This storage parameter is actually not part of the **create rollback segment** syntax. Refer to the discussion of rollback segments in this chapter.

2. B. The default options for the table in the tablespace.

Explanation All default storage parameters for table objects are specified as part of the tablespace creation statement. A default tablespace can be named for a user on username creation, along with a maximum amount of storage in a tablespace for all objects created by the user. But there are no default storage parameters on a table-by-table basis either in the database or for a user. Refer to the discussion of tablespace creation.

3. A. Increases performance costs by forcing Oracle to place the block on freelists frequently.

Explanation A high value for **pctused** means that Oracle must keep a high percentage of each block used at any given time. Choice B is incorrect because the block will make its way to the freelist frequently, not rarely, if rows are frequently removed from the block. Choices C and D are incorrect because performance costs are increased by high **pctused**, not lowered. Refer to the discussion of space usage in the Oracle database.

4. C and E. Specify low **maxextents** and specify low **pctincrease**.

Explanation Having a database object that can acquire many extents and increase the size of each extent can make the storage allocation for a database object grow wildly. Choices D and F will facilitate that growth. Choices A and B are incorrect because **pctfree** and **pctused** control how the space usage in each block will be managed, not how many blocks will be allocated to an object total.

5. E. DBWR

Explanation At a checkpoint, LGWR signals DBWR to write changed blocks stored in the dirty buffer write queue to their respective datafiles. Choice A is incorrect because PMON resolves in-doubt transactions on distributed databases when the distributed option is used. Choice B is incorrect because SMON handles instance recovery at instance startup and periodically coalesces free space in tablespace. Choice C is incorrect because ARCH handles automatic archiving at log switches, and even though checkpoints happen at log switches, the overall process is not driven by ARCH. Choice D is incorrect because RECO handles transaction recovery in distributed transactions when the distributed option is used. Refer to the discussion of checkpoints.

6. B. Set LOG_CHECKPOINT_INTERVAL to twice the size of the online redo log.

Explanation The other three choices are incorrect because each of them actually increases the number of checkpoints that will be performed by Oracle. In addition, choices C and D indicate that values set for LOG_CHECKPOINT_TIMEOUT depend on the size of the redo log in bytes, which is not true. LOG_CHECKPOINT_TIMEOUT is a numeric value that determines the timed intervals for checkpoints. Refer to the discussion on checkpoints.

7. C. Store redo log members on different disks to reduce I/O contention.

Explanation Choice A is incorrect because storing all redo log members on the same disk increases I/O contention when log switches occur. Choices B and D are incorrect because DBWR and LGWR should be running at all times on the database. Refer to the discussion on redo logs.

8. A. TRUE

Explanation Allowing users to write redo entries to the redo memory buffer while LGWR handles the transfer of those entries to disk does reduce I/O dependency for user processes.

9. D.   Checkpoint step

Explanation   This is one of the most difficult questions in the section. At the parse step, Oracle simply develops an execution plan for the query. At the execution step, Oracle makes the change to the row in a data block *that is stored in the buffer cache.* That block is then transferred to the dirty buffer write queue. At the time the transaction is committed, an entry is simply made to the redo log that relates to the system change number (SCN) for the transaction stating that this transaction is committed. An SCN is a unique identifier for every transaction that takes place in the database. Only when the checkpoint occurs, and the dirty buffer write queue is flushed, is the change to the data block written to disk.

10. B.   Locking mechanisms

Explanation   Choices A and C refer to **select** access to the database, which technically is not considered a transaction. Choice D refers more to design and database customization than to transaction processing. Refer to the discussion of read consistency and data concurrency.

11. A.   Redo log switches.

Explanation   Choice A is the only choice given that relates to checkpoints. Refer to the discussion of checkpoints.

12. C.   DBA_SEGMENTS

Explanation   Choices A and D are incorrect because they are not actual views in the data dictionary. Choice B is incorrect because DBA_TABLES only lists information about the tables in the database, not the temporary segments created as part of a sort operation. Refer to the discussion of viewing storage information in Oracle.

13. A.   The instance will fail.

Explanation   If a disk becomes unavailable that contains all redo log members for the redo log currently being written, the instance will fail. All other choices are incorrect because they depend on the instance being fully available, which is not the case in this situation. Refer to the discussion of redo log components.

14. B.   Handled by rollback segments.

Explanation   Read consistency is the idea that the data being used by a statement or transaction should not change for the life of the transaction unless the statement or transaction is the one changing it. Choice A is incorrect because when data changes while being read by a statement, that is considered read-*in*consistent. Choice C is incorrect because the users that execute the query again and again will have read consistency only during the execution of each individual query. Remember, selection of data for viewing purposes only is not considered a transaction. Choice D is incorrect because read consistency is available in Oracle.

CHAPTER

8

Managing
Database Objects

n this chapter, you will understand and demonstrate knowledge in the following areas:

- Managing rollback segments
- Managing tables and indexes
- Managing clusters
- Managing data integrity constraints

A good deal of the DBA's daily job function is to create database objects. This fact is especially true for database administrators who manage databases primarily used for development and test purposes. But even DBAs working on production systems will find that a good deal of their time is spent exploring the depths of setting up database objects. In most large organizations, there are development and enhancement projects. The types of database objects covered in this section are found in most database environments. This discussion covers material that will comprise about 27 percent of OCP Exam 2.

Managing Rollback Segments

In this section, you will cover the following topics related to managing rollback segments:

- Rollback segment concept and function
- Creating and sizing rollback segments
- Storage and performance trade-offs
- Determining the number of rollback segments

Often, the DBA spends part of a given day "fighting fires." Many times, these fires involve rollback segments. These database objects are probably the most useful in data processing, but they can be troublesome for the DBA to maintain. Often, rollback segments need to be resized to support the execution of long-running transactions. Other problems related to rollback segments include adding rollback segments to support higher numbers of transactions executing on the database, or resolving a recovery issue related to rollback segments. Whatever the cause, the DBA is well advised to master the management of these sometimes fussy database objects.

Rollback Segment Concept and Function

Transactions cannot exist without rollback segments. In the same way that Oracle automatically provides statement-level read consistency, Oracle can also provide transaction-level read consistency with the use of rollback segments. Transaction processing makes it easy to correct large mistakes with the use of commits and rollbacks. When the user process executes a logical unit of work, the individual **update**, **insert**, and **delete** statements that may have happened in the transaction can then be committed as a group. Likewise, if the user decides that the work must be "backed out," the user can simply execute a rollback, which discards the changes made to the database in favor of the version existing before the transaction began. It is also possible to break a transaction down into logical units. This function is managed with the use of savepoints. Savepoints are statements that can be issued in the course of a transaction that act as a benchmark for the end of one transaction portion and the beginning of another one.

```
SELECT * FROM emp FOR UPDATE;
DELETE * FROM emp WHERE empid = 49395;
SAVEPOINT pointA;
UPDATE emp SET emp_lname = 'SMINT'
WHERE empid = 59394;
SAVEPOINT pointB;
ROLLBACK TO SAVEPOINT pointA;
COMMIT;
```

This extract demonstrates how savepoints can be incorporated into a session or transaction. At the beginning of the block, the rows of the EMP table are locked for the **update**. The user then deletes some data, which is the first logical unit of the transaction as noted by **savepoint pointA**. The second part of the transaction contains an **update**, which is marked as a unit by **savepoint pointB**. After that, the user process eliminates the first transaction unit by rolling back to the first savepoint, **pointA**, and then the transaction is committed. The change made to employee #59394's last

382 Oracle Certified Professional DBA Certification Exam Guide

name was *NOT* saved, but the deletion of data for employee #49395 is now permanent.

Rollback segments store all uncommitted data changes from transactions along with what the database looked like "prechange," for the purposes of read consistency and transaction concurrency. Each rollback segment has several extents allocated to it of equal size. As user processes make data changes, they must also write entries of the "before" and "after" look of the data. These entries allow other processes to issue statements and transactions that see a read-consistent version of the data at whatever time they execute.

Each entry to a rollback segment is associated with a transaction by use of a special tracking value called a *system change number,* or SCN for short. The SCN allows Oracle to group all entries associated with a particular transaction together for the purpose of identification. If a **rollback** or **commit** occurs, Oracle adds a record to the redo log saying that SCN #*X* has been committed. Oracle then knows which changes to apply to the database permanently based on the SCN used to identify the transaction. If the transactions that create entries in the rollback segment do not **commit** their changes for a long time, those entries must stay active in the rollback segment until the process commits the transaction. Once the transaction is committed, the entries in the rollback segment for that transaction are no longer active, and the space they take up in the rollback segment can be reused.

The ideal use of the rollback segment is to reuse the extents as much as possible. However, this is not always possible. Uncommitted transaction entries can span multiple extents of rollback segments. If a transaction goes on for a long time without committing data changes, the span of active rollback entries in the rollback segment corresponding to the uncommitted transaction will grow and grow over several extents. It is possible that the rollback segment will grow too large—an error will ensue, and the transaction rolls back automatically, and has to be executed again.

The most effective use of space for rollback segments is for the rollback segment to have few extents that are reused often. To support this operation, a special option is available in rollback segment storage called **optimal**. The **optimal** clause specifies the ideal size of the rollback segment in kilobytes or megabytes. This value tells Oracle the ideal number of extents the rollback segment should maintain. The **optimal** clause prevents rollback segments

from getting stretched out by one or two long-running transactions. Figure
8-1 illustrates rollback segment reusability.

At instance startup, at least one rollback segment in the SYSTEM
tablespace must be acquired by Oracle to support the database. If the user
will be creating tables in other tablespaces, then at least one more rollback
segment will be required. The number of rollback segments that the instance
tries to acquire at startup is determined by two parameters: TRANSACTIONS
and TRANSACTIONS_PER_ROLLBACK_SEGMENT. These parameters are
set by the DBA in the **init.ora** file. The TRANSACTIONS parameter
represents the average number of active transaction at any given time
anticipated by the DBA. The TRANSACTIONS_PER_ROLLBACK_SEGMENT
parameter represents the number of transactions that the DBA wants to
allocate to any given rollback segment. By dividing TRANSACTIONS by
TRANSACTIONS_PER_ROLLBACK_SEGMENT, the DBA can calculate the
number of rollback segments Oracle will allocate at startup. Normally, the
DBA wants to name certain rollback segments to be acquired at the time the

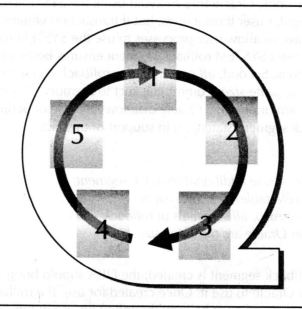

FIGURE 8-1.   *Rollback segment reusability*

instance starts. This task is accomplished with the ROLLBACK_SEGMENTS initialization parameter in **init.ora**.

Oracle's Parallel Server Option presents a unique issue to DBAs trying to configure rollback segments. Two types of rollback segments are available in Oracle: *public* and *private* rollback segments. Public rollback segments are a collection of rollback segments, any of which can be acquired by any of several instances on a database at instance startup. Private rollback segments are acquired by one and only one instance in a parallel configuration. The private rollback segment is usually acquired by name by one instance only in the Parallel Server Option. When the Parallel Server Option is not used, all rollback segments are public *and* private rollback segments, because public and private rollback segments are one in the same.

Two important reminders for setting up rollback segments are as follows. First, it benefits rollback segment performance on the system if the DBA creates at least one other rollback segment in the SYSTEM tablespace in addition to the one created by Oracle at instance startup. With two SYSTEM rollback segments, Oracle can keep one rollback segment available for all internal transactions. Oracle tries to avoid using the SYSTEM rollback segment for regular user transactions, but if transaction volume is heavy, Oracle may have to allow user processes to use the SYSTEM rollback segment. The extra SYSTEM rollback segment ensures better performance for system operations. Second, *all extents in the rollback segments of an Oracle database are the same size*. Commit this fact to memory—it's on the OCP exam in one form or another. Oracle disallows the use of **pctincrease** in the **create rollback segment** statement in support of this fact.

TIP

Create at least one additional rollback segment in the SYSTEM tablespace for system transactions. Also, all segments of rollback segments in Oracle are the same size.

Once a rollback segment is created, the DBA should bring it online in order to allow Oracle to use it. Once created for use, the rollback segment is in an offline status and must be brought online for use in the Oracle instance. Once online and in use by the users of the Oracle database, the rollback segment cannot be taken offline again until every transaction with entries in the rollback segment has completed.

Exercises

1. What function is served by rollback segments? What is the minimum number of rollback segments that must be acquired for the Oracle instance to start when the only tablespace is the SYSTEM tablespace? How does that minimum number change when more tablespaces are added to the database?

2. How does Oracle determine how many rollback segments to acquire? How can the DBA identify specific rollback segments to acquire at database startup?

3. What is the difference between a public and private rollback segment? When is there no difference between public and private rollback segments? Can **pctincrease** be 50 percent on a rollback segment? Explain.

4. What is an SCN?

Creating and Sizing Rollback Segments

Bigger is not usually better when it comes to rollback segments. The ideal size for rollback segments is large enough so that by the time the last extent fills with uncommitted transaction entries, the first extent of the rollback segment is filled with data from inactive transactions, and is thus reusable. If there are active transactions in the first extent of the rollback segment in this scenario, then the rollback segment must acquire another extent. Generally, the DBA should avoid letting Oracle stretch rollback segments out of shape like this, and the DBA has a few options to combat rollback segment stretch. First, the DBA may want to specify a value for the **optimal** clause for rollback segments. After Oracle commits the *second* transaction that causes the rollback segment to extend twice past optimal size, the database tells the rollback segment to shrink. This act will prevent a rollback segment from growing larger than required after supporting rollback entries for long-running transactions. Figure 8-2 illustrates how Oracle obtains or allocates more extents for a rollback segment.

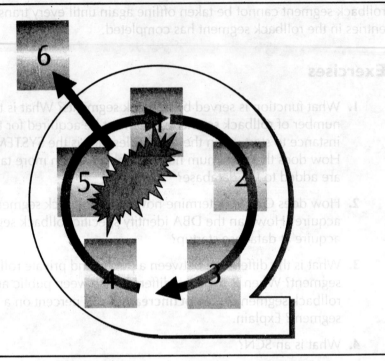

FIGURE 8-2. *Allocating more extents for a rollback segment*

Another option for managing rollback segment size is to create rollback segments of different sizes, and assign transactions to appropriately sized rollback segments. Consider a situation where almost all transactions during normal business hours on an Oracle database application handle small amounts of data. It makes sense to maintain small rollback segments in support of those transactions. But, it is important to ensure that rollback segments are not too small. If a long-running transaction cannot complete before being forced to allocate its rollback segment to acquire its maximum number of allowed extents, Oracle gives the following error: **Snapshot too old (rollback segment too small)**. The transaction that produced this error is rolled back, and has to try to execute again after the rollback segment has been resized. It is wise for a DBA to create a few rollback segments large enough to handle long-running transactions in support of batch processing for the database system.

Rollback segments are created with the **create rollback segment** statement. The created rollback segment should have *at least two* extents of equal size. The **alter rollback segment** command can be used in any case to create the different rollback segments required on the database. Size for rollback segments is determined by the storage clauses. The following list of options is available for setting up rollback segments:

- **initial**   The size in K or M of the initial rollback segment extent.

- **next**   The size in K or M of the next rollback segment extent to be allocated. Should be the same as **initial**.

- **optimal**   Total size in K or M of the rollback segment, optimally.

- **minextents**   Minimum number of extents on the rollback segment, at least two.

- **maxextents**—Maximum number of extents the rollback segment can acquire.

Exercises

1. Generally speaking, how should the DBA size rollback segments for a database? How should the DBA use the **optimal** clause?

2. When the DBA knows the size and number of transactions, what size should the rollback segments be?

3. How are rollback segments created and altered?

Storage and Performance Trade-Offs

The ideal storage management a rollback segment can attain is to have the final extent of the segment filling just as the last set of active transactions in the first extent **commit**. In this manner, the rollback segment never needs to extend. When the rollback segment does not need to extend, then it also never needs to shrink. The process of extending and shrinking causes performance degradation associated with rollback segment performance. Information about the management of shrinks and extents and the use of the **optimal** storage clause can be found in chapters covering OCP Exam 4 in this Guide. Refer to the discussion of rollback segment performance, and the V$WAITSTAT view.

Another area of rollback segment performance that must be monitored and managed carefully is ensuring that enough rollback segments are available for the transactions on the database to obtain a rollback segment when they need to place transaction entries in one. The performance of rollback segments is covered extensively in this text. At this point, however, a few key topics should be covered. The first is the concept of a *wait ratio*. If a process ever has to wait for something, Oracle keeps track of it in a special set of data dictionary views designed to track performance, called the V$ views. For example, a user may need to write several transaction entries to the rollback segment, but cannot do so because the rollback segment is busy being written to by another user. The result is that a user process has to wait for a resource to become free in order to write a rollback segment entry. Some V$ views that are used for this area are the V$ROLLNAME and V$ROLLSTAT views.

TIP

In general, a wait ratio for a database resource is calculated as the "waits" for an object divided by the "gets," times 100. The wait and get statistics come from a V$ performance view. If the wait ratio is over 1 percent, the DBA needs to do something to improve performance on the resource in question.

Most of the time, the wait ratio for any resource will be under 1 percent, based on the way it is calculated. In Unit IV, the text will elaborate on the ways to calculate wait ratios for various resources. For now, it is important to know that, when the wait ratio for any resource goes over 1 percent, the DBA must do something to improve the performance on that resource. For example, consider a performance problem on the rollback segment. Assume that the wait ratio is determined to be 3 percent for that rollback segment by data in the V$ROLLSTAT performance view. Since the wait ratio is over 1 percent, the DBA must do something. In this situation, the DBA needs to figure out which option available to her will reduce the number of times a process will wait. For example, increasing the number of extents a rollback segment has may not improve the likelihood that a process will have to wait in order to write a record to the rollback segment, because perhaps the problem is due to the fact that the disk controller for the drive containing rollback segments is frequently in use by other processes. In other words, the right option may be to increase the number of rollback segments available to the database.

Exercises

1. What happens to database performance if Oracle has to allocate extents to its rollback segments frequently without giving them up?

2. What are performance views? What is a wait ratio? What value for a wait ratio is considered a problem?

Determining the Number of Rollback Segments

Performance is made or broken not by the size of the rollback segments but by the number of them. Unfortunately, knowing there is a problem with the size is more clear-cut. If a transaction causes the rollback segment to allocate its maximum number of extents and the transaction still cannot finish, Oracle returns an error. However, if there are processes that don't exceed the maximum number of extents but do cause a lot of extents to be allocated, Oracle silently extends and shrinks, and causes phantom performance degradation that will be noticed by users and the DBA, but that will be impossible to identify without close examination of V$WAITSTAT. Worse, there may not be enough rollback segments to go around for all the processes on a busy day. This situation causes waits for the rollback segments that are available. But again, no explicit error gets written to a log file or to the screen. Performance just quietly gets worse and worse until users start complaining loudly that the processes that ran in 10 seconds two weeks ago now take several minutes. Only on close examination of performance as reflected by V$ROLLSTAT and V$WAITSTAT will the DBA identify the problem.

Using the Rule of Four

Once performance situations are identified, the DBA will most likely have to add rollback segments to the instance. Oracle has a recommended strategy for placing the appropriate number of rollback segments on a database to start, followed by careful monitoring to determine if the number of rollback segments on the database are enough to handle the job. For easy recollection, the DBA can call Oracle's rollback sizing methodology the *Rule of Four*. The basic tenet of the Rule of Four is to take the total number of transactions that will hit the database at any given time and divide by 4 to know how many rollback segments to create.

Consider this example. A DBA needs to size the number of rollback segments for the database. Initially, this database will be used for a small user rollout of an application for user acceptance testing purposes. Only about 25 users will access the database at any given time. The DBA applies the Rule of Four to the average number of transactions on the database at any given time and determines that about six rollback segments are required to support these users. The additional calculation of rollback segment size would be piggybacked into the Rule of Four calculation, taking an average of four transactions per rollback segment and multiplying it by the average size of the transactions the users will commonly execute.

There are two exceptions to the Rule of Four. The first exception is that if the quotient is less than 4 + 4, round the result of the Rule of Four up to the nearest multiple of 4 and use that number of rollback segments. In this case, the result would be rounded from 6 to 8. The second exception to the Rule of Four is that Oracle generally doesn't recommend exceeding 50 rollback segments for a database. If the Rule of Four determines that more than 50 rollback segments are needed, the DBA should start by allocating 50 and spend time monitoring the rollback segment wait ratio to see if more should be added later.

To summarize, the Rule of Four is as follows. Take the average number of user transactions that will run on the database at any given time, and divide that number by 4. If the result is less than 4 + 4 (8), round up to the nearest multiple of 4. If the result is over 50, use 50 rollback segments and monitor the wait ratio for the rollback segments to see if there is a need to add more.

Exercises

1. How does Oracle keep track of performance statistics? What is the name for the location where performance statistics for rollback segments are stored?

2. Use the Rule of Four to determine the appropriate number of rollback segments for a database with 36 concurrent users. How many rollback segments would be required if the number of concurrent users dropped by 50 percent? What if the number of concurrent users doubled?

Managing Tables and Indexes

In this section, you will cover the following topics related to managing tables and indexes:

- Sizing tables
- Sizing indexes
- Understanding storage and performance trade-offs
- Reviewing space usage

Good table and index management is critical to the success of the Oracle database in two ways. First, if tables and indexes are managed poorly, there will be problems with data storage. A database with storage problems has users constantly complaining about tables running out of room, forcing the DBA to reorganize tablespaces to accommodate unplanned growth. Eventually, the database exceeds disk capacity, forcing the DBA either to make unpleasant performance trade-offs by placing tablespaces on disks in ways that lead to contention problems, or the organization is forced to purchase new hardware to store the growing data. A well-planned database is much easier to manage than one created piecemeal. The following discussion will focus on appropriate sizing for database tables and indexes.

Sizing Tables

The tables of the database are generally its largest and most important objects. Without tables of data, there is no reason to have anything else set up, because the data is the database. Since tables have the highest storage, access, and maintenance costs, it makes sense for the DBA to plan far in advance to avoid unplanned hardware and support costs. It is far easier to store small amounts of data in large databases and watch them both grow together than it is to retrofit large tables into a small database.

The cornerstone of storage management is managing the data block. There are several different components to a data block, divided loosely into the following areas: *header and directory information, row data,* and *free space.* Each block has a special header containing information about it, including information about the table that owns the block and the row data the block contains. Row data consists of the actual rows of each data table or index. Finally, Oracle leaves an amount of space free for each row in a block to expand via data update.

There are several space utilization clauses related to block usage. Two have been covered, **pctfree** and **pctused**. The **pctfree** option specifies a small amount of space that Oracle should leave free when inserting rows in order to accommodate growth later via updates. The **pctused** option is a threshold percentage of a block that the actual contents of row data must fall below before Oracle will consider the block free for new row inserts. There are two other space utilization clauses to be aware of that control Oracle's ability to make concurrent updates to a data block. Those clauses are **initrans** and **maxtrans**. The **initrans** option specifies the initial number of transactions that can **update** the rows in a data block at once, while **maxtrans** specifies the maximum number of transactions that can perform the same function. For the most part, the default values for each of these options should not be changed. For **initrans**, the default for tables is 1, while for clustered tables the default is 2.

To estimate storage requirements for a table, several factors must be calculated about its contents. They are (1) estimate a count of the number of rows that will be part of the table, (2) determine the number of rows that will fit into each block, and (3) determine the number of blocks that will comprise the table.

Step 1: Estimating Row Counts

First, the DBA may find it useful to enlist the help of application developers with this task. In many environments, the DBA will not have the extensive application knowledge required to determine the number of rows that will populate the table. The DBA can ensure a more accurate estimate with the developer's assistance than simply taking a chance. Many DBAs find it useful having developers offer row count forecasts for today, six months out, twelve months out, and two years out. Forecasting growth for tables allows the DBA to prepare the entire database for growth, avoiding the need to make unplanned changes because the original estimate didn't take into account a factor for growth occurring 12 months down the road. The discussion will help you learn this material with an example: Say the DBA wants to create a table called DRESSES. This table has a row count estimate of 2,000 in 24 months, and three columns, called NAME—a VARCHAR2(10) column, size—a NUMBER(3) column, and description—a VARCHAR2(250) column.

Step 2: Determining How Many Rows Fit into a Block

To begin this step, the DBA should review the contents of each data block, along with some size figures attached to the components. The components of a block header, shown in Figure 8-3, include the following items, each listed with size estimates:

- Fixed block header—24 bytes

- Variable transaction header—24 bytes * **initrans** (1 for tables, 2 for clusters)

- Table directory—4 bytes

- Row directory—4 bytes * number of rows in block

All told, the space required for a block header is represented by **52 + 4(X)**, where X equals the number of rows in a block. Notice that the formula for calculating the header size depends on determining the number of rows in each block, which requires estimation. Determining how many rows fit into one block consists of the following steps:

2.1. Determine the size in bytes of each row, either as largest possible row size if the table doesn't exist or with the **vsize( )** and **avg( )** operations if the table does exist, and call the result Z:
Z = 3 + (size of column 1 + size of column 2 … + size of column n) + (number of columns with size < 250) + (3 * (number of columns with size >= 250)). Use of the **vsize( )** operation follows.

```
SELECT avg(vsize(column1)), avg(vsize(column2)), … avg(vsize(columnN))
FROM table;
```

2.2. Estimate the block row count by dividing DB_BLOCK_SIZE by Z, and call the result X:
$X = $ DB_BLOCK_SIZE $/ Z$.

2.3. Round X down to the nearest integer and use it in the following equation to determine the number of bytes available in each block for row data, and call the result Y:
$Y = $ DB_BLOCK_SIZE $- ($**pctfree**(DB_BLOCK_SIZE $- (52 + 4(X)))$

2.4. Validate X with the following equation:
$Y >= X * Z$
If the equation is not true, subtract 1 from X and repeat Step 2.4.
If the equation is true, then X is the answer to Step 2.

Resolving Step 2.1 requires analysis of the column definition for the table being created. First, it should be noted that each row in an Oracle database has three components: a row header requiring 3 bytes, column data with varying size requirements by datatype, and length bytes for each column,

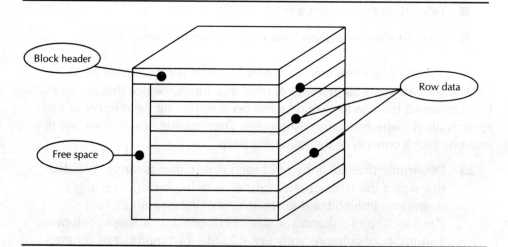

FIGURE 8-3. *Components of a data block*

depending on size (1 for columns < 250 bytes, 3 for columns >= 250 bytes). The storage requirements for datatypes are listed here:

- NUMBER—Maximum 21 bytes.

- CHAR(n), VARCHAR2(n)—Each character specified in the length as noted by (n) equals 1 byte in single-byte character sets, 2 in multibyte character sets. Maximum 255 for CHAR, 2,000 for VARCHAR2, prior to Oracle8.

- DATE—Each date column takes 7 bytes to store.

- ROWID—Fixed at 6 bytes in size.

- RAW, LONG, LONG RAW—Varies, maximum 2 gigabytes for LONG and LONG RAW, 2,000 bytes for RAW. The DBA may have difficulty sizing these rows, because chaining is inherent in using LONG datatypes in Oracle prior to Oracle8.

Return now to the example. There will be three columns in the DRESSES table, called NAME—a VARCHAR2(10) column, SIZE—a NUMBER column, and DESCRIPTION—a VARCHAR2(250) column. The maximum row length for this table is calculated as follows:

$$Z = 3 + (10 + 21 + 250) + (1 * 2) + (3 * 1)$$
$$Z = 3 + 281 + 2 + 3$$
$$Z = 289$$

Step 2.2 gives the DBA an estimated number of rows that fit into one block. This estimate disregards the presence of a row header and free space as specified by **pctfree**. This step minimizes difficulty in calculating the row count per block. Assuming a 4K database and with Z already calculated, the following estimate is calculated for X:

$$X = 4096 / 289$$
$$X = 14.173$$

Step 2.3 can now be accomplished. With an estimate for block row count represented by X, Step 2.3 tests the estimate. Assuming **pctfree** in this database is 10, the following formula is made for Y, bearing in mind the need for the DBA to round X down to the nearest integer:

$$Y = 4{,}096 - ((4{,}096 - (52 + 4(X))) * 0.1)$$
$$Y = 4{,}096 - ((4{,}096 - (52 + 4(14))) * 0.1)$$
$$Y = 4{,}096 - ((4{,}096 - (52 + 56)) * 0.1)$$
$$Y = 4{,}096 - ((4{,}096 - 108) * 0.1)$$
$$Y = 4{,}096 - (3{,}988 * 0.1)$$
$$Y = 4{,}096 - 399$$
$$Y = 3{,}697$$

Step 2.4 is used by the DBA to check her work by multiplying the estimated number of rows per block, X, by the size of each row, Z. If the result is more than Y, the estimated number of rows per block is too high. If this happens, subtract 1 from X and compare Y to $(X * Z)$ again.

$$Y >= X * Z$$
$$3{,}697 >= 14 * 289$$
$$3{,}697 >= 4{,}046 \text{ (FALSE)}$$

The result of the equation is an untrue statement, and therefore the DBA must subtract 1 from X and try again.

$$3{,}697 >= 13 * 289$$
$$3{,}697 >= 3{,}757 \text{ (FALSE)}$$

The result of the equation is still not true, so the DBA makes one more pass:

$$3{,}697 >= 12 * 289$$
$$3{,}697 >= 3{,}468 \text{ (TRUE)}$$

Therefore, the number of rows from the DRESSES table that will fit into a block on a 4K database with **pctfree** set to 10 is 12.

Step 3: Determining How Many Blocks Comprise a Table

Once the estimated row count for the table and the number of rows that will fit in a block are determined, determining the number of blocks required to store data for the table is a straightforward task. Simply divide the result of

Step 1 by the result of Step 2. In the example provided in this discussion, the number of blocks required to store the DRESSES table is 2,000 / 12, or 167 blocks. Multiply that result by DB_BLOCK_SIZE, divided by 1,024 (1,024,000 for megabytes), and the DBA has the size of the table in kilobytes. In this example, the size of the DRESSES table is (167 * 4,096) / 1,024, or 668K.

Exercises

1. Identify the general steps for estimating the size of a table.

2. How many bytes are required to store a column of type DATE? How many bytes would be required to store the *length* of a VARCHAR2(2,000) column?

3. A nonclustered table has four columns. Assuming a block size of 2K, **pctfree** equals 10, and that one-third the length of each VARCHAR2 column will be used, on average, how many rows will each block accept? The data definitions for each is listed as follows: VARCHAR2(40), NUMBER, DATE, VARCHAR2(2,000).

Sizing Indexes

There are some differences in determining indexes. The first major difference between sizing tables and indexes is the nature of data in the index. Instead of rows, indexes store *nodes* or entries of column index data from the table in conjunction with a ROWID of where to find the associated table row. The next difference is the size of the fixed block header. As discussed, a table has a fixed block header of 24 bytes and a variable block header whose size depends on the number of rows. Index headers have a slightly larger footprint of 113 bytes, and a fixed header size. The value for **initrans** in indexes is 2, not 1, so in general the total size of the index block header is 113 + (24 *2), or 161 bytes. Additionally, a node in an index has a header of 2 bytes in length. Recall that a table's row header length is 3.

Step 1: Estimating Node Counts

Placing these differences into context, revisit the example from the last discussion. The DBA is estimating size required for an index on a non-NULL column in the DRESSES table. Similar to Step 1 in the table size estimation process, the DBA now has information for node count, 2,000. The DBA can use the associated row count forecasts for the table to size the index. If the column(s) being indexed contains NULL values, that's fine, but the DBA should subtract the number of rows containing NULLS from the overall node count for the index before proceeding to Step 2.

Step 2: Determining How Many Nodes Fit into a Block

In Step 2, the number of nodes per block for the index is determined. Assume that the index will be composite, and the two elements are of type NUMBER and VARCHAR2(10). For Step 2.1, the length of each node in the index equals node header + ROWID + (column1 length + column2 length ... + columnN length) + number of columns, called Z. Note that the ROWID column does **not** have a length byte associated with it.

$$Z = 2 + 6 + (10 + 21) + 2$$
$$Z = 2 + 6 (10+21) + 2$$
$$Z = 41$$

The estimated block row count process in Step 2.2 is unnecessary for indexes. Since the index block header is static at 161 bytes, the space available in a data block is easier to calculate. With that fact established, the DBA can move on to calculating the free space available in a block for index node data in Step 2.3. Assuming that the DB_BLOCK_SIZE is the same in this example as in the previous example, and that **pctfree** is also the same, the DBA can make an initial pass at the number of rows in each block. The formula for calculating the number of bytes available for row data equals DB_BLOCK_SIZE - (**pctfree**(DB_BLOCK_SIZE - 161)), and is called Y. For the example:

$$Y = 4,096 - (0.1(4,096 - 161))$$
$$Y = 4,096 - (0.1(3935))$$
$$Y = 4,096 - 394$$
$$Y = 3,702$$

Step 2.4 is slightly modified for indexes as well. Since the index block header size is fixed, there is no guesswork in determining the result for

Step 2. The formula used for determining the number of index nodes in each block is equal to Y / Z.

$X = 3702 / 41$
$X = 90$

Step 3: Determining How Many Blocks Comprise a Table

At this point, the DBA determines the number of blocks required to store the index. There are some important differences again between indexes and tables related to the calculation of total blocks for the index. The first fact is that there will be slightly more blocks in each index than those being used to store index nodes. This fact is true because there are a certain number of special blocks in an index used to join the nodes together in the tree structure that comprises the index. A special multiplier, 1.05, can be used to determine the number of blocks required for the index. The formula for determining the number of blocks required, then, is the result from Step 1 divided by the result of Step 2, times 1.05. For this example, (2,000 / 90) * 1.05 = 24 blocks. The size in kilobytes can further be determined by taking the size of the index in blocks, multiplying it by DB_BLOCK_SIZE, and dividing that result by 1,024 (1,024,000 for megabytes). The result for this index in kilobytes is (24 * 4,096) / 1,024, or 96K.

Exercises

1. How can the DBA factor in the NULL values for a nullable column when determining the size of an index?

2. What is the difference between index block headers and table block headers? How does this change affect the method used to determine the number of index nodes that fit in a block?

3. Why will the number of blocks in an index always be larger than the number of blocks required to hold all the index nodes?

Understanding Storage and Performance Trade-Offs

Searching a table without indexes proceeds as follows. The first step is to perform a full table scan. The server process copies every block from the table into the buffer cache, one by one, and searches the contents of each row in the set of criteria given by the user until the entirety of the table is searched. Although a full table scan may only take a short while on a small table, on a large table it can take several minutes or hours. Indexes are designed to improve search performance. Unlike full table scans, whose performance worsens as the table grows larger, the performance increase on table searches that use indexes gets exponentially better as the index (and associated table) gets larger and larger. In fact, on a list containing one million elements, the type of search algorithm used in a B-tree index finds any element in the list within 20 tries. The same search using a full table scan takes anywhere from one to one million tries!

However, there is a price for all this speed, paid in the additional disk space required to store the index. To minimize the trade-off, the DBA must weigh the storage cost of adding an index to the database against the performance gained by having the index available for searching the table. The performance improvement achieved by using an index is exponential over the performance of a full table scan, but there is no value in the index if it is never used by the users.

The first step in determining the value of an index is to identify the columns that SQL statements use to access data in a table. Take, for example, a table called BANK_ACCOUNT, which has an index on the ACCOUNT_NO column. All the SQL statements issued against the table search in EMPID. Even though the index on ACCOUNT_NO provides excellent performance to queries with ACCOUNT_NO in their **where** clauses, the index provides little performance value overall because no SQL statements against BANK_ACCOUNT use ACCOUNT_NO in their **where** clauses. Therefore, the storage/performance trade-off would be better resolved with the use of an index on EMPID because the application searches the database on those values. An index does little good if users aren't using it. Since the DBA cannot simply create indexes on every conceivable column combination to ensure good performance, regardless of the **where** clause, the only alternative is to look at how the data is selected and index accordingly.

Exercises

I. What performance advantage does an index provide?

2. Describe the storage/performance trade-off DBAs make in deciding whether to index data. How can this trade-off be minimized?

Reviewing Space Usage

There are other performance trade-offs that the DBA has to consider when creating indexes. Each index on a database creates overhead for Oracle when the user wants to change data in a table. The database must update the table and the index when a record is changed, added, or deleted. Performance on data change, then, is adversely affected by the improvement of query access to the database.

Another area where this type of trade-off is encountered is in the management of space at the block level. Depending on the types of changes to data being made in a table, the DBA may want to adjust options for managing space inside each Oracle data block accordingly. The options for managing storage space within the Oracle database are **pctfree** and **pctused**. Their meanings are as follows:

- **pctfree** specifies a certain amount of space inside each block that remains free when new rows are inserted, in order to allow room for existing rows in the table to increase in size via updates.

- **pctused** specifies a threshold amount of usage under which the space utilization in a data block must fall before Oracle will consider adding more rows to the block. Note that **pctused** is not used for indexes.

These two options are treated in tandem. When added together, they should not exceed or even be close to 100. Setting these options in different ways has different effects on the database. A high **pctfree** will keep a great deal of space free in the database for updates to increase the size of each row. However, this configuration also means that some space in each block will lie dormant until the data updates to the rows utilize the space. Setting the value of **pctfree** low will maximize the number of rows that can be stored in a block. But, if a block runs out of space to store row data when the row is updated, then Oracle will have to migrate the row data to another block. Row migration degrades performance when the server process attempts to locate the migrated row, only to find that the row is in another location. Chaining is also detrimental to performance on the database, as the server process must piece together one row of data using multiple disk reads. In addition, there is performance degradation by DBWR when it has to perform multiple disk writes for only one row of data.

Settings for **pctused** create different effects on storage also. A high value for **pctused** will ensure that whenever few rows are removed from a data block, the block will be considered free and repopulated in a timely manner. However, this configuration degrades performance by requiring Oracle to keep track of blocks whose utilization falls below **pctused**, placing the block on a freelist and then taking the block off the freelist after inserting relatively few records into the block. Although space is managed effectively, the database as a whole pays a price in performance. A low **pctused** changes this situation by putting blocks on freelists only when a lot of row data can be put into the block. However, even this situation has a trade-off, which is if a lot of data is removed from the blocks, but enough to put utilization below **pctused**, that block will sit underused until enough rows are removed to place it on a freelist.

The DBA may want to specify a high **pctfree** value and a low **pctused** for online transaction processing systems experiencing many **update**, **insert**, and **delete** commands. This approach is designed to make room in each block for increased row lengths as the result of frequent updates. In contrast, consider a data warehouse where a smaller number of users execute long-running query statements against the database. In this situation, the DBA may want to ensure that space usage is maximized. A low **pctfree** and high **pctused** configuration may be entirely appropriate.

Exercises

1. On which type of statements does the presence of an index degrade performance?

2. Explain how Oracle manages space usage within a data block. What are some of the various configurations available for the options that manage space usage?

3. What is chaining? What is row migration? How do they affect performance on the Oracle database?

Managing Clusters

In this section, you will cover the following topics related to managing index clusters:

- Identifying the advantages and disadvantages of clusters
- Creating index clusters
- Using hashes
- Creating hash clusters

For the most part, the users and the DBA on an Oracle database system will find the use of standard tables and indexes to be effective in most situations. However, indexes on standard tables are not the only option available on the Oracle database for managing data to suit performance needs. The discussion in this section will cover some alternatives to traditional tables and indexing. The two options discussed will be clustered tables and hashing. Both of these options have advantages for use in certain, specialized situations. However, they are both somewhat complex to set up in comparison to standard tables and indexes. It is important to know when clustering and hashing will assist performance, but it is perhaps more important to know when hashing and clustering will adversely impact performance as well in order to avoid pitfalls.

Identifying the Advantages and Disadvantages of Clusters

Clusters are special configurations for DBAs to use when two or more tables are stored in close physical proximity to improve performance on SQL join statements using those tables. The tables in the cluster share the same data blocks as well as a special index of each table's common columns. Each unique element in the index is called a cluster key. Ideally, the rows in all tables corresponding to unique elements in the cluster key fit into one data block. The cluster can then offer I/O performance gains even over indexed tables. Even when the common column is indexed in both tables, the server process still has to perform multiple disk reads to retrieve data for the join. In contrast, the data in a clustered table is read into memory by the server process in only one disk read.

Clusters minimize disk I/O on table joins. Figure 8-4 illustrates the idea behind clustering. Assume that three tables share the same common primary key. The three tables are INVOICE, which stores general information about invoices for each purchase order; INVOICE_ITEM, which stores each line item of the purchase order; and INVOICE_DETAIL, which stores detailed information about each INVOICE_ITEM record, including part number, color, and size.

Since all rows in clustered tables use the same column(s) as the common primary key, the columns are stored only once for all tables, yielding some storage benefit. The use of clustering works well in certain situations, but has limited performance gains in others. First, effective use of cluster segments is limited to tables with static or infrequently inserted, updated, or deleted data. The location of pertinent data from several different tables in

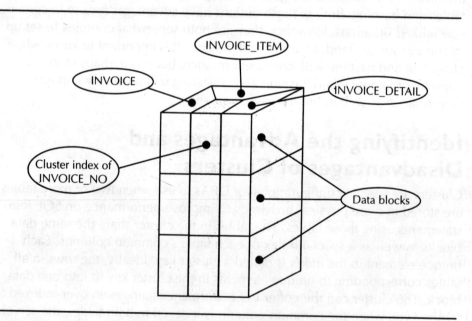

FIGURE 8-4. *Cluster keys and table distribution in cluster blocks*

one block is the biggest performance advantage cluster segments can offer. Changing data in any of the tables can throw off the tenuous balance of data in each block, potentially negating any performance value a cluster can offer by increasing disk reads. Cluster segments require more maintenance than traditional tables and indexes, especially when data is changed. Additionally, the cluster works best when several rows of data in each of the tables hang off each individual element in the cluster key. If few rows share cluster keys, the space in each block is wasted and additional I/O reads may be necessary to retrieve the data in the cluster. Conversely, cluster keys with too many rows hanging off of them causes additional I/O reads and defeat the purpose of clustering as well.

On the whole, the use of cluster segments is a fairly limited way to achieve performance gains in a few special circumstances. However, the DBA should have a full understanding of the circumstances in which clusters can improve performance, and use clustering effectively when those situations arise.

Exercises

1. What is a cluster? What advantages do clusters offer over nonclustered tables?

2. What are the limitations of clusters? What type of DML activity is particularly detrimental to clusters?

Creating Index Clusters

The DBA should begin the task of creating a cluster by treating all the data in a cluster segment as one unit. Although the logical data model and the applications may continue to treat each component as a table, from a management and maintenance standpoint, the line between each table gets blurry as soon as the tables are clustered. A major aspect of space management, **pctfree** and **pctused**, is not available in clusters. In disabling **pctfree** and **pctused** clauses for management at the table level, Oracle forces each table to take on the storage management used in the cluster. The cluster's space management is handled with the **size** option. The **size** option is determined by a complex calculation, somewhat like that used for determining an index or table:

1. Determine the amount of space each block has available for cluster data.

2. Determine the total size of all rows that will be associated with each cluster key.

3. Determine the number of blocks that will be required for the cluster.

Step 1: Determining Space Available in Each Cluster Block

As illustrated in the sections on sizing tables and indexes, the space available in each block for data storage can be expressed as DB_BLOCK_SIZE - block header. Since **pctfree** and **pctused** are not available on tables in clusters, factoring in **pctfree** when determining the space available per block is unnecessary. The block header size can be expressed as fixed header + variable header + table directory + row directory. Fixed header size for clusters is operating system specific. The DBA should refer to the components for fixed header size as listed in the V$TYPE_SIZE data dictionary view. For most systems, it will equal 57, while the variable header is determined by 23 times **initrans**(2), or 46. The table directory size is expressed by $4T + 1$, where T is the number of tables being clustered. The row directory size is determined by $2R$, where R is the number of rows per key. To simplify, the block header formula can be expressed as $104 + 4T + 2R$, making the total amount of space available in the block for clustered data expressed as DB_BLOCK_SIZE - $(104 + 4T + 2R)$.

Step 2: Determining Total Size of All Rows Associated with Cluster Keys

The space required for rows associated with cluster keys is determined in the same way as determining the row size for each row in a table. There is one exception—the columns in the cluster key must not be included in the size estimate for each row length for each table; columns in the cluster key are stored only once to support one common index for all rows in the table. The same rules for determining row length in nonclustered tables also apply to clustered tables, including the row header length of 4 bytes, the length byte of 1 for columns under 250 bytes and 3 for columns over 250 bytes in length.

At this point, the DBA should also calculate the number of rows that will hang off each key in the cluster. This is accomplished by determining how many rows are associated with each column in the cluster for each table, then adding the results. For example, if one row in the INVOICE table hangs off the cluster key, and three rows in both the INVOICE_ITEM and INVOICE_DETAIL tables, then a total of seven rows will be associated with each cluster key. Additionally, this step can be used to determine the size of all rows that associate with each key. Row size of each table is indicated by: row header + sum of column lengths except cluster key + sum of all column length bytes except cluster key.

The DBA should note that the space required for columns in the cluster key is determined separately. The cluster key length is determined in the same way as the length of each row in a nonclustered table; however, the cluster key header is 19 bytes. Also, there are no length bytes in the cluster. So, if the length of the cluster key columns is 20, the average size for each cluster key is going to be 39 bytes. This amount is then added to the space required for the size of all rows associated with the index.

Step 3: Determining How Many Blocks the Cluster Segment Will Require

After determining the size of each entry in the cluster, the DBA can then determine how many cluster entries will fit into a block. From there, the DBA determines how many blocks are required for the cluster overall. The first task is determined with the original formula representing the size available in each block. The available space is then divided by the size of each cluster element. In order to factor back in the row directory size, multiply the number of cluster elements by the number of rows associated with each cluster key. If 10 cluster elements fit into each block, and each element contains 7 rows, the number of rows overall in the block will then be 7 rows per entry times 10 entries, or 70 rows. The DBA can then factor the number of rows back into the original equation of available space per block.

Usually, there is little room left over in each block for growth. If data is inserted on all three tables with clustered rows around one entry, Oracle may have to migrate or chain row entries for this cluster. As soon as migration or chaining occurs, the performance benefit of clustering tables begins to erode. Therefore, it is best to cluster data only when the tables being clustered are **read only** or extremely static.

Once space requirement determination is complete and the **size** value determined, the DBA can then go about creating the cluster in the database. The first step to clustering the three invoice-related tables for our running example is to create the actual cluster segment for the three tables to reside in. This step is accomplished with a **create cluster** statement.

```
CREATE CLUSTER invoices_items_details
(invoice_id VARCHAR2(20))
PCTUSED 90  PCTFREE 5  SIZE 400
TABLESPACE clustered_data_02
STORAGE  ( INITIAL 1M  NEXT 1M
MINEXTENTS 2 MAXEXTENTS 100
PCTINCREASE 50 ) SIZE 400;
```

Within the syntax of the cluster creation statement, notice the presence of **pctfree** and **pctused**. Although these options are not available for the individual tables in the cluster, they *are* available for the cluster as a whole. Thus, space utilization is managed by the cluster. After creating the cluster segment, the DBA can add tables with the **create table** statement.

```
CREATE TABLE invoice (
Invoice_id      VARCHAR2(20) PRIMARY KEY,
User_account    VARCHAR2(9),
Pmt_dttm        DATE)
CLUSTER invoices_items_details (invoice_no);

CREATE TABLE invoice_item (
Invoice_id      VARCHAR2(20) PRIMARY KEY,
Part_id         VARCHAR2(4),
Item_amount     NUMBER)
CLUSTER invoices_items_details (invoice_no);

CREATE TABLE invoice_detail (
Invoice_id      VARCHAR2(20) PRIMARY KEY,
Prchs_address   VARCHAR2(20),
Purchaser_zip   VARCHAR2(10))
CLUSTER invoices_items_details (invoice_no);
```

The next step is crucial to the placement of data into the cluster. Without completing this step, the cluster is unusable, even if the table definitions and cluster definitions are in place. *In order to place data in the cluster, the DBA must create the cluster key index.*

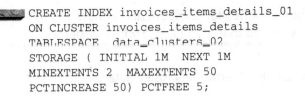

```
CREATE INDEX invoices_items_details_01
ON CLUSTER invoices_items_details
TABLESPACE data_clusters_02
STORAGE ( INITIAL 1M  NEXT 1M
MINEXTENTS 2  MAXEXTENTS 50
PCTINCREASE 50) PCTFREE 5;
```

After the index is created, the DBA can load data into the table with SQL*Loader or with some other mechanism for batch **update**. At that point, the DBA should strongly consider some form of control for limiting the amount of user **update** to the tables in the cluster. This task can be accomplished either by setting the tablespace containing the cluster to **read only** availability, limiting user **update** capability with the application, or via policy.

TIP

The tables in the cluster cannot be populated until the cluster key index is created by the DBA.

Configuring and using clusters can be complex. There are several calculations along the way that have difficult-to-find values plugged into them. After the initial determination that clustering is appropriate for this group of tables, the DBA must spend time carefully considering the implications of sizing various elements. In order to simplify the process, the following principles are offered:

- Determine the number of rows that will be associated with the cluster key first. This is a crucial element that, in the absence of completing other elements, can still help the DBA create a reasonable estimate for the cluster size.

- Remember not to include the cluster key columns in the estimation of the size for each row of the table. Although the cluster key columns appear in several different tables, the data for the key is stored only once. Calculating the columns in with the table row lengths will unnecessarily overestimate the size of each cluster entry.

- Information for most of the block header components is operating system specific, and can be found in the V$TYPE_SIZE view of the Oracle data dictionary.

- The cluster index must be created before the cluster data is populated.

- The **pctfree** and **pctused** options for each table default to the values set for the cluster, which makes sense because all tables being stored in a cluster are treated as one object.

- Attempts to issue **alter table** statements that assign values for storage options for the table, such as **pctfree**, **initrans**, or **pctincrease**, will result in an error.

- In all attempts to create a cluster, bear in mind the principles of performance improvement the cluster is designed to make.

Exercises

1. Where can the specific values of particular data elements in the cluster block header be found in the data dictionary? What is the size in bytes of the cluster key header?

2. What should not be included in the DBA's estimate on the size of each row associated with the cluster key?

3. What object must be created before any data can be populated into a cluster?

Creating Hash Clusters

Another option available for improving performance by placing data in close proximity is called hashing. Normal clustering works on the principle of hanging the data from several different tables together with one common index, and then searching the index when data from the cluster is needed. The performance improvement it offers is on disk I/O. Hashing is designed to enhance performance even more. The implementation of hashing adds two new items to the creation of a cluster—a *hash key* and a *hash function*. The hash key represents a special address in memory that corresponds to each unique cluster key value. When a user process looks for data in a hash cluster, the required data is converted into the hash key by means of the hash function. The result is an address on disk that tells Oracle exactly where to find the data requested by the user process. Ideally, performance in hash clusters can be so effective as to enable the database to retrieve requested data in as little as *one disk read*.

Hash clustering can be a very useful performance enhancement to a database. However, the DBA needs to understand when hash clusters are appropriate. In addition to restrictions on regular clusters, such as creating clusters on tables with static data, the hash cluster is only effective when the types of queries executed against it contain equality operations in their **where** clauses. Figure 8-5 demonstrates inappropriate selection of data from a hash cluster.

There are other restrictions that apply to hashing. The size and number of rows in tables in the hash cluster must be stable. A change in row data can produce data migration or chaining, which erodes the performance of the hash cluster. Also, all tables in the cluster should be searched via the cluster key. If a user process attempts to **select** data on columns not in the cluster key, the performance of the query will be worse than if the table was not clustered. Hash clusters also require lots of disk space and should not be used when storage is tight.

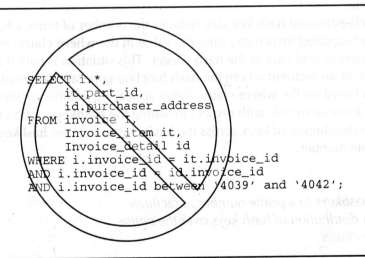

```
SELECT i.*,
       it.part_id,
       id.purchaser_address
FROM invoice I,
     Invoice_item it,
     Invoice_detail id
WHERE i.invoice_id = it.invoice_id
AND i.invoice_id = id.invoice_id
AND i.invoice_id between '4039' and '4042';
```

FIGURE 8-5.   *select statements that use ranges are not appropriate in hashing*

Sizing hash cluster requirements is similar to sizing regular clusters, with the following exception. There is an additional factor for creating a set of hash key values to which the cluster keys of the hash cluster will map. The number of hash keys should correspond to the number of blocks that are used to store the cluster. Therefore, determining the number of blocks containing cluster data is required in order to specify the hash key clause. Once sizing for a hash key is complete, the DBA then creates a hash cluster for the tables being clustered in the same way as the regular cluster is created, with the following addition to the storage clause of the cluster:

```
STORAGE ( INITIAL 1M  NEXT 1M
MINEXTENTS 2 MAXEXTENTS 100
PCTINCREASE 50) SIZE 400
HASHKEYS 250;
```

In situations where the cluster key is of the NUMBER datatype and consists of only one column, and the cluster key is a list of unique sequential or uniformly stepped integers, the DBA can use the **hash is** clause to name the cluster key. This clause names the column on which the hashing function can be applied directly in order to produce the hash key equivalent used by Oracle to find the exact block on disk where the rows corresponding to the result set of each query using the hash cluster will reside.

A well-estimated hash key size reduces the number of times a hash function is applied incorrectly onto the value in the **where** clause requested in the query to find data in the hash cluster. This situation is called a ,collision, or an incident where the hash function generates an incorrect location based on the **where** clause value appearing in different blocks. One tip Oracle recommends with respect to setting the **hashkeys** option to allow for good distribution of keys across the hash cluster is to set **hashkeys** equal to a prime number.

TIP
*Set **hashkeys** to a prime number to facilitate even distribution of hash keys over the entire hash cluster.*

If the DBA thinks cluster creation is hard, the complexity of hash clustering can encourage the DBA not to use hashing on databases. Even when the mechanisms for creating a hash cluster are well understood, there are still compelling reasons not to use hash clusters. For one thing, the performance improvements made as part of hashing can easily be diminished when considered in light of the increased storage burden for hash clustering. Hash clusters require as much as 50 percent more space to store the same amount of data as would be required if the tables in the hash cluster were placed into nonclustered tables with associated indexes. Moreover, the user would have more flexibility with nonclustered tables by querying the data using methods other than equality operations in the **where** clause and for inserting, updating, and deleting data than with hash clusters. Data in hash clusters must be absolutely static. However, although the scope is limited, there is often opportunity to use hash clustering on data warehouses with **read only** data. In these situations, hash clustering can yield dramatic performance results.

Exercises

1. What is hashing? What are the advantages of using hashing? What are the limitations or disadvantages of hashing?

2. What two items are added to the cluster architecture in order to support hashing?

3. What does Oracle recommend when specifying a value for **hashkeys**?

Managing Data Integrity Constraints

In this section, you will cover the following topics related to managing data integrity constraints:

- Types of declarative integrity constraints
- Constraints in action

- Managing constraint violations
- Viewing information about constraints

One of Oracle's greatest assets is its ability to manage data integrity from within the object definition of a table. The use of declarative integrity constraints allows the DBA to specify all but the most complicated data integrity rules in the database at the table definition level. Furthermore, the existence of declarative integrity constraints allows the DBA to view all constraints defined on the database easily using data dictionary views rather than by sorting through sometimes complex PL/SQL blocks contained in triggers throughout the database. Finally, declarative constraints allow for several different types of integrity checking, from simple valid value references, to uniqueness within a table, to foreign-key lookups in other tables. However, declarative constraints cannot do everything. For example, a declarative constraint cannot perform a foreign-key verification operation on different tables in the database depending on the value specified in the column. Additionally, a declarative integrity constraint cannot perform a PL/SQL operation, nor can it **insert** data into another table if the data does not exist there already. However, most business rules can be modeled using declarative integrity constraints if the logical data model is constructed well.

Types of Declarative Integrity Constraints

Several different options exist in Oracle for declarative integrity constraints. The first type of integrity constraint available in the Oracle architecture, and perhaps most central to the theory of relational databases, is the *primary-key constraint*. The primary key of a database table is the unique identifier for that table that distinguishes each row in the table from all other rows. A primary-key constraint consists of two data integrity rules for the column declared as the primary key:

- Every value in the column declared to be the primary key must be unique in the database.

- No value in the column declared to be the primary key is permitted to be NULL.

Primary keys are considered to be the backbone of the table. As such, the DBA should choose the primary key for a table carefully. The column or columns defined to be the primary key should reflect the most important piece of information that is unique about each row of the table. Primary keys are one of two integrity constraints in the Oracle database that are created with an associated index. This index helps to preserve the uniqueness of the primary key and also facilitates high-performance searches on the table whenever the primary key is named in the **where** clause.

The next integrity constraint to be discussed is the *foreign-key constraint*. The DBA should ensure that foreign keys on one table refer only to primary keys on other tables. The creation of a foreign-key constraint from one table to another defines a special relationship between the two tables that is often referred to as a parent-child relationship. The parent table is the one referred to by the foreign key, while the child table is the table that actually contains the foreign key. In order to better understand this relationship, refer to Figure 8-6. Unlike primary-key constraints, defining a foreign-key constraint on a column does not prevent user processes from setting the value in the foreign-key column of the child table to NULL. In cases where the column is NULL, there will be no referential integrity check between the child and the parent.

A third type of integrity constraint available in Oracle is the *unique constraint*. Like the primary key, a unique constraint ensures that all values in the column that the unique constraint is defined on are not duplicated by other rows. In addition, unique constraints are the only other type of constraint that has an associated index created with it when the constraint is named. The fourth integrity constraint defined on the Oracle database is the *NOT NULL constraint*. This constraint ensures that NULL cannot be specified as the value for a column on which the NOT NULL constraint is applied. Often, the DBA will define this constraint in conjunction with another constraint. For example, the NOT NULL constraint can be used with a foreign-key constraint to force validation of column data against a "valid value" table. Also, the NOT NULL constraint and a unique constraint are defined together on the same columns—they provide the same functionality as a primary key.

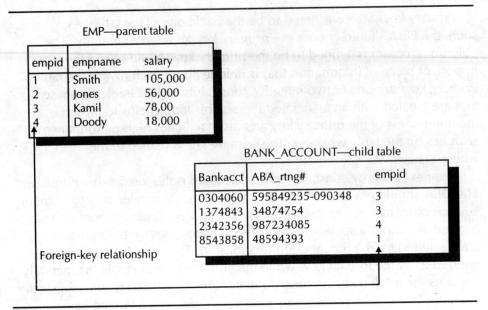

EMP—parent table

empid	empname	salary
1	Smith	105,000
2	Jones	56,000
3	Kamil	78,00
4	Doody	18,000

BANK_ACCOUNT—child table

Bankacct	ABA_rtng#	empid
0304060	595849235-090348	3
1374843	34874754	3
2342356	987234085	4
8543858	48594393	1

Foreign-key relationship

FIGURE 8-6. *Creating parent-child table relationships using foreign keys*

The final type of integrity constraint that can be defined on a database is the *check constraint*. Check constraints allow the DBA to specify a set of valid values allowed for a column, which Oracle will check automatically when a row is inserted with a non-NULL value for that column. This constraint is limited to hard-coded valid values only. In other words, a check constraint cannot "look up" its valid values anywhere, nor can it perform any type of SQL or PL/SQL operation as part of its definition.

Exercises

1. What is declarative data integrity?

2. Name the five types of integrity constraints used on the Oracle database. What are some uses for each? How is each defined?

3. Which integrity constraints have indexes associated with them?

Constraints in Action

Constraint definitions are handled at the table definition level, either in a **create table** or **alter table** statement. Whenever a constraint is created, it is enabled automatically unless a condition exists on the table that violates the constraint. If this is the case, then the constraint is created with a disabled status and the rows that violated the constraint are written to a special location. The data in a table should not be populated before the primary key is created.

The primary key is defined with the **constraint** clause. A name must be given to the primary key in order to name the associated index. The type of constraint is defined on the next line. The type of constraint defined with this clause will either be a primary key, foreign key, unique, or check constraint. The tablespace to which the associated index will be created is named in the **using tablespace** clause. Oracle allows the DBA to specify a separate tablespace for indexes and the tables for which they index because it improves performance on **select** statements if the index and table data are in separate tablespaces on different disks. The code block here illustrates the creation of a table with constraints defined:

```
CREATE TABLE emp
( empid          NUMBER           NOT NULL,
  empname        VARCHAR2(30)     NOT NULL,
  salary         NUMBER           NOT NULL,
  CONSTRAINT             pk_emp_01
  PRIMARY KEY           (empid)
  USING TABLESPACE      indexes_01)
TABLESPACE data_01;
```

A foreign key is also defined in the **create table** or **alter table** statement. The foreign key in one table refers to the primary key in another, which is sometimes called the parent key. Another clause, **on delete cascade**, is purely optional. When included, it tells Oracle that if any deletion is performed on EMP that causes a bank account to be orphaned, the corresponding row in BANK_ACCOUNT with the same value for EMPID will also be deleted. Typically, this relationship is desirable because the BANK_ACCOUNT table is the child of the EMP table. *If the **on delete** cascade option is not included, then deletion of a record from EMP that has a corresponding child record in BANK_ACCOUNT with the EMPID defined* *will not be allowed.* Additionally, in order to link two columns via a foreign-key constraint, the names do not have to be the same, but the datatype for each column must be identical.

```
CREATE TABLE bank_account
(bank_acct       VARCHAR2(40)        NOT NULL,
 aba_rtng_no     VARCHAR2(40)        NOT NULL,
 empid           NUMBER              NOT NULL,
 CONSTRAINT               pk_bank_account_01
 PRIMARY KEY              (bank_acct)
 USING TABLESPACE         indexes_01,
 CONSTRAINT               fk_bank_account_01
 FOREIGN KEY              (empid) REFERENCES (emp.empid)
 ON DELETE CASCADE)
 TABLESPACE data_01;
```

TIP
In order for a foreign key to reference a column in the parent table, the datatypes of both columns must be identical.

The method used to define a NOT NULL constraint is as follows. The existence of this clause in the definition of the table will ensure that the value for this column inserted by any row will never be NULL. In order to illustrate the definition and usage of the NOT NULL constraint, consider the data definition statement next, which is identical to the statement used to illustrate the foreign-key constraint. However, this time the definition for the NOT NULL constraint is highlighted.

```
CREATE TABLE bank_account
(bank_acct       VARCHAR2(40)        NOT NULL,
 aba_rtng_no     VARCHAR2(40)        NOT NULL,
 empid           NUMBER              NOT NULL,
 CONSTRAINT pk_bank_account_01
 PRIMARY KEY (bank_acct)
 USING TABLESPACE indexes_01,
 CONSTRAINT fk_bank_account_01
 FOREIGN KEY (empid) REFERENCES (emp.empid)
 ON DELETE CASCADE)
 TABLESPACE data_01;
```

Defining a unique constraint is handled as follows. The DBA decides to track telephone numbers in addition to all the other data traced in EMP. The **alter table** statement can be issued against the database. As in a primary key, an index is created for the purpose of verifying uniqueness on the column. That index is identified with the name given to the constraint.

```
ALTER TABLE emp
ADD (home_phone    VARCHAR2(10),
     CONSTRAINT    uk_emp_01
     UNIQUE        (home_phone));
```

The final constraint considered in this example is the check constraint. The fictitious company using the EMP and BANK_ACCOUNT tables places a salary cap on all employees of $110,000 per year. In order to mirror that policy, the DBA issues the following **alter table** statement. The constraint takes effect as soon as the statement is issued. If there exists a row in the table whose value for the column with a check constraint against it violates the constraint, the constraint remains disabled.

```
ALTER TABLE emp
ADD CONSTRAINT ck_emp_01
CHECK (salary <=110000);
```

Exercises

1. What condition must be true regarding datatypes when defining foreign-key constraints?

2. What statement is used to create integrity constraints on a new table and on an existing table?

Managing Constraint Violations

The only foolproof way to create a constraint without experiencing violations on constraint creation is to create the constraint before any data is inserted. If this is not done, then the DBA must know how Oracle works with constraint violations. The first and most important step to managing the violations that may arise from creating constraints on tables with data already populated is to create a special table called EXCEPTIONS by running a script provided with the Oracle software distribution called **utlexcpt.sql**. This file is usually found in the **rdbms/admin** subdirectory under the Oracle software home directory.

EXCEPTIONS contains a column for the ROWID of the row that violated the constraint and the name of the constraint it violated. In the case of constraints that are not named explicitly by the DBA, such as NOT NULL, the constraint name is listed that was automatically created by Oracle at the time the constraint was created. One method the DBA can use to discover the root cause of the problem is to review the constraints created against the database to determine which constraints are disabled by attempting to reenable the constraint with the **exceptions into** clause.

```
ALTER TABLE table_name
ENABLE CONSTRAINT constraint_name
EXCEPTIONS INTO exceptions;
```

This statement will cause the constraint to fail again and place each ROWID for offending rows into the EXCEPTIONS table. The DBA can then issue a **select** statement on the EXCEPTIONS table. By substituting the column name with the column(s) on which the disabled constraint was defined, the DBA should have a better understanding of the problem that caused the constraint to remain disabled after database creation.

```
SELECT e.constraint, x.column_name, …
FROM exceptions e, table_name x
WHERE e.row_id = x.rowid;
```

In order to correct the problem, the DBA must change the data in the offending row to be in compliance with the constraint, or remove the offending row. This step is accomplished by issuing an **update** or **delete**, with the ROWID of the offending row(s) specified either explicitly in the **where** clause or via a join statement with the EXCEPTIONS table.

Exercise

The DBA defines an integrity constraint associated with a table, which fails on creation. What can be done to determine which rows in a table violate an integrity constraint?

Viewing Information About Constraints

There are several ways to access information about constraints. Many of the data dictionary views present various angles on the constraints. Although each of the views listed are prefixed with DBA_, the views are also available in the ALL_ or USER_ flavors, with data limited in the following ways. ALL_ views correspond to the data objects, privileges, etc. that are available to the user who executes the query, while the USER_ views correspond to the data objects, privileges, etc. that were created by the user.

- **DBA_CONSTRAINTS** Lists detailed information about all constraints in the system. The constraint name and owner of the constraint are listed, along with the type of constraint it is, the status, and the referenced column name and owner for the parent key if the constraint is a foreign-key constraint. One weakness lies in this view—if trying to look up the name of the parent table for the foreign-key constraint, the DBA must try to find the table whose primary key is the same as the column specified for the referenced column name.

- **DBA_CONS_COLUMNS** Lists detailed information about every column associated with a constraint. The view includes the name of the constraint and the associated table, as well as the name of the column in the constraint. If the constraint is composed of multiple columns, as can be the case in primary, unique, and foreign keys, the position or order of the columns is specified by a 1,2,3,....n value in the POSITION column of this view. Knowing the position of a column is especially useful in tuning SQL queries to use composite indexes, when there is an index corresponding to the constraint.

- **DBA_INDEXES** Lists more detailed information about all indexes in the database, including indexes created for constraints. Most of the information about constraints that are indexed, including the position of the column in the composite index, is duplicated in the DBA_CONS_COLUMNS view. However, for the DBA who needs more detailed information about the indexed constraint (perhaps to determine if there is a problem with the index), this is the data dictionary view to use.

Exercise

Where in the data dictionary can the DBA look to find out whether a constraint's status is enabled or disabled?

Chapter Summary

This chapter covered topics related to database administration of database objects in the Oracle architecture. The areas covered are management of tables and indexes, management of the two types of cluster segments (regular and hash), the management of rollback segment resources that allow for transaction processing, and creation of integrity constraints that aid in storing the right data on the database. These sections comprise material representing 27 percent of questions asked on the OCP Exam 2.

The first area covered is management of rollback segments. These database objects facilitate transaction processing by storing entries related to uncommitted transactions run by user processes on the Oracle database. Each transaction is tracked within a rollback segment by means of a system change number, also called an SCN. Rollback segments can be in several different modes, including online (available), offline (unavailable), pending offline, and partly available. When the DBA creates a rollback segment, the rollback segment is offline, and must be brought online before processes can use it. Once the rollback segment is online, it cannot be brought offline until every transaction using the rollback segment has completed.

Rollback segments must be sized appropriately in order to manage its space well. Every rollback segment should consist of several equally sized extents. Use of the **pctincrease** storage clause is not permitted with rollback segments. The ideal usage of space for a rollback segment is for the first extent of the rollback segment to be closing its last active transaction as the last extent is running out of room to store active transaction entries, in order to facilitate reuse of allocated extents before obtaining new ones.

The size of a rollback segment can be optimized to stay around a certain number of extents with use of the **optimal** clause. If the **optimal** clause is set and a long-running transaction causes the rollback segment to allocate several additional extents, Oracle will force the rollback segment to shrink after the long-running transaction commits. The size of a rollback segment should relate to both the number and size of the average transactions running against the database. Additionally, there should be a few large rollback segments for use with long-running batch processes inherent in most database applications. Transactions can be explicitly assigned to rollback segments that best suit their transaction entry needs with use of **set transaction use rollback segment**.

At database startup, at least one rollback segment must be acquired. This rollback segment is the system rollback segment that is created in the SYSTEM tablespace as part of database creation. If the database has more than one tablespace, then two rollback segments must be allocated. The total number of rollback segments that must be allocated for the instance to start is determined by dividing the value of the TRANSACTIONS initialization parameter by the value specified for the TRANSACTIONS_PER_ROLLBACK_SEGMENT parameter. Both of these parameters can be found in the **init.ora** file. If there are specific rollback segments that the DBA wants to acquire as part of database creation, the names of those rollback segments can be listed in the ROLLBACK_SEGMENTS parameter of the **init.ora** file. To determine the number of rollback segments that should be created for the database, use the Rule of Four. Divide the average number of concurrent transactions by 4. If the result is less than 4 + 4, or 8, then round it up to the nearest multiple of 4. Configuring more than 50 rollback segments is generally not advised except under heavy volume transaction processing. The V$ROLLSTAT and V$WAITSTAT dynamic performance views are used to monitor rollback segment performance.

The next area discussed is management and administration of tables and indexes. These two objects are the lifeblood of the database, for without data to store there can be no database. Table and index creation must be preceded by appropriate sizing estimates to determine how large a table or index will get. Sizing a table is a three-step process: (1) determining row counts for the table, (2) determining how many rows will fit into a data block, and (3) determining how many blocks the table will need. Step 1 is straightforward—the DBA should involve the developer and the customer where possible and try to forecast table size over one to two years in order to ensure enough size is allocated to prevent a maintenance problem later. Step 2 requires a fair amount of calculation to determine two things—the amount of available space in each block and the amount of space each row in a table will require. The combination of these two factors will determine the estimate of the number of blocks the table will require, calculated as part of Step 3.

Sizing indexes uses the same procedure for index node entry count as the estimate of row count used in Step 1 for sizing the index's associated table. Step 2 for sizing indexes is the same as for tables––the amount of space available per block is determined, followed by the size of each index node, which includes all columns being indexed and a 6-byte ROWID associated with each value in the index. The two are then combined to determine how many nodes will fit into each block. In Step 3, the number of blocks required to store the full index is determined by determining how many blocks are required to store all index nodes; then, that number is increased by 5 percent to account for the allocation of special blocks designed to hold the structure of the index together.

The principle behind indexes is simple—indexes improve performance on table searches for data. However, with the improvement in performance comes an increase in storage costs associated with housing the index. In order to minimize that storage need, the DBA should create indexes that match the columns used in the **where** clauses of queries running against the database. Other storage/performance trade-offs include use of the **pctincrease** option. Each time an extent is allocated in situations where **pctincrease** is greater than zero, the size of the allocated extent will be the percentage larger than the previous extent as defined by **pctincrease**. This setup allows rapidly growing tables to reduce performance overhead associated with allocating extents by allocating larger and larger extents each time growth is necessary. One drawback is that if the growth of the table were to diminish, **pctincrease** may cause the table to allocate far more space than it needs on that last extent.

Space within a table is managed with two clauses defined for a table at table creation. Those clauses are **pctfree** and **pctused**. The **pctfree** clause specifies that a percentage of the block must remain free when rows are inserted into the block to accommodate for growth of existing rows via **update** statements. The **pctused** clause is a threshold value under which the capacity of data held in a block must fall in order for Oracle to consider the block free for inserting new rows. Both **pctfree** and **pctused** are generally configured together for several reasons. First, the values specified for both clauses when added together cannot exceed 100. Second, the types of activities on the database will determine the values for **pctfree** and **pctused**. Third, the values set for both clauses work together to determine how high or low the costs for storage management will be.

High **pctfree** causes a great deal of space to remain free for updates to existing rows in the database. It is useful in environments where the size of a row is increased substantially by frequent updates. Although space is intentionally preallocated high, the overall benefit for performance and storage is high as well, because chaining and row migration will be minimized. *Row migration* is when a row of data is larger than the block can accommodate, so Oracle must move the row to another block. The entry where the row once stood is replaced with its new location. Chaining goes one step further to place pieces of row data in several blocks when there is not enough free space in any block to accommodate the row.

Setting **pctfree** low means little space will be left over for row **update** growth. This configuration works well for static systems like data warehouses where data is infrequently updated once populated. Space utilization will be maximized, but setting **pctfree** in this way is not recommended for high **update** volume systems because the updates will cause chaining and row migration. High **pctused** means that Oracle should always attempt to keep blocks as filled as possible with row data. This setup means that in environments where data is deleted from tables often, the blocks having row deletion will spend short and frequent periods on the table's freelist. A freelist is a list of blocks that are below their **pctused** threshold, and that are available to have rows inserted into them. Moving blocks onto and off of the freelists for a table increases performance costs and should be avoided. Low **pctused** is a good method to prevent a block from being considered "free" before a great deal of data can be inserted into it. Low **pctused** improves performance related to space management; however, setting **pctused** too low can cause space to be wasted in blocks.

Typically, regular "nonclustered" tables and associated indexes will give most databases the performance they need to access their database applications quickly. However, there are certain situations where performance can be enhanced significantly with the use of cluster segments. A cluster segment is designed to store two or more tables physically within the same blocks. The operating principle is that if there are two or more tables that are joined frequently in **select** statements, then storing the data for each table together will improve performance on statements that retrieve data from them. Data from rows on multiple tables correspond to one unique index of common column(s) shared between the tables in the cluster. This index is called a cluster index. A few conditions for use apply to clusters. Only tables that contain static data and are rarely queried by themselves work well in clusters. Although tables in clusters are still considered logically separate, from a physical management standpoint they are really one object. As such, **pctfree** and **pctused** options for the individual tables in a cluster defer to the values specified for **pctfree** and **pctused** for the cluster as a whole. However, some control over space usage is given with the **size** option used in cluster creation. In order to create clusters, the size required by the clustered data must be determined. The steps required are the same for sizing tables, namely (1) the number of rows per table that will be associated to each member of the cluster index, called a cluster key; (2) the number of cluster keys that fit into one data block will be determined; and (3) the number of blocks required to store the cluster will also be determined. One key point to remember in Step 2 is that the row size estimates for each table in the cluster must not include the columns in the cluster key. That estimate is done separately. Once sizing is complete, clusters are created in the following way: (1) create the cluster segment with the **create cluster** command; (2) add tables to the cluster with the **create table** command with the **cluster** option; (3) create the cluster index with the **create index on cluster** command; and lastly (4) populate the cluster tables with row data. Note that Step 4 *cannot* happen before Step 3 is complete.

Clusters add performance value in certain circumstances where table joins are frequently performed on static data. However, for even more performance gain, hash clustering can be used. Hashing differs from normal clusters in that each block contains one or more hash keys that are used to identify each block in the cluster. When **select** statements are issued against hash clusters, the value(s) specified by an equality operation in the **where** clause is translated into a hash key by means of a special hash function, and data is then selected from the specific block that contains the hash key. When properly configured, hashing can yield required data for a query in as little as one disk read. There are two major conditions for hashing—one is that hashing only improves performance when the two or more tables in the cluster are rarely selected from individually, and joined by equality operations (**column_name** = *X*, or **a.column_name = b.column_name**, etc.) in the **where** clause *exclusively*. The second condition is that the DBA must be willing to make an enormous storage trade-off for that performance gain—tables in hash clusters can require as much as 50 percent more storage space than comparably defined nonclustered tables with associated indexes.

The final area of this chapter is the use of declarative constraints in order to preserve data integrity. In many database systems, there is only one way to enforce data integrity in a database—define procedures for checking data that will be executed at the time a data change is made. In Oracle, this functionality is provided with the use of triggers. However, Oracle also provides a set of five declarative integrity constraints that can be defined in the table definition. The five types of integrity constraints are (1) primary keys, designed to identify the uniqueness of every row in a table; (2) foreign keys, designed to allow referential integrity and parent/child relationships between tables; (3) unique constraints, designed to force each row's non-NULL column element to be unique; (4) NOT NULL constraints, designed to prevent a column value from being specified as NULL by a row; and (5) check constraints, designed to check the value of a column or columns against a prescribed set of constant values. Two of these constraints—primary keys and unique constraints—have associated indexes with them.

Constraints have two statuses, enabled and disabled. When created, the constraint will automatically validate every column in the table associated with the constraint. If no row's data violates the constraint, then the constraint will be in enabled status when creation completes. If a row violates the constraint, then the status of the constraint will be disabled after the constraint is created. If the constraint is disabled after startup, the DBA can identify and examine the offending rows by first creating a special table called EXCEPTIONS by running the **utlexcpt.sql** script found in the **rdbms/admin** directory under the Oracle software home directory. Once EXCEPTIONS is created, the DBA can execute an **alter table enable constraints exceptions into** statement, and the offending rows will be loaded into the EXCEPTIONS table. To find information about constraints, the DBA can look in DBA_CONSTRAINTS and DBA_CONS_COLUMNS. Additional information about the indexes created by constraints can be gathered from the DBA_INDEXES view.

Two-Minute Drill

- Rollback segments allow transaction processing to occur by storing changes to the database before they are actually written to the database.

- Rollback segments should consist of equally sized extents.

- **pctincrease** is not permitted on rollback segments.

- Rollback segments must be brought online in order to use them.

- A rollback segment cannot be taken offline until such time as all active transactions writing rollback entries have completed.

- Entries are associated with transactions in the rollback segment via the use of a system change number (SCN).

- When the Parallel Server option is used, the number of public rollback segments allocated by Oracle when the database is started is equal to the quotient of TRANSACTIONS/TRANSACTIONS _PER_ROLLBACK_SEGMENT.

- Specific private rollback segments can be allocated at startup if they are specified in the ROLLBACK_SEGMENTS parameter in **init.ora**.

- Number of rollback segments required for an instance is determined by the Rule of Four—divide concurrent user processes by 4; if result is less than 4 + 4, round up to the nearest multiple of 4. Use no more than 50 rollback segments.

- Monitor performance in rollback segments with V$ROLLSTAT and V$WAITSTAT.

- Table creation and index creation depends on proper sizing.

- Three steps for determining size are as follows:

  1. Determine row counts for table.

  2. Determine how many rows each block can hold.

  3. Determine how many blocks are required for the table.

- The components of a database block that affect how much space is available for row entries are: fixed block header, variable block header, table directory, and row directory. Another factor influencing space for row entries is the **pctfree** option.

- Determining space requirements for indexes is accomplished by the following:

1. Determine number of index nodes for the associated table row count.

2. Determine number of index nodes per block.

3. Determine number of blocks per index.

■ The number of blocks required to store an index is equal to the number of blocks required to store an index node, plus an additional 5 percent for linking blocks used in the index framework.

■ Clusters improve performance on queries that join two or more tables with static data by storing related data from the tables in the same physical data blocks. This reduces the number of I/O reads required to retrieve the data.

■ Determining space requirements for clusters is accomplished by the following:

1. Determine the number of rows that will associate with each individual cluster entry.

2. Determine the number of cluster entries that will fit into one block.

3. Determine the number of blocks required for the cluster.

■ Clusters should not be used to store tables whose data is dynamic or volatile.

■ The steps to create a cluster once proper sizing has taken place are as follows:

1. Create the cluster with the **create cluster** statement.

2. Place tables in the cluster with the **create table** command with the **cluster** option.

3. Create the cluster index with the **create index on cluster** command.

4. Populate tables with data. This step cannot be done until step 3 is complete.

■ In order to further improve performance on table joins, the DBA can set up hash clustering on the database.

■ Hash clustering is the same as regular clusters in that data from multiple tables are stored together in data blocks, but different in that there is an additional key to search for data, called a hash key.

■ Data is retrieved from a hash cluster by Oracle applying a hash function to the value specified in equality operations in the **where** clause of the table join. Ideally, this allows for data retrieval in one disk read.

■ Hash clusters only improve performance on queries where the data is static, and the **select** statements contain table joins with equality operations *only*. Range queries are not allowed.

■ Data integrity constraints are declared in the Oracle database as part of the table definition.

■ There are five types of integrity constraints:

   ■ *Primary key*—identifies each row in the table as unique.

   ■ *Foreign key*—develops referential integrity between two tables.

   ■ *Unique*—forces each non-NULL value in the column to be unique.

   ■ *NOT NULL*—forces each value in the column to be NOT NULL.

   ■ *Check*—validates each entry into the column against a set of valid value constants.

■ When a constraint is created, every row in the table is validated against the constraint restriction.

■ The EXCEPTIONS table stores rows that violate the integrity constraint created for a table.

■ The EXCEPTIONS table can be created by running the **utlexcpt.sql** script.

■ The DBA_CONSTRAINTS and DBA_CONS_COLUMNS data dictionary views display information about the constraints of a database.

Chapter Questions

1. **Which of the following statements are not true about primary keys?**

   A. A primary key cannot be NULL.

   B. Each column value in a primary key must be unique.

   C. Each column value in a primary key corresponds to a primary-key value in another table.

   D. A primary key identifies the uniqueness of that row in the table.

   E. An associated index is created with a primary key.

2. **Clustering tables is appropriate when**

   A. The tables in the cluster are frequently joined

   B. The tables in the cluster are frequently updated

   C. The tables in the cluster have fewer than 60 rows

   D. The tables in the cluster have no primary key

3. **The POSITION column in DBA_CONS_COLUMNS**

   A. Indicates the position of the constraint on disk

   B. Relates to the hierarchical position of the table in the data model

   C. Improves the scalability of the Oracle database

   D. Identifies the position of the column in a composite index

4. **Available space for row entries in a data block is determined by**

   A. DB_BLOCK_SIZE + header size - **pctfree**

   B. DB_BLOCK_SIZE - header size - **pctfree**

   C. DB_BLOCK_SIZE + header size - **pctused**

   D. DB_BLOCK_SIZE - header size - **pctused**

5. **Indexes improve database performance only when used as part of SELECT statements.**

   A. TRUE

B. FALSE

6. **Rollback segment shrinks can be avoided if**

   A. The **optimal** option is decreased.

   B. The DBA manually performs all rollback segment shrinks.

   C. Long-running transactions are assigned to larger rollback segments.

   D. V$ROLLSTAT is monitored carefully.

7. **How many rollback segments will be required if the value set for TRANSACTIONS is 300 and the value set for TRANSACTIONS_PER_ROLLBACK_SEGMENT is 4?**

   A. 25

   B. 50

   C. 75

   D. 100

8. **When a rollback segment is created, its availability status is set to online.**

   A. TRUE

   B. FALSE

9. **Which of the following are components of a data block? (Choose two)**

   A. Library cache

   B. Row cache

   C. Row directory

   D. Fixed header

   E. pctincrease

10. **Which of the following constraints has an index associated with it? (Choose two)**

    A. Primary key

B. Foreign key

C. Unique

D. NOT NULL

E. Check

11. All data integrity needs are handled by using declarative integrity constraints.

A. TRUE

B. FALSE

12. A low PCTUSED

A. Decreases performance on the database by requiring short, frequent placement of the blocks on a freelist

B. Increases storage costs on the database by placing a block on the freelist only when a great deal of block space is free

C. Decreases storage costs on the database by maximizing space usage in a data block

D. Increases performance on the database by forcing Oracle to populate the block with rows frequently

13. Entries in a rollback segment are bound to a transaction by

A. Number of commits performed

B. Number of rollbacks performed

C. ROWID

D. System change number

14. Hash functions

A. Are defined by Oracle only

B. Are defined by the user only

C. Can be defined by both Oracle and the user

D. None of the above

Answers to Chapter Questions

1. C. Each column value in a primary key corresponds to a primary-key value in another table.

Explanation All other statements made about primary keys are true. They must be NULL and unique, in order to allow them to represent each row uniquely in the table. An associated index is also created with a primary key. Refer to the discussion of primary keys as part of integrity constraints.

2. A. The tables in the cluster are frequently joined.

Explanation Choice B is incorrect because data in tables that are clustering candidates must be static. Choice C is incorrect because there is no limitation on the number of rows a table can have in order to be clustered, only the static update limitation. Choice D is incorrect because a table without a primary key is inappropriate for general use in Oracle, including for use on clusters. Refer to the discussion of clustering.

3. D. Identifies the position of a column in a composite index

Explanation Constraints are stored with the data definition of a table, without regard to the value stored in POSITION. Therefore, choice A is incorrect. POSITION also has nothing to do with parent/child hierarchies in the data model or with scalability, thereby eliminating choices B and C. Refer to the discussion on using dictionary views to examine constraints.

4. B. DB_BLOCK_SIZE - header size - **pctfree**

Explanation The amount of space in any block cannot exceed the size of the block. Therefore, choice B is incorrect. The **pctused** option plays no role in the determination of free space on the Oracle database, which eliminates choices C and D. Refer to the discussion of sizing tables, indexes, or clusters.

5. A.   TRUE

Explanation   If no **select** statement uses the columns in an index as part of the select criteria in the **where** clause, then the index provides no improvement to performance. Refer to the discussion of storage/performance trade-offs in index usage.

6. C.   Long-running transactions are assigned to larger rollback segments.

Explanation   By decreasing the **optimal** clause, the DBA leaves the rollback segment more vulnerable to shrinks. Therefore, choice A is incorrect.

7. B.   50

Explanation   Refer to the Rule of Four in creating rollback segments for more information.

8. B.   FALSE

Explanation   Once created, a rollback segment status is offline, and must be brought online in order to be used. Refer to the discussion of rollback segments.

9. C and D.   Row directory and fixed header

Explanation   The library cache and row cache are part of the shared pool that was discussed earlier in the unit. Therefore, choices A and B are incorrect. The **pctincrease** option is a storage clause affecting the size of extents for a database object. Refer to the discussion of sizing tables, indexes, or clusters.

10. A and C.   Primary key and unique

Explanation   Refer to the discussion of indexes created in conjunction with integrity constraints.

11. B.   FALSE

Explanation   Not every data integrity need can be handled with a declarative integrity constraint. Some complex business rules where valid values are determined based on that data are being submitted. There are no declarative integrity constraints designed to handle that situation. The method used to handle business rules that cannot be modeled with declarative integrity constraints is to create triggers.

12. B.   Increases storage costs on the database by placing a block on the freelist only when a great deal of block space is free

Explanation   A low value set for **pctused** prevents a data block from being placed on a freelist frequently, which eliminates choices A and D. However, as rows are deleted from the block, space is wasted because Oracle will not place new rows on the block until space usage dips under **pctused**, which also eliminates choice C. Refer to the discussion of space usage in tables and indexes.

13. D.   System change number

Explanation   The number of commits or rollbacks performed simply reduces the number of active transactions on the database. ROWIDs correspond to the location on disk of rows for a table. Refer to the discussion of rollback segments.

14. C.   Can be defined by both Oracle and the user

Explanation   Oracle comes configured with its own hash function. Additionally, the user can define his or her own hash function, particularly in the case when a hash key is a uniformly distributed unique integer. Refer to the discussion of hash clusters.

CHAPTER

9

Managing Database Usage

n this chapter, you will understand and demonstrate knowledge in the following areas:

- Managing users
- Managing resource usage
- Managing database access and roles
- Auditing the database

This chapter focuses on the functionality Oracle provides in order to limit database access. There are several different aspects to limiting database usage. In many larger organizations, the DBA may find *that security is handled by a security administrator*—in which case the functionality provided by Oracle in this area may not be handled by the DBA at all. As the resident expert on Oracle software, it helps the DBA to familiarize himself or herself with this subject in order to better manage the Oracle database. Bear in mind that this discussion will use the terms *DBA* and *security administrator* interchangeably, and that the main reason it is covered here is that there will be questions about security on the OCP Exam 2. Approximately 27 percent of test content on this exam focuses on database security.

Managing Users

In this section, you will cover the following topics related to managing users:

- Creating users
- Altering and dropping existing users
- Monitoring information about existing users
- Terminating user sessions

The management of users in the Oracle database consists of many activities. Usage of a database begins with the creation of new users. Once users are created, their identification methods and default database usage can be altered by the DBA or security administrator in many ways. Information about active sessions run by users can also be monitored, and those sessions can even be killed by the DBA should the need arise. In short, there are many aspects of user management that the DBA or security administrator can control with the Oracle database.

Creating New Database Users

One of the primary tasks early on in the creation of a new database is adding new users. However, user creation is an ongoing task in the Oracle architecture. As users enter and leave the organization, so too must the DBA keep track of access to the database granted to those users. Creation of new users in the Oracle database is handled with the **create user** statement.

```
CREATE USER spanky
IDENTIFIED BY rascal
DEFAULT TABLESPACE users_01
TEMPORARY TABLESPACE temp_01
QUOTA 10M ON users_01
PROFILE app_developer
DEFAULT ROLE developer_01;
```

This statement highlights several items of information that comprise the syntax and semantics of user creation. The first aspect of user creation is the name of the user itself. There are few constraints on the name assigned to users in the Oracle architecture. The first constraint is that if the DBA is using operating system authentication for allowing users to access the database, then the usernames should be preceded by default with **ops$**. In no other case is it recommended that a username contain a nonalphanumeric character, although both _ and # are permitted characters in usernames. The name should also start with a letter. On single-byte character sets, the name can be one to 30 characters long, while on multibyte character sets, the name of a user must be limited to 30 bytes. In addition, the name should contain one single-byte character according to Oracle recommendations. The username is not case sensitive, and cannot be a reserved word.

The second component is the password for the user. This item should contain at least three characters, and preferably six or more. Generally, it is recommended that users change their password once they know their username is created. A user should change his password to something that is not a word or a name, and also preferably contains a numeric character somewhere in it. As is the case with the username, the password can be a maximum length of 30 bytes. Similar to the name, the password cannot be a reserved word.

The next item in the user creation statement plays a crucial role in tablespace management in Oracle. The **default tablespace** names the location to which all database objects created by that user will be created if the object creation statement does not explicitly name another location. Including this statement in the creation of a username plays an important role in protecting the integrity of the SYSTEM tablespace. If no **default tablespace** is named for a user, objects the user creates may be placed in the SYSTEM tablespace. Recall that SYSTEM contains many database objects that are critical to database usage. Some of these items include the data dictionary and the SYSTEM tablespace. It can be detrimental to the functioning of an Oracle database if users are allowed to create all their database objects in SYSTEM; therefore, this step of defining **default tablespace** is crucial to preserving the integrity of that tablespace.

Defining a **tablespace** in which the user will place all temporary segments is crucial in the same way as defining a **default tablespace**. If **temporary tablespace** is not explicitly specified by the DBA at user creation, then the location for all temporary segments for that user will be the SYSTEM tablespace. To understand fully the impact of this situation, consider the uses of temporary segments. Typically, when a user process executes a long-running query that performs sorting functions, such as **group by** or **order by** statements as well as others, Oracle uses a special memory area called the *sort area* to perform the required sort operation on the information. If the query requires more space than the sort area allows, then Oracle will allocate temporary segments in which to sort the information for the life of the query. This frequent allocation and deallocation can cause some fragmentation in a tablespace. It may take time before the SMON process pulls smaller amounts of free space back into larger contiguous amounts of free space. Again, SYSTEM is a valuable resource that should be used directly by users as infrequently as possible.

The next line of the **create user** statement is the **quota** allocation. A **quota** is a limitation on the amount of space the user's database objects can occupy within the tablespace. If a user attempts to create a database object in a tablespace that exceeds the user's **quota** for that tablespace, then the object creation script will receive an error stating that the user's tablespace

quota has been exceeded. In this event, one of two things should happen. Either the user should drop some of the objects he already owns in the tablespace to make room for the new object under his space **quota**, or the DBA should allocate a **higher** quota in the tablespace for the user. Quotas can be specified either in kilobytes (K) or megabytes (M). A **quota** clause should be issued separately for every tablespace other than the temporary tablespace on which the user will have access to create database objects.

TIP

Users need quotas on tablespaces to create database objects only. They do not need a quota on a tablespace to update, insert, or delete data in an existing object in the tablespace, so long as they do have the appropriate privilege on the object for data being inserted, updated or deleted.

Another clause in a user creation statement is **profile**. Profiles are a bundled set of resource usage parameters that the DBA can set in order to limit the user's ability to use the system. The principle behind profiles is manifold. One driving idea behind their use is that there may be many end users of the system in the course of a day. Since the DBA may want to reduce the number of licenses required for the Oracle database, she might use the concurrent usage licensing arrangement rather than the license-per-user-created arrangement. However, in order to accommodate each user that wants to use the system and reduce the amount of errors users get when they try to log onto a system already at its usage capacity, the DBA may set up profiles for each user that limit the amount of time they can spend on the system.

The last clause for the **create user** statement is **default role**. Each user may have specific privileges that are granted to them to allow them to do their job. These privileges include access to view or change data in a table or tables, or to execute stored procedures in a database. The number of available database objects can be quite large, making the management of access to those objects difficult and prone to mistakes. In order to facilitate the management of object or system privileges, a DBA may choose to grant those privileges to special database objects, called *roles*, instead. These roles can then be granted to users directly.

Exercises

1. What statement is used to create users? Identify the need for tablespace quotas. Do users need tablespace quotas to **insert** data in existing tables? Explain.

2. What is the purpose of a temporary tablespace?

Altering and Dropping Existing Users

Once a user is created, there should be little reason to modify that user, with the exception that regular password change increases the security of the ID. This password rotation is a feature of Oracle8. Any aspect of the username can be modified by the DBA, though the aspects of the username that may be changed by the actual user are more limited. A situation may arise in regular database usage where a user must change his or her password. This situation may be that the user's password has been shared with another user, or if the DBA simply wants all users to rotate their passwords on a regular basis. The **alter user identified by** statement is used to change the user's password to something else.

```
ALTER USER spanky
IDENTIFIED BY orange#tabby;
```

Sometimes the DBA will want to reorganize things on the database in order to make more effective use of the hardware running Oracle. Perhaps this effort involves dropping some tablespaces and creating new ones. If the DBA wants to change the default tablespace used by the users for creating their database objects, the **alter user default tablespace** statement can be used. By changing a default tablespace for a user, the DBA makes it difficult for users to place objects in the SYSTEM tablespace by accidentally forgetting to specify the appropriate storage clauses. Any objects that were created in the USERS_01 tablespace by user SPANKY will continue to reside in that tablespace until they are dropped. Additionally, if user SPANKY specifies a tablespace in which to place a database object, that specification will override the default tablespace.

By the same token, the DBA may want to reorganize the temporary tablespace used by the users of a database system, and this is done using **alter user temporary tablespace**. Only the DBA can make these changes; the users cannot change their own temporary or default tablespace.

```
ALTER USER spanky
DEFAULT TABLESPACE overflow_tabspc01;
```

or

```
ALTER USER spanky
TEMPORARY TABLESPACE temp_overflow_01;
```

As with default tablespaces, if the user had created an object in the tablespace that had been originally allocated for temporary segments, any object created there will still be there after the temporary tablespace is changed. However, since temporary segments are eliminated after the statement that required their use completes, any object created in the previous temporary tablespace will not stay there for long.

With the exception of the temporary segment tablespace, any tablespace accessible to the user at user creation can have a quota placed on it. A quota can be altered by the DBA with the **alter user quota** statement. For example, the DBA may want to reduce the quota on the USERS_01 tablespace from 10 megabytes to 5 megabytes for user SPANKY. If the user has already created over 5M worth of database objects in the tablespace, no further data can be added to those objects and no new objects can be created. Only the DBA may change a user's tablespace quota; the users may not change their own quotas.

```
ALTER USER spanky
QUOTA 5M ON TABLESPACE users_01;
```

The DBA may want to create new profiles corresponding to database usage. After the new profiles are created, the DBA then must allocate the profiles to the users that resource usage will change for. The method for changing a user's profile is the **alter user profile** statement. The changes in this new profile that affect resource usage for this user will not take effect until the user drops the current session by disconnecting and reconnects with the new session profile. Only the DBA may change a user quota; the users may not change their own quotas.

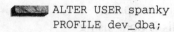
```
ALTER USER spanky
PROFILE dev_dba;
```

The final change the DBA may make to user accounts is specifying a new default role. There is no limit to the number of roles that can be granted to a user; however, if there are privileges granted to a user through a nondefault role, the user may have to switch default roles in order to use those privileges. All roles granted to a user are default roles unless another option is specified by the username creation. The **alter user default role all** statement sets all roles granted to user SPANKY to be the default role. Other options available for specifying user roles include physically listing one or more roles that are to be the default, or specifying all roles except for ones named using **all except** (*role_name* [, ...]), or **none**.

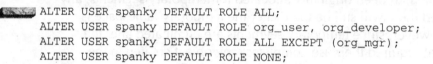
```
ALTER USER spanky DEFAULT ROLE ALL;
ALTER USER spanky DEFAULT ROLE org_user, org_developer;
ALTER USER spanky DEFAULT ROLE ALL EXCEPT (org_mgr);
ALTER USER spanky DEFAULT ROLE NONE;
```

TIP
Except for altering the password, only the DBA can change user configurations.

As personnel for an organization changes, so too should the database users that were created change. To drop a user from the database, the DBA can execute the **drop user cascade** statement. The **cascade** option provides a key function in the removal of users. If a user has created database objects, the user cannot be dropped until the objects are dropped as well. In order to drop the user and all related database objects in one fell swoop, Oracle provides the **cascade** option.

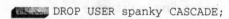
```
DROP USER spanky CASCADE;
```

Exercises

1. What statement is used for altering users?

2. What are the features of a user that the users themselves can change? What features can only the DBA change?

3. What statement is used to drop a database user? How can the objects created by the user be eliminated at the same time?

Monitoring Information About Existing Users

The DBA may periodically want to monitor information about users. Several data dictionary views may be used for the purpose of obtaining information about users. Some information a DBA may want to collect includes default and temporary tablespace information, profile information, objects created by that user, and roles granted to that user. The following data dictionary views can be used to determine this information.

- **DBA_USERS** Contains username, Oracle-generated ID number, encrypted password, default and temporary tablespace information, and the user profile that was specified in the ID creation statements or any alteration that may have followed.

- **DBA_PROFILES** Contains specific information about the resource usage parameters specified in conjunction with each profile.

- **DBA_OBJECTS** Contains the specific information about every object in the database. The DBA can determine which objects belong to which users by using the OWNER column of this view.

- **DBA_ROLES** Names all the roles created on the database.

- **DBA_ROLE_PRIVS** Names all users and the roles granted to them in the database.

- **DBA_TS_QUOTAS** Names all users and any tablespace quotas that have been created for them.

- **RESOURCE_COST** Identifies all resources in the database and their corresponding cost as defined by the DBA. Cost determines the relative importance of usage of a resource.

- **USER_RESOURCE_LIMITS** Identifies the system resource limits for individual users as determined by the profile assigned to the users.

- **V$SESSION** Provides SID and serial# to the DBA when a user session must be killed.

Exercises

1. How can the DBA determine which users own which objects?

2. How can the DBA determine which tablespaces whose access is granted to a user have quotas on them?

Terminating User Sessions

In some cases, the DBA may need to cut off a user session from running against the database. The user may not be authorized to perform a certain activity, or the DBA may need to perform some cleanup activity that necessitates eliminating sessions. The statement that a DBA can issue in order to terminate a user session is **alter system kill session** *SID, SERIAL#*. In this statement, the user's session ID (SID) must be specified, along with the serial number for the session. These two pieces of information can be extracted from the V$SESSION view by selecting the values in the SID and SERIAL# columns where the value in USERNAME equals the name of the user whose session the DBA wants to kill.

```
SELECT sid, serial#
FROM v$session
WHERE username = 'SPANKY';

SID     SERIAL#
------- ----------
34      3948

ALTER SYSTEM
KILL SESSION '34,3948';
```

The effects of issuing an **alter system kill session** are as follows. First, the user session is terminated, preventing the user from issuing any more SQL operations from the current session. Next, all SQL operations in progress are also discontinued, causing Oracle to roll back any transactions that may have been in progress with that session. As part of discontinuing all transactions related to that session, the locks held by the session are released, freeing up the associated resources. As one can see, terminating a session can be a useful emergency measure for handling a locking situation.

Exercises

1. What statement is used to kill a user session?

2. Where can the DBA look to find information needed to kill a user session?

Managing Resource Usage

In this section, you will cover the following topics related to managing resource usage:

- Understanding Oracle resource usage

- Managing profiles created for the system

- Creating and assigning user profiles

Resource usage can be managed by creating specific user profiles to correspond to the amount of activity anticipated by average transactions generated by different types of users. The principle of user profiles is not to force the user off the system every time an artificially low resource usage threshold is exceeded. Rather, resource usage should allow the users to do just about everything they have to do in order to effectively use the Oracle database. But, if a mistake should occur, or if the user should try to do something detrimental to database performance, resource usage limitation functionality provided by profiles can help reduce the problem.

Understanding Oracle Resource Usage

Oracle resource usage works on either of two principles: setting individual resource limits, or assigning resource costs and defining a composite limit. Consider the following example. A user with database **update** capability on the test database and **select** capability on the production database is attempting to perform a small test of functionality on a database application change. The user determines that he needs 2,500 rows of data populated in a table in order to complete the test. The user attempts to port production data onto the test environment using a database link, but forgets an element in the **where** clause that will limit the data selected to the 2,500 rows that he needs. As a result, Oracle attempts to execute the statement, which pulls 25,000 rows of data. This statement is running across a link and causes serious performance degradation for other users on the test database. The use of profiles to limit resource usage can help in this type of situation. Either the DBA can assign individual resource costs to limit a user's CPU time so he can't issue statements like this one, or the DBA can set a low composite limit and a high resource cost for CPU time to limit use of the CPU.

Enabling Resource Limits

In order for resource limits to be used, the DBA must specify that resource limits are to be used on the database. This step is accomplished by changing the RESOURCE_LIMIT initialization parameter in the **init.ora** file to TRUE. However, the change there will not take place until the database is shut down and restarted. To enable resource restriction used in conjunction with profiles on the current database session, the DBA should issue the following statement:

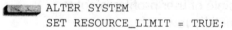

```
ALTER SYSTEM
SET RESOURCE_LIMIT = TRUE;
```

Assigning Individual Resource Limits

User profiles bundle together resource limitations into a single data object that can be assigned to a user. User profiles can control usage of specific resource usage in several areas of Oracle. A user profile can be created for the database by the DBA using the **create profile** statement.

```
CREATE PROFILE sales_emp LIMIT
SESSIONS_PER_USER 1
CPU_PER_CALL 10000
CONNECT_TIME 240;
```

A listing of the areas where usage may be limited in a profile follows:

■ *Sessions per user*—the number of sessions a user can open concurrently with the Oracle database.

- *CPU per session*—the maximum allowed CPU time in 1/100 seconds that a user can utilize in one session.

- *CPU per call*—the maximum allowed CPU time in 1/100 seconds that any individual operation in a user session can use.

- *Logical reads per session*—the maximum number of disk I/O block reads that can be executed in support of the user processing in one session.

- *Logical reads per call*—the maximum number of disk I/O block reads that can be executed in support of the user processing in one session.

- *Idle time*—the time in minutes that a user can issue no commands before Oracle times out their session.

- *Connect time*—the total amount of time in minutes that a user can be connected to the database.

- *Private SGA*—limits the amount of private memory in kilobytes or megabytes that can be allocated to a user for private storage of values returned by a query.

Resource Costs and Composite Limits

In some cases, the DBA may find the explicit setting of individual parameters for resource usage is not ideal in limiting database resource usage. An alternative known as setting composite limits works on the principle of resource cost. Resource cost is a figure determined by the DBA that reflects the relative value of that resource. Cost is specified as an abstract unit value, not a monetary resource price. For example, setting the resource cost of CPU cycles per session equal to 1.5 does not mean that each CPU cycle costs a user process $1.50 to run. Figure 9-1 demonstrates the resource costs are not necessarily monetary costs.

Rather, the cost of a resource corresponds to its importance on the system. For example, a DBA managing a database system with few CPUs available and many disk controllers may consider the **cpu_per_session** resource to be more expensive than another resource, perhaps **logical_reads_per_session**. As such, the DBA might allocate resource costs

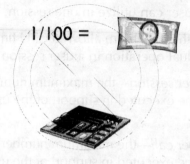

FIGURE 9-1. *Resource cost is not a monetary cost*

appropriately. The statement used for assigning a resource cost is the **alter resource cost** statement. Only certain resources can be given a cost, including **cpu_per_session**, **logical_reads_per_session**, **connect_time**, and **private_sga**. The default value for each resource cost is zero.

```
ALTER RESOURCE COST
CPU_PER_SESSION 10
LOGICAL_READS_PER_SESSION 2;
```

Once resource costs are set by the DBA, then the task of assigning a composite limit can be accomplished. Composite limits restrict the usage of database resources by forcing Oracle to keep a running total of how often a resource is used. Each time a resource is used, Oracle increments the total resource usage cost for that session until the time that the session hits the limit set by the **composite_limit** option. The SALES_EMP profile is altered by the DBA to include a composite limit with the **alter profile** statement.

```
ALTER PROFILE sales_emp LIMIT
COMPOSITE_LIMIT 500;
```

The resource costs of **cpu_per_session** and **logical_reads_per_session** are set as they appear in the **alter resource cost** statement. User SPANKY logs onto the system and proceeds to execute a query that takes 10 CPU cycles to execute. As soon as the sixth CPU cycle is complete, the user session terminates because the composite limit of 500 is exceeded by this query. Of course, setting the composite limit this low would artificially restrict the usage of the database by user SPANKY, which from the beginning was identified as not being the ultimate purpose of user profiles.

Exercises

1. What is a user profile? How can they be used to prevent excessive use of the database system?

2. What must happen before resource usage can be limited through the use of user profiles? What are the parameters that can be set to restrict database usage for individual resources?

3. What are resource costs and composite limits? How do these two features work together?

Managing Profiles Created for the System

Before creation of user profiles, the DBA should explore a special user profile that is created by Oracle at database creation. This special user profile is called DEFAULT, and it is assigned to all users on database creation if no other user profile is defined in the **create user** statement. The DEFAULT profile assigns a special identifier to all resources named above, called **unlimited**, that allows the user to have unlimited use of the resources specified in the profile. Any of these values can be changed by the DBA in order to ensure that no user can issue SQL statements that arbitrarily consume database resources. However, if the DBA does change a parameter in the DEFAULT profile, she should ensure that no other user profile is adversely impacted by the default resource usage parameter change.

TIP
*If no profile is assigned with the **profile** clause of the **create user** statement, the DEFAULT profile is assigned to that user.*

Setting a user profile to not contain explicit values for every parameter leaves the profile vulnerable to any change made in the DEFAULT profile. If the DBA plans never to change the DEFAULT profile, this scenario will work fine. However, if a change is made in the DEFAULT profile, the effects of the change will be felt in every user profile that did not specify a value explicitly for that aspect of resource usage. If the DBA doesn't plan to change settings for DEFAULT, then the creation of user profiles that do not contain explicit values set for all parameters will be fine with the default set to **unlimited**. However, the DBA should ensure that all users created are assigned to a profile other than DEFAULT in order to prevent granting unlimited resource usage to any user. If the DBA plans to allow many users to use the DEFAULT profile, then the resource parameters for DEFAULT should be changed and every user profile created should have resource usage parameters explicitly assigned.

Exercises

1. What is the DEFAULT profile? What are the default values for resource limits in the DEFAULT profile?

2. What profile is assigned to a user if one is not explicitly set by the **create user** statement?

Creating and Assigning User Profiles

With the DEFAULT profile in mind, the DBA now should consider the task of creating user profiles. This task requires considering each of the potential users in a database, and categorizing those users into several different levels of usage. For example, the DBA of database SALES_01 may determine that there are four different classes of users on this system. The first class of users is the salespeople. These users **update** their sales data on a daily basis, inputting the sales that they have generated and accessing their own profiles to find the status of sales orders when customers call them. Another class of users in this system is managers. These users have several salespeople assigned to each of them. Their job is to log onto the system and track the sales figures for each salesperson against selling goals set forth by the company. Additionally, they assign bonuses to the best salespeople in their group on a weekly basis. Finally, they compile a sales report for their team broken out by team member every two weeks.

The third class of user on this database system is the auditor. There are three auditors on the database. Their job is to review each salesperson individually to verify that the sales are legitimate, and that payment is collected for the sale. The auditor often must run ad hoc reports against the database to determine certain things per salesperson, per team, and for the sales force as a whole. The final class of user on this database system is the payroll administrator. This user executes one process weekly that determines the percentage commission for each salesperson, adds the bonus if there is one, and generates a paycheck for the salesperson for the week's worth of work. This process can take several hours, depending on how many sales were executed for the week.

The first user profile created will be called SALES_EMP. Since this profile corresponds to the salespersons that use the database to **insert** sales orders or check existing orders, the DBA can assume that most statements issued will be **select** or **insert**, and that each statement will take only a short amount of time to fulfill. Therefore, the DBA may impose limits on the CPU used per call. Since a salesperson may spend a great deal of time on the phone trying to sell to users, the DBA may not want to time the user out if the session remains idle. However, the DBA doesn't want users to simply leave their desks at the end of the day without logging off either. In order to prevent a situation where an unauthorized user submits sales entries, the DBA may limit the number of sessions the salesperson can have to one. The rest of the parameters that can be specified at user profile creation but weren't are set to the default value for that resource as detailed in the DEFAULT profile. The **create profile** statement will be used to create this profile.

```
CREATE PROFILE sales_emp LIMIT
SESSIONS_PER_USER 1
CPU_PER_CALL 10000
CONNECT_TIME 240;
```

The next profile created is for the managers. The DBA assesses resource usage by each manager in the following way. Since the manager has to review sales figures for many different users, the manager may want to review multiple salespersons' records at a time, using multiple sessions with the database. Since the manager has to generate that biweekly report, the DBA wants to make sure he will not be limited with respect to CPU or disk usage. However, since the manager has the ability to assign bonuses, the DBA does not want the manager to leave his sessions open while he is away from his desk for someone to inappropriately assign a bonus in the manager's name. Hence, the limit is placed on idle time and connect time.

All other resources that were not explicitly assigned limits for this profile will take on the default values specified in the DEFAULT profile.

```
CREATE PROFILE sales_mgr LIMIT
SESSIONS_PER_USER 3
CONNECT_TIME 480
IDLE_TIME 10;
```

For the third class of user, the auditor, the DBA must allow for a great deal of flexibility in issuing potentially long-running ad hoc queries. The DBA intentionally leaves many options off from the **create profile** statement. This is due to the fact that the DBA wants these options to default to **unlimited** as set in the DEFAULT user profile. The only item explicitly set by the statement is the limitation of sessions for the user, which is set to five.

```
CREATE PROFILE auditor LIMIT
SESSIONS_PER_USER 5;
```

The final user profile the DBA will create for the SALES database example is the profile for the payroll administrator. This profile relies on the specification of **unlimited** for all resources not explicitly identified in the creation of this statement. However, the resources that are set limit the number of sessions to one. Since the payroll administrator will be executing only one process per week to generate pay information, there is no need for her to have more than one session open at a time. Additionally, once the process is complete, there is no further need for her to be on the system. As such, if idle time exceeds five minutes, then the user is disconnected.

```
CREATE PROFILE payroll_adm LIMIT
SESSIONS_PER_USER 1
IDLE_TIME 5;
```

Once the profiles are created, they can be assigned to users that are in the process of being created with the use of the **create user** statement. In the **profile** clause of this statement, the profile should be named. As a result of this creation statement, SPANKY now has the resource usage ability to execute the types of statements that he needs in order to audit the sales records. If, however, a change is made to user SPANKY's job function, such that SPANKY is now a sales associate in the organization, the DBA may want to execute the following statement in order to reflect the change in SPANKY's resource usage needs:

```
CREATE USER spanky
IDENTIFIED BY orange#tabby
TEMPORARY TABLESPACE temp_01
QUOTA 5M ON temp_01
PROFILE auditor;

ALTER USER spanky
PROFILE sales_emp;
```

Finally, if the DBA wants to drop a user profile from the database, she can do so by executing the **drop profile** statement. As with dropping users, a profile cannot be eliminated without the **cascade** option if the profile has already been assigned to a user. Once a profile that has been assigned to a user is dropped by issuing the **drop profile cascade** command, the profile applied to the user's subsequent sessions is changed to the DEFAULT profile.

```
DROP PROFILE auditor CASCADE;
```

The act of changing a user profile may be required, particularly if user profiles in the database rely on default parameter values being set in a certain way in the DEFAULT profile. If the resource usage parameter **cpu_per_session** in DEFAULT were to be changed from **unlimited** to 20,000, then the value set implicitly for **cpu_per_session** in several of the user profiles created in the earlier example would also be changed. The DBA can issue the following statement to explicitly set this option to **unlimited** in the auditor profile.

```
ALTER PROFILE auditor LIMIT
CPU_PER_SESSION UNLIMITED;
```

Once this statement is executed, then the AUDITOR profile is no longer dependent on the configuration of the DEFAULT profile for its setup. Any option in any profile can be changed by the DBA at any time; however, the change will not take effect in user sessions currently running with the profile just changed. Instead, the profile only applies to future sessions for users with the changed profile assigned to them.

Exercises

1. What analysis tasks are required for creating user profiles? What statement is used to create a user profile? What statement is used to change a user profile?

2. What usage value is assigned to a resource in a user profile when the DBA does not explicitly assign one?

3. What statement is used to drop a profile? Can a profile be dropped if it is granted to a user? Explain.

Managing Database Access and Roles

In this section, you will cover the following topics related to managing database access:

- Granting and controlling system privileges
- Granting and controlling object privileges
- Creating and controlling roles

Once a user is allowed access to connect to the database, the actual areas the user is permitted to see and the things that the user is allowed to do are also controlled by Oracle. Use of every database object and system resource is governed by a privilege. There are privileges required to create objects, access objects, change data within tables, execute stored procedures, create users, etc. Since access to every object created is governed by a privilege, security in the Oracle database is highly flexible in terms of what objects are available to the user. There are two categories of privileges: object privileges and system privileges.

Granting and Controlling System Privileges

System privileges control the creation of all database objects, such as rollback segments, synonyms, tables, and triggers. Additionally, the ability to use the **analyze** command and to use the Oracle database **audit** capability is also governed by system privileges. Generally speaking, there are several classes of privilege that relate to each object. Those classes determine the scope of ability that the privilege grantee will have. The classes of database privileges are listed here:

create   This class of privilege allows the grantee of the privilege to create the objects managed by system privileges within their user schema. The objects managed by system privileges include every logical database object in the Oracle architecture. For example, if the user wants to create a rollback segment in their user schema, they must have the **create rollback segment** privilege.

alter   This class of privilege allows the grantee of the privilege to modify existing objects managed by system privileges within their user schema. The objects managed by system privileges include every logical database object in the Oracle architecture. For example, if the user wants to modify the size of a rollback segment in their user schema, they must have the **alter rollback segment** privilege.

drop   This class of privilege allows the grantee of the privilege to drop existing objects managed by system privileges within their user schema. The objects managed by system privileges include every logical database object in the Oracle architecture. For example, if the user wants to drop a rollback segment in their user schema, they must have the **drop rollback segment** privilege.

System privileges on database objects are a little tricky, however. The categorization listed for **create**, **alter**, and **drop** privileges does not exist for all objects. Furthermore, in some database objects like tables, the **alter** privilege is an object privilege, not a system privilege. Additionally, the **create index** privilege is an object privilege. Therefore, it may assist you to review the object privileges available in Oracle and determine first if the privilege required is an object privilege. If not, then the privilege required is probably a system privilege. In addition to the privileges required to **create** (and sometimes **alter** and **drop**) database objects within a user schema, there is a class of system privileges that allow the user to perform certain operations on any object in the database, as listed here:

analyze any	This system privilege allows the grantee to execute the **analyze** command on any database object in the database that permits the **analyze** operation on it. No equivalent exists that allows a user to use **analyze** only on the database objects in their schema.
audit any	This system privilege allows the grantee to execute the **audit** command on any database object in the database that permits the **audit** operation on it. No equivalent exists that allows a user to use **audit** only on the database objects in their schema.
audit system	This system privilege allows the grantee to execute the **audit** command on any statement or privilege issued in any session running on the database that permits the **audit** operation on it. No equivalent exists that allows a user to use **audit** only on the statements they issue within their own schema.
any	This reserved word can be added to a class of database privileges to issue the ability to perform the task anywhere or on any item in the database. For example, the **create any table** privilege allows the user to create a table in any user's schema, while the **grant any role** privilege allows the user to grant any role in the database.

There are some system privileges that don't seem to fit anywhere else in the scope of system privileges. One privilege is the **restricted session** privilege. This privilege allows the grantee to connect to the database any time that the database is in **restricted session** mode. This privilege is typically given only to the DBA. The other privilege considered is the **unlimited tablespace** privilege. This privilege allows the grantee the ability to create database objects in a tablespace using an unlimited amount of space in the tablespace. This privilege is granted typically to the user schema that will own the database objects for an application or database, the DBA, and no one else. The database objects on which at least the **create** system privilege applies appear in the following list for reference.

CLUSTER	PUBLIC DATABASE LINK	SYNONYM
DATABASE	PUBLIC SYNONYM	SYSTEM
DATABASE LINK	ROLE	TABLE
VIEW	ROLLBACK SEGMENT	TABLESPACE
PRIVILEGE	SESSION	TRANSACTION
PROCEDURE	SEQUENCE	TRIGGER
PROFILE	SNAPSHOT	USER

Exercises

1. Name some system privileges on database objects. What are some objects that do not use system privileges to let users change the object definition or create the object?

2. What are some other system privileges used to manage certain operations on any database object?

3. What is the **unlimited tablespace** privilege? What is the **restricted session** privilege?

Object Privileges Explained

The other category of privileges granted on the Oracle database is the set of object privileges. Object privileges permit the owner of four types of database objects to administer access to those objects according to the following types of access allowed. The various types of object privileges are listed here:

- **select**   Permits the grantee of this object privilege to access the data in a table, sequence, view, or snapshot.

- **insert**   Permits the grantee of this object privilege to **insert** data into a table or, in some cases, a view.

- **update**   Permits the grantee of this object privilege to **update** data into a table or view.

- **delete**   Permits the grantee of this object privilege to **delete** data from a table or view.

- **alter**   Permits the grantee of this object privilege to **alter** the definition of a table or sequence *only*. The **alter** privileges on all other database objects are considered system privileges.

- **index**   Permits the grantee of this object privilege to create an index on a table already defined.

- **references**   Permits the grantee to **create** or **alter** a table in order to create a foreign-key constraint against data in the referenced table.

- **execute**   Permits the grantee to run a stored procedure or function.

As given evidence by the **alter** and **index** object privilege, there sometimes can be a blurry line between system and object privileges. However, the point of this discussion is not to indicate nuance; rather, it is to give the DBA some general guidelines to understand about user system and object privileges. In order to grant a privilege to a user, the appropriate privilege administrator or the DBA can issue the following statement:

```
GRANT privilege ON object TO user;
```

In addition to granting object privileges on database objects, privileges can also be granted on columns within the database object. The privileges that can be administered on the column level are the **insert**, **update**, and **references** privileges. However, the grantor of column privileges must be careful when administering them in order to avoid problems—particularly with the **insert** privilege. If a user has the **insert** privilege on several columns in a table but not all columns, the privilege administrator must ensure that no other column in the table that does not have the **insert** privilege granted is a NOT NULL column. Take the following example under consideration in order to understand the implications of this rule. Table EMP has two columns, NAME and EMPID. Both columns have NOT NULL constraints on them. The **insert** access is granted for the EMPID column to user SPANKY, but not the NAME column. When user SPANKY attempts to **insert** an EMPID into the table, Oracle generates a NULL for the NAME column, then produces an error stating that the user cannot **insert** a NULL value into the NAME column because the column has a NOT NULL constraint on it. Administration of **update** and **insert** object privileges at the column level must be handled carefully, while the concept of using the **references** privilege on a column level seems to be more straightforward.

Some special conditions relate to the use of the **execute** privilege. If a user has the ability to execute a stored procedure owned by another user, and the procedure accesses some tables, the object privileges required to access those tables must be granted *to the owner of the procedure*, and *not* the user to whom **execute** privileges were granted. When a user executes a stored procedure, the user is able to use whatever privileges are required to execute the procedure. For example, **execute** privileges are given to user SPANKY on procedure **process_deposit( )** owned by user ATHENA, and this procedure performs an **update** on the BANK_ACCOUNT table using an **update** privilege granted to ATHENA. User SPANKY will be able to perform that **update** on BANK_ACCOUNT via the **process_deposit( )** procedure even though the **update** privilege is not granted to SPANKY. However, user SPANKY will *not* be able to issue an **update** statement on table BANK_ACCOUNT from SQL*Plus, because the appropriate privilege was not granted to SPANKY directly.

Exercises

1. In what situations is the **alter** privilege an object privilege? What are other object privileges?

2. What privilege is required to execute a stored procedure? To which user (the owner of the procedure or the executor of the privilege) must any object privilege related to updating a table in the procedure be granted?

Creating and Controlling Roles

Roles have the ability to take the complexity out of administrating user privileges. A role in the database can be thought of as a virtual user. The database object and/or system privileges that are required to perform a group of user functions are gathered together and granted to the role, which then can be granted directly to the users. As functions or database objects become available or required on the database, the object privileges needed for users to perform their functions are granted to the role. Since the role is already granted to the user, there is no further action required. Furthermore, if a user switches to a new job function requiring a different set of privileges, the role with those privileges granted to it can be granted to the user, while the role with the user's old privileges is revoked.

Roles are created on databases in the following manner. The DBA determines what classes of users exist on the database, and what privileges on the database can be logically grouped together into different user functions. Using the sales force example from the previous section, the DBA may determine that four different roles are required on the database, SALES_PERSON, SALES_MANAGER, SALES_AUDITOR, and PAYROLL_ADMIN. In order to create the roles that will support privilege administration of these classes of users, the following statement can be executed. Once the role is created, there are no privileges assigned to it until privileges are explicitly granted to it.

```
CREATE ROLE role_name IDENTIFIED BY role_password;
```

The use of a password to authenticate users trying to utilize a role is purely optional. If used, however, the password provides an extra level of security over the authentication process at database login. The most effective way to employ a role password is to set the role authenticated by a password to be a nondefault role. If the user needs to access the database with the set of privileges associated with the role, they must first execute the **alter user default role** role_name command, where the value set for role_name is the name of the role that must be authenticated. In this scenario, the user must provide the password for authentication once at the time the role is set as the default.

Privileges are granted to roles in the following manner. At the same time that the DBA determines the resource usage of various classes of users on the database, the DBA may also want to determine what object and/or system privileges each class of user will require. For example, a salesperson may need access to the CUSTOMER and ORDER tables to create new customers and customer orders, and may require access to the PRODUCTS table in order to determine what products are currently for sale. Instead of granting the privileges directly to the salespeople on an individual basis, however, the DBA can grant the privileges to the role, which then can be granted to several salespeople more easily.

```
GRANT SELECT, INSERT, UPDATE ON CUSTOMER TO sales_people;
GRANT SELECT, INSERT, UPDATE ON ORDER TO sales_people;
GRANT SELECT ON PRODUCTS TO sales_people;
GRANT sales_people TO spanky;
```

There are some special roles available to the users of a database as well. The roles available at database creation are CONNECT, RESOURCE, DBA, EXP_FULL_DATABASE and IMP_FULL_DATABASE. The uses of each role are listed as follows:

- **CONNECT**   Allows users extensive development capability within their own user schema, such as **create table**, **create cluster**, **create session**, **create view**, **create sequence**, and others, but not stored procedures.

- **RESOURCE**   Allows users more moderate development capability within their own user schema, such as **create table**, **create cluster**, **create trigger**, and **create procedure**.

- **DBA**   Allows user to administer and use all system privileges.

- **EXP_FULL_DATABASE**   Allows the user to export every object in the database using the EXPORT utility.

- **IMP_FULL_DATABASE**   Allows the user to import every object from an export dump file using the IMPORT utility.

Administering Privileges and Roles

Giving these privileges to users occurs in the following ways. Privileges are first given to the SYS and SYSTEM users, and to any other user created with the **grant any privilege** permission. As other users are created, they too are given privileges based on their needs with the **grant** command. For both system and object privileges, there are two ways to grant privileges to others: either as an end user or as an administrator. For example, executing the following **grant** statements gives access to create a table to user SPANKY, and object privileges on another table in the database:

```
GRANT CREATE TABLE TO spanky;                    -- system
GRANT SELECT, UPDATE ON athena.emp TO spanky;    -- object
```

At the end of execution for these two statements, SPANKY will have the ability to execute commands associated with the two prior commands, namely **create table** in his user schema and **select** and **update** row data on the EMP table in ATHENA's schema. However, the extent of user SPANKY's ability to give these privileges away is limited. User SPANKY can only create tables and **select** and **update** rows from EMP. He cannot give his privileges to others, nor can he relinquish them without the help of the DBA. In order to give user SPANKY some additional power to administer the rights granted to him to other users, the DBA can execute the following queries:

```
GRANT CREATE TABLE TO spanky WITH ADMIN OPTION;
GRANT SELECT, UPDATE ON emp TO SPANKY WITH GRANT OPTION;
```

The clause **with admin option**, when included in the general system privilege, gives the user SPANKY the ability to give or take away the same privilege to others. Additionally, it gives user SPANKY the ability to make other users administrators of that same privilege. Finally, if the item granted to user SPANKY is a role, user SPANKY can then alter the role or even remove it from the database.

For object privileges, user SPANKY has many of the same abilities as with the **admin option** of system privileges. In the previous example, user SPANKY can not only **select** and **update** data from EMP, but he can give that ability to other users as well. Also, user SPANKY can set up other users with the ability to give the **grant option** to the particular object privilege granted to them with the **grant option**. However, if user SPANKY has another object privilege, say the ability to **select** data from the CUSTOMER table, user SPANKY cannot grant that privilege to another user simply because the **grant option** was extended to user SPANKY as part of some object privileges on another table. Only the object privilege with which the **grant option** was given to user SPANKY can be given to other users by user SPANKY.

Some final notes about granting privileges. If user SPANKY creates a role after being granted the **create role** system privilege, then as the creator of that role SPANKY has the **admin option** on that role. Granting roles to users is done in the same way as granting system privileges. If user SPANKY creates a table in his own schema, he has all object privileges associated with that object as well. Additionally, there is a consolidated method for granting object privileges using the keyword **all**. Note that **all** is not a privilege unto itself, it is merely a specification for all object privileges for the database object. There may also come a time when users must have privileges revoked as well. This task is accomplished with the **revoke** command.

```
GRANT ALL ON emp TO spanky;

REVOKE CREATE TABLE FROM spanky;
REVOKE SELECT, UPDATE ON emp FROM spanky;
```

Important to note here is that revocation of the **create table** privilege also takes away the **admin** options that may have been given along with the privilege or role. No additional syntax is necessary for revoking either a system privilege granted **with admin option** or an object privilege granted **with grant option**. In the same way, roles may be revoked from users, even if the user created the role and thus has the **admin option**. The ability to revoke any role comes from the **grant any role** privilege, while the ability to grant or revoke certain system privileges comes from being granted the privilege with the **admin option**. When a system privilege is revoked, there are no cascading events that take place along with it. That is to say, if SPANKY created several tables while possessing the **create table** privilege, those tables are not removed if user SPANKY has the **create table** privilege revoked. Only the **drop table** command will remove the tables. There may be other cascading effects related to system privileges.

TIP
*Understand the following scenario completely before continuing! User X has a system or object privilege granted to her with **admin option** or **grant option**. X grants the privilege to user Y, with or without the administrative privileges. User Y does the same for user Z. Then X revokes the privilege from user Y. **USER Z WILL STILL HAVE THE PRIVILEGE.** WHY? Because there is no cascading effect to revoking privileges, only the fact that the user from whom the privilege was revoked no longer has the privilege.*

There are several considerations to make when revoking object privileges. For instance, on individual columns, if a privilege has been granted on two individual columns, the privilege must be revoked entirely and then regranted, if appropriate, on the individual column to the user. Also, if the user has been given the **references** privilege and used it to create a foreign-key constraint to another table, then there is some cascading that must take place in order to complete the revocation of the **references** privilege.

REVOKE REFERENCES ON emp FROM spanky CASCADE CONSTRAINTS;

In this example, not only is the privilege to create referential integrity revoked, but any instances where that referential integrity was used on the database are also revoked. If a foreign-key constraint was created on the EMP table by user SPANKY and the prior statement was issued without the **cascade constraints** clause, then the **revoke** statement will fail. Other cascading issues may appear after object privileges are revoked as well. In general, if an object privilege is revoked, then any item created by the user that relied on that object privilege may experience a problem during execution.

Open to the Public
The final aspect of privileges and access to the database that will be discussed involves a special user on the database. This user is called

PUBLIC. If a system privilege, object privilege, or role is granted to the PUBLIC user, then every user in the database has that privilege. Typically, it is not advised that the DBA should grant many privileges or roles to PUBLIC, because if the privilege or role ever needs to be revoked, then every stored package, procedure, or function will need to be recompiled.

Exercises

1. What is a role? How are privileges managed using roles?

2. What special options are required for system and object privileges if the user is to have administrative capability along with the privilege?

3. What cascading issues exist related to the **references** object privilege and the user PUBLIC?

Auditing the Database

In this section, you will cover the following topics related to auditing the database:

- Determining the need for auditing

- Tracking statement- and system-level access to data objects

- Understanding audit results with the data dictionary

- Managing audit information

Securing the database against inappropriate activity is only one part of the total security package Oracle offers the DBA or security administrator on an Oracle database. The other major component of the Oracle security architecture is the ability to monitor database activity to uncover suspicious or inappropriate use. Oracle provides this functionality via the use of database auditing. This section will cover aspects of database auditing use, including how to determine when auditing is necessary, how to track statement- and system-level access to database objects, using the data dictionary to monitor auditing options, and viewing and managing audit results.

Determining the Need for Auditing

Almost every database will need to be audited at one time or another. Excessive database usage by a particular user, odd changes that appear on the database at suspicious times, or simply the need to have an archive of database usage may all be reasons the database needs to be audited. Generally speaking, a database audit is most effective when the DBA or security administrator knows what he or she is looking for. Auditing is not something the DBA should just "turn on" and assume that the problem will automatically surface. Reality in database auditing is far from that, in fact. The best way to conduct a database audit is to start the audit with a general idea about what may be occurring on the database. Once the goals are established, set the audit to monitor aspects of the database related to those areas of database usage and review the results to either confirm or disprove the hypothesis.

Why must an audit be conducted in this manner? First of all, database auditing has the ability to generate LOTS of information about database access. If the DBA tried to audit everything, the important facts would get mixed into a great deal of unnecessary detail. With a good idea about the general activity that seems suspicious, as well as the knowledge of the types of statements or related objects on the database that should be looked at, the DBA can save a lot of time sorting through excess detail·later.

In addition, it is recommended that the DBA use the Oracle auditing options to conduct audits using a "top-down" approach. Auditing from the top down means that the DBA starts with an idea of suspicious database activity. From there, the DBA audits a number of general areas that may be related to the problem at hand. Once this general audit is complete, the DBA may find that auditing one or two areas produced more results than several others. From there, the DBA should conduct an audit that is much narrower in scope, perhaps focusing exclusively on the areas that displayed suspicious activity, or on one or two areas related to the suspicious activity, in order to solidify the hypothesis, but no more. Above all else in the framework of handling database audits for inappropriate activity is the importance of protecting the evidence. In order to protect evidence of improper database activity, the DBA must ensure that no user can remove records from the audit logs undetected. Therefore, a key step in auditing is to audit the audit trail.

The DBA should be mindful also that monitoring general database activity for the purpose of archiving is not the same motive as trying to uncover a problem with inappropriate database usage. In the more general situation of monitoring database activity for archiving purposes, the DBA should approach the task with two things in mind: 1) what are the key areas to focus on for auditing to produce archive information, and 2) place the audit information into an archive and clear out the online audit destination.

Lastly, it should be understood that, especially in large organizations, the DBA should not be the person ultimately responsible for managing database security, including audits. That responsibility should belong to a security administrator or manager. The DBA should, however, be familiar with the security features of the Oracle database in order to fulfill his or her role as the resident expert on Oracle software.

Exercises

1. What is auditing?

2. When might it be necessary to audit database activity?

Tracking Statement- and System-Level Access to Data Objects

As with many areas of the Oracle database, in order to begin capturing audit information, the DBA must set an initialization parameter. In this case, the initialization parameter set is called AUDIT_TRAIL. This parameter can have three values, *DB*, *OS*, or *NONE*. Each of these values corresponds to the method by which the audit will be conducted. *DB* indicates that the database architecture will be used to store audit records. *OS* indicates that the audit trail will be stored external to Oracle using some component of the operating system, and *NONE* indicates that no database auditing will be conducted at all. After changing the value set for this parameter, the database instance must be shut down and started again.

Once the database is prepared for an audit, the DBA or security administrator can set auditing features to monitor database activities related to system-level activity or statement-level activity. Some examples of system-level database activity include starting and stopping the database, and connecting to the database. Statement-level activities include the general creation or removal of database components. Additionally, statement-level activity corresponds more directly with database usage, such as updating or inserting data into a table, working with constraints, etc.

Common to all database audits are several components about which information is always recorded. These areas are directly related to the system-level activity. The areas are instance startup and shutdown, and every connection to the database of a user with database administrator privileges. However, this information must be recorded to the operating system audit trail because the database audit trail is not available until startup is complete, and will not be available after shutdown is complete. If no operating system audit trail is available, Oracle writes a special audit trail file to a location set by the parameter AUDIT_FILE_DEST. *The general syntax for initiating an audit is to state the name of the system-level or statement-level activity that is to be audited, the frequency by which to audit, and whether or not the audit should record successful or unsuccessful executions of the activity in question.*

```
AUDIT CREATE TABLE, ALTER TABLE, DROP TABLE
BY spanky
WHENEVER SUCCESSFUL;
```

This statement has three effects. First, a certain set of activities performed by user SPANKY will be recorded whenever they complete successfully. To answer the question of what activities are audited, consider the following. *Any privilege that can be granted can also be audited.* However, since there are nearly 100 system and object privileges that can be granted on the Oracle database, the creation of an audit statement can be an excessively long task. As an alternative to naming each and every privilege that goes along with a database object, Oracle allows the administrator to specify the name of an object to audit, and Oracle will audit all privileged operations. Instead of listing all privileged operations related to the type of object that would be audited, the security administrator could instead name the type of object and achieve the desired result.

```
AUDIT TABLE
BY spanky
WHENEVER SUCCESSFUL;
```

There are other options available to consolidate the specification of database activities into one easy command for auditing. These commands are listed as follows.

- **connect**   Audits the user connections to the database. Can be substituted with **session** for the same effect. Audits the login and logout activities of every database user.

- **resource**   Audits detailed information related to the activities typically performed by an application developer or a development DBA, such as creating tables, views, clusters, links, stored procedures, and rollback segments.

- **dba**   Audits activities related to "true" database administration, including the creation of users and roles, and granting system privileges and system audits.

- **all**   Is the equivalent of an "on/off" switch, where all database activities are monitored and recorded.

Related to object privileges is the ability Oracle's audit feature has to record the data change operations that happen on particular tables. This audit process adds one clause to the general audit statement, which appears as follows:

```
AUDIT UPDATE, DELETE
ON application.table
BY ACCESS
WHENEVER NOT SUCCESSFUL;
```

This statement is useful because it points out some other unique items in the audit syntax. The person setting up audits need not name particular users on which to monitor activity. Rather, the activities of this sort can be monitored every time the statement is issued with the **by access** clause. Additionally, when the **not successful** option is specified, audit records are generated only when the command executed is unsuccessful. The omission of clauses from the audit syntax causes **audit** to default to some performance feature. For example, an audit can be conducted on all inserts on table PRODUCTS, regardless of user and completion status.

```
AUDIT INSERT ON products;
```

If the person setting up **audit** wants to specify a value for the **whenever** clause but not the **by** clause, then something else has to be substituted. That substitution is the **on default** clause. Review the following statement for a clearer understanding:

```
AUDIT INSERT ON application.products
ON DEFAULT
WHENEVER SUCCESSFUL;
```

However, if the last line is left off, then all inserts on the PRODUCTS table will be recorded. Finally, the person setting up auditing can also specify that audit records are to be compiled by session. This means that **audit** will record data for audited activities in every session, as opposed to **by access**. Eliminating the **when successful** clause tells **audit** to record every table creation, alteration, or drop activity for every session that connects to the database, regardless of whether or not they were successful.

```
AUDIT TABLE
BY SESSION;
```

One final area to consider is how to disable auditing. There are two methods used. The first method is to change the initialization parameter AUDIT_TRAIL to *NONE*. On database shutdown and restart, this option will disable the audit functionality on the Oracle database. The other, less drastic, option used for changing the activities **audit** will record is called **noaudit**. This option can be executed in two ways. The first is used to turn off selective areas that are currently being audited.

```
NOAUDIT INSERT ON application.products;
```

In some cases, however, the person conducting the audit may want to shut off all auditing processes going on, and simply start auditing over again. Perhaps the auditor has lost track of what audits were occurring on the database. This statement can be further modified to limit the auditing turned off to a particular database object.

```
NOAUDIT ALL;
NOAUDIT ALL PRIVILEGES;
NOAUDIT ALL ON application.products;
```

Exercises

1. What is the general format for starting an audit? What activities in the database can be audited?

2. What initialization parameter must be changed before auditing can take place on the database?

3. How can auditing be stopped?

Understanding Audit Results with the Data Dictionary

There are some design issues to discuss in order to understand the architecture of auditing. The object in the Oracle architecture designed to handle audits is a data dictionary table called AUD$. The object is owned by the user SYS. In order to access the information provided by auditing, and to better understand the data being stored in this table, there are several views available to show various items in the architecture. The views that are available are listed as follows, along with some description of their contents and/or usage:

- **ALL_DEF_AUDIT_OPTS**   A list of all default options for auditing database objects.

- **AUDIT_ACTIONS**   A list of audit codes and their associated names.

- **DBA_AUDIT_EXISTS**   A list of audit entries generated by the **exists** option of the **audit** command.

- **DBA_AUDIT_OBJECT**   A list of audit entries generated for object audits.

- **DBA_AUDIT_SESSION**   A list of audit entries generated by session connects and disconnects.

- **DBA_AUDIT_STATEMENT**   A list of audit entries generated by statement options of the **audit** command.

- **DBA_AUDIT_TRAIL**   A list of all entries in the AUD$ table collected by the **audit** command.

- **DBA_OBJ_AUDIT_OPTS**   A list of auditing options for views, tables, and other database objects.

- **DBA_PRIV_AUDIT_OPTS**   A list of auditing options for all privileges on the database.

- **DBA_STMT_AUDIT_OPTS**   A list of auditing options for all statements executed on the database.

- **STMT_AUDIT_OPTION_MAP**   A list of type descriptions for auditing option codes.

These views are created by the **cataudit.sql** script found in **rdbms/admin** off the Oracle software home directory. This script is run automatically at database creation by the **catalog.sql** script. No additional audit information is stored anywhere else in the database, except for the special file written by Oracle that contains startup and shutdown information, unless operating system auditing is used.

Exercises

1. Where is audit data stored in the data dictionary?

2. What data dictionary views are available for viewing audit data?

3. What data dictionary views are available for viewing **audit** options and parameters?

Managing Audit Information

Once created, all audit information will stay in the AUD$ table owned by SYS. In cases where several auditing options are used to gather information about database activity, the AUD$ table can grow to be large. In order to preserve the integrity of other tables and views in the data dictionary, and to preserve space overall in the SYSTEM tablespace (where all data dictionary objects are stored), the DBA or security administrator must periodically remove data from the AUD$ table, either by deleting or by archiving and then removing the records, Additionally, in the event that audit records on an Oracle database are being kept to determine if there is suspicious activity, the security administrator must take additional steps to ensure that the data in the AUD$ table is protected from tampering.

In order to prevent a problem with storing too much audit data, the general guideline in conducting database audits is to record enough information required to accomplish the auditing goal without storing a lot of unnecessary information. The amount of information that will be gathered by the auditing process is related to the number of options being audited and the frequency of audit collection (namely, **by** *username*, **by access, by session**).

What problems can occur if too much information is being audited? The biggest problems that occur when auditing is used relate to the auditing of user connections. When the **connect** or **session** activity is audited, a record is written to the AUD$ table every time a user connects or disconnects. The amount of space in the AUD$ table is limited. The default size for AUD$ is up to 990 kilobytes—or 99 extents, each 10K in size. If the AUD$ table fills to capacity and session connections are being audited, then no user will be able to connect to the database until some room is made in AUD$.

In order to remove records from AUD$, a user with **delete any table** privilege, the SYS user, or a user to whom SYS has granted **delete** access to AUD$ must log onto the system and remove records from AUD$. Before doing so, however, it is generally advisable to make a copy of the records being deleted for archiving purposes. This task can be accomplished by copying all records from AUD$ to another table defined with the same columns as AUD$, spooling a **select** statement of all data in AUD$ to a flat file, or using EXPORT to place all AUD$ records into a database dump file. After this step is complete, all or part of the data in the AUD$ table can be removed using either **delete from AUD$** or **truncate table AUD$**.

Alternatively, if the data in AUD$ is being collected in support of suspicious activity, it is in the interest of those performing the audit to ensure that the data in AUD$ is monitored. Although this measure will keep track of the users that make changes to the AUD$ table, the only actual measure of prevention the database has against deletion is to protect the SYS user and password, and limit the number of users who have **delete** access to AUD$ to the minimum number necessary.

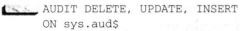

```
AUDIT DELETE, UPDATE, INSERT
ON sys.aud$
BY ACCESS;
```

Exercises

1. How can the security administrator remove data from the audit trail?

2. What problems can arise when the audit trail fills? How can data in the audit trail be protected?

Chapter Summary

This chapter covered several aspects of managing database usage that are critical to database administration. The areas discussed were creating and managing users, managing resource usage with profiles, managing database access with privileges and roles, and monitoring database activity with the **audit** command. The content discussion provided by this chapter comprises 27 percent of material covered in OCP Exam 2.

Managing users is an important area of database administration. Without users, there can be no database change, and thus no need for a database. Creation of new users comprises specifying values for several clauses. They are password, default and temporary tablespaces, quotas on all tablespaces accessible to the user (except the temporary tablespace), user profile, and default roles. Default and temporary tablespaces should be defined in order to preserve the integrity of the SYSTEM tablespace. Quotas are useful in limiting the space that a user can allocate for his or her database objects. Once users are created, the **alter user** statement can be used to change any aspect of the user's configuration. The only aspects of the user's configuration that can be changed by the user are the default role and the password.

Several views exist to display information about the users of the database. DBA_USERS gives information about the default and temporary tablespace specified for the user, while DBA_PROFILES gives information about the specific resource usage allotted to that user. DBA_TS_QUOTAS lists every tablespace quota set for a user, while DBA_ROLES describes all roles granted to the user. DBA_TAB_PRIVS also lists information about each privilege granted to a user or role on the database. Other views are used to monitor session information for current database usage as described in the chapter. An important view for this purpose is V$SESSION. This dynamic performance view gives information required in order to kill a user session with the **alter system kill session**. The relevant pieces of information required to kill a session are the session ID and the serial# for the session.

In order to restrict database usage, the DBA can create user profiles that detail resource limits. A user cannot exceed these limits if the RESOURCE_LIMIT initialization parameter is set on the database to TRUE. Several database resources are limited as part of a user profile. They include available CPU per call and/or session, disk block I/O reads per session, connection time, idle time, and more. One profile exists on the Oracle database at database creation time, called DEFAULT. The resource usage values in the DEFAULT profile are all set to **unlimited**. The DBA should create more profiles to correspond to the various types or classes of users on the database. Once created, the profiles of the database can then be granted to the users of the database. An alternative to setting usage limits on individual resources is to set composite limits to all database resources that can be assigned a resource cost. A resource cost is an integer that represents the importance of that resource to the system as a whole. The integer assigned as a resource cost is fairly arbitrary and does not usually represent a monetary cost. The higher the integer used for resource cost, the more valuable the resource. The database resources that can be assigned a resource cost are CPU per session, disk reads per session, connect time, and memory allocated to the private SGA for user SQL statements. After assigning a resource cost, the DBA can then assign a composite limit in the user profile. As the user uses resources, Oracle keeps track of the number of times the user incurs the cost associated with the resource and adjusts the running total. When the composite limit is reached, the user session is ended.

Oracle limits the users' access to the database objects created in the Oracle database by means of privileges. Database privileges are used to allow the users of the database to perform any function within the database, from creating users to dropping tables to inserting data into a view. There are two general classes of privilege: system privileges and object privileges. System privileges generally pertain to the creation of database objects and users, as well as the ability to connect to the database at all, while object privileges govern the amount of access a user might have to **insert**, **update**, **delete**, or generate foreign keys on data in a database object.

Database privilege management can be tricky if privileges are granted directly to users. In order to alleviate some of the strain on the DBA trying to manage database access, the Oracle architecture provides a special database object called a role. The role is an intermediate step in granting user privileges. The role acts as a "virtual user," allowing the DBA to grant all privileges required for a certain user class to perform its job function. When the role has been granted all privileges required, the role can then be granted to as many users as required. When a new privilege is required for this user group, the privilege is granted to the role, and each user who has the role automatically obtains the privilege. Similarly, when a user is no longer authorized to perform a certain job function, the DBA can revoke the role from the user in one easy step. Roles can be set up to require password authentication before the user can execute an operation that requires a privilege granted via the role.

The activities on a database can also be audited using the Oracle **audit** capability. Several reasons exist for the DBA or security administrator to perform an audit, including suspicious database activity or a need to maintain an archive of historical database activity. If the need is identified to conduct a database audit, then that audit can happen on system-level or statement-level activities. Regardless of the various objects that may be monitored, the start and stopping of a database as well as any access to the database with administrator privileges is always monitored. To begin an audit, the AUDIT_TRAIL parameter must be set to *DB* for recording audit information in the database audit trail, *OS* for recording the audit information in the operating system audit trail, or to *NONE* if no auditing is to take place. Any aspect of the database that must have a privilege granted to do it can be audited. The information gathered in a database audit is stored in the AUD$ table in the Oracle data dictionary. The AUD$ table is owned by SYS. Special views are also available in the data dictionary to provide views on audit data. Some of these views are DBA_AUDIT_EXISTS, DBA_AUDIT_OBJECT, DBA_AUDIT_SESSION, DBA_AUDIT_STATEMENT, and DBA_AUDIT_TRAIL. It is important to clean records out of the audit trail periodically, as the size of the AUD$ table is finite, and if there is an audit of sessions connecting to the database happening when the AUD$ table fills, then no users will be able to connect to the database until some room is made in the audit trail. Records can only be removed from the AUD$ table by a user who has **delete any table** privilege, the SYS user, or a user SYS has given **delete** access to on the AUD$ table. The records in the AUD$ table should be archived before they are deleted. Additionally, the audit trail should be audited to detect inappropriate tampering with the data in the table.

Two-Minute Drill

- New database users are created with the **create user** statement.
- A new user can have the following items configured by the **create user** statement:
  - Password
  - Default tablespace for database objects
  - Temporary tablespace
  - Quotas on tablespaces
  - User profile
  - Default role(s)
- User definitions can be altered with the **alter user** statement and dropped with the **drop user** statement. Users can issue the **alter user** statement only to change their password and default roles.
- Information about a database user can be found in the following data dictionary views:
  - DBA_USERS
  - DBA_PROFILES
  - DBA_TS_QUOTAS
  - DBA_OBJECTS
  - DBA_ROLE_PRIVS
  - DBA_TAB_PRIVS
  - V$SESSION

- The V$SESSION dynamic performance view is important to use when trying to kill a user session. The critical pieces of information given by V$SESSION for this purpose are session ID (SID) and serial#.

- Users in operating system authenticated database environments generally have their usernames preceded by OPS$ at user creation time.

- User profiles help to limit resource usage on the Oracle database.

- The DBA must set the RESOURCE_LIMIT parameter to TRUE in order to use user profiles.

- The resources that can be limited via profile usage include the following:

  - Sessions connected per user at one time

  - CPU time per call

  - CPU time per session

  - Disk I/O per call

  - Disk I/O per session

  - Connection time

  - Idle time

  - Private memory

  - Composite limit

- Profiles should be created for every type or class of user. Each parameter has a resource limit set for it in a user profile, which can then be assigned to users based on their processing needs.

- Oracle installs a special profile granted to a user if no other profile is defined. This special profile is called DEFAULT, and all values in the profile are set to **unlimited**.

- Any parameter not explicitly set in another user profile defaults in value to the value specified for that parameter in DEFAULT.

■ A resource cost is an integer value that identifies the value of the resource in the database system. High number means high value, low number means low value.

■ CPU per session, disk I/O per session, connect time, and private memory can all have resource costs assigned to them.

■ If the DBA desires, she can set limits on resource usage in the profile by specifying a composite limit. Oracle then keeps a running tab on the resource usage as determined by the frequency each resource is used times the resource cost of each usage.

■ In either individual resource specification or composite limits using resource costs, when the limit is reached, the session is over.

■ Database privileges govern access to perform every permitted activity in the Oracle database.

■ There are two categories of database privileges: system privileges and object privileges.

■ System privileges allow for the creation of every object on the database, along with the ability to execute many commands and connect to the database.

■ Object privileges allow for access to data within database objects.

■ There are three basic classes of system privileges for some database objects: **create**, **alter**, and **drop**. These privileges give the grantee the power to create database objects in their own user schema.

■ However, some exceptions exist to this rule. The **alter table** privilege is an object privilege, while the **alter rollback segment** privilege is a system privilege. The **create index** privilege is an object privilege as well.

■ Three oddball privileges here are **grant**, **audit**, and **analyze**. These privileges apply to the creation of all database objects and running powerful commands in Oracle.

■ The **any** modifier gives the user extra power to create objects or run commands on any object in the user schema.

- The final system privilege of interest is the **restricted session** privilege, which allows the user to connect to a database in **restricted session** mode.

- Object privileges give the user access to place, remove, change or view data in a table or one column in a table, as well as alter the definition of a table, create an index on a table, and develop foreign key constraints.

- When system privileges are revoked, the objects a user may have created will still exist.

- A system privilege can be granted **with admin option** to allow the grantee to administer other's ability to use the privilege.

- When object privileges are revoked, the data placed or modified in a table will still exist; however, if the user created a foreign-key constraint and the object privilege revoked is **references**, then the **cascade constraints** option must be used to complete the revocation.

- An object privilege can be granted **with grant option** to another user in order to make them an administrator of the privilege.

- The **grant option** cannot be used when granting a privilege to a role.

- Roles are used to bundle privileges together and enable or disable them automatically.

- A user can create objects and then grant the nongrantable object privileges to the role, which then can be granted to as many users as require it.

- There are five roles created by Oracle when the software is installed:

  - **CONNECT** Can connect to the database and create clusters, links, sequences, tables, views, and synonyms. This role is good for table schema owners and/or development DBAs.

  - **RESOURCE** Can connect to the database and create clusters, sequences, tables, triggers, and stored procedures. This role is good for application developers. Also has unlimited tablespace.

- **DBA** Can use any system privilege **with admin option**.

- **EXP_FULL_DATABASE** Can export all database objects to an export dump file.

- **IMP_FULL_DATABASE** Can import all database objects from an export dump file to the database.

■ Roles can have passwords assigned to them for security over usage of certain privileges.

■ Users can alter their own roles in a database session. Each role requires 4 bytes of space in the program global area (PGA) in order to be used. The amount of space each user requires in the PGA can be limited with the MAX_ENABLED_ROLES initialization parameter.

■ When a privilege is granted to the user PUBLIC, then every user in the database can use the privilege. However, when a privilege is revoked from PUBLIC, then every stored procedure, function, or package in the database must be recompiled.

■ Auditing the database can be done either to detect inappropriate activity or to store an archive of database activity.

■ Auditing can collect large amounts of information. In order to minimize the amount of searching, the person(s) conducting the audit should limit the database activities audited to where they may think a problem lies.

■ Any activity on the database can be audited, either by naming the privilege or by naming an object in the database.

■ The activities of one or more users can be singled out for audit, or every access to an object or privilege, or every session on the database, can have their activities audited.

■ Audits can monitor successful activities surrounding a privilege, unsuccessful activities, or both.

■ Starting and stopping the instance, and every connection established by a user with DBA privileges as granted by SYSDBA and SYSOPER, are monitored in every database audit, regardless of any other activities being audited.

■ Audit data is stored in the data dictionary in the AUD$ table, which is owned by SYS.

■ Several dictionary views exist for seeing data in the AUD$ table. The main ones are as follows:

  ■ DBA_AUDIT_EXISTS

  ■ DBA_AUDIT_OBJECT

  ■ DBA_AUDIT_SESSION

  ■ DBA_AUDIT_STATEMENT

  ■ DBA_AUDIT_TRAIL

■ The AUD$ table can contain up to 990 kilobytes of information in 99 extents of 10K each. If the AUD$ table fills, it must be archived and/or cleaned out.

■ If auditing is in place and monitoring session connections, and if the AUD$ fills, then no more users can connect to the database until the AUD$ table is archived and/or emptied.

■ The AUD$ table should be audited whenever in use to detect tampering with the data in it.

Chapter Questions

1. **If the DBA wishes to use resource costs to limit resource usage, the first thing she must do is**

   A. Change the value of RESOURCE_LIMIT to TRUE.

   B. Change the value of **composite_limit** in the user profile to zero.

   C. Change the value of **composite_limit** in the DEFAULT profile to zero.

   D. Change the value of the resource costs for the resources to be limited.

2. When revoking the REFERENCES privilege, the DBA must use which option to ensure success?

   A. with admin option

   B. with grant option

   C. cascade constraints

   D. trailing nullcols

3. Which line of the following statement will produce an error?

   A. create user OPS$ELLISON

   B. identified externally

   C. default tablespace USERS_01

   D. idle_time = 3

   E. default role CONNECT;

   F. There are no errors in this statement.

4. Audit trail information is stored in

   A. SYS.SOURCE$

   B. SYS.AUD$

   C. DBA_SOURCE

   D. DBA_AUDIT_TRAIL

5. Which of the following views contain data necessary to kill a user session?

   A. V$SYSSTAT

   B. V$ROLLSTAT

   C. V$QUEUE

   D. V$SESSION

6. The creator of a role is granted the use of the role WITH ADMIN OPTION.

   A. TRUE

   B. FALSE

7. To find out how many database objects a user has created, the DBA can query which dictionary view?

   A. DBA_USERS

   B. DBA_OBJECTS

   C. DBA_TS_QUOTAS

   D. DBA_TAB_PRIVS

8. On database creation, the value of the CONNECT_TIME parameter in the DEFAULT profile is

   A. 1

   B. 10

   C. 300

   D. unlimited

   E. None, the DEFAULT profile hasn't been created yet.

9. A user can change which of the following parameters with an ALTER USER statement?

   A. identified by

   B. default tablespace

   C. temporary tablespace

   D. quota on

   E. profile

   F. default role

10. A resource cost is

   A. A monetary cost for using a database resource

    B. A monetary cost for using a privilege

    C. An integer value representing the importance of the resource

    D. An integer value representing the dollar cost for using the resource

11. **The database will not continue to allow users to access the database when**

    A. The database is up and running.

    B. The AUD$ table has been filled and **session** is being audited.

    C. Restricted session has been disabled.

    D. Operating system authentication is being used.

12. **When auditing instance startup, the audit records are placed in**

    A. SYS.AUD$

    B. DBA_AUDIT_TRAIL

    C. ARCHIVE_DUMP_DEST

    D. AUDIT_TRAIL_DEST

13. **A high resource cost indicates**

    A. A less expensive resource

    B. A lower amount of resource used per minute

    C. A more expensive resource

    D. A higher amount of resource used per minute

14. **Privileges granted with the GRANT OPTION cannot be given to other users.**

    A. TRUE

    B. FALSE

Answers to Chapter Questions

1. A. Change the value of RESOURCE_LIMIT to TRUE.

Explanation   In order for any value set for a resource cost to be effective, and in order to use any user profile, the RESOURCE_LIMIT initialization parameter must be set to TRUE. Refer to the discussion of user profiles.

2. C. **cascade constraints**

Explanation   If a foreign-key constraint is defined as the result of a **references** privilege being granted, then in order to revoke the **references** privilege the **cascade constraints** option must be used. Choices A and B are incorrect because the **admin option** and **grant option** relate to the granting of system and object privileges, respectively, while this question is asking about the revocation of an object privilege. Choice D is incorrect because **trailing nullcols** refers to an option in the SQL*Loader control file covered in the next chapter. Refer to the discussion of administering object privileges.

3. D. **idle_time** = 3

Explanation   Although a user profile can be specified as part of a user creation statement, the individual options specified in a user profile cannot be. Therefore, the user creation statement will error out on line D. Refer to the section on user creation.

4. B. SYS.AUD$

Explanation   AUD$ holds all audit trail records: It is owned by user SYS. Choice A is incorrect because SOURCE$ contains source code for all stored procedures, functions, and packages. Choices C and D are dictionary views that provide access to the underlying data dictionary tables named in choices A and B. While they allow viewing of the data, the views themselves store nothing, because they are views. Refer to the discussion of auditing.

5. D.   V$SESSION

Explanation   V$SESSION contains the session IDs and the serial#s required to issue the **alter system kill session** statement. Choice A is incorrect because it contains system-wide values for statistics in V$SESSTAT for the database instance, while choice B is incorrect because it contains performance information about rollback segments. Choice C is incorrect because it contains information in the multithreaded server message queues. Refer to the discussion of killing a user session.

6. A.   TRUE

Explanation   This is a true statement. The creator of a role can do anything he or she wants to with the role, including **delete** it. Refer to the discussion of roles and the **with grant option**.

7. B.   DBA_OBJECTS

Explanation   The DBA_OBJECTS view lists all objects that are in the Oracle database, as well as the owners of those objects. Choice A is incorrect because DBA_USERS contains the actual user creation information, such as encrypted password, default and temp tablespace, user profile, and default role. Choice C is incorrect because DBA_TS_QUOTAS identifies all the tablespace quotas that have been named for the user. Choice D is incorrect because DBA_TAB_PRIVS names all the table object privileges that have been granted and to whom they have been given. Refer to the discussion of monitoring information about existing users.

8. D.   **unlimited**

Explanation   All resource limits in the DEFAULT user profile created when Oracle is installed are set to **unlimited**. Refer to the discussion of the DEFAULT profile in the managing resource usage discussion.

9. A. **identified by**

Explanation   There is only one user creation option that the created user can modify. All others are managed either by a security administrator or the DBA. Refer to the discussion of user creation.

10. C.   An integer value representing the importance of a resource.

Explanation   The resource cost is an integer that measures relative importance of a resource to the DBA. Its value is completely arbitrary, and has nothing to do with money. Therefore, choices A, B, and D are all incorrect. Refer to the discussion of assessing resource costs in the section on user profiles.

11. B.   The AUD$ table has been filled and **session** is being audited.

Explanation   If user connections are being audited and the AUD$ table fills, then no user can connect until the AUD$ table is cleared. Choice A is incorrect because the database is open for everyone's use when it is up and running. By the same token, choice C is incorrect as well, because when a restricted session is disabled the database is open for general access. Choice D is incorrect because operating system authentication is simply another means to verify user passwords; it doesn't cut users off from accessing the database. Refer to the discussion of managing the audit trail.

12. D.   AUDIT_TRAIL_DEST

Explanation   This is a difficult question. For instance startup, **audit** places the information collected in this action into a special file that is placed where background process trace files are written. The location where background processes place their trace files is identified at instance startup with the AUDIT_TRAIL_DEST initialization parameter. Since the database has not started yet, the AUD$ table cannot be the location to which instance startup information is written, eliminating choice A. Since DBA_AUDIT_TRAIL is a view on AUD$, choice B is wrong, too. Choice C is the location where archive logs are written, which is closer to the spirit of the answer but still not correct. Refer to the discussion of auditing system-level database activity.

13. C.   A more expensive resource.

Explanation   The higher the value set for resource cost, the more valued the resource is to the database system, increasing its relative "expense." Choice A is incorrect because the exact opposite is true. Choices B and D are incorrect because, although the DBA can track resource usage on a per-minute basis, there is no value added by doing so. Nor does doing so indicate the relative expense of using the resource.

14. B.   FALSE

Explanation   When an object privilege is granted with the **grant option**, the grantee of the privilege has the ability to administer the privilege to other users. Refer to the discussion of administering privileges with **grant option** and **admin option**.

CHAPTER
10

Using SQL*Loader

n this chapter, you will understand and demonstrate knowledge in the following areas:

- Introduction to SQL*Loader
- SQL*Loader operation
- SQL*Loader data load paths

Although it comprises only a small amount of the actual test material on OCP Exam 2, learning SQL*Loader has a bigger payoff in the career of a DBA than getting a few questions right. SQL*Loader is a useful tool for loading data into a table. SQL*Loader accounts for the smallest portion of OCP Exam 2—only 5 to 8 percent of the test will consist of SQL*Loader questions. But, understanding SQL*Loader is nonetheless important as you progress toward OCP DBA certification.

Introduction to SQL*Loader

In this section, you will cover the following topics related to introducing SQL*Loader:

- The control file
- The datafile

SQL*Loader is a tool used by DBAs and developers to populate Oracle tables with data from flat files. It allows the DBA to selectively load certain columns but not others, or to exclude certain records entirely. SQL*Loader has some advantages over programming languages that allow embedded SQL statements, as well. Although a programmer could duplicate the functionality of SQL*Loader by writing her own load program, SQL*Loader has the advantage of flexibility, ease of use, and performance. It allows the developer to think more about loading the data than the details of opening files, reading lines, executing embedded SQL, and checking for end-of-file markers, and dramatically reduces the need for debugging. Using

SQL*Loader consists of understanding its elements. The first is the data to be loaded, which is stored in a *datafile*. The SQL*Loader datafile is not to be confused with Oracle server datafiles, which store database objects. The next is a set of controls for data loading that are defined in a file called the *control file* (not to be confused with Oracle server's control file). These controls include specifying how SQL*Loader should read records and parse them into columns, which columns should be loaded by data appearing in each position, and other features.

The Control File

The control file provides the following information to Oracle for the purpose the data load: datafile name(s) and format, character sets used in the datafiles, datatypes of fields in those files, how each field is delimited, and which tables and columns to load. You must provide the control file to SQL*Loader so that the tool knows several things about the data it is about to load. Data and control file information can be provided in the same file or in separate files. Some items in the control file are mandatory, such as which tables and columns to load and how each field is delimited.

Example 1: A Combined Data and Control File

The following example is of a combined control file and datafile. It illustrates basic usage and syntax for control files and the effects of those specifications.

```
--variable-length, terminated enclosed data formatting
LOAD DATA
INFILE *
APPEND INTO TABLE address
FIELDS TERMINATED BY "," OPTIONALLY ENCLOSED BY '"'
(global_id, person_lname, person_fname,
 area_code,phone_number, load_order SEQUENCE(MAX,1))
BEGIN DATA
83456, "Smith","Alfred",718,5551111
48292, "Smalls","Rebeca",415,9391000
34436, "Park","Ragan",919,7432105
15924,"Xi","Ling",708,4329354
49204,"Walla","Praveen",304,5983183
56061,"Whalen","Mark",407,3432353
```

Comments can appear anywhere in the control file, and need only be delineated by two dashes. Care should be taken not to place comments in the datafile or in the data portion of the control file. The **load data** clause generally indicates the beginning of the contents of the control file. For all control files, the **infile** clause is required. It denotes where SQL*Loader can find the input data for this load. Using an asterisk (*****) denotes that the data is in the control file. The next line of the control file is the **into table** clause. It tells SQL*Loader the table to which the data will be loaded and the method by which it will be loaded. The **append** keyword denotes that these records can be inserted even if the table has other data. Other options include **insert**, which allows records to enter the table only if the table is empty; and **replace** and **truncate**, which **delete** all rows from the table before loading the new records. The **fields terminated by** clause defines how columns will be delimited in the variable-length data records. The character that separates each data element is enclosed in double-quotes. Also, an optional enclosure character is defined with the **optionally enclosed by** clause. The next line begins with a parenthesis, and within those parentheses the columns in the table to be loaded are specified. If a column from the table is not listed in this record, it will not be loaded with data from the datafile. The data loaded in each column will be selected from the data record positionally, with the first item in the record going into the first column, the second item in the second column, etc. The following example contains one special case in which an exception is made—a column denoted by SEQUENCE(MAX,1), corresponding to a column in the table that will be populated with a sequence number that is not present in the datafile. SQL*Loader supports the generation of special information for data loads, such as sequences and data type conversions. Finally, in cases where the data is included in the control file, the **begin data** clause is mandatory for denoting the end of the control file and the beginning of the data. This clause need not be present if the data is in a separate file.

Example 2: A Control File for Fixed-Width Data

Usually, however, the control file and datafile are separate. For this example, the direct path option has been set by the **options** clause, which can be used for setting many command-line parameters for the load. In a direct path load, SQL*Loader bypasses most of Oracle's SQL statement processing mechanism, turning flat file data directly into data blocks. The **load data** clause indicates the beginning of the control file in earnest. The **infile** clause specifies a datafile called **datafile1.dat**. The **badfile** clause specifies a file into which SQL*Loader can place datafile records that cannot be loaded into the database. The **discardfile** clause specifies a file in which discarded data that does not fit a **when** clause specified in the control file will be stored. A **replace** load has been specified by the **into table** clause, so all records in the tables named will be deleted and data from the file will be loaded. The column specifications in parentheses indicate by the **position** clause that the records in the datafile are fixed-width. Multiple **into table** clauses indicate that two files will be loaded.

```
OPTIONS (direct=true)
LOAD DATA
INFILE 'datafile1.dat'
BADFILE 'datafile1.bad'
DISCARDFILE 'datafile1.dsc'
REPLACE INTO TABLE phone_number
(global_id      POSITION(1:5)        INTEGER EXTERNAL,
 people_lname   POSITION(7:15)       CHAR,
 people_fname   POSITION(17:22)      CHAR,
 area_code      POSITION(24:27)      INTEGER EXTERNAL,
 phone_number   POSITIONAL(29:36)    INTEGER EXTERNAL)
INTO TABLE address
WHEN global_id !=
(global_id      POSITION(1:5)        INTEGER EXTERNAL,
 city           POSITION(38:50)      CHAR,
 state          POSITION(52:54)      CHAR,
 zip            POSITION(56:61)      INTEGER EXTERNAL)
```

Contents of **datafile.dat** are listed as follows:

```
14325 SMITH      ED      304 3924954 MILLS        VA 20111
43955 DAVISON    SUSAN   415 2348324 PLEASANTON   CA 90330
39422 MOHAMED    SUMAN   201 9493344 HOBOKEN      NJ 18403
38434 MOUSE      MIKE    718 1103010 QUEENS       NY 10009
```

Control File Keywords
The following outlines the syntax and semantics for the control file. Statements in this file can run from line to line, with new lines beginning at

any word. The control file is not case sensitive, except in strings in single or double quotes. Comments can be placed anywhere as long as they are preceded by two dashes. Column and table names can be the same as SQL*Loader reserved words as long as they appear in quotation marks.

-- comments	Any remarks are permitted.
options	Command-line parameters can be placed in the control file as options.
unrecoverable recoverable	Specifies whether to create redo log entries for loaded data. Unrecoverable can be used on direct loads only.
load continue_load	Either **load** or **continue_load** must be specified in the control file.
data	Provided for readability.
characterset	Specifies the character set of the datafile.
preserve blanks	Retains leading white space from datafile in cases where enclosure delimiters are not present.
begin data	Keyword denoting the beginning of data records to be loaded.
infile *name*	Keyword to specify name(s) of input files. An asterisk (*) following this keyword indicates data records are in the control file.
badfile *name*	Keyword to specify name of bad file. They are interchangeable.
discardfile *name*	Keyword to specify name of discard file. They are interchangeable.
discards *X*	Allows *X* discards before opening the next datafile.
discardmax *X*	Allows *X* discards before terminating the load.

insert **append** **replace** **truncate**	The table operation to be performed. **insert** puts rows into an empty table. **append** adds rows to a table. **replace** and **truncate** delete rows currently in a table and place the current data records into the table.
into table *tablename*	Keyword preceding the *tablename*.
sorted indexes	For direct path loads, indicates that data has already been sorted in specified indexes.
singlerow	For use when appending rows or loading a small amount of data into a large table (rowcount ratio of 1:20 or less).

Exercises

1. What are three components of a data load using SQL*Loader?

2. Using the information provided in this chapter, write a control file for a data load. The data in this load is made up of variable-width, pipe-delimited values to be loaded into the EMP table, which has three columns: EMPID (NUMBER), EMPNAME (VARCHAR2), and SALARY (NUMBER). A sample line from the input file is listed below:

   ```
   |3498553|SMITHY|45000|
   ```

Datafiles

Datafiles can have two formats. The data Oracle will use to populate its tables can be in fixed-length fields or in variable-length fields delimited by a special character. Additionally, SQL*Loader can handle data in binary format or character format. If the data is in binary format, then the datafile must have fixed-length fields. Figure 10-1 gives a pictorial example of the records that are fixed in length.

In contrast to fixed-length data fields, variable-length data fields are only as long as is required to store the data. Unlike in Figure 10-1, a variable-length record will have only four characters for the second field of the fourth

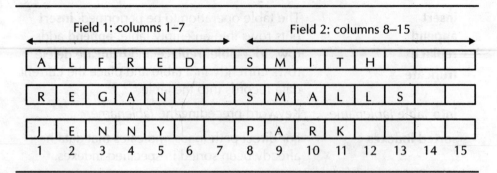

FIGURE 10-1. *Fixed-length records*

record. Typically, data fields in variable-length records are terminated by a special character or enclosed by special characters. These options are called terminated fields and enclosed fields, respectively. The following list shows the differences between terminated and enclosed fields:

Terminated fields—delimiter (,)	Enclosed fields—delimiter (|)
SMITH,ALFRED	|SMITH|ALFRED|
SMALLS,REGAN	|SMITH|REGAN|
PARK,JENNY	|PARK|JENNY|

The final thing to know about data records is the difference between physical and logical data records. In a datafile, each row of the file may be considered a record. This type of record is called a physical record. A physical record in a datafile can correspond either to a row in one table or several tables. Each row in a table is also considered a record, and the type of record each is considered to be is a logical record. In some cases, the logical records or rows of a table may correspond to several physical records of a datafile. In these cases, SQL*Loader supports the use of continuation fields to map two or more physical records into one logical record. A continuation field can be defined in the ways listed below:

- A fixed number of physical records always are concatenated to form a logical record for table loading.

- Physical records are appended if a continuation field contains a special string.

- Physical records are concatenated if a special character appears as the last nonblank character.

Exercises

1. Name and describe the two types of delimited fields.

2. What is a continuation record and how is one defined?

SQL*Loader Operation

In this section, you will cover the following topics related to SQL*Loader operation:

- Additional load files at run time

- SQL*Loader command-line parameters

Finally, SQL*Loader accepts special parameters that can affect how the load occurs, called *command-line parameters.* These parameters—which include the ID to use when loading data, the name of the datafile, and the name of the control file—are all items that SQL*Loader needs to conduct the data load. These parameters can be passed to SQL*Loader on the command line or in a special parameter file called a *parfile.*

Additional Load Files at Run Time

SQL*Loader in action consists of several additional items. If, in the course of performing the data load, SQL*Loader encounters records it cannot load, the record is rejected and the tool puts it in a special file called a *bad file*. The record can then be reviewed to find out the problem. Conditions that may cause a record to be rejected include integrity constraint violation, datatype mismatches, and other errors in field processing.

Additionally, SQL*Loader gives the user options to reject data based on special criteria. These criteria are defined in the control file as part of the **when** clause. If the tool encounters a record that fails a specified **when** clause, the record is placed in a special file called the *discard file*. The second example in the control file discussion in the previous section describes this type of load. In both cases, the tool writes the bad or discarded record to the appropriate file in the same format as was fed to the tool in the datafile. This feature allows for easy correction and reloading, with reuse of the original control file. Figure 10-2 represents the process flow of a data record from the time it appears in the datafile of the load to the time it is loaded in the database.

Recording the execution of SQL*Loader happens in the log file. If for any reason the tool cannot create a *log file*, the execution terminates. The log file consists of six elements. The header section details the SQL*Loader

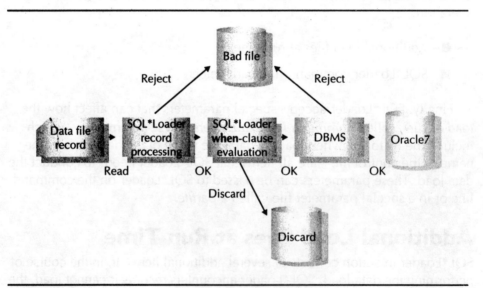

FIGURE 10-2.   *Control flow for record filtering*

version number and date of the run. The global information section gives names for all input and output files, the command-line parameters, and a continuation character specification if one is required. The table information section lists all tables being loaded by the current run, and load conditions, and whether data is being inserted, appended, or replaced. The datafile section contains details about any rejected records. The table load information section lists the number of tables loaded and the number of records that failed table requirements for loading, such as integrity constraints. Finally, the summary statistics section describes the space used for the bind array, cumulative load statistics, end time, elapsed time, and CPU time.

Exercises

1. What is the bad file? How is it produced, and what does it contain? In what format are the bad records written?

2. What are the functions and contents of the log file?

3. What is the discard file? What clause in the control file determines its contents? In what format are the discard records written?

SQL*Loader Command-Line Parameters

The following parameters are accepted by SQL*Loader on the command line. These options can be passed to SQL*Loader as parameters on the command line in the format **PARAMETER**=*value*. Alternately, parameters can be passed to SQL*Loader in another component called the *parfile*. The parameters can be identified in the parfile as **option**=*value*. The parameters available for SQL*Loader are listed below. Note that some of the parameters are duplicates of options that can be set in the control file, indicating that there are multiple methods for defining the same load using SQL*Loader.

USERID	Oracle userid and password
CONTROL	Control filename
LOG	Log filename
BAD	Bad filename

DATA	Datafile name
DISCARD	Discard filename
DISCARDS	Number of discards to terminate the load (default: **all**)
SKIP	Number of logical records to skip (default: 0)
LOAD	Number of logical records to load (default: **all**)
ERRORS	Number of errors to terminate the load (default: 50)
ROWS	Number of rows in the conventional path bind array or between direct path data saves (conventional path: 64, direct path: **all**)
BINDSIZE	Size of conventional path bind array in bytes
SILENT	Suppress messages between run (header, feedback, errors, discards)
DIRECT	Use direct path load (default: FALSE)
PARFILE	Parameter filename
PARALLEL	Perform parallel load (default: FALSE)
FILE	Datafile to allocate extents

Using Parameters

The use of parameters is now presented. Note that SQL*Loader is a separate utility from Oracle. Attempts to run it from the SQL*Plus command prompt will fail unless preceded by the appropriate command to temporarily or permanently exit SQL*Plus to the host operating system prompt. The table listing of SQL*Loader parameters presented is in a special order—if the DBA would like, she can specify the values for each option without actually naming the option, so long as the values correspond in position to the list presented. Thus, two statements executing SQL*Loader are the same, even though the parameter options may not be named.

```
Sqlldr scott/tiger load.ctl load.log load.bad load.dat
Sqlldr USERID=scott/tiger CONTROL=load.ctl DATA=load.dat
```

Additionally, a mixture of positional and named parameters can be passed. One issue to remember is that positional parameters can be placed on the command line before named parameters, but not after. Thus, the first of the following statements is acceptable, but the second is not:

```
sqlldr scott/tiger load.ctl DATA=load.dat /* OK */
sqlldr DATA=load.dat scott/tiger load.ctl /* ERROR */
```

As mentioned, another option for specifying command-line parameters is placing the parameters in a parfile. The parfile can then be referenced on the command line. The usage may be as follows.

```
Sqlldr parfile=load.par
```

The contents of **load.par** may look like the following listing:

```
DATA=load.dat
USERID=scott/tiger
CONTROL=load.ctl
LOG=load.log
BAD=load.bad
DISCARD=load.dsc
```

A final alternative to specifying SQL*Loader load parameters on the command line is specifying the command-line parameters in the control file. In order to place command-line parameters to the control file, the **options** clause must be used in the control file. This clause should be placed at the beginning of the file, before the **load** clause. Command-line parameters specified in the **options** clause should be named parameters, and can be overridden by parameters passed on the command line or in the parfile. The control file in the second example of the previous section details the use of parameters in the control file.

Exercises

   1. What are the three ways that command-line parameters can be specified for a data load?

   2. Which methods will override the others?

SQL*Loader Data Load Paths

In this section, you will cover the following topics related to SQL*Loader data load paths:

- The conventional path and the direct path

- Integrity constraints, triggers, and data loads

- Indexes and the direct path

- Data saves

SQL*Loader provides two data paths for loading data. They are the *conventional* path and the *direct* path. Whereas the conventional path uses a variant of the SQL **insert** statement with an array interface to improve data load performance, the direct path avoids the RDBMS altogether by converting flat file data into Oracle data blocks and writes those blocks directly to the database. Conventional path data loads compete with other SQL processes, and also require DBWR to perform the actual writes to database.

The Conventional Path and the Direct Path

Figure 10-3 pictorially displays the differences between conventional and direct path loads. In a conventional load, SQL*Loader reads multiple data records from the input file into a bind array. When the array fills, SQL*Loader passes the data to the Oracle SQL processing mechanism or optimizer for insertion. In a direct load, SQL*Loader reads records from the datafile, converts those records directly into Oracle data blocks, and writes them to disk, bypassing most of the Oracle database processing. Processing time for this option is generally faster than for a conventional load.

The direct load option is specified as a command-line parameter, and like other parameters, it can be specified in three different ways—on the command line as a named or positional parameter, in a parameter file, or in the control file as part of the **options** clause. At the beginning of the direct path load, SQL*Loader makes a call to Oracle to put a lock on the tables being inserted, and it makes another call to Oracle again at the end to release the lock. During the load, SQL*Loader makes a few calls to Oracle,

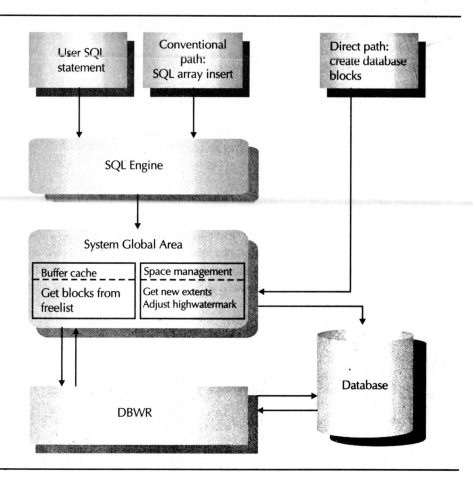

FIGURE 10-3. *Database paths for conventional and direct loads*

to get new extents when necessary and to reset the highwatermark when data saves are required. A data save is the direct path equivalent to a **commit**. A list of actions the direct path takes is given below.

■ Partial blocks are not used, so the server process is never required to do a database read.

■ No SQL **insert** commands are used.

■ The bind array is not used—SQL*Loader creates database blocks and writes them directly to storage. This feature allows the tool to avoid contending with other SQL statements for database buffer cache blocks.

- The direct path allows for presorting options, which enables usage of operating system high-speed sorting algorithms, if available. This speeds the creation of indexes and primary keys.

- Since SQL*Loader writes data directly to disk, in the event of instance failure, all changes made up to the most recent data save will be stored on disk, limiting the need for recovery.

Prior to executing the data load using SQL*Loader, the DBA must determine what type of load to use. There are two paths available for use, and the following table lists the situations for using each load type. The two types of loads available are the conventional and the direct path. Generally speaking, the conventional path is slower than the direct path because it handles all the constraints and indexing in an Oracle database as the data is loaded, essentially paying all its dues up front. On the other hand, the direct path load can make some substantial performance gains on the conventional path in certain situations by deferring payment of all its dues to the Oracle server until the load is over.

When to Use the Direct Path	When to Use the Conventional Path
Large amount of data to load in a short time frame	When loading data across a network
Need to use parallel loading to increase load performance	When loading data into a clustered table
Need to load a character set not supported in the current session, or when the conventional load of that character set produces errors	When loading small amount of data into a large indexed table or a large table with many integrity constraints—because it takes longer to drop and re-create a large index than insert a few rows to the table and index
	When applying single-row operations or SQL functions to data being loaded

The advantages of conventional path focus mainly around the fact that it is relatively nondisruptive to the underpinnings of a database table. Conventional path loads work on the same principles that normal data inserts work, only much faster. Records in a conventional path load pay their dues to the Oracle database as the records load; that is to say, the records loaded on the conventional path will update the associated indexes with a table, and generally have the look and feel of normal online transaction processing.

In contrast, direct path loading helps in the situation where a great deal of data must be loaded in a short period of time. Direct path loads bypass the "customs inspectors" of the Oracle database—namely, integrity constraints, as well as the "post office," or table indexes, of the database. Unfortunately, the safety and performance conditions provided by indexes and integrity constraints must be met at some point. Therefore, the direct path operates on a "pay me later" principle—the index updates have to happen at some point, so after the DBA completes the direct path load, he or she will need to reapply the constraints and rebuild the indexes so as to put the Oracle database back together before users can access the data loaded in the direct path.

Exercises

1. Why does a direct path load usually take less time to execute than a conventional load?

2. When will a direct path load take longer than a conventional load?

Integrity Constraints, Triggers, and Data Loads

Some types of integrity constraints can be enforced during a direct path load, but not all. Integrity constraints that can be checked include NOT NULL constraints, unique constraints and primary key constraints, and check constraints. These constraints can be checked because they typically don't refer to other tables; however, any constraint that refers to data in another table cannot be enforced by SQL*Loader during a direct path load.

These constraints include foreign key constraints. The right way to handle constraints of this type is to disable them before the load and reenable them after the load, which the tool can do automatically if specified. The syntax for specifying this option is to use the following clause in the control file:

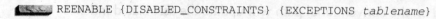

```
REENABLE {DISABLED_CONSTRAINTS} {EXCEPTIONS tablename}
```

The **disabled_constraints** keyword is optional and provided for readability; when using the **exceptions** clause, the table name specified must already exist. If this clause is not used in the data load, then the integrity constraints must be enabled manually using the **alter table** statement. When the constraint is reenabled, the entire table is checked and any errors are placed in an error table specified by the load. Similar to foreign-key constraints, default values cannot be enforced at the table level during a direct path load. Instead, the control file for the load should use the **defaultif** clause to specify the default expression. Otherwise, only data available to SQL*Loader for loading data to a column with a default specified will be inserted. If the data record for that column is NULL, then the value inserted will also be NULL.

TIP

*If a NOT NULL constraint is being used in conjunction with a default value by the table, use the **defaultif** clause in the control file to specify the default value in order to prevent a NULL from being inserted where it shouldn't.*

Triggers present a unique issue to loading data. **Insert** triggers are disabled at the beginning of the direct load, which means that the trigger does not execute for any data being inserted on the direct load. Unlike constraints, triggers are not reapplied to all table rows when the trigger is reenabled. If there is login employed by the trigger that must happen to the data loaded in the direct path, it must be duplicated in some other way by the application, either through an integrity constraint, an update trigger, or a stored procedure.

TIP
*Triggers are not reapplied after the direct load
completes. If something needs to happen in the
database when that trigger fires, try using an
integrity constraint, an **update** trigger, or a
stored procedure.*

Exercises

1. What factors do constraints present in the direct path data load?
   How should the DBA handle constraints?

2. What factors do triggers present in the direct path data load? How
   should the DBA handle triggers?

Indexes and the Direct Path

One of the reasons conventional path loads run slower than direct path
loads is because in the conventional path, the indexes are updated every
time a row is inserted. In contrast, the direct path load will rebuild the index
at the end. Ideally, data will be presorted when loaded in the direct path,
making index creation simple and fast. If this situation is the case, then
Oracle will not require temporary storage to sort and merge the index. If the
data is not presorted, however, then Oracle will require temporary space to
sort and merge the data being indexed. Use the following formula to
determine size requirements in bytes for temporary storage: **1.3**
*(*number_rows* *(10 + *sum_of_col_sizes* + *num_of_cols*)). In the equation,
1.3 represents the average number of bytes needed to sort typical lists of
unordered data. The actual range for this constant is 1.0 to 2.0, where 1.0
represents ordered input and 2.0 represents input in exactly the
opposite order.

SQL*Loader may leave an index in a state called the *direct load state* in
the event that a direct load is unsuccessful. This means that the index is
unusable and must be dropped and re-created for the data currently in the
table. A query on INDEX_NAME and status against the DBA_INDEXES data

dictionary view will show if an index was left in direct load state. The following items can cause the tool to leave an index in direct load state:

- SQL*Loader ran out of space for the index.
- Instance failure while creating an index.
- Duplicate values in a unique or primary key.
- Presorted data is not in order specified by the **sorted indexes** clause of the control file.

Exercises

1. Table EMP has three columns with the following datatypes: FNAME VARCHAR2(20); LNAME VARCHAR2(50); and SSN VARCHAR2(10). A direct load inserts 150,000 rows into a table. How large should temporary storage be, in bytes?

2. Name reasons why SQL*Loader might leave an index in direct load state.

Data Saves

SQL*Loader can save data during the direct path load with the use of data saves. Figure 10-3 shows that the direct path load accesses Oracle intermittently to request new extents and to adjust the highwatermark for the object being loaded. These activities are required as part of a data save. The frequency SQL*Loader will execute a data save is specified by the ROWS command-line parameter, and the default value for ROWS in a direct load is **all**. Although executing a data save during a direct path load reduces load performance, there are often compelling reasons to execute them intermittently rather than waiting until the load completes. A major reason for choosing the direct path is the need to load large amounts of data, so it may be wise to set ROWS such that a data save happens a few times during the load. For example, a load of 5 million rows may require a data save every million rows.

TIP
*A table's highwatermark is the maximum
amount of storage space the database has ever
used for that table. The highwatermark is reset
every time a table is truncated, but not when the
delete from table_name command is issued.*

In a direct load, full database blocks are written to the database beyond a
table's highwatermark. A data save simply moves the highwatermark.
Although similar in concept to a **commit** in regular SQL statement
processing and conventional loading, a data save is NOT the same as a
commit. Some key differences are listed here:

■   Indexes are not updated by a data save.

■   Internal resources are not released in a data save.

■   The transaction is not ended by a data save.

Exercises

1. What is a data save? To what concept in conventional path loading
   is a data save similar?

2. What is a highwatermark? How is it altered in a data save?

Chapter Summary

This chapter introduced SQL*Loader concepts and functions. SQL*Loader is
a tool that developers and DBAs can use to load data into Oracle7 tables
from flat files easily. SQL*Loader consists of three main components: a set of
data records to be entered, a set of controls explaining how to manipulate
the data records, and a set of parameters defining how to execute the load.
Most often, these different sets of information are stored in files—a datafile,
a control file, and a parameter file. SQL*Loader comprises about 5–8
percent of exam questions asked on OCP Exam 2.

Information in data records can be set into fixed-length or variable-length columns. If the data is set into fixed-length columns, the control file will contain a listing of the columns along with their start and end positions. If the data is set into variable-length columns, the control file will define the delimiters for each column in that record. There are two types of delimiters: terminating delimiters and enclosed delimiters.

SQL*Loader uses two other files during data loads in conjunction with record filtering. They are the bad file and the discard file. Both filenames are specified either as parameters or as part of the control file. The bad file stores records from the data load that SQL*Loader rejects due to bad formatting, or that Oracle7 rejects for failing some integrity constraint on the table being loaded. The discard file stores records from the data load that have been discarded by SQL*Loader for failing to meet some requirement as stated in the **when** clause expression of the control file. Data placed in both files are in the same format as they appear in the original datafile to allow reuse of the control file for a later load.

Recording the entire load event is the log file. The log filename is specified in the parameters on the command line or in the parameter file. The log file gives six key pieces of information about the run: software version and run date; global information such as log, bad, discard, and datafile names; information about the table being loaded; datafile information, including which records are rejected; data load information, including row counts for discards and bad and good records; and summary statistics, including elapsed and CPU time.

There are two load paths available to SQL*Loader: conventional and direct. The conventional path uses the SQL interface and all components of the Oracle RDBMS to **insert** new records into the database. It reliably builds indexes as it inserts rows and writes records to the redo log, guaranteeing recovery similar to that required in normal situations involving Oracle7. The conventional path is the path of choice in many loading situations, particularly when there is a small amount of data to load into a large table. This is because it takes longer to drop and re-create an index as required in a direct load than it takes to **insert** a small number of new rows into the index. In other situations, like loading data across a network connection using SQL*Net, the direct load simply is not possible.

However, the direct path often has better performance executing data loads. In the course of direct path loading with SQL*Loader, several things happen. First, the tool disables all constraints and secondary indexes the table being loaded may have, as well as any **insert** triggers on the table. Then, it converts flat file data into Oracle blocks and writes those full data blocks to the database. Finally, it reenables those constraints and secondary indexes, validating all data against the constraints and rebuilding the index. It reenables the triggers as well, but no further action is performed.

In some cases, a direct path load may leave the loaded table's indexes in a direct path state. This generally means that data was inserted into a column that violated an indexed constraint, or that the load failed. In the event that this happens, the index must be dropped, the situation identified and corrected, and the index re-created.

Both the conventional and the direct path have the ability to store data during the load. In a conventional load, data can be earmarked for database storage by issuing a **commit**. In a direct load, roughly the same function is accomplished by issuing a data save. The frequency of a **commit** or data save is specified by the ROWS parameter. A data save differs from a **commit** in that a data save does not **update** indexes, release database resources, or end the transaction—it simply adjusts the highwatermark for the table to a point just beyond the most recently written data block. The table's highwatermark is the maximum amount of storage space the table has occupied in the database.

Many parameters are available to SQL*Loader that refine the way the tool executes. The most important parameters are USERID to specify the username the tool can use to **insert** data and CONTROL to specify the control file SQL*Loader should use to interpret the data. Those parameters can be placed in the parameter file, passed on the command line, or added to the control file.

The control file of SQL*Loader has many features and complex syntax, but its basic function is simple. It specifies that data is to be loaded and identifies the input datafile. It identifies the table(s) and columns that will be loaded with the named input data. It defines how to read the input data, and can even contain the input data itself.

Finally, although SQL*Loader functionality can be duplicated using a number of other tools and methods, SQL*Loader is often the tool of choice for data loading between Oracle and non-Oracle databases because of its functionality, flexibility, and performance.

Two-Minute Drill

- SQL*Loader loads data from flat file to a table.

- There are three components: datafile, control file, and parameter file.

- The datafile contains all records to be loaded into the database.

- The control file identifies how SQL*Loader should interpret the datafile.

- The parameter file gives runtime options to be used by SQL*Loader.

- Data in the datafiles can be structured into fixed- or variable-length fields.

- The positional specifications for fixed-length fields are contained in the control file along with other specifications for the data load.

- For variable-length data fields, appropriate delimiters must be specified.

- The two types of delimiters used are terminating delimiters and enclosed delimiters.

- Two additional files can be used for record filtering: bad files and discard files.

- There are two data load paths: conventional and direct.

- Conventional loads use the same SQL interface and other Oracle RDBMS processes and structures that other processes use.

- Conventional path loading updates indexes as rows are inserted into the database, and also validates integrity constraints and fires triggers at that time.

- Direct path loads bypass most of the Oracle RDBMS, writing full database blocks directly to the database.

- Direct path loading disables indexes, **insert** triggers, and constraints until all data is loaded. Constraints and indexes are rechecked and built after data load.

■ The direct path load may occasionally leave an index in direct path state. This often is due to load failure or the loading of a data record that violates the table's integrity constraints.

Chapter Questions

1. **SQL*Loader execution parameters can be located in which of the following locations? (Choose three)**

   A. Datafile

   B. Control file

   C. Command line

   D. Discard file

   E. Parameter file

2. **Which of the following will improve performance on a data load?**

   A. Creating triggers before the load

   B. Enabling primary-key constraints before the load

   C. Specifying DIRECT=TRUE in the control file

   D. Running the load across a database link

3. **A table index should be rebuilt after running a conventional path data load.**

   A. TRUE

   B. FALSE

4. **After running SQL*Loader with the conventional path, which file contains records that could not be loaded due to violating integrity constraints?**

   A. The parameter file

   B. The bad file

    C. The discard file

    D. The log file

5. Indexes left in the direct path state after a data load must be rebuilt.

    A. TRUE

    B. FALSE

6. In which of the following operations does the direct path load use the SGA?

    A. Obtaining data blocks for writes

    B. Adjusting the highwatermark

    C. Updating the indexes

    D. Verifying integrity constraints

7. SQL*Loader can update existing rows of data in a table.

    A. TRUE

    B. FALSE

8. If a discard file is produced by SQL*Loader, in what format will the data in the file be?

    A. Fixed width

    B. Variable width

    C. Comma delimited

    D. The same as in the input file

Answers to Chapter Questions

1. B, C, and E.   Control file, command line, and parameter file.

Explanation   Choice A is incorrect because the datafile can only contain data used for input. Choice D is incorrect because the discard file contains records that were not loaded due to a user-defined restriction in the control file.

2. C.   Specifying DIRECT=TRUE in the control file

Explanation   Choice A is incorrect because firing a trigger on every record **insert** slows down the overall processing. The same is true with integrity constraints, thereby eliminating choice B. Running a load across a database link will cause SQL*Loader to perform poorly as well, eliminating choice D. The only choice that improves performance is choice C.

3. B.   FALSE

Explanation   Using a conventional load path causes SQL*Loader to use the Oracle SQL processing mechanism for data loading. This causes indexes to be updated as the data is inserted into the table.

4. B.   The bad file

Explanation   The parameter file for SQL*Loader contains runtime parameters used to control the data load, eliminating choice A. The discard file is similar in function to the bad file, but contains data rejected by user-defined reasons as part of the **when** clause, while the bad file contains rejected data for database-definition reasons, such as violating integrity constraints. This difference eliminates choice C. The log file contains information about the SQL*Loader run, such as the start and stop times and the number of records rejected, but not the records themselves. This eliminates choice D.

5. A.   TRUE

Explanation   When an index is in the direct path state, that indicates that the data loaded via direct path violated a primary or unique constraint. In order to use the index, it must be dropped and re-created.

6. B.   Adjusting the highwatermark.

Explanation   The direct path load option does not use the Oracle SQL processing mechanism or the SGA for very much of its processing, relying instead on internal mechanisms to turn flat file rows into data blocks. Choices A, C, and D are all processes that the conventional path data load uses in the Oracle database management system, but that the direct path avoids use in order to provide increased performance.

7. B.   FALSE

Explanation   SQL*Loader can only **insert** new rows into a table, not **update** existing ones.

8. D.   The same as in the input file.

Explanation   SQL*Loader produces discard files and bad files in the same format as the input file to allow for control file reuse. The input file may be in the formats named by A, B, and C, but not necessarily in every case.

UNIT
III

Preparing for OCP
DBA Exam 3: Backup
and Recovery
Workshop

CHAPTER
11

Overview of Backup and Recovery

n this chapter, you will understand and demonstrate knowledge in the following areas:

- Backup and recovery motives
- Backup methods

Mastering the art of backup and recovery is perhaps the most important area of Oracle database administration. However, this important aspect of maintaining the integrity and durability of the database with the presence of restorable copies is one of the most difficult and least-understood areas for those software professionals working with Oracle. This chapter and the unit it is part of cover required knowledge areas in backup and recovery for OCP Exam 3. Approximately 17 percent of the material in that test is covered in this chapter.

Backup and Recovery Motives

In this section, you will cover the following topics related to backup and recovery motives:

- Importance of backups
- Importance of business requirements
- Disaster recovery issues
- Management involvement
- Testing backup and recovery

Backups of the database are copies of the database that can be used in the event of an emergency. The restoration of an Oracle database depends on the presence of these backups. Without adequate backups of the database, there can be no recovery of that database. This sounds like a critical function, and it is. However, database backup and recovery is one of those "out of sight, out of mind" aspects that many developers and users ignore for the most part. The assumption made in most IT shops is that "someone else is handling backups, therefore I don't need to worry about it." That person is the database administrator. The DBA must take this role seriously, for although there won't be serious repercussions on the day a backup is missed, dropped, or forgotten, the problem will surface later when database failure occurs.

Importance of Backups

The implications of system failure for this example depend on which component is lost. Figure 11-1 illustrates the basic components of the database server used in this company. The problems created by various components in this architecture have varying solutions. For example, if the processor or memory chips of a database server were to fail, chances are that the situation, though annoying, would be recoverable with or without the presence of additional copies of data waiting in the wings for the inevitable problem to occur. The same may be said for the loss of a disk controller, the device used to manipulate the disks of a server.

Disk crashes are another story. No database recovery involving the replacement of data caused by failure of a disk can be performed without the use of a backup. Although several things can fail on a database server that will not require the database to require backups, the one thing that can happen—namely, disk failure—wreaks havoc in terms of data loss. This loss is so costly that every system, large and small, should take the necessary

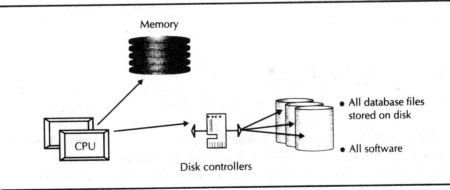

FIGURE 11-1. *Components of a database server*

precautions to ensure that the system will be recoverable to the extent that it needs to be.

Exercises

1. What is the significance of database backups?

2. In what situations will database backups be necessary?

Importance of Business Requirements

Analysis of business requirements will give the DBA and the system owners a more complete understanding of the recoverability their system requires. A needs assessment step can help the DBA determine the work outlay for bringing new systems online from a database administration perspective. The components of a template for determining the recoverability of a system may include the following:

- **Level of service** Define overall availability requirements and assign work priorities according to their impact on database availability. Identify a chain of contacts, required response, and resolution time. Create mechanisms for reporting how DBA met expectations. Agree to standards in writing.

- **Mechanisms for change** Establish an ongoing change schedule where new requirements may be evaluated.

- **Relate to DBA goals** Once business requirements are defined, align technical processes to those requirements.

Creating a Level of Service

The first step forms the core obligations of the database administration team in recovering the database in the event of many different sorts of issues. While the users of one system believe their system is highly important and any problem should be resolved in half a day or less, the DBA team has to balance the needs of any single system against the data needs for the organization as a whole. Priorities must be defined for DBAs to address different production issues effectively.

An important step to have the group recognize its successes and areas for improvement is to have quantifiable standards defined. It should be looked upon as a means to communicate about the services provided by DBAs, and whether or not that service meets the original expectations. Also, it is a time to negotiate new expectations if there seem to be areas of consistent difficulty. Agree in writing to these commitments. Without agreement on standards from all entities involved in the use and support of the system, there will always be a conflict at the time of crisis. This is because each party involved will enter the crisis with a different set of expectations. Service-level agreements are as much about maintaining good business relationships and sending a message of customer service commitment as they are about meeting the standards they define.

Mechanize Change

Any agreement on the level of service provided to a database application should be thought of as a "living" document. This means that periodically the standards agreed upon by all parties at production deployment of a system must be revisited. Due to staff turnover, a change in requirements, significant enhancements, or the changes in priorities inherent in most organizations, the level of service agreed upon by everyone involved with a database must be discussed and revised. The reprocessing of a service-level agreement should be treated with the same process for development as the original. The initial steps may not take as long, since the standards in many areas are not likely to change. The discussion of change is more likely to focus on the additions, revisions, or deletions to the service-level agreement. The modifications to reporting and the agreement of all parties in the end should follow through as well.

Relate Backup and Recovery Methods to DBA Goals

After the system requirements are laid out and the level of service is agreed upon, the DBA must plan for the worst-case—disk failure. This situation is always the worst one to encounter, for even if there is a problem with memory, CPU, or even disk controllers, ultimately the parts can be replaced. However, any loss of data has the potential to be permanent. The amount of insurance in the form of backups should relate directly to the level of importance the application has within the organization, the volatility of the data in the system, and the speed in getting the application up and running in the event of an emergency. Furthermore, the availability of certain features in Oracle can dramatically alter the requirements of users as well as the DBA's ability to provide recoverability to applications that require 24-hour operation. Some of these features include replication of data to remote machines using snapshots and the archival of redo logs to allow recovery to the point of failure. These and other features will be considered later in this unit, as mechanisms for providing backup and recovery unfold.

Exercise

Why should business requirements be considered when devising a backup and recovery strategy?

Disaster Recovery Issues

There are many issues surrounding disaster recovery that are required for any computer system, including the following:

- What disaster recovery scenarios can occur on the system?

- What disaster recovery scenarios involve recovery from data loss?

- How volatile is the data stored on the system?

- How quickly does the system need to be made available?

- How does the cost of providing recovery strategy for any scenario evaluate against the cost of losing time to reenter the data?

Computers are fragile machinery. Consider the cornerstone of any computer—the motherboard and CPU. They are vulnerable to many things, including moisture, sudden jarring movements, and dust. The amount of electricity fed to a computer is particularly important. The circuitry in a computer must be shielded both from sudden power loss and sudden power increases, both of which can cause damage. The damage these situations may cause is memory loss or damage to memory chips, or damage to the circuitry of the motherboard. Though annoying, the failure of one or more of the named components should not cause lasting damage to the applications that use the machinery unless the problem also causes data corruption on the data storage devices of the machine.

Special attention should be paid to the permanent disks used to store information on the machine. These devices are the heart and soul of the computer machinery. A memory problem may cause some trouble with the applications and the computer's ability to run, although frequent saves to disk can reduce the chance of data loss and ultimately the memory in a machine can be replaced. What often cannot be replaced is the data that is stored on the disk drives of the machine.

Some of the most crucial decisions that can be made about disaster recovery and computer systems involve the creation and execution of sufficiently frequent procedures for backing up hard disks. The processes created to take those backups should be designed to provide the recoverability that is required based on the needs of the system. For example, the frequency of backups required for support of a rapid recovery for a system that experiences a high rate of data changes would be higher than the need for backups on a system that experienced infrequent data changes and ran only once a month. Some other features for providing rapid uptime for users in the event of a disaster center around replication or mirroring of components of the database system or, in certain cases, the entire database system. If the availability of a computer system is critical to the operation of the organization, then the organization may want to consider the advantages of having a duplicate system available for use in the event of production system failure.

Providing adequate backup strategy for every situation involving any type of failure depends on the cost of losing data in a situation versus the cost of ensuring data is not lost. With enough planning and an eye on cost, it is possible to develop strategies that ensure data recovery in all but the most confounding or overwhelming situations. However, the cost of the solution provided should relate directly with the cost of the loss in the first place. It would be nice to provide daily backups to tape, which are then replicated and delivered to an offsite location for warehousing. It may also be great to have a full replica of the system waiting for the need to arise for its use. The reality of most organizations, however, is that there is neither the money nor the staff to maintain this option for every system. Furthermore, with careful planning, adequate results can be attained for far less money.

Exercises

1. What are some issues surrounding backup and recovery?
2. How might the DBA identify solutions to these issues?

Management Involvement

As with many other decisions an organization must make, the managers of an organization should be involved with the final determination of backup needs for the database applications used in the organization. Ideally, there should be management involvement in the task of defining the service-level agreement from beginning to end, so that the managers of an organization will properly assess each recovery situation as it arises. Managers often act as the best liaison for users and the DBA, although no DBA should ever be afraid of fielding their own support questions. With a proper understanding of the capacity and limitation of the backup strategy developed to handle a database application, the manager of that application can work in conjunction with all parties involved to ensure that all users' needs are met in disaster situations.

Exercise

How should managers get involved in the determination of backup and recovery issues?

Importance of Testing Backup Strategy

Nothing is worse than taking the hard work of many people to develop good plans for database backups and squandering it by failing to perform system tests to determine if the plan is adequate for the needs of the application. A good backup strategy accommodates user errors, too. The overall strategy is meant to ensure full recoverability of a database in the event of a complete system failure. The DBA shouldn't shy away from an array of options available to obtain supplemental backups during periods of high activity or when the DBA suspects there may be problems. Added backup coverage provides a value-added service that achieves additional recognition both for the DBA and for the entire IT shop. The ideal test plan consists of several areas, including a set of test case scenarios, the steps to resolve those scenarios, and a set of criteria to measure the success or failure of the test.

Only after the initial test plans are developed and executed successfully should the DBA consider implementing the backup strategy in production.

The testing of a backup strategy should not stop once the database sees live production activity, either. Good backup and recovery testing involves both formal reworking and periodic "spot-checks" to ensure that the strategy meets ongoing needs. As the focus of a database matures, so too should the backup strategy. When changes to the service-level agreement are made, the backup strategy should be tested to ensure that the new requirements are met. If they are not met, then the strategy should be rethought, reworked, and retested. However, as the DBA considers taking out some added "insurance" with special backups, the organization may also want to contemplate the power of random "audits" to ensure that the systems supported can be backed up adequately in a variety of different circumstances.

Testing backup strategy has some other benefits as well. The testing of a manual backup strategy may uncover some missing steps from the manual process, and may prompt the DBA to consider automating the backup process as well. There is no harm in automation as long as the process is tested and accommodates changes that occur in the database. Otherwise, the automated scripts will systematically "forget" to save certain changes made to the database, such as the addition of tablespaces and datafiles after the scripts are created.

Another benefit to testing the backup strategy is its ability to uncover data corruption. If one or several data blocks are corrupted in a datafile, and the physical database backup method is used for database backup, the corrupted data will be copied into the backups, resulting in backup corruption as well as corruption in the database. There is no way to verify if this is happening if there is no testing of the backups created, so the only time a DBA will discover that the backups contain corrupted data is when it's too late. Systematic data integrity checks can be accomplished with the DB_BLOCK_CHECKSUM initialization parameter and the DBVERIFY utility, both of which will be discussed later.

Exercises

1. What role should testing have in backup and recovery?

2. Name two reasons why testing the validity of backups is important.

Backup Methods

In this section, you will cover the following topics related to backup methods:

- The difference between logical and physical backups
- Mechanics of a good backup
- Implications of archiving or not archiving online redo logs
- Backup and recovery in round-the-clock operations
- Time requirements for recovery
- Time requirements for backup
- Transaction activity level and backup/recovery
- Backup and recovery for read-only tablespaces

Several methods exist for taking backups on the Oracle database. Some are handled internally using Oracle utilities and features. Others rely on the use of external or operating system-based mechanisms. The needs of a system also determine what methods are incorporated or recommended for use by Oracle. This section will discuss the use of various methods for backing up the Oracle database, along with their limitations and requirements.

Logical vs. Physical Backups

There are two types of backup available in Oracle: logical backups and physical backups. The two types of backups available in a database correspond directly to the two views of the database presented in Unit II: the logical view and the physical view. The logical database export consists of performing an export of the individual database objects available in an Oracle database. Oracle provides a utility for logical export of database objects and users called EXPORT. When EXPORT is used to create a backup of database objects, the backed-up copy of information is placed in a file called the *dump file*. A complementary application called IMPORT is designed to bring the information out of a file created by EXPORT, either into the database from which the objects were exported or into another Oracle database. Note that the format of the export dump file is compatible with the IMPORT utility only. There is no other way to use the files produced by the EXPORT utility.

Physical backups rely on the use of the operating system to copy the physical files that comprise the Oracle database from an operating system perspective. Further, for the application to incorporate changes to the database that weren't written to the database, the use of archived copies of the online redo logs must be used to ensure that appropriate changes are made to ensure a recovery up to the moment of failure. An example of the changes that exist in the instance that may not have been written to file are the changes to data blocks that are sitting in the dirty buffer write queue waiting to be written to disk as part of a checkpoint.

When deciding on a backup strategy, the DBA should bear in mind the uses for the database application and the amount of maintenance required for the backup strategy vs. the impact of lost data from the system. In general, however, it is recommended that logical backups of data in the database NOT be the primary method for ensuring that a backup exists on the database. Instead, it is recommended that physical backups of the files that comprise the Oracle database (namely, datafiles, log files, control files, and parameter files) in conjunction with the archiving of online redo log files with the **archivelog** option, be the preferred method of backup in the Oracle database. This recommendation is made because physical backups and use of **archivelog** mode allow the DBA many more options for recovery than simple logical backups. A logical backup allows for recovery only up until the point in time that the last backup was taken. In contrast, the DBA can recover a database up to the point in time of database failure when using physical database backup in conjunction with the **archivelog** mode.

TIP
When mentioned in OCP Exam 3 without a specific time reference, "point-in-time recovery" should be taken to mean the point in time that the backup was taken, NOT the point in time the database failed.

Crucial to both a logical and a physical backup is the importance of getting data off the disk or disks that are used all the time by the database and onto external storage media, such as magnetic tapes, optical drives, or even other machines. If, for example, the DBA is taking copies of datafiles and backing them up on a different directory of the same machine, then the DBA may as well not take backups at all. Consider the impact of a disk crash in this scenario—if the disk crashes, it will take both the production file and backup file with it.

Exercises

1. What is a logical backup? What utilities are available for logical backup?

2. What is a physical backup? How are physical backups taken?

Mechanics of Taking a Good Backup

First, regardless of whether or not the DBA operates the backup process manually or via the use of automated scripts, the DBA should have an intimate knowledge of the environment in which the database resides. In host system environments that use filesystems, this means that the DBA should know all the directories that the Oracle database uses in their setup, and the names and contents of each file used in their Oracle database. If need be, a map of the filesystem may be useful. Also helpful for taking backups is the use of the V$DATAFILE, V$CONTROLFILE, and V$LOGFILE performance views to determine the names of the datafiles, control files, and online redo log files, respectively.

Second, the DBA should be aware of the sequence of events that must occur in order for a good backup to happen. Each type of backup performed in the Oracle database environment requires a series of events that must happen in a certain order. If things happen out of order, then the integrity or utility of the backup may be compromised.

Finally, the DBA must know how to handle a system problem that arises during the process of database backup. The database can fail anytime, including the time a DBA is attempting to perform backups. With the knowledge of how to handle errors during backup, the DBA can ensure that the database remains recoverable in spite of the error.

Exercise

What dynamic performance views are used in determining backups?

Backup Strategies

There are several different types of backups available to the Oracle DBA. These options are used in the backing up of a database, depending on the business needs of the system. In the following section, several case studies are presented to illustrate each type of backup available. The backup options available as of Oracle7 are as follows:

- Logical export
- The offline backup
- The online backup

Logical Export

Logical export should be done outside of normal business hours to minimize impact to online database processing. The logical export of a database requires the DBA to first consider the effects of *read inconsistency*, the degree to which data involved in the transaction is unchanged by any transaction other than this one, from the start of the transaction to the finish. *This is not a condition of logical export.* Instead, the export reads data from each object in the database in turn to replicate its data in a binary file stored in a location defined by the EXPORT command-line parameters. For best results with EXPORT, use the following steps:

1. Limit database access by identifying a time for the database backup cycle to occur daily and weekly. Alternately, execute the **alter system enable restricted session** statement to allow only users with the **restricted session** privilege to connect.

2. Take the logical backup using the EXPORT tool according to the steps detailed in the next chapter.

3. After running the backup and storing the binary copy of data on a special disk dump destination, move the backup to tape.

Remember that logical backups are good for recovery to resolve user error, such as the accidental removal of a database table. However, one major limitation of the logical backup process is that they do not use archived redo logs. As such, they do not present a good solution to recovering a database to the point of failure unless a backup was taken just prior to failure. In other words, the DBA can only make recovery on the database with logical backups up to the point in time that the last backup was taken. Figure 11-2 shows the database view of a logical export.

Offline Backup

An offline backup consists of backing up the database from the operating system perspective. Since the Oracle database consists of several different files that reside in an operating system, it stands to reason that saving those files and storing them in an alternative storage form would be a viable alternative to the logical storage option. The physical database recovery model offers options for success in recovering active database systems.

Redo logs should be archived with physical backups. More information about the implications of archiving and the methods for turning on archiving is detailed later in this chapter and again in Chapter 13. From the discussion of redo logs in Unit II, you know that the redo logs store every transaction that was entered into the database. Each transaction is assigned a system change number (SCN) for the purposes of tracking the change in the rollback segment and the redo log. Once committed, Oracle stores the SCN in the online redo log, along with a message saying this transaction is committed. When

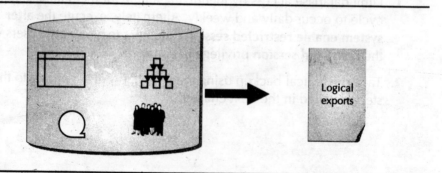

FIGURE II-2. *Database view of logical export*

archived, the online logs are stored in the archive destination specified by the **init.ora** parameter LOG_ARCHIVE_DEST. The physical database backup the DBA creates is only the first step in ensuring a recovery of committed transactions up to the point in time of failure. The successful application of data in the archived redo logs allows the DBA to insert the supplemental changes that happened on the database after the backup took place.

To ensure that all data is captured in an offline backup, the DBA should close the database using the **shutdown normal** or **shutdown immediate** statement, then begin the offline backup process. During offline backup, the database is not available to users, as shown in Figure 11-3. Archived redo logs that currently reside in the disk location are stored to tape if archiving is being used. All the files of the database that store application data are then copied and archived using the methods for file copy made available by the operating system. The following bullet points list the types of files that must be archived in order to restore the database:

- **Datafiles**   Store the tables, indexes, rollback segments, other segments, and data dictionary.

- **Redo log files**   Store the nonarchived redo log entries of the database.

- **Control files**   Store the physical-to-logical database schema translation and location information.

- **Parameter files**   Also called **init.ora**, store all parameters used for database instance startup.

- **Password files**   Store passwords for DBAs allowed to connect to the database as **sysdba**.

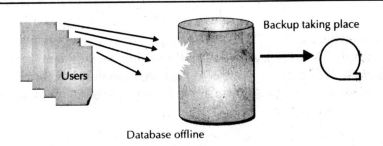

Backup taking place

Users

Database offline

FIGURE 11-3.   *Cold physical backups and the operating system*

The DBA should back up the copies of the datafiles, online redo log files, control files, password file, and parameter file to another disk, if possible, to improve recovery time. However, allocating enough space for a copy of all the files associated with a database may be difficult, especially for large databases. Ideally, however, enough space can and will be allocated to store all files on disk first, so that the backup can complete before the files are then transferred to alternate storage media such as tape. The DBA will see the best backup performance if there is enough space to store a copy of all backed-up data on a disk, then start the database to make it available to users again.

The offline backup by itself presents a good solution for minimal point-in-time recovery on database systems that the organization can afford to allow downtime on. When used in conjunction with archived redo logs, however, the recovery options for offline backups multiply to include recovery to virtually any point in time from the time the offline backup took place right up to the point in time the database experienced disk failure, and any point in time in between.

Online Backup

In globally deployed systems that require a range of availability for all hours of night and day corresponding to users in other areas of the world, the cold offline backup may not be possible. The organization may simply not be able to allocate enough time per week to allow DBAs to take the database down in **normal** mode. A **shutdown normal** process can be time-consuming, as it requires the DBA to wait until the last connected user logs off before completing the shutdown routine. As an alternative to be used in support of global operations that require round-the-clock online access, the DBA can use Oracle's online backup method, illustrated in Figure 11-4.

The online backup is an iterative process that creates backed-up copies of the database, tablespace by tablespace. Whereas in the two previous options a clear distinction was drawn between exports that take the logical view of the database (EXPORT) and backups that take the pure physical view of the database (offline backups), the online backup requires a hybrid logical-physical approach. In order to execute an online backup, the DBA must execute a command within Oracle Server Manager that prepares the

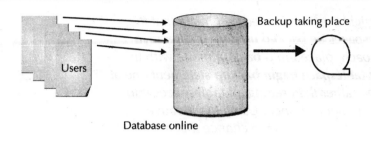

FIGURE 11-4.   *The online approach to database backups*

database for the online backup. The command is the **alter tablespace** *name*
begin backup command. An example of the command syntax in action
appears in the following code block:

```
ALTER TABLESPACE data_01 BEGIN BACKUP;
```

Once this command is issued, the DBA should immediately go to the
operating system prompt of the machine hosting Oracle and make a copy of
all datafiles associated with the tablespace. For example, if tablespace
DATA_01 has five datafiles, called **data01-1.dbf** through **data01-5.dbf**, then
after the logical database command statement in the code listing above has
been executed, the DBA must switch to the operating system and make a
copy of the five datafiles associated with the index. Once complete, the
DBA should switch back to the logical database view of Oracle and issue
the command listed in the following code block from within Server Manager:

```
ALTER TABLESPACE data_01 END BACKUP;
```

Once one tablespace is backed up, then the DBA can move on to the
next tablespace that will be backed up. However, there is no requirement to
do so. Since each tablespace is backed up independently of one another,
the DBA can formulate a practice of incremental tablespace backups or
back up all database tablespaces in their entirety.

TIP
*It is highly recommended by Oracle that the tablespaces be backed up with the iterative approach, placed into **backup** mode with the **alter tablespace begin backup** statement one at a time rather than setting all tablespaces into **backup** mode at once. Using the iterative approach minimizes the chance that a tablespace will be in **backup** mode at a time when the disk drive crashes or when the entire instance stops running for some reason.*

The online backup approach offers the DBA a distinct advantage. A complete copy of all tablespaces in the database can be obtained without shutting down database operation. This fact allows 24-hour databases the same power to back up their data as those databases that can experience downtime.

The use of online backups adds some complexity to the business of making backups in that online backups require the use of archived redo logs in order to preserve the integrity of changes made to a tablespace while the backup takes place. Remember, the database is open, available, and accepting changes during the entire time an online backup is taking place. In order to guarantee that the changes made to the tablespace while the backup took place are kept, it is required that the DBA archive redo logs that were taken during the operation of hot backups. Prior to taking the backup, the DBA should issue the **archive log list** command from Server Manager in order to determine the oldest online redo log sequence that should be saved in conjunction with the online backups being taken. Once the tablespace backups are complete, the **archive log list** command should be issued again, followed by a log switch to ensure that the current redo log entries made for the tablespaces backed up are archived properly for use by the backups should recovery be necessary. The steps to the process are listed below:

I. Execute **archive log list** from Server Manager. Note value for "Oldest online log sequence." This is the oldest redo log required for using the online backup.

2. Execute **alter tablespace** *name* **begin backup** from Server Manager. This step prepares the tablespace for online backup by freezing the headers in the datafiles for the tablespace.

3. Copy the datafiles for that tablespace using operating system or third-party products/commands. Be sure the copy resides on another disk than the production datafiles themselves.

4. Execute **alter tablespace** *name* **end backup** from Server Manager. This step completes the online backup process for that tablespace.

5. Repeat steps 2-4 for all tablespaces to be backed up.

6. Execute **archive log list** again from Server Manager. Note value for "Current log sequence" this time. This is the last redo log required for using the online backup.

7. Issue an **alter system switch logfile** to cause Oracle to create an archive of the current redo log. This archive should then be stored in the area specified by LOG_ARCHIVE_DEST. If desired, copy the archives associated with the backup to tape.

8. Create a copy of the control file. This is done with the **alter database backup controlfile** statement. Either the actual control file or a script to create it can be backed up using this statement.

TIP
A control file must be backed up whenever a change is made to the structure of a database. For example, after the creation of a new tablespace, or an addition or removal of a datafile, the control file for the database must be backed up.

Exercises

1. What is the general process for taking a logical export? Once complete, in what form is the data of a logical export?

2. What is an offline backup? What is the general process for taking an offline backup?

3. What is an online backup? What is the process for taking an online backup?

Implications of Archiving

Redo logs store every transaction that was entered into the database. Each transaction is assigned a system change number for the purposes of tracking the change in the rollback segment and the redo log. Once committed, Oracle stores the SCN in both places, along with a message saying this transaction is committed. The redo logs are an ongoing list of system change numbers and database changes. When archived, the online logs are stored when they are full to another location in the database, specified by the **init.ora** parameter LOG_ARCHIVE_DEST. The physical database backup the DBA creates is only the first step in ensuring a recovery of committed transactions up to the point in time of failure. The successful application of data in the archived redo logs allows the DBA to insert the supplemental changes that happened on the database after the backup took place.

Archiving of redo logs should be used in any production database environment where data changes are frequent and complete recovery to the point of failure is required. With archived redo logs, the potential options for database recovery are enhanced because the data changes recorded by redo logs can then be applied to the most recent backup to allow for all the committed changes that have been made since that backup to "roll forward." A roll-forward is when Oracle applies all the uncommitted changes that are stored in the redo logs to the database. Once this step is complete, Oracle then rolls back to eliminate the uncommitted changes from the database. Figure 11-5 shows the Oracle redo log architecture.

Without the archival of online redo logs, the data changes for a database are lost every time a log switch occurs. To understand why, recall the process used to write online redo logs. There are at minimum two redo logs available in the Oracle database at any given time. Each redo log may consist of one or more *members*, or copies. Ideally, the online redo log members are placed on multiple disks to minimize the Oracle database's dependency on any one disk. If a disk drive fails that contains the only member of the current online redo log, the Oracle instance will fail. Needless to say, it is important to ensure that the instance doesn't fail because of the loss of a disk containing the online redo log. The cleanup process will necessarily be incomplete if this situation occurs.

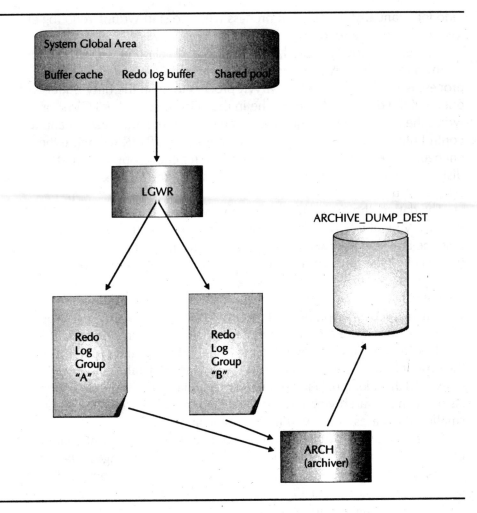

FIGURE 11-5. *Oracle redo log architecture*

When an online redo log fills, a log switch occurs. Remember that several things happen during a log switch. First of all, if archiving is enabled and the DBA has issued the **archive log start** statement from Server Manager or set the LOG_ARCHIVE_START initialization parameter to TRUE in the **init.ora** file, then the online redo log will be archived automatically by ARCH. If only archiving has been enabled, the DBA may have to archive the redo log manually. The LGWR process will also start writing redo log entries to the other online redo log.

Though not strictly related to archiving, a checkpoint will also occur during a log switch. A checkpoint is a point in time where the LGWR process issues an order to the DBWR process to flush the dirty buffer write queue of the database buffer cache in the SGA. Also, either LGWR or CKPT writes the new redo log sequence number to the datafile headers and to the control file. Flushing the dirty buffers means that DBWR will write the data changes made to database blocks in the buffer cache out to the datafiles on disk that contain copies of the blocks. These are the processes that comprise a log switch.

The data in the online redo log is always considered "junk" after the log switch. When the LGWR fills the other redo log, it will switch back to the first one and start overwriting the data changes made to the redo log prior to the switch. If the redo entries are not archived, then the redo log entries will be lost time and time again as the log switches cause Oracle to overwrite the data changes. This redo information is very useful for providing the DBA with many recovery options and should be archived wherever appropriate. The situations where archiving redo information is appropriate include any database that requires recovery to the point in time of the problem—where the cost of having users reenter lost data as part of database recovery outweighs the additional effort required to maintain archived redo information. As one can see, archiving redo logs is an appropriate option for all but the smallest databases in use within an organization.

Situations where archiving is not required include read-only databases or databases that experience a low frequency of data changes. Databases in this category may be better off using the logical backup option. For example, if it is known that a database will change only when a batch process feeds data into the system once a week, the simplest option that provides comprehensive backups for use in recovering this system is to make a backup of the database after the data changes are made. Either the logical backup approach or the offline backup will work to store the data changes made after the batch processes that update this type of system. This approach provides the needed recoverability for the system as well as requiring only nominal effort and maintenance on the backup process by the DBA. Some database types that may fit into this model include data warehouses or decision support systems.

However, any type of online transaction processing system may not be able to predict the volatility of its data in the same way that a system relying mainly on batch processing to create data changes would. In support of these online systems, Oracle recommends archiving redo logs. By saving all the data changes made to the database with the use of archived redo logs, the DBA can recover all committed data changes to the database with minimal requirements for end users to reenter data they may have placed into the trust of the database environment.

TIP
Archiving redo logs has no value in databases that rely on logical backups using EXPORT. In situations where offline physical backups are used, then archiving redo logs is recommended for the sake of applying redo changes in order to make a full recovery to the point in time of the database failure. Archiving is not required, however. When relying on hot backups due to 24-hour database availability, archiving must be used due to the reliance on archived redo information to supplement the online backup.

Exercises

1. What is archiving?
2. Why is the use of archiving significant with respect to online redo logs?
3. What recovery options are created with the use of archiving?

Backup and Recovery in 24×7 Operations

The requirements of round-the-clock databases have been mentioned in a few different areas of this chapter already. In many large organizations, the requirement that a system be available at all times is becoming more and more common. This fact holds true even for systems depending on a database that is not deployed to a global user base. The reason 24-hour operation is such an important requirement to many organizations has as much to do with batch processing as it has to do with the globalization of many businesses. In many environments, there is an entire fleet of database tables that contain validation information for applications. For example, assume there is a database that supports several applications for the human resources organization of a large company. This database contains tables that are updated daily via online users. The applications depend on an infrastructure of database tables that contain validation information such as an employee's name, organization ID, salary, start date, and address. In addition, there may be several other tables in a database that support and store validation data for any number of different reasons. Typically, this validation information is not subject to change by the applications that use the data. This doesn't mean, however, that the data never changes. For example, employees enter and leave a company all the time. The employee validation information needs to be updated for other applications that may have data populated in them on the basis of that new employee. Hence, some new data must be brought into the database on an ongoing basis. This ongoing basis is handled via batch processes. It is usually recommended that batch processing occur during time periods where few users are likely to enter data to an online application so that neither the user nor the batch process will have to share hardware resources with one another. An organization may have dozens or hundreds of batch processes that move data from one place to another, requiring several hours' processing time per night. Thus, even a suite of applications that are deployed to users in one area or country may still require 24-hour availability to handle all batch processing overhead associated with providing valid value information to the database applications.

However, systems that are deployed worldwide are even harder to support. Since the worldwide user base may log in to create transactions at any given time, there really is no specific time the DBA can earmark as available for online processing and another time for batch. These systems typically require hardware that offers enormous processing power in order to handle database transactions for both users and batch processes *at the same time*. The data integrity issues these systems present can baffle even the brightest DBAs.

Consider, for example, the situation where the database has users entering information for an application associated with an employee who is an active employee according to the database at the time the data is entered. The data entry takes place at 2 P.M. Pacific time. The application that the data is entered for has a batch process called "X" that occurs at 5 P.M. Pacific time that will only process data in this application for active employees. However, another batch process called "Y" comes along at 7 P.M. Eastern time that changes the validation data for employees. This process Y changes the employee for whom data was entered at 2 P.M. Pacific time to inactive. As a result of the change made by process Y, the application batch process X will not process the record for the employee entered at 2 P.M. because the employee is not active, even though the employee was active at the time the data was entered. This example is displayed graphically in Figure 11-6, and demonstrates the importance and difficulty of determining the beginning and end of a "business day" in terms of when batch processes will update valid values.

The difficulty of 24-hour operations extends into the world of backup and recovery as well. For a database that expects online usage during a certain period of time but requires 24-hour availability due to the need for extensive batch processing to support the validation data used to preserve data integrity in the face of online transaction processing, identifying time to perform backups is easy. The backups for this type of database should be scheduled during the same time as that allocated for batch processing. Usually, a few hours are identified in the business day, possibly early in the morning or late at night, where database activity is low. At this time, the

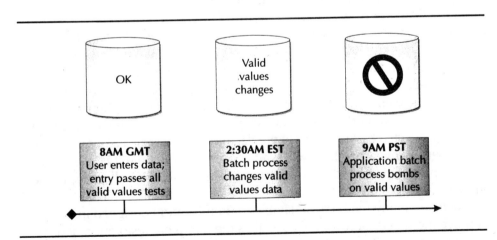

FIGURE 11-6.   *Importance of synchronicity in 24-hour databases*

DBA may schedule online backups to occur, or, alternatively, could shut down the database and take an offline backup. Online backups present the best option because they allow the database to be available on the errant chance that a user may still be working with information in the database. The overall effect of scheduling online backups during lulls in database activity is to limit the amount of redo information that must be applied to a backup, to place committed changes into the database that were made while the backup was being taken.

Using the logical backup strategy is usually not effective in 24-hour operations or for online transaction processing systems, mainly because of the volatility of the data changes. Since exports cannot be used in conjunction with archived redo information, there is no way to enact database recovery past the last point in time a logical backup was created. However, logical exports can be used for supplemental backups of individual database objects or for the recovery of a dropped object in certain cases.

The difficulties faced by backup and recovery strategies are compounded by the requirement of an application to be available 24 hours a day for online usage as well as batch processing. The same problems related to scheduling batch processes are in effect for backup and recovery. The solution with respect to obtaining good database backups is solved partially with the use of online backups to enable the database to be available during the backup period. The size and number of redo log entries that must be applied to an online backup may be high or low, depending on the level of transaction activity during the time the backup is taken. It is worth determining when the database is least active in terms of online and batch processing in this situation because the fewer the number of redo logs that need to be applied to a backup, the less time that will be spent waiting for the files to be restored from tape.

However, recovery in a 24-hour operation is another story entirely. Since the expected availability of a database system is *all* the time, the success of recovery of a 24-hour database is not simply based on the complete recovery of all data affected by the failure of the database. Time is also a consideration. Since users all over the globe will wait no matter what time it is, the DBA must be prepared to handle the recovery of the database at all times, in the shortest time possible.

There are many methods of database administration designed in order to improve the speed for recovery as well as the complete restoration of data into the database. Two of the various options used to minimize the recovery of a database in 24-hour operations include relating the frequency of a backup to the frequency of change experienced by the objects in the database and using a standby database. These two options can provide speedier recovery in different ways.

By backing up areas of the database that are updated more frequently, the DBA minimizes the recovery time required. More frequent backups minimize the number of redo logs that must be applied to the backup to bring the data in the database current to the point in time the database failure occurred. If full database backups occur infrequently, then many archived redo logs must be applied to the database in order to make current the database changes to the point in time of the failure.

The standby database provides faster recovery in another way. A standby database allows for almost instant recovery of a database by using additional hardware, along with data replication, to create a second copy of the database on another machine. When failure occurs, the DBA can switch users to the standby database for the period that the original database must be recovered. Although standby databases sound great in concept, the actual management of a standby database can be tricky. A more complete discussion of use for standby databases will appear in Chapter 15.

Exercises

1. What are the implications associated with backup in 24-hour availability database environments?

2. What are the implications associated with recovery in that same scenario?

Implications of Recovery Time

As long as there are backups of the database files, along with archived online redo logs, it is usually possible to recover the data right up to the last **commit** issued before the crash. However, the time it takes to achieve that level of availability can become an issue in and of itself. The general rule of thumb is the more time the database is expected to be available in the course of a day, the more pressure the DBA will be under to recover data in the event of a system crash. To improve recovery time, the frequency of a backup should be related to the frequency of change experienced by the objects in the database. Recovery time can also be minimized with a standby database.

Frequent backups minimize the number of redo logs that must be applied to the backup to bring the data in the database current to the point in time the database failure occurred. If full database backups occur infrequently, then many archived redo logs must be applied to the database in order to make current the database changes to the point in time of the failure. More frequent backups should be considered if the database experiences a high degree of data change in certain areas. The frequency of backups can be broken down to the tablespace level for those DBAs who use online backups as well. By backing up the database one tablespace at a time, the DBA may find it useful to back up tablespaces whose data is frequently changed. In addition, the DBA may want to back up tablespaces containing rollback segments in databases experiencing high transaction volumes.

The standby database provides faster recovery in another way. As discussed, a standby database allows for almost instant recovery of a database by using additional hardware along replication to create a second copy of the database on another machine. When failure occurs, the DBA can switch users to the standby database for the period that the original database must be recovered. Although standby databases sound great in concept, the actual management of a standby database can be tricky. In general, the use of a standby database is expensive and challenging. Although it certainly has its place in database backup and recovery, care should be taken in order to ensure that the DBA manages standby databases properly. A fuller treatment of the standby database appears in Chapter 15.

Exercises

1. What are two ways the DBA can minimize recovery time?

2. What relationship should the frequency of backups have to the frequency of data change?

Implications of Backup Time

Backing up the database has its own time implications as well. The length of time a backup may take need not be considered "lost time" in terms of productivity of availability of the system, as has already been established.

However, each style of backup has its own time considerations, as will be presented shortly.

Consider first the time requirements of the logical backup. In order to obtain a logical backup, the database must either be open to all users or set into **restricted session** mode, whereby only users with the **restricted session** privilege may access the database. Presumably, the user that connects to Oracle to take the logical backup, either a person at a terminal or a batch script, will have this privilege.

It is recommended that the **restricted session** option be used when backing up the database using the logical options presented by the EXPORT utility. The reason for this recommendation is because of EXPORT's biggest time implication—for the period of time the EXPORT is taking place, there is no guarantee of read consistency for the entire export. Due to the method Oracle uses for exporting data, the EXPORT utility does give read-consistent views of the data *in each table* while the read takes place; however, the same ability is not given across tables. Thus, if the DBA has a set of tables to back up using the EXPORT method, and users have access to the data, there is a chance that data can change in one table while the backup is saving another. Once the data export is complete, the utility will not go back to find data that may have changed while the export was running. In effect, even though the data may have changed in the table, there is still no guarantee that it was backed up.

The time implications involved with the use of EXPORT are important for the DBA to consider when scheduling and designing backups. Time impact is twofold. First, during the period of time the export takes place, the DBA should consider disallowing the users' access to the database so as to provide a read-consistent view of all objects backed up. The time trade-off with this option is that for the time the backup is taking place, the users may not access the database. The second trade-off is that if user access is not disallowed, then the data in the export may not be useful. It is conceivable that since there is no read consistency between database objects as the export takes place, if a user inserts data into a table after the data was exported, the row would not appear in the table but it would appear in the index.

Second in consideration to logical backups is the fact that the more infrequent the backup, the more time that will be required for data reentry into the database system. It has been mentioned that the logical backup is only capable of restoring the data in a database to the point in time the last backup was taken. If, for example, the last export of a database was taken at 2 A.M. on a Tuesday and the database crashed on Wednesday at 4 P.M., then the DBA will only be able to provide restoration of data to the point the export took place at 2 A.M. Tuesday. Thus, the users of the database will be required to redo work on their own time.

Physical backups have their own set of time considerations as well. An offline backup must take place while the database is closed. The first time implication for offline backups is that the backup must occur when users are not likely to be on the system. As with logical backups, this time period may be late at night or on weekends, provided that the database system does not have 24-hour availability requirements due to global user base and/or extensive batch processing.

The second fact is that for the period of time the offline backup takes place, no user may access the database system. Period. This fact is due to the database being offline while the backup takes place. Although logical backups have a similar recommendation that the database be in **restricted session** mode for the period of the backup to ensure read consistency, the offline physical backup *must* take place when the database is down. Therefore, the users of the database must necessarily be willing to accept downtime as part of the backup process.

Finally, in the event of a disaster, as with logical export backups, the physical offline backup will only restore data to the point of failure if database archiving is not used. In this situation, the users will be required to take time to redo their database work from the time the backup occurred to the time the failure occurred. It should be said at this point that the cost of recovery in the situation where users' changes are not restorable to the point in time of the database failure could grow quite costly. Even though it may take several hours to apply redo log entries onto the restored database on top of the time it takes to restore the database itself, during that time the users may be able to salvage their own productivity by doing something else until the system is available. However, if the database is available and several users must accomplish a day's worth of work to recover their own data changes (for example), then the users of the database have definitely lost time. The time loss suffered by each user, when translated into an hourly rate times the number of users who suffered the time loss, can add up to a scandalously large soft cost paid by the company to restore a database. As such, Oracle strongly recommends the use of archiving in conjunction with physical backups for any shop that must have data recovery to the point in time a failure may occur.

The final backup option whose time implications will be considered is the online backup method. As mentioned before, this option requires the use of archiving in order to obtain the data changes made to the tablespace during the online backup period. The time implications with this form of backup basically amount to showing how forgiving an online backup really is. During the period that the backup occurs, the database can and should be available for the use of any users to **insert**, **select**, **update**, or **delete** data from the tablespace being backed up. This option is designed to support 24-hour availability on a database.

The main time implication of online backups, however, is the time to recover using them. The recovery process when using archived redo logs is twofold. First, the DBA must apply the backup to the database in order to restore the database to the point in time the backup was taken. Then, in order to restore the database to the point in time that it failed, the DBA must apply the archived redo logs. This two-step process can be time-consuming, depending on the number of archived redo logs that need to be applied. If backups are infrequent and the redo logs large and many, then recovery will take a long time to accomplish. If backups are frequent and the redo logs small and few, then the same amount of data recovery will take less time.

In order to avoid the time implications created by online backups, the DBA should schedule the backups as frequently as possible without incurring excessive overhead on the database during peak hours of usage. A deeper discussion of the implications of large and voluminous archived redo logs and some potential causes for this situation will be discussed shortly.

Exercises

1. What are the time implications associated with taking various types of backups?

2. How can the DBA minimize the time spent taking backups for each of the three types of backups presented?

Backup and Recovery on Systems with Various Transaction Levels

It is not difficult to ensure that the database can have all its data restored up to the final committed transaction just prior to system failure. The difficulty starts when trying to perform said recovery in the rapid manner demanded by most online applications. To boot, the business situations that make DBAs opt to use archiving in the first place are often the same business situations that put the most pressure on DBAs to provide a rapid recovery. Often, the situation gives rise to a paradox—does the DBA emphasize recoverability of data at the expense of recovery performance, or does the organization have to suffer the potentially poor performance of a complete recovery for the sake of recovering all its data?

The size and number of redo logs that will be required for an Oracle database recovery in the event of an emergency correlates directly to two factors. The first factor is the amount of transaction activity. The number of redo logs that are generated and required to support recovery from the last backup to the most current redo log is in direct proportion to how long ago the last backup was made and how high the transaction activity has been on that tablespace since the last backup. A general rule of thumb is the higher the transaction level, the more archived redo logs that will be generated. The size of a redo log is set by the parameters specified for the database at the time a database is created. For more information about the size of a redo log, refer to the discussion of creating databases in Unit II.

The second factor is the frequency of the backups. Once a backup is taken, all the data in a tablespace at the moment in time the backup takes place is recorded in that backup. Any archived redo logs that were required to get the database to the point of the backup from a previous backup are no longer required for that point-in-time recovery. Generally speaking, the more frequent the backup, the fewer the number of redo logs that will be required by the DBA for purposes of recovery to the point in time of failure.

Transaction activity makes more or fewer redo entries, depending on how much activity the database is seeing. For example, on a database that infrequently experiences weekend activity, there will be fewer redo log entries, and thus fewer redo logs, that are produced during weekend activity. At peak periods of usage, however, when the users are adding data to the database frequently, the redo logs will grow rapidly.

In general, larger and more numerous archived redo logs coupled with infrequent backups produce longer recovery times than fewer, smaller redo logs coupled with more frequent backups. Fortunately, there are recovery alternatives that may be faster to execute. It is beneficial for the DBA to back up the database more frequently during periods of high transaction activity. This will enable the DBA to use fewer archived redo logs during database recovery to produce the same recovered data in less time. Another practice commonly applied by DBAs who are using online backups is to back up the most frequently used tablespaces most often. Since online backups are accomplished tablespace by tablespace, the DBA can easily pinpoint database objects for backup that are updated frequently by consolidating placement of those objects into tablespaces earmarked for frequent backup. The recovery of those frequently updated database objects is more convenient in the event that the disk storing those tablespaces fails.

This approach also works for those tablespaces that may not be as frequently changed. Since the changes to a tablespace may not be frequent, a large number of archived redo logs to apply may not contribute as heavily to the recovery time required for infrequently updated tablespaces. This fact is due to the existence of few redo entries in each of the archived redo logs. So, each redo log that is applied to the infrequently changed tablespace may run quickly due to the fact that there aren't many redo entries in the log to apply.

TIP
The higher the transaction activity level, the more redo log activity Oracle will generate. Back up frequently updated tablespaces often to minimize time spent applying redo log entries during recovery.

The transaction activity level will adversely impact database recovery in databases that do not use archiving as well. More frequent backups should be used when the database relies on logical backups or offline backups. Since these methods only afford the DBA the opportunity to make recovery to the point in time the backup occurred, it makes sense to back up data frequently to minimize the amount of effort the users will have to reapply to the database in the event of a database failure.

Unfortunately, in nonarchiving situations, more frequent backups require more downtime—during which the users will not be able to add or change data in the database. In reality, it may not be possible to accomplish these nonarchiving backups more often than once a day, which means there is always the possibility that users will lose at most one day's work plus recovery downtime. Especially on databases with high transaction activity, Oracle recommends archiving the redo logs in order to provide recovery to the point in time of the failure.

Exercises

1. How does a high-level of transaction activity affect the time it takes to recover a database?

2. How can the DBA minimize the impact of high transaction activity on database recovery?

3. What factor does archiving play in these scenarios?

Backup and Recovery on Read Only Tablespaces

Drawing on the points made about backup needs for less frequently changed database objects, there are special considerations that should be made for backup on the least frequently changed database objects. In cases where special "valid values" data is kept in lookup tables on the Oracle database, the tables that contain this data can be placed into special tablespaces called **read only** tablespaces. These tablespaces in the database are precisely that—the data in the tables of a **read only** tablespace may not be changed.

Data that is **read only** in a database represents the easiest effort in terms of DBA maintenance and backup for the sake of database recovery. In situations where database data is defined as **read only**, the DBA needs to back up the **read only** tablespace once for every time the data changes. The mechanics of setting a tablespace to **read only** status is covered in Unit II. Once the tablespace is **read only**, the DBA can rest assured that the data will not change. As such, repeated backup is not necessary. The data in a **read only** tablespace needs to be backed up only once.

Exercises

1. What is a **read only** tablespace?

2. What are the considerations for backup on **read only** tablespaces?

Chapter Summary

This chapter covered several areas of introduction to the business of backup and recovery on an Oracle database. The two topic areas covered in this chapter include the backup and recovery motives in Oracle and the backup methods in the Oracle database. Together, these topics comprise 17 percent of the OCP Exam 3 test content.

The first area covered in this chapter is backup and recovery motives. The DBA must remember that the data in a table cannot be recovered without backups. This is the critical nature of backups for recovery purposes. When determining the setup for a backup schedule, the DBA should keep several things in mind. First, the nature of business for this application should be remembered. Is the application meant for online transaction processing situations, where several thousand users are entering data daily? If so, then the backups taken on that type of system should reflect the volatility of the data being stored. On other systems, where data may be fed to the database on a batch schedule such as in the situation of a data warehouse, backups may be required only after said batch processes **update** data. This may be true because after that time, the database is primarily available on a **read only** basis to its users. The point being made here is that the backup and recovery strategy must be tied very closely to the overall objectives of the database being backed up.

Disaster can strike any computer system at any time. Some of the implications of disaster recovery for any system include data loss, reduced productivity for users while the computer system is recovered, and hardware costs for replacing missing or destroyed server and/or client components. Other costs to the computer system include the time it may take to manually reenter data that could not be recovered automatically due to the absence of backup components. Any or all of these issues may be deemed acceptable by the organization, depending on whether or not the organization is risk-taking or risk-averse. However, as with most decisions in organizational settings, management should be involved and ultimately responsible for making the hard decisions about backup and recovery. Oracle supports many options that can provide a high level of recoverability for database data. However, many of the options, such as backup archiving offsite or a standby database, have premium costs attached to them. Having as many options as possible at the DBA's disposal is important, but so is the cost of providing those options.

One final area of importance when considering the motives for backup and recovery is to test the backup strategy to ensure the success or failure of the strategy *before* a problem occurs. Testing backup and recovery in the organization accomplishes several goals. The first goal accomplished is that the overall strategy can be observed in several different scenarios to determine if there are flaws or weaknesses in the plan. The bonus of testing the plan is also that the plan can be remodeled in a noncritical atmosphere, with little or no consequence regarding the loss of data and subsequent frustration of the organization with its DBA. The second important consequence of periodic testing of the database backups relates to the use of physical backups. Testing backups allows the DBA to determine if there is some sort of subtle data corruption in the physical database files that is being copied into all the backups, rendering them as defective as the production database. Finally, testing the backup and recovery strategy allows the DBA to develop expertise in that area, which offers the benefit of the DBA developing well-tuned backup and recovery.

Overall, the success of a recovery is not only dependent on whether or not all data can be restored successfully. The true victory in database recovery is won when the DBA can restore all data *successfully and quickly*, so as to minimize the overall strain a database failure poses to the organization.

Backup methods is the other major area of concern covered in this chapter. The first discussion in this section identified differences between logical and physical backups. The first difference between physical and logical backups is based on the two fundamental viewpoints a DBA has on the information stored for the Oracle database on disk. From the logical perspective, the disk contains tables, tablespaces, indexes, sequences, and the like. The logical backup supports this viewpoint by allowing the DBA to handle the backup entirely within Oracle, at the level of tables, indexes, sequences, users, and the like. The tool in Oracle used to support logical backups is the EXPORT tool. The other perspective of Oracle disk usage is the perspective of the operating system. Oracle stores data in files that look the same from the operating system as other files. This is the physical view of the database. Backups from this perspective consist of copies of the files that comprise the Oracle database.

Logical database backups can be taken with the EXPORT utility provided with Oracle. Good exports start with the identification of low usage times on the database, times that are suitable for exporting data. Ideally, the users are locked out of the database by the DBA enabling the **restricted session** mode. With the users locked out of the database, the DBA can ensure that the backup made is a read-consistent view of the database at the point in time the backup is made. The proper steps for executing a backup with the EXPORT tool are detailed in Chapter 12. After the logical backup is complete, the database should be opened for general use by disabling the **restricted session** mode.

Physical database backups are divided into two categories—offline, or "cold" backups, and online, or "hot" backups. Cold backups may only be accomplished by the DBA when the database is closed, or unavailable to users. The database must be shut down using the **shutdown normal** or **shutdown immediate** statement. If the **shutdown abort** options are used to shut down the database, the next time the database is opened, Oracle will attempt instance or media recovery, respectively. Shutting the database down in **normal** mode is the method used to avoid this problem. Only when the database is closed normally is the DBA assured that all changes made to data in the database that may still be in memory have been written to disk. Once the database is closed normally, the DBA can begin the process of taking a complete copy of the physical database files in the database. These files are generally of four types. The four types are datafiles, control files, redo log files, and parameter files. Only full backups of the database are available with offline backups; it is inappropriate to back up only a few of the datafiles in this situation. To obtain a list of all the files that should be backed up in the database, the DBA can look in the following views: V$DATAFILE for datafiles, and V$LOGFILE for the redo log files. To obtain the names of the control files for the Oracle database, the DBA should execute the **show parameters control_files** command from Server Manager. Once all the database files have been backed up, the DBA can then restart the database.

The final type of backup considered is the online backup. These types of backups allow the database to be up and running during the entire time the backup is taking place. Hot backups require archiving of redo logs in order to recover the backups. Hot backups require the DBA to adopt a hybrid logical-physical view of the database. Hot backups are taken in an iterative process, one tablespace at a time. The first step in a hot backup is to place the tablespace into **backup** mode with the **alter tablespace** *name* **begin backup** statement. Once executed, the DBA can make a copy of the datafiles that comprise a tablespace to an alternate disk, or off the machine entirely to tape or other external media. Once the backup is complete, the **alter tablespace** *name* **end backup** statement is issued. Since the database was open for activity the entire time the backup took place, the DBA must archive the redo logs that were collected during the time of the backup. In order to know which redo logs were used, the DBA should execute the **archive log list** statement within Server Manager and take note of the oldest online redo log sequence. After the backup is complete, the DBA can force archival of the redo log entries saved written during the backup with the **alter system switch logfile** statement.

Discussed in this chapter also is the importance and value of archiving redo logs in the various backup situations. Archiving redo logs allows the DBA to save all redo information generated by the database. In the event of a database failure that destroys some data, the changes that were written to the redo logs can be reapplied during database recovery to allow for full re-creation of all data changes committed right up to the point the database failed. If the DBA is using the logical export options provided with the Oracle EXPORT and IMPORT utilities, then archiving is of limited value because archiving cannot be applied to recovery using logical backups. Only if the database is using physical backups can the use of archiving be applied. For any database that requires recovery of data to the point of database failure, Oracle recommends the archiving of redo logs and the use of physical database backups.

Some operations have special database availability considerations that will influence the backup options that are required for those systems. This statement is particularly true for databases that are required to be available at all times, or 24×7 databases. There are two types of situations where 24-hour availability may be required for a database. One is where the database is deployed globally to users around the world who work at different times. The other is for databases that are deployed to users on a limited range of time zones, but the application relies on periodic refreshing of data as provided by batch processing that runs during off-peak usage time periods in the day. The 24-hour database cannot be brought down or have **restricted session** enabled on it frequently enough to allow for offline or logical backup. Furthermore, their recovery requirements include the ability to recover all data up to the point of time the database failed. As such, these systems generally require online backups in conjunction with archiving of online redo logs. The online backup allows users to access the database at all times, even while the backup takes place, and the archival of redo logs allows the DBA to apply all database changes made during and after the backup up to the moment in time the database failed.

Database recovery has several implications related to time. Database recovery is a two-step process. The first step is the application of the backup to the database to restore lost or damaged information. The second part is the application of archived redo logs in order to allow for recovery to a point after the most recent backup, usually to the point in time the database failed. Depending on the type of recovery plan pursued and the number of archived redo logs that need to be applied, the database recovery can be time-consuming. Another time consideration that should be weighed into database recovery is the amount of time required by users to recover their own data changes by reentering the data lost.

The backup options pursued by the DBA have time implications of their own. Depending on the option chosen for use in the database, the DBA may require time where the users are not permitted to access the system. This requirement may be fine for systems that are expected to be available during normal business hours. In this case, logical or offline backups may be an option. However, there are situations where the database must always be available. In this case, the DBA should choose online backups in conjunction with the archiving of redo logs. The choice of backup method used to support recoverability on the database will impact the time required for recovery on the database.

Transaction volume will ultimately affect the backup and recovery of a database as well. This fact is especially true for databases that archive their redo log information. Since high transaction volumes produce large amounts of redo log information, the number of archived redo logs has a tendency to increase quickly. In order to recover all database changes made in the event of a database failure, all archived redo log entries made during and after an online backup, or after the offline backup, will need to be applied after the backup is applied. This effort of applying the redo information takes more or less time depending on the number or size of the redo logs to be applied.

The more redo logs, the longer the recovery. In order to combat the length of time it takes for database recovery with archived redo logs, the DBA should save tablespaces that experience large transaction volumes frequently. Even in environments where archiving is not used, the overall recovery time for a database, including the time it takes for users to reenter the data lost from the period of time following the most recent backup to the database failure, is improved if backups occur frequently. However, obtaining downtime on the database for an offline backup or a logical backup may not be possible more often than once a day. This fact means that the system may always be susceptible to a day's worth of downtime in the event of a database failure, plus the time it takes to perform the recovery that is possible using the offline or logical backups available.

The final area of discussion involved the opposite situation to high transaction volumes and their backup/recovery implication. That other situation is that involving **read only** tablespaces. Since the data in **read only** tablespaces cannot be changed, the backup requirements for these tablespaces are minimal. Whenever the data does change, the tablespace must be backed up. After the tablespace is set into **read only** mode, the data should be backed up once and then left alone, as the DBA can rest assured that the tablespace will not change.

Two-Minute Drill

- Without backups, database recovery is not possible in the event of a database failure that destroys data.

- The business requirements that affect database availability, whether the database should be recoverable to the point in time the database failure occurred, along with the overall volatility of data in the database, should all be considered when developing a backup strategy.

- Disaster recovery for any computer system can have the following impact: loss of time spent recovering the system, loss of user productivity correcting data errors or waiting for the system to come online again, the threat of permanent loss of data, and the cost of replacing hardware.

■ The final determination of the risks an organization is willing to take with regard to their backup strategy should be handled by management.

■ Complete recovery of data is possible in the Oracle database—but depends on a good backup strategy.

■ Database recovery consists of two goals: the complete recovery of lost data and the rapid completion of the recovery operation.

■ Testing backup and recovery strategy has three benefits: weaknesses in the strategy can be corrected, data corruption in the database that is being copied into the backups can be detected, and the DBA can improve his or her own skills and tune the overall process to save time.

■ The difference between logical and physical backups is the same as the difference between the logical and physical view of Oracle's usage of disk resources on the machine hosting the database.

■ Logical backups are used to copy the data from the Oracle database in terms of the tables, indexes, sequences, and other database objects that logically occupy an Oracle database.

■ The EXPORT and IMPORT tools are used for logical database object export and import.

■ Physical backups are used to copy Oracle database files that are present from the perspective of the operating system. This includes datafiles, redo log files, control files, the password file, and the parameter file.

■ To know what datafiles are present in the database, use the V$DATAFILE or the DBA_DATA_FILES dictionary views.

■ To know what control files are present in the database, use the **show parameters control_files** command from Server Manager or look in the V$CONTROLFILE view.

■ To know what redo log files are available in the database, use the V$LOGFILE dictionary view.

■ There are two types of physical backups: offline backups and online backups.

■ Offline backups are complete backups of the database taken when the database is closed. In order to close the database, use the **shutdown normal** or **shutdown immediate** command.

■ Online or "hot" backups are backups of tablespaces taken while the database is running. This option requires that Oracle be archiving its redo logs. To start an online backup, the DBA must issue the **alter tablespace** *name* **begin backup** statement from Server Manager. When complete, the DBA must issue the **alter tablespace** *name* **end backup** statement.

■ Archiving redo logs is crucial for providing complete data recovery to the point in time that the database failure occurs. Redo logs can only be used in conjunction with physical backups.

■ When the DBA is not archiving redo logs, recovery is only possible to the point in time the last backup was taken.

■ Databases that must be available 24 hours a day generally require online backups because they cannot afford the database downtime required for logical backups or offline backups.

■ Database recovery time consists of two factors: the amount of time it takes to restore a backup, and the amount of time it takes to apply database changes made after the most recent backup.

■ If archiving is used, then the time spent applying the changes made to the database since the last backup consists of applying archived redo logs. If not, then the time spent applying the changes made to the database since the last backup consists of users manually reentering the changes they made to the database since the last backup.

■ The more changes made after the last database backup, the longer it generally takes to provide full recovery to the database.

■ Shorter recovery time can be achieved with more frequent backups.

■ Each type of backup has varied time implications. In general, logical and offline physical database backups require database downtime.

■ Only online database backups allow users to access the data in the database while the backup takes place.

■ The more transactions that take place on a database, the more redo information that is generated by the database.

■ An infrequently backed-up database with many archived redo logs is just as recoverable as a frequently backed-up database with few online redo logs. However, the time spent handling the recovery is longer for the first option than the second.

■ **Read only** tablespaces need backup only once, after the database data changes and the tablespace is set to **read only**.

Chapter Questions

1. **Which of the following scenarios will most likely result in the need for media recovery?**

    A. Machine failure as a result of a CPU crash

    B. Disk failure that makes several tablespaces unavailable

    C. A broken disk controller

    D. A defective memory board

2. **A decrease in the transaction activity level for a database**

    A. Decreases the amount of redo log activity for the database

    B. Increases the amount of redo log activity for the database

    C. Doubles the amount of redo log activity for the database

    D. Has no effect on the redo log activity for the database

3. **In order to recover data to the point of failure, the DBA must first import the lost database objects, then apply archived redo logs.**

    A. TRUE

    B. FALSE

4. **A good plan for backups of a read only tablespace may include which of the following?**

    A. Weekly offline backups and nightly data exports

    B. Weekly data exports and monthly offline backups

C. Backing up the **read only** tablespace once

D. Backing up the **read only** tablespace daily

5. **Which three of the following are effects of archiving?**

   A. No potential for recovery to point of failure

   B. Ability to recover the database to a point in time after the last backup

   C. LOG_ARCHIVE DEST must be set in **init.ora**

   D. Ability to take online backups

6. **The number of archived redo logs produced by a database in a given time period is most closely related to**

   A. The number of tables in the database

   B. The amount of time required to execute one transaction

   C. The number of hours per day the database is available

   D. The number of transactions taking place on the database

7. **Which of the following backup strategies would be most appropriate for a database with users in 12 time zones?**

   A. Logical database backups with archiving disabled

   B. Online backups with archiving enabled

   C. Offline backups with archiving enabled

   D. Offline backups with archiving disabled

8. **In order to take an offline backup using operating system tools, the DBA should first shut down the database using NORMAL or IMMEDIATE mode.**

   A. TRUE

   B. FALSE

9. **Which three of the following objects are backed up using EXPORT?**

   A. Tablespaces

B. Sequences

C. Redo logs

D. Indexes

10. **What command is used to begin an online tablespace backup?**

   A. alter system begin backup

   B. alter tablespace begin backup

   C. alter database noarchivelog

   D. alter tablespace end backup

11. **Which of the following is not a benefit of testing backup and recovery?**

   A. Uncovering hidden corrupt data in the database propagating itself into backups

   B. Improving the performance of the overall recovery strategy

   C. Uncovering weaknesses in the backup strategy and resolving them

   D. Archiving unused data from retired applications

12. **For a database with few users and minimal data change, enabling archiving would probably be overkill.**

   A. TRUE

   B. FALSE

13. **Which of the following backup options is viable for databases that are used primarily during the hours of 8 A.M. and 5 P.M.?**

   A. Logical backups with archiving enabled.

   B. Offline backups with archiving disabled.

   C. Offline backups with archiving enabled.

   D. No backup strategy is required for this scenario.

Answers to Chapter Questions

I. B. Disk failure that makes several tablespaces unavailable.

Explanation Choice B is the most appropriate answer. If no data loss occurs as a result of the machine failure, then there is no real need for data recovery. Choices A, C, and D are inappropriate because these aspects of the database, though important for the continued operation of the database, will not necessarily cause data loss on the disks.

2. A. Decreases the amount of redo log activity for the database.

Explanation The amount of data transacted on the database directly correlates to the amount of redo log activity on the database. All other choices are logically wrong.

3. B. FALSE

Explanation Archived redo logs are not usable in conjunction with logical backup and recovery methods.

4. C. Backing up the **read only** tablespace once.

Explanation Since data cannot change in them, **read only** tablespaces need to be backed up only once. All other backup strategies are recommended for more volatile databases.

5. B, C, and D.

Explanation The only option that is not viable for this question should be obvious—there is, of course, potential for recoverability to the point in time of the database failure when archiving is used.

6. D.   The number of transactions taking place on the database.

Explanation   Although choices A, B, and C may be conditions that are present on databases that have high transaction activity, none of these conditions will necessarily lead to higher database change transaction activity. For example, a data warehouse typically has large tables, but data is rarely changed directly by users to the level that would produce large amounts of redo log information.

7. B.   Online backups with archiving enabled.

Explanation   It is altogether possible that a database with users in 12 time zones must be available 24 hours a day. With a user base so globally defined, the best option in this situation usually involves online backups. Since choice B is the only one that offers online backups as a choice, it is probably the right choice.

8. A.   TRUE

Explanation   It is true that offline backups should be taken only when the database has been shutdown using **normal** mode. If the backup is taken after shutdown in any other mode, then the backup will contain unusable data.

9. A, B, and D.

Explanation   Redo logs are never used in conjunction with logical backups.

10. B.   **alter tablespace begin backup**

Explanation   Choice A is inappropriate because it is incorrect command syntax. Choice C is inappropriate because archiving must be used for online backups. Choice D is the correct statement for ending online backups, not beginning them.

11. D. Archiving unused data from retired applications.

Explanation This selection is the only one that is not a benefit of testing backup and recovery strategy.

12. A. TRUE.

Explanation This scenario is a good candidate for offline database backup or even logical backup and recovery. Archiving redo logs, though, is always useful in allowing the DBA to make recovery to the point of failure.

13. C. Offline backups with archiving enabled.

Explanation Of the choices presented, this one represents the best option for allowing the DBA to recover the database without the requirement of 24-hour database availability.

CHAPTER
12

Logical Backup and Recovery

n this chapter, you will understand and demonstrate knowledge in the following areas:

- Failure scenarios
- Logical backups

Logical export and import are useful for many functions including migration of database objects between different Oracle databases and versions of Oracle. These activities are conducted with two tools provided by Oracle. These two utilities come with the software distribution of the Oracle database server. The two utilities provided by Oracle for the purpose of logical backup and recovery are called EXPORT, for backup of database objects, and IMPORT, for recovery of database objects in export dump files. EXPORT and IMPORT work closely together and, in fact, the only tool that can read an EXPORT file is the IMPORT utility. In addition, there is a discussion on database failure scenarios. These areas of Oracle backup and recovery comprise 10 percent of material tested in OCP Exam 3.

Failure Scenarios

In this section, you will cover the following topics related to failure scenarios:

- Statement failure
- User process failure
- Instance failure
- User error
- Media failure

Dealing with database problems is the cornerstone of the job description for DBAs. The effort required to resolve different types of database problems depends greatly on the type of problem encountered. There are several different scenarios for failure in the Oracle database. These scenarios can be divided into five general categories, which will be discussed in this section.

At a high level, the five categories include statement failure, user process failure, instance failure, user error, and media failure. Each of these categories has different implications on the need for DBA intervention in order to provide recovery from the situation. This section will provide a discussion of each area as it pertains to the effort required for resolution from the DBA perspective.

Statement Failure

In the course of normal transaction processing, many things can happen that cause problems for users executing their SQL statements. A statement failure occurs when Oracle cannot process a statement issued by a user. There are several causes for statement failure. First of all, a user may be attempting to issue a statement referencing a table that does not exist or to which they are not granted permission to use. In this case, Oracle issues the user an error that details both the phrase of the statement that contained the error and a reference to a special code, called the Oracle error message code, to help solve the problem. The user can then look the error up in the Server Messages Guide that Oracle publishes for all its database server releases. The following code listing shows the output from SQL*Plus when the user issues a statement that generates an error:

```
select employee_id, name, dob, title
from us_emp
where employee_id = 49585;

from us_emp
     *
ERROR at line 2:
ORA-00942: table or view does not exist
```

Notice that in this situation there are three components to the interactive reply Oracle gives. First, the reply repeats the portion of the data request that generated the statement error. To highlight a specific area of the statement that failed, Oracle places an asterisk (*) under the offending clause or keyword. Following the first part of the reply, there is an identification of the line number that contains the error text. Following that, there is the final component of the error that occurred. In this case, the user statement issued to Oracle contained reference to a table that does not exist within the scope of what the user can see or manipulate.

Recovery from this error situation consists of Oracle immediately rolling back any changes made by the statement automatically. The involvement of a DBA may be minimal or extensive, depending on the desired outcome. On one hand, the user may have typed in the wrong table name, thus relieving the DBA of any involvement in the solution other than to direct the user to an appropriate data model for the table layout of the database. On the other hand, the fact that this user could not issue this statement may indicate a deeper problem related to privileges and/or roles granted to this user, or perhaps even the erroneous dropping of the table that does not exist. Although in many (if not most) cases, the DBA will not be required to analyze the problem and present a solution, there could be trouble lurking behind this seemingly innocent error message.

Exercises

1. What is statement failure? How is it resolved?

2. What are the three components of the error message Oracle provides when statement failure occurs?

User Process Failure

The failure of a user process requires more intervention from the Oracle database. A user may cancel or terminate the statement they are executing. A classic example of user process failure occurs when the user is attempting to change data in a table but cannot due to some locking situation on the table. In order to regain control of the SQL*Plus session to stop waiting and move onto another task, the user may choose to execute the **cancel** command by typing a CTRL-C from from SQL*Plus. The issuance of a **cancel** command causes the user process to fail. Oracle may also issue the **cancel** command for a user process if there is something the process is trying to do that Oracle won't let it do. In most cases, the cancellation of a user process will not cause the user's session to fail, although there is a slight chance that this situation may occur.

If a user process terminates abnormally, then Oracle will have to get involved in the cleanup effort for that terminated process. Oracle has a special background process in the database architecture that handles this type of situation. The name of the process is PMON, the *process monitor* background process. When a user process fails, PMON is there to handle automatic process recovery for the database in several areas. Some of those areas are listed in the bullet points below:

- Rollback on the failed process

- Release of locks on tables and internal latches the process acquired

- Removal of that process identifier from active processes in the V$ performance views

In the event that a user cancels his or her own process, no intervention is required from the DBA. This fact is due to Oracle's ability to handle process failure recovery automatically in the areas listed in the previous bullet points. However, despite the utility it serves in the area of user process monitoring and cleanup, PMON does not do it all. If a process is killed by Oracle, then PMON will not execute any cleanup activities on it. Further, if it is an Oracle background process that has failed, the instance can no longer run. The intervention of a DBA in this situation will be to restart the instance.

Exercises

1. What is user process failure? How does the user cancel SQL statements?

2. What background process handles memory cleanup in user process failure?

Instance Failure

The discussion of PMON's inability to handle the failure of another background process and the subsequent fact that the instance will not be able to continue running in the event of background process failure provides a segue into the next type of failure that can occur in Oracle. This type of failure is called instance failure. Instance failure is a serious situation in most Oracle database environments. If the instance fails, then no users are able to access the database, and the DBA must determine the solution for the problem and restart the database.

Consider some of the potential causes for instance failure. There are many different things that may cause an instance to fail, including a problem with the memory of the host system running Oracle, a power outage, or disk corruption. Although instance failure requires the DBA to intervene in order to restart the database, the initiation and completion of the recovery of the instance is handled by the Oracle background process SMON. SMON handles several different components of instance recovery, including the rebuilding of the Oracle SGA, rolling forward all transactions in progress at the time of the crash, and then rolling back all uncommitted work that was in progress at the time the database crashed.

As mentioned, SMON handles instance recovery automatically, requiring only that the DBA restart the Oracle database. At the time that the DBA starts the database, SMON begins the tasks required to restore the instance to full operational capacity. The operations carried out by SMON may be somewhat extensive, depending on the transaction volumes that were occurring on the database at the time the database failure occurred.

The real effort involved in managing an instance failure on the part of the DBA is to figure out the problem or problems that caused instance failure in the first place. If the failure is due to a problem with the hardware of the machine hosting Oracle, then the DBA may need to work with the hardware vendor or the internal hardware support organization to ensure the installation of new parts to make the machine that runs the Oracle database operational again. If the problem that caused instance failure is due to the corruption of a disk, a few things will happen. First, since DBWR and LGWR handle the writing of data to and from disk, they are the background processes that will detect the corruption. As with all background processes, DBWR and LGWR maintain trace files that log all activities associated with their running execution. When a situation occurs that forces either of them not to be able to write data to the disk they must work with, the background process that experiences the problem writes a message to its own trace file. In addition, the process writes to the **alert** log that is maintained for the entire database instance. If the instance fails and the DBA wants to find out why, the DBA can look in the trace files for the Oracle background process(es) and/or the **alert** log. There, the message produced by the background process that encountered the error will appear, telling the DBA more information about the problem encountered. This information will require some interpretation in order to resolve hardware difficulty. Once the DBA has identified the cause of the Oracle instance failure and resolved any hardware problems that may have resulted in the instance failing, the DBA should restart the instance and let Oracle's SMON process handle the rest.

Exercises

1. What is instance failure? What causes instance failure?

2. What background process handles instance failure?

User Error

The users of an Oracle database may experience problems as a result of mistakes such as accidentally deleting data or database objects from the Oracle database. This scenario, although not high on the priority list of many organizations, can display the strength or weakness of backup and recovery skill on the part of the DBA. Sometimes the DBA can prevent the problem in production environments by not allowing users or developers any privileges that allow them to **create**, **alter**, or **drop** database objects in the application's production environment. Though it can't be done in every environment, this configuration prevents users other than the DBA from adding or taking away objects from the production database.

In all database environments, the correction of data that was changed, removed, or added in error by a user can be re-created by the user as well. The rollback segment, a tool used in conjunction with transaction processing, has an ideal role in the database that allows for easy recovery of data changes that were made accidentally. If, for example, the user issues a statement such as **delete from** *tablename* and inadvertently leaves off the **where** clause, the rollback statement allows the user to correct the mistake immediately.

There is one important thing to remember if the user has issued a statement that causes accidental alteration of data in the database. *Do not commit the change.* If, for example, a user issues a statement that changes the values stored in a column called LASTNAME for a table called EMPLOYEE from their own last name to "DOE," it is a simple task to discard the change in favor of the original data with the use of a **rollback** statement. However, if the statement is issued, then the change is committed, and then the user realizes it was a mistake, there could be a serious issue with data corruption on the database. In this situation, it pays to ensure that any user

of the database is limited by the privileges and roles they are given so they can execute only the functions they are responsible for and no more.

In order to resolve this situation, the DBA must rely on a backup strategy. There are a couple of appropriate strategies for this situation. The first, and arguably most effective, involves the use of logical backup and recovery options provided by the EXPORT and IMPORT tools. Particularly during development periods, the DBA should consider daily or weekly export of database objects using the EXPORT tool, in addition to other database backup plans in place. Alternately, the DBA can use only physical backups to obtain copies of database objects. However, if only the physical approach is used, the DBA should allocate enough hardware to allow for a point-in-time recovery of the database object(s) that were dropped or contained data that was changed accidentally. After the point-in-time recovery, the DBA will need to export the database object that must be restored on the other system. So, at some point the DBA will use EXPORT and IMPORT anyway.

The amount of time a DBA spends correcting user errors should be carefully considered. What sort of commitment does the DBA want to make for this potentially time-consuming area of work? Although it adds value to an organization to have the DBA perform this type of work, the better approach is to give users and developers minimal access to production, with progressively more access to test or development environments. In addition, the DBA may want to consider a strategy for users to develop their own database objects in a privately owned user schema, to allow for users to experiment with table creation and development in a noncritical environment.

Exercises

1. What is user error? How can the DBA resolve user errors?

2. How can the DBA prevent user errors in production environments?

Media Failure

Media failure means disk failure, the loss of information on a disk that has either been corrupted at a hardware level, erased by mistake, or suffered some other form of irreparable damage. The backup and recovery strategy of an organization is designed to act as an insurance policy against problems in the database that render the database unusable. This is generally the most time-consuming problem a DBA will face in the arena. A database recovery that occurs as a result of media failure is tied directly to the abilities of the DBA to handle database recovery both before and after the disk failure.

The success of a DBA in this area starts far in advance of a problem with losing a disk on the machine hosting the Oracle database. Good database recovery starts with sound backup strategy. The DBA must evaluate the needs of the organization and obtain buy-in from users, developers, and managers alike. Second, the DBA must execute the backup strategy like clockwork. The best backup strategy in the world means nothing if backups are not run, just as the best homeowner's insurance policy in the world means nothing if the home is robbed *before* you buy the policy.

When failure occurs, however, the clutch skills of the DBA are tested. As mentioned before, the success of a database recovery depends on both the complete recovery of data to the point of failure (or before the failure, depending on the needs of the recovery) and completion of the recovery in a timely manner. The time spent in **recovery** mode depends on several critical factors. The list following this paragraph will identify those factors:

- **Accessibility of backups**   The ability of a DBA to obtain data from the backup has a direct impact on the speed in which he or she can accomplish the recovery. Accessibility should be taken to mean both the physical availability of backups (onsite or offsite) *AND* the accessibility of backup data on the offline storage media used to archive the data. The backup data is only available to the DBA at the speed of its storage media.

- **Frequency of backups**   As mentioned in the last chapter, if backups are taken twice a month and the DBA is relying on the application of scores of archived redo logs to provide the data needed, then the backup will take much longer than if the DBA backed up the database daily.

- **Type of failure**   The amount of time the DBA will spend in recovery depends on the type of failure that has occurred. For example, if the database lost one disk drive that contained just a few **read only** tablespaces, the DBA will spend a much smaller period of time handling database recovery than if the DBA lost a disk containing several datafiles that contained highly volatile data that experienced infrequent backup anyway.

■ **Type of backups** The amount of time an organization spends in recovery depends also on the type of backup strategy used in the organization. If, for example, the business made an unwise choice to go with infrequent logical backups on a highly volatile database, then the entire organization may find itself keying in data manually as part of the recovery process.

Exercises

1. What is media failure? How is media failure managed in Oracle?
2. Name and describe the factors that determine the amount of effort required to handle recovery in the event of media failure.

Logical Backups

In this section, you will cover the following topics related to logical backups:

■ Using EXPORT

■ EXPORT modes

■ Backup strategy and EXPORT

■ Using IMPORT

■ Read-consistency and database export

■ Using the EXPORT direct path

■ EXPORT, IMPORT, and archived redo logs

■ Using the right character set

This section will cover three different topic areas. The first area of discussion will include the use of the EXPORT utility. Many of the features and uses will be discussed. Following that treatment, the use of IMPORT as the complementary utility will be discussed. After covering the highlights of features and usage for each of these areas, the discussion will turn to a number of advanced topics of discussion for EXPORT and IMPORT. Some of the limitations of EXPORT and IMPORT, such as the inability to use archived redo logs in conjunction with the logical backup and recovery strategy and other specialized areas of knowledge will be presented.

Using EXPORT

The EXPORT tool offers many options and features for backing up a database. EXPORT accepts many parameters that tell the utility what data to export and in what fashion. The end result of an EXPORT is a file that contains data according to the specifications given at the time the export is executed. The file produced by EXPORT is in binary format, usable only by IMPORT, a complementary tool designed to bring the database objects and/or table data back into a database from the export file. The exported data is commonly referred to as a "dump," although it does not bear much resemblance to the core dump many developers may already have exposure to. EXPORT is run from the operating system prompt. The parameters to be used can be identified in two ways. The DBA can identify the features to be used on the command prompt as command-line options.

```
Exp userid=ORADBA/dbapass full=y file='/oracle/export/dump'
```

Alternatively, the DBA can run EXPORT with a list of parameter options specified in a parameter file. The extension of the parameter file should be *parfilename.par*. There is also a graphical user interface available with EXPORT. Many UNIX users of the Oracle database may opt to stick with the command-line interface. However, the segment of Oracle databases running on Windows NT continues to climb. As such, it is expected that DBAs will become more familiar with Oracle with a graphic front end as time goes on. The following code block demonstrates the use of EXPORT in conjunction with a parameter file.

```
Exp parfile=EXPORT_120198.par
```

TIP
*To use EXPORT and IMPORT, the **catexp.sql** utility script stored in the Oracle software home directory under **rdbms/admin** should be executed. This script creates several views required for the execution of EXPORT and IMPORT, as well as the EXP_FULL_DATABASE and IMP_FULL_DATABASE roles required to run these utilities.*

Within the parameter file, there may be several different parameters listed, along with specified values. The parameters given either at the command line or in the parameter file determine several things about the database export. For example, the objects that will be exported in this execution of EXPORT, the name and location of the exported data file, and the name and password for the username EXPORT will use for execution, are all options that can be defined by command-line parameters. A sample listing of the parameters EXPORT can handle is displayed in the following table:

USERID (*name/pass*)	The user and password under which EXPORT will execute.
BUFFER (*number*)	Defines a buffer size EXPORT will use to fetch rows for the export file.
FILE (*filename*)	Identifies the name and location of the export file produced.
GRANTS (Y/N)	Indicates whether table grants should be included in the export.
INDEXES (Y/N)	Indicates whether table indexes should be included in the export.
ROWS (Y/N)	Indicates whether table rows should be included in the export.
CONSTRAINTS (Y/N)	Indicates whether table constraints should be included in the export.
COMPRESS (Y/N)	Indicates whether EXPORT will place all rows of the table into one initial extent in the export file.
FULL (Y/N)	Indicates whether EXPORT should export the entire database.
OWNER (*name*)	Indicates a list of users whose database objects should be exported (**user** mode).
TABLES (*list*)	Indicates a list of tables that should be exported (**table** mode).

RECORDLENGTH (*number*)	Lists the size of each data record in the export file. If the DBA wants to import the exported file onto a database in another operating system, this value must be modified to the proper value for that operating system.
INCTYPE (*keyword*)	Accepts the keywords **complete**, **cumulative**, or **incremental** to indicate the type of EXPORT executed.
HELP (Y/N)	Displays a help message with all features of EXPORT described.
RECORD (Y/N)	Will specify information about the export in one of the following SYS tables used to track export information: INCVID, INCFIL, INCEXP.
LOG (*filename*)	Specifies the name of a file containing runtime details and error messages for the given export.
CONSISTENT (Y/N)	Allows the cumulative or full export to obtain a read-consistent view of all data exported. Requires large rollback segment. Effect can be duplicated by the DBA enabling **restricted session** mode before beginning export.
FEEDBACK (*number*)	When set, displays a dot to indicate progress on rows exported per table.
STATISTICS (*keyword*)	Accepts the **estimate**, **compute**, or **none** keyword. Used to generate statistics for cost-based optimization on the database.
MLS (Y/N)	Used for Trusted Oracle. Stores the multilayer security label for tables and rows in the export.
MLS_LABEL_FORMAT	Used for Trusted Oracle. Redefines the default format for multilayer security labels.
DIRECT (Y/N)	Allows the DBA to run faster exports using the direct path. Similar in function to direct path in SQL*Loader.

Exercises

1. What are the different methods for running EXPORT?

2. What are the different ways to specify parameters for running EXPORT?

EXPORT Modes

There are three modes for using EXPORT. They are the **user** mode, the **table** mode, and the **full** mode. The emphasis for using each is different, and the discussion that follows will present the similarities and differences. In addition to the modes allowed with the EXPORT tool, there are several types of backups that can be used for the database to give a full range of options for backup and recovery.

USER Mode

EXPORT allows the DBA to move data objects from a database according to categories. In order to set up EXPORT to export the objects that are owned by a user, the DBA should provide a list of one or more users whose objects will be taken in the export. This option is useful in database situations where the DBA has configured several applications within the same database that use different usernames as schema owners for the database objects of their application.

```
Exp userid=DBA/password owner=HRAPL file='/oracle/export/hrapl10298.dmp'
```

The export of database objects in **user** mode takes a backup of all objects specified by the other command-line parameters given. In the prior example, no values were specified for any of the parameters that determine which database objects are exported. Some of these parameters include GRANTS, INDEXES, ROWS, and CONSTRAINTS. Since the default for these parameters is Y, however, there is no need to specify the parameters unless the DBA specifically *doesn't* want the objects included in the export. This point illustrates a fact about EXPORT—each parameter has a default value, and the default value is the one used for the export if the DBA doesn't specify a value for it at either the command line or in the parameter file. Figure 12-1 illustrates EXPORT tool usage in **user** mode.

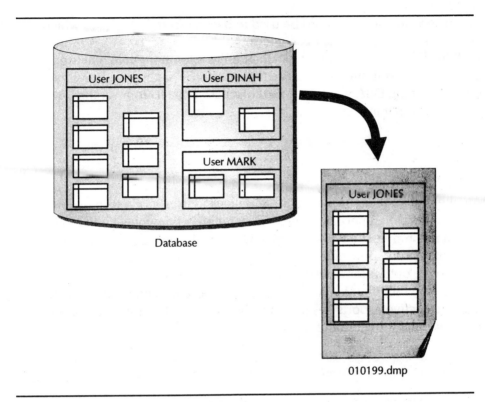

FIGURE 12-1.   *Exporting in **user** mode*

Consider the impact of exporting several database objects associated with a particular owner. If, for example, the DBA understands that a particular application in the database is undergoing schema changes, the DBA may want to take daily backups of that schema to ensure that the database objects are recoverable in the event of accidentally being dropped. Figure 12-1 illustrates the principle of exporting in **user** mode. There are database objects owned by several users in the database, but since the OWNER parameter is used, the user specified for that parameter is the only one whose objects will be exported. This operation typically is not considered an effective overall backup strategy, but does allow the DBA to take supplemental backups if the need arises to offer value-added service (mainly to developers who are modifying their database schemas).

Alternately, this service could be used to back up certain tables in which users make changes to the data in error.

If the DBA wants to export database objects for more than one user, this is possible as well through the use of the OWNER parameter. The schema owners that the DBA wants to export database objects from can be listed in the OWNER parameter easily.

```
Exp userid=DBA/dbapass owner=HRAPL,FINAPL file='/oracle/export/hrapl10298.dmp'
```

TABLE Mode

An alternative to exporting database objects in **user** mode is to export those objects on a per-table basis. This option is known as **table** mode. With **table** mode, the DBA can specify very selective exports that only draw data from a few different tables. This option is not appropriate as a full-service option for database backup and recovery. However, the DBA can use the **table** mode EXPORT for the purpose of highly supplemental, highly selective exports designed for the purpose of restoring a specific table or other object to the database.

```
Exp userid=DBA/dbapass tables=HRAPP.EMPLOYEE indexes=N file='hrapl10298.dmp'
Exp userid=DBA/dbapass tables=EMPLOYEE indexes=N file='hrapl10298.dmp'
```

Consider the situation presented in the beginning of the chapter, in the discussion of user errors. In these situations, the data, or the table itself, may have been changed or removed in error. In this type of situation, the DBA will find the table mode offered by EXPORT to be useful. In the code example provided above, there are two situations illustrated by the specification in the TABLES parameter. In the first example, the EMPLOYEE table is prefaced by mention of the schema that owns this table. If no schema is mentioned, EXPORT will do one of the following things. It will either try to find the table in the schema of the user specified under which the export will run, or EXPORT will look for all tables that the user it is running under can see to find the specified table.

If, for example, there are two EMPLOYEE tables in the database, one owned by HRAPP and one owned by DBA, then the first example in the code block above the preceding paragraph will export the EMPLOYEE table owned by HRAPP, while the second will export the table owned by DBA. In general, when using EXPORT in **table** mode, the DBA should bear in mind the schema owners of each table in order to avoid exporting unwanted information.

For these examples, also notice that the DBA has chosen not to export the indexes. Since read consistency cannot always be guaranteed on an export, the DBA may choose not to export the indexes for a table, instead opting to re-create the index on the database after the table and/or its data have been imported. Remember that the default options for all database object parameters is Y for every run of EXPORT. That is to say, if EXPORT runs with GRANTS=N, and then run again without GRANTS specified, then the default value of Y is used for the GRANTS parameter the second time.

FULL Mode

The final option for running EXPORT is to do so in **full** mode. This mode will export all tables from all user schemas. In order to use **full** mode, the FULL parameter must be set to Y either at the command line or in the parameter file. Unlike **table** or **user** mode, **full** mode for database export is used in order to provide a full database backup and recovery option with logical methods.

```
Exp userid=DBA/password FULL=Y file='hrapl10298.dmp'
```

In order to provide a full solution to the need for backup and recovery using EXPORT, the DBA should operate the utility in **full** mode with the FULL=Y parameter specified. The default value for this parameter is N, however, so it is important that the DBA ensure FULL=Y is explicitly stated each time EXPORT is run, either on the command line, or more preferably in a parameter file. Neglecting to do so will simply run the export in either **table** or **user** mode.

In order to use EXPORT in **full** mode to provide a complete backup and recovery option using logical means, the DBA must first understand an important concept. The concept is that there are several types of exports that can be executed when the database is running in **full** mode. The types of exports that can be used are *complete, cumulative,* and *incremental.* The type of full export taken depends on setting the INCTYPE parameter to either **complete, cumulative,** or **incremental.** Together, these exports can operate in a plan to provide the complete backup solution required for databases.

There are a few other restrictions to understand before discussion of the three types of full exports can be explained. The first restriction involves the situation of parameter conflict. There are three export modes available in

EXPORT, which are specified using the OWNER, TABLES, and FULL parameter specifically. Consider the example that follows this paragraph.

```
Exp userid=DBA/password full=Y tables=EMPLOYEE
file='hrapl10298.dmp'
```

In the following example of running EXPORT, there is a conflict of interest between two of the parameters. The FULL=Y parameter indicates that the user wants to perform a full export of the database using EXPORT; however, the TABLES parameter also indicates that the EMPLOYEE table is the only table the DBA wants to export. The conflict arises because EXPORT cannot simultaneously back up the full database and the EMPLOYEE table only. In general, the DBA must be careful to avoid conflicts between the parameters used on database exports. Also, no one can execute a full export without the EXP_FULL_DATABASE role granted to her.

COMPLETE EXPORTS　　A complete export is one that produces an export file containing all database objects in the database. A complete export allows the DBA to make a complete recovery on the database as well. Complete exports are a required component for the full backup and recovery strategy that will be discussed later in the section. In order to take a complete export while the database is in **full** mode, the DBA should use the INCTYPE parameter either at the EXPORT command line or in a parameter file. The following code block demonstrates usage of EXPORT to produce a complete export of data from the database:

```
Exp userid=DBA/password full=Y inctype=complete
file='010199cmpl.dmp'
```

The INCTYPE parameter can only be used in conjunction with **full** mode. The three permitted values for INCTYPE are **complete, cumulative,** and **incremental**. At the end of this section, there will be a discussion defining the use of these three types of full exports for the purpose of database backup and recovery.

CUMULATIVE EXPORTS　　Unlike the complete export, which creates a backup of every logical database object in the database, the cumulative export creates a copy of only the database objects that have been changed

in the database since the last time a cumulative or complete database export
was taken.

```
Exp userid=DBA/password full=Y inctype=cumulative
file='010399cml.dmp'
```

Cumulative exports do not take complete exports of all objects in the
database. Instead, the cumulative export will copy only the database objects
that have changed since the last complete or cumulative export. Consider
the following list to understand the implications of a cumulative export:

- There are five tables in a database.

- The database was backed up using a complete export three days ago.

- Only two of the tables have had rows added or changed since then.

- The cumulative export run will only contain the two tables that
  have changed.

Cumulative exports generally take less time to run than complete
exports, because they export less data than the complete export. The two
types of export are designed to work together to produce an overall recovery
option. It is important to remember that if the data in a table has changed
since the last complete export, then the *entire table* will be included in the
cumulative export. EXPORT is not designed to back up individual rows for a
table. The ROWS parameter simply instructs EXPORT to back up all rows for
the table or none of the rows at all. Cumulative exports can be thought of as
exports that bundle together the data changes saved in all incremental
backups that take place between cumulative or complete exports.

INCREMENTAL EXPORTS   An incremental export consists of all
database objects that have changed since the last cumulative, complete, or
incremental export run on the database. In other words, an incremental
backup saves all database objects that occurred since the last backup of any
type. A complete presentation of all three backups in action as part of a
full-service backup and recovery strategy using logical means will appear at
the end of this section. For now, the DBA should understand fully the

implications of incremental export. An example for using EXPORT and specifying an incremental export appears in the following code block:

```
Exp userid=DBA/password full=Y inctype=incremental
file='010299inc.dmp'
```

Exercises

1. What objects are exported when EXPORT is run in **user** mode? What objects are exported when EXPORT is run in **table** mode?

2. What parameters are set for each of the three modes of EXPORT?

3. What are the three types of exports made in **full** mode?

Using EXPORT for Backups

With all export options presented, the DBA should now consider how the full export options work together to provide a full-service backup and recovery solution using logical means. First, the DBA must create a benchmark backup for the purposes of initiating a complete recovery, if need be. However, since complete backups can take a long time to execute and a lot of room to store, the incremental backup is a viable option for conducting backups in between. A sample backup schedule using all backup options presented in this discussion appears in Figure 12-2. First of all, since complete exports take a long time, an organization using EXPORT to handle their backups may prefer to run complete exports only on the weekends, when the database experiences low or nonexistent activity from end users. During the week, however, users are on the database frequently. As such, the backup strategy includes a daily incremental backup to save the objects that experienced changes that day. Finally, the use for cumulative backups is illustrated by the midweek backup. This is designed to reduce the number of exports that must be applied in the event that a recovery is necessary to restore damaged files. The cumulative export, then, collects all data that was saved in the incremental exports taken Sunday, Monday, and Tuesday and bundles all that information into the cumulative export. Essentially, a cumulative export can be considered redundant effort. However, the cumulative export reduces the number of backups required for recovery.

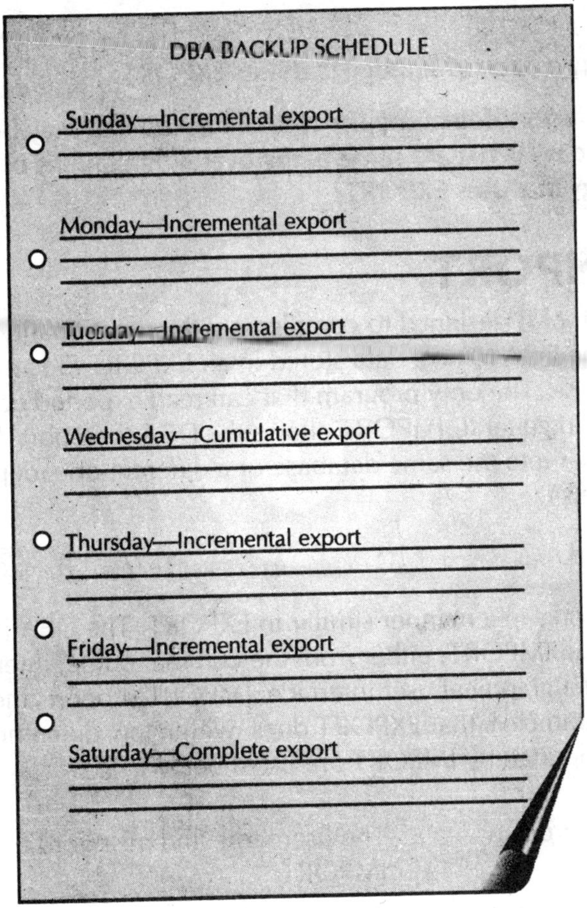

FIGURE 12-2. *Sample backup schedule using EXPORT*

The EXPORT tool is useful for devising a backup strategy based on the logical view of the database. The three types of full backups are most effective for an overall backup strategy, while the **user** and **table** modes allow for highly specialized data storage for recovery purposes. Important to note, however, is that *it is only possible to recover the database to the point in time that the most recent backup was taken*. If a situation arises where the recovery of data entered after the most recent recovery was performed is required, then the users must reenter the data manually.

Exercises

1. Identify a backup strategy that uses EXPORT.

2. What factors determine the type of backup that may be taken on any given day? What are some of the overall limitations of a backup strategy that uses EXPORT?

Using IMPORT

The IMPORT tool is designed to complement the functionality of EXPORT by allowing the DBA to take data stored in an EXPORT file and draw it back into the database. The only program that can read exported data is the IMPORT tool. In general, IMPORT allows the DBA to import data from an export file either into the same database or a different one, depending on the needs of the DBA.

```
Imp userid=DBA/password full=y file='/oracle/export/010199exp.dmp'
```

IMPORT works in a manner similar to EXPORT. The DBA issues the command to run IMPORT, either from the command line, interactively, or with the use of a graphical user interface. IMPORT supports the use of many of the same parameters that EXPORT does, with a few differences. All of the parameters supported by IMPORT are listed below:

USERID (*user/pass*)	The username and password used to run the IMPORT.
BUFFER (*number*)	Parameter that defines the number of rows inserted into a database at one time.
FILE (*filename*)	Determines the name of the export file to use for the input.
SHOW (Y/N)	Displays the contents of the export file but doesn't actually cause IMPORT to import anything.
IGNORE (Y/N)	Specifies whether to ignore errors that occur during import.

GRANTS (Y/N)	Specifies whether grants in the export file should be imported.
INDEXES (Y/N)	Specifies whether indexes in the export file should be imported.
ROWS (Y/N)	Specifies whether rows in the export file should be imported.
FULL (Y/N)	Determines whether the import will be in **full** mode.
FROMUSER (*name*)	The names of schema user database object owners for the objects in the export file that should be imported.
TOUSER (*name*)	Identifies the user schema into which database objects should be placed if the IMPORT is running in **user** mode.
TABLES (Y/N)	Specifies whether tables in the export file should be imported.
RECORDLENGTH (*number*)	Identifies the length in bytes of the each record in the export dump. Must be specified properly.
INCTYPE (*keyword*)	Defines the type of import that will occur. Valid values are **system** and **restore**.
COMMIT (Y/N)	Specifies whether IMPORT should **commit** after each time a buffer's worth of data is written to the database.
HELP (Y/N)	Indicates whether IMPORT should display help information about the parameters and their meanings.
LOG (*filename*)	Indicates the name of a file into which all IMPORT runtime information and errors will be stored.
DESTROY (Y/N)	Indicates whether IMPORT should reuse the datafiles that exist in the database for storage of imported objects.

INDEXFILE (Y/N)	Indicates whether IMPORT should create a file that contains a script to create the index for a table rather than creating the index itself.
FEEDBACK (Y/N)	IMPORT gives the same dot notation to indicate progress in the importation of data.
MLS	Used in conjunction with importing data into Trusted Oracle.
MLS_LISTLABELS	Used in conjunction with importing data into Trusted Oracle.
MLS_MAPFILE	Used in conjunction with importing data into Trusted Oracle.

Data is imported from the export dump file in the following way. First, the table definitions are brought into the database from the export file in order to create the table objects. Next, the actual row data from each table is brought into the database from the export file, indexes are created, the row data is brought into the database, and then the index data for the table is imported. The last items to be brought into the database from the export file are the integrity constraints and the triggers. There are some implications for the database objects that are created as a result of the order in which they are created. First, the data in an index must correspond to the data in the table or the index data could be corrupted. Secondly, if the integrity constraint should fail when imported, then there will be no data inserted into the table. Although the chances of this happening can be minimized with the placement of the database into **restricted session** mode, there is still the chance of a problem. Disabling integrity constraints manually during export will compound the problem.

However, the biggest problem the DBA may encounter with respect to the data inconsistency of a database relates to the trigger. If, for example, there is a trigger on a database that populates data or applies some business rule as a result of the change of data in a table, then that activity will not occur when the object is imported. This is because the trigger is imported last, and as such, it will not fire for each row as the row data is imported. There are ways to circumvent the problem; however, the DBA must be aware of object import order in order to understand that there could be problems related to the consistency of data imported from an export file.

However, even though the order of object importing is fixed, the DBA can eliminate certain steps by setting certain parameters. The parameters include TABLES, which indicates a listing of tables that are to be imported. Other parameters are assigned flag values Y or N, depending on whether the DBA does (Y) want to import that type of object, or not (N). The first parameter of this type is INDEXES, which indicates whether or not the indexes that correspond to tables should be imported. Another example is the GRANTS parameter, which determines if user object privileges should be imported from the export file. The final two are CONSTRAINTS and TRIGGERS, which determine whether or not constraints and/or triggers are imported, respectively. Another condition for the import of these objects is the fact that they are present in the export file. In other words, the DBA can specify Y or N for any of these parameters, but if the object is not in the export file, the object will not be imported.

Like EXPORT, IMPORT has the ability to run in a few different modes, such as **user** and **table** mode. IMPORT runs in **user** or **table** mode with the use of certain parameters. The parameter for table mode has already been introduced. That parameter is TABLES. The DBA can provide a list of tables for which IMPORT should draw from the export dump file into the database. However, the parameter must contain listed tables that are part of the export file or else the tables in the TABLES parameter listing will not be imported.

```
Imp userid=DBA/password file='010199exp.dmp' tables=EMPLOYEE
```

There are some slight differences in the way IMPORT handles **user** mode. First of all, the parameters for IMPORT's **user** mode are slightly different than those for EXPORT. The parameters used in IMPORT **user** mode are called FROMUSER and TOUSER. In EXPORT, the user(s) listed in the OWNER parameter for the execution of the export determine which user's objects are exported. With IMPORT, however, two things must be determined. First, the DBA must specify the user schema whose objects will be drawn in from the export file. This step is done by listing the user schema(s) in the FROMUSER parameter. The second part is to determine who will own the database object once it is imported. This step is particularly important in the situation where the user schema that owned the database object in the database from which the export was produced doesn't exist in the database to which the export is applied. For this step, the TOUSER parameter is used.

```
Imp userid=DBA/password file='010199exp.dmp' fromuser='MILON' touser='SHUG'
```

TIP
*IMPORT can run in **table** or **user** mode to import database objects from dump files made by EXPORT running in **full** mode. IMPORT cannot run in **full** mode, however, when the dump file was made with EXPORT run in **table** or **user** mode.*

IMPORT in **full** mode is also an option: however, the values available for the INCTYPE parameter are slightly different. The first is **system**. When INCTYPE is set to **system**, this means that the import will draw data from the export file specified that are system objects, except for those objects owned by SYS. When INCTYPE is set to **restore**, all database objects in the export file are imported by the IMPORT execution.

When data is imported, the order on which the export files are applied is critical to the success of the IMPORT run. First of all, in order to recover a database using an export file, the DBA must first apply the most recent complete export. If the backup schedule that was illustrated in Figure 12-2 is in place for the organization, then the last complete export file produced would generally be from the Saturday export. After the complete export is applied, then the most recent cumulative export can be applied. After that import from the cumulative export has been applied, then the DBA can apply all incremental export files produced up to the time that the data should be restored. If there are additional data changes that were made after the last incremental export, then those changes must be entered manually.

The order in which database export files are applied is relaxed somewhat in the situation where the DBA wants only to import objects in **table** or **user** mode. In this case, only one export file is needed, the one containing the data current to the time that the DBA wants to import. Use of IMPORT is similar to use of EXPORT in this situation, with the DBA using the TABLES or FROMUSER and TOUSER parameters appropriately to identify the tables or owners in the export file that will be extracted and the user schema to which they will belong once populated into the database.

In order to find out what export file to use to draw certain data into the database, there are a couple of options. The first option is the SHOW parameter. This special parameter can be used in conjunction with the FILE parameter to find out the names of the database objects that are contained in the EXPORT dump file.

```
Imp user=DBA/password show=Y file='010199exp.dmp'
```

Another option for determining the contents of an export file, or the location of a database object in a particular export file, is as follows. There are some special dictionary views that the DBA can use to determine the location of database objects in export files, the unique tracking ID for a particular export, and the identification for the last export from the database. These three views are called INCEXP, INCFIL, and INCVID. They are owned by the user SYS.

Using INCEXP

The INCEXP view contains a listing of all database objects that have been exported and the export files that contain them. The columns in this table include the owner's unique ID for their username, the name of the database object, and the export ID number that contains the object.

Using INCFIL

The INCFIL view contains a listing of all database exports and their corresponding export IDs for tracking information. The columns include the unique ID for the export, the name of the user that created it, the date and time it was created, and the type of export it is.

Using INCVID

This view is very small—one column, in fact. The contents are the export ID number for the last export that ran. This view is used to generate the export IDs. There are some constraints for using IMPORT. First, the user must have the IMP_FULL_DATABASE role granted to them. This role is created at the time the database is created, with the execution of the **catexp.sql** script. Also, the user that runs IMPORT must have the appropriate privileges to create the database objects that will be brought into the database as a result of the import. Finally, the version of IMPORT must match the version of EXPORT that created the export file.

Database Recovery with IMPORT

Database recovery with IMPORT occurs in the following way. First, the DBA must take the most recent database export and re-create the data dictionary and other database internals with the use of IMPORT running with the FULL=Y and INCTYPE=**system** parameters set. Following this critical step, the DBA must run IMPORT again with FULL=Y and INCTYPE=**restore** parameters set using the most recent complete database export. After that, the DBA imports all cumulative exports, starting with the first cumulative export after the most recent complete export, then the next cumulative export. After all cumulative exports are applied to the database, in order, the DBA then applies all incremental exports, in order, starting with the incremental export that followed the most recent cumulative export, then the next one, etc. With the DBA using the backup strategy as indicated in Figure 12-2 in mind, the following steps (with examples) are presented as a note of final clarity on the order required for media recovery using the IMPORT option.

1. On Friday morning, a database failure occurs that requires media recovery. The DBA ran the most recent export Thursday night, an incremental. This export is the first that should be applied.

   ```
   Imp file='thursdayinc.dmp' userid=DBA/password full=y
   inctype=system
   ```

2. The next step the DBA must accomplish is to apply the most recent complete export. In this backup strategy, complete backups are taken Saturday nights.

   ```
   Imp file='saturdaycmpl.dmp' userid=DBA/password full=y
   inctype=restore
   ```

3. Only one cumulative export is taken in this backup strategy, on Wednesday evenings. This is the next backup to be applied.

   ```
   Imp file='wednesdaycmlt.dmp' userid=DBA/password full=y
   inctype=restore
   ```

4. Since the problem occurred Friday morning, only one incremental export has taken place. Therefore, only one incremental must be applied. The following code block illustrates:

```
Imp file='thursdayinc.dmp' userid=DBA/password full=y
inctype=restore
```

Notice that, when using IMPORT, the most recent export backup created in the backup strategy is applied twice. The main difference between the two executions is the value set for INCTYPE. In the first, the SYSTEM import is run to re-create the database objects that are necessary for the database to run, which are stored in the SYSTEM tablespace. This includes data dictionary information that is vital to the proper execution of the Oracle database after the recovery is complete. If this step is omitted, the recovery will be unusable, and the Oracle database will need to be recovered again before usage is possible. Get it right the first time by remembering to set INCTYPE=**system**.

Exercises

1. What are the three modes IMPORT runs in? How is the mode of an IMPORT run determined? What two options are available for parameter passing for IMPORT?

2. What are the two types of **full** import? What database information does each one import? What parameter determines the type of import taken?

3. What parameters determine which types of database objects are imported?

4. Identify a recovery strategy that uses IMPORT. How is the overall recovery performed? What are some of the overall limitations of a recovery strategy that uses IMPORT?

Read Consistency and Database Export

Read consistency is the idea that a statement or transaction has a consistent view of data during the period of time the statement or transaction executes.

Oracle provides read consistency at the statement level automatically. In addition, with the use of database locks, the user can establish transaction-level read consistency on the database as well. The use of rollback segments is crucial for the successful application of transaction-level read consistency.

Read consistency is useful at the export level as well. It can be approximated with the use of the CONSISTENT parameter, which has the Y or N flag value set for it by the DBA at run time, either with a command-line parameter or in the parameter file. In order to give an EXPORT run a read-consistent view of the database, several things must happen. First, the DBA must ensure that there is adequate rollback segment space allotted to the export. In essence, the export can be thought of as one giant "transaction" in this way. As such, it is necessary to ensure that a large rollback segment is available for the export to support the additional transactions as they make changes to the database.

First, only the complete export and the cumulative export can use the CONSISTENT parameter. This option is simply not available for incremental exports. Read consistency, or a lack of it, can be a problem for the DBA using the logical methods offered by IMPORT and EXPORT for the management of backup and recovery in the Oracle database. In some cases, data changes in the database that happen while the export is taking place may cause problems for IMPORT. This situation is a particular problem with referential integrity that is not enforced by the database constraints, but it can be a general problem related to the database as well. The best method for reducing the problem posed by the inability of EXPORT to guarantee the read consistency of the export is to put the database into **restricted session** mode before running the export. This step is accomplished with the **alter system enable restricted session** statement.

```
ALTER SYSTEM ENABLE RESTRICTED SESSION;
```

Without the critical step of locking users out of the database before running the export, there can be some serious implications. First of all, the database import later may contain inconsistencies such as rows in the index that are not in the table. The indexes of a database are exported after their associated tables are. This may lead to problems with finding no data in tables even when the values are there in the indexes. Another common problem with exports that are performed without read consistency is the fact that data changes that are happening while the export occurs are not being saved in the export. Bear in mind that once an export has saved the data and the definition of a database object such as an index, there is no going back to it at the end. If read consistency is not in place, there will be data inaccuracy in the export dump file.

Exercises

1. Explain the usage of the CONSISTENT parameter for database exports.

2. What are the requirements of the CONSISTENT parameter? What are its limitations?

Using the EXPORT Direct Path

In many cases, high-performance export of the database objects is a crucial factor in the overall strategy of the database recovery. In order to improve the performance of a database export, the DBA can opt to use the direct path for the export. As with the direct path for SQL*Loader covered in Chapter 10, the direct path for EXPORT speeds the creation of the export file considerably by skipping over many of the steps required in normal database processing when handled conventionally, as is the case for users.

The direct path is specified by the DBA to be used for the run of EXPORT with the use of the DIRECT parameter. This parameter, which can be set to Y or N, has a default value of N and can be set by passing it on the command line of the EXPORT run or in a parameter file specified by the run. As the default value for DIRECT is N, the direct path export will not happen automatically. Instead, the direct path export happens only when the DIRECT parameter specifies it.

The direct path of a database export works in the following way. First, in a conventional path export, Oracle obtains the data from the database using standard SQL statements, which then are designed to run in the same way as the statement would run if a user had issued the statement directly from SQL*Plus. In contrast, the direct path export handles the unloading of data from the database in a more efficient way. EXPORT creates a **select** statement to obtain the data definition and data that is optimized to skip some of the steps involved in processing user SQL. The result of this optimization is a faster process that extracts data from the database into the export dump file.

The following factors are involved in the high performance of the direct path export. The BUFFER parameter is not used for direct path exports because the buffer defines an area into which data will be placed as part of the conventional path data fetch. There is also some interesting information the DBA should understand about the direct path export and the export file it produces, related to the size. The size of a conventional path export file and the direct path export will almost invariably be different. This fact is true even when the objects exported are exactly the same. The differences are related to the way EXPORT pads the length of each data record in the export binary and in the way a column may be split by the export in direct path exports. Although the differences shouldn't be of major consequence, it is worth bearing the fact in mind in usage situations.

Exercises

1. Explain the use of the DIRECT parameter for database exports. What value is added when this parameter is used?

2. What parameters may not appropriate for use in conjunction with DIRECT?

Using the Right Character Set

There are some other conditions that the DBA should consider when using IMPORT and EXPORT related to national language support. The character set data is saved in an export file. The character set for the export file must be the same as that for the database. If the character set for the session of the user is different than that used in the database, then the user must switch the character set of the session to that of the database or the export will fail.

With respect to importing data later, the character set of the export file can be the same or different than the character set of the database. In this situation, the import will perform an automatic character conversion on the export file as the data is imported. This degrades performance, so the DBA should expect that imports will take longer in the situation where the database receiving data has a different character set than the exported data does.

Exercises

1. Is it possible to import data from an export file if the character sets on the source database and destination database are different?

2. What character set will be used in the export dump file, the source database's character set or the character set of the session executing the export?

EXPORT, IMPORT, and Archived Redo Logs

In order to understand the abilities for data restoration that are provided by the logical backup and recovery options available using EXPORT and IMPORT, the DBA should recall the difference between physical and logical backups. Logical backups, on one hand, consist of taking the perspective of the logical database objects as they are stored within Oracle. These tools provide the DBA with the ability to store and re-create the objects in an Oracle database with accuracy up to the point in time that the export completed. However, from that point on, there is no way to recover data until the next logical backup is run.

Consider the other alternative viewpoint for the space Oracle takes to store data on disk drives. The information Oracle stores is in files. This file and directory viewpoint is the physical viewpoint of an Oracle database. The DBA can choose to back up the database from this perspective as well, using operating system methods or third-party products. As with logical backups, the physical backup allows the DBA to recover a database to the point in time the backup was taken as well.

However, there is another method for data backup that is available as well. This method is the redo log. As the DBA knows, the redo log stores database change entries. As the user and batch processes execute their database change statements on the Oracle database, Oracle's LGWR process writes those changes to an online redo log. Oracle allows the DBA the ability to archive the redo logs produced. If there is a situation where the database fails, if the DBA has been archiving redo logs and running the right type of backup, the DBA can recover data to the last committed transaction that ran against the database before the media failure occurred. That "right type of backup," however, is the key to the whole equation.

Logical backups do not allow for recovery to the point of media failure. The fact is plain and simple. In order to provide recovery to the point of failure, the backup must work in conjunction with the archived redo logs. This is something that EXPORT and IMPORT simply cannot do.

When considering the backup strategy for a database, the DBA must be keenly aware of the need for that database to recover to the point in time of the failure. In some cases, that ability may not be deemed necessary by the organization running the database. Sometimes, the database may only be used by a few people, or may contain relatively static data. In this case, the DBA can usually guarantee that the database will not lose more than a day's worth of changes when a disk crashes if the plan for backup and recovery presented in Figure 12-2 with IMPORT/EXPORT is used in the database. However, for those organizations that have highly volatile data and/or many users, the DBA should consider physical backup and recovery covered in Chapters 13, 14, and 15 in conjunction with archiving redo logs. Physical backups and archived redo logs are required to provide the recovery to point of failure.

Exercise

Should archiving redo logs be used in conjunction with the EXPORT and IMPORT backup strategy? Explain.

Chapter Summary

This chapter covers subject matter related to the function and purpose of logical backup and recovery. The subject matter in this area includes identifying failure scenarios and coverage of the methods and practices used for logical backup and recovery. Topics discussed include the meaning of the various failure scenarios, such as user error, statement failure, process failure, instance failure, and media failure. For logical backup and recovery, several topic areas were presented. First, an in-depth presentation of EXPORT usage and IMPORT usage was discussed, along with discussions on the impact of read consistency on the data quality of the exported information. After that, the usage of the direct path was presented. The irrelevance of archiving redo logs and the use of the logical backup and recovery, and the considerations of the character set used in the databases between which exported data is shared are topics of discussion in this chapter as well. In total, this chapter comprises about 10 percent of the material tested in OCP Exam 3.

The first area of discussion involves descriptions of the various failure scenarios a DBA may encounter in the course of administering an Oracle database. The first failure scenario is that of statement failure. Statements fail for many reasons. For one thing, the user issuing the statement may have spelled a table name incorrectly, causing Oracle to return a "table does not exist" error. Another reason for statement failure is the inability of the user to see the database object he or she is trying to access. Often, the cause for this problem is the fact that the user is missing or denied an object privilege, or that the object truly does not exist in the database.

Another type of failure scenario that the DBA may encounter is user process failure. In this situation, an entire process executing on the database fails. Oracle handles many aspects of process recovery after statement failure with the use of the PMON process. PMON is process monitor, a process that monitors the activities of user processes to clean up after processes that fail. Some of the things PMON handles include release of locks the statement may have had, rollback of any transaction activity the process may have generated, and removal of that process from the list of active processes maintained in the V$ dynamic performance views.

The next failure scenario considered in the chapter is the user error. This type of failure is generally caused when someone inadvertently deletes or changes data in the database and commits the change. Alternately, the situation may arise when the user or developer truncates or drops the table in error. Data definition language statements such as truncation and table drops are not recoverable with the use of the rollback segment in the same way that an **update**, **insert** and **delete** are. The DBA may need to intervene in this situation by providing data or object recovery. Although logical database backups for the supplemental support of user error is the ideal approach to this failure scenario, it is possible to make a point-in-time recovery using physical backup followed by an export of the database object that was changed or dropped.

Another scenario explored in the chapter is that of instance failure. This scenario occurs when there is some problem with the hardware of the host machine running Oracle that causes the database to shut down unexpectedly. Additionally, instance failure occurs when the **shutdown**

abort command is used to shut down the database. Finally, instance failure can occur when there is some power failure on the host machine running Oracle that causes the instance to terminate abnormally. The SMON (system monitor) background process handles instance recovery the next time the Oracle instance is started if the database shows signs of instance failure. The most that is expected of the DBA in this situation is to identify the cause of the instance failure and resolve it. At any rate, if the DBA handles the hardware situation that creates instance failure, Oracle will handle the rest automatically once the instance is restarted.

The final situation that a DBA may encounter is media failure. Media failure, also known as disk failure, is the result of a problem with the disk drive that stores Oracle data. If there is a situation where the disk is irreparably damaged, or something happens that renders Oracle's access to its physical database files impossible, then the DBA will have to obtain new hardware for the database to use to store information and also recover the files that were lost by using the backups the DBA keeps in the event of this type of an emergency. This situation is generally the most manual intensive for DBAs to handle out of all the failure scenarios. It is also the most destructive. In a situation of media failure, there is always the chance for permanent loss of data. The DBA must institute an effective strategy for database backup and recovery in order to guarantee that the users of the database do not experience loss of their data.

With possible failure scenarios established, the DBA should turn attention to the option of logical backup and recovery. The utility used for logical database backup is called EXPORT. This utility is included in the distribution of Oracle database software, and can be executed by the DBA or another user who has the EXP_FULL_DATABASE role granted to their username. This role is created by the **catexp.sql** script, which is run automatically at Oracle software installation time.

In order to manage the execution of EXPORT, the DBA passes a variety of parameters to the tool at the time the export is taken. These parameters control virtually every aspect of the export, from the name of the export dump file produced to the objects it will contain. Some of the parameter names that are crucial are FILE, USERID, OWNER, TABLES, and FULL. In order to execute, EXPORT must be able to log onto Oracle with a username and password.

The final three parameters mentioned above have the purpose of determining the mode that EXPORT will run in. The three modes available to EXPORT are **user**, **table**, and **full**. **User** mode is where EXPORT accepts the name of a user in the database who owns some database objects. The objects owned by that user schema are then the only objects that will be exported. **Table** mode is another mode where EXPORT is passed a list of specific tables that it will store in the export file. In both of these cases, the DBA can further limit the database objects that are taken for backup with the use of parameters. These parameters specify whether or not the classes of objects they represent will be exported into the dump file. These object parameters include INDEXES, CONSTRAINTS, TRIGGERS, and ROWS.

Full mode is specified with the FULL parameter set to Y. In order to run EXPORT in **full** mode without conflict, it is important that the DBA not set the OWNER or TABLES parameter in conjunction with setting the FULL parameter. There are three types of full exports available to the DBA. They are *complete*, *incremental*, and *cumulative*. The type of EXPORT made in **full** mode depends on the setting the INCTYPE parameter to either **complete**, **cumulative**, or **incremental**. Complete exports save the information one would expect they would save—the entire database, minus any database objects specifically omitted by the INDEXES, CONSTRAINTS, and other parameters identified above. Incremental exports store only the database objects that have experienced changes since the last export *of any type* was taken. Note that the incremental export stores a copy of the entire object, not simply the data that was changed. In other words, if one column in one row in a million-row table was altered, the whole table is exported. Cumulative exports store all database objects that have changed since the last full or cumulative export was taken. In a sense, cumulative exports are somewhat redundant because they export the same data that is stored on incremental exports, which may have been taken prior to the cumulative export but after a complete or cumulative export. However, in this situation, cumulative exports provide the value of consolidating the data backed up on several incremental exports into one file.

Once exported, the data in an export file can be imported to the same database or to another database. This "recovery" of backup data is handled with the IMPORT utility. This utility complements EXPORT. IMPORT accepts several different parameters that modify how the IMPORT will operate. Like EXPORT, IMPORT runs in three modes. Those modes are **user**, **table**, and **full**. An important difference to note here is that IMPORT can run in **user** or **table** mode using an export dump file, regardless of the mode EXPORT ran in to produce the export dump. As long as the database object is there for IMPORT to use, IMPORT can specify it to be imported any way the DBA sees fit.

User mode for IMPORT is slightly different from the **user** mode for EXPORT. There are two parameters that manage the use of IMPORT in **user** mode. Those parameters are FROMUSER and TOUSER. The FROMUSER parameter corresponds to OWNER in EXPORT insofar as the database objects in the export dump have a schema owner. If the DBA wants to import the objects owned by a particular user stored in the export file, the DBA specifies that user schema in the FROMUSER parameter. However, the DBA must also specify the TOUSER parameter for the execution of IMPORT as well. This fact is due to the situation where the user on one database from which the database objects were extracted does not exist on the database to which the database objects will be imported.

There is a difference between the options used to run full imports as well. First, there are only two different types of full imports specified as values for the INCTYPE parameter, **system** and **restore**. The import must be run with FULL=Y and INCTYPE=**system** first using the last export created on the database before a media failure, and is critical to the successful recovery of the database. This run of IMPORT re-creates vital data dictionary and other SYSTEM tablespace information. Then IMPORT must be run to recover the database objects stored in all the different types of exports—namely, complete, cumulative, and incremental. The proper order for applying exports to the database for recovery purposes after the most recent export is applied in the SYSTEM import, is listed as follows. First, apply the most recent complete export. Next, apply all cumulative exports since the complete one in least- to most-recent order. Finally, apply all incremental exports taken since the most recent cumulative export.

Bear in mind that the logical backup and recovery services provided by EXPORT and IMPORT have the limitation of only being able to provide recovery to the point in time of the most recent database export. In other words, if there have been several database changes since the most recent export, those changes will be lost. To recover those changes, the users will have to reenter the data.

In order to determine which exports contain which database objects, the DBA has several dictionary tables at his or her disposal. The three tables in the data dictionary that are used to determine the contents of export files are called INCEXP, INCVID, and INCFIL, and all are owned by SYS. INCEXP contains a listing of all the database objects that are stored in exports and the schema containing the object. INCFIL is a catalog of all database exports, their ID numbers, and all information pertaining to the creation of the export, such as time and date and the user who created it. INCVID contains the information for the last export that was created. INCVID is used for the purpose of creating an ID for the next export that is created on the database.

Read consistency for database exports is a topic of discussion in this chapter. Read consistency has been defined so far at the statement and transaction levels as the consistency of data in the database during the period of time the statement or transaction executes. It is specified when using EXPORT with the CONSISTENT parameter. When specified, it allows the complete or cumulative export occurring in the database to have read consistency during the period of time of the export. Depending on the number of objects in the database, the time it takes the export to complete, and the number of transactions that are changing data in the database, the rollback segment space that is required to sustain the export can be quite large. In addition, read consistency is not possible for use with incremental exports.

Read consistency with the CONSISTENT parameter promises a lot, but in reality does not always measure up. Since the parameter cannot be used with incremental exports, the DBA must secure other methods for ensuring that the read consistency of the database is not compromised during the export. One popular method for doing so involves the use of Oracle's **restricted session** mode. When the DBA issues the **alter system enable restricted session**, only the users that have the **restricted session** privilege granted to them may access the database. Ideally, this privilege is only granted to the DBA. Since no other users can access the database during this time, there are two factors that should be considered. First, the export should take place when there are few users on the database, considering the full-service backup and recovery approach offered in Figure 12-2. Second, the **restricted session** mode will prevent users from making database changes while the export runs, effectively creating read consistency.

As mentioned on a few different occasions, the goal of a database recovery is not only to restore lost data, but to do so quickly. A parallel objective involves the fast backup of data as well. Due to the fact that the export is generally conducted on a database in **restricted session** mode in order to avoid the read inconsistency issues raised by leaving the database open to user changes and messing with the CONSISTENT option, the backup of a database using EXPORT should happen as quickly as possible.

This can be assured when the DBA incorporates the DIRECT parameter into the usage of EXPORT. EXPORT uses the same SQL processing mechanism used by regular user queries to obtain data from the database. The direct path eliminates some of the processing that regular queries and the conventional export path incorporate. The direct path optimizes the queries used to obtain data from the database as well.

One of the biggest drawbacks of the logical backup and recovery options provided by IMPORT and EXPORT include their inability to restore data changes that were made after the most recent backup was taken. Generally, this function is provided with the application of archived redo logs, as will be discussed in the next three chapters. However, the export files that are created with EXPORT are incompatible with archived redo logs. As a result, it adds no value to database backup and recovery to archive redo log information. Logical backup strategy is most effective in situations where the database user population can withstand the inevitable data loss.

The final area covered in this chapter involves the use of national language support. When an export takes place, EXPORT uses the character set for the database to store the exported data for that database. The IMPORT tool can import data from that character set even if the target database uses a different character set, due to the fact that the IMPORT tool can perform a character set conversion on the fly. However, this conversion will increase the amount of time required for the import to finish. If the DBA tries to export the data from the database in a character set other than the character set for that database, the export will fail.

Two-Minute Drill

- The types of database failure are user error, statement failure, process failure, instance failure, and media failure.

- User error comes when the user permanently changes or removes data from a database in error. Rollback segments give supplemental ability to correct uncommitted user errors.

- Statement failure occurs when there is something syntactically wrong with SQL statements issued by users in the database. Oracle rolls back these statements automatically.

■ Process failure occurs when a statement running against the database is terminated either by Oracle or by the user. Statement rollback, release of locks, and other process cleanup actions occur automatically by PMON.

■ Instance failure occurs when there is some problem with the host system running Oracle that forces the database to shut down. Recovery from this problem occurs when the instance is restarted. Instance recovery is handled automatically by the SMON process.

■ Media failure occurs when there is some problem with the disks that store Oracle data that renders the data unavailable. The DBA must manually intervene in these situations to restore lost data using backups.

■ Logical backup and recovery with EXPORT and IMPORT is one means by which the DBA can support backup and recovery.

■ EXPORT and IMPORT both accept certain parameters that will determine how the processes run.

■ These parameters are divided according to function.

■ There are parameters that handle the logistics of the database export. These parameters are USERID, FILE, CONSISTENT, and BUFFER.

■ There are parameters that limit the database objects that will be exported. These parameters are INDEXES, CONSTRAINTS, TRIGGERS, and GRANTS.

■ There are parameters that determine what mode the export will run in. These parameters are OWNER, TABLES, FULL, and INCTYPE.

■ Database export can happen with the EXPORT tool in three modes — **table**, **user**, and **full**.

■ In **table** mode, the DBA specifies a list of tables that will be exported by EXPORT.

■ In **user** mode, the DBA specifies a list of users whose database objects will be exported.

■ In **full** mode, the DBA will export all database objects, depending on certain factors.

- There are three types of full exports. They are complete, cumulative, and incremental.

- The type of export depends on the value specified for the INCTYPE parameter. Values are **complete**, **cumulative**, and **incremental**.

- Complete exports save all database objects in the export file.

- Incremental exports save all database objects that have been altered or added since the last export of any type was taken.

- Cumulative exports save all database objects that have been altered or added since the last complete or cumulative export was taken.

- There are parameters that handle the logistics of the database import. These parameters are USERID, FILE, CONSISTENT, and BUFFER.

- There are parameters that limit the database objects that will be imported. These parameters are INDEXES, CONSTRAINTS, TRIGGERS, and GRANTS.

- There are parameters that determine what mode import will run in. These parameters are FROMUSER and TOUSER for **user** mode, TABLES for **table** mode, and FULL and INCTYPE for **full** mode.

- Database export can happen with the IMPORT tool in three modes—**table**, **user**, and **full**.

- In **table** mode, the DBA specifies a list of tables that will be imported by IMPORT.

- In **user** mode, the DBA specifies a list of users whose database objects will be imported.

- In **full** mode, the DBA will import all database objects, depending on certain factors.

- There are two types of full imports. They are system imports and restore imports.

- The type of export executed depends on the value specified for the INCTYPE parameter mentioned. Values are **system** and **restore**.

- Imports with FULL=Y and INCTYPE=**system** restore database objects in the export file for the data dictionary. This complete import should always be the first performed in the event of a database recovery. The most recent export should be used.

■ Imports with FULL=Y and INCTYPE=**restore** restore all other database objects in the export file to the damaged database.

■ There is a particular order required for database import.

   ■ First, the last export taken should be applied using the **system** import.

   ■ Next, the most recent complete export should be applied using the **restore** import.

   ■ Then, all cumulative exports taken since the complete export, starting from least to most recent, should be applied using the **restore** import.

   ■ Finally, all incremental exports taken after the most recent cumulative export should be applied, from least to most recent incremental export, using the **restore** import.

■ There are three dictionary views used to track exported data.

   ■ INCEXP lists all exported database objects and the exports that contain them.

   ■ INCFIL lists all database exports by export ID number.

   ■ INCVID lists the most recent export ID number for the purpose of generating a new export ID number.

■ Read consistency is established when data doesn't change for the life of a statement or transaction.

■ The CONSISTENT parameter handles read consistency for the database export.

■ Use of the CONSISTENT parameter is only permitted with the complete or cumulative export.

■ Read consistency can also be established by barring user access to the database during the time the backup is taken. This is done by issuing **alter system enable restricted session**.

- Export obtains data from the database using the SQL execution mechanism that all other user processes use.

- For better performance, the export can be run with the direct path, eliminating some of the steps required to handle standard SQL statements while optimizing the processing of other steps.

- Direct path is specified using the DIRECT parameter. When using the direct path export, the BUFFER parameter is not valid.

- Logical exports do not work in conjunction with archived redo logs. This has two implications. First, without archived redo logs, it is not possible to recover database changes to the point in time the database failed. Second, there is no value added by archiving redo logs.

- Exports are in the same character set as the database from which the data came.

- Data from a database can only be exported in the same character set as the database the data came from.

- Data can be imported into another database using that database's character set. If the character sets are different, IMPORT will execute a data conversion, which will lengthen the time required for the import.

Chapter Questions

I. **The DBA is conducting an export. Which of the following actions guarantees read consistency during all types of exports?**

A. Setting CONSISTENT=Y in the parameter file for the export

B. Issuing the **alter system enable restricted session** statement

C. Issuing **startup mount** on the database

D. Issuing **shutdown abort** on the database

2. Setting the value of the BUFFER parameter to zero will allow EXPORT to

   A. Export row data from the database continuously

   B. Export no row data from the database

   C. Export row data from the database in one try

   D. Export row data from the database, one row at a time

3. Which of the following options are valid values for INCTYPE during a run of IMPORT? (Choose two)

   A. complete

   B. cumulative

   C. system

   D. incremental

   E. restore

4. To export the indexes, constraints, and triggers associated with only one particular table, the DBA should use which set of parameters?

   A. USERS=Y, INDEXES=Y, CONSTRAINTS=Y, TRIGGERS=Y

   B. OWNERS=Y, INDEXES=Y, CONSTRAINTS=Y, TRIGGERS=Y

   C. TABLES=Y, INDEXES=Y, CONSTRAINTS=Y, TRIGGERS=Y

   D. FULL=Y, INDEXES=Y, CONSTRAINTS=Y, TRIGGERS=Y

5. IMPORT can only import export files that are the same character set as the target database.

   A. TRUE

   B. FALSE

6. **The DBA is about to run IMPORT. The first step for database recovery using IMPORT should always be to**

    A. Apply the most recent complete export

    B. Apply all cumulative exports

    C. Apply all incremental exports

    D. Apply the most recent export of any type

7. **Which of the following lists only the mandatory parameters set for the first step of database recovery using IMPORT?**

    A. BUFFER, USERID, FILE

    B. FILE, FULL, TABLES

    C. FILE, FULL, INCTYPE

    D. CONSISTENT, FROMUSER, TOUSER

8. **Instance recovery is handled**

    A. Manually with intervention from the DBA

    B. Automatically using PMON

    C. Automatically using ARCH

    D. Automatically using SMON

9. **Process failure can occur when**

    A. The user issues the **CTRL-C** command

    B. The user misspells the name of the table in the **from** clause

    C. The user does not have object privileges on the database object

    D. The database object does not exist

10. If the objects imported into a database are owned by a schema that doesn't exist on the target database, which of the following parameters should be set?

    A. CONSISTENT

    B. USERID

    C. TOUSER

    D. OWNER

11. Setting DIRECT=Y will cause EXPORT to use the conventional path.

    A. TRUE

    B. FALSE

12. Setting INCTYPE=system on the first import is crucial to the success of database recovery using IMPORT.

    A. TRUE

    B. FALSE

Answers to Chapter Questions

1. B.   Issuing the **alter system enable restricted session** statement

Explanation   Choice A is incorrect because the CONSISTENT parameter does not work in conjunction with incremental exports. Choices C and D are incorrect because the database must be open and available at least in **restricted session** mode in order for the logical database backup and recovery options to work.

2. D.   Export row data from the database, one row at a time.

Explanation   Since all options present different scenarios based on the same idea, only one of these choices can be correct. Recall that the BUFFER parameter is used in conventional path exports to determine the size of the buffer that will be used to move row data from the database to the export file. The larger the buffer, the more rows that can be selected. Setting BUFFER to zero means that only one row will be moved from the database at a time. Therefore, choice D is correct.

3. C and E.   **system** and **restore**

Explanation   Choices A and B are incorrect, as they list the values that can be set for INCTYPE on runs of EXPORT. Choice D is incorrect because FULL is a parameter used to take full imports, not a value for the INCTYPE parameter.

4. C.   TABLES=Y, INDEXES=Y, CONSTRAINTS=Y, TRIGGERS=Y

Explanation   For an export of one particular table and its indexes, constraints, and triggers, the DBA can set the INDEXES, CONSTRAINTS, and TRIGGERS parameters to Y. However, to ensure that only one particular table is exported as the question requires, **table** mode should be used. **Table** mode is set with the TABLES parameter. Choice A is incorrect because there is no USERS parameter. Choice B is incorrect because the OWNERS parameter is used to set the **user** mode for EXPORT. Choice D is incorrect because FULL is used to set EXPORT into **full** mode.

5. B. FALSE

Explanation Import can perform character set conversions on data as it comes out of the export dump file and into the target database.

6. D. Apply the most recent export of any type.

Explanation The first step in logical database recovery using IMPORT is to apply the most recent database export of any type using parameters FULL= Y and INCTYPE=system. All other choices offered are for steps that occur later in the recovery process.

7. C. FILE, FULL, INCTYPE

Explanation These parameters must be set on the first application of the most recent export in order to complete the database recovery using IMPORT. Choice A is incorrect because BUFFER need not ever be specified to run any export or import of data. Choice B is incorrect because the specification of TABLES and FULL conflict. Choice D is incorrect because the parameters FROMUSER and TOUSER are generally associated with the import of data in **user** mode.

8. D. Automatically using SMON

Explanation Choice A is incorrect because the DBA needn't do anything manually within Oracle to perform instance recovery on the database. Choice B is incorrect because PMON handles process failure, not instance failure. Choice C is incorrect because ARCH handles the movement of archived redo logs into the archive destination.

9. A. The user issues the CTRL-C command.

Explanation Choices B, C and D are all incorrect because they are symptoms of statement failure.

10. C. TOUSER

Explanation The use of TOUSER is to specify a new schema owner for a database object where the schema owner of that object contained in an export file does not exist on the target database. Choice A is incorrect because CONSISTENT specifies read consistency on complete or cumulative exports. Choice B is incorrect because USERID specifies the username and password that should be used to execute the import. Choice D is incorrect because OWNER is a parameter used in the running of EXPORT to produce the export file.

11. B. FALSE

Explanation Setting DIRECT=Y specifies that EXPORT will use the direct path, thereby improving performance on the database export.

12. A. TRUE

Explanation Setting INCTYPE to **system** in order to recover the database dictionary data values is critical to the success of database recovery. It should be the first step executed at the recovery of a database.

CHAPTER 13

Physical Recovery
Without Archiving

n this chapter, you will understand and demonstrate knowledge in the following areas:

- Recovery theory
- Database recovery without archiving
- Archiving redo logs

The purpose of this chapter is to present the DBA with the capabilities of Oracle to handle database recovery. The first portion of the discussion will focus on introducing database recovery. The various types of database failure that may occur will be illustrated, along with the need for the DBA to communicate effectively in this time of crisis. The discussion will also present the types of recovery available in Oracle. This discussion will identify the type of recovery, the backup requirements that type of recovery presents, and more. The remainder of the chapter will focus on the methodology required for restoration of a database that has experienced a problem when the redo logs are not archived. Recall that redo logs contain records of all transactions that have occurred on the database. The redo logs can be archived to assist in database recovery only when the DBA uses physical backups as the method for storing copies of the database. Approximately 27 percent of the OCP Exam 3 content is material presented in this chapter.

Recovery Theory

In this section, you will cover the following topics related to recovery theory:

- Failure scenarios
- Managing database failure
- Managing database recovery
- Role of database archiving
- Types of recovery

In order to master the art of database recovery, the DBA should be mindful of both the technical requirements of various aspects of database recovery and the need to communicate effectively in times of crisis. This section focuses on failure scenarios, managing database failure, recovering the database without archiving, and the importance of using and startup of database archiving.

Failure Scenarios

There are several different scenarios for failure in the Oracle database. These scenarios can be divided into five general categories, which will be discussed in this section. The five categories include statement failure, user process failure, instance failure, user error, and media failure. Each of these categories has different implications on the need for DBA intervention in order to provide recovery from the situation.

Statement Failure

When Oracle cannot process a statement issued by a user, this situation is generally known as statement failure. There are several causes for statement failure. First of all, a user may be attempting to issue a statement referencing a table that does not exist, or to which they are not granted permission to use. In this case, Oracle will issue the user an error that details both the area of the statement that contained the error and a reference to a special code, called the Oracle error message code. Recovery from this error situation consists of Oracle immediately rolling back any changes made by the statement automatically.

User Process Failure

The failure of a user process requires more intervention from the Oracle server. In some cases, the user may cancel or terminate the statement or process they are running with a **CTRL-C** command from SQL*Plus. If a user process terminates, then the *process monitor* (PMON) background process has to intervene. When a user process fails, PMON is there to handle automatic process recovery for the database in several areas. Some of those areas are listed here:

- Rollback on the failed process

- Release of locks on tables and internal latches the process acquired
- Removal of that process identifier from active processes in the V$ performance views

Instance Failure

There are many different things that may cause an instance to fail, including a problem with the memory of the host system running Oracle, a power outage, or disk corruption. Although instance failure requires the DBA to intervene in order to restart the database, the recovery of the instance is handled by the Oracle background process system monitor. SMON handles the rebuilding of the Oracle SGA, rolling forward all transactions in progress at the time of the crash, and then rolling back all uncommitted work that was in progress at the time the database crashed. When the DBA starts the database, SMON begins the tasks required to restore the instance to full operational capacity. SMON may take a while to recover the instance, depending on the transaction volumes on the database at the time of database failure.

User Error

Several situations may arise as a result of mistakes produced by users, such as accidentally deleting data or database objects from the Oracle database. This situation can test the limits of a backup and recovery strategy. If the problem is related to data change, the user may be able to recover using the **rollback** command. However, the dropping of tables or other objects may require DBA intervention, recovering the entire database to another machine, exporting the dropped object, and then restoring the object to the appropriate environment. To avoid this problem in production, only the DBA should be allowed to create database objects, or the task should be given to a privileged user.

Media Failure

Media failure means the loss of information on a disk that has either been corrupted at a hardware level or suffered some other form of irreparable damage. There are two types of media failure that may occur on the database: temporary and permanent media failure. If the disk is temporarily unavailable because a disk controller card failed, the problem should be easy and fast to correct with simple hardware replacement. Permanent media failure is caused by physical or magnetic damage to the casing in which the disk is stored or other corruption of data stored on disk. Permanent media failure requires the DBA to restore the file(s) lost from backup copies of the database as well as any database changes made after the most recent backup with the application of archived redo log information, if archiving is used. Backup and recovery strategy of an organization is designed to act as an insurance policy against problems in the database that render the database unusable. Database recovery requires a strong understanding of operating-system-specific commands and processes for physical Oracle file manipulation, as well as an understanding of Oracle's recovery mechanisms. The time spent recovering the database depends on several critical factors:

- **Accessibility of backups**   Both the physical availability of backups (onsite or offsite) *AND* the accessibility of backups on hardware storage media. Disk is fastest; tape is slower.

- **Frequency of backups**   More frequent backups mean faster recovery, because fewer archived redo logs need to be applied for the same amount of recovered data.

- **Type of failure**   Some types of failure are easier to fix and less time consuming than others. For example, if the database lost one disk drive that contained only a few **read only** tablespaces, the DBA will spend less time recovering than if the DBA lost several disks of volatile data that were backed up infrequently.

- **Type of backups**   Physical backups provide better recoverability than logical exports, because archived redo can be applied to handle the changes made after the most recent backup was taken.

Exercises

1. For review, what are the five types of failure that may occur on an Oracle database?

2. What is the difference between temporary media failure and permanent media failure?

Managing Database Recovery

Database recovery is the most critical skill a DBA can master to provide value to an organization. However, it is not a skill that is easily encapsulated into one or two commands or parameters in the way that dropping database objects can be reduced to a statement. Of all areas of Oracle database administration, the mastery of database recovery is the trickiest. Not only must a DBA have the experience it takes to develop seasoned, instinctive approaches to recovery of a database, but the DBA must also be a facilitator of good communication. Most DBAs in larger IT organizations with many databases will know the intricacies of every application using the database. Knowing who to contact is as important as technical skill. For recovery requiring a lot of downtime, the decision to recover must be made in consensus. In crisis situations, users and managers generally have a few specific questions they need to have answered. Those questions are as follows:

- What caused the problem?

- Who is affected by this problem?

- What steps are required to correct the problem?

- How long will it take to correct this problem?

- Can this problem be prevented?

A few cases of hands-on experience provide the best instruction for DBAs who want to know the right things to communicate in the organization when a database crisis arises. However, the DBA with the technical expertise and strong communication skills will be effective in crisis situations quickly.

TIP
In crisis situations, the DBA should get the right people involved in consensus decisions for recovering databases. The DBA should neither gloss over important facts nor dwell on details when explaining the steps required for resolving the crisis. Communication is the best means to build support for the solution to a database problem.

Exercise

How important is communication on the part of the DBA in media failure scenarios?

Role of Archiving

With physical backups, it is an excellent idea to use the **archivelog** option of Oracle. The method for turning archiving on is covered shortly. Archiving of redo logs should be used in any production database environment where data changes are frequent and complete recovery to the point of failure is required. With archived redo logs, there are more options for database recovery. Data changes made after the most recent backup are recorded by redo logs that can then be applied to the database after that backup is restored, for full database recovery. Without the archived redo logs, the data changes for a database are lost every time a log switch occurs. Recall the process used to write online redo logs. Two or more redo logs store online redo taken from the redo log buffer and copied to disk by LGWR. Each redo log may consist of, ideally, more than one *member*, mirrored (or "multiplexed") on multiple disks to minimize the Oracle database's dependency on any one disk. If a disk drive fails that contains the only member of the current online redo log, the Oracle instance will fail.

When an online redo log fills, a log switch occurs. Old redo logs will be archived automatically by ARCH if the DBA has issued the **alter system archive log start** statement from Server Manager or if the LOG_ARCHIVE_START initialization parameter is set to TRUE before instance startup. LGWR or CKPT will write the current redo log sequence information to the datafile headers and to the control file, then LGWR will start writing redo log entries to the other online redo log. A checkpoint also occurs. LGWR tells DBWR to flush the dirty buffer write queue of the database buffer cache in the SGA. Flushing the dirty buffers means that DBWR will write the data changes made to database blocks in the buffer cache out to the datafiles on disk that contain copies of the blocks. Once archived, data in the online redo log is no longer required.

Situations where archiving may not be required include **read only** databases, or databases that experience a low frequency of data changes. Databases in this category may be better off using logical exports for backup, or offline physical backups. Either approach will work to store the data once changes are made, providing needed recoverability for the system with only nominal effort and maintenance on the backup process by the DBA. However, any type of online transaction processing system with data volatility should archive redo logs. By saving all the data changes made to the database with the use of archived redo logs, the DBA can recover all committed data changes to the database with minimal requirements for end users to reenter data they may have placed into the trust of the database environment.

Exercises

1. What role does archiving play in the backup and recovery strategy of an Oracle database?

2. In what situations might archiving be used? When might archiving not be required?

Types of Recovery

In general, there are two categories for database recovery: recovery with archiving and recovery without. Without archiving, the database can be recovered to the point in time where the last database backup took place. With archiving enabled, the DBA has more options in the event of a disaster. Usually, the DBA will perform a database recovery to the point of failure on the database. This is *complete* recovery. To have complete recovery, the DBA needs the most recent database backup and a full set of archived redo logs for that backup to the time of failure. There are other options for incomplete recovery as well. Incomplete recovery is the recovery option available when the DBA is missing archived redo logs, or if the DBA plans to recover the database to a point in time in the past.

Complete Recovery

Database recovery is handled with the **recover** command. The **recover** command is available from the Server Manager utility or in conjunction with the **alter database** statement. There are three different types of media recovery that can be performed on the database with respect to the scope of recoverability required for the database. The first type of recovery available in situations where archiving is enabled is database-wide recovery. The command for database-wide recovery is the **recover database** command. A database that requires database-wide recovery cannot be available for use by the applications and users. When the **recover database** command is issued, Oracle will examine all tablespaces and datafiles of the database and apply archived redo log information to those areas that require recovery. The instance must be mounted in **exclusive** mode. Otherwise, the database should remain closed. An example for specifying the database recovery command appears in the following code block. Note that the database name need not be specified either in the **shutdown** or the **recover** command, as Oracle will operate on the database that is mounted to the instance. From Server Manager, the following commands may be issued:

```
SHUTDOWN ABORT
STARTUP PFILE=orgdb01.ora MOUNT EXCLUSIVE orgdb01
ALTER DATABASE orgdb01 RECOVER DATABASE;
```

A more localized option is the recovery of a tablespace. This option is accomplished with the **recover tablespace** command within Server Manager. Recovering a tablespace allows the database to be open for use while the recovery takes place. The only area of the database that is not available during the period of tablespace recovery is the tablespace itself, which must be offline for the duration of the restoration. A tablespace can be brought offline using the **alter tablespace offline** SQL statement, either from Server Manager or from SQL*Plus. Even more localized is the recovery of an individual datafile for a tablespace. This option is accomplished with the **recover datafile** command from Server Manager, and can be compared to laser surgery in that it offers the DBA a highly selective option to restore lost data while the rest of the database stands untouched. This operation, along with the overall requirements for recovery while leaving the database online, will be discussed in Chapter 15, in the section on minimizing the downtime of a database. The following code block demonstrates the online recovery of a tablespace:

```
ALTER TABLESPACE data_301 OFFLINE;
ALTER DATABASE orgdb01 RECOVER TABLESPACE data_301;
```

Database recovery is handled in an interactive manner when archived redo logs are involved. Oracle expects that all archived redo logs required for database recovery will be located in the LOG_ARCHIVE_DEST location specified as part of the **init.ora** parameter file. If the redo logs are restored from archive at another location due to space constraints, the DBA should specify the new location.

Incomplete Recovery

There are three types of incomplete database recovery: *change-based*, *time-based*, and *cancel-based* recovery. All three of these types of recovery are incomplete forms of recovery because they will limit the number of archived redo logs that are applied to the database, either by time, by change, or by cancellation. These three types of recovery will take place generally only when the database has been mounted in **exclusive** mode and otherwise left closed.

CHANGE-BASED RECOVERY   In change-based recovery, Oracle will restore database changes made up to the change that is specified by the DBA as part of the command that initiates the recovery. The DBA may, in some cases, use the change-based recovery option to identify the last known good transaction to have taken place for the purpose of recovering the database to the point just after that transaction was committed. The change that indicates the end of the recovery to Oracle is defined with the use of a system change number, or SCN. The SCN is a number that Oracle assigns to every transaction that occurs in the database. This "transaction ID number" is then attached to every statement that executes as part of the transaction. The change information can then be tracked both in the rollback segments and the online redo logs, gathering all statements that make changes together as one transaction. The SCN is specified as an integer. To find the last SCN archived by Oracle or what the SCN that was written at the last checkpoint was, the DBA can query the V$DATABASE dynamic performance view. The following code block demonstrates the specification of change-based recovery:

```
ALTER DATABASE orgdb01 RECOVER DATABASE UNTIL CHANGE 4043;
```

TIP
The SCN of the last transaction conducted at a checkpoint or archived can be found in the V$DATABASE dynamic performance view. To find the SCN of a particular transaction in an archived redo log, the V$LOG_HISTORY performance view can be used.

TIME-BASED RECOVERY   The incomplete database recovery may be conducted to a certain point in time. This type of recovery is considered to be a time based recovery. Time-based and change-based recoveries are similar in that Oracle will restore data to the database to some point in the past. The appropriate format for the time a DBA can specify is a four-digit year, followed by a two-digit month, followed by a two-digit date. These three items are separated by a hyphen. Immediately following the date should be a colon, followed by the hour of the day in 24-hour format, followed by the minute, followed by the second. The time components should be separated by colons. A sample **alter database** statement with recovery to a point in time identified is listed in the following code block:

```
ALTER DATABASE orgdb01 RECOVER UNTIL '1999-12-05:14:34:00';
```

CANCEL-BASED RECOVERY   The final type of incomplete recovery considered is the cancel-based recovery. This type allows the DBA to conduct database recovery until a **cancel** command is issued. Cancel-based recovery requires the DBA to monitor the recovery process. In order to demonstrate the usage of cancel-based recovery, the following code block illustrates an **alter database** statement that specifies cancel-based recovery. In order to cancel recovery, the DBA can issue the **cancel** command as Oracle interactively requests the DBA to confirm the application of suggested redo logs.

```
ALTER DATABASE orgdb01 RECOVER UNTIL CANCEL;
```

LOG_ARCHIVE_DEST
During normal operation of the database when archiving is enabled, the archived redo entries are moved to a location specified by the

LOG_ARCHIVE_DEST parameter. This parameter is declared in the **init.ora** file, which is used at instance startup. The archived redo logs will then be taken out of the LOG_ARCHIVE_DEST and stored on offline storage media, usually tape. When database recovery is required, then the DBA must put the required redo logs back into the LOG_ARCHIVE_DEST. However, there may be situations where all the archived redo information required for the database recovery will not fit into the location specified for LOG_ARCHIVE_DEST. In this case, the DBA may specify an alternate location for putting archived redo information with the **set logsource** command from within Server Manager before the issuance of the **alter database recover** command. An example for using this command within Server Manager at the command prompt is listed here:

```
SET LOGSOURCE '/u01/oracle/archive/bkp'
```

Alternatively, the DBA can specify a location for the archived redo log information in the statement used to recover the database. The syntax for this command used is the **from** keyword. An example of this clause appears in the following code block:

```
ALTER DATABASE orgdb01
RECOVER FROM '/u01/oracle/archive/bkp'
DATABASE UNTIL CANCEL;
```

Discarding Archives at Startup

Once incomplete recovery is complete, the database will reflect the changes made to it up to the specified point in time in the past. All archives of changes made to the database after that point in time must be discarded. To dispose of unneeded redo information after database recovery has taken place, open the database with of the **resetlogs** option. The redo log number is reset to one (1), and Oracle starts writing a new set of redo logs according to LOG_ARCHIVE_FORMAT. Examples for discarding and not discarding redo logs at the time the database is opened appear in the following code block:

```
ALTER DATABASE OPEN RESETLOGS;
ALTER DATABASE OPEN NORESETLOGS;
```

Automatic Recovery Using Recommended Archived Logs

The course of conducting database recovery is an interactive one within Oracle. As the recovery proceeds, Oracle prompts the DBA to specify which archived redo log to apply next. Based on information supplied to the database by LOG_ARCHIVE_DEST for the location of the archived redo logs and LOG_ARCHIVE_FORMAT for the naming convention of the archived redo log files, Oracle can recommend to the DBA the next archived redo log to apply as part of the database recovery. However, the DBA must give some manual intervention, either by confirming that "suggestion" or specifying the appropriate file. It is during this interaction between Oracle and the DBA that the DBA may also choose to cancel the recovery altogether in the case of cancel-based incomplete database recovery. However, if desired, the DBA can also bypass the interaction between Oracle and the DBA entirely with the use of automatic recovery. When automatic recovery is used, Oracle will prompt the DBA with its suggested next archived redo log to apply, and then Oracle will automatically apply that redo log suggestion. This utility reduces the need for the DBA to interact with the database, especially when all archived redo logs are in place specified by LOG_ARCHIVE_DEST and Oracle can correctly identify them using LOG_ARCHIVE_FORMAT. The following code block identifies the correct syntax and semantics for using automatic recovery:

```
ALTER DATABASE orgdb01
RECOVER AUTOMATIC
DATABASE UNTIL CHANGE 39455;

ALTER DATABASE orgdb01
RECOVER AUTOMATIC
DATABASE UNTIL TIME '1999-01-20:20:04:00';
```

Exercises

1. What is complete recovery? What statement is used to recover the database? A tablespace? A datafile?

2. What is incomplete recovery? Name the three types of incomplete recovery that are offered in Oracle? How are redo logs discarded after incomplete recovery?

Database Recovery Without Archiving

In this section, you will cover the following topics related to database recovery without archiving:

- Using a full physical backup

- Recovering **read only** tablespaces

This discussion focuses on the tasks required to recover a database using a full physical backup without archiving. The advantage to not use archiving is simplicity in database recovery. Only the most recent full backup need be applied to the database. On the other hand, if archiving is not enabled on the database, then all changes that have taken place since the most recent full backup will not appear in the database after the recovery takes place. Additionally, the requirements for recovering a **read only** tablespace will be addressed.

Using a Full Physical Backup

The DBA must conduct a complete recovery from full backup if the database does not have archiving enabled to resolve problems of media failure. The database cannot be open for use during complete recovery. If the database is not shut down already, the DBA can issue **shutdown abort** to shut it down. At the command line within Server Manager, the following statement can be executed by the DBA while connected as a user with the **sysdba** privilege granted.

 SHUTDOWN ABORT;

Media failure usually requires some sort of hardware repair or replacement. In order to restore the database to its full functionality, the DBA should ensure that the disk hardware that was damaged—the initial cause for the media failure—is fixed. Alternatively, the DBA may choose to circumvent the problem by restoring the database using another disk to store the different files of the database. Assuming the disk has been replaced, the following steps are necessary to perform complete recovery:

1. Restore all files from the complete backup, datafiles, redo log files, and control files. All files must be restored, not just damaged ones, in order for the entire database to be read consistent to a single point in time of the last database backup. Operating system copy commands available on the host machine running Oracle are used to handle this step.

2. Reset redo logs with the **resetlogs** option for the **startup** command. After full backup has been applied, the DBA will open the database for access by the users with the following statement. As discussed earlier, this step resets the redo log sequence to one (1).

   ```
   ALTER DATABASE OPEN RESETLOGS;
   ```

If the disk cannot be replaced, then the DBA may need to move the files to other disks, and update the control file accordingly. The following steps can be used for this purpose.

1. Restore all files from complete backup, datafiles, redo log files, and control files. Files that were located on the damaged disk should be restored to another disk at this time. All files are restored, not just damaged ones, in order for the entire database to be read-consistent to the point in time of the last database backup. Operating system copy commands available on the host machine running Oracle are used to handle this step for recovery.

2. Move the control file specification as noted by the CONTROL_FILES parameter of the **init.ora** file. The path and filename may be changed to reflect a new location for the control file of the Oracle database if the control file was lost in the disk failure.

3. Mount the database in **exclusive** mode.

4. Update the control file to reflect new locations for datafiles or redo log files to other disks. To move a datafile or redo log file, the DBA must use the **alter database** statement with the **rename file** option from Server Manager. Full pathnames for the datafile at old and new locations should be specified. Examples for executing this operation appear in the following code block:

```
ALTER DATABASE orgdb01
RENAME FILE '/u01/oracle/data/data_301a.dbf'
TO '/u02/oracle/data/data_301b.dbf';

ALTER DATABASE orgdb01
RENAME FILE '/u01/oracle/ctl/rdorgdb01'
TO '/u02/oracle/ctl/rdorgdb01';
```

5. Back up the database in the same manner detailed for offline backups in Chapter 11.

6. Discard redo logs with the **resetlogs** option for the **startup** command and open the database. The following code block gives an example:

```
ALTER DATABASE OPEN RESETLOGS;
```

Exercises

1. What steps are required for recovery in conjunction with a full physical backup?

2. What additional steps are required if database files must be moved for media recovery?

3. What shutdown method causes Oracle to require media recovery after shutdown is complete? Identify the importance of resetting the redo log sequence number after recovery using full backups.

Recovering Read Only Tablespaces

The read and write status of the tablespace is recorded in the control file for the database. Changing the status of a tablespace from read-write to **read only** or vice versa should *always* be followed by a full backup of the tablespace. If the backup of the database was taken *after* the status of the tablespace was changed from **read only** to read-write, there should be no problem with database recovery because the status of the tablespaces for the database is reflected accurately in the control file. The DBA should be sure to recover the control file along with the other database files that are used for the complete database recovery. However, if the tablespace status was changed after the most recent backup and no subsequent backup was taken, then the DBA may have to restore the tablespace in the state it was in when the backup was taken, and then change the status manually. This method is consistent with the overall requirement in restoring databases where archiving is disabled, in that all changes that took place after the most recent backup must be reentered.

TIP
*Always take a backup of the control file whenever the status of a tablespace changes from read-write to **read only** and vice versa.*

Oracle behaves a little differently in situations where recovery of **read only** tablespaces takes place on databases that archive their redo logs. As with databases that leave archiving disabled, the DBA should always back up the database, particularly the control file for that database, *after* the status change is made to a tablespace. However, with archiving enabled, there are some steps that must be taken in order to recover the database. If the database has been backed up since the status was changed, the backup taken can be used to aid recovery. After recovering the datafile(s) that comprise the tablespace, which were lost in the media failure, the DBA should apply redo log information. Although no data will be changed in the **read only** tablespace, Oracle may need to set other information in the database appropriately. In any case, Oracle will prompt the DBA with the suggested redo log. The same process of restoring the datafile backup and applying archived redo information is required even when the status of the tablespace has changed since the most recent backup was taken. This is because the archived redo information for that tablespace will contain, among other things, the status change of the tablespace. The steps required for database recovery of a **read only** tablespace with the original control file in place, regardless of whether a backup of the database was taken before or after the tablespace writability status was changed, is listed:

1. Restore the **read only** tablespace datafile(s) that were lost in the media failure.

2. Apply the required redo logs. This step is required mainly when the status of the tablespace changed after the tablespace or database backup was taken.

The importance of backing up control files after the status of a tablespace is changed becomes more pronounced if **read only** tablespace recovery is required due to the failure of a disk that also contained a control file. There are some factors to remember with respect to the control file and recovery of a **read only** tablespace. If the recovery is using a backed-up control file, Oracle cannot recover a **read only** tablespace. The DBA must take the **read only** tablespace offline in order to conduct the recovery. After the archived redo logs are applied, the DBA must apply the current online redo log as the last step in recovery, and then the rest of the database recovery completes. After that, the DBA can bring the **read only** tablespace online and things should work well. The steps required for recovery with a backed-up control file are as follows:

1. Take the **read only** tablespace offline.

2. Conduct the recovery with the **alter database recover database using backup controlfile** command.

3. Apply archived redo logs as appropriate. Apply the online redo log last.

4. Bring the **read only** tablespace online.

5. Open the database.

Exercises

1. Identify the procedure for recovering the database after a **read only** tablespace.

2. What is the importance of backing up the control file after setting the write status of a tablespace?

Archiving Redo Logs

In this section, you will cover the following topics related to enabling archiving:

■ Displaying archive mode

■ Enabling archiving

■ Using the ARCH background process

■ Displaying a list of archived redo logs

■ Selectively archiving redo logs

■ Taking backups after enabling archiving

The archiving or backup of redo information is Oracle's innate method for backing up the database. If archiving is enabled and all archives are stored properly, the emphasis on backups for database recovery that are present in both the logical and the offline physical (full) backup strategies (presented in Chapters 11 and 12) is reduced for a backup and recovery strategy. Database recovery options are vastly more flexible when archiving of redo log information is enabled in Oracle. Every transaction in the database writes redo log entries. These entries are stored in the SGA until LGWR copies the redo entry to the online redo log, which resides on disk and is mirrored on several disks, ideally. There are at least two sets of mirrored redo log files on the Oracle database that are online or available for LGWR to write entries at any time. When a redo log fills with redo information, a log switch occurs. LGWR starts writing redo to another set of online redo logs. A checkpoint also occurs at a log switch. LGWR tells DBWR to flush the buffer cache's dirty buffer write queue of all buffers containing database changes. LGWR also writes log switch information to datafile headers and to the control file. The last thing that optionally happens if the DBA has set up automatic archiving is that the ARCH background process will copy the online redo log to the archive log destination as denoted by LOG_ARCHIVE_DEST. Automatic archiving is enabled with LOG_ARCHIVE_START set to TRUE in the **init.ora** parameter file or with the **alter system archive log start** command in Server Manager. Starting archiving will be discussed in this section.

Displaying Archive Mode

The first and most basic step to understanding whether or not archiving is enabled on the Oracle database, the DBA must display the status of archiving on the Oracle database. There are a number of different methods that may be used for displaying archiving information. The most prevalent for DBAs is a command run out of Server Manager called **archive log list**. In addition to whether Oracle is archiving redo logs, this command displays extensive information about the actual redo log being written and whether automatic movement of archives to the archive destination is being done. The following code block illustrates the use of this command:

```
SVRMGR> ARCHIVE LOG LIST
Database log mode              NOARCHIVELOG
Automatic archival            DISABLED
Archive destination           /DISK01/Oracle/home/arch/
Oldest online log sequence    20
Next log sequence to archive  21
Current log sequence          21
```

Note several different things about the list of information for archiving. First of all, the database log mode is the item that denotes whether the database has archiving of redo logs enabled. This information is supplied in the database log mode line. Another important feature of information displayed by this command is whether the DBA has set up Oracle to move archives to their archiving destination automatically or whether the DBA has chosen to move archives to their destination manually. A complete discussion of automatic vs. manual movement of archived redo logs to the archive destination is presented later in this section. If archiving is enabled, there will be a destination detailed in the archive log destination line of the output for **archive log list**. This pathname is taken from a parameter in the **init.ora** file of the database called LOG_ARCHIVE_DEST. The last three lines of output detail information about the sequence number of the online redo logs that have been written or are being written in the database. When the DBA opens a database using the **resetlogs** option, the numbers being reset are the values for these three lines. Also, when a log switch occurs, the number for the current log sequence is incremented.

Another method that may be used to obtain only the status of archiving on the Oracle database comes from using a dynamic performance view called V$DATABASE. This view contains several columns detailing system change number information. Its use has been mentioned in the context of presenting the requirements of change-based incomplete recovery, a method of database recovery that will be discussed in greater depth in Chapter 14. V$DATABASE has several columns, including one called LOG_MODE that contains the archive log mode for the database, either

noarchivelog or **archivelog** mode. The following code block contains a query and the output that can be used to determine the archiving information for a database:

```
SELECT name, log_mode
FROM v$database;

NAME        LOG_MODE
---------   --------------------------
ORGDB01     NOARCHIVELOG
```

The information for this query, indeed all information for the V$DATABASE view, comes from the control file of the database. One other method that can be used for determining what archiving mode the database is in is to use the control file for the database itself. If the DBA was in a pinch and none of the other options were available, such as in the situation where the instance was shut down, the DBA may look in the control file to determine the archiving status of the database as well. However, this method is really only useful as a last resort since the other two methods detailed earlier should suffice in almost all situations.

One last area that should be presented here is the use of V$LOG to identify whether specific online redo log groups have been archived. The V$LOG performance view identifies several items of information about the current status of the online redo log, including the SCN range for the online redo log and the archiving status of the redo log. The ARCHIVED column of the V$LOG performance view will identify whether or not the redo log has been archived.

Exercise

Describe some different methods the DBA may use to identify the archiving mode for the database.

Enabling Archiving

If a physical backup strategy is in place on the database and the DBA needs to ensure several different recovery options are in place, including recovery to the final committed transaction before the media failure occurred, then the DBA should enable archiving on the Oracle database in question.

Archiving makes all sorts of recovery strategies possible, including complete recovery and several forms of incomplete recovery. Without archiving, recovery is only possible to the point in time of the last backup, whether it is complete in the case of a full offline physical backup or partial as in the use of the backup strategy presented for use with EXPORT.

If the methods described for determining whether archiving is in use on the database denote that archiving is not in use on the database, and the DBA determines that archiving should be activated for the database, then the DBA can enable archiving with the following methods. There are two points in time that the DBA can enable archiving on the Oracle database. The first point is at the time the database is created. If the DBA determines that archiving should be used, the DBA can create the database with archiving already in place. The DBA can set archiving to be enabled as part of the **create database** statement. At some point in this statement, the DBA should include the keyword **archivelog** to enable archiving. The placement of this keyword is not important, so long as its appearance does not disrupt the syntax of other options such as the specification for datafiles or redo log files. A sample **create database** statement with archiving enabled at database creation appears in the following code block:

```
CREATE DATABASE newdb01
CONTROLFILE REUSE
LOGFILE GROUP 2 (log01,log02)
DATAFILE (users01.dbf, data01.dbf, index01.dbf)
ARCHIVELOG;
```

If the **archivelog** option is not included in the database creation statement, Oracle defaults to disabling the archiving of redo logs, or **noarchivelog**. It is possible to switch the archiving status of a database after the database has been created. This operation is essentially an alteration of the database, and as such it uses the **alter database** statement. Altering the database to begin archiving redo logs can be executed along with any other database alteration, so long as the syntax is correct for the statement when issued. An example for altering the database to archive redo log information without altering any other aspect of the database appears in the following code block:

```
ALTER DATABASE orgdb01 ARCHIVELOG;
```

In general, it is recommended that the DBA back up the database when archiving is enabled or disabled. A more complete discussion of the implications of this recommendation is presented later in the section.

Exercises

   1. How does the DBA put the database into **archivelog** mode as part of database creation?

   2. How does the DBA put the database into **archivelog** mode after database creation?

   3. What crucial action should be performed by the DBA after archiving is enabled on a database?

Using the ARCH Background Process

When archiving is enabled on the Oracle database, there must be some process by which archived redo logs are copied to an archive destination. The DBA can handle the process manually using operating system copy commands to move the files to the destination determined to be appropriate. The archiving of online redo logs must be handled as the redo logs fill. In order to archive an online redo log manually, the DBA must issue the **alter system archive log all** statement. The usage of this statement appears in the following code block. The following statement archives all full online redo logs that have not already been archived. The archive is specified in the pathname that is provided in quotes in the **to** clause of the statement.

```
ALTER SYSTEM ARCHIVE LOG ALL TO '/u01/Oracle/arch'
```

Manual archiving of redo logs may work fine for the DBA who manages a smaller or more static database who wants a hands-on approach to managing archived redo information. However, this method can be time consuming, and ultimately a performance problem. Since the DBA must manually enter this statement or develop and test a script that enters this statement, there is some effort involved. Also, if the DBA does not handle the manual archival of online redo logs before all online redo logs fill, the DBA will create a performance problem on the database. If archiving is enabled, archiving is handled manually, and all online redo logs are full,

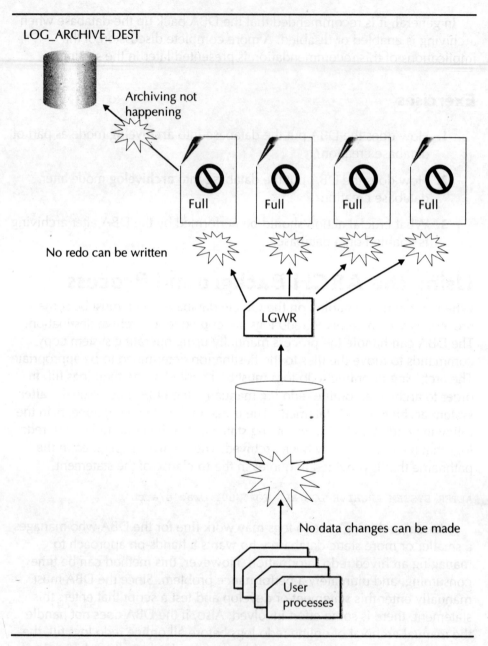

LOG_ARCHIVE_DEST

Archiving not happening

No redo can be written

LGWR

No data changes can be made

User processes

FIGURE 13-1. *When all online redo logs fill*

then Oracle will not be able to continue running until the DBA archives the data in the online redo logs so that LGWR can switch to writing redo to another log. Figure 13-1 demonstrates the result of Oracle filling all online redo logs and the DBA failing to manually archive the redo information.

In order to reduce any problems that may come about as a result of manually archiving redo log information, the DBA can have the database automatically handle archiving of redo information. This process is called *automatic archiving*. When Oracle handles archiving of online redo logs automatically, there is little chance that the database will cease to run due to the fact that an online redo log was not archived. Automatic archiving creates a new background process that runs in the Oracle database. This process is called ARCH, for archiver. The ARCH process executes the copying and movement of recently filled online redo logs to the archive destination specified. To enable automatic archiving, the DBA must execute another **alter system** statement, this time with the **start** option. The proper syntax for this option appears in the first statement of the following code block. To stop the automatic archival of online redo logs, the second statement in the following code block may be used.

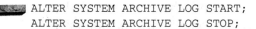

```
ALTER SYSTEM ARCHIVE LOG START;
ALTER SYSTEM ARCHIVE LOG STOP;
```

When this statement is issued, a parameter within the instance is set to TRUE. That parameter is called LOG_ARCHIVE_START. If the DBA so desires, she may also set the parameter within the **init.ora** parameter file. In this manner, the automatic archiving of redo log entries will be in effect every time the instance is started. There are two major points to consider in the configuration of automatic archiving for redo information. These points include defining the destination for all archived copies of redo information and the format ARCH should automatically apply when moving redo log files to the archive destination. These two items are handled with parameters called LOG_ARCHIVE_DEST and LOG_ARCHIVE_FORMAT, respectively. These parameters can be identified in the **init.ora** initialization parameter file, which is used at the startup of the database instance.

LOG_ARCHIVE_DEST
The location of the database archive for redo log information is specified to Oracle using the LOG_ARCHIVE_DEST. There must be a value for this

initialization parameter at instance startup. If the DBA should wish to specify another archive destination, the DBA can issue the **alter system archive log start** with a destination specified at the time the statement is issued. The following code block illustrates this point:

```
ALTER SYSTEM ARCHIVE LOG START '/u02/Oracle/archive';
```

In order to specify an archive destination for the LOG_ARCHIVE_DEST parameter, the DBA should use the absolute pathname for the destination directory or area of the filesystem. An example for specifying this parameter in the **init.ora** file is listed in the following code block:

```
LOG_ARCHIVE_DEST='/Oracle/archive'
```

LOG_ARCHIVE_FORMAT

This parameter is also specified in the **init.ora** file. It handles the identification of a naming convention for ARCH to use when moving online redo logs to the archived redo log location. The format for redo information is arbitrary, and dependent on the filename formats supported by the operating system of the machine hosting the Oracle database. However, since the archived redo logs will essentially be a sequence of files, there are some formatting options available with Oracle that can be used in the LOG_ARCHIVE_FORMAT parameter to ensure that the sequence of numbers for each redo log archived will be consistent and in a manner prescribed by the DBA. The four formatting conventions that are usable with LOG_ARCHIVE_FORMAT are listed here:

- **%T** Thread number for the redo logs of that instance within the Oracle Parallel Server architecture, padded with zeros to the left. A thread is a running set of redo log information for one instance within a parallel database server.

- **%t** Thread number for the redo logs of that instance within the Oracle Parallel Server architecture, not padded to the left with zeros.

- **%S** Log sequence number, a sequential number representing the number of redo logs that have been written and archived since archiving began, instance started, or sequence reset by **resetlogs**, padded to the left with zeros.

- **%s** Log sequence number, not padded to the left with zeros.

The format specified for the LOG_ARCHIVE_FORMAT must conform to any naming conventions required for files at the operating system. It will generate archived redo logs that are similar in form to the sample filenames listed after the specification for the variable. Typically, the archived redo logs will carry the **.arc** extension as well.

```
LOG_ARCHIVE_FORMAT = Log%S.arc
Log0023.arc
Log0024.arc
Log0025.arc

LOG_ARCHIVE_FORMAT = Arch-%t-%S.arc
Arch-3-0001.arc
Arch-3-0002.arc
Arch-3-0003.arc
```

During database recovery, the suggestions that Oracle formulates for the DBA to confirm are based on the value of the LOG_ARCHIVE_FORMAT parameter. The automatic archiving destination specified by LOG_ARCHIVE_DEST can be overridden during a manual archive by specifying a destination in the **alter system archive log** statement. However, the automatic archiving destination will still default to the LOG_ARCHIVE_DEST location.

Exercises

1. What is ARCH? How is it enabled?

2. Identify two initialization parameters for automatic archiving.

Displaying the List of Archived Redo Logs

Once the redo logs are archived either automatically or manually, there are several ways to identify which redo logs exist and what their contents are. The V$LOG_HISTORY dynamic performance view provides a listing of all archived redo logs for the database, along with detailed information about the transactions in each of the redo logs identified by system change number. The ARCHIVE_NAME column of the V$LOG_HISTORY performance view will identify the name of the archived redo log according to the format specified by the LOG_ARCHIVE_FORMAT parameter or by the filename used when the DBA manually archived the online redo log file. The following SQL query allows the DBA to identify the filename, the transactions in the redo log by SCN, and the sequence and thread numbers for the archived redo log:

```
SELECT archive_name,
    to_char(low_change#) || '..' || to_char(high_change#) SCN_RANGE,
    sequence#, thread#
FROM v$log_history;
```

In addition, the DBA can use the **archive log list** command to display detailed information about the archiving of redo logs. The usage of this feature is detailed earlier in the section—refer to the discussion of identifying the mode for archiving that was presented in the section.

Exercise

How can the archived redo logs of a database be displayed?

Selectively Archiving Redo Logs

In general, the DBA will find the use of automatic archiving with the ARCH background process to be sufficient for archiving purposes. Likewise, the DBA may want to manage manual archiving with the **alter system archive log all** statement to get all online redo logs archived that have not been archived already. However, archiving of redo logs is actually a full-featured function, complete with many different options that allow for the selective archiving of online redo logs. Several options are available for selectively archiving online redo log information. Some of the options that are available for selectively archiving redo logs with the **alter system archive log** statement include specifying a particular online redo log sequence, system change number, current redo log group, and several others. In addition to archiving all redo logs with the **alter system archive log all** statement identified earlier, the different options available with this statement are as follows: **seq**, **change**, **current**, **group**, **logfile**, and **next**. Each term will now be explained.

SEQ

This option is used to manually archive online redo logs according to sequence number. The sequence number for a given current log group is displayed when the DBA executes the **archive log list** command. Alternatively, the DBA can determine current redo log sequence and thread information using the V$LOG dynamic performance view. The sequence number for the redo log to archive is specified after the **seq** keyword option. An example for archiving according to the sequence number appears in the following code block:

```
ALTER SYSTEM ARCHIVE LOG SEQ 39;
```

CHANGE

This option is used to manually archive logs according to a system change number, or SCN. To obtain the range of transaction system change numbers for a given set of online redo logs, the DBA can query the V$LOG dynamic performance view. The columns that define the range of system change numbers available on the database are LOW_CHANGE# and HIGH_ CHANGE# in V$LOG, respectively. If the DBA wants to archive a specific redo log based on a system change number, the following statement can be used for that purpose:

```
ALTER SYSTEM ARCHIVE LOG CHANGE 450394;
```

CURRENT

This option is used to manually archive the redo log that is currently being written by the instance. In effect, issuing the **alter system archive log** statement with the **current** option forces Oracle to conduct a log switch. The same effect can be created if the DBA uses automatic archiving of redo log entries and issues the **alter system switch logfile** statement. For an example of using this option, the following statement illustrates the syntax of this **alter system** option. Its usage is straightforward.

```
ALTER SYSTEM ARCHIVE LOG CURRENT;
```

GROUP

This option is used to manually archive redo log information according to the online redo log group that has the value specified by the integer that follows this option in the **alter system archive log** statement. The DBA can obtain group information from the V$LOG performance view in the GROUP# column. The syntax and semantics for using this option are illustrated by the following **alter system** statement:

```
ALTER SYSTEM ARCHIVE LOG GROUP 3;
```

LOGFILE

This option is used to manually archive redo log information according to the online redo log group containing the member identified by the filename specified as part of the **logfile** option. The value specified for **logfile** must be a filename for one of the members of a log file group. The members of a log file group are specified as part of the **create database** command, but that information can be obtained from the V$LOGFILE dynamic performance view. Meanwhile, an illustration for usage of the **logfile** option appears in the code block here:

```
ALTER SYSTEM ARCHIVE LOG LOGFILE 'LOG1A';
```

NEXT

This option is used to manually archive the most recent online redo log that has filled but not been archived. If all online redo logs have been filled, then there is nothing to archive. Usage of this option appears in the following example:

```
ALTER SYSTEM ARCHIVE LOG NEXT;
```

Exercises

1. How can the DBA archive redo logs selectively?

2. What statement and parameters are available for the task of selectively archiving redo logs?

Taking Backups After Enabling Archiving

Archiving offers the added protection of knowing that all changes in the database are recorded for posterity in the online redo log, and all online redo logs that are created by Oracle are archived for protection. However, the DBA cannot simply rely on archived redo logs to save the day. Recovery with archiving is slow. In almost all cases, the more recent the backup a DBA has to recover lost information and the fewer the number of archived redo logs there are to apply, the faster database recovery will run. For this reason, backing up the database frequently is still an important feature of database recovery, even when the added protection of archiving is used.

There is an important time for backups in the operation of a database for the DBA to be aware of when using archiving. The DBA must always remember that a backup must be taken of the database immediately after the status of archiving is changed from enabled to disabled, or **archivelog** to **noarchivelog**. This step is important mainly because Oracle writes special information to the backup of a database related to archiving or not archiving. If archiving is enabled but the most recent backup used to recover the database was taken at a time when archiving was not enabled, then archived redo logs may not be applied to the database as part of recovery from that backup. So, in essence, if the DBA enables archiving on a database but does not create a backup of the database when it is in **archivelog** mode status, the archived redo log information is worthless for use in recovery. The DBA should remember to always take a backup of the database after the archiving status of the database changes.

TIP
*Always take a backup of the database after enabling or disabling **archivelog** mode!*

Finally, it may be valuable to the DBA to keep backups of the archived redo logs. Recall earlier in the chapter that if a redo log archive is lost, the database can only be recovered to the point in time just prior to the lost redo log. Therefore, the only choice a DBA will have in this situation is a forced incomplete recovery. Once archived redo logs are placed in the LOG_ARCHIVE_DEST, the DBA is free to move the archives offline or copy them in any manner permitted by the operating system copy commands available on the host machine running Oracle.

Exercise

What is the relationship between backups and archived redo logs?

Chapter Summary

This chapter covers some important areas of Oracle database recovery. There are three main areas this chapter presents, including an introduction to database recovery, the requirements of database recovery without the use of archival of online redo logs, and enabling **archivelog** mode on the Oracle database. The introduction to database recovery covers several different areas, including a review of the various failure scenarios occurring in Oracle and the role of communication in crisis situations. The role of archiving and the various types of database recovery are also presented. This chapter also offers guidance on the steps required for the recovery of a database using full database backups taken offline when archiving is disabled. A special presentation on recovering **read only** tablespaces is also included. Finally, the requirements for initiating archiving on the database are presented. Overall, this chapter is a lengthy one, comprising 27 percent of test material on OCP Exam 3.

The first discussion in this chapter reviewed failure scenarios. There are five different types of failure scenarios in an Oracle database. They are statement failure, process failure, user error, instance failure, and media failure. Statement failure is something that generally occurs as a result of a syntax error on the part of someone issuing a statement against the database. There is usually no need for intervention on this problem, as people must correct the issue for themselves.

Process failure arises as the result of cancellation of a user SQL statement that otherwise was running. The process may have been canceled either by the user, manually, or by Oracle automatically. In order to handle user process failures, Oracle has a built-in process called PMON that monitors user processes. If one should fail, PMON handles cleanup activities like releasing locks the process acquired, rolling back the incomplete transaction, and taking the process off the active process list.

User error is a unique situation on the database whereby some user of the database inadvertently changes data or eliminates a table. Depending on whether the organization has made a commitment to support this situation, the DBA may need to formulate a strategy for handling user error. Generally, the solution for user errors requires the use of backup and recovery. Whatever the commitment for resolving user error, the DBA should ensure that it fits into the overall strategy for backup and recovery on the database.

Instance failure arises when, for some reason, the Oracle instance cannot continue running. Some potential causes for this situation include hardware failure or a power outage. When instance failure occurs on the database, the DBA must identify the root cause of the failure and resolve it before restarting the instance. However, once the instance is restarted, the DBA needn't put that much effort into the instance recovery because the SMON background process will handle the recovery automatically.

Media failure is the problem to watch out for. It is related to the failure of a disk drive on the machine that hosts Oracle. There are two categories for media failure: temporary and permanent. Temporary media failure occurs when something happens that prevents access to database files on a particular disk, but no permanent damage to those files has occurred. For example, the failure of a disk controller device may cause the disk to be inaccessible temporarily. But, when the problem is corrected, the data will again be available for use by Oracle. Permanent media failure occurs when the database disk drive becomes damaged or destroyed and the data on the drive is rendered inaccessible. In this case, the DBA must usually recover the data that was lost from a backed-up version of the database.

The importance of communication, though not critical knowledge for certification, is a real-world skill that a DBA should master. During the crisis event, which produces the need for a database recovery, tempers often flare and there is a serious need for strong communication skills. The DBA should be able to address communication issues in the situation of a crisis so that the users of the database are not left wondering what is happening to recover the damaged system. The importance of speaking to the level of technical understanding for other people in the organization, such as users and managers, was also identified. These groups of people usually have a technical language all their own, which is not similar to the technical language of the DBA. The DBA must bear the information needs of the audience in mind when dealing with crises that create a need for database recovery.

The importance of archiving was again highlighted as an integral part of database recovery. The overall architecture of archiving was detailed for review in this discussion. The architecture for redo log archiving consists of many different components. The first component for redo log archiving is the redo log buffer, a memory area designed to capture the redo information produced by statements changing data in the database. This redo information is written to a disk file, called the online redo log, by a special background process called LGWR. There must be at least two of these online redo log groups in order for Oracle to function properly. LGWR writes data to the redo log group, switching back and forth between them. When one log group fills, LGWR writes to the other log group. This design forces LGWR to overwrite redo information unless the DBA chooses to archive redo log information. When archiving is enabled, then Oracle allows for the archiving, or saving, of redo information. The movement of this data is handled either manually by the DBA or automatically by the ARCH background process.

The DBA should strongly consider archiving redo log entries because it allows for many different options when the need arises to make database recovery happen with the backups available. When archiving is used and recovery is required, Oracle makes the recovery an interactive process with the DBA. Along the way, Oracle suggests archived redo logs to apply based on the contents of its V$ performance views for redo logs, namely V$LOG and V$LOG_HISTORY. The DBA can confirm these suggestions or supply her own recommendation, which Oracle will then use to execute the recovery. In addition, the DBA can use automatic recovery, whereby Oracle will simply apply its suggestions for recovery, bypassing the interactive portion of the recovery.

There are several different types of recovery available to the DBA. One division of recovery options into categories is complete and incomplete recovery. Within complete recovery, there is generally only one type of recovery that is complete. That is the complete recovery made possible with archived redo logs to recover database changes to the moment of the database failure.

Forms of incomplete recovery include any type of recovery that takes place by applying archived redo logs to a point in time in the past. There are three types of incomplete recovery: change-based, time-based, and cancel-based. These three types of database recovery are designed to allow the DBA to recover the database to a point in time in the past, specified by a variety of different methods. The first of these methods is cancel-based recovery. A cancel-based recovery is one that runs based on the interactive part of database recovery with archived redo logs. The recovery will continue to apply archives until Oracle makes a suggestion for the next redo log and the DBA issues the **cancel** command.

Another type of incomplete recovery is the change-based recovery. This recovery is based on the system change numbers (SCN) that Oracle applies to every transaction that runs on the database. When issuing the command for change-based recovery, the DBA must supply a system change number that Oracle will use to determine the stopping point for the recovery. When Oracle completes application of the redo log information for the SCN for the log containing that SCN, the recovery will end automatically. The result is a database that is recovered to a point in time in the past at which the final transaction is the one whose SCN is the one defined at recovery time by the DBA.

The final type of incomplete recovery that uses archiving is the time-based recovery. Perhaps the most straightforward of all incomplete recoveries, the time-based recovery requires the DBA to specify a time to which the database should be recovered. When Oracle has applied enough archived redo information to recover the committed transactions to the point in time specified for time-based recovery, Oracle will automatically cease the recovery effort.

Although there are only the three incomplete recoveries described that work in conjunction with archived redo logs, other types of database recovery that do not work with archived redo also may be considered "incomplete" because they are only capable of recovering data to a point in time in the past. These types of recovery are database imports, described in Chapter 12, and physical recovery based on the full physical offline backups that were explained in Chapter 11. A full recovery from complete backup is handled in the following way. The database must first be shut down. The DBA replaces *all* files in the Oracle database with the backup versions. If need be, the name and/or location of the control file may be changed in the **init.ora** file before mounting the database. At this point, the database can be mounted, but if there was some movement of datafiles or redo log files from one disk to another, the DBA should use the **alter database** statement at this time to ensure Oracle's awareness of the change. Finally, the DBA should open the database using the **resetlogs** option to discard all online redo information.

There are special considerations the DBA must make for recovery of **read only** tablespaces. The golden rule for facilitating recovery on **read only** tablespaces is to always make a backup of the control file after the status of a tablespace changes from **read only** to read-write, or vice versa. Without this backup of the control file, there are always extra steps to manage the recovery of **read only** tablespaces.

The mechanisms to enable archiving were also covered in this chapter. There are several aspects to setting up the database to handle archived redo log information. The first of these items covered is determining whether or not archiving is enabled on the database. One method for handling this step is to look in the V$DATABASE dynamic performance view. Another is to issue the **archive log list** command from within Server Manager. The output from this command not only gives the DBA information about the archiving status, but also gives a great deal of information about the archived redo logs themselves. Finally, if archiving is enabled, the V$LOG view gives information about whether the individual online redo logs have been archived.

Putting the database into **archivelog** mode is perhaps the greatest and simplest step a DBA can take to ensure the recovery of the Oracle database. Archiving is enabled in two ways. First, at the creation of a database with the **create database** statement, the DBA can include the **archivelog** option to begin archiving of redo log entries right away. Alternatively, the DBA can issue the **alter database archivelog** statement to change a previously nonarchiving database into one that archives its redo logs. To change the database into **noarchivelog** mode, the DBA can issue the **alter database noarchivelog** statement. It is important that the DBA take a complete backup of the entire database after changing the archiving status of the database to **archivelog** mode in order to ensure that the database archived redo logs are useful in database recovery. Archived redo logs *cannot* be applied to a database that has been recovered from a backup taken of the database when it was not in **archivelog** mode.

Once the DBA has set the database to **archivelog** mode, she can either handle the archiving of redo logs manually with the **alter system archive log all** statement or by setting Oracle up to handle automatic archiving with the use of the ARCH background process. Automatic archiving is started using the **alter system archive log start** statement. When enabled, the ARCH background process archives redo information automatically every time a log switch occurs, placing them into a destination specified by the value for the LOG_ARCHIVE_DEST in the **init.ora** file. The name ARCH will file the archive under its contingent on the value specified for the LOG_ARCHIVE_ FORMAT parameter, also specified in the **init.ora** file.

To view the archived log list, the DBA may look in the V$LOG_ HISTORY performance view. The ARCHIVE_NAME column contains the name assigned to the archived redo log sequence and thread, based on automatic archiving using the LOG_ARCHIVE_FORMAT parameter. Finally, the DBA can selectively archive redo log information by manually archiving redo with the **alter system archive log** statement. There are several manual options available for selective archiving. They are **seq, change, current, group, logfile**, and **next**. The **seq** option allows the DBA to archive redo logs according to sequence number. Each redo log is assigned a sequence number as LGWR fills the online redo log. The **change** option can be used to archive a redo log that contains a certain SCN. The **current** option archives the redo log that is currently being written by LGWR, which forces Oracle to perform a log switch. The **group** option allows the DBA to specify a redo log group for archiving. The **logfile** option allows the DBA to archive redo logs by named redo log member files. The **next** option allows the DBA to archive redo information based on which redo log is next to be archived. Also, it should be noted that **thread** is also an option for archiving redo logs. A **thread** is a number representing the redo information for a single instance in a multi-instance parallel server setup using Oracle's Parallel Server Option. The **thread** option can be set for any of the options for manually or automatically archiving redo log information using the **alter system archive log** statement.

Two-Minute Drill

- There are two types of media failure: temporary and permanent.

- Temporary media failure is usually the result of hardware failure of something other than the actual disk drive. After it is corrected, the database can access its data again.

- Permanent media failure is usually the result of damage to the disk drive itself. Usually, the drive will need to be replaced and the DBA will need to recover the data on the disk from backup.

- In crisis situations, it is beneficial to the DBA to have strong communication skills to facilitate important decisions in tough situations with input from users and managers.

■ There are several different types of recovery. With archiving in place, the DBA has more options to choose from.

■ Two categories of recovery exist: recovery with archiving and recovery without.

■ In recovery with archiving, there are two categories: complete recovery to the point in time of the database failure, and incomplete recovery to some point in time before the failure occurred.

■ There are three types of incomplete recovery when the database runs in **archivelog** mode: change-based, cancel-based, and time-based.

　■ Change-based recovery is where the DBA specifies a system change number that Oracle should use to denote the end of database recovery.

　■ Time-based recovery is where the DBA specifies a date and time that Oracle should use to determine the end of database recovery.

　■ Cancel-based recovery runs until the DBA issues the **cancel** command, taking advantage of the interactive process that happens as Oracle restores archived redo log information.

■ Automatic recovery can be used to reduce the amount of interaction required for database recovery. When enabled, Oracle will apply its suggestions for archive logs to apply automatically.

■ When the DBA opens the database after recovery, the **resetlogs** option can be used to discard online redo logs and to reset the sequence number.

■ Database recovery can be accomplished from full offline backups. The DBA should ensure that all files are restored from backup, not just damaged ones, to ensure that the database is consistent to a single point in time.

- When restoring **read only** tablespaces, it is important that a backup of the control file be made after the status of the tablespace was changed to read-write or to **read only**.

- There are two methods for determining the archive status of the database: the DBA can look in V$DATABASE or execute **archive log list** from Server Manager.

- The DBA can set archiving on or off using the **archivelog** or **noarchivelog** options in **create database** or **alter database** statements.

- There are two methods available for archiving redo logs: manual and automatic.

- Automatic archiving is started with the **alter system archive log start** statement. Substitute **stop** for **start** to shut off automatic archiving.

- If manual archiving is used, the DBA must make sure to archive redo logs before LGWR runs out of online redo logs to write information to. If archiving is used, LGWR will not overwrite an online redo log until it has been archived. If Oracle runs out of online redo logs for LGWR to write redo information to, no user can make database changes until archiving happens.

- Automatic archiving needs the LOG_ARCHIVE_DEST and LOG_ARCHIVE_FORMAT parameters to be set in **init.ora**.

  - LOG_ARCHIVE_DEST determines where redo log archives will be placed.

  - LOG_ARCHIVE_FORMAT determines the nomenclature for the archived redo information.

- Information about the archived redo log files is listed in the V$LOG_HISTORY dynamic performance view.

- Selective archiving of redo information is possible with the use of several options for manual archiving. Those options are **seq**, **change**, **current**, **group**, **logfile**, **next**, **thread**, and **all**.

- **seq** allows the DBA to archive redo logs according to sequence number. Each redo log is assigned a sequence number as LGWR fills the online redo log.

- **change** can be used to archive a redo log that contains a certain SCN.

- **current** archives the redo log that is currently being written by LGWR, which forces Oracle to perform a log switch.

- **group** allows the DBA to specify a redo log group for archiving.

- **logfile** allows the DBA to archive redo logs by named redo log member files.

- **next** allows the DBA to archive redo information based on which redo log is next to be archived.

- **thread** is also an option for archiving redo logs. A thread is a number representing the redo information for a single instance in a multi-instance parallel server setup using Oracle's Parallel Server Option.

- The **thread** option can be set for any of the options for manually or automatically archiving redo log information using the **alter system archive log** statement.

- The **all** option specifies archival of all redo logs that are currently in need of being archived.

Chapter Questions

I. The type of failure most likely to require recovery from backup is

   A. User error

   B. Statement failure

   C. Process failure

   D. Instance failure

2. **ALTER DATABASE RECOVER AUTOMATIC begins automatic archiving.**

      A. TRUE

      B. FALSE

3. After executing which three situations should the DBA consider backing up the datafiles of a database?

      A. Taking a tablespace offline.

      B. Changing a database to **archivelog** mode.

      C. After a database experiences many data changes.

      D. After substantial numbers of tables are added to the database.

4. The integer assigned to each transaction that takes place in the database is called a

      A. Sequence number

      B. Thread number

      C. System change number

      D. Userid number

5. To put the database into ARCHIVELOG mode, the DBA should issue the _____ statement.

      A. alter database archivelog;

      B. alter system archivelog;

      C. alter database archive log start;

      D. alter system archive log start;

6. Which view contains information about the archiving mode of the database?

      A. V$LOG

      B. V$LOGFILE

      C. V$LOG_HISTORY

      D. V$DATABASE

7. In order to provide a consistent view of the database, the DBA should restore only damaged files when recovering a database from a full, offline backup.

   A. TRUE

   B. FALSE

8. Which two of the following parameters must be set for using automatic archiving?

   A. LOG_ARCHIVE_DEST

   B. BACKGROUND_DUMP_DEST

   C. LOG_ARCHIVE_FORMAT

   D. LOG_ARCHIVE_TIME

9. The name of the background process that handles archiving redo logs is

   A. LGWR

   B. DBWR

   C. ARCH

   D. RECO

10. To selectively archive a redo log entry according to the sequence number, which of the following statements should be issued?

    A. alter system archive log start;

    B. alter database archive log;

    C. alter system archive log seq 34;

    D. alter system archive log current;

11. To view the list of archived redo logs, which operation is appropriate?

    A. Archive log list

    B. select * from v$log_history;

    C. alter system list archive logs;

D. select * from log;

12. **If automatic archiving is not enabled, what will happen on a database in ARCHIVELOG mode if the DBA does not archive in a timely manner?**

    A. Nothing, archiving is handled automatically.

    B. Database performance will degrade slightly.

    C. Database performance will degrade substantially, but will not stop.

    D. The database will not be able to accept any more changes until archiving occurs.

13. **Automatic archiving is enabled. An example filename for a redo log archived is Rdo-3-0003.arc. What is the value for LOG_ARCHIVE_ FORMAT?**

    A. ARCH%T%s.arc

    B. Rdo%T-%s.arc

    C. Rdo-%t-%S.arc

    D. Rdo%t%s.arc

14. **Archived redo logs can be applied to a database if the database was restored from a backup taken when the database was in NOARCHIVELOG mode.**

    A. TRUE

    B. FALSE

15. **To discard redo logs and set the sequence number back to 1 upon opening the database, the DBA should use which of the following options?**

    A. archivelog

    B. resetlogs

    C. exclusive

D. parallel

16. The interactive aspect of database recovery can be eliminated with the use of which of the following options to the ALTER DATABASE statement?

   A. archivelog

   B. resetlogs

   C. automatic

   D. start

Answers to Chapter Questions

I. A.   User error

Explanation   The cause of user error is when a user accidentally makes a permanent change of some sort to the database. To recover from gross user error, the DBA must usually rely on the backups available on the database. Choices B, C, and D are incorrect because recovery from backup is not usually necessary for recovery from these problems.

2. B.   FALSE

Explanation   The **alter database recover automatic** statement initiates database recovery without the interaction between DBA and Oracle to determine which archived redo log to apply. Instead, when **recover automatic** is used, Oracle will simply apply its redo suggestions automatically.

3. B, C, and D.

Explanation   Choice A is inappropriate because the database doesn't necessarily need to be backed up after a tablespace is taken offline.

4. C.   System change number

Explanation   Every transaction on the Oracle database is assigned an SCN. Choices A and B are incorrect because sequence numbers and threads are assigned to redo logs, while choice D is incorrect because userid numbers are assigned to users that are created in Oracle.

5. A.   **alter database archivelog;**

Explanation   Choices B and D are both incorrect because only the **alter database** command can be used to enable archiving of redo logs. **Alter system** is used to handle the act of archiving redo logs. Choice C is incorrect for the very reason that **alter system** is used to handle the act of archiving redo logs, not **alter database**.

6. D.   V$DATABASE

Explanation   Choice A is incorrect because V$LOG contains information about the online redo logs for the database. Choice B is incorrect because V$LOGFILE contains information about the members of each of the online redo log groups in the Oracle database. Choice C is incorrect because V$LOG_HISTORY contains information about all redo logs archived for the database.

7. B.   FALSE

Explanation   In order to provide a read-consistent view of the database, the DBA should restore all files from the full offline backup.

8. A and C.   LOG_ARCHIVE_DEST and LOG_ARCHIVE_FORMAT

Explanation   Choice B is not correct because BACKGROUND_DUMP_DEST has no relevance to archiving except to identify where the **alert** log is, a fact not required for this question. Choice D represents a fictional initialization parameter, and therefore is not correct.

9. C.   ARCH

Explanation   LGWR handles writing redo entries to the online redo log, and therefore choice A is wrong. DBWR handles the transfer of datafile blocks to and from the buffer cache, and therefore choice B is wrong. RECO handles recovery on transactions between different database nodes on a distributed database format, and therefore choice D is incorrect.

10. C.   **alter system archive log seq 34;**

Explanation   In order to use the **seq** option, an integer representing the sequence number must be included. Choice A is incorrect because the **start** option is used to initiate automatic archiving of redo logs. Choice B is incorrect because the DBA must specify some option for archiving redo logs with the **alter system archive log** statement. Choice D is incorrect because the **current** option archives the current redo log being written regardless of sequence number, which is not what the question asked for.

11. B.   **select * from v$log_history;**

Explanation   Choice A is incorrect because the **archive log list** statement is designed to list information about archiving redo information. Choice C is incorrect because the statement is fictitious. Choice D is incorrect because V$LOG contains information only about the current set of redo logs.

12. D.   The database will not be able to accept any more changes until archiving occurs.

Explanation   With choice D correct, all other choices are logically incorrect. The reason choice D is correct is because all transactions must write redo information, and Oracle will not overwrite a redo log until it has been archived if archiving is enabled. Thus, if the DBA does not use automatic archiving or manually archive redo in a timely manner, then the database operations will halt except for **select** statements until archiving is performed.

13. C.   Rdo-%t-%S.arc

Explanation   This format is the only one that ARCH could use to produce an archived redo log with a filename similar to the one listed. Recall that the formatting conventions for thread and sequence numbers are uppercase for left-padded numbers and lowercase for nonpadded numbers. All other characters in the name of the file must appear in the format where the DBA would like them to appear in the filename ARCH gives to the files.

14. B.   FALSE

Explanation   In order for archived redo information to be applicable to datafiles, the datafiles themselves must be in **archivelog** mode. If the datafile was lost in a media failure and the only backup of that datafile was taken when the database was not in **archivelog** mode, then the archived redo logs may not be used for database recovery.

15. B.   resetlogs

Explanation   The **resetlogs** option is used at database opening time to reset the log sequence number. **Archivelog** is used in the **alter database** statement, and is not applicable to how the database should be opened. Therefore, choice A is incorrect. **Exclusive** refers to the mode in which the database should be mounted during recovery, not opened. Therefore, choice C is incorrect. **Parallel** refers to an option for running the Oracle database and does not relate to how the DBA should discard redo logs and reset the sequence number. Therefore, choice D is incorrect.

16. C.   automatic

Explanation   **Archivelog** is used in the **alter database** statement, and is not applicable to how the database should be opened. Therefore, choice A is incorrect. **Resetlogs** relates to how the DBA should discard redo logs and reset the sequence number. Therefore, choice B is incorrect. **Start** is an option used in the **alter system archive log** statement to begin automatic archival of online redo logs, which doesn't relate to the disabling of interaction between the DBA and Oracle during database recovery. Therefore, choice D is incorrect.

CHAPTER
14

Backup and Recovery Options with Archiving

n this chapter, you will understand and demonstrate knowledge in the following areas:

- Supporting 24-hour operations
- Complete recovery with archiving
- Incomplete recovery with archiving

There are several areas that this chapter focuses on. First, an in-depth discussion will be presented on the methods used for backing up the database that must be available 24 hours a day. The methodology presented for backups on 24-hour operations is only available when archiving is used. After covering the concepts and functions involved in backup on 24-hour databases, the discussion will focus on methods for complete recovery of all committed transactions to the time the database experienced media failure when archiving is enabled. The steps involved for this task, along with explanations and examples, will be presented. Finally, the potential for incomplete recovery with archiving will also be presented. These three main context areas comprise approximately 35 percent of the test, making understanding this chapter most critical for your passing the OCP DBA Exam 3.

Supporting 24-Hour Operations

In this chapter, you will cover the following topics related to supporting 24-hour operations:

- Online vs. offline backups
- Online backup methods
- Online backup of the control file

Today's corporations need more database availability for a global user base and/or a 24-hour workforce. They need databases that are available on a 24-hour basis as well. Supporting organizations with high availability requirements puts intense pressure on the DBA in two ways. First, many of the options presented, such as database export or offline full backups, are not viable strategies for database recovery. The only viable option is the one that takes advantage of archiving—online hot backups. The second factor is the additional pressure on the DBA to recover the database as quickly as possible. Since the database has users at all hours of the day, the DBA has pressure to restore the 24-hour database at all times, day or night.

Online vs. Offline Backups

A live database is always in flux. Data is stored to disk at times determined by the background processes DBWR and LGWR. Data from transactions that have been committed may not have actually been stored to database files. In order to ensure that all data is captured in a cold backup, it is required that the DBA close the database using **shutdown normal** from the Server Manager prompt. After the database has been shut down, all database file components are then copied and archived using operating system commands. The following bullet points list the five types of files that must be archived in order to restore the database:

- **Datafiles**   Store the tables, indexes, rollback segments, other segments, and data dictionary.

- **Redo logs**   Store the nonarchived redo log entries of the database.

- **Control files**   Store the physical database location data.

- **Parameter files**   Also called **init.ora** files, store all parameters used for database instance startup.

- **Password file**   Stores encrypted password information for DBAs on the system when Oracle password authentication is used.

Allocating enough space for a copy of all database files may be difficult, especially for large databases. Ideally, enough space can be allocated to store all files on disk first to complete the backup before transferring files to offline storage. This method not only minimizes downtime for the offline backup, but also improves recovery time if the DBA can keep some of the backups on disk in case of media failure. Offline backups by themselves offer coverage for minimal point-in-time recovery on database systems. With archived redo logs, the recovery options for offline backups expand to include recovery to any point in time up to point of disk failure. It is important for the DBA to use archiving with offline database backups for systems requiring more options than point-in-time recovery.

In globally deployed systems that require a range of availability for all hours of night and day corresponding to users in other areas of the world, offline backup may not be possible. The organization simply may not be able to allocate enough time per week to allow DBAs to take the database down in **normal** mode. As an alternative to be used in support of global operations that require round-the-clock online access, the DBA can use Oracle's online backup method. Executing an online backup is an iterative process that creates backed-up copies of the database, tablespace by tablespace. In order to execute a hot backup, the DBA must execute the **alter tablespace** *name* **begin backup** command in Server Manager. An example of the command syntax in action appears in the following code block:

```
ALTER TABLESPACE data_01 BEGIN BACKUP;
```

After issuing this command, the DBA makes a copy of all datafiles associated with the tablespace using operating system copy commands. The DBA issues the **alter tablespace** *name* **end backup** command from Server Manager.

```
ALTER TABLESPACE data_01 END BACKUP;
```

TIP
*It is highly recommended by Oracle that the tablespaces be backed up with the iterative approach, placed into **backup** mode with the **alter tablespace begin backup** statement one at a time, rather than setting all tablespaces into **backup** mode at once. Using the iterative approach minimizes the chance that a tablespace will be in **backup** mode at a time when the disk drive crashes or when the entire instance stops running for some reason.*

Exercises

1. Identify the two areas DBAs are typically pressured to perform or deliver with respect to backup and recovery support for 24-hour database operations.

2. Identify differences between online and offline backups. Determine the appropriateness of using archiving for recovery with both online and offline backups. Which backup option requires archiving?

Online Backup Methods

In order to guarantee that the changes made to the tablespace while the online backup took place are kept, it is required that the DBA archive redo logs that were taken during the operation of online backups. Prior to taking the online backup, the DBA should issue the **archive log list** command from Server Manager in order to determine the oldest online redo log sequence that should be saved in conjunction with the online backups being taken. Once the tablespace backups are complete, the **archive log list** command should be issued again, followed by a log switch to ensure that the current redo log entries made for the tablespaces backed up are archived properly for use by the backups should recovery be necessary. The steps to the process are listed below:

1. Execute **archive log list** from Server Manager. Note value for "Oldest online log sequence." This is the oldest redo log required for using the online backup.

   ```
   SVRMGR> ARCHIVE LOG LIST
   ```

Database log mode	ARCHIVELOG
automatic archival	ENABLED
Archive destination	/u01/oracle/home/arch
Oldest online log sequence	21
Next log sequence to archive	25
Current log sequence	25

2. Execute **alter tablespace** *name* **begin backup** from Server Manager. This step prepares the tablespace for online backup.

   ```
   SVRMGR> ALTER TABLESPACE users_01 BEGIN BACKUP;
   ```

3. Copy the datafiles for that tablespace using operating system commands or third party products. Be sure the copy resides on another disk than the production datafiles themselves.

4. Execute **alter tablespace** *name* **end backup** from Server Manager. This step completes the online backup process for that tablespace.

```
SVRMGR> ALTER TABLESPACE users_02 BEGIN BACKUP;
```

5. Repeat steps 2–4 for all tablespaces to be backed up.

6. Execute **archive log list** again from Server Manager. Note value for "Current log sequence" this time. This is the last redo log required for using the online backup.

```
SVRMGR> ARCHIVE LOG LIST
```

```
Database log mode              ARCHIVELOG
automatic archival             ENABLED
Archive destination            /u01/oracle/home/arch
Oldest online log sequence     21
Next log sequence to archive   33
Current log sequence           33
```

7. Issue an **alter system switch logfile** to cause Oracle to create an archive of the current redo log. This archive should then be stored in the LOG_ARCHIVE_DEST area. If desired, copy the archives associated with the backup to tape.

```
SVRMGR> ALTER SYSTEM SWITCH LOGFILE;
```

8. Create a copy of the control file. This is done with the **alter database backup controlfile** statement.

TIP

A control file must be backed up whenever a change is made to the structure of a database. For example, after the creation of a new tablespace, or an addition or removal of a datafile, the control file for the database must be backed up.

It is possible to perform parallel online backups of the tablespaces of the database. The code block following this paragraph will illustrate parallel online tablespace backup. However, this method *is not recommended.*

Taking tablespace backups iteratively allows less time between the beginning and the end of a tablespace backup. Minimizing backup time is important because less time for backup means there is less time when the database is exposed to the problems caused by database failure while a backup is taking place. The second reason for taking online tablespace backups iteratively is that the amount of redo information written is larger and more extensive during online backups than during normal operation of the database.

```
ALTER TABLESPACE users01 BEGIN BACKUP;
ALTER TABLESPACE data01 BEGIN BACKUP;
ALTER TABLESPACE index01 BEGIN BACKUP;
...
ALTER TABLESPACE users01 END BACKUP;
ALTER TABLESPACE data01 END BACKUP;
ALTER TABLESPACE index01 END BACKUP;
```

TIP
*Two reasons not to take online tablespaces in parallel are that during the period of time a backup is occurring, the database is vulnerable to a system crash. To avoid leaving the system vulnerable for extended periods of time, the DBA should run online backups iteratively. The second reason for performing backups in this way is that redo log information is more substantial for transactions on tablespaces when the tablespace is in **backup** mode.*

Exercises

1. What are the steps required for taking an online backup?

2. What is the difference between taking online backups in an iterative fashion and taking them in a parallel fashion?

3. What are the advantages and drawbacks for parallel tablespace backups?

Online Backups of the Control File

Taking an online backup of the control file is accomplished in two different ways. The first way provides the DBA with a backup of the actual database control file, which is then used if there is a media failure that causes damage to a control file on the database. The method used to handle backup of this control file is the **alter database backup controlfile** statement. An example of usage for this statement appears in the following code block:

```
ALTER DATABASE orgdb01 BACKUP CONTROLFILE TO name;
```

There is another method available for database backup of control files as well, using the same syntax with the addition of a special keyword called **trace** to use in place of *name*. In this situation, Oracle creates the script required to create the control file. This file is created in the trace file directory specified by the BACKGROUND_DUMP_DEST parameter of the **init.ora** file. An example for usage of the **trace** option is described in the following code block:

```
ALTER DATABASE orgdb01 BACKUP CONTROLFILE TO TRACE;
```

Exercise

What are the two options for backups of control files?

Complete Recovery with Archiving

In this section, you will cover the following topics related to complete recovery with archiving:

- Complete recovery methodology
- Complete recovery scenarios

Complete recovery can be accomplished in two different ways: with offline backups or with online tablespace backups. Either way, however, the DBA must have all redo logs written by Oracle after the database was restarted for full offline backups, or all redo logs written during the database backup and after the backup to the point in time of the failure in the case of online backups. If the criteria for either scenario are met, the DBA can run a complete recovery of the database. This section will describe the process of making complete recovery happen to the point in time of a database failure using both online and offline backups, and the application of archived redo logs. It will also illustrate those processes with examples for each.

Complete Recovery Methodology

Recovery to the point of media failure on the Oracle database requires two things. First, the DBA requires some sort of database backup for the files that were lost in the media failure. This backup can either be online tablespace backups or offline database backup. The other component is a complete set of archived redo logs for the period of time following the backup, and in the case of hot online backups, redo information that was taken during the period of the backup. The requirements for backups and archived redo logs for complete recovery are illustrated in Figure 14-1.

After restoring the database from backup components, the recovery takes place. Oracle looks for archived redo logs in the location specified by the LOG_ARCHIVE_DEST parameter of the **init.ora** file. An alternate location for the archived redo logs can be specified manually by the DBA using the **from** clause in the **alter database recover** statement. An example for usage of **alter database recover** in which an alternate location for archived redo log files is specified appears in the following code block:

```
ALTER DATABASE RECOVER FROM '/u03/archive/alt' ... ;
```

Backup datafiles, redo logs, control files

Archived redo logs

FIGURE 14-1. *Requirements for complete recovery*

The database cannot be open for use during a full recovery. The DBA can shut it down using **shutdown abort**. Using this option forces Oracle to require media recovery the next time the database is opened.

```
SHUTDOWN ABORT;
```

Complete Recovery with Disk Replacement

After making any hardware repairs or replacements necessary, the following steps are necessary to make complete recovery. These steps are accomplished only when the disk media that failed is replaced before recovery begins.

1. Restore all files from the complete backup taken, including datafiles, redo log files, and control files. All files should be restored—not just damaged ones—in order for the entire database to be read consistent to a single point in time, unless complete recovery using archive logs will be performed. In this case, only lost files should be recovered. Operating system copy commands are used to handle this step.

2. Recover the database using archived redo log information. The command syntax for this process is the **alter database recover database** statement. This statement will begin the interactive process of applying redo log information:

```
ALTER DATABASE RECOVER DATABASE;
```

3. Take a full backup of the database. Use operating system copy commands for this step.

4. Open the database for use with the **resetlogs** option.

```
ALTER DATABASE OPEN RESETLOGS;
```

Complete Recovery Without Disk Replacement

It may not be possible to secure a repair or replacement for the disk(s) that failed. In these situations, the DBA may need to recover the database by placing files that were on the damaged disk onto other disks. The database must be closed for this process, and the other steps are listed.

1. Restore all files from the complete backup taken, including datafiles, redo log files, and control files. It is important that all files be

restored—not just damaged ones—in order for the entire database to
be read consistent to a single point in time (the point in time of the
last database backup), unless complete recovery using archive logs
will be performed. In this case, only lost files should be recovered.
Operating system copy commands are used to handle this step for
database recovery from a full backup.

2. Move control files to other disks if they were lost in media failure.
Change the location of control files as specified in the
CONTROL_FILES parameter of the **init.ora** file to reflect a new
location for the control file of the Oracle database.

3. Mount the database in **exclusive** mode.

4. Move datafiles and redo log files onto other disks with the **alter
database rename file** statement from Server Manager. The full
pathnames for the datafile at the old and the new locations should
be specified in the statement.

```
ALTER DATABASE orgdb01
RENAME FILE '/u01/oracle/data/data_301a.dbf'
TO '/u02/oracle/data/data_301b.dbf';

ALTER DATABASE orgdb01
RENAME FILE '/u01/oracle/ctl/rdorgdb01'
TO '/u02/oracle/ctl/rdorgdb01';
```

5. Recover the database using archived redo log information. The
command syntax for this process is the **alter database recover
database** statement. This statement will begin the interactive process
of applying redo log information:

```
ALTER DATABASE RECOVER DATABASE;
```

6. Back up the database.

7. Open the database using the **resetlogs** option.

```
ALTER DATABASE OPEN RESETLOGS;
```

Tablespace Recovery

Recovery can be performed on individual tablespaces in addition to the entire database. The DBA can execute a tablespace recovery using the **alter database recover tablespace** statement. The database must be open in order to accomplish a tablespace recovery, so that Oracle can view the contents of the database while the tablespace recovery occurs. However, the tablespace itself must be offline. A benefit to tablespace recovery is that the DBA can allow users to access other tablespaces while the offline tablespace is restored. In this example, assume that the USERS01 tablespace needs to be recovered.

1. Open the database if it is not already open.

   ```
   ALTER DATABASE OPEN;
   ```

2. Take the tablespace on the disk(s) that failed offline.

   ```
   ALTER TABLESPACE users01 OFFLINE;
   ```

3. Restore damaged datafiles with their respective backup copies using operating system commands, assuming hardware problems have been rectified. If the hardware problem has not been rectified, or if the DBA decides to move the files of the tablespace to another disk, the DBA should issue the appropriate **alter database rename file** command.

   ```
   ALTER DATABASE
   RENAME FILE '/u01/oracle/home/data01.dbf'
    TO '/u02/oracle/home/data01.dbf';
   ```

4. Recover the tablespace. To minimize the amount of interaction required between DBA and Oracle, the DBA can include the **automatic** keyword in the **alter database** statement, allowing Oracle to automatically apply its own suggestions for redo logs.

   ```
   ALTER DATABASE RECOVER AUTOMATIC TABLESPACE users01;
   ```

5. Back up the database.

6. Bring the tablespace online using the **alter tablespace online** statement.

   ```
   ALTER TABLESPACE users01 ONLINE;
   ```

Datafile Recovery

Recovery can be performed on individual datafiles in the tablespace with the **alter database recover datafile** statement. The database and tablespace must be open in order to accomplish datafile recovery so that Oracle can view the contents of the database while the datafile recovery occurs. However, the datafile itself must be offline. A benefit to datafile recovery is that the DBA can allow users to access other tablespaces while the offline datafile is restored. In this example, assume that the **users01a.dbf** datafile needs to be recovered.

1. Open the database if it is not already open.

   ```
   ALTER DATABASE OPEN;
   ```

2. Take the datafile on the disk(s) that failed offline.

   ```
   ALTER DATABASE DATAFILE 'users01a.dbf' OFFLINE;
   ```

3. Restore damaged datafiles with their respective backup copies using operating system commands, assuming hardware problems have been rectified. If the hardware problem has not been rectified, or if the DBA decides to move the file to another disk, the DBA should issue the appropriate **alter database rename file** command.

   ```
   ALTER DATABASE
   RENAME FILE '/u01/oracle/home/data01a.dbf'
    TO '/u02/oracle/home/data01a.dbf';
   ```

4. Recover the datafile. To minimize the amount of interaction required between DBA and Oracle, the DBA can include the **automatic** keyword in the **alter database** statement, allowing Oracle to automatically apply its own suggestions for redo logs.

   ```
   ALTER DATABASE RECOVER AUTOMATIC DATAFILE 'users01a.dbf';
   ```

5. Back up the database.

6. Bring the tablespace online using the **alter database datafile online** statement.

   ```
   ALTER DATABASE DATAFILE 'users01a.dbf' ONLINE;
   ```

Exercises

1. What database recovery procedure is performed when damaged disks are replaced? What database recovery procedure is performed when datafiles of other database files must be moved? Can the database be available?

2. What is the procedure for tablespace recovery? Can the database be available?

3. What is the procedure for datafile recovery? Can the database be available?

Complete Recovery Scenarios

The following discussion will present an example of a crisis situation that requires database recovery. A permanent media failure has occurred on two disks, which destroyed several datafiles for two different tablespaces, DATA01 and INDEX01. Hardware support has installed and formatted replacement drives for the disks that failed, thereby eliminating the DBA's need to move the tablespaces to different disks. For this example, the DBA should assume that all the backups are available, along with all archived redo logs.

Scenario 1: Full Offline Backups

The first step required in this situation is to restore the appropriate files from backup to the disks that were replaced. There are three datafiles corresponding to one of the tablespaces that failed, **data01a.dbf**, **data01b.dbf**, and **datao1c.dbf** for DATA01. The other tablespace, INDEX01, consists of only one datafile, **index01a.dbf**. The DBA must first restore all copies of the database datafiles to the empty disks. However, since the DBA uses full offline backups as the cornerstone of the database recovery strategy, the DBA must restore all datafiles to all appropriate disks in order to maintain a read-consistent database. This step is accomplished manually, as illustrated in Figure 14-2.

Once all datafiles are copied into their proper locations, the DBA can then initiate recovery of the entire database. This step allows Oracle to rewrite all database changes made after the full backup was taken. This step is accomplished with the use of the **alter database recover database** statement

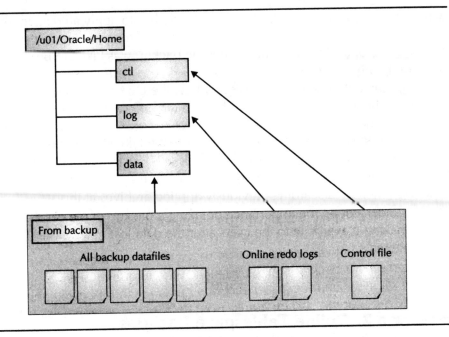

FIGURE 14-2. *Recovering all datafiles using full offline backups*

from SQL*Plus, or simply the **recover database** command from Server Manager. The DBA can issue this statement from either tool according to the syntactic requirements illustrated in the following code block:

```
SQL> ALTER DATABASE orgdb01 RECOVER DATABASE;
SVRMGR> RECOVER DATABASE;
```

Oracle will prompt the DBA to specify archived redo logs to apply in order to facilitate the complete recovery. To ease the effort required from the DBA, Oracle will provide suggested names of archived redo logs to apply based on the values for the LOG_ARCHIVE_DEST, LOG_ARCHIVE_FORMAT, and the V$LOG_HISTORY dynamic performance views. If the archived redo log Oracle suggests the DBA apply is appropriate, the DBA need only press the ENTER key. Otherwise, the DBA can manually key in the appropriate redo log to apply. The database recovery may run for a long time, depending on how many redo logs there are to apply to the database. Another factor that increases the time recovery will take in this situation is the fact that Oracle has to apply all data in the archived redo logs to all tablespaces. The recovery from backup in this case causes all database changes made after the backup was taken to be discarded, only to be reentered from archived redo entries.

When the database recovery is complete, the DBA should take a full backup of the recovered database. This step will allow a full recovery at least to the moment in time the database was restored. The steps required for a full backup are detailed in Chapter 11. After taking the full backup, the DBA will be able to open the database. This step can be done with the **alter database open** statement. It should be noted that the DBA should reset the redo logs, thereby discarding previously applied archives at this stage, and thereby underscoring the importance of taking a backup of the database before making it available to the users after the data lost in a disaster has been restored.

```
ALTER DATABASE orgdb01 OPEN RESETLOGS;
```

Scenario 2: Online Tablespace Backups

This scenario requires several things from the DBA: a backup copy of the datafiles for each tablespace lost and all archived redo logs taken during the online tablespace backup *and* the archived redo information taken after the backup was completed. With these items available, the recovery can begin. The first thing required of the DBA is to put the datafiles onto the new disks that replaced the disks that failed. This step, like the complete recovery of a full offline backup, is accomplished using the commands and/or utilities available from the operating system.

After this step is complete, the DBA must recover the tablespaces to the same point in time as other tablespaces in the database. To do this, recall that the database must be open. If the database is not open already, the following statement can be issued:

```
ALTER DATABASE orgdbo01 OPEN;
```

Recall, however, that the tablespace that is being recovered cannot be available for regular usage. In this case, there are two tablespaces that cannot be available. As a result, the DBA must take these tablespaces offline. The command syntax for doing so lies in the **alter tablespace** statement in the following code block:

```
ALTER TABLESPACE data01 OFFLINE;
ALTER TABLESPACE index01 OFFLINE;
```

Now that the prerequisites for completing recovery specifically for the tablespaces lost in the database failure are complete, the DBA can pursue the recovery of those tablespaces lost with the **recover tablespace** command run from Server Manager, or the **alter database recover tablespace** statement run from SQL*Plus. The statement in the following code block will initiate the interactive process between Oracle and the DBA to recover the database to the point where media failure damaged the tablespaces irreparably:

```
ALTER DATABASE orgdb01 RECOVER TABLESPACE data01, index01;
```

Overall, the recovery of the individual tablespaces is faster than the time required for a database recovery, even though both recovery strategies use the same archived redo information. The reason for this brevity in producing a recovered database with the **recover tablespace** option is due to the fact that Oracle will not apply as much redo from the archived redo log to recover a tablespace as it would in recovery of a full database.

After tablespace recovery is complete for DATA01 and INDEX01, the DBA can bring the tablespaces back online with the **alter tablespace** *name* **online** statement. Also, the DBA may want to take an online backup of the tablespaces that were damaged as part of the media failure. This additional precaution allows the DBA to recover the tablespaces just recovered more easily in the event of some emergency. In fact, the DBA may want to take online backups for all tablespaces at this time.

In general, online backups offer the DBA a great deal of flexibility for backup strategies that must work around 24-hour database availability requirements. When the need arises to recover the database, the DBA has many options to reduce recovery time, and leave undamaged parts of the database untouched by the recovery effort and available to the users of the database. However, one option that online backups of tablespaces do not grant is incomplete recovery. The reason incomplete recovery is impossible is because it would leave the recovered portion of the database in an inconsistent state with the rest of the database, which was undamaged by the database media failure and therefore untouched by the database recovery.

In order to provide the users with incomplete recovery, the DBA must employ other options. One strategy the DBA may want to use is a periodic complete backup with the database offline. Usually, all databases but the ones to which 24-hour availability is most mission-critical should be able to sustain downtime at some point in a weekly or monthly cycle. However, for those databases that cannot, the DBA may have to employ a strategy whereby he or she recovers the database to another machine with the use of online backups, then exports the objects that must be recovered to a point in time in the past. This strategy is also useful in situations where user error requires the DBA to correct an improper data change.

Exercises

1. Which recovery scenarios in this discussion minimize downtime?

2. What initialization parameters does Oracle use to formulate the recommendations for applied archived redo logs?

Incomplete Recovery with Archiving

In this section, you will cover the following topics related to incomplete recovery with archiving:

- When to use incomplete recovery

- Why incomplete recovery may be necessary

- The incomplete recovery process

- Incomplete recovery and recreating the control file

The DBA may have to recover the database to a point in time in the past, at which time a backup may or may not have been taken. Archiving allows the DBA to make incomplete recovery. This discussion will present several aspects of incomplete recovery, from understanding what situations will require the DBA to execute incomplete recovery to the processes required for executing incomplete recovery. Also, the implications of incomplete recovery when the control file must be re-created will be a topic of presentation as well.

When to Use Incomplete Recovery

Incomplete recovery is recovery to a point in time in the past, before a media failure occurred. By definition, any database recovery that does not involve the application of archived redo information is an incomplete recovery. This fact is true because it is the application of archived redo information that brings the database to a state of complete recovery. Logical backup and recovery methods using EXPORT and IMPORT do not permit the possibility of complete recovery, for although database exports can be imported to provide recovery to a point in time, the DBA cannot necessarily pick an arbitrary point in time to recover the database to. Rather, that point in time is determined by when the backup completes.

TIP
The status of the datafiles in a database that may need to be recovered can be determined with use of the V$RECOVERY_FILE_STATUS dynamic performance view. The status of a database recovery overall may be determined using the V$RECOVERY_STATUS view.

Just as archived redo log information allows the DBA a great deal of flexibility in allowing complete recovery to the exact point in time the database media failure occurred, archived redo information also allows the DBA to perform recovery to just about any point in between. The point, then, can be specified in a variety of ways, allowing the DBA to perform both complete recovery to the point in time of the database failure as well as incomplete recovery to any point in time desired.

There are three other types of database recovery that have already been introduced. These three types of recovery are change-based recovery, cancel-based recovery, and time-based recovery. These types of recovery are based entirely on the availability of archived redo logs for the purpose of restoring changes made. These categories for database recovery are named based on the mechanisms that Oracle and the DBA will use to end the recovery. These three types of recovery will generally take place only when the database has been mounted in **exclusive** mode and otherwise left closed.

Change-based recovery is the first type considered. In change-based recovery, Oracle will restore database changes made up to the change that is specified by the DBA as part of the command that initiates the recovery. The DBA may in some cases use the change-based recovery option to identify the last known good transaction to have taken place, for the purpose of recovering the database to the point just after that transaction committed. The change that indicates the end of the recovery to Oracle is defined with the use of a system change number, or SCN. The SCN is a number that Oracle assigns to every transaction that occurs in the database. This "transaction ID number" is then attached to every statement that executes as part of the transaction. The change information can then be tracked both in the rollback segments and the online redo logs, gathering all statements that make changes together as one transaction. The SCN is specified as an integer. To find the last SCN archived by Oracle or what the SCN that was written at the last checkpoint was, the DBA can query the V$DATABASE dynamic performance view. The following statement illustrates how the DBA may use the change-based recovery. The number 4043 is the SCN for a transaction in the online redo log. When the recovery procedure reaches transaction number 4043, Oracle will apply the database changes that were committed as part of that transaction. After that point, Oracle will terminate the recovery automatically.

```
ALTER DATABASE orgdb01 RECOVER DATABASE UNTIL CHANGE 4043;
```

TIP

The SCN of the last transaction conducted at a checkpoint can be found in the V$DATABASE dynamic performance view. To find the SCN of a particular transaction in an archived redo log, the V$LOG_HISTORY performance view can be used.

Rather than restoring to a system change number, which may be hard for the DBA to ascertain, the incomplete database recovery may be conducted to a certain point in time instead. This type of recovery is considered to be a time-based recovery. Time-based and change-based recoveries are similar in that Oracle will restore data to the database to some point in the past. The big difference is that the DBA can identify a point in time rather than dig through the database to identify the system change number for the last transaction committed at a point in time. Once the recovery has applied redo information for *all committed* transactions through the time named, the recovery will end automatically. If uncommitted data was written in order to supply the database with all committed information to the time named, then the uncommitted transaction data will be rolled back before the recovery ends. The final type of incomplete recovery considered is the cancel-based recovery, which allows the DBA to run a database recovery for an indefinite period, defined on the fly by the DBA as the recovery executes. During the course of the recovery, the DBA may choose to issue a **cancel** command, and the recovery will stop. The cancel-based recovery offers the DBA unmatched control over the execution of database recovery; however, it carries with that control the responsibility of the DBA to monitor the recovery process. More details about these types of database recovery are discussed a little later in this chapter.

Exercises

1. What are the three types of incomplete recovery?

2. Which type of incomplete recovery cannot be run in conjunction with automatic recovery?

3. Can the database be available during incomplete recovery? Why or why not?

Why Incomplete Recovery May Be Necessary

The DBA may use incomplete recovery for several reasons. In a system fed daily with valid value or core data, an incorrect feed of information may cause transactions to be conducted based on incorrect information. However, there are other situations where the database may require incomplete recovery. For example, in the situation of a user error, a database might require recovery to the point where a database object existed in one state such that the DBA can export that singular database object. The DBA may restore the information to a duplicate database and populate the production version of the database with the object as it appeared in the past, thus correcting a user error.

Incomplete recovery may be the result of a lack of choice on the part of the DBA. Somewhere along the line, an archived redo log may get lost or damaged. If a situation arises where the redo information for a database on a specific redo log sequence is lost, then the database cannot be recovered beyond that point via the application of archived redo logs. Thus, unless there is a baseline backup to work with that was taken after the missing archived redo log, the database cannot be recovered past the point in time representing the gap in redo log information. So, if an archived redo log is lost, the DBA may have no choice but to perform incomplete recovery.

Exercises

1. What are some reasons incomplete recovery with archiving might be used by the DBA?

2. Why is incomplete recovery with archiving better than recovery without archiving for point-in-time recovery?

Incomplete Recovery Process

The command used to perform database recovery is the **alter database recover** statement issued from SQL*Plus, or the **recover** command in Server Manager. At the time one of these commands is issued, the database cannot be opened or available for use, and must be mounted by only one database instance. The DBA may want to issue the following statements to prepare the database for incomplete recovery, executed from within Server Manager:

```
SHUTDOWN ABORT;
ALTER DATABASE MOUNT EXCLUSIVE;
```

Incomplete recovery should be executed on the entire database. An incomplete recovery cannot be performed on only one tablespace in Oracle7, because the database would then be left in a read-inconsistent state. By performing the incomplete recovery on the entire database, the DBA keeps the database read consistent with a moment in time in the past. The next step in incomplete recovery is to restore the database from a backup copy. This step must be done with a full backup, to create a benchmark copy of the

Oracle database at a point in time. Alternately, several tablespace backups can be used, as long as all the backups were taken at a point in time prior to the point to which the DBA wants to recover.

In case of media failure associated with the need for incomplete recovery, the DBA may have to place datafiles on alternate disk media. If this is the case, the DBA may want to issue some **alter database rename file** statements to update the control file with the location changes. For the purposes of this discussion, assume that all datafiles will stay in the same location. After recovering the datafiles from the operating system perspective, the DBA can then move onto complete the recovery from the perspective of Oracle by applying the archived redo log information. Provided that Oracle has handled archiving automatically, the location from which Oracle will pull archived redo log files is specified by the pathname in the LOG_ARCHIVE_DEST parameter in the **init.ora** file. If automatic archiving has not been used, the LOG_ARCHIVE_DEST parameter may or may not be specified. To specify a location from which to draw archived redo information, the DBA can include a **from** clause. Consider the following code block:

```
ALTER DATABASE orgdb01
RECOVER FROM '/u02/oracle/archive' … ;
```

As stated before, the incomplete recovery must be a database-wide recovery involving the application of archived redo information to all datafiles of all tablespaces. This process requires the use of the **database** clause in the **alter database** statement. The following code block demonstrates the proper use of the database clause:

```
ALTER DATABASE orgdb01
RECOVER FROM '/u02/oracle/archive
DATABASE UNTIL …;
```

The three incomplete recovery processes begin to differentiate after the **until** keyword. The specifications for each of the incomplete recovery processes appear after this keyword, and tell Oracle when and how to identify the moment recovery is over. To refresh the discussion, recovery can be stopped on the application of a specific system change number (SCN). Alternately, database recovery can cease at a point in time in the past, or via an explicit **cancel** issued by the DBA in the interactive process between Oracle and the DBA that marks the application of archived redo information during database recovery.

Change-Based Recovery

Oracle will restore database changes made up to the change that is specified by the DBA as part of the command that initiates the recovery. The change that indicates the end of the recovery to Oracle is defined with the use of a system change number, or SCN. The SCN is a number that Oracle assigns to every transaction that occurs in the database. The SCN is specified as an integer. To find the last SCN archived by Oracle or what the SCN that was written at the last checkpoint was, the DBA can query the V$DATABASE dynamic performance view. The following statement illustrates how the DBA may use the change-based recovery. The number 39983 is the SCN for a transaction in the online redo log. When the recovery procedure reaches transaction number 39983, Oracle will apply the database changes that were committed as part of that transaction. After that point, Oracle will terminate the recovery automatically.

```
ALTER DATABASE orgdb01
RECOVER AUTOMATIC FROM '/u02/oracle/archive'
DATABASE UNTIL CHANGE 39983;
```

In the database recovery statement listed in the code block above, several things are happening. First, the database will be recovered automatically, meaning that interaction between Oracle and the DBA will be minimized during the database recovery. Instead of prompting the DBA to supply names of archived redo logs while simultaneously offering suggestions for redo to apply, Oracle will simply apply its own redo log suggestions and inform the DBA if there is a problem. Once transaction 39983 has been applied in its committed entirety, the database recovery is complete and Oracle concludes the recovery automatically.

Time-Based Recovery

The incomplete database recovery may also be conducted to a certain point in time. This type of recovery is considered to be a time-based recovery. The point in time should be identified to a precision in seconds. The appropriate format for the time a DBA can specify is a four-digit year, followed by a two-digit month, followed by a two-digit date. These three items are separated by a hyphen. Immediately following the date should be a colon, followed by the hour of the day in 24-hour format, followed by the minute, followed by the second. The time components should be separated by colons. A sample **alter database** statement with recovery to a point in time identified is listed in the code block following the paragraph. Note also that in addition to the formatting constraints described above, the date must be enclosed in single quotes. Once the recovery has applied redo information for *all committed* transactions through the time named, the recovery will end automatically. If uncommitted data was written in order to supply the database with all committed information to the time named, then the uncommitted transaction data will be rolled back before the recovery ends.

```
ALTER DATABASE orgdb01
RECOVER AUTOMATIC
UNTIL '1999-04-15:22:15:00';
```

In the database recovery statement listed in the code block above, several things are happening. First, the database will be recovered automatically, meaning that interaction between Oracle and the DBA will be minimized during the database recovery. Instead of prompting the DBA to supply names of archived redo logs while simultaneously offering suggestions for redo to apply, Oracle will simply apply its own redo log suggestions and inform the DBA if there is a problem. Once transaction information has been applied , the database recovery is complete and Oracle concludes the recovery automatically.

Cancel-Based Recovery

The final type of incomplete recovery considered is the cancel-based recovery. This type of recovery allows the DBA to run a database recovery for an indefinite period, defined on the fly by the DBA as the recovery executes. During the course of the recovery, the DBA may choose to issue a **cancel** command, and the recovery will stop. The cancel-based recovery offers the DBA unmatched control over the execution of database recovery; however, it carries with that control the responsibility of the DBA to monitor the recovery process. In order to demonstrate the usage of cancel-based recovery, the following code block illustrates an **alter database** statement that specifies cancel-based recovery. In order to cancel recovery, the DBA can issue the **cancel** command as Oracle interactively requests the DBA to confirm the application of suggested redo logs.

```
ALTER DATABASE orgdb01
RECOVER UNTIL CANCEL;
```

In the database recovery statement listed in the code block above, several things are happening of note. First, the database cannot be recovered automatically, meaning that interaction between Oracle and the DBA cannot be minimized during the database recovery. Because cancel-based recovery requires the DBA to specifically tell Oracle when to stop applying redo information, the DBA cannot use the **automatic** option in conjunction with cancel-based recovery. Once transaction information written to the database as of the moment has been applied in its committed entirety, the database recovery is complete and Oracle concludes the recovery when the DBA issues the **cancel** command at an interactive prompt.

After the execution of whichever incomplete recovery option the DBA must use in order to obtain the desired recovery result, the DBA may want to back up the database before allowing the users access to it. The DBA should conduct a full offline backup of the database before allowing the database to be accessed by the users. After obtaining the full offline physical backup using means identified in Chapter 11, the DBA can now allow the users access to the database while simultaneously discarding the archived redo log information with the use of the **resetlogs** option. Discarding archived redo log information underscores the importance of taking a full backup of the database after recovery is complete, and is done with the **alter database open resetlogs** statement.

```
ALTER DATABASE OPEN RESETLOGS;
```

Steps for Incomplete Recovery
Here is a list of the steps required for incomplete recovery:

I. Prepare the database for incomplete recovery by disallowing user access and mounting the database to only one instance.

```
SHUTDOWN ABORT;
ALTER DATABASE orgdb01 MOUNT EXCLUSIVE;
```

2. Restore all datafiles for all tablespaces using commands or utilities provided by the operating system.

3. Execute the incomplete recovery with the **alter database recover database** statement, specifying the appropriate incomplete recovery method, depending on the needs of the DBA in the **until** clause of that statement.

```
ALTER DATABASE orgdb01
RECOVER AUTOMATIC
DATABASE UNTIL scn;

ALTER DATABASE orgdb01
RECOVER AUTOMATIC
DATABASE UNTIL 'yyyy-mm-dd:hh24:mi:ss';

ALTER DATABASE orgdb01
RECOVER AUTOMATIC
DATABASE UNTIL CANCEL;
```

4. After recovery is complete, the DBA should perform a full backup of the database using operating system methods.

5. Finally, the DBA can make the database available to the users with the **alter database open resetlogs** statement, simultaneously opening the database and discarding the online redo information. This step underscores the importance of the full backup taken in Step 4.

```
ALTER DATABASE OPEN RESETLOGS;
```

Exercises

1. Describe in detail each type of incomplete recovery process. What are the similarities between each incomplete recovery process? How are they different?

2. How does the DBA open the database while simultaneously discarding redo information?

Incomplete Recovery and Re-Creating the Control File

Executing database recovery can be done with a control file other than the "live" one currently being used. If the DBA should need to perform incomplete recovery of the database without the control file that existed on the database, the DBA can create a new one using the **create controlfile** statement. In order to create a new control file to replace one that was lost in the media failure, the DBA should issue the **create controlfile** statement and specify all online redo logs and all datafiles that are part of the Oracle database in the **create controlfile** statement. There are two special options that should also be included. The first is **resetlogs**, used to reset the online redo log sequence number in order to make the control file current and therefore usable with the recovery effort, and the other is the **archivelog** option to inform Oracle that archiving is enabled. An example **create controlfile** statement may look similar to the statement in the following code block:

```
CREATE CONTROLFILE DATABASE orgdb01
LOGFILE GROUP 1 ('disk1name', 'disk2name', 'disk3name') SIZE 1M,
        GROUP 2 ('disk1name', 'disk2name', 'disk3name') SIZE 1M
RESETLOGS
DATAFILE ('datafile1name', 'datafile2name')
ARCHIVELOG;
```

Once this control file is created, the incomplete database recovery can commence using the steps outlined in the prior discussion. For refreshing, the steps required, including the creation of a control file, are listed as follows:

1. Re-create the control file for the database using the **create controlfile resetlogs archivelog** statement.

2. Prepare the database for incomplete recovery by disallowing user access and mounting the database to only one instance.

   ```
   SHUTDOWN ABORT;
   ALTER DATABASE orgdb01 MOUNT EXCLUSIVE;
   ```

3. Restore all datafiles for all tablespaces using commands or utilities provided by the operating system.

4. Execute the incomplete recovery with the **alter database recover database** statement, specifying the appropriate incomplete recovery method, depending on the needs of the DBA in the **until** clause of that statement.

```
ALTER DATABASE orgdb01
RECOVER AUTOMATIC
DATABASE UNTIL scn;

ALTER DATABASE orgdb01
RECOVER AUTOMATIC
DATABASE UNTIL 'yyyy-mm-dd:hh24:mi:ss';

ALTER DATABASE orgdb01
RECOVER AUTOMATIC
DATABASE UNTIL CANCEL;
```

5. After recovery is complete, the DBA should perform a full backup of the database using operating system methods.

6. Finally, the DBA can make the database available to the users with the **alter database open resetlogs** statement, simultaneously opening the database and discarding the online redo information. This step underscores the importance of the full backup taken in step 5.

```
ALTER DATABASE OPEN RESETLOGS;
```

Database Recovery Using a Backup Control File

In some cases, the DBA may instead need to perform a database recovery using a backup copy of the control file. The syntax for this option is to add the **using backup controlfile** clause to the **alter database recover database** statement used when the statement commencing incomplete recovery is issued. Also, the step for re-creating the control file should be eliminated. The steps for this process are listed as follows:

1. Prepare the database for incomplete recovery by disallowing user access and mounting the database to only one instance.

```
SHUTDOWN ABORT;
ALTER DATABASE orgdb01 MOUNT EXCLUSIVE;
```

2. Restore all datafiles for all tablespaces using commands or utilities provided by the operating system.

3. Execute the incomplete recovery with the **alter database recover database** statement, specifying the appropriate incomplete recovery method, depending on the needs of the DBA in the **until** clause of that statement.

```
ALTER DATABASE orgdb01
RECOVER AUTOMATIC
DATABASE UNTIL scn
USING BACKUP CONTROLFILE '/u01/oracle/bkp/backup.ctl';

ALTER DATABASE orgdb01
RECOVER AUTOMATIC
DATABASE UNTIL 'yyyy-mm-dd:hh24:mi:ss'
USING BACKUP CONTROLFILE '/u01/oracle/bkp/backup.ctl';

ALTER DATABASE orgdb01
RECOVER AUTOMATIC
DATABASE UNTIL CANCEL
USING BACKUP CONTROLFILE '/u01/oracle/bkp/backup.ctl';
```

4. After recovery is complete, the DBA should perform a full backup of the database using operating system methods.

5. Finally, the DBA can make the database available to the users with the alter database open **resetlogs**, simultaneously opening the database and discarding the online redo information. This step underscores the importance of the full backup taken in Step 4.

```
ALTER DATABASE OPEN RESETLOGS;
```

Exercises

1. How is a control file created? When is it useful to do so in conjunction with incomplete recovery? What is the syntax for recovery using a control file backup?

2. What dynamic performance views may be used to determine the status of database recovery for the database and for the datafiles?

Chapter Summary

This chapter covers several aspects of database recovery related to archiving and backup methods on a 24-hour database. The three topics covered include complete recovery with archiving, incomplete recovery with archiving, and online database backups for databases that require 24-hour availability. This chapter covers about 30 percent of the material tested in OCP Exam 3.

The first area of discussion is online database backup facts and methods for databases that must be available 24 hours a day. This section presents methods for distinguishing online backups from offline ones. As a point of fact, an offline database backup is usually just that—a backup of the database. Thus, when the DBA is examining a full database backup, it is usually one that contains all datafiles, redo log files, control files, and parameter files. A full backup is usually taken while the database is offline so that the backup is read consistent to a single point in time. Online database backups, however, are slightly different. An online backup is usually taken tablespace by tablespace. As such, the online backup usually only consists of the datafiles for each tablespace, rather than all datafiles for all tablespaces. Of course, there is nothing that says the DBA cannot take a backup of all tablespaces one at a time or in parallel on each occasion that online backups are performed.

In order to take online backups of the database, archiving of redo logs must be used. The database is open, available, and accepting changes during the entire time a hot backup is taking place. In order to guarantee that the changes made to the tablespace while the backup took place are kept, it is required that the DBA archive redo logs that were taken during the operation of hot backups. Prior to taking the hot backup, the DBA should issue the **archive log list** command from Server Manager in order to determine the oldest online redo log sequence that should be saved in conjunction with the online backups being taken. Once the tablespace backups are complete, the **archive log list** command should be issued again, followed by a log switch to ensure that the current redo log entries made for the tablespaces backed up are archived properly for use by the backups should recovery be necessary.

The steps to the process are as follows. Execute **archive log list** from Server Manager. Note the value for "Oldest online log sequence." This is the oldest redo log required for using the online backup. Execute **alter tablespace** *name* **begin backup** from Server Manager. This step prepares the tablespace for online backup. Copy the datafiles for that tablespace using operating system commands or third-party products. Be sure the copy resides on a disk other than the production datafiles themselves. Execute **alter tablespace** *name* **end backup** from Server Manager. This step completes the online backup process for that tablespace. Repeat for all tablespaces to be backed up. Execute **archive log list** again from Server Manager. Note the value for "Current log sequence" this time. This is the last redo log required for using the online backup. Issue an **alter system switch logfile** to cause Oracle to create an archive of the current redo log. This archive should then be stored in the LOG_ARCHIVE_DEST area. If desired, copy the archives associated with the backup to tape. Create a copy of the control file. This is done with the **alter database backup controlfile** statement.

The final step in the online backup of a database is an important one that merits special consideration. There are two different types of backups of database control files. The first is a backup created of the actual control file, ready for use on the Oracle database. Should the production version of the control file be destroyed, the DBA can simply put the backup in place and move forward. The **alter database backup controlfile to** *filename* statement can be used in this case to ensure that a usable backup copy of the control file is available in the event of an emergency. The other option is to use a special keyword in place of *filename* in the **alter database backup controlfile** statement. This keyword is called **trace**. The use of this keyword allows the DBA to obtain a special backup of the control file. Rather than backing up the control file itself, this statement backs up a copy of the script that can be used to create the control file. If the DBA has space considerations or wishes to create the control file on a database running under a different operating system, this option will provide the backup required.

The next section of discussion in this chapter is complete recovery with database archiving. To perform complete recovery, there are two things required. The first thing required is the backup. The discussion takes into account that there are two different types of database backups that a DBA might use to execute a database recovery: the offline backup and the online backup. Complete recovery also requires a complete set of archived redo logs from the period of time the backup was taken to the present. In addition, the DBA may require the archived redo log information taken while the online backup was taking place if online backups are used on the database.

The first step required in complete database recovery using offline backups and archived redo logs is to make the database unavailable to the users. This step can be accomplished with the **shutdown abort** statement executed within Server Manager. The database cannot be available to the users during recovery from offline backups because a full database recovery is required to bring the contents of the database up to the point in time the media failure occurred, which requires Oracle to write a lot of redo information. The same condition is not required for database recovery from online backups, however, because database recovery from online backups need only consist of tablespace recovery, which means the rest of the database can be available for use during the period of time the recovery is taking place.

Once the database is offline (if it needs to be), the DBA needs to handle the restoration of the database files from backup. This step requires the DBA to replace the files lost in the database media failure with backed-up copies using operating system commands and/or utilities. If need be, the DBA may also need to replace the failed media device, although this is not always required. In some cases, the DBA instead might simply move the files onto other disks.

When the task of restoring backed-up copies of lost files to their proper places on replaced disks is complete, the DBA can then set forth with the task of mounting (but not opening) the database if offline backups were used, or simply leaving the database available for use if online backups were used. If the DBA does move the files to another disk, it is at this point that the DBA should issue the **alter database rename file** statement to change the Oracle control file so that Oracle will know where all the physical database components are.

At this point, the task of replacing lost or damaged files with backup copies is complete. The second part of complete recovery can now begin. This is the part where archived redo is applied to the backups to make the database consistent to the point in time that the database failed. This step requires the DBA to issue an **alter database recover database** command, in the case of complete recovery from offline database backups, or the **alter database recover tablespace** command in the case of recovery from online backups. Oracle will expect that the archived redo information will be located in the place on the machine specified by the parameter called

LOG_ARCHIVE_DEST in the **init.ora** file. If automatic archiving is not used, or if another location contains the archives, the DBA should instruct Oracle to use another location by specifying the pathname containing the archived redo information with the **from** clause of the **alter database recover** statement.

Application of archived redo logs is handled interactively by Oracle. The database prompts the DBA to supply the name of the next archive to apply, while also issuing a suggestion for which redo log to apply. This suggestion is based on the V$LOG_HISTORY dynamic performance view, the LOG_ARCHIVE_FORMAT parameter, and the LOG_ARCHIVE_DEST parameter. If the DBA desires, he or she can specify Oracle to apply its own suggestions automatically during database recovery by including the **automatic** keyword in the **alter database recover** statement.

All archived redo information will be applied by Oracle to execute a complete recovery. When Oracle is complete, the DBA can open the database for usage by issuing the **alter database open resetlogs** statement. The **resetlogs** option indicates that the DBA wishes to reset the log sequence number for the database online redo logs to 1. It is generally recommended that prior to opening a newly recovered database, the DBA take a full backup of the recovered database in the event of an emergency.

As a point of reference, to minimize downtime during database recovery, it is faster to use online tablespace backups. This is because tablespace recovery runs faster than full database recovery required for offline backups, and also allows the DBA to leave the unaffected parts of the database available to users while fixing the damaged portion.

The final subject for discussion in this chapter is facts and methods for incomplete recovery using archived redo information. There are several situations that may force the DBA to recover the database to a point in time in the past using incomplete database recovery methods. Some of these reasons include an errant batch process or feed that contains bad data, which causes some improper information to enter the database. Another situation where incomplete recovery may occur simply involves bad luck, where the DBA loses an archived redo log file or finds that the file has been damaged. In any event, incomplete recovery is the recovery of a database to some point in the past.

One of the things that makes incomplete recovery involving archived redo logs better than incomplete recovery involving backups that do not work in conjunction with archiving, or backups on a database that does not use archiving, is choice. The DBA can choose the point in time to which incomplete recovery will occur (barring loss of archived redo logs) when archiving is used. In contrast, the only "point in time" to which a database can be restored is the point in time when the last backup completed.

To accomplish incomplete recovery, the DBA requires two things. The first is a complete backup of the system. Incomplete recovery is a complete database recovery operation. Incomplete recovery from online tablespace information, and the tablespace recovery operation, is not allowed. This is because incomplete recovery of an individual tablespace would put the entire database into a read-inconsistent state. The second item required is archived redo log information. As stated, incomplete recovery may be the result of lost archived redo logs. If, for example, consider that there are three archived redo logs for a database, numbered 1, 2, and 3, and each archive contains information for 30 transactions, whose SCNs are from 0–9, 10–19, and 20–29. If archive sequence 3 is lost, the DBA can only recover the database through SCN 19, or archive sequence 2. If 2 is lost, then the DBA can only recover the database through SCN 9, and if archive sequence 1 is lost, then *no* archived redo log information can be applied.

There are three types of incomplete recovery. Those three types are change-based, time-based, and cancel-based. The change-based incomplete recovery allows the DBA to specify a system change number (SCN) of a transaction at which, once its full set of committed operations are applied, Oracle will stop running the database recovery automatically. The time-based incomplete recovery allows the DBA to specify a date and time later in the past than the database backup, to which the database will be recovered. When Oracle applies redo information to that point in time specified by the time-based recovery, Oracle will automatically stop the recovery process. The final type of database incomplete recovery is the cancel-based recovery. This recovery allows the DBA to arbitrarily decide when to end the recovery by issuing a **cancel** command when Oracle prompts the DBA to enter the name of the next archived redo log entry to be applied. This option gives the DBA complete control over when to end a database backup, but requires the DBA to interact with Oracle during the recovery at all times.

As with complete recovery using offline backups, the DBA cannot allow users to have access to the database while the incomplete recovery is taking place. As such, the database should be mounted in **exclusive** mode to prevent other instances from opening it, but not opened by that instance either. The DBA can then place all datafiles in place on their respective disks from backup and issue the **alter database recover database until** statement. Following the **until** clause, the DBA can specify the exact form of incomplete recovery that will be employed, either using **change** followed by the SCN, a date and time, or simply the **cancel** keyword. If the DBA wants to limit the interactive portion of recovery where Oracle prompts the DBA for names of archived redo log files to apply, the DBA can use the **automatic** keyword in the **alter database recover** statement, except in the case of using the cancel-based recovery option. When using cancel-based recovery, the DBA must interact with Oracle during application of redo logs in order to issue the **cancel** command.

After recovery is complete, it is recommended that the DBA perform a full database backup before allowing the users to access the database. After that, the DBA can allow the users access to the database by executing the **alter database open resetlogs** statement. Using the **resetlogs** keyword means that Oracle will reset the log sequence number to 1, effectively discarding all archived redo information taken before the recovery and underscoring the importance of taking a backup before allowing user access to the database again.

Of particular importance in running incomplete database recovery is the manipulation or creation of a new control file in the event that a new one is required. If the control file is damaged, and there is no backup to it that will allow the DBA to perform complete recovery on the Oracle database, the DBA may be forced to create a new control file as part of the recovery process. This process is accomplished with the use of the **create controlfile** statement. In it, the DBA will identify the location of all redo logs and datafiles, as well as specifying the **resetlogs** option to discard any online redo information (also to make the control file usable for recovery). The DBA should also remember to specify the **archivelog** option because, after all, the database *is* archiving redo. If the DBA ever used the **alter database backup controlfile to trace** option for control file backup, the script backed up could be modified (if necessary) and executed in lieu of formulating a new one.

Finally, in the event that the DBA is using an actual backup of the control file and needs to execute recovery from it, the DBA can issue an **alter database recover** statement using a special clause that tells Oracle to use the backup control file. The full statement would be **alter database** *dbname* **recover database using backup controlfile** *ctlname*.

Two-Minute Drill

- Offline backups usually are full backups taken with the database offline. They are required for complete database recovery using the **recover database** option and for incomplete recovery.

- Online backups are usually tablespace backups taken with the database online. They are required for complete recovery using the **recover tablespace** option. Tablespace recovery is not an option for incomplete recovery.

- Online backups of tablespaces are taken in the following way:

  1. Prepare the database for backup using the **alter tablespace begin backup** statement.

  2. Make backups of the tablespace datafiles using operating system commands.

  3. End the tablespace backup using the **alter tablespace end backup** statement.

- Due to the increased archive redo information taken during online backups, and to the increased damage caused by database failure during a backup, it is recommended that online backups be taken one tablespace at a time, rather than doing them in parallel.

- A control file can be backed up in two ways. The first creates an actual usable control file for the DBA to incorporate. This backup is created with the **alter database backup controlfile to** *filename* statement. The second creates a script that can be run to create the control file. This backup is created with the same statement, replacing *filename* with the keyword **trace**.

- Complete database recovery with archiving is when the DBA can recover the database to the point in time of a database failure. Incomplete recovery is recovery to any point in time in the past.

- There are three types of incomplete recovery: time-based, change-based, and cancel-based. They are differentiated in the **recover database** option by what follows the **until** clause.

Cancel-based uses **until cancel**, change-based uses **until change** *scn*, and time-based uses **until** *'yyyy-mm-dd:hh24:mi:ss'*.

■ Information about the status of a recovery can be found in two dynamic performance views on the database: the V$RECOVERY_FILE_STATUS and V$RECOVERY_STATUS performance views.

■ Information about system change numbers contained in each archived redo log can be found in V$LOG_HISTORY.

■ Database recovery is an interactive process where Oracle prompts the DBA to supply the names of archived redo logs to apply while also making suggestions based on V$LOG_HISTORY and the two parameters for automatic archiving: LOG_ARCHIVE_DEST and LOG_ARCHIVE_FORMAT.

■ The DBA can automate this process by specifying the **automatic** option in the **recover database** statement. This option may *not* be used in conjunction with cancel-based recovery.

■ For complete recovery using offline backups, or for incomplete recovery, the database cannot be available for users. For complete recovery of a tablespace only, the undamaged or unaffected parts of the database can be available for use.

■ In some cases, it may be necessary to move datafiles as part of recovery. The control file must be modified, if this is required, with the **alter database rename file** statement.

■ Complete recovery is accomplished with offline backups in the following way:

1. Have the database mounted in **exclusive** mode but not opened.

2. Restore all backup copies of datafiles.

3. Specify new locations of datafiles if any were moved.

4. Execute the **recover database** operation, applying appropriate archived redo logs.

5. Take a complete backup of database.

6. Open the database using the **resetlogs** option to discard archives and reset sequence number.

- Complete recovery is accomplished with online backups in the following way:

  1. The database can be open for use, but the damaged tablespace must be offline.

  2. Restore all backup copies of datafiles.

  3. Specify new locations of datafiles if any were moved.

  4. Execute the **recover tablespace** operation, applying appropriate archived redo logs.

  5. Bring the tablespace online.

  6. Take an online backup of tablespace.

- Situations that require incomplete recovery include when a data change is made in error at some point in the past and many other changes are made as a result, in effect, batch processing.

- Incomplete recovery may be required when the DBA loses an archived redo log file. To illustrate, there are three archived redo logs for a database, numbered 1, 2, and 3. Each archive contains information for 10 transactions (SCN 0–9, 10–19, and 20–29), for a total of 30 transactions. If archive sequence 3 is lost, the DBA can only recover the database through SCN 19, or archive sequence 2. If 2 is lost, then the DBA can only recover the database through SCN 9, and if archive sequence 1 is lost, then *no* archived redo log information can be applied.

- Incomplete recovery is accomplished with offline backups in the following way:

  1. Have the database mounted in **exclusive** mode but not opened.

  2. Restore all backup copies of datafiles.

  3. Specify new locations of datafiles if any were moved.

  4. Execute **recover database** operation, applying appropriate archived redo logs. Use the appropriate **incomplete recovery** option: Cancel-based uses **until cancel**, change-based uses **until change** *scn*, time-based uses **until** '*yyyy-mm-dd:hh24:mi:ss*'.

  5. Take complete backup of database.

6. Open the database using the **resetlogs** option to discard archives and reset sequence number.

■ Create a new control file, if required, before initiating recovery using the **create controlfile** statement. Be sure to specify **resetlogs** and **archivelog**. If available, use the control file script created when the **trace** option is used in backing up the control file.

Chapter Questions

1. Characteristics of a change-based recovery include

   A. Recovery to the point in time of a database failure

   B. Usage of the **recover tablespace** option

   C. Recovery by system change number

   D. Availability of the database during recovery

2. The DBA takes a backup of the control file daily. A situation arises where the control file must be recovered. To do so, the DBA uses the CREATE CONTROLFILE statement in conjunction with her backup. Which of the following correctly describes her control file backup methods?

   A. The DBA's backup method for control files puts the backup in a trace directory.

   B. The DBA's backup method for control files creates a usable control file.

   C. The DBA's backup method for control files uses an **alter tablespace** statement.

   D. The DBA's backup method for control files uses the **alter database backup controlfile to dbase.ctl** statement.

3. In order to execute a complete recovery using a full backup, the DBA should first

   A. Open the database in **restricted session** mode

   B. Restore only the damaged datafiles from backup

   C. Use **resetlogs** to reset the redo log sequence

   D. Mount but not open the database

4. **The DBA must perform incomplete recovery. Characteristics of a cancel-based recovery include**

   A. Automatic application of Oracle's archive redo suggestions

   B. Use of the **alter database recover database until cancel** statement

   C. Tablespace recovery with online backups

   D. Availability of the database during the recovery process

5. **When conducting online backups, it is usually best to take backups of tablespaces in parallel.**

   A. TRUE

   B. FALSE

6. **The DBA is conducting a closed database recovery using full offline backups. The DBA realizes that archived redo log sequence #34 is missing. What can the DBA do to execute the proper recovery?**

   A. Check the V$LOG view to find the beginning SCN for log sequence 34, then issue the **alter database recover tablespace until change 34** statement.

   B. Issue the **alter database recover database using backup controlfile** statement.

   C. Check V$LOG_HISTORY for the beginning SCN of log 34, issue **alter database recover database until change** N, where N equals the beginning SCN minus 1 for log 34.

   D. Use IMPORT to recover the database from the most recent database export.

7. **Which of the following RECOVER DATABASE statements should not use the AUTOMATIC option?**

   A. **until change** 495893

   B. **until** '2000-01-31:22:34:00'

   C. **until resetlogs** 1

   D. **until cancel**

8. **The RECOVER DATABASE method requires that the database not be available to users during recovery.**

   A. TRUE

   B. FALSE

9. **Three characteristics of offline backups are**

   A. Complete set of all files in the Oracle database

   B. Obtained after issuing the **alter system enable restricted session** statement

   C. Taken when the database is closed

   D. Used in conjunction with incomplete recovery

10. **If the DBA must re-create the control file as part of database recovery, she should do it**

    A. After opening the database

    B. After backup datafile restoration

    C. Between restoring backups and applying redo logs

    D. Before closing the database to user access

11. **A system change number is**

    A. The number assigned to every redo log in the database

    B. The number of each transaction executed in the database

C. The number of every user created in the database

D. The number of each backup taken of the database

12. **Which of the following steps is inappropriate for complete recovery?**

    A. Mount the database in **exclusive** mode

    B. Restore backup copies of datafiles

    C. Issue the **cancel** command when the DBA runs out of redo to apply

    D. Open the database using the **resetlogs** option

13. **Which of the following are characteristics of online backups? (Choose two)**

    A. Initiated with **alter tablespace begin backup** statement

    B. Run on databases in **archivelog** mode

    C. Contain all files for the database

    D. Contain only changes made since last backup

14. **Incomplete recovery can be accomplished with the RECOVER TABLESPACE statement.**

    A. TRUE

    B. FALSE

15. **Which of the following recovery methods require use of archiving? (Choose three)**

    A. Recovery from full offline backup

    B. Cancel-based recovery

    C. Complete recovery

    D. Change-based recovery

Answers to Chapter Questions

I. C. Recovery by system change number

Explanation Change-based recovery is an incomplete recovery option, and all incomplete recoveries are database recoveries in order to prevent problems with read consistency. Hence, Choices A and B are incorrect, because incomplete recovery by definition does not handle recovery to the point of failure, and tablespace recovery is not used. Choice D is incorrect because incomplete recovery is a "closed database" recovery, meaning that the database is unavailable to users.

2. A. The DBA's backup method for control files puts the backup in a **trace** directory.

Explanation The tip-off in this question is the use of **create controlfile** to restore the control file to the database. There are two ways to back up the control file, one that creates a copy of the control file, and the other that creates a script that can be used to create the control file. The method of creating a script for creating a control file is the **alter database backup controlfile to trace**. This operation and this operation alone puts the backup control file creation script in the trace directory of the database. Therefore, choice A is correct.

3. D. Mount but not open the database.

Explanation Complete recovery from full backup means that the database cannot be available for users during recovery. Choice A is incorrect because **restricted session** mode is used generally when taking backups of database using the EXPORT tool. Choice B is incorrect because a database recovery using full backups would restore all datafiles, not just damaged ones. Choice C is incorrect because **resetlogs** is not a factor at this stage of database recovery.

4. B. Use of the **alter database recover database until cancel** statement

Explanation Cancel-based recovery is a type of incomplete database recovery, not tablespace recovery, and since database recovery means that the users cannot access the database, choices C and D are incorrect. Choice A is wrong because the DBA cannot use automatic recovery in conjunction with the cancel-based option, because the DBA needs to interact with Oracle to notify the database when the recovery should end.

5. B.   FALSE

Explanation   Online backups have two effects. The first is that they increase the amount of redo information Oracle produces. Second, a database failure during execution of an online backup leaves Oracle particularly vulnerable when trying to recover that tablespace. If all tablespaces are in **backup** mode and the database fails, then the DBA will have to address the problem for all tablespaces instead of only one. Furthermore, taking tablespace backups one at a time helps to limit the redo information produced during backup. Therefore, DBAs should not take online backups in parallel.

6. C.   Check V$LOG_HISTORY for the beginning SCN of log 34, issue **alter database recover database until change** N, where N equals the beginning SCN minus 1 for log 34.

Explanation   In general, it helps to read each answer choice to a question carefully in order to eliminate wrong answers. This question is a good example. This question boils down to one about incomplete recovery. Choice A is incorrect because incomplete recovery cannot be conducted on a tablespace, only on an entire database. Choice B is incorrect because there was no mention of the need to recover from a backup control file. Choice D is grossly incorrect because it refers to logical backup and recovery, a topic covered elsewhere.

7. D.   **until cancel**

Explanation   The rule is plain and simple—never use the **recover automatic** option to limit interaction between the DBA and Oracle if the DBA wants to execute cancel-based recovery. To execute this incomplete recovery method, the DBA has to interact with Oracle to tell it when to stop the recovery. Automatic recovery minimizes the interaction, and therefore shouldn't be used.

8. A.   TRUE

Explanation   The recover database method of database recovery requires that the database be mounted exclusively to the instance recovering it, and otherwise be unavailable for use during the recovery process. The answer to this question is TRUE.

9. A, C, and D.

Explanation   The **restricted session** statement is typically only used in conjunction with logical database backup using EXPORT. Offline backups are typically full backups of the physical database files, taken when the database is offline, and can be used in conjunction with complete or incomplete recovery.

10. D.   Before closing the database to user access

Explanation   This question is tricky, and requires careful reading of the question as well as thorough knowledge of the Oracle database recovery process. Creation of a control file for the database recovery process should be accomplished *first*. Choices A, B, and C are all incorrect because they place the creation of control files later in the recovery process.

11. B.   The number of each transaction executed in the database

Explanation   A system change number is an identification number assigned to each transaction executing on the database. Choice A refers to a sequence number and/or a thread number. Choice C refers to a userid, while there really isn't a unique number assigned to a database.

12. C.   Issue the **cancel** command when the DBA runs out of redo to apply

Explanation   This answer is not appropriate for a complete database recovery, which applies all archived redo information to recover the database to the point in time of the failure.

13. A and B.

Explanation Online backups only back up datafiles one tablespace at a time. As such, they typically don't consist of the entire database, eliminating choice C. The only backups that contain database changes made since the last backup was taken are the cumulative and incremental exports taken with the EXPORT utility.

14. B. FALSE

Explanation Incomplete recovery can only be accomplished using the **recover database** method. If **alter tablespace** were used, the database would be left in a read-inconsistent mode, which would cause problems.

15. B, C, and D.

Explanation Recovery from full offline backup is the only one that can be performed without archiving enabled on the database. The other three options are simply variants on complete or incomplete recovery, all of which require archiving.

CHAPTER
15

Advanced Topics of
Oracle Backup
and Recovery

n this chapter, you will understand and demonstrate knowledge in the following areas:

- Minimizing downtime
- Troubleshooting
- The standby database

The final areas of Oracle backup and recovery that the DBA should understand are database troubleshooting, minimizing database downtime, and the use of the standby database feature of Oracle. The first advanced topic of backup and recovery—minimizing downtime—will consist of several discussions. These discussions include system startup after database failure. This section also includes discussion of starting up the database in situations where parts of the database are damaged. A continuation of the discussion started on the topic of leaving the database open during tablespace recovery will be included as well. Finally, related to minimizing downtime, the parallel recovery option will be discussed. Troubleshooting will also be presented. The usage of the **alert** log and process trace files is discussed, as is a further discussion of the dynamic performance views. The detection and resolution of corrupt data in online redo logs is also presented in this chapter. For this discussion, the use of DBVERIFY will be presented. Finally, the usage and functions of the standby database feature in Oracle will be presented. These three topics comprise the advanced topics of Oracle backup and recovery covered by the OCP Exam. These three topics comprise 12 percent of OCP Exam 3.

Minimizing Downtime

In this section, you will cover the following topics related to minimizing downtime:

- Database startup after system failure
- Starting the database when missing database files

- Initiating partial recovery on an open database
- Parallel recovery

Minimizing downtime is one of the most important goals for every database administrator. The first portion of this chapter covers everything you need to know about this key function for OCP Exam 3.

Database Startup After System Failure

When a database crashes, several things go wrong at the same time. A hardware failure prevents Oracle from using one of the disks on the hardware hosting Oracle. Alerts are written in their proper places, and the DBA realizes there is a problem. As mentioned, it is important to get the database back into the state of being open and available for use. However, a parallel goal that the DBA should have for recovering the database is to recover the database as quickly as possible.

One feature of the Oracle database allows it to start quickly after database failure occurs. This feature makes the database open after the failure in a manner that quickly gets the database recovery going so that the DBA can get off to a good start performance-wise with the database recovery. This feature is called *fast transaction rollback*.

To understand the process of database recovery and how fast transaction rollback works, consider the following presentation. The architecture of the Oracle database is such that recovery occurs in two processes. Recall that issuing the database **shutdown** command from Server Manager with the **abort** option will force database media recovery after the database restarts. The first process in that media recovery is called *rolling forward*. In Figure 15-1, there is a demonstration of the activity Oracle undergoes during the rolling forward process. Consider the act of complete recovery with archiving, as presented in Chapter 14. Oracle will roll forward all the database transactions that have been exchanged with users. This process will happen until all redo entries have been applied that were present in the online redo log after database startup.

After that point, the second process will kick in—the database will engage in the process of **rollback** of all transactions that were not committed at the time the **shutdown abort** was issued. This process is also demonstrated at a high level in Figure 15-1. Any transaction that was still

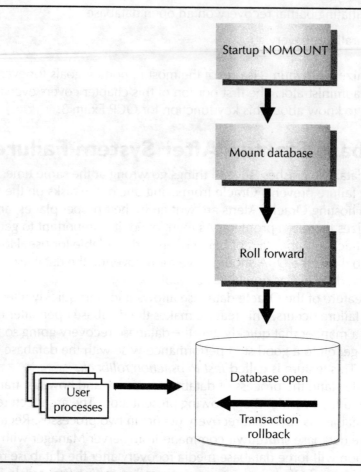

FIGURE 15-1. *Database startup after media failure*

being engaged by a user process when the database was shut down is considered uncommitted, while those transactions that had a **commit** statement issued to end them are considered committed. The second part of the recovery is designed to eliminate the in-progress information for uncommitted transactions from the data dictionary required for transaction rollback.

TIP
*The media recovery process after a **shutdown
abort** statement is accomplished in two steps:
rolling forward, or application of all
transactions in the online redo logs to the
database after startup, and rolling back all
uncommitted transactions.*

The fast transaction rollback feature of the Oracle database is designed to improve performance of the second part of this process. It accomplishes the process of rolling back in a manner that is more efficient than normal database rollback. The efficiency is created in several ways. In earlier versions of Oracle, the database could not be opened for use by the users until Oracle had resolved everything related to the transactions that failed in the media failure and subsequent database abort. Oracle would first roll everything forward, then roll back, then open the database. With fast transaction rollback, Oracle will open the database for use after the roll forward occurs, making the database open for users to execute transactions on the vast majority of the database.

What effect does this fast transaction rollback have on the rest of the database? Recall that there are several things a database does in order to facilitate transaction processing. The items that facilitate transaction processing include rollback segments, locks, and transaction marker statements such as **begin transaction**, **commit**, and **rollback**. First of all, each transaction is assigned to a rollback segment that stores any database changes the transaction makes, along with what the database looked like before the changes were made. These changes are stored in order to make it easy for the user process to discard the database transaction right up to the moment it is committed. Recall also the use of locks in transaction processing. In order to obtain read consistency for the life of a transaction, there are several locks a user process may acquire while the transaction operates. The user process holds *all* of them until the transaction ends.

When media recovery occurs, Oracle will go through the process of applying all the changes made to the database to the point in time of the failure, only to roll the uncommitted ones back. To do so, the database must both use the rollback segment entries made for the uncommitted transactions to put the database back the way it was, and force those uncommitted transactions to give up their locks. With the fast transaction rollback feature in place, allowing users to access the database after Oracle rolls forward, there are other user processes that are simultaneously accessing the database resources while these other things related to transaction rollback takes place. The impact may be felt by the user processes in the following ways:

- Rollback segments involved in the fast transaction rollback are in a *partly available* state. Transactions that operate on the database while fast transaction rollback takes place will have fewer rollback segments at their disposal.

- Locks held by transactions active at the time of failure will still be held until Oracle can force their release. This means that the rows or tables that may have been used in transactions that are in the process·of rolling back are still locked. So, even though the database is technically open and available for use, if the user processes attempt to change the tables or rows that are held in locks awaiting fast transaction rollback, those processes will wait until the locks are released.

Essentially, the benefit of fast transaction recovery is to allow the user processes to work on the database without affecting the data manipulated by the transactions in progress when the failure occurred. But, for those users who may want to rerun the same transactions that were running when failure struck, or those users who want to use the same data that was being manipulated by the active transactions at the time of the failure, they will have to wait.

Fast transaction rollback has the potential to minimize downtime for the database after an instance failure. The fast transaction rollback accomplishes its goal by opening the database immediately after the roll-forward process occurs, rather than waiting until the database has had the chance to roll back also. Although this feature has the advantage of allowing the database to open sooner, the benefit is mixed, depending on the amount and types of transactions running at media failure time. The parts of the database that were involved in transaction processing at the time the failure occurred (rollback segments and locked rows/tables) will continue to be unavailable until fast transaction rollback completes. However, the users that do not require those resources in process of recovery will fare better performance-wise than the users that try to use the resources that are being recovered. Overall, the use of fast transaction recovery is helpful for the DBA who tries to minimize downtime for the organization.

Exercises

1. What database feature enables Oracle to start more quickly after a database has experienced media failure? How does this feature accomplish its goals?

2. What potential limitations may the database users experience who access the database soon after it opens?

Starting the Database When Missing Database Files

Many times, the DBA will need to make the database available during the course of the recovery. In many organizations where several applications share the same database instance, a media failure causes one disk to crash containing data for one application while several other applications remain unaffected by this failure. If this is the case, it makes sense that the database be available for those other applications while the DBA handles recovery of the disk information for the affected application.

The next discussion will present information about handling the recovery process for a database that must be available to the users while the damaged or affected areas of the database are fixed. This discussion will focus on opening a database that is missing some of its datafiles, or even entire tablespaces, so that it is available for use while the DBA performs recovery.

It is possible to open a database that is missing datafiles. To understand how to do so, first the three database availability states will be reviewed. The three database availability states are **nomount**, **mount**, and **open**. There are different activities that Oracle engages in when the database is in each of these three states. Figure 15-2 demonstrates these pictorially. If the DBA

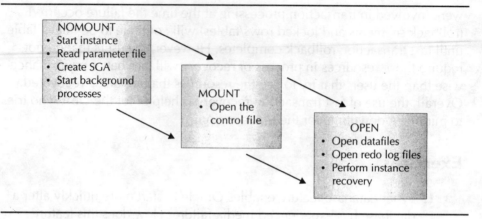

FIGURE 15-2. *Database availability states and their corresponding activities*

puts the database into **nomount** state with the **startup nomount** command issued from Server Manager, then the Oracle instance will start the execution of all background processes and create the system global area, or SGA. As part of these tasks, the database parameter file **init.ora** will be read.

Several other things happen when the database is mounted. To mount the database and start the instance all at the same time, the DBA can issue the **startup mount** command from Server Manager, or use the **alter database mount** statement to mount a database to a previously started instance without a database mounted to it. When the database is mounted, the instance opens the control file containing the physical database specification of all files associated with the database. However, the database still cannot be accessed, and will not be accessible until the DBA opens it.

To open the database, the DBA can either issue the **startup open** command from Server Manager or the **alter database open** statement from SQL*Plus. The first statement allows the DBA to start the instance, mount, and open a database, all in one statement. The second allows the DBA to open a previously mounted database. Only when the database is open can users access the logical database objects like tables, indexes, and sequences that comprise the Oracle database.

In order to open a database that has had damage done to one or more of its datafiles as part of media failure, the DBA must engage in the following tasks. First, the Oracle instance must be started and the database must be mounted to it, but not opened. At this point, the database is not available for use. In order to open the database with a datafile missing, the DBA at this point should take the tablespace offline using the **alter tablespace offline** statement executed from the SQL*Plus or Server Manager command prompt. For the following example, assume that a media failure has damaged a datafile called **index01.dbf**, the only datafile for tablespace INDEX01. In order to open the database to other users while simultaneously performing database recovery on the damaged tablespace, the following code block can be used by the DBA:

```
STARTUP MOUNT;
ALTER TABLESPACE index01 OFFLINE;
RECOVER TABLESPACE index01 … ;
```

A few items related to open database recovery must be understood by the DBA. Recall that only complete tablespace recovery can be executed on an open database. Incomplete recovery in particular, which is a full database recovery, or complete database recovery, may not be executed while the database is open. Datafile recovery can be conducted either with the database available or without the database being available. Finally, redo logs *must* be archived in order to conduct online database recovery.

Exercises

    1. What options must be used to start a database that has datafiles missing?

    2. When might it be useful to do this?

Initiating Partial Recovery on an Open Database

After issuing the appropriate commands to open the database for use, being sure to take the tablespace offline that contains damaged datafiles, open database recovery can commence. To refresh the discussion, the DBA must understand that the only option she may pursue for open database recovery is the complete recovery of a tablespace using both a backup copy of the datafiles that comprise the tablespace and all archived redo information, taken both during the backup and after. Remember, online backups require use of archiving to capture the data changes made to the datafiles of a tablespace while the database was open during the database backup.

One of the main reasons to engage in open database recovery is to support database availability. The steps for tablespace recovery have been covered in Chapter 14. To refresh the discussion, the database must be open in order to accomplish a tablespace recovery. This is so that Oracle can view the contents of the database while the tablespace recovery occurs. However, the tablespace itself must be offline. An added benefit to using tablespace recovery is the fact that the DBA can allow users to access other tablespaces while the offline tablespace (presumably on the disk that failed) is being restored. In this example, assume that the INDEX01 tablespace needs to be recovered.

1. If the database is already running, leave it that way. If not, start it in **mount** mode.

   ```
   ALTER DATABASE MOUNT;
   ```

2. Take the tablespace on the disk(s) that failed offline.

   ```
   ALTER TABLESPACE index01 OFFLINE;
   ```

3. Assuming that any hardware problems have been rectified and the path listed for the related tablespace datafiles is available, replace the damaged datafiles with their respective backup copies using operating system commands or utilities. If the hardware problem has not been rectified, or if the DBA decides to move the files of the tablespace to another disk, the DBA should issue the appropriate **alter database rename file** command.

   ```
   ALTER DATABASE OPEN;
   ALTER DATABASE
   RENAME FILE '/u01/oracle/home/index01.dbf'
   TO '/u01/oracle/home/index01.dbf';
   ```

4. Issue the appropriate tablespace recovery command to apply archived redo information for that tablespace, both from the period of time the backup was taken and from the period of time database changes were made after the backup. Oracle's interactive process for applying redo logs will then commence. To minimize the amount of interaction required between the DBA and Oracle, the DBA can include the **automatic** keyword in the **alter database** statement,

allowing Oracle to automatically apply its own suggestions for redo logs.

```
ALTER DATABASE RECOVER AUTOMATIC TABLESPACE users01;
```

5. Finally, the tablespace should be brought online using the **alter tablespace online** statement.

```
ALTER TABLESPACE users01 ONLINE;
```

Note that after database recovery, it is always a good idea to conduct a database backup. Though it is certainly possible to recover the database again if there should be another failure after recovery is complete (after all, the DBA performed just that), it speeds things greatly if the DBA can move forward with the certainty of knowing that all the work she just performed can be recovered more easily.

Exercises

1. What is open recovery?

2. What processes are used by the DBA to engage in open recovery?

Parallel Recovery

A final method DBAs may use to improve database recovery performance is the parallel recovery feature of the Oracle database. The DBA can run a recovery in parallel, which dedicates more processing power and database resources to accomplish the database recovery faster, thus minimizing downtime while also taking better advantage of the resources of the host machine running Oracle.

Parallel recovery requires Parallel Query to be in place on the Oracle database. The database must be running in parallel in order to run parallel recovery. When parallel recovery is used, the process from which the parallel recovery statement is issued will be the master process, or coordinator of the recovery. Oracle will allow the master process to create several slaves that execute the recovery in parallel according to several different parameters. In order to execute a parallel recovery, the DBA must issue the **recover parallel** statement from Server Manager, with several options specified. The DBA can execute parallel recovery using any of the recovery options available in Oracle: **recover database parallel**, **recover tablespace parallel**, and **recover datafile parallel**. The available options will now be discussed.

RECOVERY_PARALLELISM

Parallel recovery is limited to the resources available to the database from the host machine running Oracle. The resources of the Oracle database that are available for parallel recovery are limited by an initialization parameter in the **init.ora** file called RECOVERY_PARALLELISM. This parameter represents the total number of parallel processes that can be used to execute a parallel recovery. The value for this parameter cannot exceed the value specified in another **init.ora** parameter set for database parallelism, PARALLEL_MAX_SERVERS.

DEGREE

When the DBA issues the parallel recovery command, she can specify the degree of parallelism to which the recovery should be executed. The degree of parallelism is synonymous with how many processes will operate in tandem to recover the database. That is, the degree of parallelism specified by the **degree** clause of the recovery operation represents the number of processes that will execute the recovery operation at the same time.

INSTANCES

When the DBA issues the parallel recovery command, she can specify the instances that will be dedicated to the task of database recovery. In order to use the **instances** clause, the database must be mounted and opened in parallel by more than one instance. As opposed to database recovery, for which the database may be mounted to only one instance and not opened, parallel online tablespace recovery can be executed on an open database. The **instances** clause acts as a multiplier for the **degree** clause, allowing the DBA to apply a specified **degree** number of processes or degrees to database recovery for every instance specified for the **instances** clause. The total number of processes that can be applied to the database recovery equals **degree** times **instances**.

Executing the recovery of the Oracle database involves the following process. The DBA issues the **recover database parallel** statement with values for the **degree** and **instances** clauses, being careful not to exceed the value set for RECOVERY_PARALLELISM. The following code block can be used:

```
RECOVER DATABASE PARALLEL DEGREE 3 INSTANCES 2;
```

The following points should be made about the benefits of parallel recovery. First, parallel recovery works best in situations where a media failure may have damaged information on two or more disks. In this way, the recovery can operate on the two or more disks in parallel, rather than the DBA having to execute the recovery of each disk serially. However, the real performance benefit of parallel recovery depends on the operating system's ability to have two or more processes writing I/O to the same disk or to different disks at the same time. If the operating system on the machine hosting Oracle does not support this function, then the performance gain made by parallel recovery may be limited.

The discussion in these four areas is designed to help minimize downtime. DBAs in 24-hour database operations environments may be required to know these techniques in order to obtain maximum performance on their database recovery techniques. Remember, the goal of database recovery is two-fold: to get the database operational with no loss of data, and to get it that way in the shortest time possible.

Exercises

1. What is parallel recovery? What are the parameters that must be used in conjunction with parallel recovery?

2. What may limit the performance benefits granted with parallel recovery?

Troubleshooting the Oracle Database

In this section, you will cover the following topics related to troubleshooting the Oracle database:

- Using trace files and the **alert** log
- Using the V$ performance views to identify problems

- Detecting corruption in online redo logs
- Clearing corruption in online redo logs
- The DBVERIFY utility

Fundamental to the resolution of a problem in the Oracle database is the ability to identify it. In order for the DBA to solve a problem involving any aspect of the Oracle database, the DBA must know the problem exists. This fact is true even when backup and recovery are not required as a solution to whatever problem arises. Knowing how to identify problems that arise in Oracle is the topic of discussion in this section. This discussion will consist of several different topics. The first topic is identifying errors using trace files. Included in this part is a discussion of a special trace file for the entire Oracle database called the **alert** log, which can be used to identify many different types of problems in the Oracle database. This discussion will also give introductory usage instruction for the dynamic performance views of the Oracle database. Dynamic performance views give real-time information about the Oracle environment and are located in the data dictionary, and they are identified by a special prefix to their name called V$. This discussion provides introduction to the more detailed information about V$ that will appear in the next unit covering OCP Exam 4. This section will also present how to detect and resolve corruption in the online redo logs of the Oracle database, and the special problems redo log corruption creates. Finally, a discussion of using the DBVERIFY utility will be presented.

Using Trace Files and the Alert Log

The first topic to be presented in this section is the concept, function, and process of identifying errors using special files for background processes called trace files. Trace files can be used to identify many different things about the runtime activities of a process in the Oracle database. Any process, be it a user process, a server process, or an Oracle background process, can have a trace file. This trace file collects many different things about the process, including the input to the process as well as its output. These trace files can also list any errors that the process may have encountered during their execution. In the next unit, covering OCP Exam 4, the text will cover some uses for trace files in conjunction with user processes to determine any performance problems that may be occurring on the Oracle database. For this section, however, the discussion will focus on the use of trace files in conjunction with Oracle's background processes, and how these trace files help the DBA identify problems that may arise during database usage.

Included in this part is a discussion of a special trace file for the entire Oracle database called the **alert** log, which can be used to identify many different types of problems in the Oracle database. The Oracle database has a special trace file that covers the entire database operation. This special trace file is the **alert** log, and it contains a great deal of runtime information about the execution of the Oracle database. If the DBA has any questions about what's going on inside Oracle at any given point, the DBA can use the **alert** log to find out what is happening. Often, when a problem has occurred, the **alert** log is updated. The **alert** log is designed to act as a running log of any and all problems that occur on the database. There are several different things that are marked in the **alert** log. These factors include the following list of items:

- Initialization parameters at the start of the Oracle instance

- Information about the execution of all database, tablespace, and rollback segment creation statements

- Information about all startup and shutdown statements issued by the DBA

- Descriptive information about recoveries that may have been performed and the enabling/disabling of redo log archiving

- Many different types of error messages, along with a descriptive explanation of their cause

The location of trace information and the **alert** log vary by database instance. The DBA can control where the files are placed with the use of several different parameters in the Oracle instance. The two parameters used are called BACKGROUND_DUMP_DEST and USER_DUMP_DEST. These parameters can be specified in the **init.ora** file and will be set at the time the instance is started. The locations specified for the parameters must conform to operating system specifications.

The location specified by the BACKGROUND_DUMP_DEST parameter identifies where Oracle will place the trace information for Oracle background processes like LGWR, DBWR, SMON, and PMON. In addition, the location specified by the BACKGROUND_DUMP_DEST parameter will also be where Oracle places its **alert** log. The USER_DUMP_DEST process is the location where Oracle will allow server processes to write trace files (that will be discussed later in the coverage of OCP Exam 4) for the purpose of identifying problems with performance in application code or SQL statements. The following code block illustrates the contents of an Oracle database **alert** log. Notice that each item in the **alert** log contains a time stamp for its activity. This **alert** log illustrates a startup and shutdown of an Oracle database, with no problems encountered. Notice that all activities associated with startup and shutdown are listed, along with the specified values for the initialization parameters for the database, and the activities of archiving on the database as well.

```
Dump file C:\ORANT\RDBMS733\trace\orclALRT.LOG
Mon Feb 16 10:39:10 1998
ORACLE V7.3.3.0.1
vsnsta=0
vsnsql=a vsnxtr=3
Windows NT V4.0, OS V192.0, CPU type 586
 Starting up ORACLE RDBMS Version: 7.3.3.0.1.
 System parameters with non-default values:
 processes                 = 50
 license_max_sessions      = 1
 control_files             = C:\ORANT\DATABASE\ctl1orcl.ora
 db_block_buffers          = 200
 compatible                = 7.3.0.0.0
 log_buffer                = 8192
 log_checkpoint_interval   = 10000
 db_files                  = 20
 sequence_cache_hash_buckets= 10
 remote_login_passwordfile= SHARED
 mts_servers               = 0
 mts_max_servers           = 0
 mts_max_dispatchers       = 0
 audit_trail               = NONE
 sort_area_retained_size   = 65536
 db_name                   = orgdb01
 snapshot_refresh_processes= 1
 background_dump_dest       = %RDBMS733%\trace
```

```
  user_dump_dest             = %RDBMS733%\trace
  max_dump_file_size         = 10240
Mon Feb 16 10:39:10 1998
 PMON started
Mon Feb 16 10:39:11 1998
 DBWR started
Mon Feb 16 10:39:12 1998
 LGWR started
Mon Feb 16 10:39:14 1998
 RECO started
Mon Feb 16 10:39:16 1998
 SNP0 started
Mon Feb 16 10:39:18 1998
ALTER DATABASE MOUNT EXCLUSIVE
Mon Feb 16 10:39:19 1998
Completed: ALTER DATABASE MOUNT EXCLUSIVE
Mon Feb 16 10:39:19 1998
alter database open
Mon Feb 16 10:39:21 1998
Thread 1 opened at log sequence
Mon Feb 16 10:39:21 1998
   Current log# 1 seq# 3 mem# 0: C:\ORANT\DATABASE\log2orcl.ora
Mon Feb 16 10:39:21 1998
SMON: enabling cache recovery
Mon Feb 16 10:39:27 1998
SMON: enabling tx recovery
Mon Feb 16 10:39:27 1998
Completed: alter database open
Mon Feb 16 10:40:25 1998
Thread 1 advanced to log sequence
Mon Feb 16 10:40:26 1998
   Current log# 2 seq# 4 mem# 0: C:\ORANT\DATABASE\log1orcl.ora
Mon Feb 16 10:42:52 1998
   Shutting down instance (normal)
Mon Feb 16 10:42:52 1998
License highwatermark = 2
Mon Feb 16 10:42:53 1998
alter database close normal
Mon Feb 16 10:42:55 1998
SMON: disabling tx recovery
Mon Feb 16 10:42:56 1998
SMON: disabling cache recovery
Mon Feb 16 10:42:57 1998
Thread 1 closed at log sequence 4
Mon Feb 16 10:42:57 1998
```

```
    Current log# 2 seq# 4 mem# 0: C:\ORANT\DATABASE\log1orcl.ora
Mon Feb 16 10:42:57 1998
Completed: alter database close normal
Mon Feb 16 10:42:57 1998
alter database dismount
Mon Feb 16 10:42:57 1998
Completed: alter database dismount
```

   The **alert** log of an Oracle database is highly useful for identifying the
activities of many different parts of the Oracle database at one time, in much
the same way as a console window is useful for identifying runtime activities
on other types of systems. Additionally, there is important information
captured in the individual trace files for each Oracle background process.
These processes have their trace information stored in the same location,
but the trace files themselves generally contain only information for the
individual process, while the **alert** log captures information for the database
overall. Two trace files that are useful to look at if disk failure is suspected
are the trace files for the LGWR and DBWR processes. Since these two
Oracle background processes interact with disk I/O extensively, it is likely
that the DBA will see a problem with disk I/O be detected by those two
processes, and errors indicating those problems will therefore appear in their
associated trace files.

Exercises

   1. What is a trace file?

   2. What is the name of the special trace file where error messages,
      archiving information, and database startup and shutdown
      are stored?

Using the V$ Performance Views to Identify Problems

The dynamic performance views of the Oracle database are highly useful for
DBAs to understand what is happening on the Oracle database. This
discussion will give introductory usage instruction for the dynamic
performance views of the Oracle database. Dynamic performance views
give real-time information about what Oracle is doing, and they are located

in the data dictionary, identified by a special prefix to their name called V$. This discussion provides an introduction to the more detailed information about V$ that will appear in the next unit covering OCP Exam 4.

The dynamic performance views of the Oracle database can be used in several ways. First, they can themselves be accessed as long as the Oracle instance is active. Dynamic performance view information is generally valid for the life of the instance. Since it is information that is designed to give the DBA an understanding of the runtime performance of the Oracle database, the data in V$ performance views is not carried over from the execution of one instance to the next. Instead, the DBA must find other means to track that information across instances if it is something desired.

There are dozens of V$ performance views in the Oracle database. These views fall into several different categories, depending on the type of monitoring they are designed to provide. There are several different performance views designed to provide information about the database in several areas, some of which are listed in the following set of bullets:

- Archived redo log information

- Locks, latches, and other points of contention

- Oracle internal components such as the SGA, disk I/O and files, and database processes

- Any sort of database activity

The use of V$ views to help diagnose problems is as follows. The database, as discussed, is comprised of many datafiles, redo logs, parameter files, and control files. The DBA can detect a problem with Oracle's ability to write to a datafile using the V$DATAFILE performance view. One of the columns in this view is a status column. The status column indicates what the status of the datafile is. There are several different status possibilities, such as ONLINE or OFFLINE. One status, the RECOVER status, indicates that this datafile is one that is in need of recovery. Working in conjunction with the dynamic performance view V$DATAFILE, the DBA should first identify which datafiles are unavailable. Then the DBA should try to access that disk using appropriate operating system commands. If the access to that disk proves unsuccessful, the DBA may have identified a disk with a problem.

Of course, disks containing datafiles are not the only ones with the capacity for media failure. Any disk, as a matter of fact, can experience media failure that will render the disk inaccessible, and thus requiring the DBA to execute database recovery. In addition to V$DATAFILE, there is a dynamic performance view called V$LOGFILE, which identifies information about the online redo log files of the Oracle database. This performance view contains a status column as well, one that has several different possibilities regarding the states a log file may be in. One of those states is INVALID—meaning that the redo log file is inaccessible by the LGWR process. If a DBA spots one of her log files reading the INVALID state in the V$LOGFILE performance view, she may have a problem with media failure that requires attention. As such, it is always a good idea to multiplex redo log files, or specify several different log file members, each placed on a different disk. Multiplexing redo log information prevents the possibility that the failure of a disk containing the only redo log file for the log currently online causes the entire instance to crash.

TIP
Always multiplex online redo log file members.
If only one member of the online redo log is
used and that member is on a disk that
experiences media failure, and LGWR cannot
write to that redo log as a result, the database
instance will crash—requiring both instance
recovery and media recovery.

Finally, the DBA must pay attention to the possibility of disk failure eliminating one of the control files for the database. The instance is aware of the database's control files through the use of the CONTROL_FILES parameter in the **init.ora** file. If any of the control files specified in this parameter should be damaged by a media failure, then the DBA must shut down the instance and restore the control file. Since the control file is such an important link for Oracle to know what the physical side of the database looks like, it is important that the DBA allow Oracle to maintain multiple copies of the control file. In order to detect problems with media failure that may have damaged a control file, the DBA usually has to look in the **alert** log.

In addition to accessing the dynamic performance view information directly as the DBA would for another table in the data dictionary or in the database, the DBA can access the information from dynamic performance views using the Oracle Server Manager database monitoring tools. The Server Manager tool allows access to the V$ performance tables without dealing with the actual access to those views. Instead, the Server Manager program gathers data from these views and presents the data to the DBA in a graphical user interface.

Exercise

Name some dynamic performance views that contain status information about the files of the database.

Detecting Corruption in Online Redo Logs

Normal redo log operation consists of LGWR writing redo log buffer information to the online redo log. Optional but highly recommended to this process is the archival of redo log information. One situation that Oracle may encounter in the process of writing redo log information is the corruption of a data block within the online redo log, containing redo information. This scenario is highly detrimental to the recoverability of a database. The reason this is so damaging is that if undetected, a redo block corruption will get propagated silently to the database archived redo logs. Only when Oracle attempts to recover the database using the archived redo log will Oracle discover that the archived redo information is corrupted. However, by then it is too late—the database has failed and complete recovery is questionable.

For added protection, the DBA can specify redo log checksums to ensure that data block corruption does not occur within archived redo logs. This feature verifies each block by using checksums of values for each data block. If Oracle encounters unexpected values from this operation, Oracle will read the data in the corrupted data block of one online redo log member from another member in the redo log group. Hence the benefit of multiplexing redo log groups is twofold—Oracle is more likely to obtain good archived redo log information, and is likely not to have instance failure occur as a result of a media failure taking with it the only copy of an online redo log.

Checking redo log file blocks for data corruption is conducted only when the checksum operation is active. To activate this feature, the DBA must set the LOG_BLOCK_CHECKSUM initialization parameter to TRUE. This parameter is set by default to FALSE, rendering redo block checksum inactive by Oracle's default behavior. When set to TRUE, Oracle will check every redo log block at archive time, substituting copies of corrupted blocks in one member with the same uncorrupted blocks from another redo log member. As long as the data block is not corrupted in every redo log member, the process will complete. If the block is corrupted in all members, however, Oracle will not be able to archive the redo log.

There are some points to be made about this feature. First of all, the use of log block checksums is irrelevant unless archiving is enabled. If the DBA is not archiving the redo log information for the database, she might as well not use the checksum feature. Second, there is some performance degradation that may be experienced as a result of checking sums. The checksum process occurs at each log switch, at the same time the archiving of redo logs takes place. The performance loss would occur at this point. If online redo logs are filling fast due to heavy database usage activity, there might be some overall impact on performance. For the most part, however, the benefit of using LOG_ARCHIVE_CHECKSUM outweighs any performance hit. It is recommended that this feature be used on the Oracle database.

Exercise

How can the DBA identify corruption in data blocks in the online redo logs to prevent propagation of block corruption to archives?

Clearing Corruption in Online Redo Logs

If data block corruption is detected in an online redo log, Oracle will automatically try to obtain the same block from a different member of the online redo log group. So long as the group is multiplexed using several different members, this will minimize problems with data block corruption in the redo logs, because it is unlikely that the same block will be corrupted in two or more redo log members on two or more disks.

If for some reason the same redo data block is corrupt in all members of the online redo log (or if there is only one member in the online redo log), then Oracle cannot archive the redo log. Furthermore, there is some manual intervention that the DBA must engage in order to correct the problem. Recall the discussion about archiving redo logs manually in Chapter 13. If a redo log does not get archived manually and all online redo logs fill with redo information, Oracle will not accept any database transaction activity until the redo logs are archived. Since the redo log containing block corruption cannot be archived, an alternate step must be accomplished by the DBA. That alternative is that the online redo log must be cleared.

To clear an online redo log, the DBA must accomplish the following step. The DBA must issue an **alter database clear logfile group** statement. The following code block demonstrates the clearing process of an online redo log. In order to clear an unarchived redo log, the DBA must remember to specify the **unarchived** keyword in the statement. The issuance of this statement will eliminate all redo information in the database redo log group specified. An example of the statement is demonstrated in the code block following this paragraph. This statement must be issued by the DBA in a timely fashion if Oracle is unable to archive a redo log in the event that every member has a block corruption in the same place.

```
ALTER DATABASE orgdb01
CLEAR UNARCHIVED LOGFILE GROUP 5;
```

In the event a redo log is found to be corrupt by the checksum process, the DBA must back up the database. If a database backup does not take place, the DBA will not have a complete set of archives from which to conduct a complete database recovery. Without that complete set of archives, the DBA will have only enough data to conduct an incomplete recovery, which results in a loss of data in the event of a database failure. The best method for handling the situation is simply to take a new backup, start archiving again, and be done with it.

Any redo log can be cleared, not just the one currently online. For example, if the DBA would like to clear the redo log that was just archived, she can issue the **alter database clear logfile group** statement to do so. If the redo log being cleared has already been archived, then the DBA should *not* use the **unarchived** keyword from the previous example. A demonstration of usage for this statement is offered in the following code block. Assume in this example that Oracle is currently writing to online redo log group 5, having just finished on group 4. An archive of group 4 is then created. Afterward, the DBA decides to clear the redo log group. She can do so with the following statement:

ALTER DATABASE orgdb01 CLEAR LOGFILE GROUP 4

Exercise

How does the DBA remove corruption from the online redo logs?

The DBVERIFY Utility

The verification process offered with respect to the database online redo log data blocks is a useful process for ensuring that bad data does not get propagated to the backup copies of a database. However, the LOG_ARCHIVE_CHECKSUM parameter does little to check any other aspect of the database. Suppose the DBA wants to verify the integrity of other database files. Verification of structural integrity of Oracle database files is done with the DBVERIFY utility.

DBVERIFY Parameters

DBVERIFY is a utility that verifies the integrity of a datafile backup or production file. It can be used either to verify that a backup is usable, to verify the usability of a production database, or to diagnose a situation where corruption is suspected on a datafile or backup. DBVERIFY is usually run from the operating system command line, and is a stand-alone utility. It operates on a datafile or datafiles of a database that is currently offline. As such, it usually runs with good performance. Like other Oracle utilities, it runs from the command line according to the parameters that are identified for it. There are several parameters that can be specified. They are FILE, START, END, BLOCKSIZE, LOGFILE, FEEDBACK, HELP, and PARFILE. The following presentation will describe briefly each of the parameters that can be used with DBVERIFY.

FILE   This parameter specifies the name of the datafile that DBVERIFY will analyze. Without this parameter, the utility can do nothing.

START   This parameter specifies the start address in the Oracle blocks where DBVERIFY will begin its analysis. If no value for START is specified, then the utility will assume the start of the file.

END This parameter specifies the end address in the Oracle blocks where DBVERIFY will end its analysis. If no value is specified, the utility will assume the end of the file.

BLOCKSIZE This parameter specifies the database block size for the database. It should be specified explicitly in all cases where the block size for the Oracle database is not 2K, or 2,048 bytes. The value should be specified in bytes. If the database is not 2K and a value is not specified for this parameter, an error will occur and the run of DBVERIFY will terminate.

LOGFILE This parameter identifies a file to which all output from DBVERIFY will be written. If no filename is specified, then DBVERIFY will write all output to the screen.

FEEDBACK This parameter allows the DBA to use an indicator method built into the utility that indicates the progress made by the utility. The indicator works as such. An integer value is assigned to the FEEDBACK parameter, which represents the number of pages that must be read of the datafile before DBVERIFY will display a period (.) on the output method, either the terminal or the log file. If FEEDBACK=0, then the function is disabled.

HELP When DBVERIFY is run with HELP=Y, the utility will print out a help screen containing information about the parameters that can be set for this tool.

PARFILE As with other Oracle utilities, all parameters can be included in a parameter file that is named by the PARFILE parameter. This parameter identifies a parameter file for use by the utility in this run.

The DBVERIFY tool is a stand-alone program that, again, should be run from the command line. The name for the command that runs the utility varies from one operating system to the next, but the functionality is the same. If the DBA encounters any errors when running DBVERIFY, it is recommended that the DBA contact Oracle Worldwide Support. On many systems, the utility is referred to on the command line as **dbv**. The following code block demonstrates usage of this utility from a UNIX prompt:

```
$ dbv file=users01.dbf blocksize=4096 logfile=users01.log feedback=0
```

Alternatively, the DBA can execute the utility with the use of a parameter file, as follows:

```
$ dbv parfile=users01.par
```

The contents of the parameter file are listed as follows:

```
file=users01.dbf
blocksize=4096
logfile=users01.log
feedback=0
```

Typically, the DBVERIFY utility is only used in cases where the DBA is trying to identify corruption problems with the data in a datafile. Its output should be interpreted with the assistance of Oracle Worldwide Support. In fact, its use is often under the guidance of Oracle Worldwide Support. However, it, like all other troubleshooting methods identified herein, can be quite useful in resolving database problems.

Exercises

1. Describe the use of DBVERIFY.

2. What parameters may be used in conjunction with DBVERIFY?

Standby Database Feature

In this section, you will cover important topics related to the standby database feature of Oracle:

- Standby database configuration
- Deployment of the standby database when disaster strikes
- Switching back to the principle database

All preparation for database recovery with configuring, reading, testing, and tuning, pays off when disaster strikes. With tensions running high in the organization when a database crashes, the assumptions made are that the database will be available, and soon. And the sooner it can be made available, the better for everyone. The final area of discussion in this chapter is the use of the standby database. Introduced in Oracle7.3, the standby database offers an additional option for minimizing downtime. So minimal is downtime with the standby database that some may consider the high cost for operation and challenge of maintenance to be a small price to pay. Those organizations tend to be large ones, where a lot of time and money are riding on the availability of a machine hosting a database.

Standby Database Configuration

The standby database feature of Oracle allows DBAs to configure and maintain an operational clone of a mission-critical database within an organization. When disaster strikes, the DBA can use the standby database to minimize downtime for the organization by having a fully functional and up-to-the-minute copy of the database on hand. The DBA in this situation need only switch to the standby database in order to handle short-term goals for database recovery like minimizing downtime and having the database available for the users again on short notice.

The standby database is an exact replica of the current production database. To make the match even more identical, it is usually recommended that the DBA use identical hardware and operating system versions for the standby database in order to avoid any unplanned inconsistencies between versions at the time a disaster strikes. Obviously, this may be an expensive proposition—for example, the organization running on the latest and greatest hardware that cost $100,000 for the main system alone, without an identical backup system. If a decision is made to run the standby database feature to ensure 100 percent availability for a mission-critical database, that decision effectively doubles the cost of database hardware and software for the production machine, not to mention the cost of additional maintenance. However, the extra cost for hardware, software, and maintenance may be a small price to pay for the security of knowing the DBA has a spare database on hand to minimize the downtime and data loss to the period of time it takes users to connect to a new machine.

The standby database operates in the following way. To first create the standby database, the DBA should take a full offline backup of the primary database and create a special control file for the standby machine. The statement used to create that control file is **alter database create standby controlfile as** '*filename*'. Finally, the DBA should archive the current redo logs using **alter system archive log current**. Refer to Figure 15-3 for more information.

The following list demonstrates the activities in a step-by-step format:

I. Create a full backup of the primary database using either the offline or online method. If offline methods were used, restart the database.

2. Create a standby database control file with the statement in the following code block:

```
ALTER DATABASE orgdb01
CREATE STANDBY CONTROLFILE
AS 'stbydb.ctl';
```

3. Archive redo logs with the statement in the following code block. This will start the transfer of redo log information to the standby database.

```
ALTER SYSTEM ARCHIVE LOG CURRENT;
```

After the necessary backups have been made, the DBA should transfer the standby database backup files and restore the primary database on the standby machine. At this point, the DBA has a baseline copy of the required database objects and information. From there, the maintenance of transaction information between the primary and standby database is

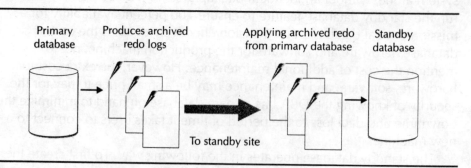

Primary database — Produces archived redo logs — To standby site — Applying archived redo from primary database — Standby database

FIGURE 15-3. *Data movement between primary and standby database*

accomplished with the use of archived redo logs. Redo logs are generated as information is entered into the primary database. The redo logs are then archived and a copy is sent to the standby database, where it will be restored to the standby database. Essentially, the standby database is always in **recovery** mode. Ideally, the continuous process of recovery required to apply an ongoing amount of archived redo information prompts the DBA for the standby and primary database to devise some sort of automated method for moving and applying archived redo logs between the two and restoring the data on the standby database. The following steps should be engaged to begin the perpetual recovery of the standby database:

1. Start and mount the database using **startup nomount** from Server Manager, followed by **alter database mount standby database exclusive**. This puts the standby database in the appropriate state.

   ```
   STARTUP NOMOUNT;
   ALTER DATABASE MOUNT STANDBY DATABASE EXCLUSIVE;
   ```

2. Initiate the recovery of the standby database using archives from the primary database using the **recover standby database** statement from Server Manager. Note that the **from** clause in the statement in the following code block is optional, and should be specified when the LOG_ARCHIVE_DEST initialization parameter does not contain the archives needed for standby database recovery.

   ```
   RECOVER FROM pathname STANDBY DATABASE;
   ```

For purposes of ensuring data consistency between the primary and standby database, it is important the DBA bear some things in mind. First, the DBA must always ensure that every data change made in the primary database finds its way onto the standby database. In general, as long as redo information is generated on whatever activity takes place on the primary database, the standby database will be updated as well. Archiving must be used in conjunction with the standby database. Some activities should be avoided, particularly those activities that do not produce redo log information. Such activities include creating database objects with the **unrecoverable** option. The performance benefits of creating database objects with the **unrecoverable** option will be discussed in the next unit covering OCP Exam 4. At this point, it should be said that the performance gain using this option is made at the expense of creating archived redo information for the database operation. The use of a standby database for recovery purposes cannot afford this performance improvement, and for this reason the DBA should *never* use the **unrecoverable** option when creating database objects or making other changes to the database.

A few final remarks about the use of a standby database will be made. It is important that the flow of archived redo log information from the primary database to the secondary database be constant. Any interruptions, such as the need to clear an online redo log because of block corruption, make it necessary for the DBA to rebuild the standby database from backup. Since this will require that the standby database not be available for recovery, the database is particularly vulnerable to disaster during the period of time the standby database is being rebuilt.

Exercises

1. What is a standby database?

2. What special statements are used for setting one up? What costs are involved?

Deployment of the Standby Database

In the situation where the primary database experiences disaster, the DBA can switch to using the standby database in the following way. First, any remaining archived redo information from the primary database must be applied to the standby database as part of the ongoing recovery that creates the standby database. This step should include the online redo logs from the primary database, if possible, so as to allow the standby database to contain every committed transaction to the point in time of the failure. Next, when the recovery is complete, the DBA must activate the standby database so that it may be used in a production capacity. This step is accomplished with the **alter database activate standby database** statement. After activating the standby database, the DBA can handle any last-minute changes to tablespaces, such as putting them into **read only** status or bringing them online or offline, depending on the status they had in the primary database. The final step is to have users point their connections to the new production machine. Depending on the application, there may (and perhaps should) be some centralized method for automating this task in order to prevent a rash of users pointed to an invalid or offline database, then calling the DBA or some other help desk group to figure out what to do. The steps for this process are listed here for reinforced understanding:

1. Start and mount the standby database, and recover the standby database using the final archives and online redo logs from the primary database.

```
STARTUP MOUNT;
ALTER DATABASE RECOVER;
```

2. When step 1 completes, the DBA activates the database using the statement in the following code block:

```
ALTER DATABASE
ACTIVATE STANDBY DATABASE;
```

3. At this point, the database is ready and waiting for users to use it as the production database. The DBA can handle any last-minute tablespace changes at this point, along with any operations required to point users from the old invalidated production database to the new one.

Exercises

1. How are data changes on a primary database moved onto the standby database?

2. What mechanisms should be designed to facilitate this?

Switching Back to the Principle Database

It is important that the DBA understand that once the standby database is activated and used by the users, it becomes the production database. The original production database can then be built from the new database and it will become the new standby database. The same procedures for creating the original standby database apply to the creation of the new standby database. However, the DBA must understand that there is no point in time where the DBA switches the database activity back to the original production database. After the standby database is activated and used, there is no further link between the production and the standby database. This operation occurs again and again.

The main benefit of using the standby database is to minimize downtime in the event of media failure. However, the standby database essentially requires the DBA to maintain two copies of the organization's data at all times, on two separate machines, which increases hardware, software, and maintenance costs substantially. For many organizations, such as national or worldwide operations where 24-hour, 99+ percent availability is a requirement (not a nice feature), the standby database is an integral tool for delivering that requirement. However, the standby database is also the most expensive option for backup and recovery. The use of a standby database should be tested thoroughly in order to understand the impact of relying on this method to minimize downtime. The importance of testing the use of this option is greater than the testing of other backup and recovery options for one reason—an organization even considering use of the standby database must have critical needs for that database to be available at all times.

Exercises

1. When disaster strikes a primary database, what happens to the standby?

2. When does the DBA switch back to the primary database?

Chapter Summary

The focus of database recovery is to minimize downtime and minimize data loss. In this chapter, several areas of maintaining a database from the perspective of backup and recovery are discussed. The first advanced topic of backup and recovery—minimizing downtime—will consist of several areas. These discussions include system startup after database failure. This section also includes discussion of starting up the database in situations where parts of the database are damaged. A continuation of the discussion started on the topic of leaving the database open during tablespace recovery is included as well. Finally, related to minimizing downtime, the parallel recovery option is discussed. Troubleshooting is also presented. The use of the **alert** log and process trace files is discussed, as is a further discussion of the dynamic performance views. The detection and resolution of corrupt data in online redo logs is also presented in this chapter. For this discussion, the use of DBVERIFY is presented. Finally, the usage and functions of the standby database feature in Oracle are presented. These three topics comprise the advanced topics of Oracle backup and recovery, and together comprise 12 percent of OCP Exam 3.

The first area of discussion within the topic of minimizing downtime is starting the database after system failure. The database startup after system failure will be faster than a typical database startup. This is due to the use of fast transaction rollback when opening the database in media recovery situations. Database recovery consists of two general steps: rolling forward and rolling back. The roll-forward process consists of applying all transactions, committed and uncommitted, to the database, while rollback consists of discarding those transactions that were not committed to the database at the time of the failure. Opening the database with fast transaction rollback consists of several items. First, Oracle will not open the database until the roll-forward process completes. However, the database will not wait until the rollback completes. Instead, Oracle will open the database for regular use after the roll-forward takes place, rolling back uncommitted transactions at the same time users are accessing the database objects. A couple of situations may arise from this. First, if a user process attempts to change a row or table that is involved in the rollback process, the transaction that failed may still hold a lock to that object, forcing the user to wait. Second, there will be fewer rollback segments available to user processes while the fast transaction rollback takes place, due to the fact that the rollback segments that were being used by transactions that failed in the database failure will be involved in the fast transaction rollback effort. However, fast transaction rollback does allow the DBA to open the database sooner than would otherwise be permitted in a database recovery situation. Thus, downtime can be minimized.

Another area of minimizing downtime comes with the ability to open the database for use when datafiles are damaged or missing as a result of a media failure. In order to do this, the DBA must first mount but not open the database. At this stage, the DBA can take the tablespace(s) containing lost datafiles offline. Then, the DBA can open the database. By opening the database even while parts of it are damaged, the DBA allows users of the database to access undamaged parts of the database while damaged parts are being fixed.

The DBA can then initiate a complete tablespace recovery on the damaged tablespaces with the use of online tablespace backups and a full set of archived redo logs. The types of organizations that benefit most from this sort of recovery are those with multiple applications running on the same database. A media failure in this situation may damage the datafiles associated with only one of the applications, implying that other applications should not have to suffer downtime because of damage to another application. This operation is usually accomplished with the **recover tablespace** option. Recall that the **recover tablespace** option requires a complete recovery to be performed to the point in time of the database failure.

A final area covered with respect to minimizing downtime is the use of the parallel recovery feature of Oracle. Parallel recovery can improve the performance of a database recovery when two or more disks have been damaged, or a great deal of redo must be applied as part of the recovery. The parallel feature is incorporated into recovery with the use of the Server Manager **recover database parallel** command. The DBA can issue this statement from Server Manager line mode or using the graphical interface. Parallel recovery requires two clauses to be specified as part of the recovery. The first is called **degree**. The integer specified for this parameter represents the degree of parallelism for the database recovery, or the number of processes the database will have actively attempting to recover the database. The second clause is called **instances**. The integer specified for this parameter indicates the number of instances that will accomplish the recovery. Each instance involved in the parallel recovery can have the number of processes dedicated to recovery indicated by degree, so in a sense the **instances** parameter is a multiplier for the **degree** clause. Because of the multiplier effect, it is important to remember that the number of processes that can be used to handle parallel recovery may not exceed the value set for RECOVERY_PARALLELISM, an initialization parameter set at instance startup in the **init.ora** file. Further, database recovery is more effective when the operating system of the machine hosting the Oracle database supports *synchronous I/O*. Otherwise, there will be limited gains in recovery performance using **recover database parallel**.

The next area of discussion in this chapter is the technique of troubleshooting a database to identify issues requiring recovery from backup. The first technique is mastering the use of trace files and the **alert** log for identifying problems with the operation of the database. As presented first in the second unit of the book covering OCP Exam 2, the Oracle database has several background processes handling various functions for the database, such as the operation of moving redo information or database blocks from and to the disks, various recovery activities, and other operations. Each of these background processes writes a log of its activities, detailing any errors it may have encountered, when it started running, and other things. These logs are called trace files, and they are stored in a location identified to Oracle by the use of the initialization parameter in **init.ora** called BACKGROUND_DUMP_DEST. Each of the user processes connecting to the database requires a server process to run Oracle database transactions on its behalf. These processes also create an activity tracing log. This log is stored in another location, specified with the use of the initialization parameter in **init.ora** called USER_DUMP_DEST. A final, and perhaps most important, log mechanism is the overall log of activity for the Oracle database, called the **alert** log. This file contains all error messages encountered by the database in its normal activity, along with startup and shutdown times, archiving information, and information about the startup and shutdown of background processes. If the DBA suspects there is a problem with the operation of the database, the **alert** log should be the first place she looks.

Another method the DBA can incorporate into the detective work required for the identification of database problems is the use of the dynamic performance views in the Oracle data dictionary. These views track performance information for the database, and their names are usually prefixed with either V$ or X$. Several of these views identify the status for various components of the database, such as the datafiles and redo log file of that database. If there is a problem with the status of a datafile or redo log file arising from the failure of a disk, Oracle will mark the file with the appropriate status in the appropriate dynamic performance view. There are several performance views involved in the task of backing up and recovering the database. Some of these have already been identified. The two views emphasized in this discussion are the V$DATAFILE and the V$LOGFILE views. Both of these dynamic performance views contain status information for each of the files they represent. These files are datafiles and redo log files, respectively. If the DBA should find a datafile with a status of RECOVER or a redo log file with a status of INVALID, the DBA may want to investigate a problem with accessing the disk containing the datafile and/or log file using operating system means. These methods may be used to check the status of the database for recovery issues.

One particular issue for DBAs that may arise in the need to identify damage to the database is the need for verification mechanisms of the database. There are a few mechanisms available for the DBA to do just that. The first pertains to the verification of operation on the online redo logs. There is a feature that will verify the blocks of an online redo log before archiving, or before applying an archived redo log as part of database recovery, to prevent the propagation of corrupted data blocks in the backup and recovery of an Oracle database. To use this feature, the DBA needs to set the LOG_ARCHIVE_CHECKSUM initialization parameter to TRUE. If the DBA is using archive checksums to confirm the integrity of the blocks in an online redo log, the following process will occur. When Oracle reaches a log switch, it will check the online redo log for corruption in the data blocks of the online redo log to archive. If Oracle finds corruption in an online redo log, it will try to write archive information using a different redo log file. If all members contain the corruption in the same data block, Oracle will not be able to archive that redo log and archiving will stop.

At this point, the DBA must intervene in the archiving process. The redo log containing the corrupt data block will need to be cleared using the **alter database clear unarchived logfile group** statement. Since the log has not been archived, the DBA will also need to include the **unarchived** option as previously described. Any redo log group can be cleared, depending on the desires of the DBA. For example, a redo log can be cleared after archiving by using the statement identified earlier for clearing online redo logs, but since the statement has been archived, the **unarchived** option can be eliminated. However, once a redo log is cleared, the DBA no longer has a complete set of archived redo logs for database recovery. Unless the DBA backs up the database at this point, the DBA will only be able to execute incomplete recovery from database failure. The DBA should be sure to back up the database in the event of clearing online redo logs.

Another tool available for the DBA to use in verification of other types of files such as datafiles is the DBVERIFY utility. This utility will take an offline datafile and inspect it for block corruption. DBVERIFY is a stand-alone utility that operates in the same way as other utilities discussed in Oracle. To run it, the DBA supplies a set of parameters. Some parameters the DBA can identify for running DBVERIFY are listed: FILE, START, END, BLOCKSIZE, LOGFILE, FEEDBACK, HELP, and PARFILE. The FILE parameter is used by the DBA to name the file that DBVERIFY will operate on, while START and END are used to tell DBVERIFY where in the file to start and end the verification. The defaults are the beginning and end of the file, respectively. The BLOCKSIZE parameter specifies the size of Oracle blocks in the database, in bytes. The LOGFILE parameter names a file to which the output of DBVERIFY will be written. If no log file is specified, DBVERIFY writes its output to the screen. The FEEDBACK parameter can be assigned an integer that specifies how many pages of the datafile will be read before DBVERIFY puts some notification of its progress on the screen. Setting the HELP parameter to 'Y' will cause DBVERIFY to display information the DBA can use for setting other parameters. Finally, the PARFILE parameter can be used to name a parameter file containing values for other parameters used in DBVERIFY. Due to the fact that DBVERIFY identifies problems involving database corruption, use of it may be best undertaken with the guidance of Oracle Worldwide Support.

The final topic covered in this chapter is the use of the standby database feature of Oracle. DBAs who need to provide a high degree of availability for the users of a database may incorporate a standby database into the overall backup and recovery strategy. A standby database is an identical twin database for some other database, and it can be used in the event of a disaster. In order to use the standby database feature of Oracle, the DBA must use archiving in both databases. The reason archiving is necessary is because the standby database is updated with data changes on the primary database by applying the archive logs generated by the primary database.

To create a standby database, the DBA must execute the following steps. First, the DBA should acquire a machine to host the standby database that is identical to the machine hosting the primary database. Next, the DBA needs to take a complete backup of the primary database. After that, the DBA must create a special control file for the standby database using the **alter database create standby controlfile as** '*filename*'. Finally, the DBA should archive the current set of redo logs using the **alter system archive log current** statement.

With the archived redo logs, datafile backups, and standby control file, the DBA can create a baseline standby database. After creating the standby database, it must be perpetually standing by for database recovery in order to keep the standby database current with the changes made in the primary database. To do so, the DBA should use the **startup nomount** statement in Server Manager, followed by the **recover standby database** statement. Archive logs generated by the principle database should be placed in the location specified by LOG_ARCHIVE_DEST on the standby database, or, alternatively, the **from** clause can be used in conjunction with the **recover standby database** statement. Ideally, the process of moving archive logs from the primary database to the standby will be automated in order to keep the standby database as current with changes in the primary database as possible.

When disaster strikes the production database, the DBA must do the following to get users on the standby database as quickly as possible. First, the application of all archived redo logs on the standby database must complete as quickly as possible. Next, the DBA should shut down the standby database and restart it using **startup mount**. From there, the DBA should execute a **recover database** statement, being sure to omit the **standby** clause. As part of this recovery, the DBA should try to apply the current online redo logs on the production database to the standby database in order to capture all transaction information up to the moment of failure on the other database. After recovery of the standby database is complete, the DBA can execute the **alter database activate standby database** statement. From this point on, the standby database is the production database. Switching back to the original production database, then, will not happen unless the production database is made into the standby of the new production database and the new production database fails.

Standby databases can offer enormous benefit to the organization requiring 24×7 database availability with little or no option for downtime. However, standby databases are a costly solution to database recovery. The costs of a standby database are usually twice the price of the production database hardware and software, plus added expenses for maintaining both databases. Of course, the price of downtime per minute on a mission-critical database system can be far, far higher, thereby justifying the additional costs.

Two-Minute Drill

- The reason the database will start quickly after a system failure is due to the fast transaction rollback feature of the Oracle database.

- There are two general parts to database recovery: roll forward and rollback. Fast transaction recovery allows Oracle to open the database after roll forward is complete, executing the rollback while users access the database.

- Fast transaction recovery eliminates the wait for a database to open after system failure, minimizing downtime so the DBA can initiate recovery quicker. However, users entering the database may still encounter delays due to rollback segments still being involved with recovery, and locks on tables and rows that are still held by dead transactions.

- In some organizations, a media failure may not impact all users.

- To allow the users who are not impacted to continue using the database even when datafiles are missing, the DBA can open the database in the following way. First, the DBA should use **startup mount** from Server Manager to start the instance and mount the database. From there, the DBA can take the tablespaces containing missing or damaged datafiles offline with the **alter tablespace offline** statement. After that, the DBA can open the database with the **alter database open** statement.

- Recovery on parts of a database that are missing can be accomplished using the methods for complete tablespace recovery. The DBA will require an online backup and all appropriate archived redo logs. For this recovery, the tablespace must be offline.

- When the DBA is done recovering the tablespace damaged, while the rest of the database is used by the users, the DBA can back up the recovered tablespace or the entire database.

- Parallel recovery can be used to improve recovery time for the Oracle database. To engage in parallel recovery, the DBA can use the **recover database parallel** statement from Server Manager.

- There are two clauses that must be set for parallel recovery: **degree** and **instances**.

■ The **degree** option indicates the degree of parallelism for the recovery, or the number of processes that will be used to execute the recovery.

■ The **instances** option indicates the number of instances that will engage in database recovery.

■ The total number of processes that will engage in parallel recovery equals **degree** *times* **instances.** This value may not exceed the integer set for the RECOVERY_PARALLELISM initialization parameter set in the **init.ora** file.

■ Troubleshooting the Oracle database can be accomplished by looking in trace files or the **alert** log.

■ Every background process writes its own trace file, containing information about when the background process started and any errors it may have encountered.

■ A special trace file exists for the entire database, called the **alert** log. This file contains trace information for database startup and shutdown, archiving, any structural database change, and errors encountered by the database.

■ The V$ performance views may also be used to detect errors in the operation of the database.

■ The V$DATAFILE view carries information about the datafiles of the database. One item it contains is the status of a datafile. If the status of a datafile is RECOVER, there may be a problem with media failure on the disk containing that datafile.

■ The V$LOGFILE view carries information about the redo log files of the database. One item it contains is the status of a log file. If the status of the logfile is INVALID, there could be a problem with media failure on the disk containing that redo log.

■ Another cause of problems in the Oracle database is the problem of data integrity. If there is a corruption in the online redo log of the database during archiving or an archived redo log during recovery, the DBA risks having an unusable set of backups for database recovery.

- To minimize risk of storing corrupt archived redo information, the DBA can use a verification process available for redo logs. To use this verification process, the DBA should set the LOG_ARCHIVE_ CHECKSUM parameter in the **init.ora** file to TRUE and restart the database.

- The redo log verification process works as follows. At a log switch, Oracle will check every data block in the redo log as it writes the archive. If one is corrupt, Oracle will look at the same data block in another redo log member. If that data block is corrupt in all members of the online redo log file, Oracle will not archive the redo log.

- If Oracle does not archive the redo log, the DBA must intervene by clearing the log file. This step is accomplished with the **alter database clear unarchived logfile group** statement. If the log file group has been archived, the **unarchived** clause can be eliminated.

- Verifying the integrity of a database can also be executed on its datafiles using the DBVERIFY utility. DBVERIFY is a stand-alone utility that verifies a file or files of an offline database or tablespace.

- Operation of DBVERIFY involves specifying parameters to manage its runtime behavior. The parameters that may be specified include FILE, START, END, BLOCKSIZE, LOGFILE, FEEDBACK, HELP, and PARFILE.

- FILE is used to identify the filename of the datafile that DBVERIFY will analyze.

- START is used to identify the Oracle block where DBVERIFY will start analysis.

- END is used to identify the Oracle block where DBVERIFY will end analysis.

- BLOCKSIZE is used to identify the size of blocks in the datafile.

- LOGFILE is used to identify a file that DBVERIFY will write all execution output to. If not used, DBVERIFY writes to the screen.

- FEEDBACK is a special feature whereby DBVERIFY writes out dots on the screen (or logfile) based on progress, or the number of pages it has written.

- HELP is used to obtain information about the other parameters.

- PARFILE is used to place all other parameters in a parameter file.

- The standby database is used by DBAs to create and maintain a clone database for the purpose of minimizing downtime in the event of a disaster.

- The hardware used to support the standby database should be identical to the machine that supports the production database.

- To create a standby database, the DBA must do the following. First, take a full backup of the database, either offline or online. Then, create a standby database control file with the **alter database create standby controlfile as** '*filename*'. Finally, the DBA should archive the current set of redo logs using the **alter system archive log current** statement and move it all to the standby machine.

- After creating the standby database on the other machine, the DBA should put the standby database into perpetual **recovery** mode. The first step is to use the **startup nomount** option to start the database with Server Manager. Then, the DBA must issue the **recover standby database** statement. At this point, the database will apply archived redo logs from the primary database to the standby database.

- When a disaster strikes, the DBA can recover the final transactions made to the primary database and move data to the standby database. Starting the standby database is accomplished in the following way. The DBA should shut down the standby database and restart it using **startup mount**. From there, the DBA should execute a **recover database** statement, being sure to omit the **standby** clause.

- As part of this recovery, the DBA should try to apply the current online redo logs on the production database to the standby database in order to capture all transaction information up to the moment of failure on the other database. After recovery of the standby database is complete, the DBA can execute the **alter database activate standby database** statement.

■ From this point on, the standby database is now the production database. There is no step later where the DBA switches it back, unless the original database is turned into a standby for the new production database and the new production database fails.

■ The standby database, though costly, is the best option for minimizing downtime to make a fast recovery.

Chapter Questions

1. **In order to detect online redo log corruption, the DBA should**

    A. Run DBVERIFY on the redo log file

    B. Run DBVERIFY on the datafile

    C. View the contents using Server Manager

    D. Set LOG_ARCHIVE_CHECKSUM to TRUE

2. **Which of the following statements is appropriate for creating a control file for a standby database?**

    A. alter database backup controlfile to 'orgstby.ctl';

    B. alter database backup controlfile to standby;

    C. alter database create standby controlfile to 'orgstby.ctl';

    D. alter database create controlfile;

3. **The DBA believes there is a media failure on the disk containing the DATA01 tablespace. In the trace file for which background process might the DBA look for an error message?**

    A. LGWR

    B. DBWR

    C. SMON

D. PMON

4. Which of the following statements is used to recover the database when the DBA wants to let users access undamaged areas of the database while recovery takes place?

   A. recover tablespace

   B. recover database

   C. recover parallel

   D. recover until cancel

5. If archiving has stopped due to corruption of a data block in all redo log members, which of the following statements is appropriate for resolving the problem?

   A. shutdown abort

   B. alter database archivelog

   C. alter database clear unarchived logfile group

   D. alter system archive log current

6. Archiving must be used in conjunction with the standby database.

   A. TRUE

   B. FALSE

7. Which of the following items most directly improves the performance of parallel recovery?

   A. Synchronous I/O

   B. Decreasing **instances**

   C. Decreasing **degree**

   D. Increasing RECOVER_PARALLELISM

8. To identify the time archiving was turned off, the DBA should use

   A. The V$LOG view

   B. The **alert** log

   C. The V$LOGFILE view

   D. The redo log

9. **Which of the following is most likely the reason why a database starts faster after system failure?**

   A. Hardware upgrade

   B. Lower memory usage

   C. The DBVERIFY utility

   D. Fast transaction rollback

10. **Multiplexing redo log members reduces the possibility of having to clear an online redo log.**

   A. TRUE

   B. FALSE

11. **If RECOVERY_PARALLELISM=15, which of the following are appropriate settings for parallel recovery?**

   A. instances=4, **degree**=4

   B. instances=2, **degree**=5

   C. instances=3, **degree**=6

   D. instances=5, **degree**=4

Answers to Chapter Questions

1. D. Set LOG_ARCHIVE_CHECKSUM to TRUE

Explanation To verify the integrity of a database redo log file, the DBA should use the checksum verification method specified by setting the LOG_ARCHIVE_CHECKSUM initialization parameter to TRUE. DBVERIFY is best used for the datafiles of the database, thus eliminating choices A and B. Choice C is incorrect because it is not possible to view the contents of an online redo log using Server Manager.

2. C. **alter database create standby controlfile as** 'orgstby.ctl';

Explanation A special control file must be created for standby databases. Choice C indicates the statement that is used to create that special control file. Choices A and B are incorrect because the statements they list are used to back up a control file, not create a standby one. Choice D is incorrect because it is used to create a new control file for a primary database, not a standby.

3. B. DBWR

Explanation Since DBWR is the background process that writes data blocks between user and application tablespaces—which according to standard nomenclature, a tablespace called DATA01 most likely contains—this background process is the one most likely to encounter errors stemming from media failure on the disk containing datafiles from the DATA01 tablespace.

4. A. **recover tablespace**

Explanation Choices B and D are both recoveries that require the database to be closed. Choice C is incorrect because the parallel recovery doesn't specify which type of recovery, either tablespace, database, or datafile.

5. C. **alter database clear unarchived logfile group**

Explanation   When a redo log cannot be archived due to data block corruption, the solution is to clear the online redo log. Choice C correctly identifies the statement for clearing the online redo log. Choice A is incorrect because although aborting the instance will alleviate the problem at hand, it will also create many other problems arising from incomplete media recovery that will ensue. Choice B is incorrect because ceasing to archive redo logs is an inappropriate action for reasons similar to choice A—overkill. Choice D is incorrect because Oracle will not allow the DBA to archive the current redo log because of data block corruption.

6. A. TRUE

Explanation   Archiving redo information is the method data in the primary database is restored into the standby. Archiving is therefore required.

7. A. Synchronous I/O

Explanation   Choice A identifies the feature upon which the benefits of parallel recovery depend most heavily. Choices B and C are incorrect because decreasing either parameter reduces the number of parallel processes that will work on the recovery. Choice D reduces the total number of processes that can be used in parallel recovery as well, thereby worsening performance.

8. B. The **alert** log

Explanation   The **alert** log lists the time at which many major events take place on the database. Choices A, C, and D are all incorrect because these options don't enable the DBA to know what time any of these things happened.

9. D. Fast transaction rollback

Explanation   Although choices A and B may have some effect on better performance for database startup, the reason that will most heavily impact the performance of system startup after a database failure is choice D. The DBVERIFY utility answer for choice C has no relevance in system startup after database failure.

10. A. TRUE

Explanation If redo logs are multiplexed, then Oracle has more members of a redo log group to choose from if there is a problem with corruption in a data block. Thus, it makes sense to have more members of a redo log available for Oracle to choose from if it encounters a corrupt data block.

11. B. **instances**=2, **degree**=5

Explanation The constraint on the number of parallel processes that can execute on a recovery is limited by RECOVERY_PARALLELISM. The number of processes that will operate according to the options **instances** and **degree** is based on the two values multiplied by one another. Choice A is incorrect because $4 \times 4 = 16$, while RECOVERY_PARALLELISM = 15. Choice C is incorrect because $3 \times 6 = 18$, $18 > 15$. Choice D is incorrect because $5 \times 4 = 20$, $20 > 15$.

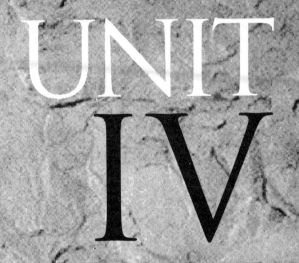

UNIT
IV

Preparing for OCP
DBA Exam 4:
Performance Tuning
Workshop

CHAPTER 16

Introducing Database Tuning

n this chapter, you will understand and demonstrate knowledge in the following areas:

- Tuning overview
- Diagnosing problems

This chapter is an introduction to tuning. OCP Exam 4 covers many aspects of tuning the Oracle database, and this chapter will set the stage both for your high-level understanding of the Oracle tuning process and for the material to come in the rest of Unit IV. This chapter will begin your exploration of tuning the Oracle database and the applications that use the Oracle database. Both the methodology for tuning and the tools for executing the tuning process will be discussed. The material in this chapter comprises about 15 percent of test questions asked on OCP Exam 4.

Tuning Overview

In this section, you will cover the following topics related to tuning overview:

- Discussing the nature of tuning
- Outlining a tuning methodology
- Identifying diagnostic tools

The Oracle database server is designed to meet the needs of different applications, including those applications that have large user populations who execute many transactions to put data into the database and modify existing data in that database. Oracle also serves the needs of organizations that require large amounts of data to be available in a *data warehouse*, or an application that contains vast amounts of data available primarily for read access and reporting. In order to meet the needs of these different types of applications, Oracle offers a great deal of flexibility in the way it can be configured. The ongoing tuning process is used by DBAs to run the Oracle server in such a way as to maximize query performance, storage management, and resource usage according to the needs of the application. This section will begin the discussion of the nature of tuning, allowing you to make the most of Oracle.

Discussing the Nature of Tuning

Tuning is done for many reasons on an Oracle database. Users often want their online applications to run faster. The developers may want batch processes to run faster as well. Management in the organization often recognizes the need for faster applications and batch processing on their Oracle databases. One solution to the problem of performance is to invest in the latest hardware containing faster processors, more memory, and more disk space. To be sure, this is often an effective solution, and methods for maximizing the hardware on the machine hosting the Oracle database will be presented in this unit in order to improve your understanding in this area for OCP. However, the latest and greatest machines are also the most expensive. Organizations generally need to plan their hardware purchases some time in advance also, which means that acute problems with performance are not usually resolved with the hardware purchase approach. Instead, the DBA must determine other ways to improve performance.

In order to meet the needs of an ongoing application that sometimes encounters performance issues, the DBA must know how to resolve those issues. Many problems with performance on an Oracle database can be resolved with three methods, the first being the purchase of new hardware described. The second and third are effective database configuration and effective application design. It should be understood by all people who use Oracle databases that by far the greatest problems with performance are caused by the application—not the Oracle database. Poorly written SQL statements, the use of multiple SQL statements where one would suffice, and other problems within an application are the source of most performance issues. The DBA should always place the responsibility of the first step in any performance situation onto the application developers to see if they can rewrite the code of the application to utilize the database more effectively.

Only after all possibility for resolving the performance issue by redeveloping the application is exhausted should the DBA attempt any changes to the configuration of the Oracle database. This consideration is designed to prevent the impromptu reconfiguration of the Oracle database to satisfy a performance need in one area, only to create a performance problem in another area. Any change to the configuration of the Oracle database should be considered carefully. The DBA should weigh the trade-offs she might need to make in order to improve performance in one area. For example, when changing the memory management configuration for the Oracle database without buying and installing more memory, the DBA must be careful not to size any part of the Oracle SGA out of real memory. Also, if the Oracle SGA takes up more existing memory, other applications that might be running on the same machine may suffer. The DBA may need to work in conjunction with the systems administrator of the machine to decide how to make the trade-off.

Exercises

1. Why must a database be tuned?

2. What is the cause of most performance problems on Oracle databases?

Outlining a Tuning Methodology

Before the DBA begins tuning Oracle, he or she should have an appropriate tuning methodology outlined. This methodology should correspond directly to the goals the DBA is attempting to reach regarding the use of each application and other needs identified by the organization. Some common goals include allowing an application to accept high-volume transaction processing at certain times of the day, returning frequently requested data quickly, or allowing users to create and execute ad hoc reports without adversely affecting online transaction processing. These goals, as well as the many other performance goals set before DBAs, fall into three general categories:

■ To improve performance of specific SQL statements running against the Oracle database

■ To improve performance of specific applications running within the Oracle database

■ To improve overall performance for all users and applications within the Oracle database

Oracle has its own four-step process that every DBA should use for performance tuning. In general, it is best to start with step 1 in every situation, in order to avoid creating problems as you attempt to solve them. Also, notice that progressing from step to step directly translates to an increase in the scope and impact of the proposed change. The steps of the process are to start by tuning the performance of applications using the Oracle database, then to tune the memory usage of the Oracle database. If there are still problems, the DBA can tune the disk I/O and utilization of the Oracle database, and finally, the DBA should tune locks and other contention issues. A full presentation of each area follows.

Step 1: Tune the Application

The importance of tuning the application SQL statements and PL/SQL code cannot be overstated. Most often, poorly written queries are the source of poor performance. DBAs should play an active part in encouraging developers to tune the application queries before engaging in other steps of the tuning process. Some of the tools available for developers are described shortly, including SQL Trace and the **explain plan** command. More detailed information about application tuning appears in Chapter 17.

Step 2: Tune Memory Structures

After application tuning, appropriate configuration and tuning of memory structures can have a sizeable impact on application and database performance. Oracle should have enough space allocation for the SQL and PL/SQL areas, data dictionary cache, and buffer cache to yield performance improvement. That improvement will be in the following areas:

- Retrieving database data already in memory

- Reduction in SQL parsing

- Elimination of operating system paging and swapping (the copying of data in memory onto disk that has detrimental impact to application performance)

More detailed information about memory tuning appears in Chapter 18.

Step 3: Tune Disk I/O Usage

Oracle server is designed in such a way as to prevent I/O from adversely impacting application performance. Each of its features such as the server, DBWR, LGWR, CKPT, and SMON background process contributes to the effective management of disk usage, and is designed to reduce an application's dependency on fast writes to disk for improvements in performance. However, there are situations where disk usage can have an adverse impact on an application. Tuning disk usage generally means distributing I/O over several disks to avoid contention, storing data in blocks to facilitate data retrieval, and creating properly sized extents for data storage. More information about disk I/O tuning appears in Chapter 19.

Step 4: Detect and Eliminate Resource Contention

As in the case of tuning disk I/O, Oracle server is designed in such a way as to minimize resource contention. For example, Oracle can detect and eliminate deadlocks. However, there are occasions where many users contend for resources such as rollback segments, dispatchers, or other processes in the multithreaded architecture of Oracle server, or redo log buffer latches. Though infrequent, these situations are extremely detrimental to the performance of the application. More information about resource contention tuning appears in Chapter 20.

As stated, the steps listed above should be used in the order listed in the event of a tuning emergency. However, the proactive DBA should attempt to tune the database even when everything appears to be running well. The reason proactive tuning is necessary is to reduce the amount of time the DBA spends in production support situations. Proactive tuning also increases the DBA's knowledge of his or her applications, thereby reducing the effort required when the inevitable production emergency arises.

Exercises

1. What are the three general categories of performance goals?

2. Where are the four steps for performance tuning? In what order should the DBA engage in these steps? How does scope relate to this order?

Identifying Diagnostic Tools

The most important step in solving performance issues is discovering them. While the easiest way to discover performance issues is to wait for developers or users to call and complain, this method is not very customer-oriented, and has proved very detrimental to the reputation of many information technology departments. This approach of taking performance problems on the chin is a reality that is not required, given the availability of tools from Oracle to help monitor and eliminate performance issues. Here are some utilities designed to assist in tuning the Oracle instance.

UTLBSTAT   This creates tables to store dynamic performance statistics for the Oracle database. Execution of this script also begins the statistics collection process. In order to make statistics collection more effective, the DBA should not run UTLBSTAT until after the database has been running for several hours or days. This utility uses underlying V$ performance views (see V$ views below) to find information about the performance of the Oracle database, and the accumulation of useful data in these views may take some time.

UTLESTAT   This ends collection of statistics for the instance. An output file called **report.txt** containing a report of the statistics is generated by the UTLBSTAT utility. To maximize the effectiveness of these two utilities, it is important that UTLBSTAT be allowed to run for a long time before ending statistics collection, under a variety of circumstances. These circumstances include batch processing, online transaction processing, backups, and periods of inactivity. This wide variety of database activity will give the DBA a more complete idea about the level of usage the database experiences under normal circumstances.

SERVER MANAGER   Oracle's Server Manager tool contains several menu options for monitoring the database and diagnosing problems. This menu is usable when Server Manager is run in GUI mode. Since most Oracle DBAs who use UNIX as the operating system to support Oracle run Server Manager in line mode, this option may not be as familiar to them as other options that take advantage of line mode operation.

EXPLAIN PLAN   This command enables the DBA or developer to determine the execution path of a block of SQL code. The execution plan is generated by the SQL statement processing mechanism. In Oracle7, this command can be executed by entering **explain plan set statement_id = 'name' into plan_table for** *SQL_statement* at the SQL*Plus prompt. The execution plan shows the step-by-step operations that Oracle will undertake in order to obtain data from the tables comprising the Oracle database. This option is provided mainly for developers and users who write SQL statements and run them against the database to avoid running inefficient SQL. The output of this information is placed into a special table created by running the **utlxplan.sql** script found in the **rdbms/admin** subdirectory under the Oracle software home directory. This table is called PLAN_TABLE. An example of an operation that obtains data from the database inefficiently is a *full table scan*. The execution information can be retrieved from PLAN_ TABLE using a special query provided by Oracle—this query will display the information in PLAN_TABLE in a certain way that requires interpretation of the innermost indented operation outward, and then from top to bottom. More information about using **explain plan** will be presented in Chapter 17.

ENTERPRISE MANAGER PERFORMANCE PACK   This set of utilities contains products that will help the DBA identify performance issues. This package is available mainly to organizations using Oracle on servers running Windows operating systems. This option may not be as well known to DBAs in organizations using Oracle in UNIX environments, because many DBAs use Oracle database management tools in line mode.

SQL TRACE   This tool extends the functionality provided by **explain plan** by giving statistical information about the SQL statements executed in a session that has tracing enabled. This additional statistical information is provided in a dump file. This utility is run for an entire session using the **alter session set sql_trace = true** statement. Tracing a session is especially useful for analyzing the full operation of an application or batch process containing multiple transactions, where it is unclear which part of the application or batch process is encountering performance issues.

TKPROF   The dump file provided by SQL Trace is often hard to read. TKPROF takes the output in a trace file and turns it into a more understandable report. The relationship between SQL TRACE and TKPROF is similar to the relationship between IMPORT and EXPORT, as TKPROF only operates or accepts as input the output file produced by SQL TRACE. The contents of the report produced by TKPROF will be discussed.

V$ VIEWS   These are views against several memory structures created by the Oracle SGA at instance startup. These views contain database performance information that is useful to both DBAs and Oracle to determine the current status of the database. The operation of performance tuning tools, such as those in the Oracle Enterprise Manager or Server Manager utilities running in GUI mode as well as utilities available from third-party vendors, use the underlying V$ performance views as their basis for information.

Exercises

1. Identify the usage of the UTLBSTAT and the UTLESTAT tools. Which tool produces **report.txt**?

2. Identify the tool that identifies the execution plan of a given SQL query. In what step of Oracle's recommended tuning methodology might this information be useful?

3. What are the V$ views, and how are they used in the database?

Diagnosing Problems

In this section, you will cover the following topics related to diagnosing problems:

- Running UTLBSTAT and UTLESTAT

- Describing contents of **report.txt**

- Understanding latch contention

- Checking for events causing waits

In order to solve performance issues, the DBA must be able to pinpoint their source. Often, the performance issue may occur in conjunction with another event. For example, a DBA may get a performance-related support call from users of an online transaction processing system who experience noticeably slower performance at 3 P.M. The DBA may think that there is a performance issue with the application until she discovers that there are a series of ad hoc reports that are scheduled to deploy at around that time. Unfortunately, performance issues sometimes happen infrequently or at irregular intervals. The task of identifying the problem can involve a detailed review of what was happening in the database at the time the performance issue arose. A real-time database monitoring tool that uses V$ dynamic performance views as the basis of reflecting database usage can tell the DBA when the performance issue happened. However, the tool will only be able to tell when the problem occurred in real time. The DBA or someone else must actually be observing the performance monitor when it reflects the change in performance. This can be time consuming and prone to human error such as momentary distraction. The answer to this problem is to maintain a history of performance statistics. This section will describe how the DBA can do this.

Running UTLBSTAT and UTLESTAT

These two utilities, mentioned earlier, provide the functionality required to maintain a history of performance information. To review, UTLBSTAT creates several statistics tables for storing the dynamic performance information. It also begins the collection of dynamic performance statistics. Typically, the script containing this utility is called **utlbstat.sql** and is found in the **rdbms/admin** directory under the Oracle software home directory, and is executed from within Server Manager. Though it is not necessary to execute the **connect internal** command before executing this query, the DBA should connect to the database as a user with **connect internal** privileges prior to running the query. The database overhead used for collecting these statistics, though not sizeable (depending on the platform running Oracle), can have an impact on the system as high as 10 percent. UTLBSTAT creates tables to store data from several V$ performance views including:

V$WAITSTAT	V$SYSTEM_EVENT	V$SYSSTAT
V$ROLLSTAT	V$ROWCACHE	V$LATCH
V$SESSION	V$LIBRARYCACHE	V$SESSION_EVENT

TIP
*In order to execute UTLBSTAT, the TIMED_STATISTICS parameter must be set to TRUE for the Oracle instance in the **init.ora** file. Certain information will not be captured by the utility if this parameter is not correctly set. Also, do not run this utility against a database that has not been running for several hours or more, as it relies on dynamic performance views that will not contain useful information if the database has not been running for some time.*

UTLESTAT ends the collection of performance statistics from the views named above. Typically, the script is called **utlestat.sql** and is found in the same location as UTLBSTAT, in the **rdbms/admin** directory under the Oracle software home directory, and it is executed from Server Manager. Though it is not necessary to execute the **connect internal** command before executing this query, the DBA should connect to the database as a user with **connect internal** privileges prior to running the query. This utility will gather all statistics collected and use them to generate an output file called **report.txt**. After generating **report.txt**, the utility will remove the statistics tables it used to store the performance history of the database. The contents of **report.txt** will be discussed shortly.

Care should be taken not to shut down the database while UTLBSTAT is running. If this should happen, there could be problems with interpreting the data, and since the database must be running for several hours in order for the V$ views that UTLBSTAT depends on to contain useful data, all work done by UTLBSTAT will be useless. The best thing to do in this situation is to run UTLESTAT as soon as possible to clear out all data from the prior run, and wait until the database has been up long enough to attempt a second execution.

Exercises

1. What is the purpose of the UTLBSTAT utility? What database initialization parameter should be set to TRUE before UTLBSTAT is executed?

2. What is the purpose of the UTLESTAT utility? What is the name of the output file produced by this utility?

Describing Contents of report.txt

There are several important areas of information provided by the **report.txt** file. The **report.txt** file provides a great deal of useful information in the following areas. First, it provides statistics for file I/O by tablespace and datafile. This information is useful in distributing files across many disks to reduce I/O contention. SGA, shared area, dictionary area, table/procedure, trigger, pipe, and other cache statistics. **report.txt** is also used to determine if there is contention for any of several different resources. This report also gives latch wait statistics for the database instance and shows if there is contention for resources using latches. Statistics are also given for how often user processes wait for rollback segments, which can be used to determine if more rollback segments should be added. Average length of a dirty buffer write queue is also shown, which the DBA can use to determine if DBWR is having difficulty writing blocks to the database. Finally, the **report.txt** file contains a listing of all initialization parameters for the database and the start and stop time for statistics collection. An example of **report.txt**, slightly modified for readability, is listed here:

```
SVRMGR> Rem Select Library cache statistics. The pin hit rate should be high.
SVRMGR> select namespace library, gets,
    2>      round(decode(gethits,0,1,gethits)/decode(gets,0,1,gets),3)
    3>       gethitratio, pins,
    4>      round(decode(pinhits,0,1,pinhits)/decode(pins,0,1,pins),3)
    5>       pinhitratio, reloads, invalidations from stats$lib;
```

LIBRARY	GETS	GETHITRATI	PINS	PINHITRATI	RELOADS	INVALIDATI
BODY	2	1	2	1	0	0
CLUSTER	0	1	0	1	0	0
INDEX	0	1	0	1	0	0
OBJECT	0	1	0	1	0	0
PIPE	0	1	0	1	0	0
SQL AREA	5098	.605	18740	.772	185	0
TABLE/PROCED	7762	.989	15138	.982	186	0
TRIGGER	0	1	0	1	0	0

```
SVRMGR> Rem The total is the total value of the statistic between the time
```

```
SVRMGR> Rem bstat was run and the time estat was run. Note that the estat
SVRMGR> Rem script logs on as "internal" so the per_logon statistics will
SVRMGR> Rem always be based on at least one logon.
SVRMGR> select n1.name "Statistic", n1.change "Total",
     2>       round(n1.change/trans.change,2) "Per Transaction",
     3>       round(n1.change/logs.change,2) "Per Logon"
     4>   from stats$stats n1, stats$stats trans, stats$stats logs
     5>   where trans.name='user commits'
     6>    and logs.name='logons' and n1.change != 0
     7>   order by n1.name;
```

   0 rows selected.

```
SVRMGR> Rem Average length of the dirty buffer write queue. If this is larger than
SVRMGR> Rem the value of the db_block_write_batch init.ora parameter, consider
SVRMGR> Rem increasing the value of db_block_write_batch and check for disks that
SVRMGR> Rem are doing many more IOs than other disks.
SVRMGR> select queue.change/writes.change "Average Write Queue Length"
     2>   from stats$stats queue, stats$stats writes
     3>   where queue.name  = 'summed write queue length'
     4>    and  writes.name = 'write requests';
```

   0 rows selected.

```
SVRMGR> Rem I/O should be spread evenly across drives. A big difference between
SVRMGR> Rem phys_reads and phys_blks_rd implies table scans are going on.
SVRMGR> select * from stats$files order by table_space, file_name;
```

TABLE_SPACE	FILE_NAME				
PHYS_READS	PHYS_BLKS_RD	PHYS_RD_TIME	PHYS_WRITES	PHYS_BLKS_WR	PHYS_WRT_TIM
DATA	/u01/oradata/norm/data01.dbf				
303	405	0	108	108	0
INDEX	/u03/oradata/norm/index01.dbf				
200	189	0	56	56	0
RBS	/u04/oradata/norm/rbs01.dbf				
7	7	0	202	202	0
SYSTEM	/u02/oradata/norm/system01.dbf				
1072	3731	0	367	367	0
TEMP	/u05/oradata/norm/temp01.dbf				
3	34	0	280	280	0
USERS	/u05/oradata/norm/users01.dbf				
0	0	0	0	0	0

```
SVRMGR> Rem sum over tablespaces
SVRMGR> select table_space, sum(phys_reads) phys_reads,
    2> sum(phys_blks_rd) phys_blks_rd,
    3> sum(phys_rd_time) phys_rd_time,  sum(phys_writes) phys_writes,
    4> sum(phys_blks_wr) phys_blks_wr,  sum(phys_wrt_tim) phys_wrt
    5> from stats$files group by table_space order by table_space;
```

TBLE_SPACE	PHYS_READS	PHYS_BLKS_RD	PHYS_RD_TIME	PHYS_WRITES	PHYS_BLKS_WR	PHYS_WRT
DATA	303	405	0	108	108	0
INDEX	200	189	0	56	56	0
RBS	7	7	0	202	202	0
SYSTEM	1072	3731	0	367	367	0
TEMP	3	34	0	280	280	0
TOOLS	1	1	0	0	0	0
USERS	0	0	0	0	0	0

```
SVRMGR> Rem Sleeps should be low. The hit_ratio should be high.
SVRMGR> select name latch_name, gets, misses,
    2> round(decode(gets-misses,0,1,gets-misses)/decode(gets,0,1,gets),3)
    3> hit_ratio, sleeps, round(sleeps/decode(misses,0,1,misses),3) "SLEEPS/MISS"
    4> from stats$latches where gets != 0 order by name;
```

LATCH_NAME	GETS	MISSES	HIT_RATIO	SLEEPS	SLEEPS/MISS
cache buffer handl	532	0	1	0	0
cache buffers chai	1193540	203	1	514	2.532
cache buffers lru	20200	145	.993	332	2.29
dml lock allocatio	1016	0	1	0	0
enqueues	3601	0	1	0	0
library cache	133513	853	.994	1887	2.212
messages	1998	0	1	0	0
multiblock read ob	5265	0	1	0	0
process allocation	14	0	1	0	0
redo allocation	3776	4	.999	15	3.75
row cache objects	150451	266	.998	633	2.38
sequence cache	170	0	1	0	0
session allocation	1430	1	.999	1	1
session idle bit	37204	7	1	11	1.571
shared pool	87978	447	.995	931	2.083
system commit numb	7702	4	.999	9	2.25
transaction alloca	578	0	1	0	0
undo global data	442	0	1	0	0
user lock	30	0	1	0	0

```
SVRMGR> Rem Statistics on no_wait latch gets. No_wait get does not wait for the
SVRMGR> Rem latch to become free, it immediately times out.
SVRMGR> select name latch_name,
    2>     immed_gets nowait_gets,
    3>     immed_miss nowait_misses,
    4>     round(decode(immed_gets-immed_miss,0,1,immed_gets-immed_miss)/
    5>        decode(immed_gets,0,1,immed_gets),3) nowait_hit_ratio
    6> from stats$latches where immed_gets != 0 order by name;
```

LATCH_NAME	NOWAIT_GETS	NOWAIT_MISSES	NOWAIT_HIT_RATIO
cache buffers chai	87950	109	.999
cache buffers lru	580277	18656	.968
library cache	555	45	.919
row cache objects	649	60	.908

```
SVRMGR> Rem Waits_for_trans_tbl high implies you should add rollback segments.
SVRMGR> select * from stats$roll;
```

UNDO_SEG	TRANS_T_G	TRANS_T_W	UNDO_BYT_WR	SEGMENT_SIZE_BYT	XACTS	SHRINKS	WRAPS
0	6	0	0	180224	0	0	0
2	68	0	10915	10645504	0	0	0
3	28	0	4857	10645504	·0	0	0
4	65	0	14027	10645504	0	0	0
5	18	0	1786	10645504	0	0	0
6	10	0	1530	10645504	-1	0	0
7	58	0	18306	10645504	1	0	0
8	50	0	8018	10645504	-1	0	0
9	39	0	13020	10645504	0	0	0
10	6	0	0	10645504	0	0	0
11	6	0	0	10645504	0	0	0
12	51	0	12555	10645504	0	0	0
13	61	0	10194	10645504	0	0	0
14	57	0	10081	10645504	-1	0	0
15	8	0	938	10645504	-1	0	0
16	29	0	3369	10645504	-1	0	0
17	20	0	3267	10645504	0	0	0
18	68	0	58861	10645504	0	0	0
19	12	0	6187	10645504	0	0	0
20	6	0	0	10645504	0	0	0
21	6	0	0	10645504	0	0	0

```
SVRMGR> Rem The init.ora parameters currently in effect:
SVRMGR> select name, value from v$parameter where isdefault = 'FALSE'
```

```
    2> order by name;
```

NAME	VALUE
audit_trail	NONE
background_dump_dest	$ORACLE_BASE/admin/norm/bdump
control_files	/u02/oradata/norm/control.ctl
core_dump_dest	$ORACLE_BASE/admin/norm/cdump
db_block_buffers	6000
db_block_size	4096
db_file_multiblock_read_count	8
db_file_simultaneous_writes	8
db_files	200
db_name	norm
distributed_transactions	61
dml_locks	750
enqueue_resources	5000
gc_db_locks	6000
ifile	/u07/app/oracle/admin/norm/pfile/config
log_archive_dest	$ORACLE_BASE/admin/norm/arch/arch.log
log_archive_format	'log%S%T.arch'
log_checkpoint_interval	4096
log_checkpoints_to_alert	TRUE
log_simultaneous_copies	0
max_dump_file_size	10240
max_enabled_roles	22
mts_servers	0
nls_sort	BINARY
open_cursors	255
optimizer_mode	RULE
pre_page_sga	TRUE
processes	200
resource_limit	TRUE
rollback_segments	r01, r02, r03, r04, r05
row_locking	ALWAYS
sequence_cache_entries	30
sequence_cache_hash_buckets	23
sessions	225
shared_pool_size	31457280
sort_area_retained_size	131072
sort_area_size	131072
temporary_table_locks	225
transactions	206
transactions_per_rollback_segment	42
user_dump_dest	$ORACLE_BASE/admin/norm/udump

SVRMGR> Rem get_miss and scan_miss should be very low compared to the requests.
SVRMGR> Rem cur_usage is the number of entries in the cache that are being used.
SVRMGR> select * from stats$dc
   2> where get_reqs != 0 or scan_reqs != 0 or mod_reqs != 0;

NAME	GET_REQS	GET_MISS	SCAN_REQ	SCAN_MIS	MOD_REQS	COUNT	CUR_USAG
dc_tablespaces	45	0	0	0	0	15	12
dc_free_extents	1300	53	64	0	133	311	302
dc_segments	2789	21	0	0	51	315	310
dc_rollback_seg	264	0	0	0	0	24	23
dc_used_extents	65	40	0	0	65	62	54
dc_users	134	0	0	0	0	36	24
dc_user_grants	59	0	0	0	0	58	19
dc_objects	7837	109	0	0	0	984	983
dc_tables	21636	15	0	0	0	415	412
dc_columns	62063	2272	3001	522	0	11106	11100
dc_table_grants	18080	113	0	0	0	956	938
dc_indexes	3620	39	2742	12	0	849	848
dc_constraint_d	554	82	61	9	0	536	535
dc_constraint_d	0	0	41	2	0	1	0
dc_synonyms	2524	85	0	0	0	510	509
dc_usernames	3010	0	0	0	0	44	40
dc_sequences	156	3	0	0	24	46	43
dc_sequence_gra	98	4	0	0	0	124	123
dc_tablespaces	38	0	0	0	38	16	8
dc_profiles	14	0	0	0	0	8	1

SVRMGR> Rem The times that bstat and estat were run.
SVRMGR> select * from stats$dates;

STATS_GATHER_TIMES

28-JUN-99 15:20:42
28-JUN-99 16:30:40

An important facet of performance tuning lies in knowing how to set initialization parameters. Knowing the values of these parameters often becomes an issue when trying to identify and solve problems. Although the DBA can find the values of initialization parameters by reading the **init.ora** file used to start the database instance, this method of determining initialization parameters for the instance isn't the most accurate. Instead, the DBA should use the **show parameter** command available in Server

Manager. Alternately, the following **select** statement using the V$PARAMETER view will show the initialization parameters for the instance:

```
SELECT name, value
FROM v$parameter;
```

The next four chapters on performance tuning that comprise this unit utilize information from dynamic performance views on the Oracle database. These views are the cornerstone of statistics collection for the Oracle database and are used by many performance monitoring tools such as Server Manager. Access to these views, whose names generally start with either V$ or X$, is as follows: V$ views can be accessed either by the DBA logging in as the owner (SYS) or as a user with the **select any table** privilege granted to it. The X$ views can be accessed only by user SYS.

TIP
*In Oracle7, V$ performance views are accessed by any user with **select any table** object privilege granted to them. X$ views are accessed only by user SYS. However, the **select any table** object privilege doesn't have to give access to V$ views in Oracle8—see Chapter 25 for details.*

Exercises

1. The output for the **report.txt** file shows a great deal of *hit* and *wait* information. What do you think this information means? What sorts of values (high or low) for hits and waits do you think indicate good or poor database performance?

2. You are the DBA on a database experiencing performance problems accessing information from many dictionary views. The database has been running for a while. You use the UTLBSTAT and UTLESTAT utilities to pinpoint the cause of the performance degradation. In what area might you look in the output file to see if there is a problem?

3. Name the sections of the **report.txt** file and identify uses for each.

Understanding Latch Contention

To monitor and control access to most Oracle system resources, there are mechanisms called *latches* that limit the amount of time and space any single process can command the resource at any given time. Monitoring the latch that controls access to the resource is the method used to determine if there is a problem with contention for the resource. A latch is simply an object in the Oracle database that a process must obtain access to in order to conduct a certain type of activity.

TIP

Contention is when one process in the Oracle database wants a resource to which another process has access. There is always some amount of contention for resources in the database. As long as those processes that hold access to resources via the latch do not hold it for a long time, things on the Oracle database should run smoothly. It is when processes contend for resources for a long time that the DBA must intervene to solve the problem.

Latches Available in Oracle

As with any other monitoring exercise, there are V$ dynamic performance views provided by Oracle to assist in the task of observing the performance of the resource. In this case, there are two views that accomplish the task. They are V$LATCHHOLDER and V$LATCH. V$LATCH gives statistical information about each latch in the system, like the number of times a process waited for and obtained the latch. There are approximately 40 different latches in Oracle (possibly more, depending on the options installed and used). V$LATCHHOLDER tells the DBA which latches are being held at the moment, and identifies the processes that are holding those latches. Unfortunately, this information is stored in V$LATCHHOLDER and V$LATCH according to latch number, while the actual names of the latches corresponding to latch number are stored only in V$LATCHNAME.

The following code block shows the contents of V$LATCHNAME, a dynamic performance view that contains the names of all latches in the database, along with their corresponding latch numbers. The name of the latch is stored in this view only, and can be joined with data stored in the other V$ views on latches by latch number. This listing should give an idea about the types of latches that are available in Oracle:

```
SELECT * FROM v$latchname;

LATCH# NAME
--------- ----------------------------
       0 latch wait list
       1 process allocation
       2 session allocation
       3 session switching
       4 session idle bit
       5 messages
       6 enqueues
       7 trace latch
       8 cache buffers chains
       9 cache buffers lru chain
      10 cache buffer handle
      11 multiblock read objects
      12 cache protection latch
      13 system commit number
      14 archive control
      15 redo allocation
      16 redo copy
      17 dml lock allocation
      18 transaction allocation
      19 undo global data
      20 sequence cache
      21 row cache objects
      22 cost function
      23 user lock
      24 global transaction mapping table
      25 global transaction
      26 shared pool
      27 library cache
      29 virtual circuit buffers
      30 virtual circuit queues
      31 virtual circuits
      32 NLS data objects
      33 query server process
      34 query server freelists
      35 error message lists
```

```
36 process queue
37 process queue reference
38 parallel query stats
```

The latches in the list above manage many different resources on the Oracle database. Those resources, along with some of the latches from above that handle management of that resource, are listed below:

- **Buffer cache**   Cache buffers chain, cache buffers LRU chain, cache buffer handle, multiblock read objects, cache protection latch

- **Redo log**   Redo allocation, redo copy

- **Shared pool**   Shared pool, library cache, row cache objects

- **Archiving redo**   Archive control

- **User processes and sessions**   Process allocation, session allocation, session switching, session idle bit

Obtaining Latches

To obtain any of the resources listed in the previous code block, the process must first acquire the latch. Processes that request latches to perform activities using Oracle resources do not always obtain the latch the first time they request them. There are two behaviors that processes will undertake when they need to use a latch and find that the latch is not available for their use. One is that the process *will wait* for the latch to become available for the process's use. The other is that the process *will **not** wait* for the latch to become available, but instead will move on within its own process.

V$LATCHHOLDER handles identifying the processes running on the database that are holding latches. These particular processes may be causing waits on the system. A query against V$LATCHHOLDER will allow the user to identify the process IDs for all processes holding the latch. Since the period of time that any process will hold a latch is very brief, the task of identifying waits on the system, as discussed earlier, can be accomplished by continuously monitoring V$LATCHHOLDER to see which users are holding latches excessively. If there are processes that are holding latches for a long while, that process will appear again and again. Performance for all processes that are waiting for the latch to be free will wait as well.

Unfortunately, each of these views uses a rather cryptic method of identifying which latch is currently being held. A listing of the columns in each table and their meaning follows this discussion. One solution to the problem of cryptic latch numbers used to identify the latch being used is to use V$LATCHNAME. This view maps the latch number to a more readable name that the DBA can associate with a latch. A sample query is given below that will list out the latches that are currently being held by a process, as well as the name of the latch being held:

```
SELECT h.pid, n.name
FROM v$latchholder h, v$latchname n, v$latch l
WHERE h.laddr = l.addr
AND l.latch# = n.latch#;

H.PID      N.NAME
---------  ----------------------
34         redo allocation
12         library cache
...
```

Note that this query performs a join through the V$LATCH performance view. This is because the link from the latch name in V$LATCHNAME and the latch address that is given in V$LATCHHOLDER can only be made through the latch number, which is present in V$LATCH. More information about the contents of each performance view designed to store latch statistics can be found in Figure 16-1.

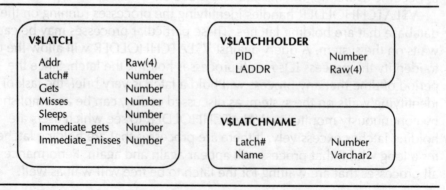

FIGURE 16-1. *V$ performance views storing latch statistics*

Exercises

1. Identify several different latches in the database. What resource do the redo allocation and copy latch handle resource management for?

2. What are two different ways a process may request access to a latch?

3. What are three dynamic performance views showing information about latches?

Checking for Events Causing Waits

The V$LATCH can be used as a link between latch views to obtain latch numbers corresponding with latch addresses. Sometimes this link is useful for tying in another important piece of information related to latches. This important piece of information is the wait ratio for the latch—the number of times processes waited for latch access in proportion to the overall number of times processes requested the latch. The wait ratio for latches helps to determine if there is a more serious problem associated with latch waits on the system. The following code block shows how to obtain the latch wait ratio using appropriate views:

```
SELECT h.pid, n.name, (l.misses/l.gets)*100 wait_ratio
FROM v$latchholder h, v$latchname n, v$latch l
WHERE h.laddr = l.addr
AND l.latch# = n.latch#;

H.PID  N.NAME               WAIT_RATIO
------ -------------------- -------------
    34 redo allocation      1.0304495
    12 library cache        0.0403949
...
```

This new feature of the latch holder query adds in the ratio of times a process did not obtain the latch vs. the total number of times the latch was requested. Consistent monitoring of these V$ performance views yields the following: If the same process shows up time and time again as holding the latch named, and the wait ratio is high for that latch, then there could be a problem with an event causing a wait on the system.

To find out more about the events or processes that are suffering as a result of an event causing waits, the V$PROCESS view can be put into play.

V$PROCESS has a special column associated with it that identifies the address of a latch for which that process is currently experiencing a wait. This column is usually NULL, but if there is a value present for it then there is a wait happening. Associating the latch name and wait ratio can be accomplished with an extension of the query already identified. The following code block demonstrates this:

```
SELECT p.pid, n.name, (l.misses/l.gets)*100 wait_ratio
FROM v$process p, v$latchname n, v$latch l
WHERE p.latchwait is not null
AND p.latchwait = l.addr
AND l.latch# = n.latch#;

P.PID   N.NAME              WAIT_RATIO
-------  -------------------  -------------
     34 redo allocation  1.0304495
```

The execution of this query produces the process identifier for a process experiencing the wait, the name of the latch that is currently held by another process, and the wait ratio for that latch overall. The functionality that these V$ views give can be better managed with use of the MONITOR LATCH menu item present in Oracle's utilities for database administration, Server Manager. This feature is not available in Oracle8.

There are two types of requests for latches. The distinction between each type of request is based on whether the requestor will continue to run if the latch is not available to that process. Some processes are willing to wait for the latch, while others are not. If a process will wait for the latch, the following series of events will take place:

1. The process will request the latch.

2. If the latch is available, the process will obtain it.

3. If the latch is unavailable, the process will wait a short period of time and ask for the latch again. This period of wait time is called a *sleep*. The process will continue its cycle of asking and sleeping until the latch becomes available.

Unlike those processes that are willing to wait until a latch becomes available, there are other processes that will not wait until the latch is free to continue. These processes require the latch immediately or they move on.

The V$LATCH dynamic performance view captures statistics on both types of latch requests. The following chart depicts the columns of V$LATCH, the explanation of the column, and the corresponding type of request it reflects:

GETS	Willing to wait	The number of latch requests that resulted in actually obtaining the latch
MISSES	Willing to wait	The number of latch requests that did not result in actually obtaining a latch
SLEEPS	Willing to wait	The number of times a process waited for the latch, then requested to obtain it again
IMMEDIATE_GETS	Immediate	The number of latch requests that resulted in immediately obtaining the latch
IMMEDIATE_MISSES	Immediate	The number of latch requests that were unsuccessful in obtaining the latch

Consider a couple of examples of obtaining latches to understand the process Oracle uses to maintain latch statistics better. Assume a user process puts forth an immediate request to obtain a latch. The latch is available, so the request is granted and the user process obtains the latch. The IMMEDIATE_GETS column on V$LATCH corresponding to the row entry for that latch will be incremented by one (1). Using that same example, let's say now that the latch was busy. Instead, Oracle will now update the IMMEDIATE_MISSES column on the corresponding row entry in V$LATCH for that latch. This example illustrates that the statistics compilation process for immediate requests for latches is straightforward.

Now, let us consider the more involved process of compiling statistics for willing to wait requests. A user process makes a willing to wait request for a latch. The latch is available, so the process obtains the latch. The GETS column from V$LATCH is incremented by one (1). Using the same example, the user process requests a latch, but this time the latch is unavailable. The user process has to wait. So, the user process goes to sleep. The MISSES column is incremented and the SLEEP column is incremented, and the process doesn't get its latch. After a short period, the process wakes up and asks for the process again. The latch is now available, so the GETS column in V$LATCH for that latch is incremented as well. One can see that the numbers will add up on those columns corresponding to willing to wait requests if latches become tough to obtain.

The next important aspect of latches to cover is calculation of the wait ratio for a latch. The DBA can obtain the wait ratio for a given latch by executing the following query against Oracle:

```
SELECT n.name,
(l.misses/l.gets)*100 w2wait_ratio,
(l.immediate_misses/l.immediate_gets)*100 immed_ratio,
FROM v$latch l, v$latchname n
WHERE n.name in ('redo copy','redo allocation')
 AND n.latch# = l.latch#;

N.NAME            W2WAIT_RATIO    IMMED_RATIO
---------------   -------------   -------------
redo allocation   1.0304495       2.9405949
```

Any of the names for latches listed in the code block displaying the contents of V$LATCHNAME can be used as part of the **in** clause in this statement. However, as we will learn in this unit, the latches that manage access to the redo log resources are particularly important because there are few of them, and every process that makes changes to data needs access to them. If either the wait ratio on willing to wait or the immediate latch requests for the latch named by the DBA in the query are greater than 1, then there is a problem with latch contention in the database.

Exercises

1. What is a willing to wait request for a latch? How does it differ from an immediate request for a latch?

2. What is a wait ratio? What are the two types of wait ratios associated with latches? How can the DBA find out what the wait ratio is? If the wait ratio is 6, is there an issue with latch contention in the database?

Chapter Summary

In this chapter we have covered the fundamentals in this advanced area of performance tuning as evaluated by OCP Exam 4. These areas are the tuning overview and problem diagnostics. These two topics comprise 15 percent of OCP Exam 4 content. The beginning of this chapter focused on the nature of database tuning. The text outlined three goals for any DBA approaching the task of performance tuning. They are improving performance of certain queries running against the Oracle database, improving performance of certain applications running against Oracle, and improving Oracle's overall handling of database user and application load. The text also covered why DBAs should always begin the tuning process by trying to achieve the first goal, that of tuning the SQL queries first. Only when that approach does not work should higher levels of performance tuning be sought.

The following steps were also presented as the outline of an appropriate tuning methodology for DBAs. Step 1 is to tune the applications. Step 2 is to tune memory structures. Step 3 is to tune disk I/O usage. Step 4 is to detect and eliminate I/O contention. These steps are the Oracle-recommended outline of tasks to execute in all tuning situations. The DBA is encouraged to use these steps when he or she isn't sure of the cause for poor performance on the Oracle database. Following the logical hierarchy or scope of each change is the important feature to remember from this section. OCP Exam 4 will focus some attention on taking the most appropriate tuning measure without making sweeping changes to the database in order to avoid causing more problems than were solved.

The tools used to diagnose and solve performance issues were also discussed in this chapter. One important method the DBA will use to determine performance issues on an Oracle database involves the use of the statistics gathering utilities UTLBSTAT and UTLESTAT. The names of the scripts containing these utilities are **utlbstat.sql** and **utlestat.sql**, respectively. The location of these utilities on the Oracle distribution is usually the **rdbms/admin** subdirectory under the Oracle software home directory. UTLBSTAT begins statistics collection for observing database performance over an extended period of time. When executed, this process will create the necessary data dictionary tables to store performance data history, and then it will begin collecting those historical performance statistics. UTLESTAT is the statistics collection end utility. On execution, it takes the statistics gathered in the tables UTLBSTAT created and creates a report based on that data. The report name is **report.txt**, and it can be found in the current directory. The **report.txt** file consists of several parts, which are described and illustrated in the chapter body.

These tools are dependent on performance data collected by the V$ views in the Oracle data dictionary. That data is valid only for the current Oracle instance; the data is not carried over when an instance is shut down. Since it takes some time for those statistics gathered to have any meaning, it is wise to hold off running UTLBSTAT and UTLESTAT until the database instance has been available for several hours.

Also covered by this chapter was the topic of latch contention in the Oracle instance redo log. Similar to locks, latches exist to limit access to certain types of resources. There are at least 40 different latches in the Oracle database. Two important latches in the database manage the redo log resource. They are the redo copy and redo allocation latch. Latches can be monitored by using the dynamic performance views V$LATCH, V$LATCHHOLDER, and V$LATCHNAME. The statistics to monitor about latches are the number of times a process has to wait for Oracle to fulfill a request it makes to obtain a latch vs. the times a process requests a latch and obtains it. A process will generally do one of two things if it is denied access to a latch. Its request is either *immediate* or *willing to wait*. These two types of process requests affect the collection of V$LATCH statistics in the following way. V$LATCH tracks the number of GETS, MISSES, and SLEEPS for processes willing to wait on a request for a latch. A process will sleep if its latch request is denied and the process wants to wait for it to become available. V$LATCH also calculates the number of IMMEDIATE_GETS and IMMEDIATE_MISSES for those processes requesting latches that want the latch immediately or the process moves on. Latch wait time for processes willing to wait is based on the number of MISSES divided by GETS, times 100, or (MISSES/GETS)*100. Latch wait time for processes requiring immediate access to latches or the process will move on is based on the number of IMMEDIATE_MISSES divided by IMMEDIATE_GETS, times 100, or (IMMEDIATE_MISSES/IMMEDIATE_GETS) *100.

Looking for events causing waits was also covered. Events that are causing waits appear in both the V$LOCK dynamic performance view and the V$LATCHHOLDER view. Both these views list information about the processes that are currently holding the keys to access certain resources on the Oracle database. If there are high wait ratios associated with a process holding a latch or lock, as reflected by statistics gathered from V$LATCH or hy the presence of a process ID in the V$LOCK view, then there could be a contention issue on the database.

Two-Minute Drill

- Three goals of performance tuning are improve performance of particular SQL queries, improve performance of applications, and improve performance of the entire database.

- The four steps of performance tuning are as follows:

    1. Tune applications

    2. Tune memory structures

    3. Tune I/O

    4. Detect and resolve contention

- Performance tuning steps listed above should be executed in the order given to avoid making sweeping database changes that cause things to break in unanticipated ways.

- The UTLBSTAT and UTLESTAT utilities are frequently used by DBAs to identify performance issues on the Oracle database.

- UTLBSTAT is the begin statistics collection utility. Executing this file creates special tables for database performance statistics collection and begins the collection process.

- UTLESTAT is the end statistics collection utility. It concludes the statistics collection activity started by UTLBSTAT and produces a report of database activity called **report.txt**.

- The **report.txt** file consists of the following components:

    - Statistics for file I/O by tablespace and datafile. This information is useful in distributing files across many disks to reduce I/O contention.

    - SGA, shared pool, table/procedure, trigger, pipe, and other cache statistics. Used to determine if there is contention for any of the listed resources.

- Latch wait statistics for the database instance. Used to determine if there is contention for resources using latches.

- Statistics for how often user processes wait for rollback segments, which is used to determine if more rollback segments should be added.

- Average length of dirty buffer write queue, which is used to determine if DBWR is having difficulty writing blocks to the database.

- Initialization parameters for the database, including defaults.

- Start time and stop time for statistics collection.

■ Latches are similar to locks in that they are used to control access to a database resource. Latch contention is when two (or more) processes are attempting to acquire a latch at the same time.

■ There are approximately 40 different types of latches in the Oracle database.

■ Latches are used in conjunction with restricting write access to online redo logs, among other things. The two types of latches for this purpose are redo allocation latches and redo copy latches.

■ Some processes make requests for latches that are willing to wait for the latch to be free. Other processes move on if they cannot obtain immediate access to a latch.

■ V$LATCH is used for latch performance monitoring. It contains all GETS, MISSES, SLEEPS, IMMEDIATE_GETS, and IMMEDIATE_MISSES statistics required for calculating wait ratios.

■ V$LATCHNAME holds a readable identification name corresponding to each latch number listed in V$LATCH.

■ V$LATCHHOLDER lists the processes that are currently holding latches on the system. This is useful for finding the processes that may be causing waits on the system.

■ V$LOCK lists the processes that are holding object locks on the system. This is useful to find processes that may be causing waits on the system.

- Latch performance is measured by the wait ratio. For processes willing to wait, the wait ratio is calculated as MISSES / GETS * 100.

- For processes wanting immediate latch access, the wait ratio is calculated as IMMEDIATE_MISSES / IMMEDIATE_GETS * 100.

Chapter Questions

1. **The DBA is about to begin performance tuning. Which utility script can be run by the DBA in order to begin tracking performance statistics on the database instance?**

   A. UTLESTAT

   B. UTLBSTAT

   C. UTLMONTR

   D. UTLLOCKT

2. **Which of the following is not part of REPORT.TXT?**

   A. Redo log and rollback segment entries

   B. Database instance initialization parameters

   C. Dirty buffer write queue statistics

   D. Statistics collection start and stop times

3. **What area of the database should the DBA tune before tuning memory structures?**

   A. Disk I/O

   B. Contention

   C. SQL statements

   D. Latches and Locks

   E. Dispatchers and shared servers

4. Output for the EXPLAIN PLAN command is stored in

   A. PLAN_TABLE

   B. report.txt

   C. TRACE files

   D. init.ora

   E. Nowhere

5. The DBA is preparing to analyze database performance statistics using UTLBSTAT and UTLESTAT. In order to increase the likelihood that UTLBSTAT will capture meaningful statistics,

   A. The instance name should be fewer than eight characters.

   B. The instance should be running for several hours before starting UTLBSTAT.

   C. The shared pool should be flushed.

   D. The SYSTEM tablespace should be reorganized to reduce fragmentation.

6. The most efficient and effective way to find out the database instance parameters is to

   A. Run UTLBSTAT/UTLESTAT

   B. Read the **init.ora** file

   C. Execute the **show parameter** command

   D. Read **report.txt**

7. Which of the following is NOT a tool used for diagnosing tuning problems on the Oracle instance?

   A. Server Manager

   B. V$ performance views

   C. SQL*Loader

   D. TKPROF

   E. DBMS_APPLICATION_INFO

8. **Which two views are used to track latch performance statistics?**

   A. V$LATCH

   B. V$LATCHWAIT

   C. V$LATCHNAME

   D. V$LATCHHOLDER

   E. V$LATCHLOG

9. **SQL operations listed as output from EXPLAIN PLAN**

   A. Are executed from top to bottom, from outside in

   B. Are executed from bottom to top, from outside in

   C. Are executed from top to bottom, from inside out

   D. Are executed from bottom to top, from inside out

10. **Dynamic performance views in the Oracle instance are owned by**

   A. SYSTEM

   B. sysdba

   C. osdba

   D. SYS

Answers to Chapter Questions

1. B.   UTLBSTAT

Explanation   UTLBSTAT is the begin statistics collection utility. Choice A is incorrect because UTLESTAT is the script run to end statistics collection on the database. Choice C is incorrect because the UTLMONTR script is incorporated in the installation of Oracle. Choice D is incorrect because UTLLOCKT creates a package used to manage locks. Review the discussion of the UTLBSTAT and UTLESTAT utilities in the "Diagnosing Problems" section.

2. A.   Redo log and rollback segment entries

Explanation   All other choices are contained in **report.txt**. Redo log entries are contained in the redo log, and rollback segment entries are contained in the rollback segments. Review the tour of **report.txt** in the "Diagnosing Problems" section.

3. C.   SQL statements

Explanation   SQL statements are the first area the DBA should tune on the database. Choice A is incorrect because disk I/O is tuned after memory usage according to the tuning methodology. The same is true of contention, choice B. Choices D and E are both tuned as part of tuning memory usage. Review the discussion of tuning methodology.

4. A.   PLAN_TABLE

Explanation   PLAN_TABLE stores all execution plan information generated by the **explain plan** command. Choice B is incorrect because **report.txt** contains output from the UTLBSTAT/UTLESTAT statistics collection utilities. Choice C is partly correct because trace files contain the execution plan for statements executed during the traced session, but user session trace files are not the only type of trace file on the database. Review the discussion of available diagnostic tools.

5. B. The instance should be running for several hours before starting UTLBSTAT.

Explanation The database must be running for several hours in order for the performance views that feed UTLBSTAT to contain meaningful information. Choice A is incorrect because, although the instance name should be eight characters or fewer, it does not improve performance to have that instance name under eight characters. Choice C is incorrect because the shared pool does not need to be flushed to improve statistics collection performance. Choice D is incorrect because correcting tablespace fragmentation defeats the purpose of statistics gathering to determine the problem. Review the discussion of UTLBSTAT and UTLESTAT.

6. C. Execute the **show parameter** command

Explanation The **show parameter** command from Server Manager is the easiest and fastest way to obtain all initialization parameters, including defaults. Running UTLBSTAT and UTLESTAT to generate initialization parameters in **report.txt**, but it takes longer to execute than showing the parameter block; therefore, choices A and D are incorrect. Choice B is incorrect because **init.ora** only shows the parameter that the DBA sets for the instance, not all initialization parameters. Review the discussion of **report.txt**.

7. C. SQL*Loader

Explanation Server Manager gives a graphical interface to the V$ performance views, so choices A and B are not correct. Choice D is incorrect because TKPROF produces a report on SQL performance based on trace file statistics. Choice E is incorrect because DBMS_APPLICATION_INFO is used to track performance of modules registered with the Oracle database. These statistics are gathered on the V$ performance views. Review the discussion of available diagnostic tools.

8. A and D. V$LATCH and V$LATCHHOLDER.

Explanation V$LATCH tracks the statistics used to calculate hit ratios for latches, while V$LATCHHOLDER identifies processes that are holding latches and the processes that are waiting for the latches to become free. The V$LATCHNAME associates a descriptive name for a latch with its latch number and tracks no pertinent statistics for performance tuning; therefore, choice C is incorrect. V$LATCHWAIT and V$LATCHLOG are not performance views in the Oracle instance; therefore, choices B and E are incorrect. Review the discussion of latch contention.

9. C. Are executed from top to bottom, from inside out.

Explanation When the execution plan is pulled from the PLAN_TABLE using the script Oracle provides, the user must read the results from top to bottom, with output from inner operations feeding as input into outer operations. Review the explanation of **explain plan** in the available diagnostic tools section.

10. D. SYS

Explanation SYS owns all dynamic performance views in the Oracle database. SYSTEM can access the performance views, but does not own the views; therefore, choice A is incorrect. **sysdba** and **osdba** are privileges granted on the database to the DBA that allow access to the views, but again, access does not mean ownership. Therefore, choices B and C are also incorrect. Review the concluding points from the tour of **report.txt**.

CHAPTER
17

Tuning Database
Applications

n this chapter, you will understand and demonstrate knowledge in the following areas:

- Tuning for differing application requirements
- How to tune applications

The first areas of any database that require tuning, in most cases, are the queries and applications that access the database. By far, the greatest improvement to performance that can be made is achieved through this critical tuning step. Other areas of tuning, like memory and disk usage, though beneficial to the database as a whole, don't have as dramatic results as a change in the SQL statements of an application. When there is a performance issue on the machine, the DBA's first inclination should be to work with the application developer. In fact, this material may actually be of more use to developers than DBAs. However, the DBA should grow accustomed to serving in the role of Oracle guru around the office. And, of course, the OCP certification series for DBAs requires that the DBA know how to tune applications—about 10 percent of OCP Exam 4 content will be on these areas of performance tuning.

Tuning for Differing Application Requirements

In this section, you will cover the following topics related to tuning for different application requirements:

- Demands of online transaction processing systems
- Demands of decision support systems
- The requirements of client/server environments
- Configuring systems temporarily for particular needs

The design of a database should take into consideration as many aspects of how the production system will work as possible. This discussion will focus on the design characteristics of different types of databases that facilitate those strategies already covered. First, understand some different types of applications organizations use in conjunction with Oracle. Three common ones are *online transaction processing applications*, *decision support systems*, and *client/server applications*.

Demands of Online Transaction Processing Systems

Online transaction processing, or OLTP, is a common system in many organizations. When you think about data entry, you are thinking about OLTP. These types of applications are characterized by high data change activity, such as inserts or updates, usually performed by a large user base. Some examples of this type of system include order entry systems, ticketing systems, timesheet entry systems, payments received systems, and other systems representing the entry and change of mass amounts of data. Figure 17-1 shows information about data volume and direction on OLTP systems.

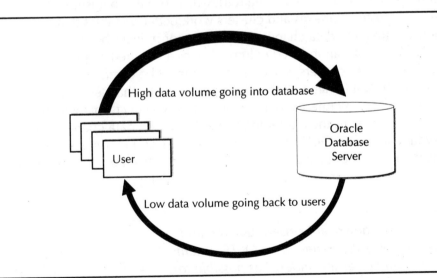

FIGURE 17-1. *Data volume and direction in OLTP applications*

Data in these systems is highly volatile. Because data changes quickly and frequently, one design characteristic for OLTP systems is the ability to enter, change, and correct data quickly without sacrificing accuracy. Since many users of the system may manipulate the same pieces or areas of data, mechanisms must exist to prevent users from overwriting one another's data. Finally, because users may make changes or additions to the database based on existing data, there must be mechanisms to see changes online quickly.

There are several design paradoxes inherent in OLTP systems. First, OLTP systems need to be designed to facilitate fast data entry without sacrificing accuracy. Any mechanism that checks the data being entered will cause some performance degradation. Oracle provides a good structure for checking data entry in the form of integrity constraints, such as check constraints and foreign keys. Since these mechanisms are built into the data definition language, they are more efficient than using table triggers to enforce integrity. Oracle then solves this paradox for all but the most complex business rules that must be enforced with triggers.

Typically, OLTP systems have a need to see the data in real time, which creates one of the largest design paradoxes in OLTP systems. Oracle uses several mechanisms to facilitate data retrieval. Those mechanisms are indexes and clusters. Indexes and clusters work better on tables that experience infrequent data change. This is true for indexes because every table data change on an indexed column means a required change to the index. In the case of clusters, since the cluster must be carefully sized to allow so much data to hang off the cluster index, data changes in clustered tables can lead to row migration and chaining—two effects that will kill any performance gains the cluster may give. However, data change is the primary function of an OLTP system. The designers and DBAs of such systems then must work with users to create an effective trade-off between viewing data quickly and making data changes quickly.

TIP
*Indexes slow down table **insert**, **update**, and **delete** statements; therefore, on OLTP systems, there should be as few indexes as possible to minimize impact on data change activity.*

This goal can be accomplished through data normalization. By reducing functional dependency between pieces of information as part of the normalization process, the database can store pieces of data indexed on the table's primary key. This design feature, used in combination with a few appropriately created foreign keys to speed table joins, will provide data retrieval performance that is acceptable in most cases.

If possible, DBAs should participate in the data modeling process to better understand which tables are frequently updated. In general, it is wise for the DBA to put tables that are frequently updated in a special data tablespace that is backed up frequently. Also, that tablespace can have default settings for data blocks with a high **pctfree** and a low **pctused** to reduce the chances of data migration and row chaining. Although configuring data blocks in this way can waste disk space, for reasons to be explained later, the desired effect of preventing row migration is obtained. Finally, keep use of indexes as low as possible to prevent the overhead involved in updating both the table and the index.

Exercises

1. What is online transaction processing?

2. What are some of the requirements for an OLTP system? What are some of the paradoxes inherent in the design requirements of an OLTP system?

Demands of Decision Support Systems

Decision support systems, sometimes referred to as DSS, offer some challenges that are different from OLTP systems. Decision support systems are used to generate meaningful report information from large volumes of data. A DSS application may often be used in conjunction with an OLTP system, but since their design needs differ greatly, it is often a bad idea to use an OLTP system for decision support needs. Whereas the user population for an OLTP system may be large, the user population for a DSS application is usually limited to a small group. Some decision support system examples include cash flow forecasting tools that work in conjunction with order entry systems that help an organization determine how large a cash reserve they should hold against anticipated returns. Another example is a marketing tool working in conjunction with an order entry system.

The key feature of a decision support system is fast access to large amounts of data. The trade-off between accessing data quickly and updating it quickly is a key point from OLTP systems that should be discussed here. As part of the design process, it should be determined what mechanisms will update the data in the decision support system. Usually, data flows from the OLTP system (or some other source) into the decision support system on a batch schedule. Users of the decision support system rarely, if ever, **update** or **insert** new data into the system, as it is designed for query access only. Figure 17-2 illustrates data volume and direction in DSS applications.

Since the decision support system data is updated on a regular batch schedule, the DBA has more options available for performance tuning. Heavy usage of indexes and clusters are both options because data updates happen less often. A process for re-creating indexes and clusters can be designed in conjunction with the batch **update** so as to prevent the ill effects of updating indexed or clustered data. In some cases, the DBA may find that some tables never change. If this is the case, the DBA may assess that it makes sense to gather those tables into a special tablespace and make the tablespace access **read only**.

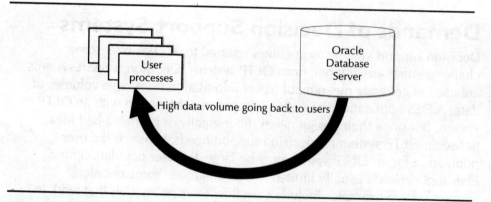

FIGURE 17-2. *Data volume and direction in decision support systems*

Exercises

  1. What is a decision support system?

  2. What are the design requirements for decision support systems?

Requirements of Client/Server Environments

The name "client/server" implies that there are two components for these types of systems. Those components are a client process and a server process. The term *process* is operative here. Client/server describes a relationship between two processes that are communicating with one another as they execute. These two processes can execute on separate machinery, utilizing the advantages inherent in having multiple CPUs dedicated to the task of solving problems and running the process. The client consists of user processes, executing most often on desktops, that may have some graphical user interface that enables the application to be more friendly in its interaction with users. The server, in this case, is the Oracle database with all of its background processes, memory areas, disk utilization, etc. Figure 17-3 illustrates the question of how many components comprise a client/server application.

  What is the missing link in Figure 17-3? The name "client/server" leaves out the most important facet of the client/server architecture—that unseen feature that allows for communication between the two processes. That feature is a network interface. The complete architecture must include a network component that allows for two processes to pass information back and forth between them. The completed architecture is given in Figure 17-4.

FIGURE 17-3. *Are there two main components in client/server?*

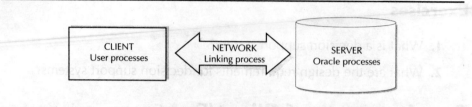

FIGURE 17-4. *Three main components of client/server networks*

With this three-piece architecture in mind, the discussion proceeds by identifying what role Oracle plays in the communication process. Simply having a TCP/IP network connection between the machine running client software and the machine running server software is incomplete. While the hardware and connectivity are there, a language barrier still prevents effective communication. Oracle offers a solution to this issue with a product called SQL*Net. This application is used by both clients and servers to communicate with one another. Without the SQL*Net layer acting as the interpreter, the client process and the server process are unable to interconnect.

Consider the client/server architecture created with the use of SQL*Net in some detail. The cornerstone of SQL*Net is a process called a *listener*. This process does just that—it listens to the network connection for requests from the client to come in and request data. A listener can be thought of as similar in many ways to a radio. The listener tunes into a particular "frequency" to listen for connections on the type of network being used, and "hears" requests issuing from only that network. In heterogeneous networking environments, there may be several different listeners in place on the machine running Oracle Server.

Once the listener "hears" a request for information, one of two things can happen, depending on whether the DBA has opted to use dedicated servers on the Oracle database, or whether the DBA has chosen to use the multithreaded server (MTS) option. In the dedicated server configuration, the user process that the listener has just "heard" is now routed to a server process. Recall in Unit II the discussion of the server process, which obtains data from disk on behalf of the user. In the dedicated server architecture, there is a one-to-one relationship between user processes and the server process, effectively giving every user its own server.

The dedicated server configuration can take a lot of memory to run on the Oracle database, particularly if a lot of users are connected. Oracle offers an alternative to the dedicated server option with the use of MTS. In the MTS architecture, Oracle has another process running called a *dispatcher*. When the SQL*Net listener hears a user request, it routes the user process to a dispatcher, which then finds a server process for the user process. One "shared" server process handles data requests for multiple user processes, thereby reducing the amount of memory required for server processes running on the Oracle database when a lot of users are connected. Figure 17-5 illustrates the path a user process will take from initially contacting Oracle with a data request, to being heard by the listener, to being given to a dispatcher, and being routed to a shared server. The rest of the discussion on client/server will assume the DBA is taking advantage of the MTS architecture.

In client/server environments using MTS where listeners and dispatchers are used to broker database services to multiple client requests, the database can be optimized to handle those client requests with a minimal number of

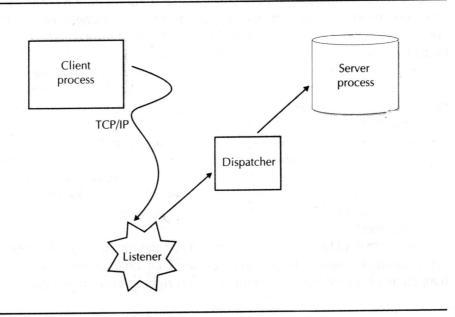

FIGURE 17-5. *Interprocess communication*

processes on the server. This task can be accomplished with the MTS option running on the Oracle database. More discussion on the multithreaded server option on the Oracle database will appear in Chapters 18, 20, and 25.

Exercises

1. What are the three components of client/server? What is SQL*Net?

2. Explain the use of dedicated server processes on the Oracle database? How does this configuration differ from the use of the multithreaded server architecture?

Configuring Systems Temporarily for Particular Needs

In general, the DBA will focus most of his or her tuning energy on tuning the production needs for a particular application. Sometimes, however, those systems will require some special tuning or configuration based on a temporary need. That need may take many forms. For example, an OLTP application may expect that there will be a window of time when usage will be particularly heavy. In this case, the DBA may plan in advance for that anticipated increase in user activity. Some steps the DBA might take could be to increase the number of rollback segments available on the system, reconfigure some initialization parameters related to redo log usage, etc.

One approach the DBA may take in preparing for the increase in database usage may be to alter the **init.ora** file to reflect the necessary parameters for the configuration change. However, making some changes to the database to suit anticipated needs of the system may not be in the best interests of the current needs of that system. In some cases, the DBA is better off waiting until the last possible moment to make the changes to suit a particular need.

The method a DBA may use in order to suit the different needs of the applications at different times is to place any DDL changes that need to happen in a script to be run when the time is right to make the changes, keeping another set of scripts on hand that will reverse the changes. This plan may include having a few different copies of the initialization script **init.ora** on hand, each with different settings appropriate to different usage situations, in order to facilitate the process of reconfiguring the database on short notice.

In order to reconfigure the database with a new set of parameters, the parameters should be placed in another version of **init.ora** that contains the specifications that must stay the same, such as DB_NAME, CONTROL_FILES, DB_BLOCK_SIZE, and other parameters that identify a unique database. When the database must be altered to handle a particular situation, the DBA can bring down the database instance and restart it using the copy of **init.ora** especially designed for the situation. Additionally, the DBA can execute the scripts prepared for altering other aspects of the database for the particular situation. When the need passes, the DBA can set the database to run as it did before by executing the scripts designed to reverse whatever alterations took place, bring down the database, and restart with the old **init.ora** file.

Another example of when the approach of having special **init.ora** files on hand to configure the database for specific needs is when the DBA needs to set up the database for maintenance. Since having the database tuned to handle online transaction processing, decision support, and other application needs could interfere with the upgrade or maintenance activities a DBA must perform, it is advisable to have a mechanism that easily reconfigures the database in such a way as to allow the DBA to perform maintenance quickly. Usually, DBAs have only a short time to perform maintenance activities like reorganizing tablespaces or distributing file I/O. The DBA should ensure the database is configured to make maintenance go quickly.

Exercises

1. What are some ways the DBA can reconfigure the instance on a temporary basis for different needs?

2. Identify some of the parameters in the **init.ora** file that uniquely identify a database.

How to Tune Applications

In this section, you will cover the following topics related to tuning applications:

- Tuning SQL statements
- Identifying inefficient SQL
- Using tools to diagnose problems
- Using the DBMS_APPLICATION_INFO package

To highlight the importance of tuning applications, consider the following situation that actually happened to a Fortune 500 company that used Oracle. One of their applications was used by nearly two-thirds of the over 70,000 employees of this company, and had several batch processes feeding data into it. Over the course of several weeks, during which time several thousand employees were added to the system, the execution of one batch process went from 4 hours to 26 hours. The company had grown accustomed to long-running batch processes, but this process ran so long that it couldn't be considered a daily job anymore. Apparently there were some poor comparison operations specified that caused a table to be joined to itself about 15 times before any results could be obtained. The solution wasn't a famous "one-line code fix," but it didn't take long to figure out what the solution was, and once implemented, the 26-hour process became a 30-minute one. One year later, the organization doubled its user base, as well as the amount of data being fed through this batch process, and it still ran in under 40 minutes. Such is the power of application tuning.

Tuning SQL Statements

Of all areas in performance tuning, none is more important than tuning the application. Often, the first and last word in turning an application that drags its feet and turning it into one that runs like a well-oiled machine is "TUNE SQL FIRST." Since the solution to most performance situations is a change in the query that causes poor performance, Oracle recommends that all DBAs consider any changes to the SQL statements themselves as the first step in every tuning situation, except ones that are obviously not related to specific SQL statements.

The reason that the importance of SQL statement tuning cannot be overstated is because most performance problems that occur can be solved with a change related to the statement. In fact, the largest performance improvements that can be gained in performance tuning are made when the DBA or developer analyzes how the SQL statement is executing and determines simply if an index can be used. By simply spending the time it takes to determine that a query is not using an index properly and changing the query so that it does, the DBA can prevent a frustrating trip through the SGA, disk I/O, and performance views related to contention, making sweeping changes that break other queries, only to find that the original problem was simply that an index was dropped causing the query to perform a full table scan on a table with 1,000,000 rows.

So, another important point to make about tuning SQL first is scope. Unless it can be determined that all SQL statements are affected by some adversity on the Oracle database configuration, the DBA should remain focused on limiting his or her scope to the possibility that this query is the only one having a problem, and should try to find a localized solution for that one query. Later in this section, some tools will be introduced to help the DBA do just that.

The final point to make about the importance of SQL statement tuning is one of user satisfaction. If queries are humming along, no one will complain. As soon as a query breaks, the user who was executing it will have a support issue. The faster the SQL statement can be fixed with minimal impact on everyone else on the database, the better off everyone using the system will be, including the DBA.

Exercise

What is the primary importance of SQL statement tuning?

Identifying Inefficient SQL

Several things are happening behind the scenes when Oracle is executing a SQL statement. First, the SQL engine takes the statement and breaks it into a set of operations Oracle will perform in order to obtain the data. Depending on how a table is configured, and on the SQL statement being performed, those activities may include the following:

- Table accesses
- Index accesses

- Data filters
- Operations to join multiple data
- Set operations like **union, intersect,** and **minus**
- **Cluster** and **hash** operations

Oracle is highly flexible in that the user can specify the fast way and the slow way to select data in the system. The key to selecting data quickly every time is to (1) have the data appropriately configured in the database for fast selection, and (2) know how the data is configured for fast selection and use the access path laid out by that configuration. Generally, it is easier to set up an application that uses efficient SQL statements to select data than it is to allow users to select their own data using ad hoc queries. The developer can predict the behavior of an application's query and plan the database for that activity better than he or she can predict how a user may want to perform self-written queries against the system.

The first possible cause for inefficient SQL activity in the database is when a database performs a *full table scan* to find the data requested by the query. Recall from Unit II that a full table scan is when Oracle goes through every row in a table to find the data a query is asking for. The full table scan is the ultimate level of nonselective data querying. The length of time required to execute this type of query is in direct proportion to the number of rows the table has. Obviously, queries that produce full table scans on large tables are going to see the biggest performance hit.

What are some reasons that a query's execution produces a full table scan? A query that uses nonindexed columns in the **where** clause will produce a full table scan, as will a query that uses an indexed column but performs some operation on the column. For example, assume that table EMP has an index on column EMPID, which is of a VARCHAR2 datatype. The following statement will produce a full table scan, even though the appropriate column was indexed:

```
SELECT *
FROM emp
WHERE nvl(empid,'00000') = '65439';
```

Even though the EMPID column was indexed, the index will not be used because the **where** clause performs a data operation on the indexed column. This operation forces Oracle to use a full table scan for that query. Other reasons a full table scan may occur include the lack of a **where** clause on the query, selecting an indexed column value based on an inequality or a comparison to NULL, and querying a table based on a composite index but placing the columns in the composite index in the wrong order (not the order they are stored in on the index). An example of misusing a composite index that results in a full table scan follows. If the EMP table has a three-column composite index defined as EMPID, LNAME, and FNAME, the query in the following code block will not use the index on the primary key:

```
SELECT *
FROM emp
WHERE lname = 'FULLER'
AND empid = '439394';
```

Oracle is very particular about order in cases where composite indexes are available. In order for the above query to use the index, the **where** clause should have the columns in the order that they are indexed.

```
SELECT *
FROM emp
WHERE empid = '439394'
AND lname = 'FULLER';
```

Queries that use full table scans decrease database performance in other ways. Recall the discussion in Unit II of the algorithm used to pull data blocks from disk. The server process moves blocks into the buffer cache from the table for the query. If there isn't enough room, Oracle uses the *least recently used* (LRU) algorithm to determine which blocks to get rid of to make room for new buffers. Blocks selected for full table scans are placed at the end of that LRU list so that those blocks are paged out of memory first. Although this algorithm prevents blocks in use by other queries from being paged out of the buffer cache, it can also slow down other queries looking for blocks used in the full table scan. It may take multiple reads for other queries using the block's data to keep the block in memory.

Some queries run inefficiently due to other reasons as well. A **select** statement that uses a B-tree index may still perform poorly if there are few unique values in the index. Recall the discussion for using B-tree and bitmap indexes in Unit I. Oracle refers to the uniqueness of values in an index as the index's *cardinality*. An example of an index with low cardinality would be an index on employee gender, using the EMP table example. Since there can be only two unique values, male and female, the cardinality or uniqueness of values in this index would be low. In fact, in some cases a query may experience improved performance if the statement used a full table scan rather than the index with low cardinality. If you must index a column with low cardinality, do not use the traditional B-tree index. Instead, use a bitmap index.

Another cause for poor performance on a query can be the use of views in the query. In trying to obtain the data for a query that has reference to a view in conjunction with joins from other tables, sometimes Oracle will attempt to resolve the view before resolving the rest of the query. This act will produce a large result set for the view, to which Oracle will then apply the rest of the **where** clause as a filter. If the dataset produced by resolving the view is large, then the performance of the query will be poor.

Exercises

1. What is a full table scan? Name some reasons queries that produce full table scans perform poorly? What are some reasons a query will result in a full table scan?

2. What is cardinality? Identify some poor candidates for indexing based on cardinality.

3. What should SQL developers remember when writing SQL queries designed to use composite indexes to obtain data from tables?

Tools to Diagnose Problems

There are several tools that help in the performance tuning process. These tools can be used to identify how the Oracle optimizer handles certain queries based on several criteria, such as the existence of indexes that can be used, whether the table is clustered, whether there are table performance statistics available, or whether rule-based or cost-based optimization is in use. One of the tools the DBA can use to tune Oracle queries has already been identified, the **explain plan** statement. In this section, more details about interpreting execution plans, along with common tuning techniques will be presented.

Explaining the Execution Plan

DBAs can use the **explain plan** statement to determine how the optimizer will execute the query in question. The DBA or developer can submit a query to the database using **explain plan**, and the database will list the plan of execution it determines it will take based on the many different factors listed at the beginning of the section. To use **explain plan**, a special table must exist in the user's schema. The name of that special table is PLAN_TABLE. This table can be created in the user's schema with the **utlxplan.sql** script provided in the **rdbms/admin** directory under the Oracle software home directory. Once the PLAN_TABLE is in place, the DBA is ready to begin using **explain plan** to optimize query performance.

The syntax requirements for **explain plan** are as follows. First, the **explain plan** clause identifies the statement as one that should have the execution plan created. The following clause is the **set statement_id** clause. It is used to identify the plan for later review. Neglecting to specify a STATEMENT_ID for the execution plan will make it difficult to obtain the plan. Finally, the **into** *table_name* **for** clause identifies the table into which **explain plan** will put the execution information. The **explain plan** statement needn't use the PLAN_TABLE, so long as an alternate table is specified that contains the same columns specified as PLAN_TABLE.

```
EXPLAIN PLAN
SET STATEMENT_ID = 'your_statement_id'
INTO plan_table FOR
SELECT *
FROM emp
WHERE empid = '43355';
```

After executing the **explain plan** statement, the DBA can recall the execution plan from the PLAN_TABLE (or other appropriately defined location) using a query similar to the following, modified from a utility provided in the Oracle release software:

```
SELECT  LPAD(' ',2*level) || operation || ' '
  || options || ' ' || object_name AS  query_plan
FROM plan_table
WHERE statement_id = 'your_statement_id'
CONNECT BY PRIOR ID = parent_id and statement_id =
'your_statement_id'
START WITH ID=1;
```

This query will produce the plan for the query just explained. The **connect by** clause joins the retrieved rows to the user in a hierarchical format. In the example used above, the resulting set that will come out of PLAN_TABLE when the retrieval query is executed will be similar in content to the listing that appears below:

```
query_plan
-------------------------------------------------
TABLE ACCESS EMP BY ROWID
   INDEX RANGE SCAN PK_EMP_01
```

The execution plan is interpreted in the following way. Innermost rows are the first events taking place in the execution plan. From there, the plan is evaluated from inside out, with the result sets from inner operations feeding as input to the outer operations. For multiple hierarchies as indicated by an additional series of inserts, often appearing in execution plans for join queries, the resulting execution plan is also read from top to bottom. In our example above, we have good usage of an index driving the overall table access operation that will produce the data the query has asked for. If the query had not used an index, however, the execution plan would have consisted of one statement—a full table scan on table EMP.

Common SQL Operations and Their Meanings

To understand some other SQL statement processing operations that may appear in an execution plan, refer to the following listing:

Operation	Meaning
TABLE ACCESS FULL	Oracle will look at every row in the table to find the requested information. This is usually the slowest way to access a table.
TABLE ACCESS BY ROWID	Oracle will use the ROWID method to find a row in the table. ROWID is a special column detailing an exact Oracle block where the row can be found. This is the fastest way to access a table.
INDEX RANGE SCAN	Oracle will search an index for a range of values. Usually, this event occurs when a **range** or **between** operation is specified by the query or when only the leading columns in a composite index are specified by the **where** clause. Can perform well or poorly, based on the size of the range and the fragmentation of the index.
INDEX UNIQUE SCAN	Oracle will perform this operation when the table's primary key or a unique key is part of the **where** clause. This is the most efficient way to search an index.
NESTED LOOPS	Indicates that a join operation is occurring. Can perform well or poorly, depending on performance on the index and table operations of the individual tables being joined.

Using Autotrace

Another method available for generating execution plans in Oracle is the **set autotrace on** command. Executing this command will effectively execute an **explain plan** for every SQL statement executed in the session for as long as the **autotrace** feature is set on. The primary difference between this feature and simply executing the **explain plan** feature is ease of use and availability of execution plan. Using **autotrace** for an entire SQL session with the Oracle database is much easier than manually keying in the **explain plan** syntax every time you execute a query, followed by actually executing the query against the database. Remember, when you specify a query using **explain plan**, you don't actually execute the query against the database. However, there is a trade-off involved. When using **autotrace**, the execution plan for any query is not available for review until the actual query is complete. This fact somewhat defeats the purpose of performance tuning, because the DBA will not know what the execution plan for that query was until the database has actually executed the plan. Eventually, the DBA will know what went wrong, but not before the problem actually occurs. However, the ease of use that **autotrace** affords may outweigh the timeliness in which it provides execution plans.

Using SQL Trace and TKPROF

The database provides a pair of tools to monitor query performance for tuning purposes called SQL Trace and TKPROF. SQL Trace puts hard numbers next to the execution plan of SQL statements to identify other problem areas in the system, creating a file detailing the appropriate statistical raw data. TKPROF is then executed on the output file, turning raw data into formatted output. SQL Trace provides the following pieces of information to aid in the SQL statement tuning process:

Parse, execute, fetch counts	Number of times the **parse**, **execute**, and **fetch** operations were processed in Oracle's handling of this query
Processor time Elapsed query time	The CPU and real elapsed time for execution of this statement
Physical/logical reads	Total number of data blocks read from the datafiles on disks for **parse**, **execute**, and **fetch** portions of the query
Rows processed	Total number of rows processed by Oracle to produce the result set, excluding rows processed as part of subqueries
Library cache misses	Number of times the parsed statement had to be loaded into the library cache for usage

SQL Trace can analyze SQL statements on a session-wide and instance-wide basis. If tracing Is started instance-wide, then every session that connects to the instance will have tracing enabled for it. If tracing is started session-wide, then only the session that has enabled SQL Trace will have trace activity captured for it.

There are three initialization parameters that must be set properly in order for Trace to work effectively on the instance or session. The first parameter is TIMED_STATISTICS. This parameter must be set to TRUE in order to use SQL Trace either on an instance-wide or session-wide level. Without this parameter set to TRUE, the collection of CPU statistics and elapsed time will not be enabled for the trace. Since setting this statistic to TRUE causes some additional overhead at the processor level, some DBAs choose only to set this parameter to TRUE when statistics collection is necessary. As such, use of this parameter sets forth the whole idea of having multiple **init.ora** files for fast reconfiguration of the database when certain needs arise.

The next parameter that should be considered is MAX_DUMP_FILE_SIZE. Output file size for the session's trace file is in operating system blocks. In some cases, the SQL Trace output trace file will not contain all data that is captured by the tracing utility and may appear truncated. The default value for this setting is 500, which can translate into 500 operating system blocks' worth of bytes that can be stored in the trace file. If Trace is enabled on the database yet the desired statistics that it generates do not seem to be present, and if the file itself looks cut off, the DBA should adjust the value of this initialization parameter and try executing the tracing process again.

The final parameter is USER_DUMP_DEST. The parameter simply tells Oracle where to put the trace file (indeed, all dump files) on the machine's filesystem. The key point of note here is that the destination should be specified as an absolute directory pathname.

Setting trace on an instance-wide level requires setting the SQL_TRACE parameter to TRUE in the **init.ora** file, and then restarting the instance. Setting Trace on a session-wide level overrides the instance-wide trace specification, and can be executed in several ways. The first way utilizes the **alter session** statement.

```
ALTER SESSION SET SQL_TRACE=TRUE;
```

The second method uses a special package available that is called DBMS_SESSION. Within this package is a special procedure called

set_sql_trace( ). The user can execute this procedure in order to start tracing statistics on SQL statements in the session as well. Another method to set tracing in the current session, and the only non-instance-wide way to set tracing for sessions other than the current one is to execute another procedure in DBMS_SYSTEM, the **set_sql_trace_in_session( )** procedure. The user executing this process should obtain the appropriate values in the SESSION_ID and SERIAL# columns from the V$SESSION view for the session to have tracing enabled. These two values must be passed into the procedure along with the SQL_TRACE setting (TRUE or FALSE).

After setting trace to run on the instance or session, Oracle will generate output to the trace file for all queries executed for the session. The trace file output will be hard to interpret by itself, so in conjunction with using Trace to gather statistics, the user should execute TKPROF to turn those statistics into answers to tuning questions. TKPROF takes as input the trace file and produces an output file named according to the specifications of the user. TKPROF has many options for its different features, including several used to specify sort order for query statistics and the capability to insert statistics records into the database. The typical output for TKPROF may consist of the following components. First is the SQL statement text and the execution plan. Next, TKPROF will display trace statistics such as CPU time and elapsed time, then rows fetched. Finally, TKPROF will display library cache misses for parsing and executing the statement.

Exercises

1. Where does **explain plan** put the execution plan for a query?

2. What are the ways a user can invoke SQL Trace for their session? For the entire database?

3. What initialization parameters are associated with setting up trace? In what way is TKPROF used in conjunction with SQL Trace?

Using the DBMS_APPLICATION_INFO Package

In complex development environments, it can sometimes be hard to track the activities of certain stored procedures, packages, Pro*C programs,

Oracle Forms programs, and more using conventional methods for performance tuning like **explain plan** and SQL Trace. Oracle provides enhanced features in a package called DBMS_APPLICATION_INFO that allow developers and DBAs the ability to track the performance of different applications using more advanced debugging techniques that utilize dynamic performance views native to the Oracle environment. The dynamic performance views that Oracle will use to track performance for these processes are V$SESSION and V$SQLAREA.

The process of employing the DBMS_APPLICATION_INFO features comprises an important development step known as registering the application with Oracle. Once the procedures of this package are utilized in the program, the DBA, developers, or other persons dedicated to the task of tuning can use this registration information to track the performance of registered applications and recommend areas for tuning improvement. The following subsections give the names of each procedure, the accepted parameters, and an example of the procedure in a sample PL/SQL block for the various procedures available in DBMS_APPLICATION_INFO. Please note that the functionality on the procedures can be duplicated with queries on the V$SQLAREA view using the MODULE column.

SET_MODULE( )

Identifies a module name for the block of code to Oracle.

Parameters

```
Module_name IN VARCHAR2
Action_name IN VARCHAR2
```

Module_name names the code block about to occur. *Action_name* identifies the SQL action taking place.

Example

```
DBMS_APPLICATION_INFO.SET_MODULE(
  Module_name => 'add empl expense info',
  Action_name => 'update empl_exp table');
```

SET_ACTION( )

Sets or alters the current action on the database.

Parameter

```
Action_name IN VARCHAR2
```

Action_name identifies the SQL action taking place.

Example

```
DBMS_APPLICATION_INFO.SET_ACTION(
  Action_name => 'delete temp_exp info')
```

SET_CLIENT_INFO( )

Allows supply of additional information about the code executed.

Parameter

```
Client_info IN VARCHAR2
```

Client_info allows 64 bytes of additional data about the action.

Example

```
DBMS_APPLICATION_INFO.SET_CLIENT_INFO(
  Client_info => 'Forms 4.5 app');
```

READ_MODULE( )

Reads active module and action information for the current session.

Parameters

```
Module_name OUT VARCHAR2
Action_name OUT VARCHAR2
```

Module_name names the code block about to occur. *Action_name* identifies the SQL action taking place.

Example

```
DBMS_APPLICATION_INFO.READ_MODULE(
  Module_name OUT VARCHAR2,
  Action_name OUT VARCHAR2);
```

READ_CLIENT_INFO( )
Reads active client information for the current session.

Parameter

 Client_info OUT VARCHAR2

Client_info allows 64 bytes of additional data about the action.

Example

DBMS_APPLICATION_INFO.READ_CLIENT_INFO(
Client_info OUT VARCHAR2);

Exercises

1. What functionality is provided by DBMS_APPLICATION_INFO?

2. What are the functions available in DBMS_APPLICATION_INFO? How does it relate to performance tuning?

Chapter Summary

This chapter covers material related to tuning for differing application needs and tuning SQL statements portions for OCP Exam 4. These areas comprise a total of 10 percent of the exam. Some of the application types covered were online transaction processing applications, decision support systems, and client/server applications. Online transaction processing (OLTP) applications are database change intensive, and commonly have a large user base driving those database changes. The performance need on these systems is for immediate response on queries that **update**, **insert**, or **delete** data on the database. This performance gain is made by reducing any overhead on those types of transactions. Some examples of performance overhead for updates, inserts, and deletes are heavy usage on indexes on tables being modified, as well as any issue causing slow performance on rollback segments and redo log entries.

Decision support systems (DSS) pose several different needs on the database than OLTP applications. Decision support systems typically store large amounts of data that is available for a small user base via reports.

These reports may be intensive in the amount of CPU time they take to execute. Fast access to volumes of data and well-tuned SQL queries as the underlying architecture for reports are the keys to success in DSS applications. Mechanisms that enhance query performance, such as clustering and indexes, are commonly employed to produce reports quickly. Since data changes will most likely be handled by batch processes at off-peak usage times, the performance overhead on change activities will probably not affect database performance or user satisfaction. Decision support systems often coexist with OLTP systems, as a reporting environment, archive repository, or both.

The other major type of application discussed is the client/server application. Often in client/server architectures, there are many client processes attempting to request data from only one server. As such, DBAs often use the multithreaded server options that are available with Oracle. Although two of the major components in the client/server architecture are identified by the name, there is an unseen element to the architecture that is as important to the success of the system as the client and the server. That component is the network that transports communication between client and server processes. However, it was explained that simply having a connection between two machines isn't enough; the processes require a common "language" to use for interprocess communication. Oracle offers a solution to this issue with SQL*Net, a program designed to facilitate communication at the network layer between clients and Oracle. One of the main components of SQL*Net is the *listener* process. This process is designed to listen to the network connection for incoming data requests from client processes.

When such a request comes across the network, the listener process takes the request and routes it along in the database to a server process that will handle such tasks as obtaining data from Oracle datafiles on behalf of the user process. There are two ways that server processes run in Oracle. The first way is known as *dedicated servers*. In the dedicated server configuration, every user process that access Oracle has its own server process handling disk reads and other Oracle database processing. The relationship between Oracle server processes and user processes is therefore one to one. However, it was discussed that this configuration requires extra memory on the database. The second way is for the DBA to use the multithreaded server (MTS) configuration. In this architecture, Oracle has a limited number of server processes that handle disk reads for multiple user processes, such that the relationship between server processes and user processes is many to one. In the MTS architecture, access to the server processes are brokered by another process called a *dispatcher*. User processes are connected to the dispatcher by way of the listener, and the dispatcher connects the user process to a *shared server* process.

This chapter covered material related to tuning SQL statements and applications in the Oracle database. Since SQL tuning often produces the most noticeable benefits for an application or query, it is generally the best place to start when tuning for performance gains. It also is the best place to start because of scope reasons. The DBA should determine that everything has been done to optimize the SQL statement before making sweeping changes to memory-, I/O- and contention-related areas that have the potential to break the database in other areas. Simply adding an index or ensuring that an index is being used properly can save problems later. Potential causes for inefficient SQL start with ineffective use of indexes associated with large tables, or lack of existence of those indexes for large tables. If there is no index present for queries against large tables to use, or if all data is selected from the table, or if a data operation (such as **nvl**, **upper**, etc.) is performed on an indexed column name in the **where** clause, then the database will perform a full table scan against the database in order to obtain the requested information. The performance of this query will be in direct proportion to the number of rows in the table.

Another cause for inefficient SQL is use of B-tree indexes of columns that contain few unique values. This low uniqueness, or *cardinality*, causes the index search to perform poorly. If a column with low cardinality must be indexed, the DBA should use a bitmap index rather than a B-tree index. More information about bitmap indexes appears in Chapter 4. Another cause of poor SQL statement performance involves views. If a view is utilized in a query, the best performance will occur if the underlying view selection statement is resolved as a component of the overall query, rather than the view resolving first and then the rest of the query being applied as a filter for the data returned. Finally, another cause for poor performance on a table that uses indexes consisting of multiple columns from the table, sometimes called concatenated or composite indexes, is the user's use of those columns in the composite index in the wrong order on the SQL **where** clause. When using composite indexes to search for data, the query must list all columns in the **where** clause in the order specified by the composite index. If the user is unsure about column order in a composite index, the user can consult the ALL_IND_COLUMNS data dictionary view for that table's indexes and the column order.

To better tune query performance, it helps to use the **explain plan** statement offered by Oracle in conjunction with the database's SQL processing mechanism. Any user can use the **explain plan** statement in conjunction with the Oracle database provided they have a special table called PLAN_TABLE created in their user schema. This table can be created using the **utlxplan.sql** script found in the **rdbms/admin** directory off the Oracle software home directory. The results of the **explain plan** command are stored in the PLAN_TABLE. It is important to include a unique *statement_id* in the **explain plan** command syntax to facilitate retrieving the execution plan for the query.

The query listed in the text is used to retrieve the execution plan data from the PLAN_TABLE. The execution plan itself is read from the top of the plan downward, with results from inner operations feeding as input into the outer operations. It is important to watch out for full table scans, as these are the operations that are so detrimental to query performance. The database session can also be configured to generate execution plans using the **set autotrace on** command. There are advantages and drawbacks to using this approach. One advantage is that the user does not need to specify the **explain plan** syntax for every statement executed during the session; **autotrace** simply generates the plan and stores it. However, the execution plan for a query will not be available until the statement completes, making it difficult to proactively tune the query.

Other tool options for tuning SQL statements include the SQL Trace feature used in conjunction with TKPROF. SQL Trace tracks performance statistics for SQL statements, placing numbers next to the operations provided by **explain plan**. These statistics include the number of times the statement is parsed, executed, and how often records are fetched if the statement is a **select**; and CPU elapsed time and real elapsed time for the query, block reads, processed rows, and library cache misses. SQL Trace must be used in conjunction with proper settings for the TIMED_STATISTICS, MAX_DUMP_FILE_SIZE, and USER_DUMP_DEST parameters. The output of a SQL Trace dump file is difficult to read, giving rise to the need for TKPROF. This tool takes the trace file as input and produces a report of statistics named above for queries executed in the given session. Tracing can be specified on a session basis or for the entire instance. To enable tracing, alter the SQL_TRACE parameter either with the **alter session** statement (session-wide) or by specifying it in the **init.ora** file (instance-wide) and restarting the instance.

To track performance statistics in large, complex code environments, it helps to register code components with the database using the DBMS_APPLICATION_INFO package. This package provides functionality to name various modules of code and identify the actions they perform. Statistics for the execution of various actions within modules and the modules themselves can then be tracked using the dynamic performance views V$SESSION and V$SQLAREA.

Two-Minute Drill

- Online transaction processing (OLTP) applications are systems used generally by large user populations that have frequently updated data and constantly changing data volume.

- OLTP application performance is adversely affected by increases in processing overhead for data changes. This includes excessive usage of indexes and clusters.

- Decision support systems (DSS) are systems that store large volumes of data available for generating reports for users.

- DSS system performance is adversely affected by processing overhead associated with complex **select** statements. This may include a lack of proper indexing, clustering, data migration, or chaining.

- Client/server applications are distributed processing applications that have a client process usually residing on one machine and a server process usually residing on another.

- The additional processors used to handle client/server processing can speed the execution of processes on both ends.

- The unseen partner in client/server processing is a network connection.

- In addition to a physical connection, Oracle requires a common "language" to be spoken between client and server in order for interprocess communication to proceed.

- Oracle provides interprocess communication with the SQL*Net tool for clients and servers.

- SQL*Net provides a listener process that monitors the database connection for requests from clients.

- When a client request comes in, Oracle must route the user process to a server process in one of two ways, depending on whether the DBA uses dedicated servers for user processes or if the DBA uses the multithreaded server architecture (MTS).

- For dedicated servers, the SQL*Net listener connects each user process to its own private or "dedicated" server process.

- For a multithreaded server, the listener routes that request to a dispatcher, which will broker the client's access to a limited number of shared server processes.

- Systems can be reconfigured on a temporary basis for application requirements.

- Multiple copies of initialization parameter files (**init.ora**) can manage this on-the-fly reconfiguration need.

- SQL tuning is the most important step in all database performance tuning, and should always happen as the first step in that tuning process.

- Possible causes for inefficient SQL stem mainly from improper or lack of index usage on data queries involving large tables or multiple table joins.

- The **explain plan** statement is used to assist the DBA or developer in determining the execution plan for a query. The execution plan is the process by which the SQL statement execution mechanism will obtain requested data from the database.

- The session can be set to generate execution plans for all executed queries by using the **set autotrace on** command.

- More information about the execution of a query can be obtained through using the SQL Trace and TKPROF utilities.

- SQL Trace can be enabled at the instance level by setting the SQL_TRACE parameter to TRUE and starting the instance.

- SQL Trace can be enabled at the session level with the **alter session set sql_trace=true** statement.

- SQL Trace tracks the following statistics for SQL statements: CPU time and real elapsed time; **parse**, **execute**, and **fetch** counts; library cache misses; data block reads; and number of rows processed.

- To use SQL Trace properly, several initialization parameters must be set in the **init.ora** file:

  1. TIMED_STATISTICS = TRUE

  2. MAX_DUMP_FILE_SIZE=(appropriate size to capture all contents, default 500, expressed in operation system size blocks)

  3. USER_DUMP_DEST=*absolute_pathname_on_your_system*

- TKPROF takes as input the trace file produced by SQL Trace and produces a readable report summarizing trace information for the query.

- DBMS_APPLICATION_INFO is used to register various blocks of code with the database for performance tuning purposes.

- DBMS_APPLICATION_INFO.**set_module( )** sets the module and action name for the current code block.

- DBMS_APPLICATION_INFO.**set_action( )** sets the action name for the current code block.

- DBMS_APPLICATION_INFO.**set_client_info( )** sets additional client information about the code block.

- DBMS_APPLICATION_INFO.**read_module( )** obtains module and action names for current active code block.

- DBMS_APPLICATION_INFO.**read_client_info( )** obtains additional client information for current active code block if there is any available.

Chapter Questions

1. Table EMP has one index, on EMPID. Which SQL statement will yield the worst performance?

    A. **select** EMPID **from** EMP **where** EMPID = '604';

    B. **select** * **from** EMP **where** nvl(EMPID,0) = '604'

    C. **select** EMPID **from** EMP **WHERE** ROWID = '021D1D1A.001.0002';

    D. **select** * **from** EMP **where** EMPID = '604';

2. Modules of code registered with the Oracle database have their performance statistics tracked in

    A. V$SYSSTAT

    B. V$SESSION

    C. V$PROCESS

    D. V$PACKAGE

3. What area of the database should the DBA tune before tuning memory structures?

    A. Disk I/O

    B. Contention

    C. SQL statements

    D. Latches and locks

    E. Dispatchers and shared servers

4. Two of the primary performance goals in OLTP systems are

    A. Fast report execution

    B. Fast **update** capability

    C. Fast **insert** capability

D. Fast ad hoc queries

E. Fast online access to data

5. **In order to improve performance on SQL statements, what operation should be avoided?**

   A. Index range scan

   B. Full table scan

   C. Index unique scan

   D. Table access by ROWID

6. **One reason for poor performance on a SELECT statement using an index may be**

   A. The query causes a TABLE ACCESS FULL to be performed

   B. The query uses an INDEX SCAN

   C. The index has only one extent

   D. The index has low cardinality

7. **Which of the following features are generally NOT found in decision support systems?**

   A. Frequent updates made by users

   B. Frequent reports generated by users

   C. Use of indexes

   D. Use of clusters

   E. Low data volatility

8. **Which of the following options makes the task of reconfiguring Oracle easier?**

   A. Many change processes done manually

   B. Use of multiple **init.ora** files

   C. The **parallel query** option

    D. Usage of SQL Trace and TKPROF to track statistics

    E. Multiple tablespaces to store index data

9. **TKPROF accepts as input**

    A. The output from UTLESTAT

    B. The output from **select * from** DBA_IND_COLUMNS

    C. The output from SQL Trace

    D. The output from EXPORT

10. **Usage of an index on a heavily updated table in an OLTP system**

    A. Decreases performance for reports and therefore shouldn't be used

    B. Decreases performance of online viewing and therefore shouldn't be used

    C. Decreases performance of ad hoc queries and therefore shouldn't be used

    D. Decreases performance of database updates and therefore shouldn't be used

11. **The process in an Oracle client/server environment that accepts user connections to the database and routes them to a dispatcher is a**

    A. Router

    B. Listener

    C. Receiver

    D. Shared server

    E. Connector

12. **Which procedure is not part of the DBMS_APPLICATION_INFO package?**

    A. read_action( )

    B. set_client_info( )

C. read_client_info( )

D. set_module( )

13. **The DBA runs SQL Trace, but the output file contains only about half of the information from the session. What should the DBA do to correct the problem?**

A. Increase the value of TIMED_STATISTICS

B. Increase the value of MAX_DUMP_FILE_SIZE

C. Run UTLBSTAT/UTLESTAT again

D. Flush the shared pool

Answers to Chapter Questions

1. B.   **select * from** EMP **where nvl**(EMPID,0) = '604'

Explanation   Both queries for choices A and D will use the index on EMPID, so these choices are incorrect. A select on ROWID is the fastest way to obtain data from the Oracle instance, so choice C is incorrect. The **nvl( )** operation
on EMPID forces Oracle not to use the index, which makes it the worst performer in selecting the row in question. Review the discussion of possible causes of inefficient SQL.

2. B.   V$SESSION

Explanation   The V$PACKAGE view does not exist in Oracle, so choice D is incorrect. V$SYSSTAT and V$PROCESS track statistics for other database resources, so choices A and C are incorrect. Review the discussion on DBMS_APPLICATION_INFO for more information.

3. C.   SQL Statements

Explanation   Tuning SQL statements should be the first step in the application tuning process. Tuning disk I/O takes place only after tuning SQL and memory have failed; therefore, choice A is incorrect. Locks and latches are part of tuning contention, so choices B and D are out. Tuning shared servers is part of tuning memory and optimizing load, so choice E is incorrect. Review the discussion of the primary importance of SQL tuning for more information.

4. B and C.   Fast **update** capability and fast **insert** capability

Explanation   Choices A, D, and E all indicate use of indexes, all of which cause processing overhead on inserts and updates, the primary function of OLTP applications. Therefore, A, D, and E are incorrect. Review the discussion of OLTP system requirements for more information.

5. B.   Full table scan

Explanation   Almost every index operation will perform better than any table operation. The only exception is a TABLE ACCESS BY ROWID, which is the fastest way to obtain data from Oracle. Therefore, choices A, C, and D are all incorrect. Review the discussion of causes of inefficient SQL.

6. D.   The index has low cardinality

Explanation   Choice A is not a true statement. The SQL processing mechanism will not perform a full table scan when an index is available and the statement does not force it to avoid the index. Similarly, the fact of using an INDEX SCAN alone does not imply poor performance; in fact, quite the opposite is true. Therefore, choices A and B are incorrect. Choice C indicates that performance on the index scan will be impressive, given a lack of dynamically allocated extents to fragment the index data. Cardinality, on the other hand, is the key to good index performance. If an index has few unique values, queries using it will perform badly. Therefore, only choice D is correct. Review the discussion of causes for inefficient SQL.

7. A.   Frequent updates made by users

Explanation   Choice A is not generally a feature on DSS systems because frequent updates can fragment an index, thereby decreasing performance for reports, online viewing of data, and ad hoc queries. Review the discussion of the needs of decision support systems.

8. B.   Use of multiple **init.ora** files

Explanation   Choice A makes the process of reconfiguring the database on a temporary basis more difficult, not easier. Choices C, D, and E have little bearing on the reconfiguration of the Oracle instance. Review the discussion of reconfiguring systems on a temporary basis for particular needs.

9. C.   The output from SQL Trace

Explanation   Choice A is incorrect because the output from UTLBSTAT/UTLESTAT is **report.txt**, which provides its own performance statistics for the instance. Choice B is incorrect as well. DBA_IND_COLUMNS is a listing of all indexed columns in the database. It can be helpful for tuning SQL queries because it identifies which columns on a table are indexed, but gives no relevant information to TKPROF. Finally, choice D is incorrect because the output from EXPORT can only be read by IMPORT.

10. D.   Decreases performance of database updates and therefore shouldn't be used

Explanation   Choices A, B, and C are all incorrect statements. In every case, an index improves performance of the operation. However, indexes also increase overhead on inserts and updates, which are the key functionality of the OLTP system. Review the discussion of the demands of OLTP systems.

11. B.   Listener

Explanation   The SQL*Net communication software provides the client/server architecture of an Oracle database with a listener process that allows user processes to establish connections with the database to obtain information. Routers, receivers, and connectors are not processes within the Oracle architecture; therefore, choices A, C, and E are incorrect. Choice D, shared servers, is a part of the multithreaded server option of Oracle. It performs operations on behalf of the user process, but does not actually establish contact with the process per se. Review the discussion of the requirements of client/server systems.

12. A.   **read_action( )**

Explanation   The procedure **read_action( )** is not from the DBMS_APPLICATION_INFO package. All other choices are actual procedures from the DBMS_APPLICATION_INFO package. Review discussion of the DBMS_APPLICATION_INFO package.

13. B.   Increase the value of MAX_DUMP_FILE_SIZE.

Explanation   MAX_DUMP_FILE_SIZE is the maximum size permitted for trace files. If the output of a trace file is cut off, this value should be increased. Choice A is incorrect because TIMED_STATISTICS is a parameter that usually has TRUE or FALSE assigned to it. Choice C is incorrect because UTLBSTAT/UTLESTAT were not run at this point to produce a trace file. Choice D is incorrect because the shared pool does not need to be flushed in order to run traces. See the discussion on SQL Trace and TKPROF as part of the section on diagnosing application performance problems.

CHAPTER
18

Tuning Memory
Utilization

n this chapter, you will understand and demonstrate knowledge in the following areas:

- Tuning the shared pool
- Tuning redo mechanisms
- Tuning the buffer cache

After tuning SQL statements and the applications that use them, tuning memory can yield the greatest performance benefit on the database. Unfortunately, upon leaving the insulated world of SQL tuning for the adventure of exploring SGA, the DBA leaves behind the advantage of knowing that the changes he or she is making won't adversely affect another area of the database. Tuning memory utilization on the Oracle database is tricky because memory (and disk I/O) resources are a global need—and if that global need is changed in a way that doesn't work, it is a problem for everyone using the Oracle database. Tuning memory utilization comprises a major component of the DBA's skills, and is also the largest percentage component of Oracle Certification in the area of performance tuning. The material in this chapter covers about 30 percent of OCP Exam 4.

Tuning the Shared Pool

In this section, you will cover the following topics related to tuning the shared pool:

- Identifying objects kept in the shared pool
- Measuring the shared pool hit ratio
- Monitoring latches to detect shared pool contention
- Sizing the shared pool
- Pinning objects in the shared pool

This section covers several different topics related to the area of the Oracle SGA called the shared pool. This section will cover several different discussions related to the shared pool. The first is identifying objects kept in the shared pool. After identifying the objects in the shared pool, the DBA will learn about measuring the shared pool hit ratio. Next, monitoring latch performance to detect shared pool contention is covered. After that topic, the DBA learns about sizing the shared pool. Finally, the topic of pinning objects in the shared pool is covered.

Identifying Objects in the Shared Pool

One of the two main memory structures in Oracle is the System Global Area, or SGA. The SGA consists of several components, as indicated in Figure 18-1. Those components are the shared pool, the redo log buffer, and the buffer cache. The ordering of items in this statement is not coincidental. Oracle recommends that priority be given when allocating memory in

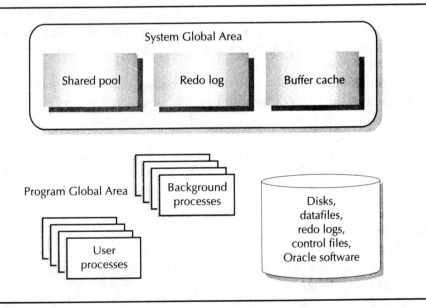

FIGURE 18-1.   *Review of the Oracle architecture*

database configuration to the memory structures in the order they are listed. The rationale is as follows. Users are the most important feature of any database system. At the database memory level, this design translates to the ability for users to run the application that they are capable of running; that is, memory should not be the restricting factor on the types of queries or application activities users run. The areas of memory dedicated to running the processes of users—that is, the shared pool and the buffer cache—should have first priority when the DBA attempts to size the memory allocation of the database.

In this discussion, we will explore the contents of the shared pool itself and various components of understanding and tuning the shared pool. The shared pool contains three main elements: the *row cache* (also called the *dictionary cache*), the *library cache*, and *control structures* such as network security attributes.

In turn, each of these structures contain some elements. The library cache contains the *shared* SQL area, PL/SQL packages and procedures, and certain *control structures* like locks, library cache handles or addresses in memory. The shared SQL area is a place in memory where SQL statements are turned into a series of operations for Oracle to perform in order to obtain requested data. The PL/SQL packages are stored in the library cache in their compiled form as well. Finally, certain control structures such as locks are also stored in the library cache.

The purpose of the row cache is to store rows of information from the data dictionary in memory for faster access. Since both users and Oracle use the data dictionary heavily, the row cache is designed to give fast access to that data. The row cache is designed to hold the actual rows of data from objects in the data dictionary. While this data is held in the row cache, the users of the database may access that information more quickly than if Oracle had to read the data into memory from disk.

Exercises

1. To what area of the SGA do the library cache and the row cache belong?

2. What structures does the library cache contain?

3. What does the row cache contain?

Measuring the Shared Pool Hit Ratio

The hit ratios for each component of the shared pool is calculated based on performance information from the V$ performance views in the data dictionary. This discussion will present the views used for calculating those hit ratios, along with the appropriate formulas.

Hits on the Row Cache

Activity in the row cache is monitored by a dynamic performance view called V$ROWCACHE. This dynamic performance view stores statistics about row cache performance. As with other dynamic performance views, the V$ROWCACHE view is accessed only by those users granted the **select any table** object privilege and the owner of the dynamic performance view, SYS. Some examples of users with the **select any table** privilege are those users with the **sysdba** privilege granted to them.

TIP
V$ROWCACHE stores performance data for the row cache. Since sometimes the row cache is referred to as the "dictionary" cache, it is one of the few performance views whose name doesn't always correspond well to the statistics it captures. Spend some extra time to memorize what this performance view describes.

Monitoring performance using the V$ROWCACHE view is accomplished by checking the rows in the view that correspond to the row type the DBA wishes to monitor. The statistics maintained for each row in the V$ROWCACHE view correspond directly to the use of that particular item in the row cache. The columns for determining row cache performance are PARAMETER for identifying each row in V$ROWCACHE with a meaningful name, and CACHE#, which is the unique identifier for each row in V$ROWCACHE. There is a naming convention associated with the PARAMETER column. Not only are all values in this column stored in lowercase, but they are also prefixed by a 'dc_.' It is important to note the convention used in the event that the DBA is attempting to find something in the V$ROWCACHE view and can't.

Data in V$ROWCACHE is treated as an aggregate. The DBA will base all statistical calculations on the sum of the GETS column and the GETMISSES column data for all rows in the view. The first column contains performance data of a somewhat dissimilar nature to what the meaning that its name suggests. The GETS column contains the number of times a process or Oracle asked for the item named in the PARAMETER column. This column tracks statistics for the total number of requests for a particular item made by users on the database and Oracle itself. Notice that this definition says *total number*, not just the ones that ended with a successful "get." The other column, GETMISSES is the number of times a request for information from the row cache ended in a *cache miss*. A cache miss means that a server process had to go out to the SYSTEM tablespace to retrieve data dictionary rows corresponding to that named entry on V$ROWCACHE. Retrieving data from disk decreases system performance and creates additional I/O overhead.

Usage of V$ROWCACHE for deriving the necessary row cache hit ratio will now be discussed. The data in the V$ROWCACHE dynamic performance view of row cache should be treated as an aggregate pool of statistical information for the row cache as a whole. This ratio, as with other hit ratios that will be discussed, represents the number of times an object was requested and not in memory vs. the total number of requests for that data. The general formula is **(MISSES/TOTAL REQUESTS)*100**. Misses is represented by the statistic collected for each row within the GETMISSES column and total requests is represented by the statistic collected in the GETS column. The ratio required for determining performance on this cache can be derived by executing the following query under the appropriate user, as detailed in the discussion earlier about access privileges and the buffer cache:

```
SELECT (SUM(getmisses)/SUM(gets))*100 dc_hit_ratio
FROM v$rowcache;
```

Oracle recommends trying to keep the hit ratio around 10–15 percent. To improve dictionary cache performance, add memory to the shared pool by increasing the value set for SHARED_POOL_SIZE. However, this method simply adds to the size of the entire shared pool for the database and is not precise enough to add space specifically to the row cache. Another problem with this method is determining how much space to add. SGA usually takes up most of the memory on an Oracle database server. The DBA will want to spend some time making sure that the additional size added to the shared pool does not increase the SGA to a size larger than real memory can handle. If the SGA requires virtual memory, there is a bigger memory performance issue at hand than the row cache.

Hits on the Library Cache

The other major component to the shared pool of the Oracle System Global Area is the library cache. This area of memory is utilized by all applications and user processes of the database, as well as the SQL execution mechanism of the Oracle database. The library cache stores all shared SQL and PL/SQL blocks, along with their parse trees. The library cache represents a unique approach to attempting to manage memory size as efficiently as possible. Oracle attempts to minimize the amount of memory a database user requires by creating a memory structure that permits the sharing of part of the SQL queries being executed. Of course, the values placed in a SQL statement bind variable will not be available to other users, to maintain security and data integrity in the database.

Effective performance in the library cache benefits the user population overall in the following way. If many users are writing or executing the same blocks of code, say an ad hoc report or a data **update**, **insert**, or **delete** statement, or a stored procedure, then the parse tree for that block of code is created once and then reused until it is eliminated from the library cache. In high-usage environments, such as OLTP environments where great numbers of users are entering and changing data, there is a great chance for overlapping the parse and execute needs of those different queries. Such an overlap in the library cache is called a library cache hit. However, even if many users execute the same queries on the database, there may be a chance that the users will experience a performance lag because the parse information they need has been eliminated from the library cache. In these cases, a user coming along with SQL to execute that is not already in the shared pool will experience a library cache miss. This miss results in the user's need to have the SQL they are executing reparsed by the Oracle SQL execution mechanism.

Key to ensuring the performance of the Oracle library cache is monitoring the activity of that cache. The view used for monitoring statistics on the library cache is called V$LIBRARYCACHE. As with other V$ views, access to the V$LIBRARYCACHE is limited to those users with **select any**

table access and the owner of the view, SYS. Each record in this view tracks statistics associated with library cache hits and misses associated with different types of SQL code blocks.

There is an associated cache hit ratio that can be calculated to ensure good performance on the cache. The library cache is no exception. The V$LIBRARYCACHE consists of several columns, three of which are useful for this discussion of how to obtain the library cache hit ratio. Those three columns are the NAMESPACE, PINS, and RELOADS columns. The NAMESPACE column allows for easy identification of different types of library cache activity associated with SQL statements and other structures Oracle maintains for internal purposes. The most common row values for the NAMESPACE columns that the DBA will use to gauge performance on will be the *SQL AREA, TABLE/PROCEDURE, BODY,* and *TRIGGER SQL* types. Unlike its cousin used for tracking statistics associated with the row cache, the NAMESPACE column attempts to put a friendly name on each row and also represents the unique identifier for that row.

The statistic tracked in the PINS column of each row corresponds to the number of times a SQL statement, PL/SQL block, table, or trigger was accessed for execution in the library cache. Every time a block of SQL code is executed as part of a process, if it has not been parsed already and is sitting in the library cache, Oracle will parse the statement and add it to the library cache. Finally, the last column to be discussed is the RELOADS column. It tracks the number of times a user attempted to execute a previously parsed statement only to find that the parsed statement had been flushed from the cache. This is also known as an *execution miss.* If there is a time lag between statement parsing and execution, the execute portion may have to reload the parse. Reloading the parse essentially consists of reparsing the statement, and costs the Oracle database some loss of performance.

Determining the library cache miss ratio from the V$LIBRARYCACHE dynamic performance view is similar in formula to that of every other hit ratio calculation, namely **(MISSES/TOTAL REQUESTS)*100**. The value from the MISSES column in this equation equals the sum of the number of reloads for all rows in V$LIBRARYCACHE and the total requests is equal to the sum of the number of pins for all rows in the same dynamic performance view.

```
SELECT (SUM(reloads)/SUM(pins))*100 lc_hit_ratio
FROM v$librarycache;
```

Reloads are bad for performance of SQL statements. Ideally, the library cache miss ratio should be under 1 percent. The higher the number of reloads, the higher the hit ratio, and the faster the rate that Oracle is eliminating parse trees from the library cache before users and other processes can execute based on the parse. Assume, for example, that the sum of pins is 177,392 and the sum of reloads is 4,503. The resultant library cache hit ratio for this example will be 2.5 percent, much higher than the DBA should like to allow.

Two methods are available for improving library cache hits on the database. The first is similar to the only method offered to improve hits on the row cache—increase the size of the shared pool as reflected by increasing the value set in the SHARED_POOL_SIZE database instance initialization parameter. This method primarily addresses the problem of high numbers of reloads appearing as a result of parse trees getting eliminated from the buffer cache. Additional space can be allocated by increasing the number of cursors allowed per session with the OPEN_CURSORS initialization parameter.

The other method requires more work and most likely will not be accomplished by the DBA alone. This method is to set it up such that the applications accessing the database execute more identical SQL queries. Since a SQL query must be identical for the principle of overlap that the library cache design thrives on to work properly, the more queries that are identical, the lower the number of misses on parse calls that will occur

TIP

*When Oracle says that two SQL statements must be identical for parse tree sharing to occur, they **mean** identical—character for character, space for space—**including** case sensitivity!*

Exercises

1. What dynamic performance views are used to collect statistics on the components of the shared pool? How is performance measured on each component?

2. What is an execution miss? What dynamic performance view and statistic is used to reflect execution misses? How might performance be improved if too many execution misses are occurring?

Monitoring Latches to Detect Shared Pool Contention

The shared pool is a resource that is sought after by much of the Oracle instance. Processes are always looking for space in the shared pool to set up their SQL parsing, or are looking to use an existing parse tree if one is available to them. However, like other Oracle resources, there have to be limits to the usage in order to avoid problems with the integrity or availability of the resource. With most Oracle system structures, there are control mechanisms called *latches* that limit the amount of time and space any single process can command the resource at any given time. An introduction to the use of latches is included in Chapter 16. Monitoring database resources to determine if there is a problem with contention is accomplished by monitoring the latch that corresponds to the resource.

As with any other monitoring exercise, there are V$ dynamic performance views provided by Oracle to assist in the task of observing the performance of the resource. In this case, there are two views that accomplish the task, a discussion of which appears in Chapter 16. They are V$LATCH and V$LATCHHOLDER. V$LATCH gives information about each latch in the system, like the number of times a process waited for and obtained the latch. Processes that request latches to perform activities using Oracle resources do not always obtain the latch the first time they request them. There are two behaviors that processes will undertake when they need to use a latch and find that the latch is not available for their usage. These behaviors are (1) the process will wait for the latch to become available for the process's usage, or (2) the process will not wait for the latch to become available, but instead will move on within its own process.

The other dynamic performance view, V$LATCHHOLDER, handles identifying the processes running on the database that are holding latches. These particular processes can be elements causing waits on the system. A query against V$LATCHHOLDER will allow the user to identify the process ID for all processes holding the latches. Since the period of time that any process will hold a latch is very brief, the task of identifying waits on the system, as discussed earlier, can be accomplished by continuously monitoring V$LATCHHOLDER to see which users are holding latches excessively. If there are processes that are holding latches for a long while, then performance for all processes that are waiting for the latch to be free will wait as well. This fact is an important piece of information related to latches that helps determine if there is a more serious problem associated with latch waits on the system. The following code block illustrates how to obtain the name of each latch, the process holding it, and the wait ratio for all latches in the database:

```
SELECT h.pid, n.name, (l.misses/l.gets)*100 wait_ratio
FROM v$latchholder h, v$latchname n, v$latch l
WHERE h.laddr = l.addr
AND l.latch# = n.latch#;
```

Consistent monitoring of these V$ performance views yields the following: If the same process shows up time and time again as holding the latch named, and the wait ratio is high for that latch, then there could be a problem with an event causing a wait on the system.

To find out more about the events or processes that are suffering as a result of an event causing waits, the V$PROCESS view can be incorporated into play. V$PROCESS has a special column associated with it that identifies the address of a latch for which that process is currently experiencing a wait. This column is usually NULL, but if there is a value present for it then there is a wait happening. Associating the latch name and wait ratio can be accomplished with an extension of the query already identified. See the following:

```
SELECT p.pid, n.name, (l.misses/l.gets)*100 AS wait_ratio
FROM v$process p, v$latchname n, v$latch l
WHERE p.latchwait is not null
AND p.latchwait = l.addr
AND l.latch# = n.latch#;
```

The execution of this query produces the process ID for a process experiencing the wait, the name of the latch that is currently held by another process, and the wait ratio for that latch overall. The functionality that these V$ views give can be better managed with use of Server Manager.

Exercises

1. What is the significance of keeping the entire Oracle SGA within the real memory available on the machine.

2. What are the views used to detect latch performance?

Sizing the Shared Pool

To improve the performance of the dictionary cache or the library cache, add memory to the shared pool. This is done by increasing SHARED_POOL_SIZE. However, this method simply adds to the size of the entire shared pool for the database and is not precise enough to add space specifically to the row cache. This same method can be used to improve hits on the row cache. This method primarily addresses the problem of high numbers of reloads appearing as a result of parse trees getting eliminated from the library cache. Additional space can be allocated by increasing the number of cursors allowed per session with the OPEN_CURSORS initialization parameter.

The most effective way to add memory to the shared pool without adversely impacting the database instance or the rest of the processes on the machine (if any) is to add real memory to the machine hosting Oracle. Memory is added by placing memory chips or cards to the actual hardware of the system, then allocating that new memory to the Oracle shared pool. However, real memory costs money and funds can be in short supply. The DBA sometimes must juggle the available memory away from another part of the SGA temporarily from another part of the database in order to give it to the shared pool. One area the DBA may take space from is the database buffer cache. The mechanics for resizing the buffer cache are covered in the section titled "Tuning the Buffer Cache."

Another aspect of appropriate sizing for the shared pool with the SHARED_POOL_SIZE parameter involves the relationship between the contents of the shared pool. The two elements of the shared pool—the row cache and the library cache—eliminate the oldest data when the cache is full and space is needed to store new information corresponding to their various roles. The row cache stores records from the data dictionary tables in memory. Since this data is a bit more static and small, the DBA may find that a properly sized shared pool will store a great deal of dictionary data in memory In contrast, the library cache area may be somewhat more volatile. The information in the library cache has a tendency to spend less time in memory, depending on the frequency that the SQL statement is duplicated by multiple user processes in the system. The frequency of duplication depends on several factors:

- *Ability of users to execute SQL ad hoc vs. usage of "canned" SQL.* If the users on the database mostly have the ability to type in their own queries and run them, there may be little opportunity on the system for SQL sharing. This setup will cause statements in the library cache to be flushed from memory faster than if everyone accessed the same limited selection of stored procedures or SQL embedded in a front end. In this scenario, there can be much sharing of SQL.

- *Size and number of applications permitted access to the database.* If there is a large number of applications that can execute different pieces of code against the database, then the potential for library sharing may be diminished. Likewise, if there is only a small application in use on the database containing limited amounts of SQL and PL/SQL blocks, then there can be a high degree of SQL statement parse information library sharing using the library cache.

- *Associated transaction volumes on the system.* On large systems with many users that utilize different applications, there may be little opportunity to reuse or share SQL parse information because so many users are accessing the system that shared SQL gets eliminated quickly from the system. In this case, there may even be a problem with the amount of reloads taking place in the system as well. In contrast, on databases with fewer distinct queries being put against the data, there could be a high amount of reuse. ·

In general, the data in the library cache will be eliminated faster than data in its shared pool cousin, the row cache, due to the decreased amount of data and change volatility that the row cache will deal with.

Finally, the importance of making sure that the entire SGA fits into real memory can never be overstated. Real memory is memory space that is actually contained on memory chips or cards. Virtual memory is stored on the system disks as swap space. If the SGA uses any virtual memory at all, the system can take a major performance dive as Oracle attempts to page blocks between memory and swap disk space while it attempts to **update** data blocks. The result is that the database will spend a great deal of time "thrashing" data between memory and swap space, creating a major performance problem.

Exercise

Identify some issues associated with sizing the shared pool.

Pinning Objects in the Shared Pool

At times, performance may be crucial for a certain block of code. For example, an organization may have a mission-critical data feed that needs to happen in a short period of time. There may also be problems with fitting large PL/SQL blocks into shared memory in order to even parse and execute the code. Whatever the reason, it may be necessary to place objects into the library cache in such a way that the shared SQL will not be paged out of the shared pool. This method is known as *pinning* the shared SQL in the shared pool.

The process for pinning shared SQL into the shared pool is accomplished as follows. There are several stored procedures provided by Oracle as part of the software release that can be used for the purposes of manipulating the shared pool. The package name containing these stored procedures is DBMS_SHARED_POOL. This package must be created before using it. From within Server Manager, execute the following SQL scripts located in the **rdbms/admin** subdirectory of the Oracle software home directory: **dbmspool.sql** and **prvtpool.sql**.

```
Svrmgr> @dbmspool
Package created.
Svrmgr> @prvtpool
Package body created.
Svrmgr>
```

TIP
*Pin objects in the shared pool using the
following method: Set up DBMS_SHARED_
POOL, then flush the shared pool or shut down
and restart the Oracle instance, then reference
the SQL or PL/SQL code to load it into the
shared pool, then pin it using
DBMS_SHARED_POOL.**keep**( ).*

Once the DBMS_SHARED_POOL package is created in the database,
the DBA can then pin objects into the shared pool. But first, the DBA
should rid the shared pool of all shared SQL information and all cached
dictionary objects. This "flush" temporarily frees all space in the shared pool
for new SQL statements to come in and parse; however, it temporarily
reduces performance for other statements running on the system. The
statement for flushing the shared pool that the DBA must use is **alter system
flush shared pool**.

```
ALTER SYSTEM
FLUSH SHARED POOL;
```

After restarting the instance, the DBA should reference the object code in
some way, either by executing all of it or some portion of it. This execution
causes Oracle to parse the code—either a cursor, procedure, or trigger—
which places the code in the shared SQL pool. *Only when the code is in the
shared pool can it be pinned.* Once the shared SQL code is in the shared
pool, the DBA executes the **keep( )** procedure.

```
set serveroutput on size 5000;
exec DBMS_SHARED_POOL.KEEP(obj,type);
```

Interpreting this statement is as follows. The **set serveroutput on**
command allows Oracle to give printed feedback to the session from a

stored procedure. The **set serveroutput on** command enables the feedback functionality, and the SIZE parameter sets the size of the output buffer in bytes to whatever number is specified. The *obj* and *type* variables passed to the **keep( )** procedure mean the following: *obj* is the name of the object being pinned and *type* defines what kind of object is being pinned. Acceptable values for the *type* variable are P—for procedure, C—for cursor, and R—for trigger.

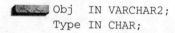

```
Obj   IN VARCHAR2;
Type IN CHAR;
```

Exercises

1. What procedure is taken by the DBA if it important to keep a parsed shareable copy of an SQL or PL/SQL code block in memory? What is flushing the shared pool?

2. What is DBMS_SHARED_POOL? How is it created?

Tuning Redo Mechanisms

In this section, you will cover the following topics related to tuning redo mechanisms:

- Determining contention between ARCH and LGWR
- Setting appropriate checkpoint intervals
- Determining contention for the redo log buffer
- Sizing the redo log buffer
- Relieving contention for the redo allocation latch

Every SQL change operation on the database requires the online redo log resource in order to complete its transaction. The pressure on availability for the online redo log is in direct proportion to the number of users making changes to the database at any given time. Contention for redo log resources is particularly detrimental to the system as a whole because of the heavy dependence every process has on redo logs.

Determining Contention Between ARCH and LGWR

Consider the roles of two background processes in the important activity of redo log archiving. These processes are LGWR and ARCH. As transactions change data, they must also write redo information to the redo log buffer. Once those transactions **commit**, or when the redo log buffer fills, LGWR assigns each transaction a system change number (SCN) and writes redo log entries to the online redo log group on disk. When *automatic* archiving of redo information is used, ARCH copies the filled redo logs to an archival destination when a log switch occurs. For more on automatic archiving, review the discussion of enabling archiving that appears in Chapter 13.

Log switches occur during the normal processing of a database that archives its redo logs automatically. At the point of a log switch, LGWR stops writing redo information to the current redo log group, because the redo log is full, and starts writing information to another group. When the log switch occurs, ARCH is then able to write the recently filled online redo log to LOG_ARCHIVE_DEST. As demonstrated in Figure 18-2, if all online redo logs are stored on the same disk, the LGWR and ARCH processes will contend as ARCH attempts to archive the filled redo log and LGWR attempts to write the online redo log. To resolve this situation, the DBA must multiplex the members of each redo log group onto separate disks.

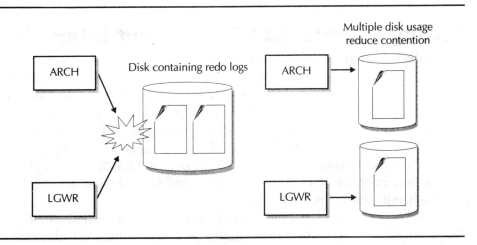

FIGURE 18-2.   *Contention between ARCH and LGWR*

Another form of "contention" may occur between ARCH and LGWR. If for some reason, such as block corruption or disk unavailability, the ARCH process cannot write the recently filled redo log to LOG_ARCHIVE_DEST, then ARCH will attempt to write the archive from another redo log member. If ARCH cannot write a redo log archive from any redo log member, then archiving stops. LGWR will continue writing redo log information to the online redo logs until it fills all redo logs. Since archiving is enabled, LGWR cannot overwrite any online redo log that hasn't been archived. So, if all redo logs fill and archiving has stopped, LGWR cannot write redo information out of the redo log buffer, and database operation must cease until archiving can be restarted. Thus, the ARCH and LGWR processes will contend if for some reason a redo log cannot be archived. The way to avoid this conflict is to ensure that ARCH is archiving redo logs faster than LGWR can fill them. Usually, this situation will be the case unless there is some data corruption in the redo log that forces ARCH to be unable to write the archive.

Exercises

1. After what event does ARCH archive an online redo log? How might LGWR and ARCH contend in this situation?

2. What happens on the database if ARCH cannot archive an online redo log?

Setting Appropriate Checkpoint Intervals

One of the events that occur at the time of a log switch is a checkpoint. When a checkpoint occurs, several things are done by LGWR. First, LGWR writes the redo log sequence number to the datafiles and the control files of the database. Each redo log is assigned a sequence number to identify it uniquely to Oracle for archiving and recovery purposes. Also, LGWR tells DBWR to write the blocks in the dirty buffer write queue to the appropriate datafiles of the database. When a checkpoint occurs, LGWR momentarily stops writing information from the redo log buffer to the online redo log in order to handle these other activities.

More frequent checkpoint intervals decrease the recovery time of the database because dirty buffers in the buffer cache are written to disk more frequently. In the event of an instance failure, the dirty buffers that are still in the buffer cache are lost by Oracle, and must be recovered from online redo log information. More frequent checkpoints means that fewer of these dirty blocks must be recovered during instance recovery, thus improving recovery time. However, more time spent handling checkpoints is less time spent writing redo information from memory to disk by LGWR, potentially slowing database processing time if there is a high amount of transaction activity.

On one hand, users want their transactions to run quickly, particularly on OLTP systems. Less frequent checkpoint intervals may be used to reduce the burden on LGWR. But, on the other hand, users want fast recovery in the event of system failure. The more often the checkpoint intervals, the more efficient the database recovery. But the opportunity cost is in the application code that has to wait until the recovery information is saved before continuing. Such is the trade-off between the reliability of having many checkpoints and poor online performance while those checkpoints happen. This trade-off may be particularly painful on OLTP systems, giving rise to a certain paradox. Users want maximum online performance, pushing DBAs to reduce the number of checkpoints performed. But, users also want maximum database availability, pushing DBAs to increase the number of checkpoints performed in order to minimize downtime.

TIP

The paradox of checkpoints in action states that a gain in recoverability translates into a loss in performance, which gives rise to the following dilemma in OLTP systems: Should the type of application that has the most volatile (and therefore difficult to recover) data sacrifice that recoverability in order to satisfy performance needs associated with high data change activity?

There are two solutions for improving the way LGWR handles checkpoints. The first is to give LGWR some help. In order to reduce the burden on LGWR to handle checkpoints, the DBA can allow the checkpoints to be handled by a special Oracle background process called CKPT. This process handles the writing of log sequence numbers to the datafiles and control files when it is enabled, allowing LGWR to return to the task of writing redo information from the redo buffer to disk after telling DBWR to write the dirty buffers. If the data in the system is volatile yet requires fast instance recovery, starting the CKPT process can allow the DBA to perform frequent checkpoints without diminishing online transaction processing performance. To enable CKPT, set the value for the CHECKPOINT_PROCESS initialization parameter to TRUE and restart the instance.

Alternatively, decreasing the number of checkpoints reduces the number of times LGWR must perform the tasks involved. Although during the checkpoint itself, performance will still degrade, this event will occur less frequently. The changing of checkpoint intervals is accomplished by adjusting the LOG_CHECKPOINT_INTERVAL to a size higher than the largest redo log file or by setting the LOG_CHECKPOINT_TIMEOUT to zero in order to eliminate checkpoints based on time. Of course, there is no way to eliminate checkpoints entirely. Since checkpoints occur every time a log switch occurs, the only further reduction to the number of checkpoints is to increase the size of the redo log files, which reduces the frequency of checkpoints because the redo logs take more time to reach their capacity.

Exercises

1. What performance impact does frequent checkpoints have on the Oracle database? What benefit does frequent checkpoints provide? How can the number of checkpoints be reduced?

2. What is the paradox of checkpoints with respect to OLTP systems?

Determining Contention for the Redo Log Buffer

Every user process in the database must write redo information to the redo log buffer. In order to write that redo information, the user process must acquire the redo log resource by requesting and obtaining the redo allocation latch. There are two types of requests for the redo allocation latch, based on whether the process can stop whatever it is doing and is *willing to wait* for the latch, or whether the process requires *immediate* access to the latch, and will not wait if it cannot acquire the latch.

"Willing-to-wait" processes will do the following when requesting the redo allocation latch:

1. The process will request the latch.

2. If the latch is available, the process will obtain it.

3. If the latch is unavailable, the process will *sleep* for a short period of time and ask for the latch again. The process will continue its cycle of asking and sleeping until the latch becomes available.

The next important aspect of finding out if poor process handling of the redo allocation latch is causing other processes to wait to write redo log entries is calculation of the wait ratio for a latch. The DBA can obtain the wait ratio for the given latch by executing the following query against Oracle. If either the wait ratio on willing to wait or the immediate latch requests for the latch named by the DBA in the query are greater than 1 percent, then there is a problem with latch contention in the database.

```
SELECT n.name,(l.misses/l.gets)*100 w2wait_ratio,
(l.immediate_misses/l.immediate_gets)*100 immed_ratio,
FROM v$latch l, v$latchname n
WHERE n.name in ('redo allocation')
 AND n.latch# = l.latch#;
```

Within the redo log buffer, there can be issues with available space for writing of redo log entries to the online redo log. A redo log entry is usually not written to disk until the user process commits it. If the user has a long-running process and there are a lot of other processes that need the space, Oracle may *flush* the redo log buffer to reduce the number of redo log buffer waits that are occurring on the database. Flushing the redo log buffer causes LGWR to write all data in the redo log buffer to the online redo log, whether the transaction has been committed or not. A statistic is tracked by the Oracle performance view V$SYSSTAT that maintains the number of times that user processes wait to obtain space in the redo log buffer in order to write their redo log entries. This statistic is obtained by executing a **select** on the NAME and VALUE columns from V$SYSSTAT where the name is **'redo log space requests'**.

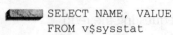
```
SELECT NAME, VALUE
FROM v$sysstat
WHERE NAME = 'redo log space requests';
```

Exercises

1. When is data written from the redo log buffer to the online redo log? What happens if the redo log buffer is full?

2. What dynamic performance view is used to detect if processes are waiting for space in the redo log buffer? How can that view be queried?

Sizing the Redo Log Buffer

Depending on how often user processes have to wait for the redo log buffer to free up some space, the DBA may want to consider increasing its size. Oracle recommends that DBAs monitor the V$SYSSTAT view regularly for increases in the number of redo log space requests. If those redo log space requests increase rapidly and consistently over time, then an increase to the size of the redo log buffer may be required. Increasing the size of the redo log buffer is accomplished by changing the value for the initialization parameter LOG_BUFFER, which is expressed in bytes.

As with any increase in the size of a portion of memory, care should be taken in order to avoid sizing the SGA out of real memory. If the SGA uses any virtual memory at all, the system can take a major performance dive as Oracle attempts to page blocks into memory and onto swap disk space while it attempts to **update** blocks. The result is that the database will spend a great deal of time "thrashing" data between memory and swap space, creating a major performance problem.

Exercise

What parameter is used to change the size of the redo log buffer?

Relieving Contention for the Redo Allocation Latch

Recall from earlier in this discussion and in Chapter 16 that database change information must be recorded in the redo log buffer by user processes. A user's ability to write redo to the redo log buffer is moderated by the *redo allocation latch*. The user process must first obtain the redo allocation latch to allocate space in the buffer. There is only one redo allocation latch in the Oracle instance. This design choice was made to ensure sequential database redo for database recovery. After obtaining the latch, the user process updates the redo log buffer.

The space in the redo log buffer allocated by the redo allocation latch for a user process's redo is determined in bytes at instance startup with the LOG_SMALL_ENTRY_MAX_SIZE initialization parameter. If the redo information the user process must write exceeds the value set by LOG_SMALL_ENTRY_MAX_SIZE, the user process must acquire the *redo copy latch* in order to write the redo information to the redo log buffer as well. The range of values, as well as the default for this initialization parameter, depends on the operating system. The DBA should keep the time that any process holds the latch as short as possible to avoid contention problems by reducing the value for LOG_SMALL_ENTRY_MAX_SIZE. Reducing this value means that a smaller number of redo log entries can be copied to the redo log buffer when the redo allocation latch is obtained, and the allowed size of the redo log entry written on the latch is smaller as well.

Since there can be only one redo allocation latch on the database, the DBA should minimize the time any user process holds the latch. To reduce the time each user spends writing redo log information while it holds the redo allocation latch, the DBA can configure Oracle to require user processes to build their redo log entries before requesting the redo allocation latch. This process is known as prebuilding the redo log entry. To configure Oracle to require user processes to prebuild redo entries, the DBA can set LOG_ENTRY_PREBUILD_THRESHOLD to an appropriate size. This initialization parameter is expressed in bytes. By default, its value is zero, hence no prebuilding occurs by default in the Oracle database. When this initialization parameter is set to a value greater than zero, all redo entries smaller than that threshold specified will be prebuilt by the user process before the latch request is made.

Exercises

1. How many redo allocation latches are available on the Oracle database?

2. What parameter determines how long a process will hold onto the redo allocation latch?

3. How can the time that each process holds the redo allocation latch be changed?

Tuning the Buffer Cache

In this section, you will cover the following topics related to tuning the buffer cache:

■ Calculating the buffer cache hit ratio

■ Determining whether to resize the buffer cache

■ Using table caching

■ Monitoring the buffer cache

After the shared pool, the buffer cache is the most important part of the Oracle instance. The buffer cache consists of several, sometimes hundreds of, memory buffers, each the same size as DB_BLOCK_SIZE. These buffers are each designed to store one block from disk. User processes never need to deal with disk I/O in Oracle as a result of the buffer cache. The associated server process reads the data blocks into the buffer cache on behalf of the user process and DBWR writes the changes back to disk, if there are any. This section will discuss how to tune the database buffer cache.

The Buffer Cache Hit Ratio

Information in memory can be accessed faster than data in datafiles on disks. It makes sense from a performance perspective for Oracle to keep as many data blocks stored in memory as it can without exceeding the amount of physical memory available on the host machine. Hence, Oracle has the database buffer cache. However, simply having the space to store thousands of data blocks isn't enough. Oracle attempts to store the right data blocks, those blocks used most frequently by user processes.

The size of the database buffer cache is determined by the DB_BLOCK_BUFFERS initialization parameter. To change the size of the buffer cache, alter the value for this parameter and restart the instance. The size of each buffer depends on the size of blocks in the database, determined by the DB_BLOCK_SIZE parameter. Blocks enter the buffer cache by means of server processes acting on behalf of user processes. The DBWR process writes changed buffers back to disk and eliminates other unnecessary blocks. DBWR writes changed, or "dirty," buffers to disk when one of the three following conditions is TRUE:

- The DBWR time-out occurs (every three seconds)
- A checkpoint occurs
- When a scan of the buffer cache shows that there are no free buffers

When a scan of the buffer cache shows that there are no free buffers, DBWR determines which blocks to eliminate based on a *least recently used* algorithm, or LRU. The LRU is based on the idea that blocks recently accessed are more likely to be used repeatedly than blocks that haven't been accessed in a while. Having a block required by a user process in the buffer cache already is called a *buffer cache hit*. Hits are good because they reduce the amount of disk I/O required for the user process.

To determine buffer cache hits, the DBA can use the V$SYSSTAT dynamic performance view to calculate the *buffer cache hit ratio*. The V$SYSSTAT dynamic performance view is available only to users with **select any table** access and to the SYS user. There are three statistics tracked in that performance view that are of use in calculating hit statistics: *database block gets, consistent gets*, and *physical reads*. The hit ratio is determined by the sum of the two "get" statistics (the total number of instance data requests), divided by the number of physical reads. The formula is as follows: **(physical reads/(db block gets+consistent gets))*100**. Since all data for this query comes from the V$SYSSTAT view, it is simple to pull all data required for this calculation by selecting the NAME and VALUE columns from V$SYSSTAT view where the name is either **'db block gets'**, **'consistent gets'**, or **'physical reads'**. Make sure to key in the names in lowercase and put spaces between each word.

```
SELECT decode(name,'physical reads',value)/
(decode(name,'consistent gets',value)+decode(name,'db block gets',value))
AS hit_ratio
FROM v$sysstat
WHERE name IN ('db block gets','consistent gets','physical reads');
```

A higher hit ratio according to this formula means the database is accessing a high number of data blocks in memory, performing few physical reads. A low hit ratio means that the database is not storing many blocks in memory that it requires for SQL statements being processed, which requires it to perform many physical reads of data blocks into the buffer cache. The breakdown of value ranges for database buffer cache hit ratios and their meanings are listed here:

95–100%   Buffer cache is experiencing few physical reads. Current size is optimal, if a bit high. It should be OK to remove buffers from the buffer cache if memory is needed elsewhere.

70–94%   Buffer cache is experiencing low to moderate number of physical reads required to access data blocks. DBA may want to resize only if there is a serious problem with memory on the Oracle database.

60–69%   Buffer cache is experiencing moderate to high number of physical reads. DBA should consider adding more buffers to the database buffer cache to improve the hit ratio.

Exercises

1. What performance view contains statistics required to calculate the buffer cache hit ratio? What is the formula for calculating that ratio?

2. What are some appropriate measures to take when the buffer cache hit ratio falls below 65 percent? What action may a DBA consider if the hit ratio was 96 percent?

3. Name the parameter used to determine the size of the database buffer cache. What would happen if this parameter were sized such that Oracle's memory structures no longer fit into real memory?

Determining Whether to Resize the Buffer Cache

If the buffer cache hit ratio is extremely high or low, or if there is a problem with memory allocation on the database, the DBA may need to resize the buffer cache in order to balance memory allocation to the different components of the SGA. In order to determine the effects of resizing the buffer cache, the DBA needs some means of comparison to determine how adding or subtracting buffers will impact the number of buffer cache hits that occur on the database. This means of comparison may help the DBA to weigh the trade-off of juggling available memory or swallowing the expense for adding additional memory for the host machine running Oracle.

Raising Buffer Hits with X$KCBRBH

In cases where the buffer cache hit ratio is low, it may help the DBA to add space to the buffer cache by increasing DB_BLOCK_BUFFERS. To understand better the impact of increasing DB_BLOCK_BUFFERS, Oracle offers a feature that can collect statistics that allow for estimation of the gain in performance that would come as a result of adding more space to make the buffer cache larger. This functionality is provided by a special performance view called X$KCBRBH, owned by user SYS. Unlike V$ performance tables, which can be accessed by users granted the **select any table** privilege, X$KCBRBH can only be accessed by logging onto the database as the owner of the view, SYS. Each row in this view offers the relative performance gain of adding more buffers to the buffer cache.

The X$KCBRBH table has two columns on it. The first column discussed is INDX. For each row of data, INDX stores a sequential value that equals the number of buffers that could be added minus 1. According to this definition, the first row of X$KCBRBH will contain an INDX value of 0, the next row 1, and so on. The other column stored in X$KRBRBH is called COUNT. This column stores a statistic that corresponds to each INDX value that represents the number of estimated cache hits that can be obtained by adding a number of buffers to the database buffer cache equal to INDX+1.

INDX	COUNT
0	3
1	14
2	28
3	34
4	50
5	90
6	40
7	39

As the INDX value goes up, the count also increases, but only to a certain point. After that point, the count goes back down again. Although the previous data is only an example, it illustrates an interesting twist on the economic principle of diminishing marginal utility. In fact, there is a threshold where it does not matter how much new space is added to the buffer cache—the hit ratio simply won't increase appreciably. It is by taking note of where this threshold occurs that the DBA is able to identify how many blocks to add to the system.

Collection of the statistics that X$KCBRBH displays is driven by the use of the DB_BLOCK_LRU_EXTENDED_STATISTICS instance initialization parameter. This parameter accepts an integer value. The default integer specified for this parameter is zero (0). As such, the X$KCBRBH performance view will not collect statistics enabling the DBA to identify the benefits of adding more buffers to the cache. However, since the collection of statistics to this view costs the Oracle instance some processing power, it is usually worth leaving the value for DB_BLOCK_EXTENDED_LRU_ STATISTICS alone, unless the DBA wants to use this performance view to determine the right number of buffers for the purpose of sizing the buffer cache. When doing so, there should be some advance planning involved. The statistics collected in X$KCBRBH rely on statistics collected in the V$SYSSTAT view, any data collected in any performance view is valid for only the current instance. With those things in mind, setting the initialization parameter DB_BLOCK_LRU_EXTENDED_STATISTICS to a nonzero value will allow the underlying performance views to gather meaningful data. Once that data is gathered, however, there is no further reason to keep collection data for the X$KCBRBH view. One final note: The value chosen for the initialization parameter DB_BLOCK_LRU_EXTENDED_STATISTICS will be the number of rows collected by X$KCBRBH.

Simply listing out the number of additional buffer cache hits that would occur as a result of adding one extra buffer to this table is not the only feature of this information in X$KCBRBH. Each row shows the additional buffer cache hits that would occur *as a result of adding just that one extra buffer*. The DBA can use that information as a statistical base to derive how many additional hits would occur if the DBA added lots of extra buffers. For example, the DBA may use the X$KCBRBH view to determine how many additional cache hits would occur as a result of adding 50 extra buffers.

```
SELECT SUM(count) addtl hits
FROM X$KCBRBH
WHERE indx < 50;
```

Notice that the **where** clause only specifies collecting the sums for COUNT if the value for INDX is less than 50, not including 50. Since INDX represents the number of buffers potentially being added to the cache, minus one, it is important to remember that there will be a statistic for INDX = 0, or the situation of adding one buffer to the cache. The DBA can then put the additional number of hits given by the larger block buffer size into the larger context of the database buffer cache hit ratio. Assuming the DBA is considering an addition of 100 buffers to the database buffer cache, the data in the V$SYSSTAT view related to the buffer cache hit ratio can be combined with the data in X$KCBRBH.

```
SELECT (decode(v.name,'physical reads',v.value)-SUM(x.count))/
(decode(v.name,'consistent gets',v.value)+decode(v.name,'db block gets',v.value))
AS hit_ratio
FROM v$sysstat v, x$kcbrbh x
WHERE v.name IN ('db block gets','consistent gets','physical reads')
AND x.indx < 100;
```

Notice that the number of physical reads in the calculation of the buffer cache hit ratio is reduced by the number of additional hits produced by adding buffers to the buffer cache. This data comes from X$KCBCBH. Figure 18-3 demonstrates a formula for recalculating the buffer cache hit ratio based on the additional cache hits that would occur when the buffer cache is increased.

$$\frac{\text{Physical reads} - \text{Additional hits}}{\text{Db block gets} + \text{Consistent gets}} * 100$$

FIGURE 18-3. *Calculating the hit ratio changed by adding blocks*

Although these methods use the X$KCBRBH view appropriately to determine the proper number of blocks to add to the buffer cache, there are other ways to manipulate the data in X$KCBRBH that better demonstrate the power of these statistics. This data can be grouped together to provide the DBA with the number of hits that would be the result of adding different ranges of buffers to the buffer cache. The following query demonstrates how the statistics in this view may be better manipulated to make an informed decision about adding buffers to the buffer cache without the stepwise refinement that is inherent in the process previously outlined:

```
SELECT 100*TRUNC(indx/100)+1|| '-'|| 100*(TRUNC(indx/100)+1 range,
       SUM(count) addtl_hits
FROM x$kcbrbh
GROUP BY TRUNC(indx/100);
```

```
Range     addtl_hits
-------   ----------
1-100     56003
101-200   105033
201-300   1756
```

The number 100 represents the interval by which the user would like to break out the statistics in order for comparison. The 100 can be substituted with a different number to break the results out according to different range specifications. Each row returned by this query indicates a range of values that could be added to the buffer cache for a gain in cache hits, as indicated by the ADDTL_HITS column. For this example, the DBA may determine that the biggest performance gain is made with an addition of about 200 buffers. Adding more buffers, however, may serve no purpose other than to take up memory unnecessarily.

Crushing Buffer Hits with X$KCBCBH

In some cases, performance in some other area of memory may be hindered, and the DBA may want to determine where to make memory allocation trade-offs. In that situation, the buffer cache hit ratio may be high enough (say, around 90 percent or higher) that it may be worth taking some memory allocation from the buffer cache and putting more memory toward the shared pool, for example. A related view is available from Oracle that will help determine the effects of buffer removal. This view is known as X$KCBCBH.

TIP
*It may get difficult to remember which X$ view corresponds to which buffer cache tuning activity. If this is the case, remember the three-letter rule of X$: X$KCB**CBH** crushes buffer hits, while X$KCB**RBH** raises buffer hits.*

X$KCBCBH has two columns called INDX and COUNT. The INDX column is the number of buffers currently in the buffer cache, treating the first buffer of the cache as buffer number 0. As a result, there are as many rows in this performance view when it is enabled as there are database block buffers in the database. The COUNT column stores the number of hits that can be directly related to the presence of the corresponding buffer in the cache. The initialization parameter that starts usage of X$KCBCBH is DB_BLOCK_LRU_STATISTICS. This parameter can be set to either TRUE or FALSE. When set to FALSE, statistics for buffer cache hits per buffer will not be collected, while setting the parameter to TRUE enables collection of buffer cache statistics. There is some overhead associated with the statistics gathering process, and it should only be undertaken when sizing the buffer cache or other memory structures.

Reading statistics from X$KCBCBH is done as follows. The generated values refer to cache misses, the additional number of misses that would occur with a smaller number of buffers in the buffer cache. The statistics in this view demonstrate the additional cache misses that will be incurred by reducing the number of buffers in the buffer cache. Refer to the following code block containing SQL code that can be used to assess the impact on the buffer cache hit ratio of reducing the size of the buffer cache. As before, assume that the DBA is considering the impact of a reduction in the hit ratio of the buffer cache for a removal of 100 buffers. The reduction in the buffer cache hit ratio in this case is reflected by a formula demonstrated in Figure 18-4.

```
SELECT (decode(v.name,'physical reads',v.value)+SUM(x.count))/
(decode(v.name,'consistent gets',v.value)+decode(v.name,'db block gets',v.value))
AS hit_ratio
FROM v$sysstat v, x$kcbcbh x
WHERE v.name IN ('db block gets','consistent gets','physical reads')
AND x.indx < 100;
```

The additional misses estimated by X$KCBCBH are added to the number of physical reads because an additional miss in the buffer cache will resolve in the V$SYSSTAT view as an additional physical read. Using a similar method as before with the query listed in the following code block, the DBA can eliminate some of the guesswork inherent in the stepwise refinement process covered by producing a report that lists ranges of buffers that could be eliminated along with their corresponding additional cache misses.

```
SELECT 100*TRUNC(indx/100)+1|| '-'||
100*(TRUNC(indx/100)+1 range,
SUM(count) addtl_misses
FROM x$kcbcbh
WHERE indx > 0
GROUP BY TRUNC(indx/100);
```

$$\frac{\text{Physical reads} + \text{Additional hits}}{\text{Db block gets} + \text{Consistent gets}} * 100$$

FIGURE 18-4. *Recalculating hit ratio after subtracting blocks*

The number 100 represents the interval by which the user would like to break out the statistics in order for comparison. This value can be changed. For example, specifying 30 in place of 100 may produce output similar to the following:

```
Range   addtl_misses
-----   ------------
1-30    763
31-60   1034
61-90   900
```

Based on this example, the DBA can then determine if there are buffers that are appropriate for removal. In this case, all ranges seem to contribute heavily, and as such the DBA may find that shedding buffers from the buffer cache is not a wise idea. However, if the numbers for the 61–90 range had been much lower, say around 100, then the DBA may have found reason to eliminate those buffers based on the fact that the number of misses produced would not reduce the hit ratio significantly.

Exercises

1. What dynamic performance view is used to determine the impact of adding more buffers to the database buffer cache? What initialization parameter is used to control usage of that performance view?

2. What dynamic performance view is used to determine the impact of removing buffers from the database buffer cache? What is the initialization parameter used to control usage of that view?

3. The DBA is considering adding buffers to the buffer cache to improve performance. The following information is at the DBA's disposal. How many buffers would be appropriate to add to the system for maximum cache hit performance for the least amount of memory?

```
Range     addtl_hits
-------   ------------------
1-50      506
51-100    1179
101-150   214
151-200   95
```

Using Table Caching

As stated earlier, the database uses an algorithm to determine how long to keep any given block in the buffer cache, based on the last time it was used. The older a block gets in the buffer cache without being used, the more likely it is that Oracle will eliminate it. This structure is designed to make room for new blocks that processes are requesting while simultaneously keeping each block in the buffer cache long enough in case there is another user who needs it.

There are, however, certain exceptions to this LRU algorithm of buffer cache management. One major exception is made for how Oracle will handle blocks from a table that is currently undergoing a full table scan. If the least recently used algorithm in its purest form is applied, Oracle would eliminate other blocks in the buffer cache while performing a full table scan. Although this algorithm will not cause too many problems if the table is small, the algorithm may eliminate most or all existing blocks from the buffer cache if the table being scanned is large. If the LRU algorithm were not modified, full table scans would be extremely disruptive to other processes simply trying to get a small amount of data. Oracle would have to perform multiple reads in order to satisfy the one process's request for data while simultaneously trying to satisfy the full table scan's insatiable appetite for more block buffers. In order to spare other users on the system, Oracle places the blocks that come into the buffer cache as a result of full table scans onto the end of the least recently used list of blocks, so that the full table scan process's buffers get eliminated first. This *last in-first out* treatment works for the other processes as well as the full table scan, because the full table scan will only need to look at any buffer that is brought into the buffer cache once.

In some cases, however, the last in-first out handling of blocks associated with full table scans is detrimental to performance on the system. Sometimes it does not make sense for a table to use extensive indexing, particularly if it is a table that contains validation values and has very few rows. In these cases, the performance of a full table scan is only slightly less effective than an indexed search, and the storage space in the INDEX tablespace benefits from not having to contain an index for that table containing valid values. However, the buffer cache will have to undergo numerous physical reads in this situation because many processes are looking for those valid values, but the blocks are being eliminated by Oracle as fast as the database can put them in the cache.

The answer to this situation is table caching. Oracle makes it possible to keep the entire contents of a table in the buffer cache when a full table scan occurs. Use of this feature should be well planned, as the blocks of the table being cached will become fixtures in the database buffer cache for as long a period of time as it takes for the LRU algorithm to eliminate them in the way it eliminates blocks brought in as part of indexed searches. Proper research on the number of blocks containing table data for the table being cached should be performed. After obtaining the number of blocks containing table data for the table being cached, the number of cache misses should be calculated for the buffer cache again, using X$KCBRBH in order to determine what the buffer cache hit ratio will be for the reduced number of available database buffers. It may take a few iterations of monitoring V$SYSSTAT to verify how many physical reads are reduced by caching the database table along with the increase in physical reads required to make up for cache misses on buffers that have the cached blocks stored in them. In any event, this approach should only be pursued if the buffer cache hit ratio shows a clear improvement as a result of caching a table containing valid values. After deciding to cache a database table, **alter table** *tablename* **cache** can be used to set up this operation:

```
ALTER TABLE empl_dept CACHE;
```

One potentially confusing aspect of this operation is identifying the time that table's blocks are actually introduced into the buffer cache. Those blocks associated with the table being cached are not read into the buffer cache at the time the statement is executed. Rather, the table is simply earmarked such that, at the time of the next table scan, the blocks read into the buffer cache will be placed in the beginning of the list Oracle maintains to determine which buffers were least recently used.

Obviously, this use of caching is not appropriate for tables with large numbers of rows. However, some of the applications developed on the Oracle database may have great use for this technique in order to reduce the number of physical reads on the buffer cache.

Exercises

1. What is table caching? When might it be appropriate to cache a table?

2. What statement can be used to set up table caching? After issuing this statement, is the table cached in memory? Explain.

Monitoring the Buffer Cache

The best indicator of buffer cache performance is the buffer cache hit ratio. Determining the buffer cache hit ratio depends on the proper use of the performance view V$SYSSTAT. The main statistics to refer to on this view are the **db block gets**, **consistent gets**, and **physical reads**. The DBA needs to remember that the buffer cache hit ratio will *NEVER* be 100. Even if your host machine has gigabytes of memory allocation or more, there will probably still be far more space available on disk.

Exercise

What is the name of the performance view used to monitor the performance of the buffer cache?

Chapter Summary

The contents of this chapter cover the tuning of memory structures in the Oracle database. This discussion covers aspects of performance tuning for the shared pool, the redo log buffer, and the buffer cache. These topics are important ones on the OCP Exam 4, so care should be taken to review the material and answer the questions. This chapter covers 30 percent of the material on OCP Exam 4.

The first area of discussion in this chapter was the tuning of shared pool elements of the SGA. The shared SQL pool consists of some major components required by users of the database. The two major structures that exist in the shared pool are the dictionary, or "row," cache and the library cache. The dictionary cache stores data from rows in data dictionary tables in memory for use by user processes to improve the performance of queries against the data dictionary. The library cache contains several elements, including parsed SQL statements, for the purpose of minimizing storage costs of the parse information and speeding the execution of SQL in the event that multiple users are executing the same statements. Additionally, the library cache contains executable versions of PL/SQL packages and procedures. Finally, the library cache contains control structures like locks and cache handles, or addresses in memory.

Each object in the shared pool is designed to produce improvements in performance on various aspects of the Oracle database. The performance of each of these objects is quantitatively determined using a calculation of a hit ratio. "Hits" are defined relative to the object being quantified. In the case of the row cache, a hit is when a process or Oracle looks for data from the data dictionary and finds it in the row cache. On the library cache, hits are defined as when a process needs to execute a SQL statement and finds it already parsed and waiting in the library cache.

Quantification of the performance for the library cache is accomplished by calculating a hit ratio. The hit ratio is determined first by pulling the relevant statistics from the appropriate dynamic performance view. In this case, the DBA will need to work with the V$LIBRARYCACHE performance view to obtain the statistics collected for the PINS and RELOADS columns on the library cache. A pin is when the user process needs to parse a statement in the library cache only to find that a parsed version of it already exists in the cache. Since this find occurred, and thus the parse tree was recently used, the parsed statement will stay "pinned" in the buffer cache as a most recently used object. RELOADS represent the number of times Oracle had to reparse a statement because the period of time between the parsing of the statement and the execution of the statement were spaced far enough so that Oracle had actually eliminated the parse tree from the library cache in order to make room for another statement. Reloads indicate that there is either a great deal of activity on the database or a great many unique statements being executed—for example, in the case of many users permitted to run ad hoc SQL against the database. The reload and pin statistics come from the RELOAD and PIN columns of the dynamic performance view V$LIBRARYCACHE. The formula for calculating the hit ratio for the library cache is defined as **(RELOADS/PINS)*100**.

In order to quantify this occurrence on the row cache, the dynamic performance view V$ROWCACHE must be queried for the statistics in the GETS and GETMISSES columns to calculate the hit ratio for the row cache. The formula for calculating the hit ratio is **(GETMISSES/GETS)*100**. If the result of this query is under about 10–15, then the hit ratio and performance for the library cache should be satisfactory. A value above 15 may not produce satisfactory performance, either for Oracle or for the user processes.

When there is a performance issue with the library cache or the dictionary cache, the shared pool must be resized. The shared pool needs to be sized in an appropriate manner. The initialization parameter that handles increases of shared pool size is SHARED_POOL_SIZE. This parameter is measured in bytes. Care should be taken when performing operations that increase the size of any Oracle memory structure to make sure that no part of the SGA is sized out of the real memory that is available for the system. The best approach to increasing the size of the shared pool is to keep the overall size of the SGA the same as before, and simply reallocate memory from one area of the SGA to another, or to add physical memory to the hardware and allocate it to Oracle.

It may become useful in some instances to place objects in the shared pool for a long-term basis. The types of objects that the DBA may want to place in the shared pool on that longer-term basis are objects that go in the library cache. This structure stores parsed statement information that can be reused by identical statements executing within the Oracle database. One reason for pinning objects in the shared pool is to increase performance for a statement not used frequently enough for Oracle to pin the SQL statement parse information in the system according to the LRU algorithm used to eliminate older SQL parse information. Also, there may be a memory fragmentation issue that prevents a large SQL or PL/SQL block from entering the library cache for parsing. In general, the steps required for pinning objects in the shared pool are:

1. Free all space in the shared pool, either by flushing the shared pool or by restarting the instance

2. Reference the object to be pinned

3. Execute the **keep( )** procedure in the DBMS_SHARED_POOL package, passing it the name of the object and a flag indicating what type of SQL code block it is, either P, C, or R for procedure, cursor, or trigger, respectively.

Redo log mechanisms are the next critical portion of the SGA for which tuning was covered in this chapter. The primary function of the redo log buffer is to store redo entries in memory until LGWR writes them to disk. It is recommended in all but the least critical database application situations to save the redo log files in the form of using the **archivelog** feature of the Oracle database. Archiving is often handled automatically with the use of the ARCH process, which handles the copying of online redo logs on disk to the archived destination. Archiving is highly recommended; however, there are some performance considerations that the DBA should be aware of that may put the LGWR and ARCH process in contention. If for some reason ARCH cannot archive a redo log, and LGWR fills all the online redo logs with redo information, operation on the database will stop until the DBA takes care of the archiving issue.

The issue of determining checkpoint intervals presents another interesting set of considerations for the DBA. During normal database operation, LGWR writes redo entries from the redo log buffer to disk whenever user processes **commit** their transactions. A checkpoint is a point in time when LGWR stops writing redo information in order to write the redo log sequence to datafile headers and to the control files of the database, and to tell DBWR to write dirty buffers from the dirty buffer write queue to disk. At the time a checkpoint occurs, performance of online applications may momentarily drop as LGWR stops writing redo log entries. The more frequent the checkpoints, the more often this performance hit will occur. However, the more checkpoints, the more current the datafiles, and the more effective the instance recovery will be in the event of a failure on the database. Decreasing the number of checkpoints is done by increasing the LOG_CHECKPOINT_INTERVAL to a number higher than the size of the largest online redo log or by eliminating time-based checkpoints by setting LOG_CHECKPOINT_TIMEOUT to zero. Also, checkpoints can be reduced in frequency by increasing the size of redo log files, which effectively makes the redo log files accept more entries before reaching capacity and making a switch. Finally, the CKPT process can be enabled to handle writing log sequence information to the datafile headers and the control files in place of LGWR by setting the CHECKPOINT_PROCESS to TRUE.

If user processes write redo information to the redo log buffer faster than the LGWR process can copy the redo log entries to disk, user processes may be temporarily unable to write records to the redo log buffer. If such a wait situation occurs too frequently, the space allocated to the redo log buffer can be increased. In order to determine if the user processes are waiting for space in the redo log buffer, the DBA can query the V$SYSSTAT performance view to find information in the NAME and VALUE columns, where the name in the NAME column is '**redo log space requests**'. Ideally, this statistic should be stable, and as close to zero as possible. If it is high or increasing, the DBA should increase the space allotted to the redo log buffer by changing the value for the initialization parameter LOG_BUFFER, which is expressed in bytes. However, as with resizing the shared pool size, care should be taken so as not to increase the size of the SGA and make it larger than what can fit in real memory.

In conclusion to this treatment of the redo log buffer, access to write redo log entries is controlled by two latches, called the *redo allocation latch* and the *redo copy latch*. There is one redo allocation latch in the entire Oracle database to ensure sequential entries to the online redo log. In heavy transaction processing application environments, there can be some contention for the redo allocation latch. Some approaches for solving that contention problem center around shortening the amount of time any process can hold the latch. There are two ways to do this. One is to reduce the size of the entry any process can write to the online redo log. This task is accomplished by the DBA by decreasing the value, expressed in bytes, for the LOG_SMALL_ENTRY_MAX_SIZE parameter. The other method is to require processes to build their redo log entry before calling Oracle for the redo allocation latch. This task is also accomplished by the DBA by setting the LOG_ENTRY_PREBUILD_THRESHOLD initialization parameter to a value in bytes that is high enough such that any redo log entry that falls below that threshold will have to be prebuilt.

The final area of tuning the Oracle SGA is the buffer cache. This area of memory is used to store a number of recently used database blocks. One principle behind the buffer cache is that more recently used buffers may be used again by the database, and if so, Oracle can speed the performance of queries requiring them by caching the blocks in memory. In order to determine if the size of the buffer cache is effective, the buffer cache hit ratio can be calculated using statistics gathered from the V$SYSSTAT dynamic performance view on the Oracle database. The statistics to be gathered are contained in this view as statistics in the VALUE column, corresponding to where the name in the NAME column equals **'db block gets'**, **'consistent gets'**, and **'physical reads'** from this view. The calculation of the hit ratio for the buffer cache is **PHYSICAL READS/(DB BLOCK GETS +CONSISTENT GETS)*100**.

As stated earlier, there are situations where the buffer cache may need to be increased or decreased, depending on the amount of memory available or added to the system and the memory requirements of other areas of the SGA. If real memory doesn't change, and if the size of another area of SGA changes, the DBA should first consider altering the size of the buffer cache to compensate. There are two performance views that are used to determine the impact of adding or removing buffers from the buffer cache. The names for these structures are X$KCBCBH and X$KCBRBH. The method to distinguish which view assists in which function is the *three-letter rule of X$*: X$KCB**RBH** *raises buffer hits* by examining increases to the buffer cache, while X$KCB**CBH** crushes buffer hits by examining decreases to the buffer cache. Use of the X$KCBRBH view is enabled by setting the DB_BLOCK_LRU_EXTENDED_STATISTICS instance initialization parameter to TRUE, while use of the X$KCBCBH view is enabled with the DB_BLOCK_LRU_STATISTICS parameter set to TRUE.

The method by which Oracle manages space in the buffer cache was also discussed. Oracle eliminates data blocks from this cache based on the premise that blocks used least recently can be eliminated. One exception exists to prevent full table scans on large tables from eliminating all other blocks potentially being used by other processes, in that blocks loaded into the buffer cache as a result of full table scans will be eliminated first. In some cases, however, small nonindexed tables may be used to store information such as valid values that may be useful to many processes. In order to prevent the database from eliminating those blocks quickly, the DBA can identify tables that should be cached in the event that they are used via full table scan by issuing an **alter table** *tablename* **cache** statement.

Finally, it is important for the DBA to always remember to keep the SGA sized such that it always fits into real memory. If the SGA is sized out of real memory, the resultant paging between memory and disk will be extremely detrimental to the overall performance of the database.

Two-Minute Drill

- Oracle SGA consists of three parts: the shared pool, the redo log buffer, and the data block buffer cache.

- The shared pool contains two structures: the dictionary, or "row," cache and the library cache.

- The dictionary cache stores row data from the Oracle data dictionary in memory to improve performance when users select dictionary information.

- Performance on the dictionary cache is measured by the hit ratio, calculated from data in the V$ROWCACHE view. Hit ratio is calculated as **SUM(GETMISSES)/SUM(GETS)*100** from that view.

- If the row cache hit ratio is greater than 15 percent, there could be a performance issue on the database. This ratio is improved by increasing the initialization parameter SHARED_POOL_SIZE.

- The library cache stores parse information for SQL statements executing in the Oracle database for sharing purposes.

- Library cache performance is measured by the V$LIBRARYCACHE view.

- Library cache hit ratio is calculated as **SUM(RELOADS)/SUM(PINS)*100** from the V$LIBRARYCACHE view.

- A pin is when a statement executing against Oracle uses an already parsed shared version from the library cache. A reload is when the execution of a SQL statement requires reparsing that statement because the parsed version for some reason has been eliminated by Oracle from the library cache.

- The library cache hit ratio should be below 1 percent. This ratio is improved by increasing SHARED_POOL_SIZE or by using more identical SQL queries in the database.

- The redo log buffer cache stores redo entries in memory until LGWR can write them to disk.

- The ARCH process writes redo logs automatically from the online location to the archived location specified by LOG_ARCHIVE_DEST.

- If ARCH fails to write redo information to LOG_ARCHIVE_DEST, LGWR will fill all online redo logs and be unable to continue writing redo entries. All database change activity will cease until the DBA handles the situation.

- If the redo log buffer fills with redo information faster than LGWR can write it to online redo logs, user processes will not be able to write redo information to the redo log buffer.

- If user processes cannot write redo information to the redo log buffer, the DBA can identify the situation with the V$SYSSTAT performance view by selecting the statistic in the VALUE column where the NAME column equals **'redo log space requests'**.

- If the value for redo log space requests is not near zero, the DBA should increase the redo log buffer cache by 3–5 percent until redo log space requests near zero. The redo log buffer cache size is determined by the parameter LOG_BUFFERS.

- Checkpoint interval frequency represents a trade-off between online transaction processing performance and database recovery performance. Decreasing the number of checkpoints is accomplished by:

  1. Set LOG_CHECKPOINT_INTERVAL to a value larger than the size of the online redo log file.

  2. Set LOG_CHECKPOINT_TIMEOUT to 0.

  3. Increase the size of redo log files.

  4. Setting CHECKPOINT_PROCESS to TRUE.

- Access to write redo log entries is managed by the redo allocation latch. There is one redo allocation latch in the entire Oracle database. Contention for this latch can be reduced by decreasing the amount of time any process in the database can hold the latch. This is done by:

  1. Decrease LOG_SMALL_ENTRY_MAX_SIZE, the initialization parameter that determines the size of the redo log entry a process can write while holding the redo allocation latch.

  2. Increase the LOG_ENTRY_PREBUILD_THRESHOLD, the initialization parameter whereby if a process's redo log entry is less than this threshold, the process must prebuild the entry before it can request the redo allocation latch.

Chapter Questions

1. **The database is experiencing problems with performance. Decreasing the value set for the LOG_SMALL_ENTRY_MAX_SIZE**

   A. Slows performance for writing rollback segment log entries

   B. Slows performance for writing redo log entries

   C. Speeds performance for writing rollback segment log entries

   D. Speeds performance for writing redo log entries

2. **The maximum number of redo allocation latches for the Oracle instance is**

   A. 0

   B. 1

   C. 10

   D. Twice the number of CPUs on the machine hosting the Oracle instance

3. **The DBA is about to begin performance tuning. Which of the following items is not part of the Oracle SGA?**

   A. ROWID cache

   B. Library cache

   C. Row cache

   D. Buffer cache

4. **The shared pool contains which of the following structures? (Choose two)**

   A. Dictionary cache

   B. Shared SQL areas

   C. Dirty buffers

   D. Redo entries

5. **Library cache hit information is calculated from statistics found in which view?**

   A. V$LIBRARY

   B. V$ROWCACHE

   C. V$SYSSTAT

   D. V$LIBRARYCACHE

6. **What is the name of the procedure used to pin objects in the shared pool?**

   A. DBMS_PACKAGE.keep( )

   B. DBMS_SHARED_POOL.keep( )

   C. DBMS_PACKAGE.pin( )

   D. DBMS_SHARED_POOL.pin( )

7. **The dynamic performance view X$KCBCBH is commonly used for**

   A. Decreasing the number of hits on the redo log buffer

   B. Increasing the number of hits on the buffer cache

   C. Decreasing the number of hits on the library cache

   D. Decreasing the number of hits on the buffer cache

8. **To decrease wait time processes experience when writing redo log entries, the DBA should increase**

   A. The LOG_SMALL_ENTRY_MAX_SIZE parameter

   B. The SORT_WRITE_BUFFERS parameter

   C. The LOG_BUFFERS parameter

   D. The number of redo allocation latches

   E. The DB_BLOCK_SIZE parameter

9. What is the name of the dynamic performance view that tracks dictionary cache performance?

   A. V$ROWCACHE

   B. V$DICTCACHE

   C. V$DICTIONARY

   D. V$DATACACHE

10. To increase the time Oracle keeps data blocks in the buffer cache from FULL TABLE SCANS on the EMP table,

   A. Run full table scans before running other queries

   B. Join data from tables accessed via full table scan with data from indexed tables

   C. Decrease the DB_BLOCK_BUFFERS parameter

   D. Execute the statement **alter table** EMP **cache;**

11. Which of the following steps will not reduce the number of checkpoints on the system?

   A. Set LOG_CHECKPOINT_INTERVAL to value larger than the size of the online redo log file

   B. Set LOG_CHECKPOINT_TIMEOUT to 0

   C. Set LOG_MAX_CHECKPOINTS to the number of CPUs available to Oracle

   D. Increase the size of redo log files

12. What initialization parameter must be set in order to use the X$KCBCBH dynamic performance view?

   A. ENABLE_KCBCBH

   B. DB_BLOCK_LRU_STATISTICS

   C. DB_BLOCK_BUFFERS

   D. LOG_BUFFER

13. **DBWR write dirty buffers to disk when**

   A. Told to do so by ARCH

   B. When a time-out occurs

   C. When LGWR writes redo entries to disk

   D. Never, dirty buffers are written to disk by the server process

14. **Which of the following describe events that occur as the result of a checkpoint? (Choose two)**

   A. Redo information is written to disk.

   B. Dirty buffers are written to disk.

   C. Redo log sequence numbers are written to the control file.

   D. The server process reads data into the buffer cache.

Answers to Chapter Questions

1. D. Speeds performance for writing redo log entries

Explanation LOG_SMALL_ENTRY_MAX_SIZE specifies the redo log entry size a process can write while holding the redo allocation latch. Choices A and C are wrong because the redo allocation latch does not regulate rollback segment activity. Choice B is incorrect because decreasing the value for LOG_SMALL_ENTRY_MAX_SIZE increases the performance of redo log writes, because each process holding the latch holds it for less time. Review the discussion of redo allocation latch configuration.

2. B. 1

Explanation There is only one redo allocation latch in the Oracle database. Review the discussion of the redo allocation latch configuration.

3. A. ROWID cache

Explanation The library cache and row cache are both part of the shared pool of the Oracle SGA. The buffer cache is another component of the SGA. Therefore, choices B, C, and D are incorrect. Review the discussion of the memory structures comprising the Oracle instance.

4. A and B. Dictionary cache and shared SQL areas

Explanation The shared pool contains the dictionary cache and the library cache. Since the shared SQL area is part of the library cache, choices A and B are correct.

5. D. V$LIBRARYCACHE

Explanation The library cache hit ratio is calculated from the statistics in the PINS and RELOADS columns in the V$LIBRARYCACHE view. The other three choices are incorrect. Review the discussion of obtaining the library cache hit ratio.

6. B. DBMS_SHARED_POOL.**keep( )**

Explanation DBMS_PACKAGE is not a package in the Oracle database, eliminating choices A and C. Choice D is wrong because although the process is called *pinning*, the procedure to do it is called **keep( )**. Review the discussion of pinning objects in the shared pool.

7. D. Decreasing the number of hits on the buffer cache

Explanation X$KCBCDIH is used to estimate the number of misses that would occur with removal of various numbers of buffers from the buffer cache. It has no use in the redo log or the shared pool; therefore, choices A and C are incorrect. The X$KCBRBH performance view is used to gauge the effects of adding buffers to the buffer cache. Refer to the discussion of examining the impact of removing or adding buffers.

8. C. The LOG_BUFFERS parameter

Explanation Increasing the LOG_SMALL_ENTRY_MAX_SIZE parameter increases the wait time each process experiences when writing redo log entries. Therefore, choice A is out. The number of redo allocation latches on the database is fixed at one, and the value of DB_BLOCK_SIZE is fixed at database creation; therefore, choices D and E are out. The SORT_WRITE_ BUFFERS parameter determines the number of buffers used for sort direct writes, which is unrelated to the redo allocation latch, so choice B is also incorrect. Refer to the discussion of setting parameters for reducing redo allocation latch contention.

9. A. V$ROWCACHE

Explanation Choices B, C, and D are incorrect because those dictionary views are not present on the Oracle database. Review the discussion of the row cache in the shared pool.

10. D. Execute the statement **alter table** EMP **cache;**

Explanation The **cache** option on the table means that, when blocks are loaded for that table into the buffer cache via full table scan, they will be kept in the cache according to the least recently used rule instead of being paged out almost immediately. Running table scans before other queries simply pages the blocks out faster. Decreasing the size of the buffer cache will have no effect, nor will joining the data in a full table scan with the indexed data from another table. Refer to the discussion on appropriate use of table caching.

11. C. Set LOG_MAX_CHECKPOINTS to the number of CPUs available to Oracle

Explanation   This choice, of course, is utter fiction. There is no LOG_MAX_ CHECKPOINTS parameter. All other choices will reduce the number of checkpoints on the Oracle instance. Refer to the discussion of setting checkpoint intervals properly.

12. B. DB_BLOCK_LRU_STATISTICS

Explanation   LOG_BUFFERS increases the size of the redo log memory area, which has no impact on X$KCBCBH, which eliminates choice D. The DB_BLOCK_BUFFERS parameter sets the size of the buffer cache, the value of which is being considered for change when the DBA uses either X$ performance view. ENABLE_KCBCBH is not an actual initialization parameter.

13. B. When a time-out occurs

Explanation   The DBWR process writes dirty buffers to disk in three situations: when LGWR tells it to as a result of a checkpoint, when a scan of the buffer cache shows that there are no free buffers to write a block required by a user process, or every three seconds as the result of a DBWR time-out.

14. B and C.

Explanation   When a checkpoint occurs, LGWR tells DBWR to write dirty buffers to disks. Either CKPT or LGWR also handles writing redo log sequence numbers to datafile headers and to control files.

CHAPTER
19

Tuning Disk Utilization

n this chapter, you will understand and demonstrate knowledge in the following areas:

- Database configuration
- Tuning rollback segments
- Tuning Oracle block usage

Disk utilization is one of the strongest features Oracle has developed into its database product. By using background processes and memory areas for the movement of data from memory to disk, Oracle prevents users from having to worry about disk usage during the execution of their processes on the database. This configuration frees user processes from being bound by I/O constraints on all but the most transaction-intensive OLTP systems with large amounts of users. This chapter will focus on several areas of Oracle disk usage tuning, including database configuration, tuning rollback segments, and Oracle block usage. These areas comprise 25 percent of the material tested by OCP Exam 4.

Database Configuration

In this section, you will cover the following areas of database configuration:

- Identifying inappropriate use of SYSTEM, RBS, and TEMP tablespaces
- Configuring rollback segments
- Designing for specific backup needs
- Distributing files to reduce I/O contention
- Using disk striping

The foundation of a well-tuned database is a well-configured database. Since many performance issues stem from improper configuration, this section is designed to explain Oracle's recommendations on database configuration. The OCP examination for performance tuning also focuses on this area. Good database configuration starts with the effective use of the tablespaces that are part of the instance.

Use of SYSTEM, RBS, and TEMP Tablespaces

A typical database might have five different types of tablespaces in use to store its objects. Those tablespaces might include SYSTEM, RBS, DATA, INDEX, and TEMP tablespaces. Some of these tablespaces must be created by the DBA before they are available for use. One tablespace, SYSTEM, is automatically generated at database creation. It contains items vital to the Oracle instance, such as the data dictionary. Without exception, the instance must have one rollback segment allocated to it from the SYSTEM tablespace. Consider first the use of the SYSTEM tablespace. SYSTEM contains dictionary objects and SYSTEM rollback segments. This tablespace should not be used for storing other database objects such as tables. As soon as other objects are placed in the SYSTEM tablespace, there can be problems. For example, placing a frequently used table in the SYSTEM tablespace opens up the database to I/O contention every time a user or DBA accesses the data dictionary.

Next, consider the RBS tablespace. RBS stands for *rollback segment*. As discussed in Unit II, rollback segments contain changed and original versions of data from uncommitted transactions. Since rollback segments frequently acquire and relinquish additional extents, they have a tendency to fragment a tablespace. They can be disruptive to other objects in the tablespace like tables and indexes, which also require contiguous blocks of free space for extents. Placing rollback segments in their own tablespace can alleviate some of the disruptions they create for other objects.

Two other important types of tablespaces are the DATA and INDEX tablespaces. The first type of tablespace can be used to store table data. Typically, the DBA creates several different DATA tablespaces, each containing database tables. If the database contains objects supporting multiple applications, the database tables for each of those applications may be placed in different tablespaces. The other tablespace discussed is the INDEX tablespace. This tablespace contains indexes that correspond to the tables stored in the DATA tablespaces. There are benefits to having separate tablespaces for data objects and indexes. Separate DATA and INDEX tablespaces on different disks can speed retrieval of information.

The final tablespace considered in this discussion is the TEMP tablespace. This tablespace is used for temporary storage of sort information being manipulated by a user process. A user process trying to manage a large sort or a **select** statement containing the **order by** clause might utilize temporary storage. Since this type of data is very dynamic, the DBA is again confronted with the issue of a fragmented tablespace, which can be disruptive to other objects as they attempt to allocate additional extents. By default, a user's temporary storage tablespace is the SYSTEM tablespace. Here, the DBA can avert a performance issue simply by creating all users with a named temporary tablespace. Additionally, the DBA can create users with a named tablespace as the default tablespace. Since the default tablespace for any user when one isn't explicitly defined by the **create user** statement is the SYSTEM tablespace, this act reduces the chance of a data object finding its way into a location that may cause problems later. Figure 19-1 indicates proper protocol for user creation.

When specifying object placement in a tablespace, there are several factors to consider to find the appropriate choice. Placing an object in an appropriate tablespace can improve performance on the database and reduce the amount of maintenance required to keep the database optimally tuned. There is an entire school of thought around the proper placement of tablespaces on different disks to avoid disk contention. The highlights of these theories will be covered in a discussion of minimizing I/O contention that will appear later in this section.

```
CREATE USER smith          CREATE USER smith
IDENTIFIED BY sally;       IDENTIFIED BY sally
                           DEFAULT TABLESPACE data01
                           TEMPORARY TABLESPACE temp01;
```

Wrong   **Right**

FIGURE 19-1. *Protocol for user creation*

Exercises

1. Identify the contents of the RBS and TEMP tablespaces. Why is it inappropriate to place tables and indexes in RBS and TEMP tablespaces? Why is it inappropriate to place the contents of RBS and TEMP tablespaces in other tablespaces?

2. What are some reasons not to store data objects like tables in the SYSTEM tablespace? A tablespace earmarked for rollback segments?

3. Identify inappropriate use of the SYSTEM tablespace related to default and temporary tablespace assignment, as related to user creation.

Configuring Rollback Segments

Rollback segments have many features to configure, which determine how well they perform. At the instance startup, if only the SYSTEM tablespace exists for the database, Oracle will attempt to acquire at least the one rollback segment created automatically by Oracle when the database is created. If there are more tablespaces on the database, and the DBA attempts to place objects in those other tablespaces, Oracle will acquire at least one rollback segment other than the SYSTEM rollback segment. There are two types of database rollback segments, *public* and *private*. On databases that do not use the Parallel Server option, public and private rollback segments are the same. In databases that use Oracle's Parallel Server, public rollback segments may be acquired by any instance in the parallel configuration, while private segments are acquired only by the instance that names the rollback segment explicitly. Public rollback segments will be acquired based on values specified for two parameters, called TRANSACTIONS and TRANSACTIONS_PER_ROLLBACK_SEGMENT. The TRANSACTIONS parameter can be set by the DBA to be an estimated number of concurrent transactions that will occur against the database. The other parameter is the number of transactions that should be allocated to each rollback segment that is acquired by the instance. Together, they are evaluated by Oracle to determine the number of rollback segments acquired at instance startup: **TRANSACTIONS / TRANSACTIONS_PER_ROLLBACK_SEGMENT**. If Oracle cannot acquire this number of rollback segments at instance startup, then the instance cannot start.

In addition to determining how many rollback segments are acquired at instance startup, the DBA can specify exactly which segments Oracle should acquire. This task is accomplished by using ROLLBACK_SEGMENTS. Private rollback segments are acquired using the ROLLBACK_SEGMENTS parameter. The specific rollback segments Oracle will acquire are listed as values for this parameter, such as **ROLLBACK_SEGMENTS=(rbs_01,rbs_02)**. The DBA may want to specify the rollback segments acquired by the database if there is a rollback segment designed to handle large queries, or if there are rollback segments in a specific instance that must be acquired when using the Parallel Server option.

An important item about rollback segment configuration is its size. There are many different ways to calculate the appropriate sizing of rollback segments, which are based on the number and size of the different transactions that will take place on the database. However, many times it is hard to determine for sure how many different transactions are going to happen on the database at any one time, particularly if there is a large number of users out there, or if there are users with ad hoc query capability. Generally, it is wise to create mostly rollback segments that fit several different sizes and types of queries nicely, while having a few on hand to handle long-running queries and the updates that are inherent in batch processing.

Another important feature to remember about rollback segments is to keep all extents the same size. Though configuring rollback segment extents to be the same size is not required, Oracle began partial enforcement of this recommendation in Oracle7 by eliminating the **pctincrease** clause from the syntax of the **create rollback segment** statement. When specifying the extent size for rollback segments, take the total size of the rollback segment initially and divide it by the number of extents that rollback segment will have initially.

An **optimal** size for each rollback segment is specified as well. The **optimal** size is specified by the **optimal** storage option at rollback segment creation. The value for this parameter should depend on the overall size of the transactions using the rollback segment. Some transactions require large rollback segments to store a great deal of transaction information as part of the execution of their queries. Such queries include long-running batch processes as well as some reports, particularly those selecting large amounts of data for monthly or yearly activity. Other processes require only a small amount of rollback segment space in order to complete their transactions. Some examples of this type are short-running ad hoc queries, reports of daily transaction activity, as well as OLTP **update**, **insert**, and **delete** activity where a record is being manipulated in the database. For queries that take long periods of time to execute, it is advisable to set the **optimal** storage parameter to a high value. For those queries that take shorter periods of time to execute, it is advisable to set the **optimal** storage parameter to a lower value. These are some of the main areas configured by the DBA for rollback segments.

Exercises

1. How does Oracle determine the number of rollback segments to acquire at startup? How can the DBA specify certain rollback segments that must be acquired at startup?

2. How does Oracle enforce the configuration of equally sized extents for rollback segments?

Configuring the Database for Specific Backup Needs

There are certain methods DBAs can use to configure the database to facilitate the backup needs of the Oracle database. This discussion will present the highlights of these methods, which can improve the backup processing of the Oracle database. First and foremost, *always run the database in* **archivelog** *mode*. Also, the DBA should follow these steps when archiving redo logs. Redo information should be sent to a disk location specified by LOG_ARCHIVE_DEST. The DBA can place the archived redo logs onto offline storage such as tape, optical disks, or other storage media later, perhaps on a once- or twice-daily schedule. Also, if it is discovered that an archived redo log is lost, then the DBA should execute a full backup of the database as soon as possible.

When creating backup copies of datafiles, redo logs, password files, parameter files, or control files, it is important to place those backups onto a disk other than the one containing the live production version of the file. If both the backup and the live copy exist on the same disk, then the database is not adequately protected against media failure. As with redo logs, it is usually a good idea to copy your backups to tape or other offline media, although database recovery runs faster when all backup and archive information is readily available on disk.

Another important database configuration strategy designed to improve the recoverability of the database is to create and maintain multiple copies of the control file. Oracle can maintain multiple copies of the control file as long as the names of all control files appear in the CONTROL_FILES parameter of the **init.ora** file. These control files are ideally placed on separate disks to avoid the situation where a media failure destroys the only copy of a database's control file. In addition, the control file should *always* be backed up when the DBA changes the physical structure of the database, either by adding datafiles or redo logs or removing them.

Oracle is particularly vulnerable to disk failures that damage online redo logs. If a disk fails that contains the only copy of an online redo log currently being written by LGWR, the Oracle instance will not be able to continue to run. To combat this vulnerability, Oracle allows the DBA to maintain multiple copies or members of each redo log group. Creating online redo logs with multiple members and placing those members on separate disks is known as *multiplexing* online redo logs, and is highly recommended by Oracle. In addition, it is a good idea for the DBA to make multiple copies of archived redo logs both on disk and tape, and perhaps even on two different tapes. In an ideal world, at least one copy of the archived redo logs could be kept at a remote yet quickly accessible site, preventing excessive dependence on location in the event of severe disasters such as an earthquake, a tornado, or a hurricane. Keeping archived redo logs on disk has the added advantage of speeding recovery during the roll-forward process of instance or media recovery, since restoring data from tape is often the most time-consuming process of database recovery.

Finally, many DBAs keep some disk space free by using an extra disk that is completely or partially empty. This extra space can be used during DBA maintenance when reorganizing tablespaces, or during recovery as an area to which to restore backup copies of datafiles, redo log files, and control files. In addition, the extra space can be used as a temporary place for a tablespace when a disk fails and the DBA must minimize downtime by bringing the database online as soon as possible.

Exercises

1. What are some strategies for database configuration that maximize the backup of control files? Archive logs? Datafiles?

2. What is multiplexing online redo logs? Why is it so important?

Distributing Files to Reduce I/O Contention

There are many techniques and options available for the DBA to distribute files to reduce or eliminate I/O contention. Each tablespace in the Oracle database contains resources that are used by user processes and Oracle processes to store data in the database. Many of these objects are utilized quite frequently. In addition to tablespaces, there are other resources that are used quite frequently, such as online redo logs and rollback segments. The underlying principle of distributing files to reduce I/O contention is as follows. Several Oracle database resources are used at the same time to support database activity, and to eliminate contention for those resources at a hardware level, the DBA should determine *which* resources contend and then place those resources on different disks.

Oracle prevents its database from being I/O bound by allowing user resources to treat certain areas of memory as repositories for their disk storage, while also having several background processes write the data from memory to disk when the time is right. Unfortunately, in some cases the background processes themselves contend for I/O resources because two different processes may conflict. Take, for example, the LGWR and server processes. LGWR writes redo information from memory to disk, while the server process reads data blocks from disk into the buffer cache in support of user processes. For this example, assume the online redo logs are on the same disk as datafiles supporting a tablespace containing tables in the database. In this situation, there is a chance for LGWR and server process contention because LGWR's frequent writes to disk may interfere with server processes trying to read blocks from tablespaces.

The most effective way for DBAs and organizations to reduce the frequency of Oracle background processes contending for I/O resources is to place each resource on a separate disk. However, there are often financial constraints for obtaining contention-free and recoverable Oracle databases, and often trade-offs have to be made. Though the prices of disk hardware have come down greatly in terms of cost per megabyte of disk space, it is not the space itself that reduces contention. Rather, it is the presence of multiple instruments to actually write information to storage. Another factor is that some of these resources do not take up much room on a disk drive. A control file, for instance, may only take up 250 kilobytes of memory, while the typical disk drive often can store gigabytes of data.

Ideally, a good balance can be found between the number of disk drives the database hardware will have and the number of valuable database resources each drive will store. That balance will be based on pairing appropriate noncontending resources on the same disk drives, and placing potential I/O contenders on their own drives. What are some pairings the DBA can make in order to reduce the necessary number of disks for the hardware working in support of Oracle, yet still maintain a minimal amount of I/O contention? One initial pairing that is often used is placing online redo logs on the same drives as control files. To improve recoverability, it helps to have multiple copies of the control file or a control file creation script backed up to a trace file. The reason for this pairing is that control files are updated mainly by LGWR (alternately, CKPT) once the instance is started, and since LGWR also maintains the online redo logs, LGWR has almost exclusive access to the disk containing both control files and redo logs. As mentioned in the previous discussion, the DBA should also multiplex members of redo logs on different disks for maximum recoverability, implying there is usually another disk available for control file storage as well. As long as the DBA multiplexes online redo logs, there should be no contention between LGWR and ARCH as well.

Another placement strategy used by many DBAs is to put all rollback segment tablespaces on the same disk. There should be little contention in this arrangement if the rollback tablespaces are created such that smaller rollback segments for typical user processes are placed in one tablespace while larger rollback segments for use with long-running batch processes that run outside of normal business hours are placed in another. In general, all temporary tablespaces can be placed on one disk as well. Other combinations abound. TEMP tablespaces can be placed on the same disks as DATA tablespaces, particularly if the DATA tablespaces are **read only** or contain tables that have static data. This is an acceptable match because static data in a database tends to be for validation purposes. Other recommended combinations appear in Figure 19-2.

However, there are several "DON'Ts" the DBA should bear in mind when distributing disk resources to minimize I/O contention. The recovery-minded DBA should be careful to ensure that exports, backup files, and archived redo logs don't appear on the same disks as their live production counterparts, if only for minimizing dependence on any one disk in the host machine running Oracle. These backup files should be archived to tape or some other storage media before too much time passes in order to minimize harm done by a disk crash.

Typically, it is not a good idea to put two items on the same disk if one of the items might be accessed at the same time as the other. Some "DON'Ts" include placing rollback segments on the same disks as redo logs, DATA tablespaces and INDEX tablespaces together, or the SYSTEM tablespace and DATA tablespaces together. Since rollback entries and redo log entries store almost the same thing and are created at almost the same time, having these two items on the same disk can be a major headache, both for performance and recovery. Regarding the placement of DATA tablespaces on the same disk as INDEX tablespaces, the database can run into I/O contention when a query is issued against an indexed table. Having data and indexes on two separate disks allows the database to search the index and retrieve data from the table almost in parallel, whereas having both tablespaces on the same disk can create some friction. Finally, the case for not placing DATA tablespaces on the same disk as the SYSTEM

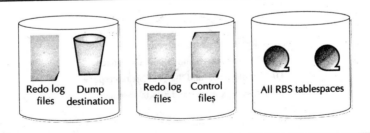

Redo log   Dump
files   destination

Redo log   Control
files   files

All RBS tablespaces

FIGURE 19-2.   *Appropriate combinations for resources on the same disk*

tablespace is this: the SYSTEM tablespace contains the data dictionary. When a **select** statement is executed against the database that contains a wildcard (*) or the **count(*)** operation, the database *must* perform a lookup of that table against the data dictionary to find out what the table's columns are. If that table is on the same disk as the data dictionary, there could be some I/O contention as the data dictionary and the tables are accessed. Combinations of disk resources that are *not* recommended appear in Figure 19-3.

Exercises

1. Describe the overall concept of using resource placement to reduce I/O contention. Why is placing every Oracle database resource on a separate disk not a good choice for real-world database design?

2. What are some good combinations of resources on disks that will not produce I/O contention? Why are they good combinations?

3. What are some bad combinations of resources on disks that will produce I/O contention? Why are they bad combinations?

Using Disk Striping

Sometimes distributing file I/O is not enough to reduce bottlenecks on systems with particularly heavy usage. Databases that can experience high levels of query and data change activity can be of all the types previously discussed. All databases in this situation may have one thing in

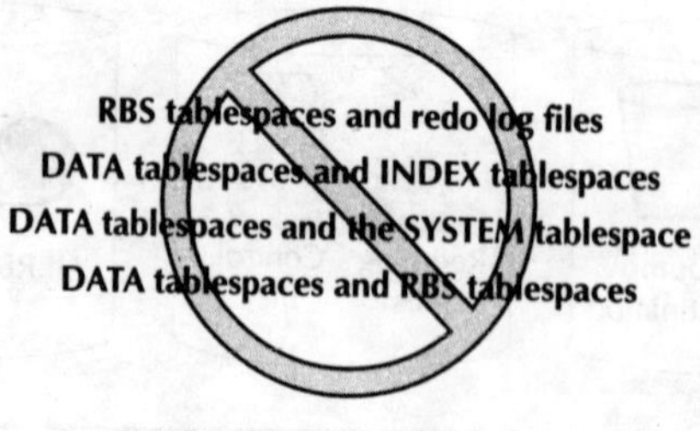

RBS tablespaces and redo log files
DATA tablespaces and INDEX tablespaces
DATA tablespaces and the SYSTEM tablespace
DATA tablespaces and RBS tablespaces

FIGURE 19-3. *Poor combinations for resources on the same disk*

common—large tables. A table's size is determined by the number of rows it has and the number and size of each column in each row. Large tables are those with hundreds of thousands or millions of rows. Access to these tables via nonindexed columns requires full table scans that can turn seemingly innocent SQL queries into database performance nightmares.

One method many DBAs use to maximize table access speed is to separate large tables into extents that span datafiles spread over several disks. In Oracle7, this task is called disk striping. A similar feature called *partitioning* is available in Oracle8, and will be discussed in Unit V. Striping is accomplished by means of several steps. First, create a tablespace to store data using datafiles of equal size placed on several disks where they will encounter little contention.

```
CREATE TABLESPACE data01
Datafile '/DISK04/oracle/data/data01_f1.dbf' size 90M,
         '/DISK05/oracle/data/data01_f2.dbf' size 90M,
         '/DISK06/oracle/data/data01_f3.dbf' size 90M,
         '/DISK07/oracle/data/data01_f4.dbf' size 90M;
```

At this point, the large table can be configured to distribute over several different datafiles. This task can be done in two ways. The first way is to create a new table with data from an existing one in the tablespace just created, using extents sized in such a way as to force Oracle to stripe automatically. This method cleanly creates data striping across several disks for the entire table. Assuming that the table being striped is 150 megabytes, the table storage parameters can be set such that the extents are all 80 megabtyes, allowing Oracle to place only one extent in each datafile. A public synonym can be used to disguise the new large table as the old large table in order to avoid referencing problems for existing applications and SQL statements.

```
CREATE TABLE new_large_table
...
STORAGE   (INITIAL 80M
           NEXT 80M
           PCTINCREASE 0
           MINEXTENTS 2)
AS SELECT * FROM old_large_table;

CREATE OR REPLACE PUBLIC SYNONYM large_table
FOR new_large_table;
```

After this table is created and the data loaded, the table will have two extents in two datafiles striped over two disks. Additionally, there is room for table growth that is properly configured to continue data striping. Generally, this approach is designed with large table storage in mind and in a situation where the DBA can have the database available in **restricted session** mode, ideally during a DBA maintenance period. Unlike the usual approach DBAs take with tablespace creation, which is to create large tablespaces designed to accommodate storage of multiple objects, the striping approach generally means creating tablespaces designed to store only a large table. Trying to use striping for small tables is an approach that will lead to a messy tablespace layout, and is generally not advised. Instead, the DBA should simply try indexing the smaller table and placing the index on another disk to alleviate I/O contention.

The other approach to striping tables is to alter an existing table to allocate an extent in a datafile on another disk. This approach can be executed at any point in database operation, since no extensive data manipulation is required to allocate an extent. Though haphazard, this approach may work in a tight situation; however, striping works best when tablespace layout is considered carefully. One drawback to altering an existing table to allocate an extent in a datafile on another disk is that I/O contention in older extents remains unresolved.

```
ALTER TABLE large_table ALLOCATE EXTENT
(DATAFILE '/u06/oracle/data/data01_f3.dbf');
```

The largest performance advantage gained by tuning I/O contention with table striping is when the DBA has set Oracle to use the Parallel Query Option. In fact, to even use parallel query, the machine running Oracle must have enough CPUs and I/O distribution at its disposal. If the machine is already CPU- or I/O-bound, then using parallel query will not help, and may even hurt the situation. But if the hardware resources of the Oracle database are not overburdened by the system, using parallel query will speed query access to nonindexed columns of large striped tables that previously ran long due to full table scans, as demonstrated in Figure 19-4.

This approach to data striping is the one method available from Oracle for distributing data across disks. Other methods are operating system dependent. It will benefit the DBA greatly in planning maintenance activities to have a strong understanding of the options provided by the system on which Oracle runs. For example, many hardware manufacturers now

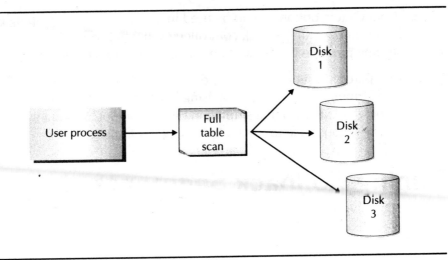

FIGURE 19-4. *Distributing I/O using parallel queries*

provide data striping products that utilize RAID technology. RAID allows
both for file I/O distribution and for data mirroring. RAID and other similar
hardware options have a distinct advantage over tablespace striping in that
RAID is somewhat easier to manage and provides cleaner I/O distribution,
and also allows for the disk mirroring capabilities that are not possible using
the Oracle striping method. Still, table striping in Oracle does have the
advantage of Oracle being the tool used to manage placement and
distribution of data. Oracle's striping methods may be used over RAID
in many situations because of the following reasons:

- RAID is more expensive than support costs for table striping in
  Oracle.

- Only a few tables in the Oracle database are large enough to require
  striping.

Exercises

   1. Explain the concept of striping. How does it reduce I/O contention?

2. What Oracle option should be used in conjunction with striping to better utilize multiple disk controllers? On what type of query will striping produce the greatest performance improvement?

3. Compare striping in the Oracle database to hardware options for data striping. What things can using hardware solutions for data striping accomplish that striping in Oracle cannot? When might it still be a good idea to use table striping in Oracle?

Tuning Rollback Segments

In this section, you will cover the following topics related to tuning rollback segments:

- Using V$ views to monitor rollback segment performance
- Modifying rollback segment configuration
- Allocating rollback segments to transactions

Rollback segments store original and change information for uncommitted user transactions. This information is helpful in the event that the process needs to eliminate an **update** it made against the database. Important to remember about rollback segments is the fact that *every update, insert, or delete statement executed on the database tables will produce a rollback segment entry.* Rollback segments, then, are an important and heavily used resource. Proper configuration of rollback segments will ensure that user processes attempting to create rollback entries will operate smoothly. If these resources are not configured to run at an optimum level, the backlog of processes needing to write rollback entries will grow quickly, causing a problem for all users on the database.

Using V$ Views to Monitor Rollback Segment Performance

Contention for the rollback segment resource is indicated by contention in memory for the buffers containing blocks of rollback segment information. The dynamic performance view V$WAITSTAT can be used to detect this type of contention. This view is available to users with **select any table** privileges, such as SYS and SYSTEM. To let another user access this view, the DBA can connect to the database as SYS and grant **select** privileges on this view to a named user or role.

There are four types of blocks associated with rollback segments that are important to monitor in conjunction with detecting contention on rollback segments. They are the *system undo header, system undo block, undo header,* and *undo block.* The first type or class of block associated with rollback segments that needs to be considered is the system undo header. Oracle maintains a statistic on the V$WAITSTAT view that corresponds to this type of block. The value for this statistic corresponds to the number of times any process waited for buffers containing header blocks from the rollback segment in the SYSTEM tablespace. There will always be one rollback segment for the database instance contained in the SYSTEM tablespace.

The next block class associated with rollback segments that needs to be considered is the system undo block. The statistic represented by this type of block corresponds with the system undo header insofar as both numbers represent waits on rollback buffers in the SYSTEM tablespace. However, the system undo block represents the number of times a process waited for buffers containing blocks other than the header from the rollback segment in the SYSTEM tablespace for that instance.

The next two classes of blocks correspond to rollback segments in tablespaces other than SYSTEM. All instances with more tablespaces than SYSTEM are required to have two or more rollback segments allocated to them at startup, only one of which must be in the SYSTEM tablespace. The first class of block we will examine of this type is the undo header. Oracle collects statistics in V$WAITSTAT corresponding to the number of times a process waits for a buffer containing header blocks from rollback segments in tablespaces other than SYSTEM. The second class of block is the undo block. The database also collects this statistic, which corresponds to the number of times a process waits for a buffer containing blocks other than the header from rollback segments in a tablespace other than SYSTEM. The following list shows the types of blocks associated with rollback segments whose usage should be monitored by the DBA:

SYSTEM undo header   Number of times user processes waited for buffers containing SYSTEM rollback segment header blocks

SYSTEM undo block	Number of times user processes waited for buffers containing SYSTEM rollback segment nonheader blocks
Undo header	Number of times user processes waited for buffers containing non-SYSTEM rollback segment header blocks
Undo block	Number of times user processes waited for buffers containing non-SYSTEM rollback segment nonheader blocks

These statistics should be monitored at times to verify that no processes are contending for rollback segments excessively. Oracle defines excessive rollback contention as a ratio of 1 percent or greater between the number of waits for any rollback block class and the total number of data requests for the system. The total number of requests for data from the database is defined as **total data requests = db block gets + consistent gets**. The information required for the calculation above can be gathered from the V$SYSSTAT dynamic performance view. To calculate the ratio of rollback buffer waits to total number of data requests, the DBA can use the following SQL statement:

```
SELECT w.class, (w.count/SUM(s.value))*100 ratio
FROM v$waitstat w, v$sysstat s
WHERE w.class IN ('system undo header','system undo block',
                  'undo header','undo block')
AND s.name IN   ('db block gets','consistent gets');
```

If a value in the ratio column for any block class in the output of this query is greater than 1, then there is an issue with contention for that block class. The DBA can reduce contention for rollback segments by adding to the number of rollback segments available to the Oracle instance. The appropriate number of rollback segments for a database instance corresponds to the average number of concurrent transactions against the database. To do so, the DBA can apply the *Rule of Four*. This rule is demonstrated in Figure 19-5.

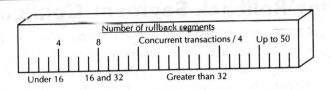

FIGURE 19-5. *Typical transaction to rollback segment ratios*

TIP.
*Use the **Rule of Four** to determine the appropriate number of rollback segments for your Oracle instance—divide concurrent transactions by 4. If result is less than 4 + 4, round up to nearest multiple of 4. Don't use more than 50 rollback segments.*

Here are some examples of the Rule of Four in action. A database handles 133 transactions concurrently, on average. By applying the first part of the Rule of Four, the DBA knows that 133 / 4 = 33 ¼, or 34. Since this result is greater than 4 + 4 and less than 50, the DBA knows that 34 rollback segments are appropriate for the instance. If that number of concurrent transactions was only 10, however, 10 / 4 = 2 ½, or 3, which should be rounded up to the nearest multiple of 4, or 4.

Exercises

1. Describe how to identify contention for rollback segments. What are the dynamic performance views involved in discovering contention for rollback segments?

2. Name four classes of rollback block classes.

3. At what block waits-to-gets ratio is the database considered to be experiencing contention for rollback segments?

4. You are trying to determine the appropriate number of rollback segments to put on a database with an average of 97 concurrent users. Use the Rule of Four to calculate the number of rollback segments your database needs.

Modifying Rollback Segment Configuration

Rollback segments are configured to be a certain size during database creation. Other features about rollback segments handled during configuration are the number and size of extents and the **optimal** size of the rollback segment. The number of active transactions using a particular rollback segment will determine that rollback segment's size. The current space allocation for any rollback segment can be determined from the V$ROLLSTAT dynamic performance view. Access to this view is granted as part of the **select any table** privilege or by executing the **utlmontr.sql** script found in the **rdbms/admin** directory under the Oracle software home directory. The V$ROLLSTAT view can be queried for the name, number of extents, **optimal** size setting in bytes, and current size in bytes for the rollback segment named. V$ROLLNAME was used to derive the associated "undo," or rollback segment number, or USN, for the rollback segment named. This number is required to derive any rollback segment information from V$ROLLSTAT.

```
SELECT rn.name, rs.extents, rs.optsize, rs.rssize
FROM v$rollname rn, v$rollstat rs
WHERE rn.name = 'rbs_name'
AND rn.usn = rs.usn;
```

Important to notice is whether or not the rollback segment has extended past its **optimal** size. For example, say a rollback segment's **optimal** size is 5M and each extent comprises 1M of the segment. If the value in the RSSIZE column of the V$ROLLSTAT view for this rollback segment is 6M, then the DBA would know that the rollback segment has extended beyond its **optimal** size. The rollback segment will try to shrink itself back to the **optimal** size when a query against the rollback segment requires it to extend a second time. Rather than waiting for the transaction to show up that makes the rollback segment extend again, the DBA may want to force the rollback segment to reduce to **optimal** size. This task is accomplished by using the **alter rollback segment shrink** statement. If the DBA does not state the size to which the rollback segment should shrink, Oracle will shrink the rollback segment to the size specified by **optimal**.

Excessive rollback segment shrinkage is an indication of a larger problem—that the rollback segment is improperly sized. If a small rollback segment routinely handles large transactions, that rollback segment will extend to the size required by the query. But if the rollback segment needs two more extents than its **optimal** size, Oracle will incur extra processing to shrink the rollback segment. The more often this happens, the worse off database performance will be. The DBA can determine if rollback segment shrinkage is causing a performance problem on the database. The information required is stored in V$ROLLSTAT. Again, since V$ROLLSTAT keeps only the rollback segment number, not the name, it is appropriate to join the two views on the USN column to obtain the necessary statistics for the following columns:

EXTENDS	This column stores the statistic for the number of times the rollback segment obtained an extent.
SHRINKS	This column stores the statistic for the number of times the rollback segment deallocated extents to return to its **optimal** size.
AVESHRINK	This column stores the average shrink size—the amount of space shed by the rollback segment when it reduced itself to the **optimal** size
AVEACTIVE	This column stores the average active extent size in bytes for that rollback segment. This statistic represents the number of bytes for the rollback segment that were part of a transaction that hadn't committed yet.

In order to determine if there is a problem with rollback segment **optimal** sizing, the statistics named above can be compared with one another. Most relevant is the comparison between SHRINKS and AVESHRINK. If the number of shrinks is high and the average shrink size is also high, there is definitely a problem with rollback shrinkage. This combination means that the rollback segment shrank often, and shed a lot of extents each time it did so. Similarly, there is a problem with rollback shrinkage if the average shrink size is low. The key point made here is that the act of shrinking is happening too often. In both these cases, the **optimal** parameter should be set higher to reduce the processing overhead. In contrast, the setting for **optimal** may be too high if there are few shrinks occurring on the database and the average shrink size is low. The final determinant in this situation is going to be the value for AVEACTIVE. If the average size in bytes of active transactions on that database is much lower than **optimal** indicated by the value for

OPTSIZE in the V$ROLLSTAT view, then **optimal** is set too high. Table 19-1 indicates the relationships between the various columns of the V$ROLLSTAT view and their meanings.

The DBA should monitor the number of times transaction information will be wrapped around in a particular rollback segment. Wrapping is an important aspect of rollback segment usage and performance. When a rollback segment wraps, it means that the current extent handling transactions is not large enough to hold those transactions in their entirety. To reduce wrapping requires an increase in the size of each extent of the rollback segment. The number of wraps occurring on the rollback segment can be identified by querying the WRAPS column of the V$ROLLSTAT dynamic performance view, and can have multiple meanings. In the event that WRAPS is high and EXTENDS is high, then the database is experiencing many active transactions that do not fit into one extent. The rollback segment is extending, therefore, and there could be an issue with shrinks and dynamic extension.

However, if an active transaction requires more room than the current rollback extent can offer, it is possible that a wrap may occur, placing information for that active transaction onto the initial rollback segment's extent. Let's reexamine the nature of rollback segments for a moment. The entire segment is designed for reusability. Ideally, when the active transactions in the last extent currently allocated to the rollback segment need more space, the transaction information in the initial extent of the rollback segment will already be committed to the database, allowing the rollback segment to reuse the space in that extent for new active

SHRINKS	AVESIZE	OPTSIZE
High	High	Too high, lower **optimal**
High	Low	Too high, lower **optimal**
Low	Low	Too low, raise **optimal** (unless nearly equal to AVEACTIVE)
Low	High	OK

TABLE 19-1. *V$ROLLSTAT Settings and Their Meaning*

transactions. In this case, a high number of wraps that is not coupled with a high number of extends is good, because it demonstrates that the rollback segment is properly sized to handle the number of transactions currently allocated to it.

However, even then there can be problems. In some cases, long-running queries will produce error **ORA-01555, "snapshot too old (rollback segment too small)."** This problem is due to the fact that too much transaction data is being stored in the rollback segment from a bad combination of long- and short-running updates and queries. As a result, the rollback has obtained and filled the maximum number of extents it is permitted to obtain, yet the transaction needs more. While the short-term solution is to increase the number of extents the rollback segment can obtain until the long-running query has enough space in rollback to complete its transaction, the true solution is to schedule the long-running batch job at a time when the rollback segment activity will be relatively quiet.

To alter the rollback segment as described, use the **alter rollback segment** statement. Any or several options may be used, including the **next, optimal,** and other options.

```
ALTER ROLLBACK SEGMENT rbs_02
STORAGE (NEXT 20M OPTIMAL 100M);
```

Exercises

1. What dynamic performance view carries rollback segment performance information?

2. How does the DBA identify if dynamic extension and shrinks are causing a performance problem on the rollback segments? What storage parameter is changed if the DBA determines there are too many shrinks occurring on the rollback segment?

3. What are wraps? When might they indicate a problem on the rollback segment? Why aren't they the best indicator of poor rollback segment performance?

4. What problem does the **ORA-01555, snapshot too old (rollback segment too small)** error indicate?

Allocating Rollback Segments to Transactions

The DBA should make every attempt to create rollback segments such that their usage is transparent to the applications and users of the database system. However, sometimes it is not always possible to size every rollback segment in the database to fit every query a user can execute. In the case of long-running transactions exhausting the available space in a rollback segment and receiving the **"snapshot too old"** error message, it is not necessarily a good solution to increase the size of that rollback segment. Most likely, it was possible that several other queries in the course of that long-running process were able to use the same rollback segment that the marathon process exhausted. In some cases, there may be only a few marathon batch jobs that run weekly that cannot fit into the average rollback segment available on the database, amidst the sea of small queries that use those rollback segments and have no problems.

It is useful to create a certain number of rollback segments that are much larger than the standard rollback segment that currently exists on the database. The larger segment can exist for the use of those marathon processes. In order to force those longer-running queries to use the large rollback segments, the user executing the process can include a statement assigning that query to the larger rollback segment. That assignment statement is the **set transaction use rollback segment** statement. Given the existence of larger rollback segments to handle the large transaction activity, this statement can eliminate cases of marathon processes receiving the dreaded **"snapshot too old"** error. At the beginning of the transaction, the process would issue the **set transaction** statement and specify the large rollback segment in the **use rollback segment** clause.

Although it is a good idea to assign marathon processes to their own rollback segments, it is not a good idea to assign every transaction explicitly to a rollback segment. In order to assign transactions to rollback segments en masse throughout the database, each process must have a complete idea of the processes running at that time, as well as the knowledge of which rollback segments are online. If too many transactions request the same rollback segment, that could cause the rollback segment to extend and shrink unnecessarily while other rollback segments remain inactive. Oracle itself can do an appropriate job at finding rollback segments for most short and medium duration transactions.

Exercises

1. What statement is used to assign transactions to a rollback segment?

2. When is it a good idea to assign transactions to rollback segments? When is it not a good idea to do it?

Using Oracle Blocks Efficiently

In this section, you will cover the following topics related to using Oracle blocks:

- Determining block size

- Setting **pctfree** and **pctused**

- Detecting and resolving row migration

- Detecting and resolving freelist contention

The foundation of all I/O activity in the Oracle database is the Oracle block. Row data for indexes and columns, rollback segment information, data dictionary information, and every other database component stored in a tablespace is stored in an Oracle block. Proper use of Oracle at the block level will go a long way in enhancing performance of Oracle.

Determining Block Size

The size of Oracle blocks is determined by the DBA and should be based on a few different factors. First and foremost, the size of Oracle blocks should be based on some multiple of the size of operating system blocks in the database. The reason this approach is a good idea is because it allows the operating system to handle I/O usage by Oracle processes in a manner consistent with its own methods for reading operating system blocks from the filesystem. Most operating systems' block size is 512 or 1,024 bytes. Usually, Oracle block size is a multiple of that. Many times, it is 2K or based on a multiple of 2K—either 4K or 8K. On certain large systems, the Oracle block size can be 16K. Oracle's default size for blocks depends on the operating system hosting Oracle, and should always be set higher than the size of operating system blocks in order to reduce the number of physical reads the machine hosting Oracle will have to perform as part of I/O activities.

Oracle block size is determined at database creation using the initialization parameter DB_BLOCK_SIZE, which is expressed in bytes. Most of the time, the default setting for Oracle blocks as provided by the operating-system-specific installation is fine. However, there are some situations where an alternate block size is worth consideration. These situations have everything to do with the operating system's ability to handle I/O and on the size of its own blocks. For example, some large machines, such as massively parallel servers or mainframes, use larger operating system blocks; hence, it is possible to set DB_BLOCK_SIZE to a higher value in Oracle at database creation time.

There is a very important fact to bear in mind about DB_BLOCK_SIZE— once it is specified and the database is created, there is no possibility to alter it without re-creating the database entirely. Therefore, it is important to make sure that the block size is correct the first time in order to prevent issues such as row chaining and migration later. DB_BLOCK_SIZE also determines the size of the buffers in the buffer cache; thus, the calculation for determining the size of the buffer cache in memory is DB_BLOCK_SIZE times DB_BLOCK_BUFFERS. Figure 19-6 gives a pictorial representation of the relationship between DB_BLOCK_SIZE and other parameters.

Exercises

1. What is the name of the variable that determines block size of the Oracle database?

2. Identify some factors on which the database block size depends.

3. Name another parameter whose value depends on the size of the database blocks.

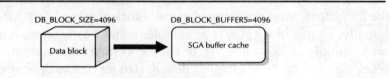

FIGURE 19-6. *Effect of block size on other parameters*

Setting PCTFREE and PCTUSED

Key to the usage of Oracle database blocks is the appropriate setting of block storage options **pctfree** and **pctused** to utilize the space within each block in an effective manner that is consistent with the needs of the Oracle object being stored. For example, the needs of a high-performance, "high response time required" OLTP application with thousands of users entering new information daily are not the same as a mostly static, complex query-intensive data warehouse system with few users. Similarly, the storage options used by database blocks within each system will not be the same, either. The two options, **pctfree** and **pctused**, determine how Oracle will fill the space in each Oracle block with table or index data. They can be configured for tables in two ways:

- Within **create table** or **alter table** and **create index** or **alter index** statements

- Within **create tablespace** or **alter tablespace** statements as default storage clause values

Storage options specified by table and index creation or change take precedence over whatever default values have been specified by the tablespace. For this reason, there is no strict database-wide configuration of Oracle data blocks—other than specifying default values for these options in the tablespace and omitting them from table and index creation, or creating all tables and indexes with the same storage options set explicitly. Nor is such an expansive approach to configuring **pctfree** and **pctused** on tables and indexes really advisable. It is generally best to fit these storage options around the needs of the database object created.

The definition of **pctfree** is the percentage of each data block that Oracle leaves empty, or free, for existing rows in the data block to expand as may be required by updates. When a process calls for row insertions on that object, Oracle will **insert** rows into the block until the **pctfree** value is reached. After a data block's **pctfree** value is reached, no more rows go into that block. At this point, the **pctused** value comes into play. The definition of **pctused** is the usage threshold that any block's current capacity must fall under before Oracle considers it a "free" block again. A free block is one that is available for insertion of new rows.

The **pctfree** and **pctused** options are configured in relation to one another to manage space utilization in data blocks effectively. When set up properly, **pctfree** and **pctused** can have many positive effects on the I/O usage on the Oracle database. However, the key to configuring **pctfree** and **pctused** properly is knowledge of a few different aspects of how the application intends to use the object whose rows are in the block. Some of the important questions that need to be answered by the DBA before proceeding with **pctfree** and **pctused** configuration are as follows:

- What kind of data object is using these blocks?

- How often will the data in this object be updated?

- Will updates to each row in the object increase the size of the row in bytes?

The range allowed for specifying **pctfree** and **pctused** is between 0 and 99. The sum of the values for these two options should not exceed 100. Consider the effects of various values for **pctfree**. For example, a **pctfree** value of 80 will leave 80 percent free from each data block used for storage, while setting **pctfree** equal to 5 means that only 5 percent of the data block is left free. Situations where lots of free space in data blocks is good are when the application will **update** row data for a table or index frequently, and the updates will produce significant increases in the size of each row being changed. For example, setting the value for **pctfree** to 40 will leave ample room for making changes to each row in the block, because once the threshold for adding new rows is reached, the block still has 40 percent of its space available for data additions on existing rows. There is one downside to setting **pctfree** high to preserve free space in each block for row growth. More blocks will be required to store row data for tables with high **pctfree** values than for tables with lower **pctfree** values. Refer to Figure 19-7 for better understanding.

Once block capacity reaches the value set by **pctfree**, DBWR will not put new rows in the block until enough data is deleted from the block for its usage to dip below **pctused**. When the percentage of space used in a data block falls below the value specified by **pctused**, then Oracle will place the block back on the *freelist*, or list of data blocks that have free space to handle row insertions. Specifying a high value for **pctused** keeps space usage as high as possible within the data blocks, forcing Oracle to manage

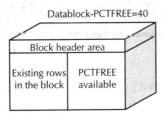

Datablock-PCTFREE=40

Block header area

| Existing rows in the block | PCTFREE available |

FIGURE 19-7. *Block example with **pctfree** specified*

data block storage allocation actively. Active storage management translates into higher resource costs associated with database **insert**, **update**, and **delete** statements. For OLTP systems, the resource cost for using a high **pctused** option can be high as well. Thus, tight disk space management is not effective for systems that have highly volatile space requirements. Usually, it is better to set the **pctused** value lower on these systems, maximizing the time a block spends on the freelist. On data warehouses containing static data, however, it may be wise to maximize disk capability by setting **pctused** high.

Examples of PCTFREE and PCTUSED Usage

It is usually not wise to set **pctfree** and **pctused** to values that add up to 100 exactly. When these two options add up to 100, Oracle will work very hard to enforce that no data block keeps more free space than specified by **pctfree**. This additional work keeps Oracle's processing costs unnecessarily high. A better approach is to set the values for **pctfree** and **pctused** to add up to a value close to 100, perhaps 90–95. This approach represents a desirable balance between higher processing costs and efficient storage management. Consider some examples of **pctfree** and **pctused** settings and what they mean.

PCTFREE=25, PCTUSED=50   This combination might be used on high transaction volume OLTP systems with some anticipated growth in row size as a result of updates to existing rows. The value for **pctfree** should accommodate the increase in row size, although it is important to assess as closely as possible the anticipated growth of each row as part of updates in order to maximize the storage of data. The value for **pctused** prevents a block from being added to the freelist until there is 50 percent free space in the block, allowing many rows to be added to the block before it is taken off the freelist.

PCTFREE=5, PCTUSED=85   This combination of values may be useful for systems such as data warehouses. The setting for **pctfree** leaves a small amount of room for each row size to increase. The **pctused** value is high in order to maximize data storage within each block. Since data warehouses typically store mass amounts of data for query access only, these settings should manage storage well.

PCTFREE=10, PCTUSED=40   Oracle assigns a default value to each option if one is not specified either in tablespace default settings or in the table and index creation statements. For **pctfree**, that value is 10. For **pctused**, that value is 40.

Exercises

  1. What is the meaning of the **pctfree** storage option? What is the meaning of the **pctused** option? How are they specified? What are the ranges for these values? What should the sum of these values add up to?

  2. The DBA is considering a change to the values for **pctfree** and **pctused** for a table for an OLTP application that experiences high **insert** activity. Existing records in the database are updated frequently, and the size of the row is rarely affected by those updates. Should the value for **pctfree** be high or low? Should the value for **pctused** be high or low?

Detecting and Resolving Row Migration

The DBA should consider the "soft" performance gain offered when considering use of higher **pctfree** values—a proactive solution to row chaining and migration. Row migration occurs when a user process updates a row in an already crowded data block, forcing Oracle to move the row out of that block and into another one that can accommodate the row. Chaining is when Oracle attempts to migrate the row but cannot find a block large enough to fit the entire row, so it breaks the row into several parts and stores the parts separately. The DBA should avoid allowing Oracle to migrate or chain rows, due to the fact that performance can drop significantly if many rows are chained or migrated in the table. The importance of avoiding row migration and chaining is demonstrated in Figure 19-8.

There are tools available with the Oracle database that detect migrated database rows. The **analyze** command offers several different parameters for use in determining everything from the validity of a table or index structure to collecting statistics for table usage that are incorporated into cost-based query optimization. It also provides the functionality required for discovering if there are chained rows in the database. The syntax for this statement is listed below:

```
ANALYZE { TABLE | CLUSTER } name
LIST CHAINED ROWS
INTO chained_rows;
```

The *name* in this context is the name of the table or cluster being analyzed for chained rows. CHAINED_ROWS is the name of the table into which **analyze** places the results of its execution. The DBA can then query the CHAINED_ROWS table to determine if there is an issue with row chaining on the database. This table is not automatically created as part of

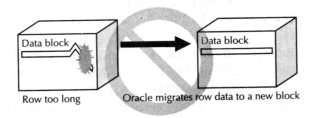

Row too long · Oracle migrates row data to a new block

FIGURE 19-8. *Avoid row migration and chaining*

database creation. Instead, the DBA must run the **utlchain.sql** script that is included with the distribution. Usually, this file is found in the **rdbms/admin** directory under the Oracle software home directory. CHAINED_ROWS is owned by the user that creates it. After running **analyze**, the original ROWID for each chained row will appear in the CHAINED_ROWS table. To determine the extent of chaining or row migration in a database table or cluster, the DBA can execute the following statement:

```
SELECT COUNT(*)
FROM chained_rows
WHERE table_name = UPPER('name');
```

Once the CHAINED_ROWS table is populated and the DBA determines that row migration for the table in question is severe enough to merit resizing the **pctfree** and **pctused** values, the DBA need not drop and re-create the table with appropriate values for those two variables. Instead, Oracle allows the **pctfree** and **pctused** variables to be adjusted by executing the **alter table** statement. The new **pctfree** and **pctused** settings will be used on all new blocks allocated by table inserts, although the new settings will not apply to blocks already created by the table. A temporary table can be created to store the rows whose head ROWIDs appear in the CHAINED_ROWS table. After creating the temporary table of chained rows and altering the original tables' block usage settings, the rows from the temporary table can then be inserted back into their original table. The DBA should use discretion when employing this option. Depending on the number of rows that were in the original table vs. the number of rows that have chained, it may be worthwhile to drop and re-create the table. The original data in this case can be preserved by using the EXPORT utility or by spooling the output of **select *** to a flat file and using SQL*Loader to populate the rows.

Finally, it is important to understand that usually it is not possible to eliminate all instances of chaining or data migration from a database. There are some cases where a single row of table data may exceed the size of a data block. For example, a table with several columns declared to be type VARCHAR2(2000) may easily exceed the capacity of a single data block's storage. The LONG datatype is another "chainer," as it can contain up to 2 gigabyte of data.

Exercises

1. Define row migration and chaining. How are these two things similar? How are they different? Describe the performance implications of row migration and chaining.

2. What command is used to identify row migration and chaining? What is the name of the table that stores information about chaining and migration?

Detecting and Resolving Freelist Contention

When a data block's row storage capacity hits the limit as expressed by **pctfree**, no more rows can be inserted into it. When the capacity for that block falls below **pctused**, the block is again considered available for row insertion. Oracle maintains records of blocks for the particular tables that have space available for data insertion. These records are called *freelists*. When Oracle needs to **insert** a new row into a block, it looks at the freelist for that table in memory to find some blocks in which to put the new record.

However, sometimes there is contention in memory for getting to those lists of free blocks. The DBA can identify freelist contention in the Oracle database by looking to see if there is contention for free data blocks within the database buffer cache of the SGA. This information is contained in the dynamic performance view that Oracle maintains called V$WAITSTAT.

Within the V$WAITSTAT view there are columns called CLASS and COUNT. This column contains the names of various classes of statistics Oracle maintains in this view. The class in this case is called **'free list'**. The value in the COUNT column identifies freelist contention—the number of times a process had to wait for free blocks in the database buffer cache since the instance was started.

The next piece of the puzzle is finding out the number of times processes issued requests for data in the same period of time. This statistic is equal to the sum of database **block gets** and **consistent gets**. The data for this statistic is gathered from another V$ performance view, this time the V$SYSSTAT performance view. By issuing a **select** against this performance view for the sum of the value column where the value of the name column is either **'db block gets'** or **'consistent gets'**, the DBA can obtain the second piece of data for calculating the wait ratio for freelists. That ratio can also be obtained by issuing the following statement against the database. The value produced for FL_WAIT_RATIO in the query should be less than 1. If it is 1 or greater, then there is an issue with freelist contention that that needs to be resolved on the database.

```
SELECT (w.count/SUM(s.value))*100 fl_wait_ratio
FROM v$waitstat w, v$sysstat s
WHERE w.class = 'free list'
AND s.name in ('db block gets','consistent gets');
```

The resolution for freelist contention on the database for that table is to add more freelists. Unfortunately, changing the number of freelists for a table is much easier said than done. The only alternative for adding more freelists for a table is to re-create the table with a higher value specified for the **freelists** storage clause in the table creation statement. Depending on the number of rows in the table, it may be wise either to use IMPORT and EXPORT to store a copy of the data while creating a new table, or to offload the table data into a flat file using **select *** and then repopulate the data once the table is re-created with higher values specified for the **freelists** clause.

Determining an appropriate value for the **freelists** storage clause in the event of detecting freelist contention for a table is as follows. Determine how many processes are concurrently adding to the table. The **freelists** clause can then be set to that number of processes that are looking for free blocks to add their data in memory. With the number of freelists set to the same number of processes adding row entries to that table, there should be little if any contention for freelists on that table.

Exercises

1. What are the two performance views used to determine the wait ratio for freelist contention?

2. How is freelist contention resolved?

Chapter Summary

This chapter discussed the many facets of tuning how Oracle utilizes its disks. The three topics in this section—database configuration, tuning rollback segments and using Oracle blocks efficiently—comprise nearly 25 percent of OCP Exam 4. The first portion of this chapter was a discussion of database configuration. Several types of database tablespaces were identified, along with the ideal contents of each. The five different types of tablespaces discussed were RBS, DATA, SYSTEM, INDEX, and TEMP. Database objects are meant to be placed into these types of tablespaces according to the following breakdown: rollback segments in RBS, tables in DATA, indexes in INDEX, temporary segments required by user processes in TEMP, and the data dictionary tables and initial rollback segment in SYSTEM. Since rollback segments and temporary segments have a tendency to fragment, it is generally wise to keep them out of the tablespaces used by tables and indexes. Particular importance is placed on the SYSTEM tablespace. Since this tablespace contains very important objects such as the data dictionary and initial rollback segment, it is unwise to place any other types of objects in this tablespace. Placing many objects like tables and indexes in SYSTEM can cause a problem. If the SYSTEM tablespace should fill, the only way to add space to it is to drop and re-create it. However, the only way to drop and re-create the SYSTEM tablespace is to drop and re-create the entire database. This act requires a full restore of all data, and generally creates huge problems. Therefore, it is inappropriate to place anything other than the data dictionary and the initial rollback segment in the SYSTEM tablespace.

The topic of rollback segment configuration was discussed. There are two types of rollback segments, public and private. In databases that do not use the Parallel Server Option, public and private rollback segments are the same. In databases that use the Parallel Server Option, public rollback segments are a pool of rollback segments that can be acquired by any instance in the parallel configuration, while private rollback segments are acquired by only the instance that names the rollback segment explicitly. The number of public rollback segments acquired at startup depends on a calculation depending on two initialization parameters, **TRANSACTIONS /**

TRANSACTIONS_PER_ROLLBACK_SEGMENT. This value produces the number of rollback segments the Oracle instance will acquire at startup. The DBA can guarantee that certain private rollback segments are acquired as part of that number by specifying a set of rollback segments in the ROLLBACK_SEGMENTS initialization parameter as well. The appropriate size for rollback segments was also covered. In order to determine that size, the DBA should attempt to find out as much as possible regarding the size of transactions that will take place in the database.

Part of database rollback segment configuration involves choosing an **optimal** size for the rollback segment. This size is specified as the **optimal** storage clause, as part of rollback segment creation. Another important feature to remember about rollback segment creation is that all extents of the rollback segment will be the same size. This design choice alleviates the possibility for a long-running query to force a rollback segment to fill the associated tablespace with its extents, making it impossible for any other object in that tablespace to obtain an extent. Oracle enforces this design by removing the **pctincrease** storage clause from the syntax of the **create rollback segment** statement.

File distribution to minimize contention was also covered. There are specific means to evaluating which Oracle resources are good to place together on the disks of the machine hosting Oracle. The most important feature of this discussion is to recall what the different components are and how they might interact (and more importantly, interfere) with one another. Some resources are best placed on separate disks to minimize I/O contention. They are DATA tablespaces and INDEX tablespaces, RBS tablespaces and redo logs, DATA tablespaces and the SYSTEM tablespace, DATA tablespaces and RBS tablespaces, and DATA tablespaces and TEMP tablespaces. Some acceptable combinations of resources on the same disk are redo logs and control files, all RBS tablespaces, and others.

For additional reduction of I/O contention in the DATA tablespaces, the option of table striping was explored. Table striping is the practice of placing different extents of a large table in datafiles on separate disks. This method has excellent benefits for SQL queries running with parallel query when searching on nonindexed columns, which results in full table scans. Parallel query makes better use of multiple CPUs and disk controllers that are available with disk striping.

This chapter also covered material regarding the tuning of rollback segments. Tuning rollback segments begins with identifying how to detect contention for rollback segments—the detection of contention in memory for buffers containing rollback segment data. The V$WAITSTAT dynamic performance view is used to determine whether this contention exists. There are four different classes of rollback segment blocks in use in the Oracle instance. They are the *system undo header block*, the *system undo block*, the *undo header*, and the *undo block*. The difference between header blocks other rollback blocks is that header blocks are ones that contain rollback block header information. The difference between system blocks and other types of blocks is that the system blocks correspond to blocks in the SYSTEM tablespace, while the other blocks are contained in other rollback tablespaces. Whether there is contention for these blocks is determined by the wait ratio, which is derived by **(WAITS / GETS) * 100**, where waits is the sum of block waits for the types of blocks listed above taken from the V$WAITSTAT performance view, and gets is the total number of data requests as represented by the sum of database **block gets** and **consistent gets** from the V$SYSSTAT performance view.

Following the discussion of how to monitor contention for rollback blocks was the discussion of how to determine the number of rollback segments required for the instance. The text documented the *Rule of Four*— divide the total number of concurrent transactions by 4. If the number of concurrent transactions is under 32, round the quotient of the previous equation up to the nearest 4. And finally, the total number of rollback segments used in any database instance should not exceed 50.

Dynamic extension of rollback segments should be avoided. The current space allocation of any rollback segment can be determined by querying either the DBA_SEGMENTS view or the V$ROLLSTAT view. Preference is given to the V$ROLLSTAT view, as it serves as the basis for more user-friendly monitoring interfaces like Server Manager, although a join on V$ROLLNAME must be performed in order to pull the statistics for a rollback segment based on rollback segment name. In order to keep the rollback segment at the **optimal** size that was specified by the **optimal** clause in rollback segment creation, the instance will perform shrinks on the rollback segment if too many extents are acquired for it. A high number of shrinks as reflected by a high number in the column of the same name in the V$ROLLSTAT performance view indicates that the **optimal** clause set for the rollback segment is too low. Since allocating or deallocating extents for rollback segments creates additional processing overhead for the Oracle instance, the DBA should carefully monitor the database rollback segment statistics and resize the **optimal** clause as necessary.

Shrinks occur in the rollback segment after a transaction commits that required the rollback segment to grow more than one extent beyond the size specified by its **optimal** storage clause. Shrinking a rollback segment can be accomplished by the DBA manually by executing the **alter rollback segment shrink** statement. If no value is specified in bytes that the rollback segment is to shrink to, the rollback segment will shrink to the size specified by the **optimal** storage parameter.

The WRAPS statistic that is also maintained in the database can be of some limited value. The number of wraps in an instance's rollback segments indicates that active transactions could not fit into the current extent, and the rollback data had to wrap across to a new extent. When a high WRAPS statistic appears in conjunction with a high value for the EXTENDS column on the V$ROLLSTAT dynamic performance view, then there is ample evidence to confirm that the rollback segments are extending often (and later shrinking) and that there could be a performance problem with excessive SHRINKS and EXTENDS occurring. However, a high number of wraps by itself indicates simply that transactions cannot fit entirely into one extent. A high number for WRAPS in conjunction with a low number of EXTENDS could indicate that the rollback segment is reusing currently allocated extents, which is a sign that the rollback segment is properly sized to handle the number of transactions assigned to it.

A problem can occur in the database rollback segments when long-running queries are attempting to access data that is volatile as a result of many smaller queries happening to the database, or if the long-running query is making many data changes to the database. If a query requires so many rollback entries to stay active in order to have a read-consistent view that the rollback segment allocates as many extents as it can, and the query still can't finish, then **ORA-01555—snapshot too old (rollback segment too small)** will appear. Although this error can be corrected by adding more space to a rollback segment, the more ideal solution is to schedule the long running job to run at off-peak times to lessen the burden on rollback segments. Alternately, this problem can be solved by assigning the transaction to a rollback segment specifically designed to accommodate larger transactions. This task is accomplished by using the **set transaction use rollback segment** statement.

Several points about tuning Oracle data blocks to perform well were also covered. The first part of this discussion focused on the size of database blocks, which is specified by the DB_BLOCK_SIZE initialization parameter at database creation time. Typically, database block size is a multiple of operating system block size to minimize the number of physical I/O reads it takes for Oracle to retrieve data. DB_BLOCK_SIZE is stated in bytes and determines the value for DB_BLOCK_BUFFERS, the size of block buffers in the database buffer cache of the SGA. Once the database is created, block size cannot be changed except by dropping and re-creating the database.

In this portion, the topic of **pctfree** and **pctused** was also discussed. These two storage options determine how Oracle inserts new rows into a database object. We learned that **pctfree** represents the portion of each data block that Oracle leaves free for growth to existing rows in the block as a result of updates to those rows. When the block is filled, Oracle takes that block off the freelist for that table. The **pctused** option is the percentage amount of the data block that must be free in order for Oracle to consider placing that block back on the freelist. The range for each value is 0 through 99, but the sum of **pctfree** and **pctused** cannot exceed 100. For performance reasons, **pctfree** and **pctused** should be set such that their total is close to, but less than, 100. The impact of setting **pctfree** is as follows:

- High **pctfree** leaves more space free in the data block for each row to expand during updates. However, it will take more blocks to store the same number of rows than it takes if **pctfree** is set low.

- Low **pctfree** maximizes block space usage by leaving less space free for existing rows to grow during updates. But, there is an increased chance of row migration and chaining if the block becomes overcrowded and the row needs to expand.

Setting **pctused** has many implications on the database. The implications of setting **pctused** are as follows:

- High **pctused** means that Oracle will try to keep the data block filled as high as **pctused** at all times. This means an additional processing overhead if the database experiences heavy data change activity.

■ Low **pctused** means that Oracle will not add rows to a data block until much of the block space is freed by data deletion. The data block will have unused room for a while before being placed onto a freelist, but once it is on the freelist, the block will be available for row inserts for a while as well.

Changing the settings for **pctused** and **pctfree** is executed by using the **alter table** statement.

Row migration and chaining were also discussed. When a row grows too large to fit into a data block, Oracle finds another data block to place it into. This process is called row migration. If there is no block available that can fit the entire row, then Oracle breaks the row into several pieces and stores the components in different blocks. This process is called chaining. These two processes are detrimental to the performance of the database. Table rows that have been chained or migrated can be identified using the **analyze** command with the **list chained rows** option. The output from this command will be placed in a special table called CHAINED_ROWS, that must be created by executing the UTLCHAIN utility script before executing the **analyze** command. The DBA can then copy the chained rows into a temporary table, **delete** the rows from the original table, change the value for **pctfree** on the table, and **insert** the rows from the temporary table. Alternately, the DBA can store the row data using EXPORT or a flat file, drop and re-create the table using a new **pctfree** setting, and repopulate the table using IMPORT or SQL*Loader.

The topic of freelist contention was also discussed. Freelists are lists that Oracle maintains of blocks with space for row insertion for a table. A freelist is experiencing contention if processes are contending for the free data blocks of that table in memory. To calculate the wait ratio for freelists, the V$WAITSTAT and V$SYSSTAT are used, **(WAITS / GETS) * 100**, where waits is V$WAITSTAT.COUNT for the associated **V$WAITSTAT.CLASS = 'free list'**, and gets is the sum of V$SYSSTAT.VALUE where V$SYSSTAT.NAME is either **'db block gets'** or **'consistent gets'**. Resolving contention for freelists is accomplished by dropping and re-creating the table with the **freelist** storage parameter set to the number of concurrent processes trying to **insert** new rows into the table. The table data can be stored and reloaded using IMPORT/EXPORT or SQL*Loader.

Two-Minute Drill

- Five types of tablespaces commonly found on the Oracle database: SYSTEM, DATA, INDEX, RBS, and TEMP.

- The SYSTEM tablespace should contain data dictionary tables and initial rollback segments only. It is inappropriate to place any other objects in them as they may fill the SYSTEM tablespace, causing maintenance problems.

- The DATA tablespaces should contain table data only. Other types of segments, such as rollback segments or temporary segments, could cause tablespace fragmentation, making it hard for the tables to acquire extents.

- The INDEX tablespaces should contain indexes to table data only.

- The RBS tablespaces should contain rollback segments only.

- The TEMP tablespaces should be available for creation of temporary segments for user queries. No other objects should be placed in this tablespace.

- Rollback segments acquire a number of public rollback segments in the Parallel Server Option according TRANSACTIONS / TRANSACTIONS_PER_ROLLBACK_SEGMENT a number of rollback segments at instance startup. The two components of this equation are initialization parameters.

- The DBA can specify the instance to acquire certain private rollback segments at startup by using the ROLLBACK_SEGMENTS initialization parameter.

- On databases that don't use the Parallel Server Option, public and private rollback segments are the same.

- Rollback segments should be sized according to the size and number of transactions occurring on the database.

- All extents of a rollback segment are the same size. This is enforced by Oracle with the removal of the **pctincrease** storage clause in the **create rollback segment** syntax.

- Rollback segments generally have an **optimal** size specified by the **optimal** storage clause.

- If a data transaction forces the rollback segment to grow more than one extent past its **optimal** setting, the rollback segment will shrink after the transaction commits.

- Shrinks and extends cause additional processing overhead on the Oracle instance.

- The DBA can query the V$ROLLSTAT dynamic performance view to determine if a high number of extends and shrinks are happening to the rollback segment.

- If a high number of shrinks are occurring as reflected by the SHRINKS column of V$ROLLSTAT, the DBA should increase the **optimal** storage clause for that rollback segment.

- If a transaction exhausts the space allowed for a rollback segment either through data change or through requiring a read-consistent data view in the case of a long-running query, **ORA-01555— snapshot too old (rollback segment too small)** error will occur.

- To fix **ORA-01555**, increase the number of extents allowed on the rollback segment the transaction uses, explicitly assign it to a larger rollback segment using **set transaction use rollback segment**, or schedule the transaction to occur during off-peak hours.

- Database resources should be distributed across multiple disks to avoid I/O contention.

- When considering which resources to place on the same disk, the DBA should evaluate what the utilization of each resource is and when it will be accessed.

- Striping is the placement of a table's extents across multiple disks to reduce I/O contention.

- Block size is determined by the DB_BLOCK_SIZE initialization parameter.

- Block size cannot be changed once the database is created.

- The size of block buffers in the SGA buffer cache, as expressed by the initialization parameter DB_BLOCK_BUFFERS, should be equal to DB_BLOCK_BUFFERS.

- Oracle block size should be a multiple of operating system block size.

- **pctfree** and **pctused** are the data block space usage options.

- **pctfree** is the amount of space Oracle leaves free in each block for row growth.

- **pctused** is the amount of space that must be freed after the block initially fills in order for Oracle to add that block to the freelist.

- A freelist is a list of blocks associated with a database object that currently have room available for rows to be added.

- A high **pctfree** means the block leaves a lot of room for rows to grow. This is good for high-volume transaction systems with row growth, but has the potential to waste disk space.

- A low **pctfree** maximizes disk space by leaving little room for rows to grow. Space is well utilized but potential is there for chaining and row migration.

- Row migration is where a row has grown too large for the block it is currently in, so Oracle moves it to another block.

- Chaining is where Oracle tries to migrate a row, but no block in the freelist can fit the entire row, so Oracle breaks it up and stores the pieces where it can.

- **pctfree + pctused** < = 100.

- Row migration and chaining can be detected by using the **analyze** command with **list chained rows** clause.

- The **analyze** command places ROWIDs for chained rows in the CHAINED_ROWS table created by **utlchain.sql**. *This table must be present for **analyze** to work.*

■ Freelist contention is when processes are contending with one another to get free data blocks when trying to **insert** new rows on the table.

■ Freelist contention is determined by selecting wait information from V$WAITSTAT, get information from V$SYSSTAT, dividing waits by total of **block gets** and **consistent gets**, and multiplying the quotient by 100. If the product is greater than 1, there is freelist contention.

■ Resolving freelist contention is done by increasing the **freelists** storage option in the table creation statement to the number of concurrent processes at any time that will **insert** rows to that table. This step usually requires dropping and re-creating the table.

Chapter Questions

1. **A high PCTFREE**

   A. Keeps the data blocks filled to capacity with table or index data

   B. Works well for both OLTP and decision support systems

   C. Maximizes performance on the database buffer cache

   D. Reduces the possibility of row chaining and data migration

2. **What is the maximum number of rollback segments recommended for an instance?**

   A. 200

   B. 100

   C. 75

   D. 50

3. **Freelist contention can be reduced by**

   A. Increasing the size of the buffer cache

   B. Increasing the size of the redo log

C. Increasing the value the FREELIST initialization parameter

D. Dropping and re-creating the table with more freelists

4. Which of the following methods can be used to detect row migration?

A. UTLBSTAT/UTLESTAT

B. analyze list chained rows

C. select count(ROWID) from V$CHAIN

D. show parameter block

5. Which of the following combinations is inappropriate for distributing disk I/O?

A. Redo logs and control files

B. DATA tablespaces and control files

C. INDEX tablespaces and DATA tablespaces

D. RBS tablespaces and the SYSTEM tablespace

6. What should not be done to resolve the error "snapshot too old (rollback segment too small)"?

A. Increase the size of the TEMP tablespace

B. Optimize the SQL statements in the transaction

C. Increase the rollback segment size

D. Run the transaction that caused the error during low database activity levels

E. Assign the transaction to a larger rollback segment

7. Which of the following lines in this SQL statement will produce an error?

A. create rollback segment RBS01

B. storage (initial 50M next 50M

C. minextents 5 maxextents 50

D. pctincrease 20

E. optimal 250M);

F. There are no errors in this statement

8. **Distributing extents of a table across multiple disk drives is called**

   A. Load optimization

   B. Striping

   C. Segmentation

   D. Condensation

9. **All rollback segments**

   A. Are placed in the RBS tablespace

   B. Are placed in the TEMP tablespace

   C. Are placed in the DATA tablespace, except those in the SYSTEM tablespace

   D. Are placed in the RBS tablespace, except those in the SYSTEM tablespace

10. **The value of DB_BLOCK_SIZE can be changed by**

    A. Resetting the DB_BLOCK_SIZE parameter

    B. Re-creating the database

    C. Resetting the value in the **next** storage option in the table

    D. Resizing the value in the **pctincrease** storage clause for the tablespace

11. **The number of times a rollback segment resizes itself according to the OPTIMAL clause is collected in which performance view?**

    A. V$ROLLSTAT

    B. V$WAITSTAT

C. V$SYSSTAT

D. V$SESSTAT

12. **The DBA creates a database and issues a CREATE TABLESPACE data_01 statement. The minimum number of rollback segments Oracle must allocate in order for the instance to start is**

   A. 2

   B. 3

   C. 4

   D. 5

Answers to Chapter Questions

I. D. Reduces the possibility of row chaining and data migration

Explanation High **pctfree** means that much space will be left empty in each data block. This doesn't keep the block filled to capacity, as choice A suggests, nor is it a good setting for decision support systems that attempt to maximize their storage capacity as choice B suggests. A high **pctfree** has little bearing on effective use of the database buffer cache; if anything, it reduces performance because fewer rows are stored per buffer in the buffer cache. Refer to the discussion of setting **pctfree** and **pctused**.

2. D. 50

Explanation This is a recommendation by Oracle. Maximum number of rollback segments should not exceed 50. Refer to the discussion of configuring rollback segments.

3. D. Dropping and re-creating the table with more freelists

Explanation Freelists are allocated per table in the Oracle instance. Increasing the size of the SGA as indicated by choices A and B will not improve freelist performance, nor will adjusting the FREELIST initialization parameter, because there is no FREELIST initialization parameter—**freelists** is a storage parameter. Refer to the discussion on detecting and resolving freelist contention.

4. B. analyze list chained rows

Explanation Choice B is the option used to discover if there is an issue with chaining and row migration. Choice A is incorrect because row chaining is not detected explicitly in UTLBSTAT/UTLESTAT. V$CHAIN is not a performance view in Oracle, thus eliminating choice C. **show parameter** will give the initialization parameters on the database, but this information is not relevant to elimination of chaining or row migration.

5. C.   INDEX tablespaces and DATA tablespaces

Explanation   Ideally, distributing INDEX and DATA tablespaces facilitates the searching of indexes and tables using two different disk controllers, reducing I/O contention and improving performance. RBS tablespaces and the SYSTEM tablespace both contain rollback segments, and in a pinch this combination can be used with acceptable results, eliminating choice D. Control files present little conflict with other database resources, eliminating choices A and B.

6. A.   Increase the size of the TEMP tablespace

Explanation   All other options will eliminate the error. See the discussion on monitoring rollback segment performance.

7. D.   **pctincrease** 20

Explanation   All extents of a rollback segment are the same size. See the discussion of configuring rollback segments.

8. B.   Striping

Explanation   The only other choice in this question that corresponds to a tuning option in Oracle is choice A, load optimization. This option corresponds to proper configuration of memory processes associated with SQL*Net and the multithreaded server configuration of Oracle.

9. D.   Are placed in the RBS tablespace, except those in the SYSTEM tablespace

Explanation   This option represents the ideal setup for rollback segments. Oracle requires at least one rollback segment to be in the SYSTEM tablespace, but the rest should be placed in specially designed RBS tablespaces. The configurations for A, B, and C involve putting rollback segments in tablespaces where their frequent allocation and deallocation of extents can disrupt other objects and cause fragmentation.

10. B. Re-creating the database

Explanation This option is the only way to change the DB_BLOCK_SIZE for the database. Any other option either doesn't relate to block size or will corrupt the database if enacted. Refer to the discussion of using Oracle blocks efficiently.

11. A. V$ROLLSTAT

Explanation This V$ performance table tracks statistics about rollback segment performance related to the rollback segment maintaining its **optimal** size. The other performance views offered track statistics for other areas of the database. Refer to the discussion of configuring rollback segments.

12. A. 2

Explanation The minimum number of rollback segments required by Oracle to start the instance is 2 when the database has more tablespaces than just SYSTEM. If the database has only a SYSTEM tablespace, the minimum number of rollback segments that must be acquired by Oracle is 1.

CHAPTER
20

Tuning Other Areas of
the Oracle Database

n this chapter, you will understand and demonstrate knowledge in the following areas:

- Monitoring and detecting lock contention
- Tuning sorts
- Optimizing load on the Oracle database

This chapter covers the final areas of tuning the Oracle database. Although each of these areas is important to understand from the perspective of day-to-day activities of the Oracle DBA, pay particular attention to tuning sorts, as the OCP Exam 4 will focus on their intricacies. All told, the materials in this chapter comprise about 20 percent of the material covered in OCP Exam 4 test questions.

Monitoring and Detecting Lock Contention

In this section, you will cover the following areas of monitoring and detecting lock contention:

- Levels of locking in Oracle
- Identifying possible causes for contention
- Using tools to detect lock contention
- Resolving contention in an emergency
- Preventing locking problems
- Identifying and preventing deadlocks

There are two objects in the Oracle architecture that manage control of access to the resources of an Oracle database. The first object is a latch, and its usage has already been discussed. Latches are used for control on Oracle internal resources, like redo logs, shared SQL buffers, the LRU list of buffers in the buffer cache, and other items that manage Oracle behind the scenes. The other devices used in an Oracle database to manage control of objects that users will encounter are called locks.

Levels of Locking in Oracle

Locks help to maintain transaction consistency on the Oracle database. A lock prevents one user from overwriting changes to the database that another user is making. Consider the necessity of transaction consistency. If two user processes are executing a series of procedures in order to make updates to the database system with no transaction consistency, there is no guarantee that data being updated by each user will remain the same for the life of that user's transaction. However, with the existence of lock mechanisms comes the ability to perform transaction processing. Locking allows users to manipulate data freely during the transaction without worry that the data will change before they are done changing it.

There are several different types of locks within the Oracle architecture. It is worth taking note of what the different types of locks are and how much scope each lock holds while it is enforced. Two different basic types of locks relate to Oracle data structures—they are the DDL locks and DML locks. DDL stands for data definition language—the statements used in the Oracle architecture for defining tables, indexes, sequences, and other devices used to define structures that are used by applications in data processing. These locks prevent the fundamental structure of a database object from changing as a user attempts to query or change data within it. For example, an **alter table** statement issued by the DBA will not complete until all user processes that are querying or changing that table have completed their query or change, and all other locks issued on that object before the DDL lock was requested have been resolved. Similarly, a DDL lock prevents a user process from querying or changing data while the object definition takes place.

The other type of locks in Oracle are the DML locks. These are the locks that user processes hold while they make changes to the database information. They allow the concept of transaction processing to exist within Oracle. Within the realm of DML locks are a few broad categories of scope that these locks will have when in action. The first scope category is the *table lock*. This lock, as one might guess, is over the entire contents of a table. During the period of time that a user process holds a table lock, no other process may make a change anywhere within that table. The next category of scope in the realm of DML locks is the *row lock*. This type of lock is more granular in that the table as a whole is left free for changes, except for certain records or rows within it. Figure 20-1 indicates the scope of table locks and row locks.

In addition to scope, there are some different access levels to which locks permit or deny access to the data being changed to other user processes. The first access level that will be covered here is *exclusive access*. Exclusive access means that for as long as the lock on a row or table is held, only the user process holding the lock can see or change the data in that row or table. The other access level is called *shared access*. This access level means that the user process holding the lock will be the only process allowed to make changes to that locked data, but other user processes will have the ability to access the data via query at all times. Exclusive access is much more controlled than shared access; however, in many situations, shared access is suitable for application needs and, as such, most Oracle default lock capability uses shared locks in some form.

Consider another subject of transaction processing—transaction-level read consistency. This term means that as a process executes a series of data change statements that constitute a transaction, the process should have a version of the data that is consistent throughout the entire transaction. With one exception, as noted below, all types of locks within the Oracle database provide transaction-level read consistency.

With those terms defined, turn attention now to the actual types of locks available in the Oracle architecture. There are five different types of locks in Oracle, and they are: *exclusive, shared, shared row exclusive, row shared,*

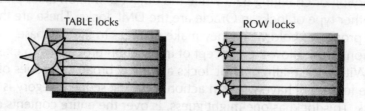

TABLE locks   ROW locks

FIGURE 20-1. *Scope of table and row locks on tables*

and *row exclusive.* The following is a more complete discussion of each type of lock in the context of the term definitions above.

exclusive **(X)**	A lock on the entire contents of the table, during which time no user other than the holder of the lock can **select** or **update** any row in the table.
shared **(S)**	A lock on the entire contents of the table that allows any user to **select** data in the table when another user holds this lock, but only the holder of the lock can actually **update** the table data.
shared row **exclusive** **(SRX)**	A lock on the entire contents of a table that allows users holding this lock to **update** data in the table. However, other processes are allowed to acquire row locks on the table, thereby *NOT* providing transaction-level read consistency.
row shared	A lock on a single row or group of rows that allows the user holding the lock access to **update** the locked row. Other users can query the row being held in a row shared lock, but only the holder of that lock can change the data.
row exclusive **(RX)**	A lock on a single row or group of rows that allows users holding this lock access to **update** the locked row. No user can query or change the row that is being held in row exclusive mode until the process holding the lock has relinquished it.

Within the Oracle database, there are two different types of methods used to acquire locks. They can be acquired by issuing a data change statement such as **update**, **insert**, or **delete**. Alternately, a process can manually acquire locks using a special package provided by Oracle called DBMS_LOCK. This package is the only method available for acquiring table locks. For row locks, locking is possible in the following statements. The first statement is **select for update**. This statement selects rows as specified by the **from** and the **where** clause and places those rows selected under a row shared lock. The other statement considered is the **update** statement. This statement places all rows affected by the **update** under a row exclusive lock. All other locks can be obtained by executing procedures in the DBMS_LOCK package.

Exercises

1. What is a lock? How do locks facilitate the use of transaction processing?

2. Describe the meaning of a shared lock and an exclusive lock. What are the two available scopes of locking within the Oracle architecture?

3. What is the name of the Oracle package that provides several different lock functions?

4. What are the five types of locks available in Oracle? How are these locks obtained?

Identifying Possible Causes for Contention

Users may sometimes have to wait to acquire locks on the database system, or wait to see data on the database that is held by a lock. This process of waiting for a lock itself is not contention, as many times a process will have to wait until another process completes its changes. However, when something happens to hold up data processing, then a lock contention issue may be the cause. One example of contention for resources as a result of locking may come from the unexpected placement of a database **update** statement in a stored procedure that is used by processes expecting to perform mainly queries against the database. In this example, the process is not expecting to perform an **update** to the database, so it does not contain any transaction completion statements like commits or rollbacks that would indicate to Oracle that the lock should be released. The effects can be particularly damaging—hundreds of locks may pile up on a table, causing performance on the table to reduce drastically, and the cleanup will require putting the database in **restricted session** mode to prevent additional locks accumulating while the DBA forces Oracle to relinquish the locks being held by user processes. Meanwhile, there is also the issue of correcting the stored procedure or embedded SQL that actually causes the problem.

Other causes of contention abound. If a process holds an exclusive lock on a database table and does not relinquish that lock, then other processes will contend with it for access to the rows of the table. The same effect will occur if the lock held is a row exclusive lock, albeit the effects are likely to be not as great, due to the limited scope of a row lock in general when compared to that of a table. As a general rule, it is ill-advised for DBAs and application administrators to start batch processes during times of heavy OLTP usage on the database because of the potential for lock contention. Figure 20-2 illustrates contention for tables that are held by table locks.

The final area to cover with respect to locking is the dangerous situation where one process holds a lock that a second process must have before the second process can give up the lock it has that the first process needs. This situation is known as a deadlock. Oracle has gone to great lengths to make sure that the database can detect situations in which deadlocking occurs. However, there are other situations where deadlocks occur and the DBA will have a great deal of difficulty detecting them.

Another possibility for contention exists within the usage of the shared row exclusive lock. Although this lock is a table lock, it allows access to the table by other processes that also have the ability to acquire row locks on the table and change data. This situation means that the holder of the original shared row exclusive lock may have to wait for other processes that acquire row exclusive locks on the table to complete their changes and relinquish the lock before the original process can proceed.

A final possibility for contention exists on client/server systems. In this environment, it is possible for network problems or process errors on the

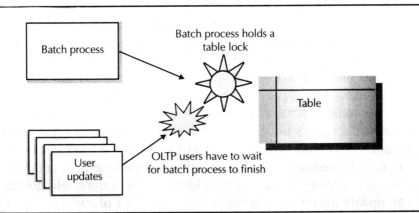

FIGURE 20-2.   *Contention for tables held by table locks*

client side to cause a process failure on the client. In some situations, there may occur a time when the user is in the process of updating a table via a row exclusive or shared lock, and the client process or SQL*Net network transportation layer fails. In this situation, although the process has terminated, the lock and the **update** have not. After a short period, Oracle will catch up to the *zombie* process and handle the cleanup and rollback portion of that process. But, in some cases there could be contention if the user does not understand that some time needs to pass before the lock they just let go actually relinquishes the resource on the table. In this situation, the user may simply restart their client process immediately after killing it and attempt to perform the same data change operation they just tried, placing a request for the same lock they still hold on another session, and *lock-wait* their own database activities.

Exercises

1. Identify a situation involving PL/SQL where lock contention might be produced. How can the contention issue be resolved?

2. Identify a situation involving SQL*Net where lock contention might be produced.

3. What is a deadlock?

Using Tools to Detect Lock Contention

Once contention starts occurring on the database, it can be hard to determine what the cause of the contention is and how to resolve it without having utilities and views at the DBA's disposal for those purposes. One tool that is commonly used by DBAs in the task of identifying contention is the UTLLOCKT utility that is provided as part of the Oracle distribution software. On most systems, this utility SQL script can be found in the **/rdbms/admin** directory under the Oracle software home directory, called **utllockt.sql**. UTLLOCKT queries the V$ACCESS and the V$SESSION_WAIT views to find the sessions and processes that are holding locks and the sessions and processes that are waiting for those locks to be relinquished so they can **update** the resource being held. UTLLOCKT places the output from that query in a readable tree graph form. This script should be run by the DBA while logged on as user SYS. Before using this script, the DBA will need to run **catblock.sql**. The output from running the **utllockt.sql** script looks something like the following code block:

```
WAITING_SESSION TYPE MODE REQUESTED MODE HELD     LOCK ID1 LOCK ID2
--------------- ---- -------------- ---------     -------- --------
8               NONE None           None                 0        0
9               TX   Share (S)      Exclusive (X)      604      302
7               RW   Exclusive (X)  S/Row-X(SSX) 50304040       19
10              RW   Exclusive (X)  S/Row-X(SSX) 50304040       19
```

One potential problem with this script is that in order to demonstrate the locks being held on the system, the script itself has to acquire some locks, thus potentially getting caught in the locking situation it is trying to help the DBA resolve. Another alternative that is available to the DBA for determining if there are contention issues, and that doesn't require logging into the database as user SYS, is a query on the DBA_WAITERS view. This view lists session information for all sessions holding locks on a table and the processes that are waiting for that table to be free. In addition, the lock mode held by the holding session and the lock mode requested by the waiter are also available from this view. To determine if there is a lock contention issue on a particular table, the DBA can execute a query against the DBA_WAITERS view.

```
SELECT holding_session, mode_held,
       waiting_session, mode_requested
FROM dba_waiters
ORDER BY holding_session;
```

Ordering the output of this query by holding session can help to identify if several processes are waiting for one session to relinquish a lock being held. The mode held will identify whether the lock holding the resource is a table or row lock, and whether the access level is exclusive or shared. This information will help the DBA resolve the contention issues in a hurry.

There is a method for determining if there are locking issues on the database. The method is to **select** information from V$SESSION where the value in the LOCKWAIT column is not NULL. Not only will this query obtain for the DBA which processes on the database are in contention, but the DBA can potentially identify what data manipulation operation is happening based on the value stored in the COMMAND column for sessions that are currently experiencing a lock wait.

Exercises

1. Identify the uses for the UTLLOCKT utility. What script must be written in order to use UTLLOCKT? What two views are used by this utility? What potential downfall does the UTLLOCKT utility have?

2. What other database view can provide information about lock contention on the database?

Resolving Contention in an Emergency

One of the only guarantees a DBA will have in the course of regular production support on the Oracle database is that emergencies will arise that require immediate resolution of locking and contention issues. There are several ways for the DBA to combat the problem of lock contention. This section will detail some of them.

One blanket solution to resolving contention is to determine what session is holding the locks that make the whole database wait, and to kill that session. The DBA can execute the query listed above on the DBA_WAITERS view to determine the session ID (SID) of the process holding the lock. The other component required for killing a session is the serial number for that session. This information can be obtained from the V$SESSION dynamic performance view with the following query. Once the SERIAL# and SID are obtained from V$SESSION, the DBA can then issue the **alter system kill session** statement. Please note, however, that this method is a blanket solution that, at the very least, does not address the underlying problem of the locking situation. However, it is important to know at least how the "solution of last resort" works.

```
SELECT sid, serial#
FROM v$session
WHERE sid in (SELECT holding_session FROM dba_waiters);

ALTER SYSTEM
KILL SESSION 'sid,serial#';
```

Exercises

1. What statement can be used to resolve lock contention in an emergency?

2. What two pieces of information does this statement require?

3. From which performance view can the DBA obtain this data?

Preventing Locking Problems

The better and more effective solution lies in the use of the DBMS_LOCK package, which was mentioned earlier in the chapter. This set of procedures allows the application to do many things. In addition to obtaining special table locks, this package has utilities that change the status of locks being held by user processes, and it also has a tool that allows the DBA to force a session to relinquish a lock. These procedures are used for resolving contention in emergency situations and should not be undertaken lightly. At the very least, the DBA should either try to contact users or management before pursuing the **alter system kill session** approach in production environments. The DBA should also ensure that the application developer follows up with a solution that ensures the locking issue will not arise in the future.

The two procedures that may be of greatest use in lock management are the **convert( )** and **release( )** procedures of the DBMS_LOCK package. The first procedure takes a lock of one type and converts it to another. For example, a process may be holding an exclusive lock on a table, in order to **update** several rows in a read-consistent manner. It may be possible to obtain the same data change information with a share lock, and by having the lock in that state, several SQL selects do not then have to wait for the process to relinquish its lock in order to simply select data. Or, if the application developer does not want other processes to see the changes it makes until the transaction completes, perhaps a reduction in lock scope from table to row is in order. By default, Oracle acquires the lowest level of locking for **select for update** and **update** statements—the shared row or exclusive row lock, respectively. For acquiring all other locks, the application developer must use the **allocate_unique( )** procedure, which identifies the lock given with a lock ID consisting of a numeric unique value. For use of the **convert( )** function, that lock ID must be passed to the procedure, as well as a numeric identifier for the lock mode requested and a time-out identifying the period of time after which the **convert( )** function will no longer attempt to change the lock mode. The **convert( )** function will return an integer value that details how the processing went for that execution. The **release( )** function simply takes the lock ID generated by

allocate_unique( ) and releases the lock. There is a return code for this function as well.

The above information about DBMS_LOCK is provided as an outline for the discussion between DBA and developer that must take place in order to prevent contention issues from occurring. Other functionality that DBMS_LOCK can provide is to ensure all processes on the system use the Oracle default locking mechanisms used in the **select for update** or **update** statement, rather than using higher levels of locking if those higher levels are not absolutely critical to the application.

Exercises

1. Identify the package that can be used to change lock status.

2. What is the lock acquired by an **update** statement? By a **select for update** statement?

Identifying and Preventing Deadlocks

Deadlocks are situations that cause painful performance problems on the Oracle database. Situations arise where sometimes one process holds a lock on a resource while trying to obtain a lock for a second resource. A second process holds the lock for that second resource, but needs to obtain the lock for the first resource in order to release the lock on the second. This catch-22 is known as a deadlock. This situation can involve more than two processes as well. Figure 20-3 illustrates a simple deadlocking situation for better understanding. Both processes in the diagram hold a lock, but they each need the other's lock to relinquish their own. Since neither process can proceed without the other giving up its lock, both processes are considered to be deadlocked. The figure is provided for information only, and does not illustrate a particular situation on the database that the DBA must watch out for. In fact, the Oracle database has several features built into it that prevent the occurrence of certain deadlocks, including the one illustrated in Figure 20-3. In reality, the DBA will have to identify and resolve far more challenging deadlock situations on the database.

There is only one solution for this situation, and that solution is the solution of last resort. The DBA must kill one or both processes in a deadlock. This solution has already been covered. When Oracle's deadlock

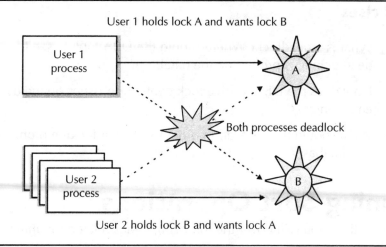

User 1 holds lock A and wants lock B

Both processes deadlock

User 2 holds lock B and wants lock A

FIGURE 20-3.   *Deadlocking in action*

detection mechanisms discover a deadlocking situation on the database, they write a message to the **alert** log for the Oracle instance. This special trace file, which is maintained by the database, contains all error messages, along with some other meaningful information about the instance. The DBA should take note of the **"deadlock detected while waiting for a resource"** error messages, and any included process information from the **alert** log sent in order to assist the DBA in determining the cause of the deadlock.

There are three final notes to make on preventing deadlocks. The DBA should recommend to developers that they should try to set their processes up such that all processes acquire locks in the same order. This will prevent the situation where processes acquire locks on resources that others need in reversed order, which has a high probability of creating deadlock situations. The second point is for applications to always specify the lowest level of locking provided by Oracle in **select for update** and **update** statements. The locking mechanisms provided by Oracle in those two data change statements should be sufficient for almost all application development needs. Finally, in the interest of preventing lock contention in OLTP systems, all long-running batch updates should be scheduled to happen outside of the normal business day's data processing.

Exercises

1. What is a deadlock? Where should the DBA look to see if deadlocking is present on the database?

2. How does the DBA resolve lock contention issues on the database in emergencies?

3. What should the DBA do in order to prevent locking problems on the database?

Tuning Sort Operations

In this section, you will cover the following topics related to tuning sort operations:

- Identify SQL operations that use sorts
- Ensuring sorts happen in memory
- Allocating temporary disk space for sorts
- Using direct writes for sorts

Relational database design traces its roots to an area of mathematics called *set theory*. E. F. Codd and C. J. Date applied the ideas behind set theory—namely, the creation of a mapping system of records to attributes—into a new relational design that acts as the cornerstone of relational databases. The names have changed, as records are now called rows and attributes are called columns, but the heart of the subject is still there in every relational database that applications may design. One other tenet in that early theory was that order does not matter in relational database design. Certainly that measure holds true within the records in any table on an Oracle database. The only time a certain order can be identified is perhaps in the situation where a table uses a sequence of numbers as the primary key. Even then, the database user may not care about the ordering of data in the database.

Identifying SQL Operations that Use Sorts

In the real world, though, order often *does* matter. Since the rows in the Oracle database usually aren't stored in any particular order, the user may want to force some order upon them. This type of operation may be used in reports or online, or within the B-tree index creation mechanism where the indexed column on the database is stored in a particular order with the intent of allowing fast access to the table on that sorted column. Hence, in the absence of storing Oracle data in a special order, often there is a need for sorting data on the database.

Several data manipulation activities will require sorts. One example is the **order by** operation. This option is commonly used in SQL selects in order to produce output from a query in an order on a certain column that is specified by the query. This option improves readability of data for the purposes of providing a more meaningful report. For example, a table dump for all employee data contains the information needed to produce a comparison report to find out who the 65 highest-paid employees are. However, since the data is provided in a haphazard format, through which the reader has to search intensively for several minutes or hours to find those 65 highly paid employees, the data really has no meaning. Instead, the report could be designed to list every employee and their salary in a department, in descending order on the SALARY column on the relevant table, using the **order by** clause of the **select** statement.

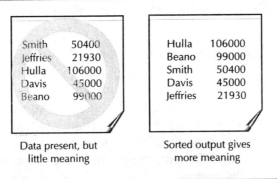

Smith	50400
Jeffries	21930
Hulla	106000
Davis	45000
Beano	99000

Data present, but
little meaning

Hulla	106000
Beano	99000
Smith	50400
Davis	45000
Jeffries	21930

Sorted output gives
more meaning

FIGURE 20-4.   *Using sorts to give data meaning*

Another SQL operation that utilizes sorts is the **group by** clause. This operation is used to collect data into groups based on a column or columns. This function can be useful in various reporting situations where a set of distinct column values may appear several times, mapped with unique values in other columns. For example, a table of states, their cities, and their cities' populations may appear in a table. To derive the population for each state, the following **group by** statement may be used:

```
SELECT DISTINCT state_name, sum(city_population)
FROM state
GROUP BY state_name;
```

Sorts are used in several different situations on the Oracle database. Both the **order by** and **group by** operations use sorts. Sorts are also conducted as part of **select**, **select distinct**, **minus**, **intersect**, and **union** statements, as well as in the **min( )**, **max( )**, and **count( )** operations. The *sort join* internal Oracle operation, run behind the scenes when a user executes a **select** statement to create a join, also uses sorts, as does the creation of indexes.

Exercises

1. What is a sort operation?

2. What SQL operations use sorts?

Ensuring Sorts Happen in Memory

There are performance considerations involved in executing sorts. Oracle requires some temporary space either in memory or on disk in order to perform a sort. If Oracle cannot get enough space in memory to perform the sort, then it must obtain space in the temporary tablespace on disk to use. In most cases, the default size for this area in memory used for sorting is enough to store the entire sort; however, there can be situations where a large sort will require space on disk. Since data in memory can be accessed faster than data on a disk, it benefits the performance on sorts to keep all aspects of the sort within memory.

The DBA should monitor sort activities. The dynamic performance view that stores information about how frequently Oracle needs to access disk space to perform a sort is called V$SYSSTAT. To find the number of sorts occurring in memory vs. the number of sorts occurring on disk, the DBA can select the NAME and VALUE from V$SYSSTAT where the name is either **'sorts(memory)'** or **'sorts(disk)'**. In the output from this query, a high value for memory sorts is desirable, while the desired value for disk sorts is as close to zero as possible.

If there is a consistently high number of disk sorts, or if number of disk sorts taking place on the database is increasing, then the DBA may want to consider increasing the space allocated for sorts in memory. This task is accomplished by increasing the value for the initialization parameter SORT_AREA_SIZE. This initialization parameter represents the greatest amount of memory a user process can obtain in order to perform a sort. Setting this value high allows the process to sort more data in fewer operations. However, as with increasing the size of any memory structure, the DBA will want to spend some time making sure that the additional size added to the sort area does not interfere with the amount of real memory available for the SGA. If the machine hosting Oracle starts paging the SGA into virtual memory on disk, there will be a bigger memory performance issue at hand associated with swapping information in real memory out to disk. One method the DBA can exercise in order to avoid problems with memory management as a result of increasing SORT_AREA_SIZE is to decrease another parameter associated with sorts, the SORT_AREA_RETAINED_SIZE. This initialization parameter represents the smallest amount of space Oracle will retain in a process's sort area when the process is through using the data that was sorted. This may help memory, but at the expense of creating some additional disk utilization to move data around in temporary segments on disk. The DBA and application administrators may also improve database performance by ensuring that batch processing does not interfere with OLTP data usage during the normal business day.

Another way to improve performance with respect to sorting is to avoid them entirely. This method is particularly useful in the creation of indexes. As stated earlier, indexes use sorts to create the binary search tree that can then be used to find a particular value in the indexed column and its corresponding ROWID quickly. Use of sorts for index creation can only be accomplished if the data in the table is already sorted in appropriate order on the column that needs to be indexed. This option is useful if the operating system on the machine hosting Oracle has a particularly efficient sorting algorithm, or if there is only a tight window available for the DBA to create the index. The **nosort** clause allows the DBA to create an index based on table data that is already sorted properly. Important to remember in this scenario is that the table data needs to be sorted on the column being indexed in order for **nosort** to work. If the data in the table whose column is being indexed is not sorted, then the index creation process will fail.

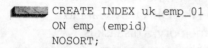

```
CREATE INDEX uk_emp_01
ON emp (empid)
NOSORT;
```

Exercises

1. For better performance, on which part of the system should sorts take place?

2. What dynamic performance view can be used to determine how frequently sorts are using the various resources of the machine hosting Oracle?

Allocating Temporary Disk Space for Sorts

When a sort operation takes place and requires disk space to complete successfully, the disk space it uses is temporary. The appropriate tablespace to allocate this space in is the TEMP tablespace. The TEMP tablespace is used for user processes that require allocating temporary segments in order to process certain SQL statements. Sorts are one type of operation that may require temporary disk storage. The **group by** and **order by** clauses are two types of SQL statements that require sorts, which then in turn may create segments in the user's temporary tablespace for the purpose of sorting. Care should be taken to ensure that the user's temporary tablespace is not set to default to the SYSTEM tablespace, as temporary allocation of segments for operations like sorts can contribute to fragmenting a tablespace. Both the default and temporary tablespaces for a user are set in the **create user** or **alter user** statement. If the tablespaces are not set in either of those statements, the user will place temporary segments used for sorts in the SYSTEM tablespace. Given the importance of SYSTEM to the integrity of the database, it is important for the DBA to minimize any problems that may occur with space management.

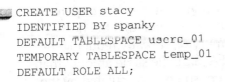

```
CREATE USER stacy
IDENTIFIED BY spanky
DEFAULT TABLESPACE users_01
TEMPORARY TABLESPACE temp_01
DEFAULT ROLE ALL;

ALTER USER DINAH
TEMPORARY TABLESPACE temp_02;
```

Exercises

1. How can the DBA ensure that users utilize the TEMP tablespace for sorts requiring temporary segments?

2. What tablespace should never be used to store temporary segments?

Using Direct Writes for Sorts

In some situations, the machine hosting the Oracle database may have extensive disk and memory resources available for effective performance on data sorts that the use of direct writes for sorting provides. This option is set up using three parameters from the Oracle initialization parameter file. Those parameters, along with an explanation of their usage, are as follows:

- SORT_DIRECT_WRITES—should be TRUE or AUTO. When TRUE, Oracle will obtain buffers in memory that are designed to handle disk writes as part of the sort.

- SORT_WRITE_BUFFERS—specified as an integer. When SORT_DIRECT_WRITES is TRUE, Oracle will obtain this number of buffers to handle disk I/O on sorts.

- SORT_WRITE_BUFFER_SIZE—value specified as an integer in bytes. When SORT_DIRECT_WRITES is TRUE, Oracle will size each buffer obtained for disk writes to be the value specified for this parameter.

It is important to remember that using SORT_DIRECT_WRITES represents a large memory and disk resource commitment for the purpose of sorting data. Specifically, this option will require memory additional to whatever sort area has been allocated as part of the SGA in the amount of SORT_WRITE_BUFFERS times SORT_WRITE_BUFFER_SIZE. The DBA should use extreme care in order to make sure that this additional memory requirement does not cause a shortage of available real memory such that the host machine pages the SGA out into virtual memory on disk. By reducing the amount of memory allocated for SORT_AREA_SIZE the same amount that the SORT_DIRECT_WRITES parameter will consume as calculated by the formula above, the DBA alleviates some of the burden on real memory that is produced by increasing SORT_DIRECT_WRITES. Oracle recommends that SORT_DIRECT_WRITES be used only in the event that the above formula is 1/10 the value specified for SORT_AREA_SIZE. If the space allocated for direct writes is any larger than 10 percent of the SORT_AREA_SIZE, then this option should not be used.

Exercises

1. Explain how direct writes boost performance on sorts.

2. What are the hardware considerations of using that option?

3. What three initialization parameters are used to configure that option?

Optimizing Load on the Oracle Database

In this section, you will cover the following topics related to optimizing load on the Oracle database:

■ Configuring the SQL*Net listener

■ Configuring and monitoring dispatchers

■ Configuring and monitoring shared servers

The basic elements of the client/server architecture have already been covered in Chapter 17. Oracle provides interprocess communication ability with a product called SQL*Net. This application is used by both clients and servers to communicate with one another. Without the SQL*Net layer acting as the interpreter, the client process and the server process are unable to interconnect. The cornerstone of SQL*Net is a process called a *listener*. This process does just that—it listens to the network connection for requests from the client to come in and request data. A listener can be thought of as similar in many ways to a radio. The listener tunes into a particular "frequency" to listen for connections on the type of network being used, and "hears" requests issuing from only that network. In heterogeneous networking environments, there may be several different listeners in place on the machine running Oracle server, each tuned to the different network protocols available. Once the listener "hears" a request for information, the listener moves the user process along in the database until it is eventually connected to a server process that will assist the user process with obtaining data from the Oracle database.

Configuring the SQL*Net Listener

The SQL*Net listener has several parameters that govern its use on the Oracle server. These parameters are set for the listeners on the database in the **listener.ora** parameter file. The first parameter is the STARTUP_WAIT_TIME parameter. This parameter identifies the maximum time period that the listener can wait before it must respond to a **status** command issued by LSNRCTL. The default value for this parameter is zero, and that value should work best on all but the slowest networks. The next parameter is CONNECT_TIMEOUT. This parameter sets the length of time that the listener will wait for the client to issue a connection request once connection is established. After the time period passes, the listener will drop the connection and continue listening for new connections to appear. SQL*Net's default value for this parameter is 10 seconds, which again should suffice for all but the slowest networks.

Another key parameter configured in the **listener.ora** file is the ADDRESS parameter. This parameter gives the SQL*Net connection description for the database connection information available for the specific database that the listener handles connections for. When using the LSNRCTL utility to manage the SQL*Net listener, the DBA must also specify the Oracle SID for the database the listener accepts connections for, the network "service" name that the host running Oracle is connected to (i.e., TCP, IPX, NETBeui, DecNet). The DBA must also specify some operating-system-specific information about the environment Oracle runs in, such as the location of the listener executable script, the Oracle software home directory, and other things.

Finally, there can be a PASSWORDS initialization parameter set into the **listener.ora** file that manages security by limiting who can administer SQL*Net on the host machine. It is recommended that this parameter be utilized in order to avoid security issues arising from the unauthorized administration of the SQL*Net listener.

The values for these parameters can be set in a few different ways. The first method that can be used to configure the SQL*Net listener is the LSNRCTL, or listener control, utility. This utility provides a graphical user interface for making changes to listener settings. The other method is to edit the listener parameter file, **listener.ora**. *Please note that the listener parameter file is NOT the same as the Oracle database instance parameter initialization file, generally known as* **init.ora**. Care should be taken to remember to differentiate between Oracle server configuration and SQL*Net configuration. In addition to the network name, node (host machine) name, and listener name (default is listener, must be unique if there are several listeners on the same machine hosting Oracle), there are several parameters that LSNRCTL must have in order to configure and run the listener.

Exercises

1. Name parameters that affect the listener process.

2. What is the tool that can be used to manage the SQL*Net listener?

3. What is the name of the initialization parameter file for the listener process?

Configuring Dispatchers

As discussed in Chapter 17, there are two ways that servers can be configured in Oracle to handle user processes. The first is the *dedicated server* configuration. In this setup, each user process that connects to the database via the SQL*Net listener has its own dedicated server process to read data into the buffer cache on behalf of the user process. The limitation pointed out for this setup was that allowing user processes to have a dedicated server process incurs a great deal of memory overhead on the Oracle database used to run a server process for every user process that connects.

Oracle's response to this situation is the multithreaded server (MTS) architecture, whereby multiple user processes can have their database reads handled by a limited number of *shared servers*. As mentioned in Chapter 17, access to the shared server processes is brokered by a *dispatcher*. Once a client process establishes connection with the SQL*Net listener, the listener passes the user process along to a dispatcher that brokers the client's access to the database. The dispatcher then connects user processes with shared server processes, which then perform operations on the Oracle database on the user processes' behalf.

Contention for dispatcher processes is an important area of tuning. Contention is indicated to the DBA either by increased wait times for dispatcher processes to respond to user processes or by a high frequency of user processes encountering dispatchers that are busy. The number of times a user process encounters a busy dispatcher is called a *busy rate*, while the number of times a user process has to wait to actually obtain a dispatcher is called a *wait time*. As with every other resource covered, there is a dynamic performance view that maintains statistics for the busy rate of the dispatchers working on each network protocol handled by a SQL*Net dispatcher. The name of that performance view is V$DISPATCHER. The formula for calculating the busy rate ratio for each network the database machine is connected to is reflected by the following formula: **(total busy time / (total busy time + total idle time)) * 100**. Total busy time is reflected by the sum of values in the BUSY column for each network, and total idle time is reflected by the sum of values in the IDLE column for each network. The method for distinguishing networks on V$DISPATCHER is represented by unique network names in the NETWORK column. Both busy and idle times are measured in 1/100 seconds. To obtain the data to place in this equation, the following query can be utilized:

```
SELECT network,
  SUM(busy) "total busy time",
  SUM(idle) "total idle time"
FROM v$dispatcher
GROUP BY network;
```

If the output of the equation used to calculate the busy rate ratio using the data provided by the V$DISPATCHER view exceeds 50 percent, there is a problem with busy rates for dispatchers on the Oracle database. This problem of busy rates for dispatchers on the Oracle database can be corrected with the addition of dispatchers to the database. This step is accomplished by increasing the number of MTS_DISPATCHERS using the **alter system set mts_dispatchers** statement.

```
ALTER SYSTEM
SET MTS_DISPATCHERS = 'protocol_name, number';
```

The value for the *protocol_name* variable corresponds to the network protocol from the query used above against the V$DISPATCHER process to obtain statistics to calculate the busy rate ratio. The value of the *number* variable for the **alter system set mts_dispatchers** statement above is the new number of dispatchers to be added. Care should be taken with adding dispatchers so as not to exceed the total number of dispatchers set for the entire database as specified in the MTS_MAX_DISPATCHERS initialization parameter. If increasing the number of dispatchers is required to improve dispatcher busy rates, then the initialization parameter MTS_MAX_DISPATCHERS should be increased as well. The highest value that can be specified for this initialization parameter is specific to the operating system hosting Oracle, but the default value for this parameter is five.

The other statistic relevant to monitoring dispatcher activity is the amount of time processes have to wait to get responses from the dispatcher while they sit in the dispatcher response queue. This ratio is calculated from statistics contained in the V$DISPATCHER performance view, as well as statistics for queue activity that are contained in the V$QUEUE performance view. The V$DISPATCHER view provides the name of the network protocol for which a wait ratio will be derived and the V$QUEUE view provides wait-time statistics and the total number of responses that have been queued for that instance. The common link between the two views is PADDR, the memory address of the dispatcher process. In order to prevent an error when Oracle divides by zero in the case of no processes having to enter the response queue, the following query also uses a **decode( )** operation. The query that can be used to derive the wait ratio for dispatcher processes is as follows:

```
SELECT d.network, DECODE(SUM(q.totalq),0,'NONE',
       SUM(q.wait)/SUM(q.totalq))
FROM v$queue q, v$dispatcher d
WHERE q.type = 'DISPATCHER' and p.paddr = d.paddr;
```

No particular value for the wait ratio is necessarily unacceptable, although the DBA should attempt to keep the value for this statistic as low as possible and also try to prevent consistent increases in this statistic. If increases in this wait-ratio statistic occur steadily on the system, the DBA should consider adding dispatchers to the database. This step is accomplished by increasing the number of dispatcher processes using the **alter system set mts_dispatchers** statement with the appropriate protocol name and number included as the value for the MTS_DISPATCHERS parameter.

```
ALTER SYSTEM
SET MTS_DISPATCHERS = 'protocol_name, number';
```

Exercises

1. What is Oracle's multithreaded server architecture? What is a dispatcher?

2. What performance views contain statistics for dispatcher performance?

3. What two aspects of dispatcher performance should the DBA monitor? What initialization parameters affect the number of dispatcher processes on the system?

Configuring Shared Servers

Shared servers handle data operations on behalf of many user processes at the same time. Their counterparts, dedicated servers, handle data operations for only one user process. The management of shared servers involves determining whether user processes are waiting excessively on the request queue for shared server processes. The statistics for this average wait-time calculation are derived from the V$QUEUE dynamic performance view, and the columns used are the same as the ones used for determining the average wait for dispatchers. The required statistics for the shared server processes are contained in the WAIT and the TOTALQ columns, and are associated with the type of queue in the TYPE column that is equal to **'COMMON'**. To calculate the average wait time from data in the V$QUEUE table, use the following formula: **total wait time / total requests enqueued**. Wait time is the statistic contained in the WAIT column associated with the row **where TYPE = 'COMMON'**. This is a total wait time for all requests. The **total requests enqueued** statistic is equivalent to the value contained in the TOTALQ column associated with the row **where TYPE = 'COMMON'**. This is the total number of requests that have been enqueued for the life of the instance. There is no particular "right" value for the quotient of this equation, but ideally, the time should be as low as possible. Also, the value for the average wait time should be tracked over time. If this average wait time increases consistently, there could be a problem with the number of shared servers on the database.

Alleviating contention for shared servers is tricky. Usually, there shouldn't be a problem with contention for shared servers because Oracle automatically increases the number of shared servers if the average wait time for the existing shared servers grows past a certain amount. However, if the maximum number of shared servers has been reached, as represented by the initialization parameter MTS_MAX_SERVERS (default 20), the DBA can increase the maximum number of shared servers by increasing this initialization parameter. After that, Oracle will automatically increase the number of shared servers. Of course, the DBA can increase the number of shared servers as well by increasing the value of another initialization parameter, MTS_SERVERS, with the **alter system set mts_servers** statement.

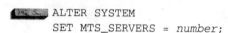

```
ALTER SYSTEM
SET MTS_SERVERS = number;
```

Exercises

1. What is the Oracle multithreaded server architecture?

2. What is a shared server process? What initialization parameters affect the number of shared server processes on the Oracle database?

3. How is shared server performance measured? What performance view contains statistics about shared server performance?

Chapter Summary

This chapter covered some miscellaneous aspects of tuning the Oracle instance. Those areas include tuning contention as demonstrated by locks, tuning sorts, and optimizing load on the Oracle database with the multithreaded server architecture. These topics cover materials that comprise 20 percent of the questions asked on OCP Exam 4.

The first area covered by this chapter was monitoring and detecting lock contention. There are five different types of locks on the Oracle database. Shared row locks entitle their holder to changing data in the locked row, but allow other users to access the locked data via query at any time. These locks are acquired automatically by **select for update** statements. Exclusive row locks entitle the holder to exclusive **select** and **update** access to the locked row. No other user can see or change data in the locked row. These locks are acquired automatically by the **update** statement. Shared locks are table locks that permit the holder of the lock the ability to change any row in the table, but any user on the database can view the data being changed at any time. Exclusive locks are table locks that permit the holder of the lock exclusive access to view or change data in a table. No other user can query or change data in that table for as long as the lock is held by that user. The final type of lock is the shared row exclusive lock. These locks are all acquired through calls to a special package that manages locks, called DBMS_LOCK.

Several possibilities for contention exist on the Oracle database. One area for contention arises from a process having a greater level lock than it needs to execute an **update**. Another example is when the application acquires a lock in an area that otherwise behaves in a "**select** only" manner, and as such never relinquishes the lock it is given. Another possibility for contention exists in the client/server architecture, when a user process drops off the database but still holds locks on the database. It takes some time before Oracle realizes the connection was lost and allows the transaction to roll back. During that time, there could be contention as the user process tries to connect again and execute the same process it was executing when connectivity was lost before.

There are utilities and views to discover what processes are experiencing and causing waits. The UTLLOCKT utility provides a tree diagram of all processes that are holding locks and all processes that are waiting for the lock to be released. Another method for updating data of this type is to query the DBA_WAITERS view of the Oracle data dictionary.

The method DBAs use to resolve contention issues in an emergency is to kill one or both of the processes in contention. For this to occur, the DBA needs the session identifier and the serial number (SID and SERIALI#

columns of V$SESSION, respectively) for the process(es) that will be killed. This information comes from the V$SESSION dynamic performance view, where the session ID equals the holding session from DBA_WAITERS. The syntax for killing a session is to issue the **alter system kill session** statement, passing the value for session ID and serial number.

The best method for preventing a locking problem is to identify and solve the problem at the application level. Typically, the problem is being caused by a process that is acquiring locks that it isn't giving up, or the process is acquiring locks that have more scope than the process really needs. The solution is to change the application to release the locks it acquires or to use locks with the least "locking power" necessary to accomplish what it is trying to accomplish.

Deadlocks are a particularly serious locking problem. Oracle is designed to resolve certain deadlocking situations automatically. The DBA can identify if these situations are occurring by checking the **alert** log for the Oracle instance for the **"deadlock detected while waiting for a resource"** error. Preventing deadlocks is accomplished by the DBA making the following two recommendations at the application level: ensure that all processes acquire locks in the same order, and always use the lock with the least amount of "locking power" required to carry out the transaction.

The next area covered in this chapter was tuning sorts. The processes that require sorts are **group by**, **order by**, **select distinct**, **minus**, **intersect**, **union**, **min( )**, **max( )**, **count( )**, and *sort join* internal Oracle operations and the creation of indexes. Sorting should be done in memory, where possible, to ensure maximum performance. The frequency of sorts occurring in memory can be assessed using the V$SYSSTAT performance view, where the value in the NAME column equals **'sort(memory)'** or **'sort(disk)'**. To increase the sorts performed in memory, the size of the sort area can be increased, although the DBA should be careful to ensure that once increased, the entire Oracle SGA still fits in real memory. See Chapter 17 for more details on what happens when the SGA is sized out of real memory. The size of the sort area is determined by the value, in bytes, of the SORT_AREA_SIZE initialization parameter.

When using sorts that require disk space, the user processes should always use the special TEMP tablespace to allocate their temporary segments for the use of sorting. The DBA can ensure this happens by configuring all users with a temporary tablespace at user creation. If the TEMP tablespace is not created or specified, the user processes will allocate temporary segments in the SYSTEM tablespace. Since temporary segments have a tendency to fragment tablespaces, and since the SYSTEM tablespace is critical to the functionality of the Oracle database, it is ill-advised to use the SYSTEM tablespace for anything other than storing data dictionary tables and the initial rollback segments of the database.

In the conclusion of tuning sorts, the topic of using direct writes for sorting was discussed. This option should only be used on systems that have extensive memory and disk resources available for improving performance on sorts. Direct writes provide the functionality of allowing Oracle to write temporary blocks for sorts directly to disk, bypassing the buffer cache of the SGA. To use this option, three initialization parameters must be used. Those parameters are SORT_DIRECT_WRITES (set to TRUE to enable), SORT_WRITE_BUFFERS (which represents the number of buffers used for sort direct writes), and SORT_WRITE_BUFFER_SIZE (which is the size of the buffers used). When using this setup for performance improvements on sorts, the DBA should ensure that there is additional memory available on the system to accommodate the SGA size plus the value of SORT_WRITE_BUFFERS * SORT_WRITE_BUFFER_SIZE. Additionally, the value of the above equation should be no more than 10 percent of the value originally specified for the SORT_AREA_SIZE or there may be little performance gain from using sort direct writes.

The last area covered in this chapter was the section on optimizing load. The first area covered in this section was the configuration of the SQL*Net listener process. Initialization parameters for this process are contained in the **listener.ora** file. The name of the SQL*Net listener is usually LISTENER, but on machines running multiple versions of listener corresponding to multiple networks connected to the Oracle database, the names of the listener must be unique. Listener has several parameters that must be configured, including PASSWORDS, SID_LIST, STARTUP_WAIT_TIME, CONNECT_TIMEOUT, TRACE_LEVEL, TRACE_DIRECTORY, TRACE_FILE, LOG_DIRECTORY, and LOG_FILE. Each parameter can be set using the LSNRCTL utility that handles listener configuration. Each parameter listed above should have the name of the listener appended to the end of it in the **listener.ora** file.

The next area to consider when optimizing load on the multithreaded server architecture is configuring the dispatchers on the Oracle server. The dispatchers act as go-betweens to map user processes coming into Oracle via the client/server architecture to shared servers that obtain data from the database on behalf of the user process. The number of dispatcher processes is determined by the MTS_DISPATCHERS initialization parameter, and its default value is five. Determining contention for dispatcher processes is based on two statistics: the busy ratio and the wait ratio. The busy ratio is calculated based on statistics from the V$DISPATCHERS dynamic performance view, while the wait ratio is calculated based on statistics from the V$QUEUE view. The busy ratio is based on the total busy time divided by (busy time plus idle time), times 100. Wait ratio is calculated from the sum of waits divided by the sum of values in the TOTALQ column from the V$QUEUE view, times 100. If the busy ratio is over 50, or if the wait ratio is increasing steadily, the DBA can increase the number of dispatchers by increasing the value set for MTS_DISPATCHERS—by executing an **alter system set mts_dispatchers** command and specifying the protocol to which to add dispatchers, and the number of dispatchers to add to that protocol. The number of dispatchers added for any protocol may not go over the total number of dispatchers allowed for all protocols, as represented by the MTS_MAX_DISPATCHERS initialization parameter. If the DBA wishes to increase the number of MTS_DISPATCHERS over the value of MTS_MAX_DISPATCHERS, then the DBA must increase the value set for MTS_MAX_DISPATCHERS as well.

The final aspect of optimizing load that was covered in this chapter was the configuration and monitoring of shared server processes. These are the processes that obtain data from the Oracle database on behalf of the user process. The number of shared servers on the database is determined by the MTS_SERVERS initialization parameter. The number of shared servers allowed on the system is determined by the MTS_MAX_SERVERS parameter, which defaults to 20. It is generally best to set MTS_SERVERS low, because Oracle will automatically add shared servers if the average wait time for a shared server by a user process goes up rapidly or consistently. The performance of shared servers is monitored by the DBA by viewing statistics collected by the V$QUEUE performance view. The average wait time is calculated by dividing the value in the WAIT column by the value in the TOTALQ column where the value in the TYPE column equals **'COMMON'**. If this statistic goes up consistently and the maximum number of shared servers has been reached, the DBA can increase the value for MTS_MAX_SERVERS in an attempt to alleviate high average wait times for shared servers.

Two-Minute Drill

- Levels of locking include row shared, row exclusive, shared, exclusive, shared row exclusive.

- Causes of lock contention are when a process doesn't relinquish a lock it holds, when a process holds a higher level of lock than it really needs, and when a user process drops while holding a lock in the client/server architecture.

- The UTLLOCKT procedure is used to detect lock contention. Additional information about lock contenders can be found in the DBA_WAITERS view.

- The method to eliminate contention is to kill sessions that are deadlocked. The Session ID and serial number from V$SESSION are required for this activity. To kill a session, execute **alter system kill session**.

- Preventing deadlocks is done at the application level by changing the application to relinquish locks it obtains or using locks with the least amount of scope required to complete the transaction.

- Oracle errors arising from deadlocks can be found in the **alert** log, a special file the Oracle database uses to track all errors on that instance. The error "**deadlock detected while waiting for a resource**" corresponds to a deadlock.

- Application developers can also prevent deadlocks by designing the application to acquire locks in the same order in all processes, and use the minimum locking capability required to complete the transaction.

- SQL operations that use sorts include **group by, order by, select distinct, minus, intersect, union, min( ), max( ), count( )**, and *sort join* internal Oracle operations and the creation of indexes.

- Sorting should be done in memory. The V$SYSSTAT view can be queried to find the number of sorts done in memory vs. the number of sorts done using disk space.

- To increase the number of sorts taking place in memory, increase the value set for the SORT_AREA_SIZE initialization parameter.

- If a disk sort is performed, the DBA should ensure that all temporary segments allocated for that sort are placed in a temporary tablespace called TEMP. This is ensured by creating users with a temporary tablespace named in **create user**. If none is named, the default tablespace used for storing temporary segments will be SYSTEM— this can lead to problems because temporary segments fragment tablespaces and SYSTEM is critical to the proper function of the database.

- If memory and disk resources permit, set the database to use SORT_DIRECT_WRITES. This parameter is set to TRUE if the database is to use direct writes to the database for sorting. The SORT_WRITE_BUFFERS parameter determines the number of buffers that will be used for direct writes and the SORT_WRITE_BUFFER_ SIZE parameter will be used to determine the size of the buffers.

- The SQL*Net listener process manages accepting connection requests from user processes. The listener is configured by the LSNRCTL utility, and its initialization parameters are stored in **listener.ora**.

- Dispatcher processes allocate user processes to shared servers. Their performance is monitored with the V$DISPATCHERS and the V$QUEUE views. Performance is measured by a busy ratio and a wait ratio. If there are contention issues with dispatchers, more can be added by increasing the MTS_DISPATCHERS setting with an **alter system** statement. In some cases, the number of the MTS_MAX_ DISPATCHERS parameter may also need to be increased if the DBA needs to add a dispatcher for a network protocol and doing so exceeds the total number of dispatchers allowed for all protocols.

- Shared server processes obtain data changes on behalf of user processes. Their performance is monitored by the DBA by calculating the average wait time for shared servers, based on statistics kept in the V$QUEUE performance view. Shared servers are added to the system automatically by Oracle. In some cases, the

DBA may have to increase the value set for the initialization parameter MTS_MAX_SERVERS in order to allow Oracle to allocate more shared servers to handle additional transaction processing burden. Or, the DBA can allocate additional shared servers by executing **alter system set mts_servers =** *num;*.

Chapter Questions

1. **The V$LATCH performance view is used for determining performance on**

   A. Latches

   B. Dispatchers

   C. Shared servers

   D. Online redo logs

2. **The name of the file containing parameters for the SQL*Net listener is**

   A. config.ora

   B. listener.ora

   C. init.ora

   D. sqlnet.ora

   E. tnsnames.ora

3. **Before using sort direct writes, the DBA should first ensure that**

   A. SORT_AREA_SIZE is larger than DB_BLOCK_BUFFERS

   B. SORT_DIRECT_WRITES is greater than 10

   C. SORT_TEMP_TABLESPACES contains the name of the tablespaces holding temporary segments

   D. All temporary segments are placed in the SYSTEM tablespace

   E. There is enough real memory to store a number of bytes equal to or greater than **SORT_WRITE_BUFFERS * SORT_WRITE_BUFFER_SIZE**

4. Increasing SORT_AREA_SIZE

   A. Has the potential to size the SGA beyond real memory capacity

   B. Improves the performance of sort direct writes

   C. Increases the size of redo log entries

   D. Alters the location of the **alert** log

5. To kill a user session requires which two pieces of information about the session?

   A. Username and session ID

   B. Username and SQL operation

   C. Session ID and SERIAL#

   D. SERIAL# and process address

   E. Username and process address

6. What is the name of the row in V$SYSSTAT that identifies the number of sorts occurring in memory?

   A. Memory(sorts)

   B. Memory, sorts

   C. Sorts(memory)

   D. Sorts, memory

7. The type of lock obtained by an UPDATE process is the

   A. Shared lock

   B. Exclusive lock

   C. Shared row exclusive lock

   D. Row shared lock

   E. Row exclusive lock

8. Which of the following SQL operations does not use sorts?

    A. group by

    B. select * from EMP;

    C. order by

    D. select count(*)

    E. create index

9. What two recommendations can DBAs make to application developers to avoid deadlocks?

    A. Use exclusive locks for all data change operations.

    B. Give different priorities to different background processes.

    C. Set all processes to acquire locks in the same order.

    D. Assign long-running transactions to large rollback segments.

    E. Set all processes to use the lowest level of locking necessary.

10. A listing of processes holding locks and processes waiting for those locks can be found in the output of which utility?

    A. UTLBSTAT/UTLESTAT

    B. EXPORT

    C. DBMS_APPLICATION_INFO

    D. UTLLOCKT

Answers to Chapter Questions

1. A. Latches

Explanation   V$LATCH tracks latch performance statistics. B is incorrect because dispatchers are monitored by V$DISPATCHERS and V$QUEUE. C is incorrect because shared servers are also tracked for performance by V$QUEUE. D is incorrect because redo log buffer performance is tracked by V$SYSSTAT.

2. B. **listener.ora**

Explanation   Choices A, D, and E correspond to other options of SQL*Net, while C is the initialization parameter for the Oracle database instance. Refer to the discussion of setting listener parameters appropriately in the section on optimizing load.

3. E. There is enough real memory to store a number of bytes equal to or greater than **SORT_WRITE_BUFFERS * SORT_WRITE_BUFFER_SIZE**.

Explanation   Choice A is incorrect because there really is no relationship between SORT_AREA_SIZE and DB_BLOCK_BUFFERS. SORT_DIRECT_ WRITES is a TRUE/FALSE variable, so choice B is also incorrect. User temporary tablespaces are set in the **create user** statement, not in an initialization parameter for the instance, so choice C is wrong. Due to the fragmentation that temporary segment allocation causes, it is not advisable to put temporary segments in the SYSTEM tablespace, so Choice D is also wrong. Refer to the discussion of sort direct writes in the tuning sorts section.

4. A. Has the potential to size the SGA beyond real memory capacity

Explanation   The SORT_AREA_SIZE parameter has little to do with redo log buffers or the location of the **alert** log, which eliminates choices C and D. The performance of direct writes depends first on setting SORT_DIRECT_WRITES to TRUE, and then properly setting values for SORT_WRITE_BUFFERS and SORT_WRITE_BUFFER_SIZE. In fact, direct write performance can be improved more by decreasing the SORT_AREA_ SIZE. Refer to the discussion of tuning sorts.

5. C.   Session ID and SERIAL#

Explanation   This question is a classic bit of Oracle trivia and is worth remembering. The username for the session to be killed is not needed, which eliminates choices A, B, and E. The process address in memory is also not required, thereby eliminating choice D. Refer to the discussion of resolving lock contention in an emergency.

6. C.   Sorts(memory)

Explanation   All row names corresponding to sorts in V$SYSSTAT are called sorts(something), and remember that sorts can be performed in two places: memory and disk. Therefore, choice C is the only one that can be correct. Refer to the discussion of keeping sorts in memory.

7. E.   Row exclusive lock

Explanation   There are two statements in the Oracle database the obtain locks automatically when they are executed. The **update** statement obtains a row exclusive lock while the **select for update** obtains a row shared lock. All other locks are obtained through executing a statement specifically for acquiring the lock, then processing the transaction.

8. B.   **select * from EMP;**

Explanation   Many statements use sorts, but statements that cause Oracle to execute *full table scans* and do not have **where** clauses or any other type of clause, such as the statement listed for choice B, usually do not perform sorts. All other options will cause a sort to occur.

9. C and E.

Explanation   Choice A is inappropriate because exclusive locks are the highest level of locking available on the instance and generally cause lock contention issues, not solve them. Choice B is entirely inappropriate because background processes are managed by DBAs (not developers) and assigning execution priorities that are not equal to background processes will cause performance problems in other areas. Choice D is a good idea as a way for developers to avoid the **"snapshot too old"** error, but will do little to prevent a deadlock. Choices C and E are the answers. Refer to the discussion of preventing deadlocks for more information.

10. D. UTLLOCKT

Explanation UTLBSTAT/UTLESTAT gives a great deal of performance information about the database, but locked processes is not an item it covers. DBMS_APPLICATION_INFO tracks module performance and may identify time periods where a process slowed down, but these options don't show exactly which process caused the poor performance for the process that performed poorly. EXPORT is a method for backing up the database structure and has no usage for lock detection. Refer to the discussion of detecting lock contention.

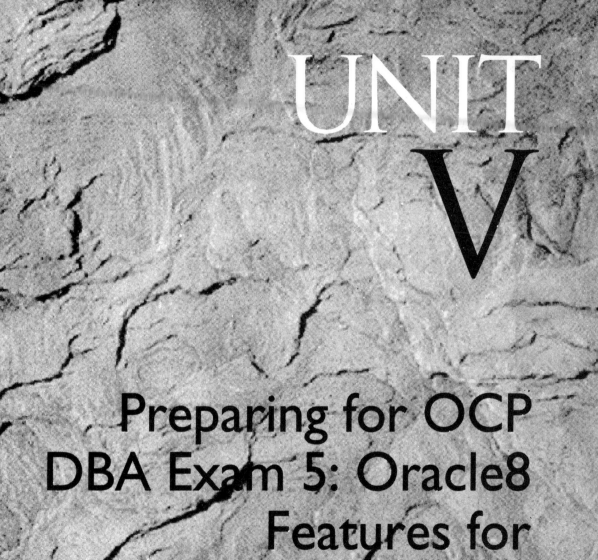

UNIT
V

Preparing for OCP
DBA Exam 5: Oracle8
Features for
Administrators

CHAPTER
21

Oracle8: Partitioning
Tables and Indexes

n this chapter, you will understand and demonstrate knowledge in the following areas:

- Overview of partitioning
- Implementing partitioned indexes
- Modifying partitioned tables and indexes
- Using Oracle utilities and partitioned objects

OCP Exam 5 is Oracle's newest addition to the OCP DBA Exam series. It is designed to test the DBA's knowledge of Oracle8's new features. Those DBAs who succeed in obtaining Oracle7 DBA certification in the OCP program can take the optional fifth exam to extend their certification into Oracle8. The next five chapters are designed to help DBAs take the OCP Exam 5 and obtain certification in Oracle8.

One of Oracle's new features for Oracle8 is the use of partitioned tables and indexes. Recall in Chapter 19 the discussion of table striping in Oracle7. This configuration allows the DBA to maximize parallelism in the database while also managing the data in a table more actively. However, the methods for table striping available in Oracle7 are only available on tables. In contrast, Oracle8 allows both tables and indexes to be partitioned. Furthermore, the mechanisms for table striping are crude in comparison to the approach Oracle8 offers with respect to partitioning. In this chapter, you will cover several areas related to partitioning database objects, including the basic facts a DBA should know about partitioning tables and indexes. The syntactic requirements for partitioning tables and indexes is also covered, as are the benefits and restrictions for partitioning tables and indexes. Finally, the impact of partitioning database objects on utilities such as SQL*Loader, IMPORT/EXPORT, **explain plan**, and **analyze** are also covered in this chapter.

Overview of Partitioning

In this section, you will cover the following topics related to overview of partitioning:

- Partitioning definition and rules
- Creating partitioned tables
- DDL and DML parallelism and partitioning
- Benefits of partitioning
- Restrictions on partitioning

This section introduces you to the methods and mechanisms of partitioning database objects. After introducing you to the basic reasons for using the feature, the section will cover the syntax and semantics of creating tables with partitions. Finally, the section will cover the benefits of partitioning database objects. This new feature of Oracle8 is relatively complex, yet the opportunities and potential for performance improvement certainly outweigh the complexity of the feature. In addition, partitioning tables promises to be a substantial portion of OCP Exam 5.

Partitioning Definition and Rules

What is a partitioned table or index? Quite simply, a partitioned table or index is similar to the table and index a DBA already understands, with one exception—the partitioned table or index is divided into several "sections," or partitions, according to some criteria. These partitions can then be managed by the DBA in many ways to improve performance on certain database operations. For example, in Chapter 19 the DBA was introduced to table striping as a way to place table data on separate disks. Partitioning a table allows the same possibility, but with a few key enhancements—one of which is that the data in each partition can correspond to a specific value in a column or columns, such as alphabetical order. A table containing employee addresses may be partitioned according to the state where the employee lives, or according to the alphabetical order of the person's last name. In contrast, table striping only allowed the DBA to divide the data in a table according to the size of the extent allocated for the table—a rather imprecise measurement.

Partitioning data in a table or index is based on a range of key values. From the addresses for employees of a company example, the key value may be the state of residence or the last name. Say, for the example, that table EMPLOYEE has three columns, EMPID, NAME, and STATE. The table can be partitioned five ways, based on the NAME column. Each partition can then be set to contain rows in several alphabetic ranges, such as A–G, H–N, O–R, S–T, and U–Z. Figure 21-1 gives a pictorial demonstration of this example for partitioning a table, though an index can be partitioned in the same way.

Partitioning represents one sign of Oracle8's commitment to support large relational databases, commonly referred to as VLDBs, or *very large databases*. VLDBs can be either online transaction processing or decision support systems, the characteristics of which were already discussed in Unit IV of this book. Although it may not benefit a database to partition a table with 50,000 rows of data, a table that has several million records storing gigabytes of data may well benefit from partitioning. Consider the following scenario: If a table with several million records is stored on one disk, the DBA may spend hours trying to recover it if that disk fails. In contrast, if

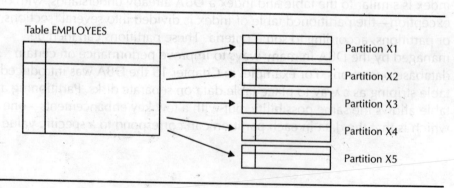

FIGURE 21-1. *Partitioned tables*

that same table was partitioned and spread over several disks, the impact of one of those disks failing is less severe, and more recoverable. Breaking the largest tables in VLDBs into manageable chunks allows for database object reorganization on part of the object as well, which can cut DBA maintenance time. Partitioning allows for extremely large growth in the Oracle database—it supports up to 64,000 partitions in a large table.

One final point about partitioned tables and indexes to be made in this discussion relates to the partitioning combinations available between tables and indexes. A nonpartitioned table can have indexes that are partitioned, and a nonpartitioned index can be created on a table with partitions. In addition, the DBA can create both indexes and tables with partitions. In short, any combination of partitioned and nonpartitioned tables and indexes is allowed. The decision to partition a table or index depends on performance and design considerations, however, which will be discussed in this section and the next.

Exercises

1. What is partitioning? How does it differ from table striping?

2. How many partitions are permitted in tables and indexes?

3. On what basis is data divided into partitions? What combinations of partitioned database objects are allowed in Oracle?

Creating Partitioned Tables

A partition of a table can be thought of as a miniature version of that table. Each partition is stored in different segments, thereby allowing the DBA to query the DBA_SEGMENTS view to find information about table partitions. Any single partition must be identical in column definition to any other partition in the table. For example, the EMPLOYEE table from before, with its EMPID, NAME, and STATE columns, cannot have a partition that has an extra column called SALARY. Additionally, no partition in the table may have a constraint that another partition does not have, so a column with a NOT NULL constraint in one partition cannot be nullable in another partition. Finally, the datatypes for all columns in the table must be the same for every attribute. The EMPID column for the table EMPLOYEES example cannot be declared as a VARCHAR2(10) column in one partition but a NUMBER(10) in another. All column definitions, constraints, and partition information (including the column or columns that can be used as the grounds for the partition) should be defined using the **create table** statement.

```
CREATE TABLE employees
(empid         NUMBER(10)        NOT NULL,
 name          VARCHAR2(30)      NOT NULL,
 state         VARCHAR2(3)       NOT NULL,
CONSTRAINT pk_employee_01
PRIMARY KEY (empid))
PARTITION BY RANGE (empid)
(PARTITION X1 VALUES LESS THAN (200000),
 PARTITION X2 VALUES LESS THAN (400000),
 PARTITION X3 VALUES LESS THAN (600000),
 PARTITION X4 VALUES LESS THAN (800000),
 PARTITION X5 VALUES LESS THAN (1000000));
```

Partitions need *not* have the same values for parameters set in the storage clause of each partition, however. Instead, the DBA can tailor the storage parameters of each partition in whatever way seems appropriate. These storage values include parameters discussed in earlier chapters like **initial**, **next**, and **pctfree**. In this way, the DBA can handle row storage on tables that allow records in static partitions to have a lower value set for **pctfree** in their partition while more dynamic partitions may have **pctfree** specified higher to prevent row migration due to **update** statements. Also, each partition can be placed in different tablespaces.

```
CREATE TABLE employees
(empid         VARCHAR2(6)       NOT NULL,
 name          VARCHAR2(30)      NOT NULL,
 state         VARCHAR2(3)       NOT NULL,
CONSTRAINT pk_employee_01
PRIMARY KEY (empid))
PARTITION BY RANGE (empid)
(PARTITION X1 VALUES LESS THAN (200000) tablespace data01
   STORAGE (10M NEXT 10M PCTFREE 10 PCTUSED 40),
 PARTITION X2 VALUES LESS THAN (400000) tablespace data02
   STORAGE (10M NEXT 10M PCTFREE 15 PCTUSED 40),
 PARTITION X3 VALUES LESS THAN (600000) tablespace data03
   STORAGE (10M NEXT 10M PCTFREE 15 PCTUSED 40),
 PARTITION X4 VALUES LESS THAN (800000) tablespace data04
```

```
STORAGE (10M NEXT 10M PCTFREE 20 PCTUSED 40),
PARTITION X5 VALUES LESS THAN (1000000) tablespace data05
STORAGE (10M NEXT 10M PCTFREE 5 PCTUSED 40)),
```

There are several components to the partition specification, including the *partition key*, the partition range specification, and the tablespace placement and storage parameters. The syntax for specifying the partition key is the **partition by range** clause of the **create table** statement. The partition key can contain more than one column. If the key contains more than one column, then the data placed in each partition will depend on values in all columns of the partition key. The ranges used for partitioning table data are defined for each partition using the **values less than** (*value*) clause, and the *value* specified in the cannot include a data operation, save for one—the **to_date( )** operation. For millennium compliance, it is best to use a four-character century indication in the character string that will be converted to a date. Thus, the **'24-SEP-02'** specification is not sufficient, but **'24-SEP-2002'** is. The value specified for the **values less than** clause is not included in the range of values allowed, and as such is referred to as the *noninclusive upper bound*. Observe that in some cases it may be difficult to define a noninclusive upper bound. For example, the **values less than ('Z')** clause will define a partition that does not accept the letter Z in the partition key. To avoid potential problems caused by this feature, the DBA can use the **maxvalue** keyword. Thus, the **values less than (maxvalue)** will encompass the letter Z in the partition. The lower bound for each partition range is either the lowest value permitted for the range or the *value* specified for the previous partition. If NULL is specified for a column in the partition key, the row data for that NULL column specified will be placed in the partition whose range includes **maxvalue**. If **maxvalue** is not specified for any partition range, then the NULL cannot be specified for the partition-key columns.

When creating multiple partitioned tables, or partitioned indexes that correspond to partitioned tables, the DBA may want to consider *equipartitioning*. Equipartitioning occurs when objects share the same partitioning definitions and column datatypes (including length, precision, and scale) for partition keys and ranges. These objects may have different storage parameters and their partitions may be stored in different tablespaces, however. Using equipartitioning helps to limit recovery and maintenance time for objects that are partitioned similarly, since other partitions can be accessed while recovery or maintenance takes place.

Each partition can be referenced according to its partition name as part of DML statements. The syntax for doing so involves the **partition** keyword along with the name of the partition. Thus, each partition in the EMPLOYEES table can be thought of as a miniature version of the table. The partition containing rows for employees whose EMPID is between 200,000 and 399,999 can be referenced as **partition** (*partition_name*). In addition, a view may be created to mask this syntax.

```
INSERT INTO employees PARTITION (X2)
VALUES (…);

CREATE VIEW empl
AS SELECT * FROM employees PARTITION X2;
```

Exercises

1. What are the components of a partition statement? Which components of a table must be the same in all partitions? Which partition components may be different in each partition?

2. What is equipartitioning?

3. How are individual partitions accessed?

DDL and DML Parallelism and Partitioning

One of the primary benefits of partitioning is its ability to take advantage of new features in the Oracle8 architecture for improved parallelism in data definition operations. Recall from previous discussion that data definition operations are specified by the data definition language, or DDL. Statements that create database objects are part of the data definition language. The DDL statements that use parallelism include **create table partition**, **create index partition**, **create table as select**, **alter table move partition**, **alter table split partition**, and **alter index rebuild partition**. The parallelism used in the object creation statements listed correlates directly to the number of partitions specified for creation in the DDL statement. However, for the object maintenance operations specified, Oracle accesses individual partitions in parallel.

Some new locks are also available in Oracle8, which are used to manage change access to partitions. These new partition locks allow the users to lock a table by partition, leaving other partitions available for change by other users. The partition locks are acquired when Oracle executes the cursor, as opposed to table locks, which are acquired at the time the cursor is parsed. For smaller transactions, however, this additional level of locking may hinder performance. To avoid that performance hit, the DBA can execute the **alter table** *name* **disable table lock** statement, which disables partition locks in addition to table locks, as implied by its syntax. However, while table locks are disabled, no **alter** statements are allowed when DML locks are disabled.

Performance has also been facilitated for statements designed to modify partitioned database objects with the use of a processing structure called the *one-step operation*. DDL statements that use this operation include **create table** statements, **alter table add partition**, the more general **alter table add** for column or constraint addition, and other operations. These operations execute quickly, but may not allow other operations in the database to run at the same time because of the higher level of locking required to complete the operation. DDL statements that use the one-step operation lock the table exclusively, thereby making other processes wait until the DDL statement is complete. Although **select** statements will continue to access the object, **update**, **insert**, and **delete** statements will have to wait until the one-step operation is complete.

The other processing structure is the three-step operation. This operation is used for many **alter table** operations like **alter table** *action* **partition**, where *action* may be any of the following actions for changing table partitions: **split**, **modify**, **exchange**, **drop**, or **move**. Other statements that use three-step operations are **create index** (global only), **alter index rebuild partition** (global only), and others. These operations take longer to execute than one-step operations such as DDL operations, but often allow other processes to operate on the object at the same time due to less restrictive share locking. The three steps in a three-step operation are as follows. First, Oracle will read the dictionary, then it will acquire the appropriate lock on a partition and make its change, and finally it will update the dictionary.

Exercises

I. What are the benefits of executing DDL and DML statements in parallel in Oracle8?

2. What new locks are available in Oracle8 to support partitions?

3. Define a one-step operation. What are some one-step operations?

4. Define a three-step operation. What are some three-step operations?

Benefits of Partitioning

There are several benefits for partitioning objects. For example, a partitioned table allows the DBA to manage each partition of the table independently of other partitions. Thus, the availability of data on a partitioned table is higher than its nonpartitioned counterpart. In addition, a situation where disk failure damages only one partition of an object will not damage the entire object, and the rest of the partitions can be available for use while the DBA recovers the damaged partition.

The DBA will also enjoy some improvements in the administration of a partitioned object. Recall that the storage parameters and tablespace location for a partitioned object can be different for each partition of that object. Partitions can also be moved from tablespace to tablespace as needed. In addition, the partition can have activities performed on it that previously were limited to objects as a whole. These activities include truncation of a partition, dropping a partition, or adding a partition. In addition, a partition can be further subdivided without disrupting other partitions in the table.

Finally, the partitioning of database objects improves performance of SQL statements against those objects. For example, if a user attempts to select data from a table that cannot be found in a particular partition according to the definition of that partition, the SQL statement processing mechanism in Oracle8 can eliminate that partition immediately. In addition, parallel processing of data in partitioned objects is improved, allowing Oracle to find requested data in partitioned objects faster than in nonpartitioned objects. This performance improvement is available in **select**, **update**, **insert**, and **delete** statements. Also, since partitions can be placed in different tablespaces, the DBA can eliminate I/O bottlenecks easily by placing partitions on different disks as well. And sort operations on queries on partitioned objects will require smaller temporary space allocation, due to the fact that the sort is applied to partitions rather than to the entire table.

Exercises

1. How does partitioning improve management and maintenance on a database object?

2. How does partitioning improve the availability of data on a database object?

3. How does partitioning improve performance in obtaining or changing data in an object?

Restrictions on Partitioning

There are several restrictions on partitioned tables. Every possible value for the column on which the partition key is defined must be accommodated by a partition. Thus, ranges of A–P, Q–Z are allowed, but ranges A–O, R–Z are not. In addition, NULL cannot be specified for a column in the partition key unless a partition is defined to accept values less than **maxvalue**. An **insert** on the table will fail if the value specified for the partition is outside any range specified for any partition on the table. The partitioned table may not contain a column declared with the LONG or LONG RAW datatypes, or any column declared with the large object (LOB) datatypes new to Oracle8. For more information on the new large object datatypes, refer to Chapter 23.

There is another restriction on partitioned tables related to changes in the partition-key values. Sometimes, it may be difficult to **update** the data in a partition key. The value in a partition-key column cannot be changed if the change will cause the row to move partitions. Thus, there is some data change allowed in partitioned tables, but the changes in partition-key values cannot be *too* drastic. If the DBA anticipates the data in a column will change, the DBA may not want to choose that column as the partition key.

There are some restrictions on referencing partitions individually in SQL and PL/SQL. First, the individual partitions of the table cannot be referenced through a database link or a synonym. However, table partitions can be referenced individually if a view has been created on the individual partition. Also, a PL/SQL block may not contain SQL that refers directly to a partition in a table. However, the user may create dynamic SQL using the DBMS_SQL package that references individual partitions in PL/SQL blocks, or may use views that reference the individual partition in the table. Finally, table partitions may only be directly referenced.

Exercises

1. What restrictions apply to specifying the partition key? Can gaps appear in partition definitions? Explain.

2. What datatype restrictions exist on partitioned tables?

3. What restrictions on partition references exist in SQL and PL/SQL? Can a partition be referenced via a database link? Explain.

Implementing Partitioned Indexes

In this section, you will cover the following topics related to implementing partitioned indexes:

- Creating partitioned indexes
- Equipartitioning and indexes
- Strategies for partitioning indexes
- Restrictions on partitioning indexes

In addition to tables, indexes on tables may be partitioned. This section will discuss the various topics of partitioning indexes in the Oracle8 database. The different types of partitioned indexes will be identified and explained, along with the syntax requirements for creating them. This section will also discuss strategies for using the various types of partitioned indexes available in Oracle8, along with the situations that justify the use of each. Finally, the restrictions on each of the partitioned indexes will be presented in this section. As with partitioning tables, understanding of index partitioning is an important new concept in Oracle database administration.

Creating Partitioned Indexes

As with tables, an index can be either partitioned or not partitioned. Since indexes on a table are never as large as the table itself, the motivation for partitioning an index for better storage management may not be as acute as it is with tables. However, there are still some compelling reasons to partition indexes, which will be covered.

In general, the DBA must answer several questions in order to determine if she should partition an index. One consideration in partitioning an index is the type of access to data required by applications and users. Partitioning indexes allows for more flexibility in terms of how users and applications can access the data. As with tables, partitioned indexes allow for a higher degree of data availability. The data in one index partition remains available in the event that another partition becomes unavailable. Management and maintenance on large indexes also run faster on partitions, leaving more data available during management or maintenance operations.

Partitioned indexes offer a higher degree of parallelism than their nonindexed counterparts as well. As with tables, the partitions of the index can be distributed over multiple tablespaces on different disks to eliminate I/O bottlenecks and improve data access. This distribution has the added benefit of reducing the dependency of a partitioned index on any one disk storing its partitions. If one disk fails, only the partition on that disk is lost, and only that data remains unavailable while the DBA recovers the partition. In general, partitioning indexes offers the same benefits for parallelism that partitioning tables offers.

There are four general categories of database indexes available in Oracle. They are *nonpartitioned indexes, global prefixed indexes, local prefixed indexes*, and *local nonprefixed indexes*. Each category has its own approach to improving overall performance, availability, and maintenance of the index. As with tables, each partition in a partitioned index can be thought of as a miniature version of the entire index, complete with its own definition, B-tree structure, and data, and stored in its own segment. A nonpartitioned index has already been covered. It is the most basic type of B-tree index that is available in Oracle7. The rest of the options available in Oracle8 covered in this discussion are partitioned indexes.

Partitions in indexes, like partitions in tables, must have a partition key, used to divide the contents of the index into ranges. The categorization of an index as prefixed or nonprefixed is related to the order of columns in the composite index and the columns used in the partition key. Recall that any index can have more than one column in it. In order for SQL **select** statements to use the index in the query, both the columns specified and the order specified in the **where** clause must correspond directly with the position of the column in the index. Special consideration must be given to determine if an index is *prefixed*. An index is prefixed if it is partitioned on a left prefix of the index columns. For example, if the EMPLOYEES table and its local index X_EMPLOYEES_01 are partitioned on the STATE column, then index X_EMPLOYEES_01 is local prefixed if it is defined on the columns (STATE, EMPID). On the other hand, if index X_EMPLOYEES_01 is defined on column NAME, then it is not prefixed. Partitioned indexes containing only one column are automatically considered prefixed. The performance advantage provided by prefixed unique indexes is that these indexes allow **select** statements against the index to access only one partition in order to find the data. If this prefixed index contains nonunique values, the index will still search only one partition for the requested data if the **where** clause specifies a value for all columns in the index. If not, then all partitions of the index must be scanned. The following block contains a definition of the table and its associated global partitioned index:

```
CREATE TABLE employees
(empid       VARCHAR2(6)      NOT NULL,
 name        VARCHAR2(30)     NOT NULL,
 state       VARCHAR2(3)      NOT NULL,
CONSTRAINT pk_employee_01
PRIMARY KEY (empid))
PARTITION BY RANGE (empid)
(PARTITION X1 VALUES LESS THAN (200000) tablespace data01
  STORAGE (10M NEXT 10M PCTFREE 10 PCTUSED 40),
 PARTITION X2 VALUES LESS THAN (400000) tablespace data02
  STORAGE (10M NEXT 10M PCTFREE 15 PCTUSED 40),
 PARTITION X3 VALUES LESS THAN (600000) tablespace data03
  STORAGE (10M NEXT 10M PCTFREE 15 PCTUSED 40),
 PARTITION X4 VALUES LESS THAN (800000) tablespace data04
  STORAGE (10M NEXT 10M PCTFREE 20 PCTUSED 40),
 PARTITION X5 VALUES LESS THAN (1000000) tablespace data05
  STORAGE (10M NEXT 10M PCTFREE 5 PCTUSED 40));

CREATE INDEX x_emp_01
ON employees (empid, name)
GLOBAL
PARTITION BY RANGE (empid)
(PARTITION ix1 VALUES LESS THAN (300000),
 PARTITION ix2 VALUES LESS THAN (700000),
 PARTITION ix3 VALUES LESS THAN (MAXVALUE))
```

Discussing prefixed indexes gives rise to a question—what about indexes where the partition key does not correspond to the columns indexed? This question is the definition of a nonprefixed index. The index may be partitioned based on range, but the partition is based on the partition key rather than on the left-most column on the index. The performance gains using this index are somewhat different. First, if **select** statements want to access data in the nonprefixed index, the index and the **where** clause must contain the partition key as part of the index key to guarantee uniqueness. If these conditions are met, then only the partition containing requested data will be searched. If the index is nonunique, then Oracle will need to search all partitions of the index in order to get the data requested. The following block contains the definition of the partitioned table and its local, nonprefixed, nonpartitioned index:

```
CREATE TABLE employees
(empid        VARCHAR2(6)      NOT NULL,
 name         VARCHAR2(30)     NOT NULL,
 state        VARCHAR2(3)      NOT NULL,
CONSTRAINT pk_employee_01
PRIMARY KEY (empid))
PARTITION BY RANGE (empid)
(PARTITION X1 VALUES LESS THAN (200000) tablespace data01
   STORAGE (10M NEXT 10M PCTFREE 10 PCTUSED 40),
 PARTITION X2 VALUES LESS THAN (400000) tablespace data02
   STORAGE (10M NEXT 10M PCTFREE 15 PCTUSED 40),
 PARTITION X3 VALUES LESS THAN (600000) tablespace data03
   STORAGE (10M NEXT 10M PCTFREE 15 PCTUSED 40),
 PARTITION X4 VALUES LESS THAN (800000) tablespace data04
   STORAGE (10M NEXT 10M PCTFREE 20 PCTUSED 40),
 PARTITION X5 VALUES LESS THAN (1000000) tablespace data05
   STORAGE (10M NEXT 10M PCTFREE 5 PCTUSED 40));

CREATE INDEX x_employees_01
ON employees (name)
LOCAL;
```

Exercises

1. What is the difference between a partitioned index and a nonpartitioned index?

2. What is the difference between a prefixed index and a nonprefixed index?

3. What are the four types of indexes?

Equipartitioning and Indexes

Notice that each of the previous code blocks used to create an index contains new keywords: **global** and **local**. Either of these keywords can be used in the **create index** statement to denote the *equipartitioning* status of the index and its underlying table. Recall that equipartitioning is when two or more objects specify identical partitioning information, including keys and ranges. When the DBA specifies the **global** keyword for the index, there is no relationship between the partitions of the index and the partitions of the table—even if those partition definitions are identical. Thus, there is no *equipartitioning* relationship between the global index and the table. When the DBA specifies the **local** keyword for the index, Oracle will maintain an equipartitioning relationship between the index and the table. All rows in a table partition will have an entry in the corresponding index partition. If there is a change in table data, or a maintenance operation on a table partition, the effect on the associated index will be limited to the corresponding partition(s). Thus, partition independence is as prevalent in the use of index partitions as it was in the discussion of table partitions. In addition, a DBA creating the equipartitioned index can leave out the name of the partition on the indexes, and Oracle will automatically name the index partitions the same thing as their table partition counterparts.

Prefixing the partition key to the index key on local indexes is often useful in searching for data on large systems in parallel based on the index key, while nonprefixed local indexes provide good search performance on columns in the partition key. The DBA should be aware of a few issues related to nonprefixed indexes and prefixed indexes. First, the nonprefixed index takes more resources to scan than a prefixed index. This is the case because Oracle can usually eliminate partitions from being scanned if the index is prefixed, but cannot if the index is nonprefixed. The following block contains the definition of the table with its local, equipartitioned index:

```
CREATE TABLE employees
(empid        VARCHAR2(6)      NOT NULL,
 name         VARCHAR2(30)     NOT NULL,
 state        VARCHAR2(3)      NOT NULL,
CONSTRAINT pk_employee_01
PRIMARY KEY (empid))
PARTITION BY RANGE (empid)
(PARTITION X1 VALUES LESS THAN (200000) tablespace data01
   STORAGE (10M NEXT 10M PCTFREE 10 PCTUSED 40),
 PARTITION X2 VALUES LESS THAN (400000) tablespace data02
   STORAGE (10M NEXT 10M PCTFREE 15 PCTUSED 40),
 PARTITION X3 VALUES LESS THAN (600000) tablespace data03
   STORAGE (10M NEXT 10M PCTFREE 15 PCTUSED 40),
 PARTITION X4 VALUES LESS THAN (800000) tablespace data04
   STORAGE (10M NEXT 10M PCTFREE 20 PCTUSED 40),
 PARTITION X5 VALUES LESS THAN (1000000) tablespace data05
   STORAGE (10M NEXT 10M PCTFREE 5 PCTUSED 40));

CREATE INDEX x_employees_01
ON employees (empid)
LOCAL
(PARTITION xe1 TABLESPACE index_01,
 PARTITION xe2 TABLESPACE index_02,
 PARTITION xe3 TABLESPACE index_03,
 PARTITION xe4 TABLESPACE index_04,
 PARTITION xe5 TABLESPACE index_05);
```

The alternative for DBAs is to create a global index—that is, an index that is not equipartitioned with its underlying table. The global index is created with the **global** keyword. When the DBA creates a global index, she forgoes the advantages of Oracle's automatic maintenance of the equipartitioning relationship between the table and index—even if the partition definitions for both objects are the same. It must also be remembered that the highest partition in the global index needs to be specified with the **maxvalue** keyword in order to allow the highest partition to catch all errant values specified for the partition key column. Usually, the SQL execution mechanism is not able to eliminate partitions from being scanned unless all columns in the partition key are specified in the **where** clause of the **select** statement. In general, global indexes are less effective than local indexes because when the associated table is modified, all partitions of a global index are affected. Finally, all global indexes are prefixed. Creating a global partitioned index on the EMPLOYEES table can be accomplished with the second statement in the following code block:

```
CREATE TABLE employees
 (empid       VARCHAR2(6)       NOT NULL,
  name        VARCHAR2(30)      NOT NULL,
  state       VARCHAR2(3)       NOT NULL,
 CONSTRAINT pk_employee_01
 PRIMARY KEY (empid))
 PARTITION BY RANGE (empid)
 (PARTITION X1 VALUES LESS THAN (200000) tablespace data01
   STORAGE (10M NEXT 10M PCTFREE 10 PCTUSED 40),
  PARTITION X2 VALUES LESS THAN (400000) tablespace data02
   STORAGE (10M NEXT 10M PCTFREE 15 PCTUSED 40),
  PARTITION X3 VALUES LESS THAN (600000) tablespace data03
   STORAGE (10M NEXT 10M PCTFREE 15 PCTUSED 40),
  PARTITION X4 VALUES LESS THAN (800000) tablespace data04
   STORAGE (10M NEXT 10M PCTFREE 20 PCTUSED 40),
  PARTITION X5 VALUES LESS THAN (1000000) tablespace data05
   STORAGE (10M NEXT 10M PCTFREE 5 PCTUSED 40));

CREATE INDEX x_employees_01
ON employees (empid, name)
GLOBAL
PARTITION BY RANGE (empid)
(PARTITION ex1 VALUES LESS THAN (500000),
 PARTITION ex2 VALUES LESS THAN (MAXVALUE));
```

Exercises

1. How does a local index take advantage of equipartitioning? What are some of the advantages local indexes offer?

2. What is a global index? What are the equipartitioning issues related to global indexes? What value must be specified in the highest partition to define the range of values stored in that partition?

Strategies for Partitioning Indexes

With so many options for defining partition keys and index keys with respect to one another, and whether to use equipartitioning on the index and corresponding table, the DBA may wonder—what strategies are available for partitioning indexes? The answer is that there are several issues that must be answered in order to determine what indexes to use on the database. The questions a DBA must answer are as follows:

- Is (are) the table's partition-key column(s) in the same order as the index columns?

- Will the index be used to search for data on a column not in the partition key?

- Can the DBA accept additional performance work by the index in order to allow for the high availability inherent in partitioning?

- Is the index to be used on decision support or OLTP systems?

If the answer to the question of whether a table's partition-key columns are in the same order as the indexed-key columns is yes, then the DBA can consider using local prefixed indexes. These indexes offer high performance, high availability, and ease of use for the DBA—in short, the local prefixed index allows the DBA to use all the advantages partitioning has to offer. Alternately, if the index will be used to search for data on a column not in the partition key, the DBA can create a global prefixed index. When doing so, the DBA sacrifices some of the ease in management inherent with partition independence, but user query performance will still be high.

If the DBA wants to index columns that are not in the partition key, but still wants to maintain the ease of use and high data availability that partition independence offers, the DBA can create a nonprefixed local index. Often, this option can be used in decision support systems such as data warehouses, where users frequently want to execute **select** statements on arbitrary search conditions that don't follow lines of partitioning. The nonprefixed local index works well when the application needs a nonunique index that conforms to lines of partitioning also. If, however, the DBA is supporting an OLTP system, a global prefixed index may be the answer. While the local nonprefixed index gives higher data availability and partition independence, the global prefixed index maximizes search performance for the **select** statement.

Exercises

1. What index can be used to support tables when the partition key is the same as the index key?

2. What index can be used to support tables where indexes are required on a column not part of the partition key?

3. What index can be used to support nonunique columns when the DBA still wants to have partition independence? What is partition independence?

Restrictions on Partitioned Indexes

With respect to creating partitioned indexes, there are certain types of indexes that may not be partitioned. One of those indexes is the index that is used in an index cluster. Another is a bitmap index. Other than that, all B-tree indexes in Oracle7 can be partitioned. Beware of partitioning incorrectly, however. A well-meaning DBA can create performance issues on the database by using the wrong type of partition. In general, if the DBA can partition the table safely, the DBA may first want to consider if it is possible to create a local prefixed index to use equipartitioning. If not, the DBA should carefully consider the other partitioned index options available.

Several situations may arise on the database that put partitions of an index in a damaged state called *INDEX UNUSABLE*. When an index partition goes into this state, the DBA must rebuild the partition. Tools like IMPORT and SQL*Loader may leave an index partition in this state if either the direct path load fails in SQL*Loader or if the conventional path load or IMPORT is manually set to bypass updates on the partitioned index. In addition, when the DBA moves a table partition such that ROWIDs for data in the partition must change with the **alter table move partition** statement, the associated index partition will be left in the *INDEX UNUSABLE* state. The same thing will happen if the DBA truncates a table partition with the **alter table truncate partition** statement, as long as the underlying table had data in it. If the DBA splits a table partition with the **alter table split partition** statement, the associated index partition will be redefined but not rebuilt, thus leaving the partition in the *INDEX UNUSABLE* state. The same situation occurs when the **alter index split partition** statement is executed. These six situations require the DBA to execute an index partition maintenance operation on local equipartitioned indexes with **alter table modify partition rebuild unusable local indexes**. For global indexes or local nonprefixed indexes in the *INDEX UNUSABLE* state, the DBA must use the **alter index rebuild partition** statement. More information about the maintenance and modification of partitioned tables and indexes will be covered in the next section.

Exercises

1. What is the *INDEX UNUSABLE* state?

2. What situations involving SQL*Loader and IMPORT will put an index partition into the *INDEX UNUSABLE* state? What situations involving table operations will put an index partition into the *INDEX UNUSABLE* state?

3. What statement will the DBA use to repair the partitions in the *INDEX UNUSABLE* state?

Modifying Partitioned Database Objects

In this section, you will cover the following topics related to modifying partitioned database objects:

■ Altering partitioned tables

■ Altering partitioned indexes

■ Privileges and restrictions for altering partitioned objects

■ Using dictionary views for partition reference

Once created, the DBA will be required to maintain the partitioned database objects available in Oracle8. Data may be added more quickly to one partition than to another, requiring the DBA to split that partition into two or more components. Data may be removed systematically from partitions on tables whose partition key is based on date of **insert**. The DBA may simply need information about the partitions on a table or index, requiring knowledge of the new dictionary views used to identify partition information for the database. This section covers these areas of Oracle8 administration of partitioned tables. The discussions in this section include altering partitions on tables and indexes, rebuilding partitioned indexes, rebuilding index partitions, and the privileges required to execute partition modification.

Altering Partitioned Tables

Partitions can be added to a table in the following way. First, the DBA must remember that partitions cannot be added to the table in the middle of the range—they can only be added onto the high end of the table. It usually works best when the DBA can add partitions based on a partition key that can increase over time, like a sequential number or a date. The following **alter table add partition** statement demonstrates adding partitions to the EMPLOYEES table where EMPID is 1,000,000 to 1,200,000:

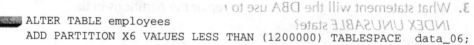

```
ALTER TABLE employees
ADD PARTITION X6 VALUES LESS THAN (1200000) TABLESPACE  data_06;
```

In addition, the DBA can rename a partition, from something obscure to something meaningful. Consider the **create table** statement presented in the first section used to create the EMPLOYEES table. The partitions on that table were named X1 through X5, which have little intrinsic meaning. The DBA may want to rename those partitions with more meaningful identifiers. The statement used to rename a table partition is **alter table rename partition**, and it is used as follows:

```
ALTER TABLE employees
RENAME PARTITION X1 TO emps_lt200000;
```

The DBA may also want to drop a partition on the database. Dropping a partition eliminates the partition definition and the data, and all data added to the table that would have been stored in the dropped partition will then be stored in the next highest partition. However, when the highest partition is dropped, information that would have been placed in that partition may no longer be added to the table. Dropping a table partition renders associated entire global indexes unusable. The syntax for dropping a partition is **alter table drop partition**, listed here:

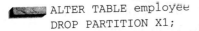
```
ALTER TABLE employee
DROP PARTITION X1;
```

Sometimes a DBA may wonder if it is better to **delete** all data from a partition before dropping the partition. When a global index is defined against the table, dropping a partition in the table will render the *entire* index unusable. If these indexes must remain available, the DBA must determine how many rows will be removed from the table (and thus the index) as a result of dropping the partition. If the number of rows removed from the table as a result of deleting the partition is high in proportion to the overall number of rows in the table, the DBA should probably drop the partition without deleting the data from it (and thus from the index). This is because the resource cost and time required to **delete** the data, plus the cost of rebuilding the index, will likely be higher than would be required simply to drop the partition and rebuild the global index. But, if the partition contains only a small number of rows in proportion to the overall table, it may be worth the while of the DBA to **delete** the rows from the partition before dropping it to save time later when rebuilding the index. Finally, the DBA may be unable to drop a partition if it is part of a parent table on which referential integrity constraints exist without first disabling the constraints or cascading the data removal into the child table.

If the DBA finds that one partition is growing at a rate much faster than others, she can split the partition into smaller partitions to balance the load of that table on any one disk. To do this, the DBA must use the **alter table split partition** statement. Splitting the partition creates a new partition named according to a value set in the statement. If the original partition contains data that will be moved into the new partition, then the corresponding local index partition will be unusable. However, if no data is present in the partition, then the resultant partitions in the index will both be valid. The index partition can be rebuilt with the **alter index rebuild partition**. A statement splitting partitions on the EMPLOYEES table appears in the following code block:

```
ALTER TABLE employees SPLIT PARTITION X5
AT (900000)
INTO (PARTITION X5A TABLESPACE data_05,
      PARTITION X5B TABLESPACE data_07);
```

The DBA can move a partition from one data segment to another, either in the current tablespace to reduce fragmentation or to a new tablespace to balance I/O load, using the **alter table move partition** statement. As discussed, moving a partition will render associated local index partitions and entire global indexes unusable. The usage of the **alter table move partition** statement is demonstrated in the following code block:

```
ALTER TABLE employees MOVE PARTITION X2
TABLESPACE data_08;
```

At some point in the existence of a partitioned table, the DBA may want to spin off a partition to its own table. Alternately, the DBA may want to convert a nonpartitioned table into the partition of another table. This type of partition exchange is accomplished with the use of **alter table exchange partition**. The exchange can be done in either direction, so long as the nonpartitioned table becoming a partition in a larger table is not clustered—and their logical definitions, including columns and constraints, must be identical. No data is moved, but the data dictionary information on both tables is modified, and all the global indexes associated with the partitioned table and any partitioned indexes on the nonpartitioned table will be rendered unusable. Corresponding local index partitions can be exchanged at the DBA's discretion with the use of the **including indexes** clause, or left unusable with the **excluding indexes** clause. The **alter table exchange partition** statement can be used to create tables out of partitions as follows:

```
ALTER TABLE employees
EXCHANGE PARTITION X1
WITH TABLE emps_lt200000
EXCLUDING INDEXES;

ALTER TABLE employees
EXCHANGE PARTITION X2
WITH TABLE emps_lt400000
INCLUDING INDEXES;
```

Recall from earlier discussion that the DBA can eliminate all data from a table quickly using the **alter table truncate** statement. This same option is available for partitions in Oracle8. Truncating a partition will render all global indexes on that table unusable if the table contained data. If not, then the index remains in VALID state. Local indexes will have the corresponding partition truncated as well, which has an added bonus of resetting the status of the index partition to VALID if it had previously been unusable. The storage for the partition can either be reused by the partition or returned to the tablespace as free, using the **reuse storage** or **drop storage** clause, respectively. An example for truncating a table partition with the **alter table truncate** statement appears in the following code block:

```
ALTER TABLE employees
TRUNCATE PARTITION X4
DROP STORAGE;

ALTER TABLE employees
TRUNCATE PARTITION X4
REUSE STORAGE;
```

The final statement available for modifying a table allows the DBA to modify many aspects of specified partitions on the table, such as physical storage parameters. The general statement that does all these things is the **alter table modify partition**. In addition, the DBA can modify the storage parameters for the entire table with the **alter table** statement. However, these physical storage parameters will not be incorporated into an existing partition; only partitions added will be impacted. The usage of the **alter table modify partition** statement to change physical storage parameters is as follows:

```
ALTER TABLE employees
MODIFY PARTITION X4
STORAGE (NEXT 10M MAXEXTENTS 20);
```

There are some other features about **alter table modify partition** that allow the DBA to perform activities related to the local partitioned indexes. It was mentioned earlier that the DBA can rebuild an index partition associated with a table partition when the index partition is in *INDEX UNUSABLE* state with the **alter table modify partition rebuild unusable local indexes** statement. In addition, the DBA can invalidate an index partition to defer maintenance on the index during data operations such as large table loads with the **alter table modify partition unusable local**

indexes. Examples for using both these statements appear in the following code block:

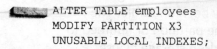

```
ALTER TABLE employees
MODIFY PARTITION X3
UNUSABLE LOCAL INDEXES;

ALTER TABLE employees
MODIFY PARTITION X3
REBUILD UNUSABLE LOCAL INDEXES;
```

The last area of this discussion concerns changing column or constraint definition on the entire table. There are several restrictions on this activity, many of which center around modification of the column(s) in the partition key. The datatype and the length of the partition-key column on the table cannot be changed, nor can this information be changed on columns used to partition indexes on the table. The partitioned table may not contain any columns defined with LONG, LONG RAW, or LOB datatypes. Finally, if any partition in the table is in a **read only** tablespace, a new column with a **default** value specified may not be added, nor can a column declared to be type VARCHAR2 be changed to type CHAR, nor can the length of a CHAR column be increased. To modify any other aspect of the table's column or constraint definition, the **alter table** statement may be used as it was in Oracle7.

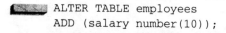

```
ALTER TABLE employees
ADD (salary number(10));
```

Exercises

1. Which of the **alter table** statements in this section will cause an index to go into the *INDEX UNUSABLE* state?

2. A table has three partitions. Partition A contains low range data, partition B contains midrange data, and partition C contains high range data. The DBA drops partition B. Later, a user inserts data that would have been placed in partition B had that partition still existed. Into which partition will Oracle place the data?

3. In the situation described in question 2, what will happen if partition C is dropped and the same event occurs?

4. What restrictions apply to changing column definitions on partitioned tables? What about restrictions on datatypes and partitioned tables? What about restrictions on tables where partitions are stored in **read only** tablespaces?

Altering Partitioned Indexes

Like tables, partitioned indexes can have many modifications made to them. The first that will be covered in this discussion is dropping index partitions. This is accomplished with the **alter index drop partition** statement. Once dropped, data that would have gone into that partition now goes into the next highest partition. Only global partitioned indexes can be dropped using this statement, and even then the highest partition cannot be dropped. Dropping an index partition effectively removes the index data that was stored in the partition. The statement used to drop an index partition is demonstrated in the following code block:

```
ALTER INDEX x_emp_01
DROP PARTITION ix1;
```

In addition, the DBA can rename a partition, from something obscure to something meaningful. The partitions on this index were named IX1 through IX3, which have little intrinsic meaning. The DBA may want to rename those partitions with more meaningful identifiers. The statement used to rename a table partition is **alter table rename partition**, and it is used as follows:

```
ALTER TABLE employees
RENAME PARTITION ix1 TO emps_lt300000;
```

If the DBA finds that one partition is growing at a rate much faster than others, the DBA can split the partition into smaller partitions to balance the load of that index on any one disk. Only global indexes may be split. To do this, the DBA must use the **alter index split partition** statement. Splitting the partition creates a new partition named according to a value set in the statement. If the partition split was unusable at the time of the split, then both partitions produced will also be unusable, and must be rebuilt. If the original partition was empty, then both partitions will be rebuilt. The index partition can be rebuilt with **alter index rebuild partition**. A statement splitting partitions on an index appears in the following code block:

```
ALTER INDEX x_emp_01 SPLIT PARTITION ix1
AT (150000)
INTO (PARTITION ix1a TABLESPACE index_01
    PARTITION ix1b TABLESPACE index_04);
```

Physical storage parameters for indexes can be changed with the **alter index modify partition** statement. Alternately, this statement can be used to change the status of an index to unusable. Both global and local partitioned indexes can have physical attributes or status changed with this feature. In addition, all partitions of an index can be marked as unusable with the **alter index unusable** statement. These statements are used as follows:

```
ALTER INDEX x_emp_01
MODIFY PARTITION ix1b
STORAGE (NEXT 5M);

ALTER INDEX x_emp_01
MODIFY PARTITION ix1a
UNUSABLE;

ALTER INDEX x_emp_01
UNUSABLE;
```

The usage of the **alter index rebuild partition** statement has already been explained. Any partitioned index can be rebuilt using this statement, allowing other partitions to continue undisturbed while the DBA handles maintenance. In some cases, however, it may run faster for the DBA to drop and re-create the index, particularly with global partitioned indexes. Optionally, the partition can be rebuilt in a different tablespace with the use of the **tablespace** keyword. Use of **alter index rebuild partition** is detailed in the following code block:

```
ALTER INDEX x_emp_01
REBUILD PARTITION ix1b;
```

```
ALTER INDEX x_emp_01
REBUILD PARTITION ix1b;
TABLESPACE index_05;
```

The parallelism with which Oracle will search for data in the index can also be set. The statement used for this process is the **alter index parallel** statement. Within this statement, there are two options that should be set: **degree** and **instances**. The **degree** option specifies how many processes can be set up to search through partitions for data. The **instances** option specifies how many instances may search in parallel for data. The total number of processes that may ever be used to search for data in parallel is **degree * instances**. Usage of the **alter index parallel** statement appears in the following code block:

```
ALTER INDEX x_emp_01
PARALLEL (DEGREE 5 INSTANCES 2);
```

The final area of index management that will be covered is the use of the **skip_unusable_indexes** option for the session. This parameter is defined as TRUE or FALSE for the current session. When it is set to TRUE, Oracle will allow the user to execute **insert**, **update**, and **delete** operations on table partitions whose corresponding *nonunique* indexes are in an unusable state. In this way, the user can make large modifications to data, deferring the index modification to a later point in time. To change the value for this parameter, use the **alter session set skip_unusable_indexes = true** statement.

```
ALTER SESSION
SET SKIP_UNUSABLE_INDEXES = TRUE;
```

Exercises

1. How does the DBA re-enable the use of an index partition after the partition is put into *INDEX UNUSABLE* status?

2. What are two uses for the **alter index modify partition** statement?

3. If the user would like to **insert** data on a table with a nonunique index in *INDEX UNUSABLE* state, what parameter must be set for the session, and how?

Privileges and Dictionary Views for Partitioned Objects

No new privileges are introduced in Oracle8 for the management of partitions. In general, the same privileges available for Oracle7 used to create tables and indexes are used in Oracle8 to create nonpartitioned and partitioned tables. The same applies to dropping tables, except for dropping or truncating partitions on tables the user doesn't own, for which the **drop any table** privilege is required. To alter table and index partitions, the privileges required are **alter table** (or **index**) *action* **partition**, where *action* can be **modify**, **rebuild**, **split**, **add**, or **move**.

In addition, there are several dictionary views that can be used to identify information about the partitioned table or index. Some of the dictionary views have already been presented, such as DBA_TABLES, DBA_INDEXES, DBA_TAB_COLUMNS, DBA_OBJECTS. Other views are new, and their uses are listed here:

- **DBA_PART_TABLES**   Gives information about how the table is partitioned for all tables in the database, including partition keys

- **DBA_PART_INDEXES**   Gives information about how the index is partitioned for all tables in the database, including partition keys

- **DBA_PART_KEY_COLUMNS**   Identifies the partition key used for all tables and indexes in the database

- **DBA_TAB_PARTITIONS**   Identifies information about the partitions of all tables in the database

- **DBA_IND_PARTITIONS**   Identifies information about the partitions of all indexes in the database

- **DBA_PART_COL_STATISTICS**   Identifies statistics for cost-based optimization for partition columns for all tables and indexes in the database

- **DBA_TAB_COL_STATISTICS**   Identifies statistics for cost-based optimization for table columns for all tables in the database

- **DBA_PART_HISTOGRAMS**   Shows the distribution of data in partitions for all partitions in the database

- **DBA_TAB_HISTOGRAMS**   Shows the distribution of the data in tables for all tables in the database

Exercises

1. Which new dictionary views give statistical information for index and table partition statistics for cost-based optimization?

2. In which new dictionary views can the DBA find information about the partition key and the partition range for tables and indexes?

Using Oracle Utilities and Partitioned Objects

In this section, you will cover the following topics for using Oracle utilities and partitioned objects:

- Using **explain plan** with partitioned objects

- Using SQL*Loader with partitioned objects

- Using EXPORT/IMPORT with partitioned objects

- Using **analyze** with partitioned objects

The addition of partitions to the Oracle table and index architecture is a major enhancement designed to support large database applications like OLTP systems and data warehouses. This addition of partitions presents some changes in the way some utilities manage table and index data. The affected utilities are those that DBAs use most frequently in conjunction with tables and indexes, such as IMPORT, EXPORT, and SQL*Loader. Since partitions affect the ways users obtain data from tables and indexes, some changes were made to utilities like **analyze** and **explain plan** as well. This section will present the changes made to several utilities as a result of the addition of partitions.

Using EXPLAIN PLAN with Partitioned Objects

The addition of partitions to the Oracle table and index architecture indicates some underlying changes to the methods Oracle will use to obtain data from those partitioned objects. New operations are used in the SQL processing mechanism, and to reflect these changes in the processing of SQL statements, the **explain plan** utility has been changed as well. The first change made is to the PLAN_TABLE. As discussed earlier, the PLAN_TABLE is used to store execution plan information generated by Oracle when a user requests this information. The new columns are PARTITION_START, PARTITION_STOP, and PARTITION_ID. The first two columns named are used to show the user which partitions Oracle will scan for the SQL statement undergoing **explain plan** activity, while the third shows the step that produced the values for the first two columns. An explanation of each column is listed below:

- **PARTITION_START** Shows the start partition of the range of accessed partitions

- **PARTITION_STOP** Shows the stop partition of the range of accessed partitions

- **PARTITION_ID** Shows the step that determines the values for the start and stop columns

In addition, there are some new operations that users of the **explain plan** feature will notice when creating execution plans for Oracle SQL statements that access partitioned tables and indexes. The new internal Oracle operation is called **partition**. Also, the existing **table access** and **index** operations have been modified to reflect the use of partitions. For the OPTIONS column currently existing in the PLAN_TABLE, some new values may appear in relation to partitions. These new values are **concatenated**, **single**, and **empty**. These values will appear as part of the execution plan in relation to the operation Oracle must execute to obtain data from the database. The first, **concatenated**, means that the **partition** step had to concatenate the results of several partitions in order to search for data. The second, **single**, means that the **partition** step will access only one partition to find requested data. The third, **empty**, indicates the partition step found no partitions to access.

For the **table access** operation, there are several new values possible for the OPTIONS column. These options are **by user ROWID**, **by index ROWID**, **by global index ROWID**, and **by local index ROWID**. These operations identify the new indexes available in Oracle8 as the source for ROWID information.

Exercises

1. What new columns have been added to the PLAN_TABLE for supporting execution plans for partitioned tables and indexes?

2. What is the new operation used in **explain plan** for handling partitions? What are the new options available with that operation? What are the new options available for the *TABLE ACCESS* operation?

Using SQL*Loader with Partitioned Objects

A few changes are noteworthy with respect to SQL*Loader and partitioned objects. For the conventional path, the DBA can load data to each partition as necessary. In addition, SQL*Loader can run multiple loads at the same time for different partitions of the same table. In the control file, the DBA must identify the partition(s) and the table to be loaded. Row data that does not belong in the partition will be placed in the bad file for later load to another partition. SQL*Loader also handles loads to all partitions of the table at the same time using the direct path. The corresponding indexes to the partitioned table being loaded are created automatically, but only one load may be run of this type on the same table at the same time. Finally, there are some changes to the direct path data load. First, a parallel direct load on one partition can be run at the same time as a parallel load on another partition. An additional parameter is included for the direct path parallel load, PARALLEL=TRUE. Global indexes should be dropped before engaging in the direct path parallel load, and the corresponding local index is rendered unusable.

Exercises

1. What changes to support partitions have been made for the SQL*Loader conventional path load? How many loads can run at the same time on the same table with five partitions?

2. What changes have been made to load all partitions of a partitioned table with SQL*Loader?

3. What option is available for improved direct path load performance using parallelism?

Using EXPORT/IMPORT with Partitioned Objects

The following changes have been made for EXPORT to handle partitions. An entire partitioned table can be exported in all modes, namely **table**, **user**, and **full**. However, a single partition can be exported only in **table** mode, specified by the following format: *table:partition*. For IMPORT, the following changes are made. The DBA can import data from a database export dump file for a partitioned table into the database as a nonpartitioned table, and vice versa. By default, IMPORT will create a partitioned table if the EXPORT was of a partitioned table. IMPORT operates in all modes, including **table**, **user**, and **full**. IMPORT can also use the **skip_unusable_indexes** option discussed earlier.

Exercises

1. What new features for EXPORT have been added to support partitioned tables?

2. What new features of IMPORT have been added to support partitioned tables?

Using ANALYZE with Partitioned Objects

The final tool considered is the **analyze** command. The DBA can collect statistics for a single table or index partition using **analyze**. The **analyze** command can also validate the structure of a single table or index partition.

Histograms can also be produced per partition. The **analyze** command can even perform the **list chained rows** feature on only one partition. As before, **analyze** can still perform its analysis on all partitions of a table or index. This is the default functionality if a specific partition is not specified, even if the index or table is partitioned.

```
ANALYZE INDEX ix1b
COMPUTE STATISTICS FOR ALL COLUMNS;

ANALYZE TABLE employees PARTITION X3
LIST CHAINED ROWS
```

Exercises

1. What new syntax is required in the **analyze** command for analyzing only the partitions of a table or index?

2. If **analyze** is executed on an index that is partitioned and no specific partition is specified, what part of the index will **analyze** work on?

Chapter Summary

This chapter covered a major new feature for Oracle8, that of partitioning tables. This area affects both the selection and change of data, as well as the administration of the indexes and tables that store data. The areas of creating partitioned tables and indexes were covered, along with the modification of those partitions once the table or index is created. The chapter discussed the benefits of partitioning tables and indexes, and the effect these new features for tables and indexes have on several utilities, such as **explain plan,** SQL*Loader, **analyze**, and IMPORT/EXPORT.

The first section covered the topic of why to use partitioning. There are several benefits for partitioning tables. Especially for large tables and indexes on data warehouses and other large-volume data systems, partitions of a table or index can be much easier to manage during maintenance operations than the entire table or index itself. This ease of maintenance translates into shorter maintenance cycles and increased data availability for the large database system, because the rest of the partitions in a table or index will continue to be available even if one of the partitions is unavailable.

Partitioned tables and indexes can be thought of as miniature versions of that same object, because the column and constraint definition for each partition of the table or index must be identical, although the storage parameters and tablespace location can be different for each partition. Also, the availability of each partition is independent of the availability of any other partition in the table or index, creating *partition independence*. Many different combinations of partitioned indexes to partitioned tables are allowed, although the most efficient combination is usually to have a partitioned table with an equipartitioned local index. Equipartitioning is when two or more objects share the same partition definition, and where data in the partition of one object appears in the partition of another object.

Equipartitioning is specified with the creation of indexes with the **local** clause. Equipartitioned database tables and their corresponding indexes have partition independence from other partitions in the database table or index to which they belong, but they also have a special relationship to the corresponding partition in the other database object. The two partitions in different database objects are related in that their partition keys and ranges are the same, and the data in one partition will have a corresponding data record in the other partition. Also, if something happens to the availability of data in the partition of the table, the availability of data in the corresponding index partition will likely be impacted.

The DBA partitions tables in the following way. The **create table** statement includes the column and constraint definition, as well as all components of the partition definition. There are three parts to the partition definition. They are the partition key, the partition range identifiers, and the partition physical storage clause. The partition key is specified with the **partition by range** (*column*) clause, where *column* equals the column used for the partition key. Usually, it is best to specify the partition key to be a column that doesn't allow NULL values. The partition key is then used to define the various value ranges that will be put into each partition. This is defined with the **values less than** (*value*) clause, where *value* equals the high end of the range permitted for that partition. The implied low end of that range is the value specified as the high end for the previous range, or the lowest possible value for the column. The highest partition has the high-end value for the column defined as its high-end range. This can either be an actual value for the column or the **maxvalue** keyword, which is a catchall keyword stating that all values for this column that do not fit in another partition go into this one. Finally, the **tablespace** clause used for partition storage can be named after the **values less than** (*value*) clause, and the physical storage options such as **pctfree**, **pctused**, **initial**, and **next** can be specified in the **storage** clause.

There are some restrictions on partitioning tables. First, a table cannot be partitioned if it has a column defined with the LONG, LONG RAW, or the new large object (LOB) datatypes. Also, data cannot be inserted into a partitioned table or index if the value for the partition key is not in the range specified by the partition key. No partition can have a column or constraint that another partition for the same table does not also have. The column(s) used for the partition key cannot have its datatype changed. However, the combinations of partitioned tables and indexes are unrestricted—a partitioned table can have nonpartitioned indexes or partitioned indexes, or even both, and a nonpartitioned table can have either nonpartitioned or partitioned indexes, or even both.

Partitioned indexes can be created with the **create index** statement. As with tables, the index is partitioned with the same three parts, a partition key specified with **partition by range** and the range specified by **values less than**. As with tables, the physical storage of index partitions can be different from partition to partition. There are four types of partitions: nonpartitioned indexes (already discussed and understood from Oracle7), local prefixed indexes, local nonprefixed indexes, and global prefixed indexes. The two general items that distinguish indexes are *global* or *local*, and *prefixed* or *nonprefixed*. A global index is one that is not equipartitioned according to its associated table (even if the partitions in both objects are identical), while a local index is equipartitioned with its table. Prefixing or nonprefixing indicates the relationship between the partition key and the overall columns in the index. An index is prefixed if it is partitioned on a left prefix of the index columns. For example, if the EMPLOYEES table and its local index X_EMPLOYEES_01 are partitioned on the STATE column, then index X_EMPLOYEES_01 is local prefixed if it is defined on the columns (STATE, EMPID). On the other hand, if index X_EMPLOYEES_01 is defined on column NAME, then it is not prefixed. A partitioned index with only one column is by definition prefixed, because the one column in the partition key is also the only column in the index key, and therefore leftmost. In contrast, if the column(s) of the partition key of the index are not in the same order as the overall order of columns in the index, then the index is *nonprefixed*. An index partition may become unusable if the associated table partition containing data is truncated, dropped, split, or otherwise modified.

Tables can be modified with the **alter table** *action* **partition** statement, where *action* can be replaced with **split** to divide one partition into two, **drop** to eliminate the partition, **add** to create another partition, or **rename** to change the name of the partition. Also, it can be replaced with **truncate** to delete all records from the partition or **move** to move a partition into another extent in the current or different tablespace. It can also be replaced with **exchange** to change a partition into a separate table or vice versa, or **modify** to change physical storage parameters (but not the tablespace) or to rebuild an unusable index. The **alter table** statement is used to add columns and modify column datatypes

Index partitions can be modified with the **alter index** *action* **partition**. Several operations are possible, including **drop** to drop the partition, **rename** to change the name of the partition, **rebuild** to fix an index partition that is no longer usable, **modify** to change the storage parameters for the index, **split** to divide the partition into two or more parts, **parallel** to set the parallelism of the index, or **unusable** to set the index as unusable.

In addition to the dictionary views used to obtain information about tables and indexes, the following new dictionary views support use of partitions. DBA_PART_TABLES gives information about how the table is partitioned for all tables in the database. DBA_PART_INDEXES gives information about how the index is partitioned for all tables in the database. DBA_PART_KEY_COLUMNS identifies the partition key used for all tables and indexes in the database. DBA_TAB_PARTITIONS offers information about the partitions of all tables in the database. DBA_IND_PARTITIONS gives information about the partitions of all indexes in the database. DBA_PART_COL_STATISTICS lists statistics for cost-based optimization for partition columns, for all tables and indexes in the database. DBA_TAB_COL_STATISTICS offers statistics for cost-based optimization for table columns, for all tables in the database. DBA_PART_HISTOGRAMS shows the distribution of data in partitions for all partitions in the database. DBA_TAB_HISTOGRAMS shows the distribution of the data in tables for all tables in the database.

Several utilities were changed to accommodate partitions. They include **explain plan**, **analyze**, SQL*Loader, IMPORT and EXPORT. For **explain plan**, three new columns were added to the PLAN_TABLE, called

PARTITION_START, PARTITION_STOP, and PARTITION_ID. A new operation called **partition** was added, along with three new options for its execution, **concatenated** (several partitions were put together to be searched for requested data), **single** (only one partition will be searched for requested data), and **empty** (the partition operation produced no partitions to search). Some new options for the **table access** operation were added as well, corresponding to the new indexes that are available. The options for TABLE ACCESS are **by user ROWID, by index ROWID, by global index ROWID,** and **by local index ROWID.**

For SQL*Loader, there are changes to the conventional path and the direct path. For conventional path, SQL*Loader may load one partition only, but several loads can operate on the same table but different partitions to execute data loads on partitioned tables more quickly. For the direct path, SQL*Loader allows the PARALLEL parameter, which is set to TRUE or FALSE depending on whether the DBA wants to load an individual partition using the direct path in parallel. If PARALLEL is used, then SQL*Loader will load records to one partition with multiple I/O processes running in parallel. Multiple loads can run on the same table but different partitions to load other partitions in parallel as well. Finally, if the DBA wants to load all partitions using SQL*Loader, she can do so with the direct path load, where SQL*Loader will load each partition sequentially. Only one load can run on the table or index at a time if this method is used.

For IMPORT and EXPORT, entire partitioned tables can be imported or exported, or an individual partition can be exported and then imported as a nonpartitioned table. Partition exports can only be done in EXPORT table mode. Partitions for tables must be specified as *table:partition*. For **analyze**, both tables and individual partitions can have this utility run on them, but to use the utility on a partition, only the partition must be named explicitly. Otherwise, the entire table will be analyzed.

Two-Minute Drill

- Tables and indexes in Oracle8 can be partitioned.

- Table and index partitions are defined with three new parts to the **create table** and **create index** statements: **partition by range** (*column*) to define the partition key, **values less than** (*value*) to define the upper bound for each partition subrange, and tablespace location and storage parameters. Only the storage parameters need be preceded by the **storage** clause.

- Tables and indexes can have up to 64,000 partitions.

- Oracle8 can store up to 512 petabytes of data.

- No table containing a column defined to be type LONG, LONG RAW, or any of the new LOB datatypes can be partitioned.

- A table's partitions can be altered in several ways.

  - The **alter table drop partition** statement drops a named partition and its contents.

  - The **alter table add partition** statement adds a partition over and above the highest range currently existing on a partition in the table.

  - The **alter table rename partition** statement renames a partition from one thing to another.

  - The **alter table modify partition** statement sets the equipartitioned local index data to *INDEX UNUSABLE* status, or allows the equipartitioned local index to be rebuilt, or allows the DBA to change physical storage parameters (but not tablespace location).

  - The **alter table truncate partition** statement deletes all data from the table partition.

  - The **alter table split partition** statement splits one partition into two.

  - The **alter table move partition** statement moves the partition to another extent in the same tablespace or into another tablespace.

  - The **alter table exchange partition** statement turns a partition into its own table, and vice versa.

- The following restrictions apply to changing column and constraint definitions on a partitioned table.

- The partition key's datatype or size cannot be changed.

- All values for the partition-key column must be accommodated by a partition, thus ranges of A–P, Q–Z are allowed, but ranges A–O, R–Z are not.

- If no partition defined for the partitioned object contains **values less than (maxvalue)**, the partition-key column cannot contain NULL values.

- An **insert** on the table will fail if the value specified for the partition is outside any range specified for any partition on the table.

- The partitioned table may not contain a column declared with the LONG or LONG RAW datatypes, or any column declared with the large object (LOB) datatypes new to Oracle8.

- The value in a partition-key column cannot be changed if the change will cause the row to move partitions.

- The individual partitions of the table cannot be referenced through a database link or a synonym.

- A PL/SQL block may not contain SQL that refers directly to a partition in a table. However, the user may create dynamic SQL using the DBMS_SQL package that references individual partitions in PL/SQL blocks, or use views that reference the individual partition in the table. Only table partitions may be directly referenced, not index partitions.

■ The **alter index drop partition** statement drops the named partition and its contents.

■ The **alter index rename partition** statement renames the partition.

■ The **alter index rebuild partition** statement fixes an *INDEX UNUSABLE* index partition.

■ The **alter index modify partition** statement changes physical storage parameters for a partition.

■ The **alter index split partition** statement splits one partition into two.

- The **alter index unusable** statement makes an index partition unusable.

- The **alter index parallel** statement defines parallelism for the index.

- The **explain plan** utility has several new features to support partitioned tables.

  - A new operation exists called **partition** that handles searching partitions.

  - Three options for **partition** operation are **concatenated**, **single**, and **empty**.

  - Three new columns for the PLAN_TABLE are PARTITION_START, PARTITION_STOP, and PARTITION_ID.

  - EXPORT and IMPORT can handle partitioned tables. EXPORT can create export files containing only the named partition if used in **table** mode.

- The **analyze** statement can be executed on either individual partitions or on entire partitioned database objects.

- SQL*Loader can run multiple conventional or direct path loads on different partitions in the object. For direct path loads, the load on each partition can be executed using the PARALLEL=TRUE parameter, which sets the direct load to run in parallel when loading one partition.

- To load all partitions of the table with one load, SQL*Loader allows a sequential load. Only one sequential load can operate on a partitioned table at one time.

Chapter Questions

1. **The SALES table is partitioned by month according to the date the sales order was taken. One of the salespeople enters a sales order dated July 31, then realizes he took the order on August 1. When he issues the UPDATE statement to modify the data, what happens?**

   A. The **update** fails because the partition-key column can never be updated.

   B. The **update** fails because a partition key column cannot be updated such that the row must move partitions.

   C. The **update** fails because a NULL value was specified for the primary key.

   D. The **update** succeeds.

2. **The most likely cause for a local index partition to be in the *INDEX UNUSABLE* state is**

   A. A user deleted one row from the table partition.

   B. The DBA issued an **alter table add partition** statement.

   C. The DBA issued an **alter index rebuild partition** statement.

   D. The DBA issued an **alter table truncate partition** statement.

3. **Which of the following operations should the DBA execute to load data into ten partitions of a table simultaneously?**

   A. Execute SQL*Loader ten times in parallel.

   B. Execute SQL*Loader once with the parameter DEGREE=10.

   C. Execute SQL*Loader once with the parameter PARALLEL=TRUE.

   D. Execute SQL*Loader five times with the parameter INSTANCES=2.

4. **The DBA creates a table called EXPENSES whose partition key is the EXPENSE_DATE column. The partitions are called EXP_JUNE, EXP_JULY, EXP_AUGUST, and EXP_SEPTEMBER. She drops the first**

partition, covering the month of June. Later, a user adds a row to the table with the EXPENSE_DATE column equal to '15-JUN-1999'. To which partition is the row added?

A. EXP_JULY

B. EXP_AUGUST

C. EXP_SEPTEMBER

D. None, the partition-key value is out of range.

5. Which of the following is not a benefit of partitioning?

A. Partition independence

B. Greater data availability

C. Inability to access one partition when another is unavailable

D. Scalable performance with data growth

6. When the DBA declares a global index with partitions identical to the table, equipartitioning is enforced automatically by Oracle.

A. TRUE

B. FALSE

7. Which of the following are not partitioned indexes available in Oracle? (Choose two)

A. Global prefixed indexes

B. Global nonprefixed indexes

C. Local prefixed indexes

D. Global equipartitioned indexes

8. The EXPENSES table uses a partition key called EXPENSE_DATE of datatype DATE, representing the date the sale was entered. The DBA splits the EXP_JULY partition of the SALES table into two partitions, EXP_JULY1-15 and EXP_JULY16-31. All rows in the EXP_JULY partition had a value greater than July 17 for the

partition key. Which of the following statements is TRUE regarding the local prefixed indexes produced by the table partition split?

A. EXP_ JULY1-15 will be unusable, but EXP_ JULY16-31 will be valid.

B. Both EXP_ JULY1-15 and EXP_ JULY16-31 will be valid.

C. Both EXP_ JULY1-15 and EXP_ JULY16-31 will be unusable.

D. EXP_ JULY1-15 will be valid, but EXP_ JULY16-31 will be unusable.

9. The DBA wants to eliminate partition X1 from table EMPLOYEES. If partition X1 contains 65 percent of the rows for the table and there are global indexes on the table, what is the fastest way for the DBA to eliminate partition X1 and make the global indexes available for use again?

A. Merge the partition, rebuild the index.

B. Drop the partition, rebuild the index.

C. Delete all rows from the partition, drop the partition, rebuild the index.

D. Split the partition, drop the partition, rebuild the index.

10. When a table partition is truncated, only the associated partition in the global index becomes *INDEX UNUSABLE.*

A. TRUE

B. FALSE

11. Which statement can be used to place partition X1 on table EXPENSES from tablespace DATA_01 to tablespace DATA_05?

A. alter table EXPENSES modify partition X1 from DATA_01 to DATA_05;

B. alter table EXPENSES rename partition X1 to DATA_05;

C. alter table EXPENSES move partition X1 tablespace DATA_05;

D. alter table EXPENSES drop partition X1 into DATA_05;

12. When the DBA executes the ALTER TABLE EXCHANGE PARTITION statement, data in the partition is physically moved into another table.

    A. TRUE

    B. FALSE

13. If the DBA wants to determine the partition key for a table, she can use which of the following dictionary views?

    A. DBA_PART_TABLES

    B. DBA_TAB_HISTOGRAMS

    C. DBA_TAB_COLUMNS

    D. DBA_TAB_COL_STATISTICS

Answers to Chapter Questions

1. B.   The **update** fails because a partition-key column cannot be updated such that the row must move partitions.

Explanation   Users may not **update** a value for a column that is part of the partition key if the **update** will cause the row to move to another partition. The row must first be deleted and then inserted again. Choices A and C are both right in that the user will not be able to **update** the row, but the reason given is incorrect. Choice D is obviously incorrect.

2. D.   The DBA issued an **alter table truncate partition** statement.

Explanation   Several operations on table partitions will cause the index partition to become unusable. One of these operations is to truncate the table partition. Adding a new table partition creates a new index partition, and since the added partition is empty, the corresponding index partition is automatically valid. Choice A will simply remove a row from the index and the table, while choices B and C create or fix indexes, leaving them valid.

3. A.   Execute SQL*Loader ten times in parallel.

Explanation   An individual SQL*Loader run can operate against a single partition of the Oracle database. Another execution of SQL*Loader can operate against a different partition at the same time. This is the best way to run a data load against multiple partitions of a table. Choices B and D are incorrect because the parameters named are not actual SQL*Loader parameters. Choice C is incorrect because the PARALLEL parameter simply runs a parallel load on the single partition, not a load on multiple partitions in parallel.

4. A.   JULY

Explanation   After a partition is dropped, all rows inserted to the table that would have been stored in that partition go into the next highest partition. If the partition dropped had been the highest partition, Oracle will not allow the row to be inserted.

5. C.   Inability to access one partition when another is unavailable

Explanation   Creating partitions creates partition independence, and this choice contradicts the definition of partition independence—namely, that the availability of each partition is independent of the availability of another partition. All of the other choices are features of partitioning.

6. B.   FALSE

Explanation   Global indexes are *not* equipartitioned; that is to say, there is not association between the partitions of a table and a global index, even if the partition key and defined ranges are identical. To create an equipartitioning relationship, the index must be local.

7. B and D.   Global nonprefixed indexes and global equipartitioned indexes

Explanation   Answering this question requires some memorization. The global nonprefixed index is not an index in the Oracle database. Since the partition key for the global index doesn't have to be tied to the partition key of the table, the DBA can create all prefixed global indexes. Choice D is a little more obvious—remember that an index cannot simultaneously be global and equipartitioned.

8. D.   EXP_JULY1-15 will be valid, but EXP_JULY16-31 will be unusable.

Explanation   When Oracle splits the table partition, a similar split occurs in the associated local (equipartitioned) index. Since one of the resultant table partitions will be empty, the associated index for that partition will be valid while the other one remains unusable. If the table partition had been empty, both resulting index partitions would have been valid.

9. B.   Drop the partition, rebuild the index

Explanation   The most efficient means for making the global index available quickly in this situation is to drop the partition and rebuild the index. Had the partition not contained so much of the row data for the table, the DBA might consider choice C. Choices A and D are both incorrect. Choice A is wrong because there is no option for merging two partitions together except by the SQL processing mechanism in a **select** statement.

10. B.   FALSE

Explanation   If any single partition in a table is truncated, all partitions of the global index will be unusable, and the DBA will have to rebuild them.

11. C.   **alter table EXPENSES move partition X1 tablespace DATA_05;**

Explanation   The **alter table move partition** statement is used to move partitions from one tablespace to another. Choice A is incorrect because the **modify** operation allows the DBA to modify other storage parameters but not to move the partition to a different tablespace. Choice B renames the partition but does not move it. Choice D is not a valid statement.

12. B.   FALSE

Explanation   Although the **alter table exchange partition** statement allows the DBA to create a table out of a partition, and vice versa, there is no data physically moved by the statement. The only change made is to the data dictionary.

13. A.   DBA_PART_TABLES

Explanation   The dictionary view containing the information about partition keys is the DBA_PART_TABLES view. Choice B, DBA_TAB_HISTOGRAMS, gives data distribution information for columns in the tables of the database. Choice C, DBA_TAB_COLUMNS, lists all columns in all tables in the database. Choice D, DBA_TAB_COL_ STATISTICS, gives column statistics for tables in the database for purposes of cost-based optimization.

CHAPTER
22

Oracle8: New Features
and Object Relational
Design

n this chapter, you will understand and demonstrate knowledge in the following areas:

- Using Oracle8's new objects
- Oracle8's new ROWID format
- Oracle8's object relational concepts

This chapter covers several new features of the Oracle database architecture. In order to accommodate other aspects of large databases, Oracle8 adds some new objects and features for data storage. These features fall into two categories: new objects and the new ROWID format. The new objects are designed to store more information, while the new ROWID format is designed to handle access to the increased amount of information stored in an Oracle database. The final category, using object relational features, is perhaps the most advanced and interesting. This area of the Oracle database represents a new way for DBAs and developers to take organizational information in new directions.

Using Oracle8 New Objects

In this section, you will cover the following areas of using Oracle8 new objects:

- Bigger databases, NLS datatypes, and new integrity constraints
- Reverse-key indexes and index-organized tables
- The large pool
- Using external procedures

Oracle8 offers the DBA many new objects in which to store data. The databases Oracle8 supports are larger than ever before. New features for national language support datatypes are present in Oracle8 as well. Also, the success of Oracle7's declarative integrity constraints has been advanced with new types of constraints and enhancements to existing constraints. This section will cover the facts related to these three areas for OCP Exam 5.

Bigger Databases, NLS Datatypes, and New Integrity Constraints

Oracle8 supports increased-size ceilings in several different areas of database administration. The first area, that of table and index partitions, offers a high level of partitioning on database tables and indexes—64,000 to be exact. Other areas of the database have received increases in capacity as well. One caveat exists for Oracle8's new capacity limits—the operating system on the host machine running Oracle8 must also support these capacity limits. These increases are as follows:

- The total capacity for database is 512 petabytes.

- The maximum number of tablespaces allowed is about 2 billion.

- The number of datafiles per tablespace is 1,022.

- The number of columns supported in a table is now 1,000.

- The maximum number of indexed columns is 32.

- The CHAR datatype now supports 2,000 bytes.

- The VARCHAR2 datatype now supports 4,000 bytes.

There are two new datatypes in the Oracle8 architecture provided for national language support as well. These two new datatypes are the NCHAR and the NVARCHAR2 datatypes. NCHAR and NVARCHAR2 are designed to store character-based data for multibyte character sets. They are identical in function and in size to their single-byte counterparts, CHAR and VARCHAR2. To access data in the columns declared to be type NCHAR or NVARCHAR2, the user must use the syntax *column* = **N**'*value*'. That letter **N** must be specified exactly as that—a capital N in front of the desired value. The columns that are declared as NCHAR and NVARCHAR2 should be used to store data in the same character set as that declared for the database in the **create database** statement.

Oracle furthers the success of declarative integrity constraints with new features for their usage. The first change made to the declarative integrity constraints in the Oracle database is the differentiation between *deferred* and *immediate* constraints. Immediate constraints are those integrity constraints that are enforced immediately, as soon as the statement is executed. If the user attempts to enter data that violates the constraint, Oracle signals an error and the statement is rolled back. Up until Oracle8, all declarative integrity constraints in the database were immediate constraints. However, Oracle8 also offers the DBA an option to defer database integrity checking. Deferred integrity constraints are those that are not enforced until the user attempts to **commit** the transaction. If at that time the data entered by statements violates an integrity constraint, Oracle will signal an error and roll back the entire transaction. The user can defer any and all constraints that are deferrable during the entire session using the **alter session set constraints=deferred** statement. Alternately, the user can defer named or all constraints for a specific transaction using the **set constraint** *name* **deferred** or **set constraint all deferred**. This form of "lazy evaluation" temporarily allows data to enter the database that violates integrity constraints. For example, in Oracle7 there was no way to **insert** data into a child table for which there wasn't also data in the parent. In Oracle8, the user can conduct the **insert** on the child table before inserting data into the parent simply by deferring the foreign-key constraint. The user may also set constraints for immediate enforcement using the **set constraint** *name* **immediate** or **set constraint all immediate** statement.

The definition of a constraint will determine whether the constraint is deferrable by users. Two factors play into that determination. The first is the overall deferability of the constraint. If a constraint is created with the **deferrable** keyword, then the constraint is deferrable by user processes until the time the transaction is committed. In contrast, if the constraint is created with the **not deferrable** keywords, then user process statements will always be bound by the integrity constraint. The **not deferrable** status is the default for the constraint. If a constraint has been created with the **not deferrable** status, then the **alter session** and **set** statements above for deferring integrity constraints cannot be used. The second factor is the default behavior of the constraint. The first option is to have the constraint deferred, defined with the **initially deferred** keyword. This option and the **not deferrable** keyword option described are mutually exclusive. The other option is to have the integrity constraint enforced unless explicitly deferred by the user process, specified by the **initially Immediate** keywords.

```
CREATE TABLE employees
(empid      NUMBER(10)     NOT NULL,
 name       VARCHAR2(40)   NOT NULL,
 salary     NUMBER(10)     NOT NULL,
 CONSTRAINT pk_employees_01
 PRIMARY KEY (empid) NOT DEFERRABLE);
```

The other new features for integrity constraints are a new status for constraints and the use of nonunique indexes to enforce unique constraints. In versions earlier than Oracle8, there are two statuses for the integrity constraints: **enable** and **disable**. Oracle8 changes the **enable** status to **enable validate** and adds a third status for integrity constraints, **enable novalidate**. The new status allows Oracle to enforce the constraint on new data entering the table (enabling), but not on data that already exists on the table (no validating). These statuses can be used with the issuance of the **alter table** *table_name* **enable novalidate constraint** *constraint_name* or **alter table** *name* **enable validate constraint** *constraint_name* statements. Also, Oracle can support unique constraints with nonunique indexes. The columns in the unique constraint should be the first columns in the nonunique index, in any order. Other columns can also be present in the index to make it nonunique. This feature speeds the process of enabling primary-key or unique constraints on the table. The nonunique index supporting the unique or primary-key constraint cannot be dropped.

Exercises

1. What is the maximum allowed size for an Oracle8 database? How large can the VARCHAR2 datatype be in Oracle8?

2. Name two new NLS datatypes available in Oracle8 that relate to the CHAR and VARCHAR2 datatypes.

3. What is the new status available for integrity constraints?

Reverse-Key Indexes and Index-Organized Tables

Several new features in the Oracle database have been created that relate to the use of traditional B-tree indexes. The first is the ability to reverse the key data of an index. Oracle has increased its support of parallel processing with the use of *reverse-key indexes*. A reverse-key index will actually reverse the order of the data in the key; thus, if a column contains data in the following set: ('SAM', 'JILL','FRANK','SITA'), the resultant reverse-key index data will look like ('MAS','LLIJ','KNARF','ATIS'). This new indexing option is used to increase Oracle's ability to retrieve and modify indexed data in parallel configurations and to minimize the chance that changes to data in the index will cause the index to be less effective in retrieving and modifying data. The index key can be reversed at index creation time with the addition of the **reverse** keyword. The index key in an already existing index can be reversed, or a reverse-key index can be placed back into its original order using the **noreverse** keyword. The following code displays the creation of a reverse-key index, the alteration of a regular index to be a reverse-key index, and the alteration of a reverse-key index to be a regular index, respectively:

```
CREATE INDEX x_empl_rev_01
ON employees (empid, name)
REVERSE;

ALTER INDEX x_sales_01
REBUILD REVERSE;

ALTER INDEX x_empl_rev_01
REBUILD NOREVERSE;
```

Another new feature available in Oracle that builds on the use of indexes is the *index-organized table*. Consider the following scenario: In Oracle7, the DBA can create a table with few columns, and index all columns in the table, effectively creating a table that is easier to search but requires significant storage for the combined size of table and index. In Oracle8, those two objects can be combined to minimize storage requirements. The resultant object is the index-organized table, an object with the structure of a B-tree index, but with all data of all columns of the table stored in it, accessible quickly by the primary key with Oracle's index scan operation.

Figure 22-1 illustrates the concept of an index-organized table. Since the data in an index-organized table is stored by indexed primary key, no SQL statement searching for data on an index-organized table will ever use a full table scan.

Index-organized tables store all data in a B-tree structure. In traditional B-tree indexes, the column data would be stored in the index, along with a ROWID for accessing the data in the table. Since the data is actually stored in the tree, however, there is no need for a correlated ROWID between table and index. Thus, row data in index-organized tables do not have ROWIDS. It is not possible to create another index on an index-organized table, so users must remember to use the primary key for all data searches on the index-organized table. Other restrictions include the inability to cluster, partition, or use LONG columns or unique constraints in index-organized tables. These database objects work best in applications that store spatial data. A good example for use of index-organized tables is to improve text searches, because the location of all copies of a particular word can be stored together in one index node for that word. An example of

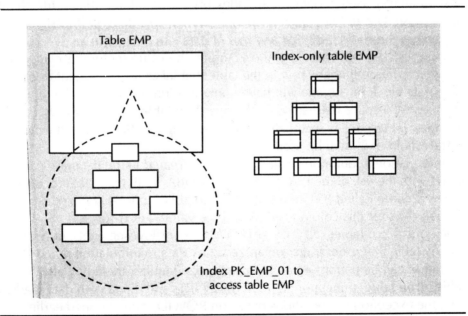

FIGURE 22-1.   *Table/index relationships and the index-organized table*

the **create table** statement used to create an index-organized table appears in the following code block:

```
CREATE TABLE prglang_keywords
(keyword VARCHAR2 CONSTRAINT pk_manual_keywords_01 PRIMARY KEY,
 page_number NUMBER(10))
ORGANIZATION INDEX
PCTTHRESHOLD 25
OVERFLOW TABLESPACE data_oflow_01;
```

There are several new keywords in this **create table** statement to discuss. First, the usage of the **organization index** keywords will be discussed. This is perhaps the most important component in defining an index-organized table, because it is the component that actually defines the table as index-organized. Prior to Oracle8, this parameter is set implicitly for all tables as **organization heap**. In Oracle8, the DBA can define the method used to organize data in regular tables using the **organization heap** keywords, but this behavior is the one Oracle uses by default. Only when **organization index** is used does Oracle create an index-organized table. The next parameter used in defining an index-organized table is the **pctthreshold** *num* clause. Use of this clause is optional. When specified, **pctthreshold** indicates a threshold limit that any row of data can occupy in an index-organized table block. In the example, the value set for this clause is 25, which means that any row in the table that takes up 25 percent *or more* of its data block for storage will have nonkey column data moved into an overflow tablespace defined using the **overflow tablespace** keywords. If **overflow tablespace** is specified without defining a **pctthreshold**, the default **pctthreshold** of 50 will be used.

Information about index-organized tables created in the database can be found with the use of the USER_, ALL_, and DBA_TABLES dictionary views. A new column called IOT stores information about index-organized tables. Data in rows for this column can have three values—IOT for index-organized tables, IOT_OVERFLOW for overflow segments, or NULL for any table that is not index-organized. Any data manipulation or load operation can be performed on index-organized tables, including **alter table**, **drop table**, truncation, EXPORT/IMPORT, and direct path data loads, with the exception of operations based on ROWID, as mentioned earlier.

Exercises

1. What is a reverse-key index? What purpose does it serve? What actually happens to data in the index key of the reverse-key index? What keyword is used in a **create index** statement to reverse the key?

2. Once reversed, what keyword can be used in an **alter index** statement to put the key back into original order?

3. What is an index-organized table? What keywords specify the organization of a table into index-organized order? What is data overflow in an index-organized table, and how Is It defined in the index-organized table?

4. What feature common to other rows of data in the Oracle database does the index-organized table not have?

The Large Pool

Oracle8 supports use of an optional new area in database SGA called the large pool. This area of memory stores session memory for the multithreaded server (MTS) configuration. Oracle allocates buffers for server I/O processes and for backup and restore operations. In creating a new area of memory, Oracle relieves the burden on existing areas like the shared pool to give up memory for caching SQL parse trees in favor of MTS session information and backup/recovery processes. One item the large pool doesn't have that other areas of memory do have is an LRU list to support paging items out of memory.

There are two new parameters used to support the creation of the large pool at instance startup in the **init.ora** file. The first is LARGE_POOL_SIZE, and the second is LARGE_POOL_MIN_ALLOC. The LARGE_POOL_SIZE parameter is used to define the size of the large pool, either in kilobytes or megabytes. The minimum size of the large pool is 300 kilobytes, while the maximum size of the large pool can be 2,000 megabytes or more, depending on the operating system. Within the large pool, there is a minimum allocation size for space in the large pool. This size is defined by the LARGE_POOL_MIN_ALLOC parameter, whose default and minimum value is usually 16 megabytes. The maximum value for this parameter is operating-system specific.

Exercises

1. What is the large pool? How might the DBA want to use the large pool? What objects may be stored in the large pool?

2. What initialization parameters are used to define the size of the large pool?

Using External Procedures

Prior to Oracle8, developers could define PL/SQL procedures that would access the Oracle database and perform operations based on data returned. Further, PL/SQL procedures allowed the developer to put data into the database. However, all code used to manipulate data or to execute in a stored procedure had to be coded "internally"—that is, the code had to be in the PL/SQL procedures. No external procedures were allowed. Oracle8 transcends this restriction using *library schema objects*. PL/SQL stored procedures can now execute other procedures written in C and stored in a shared library. The reference to the C procedure is called a *callout*, while the return of data from the external procedure is a *callback*. The C routine executes in a separate memory address space than the Oracle instance.

There are some strong benefits for using external procedures in Oracle. Instead of requiring developers to rewrite processes written in other languages such as C in PL/SQL in order to use it in the database, the original procedure can be referenced directly by a PL/SQL procedure. Although the first call to an external procedure can be costly for Oracle to process, subsequent calls will run more quickly. The process used for executing an external procedure from PL/SQL is illustrated in Figure 22-2. When a PL/SQL procedure wants to execute an external procedure, the first thing it must do is look up the external procedure using the alias that maps to the external process, also known as the library schema object. Then, the PL/SQL program passes the request to the network listener. The listener process then executes a special process called *extproc*. The **tnsnames.ora** file contains a definition called EXTPROC_CONNECTION_DATA that links the listener to extproc. This process then runs for the rest of the time the session that called

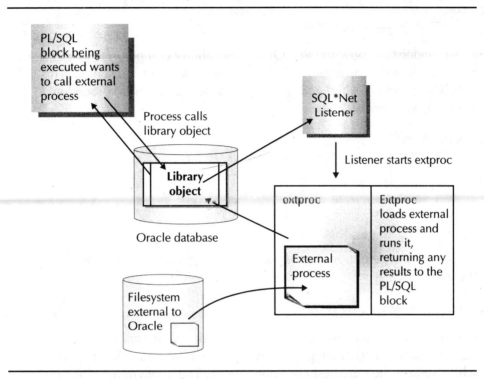

FIGURE 22-2. *Process for executing external procedures*

the external procedure runs. Extproc then loads the shared library that is used for executing the external procedure, after which time the external procedure can be run. The result of this external procedure's execution is then returned to the PL/SQL or SQL operation that called it.

The creation of the library object is accomplished with the **create or replace library** *name* **is** *path* statement, shown in the code block following this paragraph. Following the creation of the library object, PL/SQL procedures can then reference external procedures. To do so, the user must have **execute** privileges on the library object. Definitions for library objects can be found in the USER_, ALL, and DBA_LIBRARIES dictionary views. To create a library in their own schema, the user must have **create library** privileges, while to create a library anywhere in the database, the user must have **create any library** privileges. The path and filename defined for a library object is not checked until the object is referenced.

```
CREATE OR REPLACE LIBRARY sort_algorithm
IS '/DISK05/usr/bin/progsort';
```

To understand how the PL/SQL, C, and library components work in conjunction with one another, the following example is presented. This is a PL/SQL function called **gcd( )**, which registers an external procedure **c_gcd( )**, as follows:

```
CREATE FUNCTION gcd (
-- find greatest common divisor of x and y
    x BINARY_INTEGER,
    y BINARY_INTEGER)
RETURN BINARY_INTEGER AS EXTERNAL LIBRARY c_utils
    NAME "c_gcd"  -- quotes preserve lower case
    LANGUAGE C;
```

The library definition then would be created with a code block similar to the following:

```
CREATE LIBRARY c_utils AS '/DLLs/utils.so';
```

In this example, you call PL/SQL function **gcd( )** from an anonymous block. PL/SQL passes the two integer parameters to external function **c_gcd( )**, which returns their greatest common divisor. The anonymous block is listed below:

```
DECLARE
    g BINARY_INTEGER;
    a BINARY_INTEGER;
    b BINARY_INTEGER;
    ...
BEGIN
    ...
    g := gcd(a,b);  -- call function
    IF g IN (2,4,8) THEN ...
```

Exercises

1. What is a library schema object? What statement is used to create it?

2. What is the extproc process? What process executes it? How does this process know how to connect to extproc? What parameter file is this information stored in?

Oracle8 New ROWID Format

In this section, you will cover the following topics related to Oracle8 new ROWID format:

- Describing the new ROWID format
- Using the new ROWID format
- Using the DBMS_ROWID package

With new objects and greater size comes the need for accessing those new objects in a new and bigger way. In the versions that preceded Oracle8, all access to data in the database is managed with the use of ROWID data consisting of three elements: data block identifier, row number in the block, and datafile identifier. Additional reference information for objects in Oracle8—such as table and index partitions, and the increases in the amount of data Oracle8 can store—require that new components be included in the ROWID format. This section will detail those changes.

Describing the New ROWID Format

The new ROWID format uses the following conventions. It is an 18-character representation of the location of data in the database, with each character represented in a base-64 format consisting of A–Z, a–z, 0–9, + and /. The new ROWID format consists of four components, described here and in Figure 22-3:

- Database object number
- Relative datafile number
- Data block number
- Row number (also called the slot number)

ABAcZA	AA/	AxCDa+	Dbs
Object number	Relative datafile number	Data block number	Row or "slot" number

FIGURE 22-3. *Extended ROWID format in Oracle8*

Note that the name of the second component of the new ROWID format is a "relative" datafile number. Relative is the operative term. ROWID format in Oracle7 is a unique method of identification for row data for the life of the row in the database. In contrast, Oracle8 uses ROWID as a unique identifier, but not as an absolute locator address because each database object can belong to a different tablespace, and each tablespace can have the same datafile numbers as another tablespace. However, the numbering of datafiles in one tablespace must be unique. This idea of tablespace-relative addressing is crucial for the support of VLDBs. One of the key new elements in the Oracle8 ROWID format is the database object number. This feature of the new ROWID format corresponds to the value stored in the data dictionary view called DBA_OBJECTS in the OBJECT_ID and DATA_OBJECT_ID columns. With the object number, Oracle8 can identify which tablespace contains the object. Oracle increments this number as the DBA truncates the table or moves table partitions.

Exercises

1. What are the three components of the Oracle7 ROWID format? What are the four components of the Oracle8 ROWID format? What are some differences between the purpose of the ROWID in Oracle7 and the ROWID in Oracle8?

2. What notation does each character in the ROWID use?

Using the New ROWID Format

Oracle8 supports the Oracle7 ROWID format for purposes of supporting database migration. For the most part, the Oracle7 ROWID format is useful enough for locating information because Oracle can derive the tablespace in which an object is stored in, and since Oracle7 objects cannot span multiple tablespaces, the datafile number can be determined accurately. Oracle7 ROWID format cannot be used for global indexes on tables that are partitioned because tables with partitions can span more than one tablespace, making it impossible to determine absolutely which relative datafile is referenced by the datafile number in the restricted ROWID format. Oracle7 ROWID format takes 6 bytes to store.

In contrast, Oracle8 ROWID format takes 10 bytes to store. When row location must be absolute, Oracle uses the extended format provided by Oracle8 ROWIDs. The situations where Oracle uses this format is when handling global indexes on partitioned tables and in several internal processes. Backward compatibility works best, where Oracle8 can query Oracle7 ROWIDs with little difficulty. To understand Oracle8 ROWID information from Oracle7 databases, the DBMS_ROWID package must be used.

For the most part, there should be little problem with the new ROWID format used in Oracle8. However, there may arise situations where the new ROWID format may cause issues with the operation of database applications. If the application accesses data via ROWID directly, the developers of the application will have to utilize the DBMS_ROWID package to manipulate ROWID data. Also, if a table contains a column declared to be of type ROWID, there may be some migration issues. In general, if an application creates ROWID information or interprets ROWID information without the assistance of the Oracle database, then the DBMS_ROWID package must be used to ease migration concerns. Other than those situations, there should be few, if any, issues for migration related to Oracle8 ROWIDs.

Exercises

1. What are some situations where the migration of the database needn't encounter difficulty with ROWID data?

2. What are some situations where the migration of the database may encounter difficulty with ROWID data? What is the name of the package that may be used to overcome difficulties with ROWID migration?

Using the DBMS_ROWID Package

The DBMS_ROWID package is created by the **dbmsutil.sql** script, which in turn is created by executing the **catproc.sql** script. This package creates several stored procedures used for manipulating ROWIDs. There are two uses for the DBMS_ROWID package. The first is to migrate restricted

Oracle7 ROWID information to the extended Oracle8 ROWID format. The other is to interpret the ROWID information.

Migrating to Extended ROWIDs

The DBMS_ROWID functions to be used for database ROWID migration are as follows, along with explanations:

- **ROWID_TO_EXTENDED( )** Converts Oracle7 ROWID format to Oracle8

- **ROWID_TO_RESTRICTED( )** Converts Oracle8 ROWID format to Oracle7

- **ROWID_VERIFY( )** Identifies whether or not an Oracle7 ROWID can be converted to Oracle8 using the **rowid_to_extended( )** function

Perhaps the most important function of this set is the **rowid_to_extended( )** function. This function performs the actual conversion of data from the old ROWID format to the new. It is not necessary to apply this function to the tables of the database to convert the ROWID pseudocolumn present on tables to use for locating data quickly in the table. However, if the table has a column defined on it of type ROWID that contains this type of data for the application's use, the **rowid_to_extended( )** function can be used to convert these columns. There are four variables that are passed to the function: *old_rowid, schema_name, object_name,* and *conversion_type.* The *old_rowid* variable identifies the name of the table column to be converted whose datatype is ROWID. The *schema_name* variable is the name of the user who owns the table undergoing conversion. The *object_name* variable identifies the name of the table containing a column declared with datatype ROWID about to be converted. The *conversion_type* variable can have two values: 0 for an actual conversion of data stored in a ROWID column and 1 for the representation of the Oracle7 restricted ROWID in Oracle8 extended format.

The **rowid_verify( )** function uses the same parameters, but simply returns 0 if the ROWID can be converted or 1 if the ROWID cannot be converted. Conversion can run in the other direction also with the use of the **rowid_to_restricted( )** function. This function uses only two variables passed into it: *old_rowid* and *conversion_type*. The *old_rowid* variable identifies the ROWID data in extended Oracle8 format. The *conversion_type* variable is the same as above, and can have two values. 0 for an actual conversion of data stored in a ROWID column and 1 for the representation of the Oracle7 restricted ROWID in Oracle8 extended format.

DBMS_ROWID Information Functions

The DBMS_ROWID functions to be used for gaining database ROWID information are as follows, along with explanations:

- **ROWID_TYPE( )**   Returns 0 if the ROWID is the restricted Oracle7 type, 1 if the ROWID is the extended Oracle8 type

- **ROWID_OBJECT( )**   Returns the object number corresponding to the ROWID given, the first component of the extended ROWID

- **ROWID_RELATIVE_FNO( )**   Returns the relative datafile number for the ROWID given, the second component of the extended ROWID

- **ROWID_BLOCK_NUMBER( )**   Returns the data block number for the ROWID given, the third component of the extended ROWID

- **ROWID_ROW_NUMBER( )**   Returns the block row or slot number for the ROWID given, the fourth component of the extended ROWID

- **ROWID_TO_ABSOLUTE_FNO( )**   Returns the absolute datafile number for the ROWID given

All but one of these functions accept one variable as input: *row_id*, which is the ROWID the executor of the function wishes to obtain information about. The one function that accepts multiple variables as input is the **rowid_to_absolute_rowid( )** function. This function accepts a *row_id*, *schema*, and *object_name* input variables, in that order, to give the absolute location on disk for the given ROWID. The most important functions in this set of functions are the **rowid_type( )**, **rowid_object( )**, and

rowid_to_absolute_fno( ) functions, as they provide helpful information to the DBA that is useful for dissecting and interpreting ROWID data.

In addition to functions, there are two procedures in the DBMS_ROWID called **rowid_info( )** and **rowid_create( )**. The **rowid_info( )** procedure accepts one variable as input, a ROWID, and returns five variables as output. The first of the return variables is *rowid_type*, which may be equal to 0 to represent a restricted Oracle7 ROWID or 1 to represent an Oracle8 extended ROWID. The other four, *object_number*, *relative_fno*, *block_number*, and *row_number* give the four components of the extended ROWID. If the ROWID is a restricted Oracle7 format, then the return value for *object_number* will be NULL. The **rowid_create( )** procedure is useful for testing in that it creates a test ROWID.

Exercises

1. Which function converts Oracle7 restricted ROWID data to extended Oracle 8 format? What are the four input variables it accepts?

2. What procedure takes a ROWID and returns its type and all of its components?

Oracle8 Object Relational Concepts

In this section, you will cover the following topics related to Oracle8 object relational concepts:

- Defining an object relational database
- Describing the object concepts in Oracle8
- Creating a basic object type
- Reference and collection types
- Creating and using an object view

The final, and perhaps most interesting, area of Oracle8 is the introduction of the object relational database architecture, which has been called Oracle's revolutionary, or at least evolutionary, approach to the future of object-oriented database design. This section will cover several basic areas of Oracle8 object relational database design concepts, including the definition of an object relational database, the object concepts available in Oracle8, the creation of a basic object type, and the creation and use of an object view. These terms, as well as their use, will be defined shortly.

Defining an Object Relational Database

There are several features in an object relational database. Fundamental to the use of an object relational database is the existence of a system for users to define their own information or datatypes. Once defined, these types are usable everywhere Oracle uses its own predefined datatypes. In addition, the object relational database should allow the developers of applications on the database to create a layer of abstraction on the relational tables already defined in the database to support the treatment of those tables as objects. This feature is called an *object view*.

An object relational database should also support the storage of large amounts of data, along with the storage of large individual units of information. In Oracle8, they are called large objects, and several new large object (LOB) datatypes have been created to support their storage and manipulation, both inside and outside the database. Oracle has defined object relational databases to support the use of data cartridges—pieces of software that can be "plugged into" the Oracle database to support additional features. The delivery of objects to the client and manipulation of those objects via the application are also supported by Oracle in Oracle8. Finally, an object relational database should deliver improved performance for data processing applications, online transaction processing, fast SQL processing, support for large databases, and security.

Use of object technology allows for several benefits in database design. With abstract datatypes and detail hidden behind object technology, maintenance costs may be reduced and applications produced faster than using relational technology. The code produced will also offer some ability for reuse once a sufficient body of code is established.

Exercises

1. What are the features of an object relational database?

2. What are some of the benefits for using object technology in a database?

Describing the Object Concepts in Oracle8

The importance of using objects is growing in the development of database applications. In the world of software development, objects have helped developers realize the dream of data abstraction behind two concepts: attributes and methods. In relational databases, the concepts of data abstraction provided through entity-relationship diagrams and logical data models often lose their simplicity when turned into physical database design. This loss of abstraction has a great deal to do with the fundamental premise of relational database design—the tables columns, foreign keys—in short, the details of the relational database itself.

The fundamental concept behind an object relational database is the concept of an object. Objects are designed to allow developers to model business situations and real things using advanced use of types. The object methodology allows the developer to hide complexity. Instead of creating tables designed to fit the needs of one or two situations, the database can be composed of more atomic types that can be combined with other types or individual columns to define object tables. Objects are composed of two parts: *attributes* and *methods*. An attribute is to an object as table columns are to a table. Interestingly, in E. F. Codd's original presentation of relational database theory, the name for columns that comprise a "relation" (read: table) was "attributes." For example, the attributes of a paycheck object may consist of a *payee, payer, check_number, date_issued, payment_authorization, payer_account_number, routing_number,* and *payment_amount.* Even though there are hundreds of different banks and millions of payers and payees, all checks issued boil down to these components. The second area of objects is called the methods, or activities that take place in relation to the check. These methods may be written in PL/SQL, so they can operate internally within the Oracle database, or externally in C to be accessed as library objects. Some of these methods include *issue, stop_payment* and *adjust_amount.* Figure 22-4 illustrates the attributes and methods that may be used to define a check object.

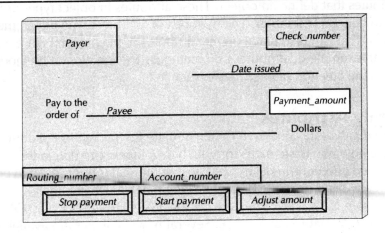

FIGURE 22-4.   *A check object with attributes and methods*

There are several key features implemented in Oracle8 to support the use of object technology. Oracle8 supports object types, which are user-defined datatypes used to define the objects. Also, Oracle8 supports the retroactive application of object technology onto existing relational database components. There are extensions to SQL and PL/SQL to handle access to object tables as well. Finally, the use of Oracle precompilers such as Pro*C continues to be possible in the face of object technology with the advent of new features to access object tables as well.

Exercises

1. What is an object? What two elements comprise objects?

2. How does Oracle8 support the application of object technology to relational database design?

3. How does Oracle8 support access to database objects?

Creating a Basic Object Type

The cornerstone of object relational design is the use of object types. Object types are user-defined datatypes, the design of which allows users to create the attributes that define an object. These attributes in object types are similar to columns for tables. The methods of an object type define the operations that can take place on the attributes of the object. Figure 22-4 defines an example of attributes and methods. The creation of methods is similar to the creation of packages in Oracle7.

Creating Attributes

The new datatypes available in Oracle8 relate to the creation of attributes. There are now two basic paths for which developers can define their types: user-defined and built-in datatypes. Most of the scalar built-in datatypes have already been defined. There are several datatypes in Oracle8 that were also available in Oracle7. They are CHAR, VARCHAR2, LONG, LONG RAW, RAW, NUMBER, and DATE. Several new datatypes are available in Oracle8. They include the new NLS datatypes NCHAR and NVARCHAR2. Oracle8 includes new methods to deal with large database objects, also called LOBs: BLOB, CLOB, NCLOB, and BFILE. More information about the datatypes in Oracle8 appears in Chapter 23. In addition to scalar datatypes, Oracle8's object programming allows for a few collection datatypes, called VARRAY (variable array) and TABLE (nested table), and a relationship datatype called REF (reference). User-defined *object types* are created as combinations of these scalar, collection, and reference datatypes. Creation of object types can be used to support several activities. Object types can be used in the following different ways:

- As columns in relational tables
- As attributes in objects
- In object views to create retroactive object databases out of relational ones
- As local variables in PL/SQL
- As type definitions in order to create object tables

The **create type** statement can be used to create object types. Several restrictions on creating object types exist. First, the object type cannot contain the LONG or LONG RAW scalar datatypes, the ROWID type, or any referential datatype created with the **%type** keyword in PL/SQL. The names of attributes must be unique in any single object type definition, but the same attribute name can be used in different object type definitions, even in the same schema. The rules governing naming object types in Oracle8 are the same rules defining the naming of columns in Oracle7, which have already been discussed. Remember, they can be no longer than 30 alphanumeric characters, including A–Z, a–z, #, $, and _. An example of the creation of an object type appears in the following code block:

```
CREATE TYPE paycheck_type AS OBJECT (
    check_number          NUMBER(20),
    payer                 VARCHAR2(40),
    payee                 VARCHAR2(40),
    date_issued           DATE,
    payment_authorization VARCHAR2(3),
    payer_account_number  VARCHAR2(20),
    routing_number        VARCHAR2(20),
    payment_amount        NUMBER(10));
```

There are three different means of identification for different user-defined types. Simple types contain all scalar, collector, and reference datatypes available in Oracle8. Composite object types have more than one attribute that is an object type. Self-referencing types contain attributes of the same object type as the one being defined. The object definition in the previous code block is a simple type, because all attributes are of the VARCHAR2, NUMBER, or DATE datatypes. Once the object type is created, a relational table can be created using the standard **create table** statement, or an object table can be defined using the **create table of** statement. A column is created implicitly in an object table to store a special value called an *object identifier*. The values stored in this column for each object can be used to identify the object as unique in the object table. No such object identifier exists in a relational table to identify unique objects. The following code block illustrates the creation of a relational table and an object table:

```
-- relational table
CREATE TABLE payroll_jul0613_reltbl
( empid        VARCHAR2(10) NOT NULL,
  emp_check  paycheck_type,
  CONSTRAINT pk_payroll_jul0613
  PRIMARY KEY (empid));

-- object table
CREATE TABLE paycheck_jul0613_objtbl
OF paycheck_type;
```

There are different ways to reference data in a relational table containing object definitions and an object table. Selection of data from attributes of the object "column" (EMP_CHECK in this case) is done using dot notation to first reference the column name and then the attribute of the column. For example, user SALLY with EMPID 59385 can obtain the paycheck number for this pay period with a **select** statement that uses dot notation to refer to the *check_number* attribute on the EMP_CHECK column of the PAYROLL_JUL0613_RELTBL table. Examples of the **select** statements used for relational and object tables in this case appear in the following code block:

```
-relational table
SELECT p.emp_check.check_number
FROM payroll_jul0613_reltbl p
WHERE empid = 59385;

-object table
SELECT check_number FROM payroll_jul0613_objtbl
WHERE empid=59385;
```

To **insert** data into an object column, the user must refer to the object type that defines the column. This reference is called a *constructor*. The constructor is used for insertion of data into object tables as well. The use of **insert** statements on a relational and object table with use of constructors is listed in the following code block:

```
INSERT INTO paycheck_jul0613_reltbl
VALUES (39283,
        paycheck_type(4596854,'Acme','HANSON','14-JUL-2002',
                'YES','59439585','00584857479',2016.96);

INSERT INTO paycheck_jul0613_objtbl
VALUES(paycheck_type(4596854,'Acme','HANSON','14-JUL-2002',
                'YES','59439585','00584857479',2016.96);
```

Creating Methods

The other component of an object is the set of methods that can be used to operate on it. Each method is a member function that contains input parameters and output values in the same way that procedures and functions have. In fact, the methods of an object are procedures and functions developed to operate specifically on the attributes defined as part of the object type. Unlike in Oracle7, however, where tables and procedures are designed, stored, and used separately, member functions and procedures are defined directly within the object type. One similarity the definition of the object type shares with something in Oracle7 is the use of package specifications and package bodies. In Oracle7, the developer can create a package specification to tell users of the package what procedures are available in the package. The body of the package is defined separately, and contains the application logic to be executed when someone references the procedure and passes the required parameters. The definition of an object type including some member functions is listed in the following code block:

```
CREATE TYPE paycheck_type AS OBJECT (
    check_number            NUMBER(20),
    payer                   VARCHAR2(40),
    payee                   VARCHAR2(40),
    date_issued             DATE,
    payment_authorization   VARCHAR2(3),
    payer_account_number    VARCHAR2(20),
    routing_number          VARCHAR2(20),
    payment_amount          NUMBER(10),
    MEMBER FUNCTION adjust_amount (check_number IN NUMBER(10),
                                   deduct_amount  IN NUMBER(10))
                                   RETURN NUMBER,
    PRAGMA RESTRICT_REFERENCES (adjust_amount, WNDS));
```

Though not necessary, the developer can identify whether the type methods will modify database tables or not using the **pragma restrict_references** clause. The developer must identify the procedure or function that **restrict_references** refers to and the restrictions on the references of the procedure or function. In this case, **wnds** was used, which stands for "write no database state." Once the type is defined both with attributes and methods, then the developer can create the code body for the procedures, defined separately in the type body.

```
CREATE TYPE BODY paycheck_type AS MEMBER FUNCTION adjust_amount
( check_number in NUMBER(20),
  deduct_amount in NUMBER(10)
) RETURN NUMBER IS
BEGIN
```

```
RETURN check_number - deduct_amount;
END; /* first end for member function end */
END;   /* second end for type body end      */
```

The applications can then refer to the methods for an object type using the same dot notation used to reference the attributes. The following PL/SQL statement demonstrates the use of a method from the PAYCHECK type to **update** the data in an attribute. The **value( )** operation in the following PL/SQL block is designed to return all attribute values stored in an object so that those values may be placed into a variable declared to be the same type as the object table.

```
DECLARE
    my_paycheck        paycheck_type;
    my_pay_amount      NUMBER(10);
BEGIN
    SELECT VALUE(p)
    INTO my_paycheck
    FROM paycheck_jul0613_objtbl p
    WHERE check_number = 4596854;

    UPDATE paycheck_jul0613_objtbl
    SET payment_amount = my_paycheck.adjust_amount(my_
                    paycheck.check_number,200)
    WHERE check_number = my_paycheck.check_number;
END;
```

The creation of object types leads to the question of how to compare them. One handy method the developer may want to consider adding to every object type is the *map* or *order* method. It is simple to compare two columns in a relational table—the user can do so based on the value for some column, defined with a scalar datatype. This operation can extend into the world of object types as well, although inefficiently because the user must compare every attribute of one object to every attribute of the other. Oracle answers this question with the use of *map* methods and *order* methods. A *map* method is designed to tell the developer where the object appears in a group of objects, while the *order* method can be used to apply order to a set of objects.

Exercises

1. What are the attributes of an object type? What are three different categories of object types? How do the attributes of the object type determine its category?

2. What are the methods of an object type? What two components are there to the definition of the methods for an object type?

3. What statement is used to create an object table? What is a constructor?

Reference and Collection Types

So far, all object types discussed have been simple types containing attributes declared with all scalar datatypes. Oracle8 also allows the definition of two new classes of datatypes, called *reference* types and *collection* types. These two datatypes are designed to allow object types to have referential integrity on a one-to-one and one-to-many level. However, reference and collection types extend the concept of referential integrity to a new level. In relational databases, foreign keys provide referential integrity between columns of the same datatype containing the same data. Reference datatypes are used to provide a one-to-one relationship between a row of an object table or object type column of a relational table and another object table or object type column of a relational table. Collection types are designed to store a grouping or collection of like-structured elements, to provide a one-to-many relationship in the same situation. This section will explain reference and collection types in further detail and provide syntax and examples for the creation of each.

Reference Types

Developers can use the reference type to define a "foreign key relationship" between two objects. The reference type can reference all columns in the table for a particular row—it is a pointer to a particular object within an object table. The definition of a reference type should include a definition of *scope*—the table to which the reference type will refer. A special keyword called **ref** should be used for defining the reference type. The definition of the reference type is demonstrated with the following code block:

```
CREATE TYPE debit_payroll_type AS OBJECT
 (acc_wd_num     NUMBER(10),
  debit          REF paycheck_type);
```

```
CREATE TABLE debit_jul0613_objreftbl
OF debit_payroll_type
(SCOPE FOR (debit) IS paycheck_jul0613_objtbl)
```

Once the reference type is defined, a special operation can be used to **insert** the pointer contained in columns defined as reference types into other tables so that the columns can reference the data for that object in another table. When handling data in conjunction with a reference type, the **ref( )** operation can be used as demonstrated in the following code block:

```
INSERT INTO debit_jul0613_objreftbl
  SELECT 1, REF(pc)
  FROM paycheck_jul0613_objtbl pc
  WHERE pc.check_number=4596854;
```

Important to remember in the example code block is that the *paycheck* object from object table PAYCHECK_JUL0613_OBJTBL whose *check_number* equals 4596854 is *not actually* inserted into object table DEBIT_JUL0613_OBJREFTBL. Instead, Oracle8 has created a *pointer to the object*! Recall, a reference type is a pointer to an object, not the object itself. Thus, table DEBIT_JUL0613_OBJREFTBL is less a table in and of itself, and more a new perspective on the PAYCHECK_JUL0613_OBJTBL table. Thus, selecting the reference type itself using the **ref( )** operation produces not the data in the object, but the pointer used to refer to the object. The user can use the pointer value created as the reference type and execute a special function called **deref( )** to produce the actual values from the pointer to those values.

```
SELECT DEREF(d.debit)
FROM debit_jul0613_objreftbl d
WHERE d.check_number = 4596854;

DEREF(D.DEBIT)
----------------------------------------------------------------
--------
PAYCHECK_TYPE(4596854,'Acme','HANSON','14-JUL-2002','NO',59439585,
00584857479, 2016.96)
```

Collection Types

Objects can be collected into types. A collection is a gathering of like-defined elements. The two types of collection types available in Oracle8 are variable-length arrays with the VARRAY type and nested tables with the TABLE type. Focus first on VARRAYs. A VARRAY can be thought of as a "list" of objects, defined to have two special attributes in addition to those attributes contained in each of the objects contained therein, called a *count* for the number of elements in the VARRAY, and the *limit* for the maximum number of elements that can appear in a VARRAY. The limit is user defined, and if the number of elements stored in the VARRAY exceeds 4K, Oracle will store the data in the VARRAY in overflow. If the amount of data stored in the VARRAY is less than 4K, the data will be stored with the rest of the information for the object. Constraints and default values may not be created for elements in a VARRAY, and once created, the user only refers to an individual element in a VARRAY with PL/SQL (although SQL can be used to access the entire VARRAY). Using the payroll examples already covered, a user-defined type can be created for each employee of an organization, along with all the paychecks the employee received for the year, by *check_number*, and the amount the check was made out for, using a VARRAY created in the following way. Once created, the developer has an object table containing three elements: the employee's unique ID, the employee name, and a 52-element array of check numbers and payment amounts.

```
CREATE TYPE pmt_rec_type AS OBJECT
(check_num       NUMBER(20),
 amount          NUMBER(10));

CREATE TYPE ann_pmt_rec_type AS VARRAY(52)
OF pmt_rec_type;

CREATE TYPE emp_paycheck_type AS OBJECT
(empid           VARCHAR2(10),
 name            VARCHAR2(40),
 emp_ann_pmt     ann_pmt_rec_type);

CREATE TABLE emp_paycheck
OF emp_paycheck_type;
```

The other collection type is the nested table. A nested table is exactly that—a table within a table. The nested table architecture is exceptionally suited for applications that in Oracle7 have parent/child tables with referential integrity. An example of the type of application suited for the use of nested tables from earlier in the Guide is the EXPENSE and EXPENSE_DETAIL tables, where the employee's expenses were identified at a high level with the EXPENSE table, and individual expenses were identified as EXPENSE_DETAIL records. Use of nested table object creation for employee expenses is demonstrated in the following code block:

```
CREATE TYPE expense_detail_type AS OBJECT
(expense_detail_num    NUMBER(10),
 expense_detail_desc   VARCHAR2(40),
 expense_detail_amount NUMBER(15,4),
 chargeback_acct       VARCHAR2(40));

CREATE TYPE expdtl_nest_tbl_type AS TABLE
OF expense_detail_type;

CREATE TABLE expense
(expense_num       NUMBER(10),
 empid             VARCHAR2(20),
 reimburse_amount  NUMBER(15,4),
 expense_details   expdtl_nest_tbl_type)
NESTED TABLE expense_details STORE AS expense_detail_nesttbl;
```

Nested tables and variable-length arrays share many similarities, but also have many differences. The differences between the nested table and a variable-length array can be identified as follows. The VARRAY works well for storing like units of information. These units ideally have few attributes, all of which may be populated and to which a specific order can be placed. Consider the example given of employee annual paycheck information. Each element in the array corresponds directly to the pay week for the year, in which order is important. With the presence of a *limit* attribute, the VARRAY also stores only a limited number of elements, while the nested table may store an unlimited number of objects, just as the base object table can. Another key difference between VARRAY and nested table data is indexing. An object column composed of VARRAY types cannot be indexed, while a nested table can be indexed. Storage for VARRAY data is also integrated with the storage segments of the data in the object table, up to a certain size. Data in nested tables is stored in another segment. In order to determine which object to use, consider the following rules of thumb:

- If the amount of data to be stored in the collection object is under 4K, well defined, and limited in number, use VARRAY; otherwise, use TABLE.

- If individual items in the collection object must be accessed, use TABLE; otherwise, use VARRAY.

- If the data in the collection object must be indexed for performance, use TABLE; otherwise, use VARRAY.

Exercises

1. What is a reference type? What is a collection type? How do reference and collection types model referential integrity? What ordinality is provided by reference and collection types within that referential integrity model?

2. What data is stored in the reference type? What special keyword must be used in conjunction with defining a reference type? What is the **deref( )** operation?

3. How is a variable-length array defined? How is a nested table defined? Identify key differences between the variable array and the nested table.

Creating and Using an Object View

The final area of object relational databases to be discussed is the process of evolving a relational application into an object application. Although there is no pressing need to migrate a relational application into an object one, the organization may want to do so for several reasons, including the fact that object applications have more features for advanced data definition and usage. To ease the transition, object views can be created to allow object applications to access relational database objects, allowing for coexistence of both types of applications using the same base data. Object views are similar to Oracle7 views in that both views provide a method for simplifying the underlying complexity of data. In addition, object views allow the user to apply object concepts to relational data. Object views even allow for advanced **update** of data in relational tables via object views using **instead of** triggers.

Creation of object views begins with the creation of relational database objects like tables. Since the object view is designed to assist in the evolution of a relational database into an object database, it is assumed the developer understands the creation of relational tables. The creation of relational tables is covered in Chapters 3 and 6.

```
CREATE TABLE employee
(empid          VARCHAR2(10)     NOT NULL,
 lastname       VARCHAR2(30),
 firstname      VARCHAR2(30),
 salary         NUMBER(15,4),
CONSTRAINT pk_employee_01
PRIMARY KEY (empid));

CREATE TABLE address
(empid          VARCHAR2(10) NOT NULL,
 street1        VARCHAR2(30),
 street2        VARCHAR2(30),
 city           VARCHAR2(30),
 state_prov     VARCHAR2(30),
 postcode       VARCHAR2(30),
 CONSTRAINT pk_address_01
 PRIMARY KEY (empid));
```

From the columns in these tables, the developer can create a more aggregate employee object view to represent the employee's name, salary, and address using user-defined types that reflect the definitions of the object. First, the creation of some object types to facilitate object design is in order. In this example, the most easily identifiable object is the collection of columns that define an address, as displayed in the example below:

```
CREATE TYPE address_type AS OBJECT
(street1        VARCHAR2(30),
 street2        VARCHAR2(30),
 city           VARCHAR2(30),
 state_prov     VARCHAR2(30),
 postcode       VARCHAR2(30));
```

After creating the object type, the developer can then create the object view, using the object type and the other columns from the original relational tables. The following block identifies that view:

```
CREATE OR REPLACE VIEW employee_obj_view AS
  SELECT e.empid, e.lastname, e.firstname, e.salary,
    address_type(a.street1,a.street2,a.city,a.state_prov,a.postcode)
  FROM  employee e, address a
  WHERE e.empid = a.empid;
```

After the view is created, the developer can create a special trigger designed to ease the insertion of data into the relational table from the object application. This trigger is called an **instead of** trigger because the syntax for defining the trigger is **create trigger instead of**. The creation of an **instead of** trigger to support insertion of data on the object view created in this section appears in the following code block:

```
CREATE OR REPLACE TRIGGER empl_trigger INSTEAD OF
  INSERT ON employee_obj_view FOR EACH ROW
  BEGIN
    INSERT INTO employee VALUES
    (:NEW.empid, :NEW.lastname, :NEW.firstname, :NEW.salary);
    INSERT INTO address VALUES
    (:NEW.street1, :NEW.street2, :NEW.city,
     :NEW.state_prov, :NEW.postcode);
  END;
```

Once the **instead of** trigger is created, the user can **insert** data into the relational tables via object views. A **constructor** (described earlier in this chapter for use during the insertion of data into object types in relational tables or object tables) can be used for inserting data into object views.

```
INSERT INTO employee_obj_view VALUES
(49384,'MANFRAN','HARVEY','90000',
 address_type('506 Pudding Street','Apt. Q','Moan','WY','70506'));
```

Exercises

1. What is an object view?

2. What device is used to **insert** data into relational tables via object views?

3. How does the use of constructors relate to the insertion of data into relational tables via the object views?

Chapter Summary

This chapter discusses three new areas of database usage operation in Oracle8. The topics include new database structures related to indexes, the new extended ROWID structure used for referencing an increased number of objects in more tablespaces and datafiles, and the new object development architecture available for server-side object relational database development.

The first area discussed was the new database structures available in Oracle8. The new release of the Oracle8 database supports larger databases than ever before. Total database capacity is 512 petabytes, the maximum number of tablespaces allowed is about 2 billion, the number of datafiles per tablespace is 1,022, the number of columns supported in a table is now 1,000, and the maximum number of indexed columns is 32. The CHAR datatype now supports 2,000 bytes and the VARCHAR2 datatype now supports 4,000 bytes, and Oracle supports national language character sets more easily with the new NCHAR and NVARCHAR types. Oracle8 also supports new features for declarative integrity constraints. This includes new **enable validate** and **enable novalidate** statuses. The **enable validate** status in Oracle8 is the same as the old **enabled** status of Oracle7. The **enable novalidate** status of Oracle8 specifies that the constraint affects the entry of new data into the database but doesn't apply to old data. These statuses can be used with the issuance of the **alter table** *table_name* **enable novalidate constraint** *constraint_name* or **alter table** *name* **enable validate constraint** *constraint_name* statements. Users now have the ability to defer the checking of integrity constraints until the time of a **commit**, rather than at the time the statement is executed. To defer all constraints that are set to be deferrable, the user can issue the **alter session set constraints=deferred** statement.

There are many new relational database objects available for the use of developers and DBAs to store and retrieve information. They include the presence of a *reverse-key index*, an index that stores key data reversed to improve index search performance in parallel configurations. Reverse-key indexes are created with the same **create index** statement as regular indexes, but the **reverse** keyword is used. An index can be reversed or unreversed with the use of the **alter index reverse/noreverse** statement. Another new feature is the index-organized table. This object stores all the data of a table in the format of a B-tree index, which is useful for storing data that will mainly be retrieved according to the primary key. Since the features of the table and the index are consolidated into one object, less space is used. An index-organized table is created with the **create table organization index** statement, to which the **pctthreshold** and **overflow tablespace** options can be added to keep key data for each row in the main index block structure while allowing extra space for row growth. An interesting point to be made here is that regular tables are created with an implicit **organization heap** clause, which can now be stated explicitly if the DBA would like.

There is an additional memory area the DBA can set up with Oracle8 called the large pool. The large pool stores session memory for the multithreaded server (MTS) configuration, I/O processes, and backup and recovery processes. Some of these processes require memory from the shared pool that can better be used to store shared SQL parse information. The large pool does not have an LRU algorithm for paging items out of memory. The large pool is configured with the LARGE_POOL_SIZE and LARGE_POOL_MIN_ALLOC parameters, which identify the size of the large pool and the minimum size a process can allocate, respectively. The defaults for these parameters are 300K and 16K, respectively, although LARGE_POOL_SIZE will default to LARGE_POOL_MIN_ALLOC if the second parameter is larger than 300K. The large pool can be at least as large as 2G, with physical/virtual memory permitting. Don't ever size the large pool such that the entire SGA cannot fit into real memory—it is a performance killer!

Another new feature of the Oracle8 database is its ability to allow PL/SQL processes to call external procedures using library objects. Library objects can be thought of as aliases to the external processes, which must be written in C or converted into C to be executed. To create a library, use the **create or replace library** *name* **as** *file* statement. To run an external procedure, the PL/SQL procedure calls the library object, which then passes the request to the listener. The listener then spawns a special new process called *extproc*, whose location and characteristics are listed in the **listener.ora** file. Extproc then loads the external procedure, executes it with any parameters specified by the PL/SQL procedure that called it, and then returns any return data (if any) to the PL/SQL procedure.

To support the increased size for the Oracle8 database, an extended ROWID format is used. The Oracle7 ROWID format consists of three elements: block identifier, row identifier, and absolute datafile identifier. In contrast, the Oracle8 extended format for ROWID information consists of an object identifier, a relative datafile identifier, a block identifier, and a row or slot number. The Oracle7 ROWID format takes 6 bytes to store, while the Oracle8 ROWID format takes 10. The Oracle8 ROWID format representation is 18 characters long, with each character in a base-64 format. The range of characters used in ROWID representation are A–Z, a–z, 0–9, + and /.

Most applications should never have to worry about the new ROWID configuration in Oracle8. However, developers with applications that either read, create, or store ROWID information in any part of the database other than the ROWID pseudocolumn used to identify rows in the Oracle7 database should be aware of the existence of a special package called DBMS_ROWID. This package is designed to convert Oracle7 ROWID (also called restricted) format to Oracle8 (also called extended) ROWID format, and to display components of the extended ROWID format for better readability. Some important functions and procedures in the DBMS_ROWID package include **rowid_to_extended( )**, **rowid_to_restricted( )**, and **rowid_info( )**.

Perhaps the most interesting new feature in the Oracle8 architecture is the set of development structures that support the object relational features. This section covered the definition of Oracle's object relational database, which is the existence of mechanisms for users to create their own datatypes, support of multimedia and large datatypes, and mechanisms called object views that allow the developer to begin building object-oriented database design on existing relational database objects. Other features of the Oracle8 object relational architecture include use of software add-ons, called cartridges, that are designed to extend the functionality of the database in whatever manner necessary, and overall support of larger databases that provide additional storage and performance for accessing data.

In the Oracle8 architecture, every object starts with the definition of an object type. An object type is created with the **create or replace type as object** statement. An object type is defined to have two parts: attributes and methods. Attributes are features of the object that store data in predefined or user-defined datatypes, while methods are features of the object that allow a prescribed action to be performed in conjunction with the object. The first part of an object type is its attributes. The attributes of an object can fall into three definition types: scalar datatypes (such as CHAR, VARCHAR2, NUMBER, and DATE), collection types (VARRAY and TABLE), and reference

(REF). The scalar datatypes are the same as Oracle7 scalar datatypes, except that an object type cannot be defined with a LONG or LONG RAW attribute, or with any of the **%type** referential datatypes used in PL/SQL. The collection types are designed to store defined arrays of data (VARRAY) inline with the object, while the TABLE collection type is designed to allow the developer to create nested tables. The final collection type, REF, is designed to allow the user to create pointers to specific data elsewhere in the database by referencing it. The attribute defined as a REF type does not actually contain the data, only a pointer to it, but the pointer can be used to derive the data with the use of the **deref( )** operation on relational tables containing columns defined with REF object types, or with the **value( )** operation on object tables defined with REF types. The **value( )** operation is used to obtain the row object, but needn't be used in conjunction only with the REF type.

Once the object type attributes are defined, the developer can focus on creating methods. Methods are defined in the type as member functions, while the executable code that is associated with the object is defined as a type body. This setup is similar in concept to the creation of packages in PL/SQL. To create the type body, the **create or replace type body** statement can be used. Once the attributes and methods for the type are defined, the developer can create relational or object tables in the database based on the type. To manipulate or **insert** data into the database, the user must use the name of the object type in the **insert** statement to identify the values as attributes for that object. This reference to the object type is called a **constructor**.

Once the appropriate types are defined, the developer can use those types to create actual database objects like object tables and object views, or incorporate the object types into relational tables. A relational table containing object types is created with the same syntax as a relational table containing predefined scalar types. An object table is created after defining the object type using the **create table** *name* **of** *object_type* statement. An object view is a special view on relational tables that allows object applications to access them as though they were relational tables containing object types. The **create view** statement can be used for defining an object view so long as an appropriately defined object type is included in the definition. To **update**, **delete**, or **insert** data into the underlying relational tables associated with the object view, the developer can use a special trigger called an **instead of** trigger. This trigger inserts data into the underlying relational tables as defined by the trigger definition. The statement used to create this trigger is **create trigger** *name* **instead of**.

Two-Minute Drill

- Oracle8 supports increased database size and new database objects, as well as a new object relational database architecture.

- Total database capacity for database is 512 petabytes.

- The maximum number of tablespaces allowed is about 2 billion.

- The number of datafiles per tablespace is 1,022.

- The number of columns supported in a table is now 1,000.

- The maximum number of indexed columns is 32.

- The CHAR datatype now supports 2,000 bytes.

- The VARCHAR2 datatype now supports 4,000 bytes.

- The NCHAR and NVARCHAR2 datatypes are new in Oracle8, and are designed for national language support.

- Declarative integrity constraints have a new status—**enable novalidate**—which is used to enforce the constraint on new data coming into the database but not on data already in the database.

- Another status for constraints in Oracle7 called **enable** has been changed in Oracle8 to **enable validate** to enable the constraint and validate existing table data based on that constraint.

- An integrity constraint can be put into **enable novalidate** status using the **alter table** *name* **enable novalidate constraint** *constraint_name* statement.

- An integrity constraint can be put into **enable validate** status using the **alter table** *name* **enable validate constraint** *constraint_name* statement.

- Constraint enforcement can be deferred until a transaction commits. Normally, constraints are enforced when a statement executes.

- The ability to defer a constraint at all is built into the **create table** statement with clauses like **deferrable** and **not deferrable**, and the constraint's default behavior is defined with the **initially immediate** or **initially deferred** clauses.

- To defer constraints in the current session, issue the **alter session set constraints=deferred**.

- Data in index keys can be reversed or set to their original order using the **alter index** *name* **reverse/noreverse** statement. The index can be created with index keys reversed using the **create index reverse** statement.

- Reversing index keys is used to make data more accessible in parallel configurations.

- To minimize storage on tables that will only be accessed via the primary key, an index-organized table can be used.

- An index-organized table contains table data stored in a B-tree index structure. No additional indexes can be created on an index-organized table. However, the storage for the index-organized table is less than the storage required for an index and a table.

- An index-organized table is created with the **create table organization index** statement. Since the index is the table, there is no need for a ROWID on the row data stored in an index-organized table.

- A threshold limit for storage of any particular row in the blocks of the index-organized table can be set using the **pctthreshold** *num* **overflow tablespace** *tblspc* clause.

- A new column on DBA_, ALL_, and USER_TABLES called IOT indicates whether the table is index-organized. This column can contain *iot* for the index-organized table segment, *iot_overflow* for the index-organized table overflow segment, and NULL for any other table.

- The large pool is a new memory object in Oracle8 designed to store session information for multithreaded server and parallel server configurations. It can also support I/O processes and backup/recovery processes.

- Total large pool size is determined by the LARGE_POOL_SIZE initialization parameter.

- Minimum allocation of large pool space is determined by the LARGE_POOL_MIN_ALLOC initialization parameter.

- Maximum size of the large pool can be 2G or more. DBAs should be careful not to size the large pool such that the SGA will be larger than real memory can support.

- PL/SQL can call external procedures written in C using library objects.

- A library object is created with the **create or replace library** statement.

- The PL/SQL process calling the external procedure via the library object triggers the library object to call the listener process.

- The listener process spawns another process, called extproc, that actually loads and runs the external process, passing it any parameters supplied from PL/SQL. Extproc can also pass return values to the library object to be used by the PL/SQL process calling the database.

- The specification for loading and executing extproc can be found in the **listener.ora** file.

- Oracle8 supports a new extended ROWID format for accessing more data. This format consists of an object identifier, a relative filename identifier, a block identifier, and a row or slot identifier.

- Extended ROWID information is represented with 18 characters of base-64 format, with values in the ranges A–Z, a–z, 0–9, +, and /.

- Developers needn't worry about the changes to ROWID format unless they have an application that creates, reads, or stores ROWID data directly.

- If the application creates, reads, or stores ROWID data directly, then the DBMS_ROWID package can be used to manage transition.

- Key functions in DBMS_ROWID include **rowid_to_extended( )** and **rowid_to_restricted( )**, used to convert a ROWID to extended (Oracle8) or restricted (Oracle7) format.

■ A key procedure in DBMS_ROWID is **rowid_type( )**, which takes a ROWID as input and returns the components of that ROWID for easy readability.

■ Oracle8 supports object relational databases with the incorporation of object types for definition of user-defined datatypes, more built-in datatypes, larger capacity, faster performance, and use of data cartridges for add-on functionality.

■ Users may define their own datatypes with object types.

■ The two components of an object type are attributes and views. Object types are created with the **create or replace type** *name* **as object** statement.

■ Attributes are data storage components of the object defined to have either predefined scalar, collection, and reference datatypes, or other user-defined types.

■ A scalar datatype is any datatype available in Oracle7 (object types cannot include LONG, LONG RAW, NCHAR, and NVARCHAR2 attributes or attributes defined with referential datatypes using the **%type** keyword) and the new LOB datatypes available in Oracle8.

■ A collection datatype can be either a variable-length array (VARRAY) or a nested table (TABLE).

■ Though similar in that both variable arrays and nested tables can store multiple object "rows" in connection to a single "row" of data in another object, there are key differences between the two.

■ If the amount of data to be stored in the collection object is under 4K, well defined, and limited in number, use VARRAY; otherwise, use TABLE.

■ If individual items in the collection object must be accessed, use TABLE; otherwise, use VARRAY.

■ If the data in the collection object must be indexed for performance, use TABLE; otherwise, use VARRAY.

■ A reference type allows the developer to create pointers in one row of one object table to objects in another object table. The reference type doesn't contain the actual data; rather, it contains a pointer to the data in another object table.

- To obtain the actual data in another table using the pointer, the **deref( )** operation can be used for a relational table and the **value( )** operation can be used in object tables.

- Methods are the other component of an object type. They are used to define activities that can be performed in association with the object.

- Definition of methods is similar to use of packages, with a specification included in the type definition and a body containing the application logic. The type body is defined with a separate **create type body** statement.

- To **insert** data into a relational table or object table defined with an object type, that object type must be referenced by name in the **insert** statement. This reference is called a **constructor**.

- Object views are designed to ease transition from relational databases to object databases by creating an object structure over underlying relational tables.

- To **insert** data into the underlying relational data using object views, special triggers can be created, called **instead of** triggers. The syntax used is **create trigger** name **instead of**.

Chapter Questions

1. During normal database operation, the DBA notices that session information for shared servers crowds out shared SQL parse information in the shared pool. To combat this situation, the DBA can use which of the following methods?

    A. Increase value set for DB_BLOCK_BUFFERS

    B. Use dedicated servers

    C. Increase value set for DB_BLOCK_SIZE

    D. Increase value set for LARGE_POOL_SIZE

2. The best choice for decreasing size requirements for tables that need only be accessed via the primary key is

   A. Create more indexes on the table

   B. Create an index-organized table to store the data

   C. Drop the primary key

   D. Increase the **pctfree** value set for table blocks

3. Which of the following statements do *not* describe features of the VARRAY type? (Choose three)

   A. VARRAY allows indexes on attributes.

   B. VARRAY limits the number of elements placed in the object.

   C. VARRAY stores data in extents separate from the main object.

   D. VARRAY stores all data over 4 kilobytes inline.

4. The DBA has an Oracle7 relational table with a column containing ROWID data. What step may be required when migrating this table to Oracle8?

   A. Execute the **rowid_to_extended( )** function on the data in the column.

   B. Execute the **rowid_to_restricted( )** function on the data in the column.

   C. Execute the **rowid_type( )** procedure on the data in the column.

   D. Nothing—Oracle8 converts the ROWID automatically.

5. The user attempts to INSERT data into a column that would violate a nondeferrable constraint. The user has issued the ALTER SESSION SET CONSTRAINTS=DEFERRED statement. What happens on INSERT?

   A. The **insert** succeeds at the time it is issued, but the transaction will roll back later.

B. The **insert** fails at the time it is issued and the transaction will end.

C. The **insert** succeeds at the time it is issued and the transaction will not roll back later.

D. The **insert** fails at the time it is issued, but the transaction will continue.

6. The value stored in an index for a column is '596849'. The DBA then issues the ALTER INDEX REVERSE statement. What does the data in the index now look like?

    A. '596849'

    B. '849596'

    C. '948695'

    D. '695948'

7. The DBA needs to find information about how EXTPROC is being called. To find out more information, the DBA may want to look in which file?

    A. init.ora

    B. config.ora

    C. orapw*sid*.ora

    D. listener.ora

8. The datafile information stored in Oracle8's extended ROWID format details the absolute datafile location for that row of data.

    A. TRUE

    B. FALSE

9. Which prefix must be used when referencing values stored in columns defined with the NVARCHAR2 datatype?

    A. V

    B. N

    C. C

    D. P

10. **The DBA executes the CREATE OR REPLACE LIBRARY QUICKSORT AS '/DISK01/USR/BIN/QSORT'; but the directory named is invalid. When will an error be produced?**

    A. At the time the library is created

    B. At the time the library is dropped

    C. At the time a PL/SQL procedure calls the library

    D. At the time the external procedure attempts a callback

11. **The user attempts the following INSERT statement on the EMPLOYEES relational table defined with the address_type object type: INSERT INTO EMPLOYEES VALUES('30493','405 RIVER STREET','BARNES','OK','12345'). Which of the following reasons is most likely why the statement fails?**

    A. The **address_type** constructor was not used.

    B. The column values specified are out of order.

    C. The **values** keyword is incorrectly placed.

    D. Object data cannot be inserted into a relational table.

12. **When an attribute of an object is defined with the REF type, what data is actually stored in the attribute?**

    A. The original data

    B. A copy of the data

    C. A pointer to the data

    D. A pointer to the copy of the data

13. **A nested table is stored in the same segment as its parent data.**

    A. TRUE

    B. FALSE

14. **The DBA chooses to allow the use of objects on relational tables in an Oracle8 database. To ease the migration effort, which of the following things might the DBA create?**

    A. Object views and **instead of** triggers

    B. Scalar types and index-organized tables

    C. Reverse-key indexes and table partitions

    D. None of the above

Answers to Chapter Questions

    1. D.   Increase value set for LARGE_POOL_SIZE

Explanation   If the large pool is used, the session information from the multithreaded server environment will be stored in the large pool rather than in the shared pool, where it detracts from space available for shared SQL parse information. A change in the buffer cache won't make much difference, eliminating choice A, while using dedicated servers will actually worsen the problem, eliminating choice B. The size of data blocks cannot be changed for the life of the database, eliminating choice C. Review discussion of the large pool.

    2. B.   Create an index-organized table to store the data.

Explanation   Index-organized tables take less space to store than a comparable table-plus-primary-key setup. Since the table will only be accessed via the primary key, there is no need for additional indexes. Furthermore, for storage reasons, the DBA won't want to create more indexes, eliminating choice A. Choice C is incorrect because dropping the primary key will reduce storage·but has the unwanted effect of making data difficult to access. Choice D is incorrect because increasing **pctfree** makes a table require more storage to store the same number of rows. Review discussion of index-organized tables.

    3. A, C, and D.

Explanation   VARRAY types do not allow the indexing of elements in the object. In addition, the data is stored in the same extents as the parent table ("inline"), as long as it isn't over 4 kilobytes. If over 4 kilobytes, the data is stored in a different extent. A VARRAY type does require a limit on the number of elements that can be placed in the array. Therefore, choice B is the only one that accurately describes the VARRAY type.

4. A.   Execute the **rowid to extended( )** function on the data in the column.

Explanation   Each item of data in the column declared to be the ROWID datatype in Oracle7 will be in the restricted ROWID format. To be used in Oracle8, ROWID should be in extended format. Choice B describes the way to put an extended ROWID into restricted ROWID format, while choice C describes the procedure that takes a ROWID and returns the components in disaggregated form. Oracle8 only handles extended ROWID conversion automatically for the database, not applications that create, store, or manipulate ROWID data. Refer to the discussion of the DBMS_ROWID package.

5. D.   The **insert** fails at the time it is issued, but the transaction will continue.

Explanation   A nondeferrable constraint cannot be deferred by the **alter session set constraints=deferred** statement. Therefore, the **insert** statement will fail. But, statement failure does not cause a transaction to fail. Therefore, choice D is correct.

6. C.   '948695'

Explanation   The data in a reverse-key index is actually reversed within the index, but not in the table.

7. D.   **listener.ora**

Explanation   Information the listener needs for the extproc process is stored in the **listener.ora** file. The **init.ora** file stores parameters used for instance startup, eliminating choice A. The **config.ora** file contains information about the configuration of the Net8 (formerly SQL*Net) listener. The **orapw**sid**.ora** file most likely contains password information for DBAs.

8. B. FALSE

Explanation   The datafile information in the extended ROWID format of Oracle8 is a relative datafile identifier. Review the discussion of the components of an extended ROWID.

9. B. N

Explanation   The **N** character is used as a prefix to the data for comparison operations using data stored in the NCHAR and NVARCHAR2 datatypes. Review the discussion of the new NLS datatypes available in Oracle8.

10. C. At the time a PL/SQL procedure calls the library

Explanation   The external procedure reference is not checked at the time the library object is created, eliminating choice A. Rather, the external procedure is verified at the time it is referenced. Choice B is incorrect because once the library object is dropped, it is not important whether the library object generates errors or not. Choice D is incorrect because at the time the callback is generated, the external procedure will already have been accessed and run.

11. A. The **address_type** constructor was not used.

Explanation   When inserting data into an object type, the name of the object type must be referenced. This reference is called a **constructor**. There is no way to know the order of the attributes in an object without seeing the object type, so choice B is incorrect. The **values** keyword is properly placed, so choice C is incorrect. And, object data can definitely be put into relational tables as long as the relational table has a column defined with an object type, making choice D incorrect as well.

12. C.   A pointer to the data

Explanation   The data in a REF type is a pointer to the referenced object, not the actual data or even a copy of the data, eliminating choices A and B. Choice D is incorrect because no copy of the data is made; thus, no pointer to the copy can be made.

13. B.   FALSE

Explanation   The data in a nested table is stored in a separate segment from its parent. Review the discussion of nested tables and collection types.

14. A.   Object views and **instead of** triggers

Explanation   The use of object views and **instead of** triggers is designed to support easier migration to object applications. The use of scalar types, index-organized tables, reverse-key indexes, and partitions are all relational in nature, and therefore not part of the transition to object relational databases, eliminating choices B and C. Obviously, choice D is also incorrect.

CHAPTER
23

Oracle8: Parallel DML, LOBs, and Advanced Queuing

n this chapter, you will understand and demonstrate knowledge in the following areas:

- Parallel DML in Oracle8
- The LOB datatypes
- Advanced queuing with DBMS_QUEUE

Oracle8 supports new features in several other areas as well. To support new levels of VLDB administration, Oracle8 has some major enhancements to improve performance on **insert**, **update**, and **delete** statements on Oracle tables by making it possible for Oracle to process these statements in parallel. In Oracle7, only **select** statements could be processed in parallel. Oracle8 also supports new datatypes for large objects, the class of which is called LOBs. These LOBs are designed to support next-generation databases that use multimedia objects such as text, graphics, sound, and video. Although the predecessors to LOB datatypes, LONG and LONG RAW, are still supported in Oracle8 as they were in Oracle7, the emphasis in Oracle8 is on the LOB types. This is because LOB types are more versatile and integrate more effectively into Oracle8's other major advancement—object relational database development features. Finally, several new features have been added to Oracle8 to support the implementation of asynchronous execution of database operations, called queuing. These features are discussed in this chapter as well. Study of these areas will assist in your preparation for OCP Exam 5.

Parallel DML in Oracle8

In this section, you will cover the following topics related to parallel DML in Oracle8:

- Advantages of using parallel DML
- Enabling and using parallel DML
- Restrictions on using parallel DML
- Dictionary views on parallel DML

The first section of this chapter covers parallel DML. The overall use of parallelism in Oracle8 has increased dramatically in support of large database environments, as given evidence by the treatment of partitioned tables in Chapter 21. This increase is due to the increase in database size as a whole, both in data warehouses and in OLTP applications. As Oracle database applications advance in the organization, they also grow. Although most organizations shouldn't ever feel too constrained by the 512 petabyte size limit for Oracle8, even the data warehouse of 20 gigabytes may seem unwieldy with several database objects whose size is measured in hundreds of megabytes. Oracle7 may have difficulty accessing data in those databases as well, given the limited ROWID structure. In contrast, accessing data in Oracle8 should offer some relief with partitioning and the new ROWID structure already discussed. Oracle8 also improves the ability of users to put data into the database efficiently with parallel DML.

Advantages of Using Parallel DML

In large databases that store gigabytes of data, a single large DML operation may affect tens of thousands of rows. In data warehouse or decision support systems, where data is fed to the system in batch cycles, these updates may take several minutes to hours. Even well-tuned SQL **update**, **insert**, or **delete** statements may take a long time if the amount of data being changed is large. Though usually the amount of data being changed per statement is small in an OLTP application, there may be some situations where large amounts of data are changed at once, perhaps in a data feed operation where status on row data must be updated to reflect the feed. Parallel DML is designed to improve the overall performance of large data change operations in conjunction with the use of partitioned tables, although the **insert as select** statement is optimized to provide parallelism even on a nonpartitioned table.

Consider the performance gains granted with the use of parallel DML. A great deal of performance gained with parallel DML depends on the ability of the machine hosting Oracle to support parallel DML operations. The requirements for parallel DML include more memory to support additional I/O processes running and more CPUs to process data spread across multiple disk drives.

Parallel DML has another advantage in that Oracle8 supports it readily, without extra setup and intervention from the developer. In Oracle7, the degree of parallelism to which DML operations could be performed was up to the developer's ability to divide the data change activity across multiple sessions using ROWID or key information. Since there is no support for multisession transactions in Oracle, the developer had to manage the data change actively, checking each session to verify the success or correct the failure of each individual piece of the parallel operation. Since parallel DML is supported within one statement running in one session, the developer can define a transaction around the parallel operation. Within parallel configurations, parallel DML can run even faster because the degree of parallelism can be duplicated automatically by the number of instances connected to the same Oracle database. Parallel processes that are used in the Oracle database include parallel query, parallel **insert as select** statements on both partitioned and nonpartitioned tables, and parallel **update** and **delete** statements on partitioned tables.

Parallelism operates in different ways for different statements and in different situations. The Parallel Query option introduced in Oracle7 improves performance for **select** statements, resulting in full table scans by dissecting requested data by ROWID and directing multiple I/O processes to obtain one of the required ranges. This division of data to be selected allows Oracle to run queries in parallel, even if the parallel operations obtaining data must work on the same partition on a partitioned table or in a nonpartitioned table. Each I/O process is limited to only one partition, and cannot span partitions.

In order to process **update**, **delete**, and **insert as select** statements in parallel on multiple table partitions, Oracle maps a disk device to a partition. The closer the DBA can make the device-to-partition mapping one to one, the more effective parallel DML should operate. The parallelism in this setup is based on the number of partitions available, whereas in the other situations parallelism is defined for within partitions. Thus, in this situation, a maximum of only one slave process may operate on any single partition on behalf of the DML statement.

Finally, for **insert as select** statements to run in parallel on nonpartitioned tables, multiple I/O processes are generated and Oracle divides the number of rows to be inserted among the I/O processes equitably. These I/O processes **insert** data into the tables in the same way that SQL*Loader's direct path data load: data is put into the table over the highwatermark. However, since the parallel DML statement operates as a transaction, a **commit** resets the high watermark rather than a data save. For more on the direct path data load in SQL*Loader, review Chapter 10. Figure 23-1 illustrates the three methods Oracle8 introduces for parallel database operation.

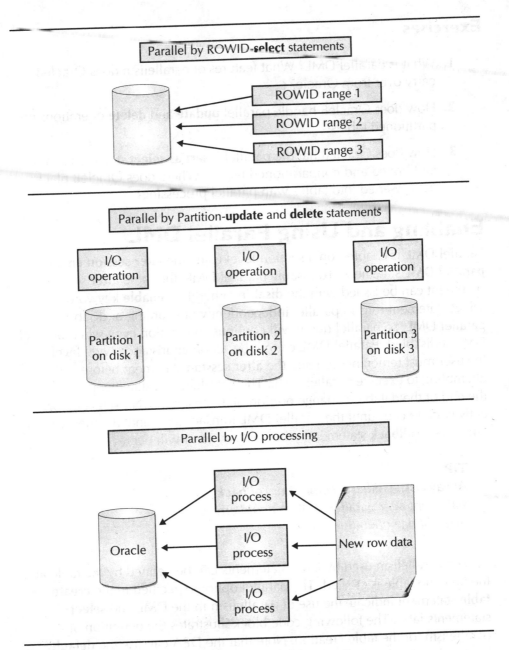

FIGURE 23-1. *Three methods for parallel data operations*

Exercises

1. What is parallel DML? What features of parallelism does Oracle8 carry over from Oracle7?

2. How does Oracle8 handle parallel **update** and **delete** operations on partitioned tables?

3. How does Oracle8 handle parallel **insert as select** statements into partitioned and nonpartitioned tables? Where does Oracle8 place data inserted into tables with parallel processing?

Enabling and Using Parallel DML

Parallel DML is enabled on a session level using the **alter session enable parallel DML** statement. To disable parallel DML, the same **alter session** statement can be issued with the **disable** rather than **enable** keyword. A **select** statement runs in parallel independently of enabling or disabling parallel DML, so parallel query will continue to function even when parallel DML is disabled. Parallel DML cannot be set on an instance-wide level, so the user must remember to issue the **alter session** statement before attempting to execute parallel DML. The parallel DML statement constitutes the end of the database change portion of a transaction. No **select** or DML activity can occur until the parallel DML transaction is ended either with the **commit** or **rollback** statement; otherwise, an error will occur.

TIP
Always issue either a ***commit*** *or* ***rollback*** *statement after parallel DML to avoid errors on data change operations later.*

The parallelism used by DML statements can be defined by the table at the time the table is created. The parallel options specified in the **create table** statement indicate the use of parallelism in the DML and **select** statements later. The following code block illustrates the definition of parallelism for the table creation. Note that the DBA can use the **default** keyword in the definition of **degree** and **instances** as part of the **parallel clause** rather than specifying a number. Also, the **noparallel** clause can be used to bypass parallelism in table creation. Finally, defining **instances** is optional, and should be used only in conjunction with a parallel configuration.

```
CREATE TABLE employees
...
PARALLEL(DEGREE 3 INSTANCES DEFAULT);
```

Even when parallel DML is enabled for the session, there is still no guarantee that it will be used when the user issues a DML statement. To ensure use of parallel DML, the user must include a special directive called a *hint*. Hints have been around for some time in Oracle7, used mainly for performance tuning. A hint is a directive sent to the Oracle SQL processing mechanism also known as the *optimizer*, telling it to process the SQL statement in a certain way. Hints can improve performance in situations where the SQL processing mechanism by default would pick an inefficient method to process the statement. Hints also override the parallelism set up in the **create table** statement. The specification of the parallel hint takes the form **/*+parallel** (*tablename, degree_parallel*) ***/** in the **update**, **insert**, or **delete** statement, as shown in the following example:

```
UPDATE /*+PARALLEL (employees,2) */
employees
SET salary = salary*1.08;

DELETE /*+PARALLEL (employees,4) */
FROM employees
WHERE to_number(substr(empid,1,1)) < 3;
```

The placement and syntax for the parallel hint is the same for **update**, **delete**, and **insert** DML operations. The parallel hint tells Oracle8 to run both the table scan to find data to change or remove and the actual data change or removal in parallel. The *tablename* and *degree_parallel* variables specified in the parallel hint of an **update**, **delete**, or **insert** statement override any values set for parallelism in the **create table** statement.

There are special considerations for parallel hints and two additional hints available for **insert as select** operations. Parallel hints can be specified both for the **insert** and **select** portions of the **insert as select** statement. The two new hints available are for **insert** statements. Those new hints are **append** and **noappend**, and they indicate to the Oracle SQL processing mechanism that the **insert** statement should use the direct path. Some examples of the uses for direct path appear in the following code block:

```
INSERT /*+APPEND */
INTO employees
AS SELECT /*+PARALLEL(people,5) */
FROM people;

INSERT /*+NOAPPEND */
INTO employees
AS SELECT /*+PARALLEL(people,5) */
FROM people;

INSERT /*+PARALLEL(employees,5) */
INTO employees
AS SELECT /*+PARALLEL(people,5) */
FROM people;
```

Parallelism is determined in light of several factors. The **degree** and **instances** options in the **parallel** clause of the **create table** statement set up default levels of parallelism, while the *tablename* and *degree_parallel* variables specified as part of the **parallel** hint for DML statements override the default parallelism. At the hardware level, the number of processors available on the machine hosting Oracle will influence parallelism as well. The number of partitions can also influence the parallelism of DML statements.

Exercises

1. How is parallel DML enabled in the Oracle database?

2. How is parallelism determined for table creation? How does it subsequently influence parallelism in DML statements?

3. What is a hint? Does the hint or the degree of parallelism specified in the table DDL take precedence in parallel DML statements?

Restrictions on Using Parallel DML

As stated earlier, parallel DML statements must be committed or rolled back before another **select** or data change operation can be issued in the session.

No **lock table** or **select for update** statements can be run in the same transaction as one containing parallel DML. No self referential integrity, **on delete cascade**, or deferred enforcement of integrity constraints may occur during parallel DML operations either. Parallel **insert** statements cannot occur on tables with global indexes, nor can parallel **update** statements operate on columns for which there are unique indexes. No parallel DML operation can execute on a bitmap index, tables containing LOBs, or clustered tables. Triggers are not fired when parallel DML occurs, so some additional PL/SQL procedures or constraints may need to be created if enforcement of constraints or replication occurs as a result of a trigger.

Failure on a transaction during instance or system recovery containing a parallel DML statement causes SMON to roll back the transaction one I/O process at a time. This means that **rollback** can take longer than the original statement took to execute. To execute **rollback** in parallel, the parallel DML statement should be rerun. This will lock the resources that failed to allow recovery in parallel so that the statement can execute again. When the parallel DML operation completes again, the user can either **commit** or roll back as necessary. If single or multiple I/O processes running in parallel fail, PMON rolls back the work of those processes one at a time while the rest of the I/O processes execute their own **rollback**. If the coordinating process fails, PMON recovers that process while all the I/O processes recover their own work in parallel.

Exercises

1. What are some of the restrictions on parallel DML related to indexes and constraints?

2. What are some of the restrictions on parallel DML related to object types and LOBs?

3. How does transaction recovery operate with parallel DML? What about process recovery in the various situations involving I/O and coordinator processes?

Dictionary Views on Parallel DML

There are several dictionary views with which the user can find information about parallel DML. The V$ performance view V$PQ_SYSSTAT can be used to find out information about parallel DML in addition to parallel queries in Oracle8. This view now contains a new statistic called "DML Initiated." The value for this statistic identifies how many parallel DML operations are running on the database. The V$PQ_SESSTAT view also has a new statistic that it captures, called "DML Parallelized," which tracks both whether parallel DML was used on the last query and on how many parallel DML statements have been issued, total, for the session. The V$SESSION view also contains a new column, called PDML_ENABLED, listing whether parallel DML is enabled for the session.

A useful, though sometimes dangerous, method can be used to speed the operation of parallel DML **insert** operations. This involves the use of the **logging** or **nologging** options, and they are set for a table—not for a transaction—using the **alter table** *name* **logging**. The **logging** keyword can be substituted with **nologging** to turn off the creation of redo log information for **insert** operations on this table. Although this process will speed the **insert** operation at hand, it will also make it impossible for the DBA to recover the transaction from archived redo log information. For compatibility with Oracle7, the **unrecoverable** option can still be specified for many operations to turn off redo log entry creation, as well.

Exercises

1. What is the performance view containing information on the parallel DML statements?

2. How can redo logs be turned off for **insert** operations on certain tables in Oracle8?

The LOB Datatypes

In this section, you will cover the following topics related to LOB datatypes:

- Creating and altering the LOB datatypes
- Comparing LONG and LOB datatypes
- Data and object management with internal and external LOBs
- Using the DBMS_LOB package

There are several drawbacks inherent in the use of LONG and LONG RAW datatypes in Oracle7 database tables. First, the use of either datatype is limited to only one column in the database table. If the object is large, the storage of that object inline with other table data almost invariably leads to chaining, which has its own host of performance issues, already discussed. Passing LONG and LONG RAW data back and forth between client and server, or between PL/SQL procedures and functions, proves difficult as well. Oracle has answered these issues by creating new and different datatypes for the storage of large objects—the LOB datatypes. This section will cover the usage and function of each of the LOB datatypes, the benefits and restrictions of each, and also some dictionary views that can be used in order to find information about the LOB datatypes used in the Oracle8 database.

Creating LOB Datatypes

Four new datatypes for storing large objects exist in Oracle8: BLOB for binary large object, CLOB for character large object, NCLOB character large object for multibyte character sets (similar to NCHAR and NVARCHAR2), and BFILE for binary files stored outside the database. All LOBs are stored within the database, except for BFILE. Thus, BLOB, CLOB, and NCLOB large objects are all considered internal LOBs while the BFILE large object is an external LOB. LOBs have two components: the *value* and the *locator*. The LOB value is the actual data that comprises the large object, while the locator is a pointer to the actual location in Oracle8 or external to Oracle8 where the data is actually stored. In cases where the LOB value is more than 4,000 bytes, only the LOB locator is stored in a table, and the value is stored in another segment external to the table—except for BFILE, which is stored outside the Oracle8 database. For LOB values less than 4,000 bytes, the value is stored inline with the rest of the table data.

LOB datatypes are used in table and variable declarations in the same way as other object types, with the definition of the type followed by the use of it. For more information on creating object types, review Chapter 22. Several attributes in an object type or table can be defined as LOBs. To populate a LOB, the DBMS_LOB package can be used, or an external application can do it with the Oracle Call Interface (OCI). LOBs can be used in table definitions, user-defined types, bind variables in SQL, host variables in programs, PL/SQL variables, and return values. The following code block illustrates the use of LOBs in object types and table definition:

```
CREATE TYPE vacation_grafx_type AS OBJECT
(picture          BLOB);

CREATE TABLE vacation_planner (
location          VARCHAR2(40),
picture           vacation_grafx_type,
itinerary         CLOB);
```

Storing Data for Internal LOBs

The VACATION_PLANNER table is then represented by five different segments: one each for the inline table data like the LOCATION column, PICTURE locator, and ITINERARY locator, and both a LOB and a LOB index segment for PICTURE and ITINERARY. The index segment is used to store locations for pieces of each LOB stored in different data blocks of the segment. Since the LOBs in this table definition are all internal, the tablespaces to store each of the identified segments and other storage options can be defined in an additional clause called **lob**. The options in this clause are defined as follows:

- **chunk** Identifies a contiguous number of blocks that will be chained to store information for the LOB. A LOB can be stored in several chunks of equal size.

- **pctversion** Identifies an amount of the LOB that must be changed before Oracle will attempt to reuse empty chunk space; it is designed to replace rollback segment usage in conjunction with LOBs.

- **cache** Tells Oracle to use the buffer cache for reading and writing LOB information.

- **nocache logging** Tells Oracle not to use the buffer cache for reading and writing LOB information, but to write changes to the redo log.

- **nocache nologging**   Tells Oracle not to use the buffer cache for reading and writing LOB information and not to write changes to the redo log.

- **tablespace**   Identifies a tablespace into which LOB value information should be placed.

- **storage**   Standard storage clause, allows for definition of **pctfree**, **pctused**, and other storage clauses.

- **index**   Storage clauses for the related index used to manage LOB storage can be identified, including **Inittrans** *num*, **maxtrans** *num*, **tablespace** *name* and **storage** *storage_clause*.

When data changes in LOBs, Oracle treats the chunk with the same read consistency as the block is treated for other database objects. For all intents and purposes, a chunk is the base unit of storage in a LOB, even though each chunk consists of many blocks. The following code block illustrates these clauses in action in the definition of LOB storage for a table:

```
CREATE TABLE book
(title              VARCHAR2(40),
 author             VARCHAR2(40),
 text               CLOB,
 author_pic         BLOB)
LOB(text,author_pic) STORE AS(
   STORAGE(INITIAL 1M NEXT 1M PCTINCREASE 0)
   CHUNK 50
   PCTVERSION 30
   NOCACHE LOGGING
   INDEX (STORAGE (INITIAL 1M NEXT 1M))
);
```

Creating and Using BFILES

Oracle is able to access data outside of its own management control with the use of BFILEs. However, Oracle may only read this data. Read access to this data must be given at the operating system level to Oracle. If a change needs to be made to the data, the user must use whatever mechanisms are required outside of Oracle to make the change. This may include text editors, graphics editors, a sound clip editor, and so on. The creation of a BFILE within the database is similar to the creation of other columns in tables of LOB types. The following code block demonstrates the use of BFILE:

```
CREATE TABLE word_processing_docs
(doc_name         VARCHAR2,
 doc_content      BFILE);
```

Since the BFILE storage is managed by the operating system and the modification by another software component, there is no need to allocate storage for a column or object of type BFILE. However, the location of the data in the BFILE must be identified to Oracle as a new object called a *directory*. The directory object specifies the pathname used to access the external object, and it can be granted to Oracle users as other object privileges are, enabling an additional layer of filesystem access security managed by Oracle. The creation of a directory object is done with the **create or replace directory** statement. Removal is done with the **drop directory** statement. The creation and removal of a directory are demonstrated in the following code block:

```
CREATE OR REPLACE DIRECTORY wp_docs
AS '/DISK01/usr/docs/wp_docs';

DROP DIRECTORY wp_docs;
```

As with the creation of library objects, there is no check at the time of directory creation that the pathname is valid. Oracle will give an error only when the directory and external file are accessed. If the directory doesn't exist when the directory object is created, Oracle will NOT create it. Access to that directory is managed by the operating system; the DBA should make sure Oracle has access to it before allowing users to refer to the LOB. System privileges to create and remove directories are consistent with other privileges: **create any directory** and **drop any directory**. There is only one object privilege, **read**, granted to users who will be able to access the BFILE. To grant the object privilege, the **grant read on directory** *name* **to** *user* statement should be used. Creation and granting read privileges on directories can both be audited as well.

TIP
Don't create directory objects for directories containing Oracle database files. It places database files in danger of being tampered with.

Exercises

1. What are the four LOB datatypes? What is the difference between an internal and external LOB type?

2. Why do storage clauses need to be specified for BLOB, CLOB, and NCLOB objects? What is a chunk? How does caching or not caching impact the LOB's use of SGA and redo log resources?

3. What is a directory object, and what statement is used to create it? What LOB type is it used in conjunction with?

Comparing LONG and LOB Datatypes

There are several key differences between LONG and LOB types that make LOB types more versatile and helpful in large object management in Oracle databases. The first difference relates to the number of columns per table and the LONG and LOB types. There can be only one LONG column in a table, because the LONG column data is stored inline. In contrast, there can be many LOB columns in a table, because in situations where the LOB value is over 4,000 bytes, only the locator data for the LOB type is stored inline with the table data—in other words, no LOB will ever require more than 4,000 bytes of space inline with other table data. Thus, **select** statements on LONG columns return the actual data, while the same statement on a LOB column returns only the locator. Oracle supports use of the LOB types in object types except NCLOB, while LONG does not. LOBs can also be larger than LONGs—4G for LOBs vs. 2G for LONGs. LOB data can also be accessed piecewise while LONG access is sequential; only the entire value in the LONG column can be obtained, while parts of the LOB can be obtained.

Exercises

1. What are some of the differences between LONG and LOB types related to size, access, and storage location?

2. What are some of the differences between LONG and LOB types and the number of columns that may be defined with each in a table?

3. How are NCLOB and LONG alike related to object types?

LOB Data Management with DBMS_LOB

Interaction with LOBs is provided in SQL, the DBMS_LOB package, and OCI release 8. The most extensive interaction with LOBs in Oracle is provided through the OCI and DBMS_LOB route, while only limited interaction is provided by SQL. The most effective way to manage access to internal LOBs is to lock the row with a **select for update** statement and access the LOB via DBMS_LOB. If the user would like to create a row in the table by populating the LOB column with NULL, the **empty_blob( )** or **empty_clob( )** operation can be used. The following code block can be used to show the population of LOB data:

```
INSERT INTO book VALUES
('Death in Venice', 'Thomas Mann', EMPTY_CLOB(), EMPTY_BLOB());
```

Later, other rows can be updated with that NULL value by referencing the LOB in the row already populated. Alternately, a host variable in embedded SQL can be used to assign the LOB to a value, so long as the type of the host variable matches the LOB type for the table column. However, the **OCILobWrite( )** operation is the fastest method to populate data to an LOB type. PL/SQL allows manipulation of LOBs directly as well. Using the DBMS_LOB.**write( )** procedure, the developer can create a PL/SQL process that updates data in the LOB. The following code block illustrates this:

```
DECLARE
    my_text_handle          CLOB;
    my_buffer               VARCHAR2(4000);
    my_amount               NUMBER  := 0;
    my_offset               INTEGER := 1;
```

```
BEGIN
    my_buffer := 'Gustave Aschenbach—or von Aschenbach, as he had
been known officially since his fiftieth birthday—had set out alone
from his house in Prince Regent Street, Munich, for an extended walk.';
    my_add_amt := length(my_buffer);
    SELECT text
    INTO   my_text_handle
    FROM book
    WHERE title = 'Death in Venice' FOR UPDATE;
    DBMS_LOB.WRITE(my_text_handle, my_add_amt, my_offset, my_buffer);
    COMMIT;
END;
```

Notice the **select** statement to obtain the locator information for the LOB. The *my_text_handle* variable doesn't actually contain the LOB data—remember, the table only stores the locator to the data. Removal of LOB data can be accomplished with the same SQL statements as used in other situations. The **alter table truncate** and **delete** statements are both useful for eliminating the LOB along with the rest of the row, or, again, the **empty_clob( )** or the **empty_blob( )** operation can be used simply to eliminate the LOB data. Dropping the table also removes the LOB. One exception is the removal of BFILE information. Even though the BFILE locator is eliminated in any of the three options put forth for deleting LOB data, the actual BFILE will still exist after they are deleted and can only be eliminated using operating system commands.

The DBMS_LOB package handles LOB operations. It is created with the **dbmslob.sql** and **prvtlob.plb** files, which are executed by running the **catproc.sql** script when the database is first created. For more information on creating a database, see Chapters 6 and 25. The maximum size for LOBs is also defined when DBMS_LOB is created to be 4,294,967,294, measured in characters for CLOB and NCLOB and in bytes for BFILE and BLOB. All locks for manipulating data in LOB columns other than BFILE need to be acquired before the call is made to a DBMS_LOB procedure. No special security is provided with DBMS_LOB; all procedures and functions in the DBMS_LOB package are run with the privileges of the owner of the procedure calling them. There are two categories for functions and procedures in this package: *mutators* and *observers*. The difference is that mutators change data in the LOB column while observers only read the LOB.

Special conditions apply to the variables used for the procedures and functions in DBMS_LOB. If a NULL value is passed as value for any variable to a function, NULL will be the return value. If a negative offset, amount, or range number is passed in, the function or procedure will return a corresponding error. The default value for offset is 1, which is the first byte or character in the LOB. Several of the procedures and functions in the DBMS_LOB package are overloaded to support CLOB, BLOB, or NCLOB types.

APPEND( )   This procedure allows the user to add the contents of one LOB to another. Both LOBs must be the same type. A destination BLOB or CLOB and a source BLOB or CLOB must be passed to **append( )** in the form **append**(*destination, source*). The return data from **append( )** will be the destination LOB.

COMPARE( )   This procedure allows the direct comparison of LOBs of the same type or BFILEs to one another for equality. The call to **compare( )** looks like the following: **compare**(*obj1, obj2, amount*). The objects passed can be BLOB, CLOB, or BFILE datatypes. The *amount* variable defines a maximum number of bytes (BLOB,BFILE) or characters (CLOB) to compare, and defaults to the maximum value permitted, 4,294,967,294. It returns an integer result: 0 if the two objects are equal, -1 if the first object is larger, and 1 if the second object is larger.

COPY( )   This function copies data from one LOB to another, either in its entirety or partially. Calls to **copy( )** look like **copy**(*destination, source, amount, destination_offset, source_offset*). If no value is specified for either object's offset, a default value of 1, for the beginning of the LOB, is used. The *amount* specifies the amount of each LOB to copy. If the offset specified for the destination is larger than the actual size of the LOB, then zero-byte or space filler is written from the end of the BLOB or CLOB to the beginning of the new data copied, respectively.

ERASE( )   This procedure eliminates a specified amount of data from the BLOB or CLOB. Calls to **erase( )** look like **erase**(*lob, amount, offset*). The *amount* is the number of bytes or characters that will be erased from the BLOB or CLOB, respectively. The *offset* tells **erase( )** where to start. The default for *offset* is 1. If there is to be data left at the end of the BLOB or CLOB when **erase( )** is done, either zero-byte or space filler will be substituted for the original data.

FILECLOSE( )   This closes a specified open BFILE. The call to **fileclose( )** is **fileclose**(*bfile*).

FILECLOSEALL( )   This closes all open BFILEs. The call to **filecloseall( )** is **filecloseall**( ).

FILEEXISTS( )   This determines if the file exists that is pointed to by BFILE. It returns 1 if it exists, 0 if not. The call to **fileexists( )** is **fileexists**(*bfile*).

FILEGETNAME( )   This identifies the directory object name and the operating system filename for a given BFILE. The call to **filegetname( )** is **filegetname**(*bfile, directory_obj, filename*). The *directory_obj* and *filename* variables are output variables, so they needn't have values set for them.

FILEISOPEN( )   This determines if the given BFILE is open. The call to **fileisopen( )** is **fileisopen**(*bfile*).

FILEOPEN( )   This opens a given BFILE. The call to **fileopen( )** is **fileopen**(*bfile, openmode*). The *openmode* variable defaults to **read only** access, because BFILEs cannot be modified in Oracle8.

GETLENGTH( )   This determines the length of BLOB, CLOB, or BFILE large object. The call to **getlength( )** is **getlength**(*lob_or_bfile*).

INSTR( )   This obtains the corresponding position of a pattern match in a given LOB or BFILE. The call to **instr( )** is **instr**(*lob_or_bfile, pattern, offset, occurrence*). Both *offset* and *occurrence* default to 1 if none are specified. The *pattern* can either be of type VARCHAR2 for CLOB or RAW for BLOB.

LOADFROMFILE( )   This copies data in an external BFILE into an internal LOB. The call to **loadfromfile( )** is **loadfromfile**(*destination, bfile, amount, destination_offset, source_offset*). The source and destination offsets default to 1 if not specified. The *amount* variable must be specified.

READ( )   This obtains data from the BFILE or LOB starting from an offset position and continuing for a specified amount of blocks. Data is then placed in a buffer. Data returned is type VARCHAR2 for CLOB and RAW for BLOB and BFILE. The call to **read( )** is **read**(*lob_or_bfile, amount, offset, buffer*).

SUBSTR( )   This returns a substring of data from the LOB or BFILE starting at the offset, including the number of bytes or characters specified by amount. It is identical in concept to the single-row operation of the same name covered in Chapter 1. The call to **substr( )** is **substr**(*lob_or_bfile, offset, amount*).

TRIM( )   This changes the amount of data in the LOB by the amount specified by *new_length*. All data past that new length is cut off. The call to **trim( )** is **trim**(*lob, new_length*).

WRITE( )   This places a specified *buffer* of data of size *amount* into the LOB starting at the position specified by *offset*. The call to **write( )** is **write**(*lob, amount, offset, buffer*).

Exercises

1. What are two methods used to **update** LOB data?

2. What is a mutator? Which procedures and functions in DBMS_LOB are mutators? What is an observer? Which procedures and functions in DBMS_LOB are observers?

3. What SQL operations can be used to write empty values to BLOB and CLOB columns?

Advanced Queuing with DBMS_QUEUE

In this section, you will cover the following topics related to advanced queuing with DBMS_QUEUE:

- Defining advanced queuing concepts

- Creating and sending messages with **enqueue( )**

- Processing messages with **dequeue( )**

- Administering the queues and the queue table

Consider the most obvious fact about an online application—you issue a command, and the application executes it immediately. This is known as synchronous, or online, processing because of the synchronization of cause and effect. You say do it, and the application does it— hence, you have an online system. Another concept in data processing is the batch processing system. Instead of happening immediately, a batch process happens as an event. Both mainframe and UNIX users should be familiar with a similar concept—job scheduling. You take a batch process, schedule it to run at a specific time via CRON or another scheduling utility, and the operating system executes the job at the appropriate time. However, without the right tool to manage scheduling, take note of any runtime errors or exceptions, and notify the appropriate person or process, no developer may ever notice when a batch job has failed until the user notices—and by then it's too late. Oracle has built on concepts of job scheduling and sending messages between processes to notify others of progress. The result is advanced queuing—the topic of this section.

Defining Advanced Queuing Concepts and Benefits

Queuing makes it possible to handle complex business process dependencies to complete or defer work. Many times, it is important that a process complete its task on time even when systems go down or other processes don't complete their work in time. Queuing is designed to fulfill this task by allowing advanced interprocess communication along with transaction monitoring capability. The result is an efficient queuing architecture within the Oracle database—eliminating the need for middleware in the delivery of effective business processing management and workflow software using Oracle8, because the software tools needed for messaging are built into the database.

In systems that don't use Oracle8 for queuing, the task of developing interprocess message flow is complex. Error checking must be coded into each component of the entire application, and connections must be built from each component into a separate message repository. The resultant "application within an application" is complex, prone to breakage, and entirely dependent on technology that may not even be designed to handle this type of work. Thus, even well-designed systems may not provide all the support an organization needs for business processing. If components are provided for messaging from different vendors, it is usually up to the buyer to design the interface between the application and the messaging software. And support burdens fall entirely on the organization that designed it.

Messages and the DBMS_AQ Package

With advanced queuing in Oracle, all application logic can exist within the Oracle database and application. Each component of the application connects to the other components with a messaging system integrated into the kernel. What is a *message*? A message is the most atomic unit of work executed within a transaction. A message consists of two parts: *data* and *control information*. The user process or application provides the data used in executing the transaction. Control information consists of the time to execute, priority, process dependencies, and other things. This control information comes from the application. Figure 23-2 illustrates the concept of advanced queuing.

This information is queued by the application and read by other applications using procedures called **enqueue( )** and **dequeue( )**, which are found in a PL/SQL package called DBMS_AQ. Messages are placed in a message queue for review by **enqueue( )** and read by other components with **dequeue( )**. A message queue is stored in a queue table in the database designed to store messages. Several queues can exist in each queue table, and several queue tables can exist in the database. The creation and management of queues and queue tables is handled by another package called DBMS_AQADM, which will be discussed later in the section.

Benefits of Queuing

The benefits of queuing are many. First, queuing and queue tables allow the identification of discrete units of work and their execution status. This information can be retained by the queue table for as long as needed,

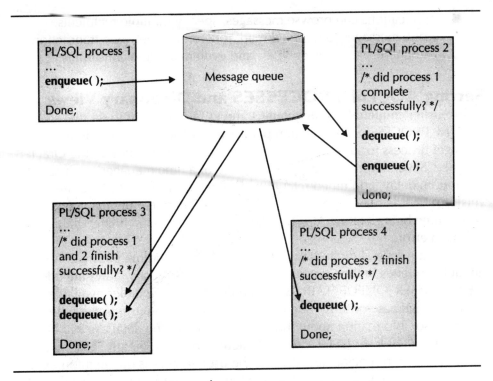

FIGURE 23-2.   *Pictorial representation of advanced queuing*

effectively keeping a repository or "message warehouse" of this information. This repository forms the foundation for event tracking and tracking relationships between messages. The business processes modeled by the application are more evident and thus more traceable. Patterns in data processing can be detected, leading to "message mining," which can then be used to identify improvements to streamline processes. A more complete list of the advantages of Oracle8 advanced queuing is given here.

■   The ordering and prioritizing of messages is possible

■   Identifiers can be used to correlate different messages

■   Reply queues can be used, along with exception queues, to identify when there are problems

■ Applications can browse messages, specify multiple recipients, group messages to form a thread, differentiate between transactions and queries, use object types, and even mark time constraints.

Setting AQ_TM_PROCESSES and Dictionary Views

Before using **enqueue( )** or **dequeue( )**, the DBA may want to set the AQ_TM_PROCESSES initialization parameter to 1 to create one time manager process to support time management on the queues on the Oracle8 instance. Several options depend on the use of a time manager, such as the expiration, delay, and timed retention. The default value is 0. In future versions, Oracle may support the use of more than one time manager, but for the time being, setting AQ_TM_PROCESSES to a value higher than 1 results in error.

There are several dictionary views available for finding information about the queues in the Oracle database. These dictionary views include DBA_ or USER_QUEUE_TABLES, which lists the queue tables available on the entire database or those queue tables owned by the user issuing the query. Also, information about individual queues in the database can be found in the DBA_ or USER_QUEUES dictionary view. Finally, each queue table has its own special view that can be used to access queue information. The name for that view will depend on the queue table, but the general format for the view name is AQ$*QUEUE_TABLE_NAME*.

Exercises

1. Define advanced queuing? What is a message? What is a message queue?

2. What package is used to place and read messages, and what are the procedures? What package is used to manage message queues?

3. What are some benefits for queuing? What is a time manager process, and how is it used? What initialization parameter is used to start it? What are the dictionary views available for finding information about queues and queue tables?

Creating and Sending Messages with DBMS_AQ.ENQUEUE

DBMS_AQ contains the **enqueue( )** procedure used to handle the placement of messages on a message queue. Privileges for using the DBMS_AQ package are given initially only to SYS, but can be granted to others in the database who have the role AQ_USER_ROLE granted to them. A call to the DBMS_AQ.**enqueue( )** procedure looks like **DBMS_AQ.enqueue(**_queue_name, enqueue_options, message_properties, payload, msg_id_**)**. All variables identified are input, except _msg_id_, which is the handle for the message enqueued and is returned by the **enqueue( )** procedure. The usage of each variable is given here.

QUEUE_NAME   This is a VARCHAR2 datatype, and it specifies the name of the queue to which this message should be enqueued. The value for _queue_name_ specified should _not_ be an exception queue, because messages are moved to the exception queue only by the queuing system itself.

ENQUEUE_OPTIONS   This is a DBMS_AQ.ENQUEUE_OPTIONS_T type. This variable is really three variables in one, because this type is a record. When using the DBMS_AQ package, the application should declare the variable used to pass values into this variable with the DBMS_AQ.ENQUEUE_OPTIONS_T type. The three subvariables are _visibility, relative_msgid_, and _sequence_deviation_. A sample definition of this variable appears in the following code block, and the explanation of their use and values follows the block:

```
DECLARE
    my_enq_opts := DBMS_AQ.ENQUEUE_OPTIONS_T;
BEGIN
    my_enq_opts.VISIBILITY           := DBMS_AQ.IMMEDIATE;
    my_enq_opts.RELATIVE_MSGID       := '02AB9AD2FG4859C5';
    my_enq_opts.SEQUENCE_DEVIATION   := DBMS_AQ.TOP;
...
```

- **VISIBILITY**   Defines transactional behavior of the queued request. Can be set to **on_commit**, meaning the enqueued message is part of the current transaction and that the operation will be complete when the transaction commits. The default value is **on_commit**. Alternatively, can be set to immediate such that the enqueued message is its own transaction, not part of the current transaction.

- **RELATIVE_MSGID**   Only relevant when **before** is used in *sequence_deviation*. This variable defines the message identifier referenced in *sequence_deviation*.

- **SEQUENCE_DEVIATION**   Identifies whether the message enqueued should be dequeued before other messages in the queue. One of the values permitted is **before**, meaning that this message should be dequeued before the message defined by *relative_msgid* above. Alternately, **top** can be specified for this variable, meaning this message is dequeued before any other messages. Alternately, NULL says this message is dequeued in regular order. NULL is default value.

MESSAGE_PROPERTIES   DBMS_AQ.MESSAGE_PROPERTIES_T type. In the same way as *enqueue_options*, the *message_properties* variable has several subvariables used to define its meaning. When using the DBMS_AQ package, the developer should declare a variable to populate with the values required for this structure using the same type as this structure uses. This variable has nine subvariables: *priority, delay, expiration, correlation, attempts, recipient_list, exception_queue, enqueue_time,* and *state*. An example for defining this variable appears in the following code block, and a description of the subvariables appears after that. In the example, a message called "DINNER TIME" is enqueued with a priority of −3 to consumers DINAH, ATHENA, and SPANKY, immediately available for their dequeuing. The message will be available for five minutes, after which time it will be placed in the NOT_HUNGRY_EXCEPTION_Q.

```
DECLARE
   my_msg_props := DBMS_AQ.MESSAGE_PROPERTIES_T;
   subscriber   := DBMS_AQ.AQ$_RECIPIENT_LIST_T;
   my_enq_opts := DBMS_AQ.ENQUEUE_OPTIONS_T;
BEGIN
   my_msg_props.PRIORITY           := -3;
```

```
my_msg_props.DELAY              := DBMS_AQ.NO_DELAY;
my_msg_props.EXPIRATION         := 300;
my_msg_props.CORRELATION        := 'DINNER TIME'
-- my_msg_props.ATTEMPTS not set at time of enqueue
   subscriber(1) := SYS.AQ$_AGENT('DINAH',NULL,NULL);
   subscriber(2) := SYS.AQ$_AGENT('SPANKY',NULL,NULL);
   subscriber(3) := SYS.AQ$_AGENT('ATHENA',NULL,NULL);
my_msg_props.RECIPIENT_LIST     := subscriber;
my_msg_props.EXCEPTION_QUEUE    := 'NOT_HUNGRY_EXCEPTION_Q';
-- my_msg_props.ENQUEUE_TIME not set by user
-- my_msg_props.STATE not set by user

my_enq_opts.VISIBILITY          := DBMS_AQ.IMMEDIATE;
my_enq_opts.RELATIVE_MSGID      := '02AB9AD2FG4859C5';
my_enq_opts.SEQUENCE_DEVIATION  := DBMS_AQ.TOP;
```

- **PRIORITY**   Specifies the priority of the message numerically. Both negatives and positives are allowed; the lower the number, the higher the priority.

- **DELAY**   Identifies a delay, in seconds, during which time the message may not be dequeued. Alternately, **no_delay** may be specified for this variable. It relies on the setting of the time manager.

- **EXPIRATION**   Defines how long the message is available for dequeuing, in seconds, after which time the message expires. Alternately, **never** may be specified for this variable.

- **CORRELATION**   Identifies the message with a name.

- **ATTEMPTS**   Number of times other consumers attempted to **dequeue( )** the message. This is not set at time of **enqueue( )**.

- **RECIPIENT_LIST**   Can be used only for queues allowing multiple consumers. Default recipients are the subscribers to the queue. Values for this variable cannot be returned in a **dequeue( )**. The recipient list can be defined with another variable, of type SYS.AQ$_AGENT, which takes three variables: *name, address, and protocol*, of datatypes VARCHAR2, VARCHAR2, and NUMBER, respectively.

- **EXCEPTION_QUEUE** Messages moved to the exception queue after value for *expiration* has passed, or if *attempts* exceed the maximum number of attempts allowed for the queue.

- **ENQUEUE_TIME** Set internally by the system as the time **enqueue( )** deposited the message.

- **STATE** The current state of the message. This has four possible values: **waiting** if the message is still in delay, **ready** if the message can be obtained via **dequeue( )**, **processed** if the message is processed and retained, and **expired** if the message moved to the location defined by *exception_queue*.

PAYLOAD   Either an object type correlated to the column of the queue table, where it will be stored, or RAW. This is the actual "message." When enqueued, the queue returns a unique message identifier to the processes using **enqueue( )**.

```
-- payload type declaration
CREATE TYPE message_type
AS object (name VARCHAR2(10), text VARCHAR2(100));

-- anonymous PL/SQL block
DECLARE
    my_msg_props := DBMS_AQ.MESSAGE_PROPERTIES_T;
    subscriber   := DBMS_AQ.AQ$_RECIPIENT_LIST_T;
    my_enq_opts  := DBMS_AQ.ENQUEUE_OPTIONS_T;
    my_message   message_type;
    my_msgid     RAW;
BEGIN
    my_msg_props.PRIORITY        := -3;
    my_msg_props.DELAY           := DBMS_AQ.NO_DELAY;
    my_msg_props.EXPIRATION      := 300;
    my_msg_props.CORRELATION     := 'DINNER TIME'
    -- my_msg_props.ATTEMPTS not set at time of enqueue
        subscriber(1) := SYS.AQ$_AGENT('DINAH',NULL,NULL);
        subscriber(2) := SYS.AQ$_AGENT('SPANKY',NULL,NULL);
        subscriber(3) := SYS.AQ$_AGENT('ATHENA',NULL,NULL);
    my_msg_props.RECIPIENT_LIST  := subscriber;
    my_msg_props.EXCEPTION_QUEUE := 'NOT_HUNGRY_EXCEPTION_Q';
    -- my_msg_props.ENQUEUE_TIME not set by user
    -- my_msg_props.STATE not set by user
```

```
my_enq_opts.VISIBILITY            := DBMS_AQ.IMMEDIATE;
my_enq_opts.RELATIVE_MSGID        := '02AB9AD2FG4859C5';
my_enq_opts.SEQUENCE_DEVIATION    := DBMS_AQ.TOP;

my_message := message_type('clause','We are hungry!');
DBMS_AQ.ENQUEUE('MY_QUEUE',
                enqueue_options=>my_enq_opts,
                message_properties=>my_msg_props,
                payload=>my_message,
                my_msgid);
```

...

MSGID   MSGID is a RAW datatype. This is the handle by which the process enqueuing or dequeuing can refer to the message.

Exercises

1. Identify the five variables for the **enqueue( )** procedure. What function does each variable serve? Which variable is output?

2. Which two of these variable have multiple subvariables to be set?

3. What are the subvariables that must be used in conjunction with a time manager?

Processing Messages with DBMS_AQ.DEQUEUE

The **dequeue( )** procedure retrieves messages from the message queue. Privileges for use of this procedure are initially only granted to SYS, but can be given to other users with the AQ_USER_ROLE. Calls to **dequeue( )** have the following variables defined: DBMS_AQ.**dequeue**(*queue_name, dequeue_options, message_properties, payload, msgid*). The *queue_name* and *dequeue_options* variables are input, while the other three are output. The messages to be dequeued are determined by the consumer attempting to **dequeue( )** the message and several subvariables of *dequeue_options*. Only messages in the **ready** state may be dequeued unless a specific *msgid* is given as a subvariable for *dequeue_options*. Order of messages dequeued is determined by the queue table unless the order was overridden in the **enqueue( )** for that message.

QUEUE_NAME   This is a VARCHAR2 datatype used to identify the name of the queue from which messages are dequeued.

DEQUEUE_OPTIONS   This is a DBMS_AQ.DEQUEUE_OPTIONS_T type. When creating variables to be passed to **dequeue( )** in the application, use the same type this variable is declared with. Seven subvariables exist for this type: *consumer_name, dequeue_mode, navigation, visibility, wait, msgid,* and *correlation.* An example for the definition of the *dequeue_options* variable is listed in the following code block, and then after that the subvariables are explained.

```
DECLARE
    my_dq_options := DBMS_AQ.DEQUEUE_OPTIONS_T;
BEGIN
    my_dq_options.CONSUMER_NAME    := 'DINAH';
    my_dq_options.DEQUEUE_MODE     := DBMS_AQ.REMOVE;
    my_dq_options.NAVIGATION       := DBMS_AQ.FIRST_MESSAGE;
    my_dq_options.VISIBILITY       := DBMS_AQ.IMMEDIATE;
    my_dq_options.WAIT             := DBMS_AQ.NO_WAIT;
    my_dq_options.MSGID            := NULL;
    my_dq_options.CORRELATION      := 'DINNER TIME';
    ...
```

- **CONSUMER_NAME**   Name of the application, process, or user receiving the message. Should be NULL for queues not set up to handle more than one consumer.

- **DEQUEUE_MODE**   Specifies locks, if any, to be acquired on the message by the **dequeue( )** process. Can be **browse** for **read only** access similar to that used in **select** statements; **locked** for the ability to write to the message during the transaction, similar to a share lock acquired in a **select for update** statement; or **remove** for the ability to read the message, updating it or deleting it. The message is retained according to properties set in queue table creation.

- **NAVIGATION**   Determines the position of the message to be retrieved, the first step in retrieving messages. The second step is applying search criteria. The *navigation* variable can have one of three values. The **next_message** value is used for retrieving the next message available that matches search criteria. Alternately, **next_transaction** is used to skip remaining messages in the current transaction group and retrieve the first message of the next transaction group. Alternately, **first_message** is used to retrieve the first message that fits the search criteria, resetting the position to the beginning of queue.

- **VISIBILITY**   Defines visibility of the message within the transaction of the application dequeuing it. Values are **on_commit** if the message dequeued is part of the current transaction or **immediate** if the message is its own transaction.

- **WAIT**   Specifies how long to wait if an attempt is made to **equeue( )** a message and there is no message to retrieve. Values are **forever**, **no_wait**, and *num*, where *num* represents the number of seconds it will wait.

- **MSGID**   The message identifier for the message to be dequeued. If specified, the message will be dequeued even if expired.

- **CORRELATION**   The name of the message to be dequeued.

MESSAGE_PROPERTIES   See the definition for *message_properties* in the discussion of **enqueue( )**. This is an output variable.

PAYLOAD   Defines the variable into which the actual dequeued message will be placed. Should be the same type as the column storing *payload* on the queue table.

MSGID   The message identifier handle corresponding to the message dequeued.

Exercises

1. What privilege or role is used to manage access to DBMS_AQ? What purpose does the **dequeue( )** procedure serve?

2. What are the five subvariables accepted by **dequeue( )**? Which ones are input? Which one defines the search information applied to the specified queue to determine which messages will be dequeued?

Administering Queues and Queue Tables with DBMS_AQADM

Configuration of a queue table and the management of queues is handled with another package called DBMS_AQADM. This package defines several procedures and functions. Initially, only the SYS user can use the procedures and functions of DBMS_AQADM. However, additional users can be given access by granting them the role AQ_ADMINISTRATOR_ROLE. Configuration of a queue should be managed tightly, as improper configuration equals poor database performance. The role should be granted only to those users who really need it, such as the DBA, the queue administrator, or privileged users. A special procedure called **grant_type_access( )** is included with Oracle8 that must be run as the first step in administering the appropriate privileges for advanced queue object types to other users. The call to **grant_type_access( )** looks like **grant_type_access(***user***)**, where *user* is the input variable specifying the name of the user that will have access to advanced queuing procedures and associated types.

Managing Queue Tables

There are two procedures for managing queue tables: **create_queue_table( )** and **drop_queue_table( )**. All options for setup and removal of the queue tables into which all queues will be placed are handled with these procedures.

CREATE_QUEUE_TABLE( )   This procedure creates the queue table designed to store all queued messages for a queue or multiple queues with the same payload type. Objects created with a queue table include the table itself, a default exception queue called AQ$*QUEUE_TABLE_NAME*_E, a **read only** view for information on the queue table called AQ$*QUEUE_TABLE_NAME*, an index for time manager operations called AQ$*QUEUE_TABLE_NAME*_T, and an index or index-organized table to handle dequeuing on queues with multiple consumers called AQ$*QUEUE_TABLE_NAME*_I. A call to **create_queue_table( )** looks like DBMS_AQADM.**create_queue_table(***queue_table, queue_payload_type, storage_clause, sort_list, multiple_consumers, message_grouping, comment, auto_commit***)**. In these four views, the *QUEUE_TABLE_NAME* variable is replaced by the actual name of the queue.

DROP_QUEUE_TABLE( )   This procedure removes an existing queue table from the database. The queues in the queue table must first be stopped and removed before the queue table can be dropped. The call looks like DBMS_AQADM.**drop_queue_table**(*queue_table, force, auto_commit*).

Managing Queues

There are five procedures for managing the queues on a queue table. They are **create_queue( )**, **alter_queue( )**, **start_queue( )**, **stop_queue( )**, and **drop_queue( )**. The descriptions and general use of each procedure follows.

CREATE_QUEUE( )   This procedure creates a queue and places it into a queue table. The queue table must first be created, or else this procedure will not be able to create the queue. There are two types of queues that can be created: *normal* queues and *exception* queues. The call to **create_queue( )** looks like DBMS_AQADM.**create_queue**(*queue_name, queue_table, queue_type, max_retries, retry_delay, retention_time, dependency_tracking, comment,auto_commit*).

ALTER_QUEUE( )   This procedure changes the definition for features of the queue. Calls to **alter_queue( )** look like DBMS_AQADM.**alter_queue**(*queue_name, max_retries, retry_delay, retention_time, auto_commit*). Currently, only these variables are supported for change through the **alter_queue( )** procedure.

START_QUEUE( )   Activates the queue for enqueuing only, dequeuing only, or both. The two variables for allowing either dequeues, enqueues, or both can be set to TRUE or FALSE. A call to **start_queue( )** looks like **start_queue**(*queue_name, enqueue, dequeue*).

STOP_QUEUE( )   This procedure deactivates the queue for enqueuing or dequeuing usage. A queue cannot be stopped if there are active transactions against that queue. The two variables for allowing either dequeues, enqueues, or both can be set to TRUE or FALSE. A call to **stop_queue( )** looks like **stop_queue**(*queue_name, enqueue, dequeue*).

DROP_QUEUE( )   This procedure removes a queue from the queue table if it has already been stopped. An active queue cannot be dropped

from the queue table. A call to the **drop_queue( )** procedure looks like
drop_queue(*queue_name, auto_commit*).

Managing the Time Manager

The following procedures can be used to manage usage of time manager
within the advanced queuing system. Available procedures are
start_time_manager( ) and **stop_time_manager( )**. The actual time manager
process is not started or stopped by these procedures, only the activity of
time manager within the advanced queuing system is modified. The time
manager process is actually started by specifying a value of 1 for the
AQ_TM_PROCESSES initialization parameter before starting the Oracle
instance. Once started, the process runs for the life of the instance.

START_TIME_MANAGER   This procedure causes the time manager to
start operating. This process does not actually start the time manager process
running; that function is handled with the AQ_TM_PROCESSES initialization
parameter. There are no variables for this procedure, it is simply called with
DBMS_AQADM.**start_time_manager**.

STOP_TIME_MANAGER   This procedure causes the time manager to
stop operating. The actual time manager process will continue to run until
the instance is shut down. There are no variables passed in the call to this
procedure. The call looks like DBMS_AQADM.**stop_time_manager**.

Managing Queue Subscribers

The addition and removal of subscribers to a queue can be managed with
two procedures in this set: **add_subscriber( )** and **remove_subscriber( )**.
Also, the set of subscribers for a particular queue can be found with the
queue_subscribers( ) function.

ADD_SUBSCRIBER( )   A subscriber is added to a queue with this
procedure. This operation is only allowed on queues that allow multiple
consumers, and takes effect immediately. Calls to **add_subscriber( )** look
like DBMS_AQADM.**add_subscriber**(*queue_name, subscriber*).

REMOVE_SUBSCRIBER( )   A subscriber is removed from the queue
with this procedure. This operation takes place immediately. The call is
DBMS_AQADM.**add_subscriber**(*queue_name, subscriber*).

QUEUE_SUBSCRIBERS( )   This function returns a PL/SQL table containing a list of subscribers for a named queue. The call is DBMS_AQADM.**queue_subscribers**(*queue_name*).

Exercises

1. What package contains procedures and functions that support the administration of queues and queue tables? What role manages execution of this package?

2. What procedure must be executed in order to allow users other than SYS to access the package to manage queues and queue tables?

3. What are the four categories of procedures and functions in this package?

Chapter Summary

This chapter covered three important areas of Oracle8 new features, including the support of parallel DML in the database, new large object types, and the use of advanced queuing to provide for deferred execution of processes and messaging between processes. The material in this chapter will be tested on OCP Exam 5.

The first area covered was the use of parallel DML in the Oracle database. With the addition of partitioning on database tables, Oracle also provides improved facilities to handle DML operations like **update**, **insert**, and **delete** in parallel. Use of parallel DML offers several benefits to users and administrators, including increased performance for large-volume database changes. Oracle also handles parallelism automatically, which simplifies the use of parallel operations. In situations where partitioning is used, the parallelism of DML operations necessitates the use of partition-to-device mapping. This coordinating operation is handled implicitly, which frees the user from having to know the relationships of instance to disk to partition explicitly.

There are three types of parallelism available. They are parallelism by ROWID, parallelism by partitions, and parallelism by I/O processes. Parallelism by ROWID ranges is used when Oracle divides the work of selecting data from the database into several ranges by ROWID, and spawns multiple I/O processes to search each range. The ranges in turn may not span a partition. Another option is parallelism by partitions. This may only be used for partitioned tables. An I/O process is spawned to work in one and only one partition. This parallelism is used for **update** and **delete** statements in partitioned tables as of Oracle8. The final option is parallelism by parallel I/O processes. This process of parallelism is used for **insert** statements on either partitioned or nonpartitioned tables. Since inserted data does not have a ROWID yet, the data is divided equitably between the I/O processes spawned. Each process inserts data above the table's highwatermark, which is then altered by the **commit** statement later.

Parallel DML must be enabled in the session before Oracle allows the user to use it. There is no instance-wide method for setup of parallel DML. The statement used to enable parallel DML is **alter session enable parallel DML**. Once enabled, parallel DML can be used for the entire session, or until the **alter session disable parallel DML** statement is issued to disable it. If a transaction contains parallel DML, the transaction must be committed or rolled back after issuing the parallel DML and before issuing another **select** or DML statement, or else an error will ensue. The DML statement may not always operate in parallel without the further issuance of a hint in the actual statement. Hints used are **parallel** for **select**, **update**, **insert**, and **delete** statements, and the **append** and **noappend** hints for **insert** statements to use direct load or not use it, respectively. One final performance improvement for parallel DML can be specified in a table. The table can be altered to specify that no redo log entries will be created by or DML statements issued on that table. The syntax for this statement is **alter table** name **logging** to turn redo logging on, or **alter table** name **nologging** to turn it off.

There are several dictionary views used to find information about parallel DML operations. The V$SESSION view contains a new column called PDML_ENABLED, which identifies if parallel DML is being used in that session. The V$PQ_SESSTAT has a new row called "DML Parallelized" to track statistics for parallel DML in sessions. Finally, a new row called "DML Initiated" has been added to V$PQ_SYSSTAT, to track system statistics in this category. Finally, transaction and process recovery for parallel DML can take a great deal more time to complete than the actual parallel DML operation. This is because the parallel DML statement must be rolled back serially in many cases.

This chapter also covered the new datatypes in Oracle8 for large objects. There are several new datatypes to support large objects in Oracle8, called binary large object (BLOB), character large object/NLS character large object (CLOB, NCLOB), and external binary file (BFILE). The differences between LONG/LONG RAW and the LOB/BFILE types are many, including twice the size allowed for LOBs, support for many LOB table and object columns(except for NCLOB), nonsequential access to data in the LOB, and storage out of line with the table data for LOBs.

A LOB consists of two components: a locator and the value. The locator is stored inline with the rest of table data, while the value is stored in another segment (BLOB/CLOB) if the size of the value is over 4,000 bytes, or external to Oracle (BFILE). LOBs have several storage aspects to be defined, such as the tablespace in which to store the LOB tablespace, the LOB index tablespace, and a host of other new storage options. Oracle supports a new unit of storage for LOBs, called a *chunk*. The chunk is composed of several contiguous blocks bound together in a segment. The number of blocks used in a chunk is specified by the **chunk** option. Although the blocks of a chunk need to be stored together, the LOB can be stored in noncontiguous chunks. If the data in a LOB is changed beyond a percentage threshold specified by the **pctversion** clause, then Oracle will reclaim unused space from the object for reuse. The use of the buffer cache in LOB read/write processing can also be specified with the **cache** or **nocache** option. Further, the redo logging of transactions that modify LOBs can be turned on or off if the **nocache** option is used with either **logging** or **nologging**.

BFILE objects are **read only**, because Oracle cannot manage the storage for the objects. For BFILE large objects, only the locator for the external object is stored in the Oracle database. An additional object is created for BFILEs, called a *directory object*, to identify the pathname to locate and read the object. A directory object is created with the **create or replace directory** *name* **as** *'path'* statement. The *path* specified is operating system specific, and there may be some issues with migrating Oracle8 database directory objects from one operating system to another. On creation, Oracle will not verify whether the directory referenced by the directory object exists. If the filesystem directory doesn't exist, Oracle will not create it. An error will be produced only at the time when the BFILE is referenced. Oracle recommends not creating directory objects that reference directories containing Oracle datafiles, redo logs, control files, password files, or the **init.ora** file.

To access the data in a LOB, the DBMS_LOB package or Oracle Call Interface can be used. An empty value can be placed in a LOB with the use of the **empty_blob( )** or **empty_clob( )** procedure. Several other procedures and functions are available in the DBMS_LOB package, divided into two categories: mutators and observers. Mutator procedures and functions include **append( )**, **copy( )**, **erase( )**, **trim( )**, **write( )**, **fileclose( )**, **filecloseall( )**, **fileopen( )**, and **loadfromfile( )**. The observer procedures include **compare( )**, **filegetname( )**, **instr( )**, **getlength( )**, **read( )**, **substr( )**, **fileexists( )**, and **fileisopen( )**.

The final area covered in this chapter is the use of Oracle advanced queuing. Queuing is the use of messages in the database to defer certain operations and to communicate execution status between two or more processes. The result is a seamless blend of database storage, application transaction processing, and messages—all managed within the Oracle architecture. A message is composed of two parts: user data and control information. The data is the actual transaction with its related data, and the control information determines things like when the message will run. Messages are stored in special database objects called queues, and they are placed into and read from queues with the use of two procedures in another new package of the Oracle architecture, called DBMS_AQ. The procedures of DBMS_AQ include **enqueue( )** and **dequeue( )**, used for putting messages into queues and reading them from queues, respectively. Several of the variables for these procedures have their own user-defined types, coming from the package as well.

As stated, queues are stored in queue tables. The management of queue tables is handled with procedures and functions in another PL/SQL package called DBMS_AQADM. The procedures of this package fall into four categories: management of queue tables, management of queues, management of time manager, and management of subscribers. The procedures and functions of this package are **create_queue_table( )**, **drop_queue_table( )**, **create_queue( )**, **drop_queue( )**, **alter_queue( )**, **start_queue( )**, **stop_queue( )**, **start_time_manager( )**, **stop_time_manager**, **start_time_manager**, **add_subscriber( )**, **remove_subscriber( )**, and **queue_subscribers( )**. Two areas related to queuing are the use of the time manager and the dictionary views for use with queuing. The time manager is used in conjunction with several features of queuing, such as delayed dequeuing and message expiration. Time manager is a process that runs as part of the Oracle instance when the AQ_TM_PROCESSES initialization parameter is set to 1. The **start_time_manager** and **stop_time_manager** processes activate and deactivate the already running time manager. The advanced queuing feature has a few dictionary views available in conjunction with its use. One is DBA_QUEUE_TABLES, to identify information about all the queue tables on the database. Another is DBA_QUEUES, to identify information about the queues on the database. The last set of views are for every queue table on the database, called AQ$*QUEUE_TABLE_NAME*, where the name of the queue table is part of the view name.

Two-Minute Drill

- Oracle8 allows DML operations to run in parallel.

- Parallel DML offers performance benefits, automatic parallelism, and affinity between partitions and disks.

- There are three types of parallelism: parallelism by ROWID range, parallelism by partition, and parallelism by I/O process.

- Parallelism by ROWID range is used in **select** statements.

- Parallelism by partition is used in parallel **update** and **delete** statements.

- Parallelism by I/O process is used in parallel **insert** statements.

- The **alter session enable parallel DML** statement is used to enable parallel DML in a session.

- There is no way to institute parallel DML for an entire instance.

- When using parallelism by partition, only one I/O process can operate on a partition.

- When using parallelism by I/O process or by ROWID range, multiple I/O processes can access a single partition, or a nonpartitioned table, at once.

- Only one parallel DML operation is allowed per transaction.

- No DML or **select** statements may be issued after a successful parallel DML operation in a transaction.

- Even though all DML statements issued after parallel DML is enabled are considered for parallelism, not all statements will be executed in parallel. To guarantee parallelism in a DML statement, use the **parallel** hint, specified with the **/*+parallel** (*tablename, degree_parallel*) **/*** syntax.

■ The degree of parallelism defined in the **create table** statement specifies the default degree of parallelism in DML and **select** statements issued on that table later.

■ Parallel hints can be specified for both the **insert** and the **select** statement in an **insert as select** statement.

■ The **append** or **noappend** hints are also available for **insert** statements, telling Oracle to use the **insert** direct path or not, respectively.

■ The **insert** direct path is similar to the direct path available in SQL*Loader.

■ New features have been added in support of parallel DML to the V$SESSION, V$PQ_SESSTAT, and V$PQ_SYSSTAT views in the form of new statistics collected in the latter two views and a new PDML_ENABLED column in the former view.

■ Redo logging can be turned on and off on a per-table basis for **insert** statements only with the **alter table** *name* **logging** and **alter table** *name* **nologging** statements, respectively.

■ Transaction and process recovery takes longer for parallel DML because usually the **rollback** process executes serially.

■ No parallel DML is allowed on bitmap indexes, tables with LOBs or object types, or clustered tables, and parallel DML must be committed or rolled back before executing another DML statement.

■ No parallel **update** on global unique indexes, and no parallel **insert** on any global index.

■ The new LOB datatypes available on Oracle8 databases are BLOB, CLOB, NCLOB, and BFILE. There is no implicit conversion between LOB datatypes.

■ LOBs have two components: value and locator.

- Differences between LONG/LONG RAW datatypes and LOB datatypes are size (2G vs. 4G), multiple LOB columns per table vs. one LONG/LONG RAW, LONG data is stored inline in the table vs. only LOB locators stored inline, and object types support LOBs (except NCLOB), not LONG/LONG RAW. Finally, access to LOB data is nonsequential, while LONG/LONG RAW data only permits sequential access to data in the column.

- LOBs have several storage considerations over and above normal objects. LOBs may have a tablespace defined to store the LOB value and another tablespace for the associated index.

- Oracle supports data storage for LOB datatypes with a new structure—a chunk. A chunk is a collection of blocks used to store LOB data. The blocks in the chunk must be contiguous, but the chunks used to store LOB data needn't be.

- The number of blocks in a chunk is defined with the object containing the LOB.

- Oracle will attempt to reclaim unused blocks in a chunk if the amount of data changed in the space of the chunk exceeds a certain threshold.

- The LOB column can have a NULL value assigned to it with either the **empty_blob( )** or **empty_clob( )** procedure.

- Access to internal LOB data is managed by the DBMS_LOB PL/SQL package or the Oracle Call Interface.

- DBMS_LOB procedures and functions are divided into mutators and observers.

- The mutators include **append( )**, **copy( )**, **erase( )**, **trim( )**, **write( )**, **fileclose( )**, **filecloseall( )**, **fileopen( )**, and **loadfromfile( )**.

- The observer procedures include **compare( )**, **filegetname( )**, **instr( )**, **getlength( )**, **read( )**, **substr( )**, **fileexists( )**, **fileisopen( )**.

- The BFILE type is not stored in the Oracle database. Only the locator is stored in the database. BFILE objects are **read only**.

■ To access an external object, a directory object must be created to identify its filesystem location. Creation of a directory object is done with **create or replace directory** *name* **as** *'path'* statement.

■ Creating a directory object in Oracle doesn't create the underlying directory path in the operating system. There is also no check at the time the directory object is created to verify if the path exists. An error only occurs at the time the BFILE is referenced.

■ Oracle8 supports advanced queuing of messages between multiple processes and the deferral of executing database operations.

■ The fundamental unit of queuing is a message.

■ Messages have two components: user data and control information.

■ Messages are stored in a queue.

■ Queues are stored in a queue table.

■ Messages are put into a queue with procedures from the DBMS_AQ package.

■ **Grant_type_access( )** must be executed by SYS in order to manage access to advanced queue object types.

■ The two procedures available in DBMS_AQ are **enqueue( )** and **dequeue( )**.

■ The management of queues and queue tables is done with the DBMS_AQADM package. The procedures of this package are **create_queue_table( )**, **drop_queue_table( )**, **create_queue( )**, **drop_queue( )**, **alter_queue( )**, **start_queue( )**, **stop_queue( )**, **start_time_manager( )**, **stop_time_manager**, **add_subscriber( )**, **remove_subscriber( )**, and **queue_subscribers( )**.

■ The roles used for managing access to the DBMS_AQ and the DBMS_AQADM packages are AQ_USER_ROLE and AQ_ADMINISTRATOR_ROLE.

■ Certain features of messaging such as dequeue delay and message expiration depend on the use of the time manager process. The time manager must be turned on as part of the start of the Oracle instance, by setting the AQ_TM_PROCESSES initialization parameter to 1.

■ Available dictionary views for queuing are DBA_QUEUE_TABLES for queue tables, DBA_QUEUES for queues, and AQ$*QUEUE_TABLE_NAME* for each queue table in the database.

Chapter Questions

1. **The DBA has run the START_TIME_MANAGER( ) process, but several of the expiration features in queuing still don't work. Which of the following may solve the problem?**

   A. The DBMS_LOB package hasn't been created.

   B. The AQ_TM_PROCESSES initialization parameter hasn't been set.

   C. The DBA ran the **grant_type_access( )** procedure.

   D. Queuing is not available in Oracle8.

2. **To execute parallel DML on the Oracle database, the DBA must**

   A. Specify **parallel** clauses in the **create table** statement

   B. Execute the **alter table** *name* **nologging** statement

   C. Execute the **alter session enable parallel DML** statement

   D. **Commit** the transaction

3. **An UPDATE statement on a partitioned table will parallelize by**

   A. Partitions

   B. ROWID ranges

   C. Slave I/O processes

   D. The **/*+append */** hint

4. **Which of the following can parallel DML not operate on? (Choose three.)**

   A. Partitioned tables

   B. Bitmap indexes

C. Clustered tables

D. Tables containing object types

5. Execution privileges on procedures in the DBMS_AQ package are managed with the

A. AQ_USER_ROLE

B. AQ_EXECUTE_ROLE

C. AQ_ADMINISTRATOR_ROLE

D. CREATE_QUEUE_TABLE( )

6. The DBA creates a directory object specifying a pathname that doesn't currently exist on the filesystem. She should expect to receive an error when

A. The **create or replace directory** statement is executed

B. The **create or replace directory** statement is committed

C. The BFILE object is created

D. The BFILE object is accessed

7. The number of blocks that comprise a chunk is defined by

A. The DB_CHUNK_SIZE initialization parameter

B. The **chunk** clause used in LOB storage definition

C. The **create tablespace** statement

D. The **create datafile** statement

8. The two components of a large object are

A. Value and type

B. Value and locator

C. Type and locator

D. Value and control

9. What parameter is used to carry a message into the queue with the ENQUEUE( ) procedure?

    A. *message*

    B. *msgid*

    C. *queue_data*

    D. *payload*

10. Oracle can write data to a BFILE object.

    A. TRUE

    B. FALSE

11. The DBA should not define a directory object on a directory in the filesystem containing which files?

    A. Oracle datafiles

    B. Operating system utilities

    C. Word processing software

    D. Web pages

12. The DBA creates a table containing two LOB columns, a BLOB and a CLOB. What is the maximum number of tablespaces that contain data for this table?

    A. 2

    B. 3

    C. 5

    D. 7

Answers to Chapter Questions

1. B.   The AQ_TM_PROCESSES initialization parameter hasn't been set.

Explanation   Several features of the Oracle advanced queuing system use time-based features. For the time-based features to work, the time manager process must be running on the Oracle instance. Although the **start_time_manager( )** process is used to activate the time manager for use, this process doesn't actually start the execution of the time manager process. Only setting the AQ_TM_PROCESSES initialization parameter to 1 can do that.

2. C.   Execute the **alter session enable parallel DML** statement.

Explanation   Parallel hints can be used in DML statements, but in order for a statement to be executed in parallel, the session must have parallel DML processing enabled.

3. A.   Partitions

Explanation   An **update** or **delete** statement on a partitioned table will parallelize by partition. Parallelism by ROWID ranges is used for **select** statements, eliminating choice B. Slave I/O parallelism and the direct path **insert** managed by the **append** hint are both used in database **insert** statements, eliminating choices C and D.

4. B, C, and D.

Explanation   Parallel DML cannot operate on bitmap indexes, tables with object types, or clustered tables. They can operate on partitioned tables. Review the limitations on parallel DML.

5. A.   AQ_USER_ROLE

Explanation   The AQ_USER_ROLE is used to administer **execute** privileges on the DBMS_AQ package. Choice B is not an Oracle-defined role, and

Choice D is a procedure in the DBMS_AQADM package used to create queue tables. AQ_ADMINISTRATOR_ROLE is used to administer **execute** privileges on the DBMS_AQADM package, eliminating choice C.

6. D.   The BFILE object is accessed.

Explanation   Oracle does not check the path specified at directory creation time to see if it exists. Therefore, choice A is incorrect. The **create or replace directory** statement is DDL, and therefore does not need to be committed, eliminating choice B. The BFILE object is created externally from Oracle, so there is no check performed at that time either, eliminating choice C.

7. B.   The **chunk** clause used in LOB storage definition

Explanation   All information, options, and clauses pertaining to the definition for storage of internal LOBs such as BLOBs, CLOBs, and NCLOBS, can be found in the storage clause of the object storage definition. Review the creation of large objects.

8. B.   Value and locator

Explanation   Every LOB has a locator, which is stored inline with the table. The locator is a pointer to the value, which is stored in a segment away from the main table information or external to the database, as in the case of BFILE.

9. D.   *payload*

Explanation   Answering this question requires experience with the **enqueue( )** and **dequeue( )** operations. Although the information carried by the queue is called a message, the variable that carries it into the queue or out of the queue is called the *payload*. Review the discussion of **enqueue( )** and **dequeue( )**.

10. B.   FALSE

Explanation   Data declared as a BFILE is stored external to the database, and therefore Oracle cannot write to it. Review the discussion on LOB types.

11. A.   Oracle datafiles

Explanation   The users of the database should not have access to the files of the Oracle database or their directories through any other method than the Oracle RDBMS. To allow access in any other way jeopardizes the integrity of the system.

12. C.   5

Explanation   A table containing two LOB columns can have as many as five tablespaces containing its data. Consider the following. The first tablespace stores the inline table data, including locator data for the LOBs. The second and third are used to store the LOB value data. The fourth and fifth are used to store index data for the LOB. Indexes are used to manage the contents of the LOB. Since table partitioning is not allowed on tables containing LOB columns, there can be no more tablespaces used than these five.

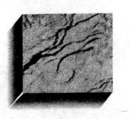

CHAPTER
24

Oracle8: Using
Recovery Manager

n this chapter, you will understand and demonstrate knowledge in the following areas:

- Introducing Recovery Manager
- Using catalog commands and reports
- Using **run** commands and scripts

Until Oracle8, the DBA required skills for database backup and recovery that blended knowledge of the underlying operating system and available Oracle tools. With the release of Oracle8 comes the introduction of a new tool to assist the DBA with executing the backup and recovery strategy for the Oracle database. This new tool is called Recovery Manager, or RMAN. The purpose of this chapter is to cover the use and features of this new tool, the language constructs it possesses, and the advantages it offers over Oracle7 backup and recovery strategy.

Introducing Recovery Manager

In this section, you will cover the following topics related to introducing Recovery Manager:

- Identifying Recovery Manager architecture and benefits
- Defining the recovery catalog
- Identifying backup types and commands
- Listing associated data dictionary views

RMAN possesses many features to ease the job of backup and recovery. This section will introduce you to the architecture and benefits of RMAN, along with the types of backups that are possible with the tool. The use of the RMAN catalog will also be presented in this section. Finally, the new data dictionary views provided to support RMAN are explained and presented.

Identifying Recovery Manager Architecture and Benefits

Recovery Manager, or RMAN, is used to manage the creation of database backups for the purpose of recovery. RMAN can be run as its own utility, or the functionality of RMAN can be used as a set of library functions that are embedded into another program or script. RMAN interfaces directly with Oracle8 to handle backup and recovery operations with the use of PL/SQL. The actual work of producing the backup or applying the recovery is done within Oracle8. RMAN also maintains a recovery catalog, or collection of backups taken to improve the DBA's ability to provide fast and effective recovery. RMAN works in conjunction with other products designed to support the mechanics of backup and recovery, such as offline storage media.

RMAN's approach to backup is as follows. The entire database can be backed up using RMAN, or it can be used for individual tablespaces and datafiles. This functionality is the same as that provided in Oracle8's predecessor. In addition, RMAN supports backup to the granularity of changed data blocks, a function not provided in Oracle7. This new feature can correlate backup time directly to the amount of change made to a database rather than to the size of the database. Consider the impact of this change—instead of backups on infrequently changed large databases for DSS or data warehouses taking hours because the database stores 20G or more of data, RMAN can complete the backup task in only a short while by targeting only the changed blocks for backup.

RMAN also eases the task of automating overall database backup and recovery. If there is a backup operation executed repeatedly, the DBA can create a backup script in an Oracle-supported utility. This utility also lets the DBA generate logs of backup and recovery activity. RMAN is well integrated with the Oracle8 database architecture, and the backup and recovery operations take advantage of several of the database's new features. These features include parallel backup and recovery, definition of conditions for backing up datafiles and targeting locations rather than simply listing the datafiles to back up and their correlated storage devices, and even compression of unused blocks.

RMAN can be run in two ways: either from the operating system command line as a batch interface or in an interactive mode, or with the graphical user interface provided by Oracle Enterprise Manager. There is even an application programming interface (API) available to allow other programming languages to use RMAN to manage Oracle backup and recovery.

Exercises

1. What is RMAN? How can DBAs interface with RMAN?

2. What new category of backup does RMAN provide?

3. Identify some benefits for using RMAN in backup and recovery.

Defining the Recovery Catalog

RMAN works in conjunction with another new feature: the recovery catalog. The recovery catalog is a collection of information about the backup and recovery operations, along with the actual backups taken with RMAN. Ideally, it is stored in a separate database from the production system whose backup and recovery processing is being handled by RMAN. The recovery catalog is not created automatically when Oracle8 is installed. The DBA must create it separately with the **catrman.sql** script provided with the Oracle database distribution software; the script is found in the **rdbms/admin** subdirectory of the Oracle software home directory. It is also recommended that a schema owner be created for RMAN to run under on the recovery catalog in order to manage the scripts and other information generated by RMAN effectively. After creating the recovery catalog in a separate database, the DBA makes that other database available to RMAN via remote links. Once created, the recovery catalog is its own database, and must be backed up as such. Thus, a symbiotic relationship is formed between the production or "target" database and the recovery catalog "backup" database; as the backup supports recovery for the production database, the production database can act as the backup for the recovery catalog database.

The contents of the recovery catalog include the following components. The physical structure of the production database is stored on the recovery catalog. Also stored in the recovery catalog are the datafiles of the database and the archived redo logs. Further, a set of copies for datafiles and archived redo logs is stored in the database. This recovery catalog is a repository of information useful to and maintained by RMAN, and is never directly accessed by the production database itself. Any structural changes to the production database should be maintained in the recovery catalog by RMAN. Instructions on how to perform this task will be covered shortly. Since a great deal of information about the structure of the database is taken from control files and rollback segments, the production database must be open in order to use RMAN to execute its processing. If for some reason RMAN attempts to execute something improperly, or attempts to use a corrupt file, there are integrity checks built into the Oracle database to prevent RMAN from causing inadvertent damage.

Oracle can also operate RMAN in the absence of the recovery catalog under certain conditions. These conditions include the maintenance of small databases where the use of an additional database to store the recovery catalog would be more trouble than it is worth. Since much of the structural information about the Oracle database maintained in the recovery catalog is taken from the control file anyway, RMAN in this case can go directly to the source for structural information about the database it maintains. There are, however, some limitations for using RMAN without the recovery catalog. For one thing, the use of automated scripts for executing routine backup operations is not supported without the recovery catalog. The operations involving a tablespace point-in-time recovery are also not supported without the use of the recovery catalog. Finally, recovery when the control file doesn't reflect the current structure of the Oracle database cannot be accomplished using RMAN without the recovery catalog. These limits can be mild or severe, depending on the level of failure encountered on the production database.

Exercises

   1. What is the recovery catalog? How does the DBA create it?

   2. What are the components of the recovery catalog?

   3. Under what situations might the DBA not want to use the recovery catalog? What are the limitations for doing so?

Identifying Backup Types and Commands

There are many features to RMAN. These features include enhanced backup and recovery operations, full-featured command syntax, changes to the control file to support RMAN, and other items covered in this discussion. The first item up for discussion is how RMAN interfaces with the database. As mentioned, RMAN uses several PL/SQL packages to interface with the different components of backup and recovery—Oracle8, the operating system, and third party backup products and/or offline storage media. With the use of these packages, Oracle can interface directly with the operating system to define the disks that need backing up and the disks that contain restore or recovery information. In this way, the DBA needn't interface with the operating system as part of backup and recovery, as was required in prior versions of Oracle. In addition, scripts can be defined to handle routine backup and recovery operations using Oracle-supported products. This increases the level of service the DBA can expect from the Oracle database. And, with the use of the RMAN API, Oracle can communicate directly with backup and recovery products offered by other vendors, making the overall backup and recovery process available with the Oracle database much improved.

There are a host of maintenance commands the DBA should understand in order to use RMAN. These commands register the production database with the recovery catalog to store all information about the production database. There are commands used for resetting the recovery catalog after performing incomplete recovery as well. Recall from the discussion of incomplete recovery in Chapter 13 that the archived redo logs from after the point-in-time recovery should be discarded, or else data corruption issues will ensue. The recovery catalog can be used to reflect changes to the structure of the production database, and to reflect the status of the backup control files.

RMAN also supports a set of commands that perform the core functionality of the tool—**backup**, **restore**, and **recover** operations. The **backup**, **restore**, and **recover** operations can be used whenever the production database needs any of these operations performed, either with the use of the **run** command whereby they are executed immediately, or through the creation of a script. The script is then kept in the recovery catalog for reuse. The script is then executed with the use of the **run** command as well, and should be backed up into a flat file that can be stored externally from the Oracle recovery catalog in the event the recovery catalog is not available and the scripted operation needs to be run.

RMAN supports the logging of **backup, restore,** and **recover** operations as well. There are two categories of logging supported by RMAN: reports and lists. A report gives information on several areas, including datafile components that require incremental backup or redundant copies, datafile components that haven't been backed up for a certain time period, unrecoverable datafile components, and unneeded backups. Reports are produced with the **report** command. A list gives information about several areas of the database backup and recovery plan, including backups and backup copies containing a given list of datafile components or datafile components belonging to a specified tablespace.

Backup Sets, Image Copies, and Tags

Backups for datafile or archived redo log components can be placed into collections called *backup sets*. There are two types of backup sets: *archivelog backup sets* and *datafile backup sets*. As the names imply, each type of backup set consists either of datafiles for database recovery or archived redo logs for recovery, but not both. Usually backup sets can be written to offline storage such as tape or online storage such as a backup disk. One suggestion is for DBAs to develop a system whereby backup sets are placed on disk and copied to tape periodically. After a specified period, the backup set on disk is eliminated to make room for more recent backup sets. In this fashion, the DBA may improve recovery time in certain situations by eliminating the often time-consuming step of retrieving backup sets from tape where the appropriate backup was on disk. RMAN also manages an important process—the segmented movement of backup sets from disk to tape and vice versa during backup and recovery. This process is called *staging*.

Datafile backup sets have several features. The first is a user-specified parameter that limits the number of datafiles backed up at the same time to the same backup set. Moderating this activity allows the DBA to strike a good balance between backing up datafile information to tape efficiently without causing undue burden on a particular datafile, thereby limiting online performance. The datafile backup set can be created from a production datafile or from a backup datafile. Full and incremental backups of datafiles are also supported with RMAN, combining incremental and full database backup and recovery features of EXPORT/IMPORT with the ability to make backups of physical database components like datafiles with redo log archives to allow complete recovery to the point of failure. More information about incremental and full backups using RMAN will be covered shortly.

Backup sets can also be multiplexed. Multiplexed backup sets contain data from many datafiles stored together. Recall that the server process reads data from datafiles into the buffer cache for use in user SQL statements. The server process also retrieves data blocks for RMAN to create backup sets. Since multiple datafiles and tablespaces can be accessed at the same time by one server process, the server process can retrieve blocks from one datafile when the datafile is less active from online processing, then switch off to another datafile when activity on the first one picks up. The data will then be ported into the backup set in a nonsequential manner, as illustrated in Figure 24-1, which can keep the stream of data flowing smoothly from the production database onto offline storage. The only impediment to smooth backup in this scenario is the need to change the tape, which is still the responsibility of the DBA or systems administrator. Control files can be included in a datafile backup set; however, the control file information will not be multiplexed with datafile information.

Once the backup set is completed, each component file of a backup set is called a *piece*. When RMAN creates the backup set out of datafiles or archived redo logs, it produces a single file of sequentially stored blocks from all datafiles or archive logs stored in the backup set for each tape volume used in the backup. If multiplexing is used, the piece will contain blocks from multiple datafiles, each file stored in nonsequential order. In order to recover a database, the necessary datafiles must first be restored

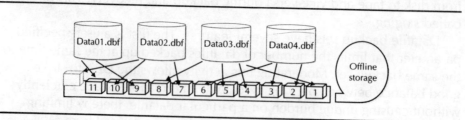

FIGURE 24-1. *Multiplexing datafile backup set information*

from pieces of the backup set. Datafile information can be distributed to different pieces on different tapes explicitly by the DBA or automatically by RMAN.

RMAN also supports the backup of individual datafiles in the database by creating image copies of these files. An image copy cannot be placed on offline storage, but can be made to disk. Unlike datafiles in backup sets, image copy datafiles needn't be restored before they are used in database recovery. RMAN allows the DBA to define a special name used in conjunction with an image copy or a backup set. This name is called a *tag*. The tag may be up to 30 characters in length, like a database object such as a table, and has similar naming restrictions. The tag can then be used in conjunction with restoring the backup set or image copy. Multiple backup objects can have the same tag. If a tag is specified for use in recovery, and more than one object corresponds to that tag, then the most recent object that is fit to use for the recovery will be the one RMAN uses.

Backup and Recovery Options with RMAN

Datafile backup sets can consist of either full or incremental backups. A full backup of a datafile consists of all blocks in a datafile, while an incremental backup of a datafile consists only of the datafile's blocks that changed since the last backup was taken. Thus, the DBA can reduce both the time it takes to obtain a backup of the database and the amount of storage that the backup will take. The DBA also has the option to take cumulative backups, which will consolidate the information stored in several incremental backups into one cumulative incremental backup of all changes made since the last full backup.

Multiple-level incremental backup strategies are also supported. Each level of incremental backup will capture data changes made according to specified time intervals. There are eight levels used in RMAN for multiple-level incremental backup strategy, numbered 0 through 7. Level 0 is a full backup of the datafile, level 1 is a monthly incremental, level 2 is a weekly incremental, level 3 is a daily incremental, and so on. The subsequent incremental backup strategy a DBA may choose to implement can take into account these different levels. Consider the following backup strategy. The baseline level 0 backup is made, followed by level 1 backups once a month, level 2 backups once a week, and level 3 backups once a day. Recovery of a datafile then consists of applying the most recent level 0 backup, then any level 1 backups occurring since then. The next step is to apply all level 2 backups made since the most recent level 1, followed by all level 3 backups made since the most recent level 2. This process continues until the supply of backups made is exhausted, at which point archived redo information taken after the most recent backup can be applied for full recovery to point of failure. RMAN also can interact with image copies of datafiles made without its assistance, such as in the case of mirrored datafiles on multiple disks used to provide highly fault-tolerant databases. However, these copies must be catalogued.

Database backup and recovery operation may also run in parallel. RMAN handles making backup and recovery operations run in parallel internally by running multiple sessions that have the ability to communicate with one another. Parallelism is used for the execution of only one command at a time. In other words, two commands (i.e., a backup on one part of the database while another is being recovered) cannot be run in parallel, but a **backup** operation can run in parallel, followed by a **recover** operation running in parallel.

A final change made to backup and recovery strategy in Oracle8 is the ability to handle point-in-time recovery of individual tablespaces. Recall from Chapter 13 that point-in-time recovery of an individual tablespace leads to read inconsistency of data in the Oracle7 database. To enact point-in-time recovery on the individual tablespace, the DBA must first create a clone of the database. It is highly recommended that this option be pursued only with the assistance of Oracle Worldwide Support, and point-in-time tablespace recovery can only be performed on non-SYSTEM tablespaces with the use of the EXPORT utility.

Preventing Problems

In order to execute a backup with RMAN, the recovery catalog database must be mounted and open, and the production database can be mounted or open. Thus, RMAN supports online backup of the Oracle database. As mentioned, to recover a damaged database, the necessary datafile and archive redo components must first be restored from backup sets. The **restore** operation may be performed with the instance open but the database not running, in the event that the control file is lost and must be re-created. As with Oracle7's use of checksums and DBVERIFY, Oracle8 has similar mechanisms that prevent the creation of corrupted backup datafiles, or the application of corrupt datafile information to the database. The occurrence of corrupt data in either place causes Oracle to write information to the control file and the **alert** log.

New Control File Features

There are several new features that are present in the Oracle8 control file, making it significantly changed from and larger than the Oracle7 control file. The Oracle8 control file stores information that is of use to RMAN. Some of this information is recycled, while other information is permanent. A new parameter called CONTROL_FILE_RECORD_KEEP_TIME allows the DBA to specify the period of time after which data in recyclable portions of the control file expire and the space in the control file that data occupies is reused. If more of this RMAN information needs to be stored, and the old information has not expired, then the control file will expand to accommodate the new data as well as the old. The value for CONTROL_FILE_RECORD_KEEP_TIME is specified as an integer, representing the number of days recyclable data will be stored before it expires. When this parameter is set to 0, the control file will not expand, allowing Oracle to expire the recyclable data as needed to make room for new data.

Exercises

1. Identify several different types of commands available in RMAN. What is a script? What is the **run** command? What is a report? What is a list?

2. What are the two types of backup sets? What is a multiplexed backup set? What is a piece? If a control file is stored in a backup set, will it be multiplexed? What is an image copy? What is a tag?

3. What is the difference between a full and incremental backup in this context? What is a multiple-level backup? Does Oracle8 support point-in-time tablespace recovery? Explain.

4. What new features and new parameter are used in conjunction with RMAN and the control file?

Listing Recovery Manager Dictionary Views

Several dynamic performance views exist in the data dictionary to support RMAN, some of which are new. Both the old and new dictionary views available are listed below:

- **V$ARCHIVED_LOG** Displays name and information in the control file about archived redo logs

- **V$BACKUP_CORRUPTION** Displays information in the control file about corrupt datafile backups

- **V$BACKUP_DATAFILE** Offers information from the control file about backup datafiles and control files

- **V$BACKUP_DEVICE** Offers operating-system-specific information about supported third-party vendors for RMAN in Oracle8

- **V$BACKUP_REDOLOG** Displays information about archived redo logs in backup sets

- **V$BACKUP_SET** Displays information from the control file about all backup sets

- **V$BACKUP_PIECE** Displays information from the control file about all pieces in all backup sets

- **V$DATAFILE** Lists information about datafiles in the Oracle8 database

- **V$DATAFILE_HEADER** Lists information about datafile headers in the Oracle8 database

Exercises

1. Which of the V$ performance views are used to store information about backup sets?

2. Which of the V$ performance views are used to store information about datafiles?

3. Which of the V$ performance views are used to store information about redo logs?

Using Catalog Commands and Reports

In this section, you will cover the following topics related to using catalog commands and reports:

- Starting Recovery Manager
- Maintaining the recovery catalog
- Generating reports and lists from the recovery catalog

In this section, an in-depth discussion of several topics already presented in the overview section will be covered. Starting RMAN and the commands for operating RMAN will be presented in greater detail, along with the details of recovery catalog maintenance. Generating reports and lists will also be covered. This section can be read as the technical specification to the topics presented in the previous section.

Starting Recovery Manager

There are four types of commands available in RMAN: recovery catalog maintenance, script maintenance and execution, report/list generation, and **run** commands. To start the RMAN utility, type **rman** at the operating system command line followed by the **target** keyword, followed by the connect string for the production database on which RMAN will operate in single- or double-quotes and press ENTER. Optionally, at the command line, four other things can be specified: the connect string location of the recovery catalog preceded by the **rcvcat** keyword, the pathname and location of a script containing commands that RMAN will process, and the keyword **cmdfile**. If a command file is used, RMAN runs in batch; otherwise, RMAN runs interactively. A name and path for a message log for the execution of RMAN can be specified at the operating system command line as well, preceded with the **msglog** keyword. RMAN can maintain an ongoing message log with the specification of the **append** keyword. An example for running RMAN in batch mode in UNIX with these specifications is shown below:

```
$/users/jcouchma/> rman target 'spanky/cat@orgdb01'\
> rcvcat 'backup/backup@orgcat01' \
> cmdfile '/usr/local/rman/cmd/lvl0bkp.cmd' \
> msglog '/usr/local/rman/msg/rman.msg' append
```

An example of running RMAN in **interactive** mode is listed below:

```
$/users/jcouchma/> rman target 'spanky/cat@orgdb01'
Recovery Manager: Release 8.0.3.0.0 - Production
RMAN>
```

RMAN terminates if it encounters an error at any point. Upon exit, RMAN will provide a return code according to its execution. If the entire operation was successful, RMAN returns **ex_succ**. If some commands succeeded, but the most recent one did not, then **ex_warn** will result. If no command processed was successful, **ex_fail** will be returned. The results of each command processed will be stored in the message file if one is defined; otherwise, the return codes will be displayed on the screen if RMAN is running interactively.

Exercises

1. What is the difference between running RMAN in **batch** mode and in **interactive** mode? What five command-line options can be specified for RMAN? Which one must always be specified?

2. What conditions cause RMAN to exit? What are the three return statuses given by RMAN, and what do they mean?

Maintaining the Recovery Catalog

There are several commands for maintaining the recovery catalog with RMAN. These commands allow the DBA to do many things, such as registering the target database with the recovery catalog, resetting information in the recovery catalog, and synchronizing information in the recovery catalog with the status of the target database. Other commands allow the DBA to change availability on a backup set or image copy, access the operating system for a backup or recovery operation to send signals through a channel, and to catalog image copies of datafiles made outside of RMAN.

REGISTER DATABASE   This process must be executed the first time RMAN is run. When executed, RMAN obtains data from the production database targeted and places necessary information into the recovery catalog. The production instance must be started and the database mounted for this operation. There are no parameters or additional clauses for this operation. The following code block shows the execution of this procedure:

```
REGISTER DATABASE;
```

RESET DATABASE   If the database has been opened with the **resetlogs** option to reset the sequence number of the online redo logs, a new incarnation, or version, of the target database information in the recovery catalog must be created with the **reset database** command in RMAN. This step must be accomplished or else RMAN will not allow further access to the recovery catalog. Occasionally, such as in the situation of point-in-time recovery, the DBA may want to reinstate a prior incarnation of the database. This is done by adding the **to incarnation** *num* clause to the **reset database** command. To obtain the value to substitute for *num*, use the **list incarnation of database** command and take the value from the column with the "Inc Key" header in the resultant output. Examples of both situations appear in the following code listings:

```
RESET DATABASE;
```

and using the **list incarnation of database** command,

```
LIST INCARNATION OF DATABASE;
RESET DATABASE TO INCARNATION 2;
```

RESYNC CATALOG   The recovery catalog is not updated when a log switch occurs, when a log file is archived, or when datafiles or redo logs are added. Thus, the **resync catalog** command must periodically be executed to keep the recovery catalog in line with the production database. This command is executed automatically when a database is registered, and after a backup, recovery, or restoration. The default is for the recovery catalog to resync against the current control file. Alternately, a backup control file may be named for the process. The following code block illustrates use of this command:

```
RESYNC CATALOG;
RESYNC CATALOG FROM BACKUP CONTROLFILE
'/home/Oracle/backup/orgdb01bkp.ctl';
```

ALLOCATE CHANNEL and RELEASE CHANNEL   These commands are used in conjunction with all major backup, restore, and recovery operations to allow communication between RMAN and the operating system for the purpose of manipulating files. The **allocate channel** *channel_name* command opens the line of communication, while the **release channel** *channel_name* command closes it. A channel can be named by adding a name in place of *channel_name*. The channel can be allocated with specific purposes in mind, such as with the **for delete** clause to delete files. Channels with specific resources in the filesystem can also be opened, both by name with the **name** "*resource_name*" clause or simply by type with the **type disk** clause. Parameters for allocating the channel and connect string for doing so can also be identified as part of the **allocate channel** command. Only one option is allowed for the **release channel** command, the name of the channel. Some examples for usage of these commands are listed in the following code block:

```
ALLOCATE CHANNEL my_channel FOR DELETE TYPE DISK;
ALLOCATE CHANNEL channel1 NAME "BKPTAPE:TAPE1";
ALLOCATE CHANNEL c1 TYPE DISK;
```

and for use of the **release channel** command,

```
RELEASE CHANNEL channel1;
```

CHANGE   The **change** command alters the availability status of a specified backup item. For backups, the **backuppiece** keyword is used. For archived redo logs, the **archivelog** keyword is used. For image copy, the **datafilecopy** keyword is used. For a control file backup, the **backup**

controlfile keywords are used. The availability statuses that can be specified are **delete**, **unavailable**, **available**, and **uncatalog**. To delete a backup object, the DBA must first issue the **allocate channel** command, because the **change** command will issue a signal to the operating system to tell it to delete the backup file. Marking a backup object **unavailable** is used to identify the backups that are missing or offsite, and therefore allowed for use in a recovery or restoration operation. Marking the object **available** means it has been found or is onsite and available again. The **uncatalog** option removes the backup permanently from the control file if it has been deleted. Both the target and the recovery catalog must be defined for this operation to work. The following code block demonstrates its use:

```
ALLOCATE CHANNEL channel1 FOR DELETE TYPE DISK;
CHANGE BACKUP CONTROLFILE '/oracle/home/bkp/orgdb01bkp.ctl' DELETE;
RELEASE CHANNEL channel1;
```

CATALOG   A datafile image copy, backup control file, or archived redo log taken using methods other than RMAN can be used by RMAN so long as they are identified to the recovery catalog. The method used for identifying these files to the recovery catalog is with the **catalog** command. Only files that are part of the database can be part of the recovery catalog for that database. Only Oracle8 files can be cataloged. Both the target database and the recovery catalog must be defined for this operation to work. For backups, the **backuppiece** keyword is used. For archived redo logs, the **archivelog** keyword is used. For image copy, the **datafilecopy** keyword is used. For a control file backup, the **backup controlfile** keywords are used. The following code block contains an example for use of **catalog**:

```
CATALOG BACKUP CONTROLFILE '/oracle/home/bkp/orgdb01bkp.ctl';
```

Exercises

1. Identify the commands used for the maintenance of the recovery catalog.

2. Which command must be issued in conjunction with the **change...delete** command?

Generating Reports and Lists from the Recovery Catalog

Another series of commands available in RMAN includes the commands used to define reports. Reports identify the database files that require backup. In addition, reports may help to identify which components of the database have not been backed up recently, and also to identify the backups that are no longer necessary for database recovery. Reports are generated with the **report** command. There are several common areas for report generation, listed here:

- **need backup**   The **need backup** clause tells RMAN to list all datafiles that are in need of a backup. The backup needed can be defined with three keywords. The **incremental** *num* keyword is for datafiles that require *num* or more incremental backups to be restored to the current state. Also, **days** *num* identifies datafiles that have not been backed up in any way for *num* or more days. Also, **redundancy** *num* identifies datafiles that require *num* backups to fulfill a minimum *num* number of redundancy.

- **obsolete**   Identifies backups that are no longer necessary.

- **unrecoverable**   Used to identify the datafiles in the database that are not recoverable with current backups available. Oracle also adds the **database** keyword to the **report** command.

The following code block illustrates use of the **report** command:

```
REPORT NEED BACKUP INCREMENTAL 5;
REPORT NEED BACKUP DAYS 3;
REPORT NEED BACKUP REDUNDANCY 2 DATABASE;
REPORT OBSOLETE REDUNDANCY 3;
REPORT UNRECOVERABLE DATABASE;
```

Lists provide a complementary function of showing which backups are available for specified datafiles, what copies exist for certain datafiles, and backup sets or image copies for datafiles belonging to a specified list of tablespaces. Lists also provide information about backup sets of archived redo logs and incarnations of the database. Lists are created with the **list** command. The clauses available are **copy of** *name*, **backupset of** *name*, and

incarnation of database *dbname*, where *name* is the name of a datafile or
tablespace, and *dbname* is the name of the database. Some example uses of
the **list** command appear in the following code block:

```
LIST COPY OF TABLESPACE "DATA01";
LIST COPY OF DATAFILE "/oracle/home/dbf/data01.dbf";
LIST BACKUPSET OF "SYSTEM";
LIST INCARNATION OF DATABASE "orgdb01";
```

Exercises

1. What is the **report** command and what are its uses? What are
   its options?

2. What is the **list** command and what are its uses? What are
   its options?

Using RUN Commands and Scripts

In this section, you will cover the following topics related to using **run**
commands and scripts:

- Channels, scripts, and attributes for **run** commands

- Using the **backup** command

- Using the **copy** command

- Using the **restore** command

- Using the **recover** command

The last two sets of commands are those used to operate backup,
restoration, and recovery of the Oracle database, and the commands used to
define scripts to execute the same. Collectively, the commands for backup
and recovery are known as the **run** commands because this keyword
precedes each of them when issued in RMAN. These operations map
directly to API calls. A more complete explanation of the uses for each of
the **run** commands appears as part of this section. The DBA can execute any
of these operations with the **run** command, following the general syntax **run**

{*command*}. There are four categories of **run** commands: **backup**, **copy**, **restore**, and **recover**. There are usually some associated **allocate channel** and **release channel** commands used for these to handle manipulation of files at the operating system level. In addition, the DBA can execute SQL DCL statements. DCL stands for data control language, the statements like **alter database enable restricted session** that set up the availability and runtime status of the database. These commands can be executed interactively within RMAN or, alternately, they can be put into a script and run with RMAN in batch. This section will cover each of these areas.

Channels, Scripts, and Attributes for RUN Commands

To execute most **run** commands, the DBA must first allocate a channel. This step establishes connection between RMAN and the operating system so that RMAN may create operating system files for backups and copies, or retrieve files for restores and recoveries. Channels can be allocated by type or by name. The syntax is **allocate channel** *channel_name*, where *channel_name* is a name the DBA assigns to the channel as a handle to refer to it later. If a channel is allocated by type such as with the **type disk** clause, then a specific device shouldn't be named by the DBA. Alternately, if the DBA allocates a channel with a specific device by name, such as with the **name** '*device_name*' clause, then the **type** clause shouldn't be used. When **name** '*device_name*' is used, an additional option called **parms** can be specified to allow the definition of port-specific parameters to be defined to allocate the channel. To operate a **run** command in parallel, the DBA must allocate a channel for each process working on the **run** command. An example for **allocate channel** is shown below:

```
RUN { ALLOCATE CHANNEL my_channel TYPE DISK };
```

Two related commands for channel allocation are **release channel** and **setlimit channel**. A channel can be released after the **backup**, **copy**, **restore**, or **recover** operation is complete. Syntax is straightforward, with only the specification of a *channel_name*. The second command is **setlimit channel** *channel_name*. It allows the DBA to set certain options on the activity of the channel. The parameters include the size of each backup piece with **kbytes** *num*, the number of blocks read per second by **backup** or **copy** commands with **readrate** *num*, and the number of files that can be open at one time by the channel with **maxopenfiles** *num*. Some examples of both statements appear in the following code block:

```
RUN { SETLIMIT CHANNEL my_channel
      KBYTES 2048 READRATE 100 MAXOPENFILES 50 };
RUN { RELEASE CHANNEL m_channel };
```

The **run** commands must be run in a script as well as interactively. When placed into a script, RMAN can execute the **run** command in batch. Scripts are created in RMAN using the **create script** command. Once created, the script is an object stored in the recovery catalog. It can be executed with the **run** command using the **execute script** command. To alter the commands in the script, the **replace script** command can be used. Deleting and printing scripts is possible as well with the **delete script** and **print script** commands, respectively. Examples of these statements appear in the following code block:

```
CREATE SCRIPT nightly_backup {
   ALLOCATE CHANNEL channel1 TYPE DISK;
   BACKUP INCREMENTAL LEVEL 3 (DATABASE 'orgdb01');
   RELEASE CHANNEL channel1;
 };
RUN { PRINT SCRIPT nightly_backup };
RUN { EXECUTE SCRIPT nightly_backup };
RUN { DELETE SCRIPT nightly_backup };
```

Attributes for the entirety of a **run** command can also be set using the **set** command. The attributes that can be defined include three clauses. The **maxcorrupt** *num* option defines a maximum number of corrupted blocks allowed in a datafile or list of datafiles extracted in a **backup** or **copy** command before RMAN terminates the **run** command. The **newname** *name* option can be used to change the name of the datafile being restored or switched. The **archivelog destination** *path* option changes the location where RMAN will look for restored redo log archives from the location specified in LOG_ARCHIVE_DEST to the location specified for *path*. The following code block illustrates its use:

```
RUN { SET MAXCORRUPT 0;
      SET ARCHIVELOG DESTINATION '/DISK1/oracle/home/arch/alt';
      ...
```

Exercises

1. What statement is used to set up lines of communication between RMAN and the operating system? What statement is used to close that line of communication? What statement defines certain features of that line of communication?

2. What statement defines an object that can be executed to process backup and recovery operations? How is the object modified and eliminated? Where is that object stored?

3. What statement defines options used throughout the **run** command?

Using the BACKUP Command

Backups for the database are created with the **backup** command. This command produces one or more backup sets into which backup copies of datafiles, archived redo logs, or control files may be placed. Password files and **init.ora** files are backed up separately. The number of backup sets created depends on the number of files backed up, the number of tapes required for the backup, the parallelism of the backup, and other factors. The parallelism of a backup depends on the number of channels allocated to the backup, and several backup sets will be the result of multiple channeled backups. The general syntax of the **backup** command consists of two parts, options and scope, and looks like **backup** *options* (*scope*). The **backup** options that may be specified include several things, such as **full**, **incremental level** *num*, **tag**, **cumulative**, **skip**, **parms**, **filesperset**, and **maxcorrupt**. The **backup** scope can be **database**, **tablespace**, **datafile**, **archivelog**, **backup controlfile**, and **current controlfile**.

The following code block illustrates an example backup. In this example, the DBA wants to create a full backup of the database. Remember that "full" in this context means that the "full" datafile, not just the changed blocks, will be backed up. The fact that the "full" database is backed up is specified with the **database** clause. The DBA explicitly defines the number of datafiles to multiplex into each backup set with the **filesperset** parameter, and defines a naming convention for the backup pieces in the **backup** command with the **format** option. Offline datafiles for the database will be skipped in the backup. These and other parameters will be explained shortly. The example is listed here:

```
RUN { ALLOCATE CHANNEL bkp_chan NAME 'tape_reel_1';
      BACKUP FULL FILESPERSET 5 SKIP OFFLINE
      ( DATABASE FORMAT 'bkp_full_orgdb01.%s.%p' );
      RELEASE CHANNEL bkp_chan;
};
```

The clauses that can be specified as *options* for the **backup** statement include those options in the following list:

- **full**   This will be a level 0 backup, in which the full datafile will be copied to the backup set.

- **incremental level**   This will be a level 1–8 backup, in which only the blocks changed since the last full backup will be taken. There must be an associated level 0 backup for the database in **available** status in the recovery catalog in order to define the baseline for the incremental.

- **tag** *name*   A name given to the backup set for identification later. It cannot be a reserved word, and is usually a meaningful identifier.

- **cumulative**   Flag for incremental backups stating that this incremental will accumulate all changes recorded in peer- or lesser-level incremental backups since the last level 0 full backup.

- **nochecksum**   No block checksum will be used in this backup to detect block corruption. It should only be used in conjunction with DB_BLOCK_CHECKSUM initialization parameter being TRUE for the instance.

- **filesperset** *num*   Explicitly defines the number of datafiles that can be multiplexed into individual backup sets.

- **maxcorrupt** *num*   Defines the maximum number of corrupt data blocks that will be backed up before the process fails.

- **skip** *option*   Defines datafile classes that will be skipped. Three options are available: **offline**, **readonly**, and **inaccessible**.

- **channel** *name*   Names the channel that should be used when creating backup sets for this process.

- **delete input**   Deletes input files after creating backup sets for them. Usable only when backing up archived redo logs.

The clauses available for defining the *scope* of the backup are listed and defined in the following set of items:

- **database**   Backs up all datafiles and the control file.

- **tablespace** *name*   Backs up all datafiles for named tablespaces.

- **datafile**   Backs up all datafiles named by name or by datafile number. If named, the name must be a datafile named in the current control file.

- **datafile copy**   Backs up all datafiles named by name or by datafile number. If named, the name must not be a datafile named in the current control file.

- **archivelog**   Backs up archived redo logs according filename pattern, sequence range, or date/time range.

- **current controlfile**   Backs up current control file.

- **backup controlfile**   Backs up a backup control file.

- **backupset**   Backs up the primary key of a backup set on disk.

Exercises

1. What command is used to perform backups?

2. What are two categories of options or clauses that can be specified with this command? What are the categories based on? What are some of the clauses in each?

3. What does the **full** clause mean? What does the **incremental level** clause mean?

Using the COPY Command

RMAN allows the DBA to create backup copies of the datafiles on the database. These copies are called image copies, and they are created with the **copy** command. The image copy can be put onto a disk only. Image copies can be made of current datafiles, datafiles copies made using any method, archived redo logs, and the current or backup control file. Once created, the image copy is immediately usable for a recovery without executing a **restore** command. General syntax for the **copy** command is **copy** *file* **to** *location*. The **allocate channel** command must precede the **copy** command, and the level of parallelism that can be used with the **copy** command relates directly to the number of channels allocated to the **copy**. Only full copies of datafiles are permitted with the **copy** command. An example of the **copy** command appears in the following code block. In this example, one copy of a single datafile is made.

```
RUN { ALLOCATE CHANNEL my_channel TYPE DISK;
      COPY DATAFILE "/DISK1/oracle/home/dbs/data01.dbf"
      TO "/DISK2/oracle/home/bkp/data01bkp.dbf";
      RELEASE CHANNEL my_channel;
```

TIP
*The **copy** command only allows channels to be allocated that specify **type disk**. All other allocate channel commands will be ignored for the **copy** command.*

Several clauses are available for use in place of *file*. These clauses are listed in the following set of items:

- **datafile**   Copies the current datafile.

- **datafilecopy** *name*   Copies an existing copy of the datafile.

- **archivelog** *name*   Copies a named archived redo log.

- **current controlfile**   Copies the current control file. Alternatively, the **current** keyword can be dropped to copy an existing control file copy, either by name or tag.

The filename and path to which the image copy will be placed is usually specified by location. Alternately, a few clauses are available for use as part of *location*. These clauses are listed in the following set of items:

- **tag**   The name of a tag assigned to the image copy.
- **level 0**   Treat this datafile copy as a level 0 backup. Subsequent incremental backups will use this image copy as a baseline.

Exercises

1. What command is used to create duplicates of database files?
2. What is the only option allowed in the channel allocation statement when this command is issued?

Using the SWITCH and RESTORE Commands

The **switch** command can be used to turn a datafile copy into the current datafile. This is done by switching the datafile name in the control file. This command creates the need for media recovery. It produces the same effect as the **alter database rename datafile** statement. General syntax for this command is **switch datafile** *name* **to datafilecopy** *new_name*. Optionally, the **to datafilecopy** portion can be dropped in favor of **all**, and all datafiles for which a new name is defined in the **run** command with the **set newname** clause will be switched. An example appears in the following code block:

```
RUN { SWITCH DATAFILE 'data01.dbf' TO DATAFILECOPY 'data01bkp.dbf'
};
```

Unlike image copies of datafiles, which are usable for recovery operations immediately, files in backup sets must be retrieved from tape and extracted from the backup set before they are available for recovery. The process to retrieve the backup is done when the DBA issues the **restore** command. When this command is issued, RMAN will either overwrite the current versions of datafiles, control files, and archived redo logs with the files from backup sets or place those files elsewhere according to the **set newname** clause. When this clause is used, RMAN recognizes the restored files as copies and marks them as such in the recovery catalog. This process can be useful if the DBA is trying to create a clone database. The **restore** command is usually not necessary for moving backup sets containing archived redo logs off tape and onto disk, but recovery performance is improved if the archives are restored. The names and locations used for archived redo logs when they are restored to disk are constructed by RMAN from the LOG_ARCHIVE_DEST and LOG_ARCHIVE_FORMAT initialization parameters set for the instance. The **set archivelog destination** clause in the **run** command overrides the location where LOG_ARCHIVE_DEST says to put the restored archives. If the entire set of files comprising the database is to be restored, then the database must be closed. General syntax for this statement is **restore** *from_clause until_clause file_clause.*

The following example shows the use of the **restore** command. In this example, the datafiles of a tablespace named are restored from the recovery catalog. No specific backup set is given, and no time range for which the backup should conform is given, so RMAN restores the most backup that will give the DBA a complete recovery automatically.

```
RUN { ALLOCATE CHANNEL my_chan TYPE DISK;
      RESTORE TABLESPACE "DATA_01";
      RELEASE CHANNEL my_chan;
  };
```

The options specified for a *from_clause* needn't be specified always and are specified in different combinations. The following options are used in conjunction with the **restore** command as the *from_clause:*

- **from backupset**   Restores files from the backup set named.

- **from datafilecopy**   Restores files from the datafile copies named on disk.

The **restore** command also supports point-in-time recovery. As such, the **until** keyword can be used. RMAN will retrieve backup copies of datafiles from the recovery catalog based on the point in time specified with **until**. This clause has three options, *time, scn,* or *log_sequence*.

Files for the entire database can be restored, or individual datafiles can be named singly or in combination with their tablespaces. The **restore** command supports these options with the *file_clause*, which has the following keywords:

- **database** Restores files for the entire database, optionally skipping named tablespaces with the **skip** clause.

- **tablespace** Restores all files for the specified tablespace.

- **datafile** Restores only named datafiles.

- **controlfile** Restores control file to location named.

- **archivelog** Restores named archived redo logs.

Exercises

1. What purpose does the **restore** command fulfill?

2. What items must be specified if the DBA wants to perform complete recovery on a datafile? A tablespace? The database?

3. What clauses are specified for restoring files to support incomplete recovery?

Using the RECOVER Command

Media or disk recovery is handled in RMAN with the **recover** command. RMAN applies incremental backups to the database in order to recover it. Only current datafiles will be recovered, and RMAN will restore archived redo logs from backup sets as needed to support the recovery operation. The recovery catalog should be available to support the **recover** command, and it must be available if the control file must be recovered. Since recovering data from incremental backup takes less time than the same recovery performed from archived redo logs, RMAN will always prefer an incremental backup over a set of archived redo logs if both are available for the recovery. If there are several levels of incremental backup available, RMAN will use the lowest level available (i.e., as close to level 0 as possible). The types of recovery available in RMAN are **database**, **tablespace**, and **datafile**. The same constraints covered in Unit III for each level of recovery apply, namely, that the target instance must be started and mounted but not open for database recovery, and open for tablespace and datafile recovery with the damaged files offline. Both complete and incomplete recovery can be performed with the **recover** command. The general syntax is **recover** *recover_clause*. The following example shows the use of the **recover** command to handle incomplete database recovery to a specific system change number, skipping the temporary tablespace:

```
RUN { RECOVER DATABASE
      UNTIL 605495694
      SKIP TABLESPACE "temp_01" ;
```

The parameters used in this option include those in the following list:

■ **database**   Recovers the database. If no **until** clause is specified for incomplete recovery, then complete recovery will be conducted. For the **until** clause, a *time, SCN,* or *redo log sequence thread* can be specified. Entire database must be closed, but mounted to the instance.

■ **tablespace**   Recovers the tablespaces identified. Database can be open, but damaged tablespace must be offline.

■ **datafile**   Recovers the datafiles identified. Database can be open, but damaged datafiles must be offline.

Exercises

1. What is the **recover** command? How does RMAN support complete database recovery? How can named tablespaces be skipped in a database recovery?

2. What is incomplete recovery? What clause is used to support it?

Chapter Summary

This chapter discusses the features of Oracle8's new architecture for backup and recovery. This new feature supports several different backup and recovery strategies, combining interfaces with the operating system and third-party backup and recovery products, enhanced tracking of backup and archived redo information, scripting for automated backup and recovery operation, all with an Oracle-supported product. This important feature will be covered heavily on OCP Exam 5.

The new backup and recovery architecture has two components: the Recovery Manager, or RMAN, and the use of a new backup feature called the recovery catalog. RMAN is a utility executed either interactively or in batch from the operating system interface. This utility has its own syntax in which backup and recovery operations are defined and run. The second part of this new feature is the recovery catalog. It is a separate database in which information about the backups taken for the production or "target" database is stored. The actual backup and archived redo is stored in the recovery catalog, along with information about the structure of the database and backup and archived redo logs. Also kept in the recovery catalog are script objects that the DBA defines to handle routine backup and recovery operations. RMAN is created with the execution of the **catrman.sql** script found in **rdbms/admin** under the Oracle software home directory.

RMAN is executed from the operating system command line with the **rman** command. There are several options that can be specified at run time for RMAN, including the username and connection string for the production or target database, the connection string and username for the recovery catalog database, a file containing RMAN commands, and a log file. Each option is specified with a keyword, **target rcvcat cmdfile** and **msglog**, respectively. To reuse the log file specified, the **append** keyword can be named after the filename specified for **msglog**.

There are four categories for the commands available in RMAN. These categories are recovery catalog maintenance commands, **report/list** commands, script commands, and **run** commands. The recovery catalog is maintained with several commands. The production target database is registered with the **register database** command. When redo log sequence numbers are reset at the time the target database is opened, the **reset database** command must be issued in RMAN to the recovery catalog as well, since there is no direct interface between the target database and the recovery catalog other than through RMAN. With the introduction of RMAN and the recovery catalog comes an accurate and easy way to identify the version of the data in the database with the **list incarnation of database** statement. After log switches on the target, the recovery catalog must be updated with the **resync catalog** command. The information in the recovery catalog can be maintained with the **change** command, used for removing or altering availability of backups or copies of files or redo logs. To remove or create files using RMAN, the DBA must use the **allocate channel** command. This command opens a line of communication between Oracle and the operating system to handle file creation, movement, and deletion. Finally, database backup files created outside of RMAN can be registered with the recovery catalog using the **catalog** command.

The next commands are **report** and **list**. These complementary reporting commands are used to provide the DBA with an accurate picture of recoverability on the database with minimal research. The **report** command tells the DBA the backup status of file components in the database. It identifies when the last backup was performed, how many incremental backups would be required to provide complete recovery, and other information. The **list** command provides a report on the names of the backups that are available that would be required to provide recovery to a specified datafile, tablespace, or database. The DBA will use these reporting functions together to determine the backup needs for the database at any point in time, or the availability of backup data for recovery purposes.

The next commands are the scripting commands. Anything that can be executed in RMAN interactively can also be executed in batch. This feature is especially important for organizations that rely on Oracle for delivery of their most important data, data that most needs to be backed up and recovered efficiently, effectively, or frequently. Scripting allows the DBA to define the most routine aspects of backup and recovery once as a script and reuse that script (or even schedule it automatically) as often as the scripted operation needs to be performed. The commands for creating, replacing, printing, or deleting a script include **create script**, **replace script**, **print script**, and **delete script**, respectively.

Once created, a script is executed using the fourth set of commands, the **run** commands. Several other items are executed with the **run** commands, including the operation of backups, copies, restores, switches, and recoveries. The **allocate channel** command must be executed before other commands in the **run** command. Backups for the database are created with the **backup** command. Several different types of backups can be run database-wide, tablespace-wide, or on particular datafiles, including full backups and incremental backups. A full backup is one that makes a complete backup copy of all blocks in a datafile. An incremental backup is one that makes a copy of only the blocks in a datafile that have changed since the last full backup. There are eight levels of incremental backups available in RMAN, corresponding to different time ranges and to a level 0 backup, which is a full backup. Backups of datafiles, control files, and archived redo logs are placed into objects called backup sets. Datafiles and control files can be stored in the same backup set, while archived redo logs are stored in their own backup set. Multiple datafiles in a backup set can be multiplexed, or stored on sequential access media such as tape such that the blocks of each datafile are not stored contiguously. However, blocks for control files and archived redo logs may not be multiplexed. Finally, if a backup is created that the DBA subsequently needs to use as part of a database recovery, the DBA must first restore the file from the backup set and then run recovery. The **restore** command is used for this task.

Another **run** command covered was the **copy** command, used to create immediately usable copies of files. This copy is also called an image copy. Copies of files are made to disk, unlike backups, which can be made directly to tape. A current database file can be switched for a backup copy using the **switch** command, also covered in this chapter. To recover a database from backup, the DBA must first restore the necessary files using the **restore** command. Finally, to recover a database with appropriate backups in place, the **recover** command is used. RMAN handles the movement of needed archived redo logs onto disk from tape automatically, but the DBA can speed recovery by restoring needed archived redo logs to disk before running **recover**. The recovery catalog usually needs to be available to execute recovery properly, in order for the RMAN to select the needed backups and archives. The recovery catalog must be available if the DBA needs to recover from a backup control file. All types of database recovery supported in Oracle7 are available with RMAN in Oracle8, including complete and incomplete recovery, tablespace recovery, and datafile recovery. There are several new features to the control file that support RMAN, and new dictionary views as well, information about which is provided in the two-minute drill following.

Two-Minute Drill

- The new architecture for backup and recovery in Oracle8 consists of Recovery Manager and a recovery catalog.

- Recovery Manager (RMAN) is a utility that allows DBAs to manage all aspects of backup and recovery using an Oracle-supported tool.

- A recovery catalog is a service run on another Oracle database that tracks all backup and archived redo logs produced for the database.

- There are some enhancements to the control file and a much larger control file in Oracle8 to support RMAN. RMAN information is stored for a period of time corresponding to the CONTROL_FILE_RECORD KEEP_TIME initialization parameter.

- RMAN is created with the **catrman.sql** script, found in **rdbms/admin** under the Oracle software home directory.

- RMAN has four sets of commands: recovery catalog maintenance commands, reporting commands, scripting commands, and **run** commands.

- To run RMAN, type **rman** at the OS command prompt. One mandatory option and four optional ones are used: **target** to identify the production or target database; **rcvcat** to identify the recovery catalog database; **cmdfile** to execute RMAN in **batch** mode with a command script; and **msglog** to keep a log of all activity with **append**, allowing RMAN to append information to an old log file for the current RMAN session.

- Communication with the operating system is possible in RMAN with the **allocate channel** command.

- Recovery catalog management commands include **register database** to register a target database, **reset database** when the target database is opened and the redo log sequence reset, **resync catalog** after log switches in target database, **change** to alter the control file or other database filenames used, **list incarnation** to show the current database data version, and **catalog** to identify copies of files made outside of RMAN.

- RMAN reporting and listing commands give information about the current database and the recovery status of it.

- Reports show information about files of the database and recoverability. One of the reports that can be used is **report need backup** to show the files of the database that need backup. Options for this report include **incremental** *num* to show the files that need *num* incremental backups to be recovered and **days** *num* to show the files that haven't been backed up in *num* days. Another report includes **report unrecoverable** to show files that are not recoverable.

- Lists show information about the backups that are available in the database. Some lists that can be used are **list copy of tablespace**, **list copy of datafile**, **list backupset**, and **list incarnation of database**.

- There are several commands available in RMAN for script creation. They are **create script**, **replace script**, **delete script**, and **print script**.

- The final set of commands in RMAN are **run** commands. These commands handle most of the processing in RMAN, such as execution of scripts, SQL, and backup/recovery operations.

- The **backup** command runs backups. RMAN creates incremental or full copies of files for the entire database, the files of a tablespace, or individual datafiles.

- The backups of files and archived redo logs are placed into collections called backup sets. A backup can contain only archived redo logs or only datafiles and control files.

- Datafiles can be multiplexed into a backup set, meaning that the blocks of datafiles are stored noncontiguously on the sequential offline storage media such as tape.

- Backup sets are composed of backup pieces. The number of pieces in a backup set depends on parallelism of backup, number of tapes required for the backup, and other factors.

- Oracle8 and RMAN support the incremental backup of datafiles, which store only the blocks of a datafile that have been changed since the last full backup. A full backup is one containing all blocks of datafiles.

- There are eight levels of incremental backups and a level 0 backup, which is a full backup.

- To recover a database component from backup, the component must first be restored.

- The **copy** command will create an image copy of a database file component. This component is immediately usable for recovery.

- The **copy** command only produces image copies to disk, while **backup** can send database file components directly to tape.

- The **switch** command will substitute a datafile copy for a current file. The datafile switched will then need media recovery.

- The **restore** command will retrieve the files from the backup copy and put them where the DBA specifies.

- The **recover** command will conduct media recovery using backups restored in combination with archived redo logs.

- Several old and new dictionary views exist in Oracle8 to support RMAN.

- V$ARCHIVED_LOG displays name and information in the control file about archived redo logs.

- V$BACKUP_CORRUPTION displays information in the control file about corrupt datafile backups.

- V$BACKUP_DATAFILE offers information from the control file about backup datafiles and control files.

- V$BACKUP_DEVICE offers operating-system-specific information about supported third-party vendors for RMAN in Oracle8.

- V$BACKUP_REDOLOG displays information about archived redo logs in backup sets.

- V$BACKUP_SET displays information from the control file about all backup sets.

- V$BACKUP_PIECE displays information from the control file about all pieces in all backup sets.

- V$DATAFILE lists information about datafiles in the Oracle8 database.

- V$DATAFILE _HEADER lists information about datafile headers in the Oracle8 database.

Chapter Questions

1. The ALLOCATE CHANNEL command used in conjunction with COPY must

   A. Name the resource explicitly

   B. Use the **disk** clause

   C. Use the **for delete** clause

   D. Be run after the **copy** is complete

2. Which of the following maintenance operations should the DBA run after adding a datafile?

   A. Register database

   B. Reset database

   C. Catalog

   D. Resync catalog

3. A full backup consists of which of the following elements?

   A. All blocks in a datafile

   B. Changed blocks in a datafile

   C. All datafiles in the database

   D. Changed datafiles in the database

4. In the absence of the recovery catalog, where can RMAN find most of the information it needs?

   A. Backup sets

    B. Datafiles

    C. Password file

    D. Control file

5. **The DBA issues the ALTER DATABASE BACKUP CONTROLFILE TO '/DISK1/Oracle/home/dbcontrol.ctl' statement. What can the DBA do to use this control file backup in conjunction with RMAN?**

    A. Issue the **catalog** command.

    B. Copy the file to tape.

    C. Issue the **copy** command.

    D. Nothing, the control file backup can be used as is.

6. **What effect does setting CONTROL_FILE_RECORD_KEEP_TIME to 0 have?**

    A. Forces Oracle8 to keep no information for RMAN

    B. Decreases backup and recovery performance

    C. Limits growth of the control file size

    D. Has no effect on control file size

7. **The DBA identifies that the backups necessary for media recovery are on tape. What command should she first execute to perform the recovery?**

    A. Copy

    B. Switch

    C. Allocate channel

    D. Restore

8. **Once the DBA defines attributes in a RUN command, how long will they be defined?**

    A. Permanently

    B. For the duration of the instance

C. For the duration of the session

D. For the duration of the **run** command

9. **By default, how many errors will occur in a RUN command before RMAN terminates?**

   A. 1

   B. 5

   C. 25

   D. Operating-system specific

10. **The DBA completes incomplete recovery to a system change number and then opens the database. What recovery catalog maintenance command must be executed?**

   A. Register database

   B. Reset database

   C. Resync catalog

   D. Change database

11. **Which command can the DBA issue to determine which datafiles in the database are in the most serious need of backup?**

   A. Report unrecoverable

   B. Report need backup

   C. List incarnation

   D. List copy of datafile

12. **Which of the following best describes multiplexing in backup sets?**

   A. One archive log in one backup set with file blocks stored contiguously

   B. Multiple control files in one backup set with file blocks for each stored noncontiguously

   C. Multiple datafiles in one backup set with file blocks for each stored noncontiguously

   D. One datafile in multiple backup sets with file blocks stored contiguously

Answers to Chapter Questions

1. B. Use the **disk** clause

Explanation The **copy** command can only work in conjunction with the **disk** specification because an image copy can be made only to disk. Review the discussion of the **copy** command. Naming the resource explicitly will not work in situations where the DBA names a tape resource, eliminating choice A. The **for delete** clause is mainly used to allocate a channel to delete a backup, eliminating choice C. The channel must be allocated before issuing the **copy** command, eliminating choice D.

2. D. Resync catalog

Explanation The catalog must be synchronized with the database every time the control file changes. This includes changes made by the log switch and changes made by adding or removing datafiles or redo logs. Choice A is incorrect because the database need only be registered when RMAN is first run. Choice B is incorrect because the database needs to be reset only when the redo log sequence is reset, as after incomplete recovery. Choice C is incorrect because **catalog** is used to include copies of database components with the recovery catalog if the copy was made using a method other than RMAN.

3. A. All blocks in a datafile

Explanation Full backup means the full datafile will be backed up, while incremental refers to the backup of only those blocks in a datafile that have changed. Thus, other choices are incorrect. Review the discussion of full and incremental backup.

4. D. Control file

Explanation The control file contains a great deal of information to support RMAN. If the maintenance of the recovery catalog is not possible, the next best thing is to let RMAN use the control file. Review introduction to RMAN and the recovery catalog.

5. A.   Issue the **catalog** command

Explanation   To include a backup file in the recovery catalog that has been created using tools other than RMAN, the DBA can issue the **catalog** command. Simply copying the file to tape will not record its existence in the recovery catalog, eliminating choice B. Executing the **copy** command on the current version of the file the DBA has already made a copy of externally is fine, but does nothing to include the first copy made by the DBA in the recovery catalog. Choice D is simply incorrect.

6. C.   Limits growth of the control file size

Explanation   The CONTROL_FILE_RECORD_KEEP_TIME initialization parameter determines how long certain time-sensitive information will be kept to support RMAN in the control file. If set to zero, Oracle will eliminate this information from the control file as often as necessary to make room for new information, thereby limiting the growth of the control file size. Review information about the enhanced Oracle8 control file support for backup and recovery.

7. C.   **Allocate channel**

Explanation   The first step on almost all **run** commands is to allocate a channel to communicate with the operating system.

8. D.   For the duration of the **run** command

Explanation   The **set** statements issued during a **run** command are valid for the entire **run** command, but no longer than that.

9. A.   1

Explanation   RMAN has low error tolerance. As soon as it encounters an error of any sort, it will terminate. This is default behavior and can't be changed.

10. B.   **Reset database**

Explanation   Incomplete recovery requires the DBA to recover the database to a point in time in the past. After completing that recovery, the DBA must discard all archived redo logs that contained changes made after that point in time by opening the database with the **resetlogs** option. After opening the database in this way, the recovery catalog must be reset with the **reset database** command in RMAN.

11. A. Report unrecoverable

Explanation This report will list all datafiles that are not recoverable with the current backups and archived redo information—the files that are in most dire need of backup.

12. C. Multiple datafiles in one backup set with file blocks for each stored noncontiguously

Explanation Multiplexing is when multiple datafiles are stored noncontiguously in a backup set to prevent the backup of any datafile from reducing online performance on that datafile. Choices A and B are incorrect because archived redo logs and control files are not multiplexed in backup sets. Choice D doesn't describe multiplexing either.

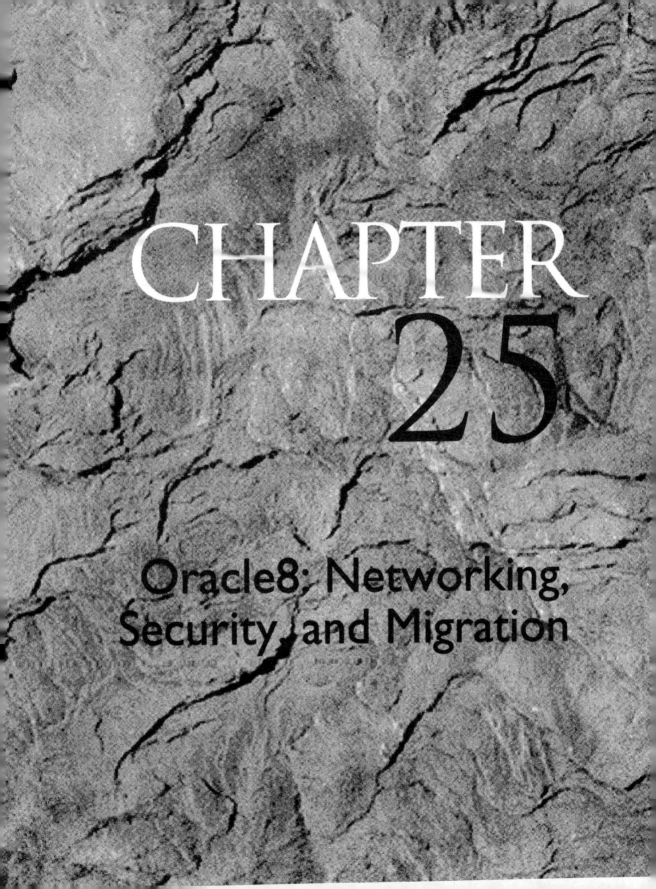

CHAPTER
25

Oracle8: Networking, Security and Migration

n this chapter, you will understand and demonstrate knowledge in the following areas:

- Oracle8 networking enhancements
- New Oracle8 security features
- Migration to Oracle8

This chapter covers the final aspects of Oracle8 new concepts. The final areas of understanding for Oracle8 covered in this Guide for the OCP Exam 5 are the networking enhancements and security features. Also, this chapter identifies the requirements and methods for migrating Oracle7 databases to Oracle8 using the Oracle migration utility. The purpose of this chapter is twofold. First, it is meant to cover the material in these areas that will be tested on OCP Exam 5. Second, it will help you with preparation for migrating to Oracle8.

Oracle8 Networking Enhancements

In this section, you will cover the following topics related to Oracle8 networking enhancements:

- Oracle8 networking new features
- Configuring the Oracle8 network
- Oracle8 network security
- Using names and simplifying management

Oracle8 offers new features for the DBA to manage connectivity between database application clients and the server. In Unit IV, in the presentation of the client/server architecture, the foundations of SQL*Net were identified. Oracle8 builds on the foundation laid by SQL*Net with Net8—the new networking tool for Oracle8 client/server applications. This section will cover the new features of Net8 and the requirements for configuring the client/server network with Net8. The new networking tool offers new features for network security as well. Finally, Net8 handles network naming and simplified management.

Oracle8 Networking New Features

The new features of Net8 are focused into several areas, including scalability, connectivity, security, performance, configuration, and administration. Net8 supports database systems with substantial user populations and provides backward compatibility with SQL*Net version 2. Net8 is designed to provide object-oriented connectivity in a utility that combines the features of Transparent Network Substrate, Secure Network Services, and Oracle Names with a new messaging layer for enhanced client/server communication. There are several challenges facing client/server systems related to scalability for large user communities. To handle the difficulties faced by client/server applications, Net8 offers features for multiplexing, connection pooling, concentration, and naming to offset or eliminate the performance degradation suffered by the addition of users. Net8 offers the DBA the ability to create a connection between Rdb and Oracle Express OLAP systems, and more compatibility with level 2 open database connectivity standards (ODBC) for direct interface to PL/SQL stored procedures.

A new component of Net8 is the Oracle Security server. It is designed to offer several improvements for database and client/server security. One of the new features of the Oracle Security server is the support of authentication using digital signatures. This usage allows for the users of the Oracle database to sign on once and have access to many different Oracle and third-party products. Further, once authenticated, the clients and servers in the Oracle network can use encryption on their SQL*Net data—but not user data—between the client and the server. The new performance features in Net8 include TNS raw transport, information for Oracle Names stored in the client, and optimization for the dispatcher process.

Exercises

1. Identify the new name for the Oracle networking utility.

2. What are some of the new networking features available with Oracle8 related to scalability? Connectivity? Authentication? Performance?

Configuring the Oracle8 Network

There are several options in Net8 designed to manage the configuration of the database network services centrally, easily, and quickly. To configure the Oracle network, the DBA can use the Net8 Assistant or the Net8 Easy Config tools. Oracle Enterprise Manager can be used to start Net8 Assistant. The Oracle Names tool handles dynamic discovery of nodes in the network. Client profiles can be defined to simplify the identification of each client in the network. For smaller Oracle installations, the DBA can use the default configuration provided with Net8. Finally, the DBAs can use the Net8 configuration utility or "wizard" to configure the full network.

One of Net8's new features for connecting user processes to shared servers in the multithreaded server (MTS) configuration is designed to reduce network traffic. Recall in the discussion of client/server configuration that the MTS architecture consists of a SQL*Net listener, which hears user requests from across the network and passes those requests to the dispatcher. The dispatcher brokers access to shared servers, and the shared servers read information from datafiles on behalf of user processes. Net8 adds a new component called the Connection Manager, which is designed to concentrate several user connections through one single transport. Connection Manager can work in conjunction with MTS. There are several advantages to using Connection Manager, namely, that it can act as a firewall for checking authorization for use and as a multiprotocol interchange (MPI) to send information sent on one network protocol to another protocol. In addition, the Connection Manager has the benefit of concentrating and multiplexing data from several user connections into one carrier. Figure 25-1 illustrates the principle of usage for Connection Manager.

The feature of multiplexing is used in Net8 as well. Since multiple user sessions connect to the database server via one physical link, the scalability of database usage can increase. The initial connection request requires its own physical transport, while the subsequent connection from the same process uses the same physical transport. So, only the new request for connection from a new client produces a higher level of network traffic, after which that new connection can be multiplexed in with existing connections.

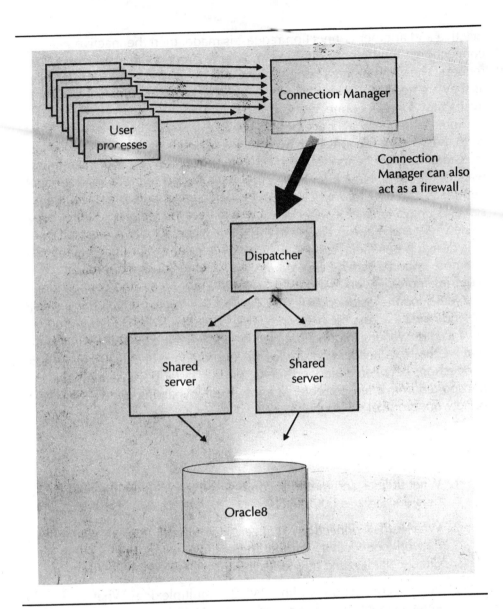

FIGURE 25-1.   *Using Connection Manager with the multithreaded server*

Connection pooling is used to reduce the burden on the network as well. Connection pooling allows the server to define a maximum number of connection sockets that can be active at any time. If one connection is inactive and another connection request is made, then the inactive connection is temporarily disabled in order to process the new connection request. The same process happens over and over—recycling sockets only as they are needed, limiting resources required while maximizing overall availability for user connections.

Some enhancements have been made to the Net8 Listener as well. The Net8 listener now supports both two-tier and *N*-tier client/server configurations. Instead of having clients make their remote procedure call (RPC) and then wait for the reply, Net8 allows the client to make the call to a third tier and terminate, allowing for asynchronous messaging and fault tolerance. If the server is unavailable or connection is terminated, the request is still queued somewhere and made available to the server when activity is reestablished. This design is beneficial for applications where scaling and load balancing are more important than a fast, connection-oriented design approach requiring more network bandwidth to support more real-time connections.

Net8 supports faster connections via TNS raw transport features. Instead of sending data across the network with a complete Net8 header and no advanced networking information, Net8 has been streamlined to automatically remove the Net8 header and use low-level protocol API calls instead. Basic connections between client and server will run faster because less data is transported from client to server at a low level, bypassing unnecessary layers of network protocol within Net8.

Exercises

1. What utilities and methods can be used to configure the Net8 network services in Oracle8?

2. What is the Connection Manager? How does it improve scalability in network connectivity without increasing network traffic? What is Oracle Names, and how does it improve network configuration?

3. What is connection pooling? What is multiplexing? What enhancements have been made to the Net8 listener process? What is TNS raw transport?

Oracle8 Network Security

To handle the increased demand for network security created with the explosion of the Web, wireless connections, and an overall increase in networking, Oracle offers several features to allow DBAs and organizations to take advantage of emerging security technologies while adding its own technological advancements to the mix. The Advanced Networking Option allows DBAs and security administrators to configure clients and servers to use encryption of data sent across a network. In addition, Net8 supports the use of checksums to detect altered or corrupted packets. Net8, in conjunction with the Advanced Networking Option, supports the use of RSA Data Security RC4 and the data encryption standard (DES) algorithms. The features of Connection Manager that handle firewalls work in conjunction with the Advanced Networking option also, which allows for secure data transfer across multiple network protocols.

Oracle offers a new product that works with Net8, the Oracle database, and Oracle clients called the Oracle Security server. This product uses public-key user authentication in an Oracle network to create digital signatures for one-time login to all areas of the Oracle network accessible to a user based on their signature. At the time of login, the user receives a set of attributes that are designed by the DBA and security administrator. These attributes are a list of privileges and roles to a component or "principal" on the Oracle network. This principal is the Oracle database, Web server, users, or other items. Finally, the DBA can set up access to distributed stored procedures on remote servers with the use of external authentication. In Oracle7, the authentication required in stored procedures or embedded SQL required the password information to be hard-coded into the source.

The Oracle Security server allows for central management of authentication data in a distributed environment based on X.509 version 1 certificates, based on public/private-key cryptography. The DBA or security administrator can use Oracle Security Manager to set up this framework. This tool is part of Oracle Enterprise Manager. Furthermore, the security management and usage can be designed into Oracle applications with the use of the security manager API called Oracle Security Server Toolkit.

Digital signatures can be administered in the following way. First, the user requests connection to the database from the Oracle Security server. The principal database or Web server sends Oracle Security Server a certificate containing an identifier for the user, a public key, and a signature of ownership. Oracle Security server responds to the user by sending its own key information and verifies the client's identification. The client will be considered authenticated if their identification checks out OK by the Oracle Security server. In this way the client is also assured that the Oracle database is authenticated. This form of third-party authentication allows both the client and the server to know that both are who they say they are. Figure 25-2 illustrates the principle of third-party authentication.

Exercises

1. What is Oracle Security server? Describe third-party authentication.

2. What is the Advanced Networking option? How does the Connection Manager use the Advanced Networking option?

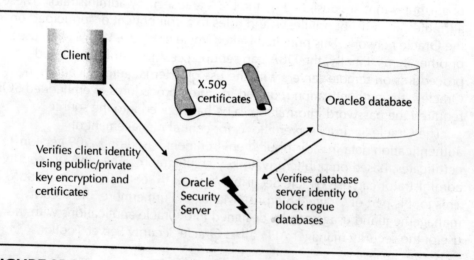

FIGURE 25-2. *Third-party authentication using Oracle Security server*

Using Names and Simplifying Management

With the use of an Oracle Names server, the DBA or security administrator can enjoy simplified configuration of network services. All destination network services such as the listener, the database, Connection Manager, and others have a name they use to register themselves with the Names server. The Names server should listen on a known port for these other services to connect and register themselves automatically. If a Names server is used, the client can find any required services available in the Oracle network by identifying the service required to all Names servers on the Oracle network. The Names server then looks in its list of names to resolve a network address based on that name. The list of Names servers available to a client is stored in the **sdns.ora** file on a client. The Names server then sends the address back to the client. With the resolved destination address, the client can then initiate contact with the appropriate resource on the network.

The Net8 Assistant can be used to configure the two types of server networks available, the Workgroup server and Enterprise server. In Workgroup server, the client connects to only one server, allowing for the definition of default information and eliminating the need to configure Net8. For Enterprise server, since clients may connect to many servers, the Net8 Assistant can use applets created from Network Manager functions to set up this type of network, or the applets themselves may be used individually.

To configure the client, there are several new options. One of these options is to change nothing at all. Oracle has attempted to set client defaults to fair values in order to enable operation in a variety of situations. Alternately, the clients and services may be able to configure by themselves automatically in the presence of a TCP/IP network working in conjunction with a Names server. Both client and server simply find the Names server and identify themselves. The Names server can manage client profiles centrally as well with the use of a client profile editor. If a default profile is present on the Names Server, Net8 on the client will load the client profile at start time from the Names server. This feature eliminates client configuration altogether. In environments where listeners on the database server using the MTS option use all defaults, the **listener.ora** file is unnecessary—simplifying configuration as well.

Client configuration of Net8 is simplified with the use of an installation guidance software interface, called a "wizard." This wizard is invoked when Net8 is first installed on the client. It locates all Names servers and places them in order, then reads client profile information from the Names server if the Names server is present to configure that client. The user has the option to override a default setting from the profile with a specific setting in an interactive fashion. Further, the default settings from the profile may be rejected altogether in favor of default settings provided by Net8. Finally, the configuration files can be modified later for enhancements, if need be.

As an alternative for organizations that feel they don't need the security options offered with Oracle Security server or the ease of configuration provided by the Names server, and are running their Oracle database client/server application over TCP/IP, the native hostname adapter can be used. The hostname adapter is usable only if the Net8 listener serves only one database. The hostname adapter works in conjunction with the local naming system on the TCP/IP network—either DNS or NIS—and returns an IP address for the hostname of the server requested by the user. No additional security services can be requested using this option. Organizations that use the native hostname adapter may do so based on having a smaller Oracle database user community, reducing or alleviating the need for additional security services, or to reduce the complexity of configuring extended security and naming options.

As a final note, Net8 uses Oracle Trace as an assistant to identifying routes taken for connections for diagnostic and troubleshooting purposes. This allows the DBA to trace a client session completely, from client to server and back again. If there is a problem with networking between client and server, Oracle Trace will identify its symptoms. Net8 does not store Oracle Trace internally; it is an external component. This reduces the overall footprint for Net8 on the client. Oracle Trace offers the following features for usage. It extracts error messages the client may have encountered and places the text for the error in a log file. It also identifies packet information and type sent between client and server, and traces statistics for client and server. In short, Oracle Trace allows for problem diagnostics without costing too much in terms of storage or execution. Net8 also offers its own applications programming interface (API) for use of the Oracle network features for connectivity needs in database and nondatabase applications. The Net8 API is called Net8 OPEN, and it offers a common interface to all industry standard network protocols. As long as Net8 is used on the network, the applications using Net8 OPEN can develop an application for one machine and port the software to another without modifying network calls.

Exercises

1. What value does having a Names server add when configuring an Oracle network? What file is used to store information about the Names servers available to the client? What is a wizard?

2. What two options are available for client configuration to use default settings? What is a client profile and where is it stored?

3. What is a native hostname adapter? When might it be used to configure the network? What conditions must be TRUE for its use? Is Oracle Trace executable software stored in Net8? What is the name of Net8's API?

New Oracle8 Security Features

In this section, you will cover the following topics related to New Oracle8 security features:

■ Managing the SYS schema

■ Authenticating users with enhanced password management

■ Creating profiles and users with password management

■ Using dictionary views for password management

The Oracle Security server is not the only enhancement made to Oracle8 to support more robust database security. There have been several changes made to the Oracle8 security architecture within the database as well. Oracle8 also allows the DBA to manage security better in many areas, such as the management of the SYS schema, expiration of passwords, enhanced user creation features and profiling to handle password expiration, and changes to dictionary views to support enhanced password management. These are areas that many DBAs may have felt Oracle lacked security in the past, but that Oracle8 now covers. This section will provide a full explanation for usage of these features to help you prepare for OCP and for Oracle8 migration.

Managing the SYS Schema

As an enhancement to the security of the SYS schema, the following changes have been made to Oracle8. First, the password provided by the DBA to access the database as **internal** or with **sysdba** privileges must match the password for SYS as it exists on the password file. Recall from Chapter 6 that the password file is used to maintain the integrity of passwords used by DBAs to connect to Oracle to perform privileged operations.

A major change in the management of the SYS schema has to do with the **any** privilege. Recall from earlier discussion that many system or object privileges can be granted with maximum scope by adding the **any** keyword to the privilege grant. For example, the following **select any table** privilege grant statement issued in Oracle7 will allow user SPANKY to see data in the SYS.AUD$ table:

```
GRANT SELECT ANY TABLE TO SPANKY;
```

In Oracle8, however, the scope of the **any** keyword no longer extends into the SYS schema, thereby eliminating unwanted side effects of granting a privilege to a user with the **any** keyword in order to allow that user to look at a SYS-owned object. This configuration is possible with a new initialization parameter in the **init.ora** file, O7_DICTIONARY_ACCESSIBILITY. By default, this parameter is set to TRUE to allow the **any** keyword to extend object privileges over the SYS schema. However, the DBA can set this parameter to FALSE, and instead manage the objects in the SYS schema by granting object privileges for the SYS schema explicitly. Alternately, access to objects in the SYS schema is managed using new roles in Oracle8 designed specifically for the purpose of managing SYS. There are three roles for managing SYS schema objects: the SELECT_CATALOG_ROLE, the EXECUTE_CATALOG_ROLE, and the DELETE_CATALOG_ROLE. These roles manage the ability to **select** data, **execute** procedures, functions or packages, and **delete** data from SYS-owned schema objects. These roles can be granted to users only by user SYS.

Exercises

1. What changes are made in Oracle8 to handle login as user SYS?

2. What changes are made in Oracle8 to the scope of the **any** keyword to minimize its use in managing SYS schema objects?

3. What new roles are available for the management of SYS schema objects?

Authenticating Users with Enhanced Password Management

Four new features exist in Oracle8 to handle password management more effectively. These features are *account locking, password aging and expiration, password history*, and *password complexity requirements*. These new features are designed to make it harder than ever to hack the Oracle8 database as an authorized user without knowledge of the user's password. This protects the integrity of assigned usernames as well as the overall data integrity of the Oracle database.

Though not required to enable password management in Oracle8, the DBA can run the **utlpwdmg.sql** script as SYS to support the functionality of password management. This script can be found in the **rdbms/admin** subdirectory under the Oracle software home directory. This script makes some additions to the DEFAULT profile identified in Chapter 9 for use with password management. These changes will be explained later. When the password management script is run, all default password management settings placed in the DEFAULT profile are enforced at all times on the Oracle8 database. This is unlike other resource limits, which still require that the RESOURCE_LIMIT initialization parameter be set to TRUE before the instance is started.

Account locking works in the following way. Account locking allows Oracle8 to lock out an account when users attempt to log into the database unsuccessfully on several attempts. Maximum allowed number of failed attempts is defined per user or by group. The number of failed attempts is specified by the DBA or security officer in ways that will be defined shortly, and tracked by Oracle such that if the user fails to log into the database in the specified number of tries, Oracle locks out the user automatically. In addition, a time period for automatic user lockout can be defined such that the failed login attempt counter will reset after that time period, and the user may try to log into the database again. Alternately, automatic lockout can be permanent, disabled only by the security administrator or DBA. User accounts can also be locked manually if the security administrator or DBA so desires. In this situation, the only way to unlock the account is manually.

A password is also aged in the Oracle8 database. The DBA or security administrator can set a password to have a maximum lifetime in the Oracle database. Once a threshold time period passes, the user must change their password or they will not be able to access the Oracle database. A grace period can be defined, during which the user must change their password. If the time of the grace period passes and the user doesn't change their password, the account is then locked and only the security administrator can unlock it. A useful technique for creating new users is to create them with expired passwords, such that the user enters the grace period on first login and must change their password during that time.

A potential problem arises when users are forced to change their passwords. Sometimes users try to "fool" the system by changing their expired password to something else, then immediately changing the password back. To prevent this, Oracle8 supports a password history feature that keeps track of recently used passwords and disallows their use for a specified amount of time or number of changes. The interval is defined within the user profile, and information on how to set it will be presented shortly.

Finally, and perhaps most important to the integrity of an Oracle user's account, is the feature of password complexity verification. There are many commonly accepted practices in the area of creating a password, such as making sure it has a certain character length, that it is not a proper name or word in the dictionary, that it is not all numbers or all characters, and so on. Too often, however, users don't heed these mandates and create passwords that are easy to decode using any of a number of products available for decoding encrypted password information. To prevent users from unwittingly subverting the security of the database, Oracle8 supports the automatic verification of password complexity with the use of a PL/SQL function to be applied during user or group profile creation to prevent users from creating passwords of insufficient complexity. The checks provided by the default function include making sure the minimum password length is four characters and not the same as the username. Also, the password must contain at least one letter, number, and punctuation character, and the password must be different from the previous password defined by at least three characters.

If this level of complexity verification provided by the given PL/SQL function is not high enough, a PL/SQL function of sufficient complexity may be defined by the organization, subject to certain restrictions. The overall call syntax must conform to the details in the following code listing. In addition, the new routine must be assigned as the password verification routine in the user's profile or the DEFAULT profile. In the **create profile** statement, the following must be present: **password_verify_function** *user_pwcmplx_fname*, where *user_pwcmplx_fname* is the name of the user-defined password complexity function. Some other constraints on the definition of this function include that an appropriate error must be returned if the routine raises an exception; if the verification routine becomes invalid, an appropriate error should be returned; and that the verification function will be owned by SYS and used in system context. The call to the PL/SQL complexity verification function must conform to the following parameter passing and return value requirements:

```
USER_PWCMPLX_FNAME
( user_id_parm       IN VARCHAR2(30),
  new_passwd_parm    IN VARCHAR2(30),
  old_passwd_parm    IN VARCHAR2(30)
) RETURN BOOLEAN;
```

To show the coding used in a password complexity function, the following example is offered. This example is a simplified and modified block of code similar to the password verification function provided with Oracle8. The function will check three things: that the new password is not the same as the username, that the new password is six characters long, and that the new password is not the same as the old one. When the DBA creates a username, the verification process is called to determine if the password is appropriate. If the function returns TRUE, then the DBA will be able to create the username. If not, the user creation will fail. This example is designed to give you some groundwork for coding your own password complexity function; bear in mind, however, that the function in the following listing is greatly simplified for example purposes only:

```
FUNCTION my_pwver (
x_user      IN  VARCHAR2(30),
x_new_pw    IN  VARCHAR2(30),
x_old_pw    IN  VARCHAR2(30)
)RETURN BOOLEAN IS
BEGIN
    IF LENGTH(x_new_pw) < 6 THEN
      RAISE_APPLICATION_ERROR(-20001, 'New password too short.');
    ELSIF x_new_pw = x_user THEN
      RAISE_APPLICATION_ERROR(-20002, 'New password same as
username');
    ELSIF x_new_pw = x_old_pw THEN
      RAISE_APPLICATION_ERROR(-20003, 'New password same as old');
    ELSE
      RETURN(TRUE);
    END IF;
END;
```

Exercises

1. Define and describe the four new features for user account protection in Oracle8.

2. What process is used to enable account protection?

3. On what feature of Oracle used to manage resource usage do the new account protection features depend?

Creating Profiles and Users with Password Management

Creating user profiles has already been discussed in Chapter 9. Oracle7 uses profiles to limit resource usage in the database, a feature that is only enforced when the RESOURCE_LIMIT initialization parameter is set to TRUE. In Oracle8, there are several new options that are specified with user profiles for password administration that are always enforced. These options include **failed_login_attempts**, **password_life_time**, **password_reuse_time**,

password_reuse_max, **password_lock_time**, and **password_grace_time**. After the **utlpwdmg.sql** script is run, these options will have default values specified for them. The DBA can specify new options using *num* to define time in days or number of attempts for the option. The other password option specified is the **password_verify_function**, for which a *function_name* value is defined. Alternately, the **unlimited** or **default** keywords can substitute for a *num* or *function_name* value on these options. A more complete explanation of each option is listed below, along with its default value:

- **failed_login_attempts**   Number of unsuccessful attempts at login a user can make before account locks. Default is 3.

- **password_life_time**   Number of days a password will remain active. Default is 60.

- **password_reuse_time**   Number of days before the password can be reused. Default is 1,800 (approx. 5 years).

- **password_reuse_max**   Number of times the password must be changed before one can be reused. Default is **unlimited**.

- **password_lock_time**   Number of days after which Oracle will unlock a user account locked automatically when the user exceeds **failed_login_attempts**. Default is 1/1,440 (1 minute).

- **password_grace_time**   Number of days during which an expired password must be changed by the user or else Oracle permanently locks the account. Default is 10.

- **password_verify_function**   Function used for password complexity verification. Default is called **verify_password( )**.

In addition to assigning a user profile that takes advantage of the preceding features, the DBA or security administrator can perform several password management operations with the **create user** or **alter user** statements. These operations include manually locking or unlocking the user account with the **alter user account lock** or **alter user account unlock** statements, respectively. On username creation, or at any time later, the DBA or security administrator may expire a password with the **create user password expire** or **alter user**

password expire statements. Some examples for the usage of these statements are included in the following example:

```
ALTER USER spanky ACCOUNT UNLOCK;
ALTER USER athena ACCOUNT LOCK;
ALTER USER dinah PASSWORD EXPIRE;

CREATE USER stacy IDENTIFIED BY attorney
DEFAULT TABLESPACE users_01
PASSWORD EXPIRE;
```

Exercises

1. Identify and describe the options that are included in the DEFAULT user profile to support password management? What must be done by the DBA in order to enforce these resource limits?

2. What are the options in the **create user** or **alter user** statements that are used to manage passwords and user accounts?

Using Dictionary Views for Password Management

There have been some changes to existing dictionary views and some additional views created in the Oracle database data dictionary to support the use of password management. The DBA_ and USER_USERS dictionary views have the following new columns on them for password management: ACCOUNT_STATUS, which may be locked, open, or expired; GRACE_DATE, which identifies the date by which the user must change their password or the account will be locked; LOCK_DATE, which is the date the account was locked (NULL for open accounts); and EXPIRY_DATE, which tells the date for account expiration.

The DBA_PROFILES view has been changed to show information about the user profile parameters. The column added is RESOURCE_TYPE, which identifies if the resource is a kernel or password resource.

Also, a new view has been created for the Oracle8 data dictionary—USER_PASSWORD_LIMITS—which has the two columns, RESOURCE_NAME and LIMIT, to show both the name of the password resource and the limit defined for it.

TIP
Some Oracle tools have been changed to support password expiration, including Server Manager (line mode) and SQL*Plus.

Exercises

I. What are the names of the dictionary views that are changed to support password management? Which view has been added to support password management?

2. What tools have been modified to support password management?

Migration to Oracle8

In this section, you will cover the following topics on migration to Oracle8:

■ Using the migration utility

■ Migrating from Oracle7 to Oracle8

Understanding how to migrate from Oracle7 to Oracle8 is perhaps the most important feature that the OCP Exam 5 can present. This section is designed to identify the concepts and steps required for converting Oracle7 applications to Oracle8, and to identify the tools available for the purpose of migration from Oracle7 to Oracle8.

Using the Migration Utility

By now, you should have a clear idea about the new features in Oracle8, and perhaps even some idea of how to incorporate these new features into your existing Oracle applications. Now, the features of the migration process are covered. In order to make room for the new features provided by Oracle8, there are many changes that are made to the data dictionary, both in terms of what the data the dictionary contains and the structure of the dictionary. Several new views are added, while others are changed. In addition, there are new features in the underlying physical structure of the Oracle8 database, the control files, redo logs, and datafiles. In order for the migration to be successful, these things must be changed. The migration process is designed to handle all of these things.

For your part as the DBA handling migration, you need to meet with people to define the following roles and responsibilities. The DBA will perform the actual migration, first backing up the Oracle7 database, then executing the migration to Oracle8, and then backing up the Oracle8 migrated database. The application developers will review the differences between Oracle7 and Oracle8 and ensure the applications are compliant. A schedule should be developed by the DBA in conjunction with the application developers and the users who will be involved with acceptance testing to ensure that critical functionality is maintained. All of these things will move smoothly with the presence of a test plan.

The migration of the Oracle7 database to Oracle8 is designed to be as easy as possible with the presence of the Oracle8 migration utility. This utility is designed to be automatic, fast, and easy on storage requirements and DBA intervention. It migrates an Oracle database by rebuilding the data dictionary in the SYSTEM tablespace and updating the structure of the datafile and the header blocks, but not the data in the database itself. Recall in the discussion of new ROWID formats in Chapter 22 that data stored in the database in Oracle7 restricted ROWID format must be migrated by the developer or the DBA. Oracle8 migration utility does not handle this. In addition, the Oracle8 migration utility is not designed to migrate databases from Oracle8 backward to Oracle7. A separate migration tool will be available for upgrade to future releases of Oracle8 as those new releases are made available.

Migration of the Oracle8 database can be handled in other ways as well. First, Oracle8 database migration can be managed using IMPORT/EXPORT, with the benefit of being able to migrate specific parts of the database independently. In contrast, the Oracle8 migration utility migrates the entire database at once. IMPORT/EXPORT also allows the DBA to migrate an Oracle8 database back to Oracle7, and compress data in the database as well. The database can also be reorganized into different tablespace configurations with IMPORT/EXPORT. However, there are disadvantages with this method. For one, IMPORT/EXPORT require additional space for storage of Oracle data in the intermediate binary format. Also, the database conversion might take many hours or days, requiring advanced scheduling and downtime.

Another method that can be used for Oracle7 migration to Oracle8 is to perform a table copy using the SQL*Plus **copy** or the **create as select** statement, as covered in Unit I. This method also allows the DBA to migrate specific parts of the database at a time, and also allows the DBA to perform database and tablespace reorganization. And it has the added advantage of allowing release migration. However, this method is even slower than IMPORT/EXPORT, and both the Oracle7 and Oracle8 databases must be available at the same time and for the duration of the migration activity.

Exercises

1. What are the basic features of an Oracle8 database migration? What are the responsibilities of the DBA, the application developers, and the users?

2. What is the migration utility? What are two other methods for conducting database migration from Oracle7 to Oracle8? What are the advantages and disadvantages for each?

Migrating from Oracle7 to Oracle8

This section covers the process of migrating from Oracle7 to Oracle8. Before conducting database migration, ensure the following aspects are complete. Everyone involved should be familiar with Oracle8's new features to the extent they need to be. The migration method should be planned and documented, along with the test plan for ensuring that the Oracle8 database is complete and a plan for migrating back to Oracle7 if there is a problem. If possible, test the migration strategy itself, perhaps by first migrating a test or development environment, then the production environment. Preparation of the Oracle7 database is important—use the **shutdown normal** procedure and execute a full offline backup. The overall database migration should consist of the following steps.

Step 1: Prepare for Migration

The first part of this step is to understand the new features of Oracle8. This is the step you are engaged in by obtaining OCP certification in Oracle8. You will need to know how Oracle8 relates to the particulars of your organization's database. After understanding the overall impact, you must decide how to conduct the migration, either with the migration utility, IMPORT/EXPORT, or table copies. Finally, identify issues that represent actions either for you, the developers, or the users. These actions include changing object names because they contain new reserved words, identifying and changing applications that use parts of the data dictionary that may have changed, determining migration strategy for columns of type ROWID, initialization parameter changes, and organizational mandates for password management.

Step 2: Make Room on Disk

There are new requirements for Oracle8 with respect to storage, memory, and processing power. First, Oracle8 requires three times as much disk space as Oracle7, and a minimum of 16M of RAM—with 32M recommended for organizations using Oracle8 in conjunction with Oracle client/server development tools. More details about these and other platform requirements can be found in operating-system-specific documentation for Oracle8. As mentioned in the previous discussion, there may be additional space requirements during the database migration, depending on which migration tool you use. The CHECK_ONLY command line parameter in the Oracle8 migration utility can be used to identify if enough space is available for storing both versions of the data dictionary in the SYSTEM tablespace. The IMPORT/EXPORT migration option requires additional space to store Oracle data in the intermediate binary format, depending on how much data is exported as well as space in the Oracle7 database. The **create table as select** statement or **copy table** command requires the same amount of disk space to store the table in both databases.

Step 3: Develop the Test Plan

This step is critical to determine the success of both your migration strategy and your migration results. There are several different categories of tests you may want to develop as part of your test plan strategy. The test of the migration strategy should involve creating a test database out of a portion of your target database. You may also want to develop some sort of minimal acceptance test to perform after the migration is complete to ensure that none of the Oracle7 database functionality or components were lost during the migration. However, don't expect to detect any serious problems with this strategy—a functional test of all components individually in the database environment and an integration test to identify how the components work together in the Oracle8 environment would be better for this purpose. Finally, to determine if Oracle8 adds value to the databases of the organization, some performance and stress testing should be planned to determine if SQL runs faster, if the database can withstand normal usage, and other things.

Step 4: Maintain the Source

In rare situations, you may find that the Oracle8 migration must be backed out in favor of the Oracle7 version of your organization's data, and that further analysis is required. To make this backout possible, the DBA should ensure that a complete offline backup is taken before migration begins of the Oracle7 database, its RBMS software, parameter files, and all other files.

Step 5: Perform the Migration

In this step, the actual migration of the database is performed. First, the DBA should delete parameters from the current **init.ora** file that are obsolete in Oracle8. Next, the Oracle8 migration utility can be used for database migration or, alternately, migration can be done with the IMPORT/EXPORT or copying of tables. The Oracle8 executable software must be installed in order to complete the migration. If table copies are used, the DBA should ensure the appropriate links are made between the Oracle7 and Oracle8 databases.

INSTALL MIGRATION UTILITY   Use of the migration utility is as follows. The DBA must install the migration utility with the ORAINST utility found in the Oracle8 software distribution. Software for the migration utility is installed in the Oracle software home directory and the **bin** and **dbs** directories under that directory. At the time of installation, there will be an option to select the utility to install. Select the **migration utility O7 -> O8** option for installation. This installation will add some new files that are required for migration and to prepare the new environment.

RUN MIGRATION UTILITY   There are several parameters required for running the migration utility. The following parameters are for use with the migration utility during database migration. At the operating system prompt, the DBA issues the **mig** command, followed by these parameters in the format PARAMETER=*value:*

- **CFILE**   Identifies the database control file to the migration utility.

- **PFILE**   Identifies the database parameter file to the migration utility.

- **CNVFILE**   Identifies the **convert.ora** file to the migration utility if standard naming is not used.

- **MIGFILE**   Identifies the **migrate.bsq** file to the migration utility if standard naming is not used.

- **DBNAME**   The name of the database to be converted.

- **NEW_DBNAME**   The new name of the database after conversion, if desired.

- **MULTIPLIER**   Identifies the multiplication factor for increasing cluster index size.

- **SPOOL**   Identifies an output file for documenting the migration utility run time.

- **NO_SPACE_TIMECHECK**   Tells Oracle not to check for space and time conditions in the Oracle7 to Oracle8 migration.

- **CHECK_ONLY**   Tells Oracle not to perform the migration—only check to make sure there is enough space in the Oracle7 database for all database objects to be converted.

INSTALL ORACLE8 SOFTWARE   As part of migration, the DBA installs the Oracle8 software with the Oracle8 installer provided as part of the migration utility. To avoid creating a new instance and database as part of the Oracle8 software installation, the DBA must select the **Install/Upgrade** option.

PREPARE ORACLE8 DATABASE   To prepare the database for conversion, the DBA must do several things. First, the Oracle7 control files must be deleted. The conversion will build new Oracle8 control files for the database. The DBA should also verify the filesystem layout is correct for Oracle8 software and database files, including datafiles and redo logs. The following parameters in the **init.ora** file must be changed as well. Set the TRANSACTIONS_PER_ROLLBACK_SEGMENT to 21 or less, and set COMPATIBLE to 8.0.0.0.0 or remove it.

EXECUTE ORACLE8 CONVERSION   There are some things that must be executed within Server Manager. First, the DBA should start Server Manager in **line** mode. The DBA should then connect as INTERNAL and start but not mount the instance, and leave the database closed. Then, the **alter database convert** command should be issued. If some failure has occurred prior to this step, do NOT issue this command. Instead, restore the Oracle7 database as it existed preconversion and start again. The following code block illustrates the commands to issue from Server Manager.

```
CONNECT INTERNAL
STARTUP NOMOUNT
ALTER DATABASE CONVERT;
```

COMPLETE ORACLE8 CONVERSION   After converting the database, the DBA should open it with the **alter database open resetlogs** command. The DBA should then run the following scripts to complete conversion of the Oracle8 database:

- **cat8000.sql**   Can be found in the **rdbms/admin** directory under the Oracle software home directory. This script converts SYSTEM tables from Oracle7 to Oracle8.

- **catalog.sql**   Also found in the **rdbms/admin** directory under the Oracle software home directory. This script has the same function in Oracle8 as it does in Oracle7—it creates the data dictionary views.

- **catproc.sql**   Also found in the **rdbms/admin** directory under the Oracle software home directory. This script has the same function in Oracle8 as it does in Oracle7—it enhances the data dictionary and executes other scripts to support PL/SQL.

There may be other scripts the DBA needs to run at this time to support other options on the Oracle database. The DBA should identify the appropriate scripts and run them at this time. After identifying and executing the appropriate scripts, the DBA should drop the MIGRATE user created as part of Oracle8 database migration, as well as any objects created in this user's schema, with the **drop user MIGRATE cascade** statement.

Step 6: Back Up, Test, Modify, Open

Following the conversion to Oracle8, the DBA should shut down the database normally and take a full backup. Then, the DBA should make the database available for users and developers to test the effects of the conversion on the online and batch applications. The DBA may need to change some connectivity options such as values in **tnsnames.ora**, or the developers may need to make these changes in the applications themselves. Once it is determined that the migration works properly, the DBA may need to convert database administration scripts used to manage the instance. This may happen over a period of time following the conversion, or even before the conversion. If there is a problem with the database conversion, the DBA will need to correct the problem, and perhaps perform the migration from Oracle7 again. This potential underscores the importance of taking a backup before and after migration.

Exercises

1. What are the six steps for database migration from Oracle7 to Oracle8?

2. Identify some of the parameters that can be used when running the migration utility? Which parameter helps to determine if there is enough space in the Oracle7 database to make the conversion?

3. What statement is issued in Server Manager to convert the database from Oracle7 to Oracle8? What SQL script is run to convert SYSTEM tables to Oracle8 after database conversion? What must happen to the MIGRATE user?

Chapter Summary

This chapter covers three important areas of understanding for Oracle8. These areas include the changes to networking that have been made by Net8 and the new security options available for network communication using Oracle databases over unsecured network connections. In addition, the new Oracle8 internal security options for managing the SYS schema and user accounts are presented. The final, and perhaps most important, area of Oracle8 presented in this chapter is the steps and factors required for migrating to Oracle8 from Oracle7. These areas are important both for passing OCP Exam 5 and for the greater purpose of using Oracle8 in your organization.

The first area is enhancements to networking. Oracle introduces the use of many new features with the Net8 product, designed to build on the foundation for networking that was established with SQL*Net in Oracle7. A higher degree of support for foreign data sources such as Rdb or Oracle Express has been integrated into Net8, along with compliance for ODBC level 2 support of stored procedures. Net8 is also designed to provide improved scalability by introducing a new component called Connection Manager, which can be used in conjunction with the multithreaded server (MTS) architecture (although Connection Manager is an independent product). This feature is designed to concentrate many user connections to the database into one physical transport. This feature reduces network traffic while supporting a substantially higher number of users. The initial user connection requires its own physical transport with the server, while subsequent communication can take place within the Connection Manager. User connections are managed more tightly with the use of connection pooling and multiplexed messages within Connection Manager.

This utility also has the capacity to operate in conjunction with the enhanced security options available in Oracle8. There are some significant enhancements in the Oracle8 network security architecture with the introduction of the Advanced Networking Option and the Oracle Security server. Advanced Networking option allows Oracle to work in conjunction with the latest technologies available for network security, such as digital signatures and external authentication. The Oracle Security server provides third-party authentication based on public/private-key encryption within the Oracle network. Other areas of enhancement are changes made to the listener process to support N-tier network configuration supporting asynchronous communication between clients and servers over large networks. However, in recognition of smaller organizations and those organizations not ready to deploy advanced networking, Net8 allows the DBA to configure it to use TNS raw transport to bypass many networking features, allowing unsecured two-tier client/server applications to operate and communicate faster.

To improve configuration of the Net8 Oracle network, Oracle has implemented advanced use of Oracle Names servers. These servers are designed to allow other services within the Oracle network to register on a Names server automatically. Clients connecting to the Oracle network can then find those services simply by referring to the Names server for assistance. The client can identify what Names servers are available by looking in the **sdns.ora** file. The Names server can also carry client profile information so that new clients needn't be configured onsite—they simply download their default configuration from the Names server and confirm those defaults with the user. Many new features for Net8, including Net8 itself and the Oracle Security server, offer an applications programming interface (API) so that developers can integrate the use of the new features into their applications. Oracle Trace can be used in association with Net8 to diagnose and resolve network connectivity issues. For those organizations not ready to deploy Net8 advanced security, the Names server, and other Net8 features, the native hostname adapter can be used to support access to Oracle via TCP/IP domain names and open security.

In addition to the Oracle Security server and external network security options working in conjunction with the Advanced Networking Option, Oracle8 offers some advancements to internal security for the SYS schema and user accounts. Oracle recommends DBAs no longer connect as **internal** without having the **sysdba** privilege. The DBA must also be part of the OSDBA group if external networking is used, or the password for SYS provided must match what is in the password file if Oracle password authentication is used. The **any** keyword used to grant maximum scope for object privileges no longer includes access to objects in the SYS schema if the new O7_DICTIONARY_ACCESSIBILITY initialization parameter is set to FALSE. New roles are available for managing access to objects in the SYS schema, called SELECT_CATALOG_ROLE for **select** access to SYS objects, EXECUTE_CATALOG_ROLE for **execute** privileges on stored procedures owned by SYS, and DELETE_CATALOG_ROLE for **delete** privileges on SYS-owned objects like the AUD$ table.

User account security has also been enhanced with the implementation of advanced password management. User accounts can now be locked to prevent unauthorized use. Passwords can now be set to expire after a period of time, and a history of passwords can be kept in order to prevent password reuse. Finally, passwords can be verified for sufficient complexity. Password management can be implemented with the execution of the **utlpwdmg.sql** script. Password management is handled with user profiles and with **create user** and **alter user** statements. Unlike resource limits, which are enforced only when the RESOURCE_LIMIT initialization parameter is set to TRUE, password limits in user profiles are always enforced.

Account locking can be accomplished manually by the DBA or the security administrator with the **alter user account lock** statement and unlocked with the **alter user account unlock** statement. Alternately, Oracle can automatically lock a user account if someone unsuccessfully attempts to log in more times than allowed by a threshold set by the **failed_login_attempts** clause set for the user profile. The duration of automatic lockout can be indefinite or it can be for a limited period of time defined by **password_lock_time**. A password will expire after a period of time as defined in the profile by **password_life_time**. After a password has expired, the user must change their password within a period of time defined by **password_grace_time**. If this time period expires before the user changes their password, the user account is locked. Other options are specified in the **create profile** statement, as defined in the chapter.

Password complexity is determined with the use of a stored PL/SQL procedure. One is provided in Oracle8, called **verify_password( )**. It verifies that the password created for a user is at least four characters long and contains one alphabet, one number, and one punctuation character. An organization can create its own password verification routine as long as it conforms to certain formats and is defined for use in the user profiles. More about these requirements is defined in the chapter. There are several new data dictionary views available in Oracle8 to support the use of password management. Columns have been added to the USER_ and DBA_USERS views, as well as to the DBA_PROFILES view, and a new view called USER_PASSWORD_LIMITS has been added to the data dictionary. Finally, some tools have been enhanced to support password management, including Server Manager and SQL*Plus.

Finally, migration to Oracle8 is covered in this chapter. The migration to Oracle8 can be performed in three ways. The first is using the Oracle8 migration utility. This tool converts existing Oracle7 databases to Oracle8 and is designed to run quickly, even on large databases. However, the migration utility only allows the DBA to convert the database up to Oracle8, not downward from Oracle8 to Oracle7. It also provides no support for database reorganization. An alternative to using the migration utility is to install Oracle8 separately and migrate the Oracle7 database using EXPORT/IMPORT. Though it requires additional space to store data from the database in intermediate binary format and more time to perform the conversion, EXPORT/IMPORT also allows the DBA to convert an Oracle8 database back to Oracle7 in the event of migration problems, and allows for partial database migration as well. A third alternative is to copy tables from Oracle7 databases to their Oracle8 counterparts. This option also allows downward migration, but takes longer, requires a great deal of space, and requires both the Oracle7 and Oracle8 versions of the database to exist simultaneously and for a connection to exist between them.

There are roles and responsibilities required of everyone in converting the Oracle8 database. The DBA is responsible for converting the database components, while the application developers are required to understand the impact that Oracle8 might have on the applications. Finally, the users should be involved in testing the applications to ensure no functionality is lost. There are six steps for migrating from Oracle7 to Oracle8. They are preparing to migrate, securing required resources, building a test plan, preserving the source database, migrating the source database, and finalizing the migration of the source database.

The actual process of migrating the database consists of several subtasks. They include installing the migration utility (if the DBA is using the migration utility), running the migration utility, and installing Oracle8 software. After these tasks, the DBA must prepare the database by removing the control file and altering the TRANSACTIONS_PER_ROLLBACK_SEGMENT to 21 and setting COMPATIBLE to 8.0.0.0.0 or blank. The actual conversion of the database is done next by connecting as **internal**, starting the instance using the **startup nomount** statement, and issuing the **alter database convert** statement. When conversion is over, the DBA should run **cat8000.sql**, **catalog.sql**, and **catproc.sql**, and then issue the **drop user MIGRATE cascade** statement. After running the migration, the DBA can back up the new Oracle8 database, execute any testing plans to ensure the migration went smooth, and then convert any database administration scripts to use Oracle8 new features. Connectivity to the database may have to be changed by modifying the **tnsnames.ora** file.

Two-Minute Drill

- Net8 networking offers enhancements in the areas of scalability, connectivity, security, performance, and configuration.

- Scalability improvements are provided with the use of Connection Manager to concentrate and multiplex multiple user connections through a single physical transport. The number of sockets to support user connections on a database server is also minimized with connection pooling.

- Connectivity is improved with support for ODBC level 2 driver for use of stored procedures and with support for foreign data sources like Rdb and Oracle Express OLAP.

- Security is improved with the use of Oracle Security server global users and roles, one-time login, public/private-key encryption, support for security servers available from other vendors, digital signatures, and the Advanced Networking Option.

- Network configuration is simplified with the use of Oracle Names servers to maintain information about the services available on the Oracle network and to support client profile distribution to manage client configuration centrally.

- New features for Oracle8 internal security over the SYS schema and password management of password information are also available.

- The new password features include account locking, password aging, password history, and password complexity verification.

- New options have been added to the user profile to support password management. These features are enforced even when resource limits are not.

- The locking and unlocking of accounts is handled with the **alter user** statement.

- The USER_, DBA_USERS, and DBA_PROFILES views have been changed to support password management, and the

USER_PASSWORD_LIMITS view has been added in support of password management as well.

- There are six steps to migrate an Oracle database: prepare to migrate, secure necessary disk resources and memory, develop the test plan, back up the Oracle7 database, migrate to Oracle8, and backup the new database.

- There are three tools available for migrating the Oracle database to Oracle8: the migration utility, IMPORT/EXPORT, and copying tables.

Chapter Questions

1. After migrating to Oracle8, the DBA must perform which of the following tasks? (Choose three)

   A. Run **catalog.sql**

   B. Issue **alter database open resetlogs**

   C. Back up the source database

   D. Install a new version of **migrate.bsq**

   E. Drop the MIGRATE user

2. The migration of the database to Oracle8 is about to begin. Which of the following is not a parameter to the migration utility?

   A. CFILE

   B. PFILE

   C. LFILE

   D. DBNAME

3. The DBA would like to implement password management on the Oracle8 database. To set up default values for password management in the DEFAULT profile, the DBA must

      A. Run the **utlpwdmg.sql** script

      B. Set RESOURCE_LIMIT to TRUE

      C. Assign users to the DEFAULT profile

      D. Start the Password Manager background process

4. Once created, a password verification function is owned by

      A. The DBA

      B. The user executing it

      C. The MIGRATE user

      D. The SYS user

5. The DBA is implementing password management. When users unsuccessfully log into the database five times, Oracle should lock the account for eight hours, after which time Oracle will unlock the account automatically. Which of the following correctly identifies both the options that must be specified and the correct value for that option?

      A. password_reuse_max 5, password_lockout 8

      B. password_login_attempts 5, password_lock_time 8

      C. failed_login_attempts 5, password_lock_time 1/3

      D. failed_login_attempts 5, password_lock_time 8

6. The DBA is deciding how to configure the Oracle networking options for the Oracle8 database. The organization uses TCP/IP with domain name service implemented. The Net8 listener will redirect connect requests for only one server. Required security is implemented at the database level using roles. What network options should the DBA use?

      A. Oracle Names server

      B. Native hostname adapter

C. Oracle Security server

D. Advanced Networking option

7. **To diagnose problems with networking between client and server, the DBA can use which of the following methods?**

A. Oracle Trace, stored external to Net8

B. Oracle Trace, stored within Net8

C. Net8 Open API, stored external to Net8

D. Net8 Open API, stored internal to Net8

8. **If additional security options are not required and the DBA would like to increase performance of communication between client and server while bypassing layers of protocol within Net8 for networking, the DBA can configure Net8 to use**

A. Connection pooling

B. TNS raw transport

C. Oracle Security server

D. Oracle Names server

9. **Which of the following are drawbacks of using EXPORT/IMPORT for migrating to Oracle8? (Choose two)**

A. Slow migration time

B. Unable to perform backward migration

C. Requires a great deal of additional disk space

D. Cannot perform database reorganization during migration

10. **The DBA must execute several scripts after migrating to Oracle8. What is the function provided by executing the CAT8000.SQL script?**

A. Creates dictionary views

B. Creates ability to use PL/SQL

C. Converts SYSTEM tables

D. Drops MIGRATE user

11. **The Oracle7 control file is compatible for use on an Oracle8 database.**

   A. TRUE

   B. FALSE

12. **Which of the following choices best describes the Oracle8 grace period?**

   A. The time limit for upgrading the Oracle server license to Oracle8

   B. The time during which the user may not reuse a password

   C. The length of time before a password expires

   D. The length of time a user has to change an expired password

13. **Which of the following complexity checks does the VERIFY_PASSWORD( ) function not perform? (Choose three)**

   A. Password is six alphanumeric or punctuation characters long, or more

   B. Password contains one letter

   C. Password contains one number

   D. Password contains one unprintable character

   E. Password contains one multibyte character

Answers to Chapter Questions

1. A, B, and E.

Explanation   Once the database is converted to Oracle8, some of the tasks the DBA must do to complete the migration include discarding redo information by issuing **alter database open resetlogs**, running **catalog.sql** to create dictionary objects, and dropping the MIGRATE user created as part of the migration utility operation. Backing up the source database should take place before executing the migration, eliminating choice C. The **migrate.bsq** file is installed along with other migration software before executing migration, eliminating choice D. Review the discussion of the steps for migrating the Oracle database.

2. C.   LFILE

Explanation   CFILE is an option for running the migration utility where the DBA tells the utility what the name of the control file is. The PFILE performs the same function, except it tells the migration utility what the parameter file is. The DBNAME parameter identifies the current name for the database migrated. Review the discussion of the migration utility in the section on migrating the Oracle database.

3. A.   Run the **utlpwdmg.sql** script

Explanation   Password management limits are set up in the DEFAULT profile using the **utlpwdmg.sql** script. Password limits are enforced for the database regardless of whether or not the RESOURCE_LIMIT parameter is set, which eliminates choice B. The users of the database are implicitly assigned to the DEFAULT profile if no other one is assigned, but even if another is assigned, any parameters not defined in the other profile will default to whatever value is set in the DEFAULT profile, eliminating choice C. Choice D is incorrect because there is no Password Manager background process.

4. D.   The SYS user

Explanation   The password complexity verification routine is compiled under user SYS in order to have it owned by that schema. Therefore, the function belongs to the SYS user. Refer to the discussion of development for the password complexity function.

5. C.   **failed_login_attempts** 5, **password_lock_time** 1/3

Explanation   Choices A and B are incorrect because they identify options for password management that do not exist. Choice D is incorrect because the **password_lock_time** value is specified in days, not hours. To configure this option to operate in terms of hours or minutes, the value specified must be a fraction. Review user profile options available in the discussion of password management.

6. B.   Native hostname adapter

Explanation   The question describes a situation where the native hostname adapter is used. The organization uses a TCP/IP network, the listener services only one database server, and there are no network security requirements for the system. These conditions are favorable for using the native hostname adapter. Choices C and D implement a higher level of security than is required by the application, while the Oracle Names server needn't be used because the TCP/IP DNS is being used. Review the discussion of usage factors for Net8 networking options.

7. A.   Oracle Trace, stored external to Net8

Explanation   Answering this question requires knowledge of two facts about Oracle. First, the DBA must know that network diagnostics are done with Oracle Trace; and second, the DBA must know that Oracle Trace is stored external to Net8 in order to reduce the Net8 executable size. This second condition eliminates choice B. Net8's OPEN API is not used for this purpose, eliminating choices C and D. Review the conclusion of the discussion for Net8 features.

8. B.   TNS raw transport

Explanation   The key to the answer to this question is bypassing levels of Net8 protocol. Although connection pooling improves performance on the Net8 networking product, it does not bypass levels of Net8 protocol the way TNS raw transport does. The Oracle Security server and Oracle Names server handle other aspects of Net 8. Review the discussion of TNS raw transport.

9. A and C.

Explanation   Using the EXPORT and IMPORT utilities for database migration to Oracle8 has some advantages—namely, the fact that the DBA can migrate down versions and can reorganize the database in the process. These facts eliminate choices B and D. Review the use of various methods and tools for database migration to Oracle8 in the section on migration.

10. C.   Converts SYSTEM tables

Explanation   Choice A is incorrect because **catalog.sql** is used to convert dictionary objects. Choice B is incorrect because the **catproc.sql** script is used to prepare the database for PL/SQL. Finally, choice D is incorrect because the DBA must execute this step manually.

11. B.   FALSE

Explanation   There are many things about an Oracle7 control file that make it incompatible with Oracle8. For example, the Oracle7 control file doesn't store all of the information about database recovery that Oracle8 requires. As part of database migration, the DBA removes the Oracle7 control file so that the migration can create a new one using Oracle8 conventions. Review the procedure for migrating a database to Oracle8.

12. D.   The length of time a user has to change an expired password

Explanation   Password lifetime is the term referred to in choice B, making it incorrect. Password reuse time is the term referred to in choice C, making that choice incorrect. There is no word or phrase for choice A. Review the options that can be specified for password management.

13. A, D, and E.

Explanation   The **verify_password( )** routine created when the DBA runs **utlpwdmg.sql** checks to see if the password is four characters or longer, and that the password contains one of each of the following: a letter, a number, and a punctuation mark. Thus, only choices B and C describe the functionality provided by this verification function.

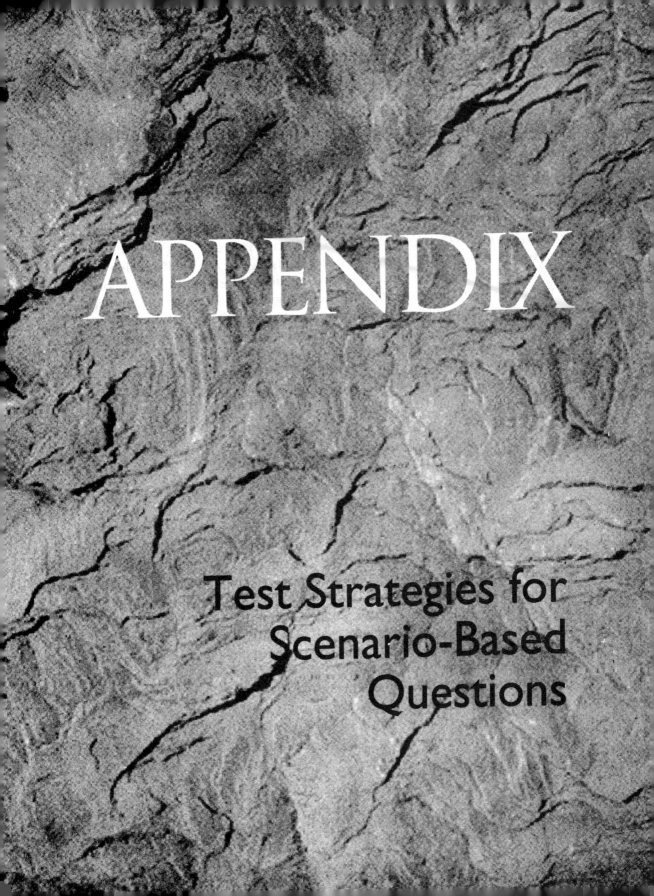

APPENDIX

Test Strategies for Scenario-Based Questions

racle has announced the introduction of scenario-based questions to the Oracle Certified Professional examination series. This announcement has a direct impact on what you have to do in order to receive your certification, because it represents Oracle's focus on making the OCP DBA certification series as experience-based as possible. Oracle's purpose is to reduce the likelihood that people with strong memorization skills but little experience with Oracle can pass the OCP exam. However, it is not entirely clear if people with strong memorization skills are not as "good" at being a DBA as people who have done it for so long their skills are mechanical, or even if scenario-based questions will serve their ends. Though it is important to know how to apply information, without knowing that a certain feature exists, one might never think to apply it. Nevertheless, in order to prepare you to pass the OCP DBA exam in light of this change, this Guide will identify what the change really means and how you can best prepare for these new questions in your goal of becoming an Oracle Certified Professional.

What Are Scenario-Based Questions?

First, some definitions. When Oracle says it is putting scenario-based questions on the OCP DBA exams, Oracle means that the questions on the exam will identify a scenario in which the DBA may find himself or herself. The questions may literally say "The DBA encounters the following situation...." Several options will be presented in multiple choice format, and from these options you must select the choice that best identifies the best plan of action, given certain facts and conditions related to Oracle that a DBA should know. Whereas originally the questions on OCP DBA exams emphasized knowledge of facts about the Oracle database, now Oracle is using assumptions the DBA should be making on those facts to answer questions. Consider the following fact-based question:

The name of the view used to analyze increases to the buffer cache is called

A. V$BUFFER

B. V$KCBRBH

    C. DBA_OBJECTS

    D. X$KCBCBH

In order to answer this question, the DBA needs to know a certain fact about Oracle—that the X$KCBRBH view can be used to compare the number of hits on the buffer cache that will be gained by increasing the size of the buffer cache. There is simply no other way to answer this question. Now, consider another question, which requires the same knowledge but asks for it in another way:

The DBA needs to increase the size of the shared pool without increasing the size of the SGA or real memory. How can you determine where to make the trade-off?

    A. Increasing SHARED_POOL_SIZE

    B. Looking in V$SYSSTAT

    C. Looking in X$KCBRBH

    D. Increasing DB_BLOCK_BUFFERS

Both of these questions require the same information—that the X$KCBRBH dynamic performance view can be used to assess the increase in cache hits on the buffer cache of the SGA. However, the second question requires that you know several related facts about X$KCBRBH, the SGA, and the buffer cache. In short, the difference between the fact- and scenario-based styles is that fact-based questions clearly define the area of database knowledge required, while scenario-based questions require you to read between the lines.

The questions presented at the end of each chapter in this Guide are split between fact-based and scenario-based questions. It may be useful for the candidate to review the questions answered and attempt to determine what other ways the question might be phrased in order to place the fact into a working scenario. For example, the DBA may know the definition of a system change number, or SCN. The DBA may also know that incomplete recovery can be conducted based on SCN. However, these two facts may require two fact-based questions for the OCP exam to determine your level of knowledge with these two items. In contrast, the equivalent level of knowledge, as well as the relationship between the two, can be detected with one scenario-based question.

A situation has occurred where extensive data corruption occurred on the database as a result of an erroneous transaction whose SCN is 4959693. What can the DBA do to alleviate the problem?

A. Drop and re-create the database

B. Issue the **recover database until 495693** statement

C. Issue the **recover database until cancel** statement

D. Issue the **recover tablespace** statement

One good exercise to study for scenario-based questions is to review the chapter summaries and Two-Minute Drills with the idea of relating facts together. Instead of remembering what a database component is, you should think about how you might have to use it.

Scenario-Based Questions: Another Take

However, although the goal of scenario-based questions is to shift emphasis away from memorization and towards experience, some of the questions in the guise of scenario format are really fact-based questions. Consider the following question:

The DBA is attempting to tune an application. What utility gives information about how Oracle will execute SQL statements?

A. Explain plan

B. UTLBSTAT

C. SQL*Net

D. EXPORT

Although this question has the right situational component to qualify as a scenario-based question, the answer is gained simply by knowing a fact—that the **explain plan** utility gives execution plan information for SQL statements. Thus, reading between the lines produces an additional result—not only should you know how to connect the facts you know about Oracle, you should also know when the "scenario" really requires knowledge of facts.

Strategies for Preparation

Scenario-based questions work to your advantage. The more information you are given in the question, the more information you have for the answer. You may find it easier to associate the information required for answering the question with a description of a situation where knowing the fact is required. One technique is for you to go back to the practice questions in the end of each chapter and write in the margin some lead-in that defines a scenario in which the fact may be necessary. The classic scenario-based lead-in would be "The DBA is attempting the _____ operation...."

Another technique for preparing for scenario-based questions is the game of association. Consider each question asked, and try to remember the scenario in which that knowledge is required. Then, reread the explanation in the "Answers to Chapter Questions" section, and review the section of the chapter that discusses this fact. Now, go back to the question and list three to five facts you need to know that are associated with the area of knowledge. Revisit the previous question:

The DBA needs to increase the size of the shared pool without increasing the size of the SGA or real memory. How can you determine where to make the trade-off?

   A. Increasing SHARED_POOL_SIZE

   B. Looking in V$SYSSTAT

   C. Looking in X$KCBRBH

   D. Increasing DB_BLOCK_BUFFERS

To answer this question, you need to know several things—the shared pool is part of the SGA, Oracle's main memory structure. There are some other parts to the SGA, such as the buffer cache and the redo log. The only memory area in which the relative effects of different sizes were considered was with the buffer cache, using the X$ views. These facts, and whatever others you may find, can be listed in the margin to help you recall the information you need to prepare for the test.

The most important thing to remember when preparing for scenario-based questions is the ability to read the question carefully, apply the appropriate facts, and, if need be, associate one set of facts to another to find the answer. Although the techniques presented here will help you to retain the facts you need to know about Oracle, there are no "magic tricks" to get scenario-based questions right. All the questions on the OCP DBA exams require a thorough knowledge about Oracle, and don't be dissuaded by the intent of the scenario-based questions. Your best method of preparation is to know Oracle thoroughly. Whatever method you come by that understanding—be it memorization, years of experience, or both—your knowledge of Oracle is your best preparation for its certification exam.

Index

Q

U

About the CD-ROM

Inside the back cover is the accompanying CD-ROM for Oracle Certified Professional DBA Certification Exam Guide, by Jason Couchman. Launching the index.htm file gives you access to the following:

- **An electronic version of the entire book in HTML format.** To view any chapter in the book, click on the "Electronic Book" button and select the appropriate chapter.

- **An electronic self-study test bank containing over 300 questions from the end of each chapter.** Click on the "Review" button and you are linked to the appropriate section of the book for further study. A correct response links you to the next question.

- **Self Assessment Test from Self Test Software** offering additional questions for test preparation.